LAW AND BUSINESS OF THE SPORTS INDUSTRIES

Volume II

Common Issues in Amateur and Professional Sports

LAW AND BUSINESS OF THE SPORTS INDUSTRIES

Volume II

Common Issues in Amateur and Professional Sports

ROBERT C. BERRY
Boston College Law School

GLENN M. WONG
University of Massachusetts

AH *Auburn House Publishing Company*
Dover, Massachusetts • London

Library of Congress Cataloging in Publication Data
Berry, Robert C.
  Law and business of the sports industries.

  Bibliography: p.
  Includes index.
  1. Professional sports—Law and legislation—United
States. I. Wong, Glenn M. II. Title.
KF3989.B47   1986   344.73'009   82–22833
ISBN 0–86569–102–9   347.30499

Printed in the United States of America

CONTENTS

Introduction   ix

CHAPTER 1
Amateur Athletic Associations   1

1.00 Amateur Sports in the Modern Age   1
1.10 Definition of Amateur   1
1.20 Amateur Athletic Associations   3
    1.21 Legal Principles   3
    1.21-1 Judicial Review   3
    1.21-2 Standing   5
    1.21-3 Injunctions   6
    1.22 Voluntary Athletic Associations   7
    1.22-1 United States Olympic Committee   10
    1.22-2 National Collegiate Athletic
        Association   15
    1.22-3 High School Athletic Associations   23
    1.22-4 State Athletic Commissions   31
    1.23 Public Responsibilities of Amateur Athletic
        Associations   32
    1.23-1 Disclosure Cases   33
    1.23-2 Funding of Public Facilities   38
    1.23-3 Delegation of a Public Responsibility   40
    1.23-4 Public Broadcast Rights   45
    1.24 Antitrust Liabilities of Amateur
        Associations   45
1.30 Constitutional Aspects of Athletics   50
    1.31 State Action Requirement   50
    1.32 Due Process   55
    1.32-1 Procedural Due Process   55
    1.32-2 Substantive Due Process   60
    1.33 Equal Protection   63
1.40 Amateur Athletic Association Authority   67
    1.41 The NCAA   67

1.41-1 The NCAA, Conferences, and Member
    Institutions   72
1.41-2 NCAA Regulation of Coaches and
    Personnel   79
1.41-3 NCAA Regulation of Recruiting   83
1.42 High School Athletic Associations   91
1.43 Other Amateur Athletic Associations   93
1.50 Scheduling   94

CHAPTER 2
The Amateur Athlete   99

2.00 Introduction   99
2.10 Individual Eligibility Requirements for Collegiate
    and High School Athletes   101
    2.11 Grade Point Average   107
    2.12 Academic Progress   109
    2.13 Transfer Rules   114
    2.13-1 College Transfer Rules   114
    2.13-2 High School Transfer Rules   122
    2.14 Redshirting and Longevity   126
    2.14-1 Redshirting   127
    2.14-2 Longevity   130
    2.15 Financial Considerations   134
    2.15-1 Scholarship and Financial Aid   134
    2.15-2 Pay   159
    2.15-3 Expenses   162
    2.16 Professional Contracts   175
    2.17 Player-Agents   177
    2.18 Individual Eligibility Requirements for
        Olympic Athletes   185
2.20 Student-Athletes' Individual Rights   189
    2.21 Freedom of Expression   189
    2.22 Hair Length   191

2.23 High School Marriages   193
2.24 Alcohol and Drug Rules   195
2.25 Handicapped Student-Athletes   196
2.30 Discipline of Individual Athletes   199
2.40 The Buckley Amendment   203
2.50 Athletes' Lawsuits for Failure to Provide an
     Education   204
2.60 Summer Camps and Outside Activities   205

CHAPTER 3
Sex Discrimination in Athletics   211

3.00 Introduction   211
3.10 Legal Principles   214
     3.11 Equal Protection   215
     3.12 Title IX   218
     3.13 Equal Rights Amendment   221
3.20 Title IX and Athletic Programs   224
     3.21 Legality of Title IX   225
     3.22 Scope and Applicability of Title IX   228
     3.23 Office of Civil Rights Title IX Compliance
          Reviews   240
3.30 Sex Discrimination   242
     3.31 One Team Only   243
     3.31-1 Contact Sports   244
     3.31-2 Noncontact Sports   247
     3.32 Women's Team, No Men's Team   253
     3.33 Both Women's and Men's Teams   256
     3.33-1 Separate but Equal   256
     3.33-2 Same Sport, Different Rules   262
     3.33-3 Same Sport, Different Seasons   265
3.40 Sex Discrimination in Athletic Employment   266
     3.41 Equal Pay Act and Title VII   266
     3.42 Coaching   267
     3.43 Sports-Related Employment
          Discrimination   272
     3.43-1 Officiating   272
     3.43-2 Participating in Professional Sports   273
     3.43-3 The News Media   273

CHAPTER 4
Tort Liability   277

4.00 Tort Liability and Its Relationship to Sports   277
4.10 Legal Principles in Tort Law   279
     4.11 Assault and Battery   280
     4.11-1 Assault   281
     4.11-2 Battery   281
     4.11-3 Defenses for Assault and Battery   282
     4.12 Negligence   284

4.12-1 Reasonable Person Standard   285
4.12-2 Standard of Care for Children   292
4.12-3 Standard of Care for Owners and
       Possessors of Property   293
4.12-4 Reckless Misconduct   297
4.12-5 Defenses for Negligence   298
4.13 Vicarious Liability   303
4.13-1 Independent Contractors   305
4.14 Defamation Law   306
4.15 Invasion of Privacy   312
4.16 Intentional Infliction of Emotional Distress
     316
4.17 Products Liability Law   317
4.17-1 Products Liability: Negligence   318
4.17-2 Products Liability: Strict Liability   319
4.17-3 Products Liability: Warranties   319
4.20 Application of Legal Principles to Persons
     Involved in Sports   320
4.21 Liability of Participants   320
4.22 Liability of Coaches and Physical Education
     Teachers   331
4.22-1 Supervision   331
4.22-2 Instruction and Training   335
4.22-3 Medical Assistance   337
4.22-4 Vicarious Liability for Actions of Fans
       and Players   340
4.23 Liability and Administrators, Schools, and
     Universities   341
4.23-1 Supervision and Personnel   342
4.23-2 Medical Assistance   346
4.23-3 Equipment   347
4.23-4 Sovereign Immunity   349
4.24 Liability of Professional Teams and
     Leagues   353
4.25 Liability of Facility Owners and
     Possessors   359
4.26 Liability of Medical Personnel   370
4.27 Liability of Officials, Referees, and
     Umpires   374
4.27-1 Intentional and Negligent Injury   375
4.27-2 Liability for Player Injury   378
4.27-3 Review of Officials' Decisions   379
4.27-4 Worker's Compensation   380
4.30 Application of Legal Principles to Defects in
     Equipment   381
4.40 Insurance   390
4.41 Liability Insurance   390
4.42 The NCAA's Catastrophic Insurance
     Plan   391
4.50 Waiver and Release of Liability   392

CHAPTER 5
Criminal Law and Sports 419

5.00 Introduction and General Considerations 419
5.10 Defining a Crime 422
5.20 Defining a Criminal Act in Athletic
Competition 422
    5.21 Justification and Excuse 423
    5.22 Responsibility for the Act 428
5.30 The Scope of Criminal Liability 432
5.40 League Disciplinary Procedure and
Sanctions 432
5.50 Proposed Legislative Solutions to Sports
Violence 434
5.60 Drug Abuse, Testing, and Enforcement 436
    5.61 Intercollegiate Athletics: Drug Abuse and
Enforcement 442
    5.62 Professional Sports: Drug Abuse and
Enforcement 452
    5.62-1 National Basketball Association 455
    5.62-2 National Football League 470
    5.62-3 Major League Baseball 473
    5.63 Olympic Games: Drug Abuse and
Enforcement 474
5.70 Gambling 477
    5.71 Intercollegiate Athletics and Gambling 477
    5.72 Professional Sports and Gambling 482
5.80 Ticket Scalping 492

CHAPTER 6
Sports and the Media 495
6.00 The "Product" of the Game 495
6.10 Nature of Rights in Transmission and
Description 495

6.11 Common Law: Misappropriation of
Property, Breach of License, Unfair
Competition 496
6.12 Communications Law 498
6.12-1 Negative Enforcement: Threat of
Loss of License 499
6.12-2 Positive Enforcement: Protection of
Private Transmissions 501
6.13 Copyright 503
6.20 Parties' Assertions of Rights to the Product 504
    6.21 Sports Teams and Leagues: Recent
Complications 504
    6.22 Players 505
    6.23 Broadcasters 506
    6.24 Conventional Television 507
    6.25 Cable 508
    6.26 Pay Cable and STV 510
    6.27 Superstations and Satellite
Transmissions 514
    6.28 Consumers 518
    6.28-1 Blackouts 518
    6.28-2 Home Taping 519
6.30 Limitations on Teams Dealing Through
Cooperative Ventures 522
    6.31 Pooling Rights in Professional Sports 522
    6.32 Amateur Sports Pooling
Arrangements 528
    6.33 New Ventures in Professional Sports 536
6.40 Rights of the Media Through the News
Function 539

Table of Cases 555

Index 573

INTRODUCTION

The scope, financial stakes, and power of amateur athletic organizations in the United States and worldwide have expanded tremendously over the last quarter of a century. In the United States alone, amateur athletics encompasses organizations that involve themselves in the lives of people from their childhood (e.g., Pop Warner Football and Little League), high school years (e.g., National Federation of State High School Associations), college days (e.g., National Collegiate Athletic Association), and beyond (e.g., United States Olympic Committee). The purpose of this introduction is to give the reader an overview of the size of amateur athletics in the United States, the involvement of the national amateur athletic organizations, and the financial impact of these organizations on amateur sports. The structure and governance of amateur athletics in the United States affects many individuals, participants, administrators, and coaches, and as such deserves close study. A particular focus will be the growth in amateur athletics and the corresponding increase in litigation, which has come about, in part, because of the rising financial stakes for amateur athletic organizations and amateur athletes.

The National Collegiate Athletic Association (NCAA)

The United States Supreme Court, in *National Collegiate Athletic Ass'n. v. Board of Regents of the University of Oklahoma and the University of Georgia Athletic Association,* hereinafter referred to as *"University of Oklahoma"* (*infra* Section 6.32) made the following observation of the NCAA:

> Since its inception in 1905, the NCAA has played an important role in the regulation of amateur collegiate sports. It has adopted and promulgated playing rules, standards of amateurism, standards for academic eligibility, regulations concerning recruitment of athletes, and rules governing the size of athletic squads and coaching staffs. In some sports, such as baseball, swimming, basketball, wrestling and track, it has sponsored and conducted national tournaments. It has not done so in the sport of football, however.
>
> The NCAA has approximately 850 voting members. The regular members are classified into separate divisions to reflect differences in size and scope of their athletic programs. Division I includes 276 colleges with major athletic programs; in this group only 187 play intercollegiate football. Divisions II and III include approximately 500 colleges with less extensive athletic programs. Division I has been subdivided into Divisions I-A and I-AA for football.

Prior to the 1984–85 academic year, the NCAA was largely financed by its percentage share of the national television contracts for intercollegiate football. However, on June 27, 1984, the Supreme Court in a 7–2 decision in the *University of Oklahoma* case struck down the NCAA's 1982–85 Football Television Plan because it violated the

Sherman Antitrust Act. (The Supreme Court's decision and other broadcasting matters are discussed in Chapter 6.) The effect of this ruling on the NCAA's budget was immediate. Estimates were that the NCAA would lose about $5 million in football television revenues, or 14 percent of its budget. In January 1985, the NCAA Executive Committee in its report to the membership reported an actual loss of $4.7 million. Fortunately for the organization, a $14-million increase in the CBS-TV fee to telecast the 1985 NCAA Basketball Championship covered the loss. A portion of this increase also went to teams in the NCAA Basketball Tournament.

The monies that the NCAA receives from its television packages are distributed mostly to the participating institutions in the NCAA championships involved. The NCAA conducts many different championships, including men's basketball, women's basketball, swimming, track and field, and baseball. While some of the revenues are retained for the NCAA's operating expenses (40 percent of the NCAA Basketball Tournament's net receipts go to the NCAA), most of the monies are distributed. For instance, participants in the 1985 NCAA Basketball Tournament received from $141,600 for first-round losers to $708,000 for the final four teams. Similarly, in intercollegiate football, the Cherry Bowl participants received $750,000 each, while the teams in the Rose Bowl collected $5.1 million each. These large stakes have put enormous pressure on coaches to succeed and some believe may be the root cause for many of the rules violations that occur.

In addition to the financial issues, a major problem facing the NCAA in recent years has been in the area of recruiting violations by member schools. "I believe there is a growing acceptance of the belief that the conditions of intercollegiate athletics are such that you have to cut corners, you have to circumvent the rules," stated Walter Byers, executive director of the NCAA. Byers added: "There seems to be a growing number of coaches and administrators who look upon NCAA penalties as the price of doing business: If you get

punished, that's unfortunate, but that's part of the cost of getting along." At one point in 1984, 13 NCAA institutions were on probation.

One of the NCAA's concerns, which involves both the financial aspects and recruiting areas, is the subject of booster organizations. Booster organizations serve as support groups for specific sports in an athletic department. Their primary purpose is to raise monies for the sport in the form of direct contributions or indirect support through the purchase of season ticket packages and dinner tickets, or by providing employment opportunities for the student-athletes on the team. While estimates are that in 1982 college sports generated approximately $700 million in revenues, only one-third of all NCAA institutions balanced their athletic budgets. Booster organizations thus become increasingly important and can play a significant role in generating additional income for athletic departments. In 1981, 11 percent of the NCAA Division I budgets are believed to have been funded by booster organizations.

Unfortunately, some booster organizations have violated NCAA rules and regulations and subsequently caused the involved programs to be put on NCAA probation. The sanctions range from total prohibition of the individual team or entire program from championship play to prohibition from television appearances to just a warning. Athletic departments rely on booster organizations for several reasons, among them the emergence of women's athletic programs, the increased costs of running programs, and the need for new or improved facilities, all of which require additional monies.

An example of the high cost of supporting a big-time athletic program can be seen at Rutgers University. In 1984, Rutgers, which is the State University of New Jersey, decided to upgrade its football program. For years it had languished at the bottom of NCAA Division I-A programs. After hiring a new coach, Rutgers immediately spent $3 million to build a new outdoor practice field, a bubble-enclosed indoor practice field, and a new $1.5 million scoreboard. The university also renovated the locker room, bought $50,000 worth of Nautilus equipment, and hired a full-time strength and conditioning coach. The next phase in upgrading the Rutgers program involves construction of a $5 million football complex consisting of a locker room, weight room, trainer's room, coaches' offices, and meeting facilities. Future plans call for installing lighting at Rutgers Stadium, increasing the seating capacity in the stadium from 23,000 to about 40,000, and building a new press box.

Another grave concern of the NCAA involves drug abuse by athletes. Drug abuse, whether recreational or sports-related, has become a very large problem for all athletic organizations, including the NCAA. In 1985, the NCAA released a drug survey of 2,000 athletes: 27 percent smoked marijuana, 12 percent used cocaine, 11 percent used major pain killers, and an overwhelming 82 percent used alcohol. NCAA research coordinator Eric Zemper noted: "I don't think the results are that surprising. The numbers are certainly higher than we hoped, but it's a pervasive problem throughout society." Drug abuse and the testing for drugs in athletes have become major areas of focus for the NCAA that seem to be leading to a new area of litigation in the 1980s. Drug testing and defending litigation will bring about additional financial problems for athletic programs. The governance authority of the NCAA is discussed in Chapter 1; litigation involving student-athletes is discussed in Chapter 2 and drug testing in Chapter 5.

NOTES _____

1. In addition to the NCAA, intercollegiate athletics has what are known as allied conferences. These are associations of NCAA member schools that agree to participate against each other in any number of sports. These allied conferences can have significant financial resources of their own and have detailed revenue distributions requirements as noted in the following excerpt from the *Pacific 10 Conference Handbook* (1984):

> *Postseason Football Income.* A member institution which participates in a postseason football game may choose between the following two revenue-sharing alternatives:
>
> (a) The participating institution will be provided a travel

allowance equal to the cost of round trip air coach fares for 150 persons. The remaining revenue will be divided into 11 equal shares, with the participating institution receiving two shares and the other nine Conference members receiving one share each; or

(b) The participating institution may elect to receive actual gross receipts from the bowl to a maximum of $450,000, with the remaining revenue being divided equally among the Conference's ten members.

FINANCIAL DISTRIBUTION

1. Football Ticket Settlement. Financial settlement of traditional rival football games shall consist of 50–50 split of the net receipts with a minimum guarantee of $75,000 and a maximum payout of $200,000.

2. Basketball Ticket Settlement. Financial settlement of traditional rival basketball games shall consist of a 50–50 split of the net receipts with no minimum guarantee or maximum payout. Financial settlement of all other Conference basketball games shall consist of a 50–50 split of the net receipts with a minimum guarantee of $7,500 and a maximum payout of $20,000.

3. Football Television. Television income resulting from an appearance by a member institution in the NCAA Football Television Plan (other than exception telecasts), after the NCAA assessment, will be divided among the Conference members according to the following formulae:

National Game of the Week (Conference Game):
40% to Pacific-10 participants
60% to Pacific-10 members (divided 10 ways)
EXAMPLE: Total payoff of $1,100,000. Two Conference participants each receive $286,000. Eight Conference non-participants each receive $66,000.

National Game of the Week (Non-Conference Game):
50% to Pacific-10 participant
50% to Pacific-10 members (divided 10 ways)
EXAMPLE: Total payoff of $1,100,000. Non-Conference participant receives $550,000. Conference participant receives $302,500. Nine Conference non-participants each receive $27,500.

Split National Game of the Week (Conference Game):
50% to Pacific-10 participants
50% to Pacific-10 members (divided 10 ways)
EXAMPLE: Total payoff of $850,000. Two conference participants each receive $255,000. Eight Conference non-participants each receive $42,500.

Split National Game of the Week (Non-Conference Game):
55% to Pacific-10 participant
45% to Pacific-10 members (divided 10 ways)
EXAMPLE: Total payoff of $850,000. Non-Conference participant receives $425,000. Conference participant receives $252,875. Nine Conference non-participants each receive $19,125.

Regional Game of the Week (Conference Game):
60% to Pacific-10 participants
40% to Pacific-10 members (divided 10 ways)
EXAMPLE: Total payoff of $600,000. Two Conference participants each receive $204,000. Eight Conference non-participants each receive $24,000.

Regional Game of the Week (Non-Conference Game):
60% to Pacific-10 participant
40% to Pacific-10 members (divided 10 ways)
EXAMPLE: Total payoff of $600,000. Non-Conference participants each receive $300,000. Conference participant receives $192,000. Nine Conference non-participants each receive $12,000.

Supplemental Series Game (Conference Game):
60% to Pacific-10 participant
40% to Pacific-10 members (divided 10 ways)
EXAMPLE: Total payoff of $350,000. Two Conference participants each receive $119,000. Eight Conference non-participants each receive $14,000.

Supplemental Series Game (Non-Conference Game):
60% to Pacific-10 participant
40% to Pacific-10 members (divided 10 ways)
EXAMPLE: Total payoff of $350,000. Non-Conference participant receives $175,000. Conference participant receives $112,000. Nine Conference non-participants each receive $7,000.

b. Incentive Fees. Incentive fees paid by the television networks for moving a site and/or date of a football game for television purposes shall be retained by the participating institution(s) and not included within the Conference's distribution of television revenue.

c. Lighting Expenses. The cost for providing necessary lighting to make an appearance on the NCAA supplemental football television series shall be deducted from the television revenue as an expense item and the remainder of the television revenues shall be distributed as per the formula set forth in this regulation.

d. Distribution of Receipts. Television income resulting from an appearance by a member institution in the NCAA Football Television Plan (other than exception telecasts) shall be sent to the Executive Director by the participating or host member institution. The Executive Director shall invest the pooled monies and the accrued interest shall be used to decrease the assessment for Pacific-10 membership. The Executive Director shall then distribute the original monies as per the formula set forth in this regulation to the member institutions.

4. Basketball Television. Television income resulting from an appearance by a member institution in the Conference's basketball television packages shall be shared, with 50% of the appearance fee going to the participant and the remaining 50% being divided equally among the ten members.

5. Football Postseason Income. A member institution which participates in a postseason football game may choose from between the following two alternatives:

(a) The participating institution will be provided a travel allowance equal to the cost of round trip air coach fares for 150 persons. The remaining revenue will be divided into 11 equal shares, with the participating institution receiving two shares and the other nine members receiving one share each; or

(b) The participating institution may elect to receive actual gross receipts from the bowl to a maximum of $450,000, with the remaining revenue being divided equally among the Conference's ten members.

6. Basketball Postseason Income.

a. NCAA Tournament. A member institution which participates in the NCAA basketball tournament shall receive $60,000 for competing in the first and/or second round, an additional $70,000 for competing in the regionals, and an additional $80,000 for competing in the Final Four. The remaining revenue will be divided equally among the Conference's ten members. The participating institution may retain all expense monies provided by the NCAA.

b. NIT Tournament. All revenue derived from the NIT basketball tournament shall be retained by the participating institution unless it reaches the semifinals or finals in New York; in that event that revenue will be distributed 60% to the participant and 40% to be shared equally by the Conference's ten members.

7. Complimentary Ticket Policies. Tickets for purchases by the visiting school will be requested in the sports of football and basketball. For all other sports the host Director of Athletics will honor a complimentary ticket request for a maximum of 30, except for baseball, which shall have a maximum of 50, and track and field which shall have a maximum of 75.

2. For further information on the subjects covered concerning the NCAA in the previous section, see the following articles:

(a) "Heading for the Big Time," *New Jersey Monthly,* September 1984, p. 82; details the upgrading of the Rutgers University football program and the associated costs.

(b) "NCAA Admits Difficulty in Catching Violators of Recruiting and Financial-Aid Regulations," *Chronicle of Higher Education,* September 5, 1984, p. 29.

(c) "Sports Boosters Help, and Sometimes Hurt, Major College Teams," *Wall Street Journal,* October 29, 1982, p. 1.

(d) "College Fund-Raisers Seek Winning Edge," *Omaha Sunday World-Herald,* January 31, 1982, p. C1.

(e) "Large Expenses for Sports Programs Lead More Colleges to Seek Funds from Donors," *Chronicle of Higher Education,* March 3, 1982, p. 5.

(f) "Colleges Come to Grips With '80's," *Boston Globe,* June 22, 1980, p. 70.

(g) "Television Footing the Bill for Huge NCAA

Payoffs," (AP Wireservice), *Asbury Park (N.J.) Press,* March 3, 1985, p. C13.

(h) "NCAA Surveys Drug Use," *New York Times,* March 17, 1985, Sec. 5, p. 3.

(i) "BC Goes Big Time," *Boston Globe Magazine,* November 25, 1984, p. 10.

3. For information on the National Association Intercollegiate Athletics (NAIA), see *Williams* v. *Hamilton,* 497 F. Supp. 641 (D.N.H. 1980), in which it is noted that:

.... NAIA is a voluntary association of 512 four-year colleges ranging in size from small (500) to moderate (1100), whose primary purpose as set forth in its constitution is "to promote the development of athletics as a sound part of the educational offerings of member institutions." The member institutions of NAIA pay dues to the Association, which are scaled by enrollment. Among other things, NAIA sets standards for recruiting and eligibility, and it sponsors post-season national championships in various collegiate sports, including soccer.

NAIA is divided into several districts, each of which is governed by a "District Executive Committee." Each district has voting representation at NAIA's Annual National Convention, at which time policy decisions are made. Also at the National Convention delegates vote for new members of the National Executive Committee, the overall governing body of NAIA....

4. For information on the National Junior College Athletic Association (NJCAA), see *Stats Ex. Rel National Junior College Athletic Ass'n.* v. *Luten,* 492, S.W. 2d 404 (Mo. Ct. App. 1973), in which it is noted that:

The National Junior College Athletic Association (hereinafter NJCAA) is a not-for-profit corporation which coordinates the scheduling and playing of intercollegiate athletics among its members schools. In 1971–72 it had 513 member schools who agree to "supervise and to control athletics sponsored by this corporation so that they will be administered in accordance with the eligibility rules ... set forth in the ... By Laws." Among its functions it issues and enforces rules relating to the eligibility of students at its schools participating in intercollegiate athletics....

5. In 1985, the *Sporting News,* in a major examination of the status of the NCAA in American sports, noted these eight major areas of concern: amateurism, cohesion, drugs, enforcement, finances, recruiting, scholarship, and television. See "What's the Future of the NCAA?" *Sporting News,* June 3, 1985, p. 16.

National Federation of State High School Associations (NFSHSA)

The National Federation consists of the 50 individual state high school athletic and/or activities associations and the association of the District of Columbia. Also affiliated are nine interscholastic organizations from the Canadian Provinces of Alberta, British Columbia, Manitoba, New Brunswick, Newfoundland-Labrador, Nova Scotia, Ontario, Prince Edward Island and Saskatchewan, as well as the Canadian School Sports Federation and the associations of the Republic of the Philippines, Okinawa, Guam and St. Thomas.

These associations have united to secure the benefits of cooperative action which eliminate unnecessary duplication of effort and which increase efficiency through the pooling and coordinating of ideas of all who are engaged in the administration of high school athletic and activities programs.

The national organization had its beginning in a meeting at Chicago on May 14, 1920. L. W. Smith, secretary of the Illinois High School Athletic Association, issued invitations to neighboring states, and state association representatives came from Illinois, Indiana, Iowa, Michigan and Wisconsin. The primary purpose of the meeting was to discuss problems which had resulted from high school contests which were organized by colleges and universities or by other clubs or promoters. In many cases, little attention was paid to the eligibility rules of the high school associations or to other school group regulations, and chaotic conditions had developed. At this first meeting, it was decided that the welfare of the high school required that a more active part in the control of such athletic activities be exercised by the high school through the state associations, and this control necessitated the formation of a national organization. A Constitution and Bylaws were adopted, and the group decided on the name "Midwest Federation of State High School Athletic Associations." Principal George Edward Marshall, Davenport, Iowa, was elected president, and Principal L. W. Smith of Joliet, Illinois, was elected secretary-treasurer.

In 1921, four states, Illinois, Iowa, Michigan and Wisconsin, continued their interest and became charter members through formal ratification of the constitution. Largely due to their efforts, the national organization grew during the early years.

In 1922, the Chicago annual meeting was attended by representatives from 11 states, and the name of the National Federation of State High School Athletic Associations was adopted. A number of college and university representatives who attended the meeting expressed sympathy for an interest in the efforts to introduce a high degree of order in the regulation of interscholastic contests.

Since that time, the National Federation has had a healthy growth to its present nationwide membership. By 1940, a national office with a full-time executive staff became necessary, and such office was established in September of that year.

The legislative body is the National Council made up of one representative from each member state association. Each representative must be a state association chief executive officer or governing board member. The executive body is the Executive Committee of at least eight members from the eight territorial sections as outlined in the Constitution. Their election is by the National Council at its summer meeting.

The purpose of the National Federation of State High School Associations is to coordinate the efforts of its member state associations toward the ultimate objectives of interscholastic activities. It shall provide a means for state high school associations to cooperate in order to enhance and protect their interscholastic programs. In order to accomplish this, the National Federation is guided by a philosophy consistent with the accepted purposes of secondary education. Member state associations' programs must be administered in accordance with the following basic beliefs:

> Interscholastic activities shall be an integral part of the total secondary school educational program which has as its purpose to provide educational experiences not otherwise provided in the curriculum, which will develop learning outcomes in the areas of knowledge, skills and emotional patterns and will contribute to the development of better citizens. Emphasis shall be upon teaching "through" activities in addition to teaching the skills of activities.

> Interschool activities shall be primarily for the benefit of the high school students who participate directly and vicariously in them. The interscholastic activity program shall exist mainly for the value which it has for students and not for the benefit of the sponsoring institutions. The activities and contests involved shall be psychologically sound by being tailored to the physical, mental and emotional maturity levels of the youth participating in them....

> The state high school associations and the National Federation shall be concerned with the development of those standards, policies and regulations essential to assist their member schools in the implementation of their philosophy of interscholastic activities.

> Nonschool activities sponsored primarily for the benefit of the participants in accordance with a philosophy compatible with the school philosophy of interscholastics may have values for youth. When they do not interfere with the academic and interscholastic programs and do not result in exploitation of youth, they shall be considered as a worthwhile supplement to interschool activities.

> The welfare of the school demands a united front in sports direction policies and the high school associations provide opportunity for this unity. They must be kept strong.

The NFSHSA's 1984 budget was $3.25 million, of which 62 percent came from the sale of printed materials and publications. Membership dues from state associations (not schools) only total $14,000.

NOTE _____

1. For further information on the NFSHSA, see *1984–85 Handbook,* National Federation of State High School Association, Kansas City, Mo. (1984).

International Olympic Committee (IOC)

The International Olympic Committee (IOC):

> ... governs the Olympic movement and exercises all rights over the Olympic Games. Every organization that plays any part in the Olympic movement must accept the authority of the IOC and be bound by the rules of the IOC.

Since the revival of the Olympic Games in 1896, the International Olympic Committee (IOC) has enforced a strict amateur code for athletes to be eligible to participate, which on occasion has given rise to litigation from athletes seeking to participate. However, in 1982, the IOC relaxes its rules and asked the individual amateur governing bodies, such as the International Football Federation, which governs the sport of soccer, to propose their own eligibility codes. At the 1984 Winter Olympic Games at Sarajevo, Yugoslavia, IOC president Juan Antonio Samaranch said: "I think the IOC must do its best to give to all the athletes from all over the world and from all the political systems the same right to participate in the Games. We are going step by step, bit by bit, but I should like to say that I wish we could go faster."

Rule 26 of the *Olympic Charter 1985,* which was instituted in 1982, to effect the change in emphasis reads:

> A competitor must observe and abide by the rules of the IOC and in addition, his or her international federation as approved by the IOC, even if the federation's rules are more strict than those of the IOC.
>
> A competitor must not have received any financial rewards or material benefit in connection with his or her sports participation except as permitted in the bylaws to this rule.

In 1985, the IOC moved even further in relaxing its eligibility rules by voting to allow professionals under the age of 23 to participate in the 1988 Winter and Summer Olympic Games in the sports of tennis, ice hockey, and soccer. Samaranch noted that: "This decision is only for 1988. After 1988 we will see. The Olympic movement must go with the times."

One major problem for the IOC, which has led to some litigation in American courts, has been the boycotting of the Olympic Games for political reasons by various countries, most significantly the United States in 1980 (Moscow Summer Games) and the Soviet Union in 1984 (Los Angeles Summer Games). The problem facing the IOC is that participation in the Olympics is volun-

tary and not compulsory. However, some have proposed that the IOC penalize countries that boycott the Olympic Games by restricting future participation.

Chapters 1 and 2 examine the Olympic movement in regards to how the American court system has handled litigation involving the governance authority of the IOC, the U.S. Olympic Committee (USOC), and the national governing bodies (NGBs) and the rights of individual Olympic athletes.

NOTES

1. For further information on the IOC and the Olympic Games, see the following articles:

(a) "Amateur Athletes: Some More Equal Than Others," *New York Times,* August 8, 1983, p. C1.

(b) "Pro-Logue to 1984—The IOC Confronts 'Creeping Professionalism,'" *Boston Globe,* March 13, 1983, p. 61.

(c) Olympics to Allow Pros in 3 Sports," *New York Times,* March 1, 1985, p. A19.

(d) "IOC Reaffirms Solid Authority of Olympic Games," *The Olympian,* February 1985, p. 24.

United States Olympic Committee (USOC)

The United States Olympic Committee (USOC) is the National Olympic Committee for the United States, representing the country's interest with the IOC. The USOC is recognized as the United States NOC pursuant to IOC Rule 24. The court in *U.S. Wrestling Federation* v. *Wrestling Div. of the AAU* noted that:

> ...each nation wishing to participate in the Olympic Games must maintain the National Olympic Committee ("NOC") recognized by the IOC. Each NOC must enforce the rules and bylaws of the IOC. The IOC recognizes the USOC as the NOC for the United States.

The USOC was formed as:

> ...a corporation chartered by the United States Congress in 1950. P.L. 81–805 (81st Cong. 2d Sess.) September 21, 1950; 64 Stat. 889. In 1978, the USOC Congressional Charter was amended by a legislative enactment popularly called "The Amateur Sports

Act of 1978." P.L. 95–606 (95th Cong. 2d Sess.) November 8, 1978; 92 Stat. 3045 ("the Act"). USOC's principal place of business is located at Colorado Springs, Colorado, and it operates in all fifty states and the District of Columbia.

The USOC operates an Olympic Training Center in Colorado Springs, Colorado. Funds for the center come primarily from corporate sponsorship. For example, the Miller Brewing Company donated $3.3 million to sponsor the Olympic Training Center in the quadrennial leading up to the 1984 Olympic Games in Los Angeles. An additional $15,081,900 was raised from corporate funds and other income sources, and the money was distributed by the USOC to the various national governing bodies to support their operations. The distribution was as follows:

Sport	Amount
Archery	$236,000
Baseball	176,300
Men's Basketball	205,800
Women's Basketball	216,900
Biathion	249,600
Bobsled	330,600
Boxing	325,000
Canoeing/Kayaking	397,000
Cycling	387.000
Diving	260,000
Equestrian	312,900
Fencing	422,600
Men's Field Hockey	361,400
Women's Field Hockey	346,600
Figure Skating	375,000
Men's Gymnastics	159,300
Women's Gymnastics	156,600
Rhythmic Gymnastics	74,500
Hockey	409,300
Men's Judo	217,400
Women's Judo	130,000
Luge	297,900
Modern Pentathion	233,000
Roller Skating	259,600
Men's Rowing	505,900
Women's Rowing	436,400
Shooting	409,500
Alpine Skiing	248,700
Nordic Skiing	413,100
Soccer	340,000
Men's Softball	133,200
Women's Softball	133,200
Speed Skating	429,700
Swimming	760,900
Synchronized Swimming	206,100
Table Tennis	184,400
Men's Team Handball	262,700
Women's Team Handball	262,700
Tennis	175,700
Men's Track & Field	943,800
Women's Track & Field	742,900
Men's Volleyball	228,300
Women's Volleyball	216,900
Water Polo	333,200
Weightlifting	333,900
Wrestling	448,300
Yachting	390,100

In comparison, between 1961 and 1964, the total development money distributed by the USOC was only $50,000. From 1965 to 1968, the sum was $300,000; from 1969 to 1972 it was $800,000; from 1973 to 1976 it was $2.2 million; and from 1977 to 1980 it was $99.2 million.

As with other amateur athletic associations, the USOC is very concerned about increasing drug use in sports. The USOC in 1985 decided to upgrade its drug-testing program to include every major athletic competition it sanctions prior to the Olympic Games, with stiff penalties for violations. The testing for drugs and controversies over drug test results may bring about increased litigation for the Olympic movement.

NOTE ————————————————

1. For more information about the USOC's concern over drug abuse in sports, see "USOC to Seek More Tests for Drugs," *New York Times,* March 24, 1985, Sec. 5, p. 1.

National Sport Governing Bodies (NGB)

The IOC, in addition to recognizing an NOC in each participating nation, also designates an International Federation which governs each Olympic sport. The International Federation establishes rules and regulations for the sport it governs, including eligibility rules for athletes. The International Federation also elects one amateur organization from each nation as its affiliate member for that nation. The selected national amateur organization is the sport's National Governing Body (NGB) for Olympic competition.

The court in *U.S. Wrestling Federation* v. *Wrestling Dir. of the AAU* noted that:

> IOC by-law V(5) to Rule 24 provides that a NOC (such as the USOC) "must not accept as members more than one national federation for each sport, and that federation must be affiliated to the relevant (international federation) recognized by the IOC."

Pursuant to its Congressional Charter and the published rules and regulations of the International Olympic Committee, the USOC recognizes one United States amateur sports organization as the national governing body ("NGB") for each Olympic sport, 36 U.S.C. section 391. The national governing body ("NGB") so recognized is the member in the United States of the international sports federation recognized by the International Olympic Committee for the purpose of administering the competitions on the Olympic program. USOC Const. Art. IV, section 4. Each NGB so recognized is the USOC's "Group A" member for its sport.

Under Section 203 of the Amateur Sports Act, 36 U.S.C. section 393, each USOC-recognized NGB is authorized to exercise certain powers, including without limitation representing the United States in the international sports federation for its particular sport.

In 1985, U.S. Committee Executive Director F. Don Miller announced that each of the United States' 38 NGBs would receive $1.132 million from the USOC from the $215 million surplus generated by the 1984 Los Angeles Olympic Games. These funds are in addition to the funds the USOC will make available from 1985 to 1988 to the NGBs from development funds, performance enhancement funds, and other resources.

NOTES _____

1. For further information on the USOC's distribution of its surplus funds, see the following article: "National Governing Bodies Will Receive $1,131,579 Each (at Least) from USOC's Share of Surplus from Olympic Games," *The Olympian*, February 1985, p. 22.

2. Typical of organization and governance powers on an NGB are those of the USA Amateur Boxing Federation which follow:

ARTICLE: NATIONAL GOVERNING BODY FOR AMATEUR BOXING IN THE UNITED STATES OF AMERICA

210.1 National Governing Body Powers. This corporation shall be the National Governing Body (NGB) for the sport of Amateur Boxing in the United States and shall exercise the following powers:

(a) Represent the United States in the AIBA.

(b) Establish national goals and encourage the attainment of those goals in the sport of boxing.

(c) Serve as the coordinating body for amateur athletic activity in the sport of boxing in the United States.

(d) Exercise jurisdiction over international amateur boxing and activities and sanction international amateur boxing competition held in the United States and sanction the sponsorship of international amateur boxing competition held outside the United States in the sport of boxing, in accordance with the provisions of these by-laws.

(e) Conduct amateur athletic competition in the sport of boxing, including national championships, and international amateur athletic competition in the United States, and establish procedures for the determination of elibility standards for the participation in such competitions, except for restricted competition referred to in the proviso herein below.

(f) Recommended to the United States Olympic Committee individuals and teams to represent the United States in the Olympic Games and Pan American Games in the sport of boxing.

(g) Designate individuals and teams to represent the United States in international amateur boxing competition (other than the Olympic and Pan American Games) in the sport of boxing and certify, in accordance with the rules of the AIBA, the amateur eligibility of such individuals and teams.

210.2 Proviso: That any sport organization which conducts amateur boxing competition, participation in which is restricted to a specific class of amateur athletes (such as high school students, college students, members of the Armed Forces or similar groups or categories), shall have exclusive jurisdiction over such competition. If such an amateur sports organization wishes to conduct international amateur boxing competition to be held in the United States, or sponsor international amateur boxing competition to be held outside the United States, it shall obtain a sanction from this corporation as herein provided.

210.3 Autonomy. This corporation shall be autonomous in its governance of the sport of boxing in that it independently shall determine and control all matters central to such governance, shall not delegate such determination and control, and shall be free from outside restraint. This provision shall not be construed as preventing this corporation from contracting with third parties for administrative assistance and support, in connection with its purposes. [*1981–84 USA Amateur Boxing Federation,* Article 12, p. 38]

The Pressure to Succeed: Impact on Coaches

The pressure to succeed in intercollegiate athletics forces a head coach and his staff to spend enormous amounts of time and money in developing a quality program, particularly in recruiting "blue chip" athletes. Maryland football coach Bobby Ross once said, "I'm not that good a coach that I can do it without the players." In explaining Boston College's system, football recruiting coordinator Barry Gallup stated: "We have a mailing list of 250, but some of the bigger programs have a much larger list."

Recruiting becomes a year-round enterprise. There is extensive travel by the staff, numerous phone calls and letters, and on-campus visits by potential players. The costs of recruiting can be enormous, and there is no guarantee that the sought-after recruits will eventually agree to attend the recruiter's institution. The athlete being recruited may visit a number of different institutions and then decide which one to attend to the exclusion of the other schools. Such uncertainty can cause a coach to look for an edge on other recruiters by providing extra inducements to the recruited athlete not allowed under NCAA rules.

The need for "blue chip" athletes has forced coaches to search worldwide for athletes. Basketball, soccer, and track and field coaches have all gone abroad to recruit athletes. The potential for abuse and confusion is greater in situations where language problems, customs, distance, and ignorance of the NCAA's rules exist. Worldwide recruiting can also prove diplomatically embarrassing. In the past, recruiters have been accused of paying recruits from other countries, among them ath-

letes who have deserted military service to enroll at American schools, to attend their institutions. Recruiters have also been accused of falsifying immigration records in order to get the recruited athlete into the country.

The problems associated with the recruitment of student-athletes and their continued athletic and academic eligibility while attending school have come under increasing examination by many of the individual schools' chief executive officers. James H. Zumberge, president of the University of Southern California, made this observation:

> Several institutions of higher learning, USC among them, have come under recent scrutiny for rules violations in the area of intercollegiate athletics. These violations appear to have been the result of malfeasance by a small number of individuals. Nevertheless, the fact that so many similar incidents should have occurred, at so many institutions, suggests that higher education may well have come to a turning point in its relationship to competitive sports. It would seem that the pressures demanding performance, in many instances, have overwhelmed the forces of responsibility and integrity within the system as a whole and within the institutions in question.

At USC an advisory committee studied these problems and in their investigative report to President Zumberge noted that:

> Higher education today may have reached a crossroads in its relationship to big-time athletics. The major spectator sports have taken on an existence and momentum entirely of their own and drifted away from the procedures and academic philosophies of the institutions which spawned them. If the present trend is allowed to continue, the potential exists for gradually undermining the integrity and credibility of the educational enterprise as a whole. Therefore, individual institutions, and the intercollegiate athletic system of which they are a part, must explore ways of restoring clear purposes and goals for competitive sports which are consistent with broader educational purposes and societal needs.

The pressures noted above, which are associated with big-time athletic recruiting and administration, take a terrific toll on the individual coaches who work under them on a daily basis. "I was on a treadmill," former University of Notre Dame football coach Ara Parseghian recalls. "You go from fall season to recruiting to fund raising to golf outings back to fall season again. The pressure I felt was just immense. There's no way to explain what your stomach feels like every day of the week." Bill Battle, former football coach at Tennessee, described the pressure in this way:

It was the staggering investment of time with uncertain results, particularly the endless recruiting dance, which I found "insane, bordering on ridiculous." You want to do what you have to do to beat the competition, so you invest months of time and effort into recruiting a prospect. Then he starts to lean the other way and you try to do what you have to do, within the bounds of your own ethics and morality, to keep him interested. I finally decided I didn't want to spend that much time trying to sign 17- and 18-year olds that your livelihood depended upon who were not necessarily the most stable guys in the world.

Marv Harshman, who retired as basketball coach of the University of Washington after the 1984–85 season, had this to say:

In the old days, I don't think any school expected to make money. Now sports has become like the professional arm of a school. We have 22 men and women sports at Washington. The money has to come from somewhere, and that somewhere is football and basketball.

I used to enjoy recruiting and talking to the youngsters, but I stopped liking it when it turned into a salesman's job. Everybody is looking for something. ...a lot of assistants will tell them anything because their job is to get players.

Joe Mullaney, who retired as basketball coach at Providence College after the 1984–85 season, noted:

Everybody has to win these days and nobody can afford to lose. It has changed recruiting....I feel sorry for assistant coaches. Recruiting is a tough way to pay your dues in order to become a head coach.

The continuous pressure on coaches exhibits itself in many ways. Fred Jacoby, executive officer of the Southwest Conference, notes that even game officials are not spared:

What a coach gets paid in salary and what he realizes is so much greater. There is a shoe endorsement, camps, clinics and speaking engagements. When a coach jumps all over an official, it's like he's saying "you're meddling with my income."

Such pressures may have led to the one-game suspension during the 1984–85 season of Indiana coach Bobby Knight, who received that penalty for tossing a chair across a basketball court after a displeasing call by an official.

Indicative of the problems facing intercollegiate athletics was the 1985 scandal involving the Baylor University basketball team. In that sad incident, Baylor basketball coach Jim Haller was secretly recorded by one of his players, reserve center John Wheeler, as he gave Wheeler a university check for $172 to make car payments and talked of having the strength coach dispense anabolic steroids to Wheeler. Coach Haller, who resigned at the end of the season, later stated:

... in my mind I know how I've lived my life and I'm not going to apologize to anybody for it. I'm not going to apologize except for a couple of situations I got myself into here lately.

...It wasn't going to help me. It wasn't gong to help our basketball team. I was doing it to help an individual.

The pressure on coaches is not limited to coaches of men's sports. With the development and expansion of women's athletic programs, female coaches have also experienced pressure. Former Louisiana Tech women's basketball Coach Sonja Hogg has stated that "there is tremendous pressure—it's do or die." Indicative of the year-long nature of recruiting is the statement of Marianne Stanley, women's basketball coach at Old Dominion University, who noted, "The camps [summer] are so valuable. I can see 250 kids at one time" The pressure may be even greater for women's sports coaches because of smaller recruiting budgets and less available information. However, at least one coach, Linda Sharp of the University of Southern California, has stated that the pressure has not reached an uncomfortable level. Sharp, who snared Cheryl Miller, the top female recruit in 1982, had this to say:

> Even though there were teams from all over the country competing for her, I don't think she received the same intense recruiting pressure as, say, a Patrick Ewing did, or a Ralph Sampson.
>
> The other day, I understood one of our assistant men's coaches had been gone eight days trying to recruit a player, watching him play in state playoffs, letting him know they're very, very interested.
>
> I haven't done that—haven't sent an assistant out for eight days just to get one individual.

Recruiting violations, sanctions against coaches and institutions, and the use of ineligible players are all sources of litigation in intercollegiate athletics. How the courts view such litigation and the effect it has on amateur athletic associations is examined in Chapter 1. Chapter 2 focuses on how these areas can affect the rights and remedies under the law of individual athletes and how courts have decided the complex and conflicting interests involved. Chapter 3 discusses the rise in intercollegiate athletic opportunities for women and the current problems that face women in athletics. Chapter 4 examines the many tort liability questions that affect coaches and athletic administrators. Chapter 5 discusses several criminal law considerations such as assault and battery, gambling, drugs, and alcohol. Chapter 6 explores the various legal issues involving the broadcasting of sporting events.

NOTES _____

1. For more information on the topics discussed above, see the following articles:

(a) "A Case of Win or Else," *Sporting News,* April 21, 1979, p. 14.

(b) "Coaches Find Recruiting Pays," *Boston Globe,* February 3, 1984, p. 42.

(c) "Sign Here, Kid," *Boston Globe,* February 3, 1984, p. 7A (about a recruit's trips to inspect and evaluate Duke and Maryland and his decision to stay at home and attend Boston College).

(d) "Texas-El Paso's Use of Foreigners Raises Questions," *New York Times,* March 21, 1982, p. 85.

(e) "The Fine Art of Recruiting Superstars for Big-Time Women's Basketball," *Chronicle of Higher Education,* March 30, 1983, p. 21.

(f) "Texas A&M Goes All Out in Recruiting," *USA Today,* February 11, 1983, p. 16.

(g) "Recruiting Now Favors the Rich," *Boston Globe,* Series on Women and the NCAA, May 5, 1983, p. 67.

(h) "Retiring Coaches Have Roots in Basketball's Simpler Past," *New York Times,* March 24, 1985, Sec. 5, p. 8.

(i) "Out with a Roar," *Dallas Times Herald,* March 9, 1985, p. C1.

(j) "A Better Game Heightens Pressure on Officials," *New York Times,* March, 3, 1985, Sec. 5, p. 1.

(k) "Knight Gets 1-Game Suspension," (AP Wireservice), *Ashbury Park (N.J.) Press,* March 3, 1985, p. C10.

(l) "Coaches, Players Split on Tougher Probation Penalties," *USA Today,* February 27, 1985, p. C3.

2. Also see *Academic Conduct, Admission, Advisement and Counseling of Student Athletes at the University of Southern California,* James H. Zumberge, president, USC, October 12, 1980.

The Pressure to Succeed: Impact on Institutions

Bill L. Atchley, former president of Clemson University, noted a few years ago that:

> The NCAA regulations remind me of the proverbial horse that was put together by a committee, and ended up as a camel. This complex body of rules must be streamlined and then disseminated with a strong educational campaign directed not only at college coaching and recruiting staffs, but also at potential recruits.

Clemson has had its share of trouble with the NCAA, including sanctions against its football team for illegal recruitment of athletes. In 1985, yet another scandal hit the Clemson athletic program, this time involving the dispensing of illegal drugs to student-athletes by Clemson coaches. Atchley resigned as an indirect result of the scandal after the University's board of trustees refused to remove the Clemson athletic director, Bill McLellan, as Dr. Atchley recommended they do because of the continuing problems with the program under McLellan.

Clemson University is not alone in having problems with its athletic department. In August 1980, the University of Southern California (USC) and four other Pacific Athletic Conference (PAC-10) member institutions had their football programs disqualified from the PAC-10 football championship. The penalty was imposed by the presidents and chancellors of the conference schools. Although the penalty was for academic violations, the study commissioned by USC following the sanction was charged with investigating all aspects of the USC athletic department. Some excerpts from that report dealing with the areas of recruitment and admissions are reprinted here:

The present crisis appears to be related to at least five major weaknesses. All of these, to one degree or another, have been manifested in the recent so-called "scandals" besetting intercollegiate athletics. Some of these weaknesses have been prevalent at USC.

First, institutional and individual integrity has not always guided action. Colleges and universities have too often taken advantage of athletes either through failing to assist those with marginal skills or failing to confront the less able early in their academic careers with an awareness that academic success may not be viable. Too often, the practice has been to admit athletes with marginal academic motivations and abilities, permit them to drift through the curriculum and, once athletic eligibility is used up, to cast them aside with neither a degree nor much hope of attaining one. The failure to offer opportunities and incentives to students to become academically successful is itself a weakness. But, the failure to confront a student-athlete early with the realities of his or her true potential for academic survival is unethical. Such practices are tantamount to exploitations and are unacceptable.

A second prominent weakness has been a failure to understand the seriousness of the present situation. A similar shakeup in college sports occurred during the early 1950s as a result of recruiting violations and classroom cheating. The proportions of the national scandal in 1980 are substantially larger and far less innocent. Today's scenario includes not only cheating and recruiting violations, but manipulations of courses by faculty and coaches, forgery of admissions credentials by outside "merchants," financial mis-

management by athletic program administrators, and more.

A third weakness has been a failure to comprehend the significance of changes that have occurred in competitive sports in America during the past three decades. Colleges and universities today must come to grips with these changes because they are the source of the malaise that afflicts intercollegiate athletics today. The earlier brief crisis of the 50s came at a time when national television played a small part; when pro-football and basketball were in a fledgling state, and big-time professional tennis and golf were almost unimaginable; when the largest pro-contracts might total $30,000 per year and agents to negotiate them were non-existent; when the egalitarian "Great Society" reforms of the 60s, which broadened higher education's accessibility, had not yet begun; when literacy levels in elementary and secondary schools were not declining; and, when Las Vegas-style gambling on collegiate sports outcomes was less prominent. Higher education must begin to comprehend the implications of these major developments if it is to begin to deal more adequately with the present crisis.

A fourth common weakness is that of failing to understand more clearly the purposes served by intercollegiate athletics. Much has been made of the importance of intercollegiate sports for institutional name recognition and fund raising. Such purposes, while often part of the institutional *raison d'etre* for sponsorship, have been largely overstated in comparison to the many individual and social values that are derived. Consequently, intercollegiate athletics have remained curiously tangential and their status indefinite. What often has been projected by institutions is doubt, uncertainty, and ambivalence about the relationship between higher education and athletics.

Excellence on the field and excellence in the classroom are not inherently incompatible. Indeed, they often are mutually reinforcing in individual development. The rapid acquisitions of new skills; the management of time and energy; the development of collaborative abilities; the development, clarification, and testing of values; and the testing of personal limits of physical and psychological endurance encountered in athletic competition all provide rare learning opportunities for the student-athlete.

Intercollegiate athletics also serve broader institutional and social interests. The role played by sports in providing a common meeting ground, in overcoming racial barriers, and in bridging the generations often have been overlooked and/or significantly understated. The importance of play in human life and education also has too often been given short shrift in discussions of the role of sports. More precision about these and other positive aspects of intercollegiate athletics should help clarify both their relationship to higher education and the reasons for institutional commitment to athletes and athletic competition.

Fifth, strong university leadership has been lacking. Presidents, coaches, athletic directors, admissions officers, academic deans, advisors, and faculty—everyone connected with the enterprise—must share in the responsibility for individual and institutional conduct. Too often, there has been a tendency to adopt an attitude of *laissez faire* toward athletes and athletics. This attitude has permitted drift within the system when the mounting pressures and abuses have called for firm action. Each individual, and most certainly presidents of institutions, must accept more active responsibility than in the past for the tenor and conduct of intercollegiate athletics within individual institutions and the system as a whole....

PRINCIPLES AND RESPONSIBILITIES OF PROPER CONDUCT

These weaknesses notwithstanding, it is abundantly clear that there is far more that is positive about intercollegiate athletics today than negative. Proper reforms, diligently implemented, can have immediate, positive effects in reversing the general drift and restoring the public's confidence in the capacity of higher education for self-correction and ethical control....

University Conduct

1. Admission standards and procedures for student-athletes should be fully consistent with University-wide standards and procedures for all students.

2. All matters of eligibility and academic progress must be under the direct supervision and control of faculty and staff outside the department of athletics....

REFORMS AND ACTIONS

Admissions

6. Responsibility for the admission of all students (including athletes) shall rest solely with the Office of Admissions acting in accordance with established University policies and procedures governing appeals and referrals.

7. The Admission Policy of the University of Southern California is to identify students who can both contribute to, and benefit from, its special ambiance by their individual excellence and intellectual promise. Admission to USC is not determined by a rigid formula. University-wide admissions standards are presently under discussion within the University Admissions Committee. A proposed policy governing regular admission has been forwarded to the President's Advisory Council. The Admission Committee will consider policies governing Special Action admissions later this Fall.

In the interim, the Office of Admissions has been directed by the President to adhere to the following criteria for Special Action: Applicants falling below a minimum high school grade point standard of 2.7 on a 4.0 scale and combined Scholastic Aptitude Test scores of 800 *normally* shall not be admitted to the University. (The average freshman today enters USC with a 3.4 high school grade point average and combined SAT scores of 1040.)

However, applicants falling below these minimums may, in certain cases, be admitted by Special Action to regular standing providing such students are able to demonstrate, through admissions credentials, potential for academic success at USC. Applicants subject to Special Action consideration shall be closely evaluated, in addition to grades and SAT (or equivalent ACT) scores, on the basis of trends in past academic performance, writing samples, personal interviews, cultural factors, class rank, extracurricular involvement, intensiveness of secondary school training, and statements of teachers and counselors regarding academic potential.

Circumstances justifying Special Action review will vary, but may include special talent, i.e., musical, dramatic, athletic, and scientific. All students admitted by Special Action are required to enter an appropriately designated support program designed to encourage academic success.

8. All student-athletes transferring after two years

at a community or four-year college or university shall satisfy standard academic admission criteria without consideration of other factors that may be taken into account for students entering as freshmen.

9. The Office of Admissions shall, in conjunction with appropriate student support personnel, determine the placement of Special Action admissions within available support programs in the USC academic support system.

PROBLEM AREAS

Admission and Retention

An *Ad Hoc* Committee on Student-Athlete Advisement and Counseling was charged with examining the current status of academic advisement and counseling of student-athletes at USC and to make recommendations for improvement, if warranted.

During its deliberations, the Committee found it appropriate to expand its inquiries and recommendations to the area of University admissions criteria and practices due to the intrinsic relationship between admissions standards and the potential for academic success. Clearly, the matter of appropriate advisement and counseling for student-athletes is closely linked to standards and practices of admission.

With regard to admission and retention it has been found that:

• For several years, the University, while adhering to NCAA admission standards for athletic eligibility, admitted some athletes who fell below normal USC standards of admission. (This practice also was aplied to some non-athlete student applications.) Between 1970 and 1980, these exceptions averaged 33 student-athletes per year (in all sports).

• Academically, marginal athletes have been admitted to USC in the past based chiefly on athletic prowess as judged by the Athletic Department, and without normal Admissions Office review.

• Although the retention and graduation rate of USC student-athletes during the past decade has been approximately the same as for the undergraduate student body as a whole, only a small number of athletes admitted as exceptions have ever graduated from the University. ["Academic Conduct, Admission, Advisement and Counseling of Student-Athletes at the University of Southern California: A Report to the USC Community," October 12, 1980]

The USC report gives an overview of many of the "academic" problems associated with intercollegiate athletics. A more individual problem in intercollegiate athletics that threatens to tarnish the image of many institutions involves drug abuse among athletes. Already noted was the case involving Clemson University athletes and coaches. Also in 1985, Arizona State University became embroiled in controversy when baseball coach Jim Brock disclosed that many of his players used a mood-altering drug dispensed by a psychiatrist who serves as a part-time consultant to the program. Vanderbilt University was involved in a drug controversy in 1985—the same year that the Tulane University gambling scandal was revealed and the underlying cause was identified as being cocaine abuse by the basketball team members.

However, although an institution can put its reputation in intercollegiate athletics at stake through involvement in academic, recruiting, or other scandals, it can also enhance its reputation by well-known programs. As an example, Georgetown University's director of annual giving, Patrick J. McArdle, credits the success of Georgetown's basketball team in recent years for "geometric" increases in contributions. Estimates are that in 1984 the Georgetown basketball team generated $3 million for the school in direct revenue. The university's 33 percent increase in admissions applications since 1983 is also indirectly credited to the team's success.

In balancing the positive and negative aspects of an intercollegiate athletic program, an institution must realize that its chances of becoming embroiled in some controveigg are quite likely. Litigation is becoming more prevalent in intercollegiate athletics and should be considered a reality by any institution. Chapter 2 examines some of the problems that face institutions in regard to these controversies.

NOTE

1. For further information on the problems facing athletic departments in U.S. colleges and universities, see the following articles:

(a) "USC: The University of Special Cases," *Sports Illustrated,* October 10, 1980, p. 19.

(b) *"Keep the Pros Out of Colleges,"* New York Times, July 4, 1982, p. 76.

(c) "Drug Scandal Forces Out Clemson Head," *New York Times,* March 3, 1985, Sec. 5, p. 1.

(d) "Clemons Head Says He Quit Over Lack of Support," *New York Times,* March 7, 1985, p. B9.

(e) "What Is at Stake When an Athletic Scandal Hits?" *New York Times,* March 10, 1985, Sec. 5, p. 2.

(f) "Grand Jury Hears Results of Clemson Drug Probe," *USA Today,* March 4, 1985, p. C4.

(g) "Use of Drug Questioned," *New York Times,* March 23, 1985, p. 45.

(h) "Inquiry Ordered," *New York Times,* March 24, 1985, Sec. 5, p. 1.

(i) "Sinking Sun Devils," *New York Times,* March 14, 1985, p. 25.

(j) "Hoya Fever, Not Hay Fever," *New York Times,* March 14, 1985, p. 45.

(k) "Net Profits: How Georgetown Is Raking It In," *Business Week,* March 25, 1985, p. 52.

(l) "Two Ex-Clemson Coaches Receive Fines, Probation," *Boston Herald,* March 12, 1985, p. 56.

(m) "Drug Scandal At Clemson Linked to 'Obsession to Win,'" *USA Today,* March 12, 1985, p. C4.

(n) "NCAA Playoffs Bring Big Bucks to Big East," *New York Daily News,* March 27, 1985, p. 53.

The Pressure to Succeed: Impact on Student-Athletes

The pressure to succeed in intercollegiate athletics can also severely affect the student-athlete. In particular, the impact of recruiting violations on student-athletes can be tremendous. It can affect all aspects of their lives, education, family, and careers. Consider this statement by Alan Page, football player for the Minnesota Vikings:

We had each spent four years in colleges with decent reputations. I remember that two of us could read the playbook, three others had some trouble with it but managed, and four of my teammates couldn't read it at all. It was embarrassing.... There were no big words and not a lot of syllables. They all understood the concept when spoken, so it's not that they were dumb. I don't think you can be dumb to play football. Maybe I'm wrong, but if you can understand the intricacies of X's and O's, then you should be smart enough to learn to read and write. The problem seems to be that these athletes—and there are many more like them, blacks and whites—were never expected to learn to read and write. They've floated through up to this point because they were talented athletes.

Ned Bolcar was one of the most sought-after high school football recruits of the 1985 recruiting season. The Phillipsburg (N.J.) High School player, who finally chose Notre Dame, made this comment about his recruitment:

Intelligent players know what recruiters are trying to do. You believe some, you let some go by. But you are always polite. If people aren't polite to me, I will hang up. I don't want any pressure. They look out for their business, and I look out for mine.

Once in college, current athletes are finding a greater emphasis on academics than in the past. In 1985, Kentucky running back George Adams noted that:

Around here, they emphasize that you get the grades and that degree. We're assigned counselors, and they keep an eye on us and our grades. Coach Claiborne keeps emphasizing that life is a bigger game, and that you can't be a player all your life.

Unfortunately for some, the new emphasis on academics causes hardship. Former University of Tennessee basketball player Gary Carter was declared academically ineligible his senior year and left school without graduating. He notes that:

I found out in December of my senior year that I was ineligible. The new rule went into effect.... I was off the team. They could have put me on probation and let me get my grades up, but they didn't. It hurt because I wanted to be drafted by the NBA.

...They could have spent more time with the players and made sure they kept their grades up, rather than wait till it's too late. Athletes know they have to get the grades, and there is emphasis on grades but you could see they really wanted you to be good in basketball.

The areas of recruitment and academic eligibility

will remain a constant problem in the years ahead for athletes and litigators. Chapter 2 examines these subjects in detail, noting the various types of litigation that can be pursued by the student-athlete.

NOTES ————————————————

1. *The Collegiate Student-Athlete Protection Act of 1983,* Hearings before the Committee on the Judiciary, United States Senate, 98 Cong. 1st Sess. 1983 (Serial No. J-98-20), involved Senate Bill S.610, which was "...designed to encourage college student-athletes to complete their undergraduate education before becoming professional athletes."

2. For further information on the above subjects, see the following articles:

(a) "College 'Factories' and Their Output," *New York Times,* January 18, 1983, p. D25.

(b) "Blitzing the USA's Future All-Americans," *USA Today,* February 11, 1985, p. C1.

(c) "Recruit: That's It, Notre Dame," *USA Today,* February 13, 1985, p. C1.

(d) "Academic Push Demands More of College Athletes," *USA Today,* March 7, 1985, p. C3.

(e) "Player's Dreams Shattered by Grade Requirement Shift," *USA Today,* March 7, 1985, p. C3.

Chapter 1

AMATEUR ATHLETIC ASSOCIATIONS

1.00 Amateur Sports in the Modern Age

Amateur sports, both inside and outside educational institutions, are an integral part of American life. Increasingly, certain amateur sports bear a resemblance to big business in that the ineligibility or unavailability of an individual athlete or program can result in a large financial loss to the institution or in the forfeiture of a chance to pursue sports as a career for the athlete.

Chapters 1 and 2 analyze the impact of the law on amateur sports and define certain basic concepts. In particular, the focus is on the development and growing power of organizations that govern amateur sports. Traditionally, these organizations have avoided legal accountability, but their pervasive influence has recently led to increasing legal scrutiny. Some argue that the result has been better protection of individual rights from arbitrary or unfair actions on the part of governing organizations, institutions, schools, coaches, and teachers.

NOTES _____

1. For further information concerning the emergence of intercollegiate athletics as big business, see the following articles:

(a) "Idaho Debates Closing a Campus and Dropping Aid for Sports," *Chronicle of Higher Education*, February 23, 1981, p. 8.
(b) "Rewards for Being No. 1," *Chronicle of Higher Education*, March 16, 1981, p. 1.
(c) "Lure of TV Money May Lead Colleges to Play on Sundays during NFL Strike," *Chronicle of Higher Education*, September, 29, 1982, p. 15.
(d) "Football without Fans, Money, or TV: The Endangered Lightweight League," *Chronicle of Higher Education*, November 17, 1982, p. 15.
(e) "Louisiana State's Athletic Program Bounces Back after a Year of Turmoil," *Chronicle of Higher Education*, December 1, 1982, p. 13.
(f) "Making It to a Football Bowl Takes More Than a Good Record," *Chronicle of Higher Education*, December 1, 1982, p. 1.
(g) "College Basketball Too Business-Oriented, Some Coaches Say," *NCAA News*, April 3, 1985, p. 3.

1.10 Definitions of "Amateur"

Each individual amateur athletic association has developed its own definition of an amateur athlete. Because the line between professional and amateur is difficult to draw, these definitions overlap to some extent. Originally, many organizations refused to allow amateur athletes to receive any money at all in compensation for their time or expenses. Increasingly, however, amateur athletes are receiving certain living, training, and competition expenses. Thus, all avenues to compensation are not closed for today's amateur athlete. Instead, the amount and the type of reimbursement allowed are determined by the governing athletic organization (see Notes 1-3).

The following definitions are representative of a variety of amateur athletic associations' attempts to define "amateur":

National Collegiate Athletic Association: An amateur student-athlete is one who engages in a particular sport for the educational, physical, mental and social benefits derived therefrom and to whom participation in that sport is an avocation. [*1985–86 NCAA Manual*, Constitution 3–1]

International Olympic Committee: An amateur is one who has participated in sports as an avocation without having received any remuneration for his participation. [Rule 26(III)(3)]

United States Olympic Committee: "Amateur athlete" means any athlete who meets the eligibility standards established by the national governing body for the sport in which the athlete competes. [Chapter 17, 36, U.S.C.A. section 373(1)]

Amateur Athletic Union: Person who engages in sport solely for the pleasure and physical, mental, or social benefits he desires therefrom and to whom sport is nothing more than an avocation. [Code/Art. 1 section 101.3(I)(1675)]

United States Swimming, 1982 Code: An amateur swimmer is one who engages in swimming solely for pleasure and the physical, mental and social benefit derived therefrom, and to whom swimming is nothing more than recreation for which no remuneration is received. [*United States Swimming Rules and Regulations 1985*, article 43 — Eligibility, section 343.1]

American Hockey Association of the United States (AHAUS): An amateur hockey player is one who is registered with the national association governing amateur hockey and is not engaged in playing organized professional hockey under contract to a professional club or on a tryout basis, or has not engaged in more than ten games in organized professional hockey in one season. He may, in accordance with the conditions involved, receive reimbursements for time lost from his regular occupation and/or general living expenses while playing hockey. A player is no longer considered an amateur the moment he signs a professional contract, regardless of when it shall become effective.

Any player having completed his contractual obligations to a professional club may apply to the AHAUS for reinstatement of his amateur status. Fee: $100. [*1982–83 Official Guide*, Rules and Regulations No. X]

United States Tennis Association (USTA): Any tennis player is an amateur who does not receive and has not received, directly or indirectly, pecuniary advantage by the playing, teaching, demonstrating or pursuit of the game (meaning that the amateur has not in any way used his tennis skills for pecuniary advantage), except as expressly permitted by the USTA. [*1982 Yearbook: Standing Orders of the USTA*, Article IIB]

NOTES

1. The Athletics Congress, America's national governing body for track, approved an agreement proposed by Eastman Kodak, by which three leading 1984 Summer Olympic medal contenders — Mary Decker, Edwin Moses, and Alberto Salazar — served as "Olympic representatives" in exchange for a consulting fee. The three appeared in television commercials as part of the deal.

2. The United States Olympic Committee, in conjunction with Canteen Corporation, operates a job opportunity program for amateur athletes. The program has serviced over 200 athletes since 1977. The job-matching service attempts to find employment for amateur athletes while they train. During the period between 1977 and 1980, athletes employed with various corporations received an average annual salary of approximately $14,500.

3. The Athletics Congress operates a trust fund by which athletes receive certain financial payments as a result of athletic activity and competition in accordance with regulations of the TAC/TRUST agreement, which has been approved by the International Amateur Athletic Federation (see Section 2.18).

4. In 1985 the International Olympic Committee voted to allow professionals under the age of 23 to participate as an experiment in the 1988 Winter and Summer Games in the sports of ice hockey, tennis, and soccer. See "Olympics to Allow Pros in 3 Sports," *New York Times*, March 1, 1985, p. A19.

5. For further information concerning the governance of amateur athletic associations, see "Government of Amateur

Athletics: The NCAA–AAU Dispute," 41 *Southern California Law Review* 464 (1968).

1.20 Amateur Athletic Associations

Amateur athletic associations are a pervasive part of American society. Individuals in the United States begin participating in such organizations at an early age (Pop Warner Football, Biddy Basketball, etc.) and can continue to do so through adulthood. This section will explore the mechanisms and principles of law as they pertain to amateur athletic associations, examine the structure of some of the organizations, and review litigation involving these organizations.

1.21 Legal Principles

Three legal principles of particular importance in the application of the law to the areas of amateur athletics include limited judicial review, standing, and type of relief. The concept of limited judicial review derives from a theory that courts should not review every legislative judgment but rather should defer to proper legislative decisions. The legal system intervenes through judicial review only when legislative actions violate rights guaranteed by the Constitution, rights granted by the institution concerned, or basic notions of fairness.

In addition to the importance of distinguishing between those occasions for which judicial review is or is not appropriate, it should be noted that federal courts possess a more limited power of review than do state courts. The federal courts may be prevented from reviewing cases that might be subject to review at the state court level. However, a case in which an action by the state violates a federal constitutional right is usually subject to judicial review at the federal level.

Another important legal concept is that of standing. Standing is a procedural device that must be demonstrated prior to the initiation of any lawsuit. The requirement of standing is based on the theory that all cases brought before the legal system must be part of a current or an ongoing controversy. Academic curiosity or contrived situations are not sufficient requisites for a plaintiff to demonstrate standing.

The third area of consideration is the type of relief to be granted. Essentially, two types of relief are commonly requested: monetary damages and injunctive relief. (See Section 1.21–3 for a further discussion of injunctive relief.) Since monetary damages do not always provide the plaintiff with appropriate or adequate relief, the equitable remedy of injunctive relief is often requested. This type of relief is particularly important in amateur sport cases. For example, it allows student-athletes to continue their sport participation during the period in which legal action involving that very participation is being tried in the courts. Time often is of the essence, and injunctive relief may be crucial to the student-athlete.

These three areas — limited judicial review, standing, and injunctive relief — are examined in greater detail in the following subsections.

1.21–1 Judicial Review

Private voluntary associations such as the National Collegiate Athletic Association (NCAA), the National Junior College Athletic Association (NJCAA), The Athletics Congress (TAC), and state high school athletic associations generally are allowed to make and enforce their own rules without interference from the courts. By becoming a member of such an organization, an individual or an institution agrees to be bound by the athletic association's existing rules as well as any others subsequently passed.

As a general rule, courts will not review a private voluntary association's rules unless one or more of the following conditions exist:

1. The rules violate public policy because they are fraudulent or unreasonable;
2. The rules exceed the scope of the association's authority;

3. The organization violates one of its own rules;
4. The rules are applied unnecessarily or arbitrarily;
5. The rules violate an individual's constitutional rights.

The harshness of a rule is not by itself grounds for judicial relief. Relief is granted only for those rules found to be in violation of one or more of the above conditions. Furthermore, even if the rule is subject to review, the role of a court is very limited. A court will not review the merits of the rule involved. It will only determine if the rule is invalid. If a violation is found, the case is remanded to the athletic association for further consideration based on directions from the court.

Constitutional violations that require judicial intervention are based on either due process or equal protection considerations. Due process involves infringements on life, liberty, or property (see Section 1.32), while equal protection involves the fair application of laws to individuals (see Section 1.33). Both of these constitutional standards require that state action be present prior to judicial review (see Section 1.31).

NOTES _____

1. The following cases represent those in which the court granted review:

(a) In *California State University, Hayward* v. *National Collegiate Athletic Ass'n.*, 47 Cal. App. 3d 533, 121 Cal. Rptr. 85 (1975), California State University at Hayward filed a request for an injunction to prevent the NCAA from designating the entire intercollegiate athletic program as indefinitely ineligible for postseason play. The NCAA argued that no substantial interest was involved that would allow judicial jurisdiction over the dispute. The court ruled that when a voluntary association such as the NCAA clearly violates one of its own rules, its decision is subject to judicial review (see Section 1.41–1).

(b) In *Estay* v. *La Fourche Parish School Bd.*, 230 So. 2d 443 (La. Ct. App. 1969), a rule prohibiting athletic participation for married students was held to be invalid because it exceeded the scope of the school board's authority and was therefore unreasonable (see Section 2.23).

(c) In *Dunham* v. *Pulsifer*, 312 F. Supp. 411 (D. Vt. 1970), a rule requiring short hair for male athletes was held to be invalid because it was beyond the school board's authority to make such a rule. Sport safety was not the issue, and even if it were, the problem could be solved by a much less intrusive measure such as requiring the wearing of headbands (see Section 2.22).

(d) In *Bunger* v. *Iowa High School Athletic Ass'n.*, 197 N.W. 2d 555 (Iowa 1972), a rule that denied eligibility to any student-athlete found in a car that also carried alcohol was held to be invalid. The rule was judged to be too far removed from the problem of high school drinking to be a reasonable exercise of authority (see Section 2.24).

2. The following cases represent those in which the court denied review:

(a) In *Kentucky High School Athletic Ass'n.* v. *Hopkins County Board of Education*, 552 S.W. 2d 685 (Ky. Ct. App. 1977), a high school student was declared ineligible for interscholastic competition when he moved his residence from his mother's to his father's house a short time after his parents were divorced. He sought to enjoin the school from enforcing the state high school athletic association bylaw under which he was declared ineligible. The court held that the bylaw was valid and that it had not been arbitrarily applied. The court reasoned as follows: "It is not the responsibility of the courts to inquire into the expediency, practicality, or wisdom of the bylaws and regulations of voluntary associations. Furthermore, the courts will not substitute their interpretation of the bylaws ... so long as [the association's] interpretation is fair and reasonable" (see Section 2.13–2).

(b) In *State ex rel National Junior College Athletic Ass'n.* v. *Luten*, 492 S.W. 2d 404 (Mo. Ct. App. 1973), a junior college filed a request for declaratory and injunctive relief, alleging that the NJCAA had misinterpreted one of its own rules. The trial court granted an injunction that was subsequently overturned by the court of appeals. The appellate court ruled that "the interpretation [of the NJCAA] being a reasonable and permissible one, and no other basis for the court's interference being present, the trial court lacked the jurisdiction to enjoin the implementation of the NJCAA ruling."

(c) In *Tennessee Secondary School Ass'n.* v. *Cox*, 221 Tenn. 164, 425 S.W. 2d 597 (1968), a lower court's review of a transfer rule based on a violation of public policy and due process was ruled invalid due to lack of jurisdiction. The court held that participation in high school athletics is a privilege, not a legally cognizable right.

(d) In *Marino* v. *Waters*, 220 So. 2d 802 (La. Ct. App. 1969), plaintiff challenged a transfer rule that denied him eligibility. The plaintiff had transferred to another school because his marriage was a policy violation of the private school he had originally attended. The plaintiff argued that the transfer rule was arbitrary. The court held that the rule was not arbitrary because it was promulgated for a legitimate purpose and was not applied in a discriminatory manner. Again, the mere harshness of a rule in its application to an individual does not make it subject to proper judicial review.

(e) In *Sanders* v. *Louisiana High School Athletic Ass'n.*, 242 So. 2d 19 (La. App. 1970), a high school student was ruled ineligible by the high school athletic association under the transfer rule because he had been "enrolled" for a period of one year. The court held that it will not ordinarily interfere with a voluntary association unless the association deprives a property right or its actions are capricious, arbitrary, or unjustly discriminatory.

(f) In *Albach* v. *Odle*, 531 F. 2d 983 (10th Cir. 1976), a high school athlete challenged the athletic association's transfer rule. Federal court jurisdiction over high school athletic programs is not proper under 42 U.S.C. 1983 unless there is a violation of due process or equal protection rights. The court held that unless the regulation denied the athlete a constitutionally protected right, the rules regarding transfer would remain within the discretion of the appropriate state board and would not be within federal jurisdiction (see Note 5b).

(g) In *Colorado Seminary* v. *National Collegiate Athletic Ass'n.*, 417 F. Supp. 885 (D. Colo. 1976), the court held that it should not act as arbiter of disputes between an athletic association and its member institutions (see Section 1.32).

3. For the proposition that harshness by itself is not grounds for judicial review, review the following cases:

(a) *State* v. *Judges of Court of Common Pleas*, 173 Ohio 239, 181 N.E. 2d 261 (1962).

(b) *Shelton* v. *National Collegiate Athletic Ass'n.*, 539 F. 2d 1179 (9th Cir. 1976) (see Section 2.15).

4. For further information, see the following articles:

(a) "Judicial Control of Actions of Private Associations," 76 *Harvard Law Review* 983 (1963).

(b) "Administration of Amateur Athletes," 48 *Fordham Law Review* 53 (1979).

(c) Lowell, "Federal Administration Intervention in Amateur Athletics," 43 *George Washington Law Review* 729 (March, 1975).

(d) "Judicial Review of Rule Making in Amateur Athletics," *Journal of College and University Law* (Fall 1977).

5. Certain statutes are commonly cited in an effort to obtain federal court jurisdiction in athletic cases:

(a) *28 U.S.C. section 1343 — Civil Rights and Elective Franchise*:

The district courts shall have original jurisdiction of any civil action authorized by law to be commenced by any person:

(1) to recover damages for injury to his person or property, or because of the deprivation of any right or privilege of a citizen of the United States, by any act done

in furtherance of any conspiracy mentioned in section 1985 of Title 42 (42 U.S.C. section 1985);

(2) to recover damages from any person who fails to prevent or to aid in preventing any wrongs mentioned in section 1985 of Title 42 which he had knowledge were about to occur and power to prevent;

(3) to redress the deprivation, under color of a State law, statute, ordinance, regulation, custom or usage, of any right, privilege or immunity secured by the Constitution of the United States or by any Act of Congress providing for equal rights of citizens or of all persons within the jurisdiction of the United States; and,

(4) to recover damages or to secure equitable or other relief under any Act of Congress providing for the protection of civil rights, including the right to vote.

(b) *42 U.S.C. section 1983 — Civil Action for Deprivation of Rights*:

Every person who, under color of any statute, ordinance, regulation, custom, or usage, of any State or Territory, subjects or causes to be subjected any citizen of the United States or other person within the jurisdiction thereof to the deprivation of any rights, privileges, or immunities secured by the Constitution and laws shall be liable to the party injured in an action at law, suit in equity, or other proper proceeding for redress.

6. For further information, review *Moran* v. *School District #7, Yellowstone County*, 350 F. Supp. 1180 (D. Mont. 1972), in Section 1.32–2, Note 2(f).

1.21–2 Standing

To establish standing in court, the plaintiff must meet three criteria. First required is a demonstration that the action in question did in fact cause an injury, whether economic or otherwise. Second, the plaintiff must establish that the interest to be protected is at least arguably within the zone of interests protected by the Constitution, legislative enactments, or judicial principles. Finally, the interest must be substantial; that is, the plaintiff must be an interested party or be otherwise directly involved. If the plaintiff has only a peripheral interest, there may be no standing, a situation that often occurs with an amateur association in which the athletes are not members of the organization. If this is so, an individual student-athlete therefore is not directly involved in the controversy because he or she is not a member of the amateur association. Consequently, the student-athlete who brings suit may be deemed to lack the necessary standing. An example is the NCAA, whose membership consists of colleges and universities and not of individual student-athletes.

NOTES _____

1. For discussion of substantiality of federal question required for federal court jurisdiction in athletic association cases, review *Fluitt* v. *Nebraska*, 489 F. Supp. 1194 (D. Neb. 1980), in Section 1.32–2.

2. In *Georgia High School Athletic Ass'n.* v. *Waddell*, 285 S.E. 2d 7 (Ga. 1981), the court held that appeals of decisions made by football officials in game conditions are not subject to judicial review. The court ruled that were the decision to be otherwise, every error in the trial courts would constitute a denial of equal protection. The court further held that courts of equity in Georgia do not have authority to review decisions of football referees because they do not present judicial controversies (see Section 4.27).

3. In *Parish* v. *National Collegiate Athletic Ass'n.*, 361 F. Supp. 1214 (W.D. La. 1973), *aff'd*, 506 F. 2d 1028 (5th Cir. 1975), the court held that the NCAA's imposition of a rule requiring a grade point average of 1.600 for athletic eligibility does not raise a substantial federal question under the Civil Rights Act such that federal court jurisdiction would be appropriate (see Section 2.11).

4. In *Watkins* v. *Louisiana High School Athletic Ass'n.*, 301 So. 2d 695 (La. Ct. App. 1974), plaintiff spectator sought an injunction preventing defendant-association from enforcing a ruling that prohibited her high school team from playing any athletic contests for one year if she was in attendance as a fan because of a dispute she had had with a referee. The Louisiana Court of Appeals held that plaintiff had a sufficient legal interest to institute the suit, assuming a valid cause of action was alleged.

5. In *National Collegiate Athletic Ass'n.* v. *Califano*, 444 F. Supp. 425 (D. Kan. 1978), the NCAA challenged the Department of Health, Education, and Welfare's jurisdiction with regard to Title IX. On appeal, the tenth circuit ruled that the NCAA had standing to challenge the application of Title IX legislation to intercollegiate athletic programs. The court based its decision on the fact that individual NCAA member institutions have the necessary standing to test the validity of Title IX regulations. The court stated that the NCAA can bring suit on behalf of its member institutions if it can show that it has their support (see Section 3.21).

6. In *Florida High School Activities Ass'n.* v. *Bradshaw*, 369 So. 2d 398 (Fla. Dist. Ct. App. 1979), the court held that neither the coach nor team players had standing to assert a denial of equal protection to an individual player.

7. In *Assmus* v. *Little League Baseball, Inc.*, 70 Misc. 2d 1038, 334 N.Y.S. 2d 982 (1972), the court held that plaintiff players who were not members of defendant corporation did not have standing to attack the alleged illegality of the defendant's rule.

1.21–3   Injunctions

For the plaintiff who has been successful on the issues of limited judicial review and standing, the next step is to request relief. If granted, equitable relief will allow the athlete to participate. The injunction is a form of equitable relief that can be used to force an athletic association to engage in, or refrain from, an action that affects an institution, an individual student-athlete, or a staff member. There are three types of injunctions: a temporary restraining order, a preliminary injunction, and a permanent injunction.

A temporary restraining order (TRO) is issued to the defendant without notice and is usually effective for a maximum of 10 days. The defendant is not bound by the TRO until actual notice is received. After receiving notice, the defendant can immediately ask the court for a review.

A preliminary injunction is granted prior to a full hearing and disposition of a case. The plaintiff is obligated to give the defendant notice and also to post a bond. The defendant is usually present at the preliminary injunction hearing. The hearing on the issuance of a preliminary injunction is informal and precedes a full and final hearing. This type of injunction is granted only in an apparent emergency and only if the plaintiff shows a likelihood of success for winning the case on the merits.

Temporary restraining orders and preliminary injunctions are granted in situations in which the injury threatened is irreparable and when money damages are either difficult to ascertain or are inadequate. The issuance of either type of relief calls for the exercise of sound judicial discretion. A judge generally considers three factors before granting or denying any form of equitable relief: the nature of the controversy, the objective of the injunction, and the comparative hardship or inconvenience to both parties.

The issuance of a permanent injunction follows a full hearing, which includes consideration of all the above factors. (Other examples dealing with injunctions are discussed in Chapter 3 of Volume 1.)

NOTES _____

1. Injunctions were denied in the following cases:
(a) In *Samara* v. *National Collegiate Athletic Ass'n.*, 1973 Trade Cases, 74,536 (E. D. Va.), two track athletes, students at NCAA schools, wished to participate in a Russian-American meet sponsored by the Amateur Athletic Union. Under NCAA bylaws, this meet was an "extra event" that must be certified by the NCAA or the participating athletes would lose their NCAA eligibility. The plaintiffs sought injunctive and declaratory relief on the basis of the Sherman Act to prevent the NCAA from imposing sanctions due to their participation. Equitable relief was denied because the plaintiffs only faced a threat; they had not suffered any injury.
(b) In *Thompson* v. *Barnes*, 294 Minn. 528, 200 N.W. 2d 921 (1972), the plaintiff had been suspended for one year from participating in interscholastic athletics, due to a second violation of the alcohol rule of the league to which his high school belonged. The plaintiff requested a temporary injunction staying his suspension until his motion for a permanent injunction could be heard. The request was denied because the plaintiff failed to show that he would have competed during the period of the suspension, that suspension would cause irreparable injury pending trial, or that the permanent injunction sought in the main action would be insufficient relief.
(c) In *Florida High School Activities Ass'n.* v. *Bradshaw*, 369 So. 2d 398 (Fla. Ct. App. 1979), an injunction was denied as improper when the plaintiff (student-athlete) failed to show personal injury.
(d) In *Kupec* v. *Atlantic Coast Conference*, 399 F. Supp. 1377 (M.D.N.C. 1975), a student-athlete's request for a preliminary injunction was ruled as improper when the plaintiff did not show actual harm, when harm would be done to the defendant by granting an injunction, and when the plaintiff did not seem likely to succeed on the merits of his claim (see Section 2.14–1).
2. Injunctions were granted in the following cases:
(a) In *University of Nevada* v. *Tarkanian*, 95 Nev. 389, 594 P.2d 1159 (1979), University of Nevada at Las Vegas (UNLV) basketball coach Jerry Tarkanian was granted a temporary restraining order and then a permanent injunction barring UNLV from suspending him from his coaching duties for two years. UNLV was directed to impose the suspension by the NCAA Committee on Infractions under the show-cause provisions of the NCAA's enforcement procedures. On appeal to the Nevada Supreme Court, the permanent injunction was reversed and remanded to the Clark County District Court for further proceedings.
(b) In *Hall* v. *University of Minnesota*, 530 F. Supp. 104 (D. Minn. 1982), the court looked to four factors to determine whether a preliminary injunction should be issued: (1) the threat of irreparable harm to the moving party; (2) the state of balance between that harm and the injury that granting the injunction would inflict on other parties; (3) the public interest; and (4) the probability that the moving party would succeed on the merits of the claim (see Section 2.12).

1.22   Voluntary Athletic Associations

All amateur athletic organizations are subject to fundamental legal principles. Many athletic organizations have been created to serve different groups of individuals in a variety of athletic activities. Other amateur athletic organizations are often distinguished on the basis of the sport — e.g., The Athletics Congress (TAC); by educational level — e.g., the National Junior College Athletic Association (NJCAA; see Note 4); or by geographical location — e.g., the local high school athletic association. Some amateur athletic organizations govern institutions, and some govern individual athletes. The NCAA, for instance, governs colleges and universities and TAC governs individual athletes.

Belonging to one amateur athletic organization does not preclude membership in another. In fact, most educational institutions belong to an allied conference — for example, the Pacific-10 Conference or the Big East Conference — in addition to a national association with a broader constituency — for example, the NCAA. Allied conferences are a subset of the larger amateur sport associations and as such, usually consist of several schools in a geographic area that have similar goals and interests. These schools compete against each other in a number of sports and often compete for conference championships (see Note 1).

In many instances, the NCAA's functions and its relationship with its members can be compared to the federal government's relationship with the state governments. This parallel is especially evident when the NCAA promulgates rules that cover minimum standards to be followed by all of its members. These rules do not, however, preclude members from creating a stricter rule on any subject already covered by an NCAA regulation. In addition, members can also make and enforce any rule that does not conflict with a stated rule or policy of the NCAA.

There are many amateur organizations besides the NCAA, such as Little League Baseball, Pop Warner Football, and the Amateur Softball Association (ASA). However, because of its strength and influence, the NCAA will be used as a representative example of a voluntary athletic association in this chapter's presentation of arguments that can be raised against or on behalf of a voluntary athletic association (see Section 1.22–1). However, note should first be taken of *Santee* v. *Amateur Athletic Union*, as this case provides a prototype for the court's traditional approach toward voluntary amateur athletic associations.

Santee v. Amateur Athletic Union of the U.S., 2 Misc. 2d 990, 153 N.Y.S. 2d 465 (1956)

This case involved Wes Santee, a track athlete who sought an injunction from the Supreme Court, New York County, against the Amateur Athletic Union of the United States (AAU). In examining the merits of issuing an injunction, the court noted:

> This is an action for an injunction brought by the plaintiff to restrain the defendants from continuing the suspension of plaintiff from participation and competition in any sports event under the jurisdiction of the AAU, and from suspending, disqualifying or punishing plaintiff in any manner and mandatorily requiring the president or secretary-treasurer of the defendant, Amateur Athletics Union, to make public announcement that the suspension of the plaintiff is terminated.
>
> The complaint alleges three causes of action: (1) that the Amateur Athletic Union Executive Committee was without jurisdiction to suspend plaintiff on charges of excessive expense accounts and other alleged violations of its regulations; and (2)

> that a quorum of the executive committee was not present at the time of the vote upon plaintiff's suspension and that the vote, therefore was void; and (3) that the defendant, Amateur Athletic Union, and its officers and members are estopped from declaring plaintiff and other outstanding athletic members of the Amateur Athletic Union professionals and ineligible to compete under AAU rules.
>
> Plaintiff is an outstanding track athlete, specializing in mile and "metric mile" runs, and up to the time of this trial had run the fastest mile in the United States.
>
> The defendant, Amateur Athletic Union of the United States, is a voluntary, unincorporated association, whose objective, in brief, is to encourage and foster athletics for sport's sake and to establish and maintain throughout the United States a uniform test of amateur standing and uniform rules for the government of amateur athletics within its jurisdiction. . . .
>
> In October, 1955 charges of excessive expense accounts were made against the plaintiff before the local registration committee of the Missouri Valley Association upon which he was found guilty by a vote of 3 to 2. On appeal to the board of managers of the Missouri Valley Association, November 20, 1955 he was acquitted of the charges by a vote of 21 to 7. A resolution was thereupon passed by the Missouri Valley Association prohibiting any appeal from their decision.
>
> On or about December 4, 1955 at the annual convention of the Amateur Athletic Union at Louisville, Kentucky, the board of governors of the AAU unanimously adopted a resolution recommending that a committee be appointed to investigate charges against the plaintiff and to report its findings to the executive committee. This investigating committee held a hearing on January 8, 1956 which plaintiff was invited to attend. Plaintiff requested that he might have counsel with him and also that he be furnished with a copy of the points to be covered. These two requests were granted. . . . Thereafter the investigating committee reported its findings to the executive committee of the defendant, AAU, which, by a vote of 14 to 1, suspended plaintiff.
>
> With respect to plaintiff's contention that the executive committee had no jurisdiction in the matter, the Court holds to the contrary. It is clear that the board of governors has not only concur-

rent original jurisdiction, but also sole appellate jurisdiction.

Article IX, subd. 3, defines as part of the duties and powers of the Board of Governors, "To impose and enforce penalties for any violation of the Constitution, By-Laws or Rules of the Union."

That the Board of Governors has interpreted this provision to mean that it has original jurisdiction is evidenced by the fact that over some 29 years in hundreds of cases, half of which had to do with excessive expense accounts, the Board of Governors exercised such jurisdiction. . . .

Indeed, it would be unrealistic and would invite disaster to the defendant, Amateur Athletic Union, if it did not, in the face of the action of the Missouri Valley Association purporting to bar an appeal from its decision, take up the charges of which Santee had been acquitted. Failure to do so could properly have brought down upon the defendant, Amateur Athletic Union, condemnation of the International Amateur Athletic Federation and exclusion of the American team from the Olympics. The defendant, Amateur Athletic Union, could properly take action to see that its laws and regulations were enforced and its integrity preserved. . . .

The court finds no merit in plaintiff's first cause of action.

In his second cause of action plaintiff contends that . . . the Executive Committee did not vote on the suspension. The uncontradicted testimony is that 15 of the 26-member Executive Committee were present at the meeting on February 19, 1956; that 14 of them expressed themselves in favor of the suspension, with one opposed; that thereafter the formal resolution of suspension was prepared and adopted, with four of the original 14 affirmatives not then present, but having their votes recorded in their absence.

To dispose first of the question of a quorum, Subdivision 3 of Article XIV of the Constitution provides that, "At any meeting of the Board of Governors a quorum shall consist of those who answer the roll call."

The same rule that governs the procedure of the board of governors would prevail in the executive committee unless the executive committee adopted different rules. The court therefore finds that a quorum of the executive committee was present at the meeting and had expressed themselves on the issue of plaintiff's suspension as indicated above. . . .

With respect to the third cause of action wherein plaintiff pleaded that defendants were estopped from enforcing the rules and regulations of the defendant, Amateur Athletic Union, with respect to excessive expense accounts, plaintiff was given every opportunity to present such evidence as he could. He declined to proceed, claiming he had not sufficient time to prepare his case. The court refused to permit the trial of the case piecemeal, and on the failure of plaintiff to proceed, dismissed the third cause of action. Acting upon such dismissal, the court refused to extend the temporary stay granted herein. The court cites the behavior of the plaintiff in his failure to proceed as indicative of his bad faith in this entire proceeding. Nowhere in plaintiff's pleading is there any allegation that as a member of the AAU, he duly abided by its rules and regulations. That point was as studiously avoided as was his appearance as a witness. He was plaintiff, he brought this action, he alleged his great desire to compete in the Olympics and to represent his country and the United States Marines. However, on the issue as to his eligibility to so compete, when confronted by his accusers, in the forum which he had chosen, he remained silent. In the face of the crushing and devastating testimony of disinterested witnesses — one a member of the Bar of the State of New York — who testified without rancor or ill-feeling and who impressed the court with their fairness and frankness, that plaintiff had frequently and consistently violated the rules of the AAU, plaintiff has, without any pretense of adhering to these rules, sought their protection. His engagement of a booking agent; his demand for moneys for the attendance of his wife at various meets and his collection of said moneys without the attendance of his wife; the excessive expense accounts for the various meets; his attempt to evade professionalism by unfairly attempting to place the onus on his clubmate, with the possibility that the latter would be guilty and the plaintiff escape; the check of $400 to his father-in-law from the promoter of a certain meet, and other matters, foreclose any serious consideration of his plea that he was harshly or unfairly dealt with. His repentance — if any — and the court thinks there is none — comes too late. Plaintiff should have thought of the Olympics and his representation of his country before he engaged his booking agent, before he accepted payments in excess of the regulated amounts, before he tried to brand his clubmate as the professional and falsely place the halo of amateurism upon himself, before he consistently violated the rules of the organization in which he desires to continue his membership. When he took out his athletic membership in the AAU he agreed to abide by the rules and regulations of the union. He has not only failed to do so, but he makes no pretence of having done so.

From this unfortunate incident some good may come to amateur athletics in the United States. Promoters of amateur athletic meets should realize that while plaintiff has, by his conduct, disqualified himself from amateur competition, the fault lies in no small part with them as a class. The record shows that in their desire for larger gate receipts, some promoters have sought to capitalize on the athletic ability of such stars. Santee eliminated himself as an amateur athlete but not without an assist from some of the "guardians" of amateur athletics.

Judgement for defendants on the merits.

NOTES

1. NCAA Division I members who form a basketball conference and wish to be eligible for automatic qualification into the NCAA postseason tournament must meet the following qualifications:

> . . . it shall be a [NCAA] conference member that determines a conference champion in at least six sports (at least two of which must be team sports. . .), and it shall conduct double round-robin, in-season conference competition before declaring its champion. A conference of 12 or more institutions may establish sub-divisions of six or more institutions to conduct divisional competition in basketball; in such cases, each institution shall conduct double round-robin, in-season competition in its own sub-division and single round-robin, in-season competition against members of the other sub-division.
>
> (a) To determine a conference champion under this legislation, at least six of the conference's member institutions shall be classified in Division I in the sport in which Division I automatic qualification is sought; further, for those conferences seeking automatic qualification in the sport of basketball under this legislation, in each of the six sports in which a conference champion is determined, at least six of the conference's member institutions shall sponsor the sport on the varsity intercollegiate level. [*1985–86 NCAA Manual*, Bylaws, 5–7 and 5–7(a)]

2. The following articles deal with the NCAA rules for institution participation eligibility:

(a) "Special NCAA Convention to Tackle Football Powers' Bid for Bigger Role," *Chronicle of Higher Education*, December 2, 1981, p. 1.

(b) "New Limits on NCAA's Top Division Fail to Satisfy Major Football Powers," *Chronicle of Higher Education*, December 12, 1981, p. 1.

(c) "Colleges without Football Will Fight NCAA's Proposal to Demote Them," *Chronicle of Higher Education*, October 27, 1982, p. 13.

(d) "NCAA's Plan to Tighten Top Division May Destroy Several Conferences," *Chronicle of Higher Education*, November 3, 1982, p. 17.

(e) "Autonomy, Federation Enhanced by Convention," *NCAA News*, January 16, 1985, p. 1.

3. The National Association of Intercollegiate Athletes (NAIA) is composed of approximately 500 small four-year colleges and universities.

4. The National Junior College Athletic Association (NJCAA) is composed of approximately 600 two-year colleges.

5. The Association of Intercollegiate Athletics for Women (AIAW), at its peak in 1980–81, had 970 members. For further information, review *Ass'n. for Intercollegiate Athletics for Women* v. *National Collegiate Athletic Ass'n.*, 558 F. Supp. 487 (D.D.C. 1983) (see Section 1.24).

1.22–1   United States Olympic Committee

The Amateur Sports Act of 1978 (36 U.S.C. sections 371–396) was passed by the U.S. Congress to reorganize and coordinate amateur athletics in the United States and to encourage and strengthen participation of U.S. amateurs in international competition. The act addresses two major areas: (1) the relationship between athletes eligible for international amateur competition and the ruling bodies that govern those competitions and (2) the relationship among the ruling bodies themselves. The act established the United States Olympic Committee (USOC) as the principal mechanism for the attainment of these goals and assigned the USOC the following 14 objectives and purposes as guidelines for its operation:

1. Establish national goals for amateur athletic activities and encourage the attainment of those goals;
2. Coordinate and develop amateur athletic activity in the United States directly relating to

international amateur athletic competition, so as to foster productive working relationships among sports-related organizations;

3. Exercise exclusive jurisdiction, either directly or through its constituent members of committees, over all matters pertaining to the participation of the United Sates in the Olympic Games and in the Pan-American Games when held in the United States;

4. Obtain for the United States, either directly or by delegation to the appropriate national governing body, the most competent amateur representation possible in each competition and event of the Olympic Games and of the Pan-American Games;

5. Promote and support amateur athletic activities involving the United States and foreign nations;

6. Promote and encourage physical fitness and public participation in amateur athletic activities;

7. Assist organizations and persons concerned with sports in the development of amateur athletes;

8. Provide for the swift resolution of conflicts and disputes involving amateur athletes, national governing bodies, and amateur sports organizations, and protect the opportunity of any amateur athlete, coach, trainer, manager, administrator, or official to participate in amateur athletic competition;

9. Foster the development of amateur athletic facilities for use by amateur athletes and assist in making existing amateur athletic facilities available for use by amateur athletes;

10. Provide and coordinate technical information on physical training, equipment design, coaching, and performance analysis;

11. Encourage and support research development, and dissemination of information in the areas of sports medicine and sports safety;

12. Encourage and provide assistance to amateur athletic activities for women;

13. Encourage and provide assistance to amateur athletic programs and competition for handicapped individuals, including, where feasible, the expansion of opportunities for meaningful participation by handicapped individuals in programs of athletic competition for able-bodied individuals;

14. Encourage and provide assistance to amateur athletes of racial and ethnic minorities for the purpose of eliciting the participation of such minorities in amateur athletic activities in which they are underrepresented. [See 36 U.S.C. section 374, Objects and Purposes of Corporation.]

The act creates a governing structure for the USOC by empowering the USOC to select one national governing body (NGB) for each Olympic or Pan-American sport. The act enumerates specific responsibilities for an NGB, including the definition of an "amateur athlete" and the determination of eligibility of each athlete for competition in that particular sport. The NGBs do the actual organizational work of developing athletes, organizing teams, instructing coaches and officials, and scheduling events. The act details explicit requirements for amateur sports organizations to become an NGB and provides a mechanism for resolution of disputes between individual organizations wishing to be recognized as the sole NGB. One important requirement of NGBs is that they have the backing of the sport's participants in the United States while also being recognized by international governing bodies. (See *United States Wrestling Federation* v. *Wrestling Division of AAU, infra.*)

Certain provisions in the act call for encouragement and assistance to "amateur athletic programs and competition for handicapped individuals" and the promotion of "physical fitness and public participation in amateur athletic activities," which would seem to warrant the inclusion of non-Olympic or non-Pan-American sports in its realm of responsibility. In the past, however, the USOC has chosen to reject this broader interpretation and has directed its efforts through the NGBs toward Olympic/Pan-American sports. Nevertheless, USOC membership remains open to any sport not falling into the Olympic/Pan-American classification.

While the USOC has chosen to concentrate on Olympic/Pan-American sports, its jurisdiction in this area is not exclusive. Not only must the NGBs be approved by an international governing body, but the USOC itself must contend with and conform to the policies and regulations of the International Olympic Committee (IOC). Furthermore, the act specifies that "any amateur sports organization which conducts amateur athletic competition, participation in which is restricted to a specific class of amateur athletes (such as high school students, college students, members of the armed forces or similar groups or categories), shall have exclusive jurisdiction over such competition." It is only when that group wishes to become involved in international competition that the USOC may play a role by granting a sanction or "certificate of approval issued by an NGB," which is required for such international competition. Even here, the USOC does not have exclusive control. For instance, when the United States hosts the Olympic or Pan-American Games, the USOC must work in concert with local and state governments and also with the organizing committee in the host city.

The act defines an amateur sports organization as a "not-for-profit corporation, club, federation, union, association or other group organized in the United States which sponsors or arranges any amateur athletic competition." Such a broad definition not only limits the jurisdiction of the USOC but allows for a comprehensive structure of many of the organizations that assume a role in the regulation of amateur athletics in the United States.

Defranz v. United States Olympic Committee, 492 F. Supp. 1181 (D.D.C. 1980), *aff'd. without decision,* 701 F. 2d 221 (D.C. Cir. 1980)

The plaintiffs, 25 athletes and one member of the executive board of the United States Olympic Committee (USOC), sought an injunction barring the USOC from carrying out a resolution not to send an American team to participate in the 1980 Moscow Olympics. The plaintiffs contended that in preventing participation, the defendant exceeded its statutory

powers and abridged the plaintiff's constitutional rights as guaranteed under the First, Fifth, and Ninth amendments.

The plaintiffs stated three causes of action. The first, a statutory claim, was that the defendant had violated the Amateur Sports Act of 1978 in the following respects:

(a) Defendant in deciding that no U.S. amateur athlete shall participate in the 1980 Olympic Games, exercised a power it did not have.
(b) Defendant breached its duty to organize, finance and control participation in the events and competitions of the Olympic Games by U.S. athletes.
(c) Defendant had denied U.S. amateur athletes the opportunity to compete for reasons other than want of athletic merit or for any sport-related determination.
(d) Defendant succumbing to political and economic pressures yielded its exclusive jurisdiction over Olympic matters to the nation's political leaders.
(e) Defendant acted in a political manner.
(f) Defendant yielded its autonomy and has succumbed to political and economic pressure.

The plaintiffs' second cause of action was based on the athletes' statutory right to compete in the Olympics. The plaintiffs asserted that the Amateur Sports Act of 1978 provides "in express terms" an athletes' bill of rights, which requires the USOC to "protect the opportunity of any amateur athlete, coach, trainer, manager, administrator or official to participate in an amateur athletic competition." Last, the plaintiffs contended that the Amateur Sports Act contains statutory language that requires the enforcement of all provisions of the act. The plaintiffs argued that such language justified their claims.

In its determination, the court carefully examined the question of the existence of state action. While the plaintiffs asserted that their constitutional rights had been violated, the court stated that before such claim could be considered, the existence of state action must be established. In its inquiry, the court examined two important factors. First, the court was concerned with the degree to which the government had become involved with the USOC. For the court the key issue was whether or not the state was now in such a position of interdependence with the USOC such that it could be considered a joint participant in the boycott. Emphasizing that the USOC receives no federal funding and that it operates and exists independently of the federal government, the court found that the requisite relationship did not exist.

The second factor that the court examined was the nature of the existing relationship as it related to the boycott. While the plaintiffs contended that "governmental persuasion" in this instance was in effect "affirmative pressure that effectively places governmental prestige behind the challenged action," the court concluded that it was incumbent upon the plaintiffs to prove that some form of control existed. Their failure to establish that such an interdependent relationship existed led the court to determine that neither "de jure" nor "de facto" control was exercised by the government over the USOC. The court qualified its decision by stating that the finding of control by the government of a private entity in this case would "open the door" and usher the courts into the difficult position of determining what level or type of political pressure would constitute sufficient federal control as to invoke federal jurisdiction.

The court then addressed the plaintiff's claims under the act. The court found that the USOC had broad powers, including those guaranteed under section 375 (a) of the act, which specifically gives the USOC the power to either accept or not accept any invitation to send an American team to the Olympics. When considering the plaintiff's contentions that the boycott violated a right to compete, the court examined the defendants' argument, which defined the right to compete as intended to protect the athlete from jurisdictional disputes between amateur groups which have often deprived athletes of the opportunity to enter certain competitions. The defendants also argued that while the act does guarantee the

enforcement of its provisions, if the USOC decides not to participate in the Olympic Games, a right to compete does not exist.

The court concluded that even if the required state action had been shown, the plaintiffs did not have constitutionally protected rights provided under the act. The court determined that the language of the act was intended to protect participation as it related to jurisdictional disputes rather than Olympic competition. Therefore, the USOC's authority to make a decision to boycott was affirmed, and the athletes were found to have no protectable right of Olympic participation.

The court adopted the attitude that the boycott was regrettable and that the plaintiffs' plight was one of "simple, although harsh facts of life," which were sadly "immutable." Although the court was sympathetic to the plaintiffs' cause, it found that since they had failed to state a claim by which relief could be granted, their claim for injunctive and declaratory relief was denied and the action dismissed.

U.S. Wrestling Federation v. Wrestling Division of AAU, 605 F. 2d 313 (7th Cir. 1979)

The U.S. Wrestling Federation (USWF) applied to the United States Olympic Committee (USOC) to be designated the USOC's national governing body of wrestling at the Olympic Games. The USOC, acting through its executive board, rejected the application, keeping in place the Wrestling Division of the AAU (WD/AAU) as the USOC's national governing body of wrestling.

Pursuant to a provision of the USOC constitution, the USWF submitted its claim to the American Arbitration Association (AAA) for binding arbitration by a panel of three arbitrators under the AAA's commercial rules. The USWF contended that it was better qualified to serve as the national governing body than the WD/AAU. The arbitrators were jointly selected by the USWF and the WD/AAU. After 17 days of hearings, the panel unanimously found for the USWF.

After the hearing, counsel for the WD/AAU discovered that the firm of the chairman of the panel, H. Blair White, had performed substantial work for Northwestern University, a constituent member of the NCAA. The NCAA, in turn, was closely affiliated with the USWF to the extent that counsel for the WD/AAU described them as the real party at interest in a meeting with the arbitrators prior to the arbitration hearings. The NCAA was the USWF's principal founder, financed and directed the arbitration proceeding against the WD/AAU, and substantially contributed financially to the USWF's activities.

As a member of the NCAA, Northwestern had paid $25,000 to the NCAA from 1975 to 1979 and had received over $1,000,000 in revenues from 1976 to 1979 from the NCAA's television football program. Northwestern also employed as its head wrestling coach Ken Kraft, one of the three original incorporators and a former president of the USWF.

White's firm, Sidley and Austin of Chicago, had represented Northwestern on a regular basis for 25 to 30 years. During the two years preceding the arbitration, between 15 and 25 attorneys at the firm had worked on Northwestern University matters, for which the firm received substantial fees. White himself was a member of Northwestern's fund-raising organization. One of White's partners served as general counsel to Northwestern. There was no evidence, however, that White or his law firm had any relation whatsoever with the NCAA, Kraft, the USWF, or the WD/AAU.

The WD/AAU argued that the ruling by the arbitration panel should be set aside on the grounds that White should have disclosed on his own motion various connections that he and his law firm had with Northwestern University. The WD/AAU further contended that White displayed evident partiality during the hearing. The WD/AAU believed that identifying the NCAA as the real party at interest should have triggered an alertness to the connection between Northwestern and the NCAA and prompted White to disclose this information to

the parties because of his direct connection with Northwestern and indirect connection to the NCAA.

The court held, however, that White's relationship to the USWF via the tenuous chain of his and his firm's relationship to Northwestern, Northwestern's relationship to Ken Kraft and the NCAA, and Kraft and the NCAA's relationship to the USWF was too "remote, uncertain and speculative" to require that the arbitration decision be set aside. The court found that White had no financial interest with any of the litigating parties nor any direct relation to them. "To embark upon disclosing relationships with nonparties who in turn might have relationships with a party, particularly when many nonparties had similar relationships, would be," the court stated, "to provide the parties with his complete and unexpurgated business biography." To require a duty of disclosure under these circumstances "would make it virtually impossible for any partner of a large firm to made [sic] adequate disclosure."

The court also rejected the WD/AAU's contention that White showed partiality during the hearings. The court found that White made rulings against both parties. The record, the court found, refuted any contention that both parties were not given a full and fair hearing before the tribunal of arbitrators.

NOTES

1. The legal counselor for the USOC advised the USWF that while the arbitration decision establishing it as the NGB of amateur wrestling had been affirmed, the group still had to be recognized by the International Amateur Wrestling Federation (FILA) before it could replace the WD/AAU as a Group A member of the USOC.

2. See Nafzinger, "The Amateur Sports Act of 1978," *Brigham Young University Law Review* 47 (1983). For further information, see Section 2.18, Individual Eligibility Requirements — Olympic Athletes.

3. In *Martin* v. *International Olympic Committee*, 740 F.2d 670 (9th Cir. 1984), the U.S. Court of Appeals for the Ninth Circuit turned down a request by 82 women athletes from 27 countries for an injunction that would order the IOC to let women compete in the 5,000 meter and 10,000

meter races at the 1984 Los Angeles Olympics. The court held that California civil rights law does not authorize the establishment of "separate but equal" events for men and women and that the IOC rule which governed the addition of new events to the games was applied equally to men and women and thus was not discriminatory. (See further Section 2.18.)

4. See Exhibit 1–1 for a listing of the National Governing Bodies which are recognized by the United States Olympic Committee.

5. See Exhibit 1–2 for a listing of the International Sports Federations which are recognized by the International Olympic Committee.

6. The USOC administers programs designed to elicit jobs and financial support for U.S. Olympic athletes from American corporations. One program, the Olympic Jobs Program, matches top amateurs with corporations which provide the athlete with full-time pay, while the athlete works part-time and trains part-time. Other corporations allow their athlete-employees to take unlimited paid vacations while traveling to competitions. Under the Olympic Gold program, corporations provide athletes with tuition and a part-time job while the athlete is enrolled in college. The corporation also reimburses athletes for time lost from their jobs while competing.

These programs were recently made possible due to more relaxed interpretations of Olympic rules. Athletes may not, however, be paid professionally for what they do athletically.

7. Following the 1984 Summer Olympic Games in Los Angeles, there was a $120-million surplus, of which the USOC received $50 million. An additional $50 million was distributed by the Los Angeles Olympic Committee to Southern California youth programs, $12.5 million to U.S. national sports governing bodies, and $7 million for a foreign exchange program. (See "Olympic Revenues," *USA Today*, February 13, 1985, p. C1.)

8. The 1988 Olympic Games will be held in Calgary, Alberta, Canada (winter), and Seoul, Korea (summer). The Calgary Winter Games are to be held February 13–28, 1988, and are budgeted to cost $450 million. (See "Calgary Has Games Plan," *USA Today*, March 7, 1985, p. C1.)

1.22–2 National Collegiate Athletic Association

The National Collegiate Athletic Association (NCAA) is a private organization made up of a voluntary membership of over 800 four-year colleges and universities located throughout the United States. Member schools agree to be bound by NCAA rules and regulations and are obligated to administer their athletic programs in accordance with NCAA rules. Over half of the NCAA's members are state-subsidized universities, and most receive some form of federal financial assistance. Operating funds for the NCAA are in part accumulated through membership dues, which are figured on a sliding scale based on the type of membership held. The annual dues range from $100 to $800, effective 9/1/82, and from $225 to $1800, effective 9/1/85, (*1985–86 NCAA Manual*, Bylaw 9–3[b & c]). A school that does not pay dues is denied a chance to vote at the annual convention and cannot enter teams in NCAA-sponsored competitions. In addition, if dues are not paid within one year, the school's membership automatically terminates.

The NCAA does not offer membership to individual student-athletes. Instead, it uses the principle of institutional control. In essence, this means that the NCAA deals only with school administrations and not with individual students. When a violation that concerns a student-athlete is discovered, the NCAA informs the school of its findings and requests that the school declare the athlete ineligible. If the school does not adhere to the request, the NCAA may invoke extensive sanctions against all, or any part of, the institution's athletic program.

The purpose of the NCAA is stated in the NCAA constitution:

Section 1. Purposes. The purposes of this Association are:

(a) To initiate, stimulate and improve intercollegiate athletic programs for student-athletes and to promote and develop educational leadership, physical fitness, sports participation as a recreational pursuit and athletic excellence;

(b) To uphold the principle of institutional control of, and responsibility for, all intercollegiate sports in conformity with the constitution and bylaws of this Association;

(c) To encourage its members to adopt eligibility rules to comply with satisfactory standards of scholarship, sportsmanship and amateurism;

(d) To formulate, copyright and publish rules of play governing intercollegiate sports;

(e) To preserve intercollegiate athletic records;

(f) To supervise the conduct of, and to establish

THE UNITED STATES OLYMPIC COMMITTEE

DIRECTORY OF MEMBER ORGANIZATIONS

Group A — Those organizations recognized by the USOC as the National Sports Governing Bodies for the sports on the program of the Olympic or Pan American Games. Each National Sports Governing Body is recognized by the USOC as the cognizant authority for exercising jurisdiction over all international amateur competition involving U.S. teams or individuals, conforming to the rules and regulations of the recognized International Sports Federations.

(10) Aquatics: Aquatics Division of the A.A.U. (A.A.U.)

(5) Archery: National Archery Association (N.A.A.)

(10) Athletics (Track and Field): Track and Field Division of the AAU (A.A.U.)

(5)* Baseball: U.S. Baseball Federation (U.S.B.F.)

(5) Basketball: Amateur Basketball Association of the U.S.A. (A.B.A.U.S.A.)

(10) Biathlon and Modern Pentathlon: U.S. Modern Pentathlon and Biathlon Association (U.S.M.P.B.A.)

(5) Bobsledding: Bobsledding Division of the A.A.U. (A.A.U.)

(5) Boxing: Boxing Division of the A.A.U. (A.A.U.)

(5) Canoeing and Kayaking: American Canoe Association (A.C.A.)

(5) Cycling: U.S. Cycling Federation (U.S.C.F.)

(5) Equestrian Sports: American Horse Shows Association (A.H.S.A.)

(5) Fencing: Amateur Fencers' League of America (A.F.L.A.)

(5) Field Hockey: Field Hockey Association of America (Men's); U.S. Field Hockey Association, Inc. (Women's)

(5) Figure Skating: U.S. Figure Skating Association (U.S.F.S.A.)

(5) Gymnastics: U.S. Gymnastics Federation (U.S.G.F.)

(5) Ice Hockey: Amateur Hockey Association of the U.S. (A.H.A.U.S.)

(5) Judo: Judo Division of the A.A.U. (A.A.U.)

(5) Luge: Luge Division of the A.A.U. (A.A.U.)

(5)* Roller Skating: U.S. Amateur Confederation of Roller Skating (U.S.A.C.R.S.)

(5) Rowing: National Association of Amateur Oarsmen (N.A.A.O.)

(5) Shooting: National Rifle Association of America (N.R.A.)

(5) Skiing: U.S. Ski Association (U.S.S.A.)

(5) Soccer Football: U.S. Soccer Federation (U.S.S.F.)

(5)* Softball: Amateur Softball Association of America (A.S.A.)

(5) Speed Skating: U.S. International Speed Skating Association (U.S.I.S.A.)

(5) Team Handball: U.S. Team Handball Federation (U.S.T.H.B.F.)

(5)* Tennis: U.S. Tennis Association. (U.S.T.A.)

(5) Volleyball: U.S. Volleyball Association (U.S.V-.B.A.)

(5) Weightlifting: Weightlifting Division of the A.A.U. (A.A.U.)

(5) Wrestling: Wrestling Division of the A.A.U. (A.A.U.)

(5) Yachting: U.S. Yacht Racing Union (U.S.Y.R.U.)

(The figures in parentheses indicate the number of delegates to the House of Delegates.)

(*) Sports on the program of the Pan American Games only.

All other summer sports except for canoeing and kayaking and modern pentathlon are on the programs for both the Olympic and Pan American Games.

Group B — Those 12 national organizations from which directly or indirectly have come substantial numbers of members of the U.S. Olympic or Pan American Teams in two or more sports and provided these organizations either hold national programs or championships, or through the constituent or related units which foster regular and nation-wide programs at a level of proficiency appropriate for the selection of athletes to represent the U.S. in international competition.

(5) Amateur Athletic Union of the U.S. (Conducting national programs in basketball, gymnastics, and volleyball) for which it is not the recognized national governing body.

(5) American Alliance for Health, Physical Education and Recreation (A.A.H.P.E.R.)

(5) Association for Intercollegiate Athletics for Women (A.I.A.W.)

(5) Catholic Youth Organization (C.Y.O.)

(5) Exploring Division of the Boy Scouts of America (B.S.A.)

(5) National Association of Intercollegiate Athletics (N.A.I.A.)

(5) National Collegiate Athletic Association (N.C.A.A.)

(5) National Federation of State High School Associations (N.F.S.H.S.A.)

(5) National Jewish Welfare Board (N.J.W.B.)

(5) National Junior College Athletic Association (N.J.C.A.A.)

(5) U.S. Armed Forces

(5) National Council of the Young Men's Christian Association (Y.M.C.A.)

Group C — Those national sports organizations, not eligible for Group A, functioning as national sports governing bodies in amateur sports which are NOT on the programs for the Olympic and Pan American Games, but are widely practiced in other countries and may therefore be eligible for inclusion in future programs of the Olympic or Pan American Games.

(1) Tae Kwon Do Division of the A.A.U.

(1) U.S. Table Tennis Association

Group D — State Olympic Organizations for each of the 50 states and the District of Columbia, recognized by the USOC for the purpose of bringing together all interested individuals, organizations and corporations to further the purposes and goals of the USOC in conducting and coordinating fund-raising activities and enhancing the USOC image by establishing broad and comprehensive communications programs for the general public.

Exhibit 1-1   National Governing Bodies Recognized by the United States Olympic Committee (*Source: The United States Olympic Commitee*)

**INTERNATIONAL SPORTS FEDERATIONS RECOGNIZED BY THE I.O.C.
AS WELL AS THE UNITED STATES MEMBER OF THE INTERNATIONAL FEDERATION (Group D)**

International Federation *For Olympic Sports*	**United States Member**
IAAF — International Amateur Athletic Federation (track and field)	Track and Field Div. — AAU
FITA — International Archery Federation	National Archery Association — NAA
FIBA — International Amateur Basketball Federation	Amateur Basketball Association of the USA — ABAUSA
FIBT — International Bobsleigh and Tobogganing Federation	Bobsled Div. — AAU
AIBA — International Amateur Boxing Association	Boxing Div. — AAU
FIAC — International Amateur Cyclists Federation	U.S. Cycling Federation — USCF
FIE — International Fencing Federation	Amateur Fencers League of America — AFLA
FIFA — International Association Football Federation (soccer)	U.S. Soccer Federation — USSF
FEI — International Equestrian Federation	American Horse Shows Association — AHSA
FIG — International Gymnastics Federation	U.S. Gymnastics Federation — USGF
IHF — International Handball Federation	U.S. Team Handball Federation — USTHBF
FIH — International Hockey Federation (field hockey)	Field Hockey Association of America (men's) — FHAA
IFWHA — International Federation of Women's Hockey Associations	U.S. Field Hockey Association, Inc. (women's) — USFHA
IIHF — International Ice Hockey Federation IIHF	Amateur Hockey Association of the U.S. — AHAUS
IJF — International Judo Federation	Judo Div. — AAU
FIL — International Luge Federation	Luge Div. — AAU
IUPMB — International Union of Modern Pentathlon and Biathlon	U.S. Modern Pentathlon and Biathlon Association — USMPBA
FISA — International Federation of Rowing Societies	National Association of Amateur Oarsmen — NAAO
UIT — International Shooting Union	National Rifle Association of America — NRA
ISU — International Skating Union (figure skating and speed skating)	U.S. Figure Skating Association — USFSA, and U.S. International Skating Association — USISA
FIS — International Ski Federation	U.S. Ski Association — USSA
FINA — International Amateur Swimming Federation (also diving and water polo)	Aquatics Div. — AAU
FIVB — International Volleyball Federation	U.S. Volleyball Association — USVBA
IWF — International Weightlifting Federation	Weightlifting Div. — AAU
FILA — International Amateur Wrestling Federation	Wrestling Div. — AAU
IYRU — International Yacht Racing Union	U.S. Yacht Racing Union — USYRU
FIC — International Canoe Federation	American Canoe Association — ACA
For Pan American Games Sports	
AINBA — The International Baseball Association	U.S. Baseball Federation — USBF
FIRS — International Roller Skating Federation	U.S. Amateur Confederation of Roller Skating — USACRS
FIS — International Softball Association	Amateur Softball Association of America — A.S.A.
ITF — International Tennis Federation	U.S. Tennis Association — USTA

Exhibit 1-2   International Sports Federations Recognized by the International Olympic Committee and U.S. Members of the International Federations

eligibility standards for, regional and national athletic events under the auspices of this Association;

(g) To cooperate with other amateur athletic organizations in promoting and conducting national and international athletic events;

(h) To legislate, through bylaws or by resolution of a Convention, upon any subject of general concern to the members in the administration of intercollegiate athletics; and

(i) To study in general all phases of competitive intercollegiate athletics and establish standards whereby the colleges and universities of the United States can maintain their athletic activities on a high level. [*1985–86 NCAA Manual*, Constitution 2–1]

In addition, the fundamental policy on which the NCAA is based is as follows:

Section 2. Fundamental policy. (a) The competitive athletics programs of the colleges are designed to be a vital part of the educational system. A basic purpose of this Association is to maintain intercollegiate athletics as an integral part of the educational program and the athlete as an integral part of the student body and, by so doing, retain a clear line of demarcation between college athletics and professional sports. [*1985–86 NCAA Manual*, Constitution 2–2(a)]

Although all members have input into new rules and revisions of old rules, the NCAA administration has overall organizational responsibility and often initiates legislation on matters of general interest to all its members. The administrative body of the NCAA consists of a 46-member council (see Note 1). The council is elected at the annual convention of the association. At least four council seats are reserved for women. Between annual meetings, the council is empowered to interpret the constitution and bylaws. These interpretations are binding after they are published and circulated to the membership via the NCAA's weekly publication (biweekly in the summer), *NCAA News*. There is a check on the power of the council in that any member can request that the next annual convention affirm a decision of the council. A simple majority of the delegates

can approve a bylaw. The council is also responsible for facilitating cooperation with other amateur organizations, such as the National Association of Intercollegiate Athletics (NAIA), The Athletics Congress (TAC), and the Collegiate Commissioners Association (CCA), and in the promotion and conducting of national or international events.

Historically, the NCAA has tried to balance the distribution of athletic talent among member institutions, act as a bargaining agent for its members concerning commercial opportunities such as television broadcasts (see Section 6.32), and conduct postseason play in intercollegiate sports, the revenue from which is distributed among eligible member institutions.

Justice v. National Collegiate Athletic Ass'n., 577 F. Supp. 356 (D. Ariz. 1983)

Four members of the University of Arizona's football team sought a preliminary injunction to prevent enforcement of the NCAA's sanctions against the football team, which would prohibit postseason play in 1983 and 1984, and television appearances for 1984 and 1985. The U.S. District Court held that

[t]he plaintiffs in this case have been deprived neither of their scholarships nor their right to participate in intercollegiate athletics. Whatever oral representations that were made by university coaches to plaintiffs regarding participation in post-season and televised athletic contests created a mere expectation or desire rather than a legitimate claim of entitlement based on contract. . . .

In sum, the rule that the plaintiffs would have this Court adopt as to the right to be free of punishment absent personal guilt is so broad that virtually any sanction or disciplinary rule, including the alternatives suggested by plaintiffs, would be struck down for "punishing" innocent persons. Indeed, under the plaintiffs' theory, the NCAA could not impose any sanction which adversely affected a football team unless *every* member of the team had violated NCAA rules. Clearly a distinction must be drawn between actions that constitute punishment without personal guilt for substantive due process purposes and actions which merely affect innocent persons adversely. This Court interprets prior case law as limiting the concept of "punishment" to deprivations of a fundamental right or liberty or property interest. This definition is consistent with the Court's discussion above of the practical problems that would accompany the broader interpretation of the concept suggested by the plaintiffs. Accordingly, the plaintiffs' loss of the opportunity to participate in post-season and televised competition, however unfortunate and personally undeserved, does not constitute a deprivation of their due process rights.

Williams v. Hamilton, 497 F. Supp. 641 (D.N.H. 1980)

The U.S. District Court denied a motion for a preliminary injunction against the National Association of Intercollegiate Athletics (NAIA) for enforcing its residency requirement rules on plaintiff soccer player because the rule did not deny due process nor equal protection. In reviewing the case, the court compared the NAIA with the National Collegiate Athletic Association with respect to the requirements of state action and noted that

> . . . [d]efendant NAIA is a voluntary association of 512 four-year colleges ranging in size from small (500) to moderate (1100), whose primary purpose as set forth in its constitution is "to promote the development of athletics as a sound part of the educational offerings of member institutions.". . . The member institutions of NAIA pay dues to the Association, which are scaled by enrollment. Among other things, NAIA sets standards for recruiting and eligibility, and it sponsors post-season national championships in various collegiate sports, including soccer.

NAIA is divided into several districts, each of which is governed by a "District Executive Committee." Each district has voting representation at NAIA's Annual National Convention, at which time policy decisions are made. Also at the National Convention delegates vote for new members of the National Executive Committee, the overall governing body of NAIA. . . .

NEC (New England College) is also a member of the National Collegiate Athletic Association ("NCAA") which divides its member schools for purposes of competition into various divisions based on the desire of a given member school to participate in a given sport at such level. Accordingly, NEC for certain sports is competing at a higher division level and following NCAA rules, while in soccer, the sport here at issue, it competes in Division III, but follows the "more stringent" requirement of the NAIA rule above quoted. The NAIA witnesses contend that the residency requirement rule is necessary to prevent "pirating" and also to prevent "tramp athletes" from moving from institution to institution for the sole purpose of participating in a given sport.

. . . Plaintiff's first argument is that he has been deprived of due process by the application of the residency eligibility requirement. Citing the so-called "NCAA cases," plaintiff urges that the action of NAIA in promulgating and enforcing such an eligibility rule comprises "state action," and thus here meets a threshold requirement to the granting of relief under 42 U.S.C. § 1983.

In *Rivas Tenorio v. Liga Athletica Interuniversitaria*, 554 F.2d 492 (1st Cir. 1977), the court had the occasion to analyze the factors upon which the NCAA cases found that state action existed for the purposes of jurisdiction. These were found to include the facts that (1) approximately 50 percent of NCAA member institutions were state or federally supported; (2) the vast majority of the capital provided NCAA came from public institutions; (3) the state instrumentalities were a dominant force in determining NCAA policy and in dictating NCAA actions; (4) the NCAA's regulations and supervision over intercollegiate athletics was extensive and represented an immeasurably valuable service for its member institutions; and (5) the NCAA negotiates television contracts in substantial sums which flow directly to participating schools, primarily the public universities . . .

Defendant argues that the NAIA cannot be analogized to the NCAA, in that the amount of state involvement in the former pales in comparison to the latter. An affidavit submitted by defendant reveals that state-supported schools comprise 33% of NAIA's membership, and pay 37% of NAIA's total dues. The Executive Committee is comprised of eleven persons, six from private schools and five from state schools. Of the six members of the National Eligibility Committee of the NAIA, four are from private schools and two are from state schools. If the state action question could be reduced to a mere numbers game in which a magic majority pushes the party into one category or the other, the solution to the problem would be easy, and defendant in this action would prevail. But as the First Circuit recognized in *Rivas*, the resolution of the state action question is not easy:

> If the NCAA was composed of solely public institutions, clearly state action would be present. In contrast, if the NCAA had no public members, its actions would be private for constitutional purposes. Drawing the line as to the requisite quantum of public participation to invoke fourteenth amendment protections is a difficult task indeed. . . .

. . . It is manifest that although the state schools do not constitute a majority of the NAIA's membership, they nevertheless contribute substantially to NAIA's financial stability and its decisionmaking process. For this reason the Court finds and rules that plaintiff has made a sufficient showing of "state action" to allow this Court to exercise its jurisdiction over this matter. . . .

Parenthetically, the Court notes that certain practices of NAIA might well be improved, *i.e.*, the six- to eight-week interval where an appeal is filed by a member institution as to the eligibility of a student might be reduced by use of such modern devices as telephone conference calls; and where, as here, the Athletic Director and the District Eligibility Chairman wear the same hat, a process providing for prompt appeal to a person in the geographical district other than a person holding such dual employment might be devised with profit to all concerned.

CASE STUDY: Walter Byers, Executive Director of the NCAA

Since he joined the association in 1951, Walter Byers' name has become almost synonymous with the letters spelling NCAA. Whether testifying before Congress, representing the association on television, or appearing before the association's national convention, over the past 30 years Byers has guided the fortunes of the NCAA and has been involved in many of its controversies and much of its litigation. The following article is reprinted to give the reader a perspective on the changes the NCAA has undergone over the period of Byers' association with the organization. ("NCAA Byers: Now a Vocal Proponent of Reform," *Chronicle of Higher Education*, November 7, 1984, p. 31).

This summer Walter Byers, executive director of the National Collegiate Athletic Association, broke his longstanding public silence on cheating in intercollegiate athletics and became a vocal proponent of reform.

It all started, he says, with a budget meeting.

In July the N.C.A.A.'s enforcement staff, which investigates violations of association rules, asked Mr. Byers for enough money to double its number of full-time investigators to 20.

"Our enforcement people said that they felt they needed more sophisticated techniques to keep up with what they considered more sophisticated techniques of circumventing the rules," Mr. Byers said in a recent interview.

Acceding to that budget request would have cost a lot of money, Mr. Byers said, so he began asking college sports personnel around the country if the funds were necessary. "It became, I think, abundantly clear that we were not keeping up with the levels of transgression," he said. "The techniques of circumventing the rules are more sophisticated and they seem to be more deliberate.

"I was surprised at first, and finally I became astonished at what I considered to be the deliberateness of strategies of getting around the rules. And I was astonished at the level of it, the level of the dollar transactions."

Mr. Byers cited one apparently common practice: The complimentary tickets to which a player is entitled are often given to his parents. A booster then buys the tickets at a prearranged, inflated price, and the money is funneled back to the player. That's a difficult practice to police, he said.

Learning that as much as $20,000 a year was being spent for the talents of a top football or basketball player, Mr. Byers decided it was time for him to go public with some reform proposals. He postponed making a decision on increasing the enforcement money.

Since then, Mr. Byers has spoken out on the state of college sports and has offered his opinions on changes that he thinks will help. He told *The Chronicle* that while much has happened to undermine college sports since he became the N.C.A.A.'s executive director, he is optimistic that integrity can be restored.

Appointed in 1951

It was in 1951 that Mr. Byers, then a 29-year-old sportswriter for United Press International, was appointed executive director of the N.C.A.A., an organization set up to administer the rules established by its members.

"I had a great attraction towards sports," Mr. Byers recalled. "I suppose I considered myself lucky to have a job and particularly lucky to be associated with college athletics."

The N.C.A.A. was a small organization in 1951, Mr. Byers said: He and a secretary were the association's only full-time staff members. "All we did was run a few championships and conduct an annual convention," he said. "That's all there was, because there wasn't any legislative authority, any enforcement, any major administrative problems associated with us at that time."

Much has changed in college sports since then. Mr. Byers still holds the same job, but now he oversees an operation that spends more than $41 million a year. The universities that belong to the association's top competitive division regularly spend millions of dollars on sports every year, and the pressure to win is often intense.

Scandals and other problems have accompanied that growth. Cars, apartments, and expensive gifts not only are eagerly doled out to players, Mr. Byers said: they are expected, and education has become secondary in importance.

What went awry? What prompted so many institutions to flout the rules?

One cause, Mr. Byers said, is the jet airplane, which "did more to complicate recruiting than any single development." Before coast-to-coast travel was so easy, most colleges recruited only in their own regions, he noted, and a coach was more likely to know a player and his family personally. Now, contacts with unknown players have become common, and the lack of personal bonds have made corruption easier, he said.

TV's Effects Dramatic

The other dramatic influence on college athletics was network television, Mr. Byers said. It has brought publicity and financial rewards, making many institutions yearn for TV exposure and willing to do whatever is necessary to get it.

Television has also served to dramatize the benefits that can come to an athlete, he said.

In addition, Mr. Byers said, "athletics has moved more into the hands of managers" and is no longer controlled by coaches. "I don't believe that, in the regular decision-making process, the people closest to athletics really have the influence and direction they used to have," he said.

A relaxation of the definition of amateurism by other associations governing athletics has also led to the deterioration of integrity in college sports, Mr. Byers said. He noted that many U.S. athletes in the summer Olympic Games could openly receive thousands of dollars and remain amateurs.

Says Rules Encourage Hypocrisy

"I think that ultimately higher education has been hurt because of the rules colleges have put in effect," Mr. Byers said. Although the N.C.A.A.'s members adopted those regulations to control athletics, he said, many of them not only fail to do the job, but often encourage hypocrisy.

Every year, he said, coaches, athletes, and college presidents sign pledges that they have abided by the rules even when there have been violations. "We're supposed to teach young people the proper, civilized way of conducting their affairs, and it is simply not right to engage them in an apparatus that is essentially deceitful."

Nor is the N.C.A.A. itself blameless, Mr. Byers said. National championships, particularly in basketball, offer a big financial incentive for winning, he said, and the rules for eligibility in different divisions create additional pressures on an institution. "I'm not sure our criteria for N.C.A.A. divisions are correct, particularly in Division I," he said.

Delegates at the next N.C.A.A. convention, in January, are expected to approve a proposal that would permit institutions in the three subdivisions of the association's most competitive division, Division I, to have much greater autonomy in deciding on policies that affect only their subdivisions.

College presidents, Mr. Byers said, could help lead the way back to respectability for athletics. "It's my view that for a number of years there have been a number of responsible chief executive officers who have been uncomfortable with the condition of college athletics. . . . There are a substantial number of responsible, thoughtful C.E.O.'s who want to change conditions."

Three areas to which presidents and chancellors should give their attention are academics, integrity, and economics, Mr. Byers said.

Academic matters are being addressed, Mr. Byers said, through the intense debate over the N.C.A.A. rule known as Proposition 48, which requires freshman athletes to meet several academic requirements in order to be eligible to play a sport in Division I. Those requirements are likely to be modified at the N.C.A.A. convention but they are still expected to be more stringent than the existing standards.

The new N.C.A.A. presidents' commission, created by last year's convention, has already raised the issues of integrity and economics, Mr. Byers said, and the commission is likely to formulate proposals to put before the January convention.

"I believe that these C.E.O.'s will take time to concentrate on the issues and reach a resolution on them and get a commitment across the country from fellow C.E.O.'s who want to operate according to those rules and in that particular division," Mr. Byers said. "And if they in turn authorize a very demanding enforcement program and stringent penalties, then I think there can be a new direction and a better day."

Punishing 'Chronic Violators'

Mr. Byers said harsher penalties are needed for the 10 to 15 per cent of N.C.A.A. institutions he calls "chronic violators."

He wants coaches at those institutions fired when violations are found, and institutions that don't take measures to prevent violations should have their athletic schedules canceled.

Mr. Byers said he was also concerned about institutions that don't want to cheat, but that skirt the rules because of competitive pressure to do so. Those institutions have to decide on a set of rules, he said, and live by them and understand that they will be penalized for deliberate violations.

The schedule of penalties should be published, he said, so that institutions will know the price they will have to pay if they cheat.

Athletes who cheat should also be subject to sanctions, Mr. Byers said, though he added that colleges that pursue athletes are more guilty than the athletes they pursue.

Ostracizing the Cheaters

Not all cheating will ever be eliminated from collegiate sports, Mr. Byers said. "There are always certain people who try to beat the rules. It seems to me our job is to deal with them in the most aggressive manner we can, and, if we can't convince them to go by the rules, ostracize them and hopefully persuade the others not to follow their example.

"Higher education is a highly constructive force in this country," Mr. Byers added. "But in addition to the search for knowledge and truth, it seems to me it has to stand for the proper conduct of human affairs. Whether you can have big-time athletics and still conduct your affairs in the proper manner, I suppose is the fundamental question.

"I think it can be done, but it will take a lot of vigilance."

NOTES _____

1. The following excerpts are from an NCAA memorandum to its member institutions, which was published by *NCAA Publications*, June 27, 1984:

President's Commission: Was created at the 1984 NCAA convention to give the chief executive officers of NCAA member institutions a greater input into association's operations. It is composed of a board of 44 college presidents who will be chosen by the NCAA. The board can propose legislation but it cannot enact it without approval of the annual convention delegates.

NCAA Council: Included 46 members, 22 from Division I, 11 from Division II, and 11 from Division III, with the NCAA president and secretary-treasurer as ex officio members. Members are elected by their respective division round tables at the annual Convention. The president and secretary-treasurer are elected by the full Convention. Geographical and conference representation requirements are the same as for the Presidents' Commission.

The Council established and directs the general policy of the Association in the interim between NCAA Conventions, and all of its actions are subject to review by the next Convention. If in effect, the Convention establishes Association law and policy, and the Council implements and applies the Convention's decisions, and with day-to-day administration provided by the staff.

Division Steering Committees: The 44 elected members of the Council represent their respective divisions as members of Council subcommittees identified as Division I, Division II, and Division III Steering Committees. Each meeting of the Council includes separate meetings of the three steering committees, as well as sessions involving the entire Council.

The steering committees consider and act upon matters relating to their respective divisions, while the Council acts as one body to deal with matters of overall Association policy and interdivision interests. The steering committees report their actions to the full Council, and any division decision stands unless overruled by a two-thirds vote of the Council members present and voting.

The steering committees also plan and conduct the division round tables at Conventions, administer surveys of division members, review legislative proposals of interest to their divisions, and encourage communication between division members and the steering committee and Council.

NCAA Executive Committee: Includes 14 members, with the NCAA president and secretary-treasurer as ex officio members. Of the remaining 12 members, eight represent Division I members, two represent Division II members, and two represent Division III members. The division vice-president automatically is one of each division's members. The five officers are elected by the Convention; the other nine members are appointed by the NCAA Council.

The Executive Committee transacts the business and administers the financial and championship affairs of the Association, including employment of an executive director (with approval of the Council) and such other staff as necessary for conduct of the Association's business.

Constitution 5–2–(c) assigns certain responsibilities directly to the Executive Committee. The committee regularly reports to the Council as to all of its activities and also submits an annual report to the NCAA Convention.

Other Committees: The other standing committees of the Association are in three general categories: Convention committees, Council-appointed (sometimes called general) committees, and sports committees (some with rule-making responsibilities and some without). The size of the respective committees is specified in NCAA Bylaw 12. In most cases, each division is represented on a committee, unless it deals specifically with a matter involving only one division. In addition, ad hoc committees frequently are appointed to deal with specific assignments.

In general, such committees report to the NCAA Council and/or the Executive Committee. Actions of any committee are subject to review by the annual Convention.

Staff: The NCAA currently employs a staff of approximately 95, including clerical personnel. The staff administers the policies and decisions approved by the Association through the annual Convention or by the Council and Executive Committee. It also serves all NCAA Committees by providing administrative services, including necessary record-keeping and continuing communications. Staff members do not serve as members of NCAA committees.

Operating under the executive director, the national office staff is organized in five departments: administration, championship, communications, enforcement, and publishing.

See also:
(a) "NCAA Presidents Get Board, Little Power," *Boston Globe*, January 11, 1984, p. 21.
(b) "Plan to Give Presidents More Power 'Undemocratic,' NCAA Office Says," *Chronicle of Higher Education*, September 14, 1983, p. 1.
2. For further information, see the following articles:
(a) Philpot, "Judicial Review of Disputes Between Athletes and the NCAA," 24 *Stanford Law Review* 903 (May 1972).
(b) "The Government of Amateur Athletes: The NCAA–AAU Dispute," 41 *Southern California Law Review* 464 (1968).
(c) "The Student Athlete and the NCAA: The Need for a Prima Facie Tort Doctrine," 9 *Suffolk University Law Review* 1340 (Summer 1975).
(d) "Battle Heats Up over Domination of Sports Group," *Chronicle of Higher Education*, November 9, 1983, p. 1.
(e) "NCAA Presidents' Panel to Back Studies of Integrity, Finances of College Sports," *Chronicle of Higher Education*, October 17, 1984, p. 23.
(f) "Proposed Autonomy for Athletic Powers Said to Have 'Pretty General Support,' " *Chronicle of Higher Education*, November 28, 1984, p. 33.
(g) Weistart, "Legal Accountability and the NCAA," 10 *Journal of College and University Law* 167 (1983–84).
(h) "Autonomy, Federation Enhanced by Convention," *NCAA News*, January 16, 1985, p. 1.
(i) "Changes Cool the Tempers at the NCAA Convention," *New York Times*, January 18, 1985, p. A22.
3. The 1984–85 NCAA budget was $41,588,000. The budget breaks down as shown in Exhibit 1–3.

1.22–3 High School Athletic Associations

High school athletic associations are voluntary associations made up of all the high schools within a state that wish to participate in association events, agree to abide by the rules of

1985-86 NCAA revenue: 75 percent will come from the Division I Men's Basketball Championship.

A. Division I Men's Basketball Championship	$37,023,000	75.0%
B. Other Division I Championships.........................	4,015,000	8.1
C. Marketing...	1,347,000	2.7
D. Football television assessments	1,200,000	2.4
E. Investments	900,000	1.8
F. Publishing department	879,000	1.8
G. Membership dues.....................................	863,600	1.8
H. Transfer from Youth/Development reserve..............	739,000	1.5
I. Transfer from 1983-84 surplus	660,000	1.3
J. Television-films......................................	645,000	1.3
K. Division II championships.............................	558,000	1.2
L. Division III championships	252,000	0.5
M. Communications department	159,000	0.3
N. General..	126,400	0.3

1985-86 NCAA expenses: 63.6 percent of total will be returned directly to member institutions.

A. Division I Men's Basketball Championship—distribution of net receipts*	$20,715,600	42.0%
B. Championships—transportation guarantees*	5,698,500	11.5
C. Championships—game expenses	2,582,400	5.2
D. Block grants to reserves*	2,200,000	4.5
E. Championships—per diem allowances*.................	1,974,000	4.0
F. Compliance and enforcement department...............	1,863,000	3.8
G. Publishing department	1,418,000	2.9
H. Legal	1,400,000	2.8
I. Administration department	1,314,000	2.7
J. Communications department	1,143,900	2.3
K. Committees	1,141,000	2.3
L. General..	1,104,100	2.2
M. Promotions...	1,007,700	2.0
N. Championships department............................	978,000	2.0
O. Films..	692,900	1.4
P. Rent...	672,000	1.4
Q. Other championships distribution*	634,500	1.2
R. Legislative services department	583,000	1.2
S. Development	618,100	1.3
T. Marketing...	503,500	1.0
U. Funded operating reserve	500,000	1.0
V. Contingency..	438,800	0.9
W. Royalties to members*	184,000	0.4

*Returned to member institutions

Exhibit 1-3   Breakdown of the 1985-86 NCAA Budget (*Source:* "1984–85 Budget Outlined," *NCAA News.*)

the association, and are accepted as members. High school associations are often given authority to organize through enabling legislation, which in effect creates a private corporation to perform a quasi-public function.

The National Federation of State High School Associations (NFSHSA) is the governing body for high school athletics. The NFSHSA as a federation has much less power than the NCAA (which has national authority). Instead, the high school athletic associations are established on an insular, state-by-state basis. Like the NCAA, they are usually funded by membership dues. Many state associations charge each school a flat fee, which includes such items as entry fees and transportation costs to association tournaments, although some states have sliding fee scales. The NFSHSA was founded on the belief that strong state and national high school organizations are necessary to protect the integrity of interscholastic programs and to promote healthy growth of those programs. Its structure is shown in Exhibit 1–4.

NFSHSA services include a press service subscribed to by editors of local, state, and national publications; a national film library; national federation publications for 13 sports; national records for more than 40,000 performances, listed in the *National Interscholastic Record Book*; sanctioning of applications for interstate and international events between schools; athletic directors conference, printed proceedings, and a quarterly magazine. The NFSHSA membership serves over 20,000 high schools, 500,000 coaches and sponsors, and 500,000 officials and judges.

The Massachusetts Interscholastic Athletic Association (MIAA) is one example of a high school association. Its members include public and private secondary schools as well as technical and vocational schools. Prior to being accepted for membership, the applicant school must be approved by the Board of Control, which administers the rules and enforces the discipline within the association. Upon acceptance of membership, the approved school agrees to be bound by the requirements set forth in the MIAA eligibility rules. Member schools are free, however, to make any other rules, including ones that are stricter than the MIAA rules, as long as they do not conflict with those of the association.

The purpose of the MIAA is clearly set forth in the MIAA constitution:

The purpose of the Association shall be to organize, regulate and promote interscholastic athletics for secondary schools of Massachusetts. In pursuing this commitment the Association shall:

A. Provide leadership and service designed to improve interschool relations in athletics.

B. Foster cooperation among voluntary institutional members and the Massachusetts Secondary School Administrators Association, the Massachusetts Department of Education, Massachusetts Association of School Committees, Massachusetts Association of School Superintendents, Massachusetts Secondary School Athletic Directors Association, Massachusetts State Coaches Association, Massachusetts Division of Girls' and Women's Sports, Massachusetts State Coaches Association and with professional organizations interested in attaining common goals.

C. Secure uniform regulations and control of interscholastic participation in athletics throughout the state to provide equitable competition for students as an integral part of the education of secondary school students.

D. Promote safety and health of participants in interscholastic athletics.

E. Develop and channel the force of opinion to keep interscholastic athletics within reasonable bounds so that it will expressly encourage all that is honorable and sportsmanlike in all branches of sports for secondary youth.

F. Provide a forum for concerns related to interscholastic athletics for institutions which become voluntary members of the association.

G. Develop uniform standards and procedures for determining championships at the end of the season. [MIAA Constitution, Article II]

Note should be made of sections D and E, which expressly designate areas of concern not explicit in NCAA policies. Here the MIAA expresses its concern for the health and safety of participating student-athletes. It also recog-

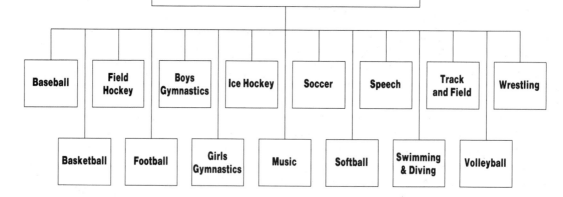

NATIONAL COUNCIL
One delegate from each of the member
high school associations

EXECUTIVE COMMITTEE
Eight members, each representing one section of the U.S.

HEADQUARTERS STAFF
Executive Director
Administrators (8)
Support Staff (12)

ACTIVITY COMMITTEES

Baseball | Field Hockey | Boys Gymnastics | Ice Hockey | Soccer | Speech | Track and Field | Wrestling

Basketball | Football | Girls Gymnastics | Music | Softball | Swimming & Diving | Volleyball

Exhibit 1-4   Structure of the National Federation of State High School Associations

nizes the particular problem of the effect of public opinion on presumably unsophisticated high school students.

The rule-making body of the MIAA is an assembly composed of the principals of the member schools. The assembly meets annually and is empowered with the authority to organize administrative committees as they are deemed necessary.

Two administrative bodies exist within the MIAA — the Board of Control and the Eligibility Review Board. The Board of Control is composed of 13 members elected from various professional, educational, and athletic associations within the state. It is authorized to hear appeals of decisions, decide the time and place of meetings, create and appoint special committees, interpret rules and fix penalties, and issue and revise rules as necessary. The Board of Control also has the power to warn, censure, or place on probation any school, player, team, coach, or game or school official who violates any rule.

The second administrative body is the Eligibility Review Board (ERB). The board is composed of five high school principals (one from each district in the state) who are appointed by, but are not members of, the Board of Control. It has the authority, when validated by a majority vote of its members, to set aside any rule. This action is permitted when the rule clearly fails to accomplish the purpose for which it was intended or when the application of the rule causes an undue hardship to an individual student. The granting of a waiver must not, however, result in an unfair advantage to the school or to the particular competitor seeking the waiver.

Using Massachusetts as an example, it is possible to generalize that other high school associations often have wide power to make decisions in the creation and interpretation of rules, in the handling of alleged violations, in determining the eligibility of individual athletes, and in administering tournaments.

Denis J. O'Connell High Sch. v. Virginia High Sch., 581 F. 2d 81 (4th Cir. 1978), *cert. den.,* **440 U.S. 936 (1979)**

This case is an appeal by the Virginia High School League from a decision by the district court enjoining the league from denying the request of Denis J. O'Connell High School to compete in league-sponsored championship athletic contests. O'Connell High School is a state-accredited, private, nonprofit Catholic high school located in Arlington, Virginia. In February 1977, O'Connell High School applied for admission to the Virginia High School League, Northern Region, but was denied on the basis that the league's constitution limits membership to public high schools. The league is an unincorporated association of public high schools in Virginia under the sponsorship of the School of Continuing Education of the University of Virginia. The league is maintained by public funds coming from the University of Virginia, local school boards, and gate receipts from league-sponsored tournaments. Although private schools are invited to league-sponsored tournaments in debate and speaking, they are excluded from tournaments involving "major" sports such as football, basketball, and baseball.

O'Connell High School brought suit against the league pursuant to 42 U.S.C. section 1983 and its jurisdictional counterpart, 28 U.S.C. section 1343(3), and alleged in its complaint that the league's refusal to admit the school solely on the basis that it is a private school was an arbitrary classification in violation of the equal protection clause of the Fourteenth Amendment. O'Connell High School also alleged that as a result of this exclusion, students who selected a private education were denied the right to compete on a tournament level in sports such as football, basketball, and baseball. These students were thus placed in a less favorable competitive position than students in public high schools to attract and receive athletic scholarships, professional bonuses, and other benefits that accrue to gifted athletes. Before trial, both parties entered into a formal stipulation which stated that action by the league in its supervision of interscholastic competition is taken under the color of state law and constitutes state action within the meaning of 42 U.S.C. section 1983.

The league defended its policy of exclusion with three basic arguments. First, the league contended that no federal question was present to support federal jurisdiction as alleged to be found under 28 U.S.C. section 1343. Second, the league argued that its limitation of membership to public schools was rationally related to the league's interest in enforcing its eligibility rules concerning transfer students. The league presented evidence that because public schools draw students from strictly defined areas, while private schools are not so limited, enforcing transfer rules with respect to private schools would be difficult. Last, the league argued that admission of a parochial school into the league would violate the establishment clause of the First Amendment.

The United States District Court for the Eastern District of Virginia found in favor of O'Connell High School and enjoined the league from barring the school from league competition. The court held that the activities of the league neither advanced nor inhibited religion, and any benefits supplied by league membership would not constitute excessive government entanglement so as to be violative of the First Amendment.

The league appealed to the United States Court of Appeals, Fourth Circuit. On appeal, the league challenged the lower court's holding that jurisdiction existed under 28 U.S.C. section 1343. The league argued that the O'Connell High School claim should not have come under the jurisdiction of the district court, as neither education nor participation in athletics, nor the speculative possibility of acquiring an athletic scholarship or professional bonus, is a right secured or protected by the Constitution and thus is not a cause of action under the cited law.

The court of appeals relied on *San Antonio Independent School District* v. *Rodriguez*, 411 U.S. 1 36 L. Ed 2d 16, 93 S.Ct. 1278 (1973), in finding that education is not a fundamental right under the Constitution and *Mitchell* v. *Louisiana High School Athletic Ass'n.*, 430 F. 2d 1155, 1158 (5th Cir. 1970), in finding that participation in interscholastic athletics is also not a fundamental right. The court went on to say, however, that these were not the rights in question. The question before the court was an alleged abridgment of the right of private school students to compete in interscholastic athletics because of the establishment of two classes of students — public and private. Relying on *Baker* v. *Carr*, 369 U.S. 186, 199 (1961), the court stated that the jurisdiction taken by the lower court was proper, as a claimed denial of equal protection by state action arises under the Constitution unless the claim is unsubstantial or frivolous, and based on the facts of this case, the claim was not without substance.

Citing *San Antonio Independent School District* v. *Rodriguez* once again, the court stated that where there is no fundamental right or suspect classification involved, the test to determine the validity of state legislation is whether the statutory classification bears some rational relationship to a legitimate state purpose. Thus the court was in agreement with the league's contention that the lower court had erred in not finding a rational basis for the provision of the league's constitution limiting membership to public schools. The court went on to say that state legislatures are presumed to have acted within their constitutional power despite the fact that, in practice, their laws result in some inequality. Citing *McGowan* v. *Maryland*, 366 U.S. 420, 425-426 (1961), the court concluded by saying that any statutory discrimination is not to be set aside if any set of facts reasonably may be conceived to justify it. In reversing the lower court, the appeals court sustained the league's argument that because of the ability of the private schools to draw from a far larger geographical area, it would be difficult to enforce eligibility rules for transfer students. Viewed in the light of these facts, the court failed to find a denial of equal protection.

In the opinion of the court, the state is justified in taking any reasonable step to prevent actual or potential abuse of student-athletes by those persons who would recruit such students for their athletic ability. Thus reasonable measures taken to reduce or remove possible temptation to make choices of schools on the basis of their respective athletic programs are justified. In the case of *Walsh* v. *Louisiana High School Athletic Ass'n.*, 428 F. Supp. 1261, 1264 (E.D. La. 1977), the court upheld the constitutional validity of transfer rules governing high school athletic associations. In its decision, the court stated that the purpose of the transfer rule was to prevent recruiting of school children by overzealous athletic coaches, fans, and school faculty. When the state finds that actions of this type may be harmful, it may take steps to prevent this harm. Adoption and implementation of a transfer rule is certainly a reasonable measure when its stated purpose is the prevention of actual and potential abuse of student-athletes. The court concluded by stating that the classification by the league made sense in light of the purpose sought to be achieved and that beyond this point of wisdom, the state must be allowed to prevail. The classification is rationally related to a legitimate state objective and thus is lawful. The decision of the lower court was reversed.

NOTES _____

1. For more information regarding the National Federation of State High School Associations, see *School Activities: The Other Half of Education*, Elgin, Illinois: NFSHSA Publications, 1978.

2. In *Snow* v. *New Hampshire Interscholastic, Etc.*, 449 A.2d 1223 (N.H. 1982), the New Hampshire Supreme Court reversed a lower court ruling that would have allowed plaintiff student to participate in a track meet. Plaintiff claimed he would have qualified for a "Meet of Champions" if he had not been fouled in a qualifying meet and finished seventh. The state association denied his appeal to compete in the championship meet. The Supreme Court supported the association's ruling, stating that the court was extremely limited in deciding such things as fouls in track meets.

3. The New Jersey State Interscholastic Athletic Association (NJSIAA) in 1983 upgraded minimum academic standards for athletes. Under the NJSIAA rule, to be eligible to play sports, a student must have passed courses with 23 credits the last school year. Since most New Jersey high school courses are five credits, at least five courses would have to be passed under the standard. The previous NJSIAA standard was that a student had to pass three courses the prior school year. Some New Jersey schools maintain higher standards than the NJSIAA requires. In Newark, for instance, a 1983 regulation requires that in addition to the NJSIAA standards, students must maintain a cumulative 2.0 or "C" average to be eligible for athletic competition. See "Academics Sack School's Season," *Newark Star Ledger*, September 14, 1984, p. 17.

4. In 1984, the Texas Legislature promulgated a "no pass, no play" rule, which was adopted by the State Board of Education in March 1985. Under the tough new academic standard, a student must have a passing grade of at least 70 in all courses to participate in sports and other extracurricular activities. Students who fail even one course in the six-week grading period must sit out the next six-week grading period. Texas Governor Mark White noted in 1985:

We in Texas don't tell our students it's OK to flunk one course.... We're going to put winners on the playing field. We're going to put winners in the classroom.... And it's going to make Texas the big winner.

For further information, see the following articles:
(a) "White Begins Reform Drive," *Dallas Morning News*, March 13, 1985, p. 1.
(b) White Vows Support for Tough Grade Law," *Dallas Times Herald*, March 14, 1985, p. 33.
(c) "Some Students Give In, Others Give Up," *Dallas Times Herald*, March 9, 1985, p. 1.
(d) "Lewis Says Grade Rule Will Stand," *Dallas Times Herald*, March 9, 1985, p. 1.
(e) "Flunk Rate Laid to Bill," *San Antonio Express-News*, March 16, 1985, p. B1.
(f) "Higher Dropout Rate Expected in Bexar," *San Antonio Light*, March 16, 1985, p. D1.

5. In *Christian Brothers Institute* v. *North New Jersey Interscholastic League*, 86 N.J. 409 (1981), a suit was instituted by a private high school against defendant league for alleged unlawful discrimination in evaluating an application for membership. The New Jersey Supreme Court, in reversing the lower court, held that a rational basis can exist for an interscholastic league limited to public schools and that such a limitation does not result per se in a denial of equal protection under the federal Constitution.

6. In *Guelker* v. *Evans*, 602 S.W. 2d 756 (Mo. Ct. App. 1980), the Missouri Court of Appeals affirmed a trial court decision ruling that plaintiff high school soccer player had

failed to meet requirements for a class action and that the appeal of that decision was moot as plaintiff had graduated and was attending college on a soccer scholarship. Plaintiff had missed 29 days of school and a major part of the soccer season while participating in a tournament sponsored by the United States Soccer Federation in Puerto Rico. This participation violated Missouri State High School Activities Association rules concerning school competition, eleven-day rule, and international competition.

7. In *State* v. *Judges of Court of Common Pleas*, 181 N.E. 2d 261 (Ohio 1962), the state high school athletic association suspended a member high school from participating in athletics for one year and declared two boys from the high school ineligible for interscholastic athletics for failure to abide by association rules. The court held that this action should not be enjoined when, although harsh, determination was not the result of mistake, fraud, collusion, or arbitrariness.

8. In *Alabama High School Athletic Ass'n.* v. *Rose*, 446 So. 2d 1 (Ala. 1984), the Alabama Supreme Court affirmed a trial court decision that granted plaintiff high school football player a preliminary injunction to compete despite an Alabama High School Athletic Association (AHSAA) declaration of ineligibility. In granting the preliminary injunction, the court noted that

> ... the burden on the challenger to overcome the presumption favoring the Association's absolute authority in the conduct of its own affairs is a heavy one. We reaffirm the ... test to the effect that the Court's jurisdiction in such matters is invoked when, and only when, the averments of fraud, collusion, or arbitrariness are supported by clear and convincing evidence; and the trial court's acceptance of jurisdiction will be affirmed only where its order makes an unequivocal factual finding of one or more of these narrow, restrictive grounds, founded upon clear and convincing evidence.
>
> The ultimate issue before us, then, given the trial court's express finding of collusion, as allegedly perpetrated upon Rose by AHSAA and its executive director, is whether this jurisdictional requisite is amply supported by the evidence. After careful review of the findings of fact, tested against the testimony of record, we are convinced that the trial court's jurisdiction was properly invoked and that its order granting a preliminary injunction was an appropriate exercise of its discretionary function.

9. At a June 26, 1984, U.S. Senate hearing on "Oversight on College Athletic Programs" (S. Hrg. 98–955, Subcommittee on Education, Arts and Humanities), Harry Edwards, Ph.D., University of California, Berkeley, Department of Sociology, gave the following testimony:

> But the problem does not start on the college campus. An exaggerated emphasis upon sports during the early school years and often in the family, leads to a situation wherein by the time many student-athletes finish their

junior high school sports eligibility and move on to high school, so little has been demanded of them academically that no one any longer even expects anything of them intellectually.

> At the high school level, the already unconscionable emphasis upon athletic development is institutionally abetted by policies which make athletic competition conditional upon minimum standards or, more typically, no standards of academic performance. As late as the Winter of 1984, it was still the case that only a handful — about forty of the nation's 16,000 plus high school districts — had set minimum academic standards for sports participation. And of those which had such standards, most required only that the student-athlete maintain a 2.0, or "C" average, or that a student-athlete's grade card show no more than one failing grade in an academic year. The problem with these minimum standards, of course, is that they have a way of becoming maximum goals. Student-athletes typically strive to achieve precisely the standards set — nothing more, nothing less.

> Only 5 percent of America's high school athletes ever participate in their sports at the collegiate level. Thus the lack of serious academic standards, seriously enforced as a condition of high school sports participation, impacts immediately upon the 95% of former high school athletes who must rely substantially upon their academic skills and records to gain college admissions. . . .

10. For further information on high school athletic associations, see the following articles:

(a) Weistart, "Rule-Making in Interscholastic Sports: the Bases of Judicial Review," 11 *Journal of Law and Education* 291 (1982).

(b) "Interscholastic Sports Eligibility — the Transfer Rule," 37 *Washington State Business News* 17 (1983).

11. In 1984, California State Senator Dan McCorquodale introduced legislation, SB 1420 High School Sports Bill, that would create a High School Athletic Development Tax Fund whose funds would be distributed to school districts throughout California for support of high school interscholastic athletics programs. The monies for the fund would have been raised by imposing a 10% tax on the gross receipts received from ticket sales and broadcast rights of professional sports events in the state. (See California Senate Bill No. 1420, introduced January 19, 1984.)

12. For further information on high school athletic governance see "High School Athletics and Due Process: Notice of Eligibility Rules," 57 *Nebraska Law Review* 877 (1978).

13. A statute requiring that all accredited high schools within a state be eligible for "open" membership in an association governing interscholastic activities at the high school level was declared constitutional in *South Dakota High School Interscholastic Activities Ass'n.* v. *St. Mary's Inter-Parochial School of Salem*, 82 S.D. 84, 141 N.W. 2d 477 (1966).

1.22–4 State Athletic Commissions

A State Athletic Commission is a state agency created by statute which generally governs and regulates a particular sport(s) as designated in its charter. Regulated sports may include boxing, wrestling, and horse, harness, dog, and automobile racing. The regulations adopted to regulate these sports vary from state to state. However, in general, the main purposes of these commissions include the regulation and oversight of eligibility of participants, referees, trainers, promoters, and the certification of competitive sites.

In amateur athletics, the primary sport regulated by state commissions is boxing. The case of *Ali* v. *State Athletic Commission* (*infra*), although dealing with professional boxing, outlines the court's general approach toward the regulatory authority of state commissions.

When issuing licenses, boxing commissions take into account factors such as personal conduct, character, physical condition, criminal record, and (primarily for promoters) financial condition. Because State Athletic Commissions are statutorily created state agencies, they are considered to be acting under color of state action and thus must meet constitutional requirements of due process.

Muhammad Ali v. Division of State Athletic Commission of Department of State of N.Y., 316 F. Supp. 1246 (S.D.N.Y. 1970)

Professional boxer Muhammad Ali moved for a preliminary injunction restraining the New York State Athletic Commission from denying him a license to box in the state of New York.

On July 20, 1967, Ali, after a jury trial, was convicted of the federal felony of refusing to submit to induction into the armed forces and was sentenced to a term of five years. Ali's conviction was affirmed by the Fifth Circuit Court of Appeals, *Clay* v. *U.S.*, 397 F. 2d 901 (5th Cir. 1968). On September 22, 1969, Ali, who was in the process of petitioning the Supreme Court for certiorari, applied to the Commission for a license to box in New York. On October 14, the commission unanimously denied his application because his "refusal to enter the service and [his] felony conviction . . . is regarded . . . to be detrimental to the best interests of boxing." In a letter to Ali, Commission Chairman Edwin Dooley advised that if the conviction should be reversed, Ali would be welcome to reapply for a license.

Ali's amended complaint charged that the defendants had arbitrarily and capriciously refused to renew Ali's license in violation of the equal protection clause guaranteed by the Fourteenth Amendment. Ali cited many cases in which the commission had granted licenses to professional boxers who had committed crimes of moral turpitude, including robbery, assault, and rape. All together, the commission's records revealed at least 244 instances in recent years in which it had licensed boxers who had been convicted of criminal or military offenses.

While the court recognized the right of the commission, a state agency, to bar convicted felons from boxing, the court held that the refusal to issue a license "should not represent the exercise of mere personal whim or caprice," but "should, and constitutionally must, have some rational basis." The court observed that had the commission denied boxing licenses to all convicted felons, Ali would have no valid basis for his demand that he be issued a license. But the court held that the commission's denial of a license to Ali was intentional, arbitrary, and capricious and thus violative of the Fourteenth Amendment.

The court suggested that a convicted murderer or rapist seemed to present more of a risk of corruptibility than would the person who openly refused to serve in the armed forces. Further, the court found it even more difficult to detect any rational basis for granting a license to a boxer who had been a deserter from the armed forces than, as here, one who refused to enter the service.

The court also rejected the defendant's argument that because Ali's conviction was recent and he had not yet served his sentence, his case differed from other boxers convicted of crimes who had been granted licenses. While the court recognized that such a distinction could be reasonable in the abstract, the commission's records revealed numerous instances in which a license had been issued to boxers within a year of their convictions of serious crimes. Further, the court noted the commission's policy that one must serve one's sentence before obtaining a boxing license penalized the convicted boxer from exercising his lawful right to appeal.

Accordingly, the court held that Ali had demonstrated a likelihood of success on the merits and enjoined the defendants from denying him a license to box in New York.

NOTES

1. In an earlier case, *Muhammad Ali* v. *Division of State Athletic Commission of Department of State of New York*, 308 F. Supp. 11 (S.D.N.Y. 1969), plaintiff's motion for a preliminary injunction was denied, but with leave for the plaintiff to replead the case. The court reasoned that the refusal of the commissioners to license the plaintiff, on the grounds that he had been convicted of draft evasion, was not irrational, unsupported by evidence, or otherwise assailable.

2. In New Jersey, the Office of State Athletics Commission was established in 1931 as a single-commissioner office to regulate the conduct and taxation of professional and amateur boxing, wrestling, and "sparring" exhibitions. The commissioner is appointed by the governor, subject to Senate confirmation, for a five-year term. The commissioner serves full time and may be removed by the governor for cause. The commissioner appoints inspectors, referees, and other officials. Regulatory control is absolute, and the commissioner's rule-making powers are restrained only by the enacting statute's parameters.

3. See also, "Interim Report and Recommendations of the State of New Jersey Commission of Investigation on the Inadequate Regulation of Boxing," *State of New Jersey Commission of Investigation Report*, March 1, 1984.

4. In 1985, New Jersey Governor Thomas Kean signed legislation that sought to reform the state's boxing industry by replacing the single athletic commissioner with a three-member Athletic Control Board and created a seven-member Medical Advisory Council. (See: "Jersey Boxing Bill," *New York Times*, March 17, 1985, sec. 5, p. 6.)

5. See Section 3.43–2, *Calzadilla* v. *Dooley* for an example of a sex discrimination case filed against a state

athletic commission, which involved the licensing of professional wrestlers.

1.23 Public Responsibilities of Amateur Athletic Associations

Amateur athletic associations as legal bodies may have certain public duties to fulfill as a condition of their corporate existence. Even a voluntary association may have a responsibility to the general public, even though it considers itself a private organization. For instance, the NCAA has the public responsibilities of maintaining amateurism in college athletics, providing competition in intercollegiate sports for both men and women student-athletes, and most recently, allowing greater access to televised football.

Greene v. Athletic Council of Iowa State University, 251 N.W. 2d 559 (Iowa 1977)

The Iowa Superior Court ruled that an amateur college association, although private in name, was "quasi-public" in character. Plaintiffs brought an action for declaratory judgment against the defendant athletic council in an effort to establish that the council meetings were subject to the open-meeting law. Plaintiffs were students at Iowa State University (ISU) and citizens and taxpayers of Iowa. A lower court ruled that council meetings did not have to be open to the public. The Iowa Supreme Court reversed the decision. The open-meeting statute became effective July 1, 1967, and its purpose was to "require [public bodies'] meetings to be open and to permit the public to be present."

The court discussed the specific statute and decided the controlling issue was "whether the athletic council was a 'council' as authorized by the laws of the state." The record showed that the ISU athletic council was an entity established by officials of the ISU to manage and control its intercollegiate athletic program. After a discussion of specific powers, the court found that the athletic council exercised powers that clearly made it a governmental entity. It went on to decide that the athletic council was granted authorization under the laws of the state that allowed the board of regents of the University to delegate responsibility to it. In conclusion, the court held that since this body was a council as authorized by the laws of the state, it was subject to the Iowa open-meeting law.

Knight v. Iowa District Court of Stony County, 269 N.W. 2d 430 (Iowa 1978)

Rolland Knight and other members of the Iowa State University Athletic Council were charged with unlawfully participating in a closed meeting of the Iowa State University Athletic Council. The Supreme Court of Iowa held that the "Open Meetings Law" as contained in the 1977 Iowa Code was unconstitutionally vague, and thus criminal provisions could not be enforced against the members without violating their rights under the due process clause of the Fourteenth Amendment. The court held that when criminal sanctions are involved for non-compliance, a higher standard of certainty is required by due process. The court held that the statute did not sufficiently specify what those within its reach must do in order to comply. The court distinguished *Greene v. Athletic Council of Iowa State* on the grounds that since the purpose of the statute was to prohibit closed meetings and the only issue in that case was whether such meetings were required to be open, the statute's provisions should be construed favorably to the public. When, however, criminal sanctions are involved, doubts must be resolved in favor of the accused.

1.23–1 Disclosure Cases

The significance of being designated a public body is that it may require an organization to be subject to any "open-meeting" or "sunshine" laws, which generally allow the public to attend meetings (with exceptions as included on a state-by-state basis). Thus, a quasi-public association may be subject to restrictions differing from those placed on a private organiza-

tion. For example, the quasi-public association may have to open its records for public inspection, while a private association would not have this obligation.

The following cases illustrate conflicts that arise concerning the right of the public to be accurately informed by athletic organizations against the need of the organization to protect the confidentiality of its files. The NCAA has argued that only through confidentiality can it investigate itself properly, maintain its amateur integrity, and fulfill this additional public responsibility. It argues that opening confidential investigation files compromises the NCAA's cooperative principles, which all member institutions agree to adhere to when they join the association (see Section 1.41).

The NCAA is a voluntary association whose members, upon joining the organization, agree to follow certain conditions and obligations, including the obligation to conduct their individual institutional athletic programs in a manner consistent with NCAA legislation. In addition, member institutions agree to be policed in regard to the organization's rule by the NCAA's enforcement staff. The key to the NCAA investigative process, such as that discussed in the following cases, is the cooperative principle, whereby the accused member institution and the NCAA's enforcement staff work together to ascertain the truth of alleged infractions.

Seal v. Birmingham Post, 8 Med. L. Rptr. 1633 (Dist. Ct. Kan. 1982)

In October 1981, Edward E. Seal instituted a defamation action in the Circuit Court of Madison County, Alabama, against the defendant newspaper and reporters Paul Finebaun and Bill Lumpkin and editor Angus McEachran. Seal's complaint alleged that the defendants falsely reported that Seal, the principal of Butler High School in Huntsville, Alabama, frequently gave money to Bobby Lee Hurt, a

Butler High School basketball star, because the player threatened to transfer to another school. In addition, the complaint alleged that the newspaper report was false in claiming that Seal ordered $100 taken from home basketball game receipts to pay for Hurt's dental work. The newspaper further reported that Hurt chose to attend the University of Alabama because of financial pressure brought to bear by a Butler High School alumnus who was linked to Seal.

The NCAA also conducted an investigation into allegations regarding Bobby Lee Hurt. *Seal v. Birmingham Post* involved pretrial procedures, separate from the libel action, concerning discovery in which the newspaper sought an issuance of subpoenas duces tecum against the NCAA for information it possessed concerning the Seal controversy. Following the issuance of those subpoenas, the NCAA moved for a protective order to prevent access to its files and employees.

The NCAA's request for a protective order concerning its files was denied by Judge Chipman of the Kansas District Court. In deciding on the motion, Judge Chipman advanced seven major reasons for denial of the NCAA request:

1. None of the parties question that this Court has jurisdiction over the parties to the action, the subject matter of the action, and there can be little question but that this Court is the proper venue. There is no question regarding the propriety of the parties. The Court concludes, as a matter of law, that the Court has *in personam* a jurisdiction of the subject matter, and that the District Court of Johnson County, Kansas is the proper venue for the hearing of this matter.

2. K.S.A.60–228(d) provides as follows: "Depositions for use in foreign jurisdiction. Whenever the deposition of any person is to be taken in this state pursuant to the laws of another state or of the United States or of another county for use in proceedings there, the District Court in the county where the deponent resides or is employed or transacts his or her business in person may, upon ex parte petition, make an order directing issuance of a subpoena as provided in K.S.A.60–245, in aid

of the taking of the deposition, and may make any order in accordance with K.S.A.60–230(d), 60–237(a) or 60–237(b)(1)."

3. In Kansas, the scope of discovery is to be liberally construed so as to provide the parties with information essential to litigation in order to insure the parties a fair trial.

4. The movants in this case do not come within any of the privileges created by the statutes of this state. Plaintiffs claim and the Court holds that trial courts are vested with broad discretion in supervising courts and scope of discovery. In the proper exercise of this discretion, the Court must weigh the interests of the private litigants in obtaining confidential relationships.

5. The United States Constitution establishes the policy that there shall be no law abridging the freedom of speech or of the press. In Kansas, only the news media enjoy any privilege to withhold information deemed to be confidential, and that privilege exists only because a failure to grant such a privilege might result in a violation of the provisions of the First Amendment.

6. Plaintiff's contention that if the information contained in its files is made public, that then the NCAA will be powerless to gain information regarding alleged violations of its rules, is outweighed by the importance of the defendants needing access to relevant information that may lead to admissible evidence to defend itself from the allegation of libel so that defendants may continue to exercise, without fear, their rights under the First Amendment to the Constitution of the United States.

7. The Court concludes that, under the facts of this case, plaintiffs have failed to show that any of the statements that may be contained in the files of the NCAA are privileged communication or that the Court should prohibit their release to the defendants for the reasons above set out.

Berst v. Chipman, 8 Med. L. Rptr. 1635, 231 Kan. 369, 653 P. 2d 107 (1982)

In May 1982, the NCAA appealed the decision in *Seal* v. *Birmingham Post* to the Kansas Supreme Court. The NCAA argued that the lower court decision should be set aside because "The documents sought relate to confidential investigations conducted by the NCAA and the Southeastern Conference of a possible infraction of NCAA rules by the University of Alabama in Huntsville, Alabama, in the recruitment of high school basketball star, Bobby Lee Hurt."

The action was filed by Edward E. Seal, then principal of Butler High School in Huntsville, Alabama. Bobby Lee Hurt, a Butler High School basketball star, also filed a libel action against the Birmingham Post Company and others for publication of alleged defamatory statements in the same newspaper.

Pursuant to a petition filed by the Birmingham Post Company in accordance with K.S.A. 60–228, Judge Chipman on April 2, 1982, caused a subpoena to issue to the NCAA, Berst, and Smith, requiring them to comply with notices to take depositions upon oral examination and to produce documents issued by the Circuit Court of Madison County, Alabama. The subpoena commanded the NCAA, Berst, and Smith to make available at their depositions "all documents and correspondence relating to the initiation, prosecution and results of any investigation by the NCAA concerning Bobby Lee Hurt, Edward Seal, Butler High School, Huntsville, Alabama or the recruiting of Bobby Lee Hurt by the University of Alabama."

On May 3, 1982, the NCAA, Berst, and Smith moved for a protective order pursuant to K.S.A. 60–226(c) directing that they "not be required to disclose the contents or results of their confidential investigation of Edward Seal, Bobby Lee Hurt, Butler High School, Huntsville, Alabama, or the University of Alabama." After a hearing the motion was denied.

The Kansas Supreme Court's abbreviated opinion ruled concerning pretrial discovery that

...the action taken by Judge Chipman was arbitrary in that an *in camera* inspection of the NCAA files tendered for examination was not undertaken upon hearing the application for a protective order.

Upon an *in camera* inspection of the confidential NCAA files by the Supreme Court of Kansas, we hold the respondents may proceed with discovery upon the following terms and conditions. State-

ments and comments of the parties litigant, their employees and fellow employees of Butler High School orally made either in person or by telephone to the NCAA investigator Dale Smith and reduced to writing in memoranda which bear the typed signature of Dale Smith, but which are otherwise not subscribed, are discoverable by the subpoena duces tecum at a time and place mutually to be agreed upon by the counsel for the respective parties litigant.

The written documents discoverable are specifically enumerated and listed by description in a separate Protective Order filed with Clerk of the Supreme Court of Kansas on this date.

The subpoena issued to the NCAA, Berst and Smith to take depositions upon oral examination and to produce documents is limited to the taking of the oral statements and comments subsequently reduced to writing in memoranda and specifically identified by the Protective Order.

The protective order was issued on May 27, 1982. It ordered that

[t]he following documents in the confidential NCAA file, specifically enumerated and listed by description, are discoverable by the subpoena duces tecum issued in the Johnson County District Court actions . . .:

1. MEMORANDUM — "Prospective Student-Athlete Bobby Lee Hurt University of Alabama" — Report of April 29, 1981, telephone call by Dale Smith to Edward Seal.
2. MEMORANDUM — "University of Alabama Prospective Student-Athlete Bobby Lee Hurt, 1980–81" — Report of May 5, 1981, telephone call by Dale Smith to Edward Seal.
3. MEMORANDUM — "Prospective Student-Athlete Bobby Lee Hurt University of Alabama" — Report of May 15, 1981, telephone call by Paul Finebaum to Dale Smith.
4. MEMORANDUM — "Prospective Student-Athlete Bobby Lee Hurt University of Alabama" — Report of May 20, 1981, interview by Dale Smith with Edward Seal.
5. MEMORANDUM — "Prospective Student-Athlete Bobby Lee Hurt University of Alabama" — Report of May 20, 1981,

interview by Dale Smith with Glen "Cotton" Johnson.

6. MEMORANDUM — "University of Alabama Prospective Student-Athlete University of Alabama, 1980–81" — Report of May 21, 1981, interview by Dale Smith with Bobby Lee Hurt.

7. MEMORANDUM — "Prospective Student-Athlete Bobby Lee Hurt, 1980–81 University of Alabama" — Report of May 22, 1981, interview by Dale Smith with Jerry Rice.

8. MEMORANDUM — "Prospective Student-Athlete Bobby Lee Hurt, 1980–81 University of Alabama" — Report of June 1 and 2, 1981, telephone call by Paul Finebaum to Dale Smith.

9. MEMORANDUM — "Prospective Student-Athlete Bobby Lee Hurt" — Report of June 15, 1981, telephone call by Paul Finebaum to Dale Smith.

10. MEMORANDUM — "University of Alabama Prospective Student-Athlete Bobby Lee Hurt" — Report of June 24, 1981, telephone call by Dale Smith to Paul Finebaum.

11. MEMORANDUM — "University of Alabama Prospective Student-Athlete Bobby Lee Hurt" — Report on June 24, 1981, telephone call by Dale Smith to John Childress.

12. MEMORANDUM — "Prospective Student-Athlete Bobby Lee Hurt" — Report of June 29, 1981, telephone call by Dale Smith to Edward Seal.

13. MEMORANDUM — "Prospective Student-Athlete Bobby Lee Hurt" — Report of August 24, 1981, telephone call by Paul Finebaum to Dale Smith.

14. MEMORANDUM — "University of Alabama Prospective Student-Athlete Bobby Lee Hurt" — Report of December 14, 1981, telephone call by Ed Seal to Dale Smith.

15. MEMORANDUM — "Case No. H43 — University of Florida — University of Alabama Case No. H70 — University of Hawaii" — Report of April 6, 1982, telephone call by Paul Finebaum to Dale Smith.

It is further ordered that the subpoena issued to the petitioners herein to take depositions upon oral examination and to produce documents is limited to the taking of the oral statements and comments, made either in person or by telephone, and subsequently reduced to writing by Dale Smith in the memoranda above enumerated and specifically identified.

Berst v. Chipman, 8 Med. L. Rptr. 2593 (Kan. 1982)

The following supplemental opinion was issued by the Kansas Supreme Court on November 12, 1982, and concerns actions involving the NCAA and *Birmingham Post*, which the court first addressed in *Berst* v. *Chipman* (see *supra*), where it ruled for Berst on terms of a protective order:

Where the petitioners have a protected interest in maintaining the confidentiality of their private investigation into possible infractions of NCAA rules undoubtedly presents a legal question of significant public interest. Substantially affected are the privacy interests of those persons to whom information in the files relates or who have passed on information to the NCAA under a pledge of confidentiality, as well as the NCAA's ability to perform one of its primary functions, that of policing its own ranks to prevent corruption in collegiate athletics. The petitioners would not have a remedy by appeal as the information sought would irretrievably have been disclosed prior to the time on which an appeal could be taken.

To fully appreciate the NCAA's high degree of interest in preserving the confidentiality of their investigation files and the identities of their sources, it is helpful to understand the self-policing function of the NCAA and how this system operates. Briefly, the NCAA is to enforce regulations governing the recruiting, admissions, financial aid, and academic standards aspects of collegiate athletics at member institutions.

Once a determination is made on the merits of an infractions case, and the case has been completed, a press release is issued by the NCAA disclosing *only* the institution involved and any sanctions imposed. All other information remains confidential.

In deciding for the *Birmingham Post*, the court noted:

We recognize this case presents a conflict between highly valued interests. On the one hand there is an interest in confidentiality, both to prevent embarrassment to persons who have relied on pledges of secrecy in disclosing information to the NCAA or about whom information in the file may relate, and to promote the public interest in the supervision of intercollegiate athletics to prevent corruption in that area and retain a clear line of demarcation between college athletics and professional sports. On the other hand is the interest in disclosure of all facts relevant to the petitioners' defense in the libel action which will contribute to a full and fair determination of the issues in that case. This case represents a situation where a compromise solution must by reached which will sufficiently serve the interests of both parties.

To protect itself from liability it was necessary for the respondent Birmingham Post Company to acquire information to support its claim that the statements published by the newspaper concerning Seal and Hurt were true. Because of its investigation into the recruitment of Hurt, the NCAA had obtained information about the involvement of both Hurt and Seal in various activities. While it may have been possible for the respondent to gather on its own the same information about the litigants which was obtained by the NCAA through its investigation, the newspaper may have had to go on a "fishing expedition" to discover who, if anyone, had knowledge of the events which were reported in the alleged libelous article. The respondents also had a limited amount of time in which to conduct an investigation and depose those persons with relevant information, as a trial was scheduled in the libel action for August 16, 1982, approximately three months after this motion was made in the court.

Therefore, while we recognize the interest in preserving the confidential nature of these memoranda is substantial, it must give way to assure all the facts will be available for a fair determination of the issues in the libel action.

We think the result reached here is fair to the interests of both parties, affording each some degree of relief.

In his dissent, one justice noted:

When I weigh the conflicting interests in the material sought to be discovered, I come down on the side of protecting the public interest. The public has an overwhelming interest in fostering and supporting the self-regulation engaged in by the Colleges and Universities under the auspices of the NCAA. Television has injected such a large amount of money into college athletic programs the temptation to cheat in recruitment of athletes is overwhelming. In the absence of NCAA regulations and sanctions, the so-called "athlete factories" consisting of twenty to thirty major universities would outbid all others for talent, then pay for it with television exposure. Such would ring the death knell of college athletics as presently constituted. I consider the present system worth maintaining. This can be accomplished only through regulation, investigation and sanctions, either by the NCAA or the government.

Since the NCAA does not have subpoena power, its investigation of complaints is dependent upon a pledge of confidentiality. The majority opinion successfully removes that technique and will ultimately eliminate NCAA regulation or force it to obtain subpoena power. I prefer self-regulation to other options, therefore I dissent.

Arkansas Gazette v. Southern State College, 620 S.W. 2d 258 (Ark. 1981)

The *Arkansas Gazette* brought suit against the Arkansas Intercollegiate Athletic Conference seeking to compel it to disclose the amount of money member institutions dispensed to student-athletes during the school year. The Supreme Court of Arkansas held that the "scholastic" exception to the public records under the Arkansas Freedom of Information Act was limited to individual education or academic records and that information maintained by the conference as to the amount of money institutions dispensed to student-athletes during the school year was not included in such exception under Arkansas Stats. paragraph 12–2803. Nor were such records protected by the federal Family Education Rights Privacy Act of 1974. The court also held that disclosure of such information did not violate students' reasonable expectation of privacy.

NOTES _____

1. In *McMahon* v. *Board of Trustees of University of*

Ark., 499 S.W. 2d 56 (Ark. 1973), the litigation involved a class action suit under the Freedom of Information Act to obtain the names of those persons who were given complimentary tickets and the number of tickets each person received for all football games in which the University of Arkansas participated in the state of Arkansas. The football seasons in question were 1969, 1970, 1971. The trial court held that such information lists "are not public records as contemplated by those statutes [Freedom of Information Act]" and dismissed the petition. The Arkansas Supreme Court affirmed the trial court's decision.

2. The Massachusetts Interscholastic Athletic Association is subject to that state's open-meeting law. See "State Ruling Makes MIAA Records Public," *Boston Globe*, January 3, 1980, p. 37.

3. In 1981 the *Mesa Tribune* (Arizona) was successful in a court challenge against the NCAA that involved the release of information about the association's investigation of the Arizona State University football program. The following excerpt is from "The Vow of Silence," *The Sporting News*, April 25, 1981, p. 14:

> The newspaper encountered harassment and "stonewalling" from the very beginning of its coverage of the Frank Kush case, according to Executive Editor Max Jennings. Kush, former Arizona State football coach, faces a $2.2 million lawsuit charging that he harassed ex-ASU punter Kevin Rutledge into quitting the team and yielding his athletic scholarship. Kush has been exonerated of Rutledge's civil charge that he punched the player during a 1978 game.
>
> "Block and delay — that's the way these public institutions deny the public the right to know," Jennings recently told the Phoenix Press Club. "It's your money and my money they're spending. . . . And the NCAA doesn't want to operate in public any more than Arizona State does."
>
> School bigwigs apparently spared no effort or expense in trying to block access to records of the investigation. The school's legal battery carried the case to the Arizona Supreme Court, claiming, among other pleas, that "the NCAA doesn't want us to reveal these documents." ASU leaders didn't bank exclusively on legal maneuvers, either. A memorandum from ASU President John Schada advised school employees to "stonewall" inquisitive reporters, Jennings said.

4. In 1984, the Miami Herald Publishing Co., the *St. Petersburg Times*, and Campus Communications, Inc., publisher of the University of Florida student newspaper, *The Gator*, had a declaratory suit filed against them in Florida State District Court by the University of Florida. The university asked the court to decide what information the university could reveal to the newspapers in response to their request that files pertaining to an NCAA preliminary investigation into the school's football program be opened

to the media. The University of Florida said that strict federal and state laws involving the confidentiality of student and employee records led to the decision to file the suit. For further information, see the following articles:

(a) "Florida Asks Court to Rule," *Washington Post*, September 5, 1984, p. C2.

(b) "U. Of Florida Asks Judge How Much Information from Unfinished NCAA Probe It Must Reveal," *Chronicle of Higher Education*, September 12, 1984, p. 31.

5. The University of Florida subsequently decided to release the information requested by the newspapers (see Note 4). The information released included a 75-page official letter of inquiry from the NCAA that listed 107 violations by Florida's football program as well as 1,700 pages of documents about the violations. These included transcripts of interviews with a number of witnesses. For further information, see "Florida Cited in 107 Violations," *New York Times*, September 12, 1984, p. D26.

6. For further information on the *Seal* v. *Birmingham Post* cases, see also:

(a) "Judge Orders NCAA to Open Its Records," *New York Times*, May 19, 1982, p. B8.

(b) "Court Tells NCAA to Release Papers Sought in Libel Suit," *Chronicle of Higher Education*, June 9, 1982, p. 14.

7. In December 1984, the University of Georgia agreed to release documents pertaining to an NCAA investigation of its athletic program. Georgia was under pressure to do so because of a request by Morris Communications Corporation, which publishes newspapers in Georgia and Florida, including the *Athens* (Ga.) *Daily News*. For further information, see these articles:

(a) "Georgia Agrees to Go Public," *Asbury Park Press*, January 8, 1985, p. D7.

(b) "Dooley Assails Charges," *New York Times*, March 3, 1985, sec. 5, p. 1.

1.23–2   Funding of Public Facilities

A recent development with respect to public responsibilities of an amateur organization is the challenge to the use of public funds. There have been challenges made to the building of sports facilities, where faculty governing bodies have been concerned that funds would be diverted from other educational areas.

While the following case was not heard on its merits and decided in a court of law, the issues raised shed light on potential problem areas in financing athletic facilities. University of Tennessee faculty members were successful in placing pressure on school officials by commencing litigation, to allow some controls and approve projects that faculty were involved with, in return for the promise not to delay the financing for Assembly Hall. "The significant thing about the settlement," said David Burkhalter, the faculty members' lawyer, "is that it's legally binding and sets a clear priority. It means that the university has recognized that the faculty has a right to say how university money should be spent, and that's unprecedented at the University of Tennessee."

Lester v. Public Building Authority of County of Knox, No. 78491, Chancery Court for Knox County, Tn. (1983)

This suit was brought by faculty members of the University of Tennessee against the university in order to block its planned funding and construction of the $30 million Assembly Center and Sports Center.

The planned arena was to be financed as follows:

State of Tennessee	$ 7 million
Knox County, Tennessee	$10 million
University of Tennessee	$13 million

The plaintiff faculty members believed they had a

special interest in this litigation in that "appropriations" from the state may be made available to satisfy the University's obligations with respect to the financing of the arena and fees may be levied on the faculty to defray the University's liabilities under the financing scheme. Specifically, the salaries of the faculty, raises and departmental budgets could be placed in jeopardy. The University had in recent years undergone severe budgetary cuts, and the faculty was concerned with a diversion of funds for the arena project that would otherwise be applied to academic programs, research and salaries.

The faculty members also argued that as Knox County residents their burden of taxation would be increased because of funding pledges made by the county and that such pledges were

made illegally and were unconstitutional. They also noted:

Moreover, arena projects, nationwide, have historically lost substantial amounts of money, and the University is to be solely responsible for maintenance and operation, the guaranty of the County's obligation in the amount of $12 million plus their pledge of $13 million.

All told, the faculty members believed "that the taxpayers will suffer substantial losses unless said illegal actions are enjoined."

The case was settled out of court. In a compromise agreement, the following was decided:

1. The University of Tennessee will make full disclosure of information concerning the funding and operation of the Assembly Center and Arena to the Faculty Senate of the University of Tennessee, Knoxville.

2. The University of Tennessee will not make any requests of the Tennessee General Assembly for additional appropriations towards construction costs of the Assembly Center and Arena over and above the $7 million dollars already appropriated and allocated by the General Assembly and the State Building Commission for construction of the Arena. The University will continue with its efforts to secure full funding for the new proposed library.

3. Construction cost overruns, if any, beyond the $30 million which the Assembly Center and Arena is expected to cost, and operation and maintenance expenses of the arena following its construction, will be funded through the Athletic Department of the University of Tennessee, Knoxville.

4. It is presently contemplated by the University of Tennessee that it will request the Tennessee State School Bond Authority to issue revenue bonds in the amount of approximately $8 million to finance a portion of the University's share of the construction costs of the arena. The University will not request of the Tennessee State School Bond Authority the issuance of bonds in excess of $8 million unless any amount in excess of $8 million dollars is secured by sufficient revenues, gifts or pledges of funds necessary to retire such bonded indebtedness. The University further agrees that all contributions presently pledged and gifts which

have been received towards construction of the arena will be solely for the arena. The University further agrees that contributions currently pledged for the arena project, future contributions specifically pledged for the arena project, unrestricted gifts to the Athletic Department, revenues derived from the operation of the arena and from other operations of the Athletic Department will be used first to retire bonds of the School Bond Authority issued for the purpose of constructing the arena.

5. The University of Tennessee Guaranty will be amended prior to execution by inserting the following provision:

> It is expressly understood and agreed however that for purposes of this Guaranty, funds legally available to the Guarantor shall not include funds appropriated by the Tennessee General Assembly for the University of Tennessee academic budgets and salaries; increases in student activity fees without consultation with the appropriate student representatives; or unrestricted gifts to Guarantor other than gifts to the Athletic Department of Guarantor.

NOTE _____

1. For further information, see "U. of Tennessee and Professors in Accord on Arena," *Chronicle of Higher Education*, April 20, 1983, p. 13.

1.23–3   Delegation of a Public Responsibility

Several questions are raised in the following three companion cases concerning the degree that an amateur athletic association can delegate its authority in light of its responsibility to the public to organize and present an annual athletic event — in this case, the Boston Marathon. The decisions reached in these cases are interesting examples as to the extent the courts will go in interpreting the law so as to protect a perceived public interest.

_____

Boston Athletic Ass'n. v. International Marathons, Inc., 392 Mass. 356, 467 N.E. 2d 58 (1984)

The Boston Athletic Association (BAA) is a nonprofit corporation incorporated under Massachusetts General Laws, G.L. chapter 180 and chapter 287 of the Acts of 88. The original purpose of the BAA was amended in 1982 to include, "the encouragement of sport and the promotion of physical exercise with particular emphasis on the sponsorship of long distance running events (especially the traditional annual BAA Marathon) and of track and field teams and events . . ."

On September 27, 1982, the BAA brought a civil action in Supreme Court seeking to enjoin International Marathons, Inc. (IMI) from representing itself to the public as BAA's agent. IMI is a Massachusetts business corporation, organized on May 1, 1981, and headed by Marshall Medoff, its sole incorporator, officer, director, and shareholder. IMI's corporate purpose is sales and sports promotions.

William T. Cloney, president of the BAA, and Medoff had initiated discussions in late 1980 about the possibility of a Medoff-headed organization that would commercially promote the Boston Marathon. At the time, the board of directors of the BAA felt that significant increases in sponsorship revenues were needed to maintain the prestige and level of organization that had always been a trademark of the marathon. At the April 1981 meeting of the BAA board of directors, a motion granting broad authority to Cloney to negotiate and execute such agreements was passed. Some members of the board did raise questions concerning the scope of authority and potential implications, but the questions were dismissed. The motion read: "That William T. Cloney, as President of the Association, be and hereby is authorized and directed to negotiate and to execute in the name of and in behalf of this Association such agreements as he deems in the best interests of the Association for the perpetuation, sponsorship or underwriting of the Boston A.A. Marathon." There was no discussion held concerning a possible involvement by Medoff.

On September 23, 1981, after a series of meetings with Medoff but without further consultation with the BAA board, Cloney entered into the following agreement with Medoff:

The agreement designates IMI as the exclusive promotor of the Marathon. IMI can make five "major" and five "minor" sponsorship contracts as well as agreements with an unlimited number of companies which would supply services to the BAA. The contract gives IMI the right to represent that the Marathon is "presented by" IMI or its assignee. With the exception of the Japanese market, all radio, television, and movie rights in the Marathon are assigned to IMI.

The exclusive promotor arrangement is accomplished through the transfer by the BAA to IMI of all right, title and interest to the exclusive use of the Boston Marathon and BAA Marathon logo(s) and name, reserving to the BAA the right to use the name and logos only in so far as such use is not inconsistent with the agreement.

The agreement also governs the conduct of the parties in carrying out their contractual responsibilities. The agreement requires the BAA to execute sponsorship agreements consistent with the terms and conditions stated herein, when IMI presents a sponsor ready, willing and able to execute and carry out the obligations of a sponsorship agreement. The BAA is bound to cooperate fully with IMI's efforts to negotiate with sponsors and is required to do all things reasonably necessary as may be requested by IMI to effectuate consummation of agreements with the sponsors. The BAA reserves the right to decline to accept any or all sponsors, but approval of a sponsor shall not be unreasonably withheld. Certain sponsors, however, are approved by the amendment to the contract and, as to these sponsors, IMI itself may execute on behalf of the BAA the sponsorship agreement, if the form of the sponsorship agreement is consistent with a form approved by prior BAA use. The BAA is solely responsible for the actual production and the expenses of the Marathon and shall lend its cooperation and support to IMI and the sponsors to make the event successful. The agreement further provides that the BAA will not make any independent sponsorship arrangements without the written consent of IMI.

According to the financial terms of the agreement, the annual sponsorship fee due the BAA is $400,000. All sponsorship revenues in excess of $400,000 are payable directly to IMI. The BAA can agree to accept less than $400,000 in a particular year if sponsorship agreements for that year total less than that amount. Every five years the sponsorship fee shall be increased by an amount equal to the average change of the Consumer Price Index for the preceding five-year term. The agreement does not require that the annual fee be paid to the BAA from revenues actually received from a sponsor.

The agreement has the following renewal provision: It shall extend and renew itself automatically and shall continue year to year so long as the annual sponsorship fee . . . is paid.

Following the agreement, Medoff negotiated and Cloney executed sponsorships for the BAA. The BAA board was not aware of the contracts. All sponsorship fees raised were paid directly to IMI. It was not until February 1982 that some of the board learned of these agreements. On September 9, 1982, the board decided that the agreement between Cloney and Medoff was beyond its authorization of September 1981. The court action was initiated by the BAA in late September 1982.

Medoff had signed contracts with nine corporate sponsors while serving as the BAA's agent for the marathon. Total revenues raised for the 1982 marathon were $700,000. The contracts entered into by Medoff varied in terms, length, and monies paid to the BAA for the corporate sponsorship. Seiko paid $400,000 for rights to be the official presenter and timer of the marathon in 1982 and agreed to raise its payment to $450,000 in 1984. The official photographer, Eastman Kodak, paid $50,000 in 1982, which was to rise to $95,000 in 1984. Medoff was also considering moving the race to Sunday, instead of the traditional "Patriots Day" Monday (a Massachusetts state holiday), to obtain broader national television exposure.

In its action, the BAA sought a preliminary injunction to have the agreement set aside. It argued that the contract was in violation of Massachusetts General Laws, chapter 68, section 21, and second, that the agreement's terms and conditions exceeded the authority delegated to Cloney.

The Division of Public Charities of the Attorney General's Office held a hearing concerning the BAA's assertion of violations of G.L. chapter 68, section 21. The hearing examiners affirmed the BAA board's decision, and IMI appealed.

Attorney General v. International Marathons, Inc., 392 Mass. 370, 467 N.E. 2d 51 (1984)

The appeals court decision was affirmed when the Massachusetts Supreme Judicial Court refused to review the hearing examiner's decision because it was a moot question. The attorney general had brought this action seeking to enforce the provisions of G.L. chapter 68, paragraphs 21 and 23, for IMI's failure to register with the Division of Public Charities and post a necessary bond.

In its decision, the appeals court noted:

1. This action should not have been dismissed as moot. An issue is moot when the parties no longer have a stake in the determination of that issue. *First National Bank* v. *Haufler*, 377 Mass. 209, 211 (1979). Although the contract between the BAA and IMI is no longer in effect, the applicability of G.L. chapter 68, paragraph 23, does not depend on the existence of a contract.

2. Although the controversy is not moot, dismissal was nonetheless proper in this case because the provisions of G.L. chapter 68 do not apply to the type of activity involved here. General Laws chapter 68 regulates the activity of professional solicitors of charitable "contributions." A "contribution" is defined in G.L. chapter 68, paragraph 18, inserted by St. 1964, chapter 718, paragraph 1, as "the promise or grant of any money or property or anything of value." A "professional solicitor" is one who solicits "contributions directly or in the form of payment for goods or services . . . for charitable purposes." Although this language is broad, it is not broad enough to include the sale of sponsorship, advertising and promotional rights. We disagree with the conclusion of the hearing examiner that as long as the goods or services received in return for a contribution are integrally related to the purposes of the charitable organization (as promotional rights invariably would be)

the contribution is charitable within the meaning of the statute.

Concerning BAA's second argument, in which it was argued that the contract was enacted in excess of Cloney's authorization, a supreme court judge in a separate action and decision on September 29, 1982, granted a preliminary injunction against IMI from using or in any way alienating any of the funds received from sponsors of the marathon. On August 29, 1983, a second superior court judge granted the BAA a partial summary judgment declaring the contract void and unenforceable. The appeals court in affirming the lower court decision ruled on the validity of the injunction and the validity of the Contract. It stated in part:

1. *The preliminary injunction.* The judge did not abuse his discretion in granting the BAA's request for preliminary relief. He made a reasonable assessment of the risk of irreparable harm to either party as a result of the issuance or denial of the injunction and the likelihood of the moving party's success on the merits. The BAA's complaint challenged the validity of its contract with IMI. As a result, it sought an injunction to prevent the dispersal of the funds prior to a determination on the merits. The harm to IMI if the injunction were denied was the risk that IMI would dispose of the funds prior to a determination on the merits. The harm to IMI if the injunction were granted was loss of use of the money pending that determination. The risk to the BAA is far greater than the risk to IMI. If IMI were ultimately to prevail on the merits, it could be compensated for loss of use of the funds by assessment of an interest payment. However, if the injunction were denied, if the BAA were to prevail, and if the money were spent by IMI, the BAA would be put to the time-consuming and sometimes difficult task of trying to exact its damages. Furthermore, the judge determined that there was a "reasonable probability" of success on the merits. He based this conclusion on the fact that the Attorney General's division of public charities had characterized the contract as subject to the provisions of G.L. chapter 68, paragraph 21. While we do not express an opinion as to whether the action of the Attorney General is

entitled to "presumptive validity," we do agree that, on balance, the BAA demonstrated sufficient likelihood of success and sufficient risk of harm to be entitled to a preliminary injunction which did no more than preserve the status quo.

2. *The validity of the contract.* We hold the contract between the BAA and IMI to be void and unenforceable. The defendant is, however, entitled to recovery in quantum meruit for the services it rendered in obtaining sponsorship contracts for the running of the Marathon in 1982.

a. *Improper delegation of authority.* Whether the board intended by its vote of April 27, 1981, to confer upon Cloney the authority to enter into the sponsorship agreement with IMI, that contract is void. The board of directors of a corporation cannot delegate total control of the corporation to an individual officer. Neither can it delegate authority which is so broad that it enables the officer to bind the corporation to extraordinary commitments or significantly to encumber the principal asset or function of the corporation.

The contract seriously encumbers the manner in which the BAA may conduct the Marathon. The BAA is obliged to produce the race in its traditional form and to pay the entire bill. But it is not entitled to "present" the race. That right, as well as the right to use the name and logo of the BAA, belongs to IMI or its assignee. The BAA may not use its own logo in any way "inconsistent" with IMI's rights pursuant to the contract. The right to enter into sponsorship agreements belongs exclusively to IMI, although the BAA can reasonably withhold its approval. The BAA may not make independent agreements without written permission from IMI. Finally, the contract between IMI and the BAA is automatically renewable at the option of IMI. Under the plain language of the agreement, there is no way for the BAA to end the relationship.

Furthermore, the contract between IMI and the BAA is especially vulnerable because it is antithetical to the BAA's nature as a nonprofit corporation in as much as this agreement turns the solicitation of sponsors from a way to support the Marathon to a way for IMI to make a profit. It is entirely inconsistent with the nonprofit nature of the organization to permit such a substantial segment of the revenue earning capacity of the Marathon to be used as a vehicle for personal gain.

For the foregoing reasons, the Board of Governors of the BAA was not empowered to delegate to Cloney the right to make this contract with IMI.

b. *Apparent authority.* IMI argues that the April 27, 1981, vote of the board conferred upon Cloney the apparent authority to enter into the disputed agreement. This argument is not persuasive. "Persons dealing with a corporation are presumed to know the extent of its powers." An officer of a nonprofit corporation cannot have apparent authority to encumber the principal function of the corporation and to divert the substantial earning capacity of the corporation to private benefit.

3. *Quantum meruit.* Although the promotion contract between IMI and the BAA is unenforceable, nevertheless as the BAA concedes IMI is entitled to recover the fair value of its services.

International Marathons, Inc. v. Attorney General, 392 Mass. 376, 467 N.E. 2d 55 (1984)

In this appeal the Supreme Judicial Court declined to review the decision of the examiners because the question was moot in light of *BAA v. IMI.* The hearing examiner had disapproved the contract between IMI and the BAA because it was:

> . . . violative of G.L. c. 68, paragraph 21, because IMI, in its capacity as a professional solicitor on behalf of the BAA, was likely to receive compensation in excess of fifteen per cent of the total moneys raised. General Laws chapter 68, paragraph 21 (a), as amended through St. 1981, c. 345, paragraph 2, provides in pertinent part: "No charitable organization . . . shall agree to pay a professional solicitor or its agents, servants or employees assigned to work under the direction of a professional solicitor, in the aggregate a total amount in excess of fifteen per cent of the total moneys, pledges, or other property raised or received by reason of any solicitation activities or campaigns, including reimbursement for expenses incurred."

NOTES _____

1. Cloney, facing forced resignation, retired from the BAA board on June 16, 1982. Cloney, however, defended his actions with IMI and Medoff: "I had authority to sign this much-maligned contract. I should note Mr. Medoff has fulfilled his end of the contract. At no time was there any question of procedures being followed, agreements being

made and contracts being signed." Clooney felt that ". . . for the first time, the BAA has a substantial cushion of some half-million dollars."

"Nobody's perfect," Cloney said under questioning from the media. "Sure, I have some regrets. I have some regrets about the latest developments [Cloney's resignation]. I have some regrets about some of the activities of some of my friends and I certainly have tremendous regrets about a profession that I hold dearly — that's the journalism profession."

For further information, see "Cloney Calls It Quits," *Boston Globe*, June 17, 1982, pp. 49, 52.

2. The following sponsors of the 1982 BAA Marathon signed contracts under IMI:

Seiko	$400,000
Chrysler	70,000
Tiger-Asics	50,000
Eastman-Kodak	50,000
Bristol-Myers	50,000
Anheuser-Busch	35,000
Sunmark	20,000
Coca-Cola	20,000
Belmont Springs	5,000
	$700,000

For further information, see "What Happened to the $700,000?" *Boston Globe*, April 13, 1983, p. 45.

3. The emphasis on corporate sponsorship by the BAA also underwent a change following the marathon's legal battles. "There's a world of difference between selling the Boston Marathon and subsidizing the race," said Timothy W. Kilduff, a spokesman for and a member of the BAA board of governors. However, Marshall Medoff continued to disagree. "This business about not commercializing the race was baloney from the start. They're intent on doing exactly the same program as we did, only they can't do it as well."

"The main difference," said Kiduff, "is that there is no interest in profit. Profit is not the objective of what we're doing." According to the BAA, many traditional sponsors of the marathon, such as the Prudential Insurance Company (at whose building the race ends) and the Bristol-Myers Company, disengaged themselves from the race after Medoff became involved. Prudential had largely under-written the race from 1965 but did not like Medoff's new plans. It terminated its involvement with the race in 1982 and only resumed a relationship after Medoff was removed from his position as agent for the BAA. Bristol-Myers explained in its termination letter in 1982 that, "The Boston Marathon sponsorship, as currently structured, does not fit into our future plans primarily because of the high cost of participation relative to the promotional value derived." Kodak, Coca-Cola, Anheuser-Busch, Inc., and Tiger-Asics also dropped out after being involved with the first race under Medoff's stewardship.

However, by the time of the 1983 race, the BAA had solved many of the corporate complaints by lowering sponsorship fees and expectations. In addition, new spon-sors were added, such as New Balance Athletic Shoe Co. and Xerox, to replace those companies that opted out of sponsorship when the BAA renegotiated all of Medoff's contracts. For further information, see "BAA's New Approach Attracts 'Contributors,' " *Boston Globe*, April 13, 1983, p. 45.

4. When dealing with an organization in which the public has placed a trust, it seems the individual should consider the higher degree of scrutiny that such involvement may receive from the courts. The NCAA in the case of *Tarkanian* v. *University of Nevada, Las Vegas* (see Section 1.41–2), discovered how difficult a court's strict scrutiny can be on an athletic organization's standards of conduct. The court stated:

In sum, what started out as an association whose members met and exceeded certain lofty goals, ended up as the NCAA-bureaucracy which looks upon its friends (sycophants) with feigned pleasure, and its enemies (those who still recognize the U.S. Constitution) with barely-concealed malevolence. The NCAA has numerous, very distinguished individuals on its various committees and its Council for public consumption, but the real power is in the hands of bureaucrats who are unknown to, and unelected by, the membership of the NCAA.

The NCAA is an association which exists for the purpose of seeing that there is fair play; it also has the obligation to play fairly.

5. For further information, see the following articles:
(a) "Cloney Survives BAA Board Meeting," *Boston Globe*, May 22, 1982, p. 27.
(b) "Always Thinking Forward," *Boston Globe*, June 16, 1982, p. 73.
(c) "He Has to Face Facts," *Boston Globe*, June 16, 1982, pp. 73, 76.
(d) "Profits Disappearing as Legal Fees Mount," *Boston Globe*, April 13, 1983, p. 45.
(e) "Dropping Out of the Race," *Boston Globe*, February 3, 1985, p. 48.
(f) "Out of Step, Dwindling Marathon Entries Point to a Busted Running Boom," *Boston Globe*, March 31, 1985, p. 39.
(g) "BAA May Offer Prize Money in '86," *Boston Herald*, February 24, 1985, p. 96.

6. In 1985, the BAA began to consider giving prize money to the top finishers of the Boston Marathon in order to compete with New York, Chicago, Pittsburgh, and other cities. The newer marathons were attracting top mara-thoners by offering prize money. See: "BAA May Offer Prize Money in '86," *Boston Herald*, February 24, 1985, p. 96.

7. In 1984 there had been 88 runnings of the Boston

Marathon which awarded no purse, had no live network television coverage, had 6,750 qualifiers to run in the field, and had a limited budget. In comparison, the New York Marathon in 1984 had conducted 15 runnings, awarded a purse of $350,000, had live television coverage by ABC-TV, had 16,315 qualifiers to run in the field, and operated on a $1.75 million budget. The Chicago Marathon in 1984 had conducted 8 runnings, awarded a purse of $450,000, had special-edited television coverage by CBS-TV, had approximately 7,500 qualifiers to run in the field, and had a $1.2 million budget. See: "Of Miles and Millions," *Boston Globe*, October 30, 1984, p. 29.

1.23–4 Public Broadcast Rights

The courts are apt to view uninterrupted broadcast of televised sports as a public right. Although decided primarily on antitrust principles, cases such as *National Collegiate Athletic Ass'n. v. Board of Regents of Oklahoma and University of Georgia Athletic Ass'n.*, have as their underlying principle the public responsibility of the NCAA not to interfere with the populace's right to view intercollegiate sports (see Section 6.32).

1.24 Antitrust Liabilities of Amateur Associations

In the past, amateur athletic organizations have not been subject to the antitrust litigation that the professional team sport industry has faced. However, with the increased prominence associated with amateur athletics and the money now involved, organizations such as the NCAA are increasingly subject to antitrust litigation. Chapter 3, Volume 1 sets forth the basic antitrust principles that are also applicable to amateur athletics.

Historically, defendant amateur athletic associations have been successful in arguing that the antitrust laws are not applicable to them since amateur athletics are not "trade" or "commerce" as defined by the Sherman Act. Amateur organizations argue that since their athletic associations are nonprofit organizations, their primary purpose is noncommercial in nature and hence not trade or commerce. However, in the cases that follow, the trend appears to be for the courts to find that amateur athletics, and especially the NCAA, are "trade" or "commerce" and therefore are subject to the antitrust laws.

College Athletic Placement Services, Inc. v. National Collegiate Athletic Ass'n., 1975 Trade Cases 60,177 (E.D. Va.)

The plaintiff was engaged in the business of locating college athletic scholarships for high school students, particularly in the less popular sports. The student or parents of the student were required to pay a contractual fee to obtain the plaintiff's services. Plaintiff had originally received assurances from the NCAA that the eligibility of the students who sought its help would not be affected, but in 1973 the NCAA drafted an amendment to its constitution that would render students who obtained information from organizations like plaintiffs, ineligible for intercollegiate competition. The amendment, Article 3, Section 1(c), reads as follows:

> Any student-athlete who agrees or has ever agreed to be represented by an agent or an organization in the marketing of his athletic ability or reputation no longer shall be eligible for intercollegiate athletics; however, a student-athlete may secure advice from a lawyer concerning a professional sports contract without violation of this provision provided the lawyer does not represent the student-athlete in negotiation of the contract. *Any individual agency or organization representing a prospective student-athlete for compensation in placing the prospect in a collegiate institution as a recipient of athletically related financial aid shall be considered an agent or organization marketing the athletic ability or reputation of the individual* [emphasis added].

Plaintiff brought suit against the NCAA, alleging a violation of the Sherman Act. Plaintiff claimed that the NCAA's action constituted a group boycott (or at least a secondary group boycott, since it is not the NCAA members themselves but rather prospective students of those institutions who would no longer avail themselves of plaintiff's services). Plaintiff alleged per se illegality.

The court found no violation. The members of the NCAA had not combined with the officials of the NCAA for the primary purpose of coercion or exclusion. Nor was their motive anticompetitive or intended to damage or eliminate plaintiff. The amendment was designed to promote amateurism in college sports and to ensure that academic admission standards of the member institutions are not compromised by an organization that has a financial interest in having a particular student admitted to a college or university.

The court applied a rule of reason analysis and found that the case at bar did not constitute a violation of the Sherman Act. In fact, it did not even come under the Sherman Act because there was no competition and hence no anticompetitive intent. Though vague in its language, the Sherman Act has been construed to deal primarily with combinations having commercial objectives. Since the NCAA was attempting to preserve educational standards in its member institutions, the court could not apply the Sherman Act to the NCAA's noncommercial objectives. Additionally, the court found no illegal boycott on the part of the NCAA, stating that the "exclusion" of plaintiff was a by-product of an NCAA mandate intended to advance a long-standing NCAA policy.

Amateur Softball Ass'n. of America v. United States, 467 F. 2d 312 (10th Cir. 1972)

The U.S. Department of Justice, through a civil investigative demand, sought inquiry as to whether the Amateur Softball Association of America (ASA) was in violation of the Sherman Anti-Trust Act, 15 U.S.C. paragraph 1. The Justice Department asked the ASA to produce several documents, but the ASA resisted, claiming (1) that it was exempt from the Sherman Act under the same provisions as professional baseball; (2) that amateur athletics are not subject to the Sherman Act, because they are amateur in nature and are not "trade" or

"commerce"; and (3) that the government had not investigated other amateur sports, and was thus discriminating against the ASA.

The court concluded that the case was not sufficiently developed to rule on the first two arguments. It indicated great doubt as to the ASA's claim to an exemption because one had been extended to professional baseball. Beyond that, it indicated that grounds existed for further exploration of whether the ASA was engaged in "trade" or "commerce" within the meaning of the Sherman Act. The third argument, concerning discrimination, was rejected by the court. The court said that inaction regarding other sports did not excuse illegal conduct, if there was such, on the part of the ASA.

Tondas v. Amateur Hockey Ass'n. of the United States, 438 F. Supp. 310 (W.D. N.Y. 1977)

Plaintiff commenced this private antitrust action for treble damages and injunctive relief pursuant to sections 4 and 16 of the Clayton Act, 15, U.S.C. sections 15 and 26. Plaintiff alleged that defendants combined, agreed, and conspired among themselves and with others to unreasonably restrain and monopolize — and have unreasonably restrained and monopolized — interstate trade and commerce in amateur hockey in violation of sections 1 and 2 of the Sherman Act, 15 U.S.C. sections 1 and 2. Plaintiff further alleged that defendants wrongfully and maliciously interfered with its franchise, contract rights, and business relations.

Three of the defendants — Amateur Hockey Association of the United States (AHAUS), Croft, and Trumble — moved for summary judgment pursuant to rule 56 of the *Federal Rules of Civil Procedure*. They alleged that (1) the plaintiff and the AHAUS were not engaged in "trade" or "commerce" within the meaning of the Sherman Act; (2) that the complaint failed to state a claim upon which relief could be granted under antitrust law; and (3) that the plaintiff lacked standing to bring the action.

The court held that the purpose of the

Sherman Act is to promote competition by preventing unreasonable restraints to interstate trade or commerce. The act specifically deals with those who conspire to restrain or monopolize commercial intercourse among the states. The act was primarily aimed at conduct that has commercial objectives. The Supreme Court, however, has indicated that organizations with other objectives can also be subject to the Sherman Act. . . .

In *Amateur Softball Ass'n. of America* v. *United States*, the court ruled that a nonprofit amateur sport association that agrees or conspires to restrain trade or commerce in commercially sold articles is subject to antitrust law. Even though the amateur association's primary purpose is noncommercial, its subsequent actions in carrying out its objectives could trigger the applicability of the Sherman Act if such conduct restrains interstate trade or commerce in an unreasonable manner. In this case, plaintiff alleged that amateur hockey is not merely a sport but a large commercial enterprise that is organized and operated for the benefit and profit of individual member teams. Defendants denied this allegation and asserted that the funds raised by the AHAUS are used solely to defray expenses and to promote the development of amateur hockey. Plaintiff, a member of the Southern Ontario Junior Hockey League, alleged that it competed for patrons with teams affiliated with the New York Penn Jr. B League, a member of the AHAUS. Defendant AHAUS disclaimed that any economic competition existed between the plaintiff and its teams.

Additionally, plaintiff alleged the AHAUS was motivated by financial considerations to eliminate it as a competing amateur hockey team in the Buffalo area. Plaintiff alleged that these financial considerations were discussed by the defendants prior to the refusal of the AHAUS to allow plaintiff to play its games in North Tonawanda. Defendants asserted that the decision of the AHAUS to withhold such permission was not motivated by any economic anticompetitive scheme or purpose, but was made in order to develop American amateur hockey and improve the quality of young American amateur hockey players. Also, defendants denied that financial considerations were discussed at meetings conducted prior to the decision of the AHAUS to refuse to permit plaintiff to play in North Tonawanda. Plaintiff alleged that AHAUS has considerable economic and market power, but defendants refuted this contention and asserted that AHAUS strictly adheres to its charitable, educational, and scientific objectives and purpose. Because of these material factual issues, summary judgment was precluded.

AHAUS, Croft, and Trumble further urged that summary judgment should be granted because the plaintiff and the AHAUS are not competitors. The AHAUS relied on *San Francisco Seals, Ltd.* v. *National Hockey League*, 379 F. Supp. 966 (C.D. Cal. 1974). That case held that a professional hockey league team does not compete in an economic sense with its league and other league members, and thus territorial restraints imposed on a member by its own league do not violate the Sherman Act. In AHAUS, the plaintiff contended that it competed for patrons with the teams affiliated with the New York Penn Jr. B League, not the teams associated with the Southern Ontario Junior Hockey League to which it belonged. The court felt that the AHAUS case was distinguishable because it involved rival leagues. The court also stated that the AHAUS was not immune from the antitrust simply because it did not see itself as a competitor of the plaintiff. A noncompetitor who agrees, contracts, or conspires with another to restrain trade or commerce is subject to the antitrust laws.

In the court's view, the AHAUS' contention that plaintiff had failed as a matter of law to state a claim pursuant to section 2 of the Sherman Act lacked merit. The court felt the market power possessed by AHAUS remained open to debate. Plaintiff's affidavits contained sufficient allegations of economic power to surmount a motion for summary judgment. All motions made by the AHAUS for summary judgment were denied.

Ass'n. for Intercollegiate Athletics for Women v. National Collegiate Athletics Ass'n., 558 F. Supp. 487 (D.D.C. 1983)

In its suit against the NCAA and its entry into the market for women's sports, the Association for Intercollegiate Athletics for Women (AIAW) charged that the contract between the NCAA and CBS for the purchase of the rights to televise the NCAA's Division I men's basketball championship was "tied" to the television rights to the NCAA's newly instituted women's basketball championships.

The evidence strongly suggested that it was the overall attractiveness of CBS's total offer rather than CBS's willingness to telecast the women's game which induced the NCAA to accept it. In fact, CBS had offered less for the women's game than its competitor NBC. The AIAW conceded that it had no personal knowledge of the NCAA's intent to condition the purchase of the men's championships upon its sale of the women's counterpart, and the court concluded that the sale of the women's championship was merely collateral to a much larger transaction that would have gone forward with or without the women's event.

With respect to the AIAW's claim that the NCAA interfered with its commercial relationship to NBC, the NCAA asserted that NBC's decision not to televise the AIAW championship was motivated by the fact that most of the "name" schools that participated in the previous AIAW tournament had expressed an intent to participate only in the NCAA tournament in 1982. The court held that the evidence as to this alleged predatory act was at best equivocal and became dispositive when the plaintiff failed to prove specific intent necessary to sustain its monopoly claim.

NOTES _____

1. In *Board of Regents, University of Oklahoma v. National Collegiate Athletic Ass'n.*, 561 P. 2d 449 (Okla.

1977), plaintiff football coaches unsuccessfully challenged under the antitrust laws an NCAA rule limiting the number of assistant football coaches (see Section 1.41–2).

2. In *National Collegiate Athletic Ass'n. v. Board of Regents, University of Oklahoma and University of Georgia*, 104 S. Ct. 2948, 82 L. Ed. 2d 70 (1984), the universities brought suit against the NCAA, alleging that the NCAA's football television contract violated sections 1 and 2 of the Sherman Act (see Section 6.32).

3. In *Jones v. National Collegiate Athletic Ass'n.*, 392 F. Supp. 295 (D. Mass. 1975), plaintiff student-athlete argued that the NCAA violated the antitrust laws by declaring him ineligible to compete in NCAA events. The court concluded that the Sherman Act does not cover NCAA members in setting eligibility standards for intercollegiate athletics (see Section 2.15–1(d)).

4. In *Hennessey v. National Collegiate Athletic Ass'n.*, No. CA 76–P–0799–W (N.D. Ala. 1976), *aff'd per curiam*, 564 F.2d 1136 (5th Cir. 1977), a limitation on school coaching staff was upheld as an "economic measure" designed to maintain athletic balance and preserve amateurism.

5. For further information on the NCAA and antitrust law suits concerning college football, see the following articles:

(a) "Big-Time College Football Powers Oppose NCAA's Exclusive Control of TV Contracts," *Chronicle of Higher Education*, June 15, 1981, p. 4.

(b) "NCAA Calls Meeting on Rules Changes, Hopes to Settle Dispute over TV Football," *Chronicle of Higher Education*, September 16, 1981, p. 1.

(c) "Football Association Retreats, But War with NCAA over Control of Television Rights Is Far from Done," *Chronicle of Higher Education*, January 6, 1982, p. 6.

(d) "NCAA Rejects Efforts by Football Group," *Chronicle of Higher Education*, January 20, 1982, p. 4.

(e) "Court Rejects Challenge to NCAA's Sway over TV," *Chronicle of Higher Education*, September 1, 1982, p. 23.

(f) "Judge Rules NCAA Television Pacts Violate Antitrust Law, Says Colleges Own TV Rights," *Chronicle of Higher Education*, September 22, 1982, p. 1.

(g) "NCAA Says Court Ruling Won't Affect TV Bans," *Chronicle of Higher Education*, October 20, 1982, p. 18.

(h) "U.S. Backs Suit on TV Football by 2 Universities," *Chronicle of Higher Education*, November 10, 1982, p. 1.

(i) "Committee to Develop Alternative TV Plan," *NCAA News*, June 1, 1983, p. 1.

(j) "NCAA Pacts to Televise College Football Violate Antitrust Law, High Court Rules"; "Ruling Is Expected to Increase Number, Variety of College Football Teams on TV," *Wall Street Journal*, June 28, 1984, p. 4.

(k) "Court Voids NCAA's TV Contracts, But Joy Doesn't Reign Supreme," *Washington Post*, June 28, 1984, p. 1.

(l) "Televised College Football: More, But for Whom?" by Don Canham, *New York Times*, July 15, 1984, Sec. 5, p. 2.

(m) "NCAA Setback on TV Poses Threat of Disorder," *New York Times*, July 15, 1984, Sec. 5, p. 6.

(n) "Football Powers Spurn NCAA's TV Proposal; Big 10 and Pac-10 Won't Join Alternative Plan," *Chronicle of Higher Education*, July 18, 1984, p. 21.

(o) "Roll-Call Vote on Amended TV Plan," *NCAA News*, July 18, 1984, p. 12.

(p) "College Football TV in Disarray as Groups Scramble for Contracts," *NCAA News*, July 18, 1984, p. 1.

(q) "College Football Powers Reject Plan for National Championship Game," *Chronicle of Higher Education*, July 11, 1984, p. 27.

(r) "Financial Report in the Black, but Budget Restraints Urged," *NCAA News*, January 9, 1985, p. 1.

(s) "Uncertain Times Ahead for NCAA," *USA Today*, September 17, 1984, p. C1.

(t) "Football Syndicators Stew While Nets Stall," *Advertising Age*, July 16, 1984, p. 6.

(u) "Colleges May Find TV's Golden Egg Is Tarnished," *New York Times*, August 26, 1984, sec. 5, p. 9.

(v) "College Football Viewing Dips 27 Percent," *NCAA News*, January 9, 1985, p. 1.

(w) "Suit Challenges College TV Pacts," *New York Times*, September 14, 1984, p. B10.

(x) "NCAA Cleared to Re-Enter Football Broadcast Fray," *Sports Industry Newsletter*, November 7, 1984, p. 179.

(y) "NCAA to Pass Up TV Role for Now," *New York Times*, November 2, 1984, p. D19.

(z) "TV Ruling Favors U.C.L.A., U.S.C.," *New York Times*, September 11, 1984, p. B13.

(aa) "Big TV Revenues Now Tougher to Get, Most College Football Powers Discover," *Chronicle of Higher Education*, January 9, 1985, p. 37.

(bb) Wong, Glenn, and Ensor, Richard J., "The Impact of the U.S. Supreme Court's Antitrust Ruling on College Football," *The Entertainment and Sports Lawyer*, American Bar Association, vol. 3, no. 3, Winter 1985, p. 3.

(cc) "Syndicators of Television Sports Receiving Fuzzy Signals," *NCAA News*, February 20, 1985, p. 9.

(dd) "CFA Signs Restrictive Contract with ABC," *NCAA News*, August 1, 1984, p. 1.

(ee) "College Football Set Free," *Boston Globe*, June 28, 1984, p. 45.

(ff) "NCAA Is Reeling, But Don't Expect a KO Any Time Soon," (AP Wireservice) *Jacksonville Times-Union and Journal*, July 1, 1984, p. D13.

(gg) "Supreme Court Opens Floodgates for TV Football," *Miami Herald*, July 1, 1984.

(hh) "NCAA Moving to Clarify TV Ruling," *New York Times*, June 29, 1984.

(ii) "U. of Miami Football Pact Renews Quarrel over TV," *Chronicle of Higher Education*, February 13, 1985, p. 44.

(jj) "Viewers Not Tuned into Football Glut," *USA Today*, November 7, 1984, p. C1.

(kk) "A Few Fumbles Aside, Ivy Football Drew Crowd," *New York Times*, November 15, 1984, p. C29.

(ll) "Court Clarifies Its Football TV Ruling," *NCAA News*, November 5, 1984, p. 1.

6. See also: Proposed, "Brief of the American Council on Education as Amicus Curiae, in Support of the Petition for Certiorari," ACE Internal Memo, August 8, 1983.

7. For further information concerning the history of the *Ass'n. for Intercollegiate Athletics for Women v. National Collegiate Athletic Ass'n.* antitrust lawsuit, see the following articles:

(a) "NCAA Votes to Widen Role in Women's Sports; Action Is Bitterly Debated, 'Power Play' Charged," *Chronicle of Higher Education*, January 19, 1981, p. 6.

(b) "NAIA, Once All-Male, Attracts Women's Teams," *Chronicle of Higher Education*, March 23, 1981, p. 5.

(c) "200 Colleges Expected to Quit Women's Sports Association," *Chronicle of Higher Education*, June 1, 1981, p. 2.

(d) "Ban Sought Against NCAA's Women's Championships," *Chronicle of Higher Education*, October 21, 1981, p. 1.

(e) "Demise of AIAW Forces Women's Teams to Shift to Competing Organizations," *Chronicle of Higher Education*, October 6, 1982, p. 19.

(f) "NCAA Tried to Drive Women's Association Out of Business, AIAW Backers Tell Court," *Chronicle of Higher Education*, October 27, 1982, p. 13.

(g) "NCAA Officer Foretold Demise of Women's Group," *Chronicle of Higher Education*, November 3, 1982, p. 17.

(h) "Court Rejects Claim of Women's Group that NCAA Violated Antitrust Law," *Chronicle of Higher Education*, March 9, 1983, p. 17.

(i) "Women's Group May Fold Unless Injunction Is Granted," *Chronicle of Higher Education*, January 6, 1982, p. 6.

(j) "Women's Sports Group Plans for Possible Dissolution," *Chronicle of Higher Education*, January 20, 1982, p. 5.

(k) "AIAW Decides Not to Appeal Court's Ruling," *NCAA News*, June 6, 1984, p. 8.

8. As events turned out for the 1984 football season, some of the individual institutions' concerns over revenue loss were unfounded. However, the manner in which the funds were generated changed dramatically from the 1983 to the 1984 season. Most institutions needed to televise their contests more frequently in 1984 than in 1983 and in addition, often had to vary and change the scheduled starting times of their games to meet the fluctuating broadcast needs of the cable television syndicated pro-

grams and network stations.

In the case of Notre Dame, for instance, the initially forecasted shortfall in funds did not materialize. Instead, Notre Dame nearly matched its 1983 total of $1.4 million in football television revenue. However, to achieve that figure Notre Dame televised eight times in 1984 as compared with three in 1983. Notre Dame also had to schedule five different starting times for its six home games.

Notre Dame was not alone in having to increase its telecast appearances in 1984 to match its 1983 income from television. Penn State (3 to 5), Washington (2 to 5), and Ohio State (4 to 7) are other examples.

Most institutions did have revenue shortfalls. Overall, Division IA football schools received a total of $43.2 million less in revenue from television appearances in 1984 than would have been anticipated from the previously negotiated NCAA contracts. See "Big TV Revenues Now Tougher to Get, Most College Football Powers Discover," *Chronicle of Higher Education*, January 9, 1985, p. 37.

9. National viewership also dropped significantly from the 1984 season, falling 27 percent from the 1983 level as rated by the A. C. Nielsen Company. (One point on the Nielsen system equals 849,000 television homes — 1 percent of the 84.9 million homes with at least one television set.) See "College Football Viewing Dips 27 Percent," *NCAA News*, January 9, 1985, p. 1.

10. In *Jones v. National Collegiate Athletic Ass'n.*, 392 F. Supp. 295 (D. Mass. 1975), plaintiff was unsuccessful in his claim that an NCAA rule making him ineligible was a secondary group boycott in violation of the Sherman Act.

1.30   Constitutional Aspects of Athletics

A student-athlete involved in a dispute with an amateur organization may decide to initiate a lawsuit based on the theory that a constitutional right has been violated. In light of the problems of limited judicial review and standing, the constitutionally based claims of due process and equal protection may be the only avenues available. In addition, however, the constitutional approach has other advantages. Most important, it enables the athlete to bring the case into a federal court, thereby utilizing the federal jurisdiction statutes. To succeed on a federal constitutional claim, however, one must show that the claim represents a state action, is not frivolous, and concerns a right of sufficient importance to be litigated in federal court. If these three points can be established, the student-athlete can then proceed generally on

an equal protection and/or a due process theory.

1.31   State Action Requirement

The constitutional safeguards of the Fifth and Fourteenth amendments of the United States Constitution apply only when state action is present. Any action taken directly or indirectly by either a state, local, or federal government is state action for constitutional purposes. In addition, action by any public school, state college, or state university or any of their officials, is construed as state action. The issue of state action arises only when alleged wrongdoers are not acting directly on behalf of the government. In order to subject voluntary, private associations to constitutional limitations, some degree of state action must be present.

Beyond the fact that the actions taken by high school and college athletic associations are generally considered state action, it may be argued that private institutions acting in compliance with these organizations are also engaging in state action. Action by strictly private individuals does not constitute state action. (See *McDonald v. National Collegiate Athletic Ass'n.* and *Arlosoroff v. National Collegiate Athletic Ass'n.*, *infra*.)

The three common methods of analysis used to determine whether or not state action exists in particular circumstances are the public function theory, the entanglement theory, and the balancing approach theory. The public function theory is somewhat limited and is traditionally confined to *essential government services that have no counterparts in the public sector*. A good example is the American Telephone and Telegraph Company, which is a private company performing an essentially public function. The NCAA has, in at least one case, been deemed a public functionary based on its comprehensive regulation of an area which would otherwise have to be regulated by the states (see Note 1). The alternative — having each state regulate college athletic programs without the existence of the NCAA — would be extremely inefficient and not a viable alternative.

The second method of analysis is commonly known as the entanglement theory. In this method, the usual focal point is the amount of state and/or federal aid directly or indirectly given to the private organization. Under this view, state action issues involve a conflict between rights, and the court must balance these rights in determining whether the Constitution mandates a preference for one right over another. The receipt of such aid may subject a recipient's action to constitutional review. For this theory to be invoked by the court, total state and/or federal control over the organization need not exist. Instead, the state or federal government must only have substantial influence over the association's activities. State and association actions must be intertwined to the extent that the organization's actions are supported or sanctioned by the government. State action is found based on the relationship of the association to the government.

Case law has held the NCAA's actions to be the equivalent of state action under this theory. In *Parish* v. *National Collegiate Athletic Ass'n.*, 361 F. Supp. 1220 (W.D. La. 1973), *aff'd*, 506 F. 2d 1028 (5th Cir. 1975) (see Section 1.21–2), and *Howard* v. *National Collegiate Athletic Ass'n.*, 510 F. 2d 213 (D.C. Cir. 1975) *infra*, the rationale typically has been that over half of the NCAA's members are state-supported schools. Some cases, such as *Williams* v. *Hamilton*, have found state action where less than half of the association's schools were not state supported (see Section 1.22–2). In addition, most NCAA member schools receive federal aid, and their students receive federal financial aid (work-study and National Defense loans). Therefore, albeit indirectly, the NCAA is supported by state and federal governments. The NCAA also provides a service that is beyond the competence or authority of any one state.

The balancing approach theory is more general and not widely accepted. Here, if the merits of allowing the organizational practice are outweighed by the limitations on asserted and/or protected rights, the courts have found state action, which allows judicial intervention for the protection of individual constitutional rights.

In addition to the above three theories, there is one situation in which the courts may intervene without a finding of state action. That is, when an organization becomes so influential and so pervasive in an area that belonging to it is an economic necessity rather than a voluntary choice, the courts will act as necessary to equitably preserve justice. (See *Board of Regents of the University of Oklahoma* v. *National Collegiate Athletic Ass'n.* in Section 1.41–2).

In most cases, NCAA activities have been found to be the equivalent of state action on the entanglement theory, although some early cases use the public function theory. The trend, however, seems to be toward holding the NCAA responsible for constitutional violations based on its omnipresence in collegiate athletics.

Most high school athletic associations are closely involved with public education and are therefore directly involved with the state. This is evident in *Kentucky High School Athletic Ass'n.* v. *Hopkins County Board of Education* (see Section 2.13–2). This direct connection usually provides a sufficient amount of state action to subject the high school association to constitutional limitations.

McDonald v. National Collegiate Athletic Ass'n., 370 F. Supp. 625 (C.D. Cal. 1974)

Plaintiff basketball players sought a preliminary injunction against two defendants, the University of California at Long Beach and the NCAA. They sought to prevent the defendants from declaring them ineligible to play intercollegiate basketball. Plaintiffs contended that the actions of the defendants could be construed as state action and that the defendants' failure to provide plaintiffs with a hearing before declaring them ineligible was a violation of their right to due process under the Fourteenth Amendment to the U.S. Constitution. The court held that since the university is a state-run institution, the actions of its administrators constitute state action. The failure of the university to invoke its own student disciplinary process was seen as violative of plaintiffs' right to due process, and the injunction against the university was granted.

In the case of the NCAA, the court held that the NCAA is a voluntary organization comprised of colleges and universities, and that the individual athletes involved were not members of the organization. The court held that "The adoption of NCAA regulations and of the benefits deriving therefrom is a decision which the institution can make independent of any interest of a particular athlete. In other words, the individual athlete has no interest — constitutionally protected or otherwise — in the institution's membership and participation in NCAA activities." Thus, the acts of the NCAA were not found to be state action in a constitutional sense. Rather, it is the voluntary concurrence of a state institution (in this case Long Beach) which is state action. If an institution is unable to concur with a voluntary organization without contravening the constitutional rights of its students, it must withdraw from that organization. "Neither Long Beach . . . nor the state of California itself can direct the NCAA to conduct itself in any manner at all. . . . the NCAA has an existence separate and apart from the educational system of any state."

The court held that the NCAA's actions were not state action; thus the complaint against the NCAA was dismissed due to lack of standing. The actions of the university were held to be state action, and the university was enjoined from imposing or continuing any sanction against the plaintiffs pending a trial or a hearing on the allegations concerning their eligibility to participate in intercollegiate athletics.

Howard University v. National Collegiate Athletic Ass'n., 510 F. 2d 213 (D.C. Cir. 1975)

Plaintiffs were a private university and an individual student-athlete seeking both injunctive and declaratory relief. The U.S. District Court found federal jurisdiction pursuant to 28 U.S.C. section 1331 (1970). The primary question for the court was whether activities by the defendant NCAA constituted state action. In its analysis, the court relied heavily on previous federal court decisions.

Citing *Parish* v. *National Collegiate Athletic Ass'n.*, the court noted that "state-supported educational institutions and their members and officers play a substantial, although admittedly not pervasive role in the NCAA's program, and that such state participation in a nominally private activity is a well-recognized basis for a finding of state action." The court then noted the many high school cases in which the activities of high school athletic associations have been determined to be the equivalent of state action under an "entanglement theory."

The NCAA relied on *McDonald* v. *National Collegiate Athletic Ass'n.*, which distinguished the NCAA from the high school athletic associations and held that the NCAA was not sufficiently state supported to be considered state action. This court, however, described several flaws in the *McDonald* analysis. First, the high school cases it cited extended constitutional scrutiny to the same types of rules as those at issue in the *Howard* case. Second, it was pointed out that the *McDonald* court did not resolve the question of whether the degree of NCAA regulation and involvement in university athletic programs, combined with the fact that approximately half the NCAA's membership is composed of public institutions, sufficiently intertwines the NCAA's and its membership's interests and affairs so that the NCAA becomes state action subject to the Fifth and Fourteenth amendments.

The court of appeals decided that state involvement in the NCAA, while not exclusive, is significant, and that all NCAA actions appear impregnated with a governmental character. The court felt if the NCAA was composed solely of state institutions, clearly state action would be present. In contrast, if the NCAA had no public members, its actions would be private for constitutional purposes. Drawing the line is a difficult task. In this case, because the degree of public participation and entanglement between the entities was substantial and pervasive, the court held that state action was present and that the district court correctly determined it possessed jurisdiction.

Arlosoroff v. National Collegiate Athletic Ass'n., 746 F. 2d 1019 (4th Cir. 1984)

The district court granted a preliminary injunction prohibiting the National Collegiate Athletic Association from enforcing one of its eligibility rules against the plaintiff, a student at Duke University. It treated the acts of the NCAA as "state action," making applicable the Equal Protection and Due Process Clauses of the Fourteenth Amendment. We reverse, for we find no state action.

The National Collegiate Athletic Association is a voluntary, unincorporated association of nearly one thousand four-year colleges and universities. Approximately one-half of its members are public institutions, state and federal.

The NCAA conducts annual conventions in which all member institutions are represented. Through these conventions, it promulgates rules to insure minimum standards for scholarship, sportsmanship and amateurism. Each participating institution must abide by the rules, and an elected council is empowered to enforce the rules and can impose sanctions upon schools and players found to have been in violation of the rules.

The plaintiff is an Israeli citizen. He was discharged from the Israeli army in March 1979 when he was twenty-two years old. Thereafter, he participated in some seventeen amateur tennis tournaments. He was a member of Israel's Davis Cup team. In August 1981, he enrolled at Duke University, and in his freshman year played the number one singles position on Duke's tennis team. After the plaintiff's freshman year, however, the NCAA declared him ineligible for further competition on the basis of NCAA Bylaw 5–1–

(d)–(3), which had been adopted by a majority vote of the member institutions at the January 1980 convention.

Bylaw 5–1–(d)–(3) provides that any participation in "organized competition in a sport during each twelve month period after the student's 20th birthday and prior to matriculation with a member institution should count as one year of varsity competition in that sport." As initially adopted, participation in organized competition while in military service was excepted. The plaintiff, however, had spent three years in organized tennis after his discharge from the Israeli army and before his matriculation at Duke. Because of that, the NCAA ruled that his freshman year was the final year of his eligibility.

This action was initially brought in a state court against Duke and the NCAA. The plaintiff asked that each be enjoined from enforcing the Bylaw. He claimed a denial of due process and equal protection. The equal protection claim is based upon an allegation that, although the Bylaw was neutral on its face, it was designed to exclude aliens from competition in the NCAA affiliated institutions.

The state court granted a temporary restraining order, but Duke and the NCAA promptly removed the case to the United States District Court for the Middle District of North Carolina. There the plaintiff requested preliminary injunctions, while Duke filed a cross claim against the NCAA seeking a preliminary injunction on due process grounds. . . .

Although the NCAA is not a public institution, most of the courts considering the matter have held that its actions are state actions subject to the limitations of the Fourteenth Amendment. *E.g., Regents of the University of Minnesota v. NCAA,* 560 F.2d 352 (8th Cir. 1977); *Howard University v. NCAA,* 510 F.2d 213 (D.C.Cir. 1975); *Parish v. NCAA,* 506 F.2d 1028 (5th Cir. 1975); *Associated Students, Inc. v. NCAA,* 493 F.2d 1251 (9th Cir. 1974). *But see McDonald v. NCAA,* 370 F.Supp. 625 (C.D. Cal. 1975). It was variously said that the NCAA performs a public function regulating intercollegiate athletics, *see Parish v. NCAA,* 506 F.2d 1032, that there was substantial interdependence between the NCAA and the state institutions that comprise about one-half of its membership, *e.g., Howard University,* 510 F.2d at 219, and that the state institutional members played a "substantial although admittedly not pervasive" role in NCAA funding and decision making. *Parish*, 506 F.2d at 1032, *see Howard University*, 510 F.2d at 219.

These earlier cases rested upon the notion that indirect involvement of state governments could convert what otherwise would be considered private conduct into state action. That notion has now been rejected by the Supreme Court, however, and its decisions require a different conclusion. *Rendell-Baker* v. *Kohn*, 457 U.S. 830, 102 S.Ct. 2764, 73 L.Ed.2d 418 (1982); *Blum* v. *Yaretsky*, 457 U.S. 991, 102 S.Ct. 2777, 73 L.Ed.2d 534 (1982).

There is no precise formula to determine whether otherwise private conduct constitutes "state action." After "sifting facts and weighing circumstances," *Burton* v. *Wilmington Parking Authority*, 365 U.S. 715, 722, 81 S.Ct. 856, 860, 6 L.Ed.2d 45 (1961), the inquiry in each case is whether the conduct is fairly attributable to the state . . .

None of the circumstances suggested by Duke and the plaintiff, however, permit an attribution of state action to the NCAA.

In a sense, the NCAA may be said to perform a public function as the overseer of the nation's intercollegiate athletics. It introduces some order into the conduct of its programs and enforces uniform rules of eligibility. The regulation of intercollegiate athletics, however, is not a function "traditionally exclusively reserved to the state.". . . The operation of a company town is subject to constitutional limitations, . . . for the governance of townships is traditionally a public function, but neither the distribution of electricity by a regulated utility nor the operation of a school, . . . is traditionally an exclusive prerogative of the state.

The fact that NCAA's regulatory function may be of some public service lends no support to the finding of state action, for the function is not one traditionally reserved to the state.

Formally, the NCAA is a private entity. Approximately one-half of its members are public institutions, and those institutions provide more than one-half of the NCAA's revenues. Those facts, however, do not alter the basic character of the NCAA as a voluntary association of public and private institutions. Nor do they begin to suggest that the public institutions, in contrast to the private institutional members, caused or procured the adoption of the Bylaw.

It is not enough that an institution is highly regulated and subsidized by a state. If the state in its regulatory or subsidizing function does not order or cause the action complained of, and the function is not one traditionally reserved to the state, there is no state action. . . .

. . . There is no suggestion in this case that the representatives of the state institutions joined together to vote as a block to effect adoption of the Bylaw over the objection of private institutions. There is simply no showing that the state institutions controlled or directed the result.

The NCAA serves the common need of member institutions for regulation of athletics while correlating their diverse interests. Through the representatives of all of the members Bylaw 5–1–(d)–(3) was adopted, not as a result of governmental compulsion, but in the service of the common interests of the members. The adoption of the Bylaw was private conduct, not state action.

NOTES _____

1. *Buckton* v. *National Collegiate Athletic Ass'n.*, 366 F. Supp. 1152 (D. Mass. 1973), was the first case to declare the NCAA to be engaged in state action. A public function analysis was employed. The public function theory has since been supplanted by other theories (see Section 1.33).

2. In *Regents of the University of Minnesota* v. *National Collegiate Athletic Ass'n*, 560 F.2d 352 (8th Cir. 1977), the court acknowledged that action taken by the NCAA has generally been accepted as the equivalent of state action (see Section 2.30).

3. In *Mitchell* v. *Louisiana High School Activities Ass'n.*, 430 F. 2d 1155 (5th Cir. 1970), the court found no state action on the part of the defendant high school athletic association. Consequently, a claim for relief based on a violation of due process rights was denied.

4. For further information, see the following articles:

(a) "State Action by State Athletic Associations," 36 *Missouri Law Review* 400 (1971).

(b) "The Student-Athlete and the National Collegiate Athletic Association: The Need for a Prima Facie Tort Doctrine," 9 *Suffolk Law Review* 1340 (1975).

5. For examples in which the court ruled that college athletic associations were acting under color of state action, see the following cases:

(a) *Rivas Tenorio* v. *Liga Atletica Interuniversitaria*, 554 F.2d 492 (1st Cir. 1977).

(b) *Parish* v. *National Collegiate Athletic Ass'n.*, 361 F. Supp. 1220 (W.D. La. 1973) *aff'd*, 506 F. 2d 1028 (5th Cir. 1975).

(c) *Associated Students, Inc.* v. *National Collegiate Athletic Ass'n.*, 493 F.2d 1251 (9th Cir. 1974).

6. For examples in which the court ruled that high school athletic associations were acting under color of state action, see the following cases:

(a) *Barnhorst* v. *Missouri State High School Athletic Ass'n.*, 504 F.Supp. 449 (W.D. Mo. 1980).

(b) *Yellow Springs Exempted School District* v. *Ohio High School Athletic Ass'n.*, 443 F.Supp. 753 (S.D. Ohio W.D. 1978), *rev'd on other grounds*, 647 F. 2d 651 (6th Cir. 1981).

(c) *Wright* v. *Arkansas Activities Ass'n.*, 501 F. 2d 25 (8th Cir. 1974) (see Section 1.32–1, Note 10).

1.32   Due Process

The constitutional guarantee of due process is found in both the Fifth and Fourteenth amendments to the U.S. Constitution. The Fifth Amendment, enacted in 1791, is applicable to the federal government. It states that "no person . . . shall be deprived of life, liberty, or property without due process of law." In 1886, the Fourteenth Amendment was ratified, reading, " . . . nor shall any state deprive any person of life, liberty, or property without due process of law . . ." This amendment extended the applicability of the due process doctrine to the states. Both amendments apply only to federal or state governmental action and not to the conduct of purely private entities. While the Constitution extends these liberties to all persons, it is also limiting in that a person must demonstrate deprivation of life, liberty, or property to claim a violation of due process guarantees.

The due process doctrine presses two inquiries. The first is procedural due process, which refers to five procedures required to ensure fairness. The second is substantive due process, which guarantees basic rights that cannot be denied by governmental action.

Claims to due process protection may be brought based not only on protections guaranteed by state constitutions and by federal and state statutes, but also on the regulations and constitutions of athletic institutions, conferences, and other athletic governing organizations.

1.32–1   Procedural Due Process

The two minimum requirements of due process are the right to a hearing and notice of the hearing's time, date, and content. The requirements are flexible, and the degree of formality depends on the nature of the right involved as well as on the circumstances surrounding the situation. If the deprivation concerned is not that of a fundamental right or is a right marginally affected by the challenged rule, only the minimal due process requirements may be necessary.

On the other hand, when a fundamental right is involved or when an infringement on personal freedom is present, the hearing must be more formal, with additional safeguards. The maximum protections of due process include notice and the right to a hearing in front of a neutral decision maker with an opportunity to make an oral presentation, to present favorable evidence, and to confront and cross-examine adverse witnesses. In addition, there may also be a right to have an attorney present during the proceedings, a copy of the transcript of the hearing, and a right to a written decision based on the record.

Although an individual may enjoy the guarantee of due process, the actual process is rarely spelled out. The type of due process protections guaranteed in a given situation are determined by a consideration of the importance of the right involved, the degree of the infringement, and the potential harm of the violation. As a general rule, the more an individual has at stake, the more extensive and formal are the due process requirements. Since a number of factors are involved, administrative agencies must examine the merits of each case to determine the required procedures on a case-by-case basis.

Behagan v. *Intercollegiate Conference of Faculty Representatives*, 346 F. Supp. 602 (D. Minn. 1972)

Two University of Minnesota basketball players who had been suspended for the season sought to enjoin the Intercollegiate Conference of Faculty Representatives (also known as the Big Ten Conference) from enforcing their suspension until they were granted due process. The court ruled that the suspension of the players from participating in practice was punitive in nature, not preventative, and could not be enforced without due process. However, suspension from intercollegiate games was upheld until the duration of such action forced it to cross the bounds from prevention to punishment, at which time it would deprive the players of their rights to due process. Thus, a stipulated time period was set for due process to be met. Upon the expiration of the set time, the lack of due process would result in the lifting of the players' suspension from games as well.

The players' suspensions developed out of an altercation in a game with a league opponent. After reviewing the incident, the Big Ten commissioner met with a University of Minnesota committee that exercised control over educational matters at the college. An agreement was reached on the suspension of the players for the rest of the season, pending further investigation.

Since the committee did not intend the players to be suspended from participating in practice, an action that the commissioner enforced, the commissioner reported the affair to the Conference Directors of Athletics Committee, as called for in the *Conference Handbook*. This committee determined that the suspension should include practice as well as games. Although the *Conference Handbook* specifically stated the "[t]he Directors shall afford the institution, its employees or students concerned an opportunity to appear at the meeting in which the Commissioner's report is made and to be heard in defense against charges," this was never done.

After further hearings by the University of Minnesota Committee on Athletics, the suspensions were lifted because the players had been denied due process, but the commissioner, acting under his power to promote the general welfare of the conference, again suspended the players. The court found it consistent with the powers of the commissioner to suspend the players temporarily, pending a hearing by the Conference Directors of Athletics Committee, if such action was not arbitrary or capricious, and was done to protect the interest of the conference. However, due process could not be denied in this case since the suspensions bordered on punitive action, with a notable concern being that the players were prevented from displaying skills that could lead to future economic rewards as professionals. The court then detailed the type of hearing that would be required.

> For guidance of the parties in any further proceedings this Court has examined those factors here and is of the opinion that the following are necessary in order for a hearing to meet the rudimentary requirements of due process. Plaintiffs should be given a written notice of the time and place of the hearing at least two days in advance. Accompanying such notice should be a specification of the charges against each, and the grounds which, if proven, would justify imposition of a penalty. The hearing should be such that the Directors of Athletics have an opportunity to hear both sides of the story. This does not require a full-dress judicial hearing, with the right to cross-examine witnesses. However, it should include the presentation of direct testimony in the form of statements by each of those directly involved relating their versions of the incident. Plaintiffs should be given a list of all witnesses who will appear, and should be allowed to hear all testimony. Plaintiffs should be given a written report specifying the Directors' findings of fact, and if there is to be any punishment the basis for such punishment. The proceedings should be recorded, and the tapes should be made available to plaintiffs in the event they wish to appeal. If these minimal standards are followed in cases of this nature, it is this Court's opinion that the requirements of due process will have been met.

Stanley v. Big Eight Conference, 463 F. Supp. 920 (W.D. Mo., W.D. 1978)

The Big Eight Conference scheduled a hearing

for November 30, 1978, to determine if Oklahoma State University (OSU), its staff members, or students enrolled in its football program had violated rules of the Big Eight Conference and of the National Collegiate Athletic Association for which sanctions or penalties should be imposed. The proposed hearing was to be conducted by a group composed of faculty representatives and directors of athletics of the member institutions and was to be based on a report prepared by Charles Neinas, commissioner of the Big Eight, of the investigation he had conducted. A copy of this report was distributed on the day prior to the proceedings. The report was based on interviews with those who may have had knowledge of the alleged infractions and was to be presented by the commissioner at the hearing.

The investigation focused on the activities of Jim Stanley, who was head football coach at OSU at the time of the alleged infractions. Stanley, who was relieved of his duties, in part because of the investigation, denied the allegations insofar as they pertained to him. At the hearing, Stanley was to be represented by an attorney and permitted to make a presentation of any information he chose, using other individuals, reports, documents, and oral evidence. All participants were to be permitted to ask questions of any other participant. The proposed hearing was not to include witnesses, and Stanley was to have no opportunity to cross-examine those making allegations against him. Nor were statements implicating Stanley to be signed or supported by affidavit.

The hearing was to be conducted in conjunction with the NCAA and upon a finding of guilt, sanctions were to be imposed under both Big Eight and NCAA rules. Though neither the Big Eight nor the NCAA could take direct action against Stanley, through sanctions against the school, the Big Eight Conference could prohibit him from coaching at any of the member institutions and the NCAA could effectively "blackball" him from coaching at any of its 830 member institutions.

In granting Stanley's request to preliminarily enjoin the hearing, Judge Russell G. Clark of the U.S. District Court of the Western District of Missouri held that the proposed hearing violated Stanley's rights to due process under the Fourteenth Amendment. In granting Stanley's request, the court held that because the Big Eight is composed solely of state-supported public universities and that because these state-supported schools have delegated to the Big Eight certain functions such as supervision over intercollegiate athletics, the activities of the Big Eight Conference constituted "state action," under which the protections of the Fourteenth Amendment could be invoked.

The court held that Stanley, who had spent his entire adult life as a head or assistant coach, had a protectable liberty interest under the Fourteenth Amendment. The court held that when state action is defamatory and the stigmatizing effect of its action will alter the right of Stanley to pursue a common occupation in life, due process guarantees can be invoked. The court held that the proposed hearing procedure of the Big Eight Conference was too susceptible to error.

Most troubling to the court was that the author of the investigative report was free to draw inferences beyond those statements of fact made to him in his interviews. The report was replete with hearsay and double hearsay. Statements within the report were not presented in a completely neutral way. Substantial allegations rested upon unnamed sources and inferences. Stanley would be in the position of refuting summaries of statements. Finally, no opportunity existed for appellate review.

Though the court left it to the Big Eight Conference to formulate an alternative procedure, the court did suggest that all statements be reduced to writing. The declarant could be requested either to sign the statement or appear before a notary to transform it into an affidavit. If the declarant declined, the investigator could note that. A summary of statements could be provided to Stanley prior to the hearing, and Stanley could be given a period of time in which to express a desire to challenge the factual statements. If the allegations were challenged, Stanley could be allowed to cross-examine the witness. Since the conference does not have subpoena power, if a witness refused to testify or appear at a deposition, the party relying on the witness could advise the other party of the reasons for such refusal.

NOTES _____

1. In *Southern Methodist University* v. *Smith*, 515 S.W. 2d 63 (Tex. Civ. App. 1974), the court held that no due process is required if the facts are not disputed, or if the issues have already been resolved (see Section 2.30 and *Graesen* v. *Pasquale*, 200 N.W. 2d 842 [1978]).

2. In *Regents of University of Minnesota* v. *National Collegiate Athletic Ass'n.*, 560 F. 2d 352 (8th Cir. 1977), the court held that due process requires notice and a hearing (see Section 2.30).

3. In *Kelley* v. *Metropolitan County Board of Education of Nashville*, 293 F. Supp. 485 (M.D. Tenn. 1968), plaintiff high school student-athlete was suspended from athletic competition by the Board of Education without being formally charged with a rule violation. The court held that due process involves the right to be heard before being condemned. Due process requires published standards, formal charges, notice, and a hearing. The court granted an injunction that prevented the enforcement of the suspension.

4. In *Pegram* v. *Nelson*, 469 F. Supp. 1134 (M.D.N.C. 1979), the court held that a short suspension (less than ten days) from participation in after-school extracurricular activities requires only an informal hearing.

5. In *Mitchell* v. *Louisiana High School Athletic Ass'n.*, 430 F.2d 1155 (5th Cir. 1970), no due process was required since the court found no state action (see Section 1.31).

6. In *O'Connor* v. *Board of Education*, 65 Misc. 2d 140, 316 N.Y.S. 2nd 799 (1970), a high school athlete was deprived of his athletic award (letter) after his coach turned him in for allegedly violating a "no drinking" rule. The court held that the process required a hearing prior to revocation of a high school athlete's letter.

7. In *Taylor* v. *Alabama High School Athletic Ass'n.*, 336 F. Supp. 54 (M.D. Ala. 1972), plaintiff high school was prohibited from hosting or participating in invitational basketball tournaments for one year due to the "misconduct and unruliness" of spectators at one of its games. The Alabama High School Athletic Association violated the plaintiff's due process rights for the following reasons:

(a) There were no preexisting standards;
(b) No punishments were provided for violation of the rules;
(c) No specific charge was made;
(d) No notice was given;
(e) There was no opportunity for an adequate hearing;

(f) The hearing was not convened as required by the association's rules.

The court also found that the penalty imposed exceeded any other previously imposed penalty.

8. In *Hamilton* v. *Tennessee Secondary Athletic Ass'n.*, 552 F.2d 681 (6th Cir. 1976), the court of appeals ruled that the privilege of participating in interscholastic athletics is outside the protection of due process.

9. In *Duffley* v. *New Hampshire Interscholastic Athletic Ass'n.*, 446 A. 2d 462 (N.H. 1982), the New Hampshire Supreme Court ruled that student plaintiff had been denied procedural due process because the New Hampshire Interscholastic Athletic Association failed to state the reasons for denial of eligibility.

10. In *Wright* v. *Arkansas Activities Ass'n.*, 501 F.2d 25 (8th Cir. 1974), the Court of Appeals ruled that a rule prohibiting football practice prior to a certain date may provide fair notice that a school may be sanctioned. However, imposition of a sanction resulting in loss of a coaching/teaching position denied the coach due process. The rule gave no notice of the fact that the coach could be subject to a sanction, resulting in unemployment.

11. In *Marcum* v. *Dahl*, 658 F.2d 731 (10th Cir. 1981), college basketball students claimed their right to due process had been violated when they were dropped from the team for disciplinary reasons without a hearing. The court held that the college had offered the opportunity for a hearing, but the students had failed to take advantage of it, thus freeing the college of any further due process responsibilities.

12. An example of a hearing and appeal process which can be made available to an athlete by an amateur sports organization is the one below implemented by United States Swimming Association:

Article 50 Hearings and Appeals

450.1.   General — As hereinafter set forth, the Corporation may censure, suspend for a definite or indefinite period of time with or without terms of probation, or expel any member of the Corporation, including any athlete, coach, manager, official member of any committee, or any person participating in any capacity whatsoever in the affairs of the Corporation, who has violated any of its rules or regulations, or who has acted in a manner which brings disrepute upon the Corporation or upon the sport of swimming. The Corporation may also conduct hearings on any matter affecting the Corporation as the national governing body for swimming.

450.2   Jurisdiction of the Local Swimming Committees (LSC) — For those matters requiring a hearing and arising solely within the geographical boundaries of an LSC, the procedure to be taken and the rules to be followed for hearing shall be as set forth in Part Five, Article 71.

450.3   Jurisdiction of the Corporation — In those

matters in which athlete(s) or other member(s) of the Corporation from more than one LSC is involved, or in matters involving such persons during a national or international athletic event, an investigation and report of the facts shall be made to the President as hereinafter set forth. If in the opinion of a majority of the elected officers of the Corporation a hearing or further investigation is then warranted, the matter shall be submitted to the National Board of Review for hearing and decision.

(1) Where persons or entities from more than one LSC are involved, the investigation and report shall be made by the Executive Director.

(2) In those matters occurring during the course of a national, regional or zone event, the Senior Division or Age Group Division, as the case may be, shall make the investigation and report.

(3) In those matters occurring during the course of an international event, the Olympic International Division shall make the investigation and report.

450.4 National Board of Review — The Board of Review shall be comprised of the General Counsel of the Corporation, all associate counsels, one (1) athlete representative from each of the four zones (elected by the Athletes committee), and such other members as may be recommended by the President and approved by the Board of Directors. The President shall appoint the chairman and shall have the authority to designate a panel of no less than three members, one of whom shall be an athlete representative, to hear and decide any case before the Board of Review.

450.5 Authority of National Board of Review — The National Board of Review has the authority to:

(1) Impose and enforce penalties for any violation of the rules and regulations, administrative or technical, of the Corporation;

(2) Determine the eligibility and right to compete of any athlete;

(3) Vacate, modify, sustain, stay or reverse any decision or order properly submitted for review, or remand the matter for further action;

(4) Investigate any election impropriety or cause for removal of a national committeeman or national officer and take corrective action;

(5) Interpret any provision of the rules and regulations of the Corporation with the exception of the technical rules (Part One);

(6) Review any revocation, suspension or reinstatement of membership to assure due process; and

(7) Reinstate any athlete to amateur status subject to ratification by no less than 2/3 vote of the House of Delegates of the Corporation.

450.6 Procedure for Review

(1) Every appeal to the Board of Review shall be instituted by a petition served upon the Executive Director and accompanied by a $50 filing fee payable to the Corporation. The fee shall be returned if the petition is upheld, but forfeited if it is rejected or abandoned. The Board of Review may assess costs against the losing party.

(2) The Executive Director shall send a copy of the petition for review to the respondent and chairman of the Board of Review immediately upon receipt. The respondent shall within 30 days following receipt of the petition file a written response with the Executive Director, the petitioner and the chairman. The petitioner may within 10 days following receipt of a copy of the response file a written rebuttal with the Executive Director, the respondent and the chairman. The Chairman may decrease or increase the time limits for any of the foregoing upon request of either party and if circumstances should warrant it.

(3) A final and binding decision shall be rendered within 75 days from date of filing of the petition by a majority of the acting panel based on the record submitted for review and on evidence submitted at such hearing as may be required by the panel. A written decision shall be sent to all parties. Petitions once reviewed and decided shall not be reopened for consideration by the Board of Review, except by direction of the Board of Directors of the Corporation, or upon showing of sufficient cause to the chairman of the Board of Review.

450.7 Appeal to the Board of Directors — Any real party in interest may appeal to the Board of Directors for review of any decision of the National Board of Review within thirty (30) days of the date of decision.

450.8 Original Jurisdiction — Upon a majority vote of the officers, the Board of Directors or the National Board of Review may be assigned original jurisdiction at any stage of any matter within the purview of this Article 50 when the best interests of the Corporation will be served thereby. If original jurisdiction is so assigned, compliance shall be made in every instance with all requirements of procedural due process as set forth in this Article 50. [1982 Code]

13. The NCAA in its recommended policies suggests in regard to the question of due process and student-athletes that:

In the administration of their athletics programs in accordance with NCAA regulations and their conditions and obligations of membership in the Association, member institutions may find it necessary, from time to time, to terminate or suspend the eligibility of student-athletes for participation in intercollegiate competition and organized athletic practice sessions. In any such case, the member institution should notify the student-athlete concerned and afford the student-athlete an opportunity for an informal hearing before the faculty athletic representative, director of athletics or other appropriate institutional authority before action is taken, it being understood that the hearing opportunity shall not delay or set aside the member's obligations required by NCAA Constitution 4–2–(a)–O–I.11 and Section 9 of the Association's enforcement procedures. This hearing opportunity will avoid possible mistaken actions affecting the student-athlete's eligibility and should satisfy due process procedures if any are required.

See *1985–86 NCAA Manual*, NCAA Recommended Policies and Practices for Intercollegiate Athletics, Policy 11, Due Process.

14. For further information, see the following article: Lowell, "Federal Administrative Intervention in Amateur Athletes," 43 *George Washington Law Review* 729 (1975).

1.32–2   Substantive Due Process

In sports cases, the interest most commonly cited is the property interest, although in some instances the personal liberty interest is involved (see hairlength cases in Section 2.22). For the purposes of the due process clause, types of property are not distinguished. Therefore, the first problem encountered in many of these cases is a determination of whether the interest involved constitutes property.

Traditionally, property has been defined as all valuable interests that can be possessed outside of oneself, which have an exchangeable value or which add to an individual's wealth or estate. Since 1972 in the Supreme Court's decision in *Board of Regents* v. *Roth*, 408 U.S. 564, 33 L.Ed. 2d 548, 92 S.Ct. 2701 (1972), property has been defined as all interests to which an individual could be deemed "entitled." Entitlements occur only if there is some form of current interest in or current use of the property. For example, a holder of a scholarship has a property right because he is currently entitled to benefits derived from it. Once this entitlement is established, there is a property right. Due process protections are triggered only when there is an actual deprivation of the entitled rights. This "entitlement" standard does not encompass wishes that do not come true or expectations that fail to

materialize; an entitlement to property must be more than an abstract need or desire for it.

The property right involved in amateur sports is the right to participate in athletic activities. The major controversy revolves around the question of whether participation is an individual protectable right or a privilege that is unprotected. This question is analyzed differently depending on whether the athletic activity is on the high school or college level. On both levels defendants have argued that participation in athletics is a privilege and therefore falls outside the parameters of the due process clause.

In the collegiate area, however, plaintiffs have been successful in claiming a property interest based on the proximity of monetary benefits currently or potentially available to the athlete. A property interest has been found in athletic participation because there exists a potential economic benefit to the athlete in the form of either a scholarship or a future professional contract. A current holder of a scholarship who would be deprived of that scholarship has a well-defined property interest based on the present economic value of the award.

A college athlete may also have a protectable interest in a future professional contract, as in *Behagen* v. *Intercollegiate Conference of Faculty Representatives* (see Section 1.32–1). Some courts, however, by looking at a statistical analysis of the percentage of people who successfully enter professional sports, have discounted a legitimate property interest in a future professional contract as being too speculative. (See *Colorado Seminary* v. *National Collegiate Athletic Ass'n.*, *infra.*) Also, at least one court has indicated that it would find a protectable property interest only if there were a professional league in that particular sport. (See *Fluitt* v. *University of Nebraska*, *infra.*)

In the interscholastic area, the right or privilege dichotomy is analyzed differently. A high school student with only the possibility of obtaining a scholarship generally has no present economic interest, and the possibility of obtaining a scholarship is too speculative an interest to receive protection. Similarly, a high school student is usually considered to have an entirely speculative interest in a future professional contract.

In high school cases, the right versus the privilege controversy involves the student's argument that he or she has a right to an education and that participation in interscholastic athletics is included in that right. The threshold issue is whether there is a right to an education. The Supreme Court has specifically denied a general constitutional right to education (see *San Antonio Independent School Dist. v. Rodriguez*, 411 U.S. 1, 36 L.Ed. 2d 16, 93 S.Ct. 1278 [1973]). Even though the right to an education is not grounded in federal law, a state may grant a right to an education either explicitly or implicitly by requiring school attendance. Through this measure, the state effectively gives each child within its boundaries an interest in the education provided. This interest has been held to be a type of property interest protected by the due process clause. (See *Pegram* v. *Nelson*, 469 F. Supp. 1134 [M.D.N.C. 1979] and *Goss* v. *Lopez*, 419 U.S. 565, 39 L.Ed. 2d 465, 94 S.Ct. 1405 [1974]). Whether a right is stated explicitly or implicitly, once it has been established, it cannot be limited or removed without due process protections.

After finding a right to education based on statutory attendance requirements, determination must be made of whether or not that right includes participation in extracurricular activities. If the right to education means a right to the "total" educational process provided by a school, the courts may find participation in athletic competition to be a right (see Section 1.32–2). The right to participate would then be protected by due process considerations. Many courts, however, interpret educational rights as encompassing only classroom learning and view all other activities as unprotected privileges (see Section 1.32–2).

Colorado Seminary v. **National Collegiate Athletic Ass'n., 417 F. Supp. 885 (D. Colo. 1976), *aff'd*, 570 F. 2d 320 (10th Cir. 1978)**

An action was brought by Colorado Seminary (Denver University) and its student-athletes to enjoin the NCAA from imposing sanctions against the institution for alleged violations of the NCAA constitution. Student-athletes had been suspended from the school hockey team at the insistence of the NCAA after it was discovered they had previously played junior A hockey in Canada. The NCAA had clarified its rule after *Buckton* v. *National Collegiate Athletic Ass'n.* (see Section 1.33), and the revised rule stated that expenses received from an outside amateur sports team or organization *in excess of necessary travel and meal expenses* for practice and game competition would be considered pay. Colorado Seminary defied the NCAA by refusing to declare any of its athletes ineligible, despite their known infraction of the outside compensation rule. Consequently, the school was placed on a two-year probation. Plaintiffs challenged this action, claiming it violated due process and equal protection rights.

The court held that the students' interest in intercollegiate athletic participation did not reach the level of constitutionally protected property or liberty interest receiving due process guarantees: "While the Court might agree that the deprivation of a previously granted scholarship would invoke the protections of procedural due process, it is of no benefit to the student-athletes in this case" [scholarships were not canceled because of graduation]. It also rejected a constitutional claim made on the opportunity to obtain a professional contract. The court judged, "the interest in future professional careers must nevertheless be considered speculative and not of constitutional dimensions."

Fluitt v. University of Nebraska, 489 F. Supp. 1194 (D. Neb. 1980)

Plaintiff Fluitt was a fifth-year student at the

University of Nebraska. Fluitt served as an assistant track coach, for which he was being paid approximately 80 percent of the dollar amount of a full scholarship. He had been on a track scholarship for four years. He had asked his head coach for one additional year of eligibility due to an injury that terminated his freshman season. The university is a member of the Big Eight Conference, and plaintiff was informed by his coach that it was too late to request a hardship ruling under Big Eight rules. Upon plaintiff's request, an appeal was made to the Big Eight commissioner.

The faculty representatives of the Big Eight Conference voted to deny Fluitt an extra year of eligibility. Plaintiff and his coach were notified by telephone of the conference's decision. Since Fluitt was not present when the decision was made, he requested and received a hearing before the faculty representatives, in which Fluitt was represented by counsel. The motion to grant an additional year was denied.

The plaintiff then brought suit against Nebraska seeking injunctive relief from the conference's decision. He complained that irreparable damage could be caused if he lost this track scholarship; the opportunity to compete; the opportunity to qualify for the 1980 Olympics; or the opportunity to defend his Big Eight title in the mile. He further complained that he was denied equal protection and due process.

In answering these charges, the University of Nebraska contended that: (1) plaintiff was on scholarship for four full years and a scholarship for the fifth year was purely speculative; (2) plaintiff was ineligible to compete according to the NCAA constitution, 3–1–(f)–(1), and therefore had lost his student-athlete status; (3) plaintiff testified that he was not precluded from competing; and (4) plaintiff could not specify what damage would occur if he were unable to defend his conference title. This title was determined not to be essential to the development of his career, especially since there was no professional league beyond college competition.

The court ruled in favor of the defendant. It reasoned that the Faculty Committee was solely responsible for all determinations of hardship, a procedure that had been followed for at least 25 years. Any denial of due process at the first hearing was remedied at the second hearing. The request for an injunction was denied.

NOTES _____

1. The following cases are examples of a property interest in intercollegiate athletics:

(a) In *National Collegiate Athletic Ass'n.v. Gillard*, 352 So. 2d 1072 (Miss. 1977), the court ruled that a player's right to play intercollegiate football is not a property right to be protected by due process guarantees. The court ruled that the denial of player's eligibility to compete for having accepted clothing at a discount did not infringe on the plaintiff's constitutional rights to due process (see Sections 1.32 and 2.30, Note 2).

(b) See *Gulf South Conference v. Boyd*, 369 So. 2d 553 (Ala. 1979), in Section 2.13–1.

(c) See *Hall v. University of Minnesota*, 530 F. Supp. 104 (D. Minn. 1982), in Section 2.12.

(d) See *Behagan v. Intercollege Conference of Faculty Representatives*, 346 F. Supp. 602 (D. Minn 1972), in Section 1.32–1.

2. The following cases are examples of the property interest argument in interscholastic athletics:

(a) In *Stock v. Texas Catholic Interscholastic League*, 364 F. Supp. 362 (N.D. Tex. 1973), the court held that the plaintiff high school student's interest in playing interscholastic football was too insignificant to justify federal court jurisdiction. The plaintiff failed to show that he had been deprived of a right under color of state law such that jurisdiction under 42 U.S.C. section 1983 should be granted. The court held that: "Nowhere in the constitution is there any guarantee of a right to play football. . . . even if the participation was thwarted under color of state law, the interest at stake was still too insignificant to justify jurisdiction."

(b) See *Gulf South Conference v. Boyd*, 369 So. 2d 553 (Ala. 1979), in Section 2.13–1.

(c) See *Scott v. Kilpatrick*, 286 Ala. 129, 237 So. 2d 652 (1970).

(d) In *Robinson v. Illinois High School Ass'n.*, 45 Ill. App. 2d 277, 195 N.E. 2d 38 (1963), plaintiff high school student was denied eligibility because he was over the age limit set by the defendant association. The court held that no property interest was sufficient to justify judicial intervention when the association's determination of eligibility did not show fraud, collusion, or unreasonable or arbitrary acts.

(e) In *Taylor v. Alabama High School Athletic Ass'n.*,

336 F. Supp. 54 (M.D. Ala. 1972), the district court held that participation in interscholastic athletics is a privilege. The mere chance of receiving a college scholarship based upon display of athletic ability at tournaments is not a protectable property right.

(f) In *Moran v. School District #7, Yellowstone County,* 350 F. Supp. 1180 (D. Mont. 1972), the court held that the right to attend school includes the right to participate in extracurricular activities. The court reasoned that sports are an integral part of the total educational process. This educational process is extremely important, and sport participation may not be denied when there is no reasonable basis upon which to distinguish among the various parts of the educational process.

3. For further information, see the following articles:

(a) "Judicial Review of Disputes Between Athletes and the National Collegiate Athletic Association," 24 *Stanford Law Review* 903 (1972).

(b) Comment, "A Student-Athlete's Interest in Eligibility: Its Context and Constitutional Dimensions," 10 *Connecticut Law Review* 318 (1975).

(c) Martin, "Due Process and Its Future within the NCAA," 10 *Connecticut Law Review* 290 (1978).

(d) "High School Athletes and Due Process," 15 *New England Law Review* 597 (1978).

(e) "NCAA, Amateurism and Student-Athletes' Constitutional Rights," 15 *New England Law Review* 877 (1978).

(f) "Entitlement, Enjoyment and Due Process of Law," 89 *Duke Law Journal* 101 (1974).

(g) "Of Liberty and Property," 62 *Cornell Law Review* 405 (1977).

(h) "Jocks Are People Too," 13 *Creighton Law Review* 843 (1979).

(i) "High School Athletics and Due Process Notice of Eligibility Rules," 57 *Nebraska Law Review* 877 (1978).

(j) "Judicial Review of NCAA Decisions: Does the College Athlete Have a Property Interest in Interscholastic Athletics?" 10 *Stetson Law Review* 483 (1981).

1.33   Equal Protection

Equal protection is the constitutional method of checking on the fairness of the application of any law. This independent constitutional guarantee governs all federal, state, and local laws that classify individuals or impact on individual rights. The equal protection guarantee is found in the Fourteenth Amendment of the U.S. Constitution. It reads: "No state shall . . . deny to any person within its jurisdiction the equal protection of the laws." It is specifically applicable only to the states, but the federal government is held to similar standards under the due process clause of the Fifth Amendment. Equal protection requires that no person be singled out from similarly situated people, or have different benefits bestowed or burdens imposed, unless a constitutionally permissible reason exists for doing so.

Different standards of review are used under equal protection analysis. The highest standard of review is that of *strict scrutiny*. Application of the strict scrutiny standard by the court means that the rule challenged will be invalidated unless the defendant can demonstrate that the rule is supported by a compelling state interest. When a rule abridges a fundamental right or makes a distinction based on suspect criteria, the defendant has the burden of proof. This standard tests only whether a classification is properly drawn — not whether an individual is properly placed within that classification. This type of review is triggered by the use of either a suspect class or fundamental interest. The Supreme Court has found three suspect classes: alienage, race, and national origin. Any time a rule impacts directly or indirectly on any of these suspect classifications, the strict scrutiny standard will be applied.

There are a number of fundamental interests, and the vast majority of these rights arise expressly from the U.S. Constitution. One interest includes all the First Amendment guarantees. The First Amendment guarantees include the right to freedom of religion, speech, and press, as well as the right to assemble peaceably and to petition the government for redress of grievances. In addition to these specific rights, the Supreme Court has found three other fundamental rights — the right to travel, the right to vote, and the right to privacy (which involves decisions about marriage, abortion, and other family choices). Some interests have been specifically found to be nonfundamental. These include subsistence and welfare payments, housing, government employment, and education.

The fact that education has been deemed a nonfundamental interest is particularly important in cases involving high school or college athletic associations. This designation makes it difficult for the plaintiff student-athlete to establish participation as a protectable property interest as evidenced in *Fluitt* v. *University of Nebraska* and in *Colorado Seminary* v. *National Collegiate Athletic Ass'n.* (see Section 1.32–2).

The second standard of review is that of *rational basis.* This standard requires only that the rule have some rational relationship to a legitimate organizational purpose. It is used in the absence of a class defined by suspect criteria or on a fundamental right. Rules reviewed under this standard are difficult for a plaintiff to challenge successfully since the defendant is generally able to present some rational relationship between the restriction and a legitimate governmental objective. The rational basis test is the most commonly applied constitutional standard.

A third standard of review, or category of classes, imposes an intermediate test, which falls between the strict scrutiny and rational basis test. It requires that rules classifying certain groups satisfy an "important," but not necessarily "compelling," interest. Two "quasi-suspect" classifications have been established — gender and legitimacy. Use of either gender- or legitimacy-based classifications will trigger this intermediate standard of review. To date, the difference between "compelling" and "important" has not been made explicit and remains the subject of much examination and speculation.

Equal protection does not bar states from creating classifications. Instead, it requires that classifications not be predicated on race, alienage, or national origin. It also requires that the criteria bear a reasonable relationship to the purpose of the law. Otherwise, the distinction is automatically suspect. Once a law is suspect, it will be held valid only if a compelling interest is established, and there is

no less intrusive means by which the same end may be achieved (see *Buckton* v. *National Collegiate Athletic Ass'n., infra*). The burden of proof is on the states to establish the compelling nature of the interest. The same analysis is used when a fundamental interest is infringed upon by a state law. In summary, the theory of equal protection is used to protect individuals by ensuring that they are fairly treated in the exercise of their fundamental rights and by assuring the elimination of distinctions based on constitutionally impermissible criteria.

The equal protection guarantee relates to classes and/or distinctions inevitably drawn whenever a legislative body makes rules relating to specific groups. One method typically employed to challenge a rule under the equal protection clause is that which claims either under- or overinclusiveness. Under- or over-inclusiveness can result in a rule being impermissibly discriminatory. Overinclusiveness means that the legislative class includes many people to whom the rule in question lacks a rational relationship. In other words, at least some of the class of affected individuals are not part of the problem addressed by the rule, and the rule as applied to these people has no relationship to its purpose. A rule's validity depends not on whether classes differ but on whether differences between the classes are pertinent to the subject with respect to which the classification is made.

Whereas overinclusiveness exists when a rule creates a class more extensive than necessary to effectuate the purpose of the rule, under-inclusiveness exists when a class does not contain all the members necessary to effectuate the rule's purpose. It is possible for a rule to be both over- and underinclusive.

The following statement is a typical example of a rule that is both over- and underinclusive: "All transfer students from public high schools will not be eligible for interscholastic play for one year from date of entry." This rule is overinclusive regarding public school transfers that were made for reasons unrelated to athletics. It would be underinclusive, however, if it permitted immediate eligibility for transfer students from private schools who might be transferring solely for athletic reasons.

It is extremely difficult to draw perfect classifications that are neither over- nor under-inclusive. In light of this, when no important constitutional rights are involved, courts can and do uphold both over- and underinclusive categories as long as they can find a rational relationship between the rule and its purpose. For example, only when an athletic association cannot demonstrate the connection between the rule and its purpose will the court find that an equal protection violation has occurred, as in *Moran* v. *School District #7, Yellowstone County* (see Section 1.32–2, Note 2).

Another reason the court will uphold rules that do not make perfect classifications is to allow athletic associations to deal with problems on an individual basis. Associations or legislatures do not have to create perfect solutions prior to attacking specific problems. In many cases, the court will not decide if the rule itself is invalid but may conclude that its application to a specific individual violates the person's civil rights. It can therefore pay deference to the legislative judgment initiating the rule, while simultaneously upholding individual rights.

Technically, there is a two-tier system for equal protection analysis. The trend, however, may be toward a sliding scale that would dissolve the absolute categories of fundamental rights and interests. The advantage of a sliding-scale approach is that it is much more flexible and will in effect create a scale of rights and/or classes that can be directly compared with the governmental interest involved (see *Indiana High School Athletic Ass'n.* v. *Raike*, 164 Ind. App. 169, 329 N.E. 2d 66 [1975], *infra*).

players, were Canadian nationals who sought an injunction to prevent the NCAA and the Eastern Collegiate Athletic Conference from declaring them ineligible and imposing sanctions as a result of their participation on Canadian major junior A hockey teams. The rule on which the declaration of ineligibility was based was attacked on equal protection grounds. The rule read: "Any student-athlete who has participated as a member of the Canadian Amateur Hockey Association's major junior A hockey classification shall not be eligible for intercollegiate athletics." Because it was determined that half of the NCAA member schools were state supported and that Boston University received state funding, the court held that state action was established.

After finding state action, the court held "these regulations constitute and impose disparate eligibility standards, one for student-athletes who have played hockey in the United States; and another for those who have played in Canada." The court noted that the mere fact that the classification separated American players from their Canadian counterparts made the rule inherently suspect. All regulations that impose such a classification are subject to the strict scrutiny standard. Under strict scrutiny, "defendants . . . bear the heavy burden of demonstrating that the classification is justified by a compelling interest."

The defendants argued that the principle of amateurism in intercollegiate sports sufficiently justified the regulation. The court found that in Canada high school players were provided with monetary support from the team, while in the United States students got fiscal support money from the high schools they attended. Therefore, the court stated that "by making the source rather than the character of the aid received the determining factor in the plaintiff's case, defendants have allowed form to prevail over substance. This, the court will not permit."

Buckton v. National Collegiate Athletic Ass'n., 336 F. Supp. 1158 (D. Mass. 1973)

The plaintiffs, Boston University ice hockey

Indiana High School Athletic Ass'n. v. Raike, 164 Ind. App. 169, 329 N.E.2d 66 (1975)

This action was initiated by a married high

school student who wanted to strike down a board of education rule that prohibited married students from participation in any extracurricular programs. The court held that the rule denied equal protection because there was no fair and substantial relationship between the classification (married students) and the objective sought (preventing dropouts). In determining the standard of review to be used, the court discussed the present two-tier system of strict scrutiny or rational basis analysis. It then went on to state:

> The rigidity of the two-tier test inevitably led to a blurring of this somewhat artificial dualism. In recent years various courts and commentators have sensed modification of the two-tier approach. They point to a new or hybrid approach to equal protection which is more flexible. By its terms, the classification must be justified by something more than any reasonably conceivable set of facts. Rather it must rest upon some ground of difference having a fair and substantial relation to the object of the legislation, so that all persons similarly circumstanced shall be treated alike.

This "new" or intermediate approach has been interpreted as being based on a "multifactor, sliding scale" analysis, with the two end points of the scale being the traditional two tiers of high and low scrutiny.

Under the traditional two-tier approach of the U.S. Supreme Court, the classification was initially examined to determine if it was "suspect" or if a "fundamental right" was violated by the statutory or regulatory scheme; if not, the low scrutiny, rational basis test was used. Judicial review of classifications will be more flexible if the "new" or intermediate approach is followed by the reviewing court. The general principle seems to be that the more important and closer the individual's interest comes to a specific constitutional guarantee, the greater the degree of judicial scrutiny. The importance of the standard of review adopted is that the result reached is in

large part a product of that initial decision.

The court went on to decide that the right to marry was not a fundamental right. Even so, it was one that required an intermediate and not merely a rational basis analysis.

NOTES

1. For an example of the application of the rational basis test, see *Mitchell* v. *Louisiana High School Athletic Ass'n.*, 430 F.2d 1155(5th Cir. 1970). This case was litigated on a theory that there was discrimination against students who chose to repeat a junior high school grade because of academic or personal reasons. The court held that allowing those who failed a year to still have four years of high school eligibility, while reducing eligibility to three years for those who chose to repeat a year, had a rational relationship with regard to the problem of redshirting (see Section 2.14–1). Therefore, it was not appropriate for the judiciary to intervene, even when the rule was unduly harsh on an individual.

2. In *Baltic Independent School District No. 115* v. *South Dakota High School Activities Ass'n.*, 362 F. Supp. 780 (D.S.D. 1973), students at a Class B high school (so classified based on its size) brought a class action claiming a denial of equal protection because the rules of the association gave Class B students a lesser opportunity to qualify for entrance into the National Debating Tournament. The court held that the association's rule of classifying high schools for speech activity was a denial of equal protection. Although no fundamental interest or suspect class was involved, there was no rational relationship between the rule and the objective of promoting fair competition. The court found the right to participate was constitutionally protected, even though debating was a voluntary extracurricular activity.

3. Rules based on national origin of athletes are subject to strict scrutiny. A foreign student eligibility rule may be held unconstitutional, as in *Howard University* v. *National Collegiate Athletic Ass'n.*, 510 F. 2d 213 (D.C. Cir. 1975) (see Section 1.31) and in *Rivas Tenorio* v. *Liga Atletica Interuniversitaria*, 554 F.2d 492 (1st Cir. 1977).

4. In *Moreland* v. *Western Pa. Interscholastic, Etc.*, 572 F. 2d 121 (3rd Cir. 1978), a high school basketball player claimed denial of equal protection when he was prohibited from competing in postseason play because he was absent from school for more than 20 days, a violation of a league rule. The court held that the rule was rationally related to the purpose of safeguarding educational values, cultivating high ideals of good sportsmanship, and promoting uniformity of standards in athletic competition.

1.40 Amateur Athletic Association Authority

The authority for amateur athletic associations to regulate its membership originates from two sources. First, as corporate bodies, amateur athletic organizations must be recognized as entities by the state. Second, in order for the association to govern, the membership must have agreed to be so regulated. In this chapter, the legal relationships between the state government, the amateur athletic associations, and membership will be examined using the NCAA as an example.

1.41 The NCAA

The National Collegiate Athletic Association (NCAA) is a voluntary association whose members, by joining the organization, agree to follow certain conditions and obligations of membership. This includes the obligation to conduct their individual institutional athletic programs in a manner consistent with NCAA legislation. This legislation is enacted by a majority vote of delegates at either the annual convention, held each January, or at special conventions called by the NCAA Council. The rules of the organization are published annually in the *NCAA Manual*, which is available to every member of the organization.

Member institutions agree, by joining the NCAA, to be policed in regard to the organization's rules by the NCAA's enforcement staff, which is given policy guidance by the NCAA's Infractions Committee. The Infractions Committee is composed of six members, one of whom serves as chair. Committee members may serve a total limit of nine years. The enforcement staff conducts all NCAA investigations based on allegation of infractions by a member institution. Some investigations may involve only one or two allegations, while others may include as many as 100 or more.

The first NCAA enforcement program was enacted by the association in 1948 and it was designed to correct recruiting abuses. The NCAA also created a Constitutional Compliance Committee, which was designed to interpret the new code and investigate violations.

The Constitutional Compliance Committee was replaced in 1951 with the Committee on Infractions. This committee was given broader investigative powers. In 1973 investigative and hearing duties were divided by the NCAA membership, with the NCAA assuming investigative responsibilities and the Committee on Infractions handling hearings. This basic structure remains the same for today's enforcement programs.

In response to increasing criticism of its enforcement procedures, the NCAA has taken steps to improve its procedures in the last few years. These steps include expanding its staff of professional investigators, many of whom are former FBI agents, and interviewing highly recruited athletes in an attempt to uncover recruiting violations as they occur. Investigators also attempt to develop close relationships with highly recruited "blue chip" athletes, hoping the athletes will inform them of any illegal offers made by recruiters.

In a step that is very likely to further heighten interest in NCAA investigations and ultimately lead to an increase in litigation, the NCAA in 1985 again took measures to strengthen its enforcement program. This step was taken in response to what was labeled by some of the association's membership as an "integrity crisis." This perceived crisis developed as a result of recent multiple scandals involving intercollegiate athletic programs. The scandals caused a great deal of pressure to be placed on the NCAA by the chief executive officers of the association's member institutions; they were worried about the direction toward which the nation's intercollegiate athletic programs were heading and wished to see reforms instituted.

As a result of the "integrity crisis," the NCAA called a special summer convention in 1985 (only the fifth in its history) and enacted stronger enforcement and penalty procedures for member schools who violate NCAA regulations. The so-called "death penalty" includes suspension for an athletic team for as long as two seasons if it is found guilty of major NCAA rule infractions twice in a five-year period (retroactive to September 1980) and sanctions against student-athletes who knowingly violate NCAA rules. The NCAA also instituted mandatory reporting requirements for member institutions in regards to student-athlete academic progress and independent financial audits of athletic department budgets. As Dr. John W. Ryan, president of Indiana University and chairman of the NCAA's President's Commission, noted at the special convention that enacted the new enforcement rules: "the nation's presidents and chancellors are going to determine the direction and major policies of college athletics and . . . we are not going to condone any failure to comply with these policies."

The key to the NCAA investigative process is the cooperative principle, in which the accused member institution and the NCAA's enforcement staff work together to ascertain the truth of alleged infractions. The process itself consists of six steps: (1) a preliminary inquiry, (2) an official inquiry, (3) a hearing by the Committee on Infractions, (4) a report of findings, (5) an assignment of penalties (if warranted), and (6) a right of appeal. These six steps are described in the following paragraphs and illustrated in more detail in Exhibit 1–5.

1. *Preliminary Inquiry.* A preliminary inquiry is initiated by the NCAA enforcement staff if alleged violations seem serious and plausible. An institution is notified through the issuance of a preliminary inquiry letter, which notifies the school that enforcment staff members will be on campus in the near future investigating alleged infractions of the NCAA's rules. This preliminary inquiry letter does not specify the nature of the allegations. If pursued further, allegations will be made specific as to time, place, and personnel. However, at no time will the source of these allegations be revealed. In some cases, the source becomes obvious, and it may involve one of the institution's own student-athletes. Additional sources of information are other institutions and coaches.

If the preliminary inquiry indicates that allegations of wrongdoing may be valid, the enforcement staff will elect either to deal with the issue with a summary procedure before the Committee on Infractions or to undertake an official inquiry.

2. *Official Inquiry (OI).* An official inquiry is authorized by the NCAA's Committee on Infractions based on the results of the enforcement staff's preliminary inquiry. The OI is primarily a second letter to the institution, which lists specific allegations of infractions and directs the school, under the terms of the NCAA membership rules, to conduct its own investigation immediately. Initially, the school has 60 days to respond, although extensions are commonly granted. The OI breaks down into the following three parts:

1. The overture consists of four questions that ask how the athletic programs are organized and administered at the accused institution.
2. The allegations, the heart of the OI, list the specific charges, cite the rules which have been violated, and give the names of those believed to be involved. Note the following allegation from a typical OI:

   Example:
   See *NCAA Manual*, Constitution 3-1-(g)-(4), 3-1-(g)-(5), and 3-4-(a)
   It is alleged that in January 1979, through the arrangements of head football coach Neils Thompson, student-athlete Charles Wright received the benefit of one-way commercial airline transportation at no cost to him between Ardmore, Pennsylvania, and Austin, Texas, in order to travel to the university following a visit to his home.

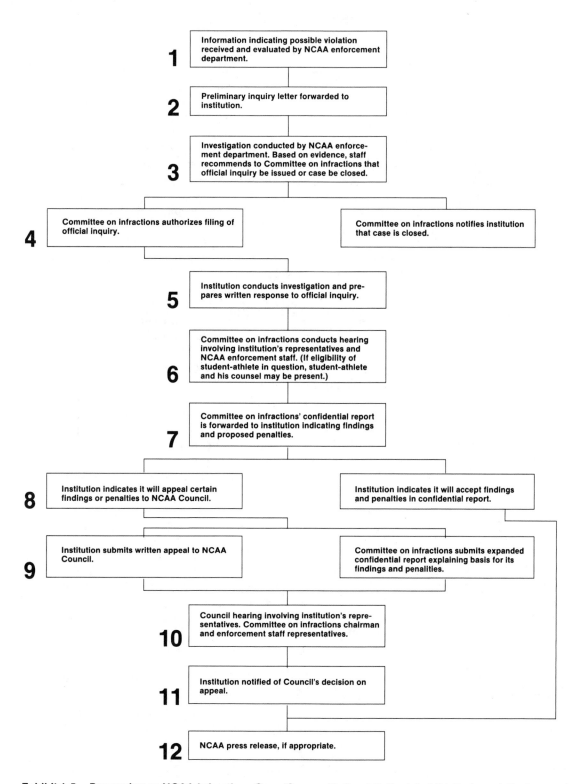

1 Information indicating possible violation received and evaluated by NCAA enforcement department.

2 Preliminary inquiry letter forwarded to institution.

3 Investigation conducted by NCAA enforcement department. Based on evidence, staff recommends to Committee on infractions that official inquiry be issued or case be closed.

4 Committee on infractions authorizes filing of official inquiry.

Committee on infractions notifies institution that case is closed.

5 Institution conducts investigation and prepares written response to official inquiry.

6 Committee on infractions conducts hearing involving institution's representatives and NCAA enforcement staff. (If eligibility of student-athlete in question, student-athlete and his counsel may be present.)

7 Committee on infractions' confidential report is forwarded to institution indicating findings and proposed penalties.

8 Institution indicates it will appeal certain findings or penalties to NCAA Council.

Institution indicates it will accept findings and penalties in confidential report.

9 Institution submits written appeal to NCAA Council.

Committee on infractions submits expanded confidential report explaining basis for its findings and penalties.

10 Council hearing involving institution's representatives. Committee on infractions chairman and enforcement staff representatives.

11 Institution notified of Council's decision on appeal.

12 NCAA press release, if appropriate.

Exhibit 1-5. Processing an NCAA Infractions Case (*Source:* National Collegiate Athletic Association)

Please indicate whether this information is substantially correct and submit evidence to support your response.

Also provide the following:

a. The actual date of this transportation.

b. The reasons Wright was provided commercial airline transportation at no personal expense to him on this occasion.

c. A statement indicating the actual cost of this transportation and the source of funds utilized to pay the resultant cost.

d. The identity of all athletic department staff members involved in or knowledgeable of these arangements for Wright, and a description of such involvement of knowledge prior to, at the time of, and subsequent to this trip.

There may be one or many of these type allegations. They can name student-athletes, potential recruits, coaches, alumni, and boosters.

3. A coda, the third part of an OI, is directed at the president of the institution. Since 1974, the NCAA has required the chief executive officer of each member institution to certify that the institution is complying with NCAA rules. In addition, since 1975, all members of an institution's athletic department staff have been required to sign a statement that they have reported their knowledge of and involvement in any violation of NCAA legislation.

The NCAA has a gag rule in effect on its involvement in an investigation. It remains in effect throughout the entire procedure (see *1985–86 NCAA Manual*, Enforcement 11). The NCAA will not even comment on the existence of an investigation unless it is in response to information released by the institution (see *1985–86 NCAA Manual*, Enforcement 12-[a]-[15]). The enforcement procedures also provide that the NCAA's primary investigator will be available to meet with the institution to discuss the development of its response and to assist in the case (see *1985–86 NCAA Manual*, Enforcement 12-[a]-[14]). The two parties attempt to reach agreement on certain facts of the case in order to streamline the hearing process. Statements of persons interviewed on behalf of the institution by the NCAA investigator will be presented as part of the institution's response to the OI. The institution must then carry out its own investigation and draft its response to the NCAA allegations. This response, which may be hundreds of pages long, is sent to the NCAA and to the members of the Committee on Infractions.

3. *Committee on Infractions Hearing.* Committee on Infractions hearings are held at the NCAA offices in Mission, Kansas. These meetings are closed and confidential and involve the members of the Committee on Infractions, the delegation from the institution, and the NCAA enforcement staff members. The procedure begins with opening statements by a spokesperson from the institution, often an attorney, who is then followed by a spokesperson for the enforcement staff. These opening statements express the overall position of the university and of the staff. The heart of the official inquiry is the detailed review of the allegations, which includes determining which allegations are and are not in dispute. The enforcement staff presents all its evidence, regardless of whether it supports or refutes the allegations. The institution's spokesperson then responds and in so doing may refer to or add to the school's written response. This procedure is informal, with frequent verbal exchanges between committee members and the university. Rigid rules of evidence are not enforced at these hearings, which may proceed for several days until all allegations have been covered. After the closing statements, the chairman of the committee advises the university of the next steps in the case, including the university's opportunity to appeal to the council if it is dissatisfied with the committee's finding, its penalty, or both. The hearing is then adjourned.

4. *Findings.* Findings are made after the members of the Committee on Infractions have deliberated over the case on an individual

basis, reviewing each allegation. Sometimes additional information is needed, either on this specific investigation or from previous cases. The NCAA has charged the committee to base its findings on information it determines to be "credible, persuasive and of a kind on which reasonably prudent persons rely on in the conduct of serious affairs." (See *1985–86 NCAA Manual*, Enforcement 4-[b]-[12].) Once a consensus of committee members is reached, all findings are put in the form of a confidential report. This report is sent to the institution's president.

5. *Penalties.* If warranted, penalties are included in the Committee on Infraction's final report. These may include prohibiting an institution's team or teams from television appearances, taking away athletic scholarships, or barring teams from postseason play (see Section 1.41–1). The latter penalty is often referred to as being put on probation. Individual coaches may also be held accountable when rule violations are discovered. Possible penalties can include freezing salary levels, limiting expense accounts, and restricting recruitment travel. At the 1983 NCAA convention, the NCAA passed a requirement that all coaches' contracts include a stipulation that the coach can be suspended without pay or fired if he or she is involved in "deliberate and serious violations of NCAA regulation." At the NCAA's 1985 special convention, penalties against coaches who violate association rules were further toughened: Any restriction imposed on an institution's coaching staff member must be applied to the coach, even if he or she is employed by an institution other than the one at which the violation occurred (see *1985–86 NCAA Manual*, Bylaw 5–6-[d]-[3]). In some cases, when violations are deemed to be less severe, the penalty imposed by the NCAA may take the form of a private reproach (see *1985–86 NCAA Manual*, Enforcement 3[a]). After the appeals process has been exhausted, the NCAA issues a press release announcing any allegations found to be true and any penalties that were imposed (see

1985–86 NCAA Manual, Enforcement 12-[f]).

6. *Appeal (optional).* An institution has an automatic right of appeal to the NCAA Council. It is heard "de novo"; that is, the matter is heard as if for the first time. The council can reverse, expand, contract, or completely change the finding of the Infractions Committee. The option also remains of appealing to the courts.

NOTES ————————————————

1. Much of the above information is from Wright, *Responding to an NCAA Investigation, or, What to Do When an Official Inquiry Comes*, a private paper, The University of Texas (July 1980), pp. 1–15.
2. For further information, see "Responding to an NCAA Investigation, or, What to Do When an Official Inquiry Comes," 1 *Entertainment and Sports Law Journal* 19 (1984).
3. The following excerpt is from the *1985–86 NCAA Manual*, Enforcement 6–(a):

The committee shall be obligated to submit a written summary statement to the Council on each case that is subject to appeal, and it shall include:
(1) Violations of NCAA requirements of questionable practices in light of NCAA requirements as determined by the committee;
(2) A statement of the committee's proposed penalty;
(3) A statement of the origin of the case;
(4) Related factors appropriate for consideration in judgment of the case, and
(5) Disciplinary or corrective actions taken by the institution or conference of any other agency involved in the particular incident.

4. For a critical analysis of the NCAA's enforcement procedures, see *Enforcement Program of the National Collegiate Athletic Association, A Report Together with Minority Views* by the Subcommittee on Oversight and Investigations of the Committee on Interstate and Foreign Commerce, House of Representatives, Ninety-Fifth Congress, Second Session, December, 1978, U.S. Government Printing Office, Washington, D.C., 1978 (see Committee Print 95–69).
5. For further information, see "NCAA Enforcement Program," Hearing Before the Subcommittee on Oversight and Investigations of House Committee on Interstate and Foreign Commerce, 95th Congress, 2nd Session (1978).
6. For further information on the NCAA's 1985 special convention and legislation that was enacted, see the following articles:

(a) "NCAA Approves Stiffer Penalties," *New York Times*, June 22, 1985, pp. 1, 49.
(b) "College Presidents Are Taking Control," *New*

York Times, June 23, 1985, sec. 5, p. 7.

(c) "What's the Future of the NCAA?" *Sporting News*, June 3, 1985, pp. 15–16, 20.

(d) "Presidents Gain NCAA Beachhead," *New York Times*, June 22, 1985, p. 49.

(e) "Going Beyond the Scandals," *New York Times*, June 25, 1985, p. C1.

(f) "NCAA Adopts Tough Line on Recruiting Ills," *New York Daily News*, June 22, 1985, p. 28.

(g) "Excerpts of Speech to NCAA Group," *New York Times*, June 22, 1985, p. 49.

(h) "Convention Success Spurs Future Commission Actions," *NCAA News*, July 3, 1985, p. 1.

1.41–1   The NCAA, Conferences, and Member Institutions

Occasionally, the NCAA will become involved in litigation with one of its member institutions over the imposition of sanctions against the member institution, one of the member institution's athletes, or against the personnel (i.e., a coach) of a member institution.

California State University, Hayward v. National Collegiate Athletic Ass'n., 47 Cal. App. 3d 533, 121 Cal. Rptr. 85 (1975)

California State University, Hayward (CSUH), brought an action to enjoin the NCAA from imposing penalties consisting of public reprimand, censure, and a probation period of not less than two years, during which it would not be allowed to participate in any postseason championship events. California State had allowed two students to compete in intercollegiate athletic events during their first year of studies, even though the students had predicted grade point averages (GPAs) lower than 1.6 on a 4.0 scale. This standard was known as the "1.6 rule" because of its reference to a freshman student's "predicted" grade point average. The students were allowed to compete after each had achieved an average above 2.0 after the first semester of study.

The 1.6 rule caused confusion and differing interpretations among NCAA members. Some, including CSUH, interpreted the rule to mean that freshmen subpredictors (those who predict below a 1.6 GPA) were eligible for in-season competition as long as they did not participate in postseason events. In addition, the assistant executive director of the NCAA was contacted and replied in a letter that the university was free to allow such students to compete during the season itself provided they were declared ineligible prior to any postseason championship competition.

At a later point in time, the NCAA published an "Official Interpretation," which imposed that the 1.6 rule made a subpredictor student ineligible to compete in intercollegiate athletics. The NCAA demanded that CSUH declare both students "currently" ineligible for one year, pursuant to "the provisions of Official Interpretation 418" and subject to an appeal by CSUH for restoration of their eligibility. CSUH at first declared the two ineligible and took an appeal, which was denied by an NCAA subcommittee and then by the NCAA Council. While the appeal was pending before the NCAA Council, CSUH declared the two students to be eligible.

The NCAA treated the two students' continuing eligibility as a further violation of the NCAA legislation, and CSUH was reported to the Committee on Infractions. The committee reached these conclusions: (1) the two students had played "while ineligible" under the 1.6 rule; (2) CSUH had defied the NCAA by declining to comply with its decisions regarding the two students' eligibility; and (3) a penalty should be imposed whereby CSUH would be "pubicly reprimanded and censored, and placed on probation for an indefinite period" (but for not less than two years), during which it would not be permitted to participate in NCAA "championship" or other postseason events.

CSUH did not challenge the committee's findings but appealed the major parts of the "proposed penalties" to the NCAA Council. After another hearing, the council denied this appeal. CSUH brought a court action two months after the appeal was denied and the probation penalty was in effect.

The superior court granted an injunction against the NCAA, which was affirmed by the court of appeals. The injunction held that the NCAA was estopped from imposing any penalties as a result of the letter from the assistant executive director. Both students, in the opinion of the court, were eligible for athletic competition under NCAA rules at the time they were permitted to compete, and that the change in interpretation of rules did not have any retroactive effect. While the courts do not generally intervene in the internal affairs of a private voluntary association such as the NCAA, they will intervene to nullify substantial disciplinary action taken against a member in violation of its constitution and bylaws. The penalties proposed by the NCAA on the university, its athletic programs, and its reputation were sufficiently substantial to warrant judicial intervention.

NOTES

1. The following excerpt is from the *1985–86 NCAA Manual*, Enforcement 7–(b):

Among the disciplinary measures, singularly or in combination, which may be adopted by the committee or Council and imposed against an institution are:

(1) Reprimand and censure;

(2) Probation for one year;

(3) Probation for more than one year;

(4) Ineligibility for one or more NCAA championship events;

(5) Ineligibility for invitational and postseason meets and tournaments;

(6) Ineligibility for any television programs subject to the association's control of administration, or any other television programs involving live coverage of the institution's intercollegiate athletic team or teams in the sport or sports in which the violations occurred;

(7) Ineligibility of the member to vote or its personnel to serve on committees of the Association, or both;

(8) Prohibition against an intercollegiate sports team or teams participating against outside competition for a specified period;

(9) Prohibition against the recruitment of prospective student-athletes for a sport or sports for a specified period;

(10) A reduction in the number of either initial or total financial aid awards (as defined by O.I. 600) which may be awarded during a specified period;

(11) Requirement that an institution which has been represented in an NCAA championship by a student-athlete who was recruited or received improper benefits (which would not necessarily render the student-athlete ineligible) in violation of NCAA legislation shall return its share of net receipts from such competition in excess of the regular expense reimbursement, or if said funds have not been distributed, they shall be withheld by the NCAA executive director, or individual or team records and performances shall be vacated or stricken; or individual or team awards shall be returned to the Association, or any combination of the preceding penalties;

(12) Requirement that a member institution which has been found in violation show cause why:

(i) A penalty or an additional penalty should not be imposed if, in the opinion of the committee (or Council), it does not take appropriate disciplinary or corrective action against athletic department personnel involved in the infractions case, any other institutional employee if the circumstances warrant or representatives of the institution's athletic interests; or

(ii) A recommendation should not be made to the membership that the institution's membership in the Association be suspended or terminated if, in the opinion of the committee (or Council), it does not take appropriate disciplinary or corrective action against the head coach of the sport involved, any other institutional employee if the circumstances warrant or representatives of the institution's athletic interests.

(iii) "Appropriate disciplinary or corrective action" as specified in paragraphs (i) and (ii) above may include, for example, termination of the coaching contract of the head coach and any assistants involved; suspension or termination of the employment status of any other institutional employee who may be involved; severance of relations with any representative of the institution's athletic interests who may be involved; the head of the department or assistant coach from any coaching, recruiting or speaking engagements for a specified period, and the prohibition of all recruiting in a specified sport for a specified period.

(iv) The nature and extent of such action shall be the determination of the institution after due notice and hearing to the individuals concerned; but the determination of whether or not the action is appropriate in the fulfillment of NCAA policies and principles, and its resulting effect on any institutional penalty, shall be solely that of the committee (or Council).

(v) Where this requirement is made, the institution shall show cause or, in the alternative, shall show the appropriate disciplinary or corrective action taken, in writing, to the committee (or Council) within 15 days thereafter. The committee (or Council) may, without further hearing, determine on the basis of such writing whether or not in its opinion appropriate disciplinary or corrective action has been taken and may impose a penalty or additional penalty, take no further action or, by notice to the institution, conduct a further hearing at a later date before making a final determination.

2. For an analysis of the effect that repeated NCAA investigations can have on a university, see "Trying to Save a University's Priceless Assets," *New York Times*, August 1, 1982, section 5, p. 2. The article discusses and includes the text of a statement made by Reverend John Lo Schiavo, S.J., president of the University of San Francisco, regarding the dropping of the school's NCAA Division I basketball program.

3. For related information concerning NCAA investigative procedures, see the following articles:

(a) "NCAA May Soon Permit Investigations of Cheating in Women's Athletics," *Chronicle of Higher Education*, October 13, 1982, p. 17.

(b) "Clemson President Bars Quarterback from Game," *Chronicle of Higher Education*, October 13, 1982, p. 17.

(c) "Deterring Cheaters in College Sports: Tougher Penalties vs. Better Policing," *Chronicle of Higher Education*, October 20, 1982, p. 15.

(d) "How the NCAA's Investigators Catch College Rule Breakers," *Chronicle of Higher Education*, October 20, 1982, p. 15.

(e) "Association Votes Itself New Powers to Penalize Institutions," *Chronicle of Higher Education*, January 20, 1982, p. 4.

(f) "Men's Athletic Program Put on a 3-Year Probation at Illinois," *Chronicle of Higher Education*, May 11, 1981, p. 8.

(g) "A Big Basketball Power Drops the Sport, Blaming Abuses by Alumni 'Boosters,' " *Chronicle of Higher Education*, August 11, 1982, p. 1.

(h) "Excessive Boosterism Plagues Sports Program at Wichita State," *Chronicle of Higher Education*, January 27, 1982, p. 5.

(i) "NCAA's Penalties Against Southern California: Does the Punishment Fit the Crime?" *Chronicle of Higher Education*, September 29, 1982, p. 15.

(j) "The NCAA: Fundamental Fairness and the Enforcement Program," 23 *Arizona Law Review* 1065 (1981).

(k) "The Enforcement Procedures of the NCAA: An Abuse of the Student-Athlete's Right to Reasonable Discovery," *Arizona State Law Review* 133 (1982).

(l) "The Enforcer," *Philadelphia Inquirer*, April 17, 1983, p. 12–E.

(m) "The Benefactor: He's Given Yale the Jitters," *Boston Globe*, July 19, 1981, p. 61.

(n) "Trouble in Loboland," *Sporting News*, December 29, 1979, p. 23.

(o) "Evolution of the NCAA Enforcement Program" (three-part series), *NCAA News*, July, 1979.

(p) "Football Teams on NCAA Probation Given Approval to Appear on TV," *Chronicle of Higher Education*, August 1, 1984, pp. 1, 22.

(q) Remington, "NCAA Enforcement Procedures Including the Role of the Committee on Infractions," 10 *Journal of College and University Law* 167 (1983–84).

(r) Brody, "NCAA Rules and Then Enforcement: Not Spare the Rod and Spoil the Child — Rather, Switch the Values and Spare the Sport," *Arizona State Law Review* 109 (1982).

(s) "Corruption in College Athletics," *The MacNeil-Lehrer Report*, September 6, 1982 (WNET/Thirteen, N.Y., N.Y., Transcript #1811).

4. In the National Association of Intercollegiate Athletics (NAIA), procedures for rules infractions are much simpler than the NCAA's. Each of the NAIA's 32 districts have an eligibility committee, usually composed of faculty members of member association schools. Most infractions involve satisfaction of academic requirements or improper institution eligibility certificates. District officials settle most cases on that level, usually by asking for an explanation from the student-athlete or athletic director from the involved college. The district eligibility committee (three members) then makes a recommendation to a national panel, which announces its decision to the NAIA's executive committee. Standard penalties include forfeiture of games, loss of the student-athlete's eligibility, and probation and suspension of athletic programs from participation in NAIA competition. For further information, see "Small-College Sports: The Unglamorous Rule-Breakers," *Chronicle of Higher Education*, October 31, 1984, p. 35.

5. The University of Florida, as a result of NCAA rules infractions which were disclosed in the fall of 1984, faced up to three years' probation, the loss of up to ten scholarships in each of two consecutive seasons, and exclusion from postseason play and television appearances for three consecutive years. For further information, see the following articles:

(a) "NCAA Hands Football Program at U. of Florida Up to Three Years' Probation, Cuts Its Scholarships," *Chronicle of Higher Education*, October 31, 1984, p. 35.

(b) "U. of Florida Asks Judge How Much Information from Unfinished NCAA Probe It Must Reveal," *Chronicle of Higher Eduation*, September 12, 1984, p. 31.

(c) "Conference Bars U. of Florida from Sugar Bowl after NCAA Sustains Charges of 59 Violations," *Chronicle of Higher Education*, November 28, 1984, p. 33.

6. The following reprint is from the University of Illinois Infractions Report, which was published in the

NCAA News in August, 1984. It details the violations of NCAA regulations by Illinois and lists the penalties imposed by the NCAA against the member institution. It is typical of the infractions reports issued by the NCAA.

The University of Illinois has been placed on probation for a two-year period by the NCAA Committee on Infractions as a result of violations occurring in the conduct of the institution's intercollegiate football program.

The NCAA penalty includes sanctions that will prohibit the university's football team from participating in postseason bowl games following the 1984 season, as well as from appearing on any "live" football telecasts during the 1984 regular season. Two representatives of the university's athletics interests will be disassociated from the athletics program during this period as a result of the Committee on Infractions' implementation of the "show cause" provision of the NCAA enforcement procedure.

Prior to the determination of the NCAA penalty, the university initiated other disciplinary actions related to the case, including: (1) a reduction of its permissible number of initial grants-in-aid in the sport of football from 30 to 20 during the 1985–86 academic year; (2) a penalty prohibiting the university's head football coach and the institution's assistant head football coach from participation in any off-campus recruiting activities during the 1984–85 academic year; (3) a prohibition against increases in the salary of the head football coach for the 1984 calendar year and the salary of the assistant head football coach prior to March 1987; and (4) an action to preclude five institutional representatives from any involvement in any activities associated with the recruitment of prospective student-athletes for a two-year period.

The actions taken by the university against its head football coach were based primarily on the responsibility of that individual for the overall supervision of the football program. The combination of NCAA and institutional penalties resulted in a total of seven institutional representatives being disassociated from the recruiting activities during the university's probationary period.

"This case was considered to be quite serious by the NCAA Committee on Infractions," said Thomas J. Niland, interim chair, NCAA Committee on Infractions, "and the committee would have imposed a more severe penalty if the institution had not already taken substantial disciplinary action on its own initiative. The committee determined that a serious penalty was warranted in light of the pattern of recruiting violations found in this case but that the penalty also should reflect the institution's thorough review of the allegations related to its football program, its corrective actions, and the commitment by institutional administrators to ensure that future activities in the conduct of the football program will be in compliance with NCAA legislation.

"Although many of the violations concerned actions involving previous coaching staff members," Niland continued, "several current members of the football coaching staff also were found in violation of NCAA legislation. The majority of the violations related to the recruitment of prospective student-athletes from junior colleges, and the institution has taken extensive corrective actions in regard to this aspect of its football recruiting program."

The Committee on Infractions found violations of NCAA legislation related to recruiting, extra benefits to student-athletes, ethical conduct and certification of compliance with NCAA legislation.

The following is a complete text of the penalty imposed upon the University of Illinois and a summary of the violations.

Penalty to be imposed upon Institution

1. The University of Illinois shall be publicly reprimanded and censured, and placed on probation for a period of two years, effective July 26, 1984, it being understood that should any portion of the penalty in this case be set aside for any reason other than by appropriate action of the Association, the penalty shall be reconsidered by the NCAA; further, prior to the expiration of this period of probation, the NCAA shall review the athletics policies and practices of the university.

2. The university's intercollegiate football team shall end its 1984 football season with the playing of its last regularly scheduled, in-season contest and the university shall not be eligible to participate in any postseason football competition.

3. During the 1984 football season, the university's intercollegiate football team shall not be eligible to appear on any television series or program subject to the administration or control of this Association or of any other television programs involving "live" coverage.

[Note: The principle set forth by the Committee on Infractions in a public statement issued by the NCAA on July 26, 1984, concerning member institutions subject to television sanctions during the 1984 football season would be applicable in this case.]

4. In accordance with the "show cause" provision of the NCAA penalty structure, the university will take disciplinary and corrective action in regard to two representatives of the university's athletics interests, which will preclude these individuals from involvement in any activities associated with the recruitment of prospective student-athletes on behalf of the university during the university's probationary period, preclude all prospective student-athletes known to the university or enrolled student-athletes from employment with any

corporation or company owned, operated or managed by these representatives during the university's probationary period, and include any further measures that the university determines to be within its authority to curtail the involvement of each individual in the university's athletics program during the probationary period.

[Additional note: The Committee on Infractions imposed the sanctions described above based upon the university's representations that the following appropriate actions have been taken by the university.

a. During the 1985–86 academic year, no more than 20 student-athletes in the sport of football shall be recipients of initial, athletically related financial aid (as set forth in O.I. 600) that has been arranged or awarded by the University of Illinois.

b. The head football coach and the assistant head football coach will be prohibited from any off-campus recruiting activities during the 1984–85 academic year, it being understood that no other individual may replace either of these coaches under NCAA Bylaw 7-1-(e) limitations during this term unless the coach no longer is employed by the university.

c. The salary of the head football coach will not be increased for the 1984 calendar year beyond his 1983 salary; further, the salary of the assistant head football coach will not be increased beyond its present level prior to March 7, 1987.

d. Five institutional representatives will be precluded from any involvement in the activities associated with the recruitment of prospective student-athletes on behalf of the university during the probationary period.]

Summary of violations of NCAA legislation

1. **NCAA Bylaws 1-1-(b)-(1) and 1-8-(g) [improper recruiting inducements and transportation]** — In January 1981, an assistant football coach arranged for a prospective student-athlete to be provided a one-way commercial airline ticket in order to enroll at a junior college in Champaign; further, an athletics association staff member provided the young man automobile transportation from Chicago to the university's campus.

2. **NCAA Bylaws 1-8-(g) and 7-1-(e) [improper transportation and use of coaching staff members]** — In January 1981, an assistant football coach arranged for a prospective student-athlete to be provided a one-way commercial airline ticket to travel to the university's campus to enroll; further, a part-time assistant football coach provided the young man automobile transportation from Chicago to the campus.

3. **NCAA Constitution 3-1-(g)-(5) and Bylaws 1-8-(g) and 7-1-(e) [extra benefits, improper transportation and use of coaching staff members]** — In January 1982, an athletics association staff member arranged for a prospective student-athlete to be provided a prepaid, one-way commercial airline ticket to travel to the university's campus to enroll; further, a part-time assistant football coach provided the young man and an enrolled student-athlete automobile transportation from Chicago to the campus.

4. **NCAA Bylaw 1-8-(g) [improper transportation]** — (a) In January 1982, the assistant head football coach purchased one-way commercial airline tickets for two prospective student-athletes in order to travel to the university's campus to enroll; (b) in August 1981, a part-time assistant football coach provided a prospective student-athlete automobile transportation from Chicago to the university's campus in order to enroll; and (c) in January 1981, an assistant football coach provided a prospective student-athlete automobile transportation from his home to an airport where the prospect boarded a plane for his flight to enroll on the university's campus; further, after arriving in Chicago, the assistant coach provided the young man automobile transportation to the university's campus.

5. **NCAA Constitution 3-1-(g)-(5) [extra benefits]** — (a) In October 1981, an assistant football coach arranged for the parents of two student-athletes to receive prepaid, round-trip commercial airline tickets between their home and the university's campus in order to attend one of the university's home football games; further, the assistant coach arranged for the parents to be lodged at a local hotel, and finally, the assistant coach arranged for the parents, the student-athletes and a friend to be entertained for a meal following the university's home football game; (b) in May or June 1982, an assistant football coach lent a student-athlete cash in order for the young man to purchase a round-trip commercial airline ticket to travel between the university's campus and the young man's home; (c) in March 1982, prior to the university's spring vacation, an athletics association staff member purchased a round-trip commercial airline ticket for a student-athlete to travel between the university's campus and the young man's home; further, approximately one week later, this staff member was reimbursed for the cost of this airline ticket upon the young man's receipt of wages for employment arranged through the athletics association; (d) during a telephone conversation with a Champaign businessman in January 1982, a representative of the university's athletics interests guaranteed to repair damages in lieu of a damage deposit for a house near the university's campus on behalf of five student-athletes; further, during the second semester of the 1981–82 academic year, this representative provided beds and a cleaning service for this house on one occasion; (e) on approximately three occasions during the second semester of the 1980–81 academic year, an assistant football coach gave a student-athlete cash for his personal use; (f) on approximately four occasions during the period January–December 1981, an assistant football coach lent a student-athlete cash for his personal

use; further, the student-athlete subsequently repaid the coach; (g) on numerous occasions during the 1980–81 and 1981–82 academic years, prospective and enrolled student-athletes received lodging at a Champaign hotel with the related expenses for their lodging billed to the university's athletics association; (h) in August 1982, a representative of the university's athletics interests provided a student-athlete transportation from the young man's home to an airport in order to fly to the university's campus; (i) on May 1981, a part-time assistant football coach provided a student-athlete automobile transportation from Chicago to the university's campus at no cost to the young man, and (j) during the second semester of the 1980–81 academic year, an assistant football coach provided several student-athletes a portable refrigerator for their dormitory room.

6. NCAA Bylaw 1-1-(b) [improper offers] — (a) In a January 1982 telephone conversation, the head football coach made statements that led a prospective student-athlete to believe that employment for his girlfriend would be arranged; further, in a subsequent telephone conversation with the girlfriend, the assistant head football coach stated that she would be contacted by a representative of the university's athletics interests to discuss employment opportunities, and finally, the representative telephoned the girlfriend to advise her that he was attempting to secure employment for her; (b) in January 1982, a representative of the university's athletics interests offered to arrange for a prospective student-athlete's girlfriend to receive one-way transportation from her home to the university's campus; (c) on at least two occasions in the fall of 1981, an assistant football coach offered to arrange for bills incurred by a prospective student-athlete at a community college to be paid; further, after the young man worked for approximately four hours on one day in January 1982, the assistant coach arranged for money to be wired in order to satisfy the young man's debt at the junior college, and (d) during the second semester of the 1980–81 academic year, an assistant football coach offered to arrange for a prospective student-athlete to be provided air transportation at a discount rate from the prospect's junior college to his home and then to the university's campus to begin employment.

7. NCAA Bylaw 1-1-(b)-(1) [improper recruiting inducements] — (a) In January 1982, a representative of the university's athletics interests promised to arrange round-trip airline transportation for the prospective student-athlete's mother between her home and the university's campus at no cost to her in order to attend the university's home football games; (b) in January 1982, a representative of the university's athletics interests made statements that led a prospective student-athlete to believe that the representative would provide the prospect an automobile at no cost to the young man;

(c) in June 1981, a part-time assistant football coach paid a prospective student-athlete's cost of tuition for summer school enrollment at a junior college; (d) in January 1982, a representative of the university's athletics interests gave a prospective student-athlete cash to share with another prospect; further, this payment was excessive in light of the amount of work performed by the prospects for the representative; (e) on two occasions in January 1982, an assistant football coach arranged for two prospective student-athletes to be lodged at a local hotel; (f) in January 1982, a member of the university's football coaching staff arranged for a prospective student-athlete to be lodged at a local hotel for two nights; (g) on one occasion during the second semester of the 1980–81 academic year, a representative of the university's athletics interests provided a prospective student-athlete cash; (h) in January 1982, a representative of the university's athletics interests gave a prospective student-athlete a portable cassette radio; (i) in January 1983, during the official paid visit to the university's campus of a prospective student-athlete, an assistant football coach purchased one sweatshirt and one pair of athletic socks for the prospect; (j) on at least one occasion during the second semester of the 1980–81 academic year, an assistant football coach provided a prospective student-athlete with a telephone credit card in order for the prospect to make personal, long-distance telephone calls, and (k) on one occasion in November or December 1981, an assistant football coach gave a prospective student-athlete several articles of clothing.

8. NCAA Constitution 3-1-(g)-(5) and Bylaw 1-1-(b)-(1) [extra benefits and improper recruiting inducements] — (a) In January 1981 and 1982, prior to and following the enrollment of six prospective student-athletes in the university, members of the university's football coaching staff arranged for the young men to be provided lodging on a total of approximately 20 nights at a local hotel; further, several of these prospects were entertained for meals and made personal, long-distance telephone calls; (b) in January 1981, members of the university's football coaching staff arranged for two prospective student-athletes to be provided lodging on a total of approximately seven nights at a local hotel; further, these prospects were entertained for meals and made several personal, long-distance telephone calls; (c) in January 1981, prior to and following the enrollment of a prospective student-athlete in the university, an assistant football coach provided the prospect lodging in the coach's home; (d) in December 1981, an assistant football coach arranged for two prospective student-athletes to receive several articles of clothing; further, the assistant coach offered and later provided one prospect another article of clothing following the prospect's enrollment in the university; (e) on several occasions in January 1981, prior to and following the

enrollment of a prospective student-athlete in the university, an assistant football coach gave the prospect cash; (f) in January 1981, a part-time assistant football coach provided a prospective student-athlete and an enrolled student-athlete articles of clothing, and (g) in January 1981 and 1982, an assistant football coach and a part-time assistant football coach provided an enrolled student-athlete and several prospective student-athletes with furnishings for the young men's apartments.

9. **NCAA Constitution 3-6-(a) [ethical conduct]** — Two former assistant football coaches acted contrary to the principles of ethical conduct inasmuch as they did not, on all occasions, deport themselves in accordance with the generally recognized high standards normally associated with the conduct and administration of intercollegiate athletics in that their involvement in the alleged violations set forth in this inquiry demonstrates a knowing and willful effort on their part to operate the university's intercollegiate football program contrary to the requirements and provisions of NCAA legislation.

10. **NCAA Bylaws 1-8-(j) and 1-8-(l) [improper transportation and entertainment]** — (a) On two occasions during the 1981-82 academic year, an assistant football coach entertained a prospective student-athlete's relatives for meals and provided local automobile transportation; (b) in December 1981, an assistant football coach provided a prospective student-athlete and his fiancee round-trip automobile transportation between the coach's hotel and a restaurant where the coach entertained the young man and his fiancee for a meal; (c) on two occasions during the 1981–82 academic year, a representative of the university's athletics interests entertained three prospective student-athletes for a meal at a restaurant; further, an assistant football coach met the representative and the young men at this restaurant; (d) on three occasions in November and December 1980, an assistant football coach provided a prospective student-athlete round-trip automobile transportation between the prospect's home and a restaurant where the assistant coach entertained the prospect for a meal; further, on at least one occasion, another prospective student-athlete accompanied this group and, on another occasion, the prospect's girlfriend accompanied this group; (e) during the 1980–81 academic year, an assistant football coach provided two prospective student-athletes automobile transportation to a local restaurant where the assistant coach entertained the prospects for a meal, and (f) on numerous occasions during the period January 13–16, 1982, athletics association staff members entertained two prospective student-athletes for meals.

11. **NCAA Bylaw 1-8-(j) [improper transportation and entertainment]** — (a) In January 1982, a prospective student-athlete and his wife were entertained for a meal on at least one occasion by an athletics association staff member; (b) on several occasions during the period January 13–17, 1982, athletics association staff members provided two prospective student-athletes automobile transportation to various locations on and off the university's campus; (c) in December 1980, an assistant football coach provided a prospective student-athlete automobile transportation from the young man's home to a restaurant where the assistant coach entertained the prospect for a meal; (d) in February 1982, an assistant football coach provided a prospective student-athlete automobile transportation from an airport to the prospect's home; (e) in December 1980, the assistant head football coach and an assistant football coach provided a prospective student-athlete automobile transportation between his home and the home of another prospective student-athlete; (f) in January 1981, an assistant football coach provided a prospective student-athlete automobile transportation from the coach's home to the university's football offices; (g) in November 1981, a representative of the university's athletics interests provided two prospective student-athletes and the prospects' friend round-trip automobile transportation between the home of one of the prospects to an intercollegiate football game, and (h) on at least one occasion in the spring or summer of 1982, a representative of the university's athletics interests provided a prospective student-athlete automobile transportation from a restaurant to the prospect's home.

12. **NCAA Bylaws 1-1-(b)-(1), 1-8-(g) and 1-8-(j) [improper recruiting inducements, transportation and entertainment]** — In January 1982, an assistant football coach provided a prospective student-athlete automobile transportation from Chicago to a hotel where the prospect was lodged for one night in the coach's room and entertained for a meal; further, on the next day, the assistant coach entertained the prospect for another meal and provided the young man automobile transportation from the hotel to the university's campus.

13. **NCAA Bylaws 1-1-(b)-(1) and 1-8-(j) [improper recruiting inducements, transportation and entertainment]** — (a) In January 1982, the wife of an assistant football coach provided the wife of a prospective student-athlete round-trip automobile transportation from the prospect's home to a grocery store where the coach's wife purchased groceries for the prospect's wife; (b) in November 1980, an assistant football coach provided a prospective student-athlete round-trip automobile transportation between the prospect's home and a football stadium where the assistant coach provided the prospect a ticket to attend a professional football game, and (c) in January 1981, an assistant football coach provided a prospective student-athlete automobile transportation from the prospect's apartment to a department store where the assistant coach purchased school supplies for the young man.

14. **NCAA Bylaws 1-1-(b)-(1), 1-8-(g) and 7-1-(e) [improper recruiting inducements, transportation and**

use of coaching staff members] — (a) In January 1981, a part-time assistant football coach provided two prospective student-athletes round-trip automobile transportation from Chicago to the university's campus; further, this coach also arranged for the young men to be provided lodging for one night at a hotel and on the following day, this coach provided the young men automobile transportation from the hotel to a campus dormitory, and (b) in January 1981, a part-time assistant football coach provided two prospective student-athletes automobile transportation from Chicago to the university's campus; further, this coach also arranged for the young men to be provided lodging for approximately three nights at a hotel.

15. NCAA Bylaw 1-8-(j)-(3) [excessive entertainment] — In December 1980, an assistant football coach provided three prospective student-athletes excessive entertainment upon the conclusion of the prospect's official paid visits to the university's campus.

16. NCAA Constitution 3-1-(g)-(5) and Bylaw 1-8-(j) [extra benefits and improper transportation] — On numerous occasions during the 1980–81 and 1981–82 academic years, an athletics association staff member, football coaching staff members and a representative of the university's athletics interests provided prospective and enrolled student-athletes automobile transportation in and around the Champaign area.

17. NCAA Bylaw 1-8-(a) [unitemized expenses] — In December 1980, an assistant football coach provided two prospective student-athletes cash in excess of the actual round-trip transportation costs incurred by the young men in travelling between their homes and the university upon the conclusion of their official paid visits to the university's campus.

18. NCAA Bylaws 1-8-(j) and 7-1-(e) [improper transportation and use of coaching staff members] — On one occasion in August 1981, a part-time assistant football coach provided a prospective student-athlete automobile transportation between the young man's home and an airport in order to meet other student-athletes who were traveling to the university's campus to enroll.

19. NCAA Bylaw 7-1-(e) [improper use of coaching staff members] — (a) On two occasions in January 1982, part-time assistant football coaches provided prospective student-athletes automobile transportation to the prospects' homes upon the conclusion of each young man's official paid visit to the university's campus, and (b) on one occasion in January or February 1983, an athletics association staff member with department-wide responsibilities contacted a prospective student-athlete and his parents in person at the prospect's home.

20. NCAA Bylaw 1-8-(j)-(4) [improper use of automobile] — In December 1980, an assistant football coach provided an automobile to a student-athlete for the entertainment of three prospective student-athletes during their official paid visit to the university's campus.

21. NCAA Bylaw 1-2-(a)-(1) [improper recruiting contact] — (a) On two occasions during the 1980–81 academic year, members of the university's football coaching staff contacted a prospective student-athlete in person in excess of the permissible three occasions, and (b) during the 1981–82 academic year, two assistant football coaches contacted a prospective student-athlete in person in excess of the permissible three contacts at sites other than the prospect's educational institution.

22. NCAA Bylaw 1-2-(a)-(4) [improper recruiting contact] — In September 1981, an assistant football coach contacted the parents of a prospective student-athlete in person for recruiting purposes during a time when such off-campus contacts were not permitted.

23. NCAA Bylaw 1-8-(m) [improper entertainment of junior college and high school coaches] — (a) During 1980, 1981 and 1982, three assistant football coaches entertained four junior college or high school coaches on approximately 11 occasions with the cost of this entertainment being paid by the athletics association, and (b) in November 1981, during the official paid visit of a prospective student-athlete to the university's campus, an assistant football coach arranged for the prospect's junior college coach to be provided lodging for two nights and the assistant coach entertained the junior college coach for four meals.

24. NCAA Bylaw 5-6-(d)-(4) [improper certification of compliance] — With full knowledge at the time that certain practices of the university's intercollegiate football program were not in compliance with NCAA legislation, five members of the university's football coaching staff attested on statements filed with the chief executive officer of the university that they had reported their knowledge of and involvement in any violation of NCAA legislation involving the university.

Source: "Illinois Placed on Probation," *NCAA News,* August 1, 1984, p. 4.

1.41–2 NCAA Regulation of Coaches and Personnel

In addition to the individual member institutions and the institution's student-athletes, the NCAA regulates the activity of an institution's coaching personnel. This section examines how such regulations may impact on an institution's coaching personnel. As in the case when an institution must sanction one of its student-athletes, the NCAA also holds an institution responsible for the enforcement of

NCAA regulations against the institution's coaching personnel.

Board of Regents, University of Oklahoma v. National Collegiate Athletic Ass'n., 561 P.2d 499 (1977)

The NCAA appealed a lower court temporary injunction barring enforcement of an NCAA bylaw that limited the number of football coaches a Division I member of the NCAA could employ. The injunction had been issued upon a finding by the trial judge that the NCAA rule violated the Oklahoma statutory equivalent of the Sherman Antitrust Act.

The appellate court rejected the NCAA's contentions that judicial scrutiny of a voluntary association's internal rules was inappropriate and that the activities of the NCAA were state action and exempt from antitrust scrutiny. However, on the merits, the court concluded that the NCAA's rule appeared to be a reasonable one, rationally related to its announced objective of curtailing costs of NCAA members. The rule was neither arbitrary nor invidiously discriminatory. The court concluded that the restraint did not prevent coaches from exercising their lawful profession but merely limited the number of coaches any given member school could employ. The court ruled that the trial court abused its discretion in granting the temporary injunction.

Tarkanian v. University of Nevada, Las Vegas, Case No. A173498, 8th Judicial District Court of the State of Nevada, June 25, 1984

Plaintiff basketball coach Jerry Tarkanian brought this suit in 1977 to enjoin the enforcement of a sanction required of the University of Nevada, Las Vegas (UNLV) by the National Collegiate Athletic Association (NCAA). On October 12, 1977, Tarkanian successfully enjoined UNLV from carrying out the NCAA-mandated sanction, which required UNLV to sever all ties with basketball coach Tarkanian. The university appealed, and the

Nevada Supreme Court reversed and remanded the matter for joinder of the NCAA as a defendant.

The NCAA, for about two years prior to February 1976, conducted an investigation of UNLV and Tarkanian regarding possible violations of NCAA legislation as published in the annual *NCAA Manual*. The investigation was conducted by Samuel David Berst, a field investigator for the NCAA. Having requested and received permission from the NCAA to charge UNLV with violating NCAA legislation, Berst proceeded to author a 300-question "Official Inquiry" addressed to UNLV. Despite written and oral requests by counsel for UNLV and Tarkanian, the NCAA provided no information regarding the practice and procedures of the Committee on Infractions, before whom UNLV and Tarkanian would have to present responses to the "Official Inquiry."

Three adversarial hearings before the NCAA Committee on Infractions took place in late 1976 and early 1977. Tarkanian, having been misled by the NCAA, was not represented by counsel. Further, the NCAA produced no witnesses whose information formed the bases of the charges. The first two hearings conducted before the Committee on Infractions consisted of a comparison of the unsworn recollections of the NCAA investigator's with the recollection of UNLV and Tarkanian. The third hearing, conducted at the request of UNLV and Tarkanian, focused on the integrity and truthfulness of the NCAA investigators, in view of the diametrically opposed recollections. The NCAA Committee on Infractions, in ruling on factual disputes, found the recollections of the NCAA investigators to be accurate and truthful, and any information disputing those recollections to be inaccurate and untruthful.

The committee used no standards or guidelines regarding the burden of proof, and the district court found as an issue of fact that at least one committee member had made his mind up against UNLV before any hearing took place. On April 26, 1977, the committee issued a "Confidential Report," which listed numerous infractions of NCAA rules. The "Confidential Report" set forth an order for UNLV to sever ties with Tarkanian for two years or be subject to possible additional penalties. UNLV appealed the sanctions, and the committee presented an "Expanded Confidential Report" to the NCAA Council. This report was authored by Berst. On August 26, 1977, the NCAA notified UNLV that the NCAA Council had accepted the findings of facts and penalty imposed by the committee. On September 7, 1977, UNLV gave Tarkanian written notice that the university was going to comply with the NCAA sanction and that the severance would become effective on September 9, 1977.

The district court, in its Conclusions of Law, held that the actions of the NCAA were "state actions" and that Tarkanian had been deprived of both procedural and substantive due process. Further, the court held that the decision by the NCAA was arbitrary and capricious, and the decision of UNLV was vicariously so.

The court acknowledged that UNLV was in a difficult position: either leave the NCAA or carry out the NCAA-imposed sanctions, which UNLV thought were unjust. The court pointed out, using an NCAA official's words, that the "NCAA is the only game in town."

The court held that the NCAA, by accepting as fact all of the charges made by Berst, had acted arbitrarily and with prejudice. In one instance, the NCAA investigators alleged (and found) that Tarkanian had paid the airfare of a recruit in violation of NCAA rules. Although UNLV produced an affadavit from the recruit's high school coach that *he* had paid for the tickets, the NCAA found Tarkanian "guilty" of this alleged infraction. Further, when Tarkanian or a representative of UNLV called the NCAA for information regarding the procedure of the hearings, the NCAA secretly taped the conversations in violation of state laws. Accordingly, the district court enjoined

UNLV from carrying out the NCAA-mandated sanctions against Tarkanian.

NOTES

1. In *University of Nevada* v. *Tarkanian*, 95 Nev. 389, 594 P.2d 1159 (1979), the Nevada Supreme Court in a decision preceding the 1983 decision ruled the NCAA was a necessary party to any action brought by Tarkanian against UNLV in regard to NCAA orders barring him from association with the university's athletic program.

2. In *Hennessey* v. *National Collegiate Athletic Ass'n.*, 564 F. 2d 1136 (5th Cir. 1977), a limitation on school coaching staffs was upheld as an "economy measure" designed to maintain athletic balance and preserve amateurism.

3. In *Stanley* v. *Big Eight Conference*, 463 F. Supp. 920 (W.D. Mo. W.D. 1978), a former Oklahoma State University football coach was granted an injunction which prevented the conference and the NCAA from conducting an infractions hearing because the procedure violated his due process rights (see Section 1.32–1).

4. For further information, see the following articles:
(a) "The Authority of the College Coach: A Legal Analysis," 49 *Oregon L. Rev.* 442 (1970).
(b) "Judicial Review of the NCAA's Bylaw 12-1," 29 *Alabama Law Review* 547 (1978).
(c) "Jury Dismisses Lawsuit Against Former Coach," *Chronicle of Higher Education*, April 27, 1981, p. 1.

5. The NCAA recommends certain policies and practices in regard to a member institution's personnel and contracts with its coaching personnel. These suggestions include:

Policy 5: Personnel

Section 1. Member institutions should prohibit an athletic staff member from participating as a player, official or promoter in professional sports such as football, basketball, baseball, soccer, boxing, wrestling and ice hockey.

Section 2. Member institutions, in the employment of coaches and other athletic personnel, should emphasize the importance of successful experience at the high school level as well as proper educational training and background.

Section 3. Member institutions should encourage staff members to report to the Association any reliable information indicating a possible violation of the Association's governing legislation.

Section 4. Prior to a person's possible employment as a member of the department of intercollegiate athletics, a member institution should give careful considerations to whether the person previously has been involved in violations of NCAA legislation.

Policy 6: Coaches' Contracts

Section 1. An individual as well as an institution should recognize the moral responsibilities inherent in respecting and fulfilling contractual agreements.

Section 2. An institution should enter into a contractual agreement with a coach similar to those entered into with the other members of the faculty; and such a contract should include the assignment of faculty rank, benefits of tenure and retirement and such other rights and privileges as are enjoyed by other members of the contracting institution's faculty.

Section 3. When a contracting institution makes special concessions to a coach, these should be set forth in detail in the contract and accepted as legal and binding in the same manner as the other provisions of the contractual agreement.

Section 4. All salary agreements between a coach and an institution should be stated in the contract, and such salary should come from sources under the administrative control of the institution.

Section 5. An educational institution seeking a coach who is under contract to another educational institution is morally obligated first to contact the institution which holds the agreement with the coach and secure permission to negotiate with the individual.

Section 6. A coach should not enter into negotiations with a second institution during the term of a contract without first notifying the institution which is a party to this contractual agreement, and the coach then should keep the first institution's administration informed concerning the negotiations.

Section 7. No institution should engage the services of a coach prior to the coach's release from any contractual obligations to another institution.

[*1985–86 NCAA Manual*, "Recommended Policies and Practices for Intercollegiate Athletics," Policy 5 and 6].

6. At the 1983 NCAA Convention, the membership enacted the following rule:

Contractual agreements between a coach and an institution shall include the stipulation that the coach may be suspended for a period of time, without pay, or that the coach's employment may be terminated if the coach is found to be involved in deliberate and serious violations of NCAA regulations. (*1985–86 NCAA Manual*, Bylaw 3-6-[G])

One institution added the following clause into its coaches contracts: "You may be suspended for a period of time, without pay, or your employment by the University of _____ as a _____ coach may be terminated if you are found to be in deliberate and serious violation of NCAA regulations."

7. In August 1984, the NCAA filed a motion in the U.S. District Court in Las Vegas asking that the state court's decision in favor of Tarkanian be amended or vacated. It also filed a notice of appeal in the same court.

Tarkanian then filed a remand to have the case moved from the federal court system back to the state court system. An appeal then would be heard by the Nevada Supreme Court. See "NCAA Asks Court to Review Ruling for Tarkanian," *Chronicle of Higher Education*, August 8, 1984, p. 20.

8. In 1975, the NCAA adopted Bylaw 7-1, which designated the number of coaches that may be employed by a Division I-A football or Division I basketball program. Football teams are limited to one head coach and nine assistant coaches. Basketball teams are limited to one head coach, two assistant coaches, and one part-time assistant coach. In addition, teams may utilize the services of one uncompensated volunteer who may not receive expense money. Teams can also utilize an unlmited number of students who have finished their playing eligibility, provided they receive education expenses only, serve no more than two years, have no contractual arrangement for a later job, and, if they are former student-athletes, are continuing and/or completing requirements for a degree from the same institution at which they competed. These positions are referred to as graduate assistants, and such personnel may not scout or recruit off campus (*1985–86 NCAA Manual*, Bylaw 7-1).

9. In *Bell* v. *University of South Carolina* (Dist. Ct. S.C. 1983), plaintiff football coach filed suit against the University of South Carolina and the athletic director to recover $150,000 for the three years that remained on his contract. He had been ordered by his athletic director to fire his assistant coaches after his first year as head coach and when he refused, he was fired. The court awarded him $150,000, and his attorney described him as a hero, a lone "Paul Revere" who dared to take the consequences of disobeying an order. [*Charlotte Observer*, July 14, 1984.] The case was settled out of court.

10. In *Irwin* v. *Board of Education, Sch. Dist. No. 25*, 340 N.W. 2d 877 (Neb. 1983), plaintiff teacher/coach was fired because of alleged neglect of duty and insubordination. The court held that the plaintiff was not entitled to a hearing in regards to his coaching duties, but was entitled to one concerning his teaching position, based on due process considerations.

11. In August 1982, an Alabama state judge ruled that the "Bear Bryant Retirement Law" was unconstitutional. Under Alabama law, the then 68-year-old coach (since deceased) would have had to retire at age 70. The Alabama legislature enacted a waiver for the famous coach. Such a waiver, said the judge, was "arbitrary and capricious in every sense."

12. In 1984, the University of Louisville sought to guarantee the retention of its basketball coach Denny Crum by offering him a retroactive 10-year contract designed to keep him at the school until the end of the 1993–94 season. The 10-year sum of the contract was estimated to be $1 million and contained an escape clause for Crum, which if exercised would cost him a completion

bonus. See "Louisville Bonanza," *New York Times*, July 25, 1984, p. B8.

13. In 1984 former University of South Carolina football coach Jim Carlen reached an out-of-court settlement with the school on a breach of contract suit he brought against the institution in December 1981. Carlen had sued for $150,000 in lost fringe benefits, although he was still receiving his $67,200 annual salary through 1986. See "Settlement for Coach," *New York Times*, July 25, 1984, p. B8.

14. The University of Illinois requires that all employees adhere to the following procedure in regard to NCAA, Big Ten Conference, and Illinois rules and regulations:

RULE VIOLATIONS (TRANSGRESSIONS)
All employees of the Athletic Association of the University of Illinois are expected to follow the rules of the University of Illinois, the Athletic Association, the Big Ten Conference, and the NCAA. As a stated condition on all employment contracts, employees are subject to (1) suspension without notice and without pay and (2) termination of employment at the discretion of the Director and the Athletic Board of Control for violation of rules.

See *Policy and Procedure Manual*, Athletic Association of the University of Illinois, 1984, section IV, B, p. 1.

1.41–3   NCAA Regulation of Recruiting

The area of recruiting is a troublesome one for athletic administrators whether it be from the perspective of an NCAA enforcement officer investigating an alleged infraction, a high school coach counseling an athlete, or a college athletic director monitoring the coaching staff. Within the structure of the NCAA, the subject arouses a great deal of animosity because of penalties enforced by the association and the "big-brother" syndrome that coaches often think about while approaching a potential recruit. This worry about who is watching is not unfounded. In the case of *Tarkanian* v. *University of Nevada, Las Vegas* (see Section 1.41–2), the Nevada District Court judge gave the following illustration in his opinion:

A case in point will serve to illustrate the prejudice a member [in this case, UNLV] faces when challenged by the NCAA staff: NCAA investigators alleged (and "found") that Coach Tarkanian had, in violation of NCAA legislation, paid the air fare of one "Jeep" Kelly from his

home to Las Vegas, Nevada. [Kelly was a player being recruited by Tarkanian.] Despite the facts that UNLV produced an affidavit from Kelly's high school coach, stating that *he* had paid for the ticket; UNLV and Tarkanian produced a copy of the ticket; and the high school coach's cancelled check which showed the payment, the NCAA found Tarkanian "guilty" of this alleged infraction.

While recruiting can pose problems on all levels of intercollegiate athletics, it becomes especially troublesome on the Division I level. This is where the financial stakes are much higher, both to the institution in the form of revenue and to the coach in terms of salary and other benefits. The *Tarkanian* case offers a vivid documentation of the rewards of coaching. Testimony at the trial revealed that Jerry Tarkanian received the following compensation:

1. Tenured professor salary of $53,000.
2. Basketball coach salary of $125,000.
3. Ten percent of net proceeds received by UNLV for participation in NCAA-authorized championship games.
4. Fees from basketball camps and clinics.
5. Product endorsements.
6. Income from writing a newspaper column.
7. Income from speaking on a radio program entitled "The Jerry Tarkanian Show" and from a similar television show.

Tarkanian, who has been a basketball coach for 28 years (1984) and at that time the winningest active basketball coach in the nation, is not unique in his compensation. In 1984, Denny Crum, coach at the University of Louisville, was offered a compensation package that includes a $1 million bonus if he stays at the school for the length of his 10-year contract and that pays a base salary of $150,000 a year. Jackie Sherrill is another coach who received a lucrative contract. Named as football coach-athletic director at Texas A&M in 1982, at $287,000 a year, he made these comments following his initial 5–6 season:

"There's a difference between building a program and a winning season — I could have got some junior college players and done that," he said. "Building a solid foundation means discipline, education, and great character. I know what it takes to build a program. I built one at Pittsburgh and I have the energy to build one more.

"You're always going to have people with tunnel vision," Sherrill said. "But our faculty sees that I treat our athletes as students first, that I care about their education."

"A lot of administrators who criticize salaries are either jealous or trying to protect their own cacoon because they're doing the same thing — with deferred salaries, deferred insurance."

The rewards of big-time athletics also benefit the institutions involved. Successful programs lead to NCAA tournament and television games, bowl bids, increased student application and recognition factors, and increased alumni donations, to name a few. Recruiting violations, however, can be expensive. In 1984, the University of Illinois was placed on probation for having committed 187 recruiting violations. The following remarks from Illinois Chancellor John Cribbet, made at a news conference one day after the NCAA announced its sanctions, are indicative of the resentment felt by many who are penalized by the association: "I think it is high time that the NCAA as a whole took a very hard, detailed look at those regulations and decided whether or not they fit the present time. . . . If I were a younger man, and had nothing better to do with my life, I wouldn't mind heading the commission to revise those NCAA rules and get them in a little better shape. . . . grown men have better things to do than try to investigate whether or not somebody bought somebody a Coke."

Chancellor Cribbet, while stressing that he was not offering excuses and admitting that some of the violations were serious, said some of the original 187 NCAA allegations included buying soft drinks, pizzas, or T-shirts for prospective student-athletes. "Too much law breeds contempt for all law," said Mr. Cribbet, who resigned as chancellor on August 21, 1984, to return to teaching law. "The NCAA regulations are very much like the Internal Revenue Code." The penalties imposed on Illinois included two years' probation, a one-season ban on postseason bowl play, and a one-year television ban. In addition, the university imposed penalties that included banning Head Coach Mike White and his top assistant, Max McCartney, from on-the-road recruiting, freezing their salaries and cutting the number of football scholarships from 30 to 20 next season. (See Section 1.41–1, Note 6.)

Recruiting violations rarely themselves become issues of litigation. Rather, they are the underlying reasons that spark the suit. In the *Tarkanian* case, the reason was that UNLV was being forced to apply sanctions against its coach, growing out of recruiting violations.

Finally, and most importantly, recruiting impacts on the athlete. Teenagers who are offered shady enticements of varying degrees often carry into their college years and for the rest of their lives a jaded view of life that may affect their educational progress, personal lives, and/or future careers.

A 1982 study by the *Dallas Times-Herald* reported that only 28 percent of the football seniors in the Southwest Conference (1981 season) graduated with their classes. The graduation rates for member schools were as follows:

SMU	47%
Texas A&M	40%
Texas Tech	38%
Baylor	36%
Rice	31%
Texas Christian	29%
Arkansas	17%
Houston	13%
Texas*	11%

* 1982 Cotton Bowl winner

The low graduation rates of recruited student-athletes has become a grave concern for many NCAA members.

NOTES _____

1. In *Seal v. Birmingham Post*, 8 Med. L. Reptr. 1633 (Dist. Ct. Kan. 1982), libel defendant newspaper sought issuance of subpoenas for NCAA files for use in its defense concerning a published news story in which it reported

that plaintiff, the principal of Butler High School in Huntsville, Alabama frequently gave money to one Bobby Lee Hurt, a Butler High School basketball star because the basketball player threatened to transfer to another school. Further, the complaint alleges that the newspaper report was false in reporting that Seal ordered $100 taken from receipts from basketball home games to pay for Hurt's dental work. The newspaper further reported that Hurt chose to attend the University of Alabama because of financial pressure brought to bear by a Butler High School alumnus who was linked to plaintiff Seal.

The court ruled that the interests of the newspaper in defending themselves far outweighed the NCAA's need to keep such information confidential (see Section 1.23).

2. In *Berst v. Chipman*, 8 Med. L. Reptr. 1635, 231 Kan. 369, 653 P. 2d 107 (1982), the Kansas Supreme Court ruled, in a partial opinion, to overturn the decision in *Seal* v. *Birmingham Post*.

The Supreme Court held that the Kansas trial court erred in denying, without conducting an *in camera* examination, the NCAA's motion for protective order limiting NCAA's disclosure, in response to subpoena duces tecum filed by newspaper defendant in libel action, of confidential NCAA files concerning its investigation of a student-athlete who was subject of allegedly defamatory article.

After reviewing the files, the Kansas Supreme Court declared that only certain specific materials were discoverable by the Birmingham Post Company and not the entire file (see Section 1.23).

3. In *Berst v. Chipman*, 8 Med. L. Rptr. 2593 (Kan. 1982), the Kansas Supreme Court, in a full opinion, reiterated its partial opinion in *Berst* v. *Chipman* and affirmed the district court's decision concerning the needs of the newspaper outweighing that of the NCAA (see Section 1.23).

4. In *Hall v. University of Minnesota*, a case concerning academic progress, the court was quick to point out that the athlete had been recruited as "a basketball player and not a scholar" and that "his academic record reflects that he has lived up to those expectations as do the academic records of many of the athletes presented to this court" (see Section 2.12).

5. For further information, see the following articles:
(a) "Sherrill's Philosophy," *New York Times*, January

3, 1983, p. A7.
(b) "Illinois Head Assails NCAA," (UPI wireservice), *New York Times*, July 29, 1984, p. S13.
(c) "72% in SWC Didn't Graduate," *New York Times*, August 24, 1982, p. A7.
(d) "The Fine Art of Recruiting Superstars for Big-Time Women's Basketball," *Chronicle of Higher Education*, March 30, 1983, p. 21.
(e) "Texas A&M Goes All Out in Recruiting," *USA Today*, February 11, 1983, p. 16.
(f) "Recruiting Now Favors the Rich," *Boston Globe*, Series on Women and the NCAA, May 5, 1983, p. 67.
(g) "Coaches Find Recruiting Pays," *Boston Globe*, February 3, 1984, p. 42.
(h) "Sign Here Kid," *Boston Globe*, February 3, 1984, p. 7A.

1.41–3 (a) NCAA Recruiting Policies

The bylaws of the NCAA pertaining to recruitment are long and detailed, covering 15 pages of the *NCAA Manual*. Listed below are selected excerpts:

1985–86 NCAA Manual, Bylaw 1-1 to 1-10

ARTICLE ONE: RECRUITING

Section 1: Offers and Inducements. (a) No member of an institution's athletics staff or other representative of athletics interests shall solicit the enrollment of any prospective student-athlete except as permitted by this Association, the institution and the conference of which it may be a member. . . .

Section 2: Contacts. (a) Divisions I and II — Contact in person with a prospective student-athlete or the prospect's relatives or legal guardian off campus for purposes of recruitment (per O.I. 100) by institutional staff members and/or representatives of athletics interests is subject to the following limitations. . . .

Section 3: Evaluation Periods. The involvement of institutional staff members or representatives of athletics interests in off-campus scouting activities designed to evaluate the academic standing and playing ability of prospective student-athletes in the sports of basketball and football shall be restricted to the permissible periods for in-person, off-campus recruiting contacts in those sports except as follows: [Note: Such scouting activities related to prospective student-athletes being recruited to participate on a Division II member institution's women's intercollegiate basketball team shall be exempt from the provisions of this section until August 1, 1985. . . .

Section 4: Publicity. (a) Publicity released by an institution about the commitment of a prospective student-athlete to attend the institution shall be limited to announcing the prospective student-athlete's signed acceptance of the institution's written offer of admission as a student and/or written tender of financial assistance to be provided on the prospect's enrollment and shall be limited to communications in those media forms normally used by the institution. . . .

Section 5: Use of Funds. (a) All funds for the recruiting of prospective student-athletes shall be deposited with the member institution, which shall be exclusively and entirely responsible for the manner in which it expends the funds.

(b) An institution shall not pay any costs incurred by an athletics talent scout or a representative of its athletics interests in studying or recruiting prospective student-athletes. An institution may not place any such person on a fee or honorarium basis and thereby claim the person as a staff member entitled to expense money.

(c) No member institution shall permit any outside organization, agency or group of individuals to utilize, administer or expend funds for recruiting prospective student-athletes, including the transportation and entertainment of, and the giving of gifts or services to, prospective student-athletes or their relatives and friends.

(d) The pooling of resources for recruiting purposes by two or more persons shall constitute such a fund, except that this provision shall not apply to persons upon whom a prospective student-athlete may be naturally or legally dependent.

(e) Use of a company's funds to pay the expenses incurred in transporting a prospective student-athlete to the campus constitutes the use of pooled resources.

(f) Bona fide alumni organizations of an institution may sponsor luncheons, teas or dinners at which prospective students (athletes and non-athletes) of that immediate locale are guests. A member institution's area alumni organization may be considered a bona fide part of that institution, provided such organization is accredited by the chief executive officer of the institution and meets these additional terms and conditions:

(1) A staff member of the institution periodically shall inspect the financial records of the alumni organization and certify that the expenditures comply with the rules and regulations of the NCAA and the conference of which the institution may be a member.

(2) A club official shall be designated by the chief executive officer as the institution's official agent in the administration of the club's funds, and said club official shall file regular reports to the institution relating the manner in which the club funds have been spent in the recruiting of student-athletes.

(3) To facilitate administration of the one-visitation provision of Bylaw 1-8-(a), whenever club funds are used to transport prospective student-athletes to the campus, the club official shall file a report with the institution including the names of the student-athletes so transported.

(g) When an alumni organization is certified by the chief executive officer as being a bona fide part of the institution, said organization becomes subject to all of the limitations placed upon the member institution by NCAA legislation; a violation of such legislation by any member of the alumni organization shall be a violation by the member institution.

Section 6: Tryouts. (a) No member institution, on its campus or elsewhere, shall conduct or have conducted in its behalf any athletics practice session, tryout or test at which one or more prospective student-athletes reveal, demonstrate, or display their abilities in any phase of sport. . . .

Section 7: High School All-Star Games. (a) No member institution shall permit any coach or any athletics department staff member directly involved in the recruiting of student-athletes to participate, directly or indirectly, in the management, coaching, officiating, supervision, promotion or player selection of any all-star team or contest involving interscholastic players or those who, during the previous school year, were members of high school athletics teams. If a coach has made a contractual commitment to coach in a high school all-star game prior to being employed by a member institution and then becomes a member of the institution's staff before the game is held, the coach shall be obligated to observe this provision and disassociate himself or herself from the all-star game. . . .

Section 8: Transportation, Visitations and Entertainment. (a) A member institution may finance one and only one visit to its campus for a given prospective student-athlete. Such visit shall not exceed 48 hours. Only actual round-trip transportation costs by direct route between the student's home and the institution's campus may be paid. If commercial air transportation is used, the fare may not exceed tourist (or comparable) class. . . .

Section 9: Precollege Expense. (a) No institution or a representative of its athletics interests shall offer, provide or arrange financial assistance, directly or indirectly, for a prospective student-athlete to pay in whole or in part the costs of the prospect's educational or other expenses for any period prior to the prospect's enrollment or to obtain a postgraduate education. . . .

Section 10: Specialized Sports Camps, Coaching Schools and Clinics. (a) In operating a specialized sports camp, coaching school or sports clinic, a member institution, members of its staff or representatives of its athletics interests shall not employ or give free or reduced admission privileges to a high school or junior college athletics award winner. . . .

CASE STUDY: University of San Francisco Case Study

On July 29, 1982, the University of San Francisco (USF), which had won the NCAA Basketball Championship twice, dropped the program. It cited continuing rules violations and its inability to control cheaters as the reason for the decision. Following is the text of the statement made by Reverend John J. Lo Schiavo, president of the University of San Francisco, concerning the decision ("A Big Basketball Power Drops the Sport, Blaming Abuses by Alumni Boosters," *Chronicle of Higher Education*, August 11, 1982, pp. 1, 12):

The board of trustees of the University of San Francisco [has] decided that the men's inter-collegiate Division I basketball program at USF

should and will be discontinued. Anyone who is familiar with this institution and its proud history will understand what a painful decision this is. In all the circumstances, however, the board had no other responsible choice.

The circumstances centrally involve problems with the basketball program, which have been plaguing us, and which the university has been unsuccessfully trying to solve for many years. Those problems have put us in the position of defending ourselves before the National Collegiate Athletic Association committee on infractions twice in the past few years. The price the university has had to pay for those problems has been much greater than the heavy financial price. There is no way of measuring the damage that has been done to the university's most priceless assets, its integrity and its reputation.

In 1976 the NCAA started an investigation of the basketball program, which culminated in 1979 with the determination by the NCAA committee on infractions that a number of violations of the NCAA rules had occurred over a period of approximately six years.

The NCAA placed the university's basketball program on probation for one year, with sanctions prohibiting participation in postseason games and restricting television appearances.

In the context of hearings on those matters before that committee, the university's representatives stressed the determination of the university to administer the basketball program in a manner that would assure compliance with the NCAA requirements.

Among the measures taken by the university were the reorganization of the athletic advisory board to oversee intercollegiate athletics and report directly to the president, and consolidation of two booster organizations.

The comprehensive review was carried out, and a series of communications was effected at all levels with everyone involved with this program, to insure the university's policy of total compliance was going to be fully implemented and that everyone understood this and was committed to making the policy work.

Notwithstanding all this, within six months after the NCAA committee on infractions issued its findings in this first proceeding, and while the university's basketball program was on probation, deliberate rules violations occurred, and less than 15 months after the first proceeding the university suffered a second proceeding before the committee, resulting in another year on probation.

The director of athletics and head basketball coach and his assistant who were responsible for these violations were terminated.

A new director of athletics and a new head basketball coach were employed and every effort was made to convince everyone concerned that the university meant what it said about its policy of playing within the rules; affirmation of understanding and commitments to conform were given by everyone involved with the program.

Among the matters communicated to everyone were:

• The university simply could not suffer another proceeding before the NCAA committee on infractions.

• Anyone tempted to bend or break the rules must understand that he would be jeopardizing the entire program, because if the program were not going to be carried on strictly within the rules, there would be no choice but to terminate it.

Against that extraordinary background less than two years later we find that further deliberate and serious violations of NCAA rules have occurred. These most recent violations have involved both an enrolled student athlete and one being recruited. An alumnus, for whose actions the NCAA holds the university responsible, has paid money on numerous occasions to an enrolled student-athlete who did not work for it. Arrangements were made for another alumnus to pay high-school tuition for a student being recruited. It should be emphasized that the student was and is totally innocent; he knew nothing about the matter. Our investigation found no evidence to support other allegations of possible recruiting violations involving another high-school athlete.

The university therefore has been put in the position where it must conclude:

• There are people for whom, under NCAA rules, the university is responsible who cannot be convinced that the university's policy is right.

• These people are determined to break the rules presumably because they are convinced that the university cannot stay within the rules and maintain an effective competitive program.

• Assuming for the sake of analysis that these people are correct in that conviction, the university would have no tenable choice but to discontinue the program because the university cannot tolerate competing in any other way than within the rules.

• Whether such people are correct in that conviction or not, the university cannot afford to pay the price the basketball program is imposing on it. That price is being exacted in terms much more important than money.

The basketball program was once a source of inspiration, respect, and pride for this university and city; that tradition adds to the sadness engendered by what it has now become. Because of it we have now been perceived as being hypocritical or naive or inept or duplicitous. Or perhaps some combination of all those. We have even had to suffer the accusation that we attempted to obstruct justice in order to protect a basketball player and preserve him for the team.

However unjust those perceptions — and they are grossly unjust — everyone who cares about the USF program must realize that those perceptions have developed as a product of the basketball program. We have no responsible choice but to rid the university of the burden of them.

All the legitimate purposes of the athletic program in an educational institution are being distorted by the basketball program as it has developed. It is no solace to note that apparently we do not suffer alone. Published reports and proceedings before the NCAA committee on infractions indicate that other institutions are experiencing similar problems; some of them are even worse. That observation is not intended as an excuse or explanation for what has happened in and to our purpose.

All of us involved in these problems have to face a fundamental question: How can we contribute to the building of a decent, law-abiding society in this country if educational institutions are willing to suffer their principles to be prostituted and involve young people in that prostitution for any purpose, and much less for the purpose of winning some games and developing an ill-gotten recognition and income?

We are acutely aware of how this decision will affect our student-athletes who are presently enrolled. We will meet our scholarship commitments to them and help them in every way we can.

We also understand how the decision will affect those students, alumni, and friends of the university who have loyally supported the basketball program. We trust them to understand, after reflecting on all the factors, that in the end we had no other responsible choice.

One hundred and twenty-seven years ago, the Jesuit fathers established this university to provide a great educational resource in San Francisco. They and their successors have worked ever since providing San Francisco with a priceless asset, by educating in this community people in a range of ages from 17 to 80, from all over the world. We are determined that this mission will not be diminished by anything, and least of all by a program that compromises with the truth.

This decision is limited to men's intercollegiate basketball. All other men's and women's intercollegiate athletic programs will continue.

Finally, we hope that one day it may be possible to restore a men's intercollegiate basketball team. That possibility will depend on whether those responsible for this university are convinced that the factors that destroyed the program are not going to beset it again, and that a sound, constructive program can be developed and maintained to contribute positively to the life of USF rather than to afflict it.

NOTES

1. In July of 1983, Reverend John Lo Schiavo announced the resumption of the men's basketball program at the University of San Francisco beginning in the 1985–86 season. The following safeguards were instituted to ensure that there would be no further problems with the NCAA:
(a) The university will limit recruiting of players and scheduling of games to the West Coast.
(b) Responsibility for fund-raising for the athletic program will be shifted from the booster club, known as the Dons' Century Club, to the office of university relations.
(c) The board of trustees will create a "committee on athletics oversight" to monitor the basketball program.
(d) Basketball players will be admitted on the same basis as all other students and will be treated no differently once they are enrolled. Father Lo Schiavo said those steps did not represent a change in policy but rather a new "practice."

For further details, see "University of San Francisco Reverses Position, Will Play Basketball Again in 1985," *Chronicle of Higher Education*, June 22, 1983, p. 15.
2. Quintin Daley, an All-American guard at USF, admitted at a probation hearing on an assault charge that he received $1,000 a month from a USF alumnus. For further details, see "San Francisco Drops Its Basketball Program," *New York Times*, July 30, 1984, p. A15.
3. For further information, see the following articles:
(a) "San Francisco Drops Men's NCAA Basketball Program," *Boston Globe*, July 30, 1982, p. 41.
(b) USF Boosters Didn't Go with the Program," *Boston Globe*, July 7, 1983, p. 29.
4. Penn State football coach Joe Paterno has called recruiting by alumni "an animal out there which coaches can't control." For further details, see "Alumni Recruiting Curtailed," *New York Times*, January 13, 1983, p. B16.
5. In 1984, the University of Nebraska Board of Regents directed the institution's attorney to take legal action against anyone outside the school who causes Nebraska to violate NCAA regulations. For further details, see "Nebraska Tightens Security on Rules," *New York Times*, February 23, 1984, p. B19.

1.41–3(b)   Conference Recruiting Policies

In addition to NCAA rules concerning recruiting, many individual associated conferences have their own policies. The following excerpts are from the *1983–1984 Handbook of the Pacific-10 Conference*:

Article 8: Miscellaneous
1. *Recruiting.* The rules of the National Collegiate Athletic Association shall govern the recruiting of prospective student-athletes by Pacific-10 Conference Member institutions.

a. *Recruiting Code of Ethics.* The following code of ethics has been adoped by the Pacific-10 for guidance of the representatives of its member institutions in their activities in recruiting prospective student-athletes.

(1) Ethical conduct is required of all persons engaged in any form of recruitment of student-athletes.

(2) The enforcement of ethical recruiting practices is the responsibility of the President or Chancellor of each member institution and may not be delegated. In the discharge of this responsibility, the Presidents and Chancellors must keep in mind that a student who acts irresponsibly is

liable to penalty and that, in turn, a staff member who acts irresponsibly will have his actions and his contract reviewed.

(3) Recruiters are to observe the following guidelines in their activities:

(a) The prospective student and the student's family are considered to be individuals who have the right of free choice and the intelligence and good sense to arrive at their choice by rational means.

(b) An expressed wish of the student and/or family to be subjected to no further contact will be respected.

(c) No oral promise, either direct or implied, will indicate more benefits to the student than the institution actually will furnish.

(d) Promises of financial aid will be precise as to the qualifying conditions, terms of the aid, and duration of the aid.

(e) No inquiry will be made of the student of the terms of aid of any other institution.

(f) Strict avoidance of derogatory comments about other member institutions, their students and the quality of their educational offerings will be observed. It is only natural that a recruiter would enlarge on the advantages of attending the recruiter's institution, but the recruiter must not comment on any presumed disadvantages of attending any other institution.

(4) Under no circumstances can any offer of financial assistance be conditioned upon participation in athletics. . . .

5. *Statement of Intent.* The Council may adopt legislation by vote of a majority of its members through which a prospective student-athlete may commit himself to a member institution by means of a Statement of Intent in order to reduce conflicting recruiting pressures. Such legislation may provide that a student who has signed a Statement of Intent accepted by one Pacific-10 member institution and action on a petition for relief of penalties shall lose such eligibility for participation in Pacific-10 sports and for financial assistance as provided in such legislation.

NOTES _____

1. *The 1983–84 Handbook of the Pacific-10 Con-*

ference, Article 3, Student Eligibility, has the following provisions:

(5) *Other Eligibility Rules.* Except as otherwise provided herein, each institution shall establish the academic rules under which its student-athletes may be eligible for intercollegiate athletic competition. . . .

b. Recruiting Violations. A student-athlete whose enrollment or attendance has been solicited by the certifying institution or any representative of its athletic interests in violation of NCAA or Conference legislation as acknowledged by the institution or established through the Conference's or NCAA's enforcement procedures shall not be eligible for practice or competition in intercollegiate athletics at that institution. Restoration of the eligibility for regular-season competition may be authorized by the Conference's Eligibility Committee and for post-season competition by the NCAA Eligibility Committee.

2. The Big Ten Conference publishes a conference guide for recruiting for prospective student-athletes. The *1983–84 Big Ten Conference Guidelines for Recruiting* contained the following excerpt:

Also, you may be offered financial aid or a scholarship because of your athletic ability, to attend one of our schools.

Upon request, we will send your coach the NCAA booklet, "A Guide for the College-Bound Student-Athlete," which is a sixteen-page document about the do's and don'ts of recruiting.

Listed below are specific areas with which you should be thoroughly familiar.

Troublesome Recruiting Areas

I. *Offers of and Receipt of Illegal Items.* This section refers to offers of and/or receipt of anything used as an illegal inducement in recruiting, either before or after you choose a school.

A coach or any person representing the athletic interests of a Big Ten university may offer you a Tender (grant-in-aid) which provides a maximum of tuition and fees, room, board, and use of books. Any other offer, inducement or reward from any source, such as a coach, alumnus, booster, or friend to secure your enrollment is improper.

The following is a partial list of examples of improper or illegal offers, benefits or arrangements:

a. Cash gifts (any amount).

b. Gift of clothing and/or use of a credit card to buy clothing.

c. Gift of an automobile and/or the use of an automobile that is owned by someone other than yourself or your parents.

d. Use of charge accounts, not belonging to your

parents.

e. Special gifts or other arrangements for the benefit of your parents or legal guardians, friends, or relatives.

f. Transportation between your home, or any place else, and the campus at any time, except upon your official campus visit.

g. Transportation or other expenses for your family or friends to see games in which you may play after your enrollment.

h. An institution or its representatives shall not provide free transportation to or from a summer job unless it is the employer's established policy to transport all employees to the job site.

i. Loans, other than from an accredited lending agency, loans without interest or standard repayment schedules, and co-signed loans.

j. Loans of university athletic equipment in the summer prior to freshman year.

k. Arrangements for you to sell your complimentary athletic game tickets.

l. Promise of financial aid for a period beyond one year, or for post-graduate education.

m. Off-campus housing at no expense, or reduced expense.

3. Finances play a large part in the pressures associated with recruiting. Note how the table on page 92, published in the *Chronicle of Higher Education*, March 10, 1982, reflects booster athletic giving in 1980–81:

4. For further information, see the following articles:
(a) "College Fund-Raisers Seek Running Edge," *Omaha World-Herald*, January 31, 1982, p. C1.
(b) "Women's Sports Caught Up in (Costly?) Transition," *Boston Globe*, May 1 1983, p. 73.
(c) "The Money Crunch," *Boston Globe*, May 24, 1981, p. 43.
(d) "UNLV Is Not Running Smoothly," *Boston Globe*, February 12, 1984, p. 55.
(e) "Sports Boosters Help, and Sometimes Hurt, Major College Teams," *Wall Street Journal*, October 29, 1982, p. 1.

1.42 High School Athletic Associations

Each of the fifty states has its own high school athletic association to govern interscholastic athletics. Generally, membership to the association is open to all high schools in the state approved by the appropriate state department of education, secondary education, or public instruction. Typical of the purposes of such associations is the following:

The purpose of this Association shall be: To promote, develop, direct, protect, and regulate amateur interscholastic athletic relationships between member schools and to stimulate fair play, friendly rivalry, and good sportsmanship among contestants, schools, and communities throughout the state. [1981–82 *Constitution and Bylaws of the Iowa High School Athletic Association*, II, Purpose]

Florida High School Activities Ass'n. v. Thomas, 409 So. 2d 245 (Fla. Dist. Ct. App. 1982)

Parents of players who were dropped from a high school football team just prior to the state championships brought this class action suit in the Florida courts seeking injunctive relief and a declaratory decree that the rules of the Florida High School Activities Association were unconstitutional. Under the rules of the association, which governed all high school interscholastic athletics, teams in championship play were to be limited to a 44-player roster. During the regular season, there were no limits on the number of players a team could carry. The association justified its rule for three reasons: to maintain order by limiting the size of each team's bench, to control cost, and to create parity among teams.

The court had no difficulty in finding that the rules and activities of the association constituted state action. The Florida High School Activities Association was responsible for the supervision and control of all facets of interscholastic athletics in the state of Florida. Its activities were so intertwined with those of the state that it was deemed an arm of the state in the constitutional sense.

The plaintiffs' sons' interest in playing football was merely a privilege and not a right. But even so, the classification of an activity as a privilege does not give the state a right to impose arbitrary and irrational rules that deny the exercise of the privilege. Arbitrary and irrational state action violates the equal protection clause of the Constitution if it creates two disparately treated classes. In this case, the

PAC-TEN CONFERENCE

Stanford	$4,000,000
Washington	$2,000,000
UC Berkeley	$2,000,000
Southern Cal	$1,600,000
Arizona State	$1,200,000
Oregon State	$ 955,000
Arizona	$ 800,000
UCLA	$ 800,000
Oregon	$ 765,000
Washington State	$ 602,000

BIG 10 CONFERENCE

Iowa	$1,900,000
Illinois	$1,350,000
Indiana	$1,350,000
Ohio State	$1,250,000
Purdue	$1,000,000
Michigan State	$ 965,000
Minnesota	$ 550,000
Michigan	$ 400,000
Northwestern	$ 300,000
Wisconsin	not available

ATLANTIC COAST CONFERENCE

Clemson	$3,140,000
North Carolina	$3,000,000
NC State	$1,900,000
Virginia	$1,600,000
Wake Forest	$1,500,000
Maryland	$1,300,000
Duke	$1,000,000
Georgia Tech	$ 945,000

SOUTHEASTERN CONFERENCE

Georgia	$2,700,000
Florida	$1,750,000
Vanderbilt	$1,500,000
Alabama	$1,200,000
LSU	$1,100,000
Kentucky	$ 850,000
Mississippi	$ 700,000
Mississippi St.	$ 600,000
Tennessee	not available
Auburn	not available

INDEPENDENTS

South Carolina	$2,300,000
Florida State	$2,100,000
Penn State	$1,470,000
West Virginia	$1,140,000
Pittsburgh	$ 657,000
Tulane	$ 525,000
Notre Dame	not available

BIG EIGHT CONFERENCE

Oklahoma	$3,500,000
Oklahoma State	$1,500,000
Kansas State	$1,500,000
Missouri	$1,500,000
Kansas	$1,240,000
Iowa State	$ 900,000
Colorado	$ 862,000
Nebraska	$ 462,000

SOUTHWEST CONFERENCE

SMU	$1,900,000
Texas A&M	$1,800,000
Houston	$1,600,000
Arkansas	$1,500,000
Texas Tech	$1,200,000
Rice	$ 575,000
Baylor	$ 450,000
TCU	$ 450,000
Texas	not available

OTHERS

Wichita State	$1,000,000
Tulsa	$ 625,000
Texas-El Paso	$ 500,000
Brigham Young	$ 500,000
Wyoming	$ 450,000
Creighton	$ 81,000
UN-Omaha	$ 70,000

association's rule created two classes of foot-ball players. The first class consisted of the players who practiced every day and were eligible to play in both regular season and playoff games. The second class consisted of the players who practiced every day and were only eligible for regular season play without regard to their contribution to the team. As a result, the court found that the association's rule was unconstitutional.

None of the three reasons for the rule were found to have any significance by the court. Bench control had never been a problem during the entire history of the playoffs. The cost of the playoffs was not impacted by the number of players on each team. Finally, nothing in the record demonstrated that paring down the size of a team just before the playoffs had any impact on parity.

NOTES _____

1. In *School District of the City of Harrisburg* v. *Pa. Interscholastic Athletic Ass'n.*, 453 Pa. 495, 309 A. 2d 353 (1973), the school principal's admission of responsibility with respect to culpability for incidents of fighting among spectators following a football game was sufficient to sustain a finding that the school had violated athletic association rules and that sanctions then imposed were therefore justified.

2. In *Kelley* v. *Metropolitan County Board of Education of Nashville, Etc.*, 293 F. Supp. 485 (M.D. Tenn. 1968), a school board and an athletic association attempted to suspend an all-black high school's athletic program for one year. The district court granted injunctive relief to the student-athletes and held that procedural due process was violated because there was a lack of preexisting standards and regulations by which the school board could take disciplinary actions, and there was a conspicuous lack of formal charges or hearings in regards to the individual student-athletes that the school suspended.

3. In *Florida High School Activities Ass'n.* v. *Bradshaw*, 369 So. 2d 398 (Fla. Dist. Ct. App. 1979), plaintiff high school football player sought to enjoin state high school activities association from imposing a forfeiture for two games in which plaintiff participated while ineligible. The court held that in the absence of actual harm to the plaintiff and because of a lack of standing for the coach and other team members to assert denial of equal protection, the injunction was valid. The court also held that the opportunity to participate is a constitutionally protected right; therefore, the court will not intervene in

an association's discipline or sanction of its members.

4. In *Oklahoma Secondary School Act. Ass'n.* v. *Midget*, 505 P. 2d 175 (Okla. 1972), the court ruled that the judiciary will not interfere when forfeiture of games is imposed by the activities association unless it violates rules or laws of the association, public policy, or federal laws or is not imposed in good faith.

5. In *Wright* v. *Arkansas Activities Ass'n.*, 501 F. 2d 25 (8th Cir. 1974), the court found that a rule prohibiting football practice prior to a certain date may provide fair notice that a school may be sanctioned. However, imposition of a sanction resulting in the loss of a coaching/teaching position denied the coach due process. The rule made no notice of the fact that the coach could be subjected to a sanction resulting in unemployment.

6. In *Harry* v. *Bike Athletic Co., et al.*, plaintiffs, parents of high school football player who died after suffering a spinal cord or brain injury, alleged it was the duty of Louisiana High School Athletic Association to promulgate rules to prevent the situation in which medical help was delayed to the player for two hours due to cars parked blocking exits, the absence of emergency vehicles at the contest, and other contributing factors.

The Louisiana High School Athletic Association was granted summary judgment based on its claim that it was not an overseer of particular contests or individual participants. The court accepted the association's contentions that its function was as a rule maker rather than a supervisor.

1.43   Other Amateur Athletic Associations

There are numerous other amateur athletic associations in addition to those previously mentioned. The organizational structure and regulatory authority of amateur athletic associations vary considerably. One example of an organization is the United States of America Amateur Boxing Federation, Inc. Its objectives are as follows:

The purpose of the corporation shall be to foster, develop, promote and coordinate recreational and competitive amateur boxing opportunities for all member athletes and supportive participants, and to supervise such other amateur boxing matters as may properly come within this purview. These and the following additional purposes shall be consistent with the provisions of Title II, Sections 202 and 203, of the Amateur Sports Act of 1978, Public Law 95–606.

(a) To coordinate those programs and activities which contribute to the development of individual integrity, character, physical and mental fitness and personal objectives.

(b) To encourage, support, aid and abet public participation on behalf of the development of individual skills during local, regional, national and international programs and activities, regardless of race, creed, age or national origin.

(c) To resolve disputes and grievances involving participating groups and individuals.

(d) To coordinate programs and activities between participants representing the United States of America and other nations which provide valuable exchanges of cultural and other ideas, thereby enhancing international understanding and relations. [*1981–84 USA Amateur Boxing Federation Official Rules*, Section 202.1, p. 30]

The USA Amateur Boxing Federation has an "Athlete's Bill of Rights":

The Local Boxing Committee (LBC) shall respect and protect the right of every individual who is eligible under reasonable national and applicable international amateur athletic rules and regulations to participate if selected (or attempt to qualify for selection) as an athlete, coach, trainer, manager, administrator or other official, representing the United States in any international amateur athletic competition, so long as such competition is conducted in compliance with reasonable national applicable international requirements.

Disciplinary Procedures and Appeal.

(a) As hereinafter set forth, the LBC Review Section of the Registration Committee may censure, suspend for a definite or indefinite period of time, or expel any member of the LBC including any athlete or coach, official, member of any committee, delegate, or any person participating in any capacity whatsoever in the affairs of the LBC, who has contravened any of its rules or regulations.

The procedure to be taken in reference to such suspension or expulsion shall be as follows: The person charged shall be notified of the charges against him or her in detail, or of the circumstances which are believed to require answers, explanation or clarification. . . .

The written statement of charges shall also set

out the penalties which may ensue if such charges are proved; the statement shall contain a date at which time a hearing will be held with the request that the person charged shall appear before the Committee with the right to have counsel of his own choice to represent him at the hearing; the written statement to the person charged shall set a date of hearing not less than twenty (20) days nor more than sixty (60) days after the date of mailing of such notification. . . .

The statement shall also set forth the right of appellate review if the decision is rendered against the person charged.

The decision shall be rendered at the time of the hearing, or within twenty-four (24) hours thereafter.

(b) When compliance with regular procedures would not be likely to produce a sufficiently early decision to do justice to the affected parties, the Review Section of the Registration Committee, or its duly authorized agent and representative, is authorized, upon such notice, as the circumstances may dictate, to the parties concerned to hear and decide a matter relating to a scheduled boxing competition.

The individual or entity charged may be suspended from participating in any activities of the ABF whatsoever after such notice and hearing. . . .

(c) Unless original jurisdiction of the matter is assumed by the Board of Governors, the decisions of the Review Section of the Registration Committee shall be final in all cases, subject only to appeal to the Board of Governors of the LBC and thereafter to the Board of Review of the National Registration Committee.

An appeal to the Board of Governors must be taken within ten (10) days. . . . [*1981–84 USA Amateur Boxing Federation Official Rules*, Appendix ix, p. 133]

1.50   Scheduling

Traditionally, scheduling of athletic events on the intercollegiate level has been free of litigation. If for some reason — for example, a change of coaches — an institution wanted to drop a contracted commitment to play against another institution, the contest has up until now generally been dropped without much difficulty. Recently, however, some scheduling problems have resulted in threats of litigation.

In 1982, the University of Missouri bought its way out of its contract with San Diego State for $50,000. It did so by exercising the contract's forfeiture clause because Missouri felt that the revenue received would not have justified travel expenses.

Sult v. Gilbert, 148 Fla. 31, 3 So. 2d 729 (1941)

The Florida Supreme Court affirmed a trial court decision that held the Florida High School Athletic Association administrative settlement of a high school football contest scheduling dispute was sufficient review and that the courts should not interfere with the operation of voluntary athletic associations. The court noted that:

In June, 1939, Palmetto High School entered into an agreement with Sarasota High School to play a game of football in November, 1939. In April, 1940, Sarasota High School severed athletic relations with Palmetto High School and a controversy arose as to whether a football game would be played between them in November, 1940. On the reverse side of the 1939 contract, the following was inserted:

"It is hereby understood that Sarasota High School will give Palmetto High School, for the year 1940, one of the following contracts:

A. The same contract as this year;

B. A $200.00 guarantee;

c. A fifty-fifty split on the gate. (Palmetto to have the choice of accepting one of the above)"

Article Nine, Constitution of the Association, provides:

". . . A contract shall not be cancelled except by the mutual consent of the parties to the contract. In case of failure of the parties to reach agreement concerning cancellation the matter shall be referred to the Executive Secretary for adjudication. His decree, or the decree of the Executive Committee in case of appeal, shall be final. . . ."

The two high schools could not reconcile their differences so the controversy as to the 1940 game was submitted by the principal of Palmetto High School to the executive secretary of the

Association as provided in article nine of the constitution above quoted. After due consideration, the executive secretary held that the contract between the two high schools provided for but one game of football which had been played in 1939 as per agreement, that the terms written on the reverse side of the contract were doubtless intended to provide for an additional game in 1940 but not having been covered in the contract as originally executed or by subsequent provision, it could not be enforced. Palmetto High School accepted the finding of the executive secretary and did not appeal to the executive committee.

In October, 1940, Palmetto High School filed its bill of complaint in the Circuit Court praying that Sarasota High School be required to play football with it in 1940. . . .

Immediately after filing this suit, the executive secretary cited Palmetto High School to show cause why it should not be suspended from the association; after a full hearing, the executive secretary held that refusal of Palmetto High School to accept his decision as to the 1940 game with Sarasota and the institution of court proceedings to compel the game was a violation of the rules of the association for which he would be bound to suspend it for a period of one year. On appeal and full hearing by both sides, the executive committee affirmed the decision of the executive secretary.

Palmetto High School then filed its bill of complaint in which it named the Florida High School Athletic Association, Sarasota High School, Winter Haven High School, and Bradenton High School as defendants. The bill prayed that said high schools be required to play football games with complainant in 1940 as per schedule or contract with them and that complainant be not suspended from membership in the Florida High School Athletic Association.

The Court entered a temporary restraining order enjoining the suspension of Palmetto High School from the association and requiring Winter Haven and Bradenton High Schools to perform their agreements to play football with complainant. The latter part of the order was promptly obeyed and thereafter a motion to dissolve the injunction and dismiss the bill of complaint was granted. The Court further found that the suspension order was regular and in compliance with the constitution of the association and should not be disturbed. This appeal is from the order of dismissal. . . .

The constitution of the Florida High School Athletic Association shows that it is a voluntary nonprofit organization. When Palmetto High School was a member of the Association, it had a right to make contracts with member schools for athletic meets. The loss of this right was all that was lost by the suspension and that being the case, we find no showing of a contractual or property right that would authorize the courts to interfere. It was purely an internal affair of the association and there is no showing of mistake, fraud, collusion, or arbitrariness in the proceedings. . . .

NOTES _____

1. *University of Washington* v. *Florida State University* (unreported decision), a case involving football schedules, was dismissed by the district court because it lacked jurisdiction in a suit between states. Washington sued Florida State when defendant institution, citing rising travel costs, canceled a scheduled football game (the 1982 season opener at Washington). Washington sought damages of $350,000 for losses in tickets, programs, concessions, parking, and other revenues. In addition, it sought $400,000 for lost opportunity of television coverage and loss of prestige, recruiting opportunities, and early season national rankings. The plaintiff went on to argue that "If two institutions enter into a contract and one institution says 12 months before the game that it is not going to play, it's not reasonable or responsible to expect the other institution to readjust its schedule. A school needs three or four years to readjust its schedule, and if there is mutual consent, then there is no problem. But there is a terrible problem if mutual consent does not exist."

Texas El-Paso agreed to play plaintiff in place of Florida State for a guarantee of $100,000. Florida State, meanwhile, juggled its schedule and played the University of Cincinnati for its season opener. Florida State argued that travel expenses forced the cancellation of the game after Washington refused a Florida State proposal to include travel costs as part of expenses. "People have to cooperate to keep intercollegiate athletics going," stated Florida State. "Football is our biggest money-making sport. If we have a loss, it's hard to meet our athletic budget. You've got to respect other universities, and you've got to understand their difficulties and try to be as flexible and cooperative as possible." The case was dismissed by the District Court because it lacked jurisdiction in a suit between states.

2. For a further discussion of scheduling problems, see the following articles:

(a) "Athletic Director Scrambles to Fill Schedules," *NCAA News*, December 29, 1982, p. 5.

(b) "Air Control," *New York Times*, December 14, 1981, p.C2.

3. The NCAA recommends certain policies and procedures in the scheduling of athletic contests. These include:

Policy 2: Governing and Scheduling Athletic Competition

Section 1. Member institutions should conduct their athletic competition on campus grounds and in campus buildings.

Section 2. Where such campus facilities are not adequate, institutions should play only on fields or in buildings over which the college or university has complete control, management and supervision. In such instances, the institution should:

(a) Rent the facility and have complete management and control, including the use of institutional personnel if it desires for the operation of the facility and related duties during the staging of any event;

(b) Arrange to create as much collegiate atmosphere as possible by location of students and faculty, allocation of tickets, control of concession (as to type of production sold), rooting sections, cheerleaders and college bands;

(c) Require that all game officials be appointed through regular collegiate channels;

(d) Enlist local law enforcement officers to protect against scalpers and gamblers and to insure proper crowd control;

(e) Arrange proper control of dressing rooms, half-time team rooms and other facilities such as players' benches;

(f) Arrange for institutional representation on press committees for all public relations matters, and

(g) Require a complete auditor's report on all events.

Section 3. Member institutions entering into contractual agreements related to the scheduling of intercollegiate athletic competition should fulfill the responsibilities set forth in such agreements, and no member institution should breach a contractual agreement to participate in intercollegiate athletic competition with another member institution. [*1985–86 NCAA Manual*, "Recommended Policies and Practices for Intercollegiate Athletes"]

4. The NCAA has specific limitations on playing seasons in basketball, football, ice hockey, and soccer, including starting dates and closing dates for competition (see *1985–86 NCAA Manual*, Bylaw 3–2).

5. The NCAA has specific limitations on the number of contests, including scrimmages, that a member can play. The limitations in Division I are 28 basketball games, 11

football games, and 22 soccer games. Games played in Hawaii or Alaska do not count toward this number (see *1985–86 NCAA Manual*, Bylaw 3–3).

6. In 1984, Florida State University in its report on the school's athletic program (see Section 2.10), made the following recommendations regarding scheduling and practices:

Scheduling

Recommendation 4.1. After reviewing the information submitted by the Athletic Department, the Committee recommends that Florida State University administrators establish a maximum number of contests and dates of competition for each sport. The maximum numbers established should be the same as those proposed but not passed at the January 1984 NCAA Convention. The NCAA proposal was the result of a nationwide study conducted by the Special Committee on Legislative Review. The Committee concurs that such standards are necessary since "athletes are students first," and it is difficult to be a successful student while participating in a sport that takes one away from the classroom to excess. The Committee urges the NCAA to adopt this proposal at its next session and requests that Florida State representatives co-sponsor and strongly support this legislation.

Recommendation 4.2. The Committee recommends that no student athlete be allowed to miss more than nine classes per course per semester (i.e., three times the number of weekly class meetings) because of practice or competition.

Teams whose schedules have required more absences than this maximum are as follows:

Women's	*Men's*
Tennis	Tennis
Cross Country	Track and Field
Volleyball	Golf

Golf	Baseball
Diving	Basketball
	Cross Country

Teams whose schedules have not exceeded this maximum are football; men's and women's swimming; women's track and field, softball, and basketball.

Recommendation 4.3. The Committee heard reports of instances of instructors allegedly penalizing student athletes unfairly because of absences resulting from participation in athletic competition. The Committee reviewed University policy as stated in the *Faculty Handbook* and the *Bulletin* regarding class absence and concluded that the language is not sufficiently precise. We recommend that the Faculty Senate clarify this policy by including reference to absence resulting from participation in University sanctioned activities.

Recommendation 4.4. The Committee recommends that no athletic contests, with the exception of NCAA or Metro Conference championship events, be scheduled during final examination periods. In addition, all coaches and academic administrators are urged not to schedule contests two to three days immediately preceding final examination periods.

Practice

The Committee heard testimony regarding required practice time for student athletes but concluded that it is unrealistic to designate arbitrarily a maximum number of hours for daily practice for all sports. It also believes that such designation of a maximum number of hours would not be enforceable.

7. In interscholastic competition, the scheduling of the same sport in different seasons for girls and boys (i.e., girls' fall tennis, boys' spring tennis) has been held acceptable by some courts because of limited playing space at a school's athletic facility. For an example, see Section 3.33–3, *Striebel* v. *Minnesota State High School League.*

THE AMATEUR ATHLETE

2.00 Introduction

Chapter 2 focuses on the various legal considerations involving the amateur athlete. Recall from Chapter 1 that the associations define "amateur athlete" and then interpret and enforce such definitions. The impacts of those definitions, however, are obviously felt by the athlete and are the subject of examination in this chapter.

Section 2.10 discusses individual eligibility requirements for the athlete. Since much of the rule making and litigation concerns the National Collegiate Athletic Association (NCAA), Section 2.10 has been outlined with the NCAA in mind. Many of the requirements, such as grade point average (Section 2.11), academic progress (Section 2.12), redshirting (Section 2.14), and player agents (Section 2.17), are indeed problems peculiar to the NCAA. However, other eligibility requirements — transfer rules (Section 2.13), financial considerations (Section 2.15), and professional contracts (Section 2.16) — concern both the NCAA and other amateur associations.

Intercollegiate athletics, primarily football and basketball, can be extremely lucrative — the rewards are great for successful programs. All programs originate from an athletic depart-ment, and these can be set up in several different ways. Some departments operate under the university budget, in which revenues go directly to the general fund and expenses are covered as line items. Other departments operate like businesses. Still others are separately incorporated and cover their expenses entirely with revenues taken in by the department. Because the stakes in inter-collegiate athletics have become greater, the pressure to be successful and to attract top-notch athletes has also increased. Eligibility requirements have therefore become extremely important, especially to the NCAA.

The grade point average requirement (see Section 2.11) is one method the NCAA uses to ensure that entering students will be academically qualified to participate. Of course, grade point average can also be used to prevent sports participation by a student who is enrolled at the university. At issue in the courts is the type of courses that should be included in the computation of grade point average. For example, should physical education courses that involve skill teaching be included? The NCAA recently passed a controversial rule that requires in-coming freshman student-athletes to achieve both a certain grade point average and certain scores on standardized examinations (see Section 2.11). Although the rule is not to take effect until 1986, it may be challenged by universities whose enrollments have historically been composed of black students.

A second individual eligibility requirement used by the NCAA is the rule requiring sufficient academic progress by the student-athlete (see Section 2.12). The rule was promulgated when the NCAA discovered that a number of athletes were maintaining their eligibility with respect to grade point average by taking one introductory-level course after another in the university. The problem occurred after their playing eligibility expired and their scholarship funds ran out and they found themselves three or four semesters short of graduation because they had not fulfilled enough upper-level course requirements in their majors. The NCAA is not the only association concerned with this problem. Many individual conferences have also promulgated academic progress rules, and some of these are more rigorous than the NCAA's rules.

A third eligibility requirement deals with transfer rules (see Section 2.13), which place restrictions on certain student-athletes who transfer from one school to another. The intent of transfer rules is twofold: first, to discourage coaches from recruiting athletes who are enrolled in another school; and second, to prevent athletes from jumping from school to school solely for athletic reasons. Many transfer rules are broadly written and prevent all transfers from immediate participation in athletics. Such rules can be overinclusive by penalizing those student-athletes who transfer for reasons other than athletics. Many students have sued amateur athletic associations in an attempt to obtain immediate eligibility. The frequency of such litigation has caused many amateur athletic associations to redefine transfer rules more narrowly. While the revised rules may still be overinclusive, they are often more reasonable in determining who may be granted immediate athletic eligibility.

A fourth individual eligibility requirement is the practice of redshirting (see Section 2.14). Redshirting is a term used to describe the practice of extending the playing career of a student-athlete by postponing or passing over a year of interscholastic or intercollegiate participation while not affecting the athlete's maximum allowable time for participating in high school or college athletics. The reasons for redshirting are varied and include medical, academic, and coaching factors. Many of the challenges on the intercollegiate level deal with situations in which athletes are requesting either an additional redshirt year or a redshirt year in a season in which they have already participated to some degree.

A fifth area of individual eligibility requirements concerns financial considerations (see Section 2.15). The NCAA has promulgated guidelines affecting scholarships (Section 2.15–1), financial aid (Section 2.15–1), and pay (Section 2.15–2). A university found to be in violation of any of these rules may forfeit games and/or face NCAA sanctions and penalties. An athlete who has violated the rules may be ruled ineligible for NCAA competition. For example, a student-athlete who is deemed to have received pay from a professional team is considered a professional and will no longer be eligible for intercollegiate athletics in that particular sport. If that athlete participated in NCAA games after receipt of money from a professional team, the university will have to forfeit those games.

The key legal issue with respect to athletic scholarships is whether they are to be construed as contracts. The ramifications of determining whether an athletic scholarship is in fact an employment contract are immense. The value of the scholarship becomes taxable income for the student-athlete, and as a result of receiving income, the student-athlete may no longer be deemed an amateur athlete in accordance with NCAA regulations. In addition, the student-athlete may be eligible for worker's compensation benefits, and the university athletic departments may be responsible for obtaining worker's compensation insurance.

A sixth individual eligibility requirement deals with professional contracts (see Section 2.16). In addition to the aforementioned increased stake in a successful intercollegiate athletic program, there has been a concomitant rise in professional sports salaries. Larger television contracts, cable television, increased attendance, increased ticket prices, and competing leagues have all contributed to the pressure of placing a successful professional team on the field and to the expectations of many intercollegiate student-athletes of receiving lucrative professional salaries upon leaving school. Therefore, the teams and leagues that compete for these athletes may sign or attempt to sign the athletes before their college eligibility has expired. This practice, of course, can lead to a violation of the NCAA rules governing amateurism.

A seventh and final individual eligibility requirement deals with player-agents (see Section 2.17). Because the stakes for professional teams have increased and the professional athletes have demanded and won an increase in the salaries they are paid, the representation of these athletes has become a very lucrative area. The competition among player-agents for student-athletes has therefore become extremely intense. As a result, some player-agents have signed student-athletes before their intercollegiate eligibility has expired, thus rendering them ineligible for future NCAA competition and possibly causing forfeiture of past school victories and/or loss of financial receipts from NCAA-sponsored championships.

NOTES _____

1. For further information see, "Administration of Amateur Athletics: The Time for an Amateur Athlete's Bill of Rights Has Arrived," 48 *Fordham Law Review* 53 (1979).

2. See also Weistart and Lowell, *The Law of Sports*, 1979, Charlottesville, Va.

2.10 Individual Eligibility Requirements for Collegiate and High School Athletes

Individual student-athletes must maintain many standards to be eligible for intercollegiate competition. Each conference, league, or organization such as the NCAA has rules and regulations that extend its authority to various areas surrounding sports activities. For collegiate and high school athletes there are usually academic standards, rules governing personal conduct, and rules for each individual sport. The following excerpts from a report by Florida State University on its student-athletes reflect these various rules.

CASE STUDY: Student Athletes at the
Florida State University:
Planning Responsibly

*A Report Submitted by the President's Committee on
the Student Athlete (Excerpts)*

Florida State University,
Tallahassee, Florida
April 17, 1984

The report, "Student Athletes at The Florida State University: Planning Responsibly," is the response to the memorandum of 25 March 1983, creating the Committee on the Student Athlete. In that action, we were asked to determine what policies and procedures needed to be developed to bring student athletes into the mainstream of student life and to assure them full and complete access to student services at Florida State.

This report reflects hundreds of hours of committee, subcommittee, and individual work. It is perhaps the most thorough study that any Division I-A school has made with regard to its student athletes. We recommend that the Athletic Board review annually the subject areas we have studied. We recommend further that a committee similar to ours review and evaluate the athletic program at least once every five years.

INTRODUCTION

This report is concerned with institutional responsibility. The word responsibility is a moral term. Basic to any moral understanding of responsibility, institutional or otherwise, is the question, "To whom or to what are we responsible?" We assume that the officers, faculty, and staff of The Florida State University are primarily responsible to their respective academic disciplines and professional communities, to their students, to the people of Florida through their elected and appointed representatives, and to others whose welfare is affected by their policies and performance.

The primary responsibilities of the University community are academic research, teaching, and service. All other responsibilities are secondary. The educational mission at Florida State is the unifying cause to which we are loyal, and all other activities must be ordered under this primary loyalty. It is from this primary commitment that we should view our participation in inter-collegiate sports.

Contemporary intercollegiate sport, played at Division I-A level, is characterized by specialization, commercialization, and bureaucratic organization. Sport participation makes increasingly totalistic claims on the student athlete's life. Florida State currently has 388 young women and men who are participating in varsity athletics. Our student athletes are receiving $1,113,600.00 in scholarship aid. The athletic budget for the academic year 1983-84 is $7,121,988.00.

Concern has been expressed from a variety of sources that programs of such size can virtually become autonomous units, thus subverting the University's primary mission. There is an increasing demand for assurance that the faculty and administration are in control of the non-athletic dimension of the student athlete's university experience and that neither institutional nor academic integrity are compromised.

Our work has required that we address the following questions: (1) What is Florida State's responsibility to student athletes? (2) How are we presently meeting this responsibility? (3) What changes need to be made with regard to policies toward student athletes?

Our study uncovered neither scandal nor ticking time bombs. In general, we are doing rather well, but we can improve. We intend that this report be anticipatory, not just reactive. Our perspective emphasizes planning for an increased level of institutional responsibility in dealing with our student athletes.

CHAPTER ONE:
HISTORY AND PHILOSOPHY

. . . In the fourteen years since 1970, the Florida State program has undergone several significant alterations. In the first three years of the Seventies the football program was successful, and basketball and baseball reached the finals of national championships. In 1973, however, the football team went 0-11 and subsequently faced a serious financial crisis. In the mid-seventies three disastrous football years created a budget crunch that led to serious talk of dropping non-revenue sports. The eventual decision, however, was to retain all eight sports and to continue to play major college schedules.

In the mid-Seventies two developments produced important alterations in this picture. The rejuvenated Seminole Boosters, Inc., began to raise a great deal more money for athletics than it had before. In 1976, Bobby Bowden became head football coach, and the grid program quickly became one of the nation's most successful.

The other major change of the Seventies was the rise in women's sports. Intercollegiate athletics for women at Florida State had been insignificant. Title IX led to greatly increased funding in a relatively brief period. Competition in eight sports was initiated, and by the early Eighties all women's sports were playing major-college schedules. This schedule was basically regional, but it also included contests that took the Lady Seminoles to all corners of the country.

In 1984 Florida State competes in sixteen sports, eight for men and eight for women. The competition in all sixteen is with major institutions with national recognition and national titles at stake. While regional rivalries and increased travel costs have determined that most competition remains in the South, the University's athletic teams compete from New York to Hawaii.

For almost four decades Florida State University varsity teams have competed at the major-college level. Under the NCAA's reorganization, Florida State has competed in Division 1-A in eight men's sports and now in eight women's sports. Florida State's athletic record has aided attempts to increase and to improve its state, regional and national visibility, financial support, and student recruitment. Intercollegiate athletics has been an integral part of the life of this thirty-six-year-old University.

This athletic program has been under the control of the president as the University's chief executive officer. The program should remain under the control and direction of the president and every effort should be made to integrate it further into the academic structure. The young men and women who compete are "student athletes," and this institution should be a national leader in recognizing the athlete as a student. Academic matters involving student athletes should continue to be under academic control. The University should provide every opportunity for all sports programs to strive for excellence within established admission, academic, and financial guidelines.

Some academic institutions in this country have sacrificed academic standards and have spent money recklessly striving for athletic superiority. Others have abandoned the chase and de-emphasized athletics. The Florida State University should take a position between these two extremes. Our athletic program is not valuable enough to turn the institution into an "athletic factory." On the other hand, it is far too important to de-emphasize athletics and abandon competition in Division 1-A. Florida State should strive to maintain a broadly competitive athletic program while maintaining its commitment to academic excellence.

CHAPTER TWO:
RECRUITING AND ADMISSIONS

Recruiting

The recruiting of student athletes is of major importance. Considerable staff time, energy, and departmental money are appropriately expended in this effort.

Successful recruiting should be measured by both athletic victories and by the academic progress of student athletes. Given the institution's decision to raise admissions standards and the recent legislative efforts to improve the quality of education, athletic recruiters must strive even harder to sign athletes who have the ability to pass standardized examinations and to compete in the classroom. All recruiters should be knowledgeable about the University and its programs. At the time of campus visits, athletic recruiters should enlist the aid of members of the academic community.

All those recruiting in behalf of Florida State should make certain that honesty and clarity are a part of their activities. As far as is possible, they should ensure that there are no major surprises for the student athlete upon his or her arrival at the University. NCAA rules must be observed at all times during the recruiting process.

The coordination of recruiting activities with admissions procedure is vitally important. This coordination should ensure that conflicts leading to refused or delayed admission of signees are avoided. The admissions exceptions policy proposed below should facilitate that coordination. There must be a continuous monitoring of recruiting practices to assure that all those involved adhere to established University and athletic governance rules and regulations.

Admissions

Recommendation 2.1: The admissions policy for athletes at Florida State should permit twenty-five automatic exceptions per year. An exception is defined as a student who scores below the Florida Board of Regents' minimum of an 840 SAT score and a 2.0 high school grade point average (GPA). Fifteen exceptions will be for men, slightly fewer than in recent years, and ten exceptions for women, the average over the past four years. The greater number for men reflects the larger number of athletes recruited by the football program. These twenty-five exceptions are considered necessary if Florida State is to continue to compete at Division 1-A level in the 1980s. With these exceptions announced in advance, coaches can recruit knowing exactly how many exceptions they will have every year and will also know that when that number is exhausted they will have no more.

These twenty-five exceptions will be granted automatically and will not be subject to review by any University body. Twenty-five should be the maximum number, and we urge the administration not to grant any further athletic exceptions.

More than twenty-five annual exceptions (125 over a five-year period) would strain the University's advising and academic support resources beyond capacity. Indeed, the 125 will necessitate an increase and improvement in resources presently available.

The twenty-five annual exceptions will be awarded to the respective sports by the Athletic Department. The only directive to the department will be that fifteen exceptions must go to men and ten to women. The Athletic Department should prepare a yearly report of test scores and high school GPAs of newly-enrolled athletes to be sent to the vice president for academic affairs and to the Athletic Board.

Recommendation 2.2: Every athlete admitted to Florida State as an exception (below 840/2.0) should be mandated to participate in an enrichment program administered by the Office of the Dean of Undergraduate Studies. There will be no exceptions to this rule.

In addition to involving academic exceptions in an enrichment program, the Athletic Department and the University are urged to provide greater counseling and academic support for these young men and women. Finally, the department must make an annual report to the vice president for academic affairs and the Athletic Board on the academic progress towards a degree of each athlete who was admitted as an exception.

CHAPTER THREE:
ACADEMIC ISSUES

Academic Advisement for Basic Studies and Undeclared Majors

The academic advisement of student athletes currently falls under the control of athletic program administrators. The department hires academic advisors who provide in-house academic support services. While this method has been somewhat successful, it is causing growing concern among faculty. The report of the Committee on Academic Support Services suggested this, and the faculty survey conducted by this Committee confirmed that this concern is prevalent. It is the Committee's recommendation that, in this day of increasing academic standards,

the hiring, training, and ultimate responsibility for academic advisors for all students must rest with the academic administration. Academic advisors should continue to work with student athletes in the current manner, but the lines of authority must flow clearly from the academic administration.

Recommendation 3.1: We concur with the Committee on Academic Support Services that academic advising of student athletes should be under the ultimate control of the proposed Dean of Undergraduate Studies. Until this office is operational, however, the existing athletic advising program should remain intact.

Recommendation 3.2: After the Office of the Dean of Undergraduate Studies has assumed responsibility for academic advising, academic support personnel may continue to be employed by the Athletic Department to provide additional academic support services for student athletes. These services should augment programs offered by Undergraduate Studies and be designed in consultation with the dean.

Recommendation 3.3: The implementation of Recommendation 3.2 will necessitate co-operation between Undergraduate Studies and the Athletic Department. The Athletic Department should continue to fund academic support programs, but Undergraduate Studies should share the financial burden so that this important function is adequately funded. . . .

Recommendation 3.4: The Committee recommends that the Budget and Analysis Department, in conjunction with the Registrar's Office and the Athletic Director's Office, conduct similar studies annually. These studies should report at least the following: retention rates, degrees awarded, grade point averages, and progress towards a degree. The University administration should review the findings to monitor the academic progress of our student athletes.

Course Composition

Recommendation 3.5: The Committee recommends that while some courses designed to improve academic competencies may be advisable for selected student athletes with special academic needs, no course sections should be comprised predominantly of student athletes. Academic advisors should, as a general rule, ensure that student athletes enroll in courses having a representative mix of student athletes and non-athletes.

Directed Individual Study

Recommendation 3.6: The Committee recommends that student athletes be assigned directed individualized study (DIS) only when there is a clear academic need related to progress towards graduation. The use of DIS to maintain eligibility should be discouraged and closely monitored by the student's academic advisor.

Correspondence Courses

Recommendation 3.7: The Committee recommends that student athletes be assigned correspondence courses only when there is a clear academic need related to progress towards graduation. The use of correspondence courses to maintain eligibility should be discouraged. Even after a correspondence course is deemed necessary, the course's academic requirements and the student's progress in the course should be closely monitored by the student's academic advisor.

Participation Credit

Recommendation 3.8: The Committee recommends that students who participate in varsity sports should receive a maximum of four credits for their participation at a rate of one credit per semester. This is an increase from the present allowable maximum of two credits.

Reduced Loads

Recommendation 3.9: The Committee recommends that Florida State co-sponsor and support NCAA legislation which would permit student athletes whose time required by their sports exceeds twenty hours weekly to take an under-load during their seasons of competition. Practice, competition, and travel time should be included in the time calculation. These students should be required, however, to achieve the normal academic progress each academic year in accordance with NCAA guidelines.

Improved Communication

Recommendation 3.10: Testimony before this Committee and the results of the faculty survey ... indicate a lack of effective communication between the athletic administration and faculty. The Committee recommends that the president charge the Athletic Board to devise strategies to improve communication between these groups. . . .

NOTES

1. At the 1985 Special NCAA convention, the association's member institutions adopted many of the reforms advocated in the Florida State self-study, including the following:

> *Budget control.* Approved a requirement that each member institution's annual budget for intercollegiate athletics be controlled by the institution and subjected to its normal budgeting procedures and that the budget be approved by the institution's CEO or the CEO's designee.
>
> *Annual audit.* Approved a requirement that each member institution conduct an annual audit of its intercollegiate athletic program, to be prepared by an individual from outside the institution, selected for the assignment by the institution's CEO or the CEO's designee.
>
> *Playing seasons.* Approved a resolution stating that the membership does not favor an increase in the permissible number of regular-season contests or dates of competition in any sport, specifically including basketball and football.

For further information, see the following articles:
(a) "Special Convention Legislation Examined in Detail," *NCAA News*, June 19, 1985, p. 4.
(b) "A Summary of Roll-Call Voting on 12 Convention Proposals," *NCAA News*, July 3, 1985, p. 4.
2. For further information, see the following articles:
(a) "Judicial Review of Disputes Between Athletes and the National Collegiate Athletic Association," 24 *Stanford Law Review* 903 (1972).
(b) Springer, "A Student-Athlete's Interest in Eligibility: Its Context and Constitutional Dimensions," *Connecticut Law Review* 318 (1977).
(c) "Judicial Review of NCAA Decisions: Does the College Athlete Have a Property Interest in Interscholastic Athletics?" 10 *Stetson Law Review* 483 (1981).
(d) "Collegiate Athletic Participation: A Property or Liberty Interest?" 15 *Pacific Law Review* 1203 (July 1984).
(e) Waicukauski, "The Regulation of Academic Standards in Intercollegiate Athletics," *Arizona State Law Journal* 79 (1982).
3. See Exhibit 2–1.

Name _____ University _____

Home Town and State _____ Date_____

Date of Birth_____ Social Security Number _____

Sport _____ School Year of Residence _____ Course of Study _____

Date of Entrance At This University _____ Date of First Entrance at Any College of University_____

Number of Previous Seasons of Competition: Here _____ Elsewhere _____

1. Have you ever registered in, enrolled in or attended any classes in any other college, university, junior college, or any other institution above high school grade, or practiced or competed in any varsity or varsity reserve intercollegiate athletic contest?

    _____
    (IF SO, STATE NAME OF SCHOOL, DATES, YEARS OF VARSITY INTERCOLLEGIATE COMPETITION, ETC.)

2. Have you ever participated as an individual or as a representative of any team in organized competition in a sport after your 20th birthday and prior to entrance at an NCAA institution?

    _____
    (IF SO, STATE SPORT, NAME OF TEAM OR TOURNAMENT, DATES, ETC.)

3. Have you ever used, directly or indirectly, your skill in your sport for financial gain?

    _____
    (IF SO, STATE NAME OF ORGANIZATION AWARDING FINANCIAL GAIN, ADDRESS, DATE, AMOUNT, SPORT, ETC.)

4. Have you ever taken part in an athletic contest in your sport in which a money prize was offered (regardless of the disposition of this prize), or received expense money based upon meet results?

    _____
    (IF SO, STATE SPORT, NAME OF TEAM, ADDRESS, DATES, OFFERING ORGANIZATION, AMOUNT OF PRIZE)

5. Have you ever received any remuneration for participating in an athletic contest in your sport (excluding expenses actually incurred as a participant or reasonable salary for services actually rendered on a job)?

    _____
    (IF SO, STATE SOURCE, ADDRESS, DATE, AMOUNT, TYPE OF CONTEST, SPORT, ETC.)

6. Have you ever lent your name to any form of commercial advertising?

    _____
    (IF SO, STATE NAME OF COMPANY OR ORGANIZATION, TYPE OF ADVERTISING, AMOUNT RECEIVED, DATE, ETC.)

7. Have you ever signed a professional athletic contract in your sport, or been represented by an agent?

    _____
    (IF SO, STATE NAME OF TEAM OR AGENT, ADDRESS, DATE, SPORT, ETC.)

8. Have you ever played in any game under an assumed name? _____

9. Have you since entering this university participated in any athletic contest, other than during summer vacations, as a representative of any team or organization other than this university? _____
    (IF SO, STATE SPORT, NAME OF TEAM, ADDRESS, DATES, ETC.)

10. Did you play organized basketball last summer?

    _____
    (IF SO, STATE NAME OF TEAM, ADDRESS, NAME OF LEAGUE, PRIZES OR AWARDS RECEIVED, SITES OF TOURNAMENTS, ETC.)

11. Did you, after completion of your high school eligibility in your sport, and before graduation from high school, participate in any All-Star football or men's basketball games? _____
    (IF SO, STATE SPORT, CITY AND STATE, SPONSOR, DATES, ETC.)

12. Did you, after graduation from high school, and before entering college, participate in any All-Star football or men's basketball games?

    _____
    (IF SO, STATE SPORT, CITY AND STATE, SPONSOR, DATES, ETC.)

I certify, upon penalty of ineligibility for intercollegiate athletics, that the above statements are complete and accurate.

(Signed) _____

(Signed) _____ (Approved) _____
COACH   FOR FACULTY COMMITTEE

Exhibit 2-1 Statement of Eligibility (*Source:* Big Ten Conference)

2.11   Grade Point Average

To represent an institution in intercollegiate athletics, a student must be admitted in accordance with the university's regular admissions standards. Additionally, to be eligible for intercollegiate competition and athletic financial aid for the first academic year, the student must graduate from high school with a 2.0 average. The NCAA defines a student with a 2.0 average as

> one who is a high school graduate and at the time of graduation from high school presented an accumulative six, seven or eight semesters' minimum grade-point average of 2.0 (based on a maximum of 4.0) as certified on the high school transcript or by official correspondence. [*1985–86 NCAA Manual*, Bylaw 5-1-(j)]

An incoming freshman who was actively recruited but did not have the minimum 2.0 would be ineligible for athletic financial aid, regular season competition, or practice for one academic year (*1985–86 NCAA Manual*, Bylaw 5-1-[j]-[2]). Even a student who was not recruited would be ineligible for one academic year if he or she were not a 2.0 qualifier. During that year, a minimum of 24 academic credits must be completed for the student to be considered eligible for participation the following year.

A student-athlete who is a 2.0 nonqualifier can receive a nonathletic financial aid award. The minimum of a 2.0 qualifier merely attempts to ensure the principle of amateurism by restricting college sports to students prepared to attend college. This principle is continued in requiring student-athletes to satisfactorily complete stipulated credit hours in a semester and academic year.

At the 1983 NCAA convention, the membership strengthened eligibility standards, specifically the 2.0 rule. It amended Bylaw 5-1-(j) to read (effective August 1, 1986):

> A qualifier as used herein is defined as one who is a high school graduate and at the time of graduation from high school presented an accumulative minimum grade-point average of 2.0

(based on a maximum of 4.0) in a core curriculum of at least 11 academic courses including at least three years in English, two years in mathematics, two years in social science and two years in natural or physical science (including at least one laboratory class, if offered by the high school) as certified on the high school transcript or by official correspondence, as well as a 700 combined score on the SAT verbal and math sections or a 15 composite score on the ACT.

The intent of this strengthening was to establish a specific core curriculum for which a student must present a minimum grade point average of 2.0 in high school, as well as to add for the first time minimum SAT and ACT scores in order for the athlete to become eligible for competition the student's first year at a Division I institution.

This revision was proposed by the American Council on Education, which is composed of university chief executive officers, and was sponsored at the convention through the NCAA Council. It was strongly opposed by the delegates from schools educating primarily black students. These schools believed that the new minimum requirements would discriminate against them and their student-athletes because they have traditionally educated students who initially may have low grade point averages and SAT and ACT scores. Questions by these schools were also raised on the floor of the convention concerning the validity of using SAT and ACT scores as a testing measure. These tests have been questioned before in relation to their possible bias in favor of white, middle-class high school students. The three-year period before implementation of this new eligibility standard in 1986 will be used to evaluate the complaints leveled against the new standards.

Parish v. National Collegiate Athletic Ass'n., 361 F. Supp. 1220 (W.D. La. 1973), *aff'd* 506 F.2d 1028 (5th Cir. 1975)

Plaintiff college basketball players sought injunctive relief to prevent member institutions from enforcing an NCAA rule that declared players ineligible if they did not predict a grade point average of 1.6 when entering college. The court held that the 1.6 rule limiting eligibility did not raise a federal question under the Civil Rights Act, that it had a substantial relation to a legitimate state interest, and that it was not in violation of equal protection or due process. The court ruled there was no restriction of constitutional rights that required judicial intervention for a rule that was enacted and implemented by a private, voluntary organization.

Jones v. Wichita State University, 698 F. 2d 1082 (10th Cir. 1983)

Plaintiff appellant basketball player Ozell Jones appealed from the district court's denial of a preliminary injunction. Jones had sued Wichita State University (WSU) and the National Collegiate Athletic Association (NCAA), seeking to enjoin them from declaring him ineligible to practice and compete for the WSU varsity basketball team.

The NCAA is a voluntary, unincorporated association of 870 colleges, which regulates much of the nation's intercollegiate athletics. The NCAA requires high school students to graduate with a 2.0 or better GPA to be eligible to compete in Division I collegiate athletics in their freshman year. The NCAA requires each high school to calculate the student's GPA in the same manner as the GPA would be calculated for all students at the high school. Jones's GPA, including physical education, was 2.38. Without the physical education grades, Jones's GPA was 1.59.

Near the end of the basketball season during Jones's sophomore year, the Missouri Valley Conference (of which Wichita State is a member) discovered that Jones's participation on the WSU basketball team may have been in violation of the 2.0 rule. Jones's high school did not normally include physical education in the computation of students' GPA's. On March 2,

1981, WSU declared Jones ineligible to compete on its varsity basketball team for an entire year. The trial court granted Jones a temporary restraining order that allowed him to continue competing pending a full hearing. The full hearing was held on March 12, 1981, and the trial court ruled that while a federal question existed within the purview of the Fourteenth Amendment, Jones had not demonstrated a likelihood of success on the merits. His motion for a preliminary injunction was denied.

The court of appeals disagreed with the trial court's holding that Jones's suit presented a substantial federal question. Citing *Wiley* v. *National Collegiate Athletic Ass'n.* (see Section 2.15-1(d), Note 1), the court held that ". . . the suits of student-athletes displeased with high school athletic associations or NCAA rules do not present substantial federal questions." The court of appeals also held that even if Jones's suit did present a federal question, the denial of Jones's motion for a preliminary injunction must prevail.

Jones challenged the 2.0 rule on equal protection grounds, charging that leaving the computation of the GPA to each high school constitutes a violation of the Fourteenth Amendment by creating disparate classes. Jones contended that because the computation of GPA's is left to each high school, and some include physical education grades in the computation while others do not, students may be ineligible "although they had the same academic achievement . . . as their counterparts who are eligible under that standard."

Jones conceded that the proper equal protection analysis is the rationality test rather than the strict scrutiny test because he is not a member of a suspect class. Therefore, the 2.0 rule must bear some reasonable relationship to its legitimate purposes. An NCAA official testified:

> The purposes of the 2.0 rule were to reduce the possibility of the exploitation of young athletes through the recruiting of athletes who will not be representative of an institution's student body and will probably be unable to meet the necessary

academic requirements for a degree, to foster the image of collegiate athletics as sports engaged in by athletes who are first and primarily college students, and as a recognition of the possibility that any student who cannot meet the requirements of the Rule should not engage in athletics during his freshman year but should devote his full time to study. [R. Vol. I, Morgan Affadavit at 22]

The court of appeals held these objectives to be permissible.

Jones argued that the NCAA, not each individual high school, should set the standards for the computation of high school GPA's. But the NCAA pointed out, and the court agreed, that the NCAA "does not, and should not, tell the high schools what courses or curriculum they should utilize in figuring the GPA's of their own students." Thus the NCAA has left the computation of GPA's with the high schools, on the premise, with which the court agrees, that the schools are in a better position to make this type of substantive determination. Accordingly, the court of appeals affirmed the judgment of the trial court which denied Jones's motion for a preliminary injunction.

NOTES

1. In an attempt to guarantee academic achievement for their student-athletes, a number of high schools have adopted grade point average standards. These rules serve the dual purpose of assuring sufficient academic progress and that the student-athlete is eligible for participation in intercollegiate athletics as an incoming freshman. For further information on the subject of high school academic requirements see Section 1.22-3, Note 3.

2. NCAA Bylaw 5–1–(j) formerly required that incoming freshmen predict their ability to maintain a 1.6 grade point average. The 1.6 prediction was based on a combination of high school grades or rank in class, and the Scholastic Aptitude Test score. The 1.6 rule was in effect from 1966 to 1973 and was subsequently changed to a 2.0 rule, which is just based on grades.

3. In *Associated Students, Inc. v. National Collegiate Athletic Ass'n.*, 493 F. 2d 1251 (9th Cir. 1974), students challenged the 1.6 GPA rule which limited eligibility to athletes who could predict a 1.6 average, regardless of their actual performance in college. The court held there was sufficient state action present to allow judicial review. The purpose of the regulation was to guarantee that only bona fide students would be eligible to participate in intercollegiate athletics in their first year. It also was intended to help discourage recruiting violations and to encourage weak students to concentrate on developing proper study skills prior to being involved in time-consuming intercollegiate athletics. The court found that the rule was reasonably related to its purposes even as applied to students who had earned a 1.6 GPA after the first year but had failed to predict a 1.6 GPA prior to being admitted to college.

4. Walter Berry, a high school basketball player, and St. John's University filed a federal lawsuit in 1984 against the NCAA, challenging that organization's ruling that Berry was ineligible to play basketball for St. John's because he had not graduated from high school or obtained an equivalency degree. Berry had completed a 24-credit course at St. John's, which qualified him for a degree under New York State regulations, but the program was not recognized by the NCAA. The suit was subsequently dropped when Berry elected to attend a junior college. In 1985, Berry transferred to St. John's where he qualified under NCAA regulations to immediately compete for the 1984–85 season.

5. "Proposal 48" came under increasing criticism as its 1986 implementation date approached. At the 1985 NCAA convention, major changes were proposed for the regulation. See the following articles:

(a) "Research Forecasts Effect of 'No. 48,'" *NCAA News*, August 29, 1984, p. 1.

(b) "Sport Rule Will Bar Able Blacks, NCAA Study Says," *Chronicle of Higher Education*, September 5, 1984, p. 1.

(c) "New Academic Rules Would Hit Blacks Hardest," *NCAA News*, September 10, 1984, p. 1.

(d) "Black-College Chiefs Say Study Backs Their Views, Will Spur Rule Changes," *Chronicle of Higher Education*, September 12, 1984, p. 31.

(e) "Presidents Who Backed Academic Rules for Athletes Seem Ready to Compromise," *Chronicle of Higher Education*, October 10, 1984, p. 1.

(f) " 'Index Score' Sought to Give Athletes Flexibility in Meeting Freshman Eligibility Requirements," *Chronicle of Higher Education*, October 17, 1984, p. 23.

(g) Greene, "The New NCAA Rules of the Game: Academic Integrity or Racism?" 28 *St. Louis University Law Journal* 101 (1984).

(h) Yasser, "The Black Athlete's Equal Protection Case Against the NCAA's New Academic Standards," 19 *Gonzaga Law Review* 83 (1983–84).

2.12 Academic Progress

The general rule for academic eligibility under NCAA rules (Division I) is that a student-athlete, after the first academic year, must maintain satisfactory progress toward a degree based on the member institution's academic rules of eligibility for *all* students, those specific academic eligibility rules adopted by the NCAA, or the athletic conference to which the institution belongs (Bylaw 5–1–j–[6]). The NCAA requires that an athlete must enroll every semester in at least 12 semester or quarter hours, must satisfactorily complete an accumulative total of semester or quarter hours of academic credit equivalent to the completion of at least 12 semester or quarter hours during each of the previous academic terms in academic years in which the student-athlete has been enrolled in a term or terms, or must satisfactorily complete 24 semester or 36 quarter hours since the beginning of the student-athlete's last season of competition, to be eligible for competition (Bylaw 5–1–j–[6]–[ii]). For purposes of this provision, a student-athlete shall meet the "satisfactory completion" requirement by maintaining a grade point average that places the student-athlete in good academic standing as established by the institution for all students who are at an equivalent stage of progress toward a degree (Bylaw 5–1–j–[6]–[ii]). All minimum credit hours earned to satisfy these requirements must be in a specific baccalaureate degree program (Bylaw 5–1–j–[6]–[iii]). A student-athlete shall designate a program of studies leading toward a specific baccalaureate degree at the certifying institution by the beginning of the third year of enrollment (fifth semester or seventh quarter) (Bylaw 5–1–j–[6]–[iv]). Correspondence courses are not included in the determination of academic eligibility unless the courses were completed at the school the student-athlete was last enrolled as a full-time student.

The academic progress requirement was adopted by the NCAA in August 1981 in an effort to fight the major problem of student-athletes taking the required number of credit hours necessary to maintain eligibility but not enrolling in the type of courses necessary to satisfy degree requirements. The NCAA rule is general in nature, and many individual conferences have established stricter academic guidelines to deal with this problem at their member institutions.

Allied conferences may decide their own eligibility standards as long as they meet the NCAA's minimum requirement. For example, even before it became an NCAA requirement, the Big Ten Conference Committee on Academic Progress and Eligibility declared that a student "must have earned at least 24 semester hours or 36 quarter hours which are acceptable toward meeting requirements for the student's baccalaureate degree objective" to be eligible for competition during the second school year of residence (Big Ten Conference, Rule 3–2–B). In addition, an "official interpretation" of the above rule states that "The Academic Progress and Eligibility Committee shall not grant eligibility for a second season of competition to a student who has earned less than 18 semester hours or 27 quarter hours." On entering the third year, the Big Ten requires 51 semester hours or 77 quarter hours. In the fourth year, at least 78 semester hours or 117 quarter hours are required to maintain athletic eligibility. (See *Handbook of Intercollegiate [Big Ten] Conference,* Sept. 1983, p. 27, Rule 3, Section 2.)

Another conference that has a stricter academic progress standard is the Pacific Coast Athletic Conference (Pac-10), which requires the same number of credits entering year two (24 semester or 36 quarter hours), but expressly stipulates that the courses must have been passed. This requirement is only implied in the Big Ten rules. Additionally, the Pac-10 requires that a student-athlete participating in a sport after the fall term must have completed and passed a minimum of 12 units (hours). The student-athlete is ineligible if any of these units are "conditional" or "incomplete," and must receive a letter grade showing passing marks prior to the granting of eligibility. (See *Handbook of the Pacific-10 Conference 1983–84,* p. 8, Article 3, Section 4.

Hall v. University of Minnesota, 530 F. Supp. 104 (D.Minn. 1982)

Plaintiff, a former basketball player, brought suit against the University of Minnesota for its failure to admit him to a degree-granting program, which resulted in his being ineligible to play basketball in his senior year. Big Ten Athletic Conference rules require an athlete to be enrolled in such a degree-granting program to maintain eligibility.

Hall had been enrolled in an associate-degree program for three seasons and upon application into a bachelor's level program was rejected. The university claimed that Hall had failed to meet the required academic criteria for admittance. Plaintiff contended that he had been deprived of due process in relation to the rejection. The university had initially accepted plaintiff's application but because of misconduct charges leveled against Hall in a confidential memorandum from a university official, admissions authorities reversed their decision. Plaintiff claimed that he had neither been notified of any allegations nor given a chance to respond and had, therefore, been denied due process.

The court found in favor of Hall, stating that a constitutionally protected interest was involved in the case and Hall's due process rights had been violated. The court found that the interest, "although ostensibly academic, is the plaintiff's ability to obtain a 'no-cut' contract with the National Basketball Association." The court noted that it had no hesitation in stating that the underlying reason for the plaintiff's desire to be enrolled in a degree program at the defendant university is the enhancement of his chances of becoming a professional basketball player. The court added that Hall was recruited to be "a basketball player and not a scholar" and that "his academic record reflects that he has lived up to those expectations as do the academic records of many of the athletes presented to this court." The court also felt that the case was more like an expulsion case than one of nonadmission since the ramifications of his rejection included the loss of scholarship rights, an inability to enroll at another college without suffering a one-year loss of athletic eligibility under existing transfer rules, and the exemption from registration at day classes at the University of Minnesota.

The court reaffirmed its application of due process, suggesting that it extended beyond a student's interest to the fact that plaintiff's lack of admission to a degree-granting program and resulting ineligibility would pose a "substantial threat" to his opportunity and ability to sign a professional basketball contract. Under this analysis, Hall had been denied due process as guaranteed by the Constitution. In response, the court not only ordered the restoration of Hall's scholarship money, but also mandated his immediate acceptance into a degree-granting program.

Wilson v. Intercollegiate (Big Ten) Conference, Etc., 668 F. 2d 962 (7th Cir. 1982)

Dave Wilson enrolled at Fullerton Junior College in 1977. In his first football game, prior to attending any classes, he was injured and did not play for the rest of the season. The coach advised him to drop out of Fullerton and assured him that he would still have four years of playing eligibility remaining. Wilson reenrolled at Fullerton the following year; he attended classes and played football in 1978–79 and 1979–80.

Following Wilson's first full junior college football season in 1978–79, he was recruited by the University of Illinois. After completing his second full year at Fullerton, he transferred to Illinois. Upon arriving at Illinois, he was informed he would have only one year of eligibility because he had played in a game during the 1977 season. He was also told that he would have to acquire senior academic year status before playing. Under Big Ten Conference rules, because he had not received a hardship waiver after being injured in the first game of the 1977–78 season, he had used three years of playing eligibility while playing at Fullerton. Since he had completed only two years of school, Wilson was in violation of the Big Ten's "insufficient academic progress rule," which requires that a specific number of credits be accumulated in order for an athlete to be eligible for each successive playing season. Because of those alleged rule violations, the conference's faculty representatives who govern Big Ten athletics ruled that Wilson would be eligible for one season only.

In response, Wilson brought suit against the NCAA, Big Ten, and University of Illinois. He charged that the faculty representatives had illegally overruled their own eligibility committee, which had originally determined that he would be eligible for two seasons at Illinois. Wilson also contended that he should have been granted a hearing regarding the determination of his eligibility. In addition, Wilson charged that the NCAA rules regarding transfers are discriminatory in that they apply only to Division I institutions. Division II and III colleges allow two-year college transfers who have lost a year due to injury to make up that year through the acquisition of an injury hardship waiver.

In addressing alleged academic progress violations, the plaintiff argued that NCAA eligibility requirements regarding academic progress are intended to ensure a level of academic achievement for all athletes. In this case, considering the circumstances and the fact that he had submitted transcripts and records of his academic performance, which demonstrated that he was a "serious sudent," the application of the rule was unnecessary.

Under several temporary court injunctions, Wilson was allowed to play football for the 1980 season. Wilson ultimately won the case, and although the Big Ten subsequently unsuccessfully appealed to the state supreme court, it held fast to its decision to grant Wilson only one full year of eligibility instead of the two he desired.

At the end of the 1980 season, the Big Ten began an investigation of the Wilson case and discovered irregularities in the evidence submitted to the conference for its determination of Wilson's eligibility to play football at a Division I institution. The conference found that the university had provided the Big Ten with inaccurate information not only about his high school records (an incorrect high school transcript was submitted) but also about his academic intentions at Illinois. While Illinois claimed no intentional wrongdoing was committed and that the error was a result of a case of mistaken identity, the Big Ten contended that if such information was submitted accidentally, the university had all the correct information necessary to correct any misimpressions or inaccuracies. Because the university failed to correct its mistakes until after a favorable injunction was granted, the conference imposed a three-year probation against the university, a two-year ban on postseason competition for all sports, and a two-year exclusion from sharing Big Ten revenue from televised and championship events.

The university argued that the penalty was too stiff and threatened to withdraw from the conference. After several months of negotiations between the parties, the conference reduced the penalty to a one-year probation, a one-year ban on postseason play, and a one-year exclusion from sharing revenue from television and postseason games.

Wilson filed a suit against the Big Ten seeking compensatory and punitive damages, claiming that his chances for a professional career were damaged by the conference's decision to grant him only one year of eligibility. The Big Ten had the case moved to the federal courts, where a summary judgment in favor of the conference was granted. Wilson appealed, and a federal appeals court found in his favor. An attempt by the Big Ten to bring the case to the Supreme Court failed, and the suit was returned to an Illinois state court for the determination of Wilson's claims. Wilson, having been refused eligibility for the 1981 football season, left Illinois and pursued a career in professional football.

NOTES ────────────────────

1. Mark Hall was a difficult problem for Minnesota academic officials. Thomas C. Buckley, then associate dean of the General College and Hall's freshman adviser, noted in an affidavit filed with the suit:

I saw problems right from the outset. I had never encountered a student-athlete who seemed so indifferent toward academics. . . . Mr. Hall demonstrated such an extensive disregard for, and disinterest in, the academic process, that I was compelled to include in a letter to coach Jim Dutcher a lengthy statement regarding Mr. Hall's situation. . . .

He did not want to take any fifth-hour classes because that would cause him to miss lunch, nor would he take a sixth-hour class because he would have to rush his lunch. Because of basketball practice, he could not take classes after the sixth hour. Mr. Hall also informed me that he did not want to take any classes outside of Nicholson Hall because he did not want to walk between buildings, and he severely limited any choice of courses by indicating that he did not want to be in any classes with other basketball players.

David Ekstrand, then educational skills counselor for the athletic department, noted in an affidavit:

Hall maintained the passing credits and GPA necessary to qualify for eligibility requirements until the spring of his junior year. At that time, Hall had 96 passing credits and a GPA of 1.44. In order to be eligible this fall, he had to go to summer school to raise his credit total to 117 and his GPA to 1.85. He also had to be accepted by a degree-granting program at the University of Minnesota. . . .

I had never seen an athlete with that poor of a record get into the Baccalaureate Program. . . . In my 12 years as the educational skills adviser, I have worked closely with hundreds of student-athletes at the University of Minnesota. Mr. Hall has been the most frustrating student-athlete, from an academic point of view, with whom I have worked.

For further details, see "Basketball in a Different Court," *Boston Globe*, January 31, 1982, p. 61.

2. For further information on the *Hall* and *Wilson* cases, see the following articles:
(a) "Court Orders U. of Minnesota to Admit Athlete to Degree Program," *Chronicle of Higher Education*, January 13, 1982, p. 5.
(b) "Illinois Quarterback Challenges the NCAA's Web

of Rules," *Chronicle of Higher Education*, January 19, 1981, p. 7.
(c) "Men's Athletic Program Put on 3-Year Probation at Illinois," *Chronicle of Higher Education*, May 11, 1981, p. 8.
(d) "Big Ten Conference Reduces Penalties Against U. of Illinois," *Chronicle of Higher Education*, September 2, 1981, p. 6.
(e) "The Big Ten's Big Mess," *Sports Illustrated*, May 25, 1981, p. 79.
(f) "The Mark Hall Case," (six-part series), *Morning Union*, (Springfield, Mass.), February 13–18, 1982. Articles present the hometown newspaper's viewpoint about the recruitment of hometown athletes and their subsequent problems in college.
3. For further information concerning the NCAA and academic rules, see the following articles:
(a) "Clemson U., Hit Hard by Sanctions, to Reform Sports," *Chronicle of Higher Education*, December 1, 1982, p. 13.
(b) "NCAA Names Independent Panel to Find 'Practical Solutions' to Sports Problems," *Chronicle of Higher Education*, August 11, 1982, p. 1.
(c) "26 University Presidents to Probe Sports Abuses," *Chronicle of Higher Education*, September 1, 1982, p. 27.
(d) "College Presidents' Panel to Ask NCAA to Tighten Academic Rules for Athletes," *Chronicle of Higher Education*, October 6, 1982, p. 19.
(e) "Raising Academic Standards for Athletes Tops Agenda of Sports-Reform Panel," *Chronicle of Higher Education*, October 13, 1982, p. 17.
(f) "Presidents Lobby NCAA Delegates for Tighter Academic Standards," *Chronicle of Higher Education*, Decembver 8, 1982, p. 15.
(g) "Modification of New NCAA Rules Weighed by College Presidents," *Chronicle of Higher Education*, March 9, 1983, p. 1.
(h) "Black Leaders Weigh Proposals to Revise Rules for Athletes," *Chronicle of Higher Education*, March 16, 1983, p. 1.
(i) "Academic Rules Would Affect Blacks Far More Than Whites, Study Finds," *Chronicle of Higher Education*, February 16, 1983, p. 17.
(j) "LSU to Make Sure Its Athletes Remain Students," *Chronicle of Higher Education*, December 1, 1982, p. 15.
(k) "NCAA Toughens Rules, Says Athletes Must Complete 12 Credits Each Term," *Chronicle of Higher Education*, January 19, 1981, p. 1.
(l) "Toner Gives Further Explanation of NCAA Eligibility Standards," *NCAA News*, June 1, 1983, p. 3.
(m) "Black Colleges Threaten Court Action to Alter NCAA's New Academic Rules," *Chronicle of Higher Education*, April 20, 1983, p. 13.
4. For further information on academic cheating and

phony transcripts involving intercollegiate athletics, see "The Writing Is on the Wall," *Sports Illustrated*, May 19, 1980, pp. 39–72.

5. In 1984, as NCAA Bylaw 5–1–(j)–(6)–(iii) concerning academic progress in a major was about to take full effect, a controversy developed concerning the interpretation of the rule. The following article focuses on the eligibility concerns and points out the difficulties involved in interpreting and understanding NCAA rules and regulations.

Robert M. Sweazy, directory of the water-resources center at Texas Tech University and secretary-treasurer of the College Football Association, said many coaches feared that up to 25 per cent of their football players entering their third year this fall could become ineligible.

"Many institutions' programs," he said, "require students to have an elevated grade-point average or to complete extra semester hours to get into them, or are open to just a select number of students. For example, many engineering programs require a 2.5 or 3.0 grade-point average at the junior level. A student could have a 2.3 average, which is good for athletic eligibility, but not be able to declare engineering as a major. It is not fair to place a burden on athletes that is not placed on other students."

Stephen R. Morgan, director of legislative services for the NCAA, says, however, that the association's council has already changed the interpretation. But how it was changed remains unclear. *The NCAA News* reported that "the council affirmed the current interpretation (major must be declared by start of fifth semester or seventh quarter) and agreed to sponsor legislation at the 1985 convention to enable the membership to determine the interpretation it desires."

The next paragraph, however, says that upon the recommendation of the association's academic testing and requirements committee, the interpretation would be "revised to replace references to declaring a major with reference to a 'designated program of studies leading to a baccalaureate degree." All clear? ["Sidelines," *Chronicle of Higher Education*, June 27, 1984, p. 21.

2.13   Transfer Rules

On both the intercollegiate and interscholastic levels of athletic competition, the question of athletes transferring from one institution to another is troublesome and controversial. For the athlete, the issues revolve around the individual's right to attend school and compete in athletics wherever the individual wishes. For the institution and conference, the issues

revolve around illegal recruitment, stability of programs, and a desire to avoid an image of athletes being recruited from one program to another. The following sections discuss in detail the problems and litigation associated with the transfer of athletes.

2.13–1   College Transfer Rules

Under NCAA regulations, an "enrolled student" is one who officially registers and enrolls at one institution and attends the opening day of classes in any quarter or semester with a minimum full-time academic load, one who attends one or more classes without being officially registered, or one who reports for regular squad practice (*1985–86 NCAA Manual*, Bylaw 5–1). A student-athlete who meets any or all of these criteria and then desires to change schools is considered by the NCAA to be a "transfer student."

As a transfer, regardless of the reason for changing schools, the athlete must forego intercollegiate athletic competition for one full year. In the case of Division I schools, the athlete must be enrolled at the new institution for the duration of that year. An exception to this rule is when a student-athlete who meets the 2.0 qualifier transfers from a two-year to a four-year college, having either graduated from the two-year institution or left after completion of the first year with a 2.0 average for a minimum of 24 credits.

Specific requirements of the NCAA for transfers between two four-year institutions and between a junior college and a four-year degree-granting institution for Division I institutions are as follows:

(j) . . .

(4) A transfer student from a four-year institution, who was a 2.0 qualifier or a 2.0 non-qualifier and who attended a four-year institution at least one academic year, shall be eligible for financial aid, regular-season competition and practice in a Division I institution under the rules of the institution and the conference of which the institution is a member.

(5) A transfer student from a four-year institution who was a 2.0 nonqualifier and attended the four-year institution less than one full academic year shall not be eligible for financial aid, regular-season competition and practice in a Division I institution during the first academic year in attendance at the certifying institution. . . .

(7) A transfer student from a four-year institution shall not be eligible for any NCAA championship until the student has fulfilled a residence requirement of one full academic year (two full semesters or three full quarters), and one full calendar year has elapsed from the first regular registration and attendance date at the certifying Division I or Division II institution. . . .

(i) If the first day of classes of the regular academic term (semester or quarter) in which the transfer student would become eligible at the certifying institution is earlier than the completion of the one-calendar-year requirement, and if the student has fulfilled the one-academic year requirement, then the student shall be eligible on that first day of classes.

(ii) If the date of the first scheduled intercollegiate contest falls earlier (between semesters) than the first day of classes of the regular academic term (semester or quarter) in which the student would become eligible, and if the student has fulfilled the one-academic-year requirement, then the student shall be eligible on that playing date.

(8) A transfer student from a junior college who is a 2.0 qualifier is not eligible in Division I institutions for any NCAA championships the first academic year in residence unless the student has:

(i) Graduated from the junior college and has satisfactorily completed a minimum of 48 semester or 72 quarter hours of transferable degree credit acceptable toward any baccalaureate degree program at the certifying institution, or

(ii) Presented a minimum of 24 semester hours or 36 quarter hours of transferable degree credit with an accumulative minimum grade-point average of 2.000, satisfactorily completed an average of at least 12 semester or quarter hours of transferable degree credit acceptable toward any baccalaureate degree program at the certifying institution during each academic term of attendance and spent at least two semesters or

three quarters in residence at the junior college (excluding summer sessions).

(9) A transfer student from a junior college who was a 2.000 nonqualifier is not eligible in Division I institutions for financial aid, practice, regular-season competition and for any NCAA championships the first academic year in residence unless the student has graduated from the junior college and has satisfactorily completed a minimum of 48 semester or 72 quarter hours of transferable degree credit acceptable toward any baccalaureate degree program at the certifying institution. . . .

(k) The student-athlete's eligibility for NCAA championships is affected by, and the student-athlete must conform to, the following additional transfer provisions:

(1) A student who transfers from a junior college after transferring from any four-year college must complete one calendar year of residence at the certifying institution, unless the student:

(i) Has completed a minimum of 24 semester hours or a minimum of 36 quarter hours at the junior college following transfer from the four-year college, and one calendar year has elapsed since the transfer from the first four-year college and, for Division I and Division II member institutions, has graduated from the junior college; or

(ii) Returns to the four-year college from which the student transferred to the junior college, provided the student did not have an unfulfilled residence requirement at the time of the transfer from the four-year college.

(2) If a student-athlete transfers from a four-year institution to a junior college and prior to graduation from junior college enrolls at another four-year institution, the student-athlete shall be subject to the one-year residence requirement, even though during the course of that one-year residence the student-athlete may earn sufficient credits to obtain a degree at the junior college; further, if a junior college student transfers to and attends a four-year institution, the student is subject to the one-year residence requirement of this provision at that institution, even though the student transfers back to the junior college and obtains a degree.

(3) A student who transfers from a collegiate

institution while the student is disqualified or suspended for disciplinary reasons must complete one calendar year of residence at the certifying institution.

(4) Exceptions to the one-calendar-year requirements as specified in Bylaw 5–1–(j)–(7)–(i) and (ii) shall apply to subparagraphs (1), (2) and (3) above.

(5) A transfer student from a foreign collegiate institution (college, university or junior college), except one entering as a bona fide exchange student, shall comply with Bylaw 5–1–(j)–(7). A bona fide foreign exchange student includes one who is sent by the government of the student's nation or is sponsored by the U.S. Department of State, Rotary International, the Ford Foundation, the Institute of International Education or similar organizations.

(6) A transfer student, upon completion of two full semesters or three full quarters of academic work and after a full calendar year has elapsed, shall be eligible for any NCAA championship that is in progress at the time the student completes the respective periods.

(7) In the administration of the various semester or quarter hours of transferable degree credit for a transfer student in accordance with Bylaw 5–1–(j) and its subparagraphs, all grades earned by a student in courses that would be transferable to the certifying institution shall be included in determining whether the student has earned the required average. All grades earned in courses that are not transferable to the certifying institution, irrespective of the grades earned, shall not be included in determining whether the student has earned the required average.

(8) When a student-athlete has been in residence at two or more junior colleges, the terms of residence at all junior colleges may be combined in order to satisfy the residence requirement of Bylaw 5–1–(j). All grades and all course credits that are transferable to the member institution shall be considered in determining the student-athlete's eligibility under Bylaw 5–1.

(9) The eligibility of a transfer student from a branch school which conducts an intercollegiate athletics program shall be determined by the applicable junior college transfer provisions of Bylaws 5–1–(j)–(8), (9), and (10).

(10) A transfer student from a junior college is not eligible for NCAA championship competition in a sport if the student-athlete has competed at the junior college in that sport during the same academic year.

(l) The student-athlete's status as a transfer student shall be based upon the following:

(1) A student shall be considered a transfer from a collegiate institution when its registrar or admissions officer certifies that the student was officially registered and enrolled at said institution on the opening day of classes in any quarter or semester in a minimum full-time academic load, or that the student attended a class or classes in any quarter or semester in which the student was enrolled in a minimum full-time academic load, or the athletics director certifies that the student reported for regular squad practice announced by the institution through any member of its athletics department staff prior to the beginning of any quarter or semester.

(2) A student shall not be considered a transfer:

(i) After enrollment or attendance only at classes in a summer school, night school or extension course;

(ii) After enrollment or attendance only at classes in a branch school, provided the branch school does not conduct an intercollegiate athletics program. If the branch school conducts an intercollegiate athletics program, the transferring student shall not be considered a transfer upon enrollment at the parent institution directly from the branch school.

O.I.502. A branch school is defined as an educational institution which usually offers two years of college work, does not award degrees and is wholly controlled and operated by a four-year, degree-granting parent institution.

(iii) After attendance as a freshman (plebe) only in the official summer enrollment program of the four national service academies.

(m) A transfer student from a four-year collegiate institution is not subject to the residence requirement for NCAA championships under the following conditions:

(1) Upon return to the student's original institution after participation in a cooperative

educational exchange program, provided the student is to receive a baccalaureate degree from the institution from which the student transferred to participate in the exchange program;

(2) Upon return to the student's original institution after attendance of one semester or quarter at another institution for purposes of taking academic courses not available at the original institution;

(3) Upon return to the student's original institution after attendance of one academic year at another collegiate institution in accordance with the program recommended by the appropriate academic officer at the original institution, provided the student was in good academic standing at the time the student left the original institution;

(4) If the NCAA Eligibility Committee concludes that the student is to be enrolled in the certifying institution for a specified period of time as a bona fide exchange student participating in a formal educational exchange program that is an established requirement of the student-athlete's curriculum;

(5) If the NCAA Eligibility Committee concludes that the student changed institutions in order to continue a major course of study because the original institution discontinued the academic program of the student's major;

(6) If the student is an alien who is required to transfer one or more times because of a study program predetermined by the government of the student's nation or the sponsoring educational organization;

(7) Upon return from at least 18 months of active service in the armed forces of the United States or from at least 18 months of active service on an official church mission;

(8) In a particular sport if the student changed institutions in order to continue participation in a sport because the student's original four-year collegiate institution dropped the sport (in which the student has practiced or competed at that institution in intercollegiate competition) from its intercollegiate program or never sponsored the sport on the intercollegiate level while the student was in attendance at the institution, provided the student had never attended any other collegiate institution which offered intercollegiate competition in that particular sport.

(9) In a particular sport if, subsequent to the student's initial attendance at a collegiate institution, the student transfers to the certifying institution from another four-year college and has neither practiced nor competed in that sport in intercollegiate competition, or in organized, noncollegiate, amateur competition while enrolled in a collegiate institution, for a consecutive two-year period immediately prior to the date on which the student begins participating (practice and/or competition) in that sport at the certifying institution.

(10) If the student transfers to the certifying institution and the following conditions are met:

(i) The student-athlete was not recruited per O.I.100,

(ii) No athletically related financial assistance has been received by the student-athlete and

(iii) The student-athlete has neither practiced nor competed in intercollegiate athletics prior to transfer, except that a student-athlete transferring to a Division III institution may have participated in limited preseason tryouts.

(11) In a particular sport at the certifying institution when the student enrolls at a second four-year collegiate institution, does not practice or participate in the particular sport at that second institution and returns to the certifying institution. . . .

(14) If the student transfers to the certifying institution from another four-year collegiate institution and the following conditions are met:

(i) The student has not transferred previously from one four-year college to another four-year college;

(ii) The student did not receive athletically related financial assistance or the student's athletically related financial assistance was not renewed for the ensuing academic year at the previous institution;

(iii) The student is in good academic standing and meets the satisfactory-progress requirements;

(iv) The student's previous institution certifies in writing that it has no objection to the student being granted an exception to the transfer residence requirement, and

(v) The student is a participant in a sport other than football or men's basketball.

(vi) If the student transfers to the certifying institution from a Division III member institution and meets the above conditions, he or she may be eligible to compete but shall not receive institutionally administered financial aid during the first academic year in residence at the certifying institution.

(n) A transfer student from a junior college is not subject to the residence requirement for NCAA championships under the following conditions:

(1) If the NCAA Eligibility Committee concludes that the student changed institutions in order to continue participation in a sport because the student's original junior college dropped the sport from its intercollegiate program or never sponsored the sport on the intercollegiate level while the student was in attendance at the institution, provided the student never attended any other collegiate institution which offered intercollegiate competition in that particular sport and provided the student earned at least a minimum 2.0 grade-point average at the junior college.... [1985–86 *NCAA Manual*, Bylaw 5–1–(j)–(4) to 5–1–(n)]

English v. National Collegiate Athletic Ass'n., 439 So. 2d 1218 (La. Ct. App. 1983)

English was an outstanding high school quarterback who entered Michigan State University in the fall of 1979 on a football scholarship. Realizing that his prospects for playing at Michigan State were poor, due in part to an injury, he enrolled at Allegheny Junior College in Pittsburgh, Pennsylvania. English attended Allegheny during the 1980–81 school year and graduated in the spring. He did not play football for Allegheny during the year he attended. In the fall of 1981, English enrolled at Iowa State University and was on the football team there during the 1981–82 season. Once again deciding that his prospects were poor, he enrolled at Delgado Junior College in New Orleans, where his family resides and where his father had recently taken the position as head football coach at Tulane. English graduated from Delgado in the spring,

and in August 1983 enrolled at Tulane, where he sought to play football.

While he was at Iowa State, English came across a copy of a booklet entitled "NCAA Guide for the College-Bound Student-Athlete." His attention was drawn to a particular section on eligibility:

> A student who transfers to an NCAA member institution from a junior college after transferring from any four-year college must complete one calendar year of residence at the NCAA member institution in order to be eligible for NCAA championships or post-season football games, unless the student has completed a minimum of 24 semesters or 36 quarter hours at the junior college following the student's transfer from the four-year college and also has graduated from the junior college, and one calendar year has elapsed since the transfer from first four-year college.

Although English was aware of the NCAA policy of prohibiting athletes from playing for different colleges in successive years, he interpreted "first four-year college" as Michigan State and not Iowa State. English called his father at Tulane and asked him "if there was any possibility that he could be eligible at Tulane" after explaining how he had found the wording in the "student handbook" and his interpretation of the "first four-year college" language. A day or two later, Coach English, having read the NCAA manual, called Ralph Peterson, Tulane's NCAA liaison person. Coach English asked him if a player who had attended a four-year institution for a year and then attended a junior college would be eligible to play for Tulane. When given an affirmative response, he reported to his son, "it was our feeling it was a good possibility he could be eligible."

At this point English moved to New Orleans and enrolled at Delgado. In April or May, coach English broached the subject with Tulane's athletic director, Hindman Wall. Wall told coach English there was no way his son could be eligible, but nevertheless agreed to contact the NCAA for a ruling. A letter from

Peterson to the NCAA in April was answered by a staff person, who flatly stated plaintiff was ineligible to play for Tulane in 1983. In May, Wall signed a letter prepared by English's then counsel and in Tulane's name, advocating English's position to the NCAA. This resulted in a telephone conference between the English advocates and a five-person Administrative Committee of the NCAA. English's position was thoroughly considered and rejected by the committee. On July 15, the president of Tulane wrote the NCAA president and requested reconsideration by the Administrative Committee. This request was granted, and the committee again ruled English ineligible. English appealed this ruling to the NCAA Council, which heard his case on August 17, 1983. The council affirmed his ineligibility. In the meantime, on August 7, English had begun to practice with the Tulane freshmen, an action that precluded him from returning to Iowa State to play football.

English brought suit contending that (1) he had been denied due process, (2) the NCAA's actions had been capricious, arbitrary, unfair, and discriminatory, (3) he was the beneficiary of a stipulation pour autrui between Tulane and the NCAA, which had been breached, (4) the NCAA was equitably estopped from declaring him ineligible, and (5) the NCAA had operated as a monopoly in violation of Louisiana law which prohibits combinations in restraint of trade.

English argued that his due process rights had been violated because the NCAA did not adequately inform him of the rules regarding his eligibility. He argued that the rule as quoted in the NCAA guide literally entitled him to play football with Tulane in 1983 because a year had elapsed since his transfer from the first four-year college, Michigan State, in 1980. He attacked the interpretation placed on the rule by the NCAA as being unreasonable in defining "first" to be the last four-year college. He argued further that the guide's reference to residence and semester hours completed at junior colleges further

confused the transfer rule and created additional ambiguity. Finally, he rejected the notion that he should have sought further interpretation of the rule as recommended by the guide in the introduction because it was clear to him that he was eligible.

The court found from the testimony of English's father that there had been a question in English's mind about his eligibility from the very beginning, notwithstanding the way he wanted to read the rule. He was aware of the NCAA policy of preventing a student from playing for different colleges in successive years. He was also instructed by the guide to contact the NCAA national office for answers but failed to do so, instead embarking on a course he knew to be perilous.

The court found that the rule contemplated two colleges — the first and second. A student-athlete who plays for a college one year cannot play for another college the next. The rule does not and need not concern itself with what the court described as "the bizarre situation where one had played for yet a third college in the distant past."

The court rejected English's argument that the NCAA's action was arbitrary or capricious. The court found that the NCAA, in adopting and implementing the transfer rule at issue, acted reasonably in its efforts to prevent players from jumping from one school to another. The court also rejected English's claim of discrimination. The court found that English's case was unique and that English had failed to produce proof of any case like his which would provide a basis for the charge.

The court rejected English's contention that he was a third-party beneficiary of a contract between the NCAA and Tulane. The principle that a contract made for the benefit of a third party is binding if the third party avails himself of the advantage has no application if the benefit derived is merely incidental to the contract. Tulane joined the NCAA long before English came on the scene, and the court held that whatever benefits may flow to a player like English are purely incidental to the benefits flowing to the schools.

The court also rejected English's claim that because he had relied on the literal interpretation of the guide's section on eligibility, the NCAA was equitably estopped from enforcing its own interpretation. The court held that the guide's language describing "first four-year college" could not be construed as English contended. Since English had questions in his mind, concerning the language, he was obliged by the guide's introduction to check with the NCAA before embarking on a transfer; in not doing so, his reliance was not reasonable.

Finally, the court rejected the argument that the NCAA was a monopoly in violation of Louisiana Monopolies Law because the NCAA was not engaged in interstate commerce. Even if it were, the court stated, "the NCAA transfer rule is a reasonable one deserving to be enforced."

Gulf South Conference v. Boyd, 369 So. 2d 553 (Ala. 1979)

Julian Boyd entered Livingston University (Alabama) in the fall of 1975 on a full grant-in-aid football scholarship and played during the 1975 football season. The grant-in-aid was for only one year and was renewable at the institution's discretion. During the one-year period, both the institution and Boyd fulfilled all of their commitments. At the end of the 1975–76 school year, Livingston coach Jack Crowe sent Boyd a written offer to renew his scholarship for the 1976–77 academic year, which Boyd rejected. Boyd told Crowe that for personal reasons he chose not to return.

Instead, Boyd decided to live with his father in Alabama and attended Enterprise State Junior College (ESJC). After graduating from ESJC, Boyd then enrolled at Troy State University. However, when he attempted to play football at Troy, he was ruled ineligible to compete by the commissioner of the Gulf South Conference (GSC) because of the GSC's restrictive transfer rule (see below). Livingston University and Troy State University are both members of the GSC, which is an unincorporated voluntary athletic association organized by nine colleges and universities. Troy State appealed the decision to the Faculty Appeals Committee of the GSC. The committee affirmed the decision of the commissioner.

The following GSC eligibility rules were at issue:

GSC Bylaws, Article VI, Section 7: A student-athlete who transfers from one GSC school to another will not be eligible to participate in any sport at the second school unless (1) the first one drops that sport and all other GSC rules are complied with, or (2) if the student qualifies under Bylaws Article V, Section 3, B or C, or (3) Article VIII, Section 3.

GSC Bylaws, Article V, Section 3(B) and (C): Transfers are students who enter college after having been registered at another college. (Summer school excepted.)

(B) Any student who has attended a GSC school but has not been recruited in any way, has not signed a pre-enrollment application, has received no financial aid, and has not participated, would be a transfer upon attending any other GSC school.

(C) When a GSC member does not renew the grant-in-aid of an eligible athlete according to NCAA Constitution 3–4(d), the athlete becomes a free agent and may be signed by any other GSC school as a transfer.

GSC Bylaws, Article VIII, Section 3: A student-athlete who signs a pre-enrollment application with one GSC school, that is duly processed with the GSC Commissioner, cannot participate with any other GSC school except: A prospective athlete who does not accept the grant-in-aid at that school or participate becomes a free agent at the end of two (2) years and can be signed by any GSC school.

In 1977, Boyd brought suit seeking a declaratory judgment from the court that he was eligible to compete in football at Troy State. The GSC moved to dismiss the action on the grounds that the lower court lacked jurisdiction and that Boyd's claim failed to state grounds on which relief could be granted. Boyd was unsuccessful in obtaining a decision allowing him to compete at Troy State in 1977–78.

However, the trial judge found that Boyd was entitled to participate in varsity football at Troy State for the 1978–79 season as long as Boyd was a student in good standing. GSC appealed and relied on *Scott* v. *Kilpatrick*, 286 Ala. 129, 237 So. 2d 652 (1970), which involved a high school athletic association transfer rule. In *Scott*, the complainant contended that the transfer rule of the high school athletic association was unconstitutional since the student-athlete's desire to compete in high school football involved a property right. The denied property right was alleged to be the opportunity for the student to compete for a college football scholarship. The court found that participation in high school athletics was a privilege and not a property right.

In the Boyd case, the court distinguished the *Scott* ruling, since Boyd involved college football. The court found a college scholarship to be a property right of present and definite economic value; whereas, for a high school player the possibility of receiving a college scholarship offer was too speculative to be recognized as a property right.

Additionally, GSC appealed on the grounds that the lower court did not have jurisdiction over the Boyd case because of the general perception that the courts should not interfere with the internal affairs of private associations. The court held that this did not apply in the Boyd case, because it was a situation involving a dispute between an individual college athlete and the athletic association. The athlete is not a member of the association, as is the institution, and therefore the "freedom of association" principle does not apply. The athlete has no bargaining position with the association, yet stands to be substantially affected by its decisions. The court felt that there is jurisdiction when the voluntary association is so dominant in its field that the membership is not voluntary but is a necessity.

The GSC also appealed on the grounds that the lower court's decision was erroneous because it was contrary to the terms of the GSC's transfer rule. The court found this position to be untenable, as the evidence showed Boyd to be eligible under two other GSC bylaws — Article V, Section 3(C) and Article VIII, Section 3. These bylaws made Boyd a free agent since he had refused the grant-in-aid from Livingston and had not played football for two years.

The appeals court found that the relationship between a college athlete who accepts an athletic scholarship and the college which awards the scholarship is contractual in nature. The judgment of the lower court was affirmed, and Boyd was granted eligibility.

NOTES

1. In *Williams* v. *Hamilton*, 497 F. Supp. 641 (D.N.H. 1980), plaintiff college student-athlete challenged the National Association of Intercollegiate Athletics (NAIA) transfer rule requiring him to be in residence at his new college for 16 weeks before becoming eligible for intercollegiate athletics. The rule was imposed, in part, to prevent "tramp athletes" from transferring from school to school for the sole purpose of participating in sports. The court held that the transfer rule was valid and did not deny due process or equal protection guarantees.

2. In *Weiss* v. *Eastern College Athletic Conference*, 563 F. Supp. 192 (E.D. Pa. 1983), an action was brought by Weiss, a tennis player who had transferred from Arizona State to the University of Pennsylvania. Weiss brought suit claiming the one-year loss of eligibility transfer rule violated antitrust law because the practice constituted a group boycott. Weiss also contended that as applied to this case, the rule did not fulfill its intended purpose of preventing the exploitation of college athletes by coaches attempting to raid other institutions. Weiss was neither recruited by the University of Pennsylvania nor given an athletic scholarship. The court denied the request for an injunction, finding that Weiss had not offered sufficient evidence that he would be irreparably harmed if the injunction were denied.

3. Bylaw 5–3–(f) in the *1985–86 NCAA Manual* provides for the waiving of the residence requirement for a student-athlete who transfers to a member institution for reasons of health. The institution to which the athlete has transferred is responsible for securing the waiver and must support its case by medical recommendations of that institution's team physician and/or the student-athlete's personal physician. Several universities have been successful in obtaining a waiver for a student-athlete who has

transferred for medical reasons.

4. For more information concerning the increase in the number of student-athletes who are transferring from colleges and the attendant problems, see the following articles:

(a) "The Power of Transfer," *Boston Globe*, January 16, 1983, p. 61.

(b) "Women's Sports Organization Limits Eligibility of Transfer Students with Athletic Scholarships," *Chronicle of Higher Education*, January 19, 1981, p. 7.

(c) Comment, "*Williams* v. *Hamilton*: Constitutional Protection of the Student-Athlete," 8 *Journal of College and University Law* 399 (1982).

2.13–2   High School Transfer Rules

High school athletic associations may restrict eligibility for student transfers in one of two ways. Some schools, in an effort to limit abuse, apply blanket restrictions on all students who change schools, regardless of their reasons. This approach is often overrestrictive and unduly harsh. Even so, such rules are often upheld by the courts, and plaintiffs have failed to gain judicial relief. The rules are said to be reasonably related to alleviating recruiting problems, and the courts are reluctant to get involved with private voluntary association matters.

In other high school athletic associations, eligibility is restricted but with exceptions. Exceptions are granted to students who transfer schools for reasons unrelated to athletics; they have immediate eligibility upon enrollment at the new school. Inherent in any rule that restricts eligibility with specific exceptions is the potential for inconsistency and abuse in the decision-making process. Therefore, many high school athletic associations simply find it easier to require all new students to meet a residency time period before participating in athletics.

Since there are problems with both blanket restrictions and exceptions on a case-by-case basis, some high school athletic associations have taken a third approach. The Massachusetts Interscholastic Athletic Association has allowed a number of transfer students to be eligible immediately if they meet certain criteria. To qualify for immediate eligibility, the student-athlete must not have participated on the varsity level of that sport at the previous school, and the transfer must occur prior to the start of practice in the sport. A student who fails to meet these criteria must forfeit athletic eligibility for one year.

Kentucky High School Athletic Ass'n. v. Hopkins County Board of Education, 552 S.W. 2d 685 (Ky. Ct. App. 1977)

Plaintiff Todd Shadowen, a high school student, sought a permanent injunction to stop the Kentucky High School Athletic Association (KHSAA) from denying him eligibility to participate in interscholastic athletic events during the 1976–77 school year. Shadowen's parents were divorced. Legal custody was granted to Todd's mother, who moved with Todd to a new residence where Todd was enrolled in high school and played varsity sports. In May 1976, for personal reasons, Shadowen moved from his mother's to his father's residence and enrolled in another school. He sought to compete in interscholastic sports and was denied eligibility on the basis of a KHSAA transfer rule that read:

> Any student who has represented a secondary school in a first team game in any sport and who changes schools with or without a corresponding change in the residence of his parents shall be ineligible for thirty-six school weeks. If there is a corresponding change in the residence of the parents, the Commissioner may waive the penalty in any case where there is evident injustice.

After an unsuccessful appeal of the ruling to the association, Shadowen sought and obtained an injunction. The KHSAA appealed.

The court of appeals stated that there were two questions that had to be answered — first, the validity of the transfer rule, and second, the reasonableness of the interpretation of the rule as applied to the plaintiff. The court found the rule was not invalid and referred to language found in *Bruce* v. *South Carolina High School League.*

In contending that, since they were not recruited

and the rule was designed to prevent recruiting, it should not apply to them, respondents confuse the reasons which prompted the adoption of the rule with the method adopted to accomplish the desired goal. Prohibitive administrative difficulties, as well as others, resulting from a determination in each case of the reason prompting the transfer could have properly influenced the member schools to decide that the best method to accomplish the elimination of the evil of recruiting was to bind themselves to adherence to a rule without exceptions or qualifications. The merits of such a rule or the wisdom of its adoption are not for the courts to determine.

Even though it adhered to this language, the court did discuss the relative arbitrariness of the rule as it applied to the plaintiff, especially in view of its determination that Shadowen's transfer was not related to athletics. Under Bylaw 6, the association's commissioner may waive the transfer rule "where there is evident injustice," if the student is transferring because of a change in the residence of the parents. If there is no change in the residence of the parents, the commissioner is allowed no discretion in the transfer rule's application. This objective standard was enacted by the association rather than adopting a procedure that would require a subjective inquiry into the motives of every transfer. If there is no change of residence by the parents, the transfer rule cannot be waived. If a student transfers because of a change in the residence, the transfer is involuntary since the student has no real choice but to follow the change of residence by the parents.

The court found the association did not act arbitrarily in applying the same rule when there was a change in legal custody of a student between divorced parents. If there is no change in the residence of either parent, there can be a question raised regarding the motive for the change in custody. In the Shadowen case, the plaintiff was not compelled to change his residence because of a reason beyond his control. The change of custody was the result of Shadowen's own wishes. Therefore, the court

found that the association did not act arbitrarily in applying the transfer rule to Shadowen and held that the injunction issued by the lower court must be reversed.

Walsh v. Louisiana High School Athletic Ass'n., 616 F. 2d 152 (5th Cir. 1980)

Plaintiffs, parents of student-athletes, brought this action on behalf of their children against the Louisiana High School Athletic Association (LHSAA). The suit alleged that the LHSAA's transfer rule unduly burdened their First Amendment right to the free exercise of their religion and deprived them of their Fourteenth Amendment right of equal protection. The U.S. District Court (E.D. La.) ruled the transfer rule unconstitutional. The U.S. Court of Appeals reversed the lower court's decision noting that:

The LHSAA is a voluntary association of public, private, and parochial high schools in the State of Louisiana . . . it promulgates and enforces various rules and regulations governing the competitive athletic activities of its members. The LHSAA promulgated one such rule in an effort to discourage or eliminate the recruitment of promising young athletes upon graduation from elementary or junior high schools. This rule provides in relevant part that, upon the completion of elementary or junior high school, a student is eligible to participate immediately in interscholastic athletic competition only at a high school within his home district. These home districts are the geographical areas designated as the attendance zones for the public high schools by the local school boards of the State of Louisiana. The home district for a private or parochial school is the geographical attendance zone of the public school in which the private or parochial school is situated. Under the transfer rule, a student is ineligible to participate in interscholastic athletic competition for a period of one year if he matriculates at a high school outside of his home district after completing elementary or junior high school.

Lutheran High School is the only high school in the greater New Orleans metropolitan area that is owned and operated by members of the Lutheran

Church Missouri Synod. There are seven Lutheran-affiliated elementary or junior high schools in the greater New Orleans area. However, none of these elementary or junior high schools are located in Lutheran High School's designated home district. As a result, any student who enrolls at Lutheran High School upon graduation from any of the seven Lutheran elementary or junior high schools in the metropolitan New Orleans area is ineligible to compete in interscholastic athletic competition for one year. Each [of the] plaintiffs . . . graduated from Lutheran elementary schools, enrolled at Lutheran High School, and were declared ineligible for interscholastic athletic competition during their ninth grade year . . .

The LHSAA is . . . not a regularly constituted agency of the State of Louisiana. Neither is its existence provided for by the constitution, statutes, or regulations of the State of Louisiana. The fact that its conduct constitutes state action for the purposes of the fourteenth amendment . . . does not dictate that it is not a "person" for the purposes of the Civil Rights Acts. We therefore conclude that the LHSAA is a person for the purposes of § 1983, . . . and that as to the LHSAA there exists a "civil action authorized by law" within the meaning of § 1343(3).

The defendants next contend that section 1343(3) jurisdiction is lacking because this action fails to raise a substantial federal question . . .

This court previously has held that an action alleging a violation of due process arising solely from an interference with a student's ability to participate in interscholastic athletic competition fails to raise a substantial federal question so as to clothe a federal district court with jurisdiction under § 1343(3). . . . Similarly, prior case authority in this circuit suggests that an action alleging a violation of equal protection arising from an interference with a student's ability to participate in interscholastic athletic competition fails to raise a substantial federal question unless it is alleged that the challenged classification burdens a suspect class. . . .

In this action, however, in addition to raising due process and equal protection claims, the plaintiffs alleged that the transfer rule unduly burdened their first amendment right to the free exercise of religion. It cannot be said that the first amendment claim asserted in the plaintiffs' com-plaint is "obviously without merit." . . . Neither can it be said that the first amendment claim advanced in the plaintiffs' complaint is clearly foreclosed by previous decisions of the United States Supreme Court.

Accordingly, the district court properly determined that it had subject matter jurisdiction of this action under § 1343(3). . . .

The plaintiffs argue that the transfer rule unconstitutionally burdens their free exercise of religion guaranteed by the first amendment. These parents indicate a sincere belief that Christian education is an integral part of the mission and ministry of the Lutheran church and that the family, rather than the state, is responsible for a child's education. Furthermore, they indicate that they responded to the dictates and compulsion of their religious beliefs by enrolling their children in Lutheran-affiliated schools. The district court determined that the operation of the transfer rule did not violate the first amendment. We agree.

A regulation that is neutral on its face and is motivated by legitimate secular concerns may, in its application, offend the first amendment requirement of governmental neutrality if it unduly burdens the free exercise of religion. . . .

It cannot be denied that, by imposing a cost on a parent's decision to enroll his children in Lutheran High School upon graduation from any of the seven Lutheran elementary schools in the metropolitan New Orleans area, the transfer rule places an indirect and incidental burden on the free exercise of the religious beliefs of these parents. The decisive issue is whether this indirect and incidental burden is an impermissible price to exact from these parents for the free exercise of their religious beliefs. We believe it is not.

The encroachment of the transfer rule on the free exercise of religion is both limited in scope and insignificant in magnitude. The transfer rule does not deny these parents or their children the right to actively practice the Lutheran faith. Similarly, it neither prohibits a parent from enrolling his child in Lutheran High School nor interferes with the ability of such a child to obtain the religious education provided by that school. The rule merely prevents a child from participating in interscholastic athletic competition during his ninth grade year. Even so, the ambit of the rule is limited. It does not forbid a student from participating in all athletic activities. The transfer rule does not prevent ninth graders at Lutheran High School from participating in intramural athletic competition. Neither does the rule prohibit such students from trying out for or from practicing with the Lutheran High School varsity athletic teams. It simply prevents a child from representing Lutheran High School in an interscholastic athletic contest for a period of one year. The burden placed on the free exercise of religion is *de minimis*. . . .

The due process clause of the fourteenth amendment extends constitutional protection to those fundamental aspects of life, liberty, and property that rise to the level of a "legitimate claim of entitlement" but does not protect lesser interests or "mere expectations." . . . A student's interest in participating in a single year of interscholastic athletics amounts to a mere expectation rather than a constitutionally protected claim of entitlement. . . .

The district court determined that the transfer rule as applied in Orleans Parish, Louisiana, violated the fourteenth amendment guarantee of equal protection. We disagree. . . .

Where, as here, the classification created by the regulatory scheme neither trammels fundamental rights or interests nor burdens an inherently suspect class, equal protection analysis requires that the classification be rationally related to a legitimate state interest. . . .

The classification of students created by the transfer rule is rationally related to the state's valid and legitimate interest in deterring or eliminating the recruitment of promising young athletes by overzealous coaches, fans, and faculty members. . . .

The rule adopted by the LHSAA, together with the classification that results, is rationally and logically related to the association's valid and legitimate interest. . . .

NOTES ————

1. After deciding the substantive issue, the court in *Kentucky High School Athletic Ass'n. v. Hopkins County Board of Education* discussed at length a particular problem illustrated by this appeal:

In the court's mind, this case demonstrates why courts are a very poor place in which to settle interscholastic athletic disputes, especially since this type of litigation is most likely to arise at playoff or tournament time. If an injunction or restraining order is granted erroneously, it will be practically impossible to unscramble the tournament results to reflect the ultimate outcome of the case. In almost every instance, the possible benefits flowing from a temporary restraining order or injunction are far outweighed by the potential detriment to the Association, as well as to its member schools who are not before the court. Only in a rare instance should a temporary restraining order or preliminary injunction be granted.

2. In *Albach* v. *Odle*, 531 F. 2d 983 (10th Cir. 1976), the court ruled that a high school transfer rule is not within federal court jurisdiction. Athletic governance, supervision, and regulation are within the jurisdiction of state boards, unless a substantial federal question is involved.

3. In *Marino* v. *Waters*, 220 So. 2d 802 (La. Ct. App. 1969), a public school transfer rule, excluding students from athletic competition who transfer between schools because of marriage, was upheld because it was applied in a nondiscriminatory manner and did not deny due process.

4. In *Bruce* v. *South Carolina High School League*, 258 S.C. 546, 189 S.E. 2d 817 (1972), a student who transferred voluntarily had no constitutionally protected right to participate in athletics. Therefore, the court has no right to enjoin enforcement of the transfer rule.

5. The court ruled in *Dallam* v. *Cumberland Valley School Dist.*, 391 F. Supp. 358 (M.D. Pa. 1975), that a transfer rule is not in violation of a recognized right or privilege protected by the Constitution.

6. In *Sturrup* v. *Mahan*, 305 N.E. 2d 877 (Ind. 1974), a transfer rule violated equal protection because it was overinclusive. The rule denied participation to a student who moved for reasons unrelated to athletics. The rule as applied was not rationally related to its stated goal.

7. In *Chabert* v. *Louisiana High School Athletic Ass'n.*, 323 So. 2d 774 (La. 1975), the court upheld the association transfer rule. The court reasoned that in view of the avowed purpose of the rule — to prevent the evils of recruiting — the rule should be upheld. Plaintiff student-athlete lost one year's eligibility by enrolling in a parochial school located within a public school district other than the one in which he resided. If he enrolled in a parochial school within the same public school district in which he resided, he would have been eligible immediately. The court held that the rule was not arbitrary and did not abridge religious freedom, even though there was only one parochial high school in the public high school district.

8. The court ruled in *Sullivan* v. *University Interscholastic League*, 599 S.W. 2d 860 (Tex. Civ. App. 1980), that a one-year-loss-of-eligibility transfer rule was not subject to due process claims, as no liberty or property interest was found to be involved in playing sports. Concerning the violation of plaintiff's rights under the equal protection clause, the court held that the purpose of

the rule was not directed at hindering interstate commerce.

9. In *Kulovitz* v. *Illinois High School Ass'n.*, 462 F. Supp. 875 (N.D. Ill., E.D., 1978), a rule mandating a one-year loss of eligibility due to a transfer was held not unconstitutional when the court rejected the plaintiff's claim that such a rule deprived him of a college scholarship. The court held that expectation of an athletic scholarship is not a constitutionally protected right. In addition, the court held that the right to interstate travel is not implicitly or expressly guaranteed by the Constitution, and therefore equal protection claims were not applicable to this case.

10. In *Niles* v. *University Interscholastic League*, 715 F. 2d 1027 (5th Cir. 1983), the University Interscholastic League declared student-athlete football player ineligible to compete after he moved out-of-state to live with his mother during the spring term and then returned to his original school in the subsequent fall semester to participate in football. Plaintiff contended that the decision was a denial of freedom of travel and freedom of familial choice. The U.S. Circuit Court of Appeals disagreed and upheld the district court's decision that there was no constitutional violation on which the plaintiff could base a suit.

11. In *Kriss* v. *Brown*, 390 N.E. 2d 193 (Ind. Ct. App. 1979), the Indiana Court of Appeals affirmed a trial court decision that held a high school basketball player was ineligible for competition after transferring to another school district because there was substantial evidence that a guardianship was created primarily to make him eligible and because the move was a result of undue influence. The court added that a determination of the Indiana High School Athletic Association that a student's desire for a scholarship was not a sufficient reason to excuse him or her from operation of the rules was neither arbitrary, capricious, nor unreasonable.

12. *In Re U.S. Ex Rel. Missouri State High Sch., Etc.*, 682 F. 2d 147 (8th Cir. 1982), the United States Court of Appeals reversed a district court decision and held that a Missouri State High School Activities Association transfer rule did not violate the federal Constitution. It noted that the minimal impact on interstate travel of the transfer rule did not require the strict judicial scrutiny normally applied to classifications that penalize exercise of the right to travel.

13. In the following opinion, the attorney general's office for the state of Arizona discusses the constitutionality of transfer rules:

Office of the Attorney General of the State of Arizona
Re: 182–045 (R82–014), Slip Opinion, April 2, 1982
OPINION:
You have asked whether it is constitutionally or legally permissible for the Arizona Interscholastic Association (AIA) to require students who transfer to a private school when their public school is closed to lose a year of sports eligibility when students from the same school retain their full eligibility when transferring to a public school.

As we understand, the AIA has adopted on behalf of its member high schools an ineligibility rule making a high school student who voluntarily transfers to another school ineligible to participate in interscholastic sports for one year following his or her transfer. The AIA, however, has partially waived the ineligibility rule for students who are forced to transfer to another high school because their school is being closed. The waiver is only partial, in that the waiver only applies to those who are forced to transfer and who elect to transfer to certain public schools. The ineligibility rule still applies to those students who are forced to transfer to another school because their school is being closed, but choose to transfer to a private school.

Other jurisdictions have found similar ineligibility rules as applied in particular factual situations unconstitutional in violation of the federal Equal Protection Clause. See, e.g., *Sullivan* v. *University Interscholastic League*, 616 S.W. 2d 170, 172, (Tex. 1981) (the rule providing that a student who had represented a high school other than his present high school in either football or basketball was ineligible for one calendar year after moving to another district to participate in the same sport in the school to which he changed was not rationally related to the purpose of deterring recruitment of high school athletes and hence was a violation of the Equal Protection Clause); *Sturrup* v. *Mahan*, 290 N.E. 2d 64 (Ind. App. 1972), modified, 261 Ind. 463, 305 N.E. 2d 877 (1974) (ineligibility rule violated equal protection by being unreasonably broad in excluding from eligibility many students who move for reasons unrelated to athletics). But see *Whipple* v. *Oregon School Activities Association*, 52 Or. App. 419, 629 P. 2d 384 (1981). Application of the ineligibility rule may also impinge upon the First Amendment right to free exercise of religion. But see *Cooper* v. *Oregon School Activities Association*, 52 Or. App. 425, 629 P. 2d 386 (1981).

It is not within the authority of the Attorney General to hold AIA rules constitutional or unconstitutional and any pronouncement regarding such would not be enforceable. However, we think the AIA action raises some very serious constitutional questions and that it is an issue that is clearly appropriate for legislative, as well as school board, resolution.
OPINION by: Bob Corbin, Attorney General

2.14   Redshirting and Longevity

Redshirting and longevity both relate to the length of time an athlete has to complete his or her eligibility in interscholastic or intercollegiate competition. Redshirting and longevity rules are designed to balance the need to extend or delay an athlete's eligibility to compete based on legitimate factors such as injury or academic difficulty, against potential abuse of the system by either coaches or athletes seeking to gain competitive advantage through an extension of an athlete's career.

2.14–1   Redshirting

Redshirting is a term used to describe the practice of extending the playing career of a student-athlete by postponing or passing over a year of interscholastic or intercollegiate participation while not affecting the athlete's maximum allowable time for participating in high school or college athletics. The NCAA rules state that any athlete who participates in organized competition after turning age 20 shall have that participation counted as one year (but no more than one year) of varsity competition in that sport (*1985–86 NCAA Manual*, Bylaw 5–1–[d]–[3]).

Colleges competing under NCAA governance are allowed to have their student-athletes compete in four complete seasons of play within five calendar years from the beginning of the semester in which the student-athlete first registered at an institution. There are exceptions to the five-year limit, such as time spent in the armed services, official church missions, or recognized foreign aid services of the U.S. government — for example, the Peace Corps (*1985–86 NCAA Manual*, Bylaw 4–1–[a]). And in other situations, such as the Olympics and the Pan American games, competition and training, the NCAA may waive the five-year limit (*1985–86 NCAA Manual*, Bylaw 4–1–[a]–[1]).

Designed to give athletes flexibility in completing their four seasons of allowable NCAA playing time, the five-year rule gives student-athletes the option to postpone their playing careers in any one of the five consecutive years of eligibility. The year postponed is commonly referred to as redshirting. The practice of redshirting may be initiated for a number of reasons, including the following:

1. *Medical*: A student-athlete might receive a serious injury or contract an illness in the off-season or before the start of the season. The student might decide it was advantageous to recover fully from such a problem by postponing for a year the resumption of athletic competition.
2. *Academic*: A student might become ineligible for play because of low grades or a student might wish to study abroad for a year.
3. *Transfer*: The five-year rule also protects the playing career of first-time transfer students. It allows them the opportunity to switch schools once without eliminating one of their four seasons of eligibility. The student-athlete must redshirt a year of competition while attending classes at the new institution (NCAA Division I). (*1985–86 NCAA Manual*, Bylaw 5–1–[j]–[7]; see also Section 2.13–1).
4. *Coaching Strategy*: A student-athlete might be asked by the coach to redshirt a season. The coach may want to use and schedule the player's eligibility to fit the long-term needs and requirements of the team.

To curb the allure of redshirting players for coaching reasons and to reduce expenses, the NCAA membership imposed limitations on financial aid awards, including maximum (allowable) awards (*1985–86 NCAA Manual*, Bylaw 6–5). Reducing the number of scholarships a program can award had the effect of making it less advantageous for coaches to redshirt athletes for reasons other than those made necessary because of academics or injury. The NCAA membership also voted to allow graduate students to be eligible for competition if they still have playing eligibility (*1985–86 NCAA Manual*, Bylaw 5–1–[c]).

On the interscholastic level, redshirting is not as formalized a system. It involves keeping back an athlete in grade school for an extra year before enrolling the student in high school. Such students thus have another year to develop their bodies and playing skills before entering high school competition.

Eligibility is again a key factor behind this practice. For instance, the Massachusetts Interscholastic Athletic Association (MIAA) does not allow students age 19 and above to compete in high school unless the student turns 19 after September 1 of the school year (*MIAA Blue Book*, Section II–[6]). The MIAA also restricts competition to 12 consecutive athletic seasons (fall, winter, and spring for four years) past the eighth grade. An MIAA Eligibility Review Board can authorize exceptions to the 12 consecutive season rule because of injury or illness.

Kupec v. Atlantic Coast Conference, 399 F. Supp. 1377 (M.D. N.C. 1975)

The case involved the football hardship rule of the Atlantic Coast Conference (ACC), which stated:

> Hardship is that incapacitating condition resulting from injury or illness which prevents a student-athlete from participating in more than one football game or more than three contests in other sports, provided the injury or illness occurred during the first half of the institution's regular schedule in the sport involved. [ACC Constitution and Bylaws, Article VIII, rule 18]

Kupec was a college football player who sought an injunction from enforcement of the ACC eligibility rules that would not allow him to participate for a fifth year. All parties involved agreed that Kupec played during the 1971, 1972, and 1974 seasons, and in two games during the 1973 season. In determining whether a preliminary injunction should be granted, the court made its decision based on the following four factors:

(1) Whether there is a substantial threat that the plaintiff will suffer irreparable injury if the injunction is not granted;

(2) Whether the threatened injury to the plaintiff outweighs the threatened harm that the

granting of an injunction might do to the defendants;

(3) Whether there is substantial likelihood that plaintiff will prevail on the merits;

(4) Whether the public interest would be promoted by granting or denying the injunction.

Kupec argued that if he was not able to participate in another year of collegiate football, (1) his professional career aspirations would be injured, (2) he would lose his right to a tuition-free education, and (3) the public interest would be damaged since the public wants to see him play college football. Additionally, he argued that the ACC was misinterpreting its hardship rule and depriving him of due process.

The court stated that it would not hesitate to enjoin the ACC from an illegal practice that fell within its jurisdiction. However, the court did not see any such practices involved in this case. The court found Kupec's argument about his professional career to be too speculative. It noted that the plaintiff needed only to finish an incomplete course to graduate and that the loss of tuition benefits did not cause any injury. Concerning the ACC's misinterpretation of its own hardship rule, the court stated:

> The only fact to be determined in any hardship application is whether the athlete played in more than one game. If he did, the rule is self-executing and nothing more is required. Plaintiff admittedly played in more than one game during the 1973 season and, thus, he exercised a year of eligibility. The fact that the ACC subsequently voted not to change its hardship rule was not, as plaintiff claims, a "hearing" to disqualify him at which he was not present and, therefore, denied due process. The ACC simply entered its rule with the result that the plaintiff is precluded from playing football at the University of North Carolina during the 1975 season because his years of eligibility have been exhausted.

The court saw little significance in the public interest argument made by the plaintiff. The plaintiff's motion for an injunction was dismissed, the court reasoned:

> The ACC is a voluntary association of colleges

and universities whose goal is basically to regulate university athletics and, hopefully, to keep university athletics from becoming professionalized to the extent that profit making objectives would overshadow educational objectives. In pursuance of its goals, the ACC prescribes standards which must be followed by student athletes and their schools. An injunction would have the effect of usurping the regulatory authority of the ACC and substituting for it the judgment of this Court. Such an action would decrease respect for the ACC's authority and its ability to adequately regulate university sports would thereby be weakened. Thus, the ACC will suffer harm if the injunction is granted far in excess of any harm suffered by the plaintiff if it is not.

NOTES _____

1. The NCAA has what it terms a hardship exception. It is often confused with the term redshirting. A hardship exception will be granted where:

(i) It occurs in one of the four seasons of intercollegiate competition at any four-year collegiate institution for members of Division I, or at any two-year or four-year collegiate institution for members of Division II or III.

(ii) It occurs when the student-athlete has not participated in more than 20 percent of the institution's completed events in his or her sport or has not participated in more than two of the institution's completed events in that sport, whichever number is greater, provided the injury or illness occurred in the first half of the season and resulted in incapacity to compete for the remainder of the season. Any contest (including a scrimmage) with outside competition is countable under this limitation. (Note: In applying the 20 percent limitation, any computation which results in a fractional portion of an event shall be rounded to the next whole number; e.g., 20 percent of a 27-game basketball schedule (5.4 games) shall be considered as six games.)

(iii) This provision shall be administered by the conference members of the Association or, in the case of an independent member institution, by the NCAA Eligibility Committee. [*1985–86 NCAA Manual*, Bylaw 5–1–(d)–(2)]

2. Redshirt rules were upheld in the following cases:
(a) In *Mitchell* v. *Louisiana High School Athletic Ass'n.*, 430 F. 2d 1155 (5th Cir. 1970), a redshirt rule restricting all incoming high school students who voluntarily repeat eighth grade to six semesters of competition rather than to the normal eight semesters was held rationally related to a legitimate state interest and was declared valid.
(b) The court ruled in *David* v. *Louisiana High School Athletic Ass'n.*, 244 So. 2d 292 (La. Ct. App. 1971), that a student who repeats a grade for reasons unrelated to athletics may still be validly restricted to six semesters (three years) of athletic eligibility rather than the normal eight semesters (four years).
(c) In *Murtaugh* v. *Nyquist*, 78 Misc. 2d 876, 358 N.Y.S. 2d 595 (1974), a longevity rule was held not arbitrary or unreasonable where a reasonable basis for the rule exists. Reasons such as the prevention of delay in the educational process and the prevention of injuries to younger, less developed student-athletes were adequate to support a longevity rule. The court found this to be true even in the case of a rule which denied eligibility to students held back for academic reasons.

3. Redshirt rules were not upheld in these cases:
(a) In *Florida High School Activities Ass'n.* v. *Bryant*, 313 So. 2d 57 (Fla. Dist. Ct. App. 1975), appellant association sought reversal of a final judgment finding student appellee eligible to play more than four years of interscholastic basketball. Affirming the judgment, the court of appeals held that for this student, basketball was vital because it provided the impetus for his general scholastic, social development, and rehabilitation from prior problems of juvenile delinquency. The student had presented an adequate case of undue hardship, meriting a waiver of the four-year rule.
(b) In *Lee* v. *Florida High School Activities Ass'n. Inc.*, 291 So. 2d 636 (Fla. Dist. Ct. App. 1974), plaintiff student stayed out of school for 10 months to help alleviate his family's troubled financial situation. Upon returning to school, he sought a waiver of the four-year (successive) rule to participate in athletics. It was denied by the association. The court found his participation in athletics would enhance his chances of being admitted to college and of winning a scholarship. Except for the four-year rule, plaintiff would be eligible. Therefore, the court found sufficient harshness. The denial of a waiver was ruled a violation of due process because no justification was given for denying eligibility in such extreme circumstances. The rule was unconstitutional as applied to the plaintiff.
(c) In *Cabrillo Community College Dist. of Santa Cruz County* v. *California Junior College Ass'n.*, 44 Cal. App. 3d 367, 118 Cal. Rptr. 708 (1975), an athletic residency requirement was held to be in violation of state law. The court reasoned that the rule imposed additional residency requirements on students who wished to participate in athletics, even though they fulfilled the residency requirements needed to be admitted to the institution.
(d) The court ruled in *Duffley* v. *New Hampshire Interscholastic Athletic Ass'n.*, 446 A. 2d 462 (N.H. 1982), that student-athlete plaintiff must be given

procedural due process when he was denied a waiver of a four-year rule.

(e) In *ABC League* v. *Missouri State High School Activities Ass'n.*, 530 F. Supp. 1033 (E.D. Mo. 1981), plaintiff student and league were granted an injunction by the district court stopping the Missouri State High School Activities Association (MSHSAA) from enforcing a rule that would have prevented students who transferred to private schools, which form the ABC league, from participating in athletic competition when their schools played against members of the MSHSAA. The district court found that the MSHSAA rule was arbitrary, capricious, and a violation of equal protection.

4. For further information, see "Geoff Smith Goes Distance," *Boston Globe*, April 15, 1984, p. 55.

5. At a June 26, 1984, U.S. Senate hearing on "Oversight on College Athletic Programs," (S. Hrg. 98–955, Subcommittee on Education, Arts and Humanities), Edward T. Foote II, President of the University of Maine, noted:

> The football players in a big-time program will spend as many as 30–40 hours a week during the fall semester on football. Graduation in five years, not four, for those who graduate is the norm for many football programs. The practice of "redshirting" (emphasis added) freshmen encourages five years of study.

2.14–2   Longevity

In 1980, the NCAA enacted a new Division I bylaw (5–1–[d]–[3]) designed to address problems concerning the increasing number of older athletes being recruited, especially in the sports of track and soccer. Some member institutions believed that athletes were entering intercollegiate athletics after excessive experience in amateur leagues in the United States and more frequently in foreign countries. The "longevity" rule was initiated because it was felt that these older, more experienced athletes would place younger and more inexperienced athletes at a disadvantage in competition and in trying to gain scholarship monies.

Butts v. National Collegiate Athletic Ass'n., 751 F. 2d 609 (1984)

Albert Butts is an academic senior at LaSalle, a distinguished private university located in Philadelphia. LaSalle is a member of the NCAA, and it competes at the Division I level in basketball.

As an outstanding high school basketball player in the Philadelphia area, Mr. Butts attracted the attention of recruiters from many colleges and universities. His otherwise bright prospects for participation in a major intercollegiate basketball program were clouded by his academic deficiencies, which might have rendered him ineligible to compete under NCAA academic standards, or unqualified for admission to many of its member institutions. In 1979, Mr. Butts enrolled for his senior year of high school in the Frederick Military Academy in Virginia, a private preparatory school. At the end of the 1979–80 school year, during which he played on Frederick's basketball team, Mr. Butts received his high school diploma. He stayed at Frederick for the 1980–81 school year, receiving a partial scholarship in exchange for another year of participation in the school's basketball program. According to Mr. Butts, he remained at Frederick for this additional year to upgrade his academic qualifications. During the 1980–81 Frederick basketball season he reached his twentieth birthday.

In the fall of 1981, Mr. Butts entered LaSalle on a full basketball scholarship. By the end of his freshman year, and first year of varsity basketball competition, school officials brought to his attention NCAA Bylaw 5–1–(d)–(3), which had been promulgated by the Division I schools in January of 1980, and which became effective August 1, 1980. The bylaw provides:

> Any participation by a student as an individual or as a representative of any team in organized competition in a sport during each 12-month period after his 20th birthday and prior to his matriculation at a member institution shall count as one year of varsity competition in that sport. Participation in organized competition during time spent in the armed services, on official church missions or with recognized foreign aid services of the U.S. Government shall be excepted.

Because Mr. Butts had played for the Frederick Military Academy basketball team after reaching the age of 20, and before matriculating at LaSalle, it was feared that under this bylaw this post-high school experience would be counted against his four years of college eligibility. After consulting with an attorney, Mr. Butts decided to take no action regarding the bylaw at that time in the hope, he testified, that the rule would be amended before his senior year. He continued to participate in LaSalle's basketball program during his sophomore and junior years (the 1982–83 and 1983–84 academic years), though he missed much of the 1983–84 basketball season due to a knee injury.

In the fall of 1984, after LaSalle determined that Mr. Butts was physically and academically eligible to compete during the current 1984–85 season, the question of his eligibility under Bylaw 5–1–(d)–(3) came to the fore. If his second year at Frederick is, under that rule, to count against his four years of college eligibility, then Mr. Butts has exhausted his eligibility and must sit out the year. On October 22, 1984, counsel for Mr. Butts wrote to the NCAA seeking a favorable interpretation of the bylaw. By letter dated November 15, 1984, the Assistant Executive Director of the NCAA indicated that Mr. Butts would be ineligible to play basketball during his senior year. LaSalle's first basketball game was scheduled for November 26. On November 23, Mr. Butts filed suit against the NCAA and LaSalle, seeking declaratory and injunctive relief. LaSalle then cross-claimed against the NCAA.

On November 26 the district court denied Mr. Butts a temporary restraining order that would have enabled him to compete in LaSalle's first game. On December 3, the district court conducted an evidentiary hearing on motions by Mr. Butts and LaSalle for preliminary injunctive relief. The district court denied these motions in a memorandum opinion and order dated December 5, finding that appellants had failed to establish a reasonable probability of success on the merits. On December 7 this court denied LaSalle's emergency motion for an injunction pending appeal, but ordered expedited briefing and argument on the merits of the appeal. Oral argument in this matter was held on December 14.

Though the complaints of LaSalle and Mr. Butts alleged a variety of constitutional and statutory defects in Bylaw 5–1–(d)–(3), only two are now urged before this court: (1) that the bylaw violates 42 U.S.C. § 6102 (1982) ("[N]o person in the United States shall, on the basis of age, be excluded from participation in, be denied the benefits of, or be subjected to discrimination under, any program or activity receiving Federal financial assistance."); and (2) that it violates 42 U.S.C. § 2000d (1982) ("No person in the United

States shall, on the grounds of race, color, or national origin, be excluded from participation in, be denied the benefits of, or be subjected to discrimination under any program or activity receiving Federal financial assistance.").

The district court concluded that appellants had shown a strong likelihood that the bylaw has a racially disparate impact, and thus that they could make out a *prima facie* case under § 2000d, but that the NCAA had advanced a legitimate, nondiscriminatory reason for the bylaw: "[T]he bylaw is designed and intended to promote equality of competition among its members at each level so as to prevent college athletics and access to athletic scholarships from being dominated by more mature, older, more experienced players, and to discourage high school students from delaying their entrance into college in order to develop and mature their athletic skills." The district court held that, in response to this justification, appellants had the burden of showing that it was pretextual or that "some other, less intrusive, rule would accomplish the stated objects of the present rule." The district court found that they had not shown a reasonable likelihood of being able to meet this burden.

For the purposes of its decision on the § 6102 age discrimination claim, the district court assumed that the usual administrative exhaustion requirement imposed by that statute, 42 U.S.C. § 6104 (e) (1982), would not apply where preliminary injunctive relief was necessary to prevent irreparable harm. Nonetheless, the district court concluded that under relevant regulations, 45 C.F.R. § 90.14 (1983), age combined with experience could be legitimately used as measures of the "maturity and level of athletic skill of the athlete."

Though there have been many changes since, in December of 1891, James Naismith first nailed two peach baskets to the balcony ten feet above the floor at the International Young Men's Christian Association Training School, now Springfield College, Springfield, Massachusetts, basketball is still the only major sport of strictly United States origin. The game was an almost instant success at the scholastic level. However, not surprisingly, it was the "acceptance by Yale in 1894 that induced other institutions to follow suit." In these early years the rules of the game varied greatly from institution to institution, with Cornell, for example, playing with 50 men per side. The first collegiate basketball game with five men on a side was played on March 20, 1897, between Yale University and the University of Pennsylvania. . . .

Approximately eight years after the first inter-collegiate basketball game the NCAA was born and since then it

> has played an important role in the regulation of amateur collegiate sports. It has adopted and pro-mulgated playing rules, standards of amateurism, standards for academic eligibility, regulations con-cerning recruitment of athletes, and rules governing the size of athletic squads and coaching staffs. . . .

During the eighty years since the NCAA's birth, collegiate basketball and the NCAA have grown as dominant institutions in America at a level which Naismith could never have contemplated when he invented this sport to appease the students at Springfield who were bored with "the Swedish, German and French forms of calisthenics of that period," and because he wanted to "fill the void that existed between football and baseball." (3 Encyclopedia Britannica, *supra*)

In this case we are confronted with a clash of many intensely felt interests. No one has captured the student-athlete's interests better than Professor Linda Greene in her seminal article, *The New NCAA Rules of the Game: Academic Integrity or Racism?* 28 St. Louis U.L.J. 101, 137 (1984), where she wrote that "athletic activities are an important and integral facet of the educational process. In addition, participation in sports activi-ties does bestow upon the athlete important psychological, social and physical benefits." Yet, as Professor Greene goes on to note:

> The substantiality of the interest increases at the college level. This is due in part to the economic stake of the student in certain important college sports. In addition, not only is the athlete often exchanging his prowess for an education, "the chance to display . . . athletic prowess in college stadiums and arenas throughout the country [may be] worth more in economic terms than the chance to get a college education." . . . Even if the college athlete does not reach the professional ranks, our sports-dominated culture often rewards outstanding college athletes in both tangible and intangible ways. Viewed from several different perspectives, the interests of athletes cannot be lightly disregarded. . . .

When stripped of legal verbiage, the competing interests in this case are those of: (1) a talented young man who fervently desires to show his athletic prowess — not primarily for success in academia but for what could be the success on the highly remunerative courts of the National Basket-ball Association; (2) a distinguished college that would like to demonstrate its highest excellence on the basketball floor and thereby rise as close as it can to a local, regional or maybe even a national championship; and (3) a powerful collegiate asso-ciation which, according to its brief, wants to thwart "professionalism" in college sports, "main-tain intercollegiate athletics as an integral part of the educational process," and "ensure that athletes are representative of, and thus an integral part of, the student body as a whole."

Despite the exalted nomenclature which today's basketball afficionado might use in describing the college game, with its adroit "full-court press" defensive maneuver, or the exhilarating offensive "slam dunks," "high percentage shooters" from the outside, "good moves" to the basket, and players who can go "either way," we recognize that there is far more involved in this case than merely the joy of the sport. At stake are the size of Mr. Butts' future bank account, the additional luster that could be added to LaSalle's legend of success in basketball, and the limits of the NCAA's power to curb "a persistent and perhaps inevitable desire to 'win at all costs,' " and prevent "a wide range of competitive excesses that prove harmful to students and institutions alike." . . .

Mindful of our narrow scope of review, we have carefully considered the record, Judge Fullam's thoughtful memorandum opinion, and the briefs and arguments presented by counsel in this ex-pedited appeal. We appreciate that all parties have advanced substantial factual and legal bases for their respective positions. Each party has indicated that it may wish to introduce additional evidence at trial on the merits. Thus, we do not now intimate any view of what the final disposition of Mr. Butts' and LaSalle's complaints should be. On the record as it stands, however, we cannot say that the district court abused its discretion, com-mitted an obvious error in applying the law, or made a serious mistake in considering the proof.

Spath v. National Collegiate Athletic Ass'n., 728 F. 2d 25 (1st Cir. 1984)

Robert Spath was a fourth-year student at the

University of Lowell in Lowell, Massachusetts, on an ice hockey scholarship. He was ready to begin his senior year of play (fourth year of competition) when Lowell disqualified him pursuant to NCAA Bylaw 5–1–(d)–(3). Spath, a Canadian, had played three years of intercollegiate hockey at Lowell. In addition, prior to coming to Lowell, but after his 20th birthday, Spath had played for a team in Canada for one year.

The NCAA limits intercollegiate competition for a player to four years, and under its bylaws, each year of organized competition anywhere in the particular sport after age 20 is counted as a year of intercollegiate competition. As a result, Spath was, under NCAA rules, no longer eligible to play. NCAA sanctions for playing an ineligible athlete include forfeiture of any games in which the athlete competes.

Spath brought a civil rights suit in federal court against the NCAA and the University of Lowell on the grounds that the bylaws adopted by the NCAA and enforced through its member institutions deprived him of equal protection and due process of law and against Lowell on the grounds of breach of contract. Spath applied for and was granted a restraining order by the district court. Finding that Spath seriously failed to show a likelihood of success on the merits, the court of appeals reversed.

Spath contended that Canadians, for various reasons, play more competitive hockey after age 20 and before going to college than do Americans and that the NCAA bylaw was particularly directed against foreigners. Spath argued that the bylaw under which he was disqualified should be subjected to a strict scrutiny standard under the Fourteenth Amendment's equal protection clause.

The court, however, found nothing to justify subjecting the NCAA bylaw to a heightened level of judicial scrutiny. The court held that no fundamental right was involved in playing intercollegiate hockey. The court also found that since the bylaw was neutral on its face

with respect to foreigners to sustain an equal protection argument, Spath would have to show that the NCAA purposefully discriminated against foreigners as a class. To this end, Spath presented statistics showing that Canadians were more likely to be adversely affected by the bylaw than Americans. The court held, however, that the mere fact that the bylaw disproportionately affected Canadians was not sufficient to establish discriminatory purpose.

Spath also cited statements made by opponents of the bylaw from the minutes of the NCAA debate on its adoption that the bylaw was discriminatory toward foreigners. (See *Howard University* v. *National Collegiate Athletic Ass'n.*) The court noted, however, that the drafters of the bylaw raised the age limit from 19 to 20 in recognition that the former might present problems for Canadians who attend five, rather than four, years of high school. The court also noted that although participants in the debate recognized that perhaps more foreigners, including Canadian hockey players, would be affected by an age and experience rule than would Americans, they believed that it was desirable to restrict older and more experienced players in general, with the emphasis being on experience. The court held that such evidence as Spath presented did not approach the point of establishing the constitutionally required "purposeful intent" to discriminate against foreigners because of their alienage.

The primary question, according to the court, was whether the rule was reasonable. The court found it to be so. "College athletics," the court stated, "are not professional sports . . . but are, within reason, democratic opportunities for students. Fairness suggests restrictions against those who may be excessively qualified."

The court also rejected Spath's claim that his due process rights had been violated in depriving him of a contractual "property" interest in playing ice hockey for Lowell. The court noted that Spath's scholarship was reviewed and renewed on a yearly basis and that due process rights do not attach to expectancies. Even assuming that Spath had a contractual right to play during his senior year, the court held no further procedure was required here. Lowell had appealed the NCAA ruling on his eligibility, and Spath had been given sufficient notice of the bylaw which was in effect, published, and available to anyone interested from 1980 on. The NCAA could not be charged, the court held, to give personal notice to every student.

Finally, Spath argued that his scholarship imposed upon Lowell a contractual obligation to allow him to play. The court pointed out, however, that his scholarship with Lowell made clear reference to the NCAA rules. The court thus found it difficult to conceive of how Lowell could be thought to have obligated itself to violate them.

NOTES _____

1. In *Blue* v. *University Interscholastic League*, 503 F. Supp. 1030 (N.D. Texas 1980), a 19-year-old high school football player sought to enjoin the University Interscholastic League from enforcing the 19-year-old eligibility rule. The U.S. District Court held that the rule did not violate due process nor equal protection guarantees of the Constitution.

2. At the 1984 NCAA convention, the longevity bylaw was amended to read:

Any participation by a student as an individual or as a representative of any team in organized competition in a sport during each 12-month period after the student's 20th birthday and prior to matriculation at a member institution shall count as one year of varsity competition in that sport, provided, however, that in no event shall the student be charged with more than one year of competition in that sport in any 12-month period after the student's 20th birthday. [*1985–86 NCAA Manual*, Section 5–1–(d)–(3)]

3. See also, the Bruce Smith case, which is discussed further in Section 2.30, Note 1(d).

2.15   Financial Considerations

In intercollegiate competition, financial matters such as scholarships and financial aid are often an area of dispute and litigation regarding an individual's athletic eligibility. In this section, these considerations will be examined, as well as the concept of scholarships as contracts, worker's compensation issues, letters of intent, excess financial aid, and the problems of pay, employment, expenses, and marketing the athlete.

2.15–1   Scholarships and Financial Aid

The cardinal rule concerning financial aid to a student-athlete is that the *aid* must be administered by the school (Exhibit 2–2). If it is administered by an outside source, such as an alumnus of the university, it jeopardizes intercollegiate eligibility. The school is required to distribute athletic scholarships through its regular financial aid channels. Donors are prohibited from making contributions to benefit specific athletes. No financial aid from an outside source can be based solely on athletic ability. Student-athletes, however, are permitted to receive aid from persons on whom they normally depend, such as their family or close relatives (*1985–86 NCAA Manual*, Constitution, 3–4–[a–b]).

Institutions may not pay preenrollment fees, application processing fees, room deposits, or dormitory damage deposits unless institutional policy specifies that the financial aid package or athletic scholarship covers these expenses. If such expenses are covered, the student can be reimbursed after payment or the fees may be paid by the school, as long as these are the policies that bind the entire student population.

The school financial aid mechanism is required to provide the athletic scholarship recipient with an officially signed document that stipulates the amount, duration, terms, and conditions to which the parties must adhere. This document is often referred to as the initial financial aid agreement (see Exhibit 2–3).

Athletic scholarships are technically renewable each year, but after being granted, they

1. I understand that under Conference Rule 7 I will be ineligible for intercollegiate athletics if I accept financial aid other than (a) from my family; (b) from the university under a Tender; (c) in the form of a grant-in-aid or scholarship having nothing whatsoever to do with my athletic interests; (d) work other than provided in a Tender at which I actually earn the going rate of pay; or (3) bona fide loans.

2. I also understand that if I am receiving financial aid under a Tender I must report the receipt of non-athletic grants or scholarships and term-time earnings from employment because they reduce my eligibility for aid under a Tender.

3. **The following is a record of all of the forms of financial aid I received last year, and have or will receive this year:**
   TENDER LAST YEAR ⊔   **TENDER THIS YEAR** ▢

OTHER GRANTS OR SCHOLARSHIPS, INCLUDING GOVERNMENT GRANTS

	Name of Award	Sponsor of Award	Basis of Award	Amount
This Year	_____	_____	_____	_____
Last Year	_____	_____	_____	_____

TERM-TIME EMPLOYMENT

	Name and Address of Employer	Type of Work	Rate of Pay	Hours of Work	Total Term Time Earnings
This Year	_____	_____	_____	_____	_____
Last Year	_____	_____	_____	_____	_____

LOANS

	Source and Address	Repayment Terms	Amount
This Year	_____	_____	_____
Last Year	_____	_____	_____

OTHER (Working Spouse, ROTC, Insurance, Etc.)

This Year (Explain) _____ Amount _____

Last Year (Explain) _____ Amount _____

LAST SUMMER EMPLOYMENT

Name and City and State of Employer	Type of Work	Weeks Worked	Rate of Pay	Total Earnings
_____	_____	_____	_____	_____
_____	_____	_____	_____	_____

4. I understand that if for any reason the sum of unearned financial aid, grant-in-aid, and earnings from term-time employment exceeds the maximum amount outlined in Rule 7, scholastic credits and graduation certificates may be withheld until restitution of the excess has been made.

5. I certify, upon penalty of ineligibility for intercollegiate athletics, and loss of athletic financial aid, that the above statements are complete and accurate, and that I am familiar with and in conformity with Conference Rule 7 governing financial aid to athletes.

Signed _____

6. To the best of my knowledge the foregoing is a complete and accurate statement.

Signed _____
(Coach)

Exhibit 2-2   Financial Aid Agreement (*Source:* Metropolitan Collegiate Athletic Conference)

Financial Aid Agreement

From: _____   Date _____
                    (University)
                                                    ☐ Initial   ☐ Renewal
To: _____   Date of Entrance in
                (Name of Applicant)   University _____
_____   Sport _____
                (Street Address)   College Period _____
_____
                (City and State)

1.   This Financial Aid Agreement is subject to your fulfillment of the admission requirements of this institution, and its academic requirements for athletic competition and financial aid.

2.   This Financial Aid Agreement covers the following as checked:

_____(a)   Full Grant: includes tuition and fees, room and board, and use of necessary books in your selected course of study.

_____(b)   The following items as checked:

  _____(1)   Tuition and fees in your selected course of study

  _____(2)   Board

  _____(3)   Room

  _____(4)   Use of necessary books in your selected course of study

  _____(5)   Other explanation of Award: _____

3.   You will be eligible for consideration to renew this Financial Aid Agreement according to this University's renewal policies at the end of its term if you are academically qualified for intercollegiate competition.

4.   If you wish to accept this Financial Aid Agreement it will be necessary for you to return two signed copies of this form NO LATER THAN _____

Signed _____   Signed _____
              (Director of Athletics)   (Scholarship Officer)

- -

ACCEPTANCE

I accept the Financial Aid Agreement which appears above on this form. In doing so, I certify that I have not accepted another Financial Aid Agreement from a member of the Metropolitan Collegiate Athletic Conference. I am also aware that:

(a)   I will forfeit my athletic eligibility if I receive any financial assistance from any source other than as provided for in this award, or my family and governmental agencies, or in the form of an award having nothing whatsoever to do with my athletic abilities or interests.

(b)   I am aware that any employment earnings by me during term time and any other financial assistance, except from my family, but including academic scholarships must be reported by me. Any such earnings or assistance, in combination with the aid provided through this Financial Aid Agreement, may not exceed basic educational costs at this University.

(c)   The aid provided in this Financial Aid Agreement will be cancelled if I sign a professional sports contract or receive compensation from a professional sports organization.

(d)   This Financial Aid Agreement may not be signed prior to March 1, 1977.

Signed _____   _____
                    Student   Date and Social Security Number

Signed _____   _____
              Parent or Legal Guardian   Date

- -

If you wish to accept this Financial Aid Agreement you are to sign all copies.

Exhibit 2-3   Statement of Financial Support (*Source:* Big Ten Conference)

cannot be canceled or reduced on the basis of the student-athlete's ability or contribution to the team. In addition, athletic scholarships cannot be withdrawn because of an injury to a student-athlete or for any other athletically related reason (*1985–86 NCAA Manual*, Constitution 3–4–[c]–[1]). NCAA rules do not, however, prohibit all types of scholarship revision or rescission. For example, financial aid may be canceled or reduced immediately if the student-athlete becomes ineligible for competition. Student-athletes may also lose their scholarships if they fraudulently misrepresent any information on any application or if they engage in serious misconduct sufficient to warrant a substantial disciplinary penalty. In addition, aid can be canceled or reduced at the end of the term or semester if the student-athlete voluntarily withdraws from a sport for personal reasons (*1985–86 NCAA Manual*, Constitution 3–(4)–[c]–[2]).

In order to protect the student-athlete, there are certain procedural requirements that must be followed when a scholarship change or reduction is made:

> The renewal of a scholarship or grant-in-aid award shall be made on or before July 1 prior to the academic year it is to be effective. The institution shall promptly notify each student-athlete who received an award the previous academic year and who is eligible to receive an award and has eligibility remaining under Bylaw 4–1 or Constitution 3–3–(a)–(3) for the ensuing academic year whether the grant has been renewed or not renewed. In the latter event, the institution also shall inform the student-athlete that if he or she believes the grant has not been renewed for questionable reasons, the student-athlete may request, and shall have the opportunity for, a hearing before the institutional agency making the financial award. The institution shall have established reasonable procedures for the prompt hearing of such a request. [*1985–86 NCAA Manual*, Constitution 3–4–(g)]

2.15–1(a) Scholarships as Contracts

The relationship between the student-athlete and institution has been analyzed by the courts in some cases on a contract theory. The institution can require the student-athlete to meet certain requirements. For example, most schools require that in return for athletic scholarship benefits, the student-athlete must maintain academic eligibility, attend practices, compete in games, and follow the rules and regulations of the institution, the allied conference (if applicable), and the NCAA. Therefore, both parties to the "contract" are required to perform certain duties creating "consideration." When any integral part of the agreement is not fulfilled, or if one or both parties are unable to comply with the agreed-upon terms, the courts have allowed the institution to rescind or revoke the scholarship.

Several legal and practical considerations are raised when the athletic scholarship is viewed as a legally enforceable contract between the student-athlete and the educational institution. A contract is enforceable, based on the triad of offer-acceptance-consideration. In this situation an institution extends a scholarship (offer) to the athlete who chooses to attend the institution (acceptance) and gets a scholarship (university's consideration) in exchange for participation (athlete's consideration). For consideration to exist, each party must give or promise to give something to the other. On the surface, this analysis seems simple and logical. However, more particular inquiries suggest problems inherent in this contractual analysis of athletic scholarships.

There are usually both explicit and implicit conditions to be fulfilled when an educational institution offers and a student accepts an athletic scholarship. The university relinquishes the right to demand payment for its educational services, while the student-athlete agrees to do all that is possible to maintain athletic ability, academic eligibility, and team participation in practice and in games. In essence, there is a quid pro quo, and the athlete is getting a benefit conditioned on his or her participation in athletics.

Theoretically, any compensation given to

induce participation or to reward the performance of an athletic skill is in direct violation of rules regulating amateur status, including the NCAA's own policies. A finding that athletic scholarships are contracted is arguably a violation of these rules. Also, this analysis of athletic scholarships potentially allows the institution to compel an athlete to perform only for it and to prevent an athlete from transferring to another school for the duration of the scholarship-contract. A finding of a contract would also seem to indicate the use of contract remedies, including litigation, if either party defaulted on the agreement.

Two early cases, *University of Denver* v. *Nemeth* (see Section 2.15–1[b], Note 1), and *Van Horn* v. *Industrial Accident Comm'n.* (see Section 2.15–1[b], Note 2) demonstrate another potential problem in analyzing scholarships as contracts. In both cases it was held that where a contractual relationship existed between an athlete and an institution, and where the receipt of the scholarship or other benefits is conditioned on athletic performance, the athlete is to be considered an employee of the institution for the purposes of worker's compensation. Note, however, that to create an employee-employer relationship, the scholarship must be granted in return for participation, not merely to defray educational expenses. Making the athlete an employee will effectively destroy his amateur status for all amateur athletic associations.

The last problem with a contractual analysis concerns the taxability of scholarship funds. An educational grant-in-aid is nontaxable since the award is "made in the nature of a relatively disinterested, no strings, educational grant, with no requirement of any substantial quid pro quo from the recipients" (*Bingler* v. *Johnson*, 394 U.S. 741, 89 S. Ct. 1439, 22 L. Ed. 2d 695 [1969]). If an athlete receives a scholarship in consideration for athletic participation, the award could be considered income and, therefore, taxable in accordance with the Internal Revenue Service (exclusionary rule, IRS 117[a]). Internal Revenue Service (IRS)

regulations specifically address athletic scholarships in Revenue Ruling 77–263. In that analysis, the IRS emphasizes that only when a recipient does not have to participate in athletics as a condition of the award is the award considered nontaxable.

In *The Law of Sports*, authors Weistart and Lowell suggest that the best method for avoiding the problems created by a contract analysis is to analyze scholarships whenever possible as being either conditional gifts or educational grants (see Note 6). This approach, however, can present a problem in regard to determining the enforceability of the gift. Also questionable is whether this approach is in accordance with practice, since universities rarely "give" anything without expecting something in return, whether it be athletic participation or the work responsibilities required with the receipt of many educational grants-in-aid.

Begley v. **Corporation of Mercer Univ., 367 F. Supp. 908 (E.D. Tenn. 1973)**

High school student Mark Begley agreed to attend Mercer University after the university offered to give him an athletic grant-in-aid worth $11,208 to pursue an undergraduate degree and to play basketball. Begley also agreed to abide by all university regulations, keep all training rules, maintain satisfactory progress toward graduation with a minimum cumulative average of 1.6, and abide by all NCAA rules and regulations. Later, it was discovered that the assistant basketball coach for Mercer University had made a mistake in calculating Begley's high school grade point average. The corrected GPA of 1.45 rendered Begley ineligible for basketball. As a result, Mercer withdrew its offer of a scholarship.

Begley brought suit seeking money damages for a breach of contract by Mercer. The district court granted the defendant's motion to dismiss the case, by summary judgment, since the facts proved beyond doubt that the plaintiff could not support his claim for relief. The court determined that the intentions of the parties in the contract were as follows: Mercer intended to extend financial aid to Begley for use toward completing his degree in exchange for Begley's participation in its basketball program; Begley intended to play basketball for Mercer subject to the stipulated provisions in exchange for the aforementioned financial aid.

Though Mercer made a mistake in investigating Begley's ability to compete in athletics, Begley was nonetheless unable to abide by the contract because he did not have a predicted minimum GPA of 1.6 or more as required by the NCAA for eligibility. Quoting from 17 *American Jurisprudence* 2d 791–92, Contracts, section 355, the court stated that "it is . . . the rule that where one party is unable to perform his part of the contract, he cannot be entitled to the performance of the contract by the other party. . .".

Mercer's inability to perform its part of the contract resulted from its need to abide by the rules and regulations of the NCAA. It was patent that Mercer contracted with Begley under the stipulation that he be bound by NCAA regulations. Mercer cannot be held to have assumed the risk that the NCAA would not permit it to perform its contract with Begley. Thus, the court could not hold Mercer liable for its inability to perform.

Taylor v. Wake Forest University, 16 N.C. App. 117, 191 S.E. 2d 379 (1972)

George Taylor and his son, Gregg Taylor, brought this action against Wake Forest University to recover educational expenses incurred by them after the university terminated Gregg Taylor's athletic scholarship. The superior court entered a summary judgment in favor of the university. The court of appeals affirmed the lower court's decision.

Wake Forest awarded Gregg Taylor a football scholarship, which he accepted. The scholarship was to be for four years unless the recipient failed to abide by the rules of the Atlantic Coast Conference (ACC), the NCAA, or the institution or failed to maintain eligibility for intercollegiate athletics according to ACC or institution rules.

Taylor enrolled at Wake Forest for the fall semester of 1967 and played football. At the completion of the fall semester, he had a grade point average below Wake Forest requirements for all students after completion of their freshman year. Taylor notified the football coach he would not participate in practice sessions during the spring semester of 1968 until his grades improved.

After the spring semester, Taylor improved his grade point average above the required standard. However, Taylor decided he no longer wished to play football. In the fall semester of 1968, Gregg Taylor attended Wake Forest but did not play football.

NCAA regulations permitted a college or university to terminate a scholarship during the period of the award if the recipient voluntarily rendered himself or herself ineligible for intercollegiate competition, but only if:

(1) gradation or cancellation of aid is carried out by the regular disciplinary and/or scholarship awards authorities of the institution;
(2) the student has the opportunity for a hearing; and
(3) such action is based on institutional policy applicable to the general student body.

In May 1969, Gregg Taylor was notified that the Faculty Athletic Committee would hold a hearing concerning his scholarship. Taylor attended the hearing, which resulted in a recommendation to the Scholarship Committee that Taylor's scholarship should be terminated because of his failure to participate in the football program. The Scholarship Committee accepted the recommendation and notified Taylor that his scholarship would terminate at the end of the 1968–69 academic year. Taylor continued to attend Wake Forest and graduated from the university in June 1971.

The Taylors claimed that they had an oral agreement with Wake Forest, assuring them that if Gregg did not make reasonable academic progress, his athletic involvement would be limited to the point at which his academics would not suffer. The Taylors also claimed that the agreement allowed them to judge what was reasonable academic progress.

The court of appeals ruled in dismissing the claims that the written scholarship agreement could not be construed to give the Taylors the right to determine "reasonable academic progress" for Gregg. In consideration for the scholarship grant, Gregg Taylor agreed to maintain his athletic eligibility, which meant being physically prepared and maintaining a sufficient grade point average. Since his grade point average after the spring semester of 1968 was above the eligibility requirements of Wake Forest, he was required to attend regular practice sessions and games in order to comply with his part of the contract. Since Taylor refused to participate in the football program when he was scholastically eligible to do so, Wake Forest acted properly when it terminated his scholarship. The Taylors were not entitled to recover the educational expenses incurred during the 1969–70 and 1970–71 academic years.

NOTES

1. Both *Begley* and *Taylor* were decided on the basis of a contractual analysis. However, none of the problems of viewing the scholarship as a contract are raised in the decisions.

2. In *Lohrke v. University of Louisville*, No. 84–CI–0488 (Ky. Cir. Ct. 1984), plaintiff student-athletes sought reinstatement of their football scholarships on contractual due process grounds. The Kentucky Circuit Court held for the student-athletes. The court concluded that the plaintiffs were entitled to a hearing prior to the termination of their contract for financial aid and that Louisville had also not complied with NCAA regulations (*1984–85 NCAA Manual*, Constitution 3–4–[c]–[2]) which entitled the students to their scholarships through the conclusion of the semester. The court ordered the institution to reimburse

each plaintiff for "the costs of tuition, board and fees for the fall semester of 1983 plus costs of this action, with interest from the date of this judgment."

3. For further information, see the following articles:
(a) Steinbach, "Workmen's Compensation and the Scholarship Athlete," 19 *Cleveland State Law Review* 521 (1970).
(b) "Breach of Contract Suits by Students Against Post-Secondary Institutions: Can They Succeed?" 7 *Journal of College and University Law* 191 (1980–81).
(c) "Contract Law, Due Process and the NCAA," 5 *Journal of College and University Law* 76 (1977).

4. For a critical review of practices surrounding collegiate scholarships, see the *Boston Globe's* three-part series:
(a) "The Power of Transfer," *Boston Globe*, January 16, 1983, p. 61.
(b) "Florida's Disillusioned 7," *Boston Globe*, January 17, 1983, p. 25.
(c) "Dark Side of Victory, BC Recruits Fall by Wayside as Eagles Soar," *Boston Globe*, January 18, 1983, p. 57.

5. For further information, see J. Weistart and C. Lowell, *The Law of Sports*, Bobbs-Merrill Company, Charlottesville, Va. 1979.

2.15–1(b) Worker's Compensation

Worker's compensation is a statutorily created method of providing cash benefits and medical care for employees and their dependents when the employee has suffered personal injuries or death in the course of employment. The purpose of the benefits is to provide employees and their dependents with greater protection than they were afforded by the common-law remedy of a suit for damages. Each state has its own worker's compensation act, which provides a system of money payments for the loss of earning capacity to an employee according to a scale established by the state. The act may also have provisions for furnishing burial, medical, or other expenses that the employee may have due to the injury.

The type of worker's compensation acts differs as to where the funds are derived and the method of payment used in compensating claims. Some acts require payment to be made directly to the employee by the employer. Other acts provide payment from a fund to which many different employers contribute. In still other acts, payments are made by the employer's private insurer.

The primary reason for passing worker's compensation statutes was to eliminate the inadequacies of common-law remedies. These inadequacies resulted from the requirement of the injured party to show that the employer was negligent. Proving negligence was often difficult because of the defenses available to the employer, such as contributory negligence, assumption of the risk, or co-worker negligence. Under a worker's compensation act, the injured employee need only show that the employer was subject to the act, that he or she was an employee under the act's definition, and that the injuries occurred in the course of employment. Fault or employer negligence is not a prerequisite to receiving worker's compensation benefits. Payments are made in intervals, when the injured party and the dependents need money most, instead of waiting for the end of costly litigation. To claim a right to compensation employees need only to bring themselves within the terms of the statute.

This theory of compensation shifts the burden of economic loss from the employee and the dependents under the common law to the employer under the act. The employer considers worker's compensation a production cost; it is the consumer who ultimately bears the economic burden of the cost of the benefits.

Every state's worker's compensation act has the same fundamental principle — that is, workers have a right to receive payment for injuries arising out of their employment. Although each jurisdiction varies in the details of its act, there are some general similarities. For example, all acts call for a short waiting period, during which the employee must either be totally or partially incapacitated. The reason for a waiting period is to avoid small and insignificant claims. When the period ends, the worker is eligible for compensation beginning from the date of the injury. Every jurisdiction sets its own rate schedule, proscribing minimum and maximum amounts for either total disability, partial disability, or permanent and total disability. These amounts are determined by the state legislature and may be revised yearly. An additional benefit, separate from weekly compensation, is added for every person wholly dependent on the injured provider. An additional sum may be awarded for certain specific injuries, such as loss of eyesight. Each state has its own procedure for arriving at dollar amounts, depending on that state's average wage or its economy.

Rensing v. Indiana State University, Etc., 437 N.E. 2d 78 (Ind. Ct. App. 1982)

Plaintiff Fred Rensing filed a claim for worker's compensation benefits seeking recovery for injuries and medical expenses he incurred while playing varsity football for Indiana State University. In a 1976 spring practice session, Rensing was rendered a quadriplegic following a neck injury sustained while making a tackle.

Rensing based his worker's compensation claims on the interpretation that his athletic scholarship agreement was in fact an employment contract with the board of trustees of the university. The Indiana Industrial Board rejected Rensing's claim, finding that no employer-employee relationship existed between the two parties. Rensing brought suit in state court, seeking to overturn the board.

The Indiana Court of Appeals carefully examined the issue of the athletic scholarship as employment contract and ultimately reversed the Industrial Board's decision and remanded the case back to the board for further proceedings. The court stated that worker's compensation cases should be liberally interpreted in order to satisfy public policy concerns and found that the scholarship had "constituted a case for hire . . . and created an employer employee relationship" between the parties. In its decision, the court relied upon the definition of "employee" as "every person, including a minor, in the service of another, under any contract of hire or apprenticeship, written or implied, except one whose employment is both casual and not in the usual course of trade, business, occupation or profession of the employer."

The court, in support of its finding that the athletic scholarship was a contract, stated that "any benefit, commonly the subject of pecuniary compensation, which one, not intending it as a gift, confers on another, who accepts it, is adequate foundation for a legally implied or created promise to render back its value." The financial aid agreement between Rensing and the university "clearly anticipated not only that Rensing would play football in return for his scholarship, but also provided that in the event Rensing suffered an injury during supervised play that . . . the trustees would ask him to assist in other tasks to the extent of his ability." Therefore, the court found no merit in the trustee's claim that the scholarship was only a gift or a grant. The fact that the agreement could be terminated by the school if Rensing failed to fulfill certain requirements was also considered evidence that it was an employment contract. The court also relied upon the Indiana State Legislature's recognition that "scholarships or similar benefits may be viewed as pay pursuant to a 'contract of hire' in the analogous context of unemployment benefits."

The court found that Rensing's employment with the university was "periodically regular and not casual" and that maintaining a football team was in fact "an important aspect of the university's overall business or profession of educating students, even if it may not be said that such athletic endeavors themselves are the university's 'principal' occupation." In conclusion, the court relied upon two other cases involving student-athletes and worker's compensation claims — *Van Horn* v. *Industrial Accident Commission* and *Denver* v. *Nemeth*.

Despite significant differences among *Rensing, Van Horn,* and *Nemeth,* all three cases involved a student-athlete being given a scholarship "solely because of his athletic ability and participation on a football team." The court found, in light of this fact, as well as in light of the size and importance of the football program at Indiana, and given that Rensing's involvement with the university was not by "happenstance," he must be construed as an "employee" of the university under the definition set forth by Indiana law. Consequently, Rensing should be entitled to worker's compensation benefits.

A dissent to the majority argued that while Rensing and the university had entered into a contract, the agreement was not a "contract of hire." Furthermore, while Rensing's participation in football may have very well benefited the university in a general way, he was not necessarily "in the service of the Trustees." Therefore, Rensing's athletic scholarship and subsequent participation in varsity football fell outside of the realm of coverage of Indiana's Workmen's Compensation Act.

Rensing v. Indiana State University Board of Trustees, 444 N.E. 2d 1170 (Ind. 1983)

The Indiana Supreme Court reversed the court of appeals ruling, finding that an athletic scholarship does not constitute an employment contract. In support of its decision, the court noted a number of factors that suggested the scholarship did not constitute an employment contract: (1) Rensing had not reported his benefits on his income tax returns; (2) NCAA regulations are incorporated by reference into the scholarship agreement and since these regulations prohibit payment for athletic participation, the scholarship cannot be a job contract; and (3) the employer's right to dismiss Rensing on the basis of poor performance was conspicuously absent. The court also found that since neither party had the intent to enter into an employment contract, no such contract existed. Since at least three factors "indicative of an employee-employer relationship are absent," the court found that

Rensing had enrolled at the Indiana State University as "a full-time student seeking advanced educational opportunities" and not as "a professional athlete who was being paid for his athletic ability." Rensing could not be construed as an "employee" but only a student-athlete and as such was not entitled to relief under the Workmen's Compensation Act.

Cheatham v. Workers' Compensation Appeals Board, 3 Civ. 21975 (Cal. Ct. App. 1984)

Cheatham was a wrestler who was recruited and awarded an athletic scholarship by California Polytechnic. After suffering a career-ending injury during a team scrimmage, Cheatham applied for worker's compensation.

The worker's compensation judge held for Cheatham, citing the authority of *Van Horn* v. *Industrial Accident Commission* (see Note 3), which held that a football player was an "employee" under the definition in the California Labor Code, because he engaged in athletics in exchange for consideration. The Workers' Compensation Appeals Board reversed, and Cheatham appealed to the California Appeals Court.

The court upheld the appeals board. *Van Horn* was distinguished by the court on the basis that wrestling was not shown to provide a "fair inference of economic benefit to Cal Poly." The court viewed *Van Horn* as "reflecting an unarticulated premise" that football and basketball programs are unique in the relationship between the student-athlete and the institution because those programs are expected to produce revenue. Thus, while the consideration necessary to create the employment relationship was present in *Van Horn* because the petitioner was a football player, it was not in this case, which involved a wrestler. Finally, it was noted that in response to the *Van Horn* decision, the state legislature had amended the California Labor Code to specifically exclude student-athletes from the definition of employee.

NOTES

1. Although most decisions in these cases seem to hinge on the question of whether a student-athlete held a job with the school in addition to the scholarship, the fact that the benefits provided an athlete can be distributed through salary or scholarship in proportions that are often decided by a coach or athletic administrator makes this a questionable standard on which to base a decision concerning an injured athlete's right to worker's compensation. The rationale that student-athletes do nothing to benefit their schools is also questionable when one considers the vast revenues received by athletic departments through gate receipts, broadcasting contracts, and alumni donations — revenues that would be unavailable were it not for the performance of the student-athlete.

The NCAA has recognized the need for protection for injured athletes and has developed proposed guidelines for an insurance policy that would cover athletes who have suffered catastrophic injuries. The voluntary nature of this program, however, would still leave the decision to purchase such policies in the hands of individual institutions (see Section 4.42).

2. In *University of Denver* v. *Nemeth*, 127 Colo. 385, 257 P. 2d 423 (1953), Nemeth, a student-athlete injured during football practice, was found eligible to collect worker's compensation. Evidence showing that Nemeth was given meal money and a job on campus only if he produced on the football field brought him within the worker's compensation act requirement of "injury arising out of and in the course of employment."

3. In *Van Horn* v. *Industrial Accident Commission*, 219 Cal. App. 2d 451, 33 Cal. Rptr. 169 (1963), a student (Van Horn) who had received a football scholarship from California State Polytechnic College, was killed in a plane crash while returning from a game. The Industrial Accident Commission ruled there was no contract of employment between the school and Van Horn and that his scholarship did not depend on his playing football. The California District Court of Appeals overruled the commission's findings and found a contract of employment did exist dependent on Van Horn's athletic prowess, which entitled his dependents to compensation under the act. Although Van Horn also held a job with the college, the court stressed that his scholarship alone could be construed as an employment contract.

4. In *Tookes* v. *Florida State University*, Claim No. 266–39–0855, State of Florida, Department of Labor and Employment Security, Office of the Judge of Industrial Claims (1981), a Florida State University basketball player suffered a knee injury, which sidelined him for most of the 1981–82 season. As a result, he claimed he should be entitled to worker's compensation benefits and filed suit seeking payment of medical bills and "lost salary." Tookes contended that as a scholarship athlete, he was an employee of the university.

The deputy commissioner of the Florida Department of Labor and Employment Security held that Tookes's scholarship was not in itself an employment contract. Had Tookes also held a university job, however, he would have been considered an employee. The deputy commissioner also found that Tookes's meager playing time indicated that the school did not materially benefit from his activities.

On appeal, the industrial claims judge found that no employer-employee relationship existed but asserted that were one present, Tookes must be considered a professional athlete and as such would be a member of a class of employee specifically excluded under Florida law.

5. *State Compensation Ins. Fund* v. *Industrial Comm'n.*, 135 Colo. 570, 314 P. 2d 288 (1957), involved a fatal football injury. Ray Dennison left his job at a gas station to play football for Fort Lewis A & M College after the Fort Lewis coach offered him a job and a scholarship. Dennison received a fatal head injury in a game, and the Industrial Commission of Colorado awarded death benefits to his widow. The Colorado Supreme Court reversed this decision, however, and held that no evidence existed which showed that Dennison's employment was dependent on his playing football. The court also felt it significant that the school did not make money from its football program.

6. In *Coleman* v. *Western Michigan University*, 336 N.W. 2d 224 (Mich. Ct. App. 1983), worker's compensation was denied for an injury received during the course of a college football practice. The Michigan Workmen's Compensation Board denied benefits, and the Court of Appeals of Michigan upheld the decision. The court, relying on *Askew* v. *Macumber*, 398 Mich. 212, 247 N.W. 2d 288 (1976), considered the following four factors in determining whether there existed an "expressed or implied contract for hire":

1. The proposed employer's right to control or dictate the activities of the proposed employee.
2. The proposed employer's right to discipline or fire the proposed employee.
3. The payment of "wages" and, particularly, the extent to which the proposed employee is dependent upon the payment of wages or benefits for his daily living expenses.
4. Whether the task performed by the proposed employee was "an integral part" of the proposed employer's business.

The court held that although a scholarship was "wages," the athlete receiving the scholarship was not an "employee" within the meaning of the statute. The court noted:

As to the limits on defendant's "right to control" the plaintiff's activities, plaintiff suggests that defendant had a great deal of control over plaintiff's activities as a football player. It is observed, however, that such control applied to the sports activity whether or not an athlete had the benefit of a scholarship. Plaintiff's scholarship did not subject him to any extraordinary degree of control over his academic activities. The degree of defendant's control over this aspect of plaintiff's activities was no greater than that over any other student. Moreover, the record suggests that the parties contemplated a primary role for plaintiff's academic activities and only a secondary role for plaintiff's activities as a football player. Plaintiff recognized that "you are a student first, athlete second". In this case, however, plaintiff's football playing was not essential to the business of the defendant university, which plaintiff himself recognizes "as education and research." The record supports the conclusion that defendant's academic program could operate effectively even in the absence of the inter-collegiate football program. Defendant aptly notes that "the football season lasts for only a small portion of the academic year," and contrasts this with the fact that "the greater part of the school year is devoted exclusively to obtaining a regular college education".

7. At least one state legislator has attempted to deal with some of the problems inherent in treating football as big business. Every year since 1981, Nebraska State Senator Ernest Chambers has introduced a bill (Legislative Bill No. 499) that would make all football players at the University of Nebraska employees of the university. The purpose of the bill was to provide football players with the same rights and benefits as other university employees. The rationale was that the football team created tremendous revenues for the university, and thus its members should be protected by worker's compensation insurance, as are other university employees.

The bill specifically stated that it is not to be construed in such a way as to make the players professional athletes, thereby violating NCAA rules. However, despite its intentions, some authorities believed that should such a bill be passed, the players would be deemed professional by the NCAA and would be barred from further amateur competition. The Chambers bill is scheduled to be debated for the first time by the full Nebraska legislature during its 1986 session. For further information, see the following articles:
(a) "CFA Supports Proposal to Pay Football Players," *Lincoln Star*, June 3, 1985, p. 11.
(b) "Let's Pay the Players for the Job They Do," *USA Today*, April 5, 1985, p. A8.
(c) "Chambers Pushes His Pay Plan," *Baton Rouge Morning Advocate*, May 9, 1985, p. E1.
(d) "Chambers: Make Athletes Semi-Pros," *Baton Rouge State-Times*, May 9, 1985, p. F3.
(e) "Nebraska Senator Means Business," *USA Today*, May 10, 1985, p. C2.

8. For further information concerning student-athlete worker's compensation issues, see the following articles:
(a) "Court Orders Worker Compensation for Injured

Athlete," *Chronicle of Higher Education*, June 30, 1982, p. 3.

(b) "Top Indiana Court Hears Rensing Compensation Case," *NCAA News*, December 6, 1982, p. 12.

(c) "4-Year Scholarships Proposed to Avoid Workers' Benefit Disputes," *Chronicle of Higher Education*, February 23, 1983, p. 17.

(d) "Worker's Compensation and College Athletes: Should Universities Be Responsible for Athletes Who Incur Serious Injuries?" 10 *Journal of College and University Law* 197 (1983–84).

2.15–1(c) Letter of Intent

The national letter of intent was developed to regulate the intense competition surrounding the recruitment of talented athletes, commonly referred to as "blue-chippers," to play college athletics. Letters of intent were developed first on the conference level in the late 1940s during a period when intercollegiate athletics first gained national prominence.

The guiding principle behind the letter of intent or preenrollment application is that there is agreement among member institutions that subscribe to the letter of intent to place a time limit on recruiting. On a given date, high school students can sign a letter of intent, and after the signing, no member institution subscribing to the letter will make any effort to recruit the student-athlete. A student who signs the letter, whether or not the athlete actually enrolls at the institution he or she signed with, is not eligible to compete at any other institution subscribing to the letter-of-intent plan for two calendar years of intercollegiate competition (see Exhibits 2–4, 2–5, and 2–6). However, the athlete is free to enroll at any member institution to pursue academic interests.

The letter of intent is administered by the Collegiate Commissioners Association (CCA) through the commissioners of athletic conferences. An institution must be an NCAA member to belong to the program, and the letter of intent applies only to member institutions. Independent institutions that belong to the letter-of-intent program file all necessary paperwork through an allied athletic conference of their choice.

The program in its present form was started in 1964, with 7 conferences and 8 independent institutions joining for a total of 68 schools. In 1982, a women's letter of intent was added. Today, 27 conferences and nearly 300 institutions belong to the program.

Prior to enactment of the letter of intent in 1964, similar programs had been suggested. At the 1961 NCAA convention, a compulsory national letter of intent was proposed. This proposal, and a similar one at the 1962 convention, were defeated, in part out of apprehension expressed by institutions with less developed athletic programs that the letter of intent favored the more established athletic programs.

The letter of intent is considered a pre-enrollment application by the CCA, although much of the language indicates that it may be a contract. In 1985, the men's letter of intent had four signing dates, based on sport categories of (1) football, mid-year junior college transfer, (2) football, (3) basketball, and (4) all other sports (see Exhibit 2–2). There were three women's sport categories for (1) volleyball and field hockey, (2) basketball, and (3) all other sports (see Exhibit 2–3).

In addition to the national letter of intent, many conferences have their own internal letter-of-intent program (see Note 4).

NOTES ────────────────────────

1. See Exhibit 2–4.
2. See Exhibit 2–5.
3. See Exhibit 2–6.
4. Many athletic conferences employ a statement of intent among their own members. The following example is from the *1983–84 Handbook of the Pacific 10 Conference*:

  5. Statement of Intent. The Council may adopt legislation by vote of a majority of its members through which a prospective student-athlete may commit himself to a member institution by means of a Statement of Intent in order to reduce conflicting recruiting pressures. Such legislation may provide that a student who has signed a Statement of Intent accepted by one Pacific-10 member institution and who then enrolls in another Pacific-10 institution without securing favorable action

1984   MEN'S NATIONAL LETTER OF INTENT   1984

(Administered by the Collegiate Commissioners Association)

☐ **FOOTBALL, MID-YEAR JUNIOR COLLEGE TRANSFER: Do not sign prior to 8:00 a.m. December 15, 1983 and no later than January 15, 1984**

☐ **FOOTBALL:**   Do not sign prior to 8:00 a.m. February 8, 1984 and no later than May 1, 1984

☐ **BASKETBALL:**   Do not sign prior to 8:00 a.m. November 9, 1983 and no later than November 16, 1983 OR do not sign prior to 8:00 a.m. April 11, 1984 and no later than May 15, 1984

☐ **ALL OTHER SPORTS:**   Do not sign prior to 8:00 a.m. April 11, 1984 and no later than
(Place "X" in proper box above)   **August 1, 1984**

Name of student _____
(Type proper name, including middle name or initial)

Address _____
Street Number   City, State, Zip Code

This is to certify my decision to enroll at _____
Name of Institution

IMPORTANT · READ CAREFULLY

It is important to read carefully this entire document, including the reverse side, before signing this Letter in triplicate. One copy is to be retained by you and two copies are to be returned to the institution, one of which will be sent to the appropriate conference commissioner.

---

1. By signing this Letter, I understand that if I enroll in another institution participating in the National Letter of Intent Program, I may not represent that institution in intercollegiate athletic competition until I have been in residence at that institution for two calendar years and in no case will I be eligible for more than two seasons of intercollegiate competition in any sport.

    However, these restrictions will not apply to me:

    (a) If I have not, by the opening day of its classes in the fall of 1984 (or the opening day of its classes of the winter or spring term of 1984 for a mid-year junior college entrant in the sport of football), met the requirements for admission to the institution named above, its academic requirements for financial aid to athletes, the NCAA 2.000 GPA requirement, and the junior college transfer rule; or

    (b) If I attend the institution named above for at least one academic year; or

    (c) If I graduate from junior college after having signed a National Letter of Intent while in high school or during my first year in junior college; or

    (d) If I have not attended any institution (or attended an institution, including a junior college, which does not participate in the National Letter of Intent Program) for the next academic year after signing this Letter, provided my request for athletic related financial aid for the following fall term is not approved by the institution with which I signed. In order to receive this waiver, I must file with the appropriate conference commissioner a statement from the Director of Athletics at the institution with which I signed certifying that such financial aid will not be available to me for the requested fall term; or

    (e) If I serve on active duty with the armed forces of the United States or on an official church mission for at least eighteen (18) months; or

    (f) If my sport is discontinued by the institution with which I signed this Letter.

2. I understand that **THIS IS NOT AN AWARD OF FINANCIAL AID.** If my enrollment decision is made with the understanding that I will receive financial aid, I should have in my possession before signing this Letter a written statement from the institution which lists the terms and conditions, including the amount and duration, of such financial aid.

I certify that I have read all terms and conditions on pages 1 and 2, fully understand, accept and agree to be bound by them. *(All three copies must be signed individually for this Letter to be valid. Do not use carbons).*

SIGNED _____   _____   _____
                        Student   Date & Time   Social Security Number

SIGNED _____   _____   _____
                 Parent or Legal Guardian   Date   Time

Submission of this Letter has been authorized by:

SIGNED _____   _____   _____
                 Director of Athletics   Date Issued to Student   Sport

3. **I MAY SIGN ONLY ONE VALID NATIONAL LETTER OF INTENT.** However, if this Letter is rendered null and void under item 1 - (a) on page 1, I remain free to enroll in any institution of my choice where I am admissible and shall be permitted to sign another Letter in a subsequent signing year.

4. I understand that I have signed this Letter with the **institution** and not for a particular sport.

5. I understand that all participating conferences and institutions (listed below) are obligated to respect my decision **and shall cease to recruit me once I have signed this Letter.**

6. If my parent or legal guardian and I fail to sign this Letter within 14 days after it has been issued to me it will be invalid. In that event, this Letter may be reissued. (Note: Exception is November 9-16, 1983, signing period for basketball).

7. My signature on this Letter nullifies any agreements, oral or otherwise, which would release me from the conditions stated on this Letter.

8. This Letter must be signed and dated by the Director of Athletics or his/her authorized representative before submission to me and my parent or legal guardian for our signatures. The Letter may be mailed prior to the initial signing date.

9. This Letter must be filed with the appropriate conference by the institution with which I sign within **21 days** after the date of final signature or it will be invalid. In that event, this Letter may be reissued.

10. If I have knowledge that I or my parent/legal guardian have falsified any part of this Letter, I understand that I shall forfeit the first two years of my eligibility at the participating institution in which I enroll as outlined in item 1.

11. A release procedure shall be provided in the event the student-athlete and the institution mutually agree to release each other from any obligations of the Letter. A student-athlete receiving a formal release shall not be eligible for practice and competition at the second institution during the first academic year of residence and shall have no more than three seasons of eligibility remaining. The form must be signed by the student-athlete, his parent or legal guardian, and the Director of Athletics at the institution with which he signed. A copy of the release must be filed with the conference which processes the Letters of the signing institution.

12. This Letter applies only to students who will be entering a four year institution for the first time as a full time student.

The following Conferences and Institutions have subscribed to and are cooperating in the National Letter of Intent Plan administered by the Collegiate Commissioners Association:

COMMISSIONERS OF THE FOLLOWING CONFERENCES:

Atlantic Coast	Lone Star	North Central	Southwest
Atlantic 10	Metropolitan	Ohio Valley	Southwestern
Big East	Mid-American	Pacific Coast	Sun Belt
Big Eight	Mid-Continent	Pacific-10	Trans America
Big Sky	Mid-Eastern	Southeastern	West Coast
Big Ten	Midwestern City	Southern	Western
California Collegiate	Missouri Intercollegiate	Southern Intercollegiate	Western Football
Central Intercollegiate	Missouri Valley	Southland	

DIRECTORS OF ATHLETICS OF THE FOLLOWING INSTITUTIONS:

Arkansas-Pine Bluff	Florida International	Minnesota-Duluth	Slippery Rock
Augusta	Florida Southern	Morgan State	Southeastern Louisiana
Baptist	Fordham	New Hampshire	Southwestern Louisiana
Bellarmine	Gannon	New Orleans	Southern Illinois-
Brooklyn	George Mason	Niagara	Edwardsville
Campbell	Grand Valley	North Carolina-Wilmington	Stetson
Canisius	Hofstra	Northern Kentucky	Tampa
Central Florida	Indiana-Purdue (Ft. Wayne)	Northern Michigan	Tennessee State
Central State (Ohio)	Indiana State-Evansville	Notre Dame	Texas-San Antonio
Chicago State	Iona	Oakland	Transylvania
Clarkson	James Madison	Pan American	Troy State
Dayton	Kentucky Wesleyan	Randolph-Macon	Utica
Delta State	Lake Superior	Richmond	Valdosta State
DePaul	Liberty Baptist	Robert Morris	Vermont
East Carolina	Maine (Orono)	Rollins	Wayne State
Eastern Montana	Manhattan	St. Francis (PA.)	William and Mary
Eastern Washington	Marist	Saint Leo	Wright State
Eckerd	Marquette	St. Michael's	
Fairfield	Miami (Florida)	St. Peter's (New Jersey)	
Ferris State	Michigan Tech	Siena	

Exhibit 2-4   Men's National Letter of Intent, 1984 (*Source:* Collegiate Commissioner's Association)

1984 WOMEN'S NATIONAL LETTER OF INTENT 1984

(Administered by the Collegiate Commissioners Association)

☐ **Volleyball and Field Hockey: Do not sign prior to 8:00 a.m. February 8, 1984 and no later than August 1, 1984**

☐ **Basketball: Do not sign prior to 8:00 a.m. November 9, 1983 and no later than November 16, 1983 OR do not sign prior to 8:00 a.m. April 11, 1984 and no later than August 1, 1984.**

☐ **All other sports: Do not sign prior to 8:00 a.m. April 11, 1984 and no later than August 1, 1984**

Name of student _____
(Type proper name, including middle name or initial)

Address _____   _____
Street Number   City, State, Zip Code

This is to certify my decision to enroll at _____
Name of Institution

IMPORTANT · READ CAREFULLY

It is important to read carefully this entire document, including the reverse side, before signing this Letter in triplicate. One copy is to be retained by you and two copies are to be returned to the institution, one of which will be sent to the appropriate conference commissioner.

---

1. By signing this Letter, I understand that if I enroll in another institution participating in the National Letter of Intent Program, I may not represent that institution in intercollegiate athletic competition until I have been in residence at that institution for two calendar years and in no case will I be eligible for more than two seasons of intercollegiate competition in any sport.

   However, these restrictions will not apply to me:

   (a) If I have not, by the opening day of its classes in the fall of 1984, met the requirements for admission to the institution named above, its academic requirements for financial aid to athletes, the NCAA 2.000 GPA requirement, if applicable; or

   (b) If I attend the institution named above for at least one academic year; or

   (c) If I graduate from junior college after having signed a National Letter of Intent while in high school or during my first year in junior college; or

   (d) If I have not attended any institution (or attended an institution, including a junior college, which does not participate in the National Letter of Intent Program) for the next academic year after signing this Letter, provided my request for athletic related financial aid for the following fall term is not approved by the institution with which I signed. In order to receive this waiver, I must file with the appropriate conference commissioner a statement from the Director of Athletics at the institution with which I signed certifying that such financial aid will not be available to me for the requested fall term; or

   (e) If I serve on active duty with the armed forces of the United States or on an official church mission for at least eighteen (18) months; or

   (f) If my sport is discontinued by the institution with which I signed this Letter.

2. I understand that **THIS IS NOT AN AWARD OF FINANCIAL AID.** If my enrollment decision is made with the understanding that I will receive financial aid, I should have in my possession before signing this Letter a written statement from the institution which lists the terms and conditions, including the amount and duration, of such financial aid.

I certify that I have read all terms and conditions on pages 1 and 2, fully understand, accept and agree to be bound by them. All three copies must be signed individually for this Letter to be valid. Do not use carbons.

SIGNED _____   _____   _____
Student   Date & Time   Social Security Number

SIGNED _____   _____   _____
Parent or Legal Guardian   Date   Time

Submission of this Letter has been authorized by:

SIGNED _____   _____   _____
Director of Athletics   Date Issued to Student   Sport

3. **I MAY SIGN ONLY ONE VALID NATIONAL LETTER OF INTENT.** However, if this Letter is rendered null and void under item 1 - (a) on page 1, I remain free to enroll in any institution of my choice where I am admissible and shall be permitted to sign another Letter in a subsequent signing year.

4. I understand that I have signed this Letter with the **institution** and not for a particular sport.

5. I understand that all participating conferences and institutions (listed below) are obligated to respect my decision **and shall cease to recruit me once I have signed this Letter.**

6. If my parent or legal guardian and I fail to sign this Letter within 14 days after it has been issued to me it will be invalid. In that event, this Letter may be Reissued. (Note: Exception is November 9-16, 1983, signing period for basketball.)

7. My signature on this Letter nullifies any agreements, oral or otherwise, which would release me from the conditions stated on this Letter.

8. This Letter must be signed and dated by the Director of Athletics or his/her authorized representative before submission to me and my parent or legal guardian for our signatures. This Letter may be mailed prior to the initial signing date.

9. This Letter must be filed with the appropriate conference by the institution with which I sign within **21 days** after the date of final signature or it will be invalid. In that event, this Letter may be reissued.

10. If I have knowledge that I or my parent/legal guardian have falsified any part of this Letter, I understand that I shall forfeit the first two years of my eligibility at the participating institution in which I enroll as outlined in item 1.

11. A release procedure shall be provided in the event the student-athlete and the institution mutually agree to release each other from any obligations of the Letter. A student-athlete receiving a formal release shall not be eligible for practice and competition at the second institution during the first academic year of residence and shall have no more than three seasons of eligibility remaining. The form must be signed by the student-athlete, his parent or legal guardian, and the Director of Athletics at the institution with which he signed. A copy of the release must be filed with the conference which processes the Letters of the signing institution.

12. This letter applies only to students who will be entering a four-year institution for the first time as a full time student.

The following Conferences and Institutions have subscribed to and are cooperating in the National Letter of Intent Plan administered by the Collegiate Commissioners Association:

COMMISSIONERS OF THE FOLLOWING CONFERENCES:

Atlantic Coast	High Country	North Central	Southland
Atlantic 10	Lone Star	North Star	Southwest
Big East	Metropolitan	Northern Pacific	Southwestern
Big Eight	Mid-American	Ohio Valley	Sun Belt
Big Ten	Mid-Continent	Oil Country	Trans America
California Collegiate	Mid-Eastern	Southeastern	West Coast
Central Intercollegiate	Missouri Intercollegiate	Southern	Western Collegiate
Gateway	Mountain West	Southern Intercollegiate	

DIRECTORS OF ATHLETICS OF THE FOLLOWING INSTITUTIONS:

Augusta	Georgia Southern	Nevada-Reno	Slippery Rock
Bellarmine	Grand Valley	New Orleans	Southeastern Louisiana
Brooklyn	Hawaii	North Carolina-Wilmington	Southwestern Louisiana
California-Irvine	Indiana-Purdue	Northeastern	Southern Illinois-
California-Santa Barbara	Iona	Northern Arizona	Edwardsville
Central Florida	Lake Superior	Northern Kentucky	Stetson
Central State (Ohio)	Liberty Baptist	Northern Michigan	Tampa
Chicago State	Loyola Marymount	Oakland	Tennessee State
Creighton	Maine (Orono)	Pepperdine	Troy State
Delta State	Manhattan	Randolph-Macon	Tulsa
East Carolina	Miami (Florida)	Richmond	Utah State
Eastern Montana	Michigan Tech	Rollins	Valdosta State
Fairfield	Minnesota-Duluth	St. Francis (PA.)	Wayne State
Florida Southern	Morgan State	Saint Leo	William and Mary
Fordham	Mount St. Joseph	St. Peter's (NJ)	Wright State
George Mason	Nevada-Las Vegas	San Diego	

Exhibit 2-5   Women's National Letter of Intent, 1984 (*Source:* Collegiate Commissioner's Association)

MEN'S AND WOMEN'S
1984   NATIONAL LETTER OF INTENT   1984
POLICIES AND INTERPRETATIONS
(Administered by the Collegiate Commissioners Association)

1. Each conference and participating institution agrees to abide by the regulations and procedures outlined in the National Letter of Intent Program.

2. An institution must be an NCAA member to participate in the Program, and the Letter applies only to those institutions.

3. The Steering Committee has been authorized to issue interpretations, settle disputes, and consider petitions for release from the provisions of the Letter where there are extenuating circumstances. Its decision may be appealed to the CCA, which is the final adjudication body.

4. No additions or deletions may be made to the Letter or the release form.

5. A coach is not authorized to void, cancel or give a release to the Letter.

6. A release from the Letter shall apply to all participating institutions and cannot be conditional or selective by institution.

7. When two members of the same conference are in disagreement involving the validity of a Letter, the conference commissioner shall be empowered to resolve the issue.

8. The prospect should be notified anytime his/her signed National Letter of Intent has been declared invalid or null and void.

9. In matters involving the validity of the Letter of administrative procedures between two or more institutions not members of the same conference, the appropriate conference commissioners shall take steps to ascertain the facts and apply National Letter of Intent rules. If the case cannot be settled in this manner, it shall be submitted to the Steering Committee. The prospective student-athlete may submit any information he/she desires.

10. The institution shall immediately notify a prospect if he/she fails to meet, for the fall of 1984 (or winter or spring term of 1984 for mid-year junior college transfers in the sport of football), its admission requirements, or its academic requirements for financial aid to athletes, or the NCAA 2.000 GPA requirement (or NCAA junior college transfer rule) if applicable. The institution shall immediately notify the appropriate conference commissioner of the prospective student-athlete's failure to meet any of these requirements, and the date on which the notification of such failure was sent to the prospect. The conference commissioner shall promptly notify all other participating conference commissioners.

11. The parent or legal guardian is required to sign the Letter regardless of the age or marital status of the prospective student-athlete.

12. If the prospect does not have a living parent or a legal guardian, the Letter should be signed by the person who is acting in the capacity of a guardian. An explanation of the circumstances should accompany the Letter.

13. If the NCAA or Conference declares a student ineligible for competition at the institution at which he/she signed a National Letter of Intent, he/she shall be released from the Letter, but may not sign a second letter.

14. It is presumed that a student is eligible for admission and financial aid at the institution for which he/she signed a National Letter of Intent until information is submitted to the contrary. This means that it is mandatory for the student to provide a transcript of his/her previous academic record and an application for admission to the institution where he/she signed a National Letter of Intent when requested.

15. The National Letter of Intent rules and regulations shall apply to all sports recognized by the member institution as varsity intercollegiate sports in which the NCAA sponsors championships or publishes the official playing rules.

16. The National Letter is considered to be officially signed on the final date of signature by the prospective student and his/hers parent or legal guardian. A National Letter is validated when name is listed on signing list that is circulated to all conferences. If an incomplete Letter is submitted to a conference office by an institution, the Letter may be returned and reissued. If no time of day is listed for signing of Letter it is assumed a 11:59 P.M. signing time.

17. It is a breach of ethics for an institution to sign a prospective student-athlete to an invalid second Letter for the purpose of making the prospect feel obligated to that institution.

18. If a prospect signing a Letter is eligible for admission but the institution defers his/her admission to a subsequent term, the Letter shall be rendered null and void. However, if the prospect defers his/her admission, the Letter remains valid.

19. Any prospect who signs a Letter prior to April 11, 1984 and who becomes a countable player under NCAA Bylaw 6, shall be counted in the maximum awards in the designated sport in his/her first year at the institution with which he/she signed.

20. The conditions of the National Letter of Intent Program shall not apply retroactively to an institution joining the Program.

21. A prospect who signs a professional sports contract remains bound by Letter rules when financial aid cannot be made available to him/her by the institution with which she/she signed.

22. Upon receipt of the completed Letter, the commissioner of each conference shall promptly notify the Big Ten Conference (two copies of signing lists for computer check for double signings) and one copy to the NCAA office.

23. The National Letter of Intent will carry a four year statute of limitations.

24. For a prospective student-athlete signing a National Letter of Intent as a Mid-Year Junior College Transfer, the National Letter applies for the following fall term if the student was eligible for admission, financial aid, and met the junior college transfer requirements for the winter or spring term.

Exhibit 2-6   Men's and Women's National Letter of Intent (*Source:* Collegiate Commissioner's Association)

on a petition for relief of penalties shall lose such eligibility for participation in Pacific-10 sports and for financial assistance as provided in such legislation.

(a) National Letter of Intent. The Pacific-10 annually subscribes to a voluntary National Letter of Intent program. Member institutions and any prospective student-athlete who signs such a Letter of Intent shall be bound by the regulations in effect at the time of such signing. [1983–84 *Handbook of the Pacific-10 Conference*, C8–5, p. 14]

5. In 1983, independent institutions whose women's programs participate in the program will pay a total of $150 to the conference office which processes their letters to defray expenses in administering the program — printing, mailing, telephone, maintaining records, and so forth. Each participating conference is required to pay a fee of $100 to the Big Ten Conference, plus $15 for each independent institution they serve, for maintaining a computer list of all signees nationwide. In addition, each conference office will absorb administration costs for its member institutions.

2.15–1(d) Excess Financial Aid

The amount of financial aid a student-athlete may receive from the institution or from outside sources is strictly regulated under NCAA guidelines. Scholarships may not exceed commonly accepted educational expenses (*1985–86 NCAA Manual*, Constitution 3–1–[g]), which are limited to tuition and fees, room and board, and books. A school or other donor is not allowed to pay expenses exceeding these, and the student-athlete is not allowed to have any other benefits generally unavailable to all members of the student body (*1985–86 NCAA Manual*, Constitution 3–1–[g]–[1–5]).

A student-athlete may participate in any sport in which he or she has never participated at the professional level. However, a student who is either currently under contract to a professional organization or who is receiving compensation from a professional organization may not receive financial aid. A student-athlete may never receive payment, or even a promise of payment, for playing in the chosen sport, directly or indirectly, either before enrollment in college or during the period of eligibility (*1985–86 NCAA Manual*, Constitution 3–1–[a]–[1]). Acceptance of either payment or the

promise of money automatically categorizes the student-athlete as a professional, and thus erases amateur status. The athlete is also not entitled to be paid or sponsored when not representing the institution (unless by a natural or legal sponsor). Also, the student-athlete may not receive special treatment because of athletic prowess — for example, loans on a deferred pay-back basis, automobiles, or special living quarters (*1985–86 NCAA Manual*, Constitution 3–1–[g]–[5]).

Student-athletes may not participate in any competition for cash or prizes, either for themselves or for a donation on their behalf, unless they are eligible to receive such monies under the NCAA guidelines (*1985–86 NCAA Manual*, Constitution, 3–1–[i]–[1]–[i–v]). For example, the NCAA has approved the granting of a scholarship in a student's name when selected as a player of the game. The NCAA has not approved a student-athlete's participation in events such as television's "Superstars" competition on ABC–TV. A student-athlete would also jeopardize eligibility upon receiving, for example, a country-club membership as a prize or compensation.

The rule of thumb regarding payment or receipt of expenses provides that an athlete may not receive money for expenses that are in excess of the actual and necessary expenses involved in an activity authorized by the NCAA. Examples of prohibited expense payments include travel expenses to a special location for an article on and/or photographs of a student-athlete (unless in conjunction with the receipt of an established/authorized award at that location) and expenses from an agent seeking to market the student-athlete's athletic skills (*1985–86 NCAA Manual*, Constitution, 3–1–[e]).

Under NCAA rules, a member school may allow a student-athlete a maximum of four complimentary admissions for each contest in his or her particular sport. However, the student-athlete's guests must sign for the admissions and receive no tickets (*1985–86 NCAA Manual*, Constitution 3–1–[g]–[3]).

Tickets are prohibited since the NCAA believes that they tempt the student-athlete to receive compensation by selling the tickets for greater than the face value to athletic department supporters (see Section 2.15–2, Note 1). A student-athlete, however, may receive free admission to a professional contest without endangering her or his amateur status and college eligibility.

Jones v. National Collegiate Athletic Ass'n., 392 F. Supp. 295 (D. Mass. 1975)

Plaintiff, an American ice hockey player attending Northeastern University in Boston, brought an action against the NCAA for a preliminary injunction to enjoin the NCAA from declaring him ineligible to compete and from imposing sanctions against Northeastern if the university allowed him to play.

Prior to entering Northeastern University, plaintiff Jones was compensated for five years while playing junior hockey in Canada. For the first three years, plaintiff was in high school, and the compensation was primarily in the form of room, board, and living expenses. During one of those three years, however, he was paid a weekly salary and received a signing bonus. During the two years between high school and college, he received weekly allowances, tuition expenses, and game reimbursements.

When the director of athletics at Northeastern University learned of Jones's past experience, he declared him ineligible to play ice hockey; however, the athletic director sought waivers from both the Eastern Collegiate Athletic Conference (ECAC) and the NCAA to permit Jones to participate. The ECAC granted the waiver, but the NCAA denied the request.

Jones set forth two complaints, one being for a denial of due process and equal protection and the other being for an antitrust claim for restraint of trade and monopoly. The court

denied the plaintiff injunctive relief, finding that Jones failed to show a substantial likelihood of prevailing on the merits at trial.

To arrive at this conclusion, the court determined that the plaintiff was clearly ineligible under NCAA rules, which state that a player is ineligible for intercollegiate competition if he "has directly or indirectly used his athletic skill for pay in any form in that sport; however, an individual may accept or have accepted scholarships or educational grants-in-aid administered by an educational institution that do not conflict with the governing legislation of this Association" (*NCAA Manual*, Constitution, 3–1).

The court declared that the bonus, weekly allowances, and other financial benefits paid to Jones during his five years of junior hockey constituted a violation of the NCAA constitution. In distinguishing this case from *Buckton v. National Collegiate Athletic Ass'n.* (see Note 2), in which a Canadian citizen was granted eligibility for intercollegiate competition in the United States despite having played junior hockey for pay in Canada while in secondary school, the court stated that as a Canadian citizen, Buckton had no recourse but to play junior hockey since Canadian secondary schools have no scholastic ice hockey programs. Jones, however, was an American and from an area where hockey was available in secondary school. He did not have to play for pay in order to compete. Even if Jones had received no compensation, he would still have been ineligible because the NCAA rules state that to play a sport in a foreign country for a team on which other athletes receive compensation renders the athlete ineligible to compete in NCAA events (*NCAA Manual*, Constitution, 3–1). Participation in Canadian junior hockey was not required for the plaintiff to compete in ice hockey.

In addition, Jones spent two years out of school while continuing to play hockey for pay, some of which pay was characterized as tuition expenses. On the other hand, in *Buckton*, the plaintiff was in school throughout his junior hockey career, so it was reasonable to compare the compensation he received "to the aid permissibly awarded by American schools in the form of athletic scholarships." Jones received so-called "tuition expenses" even when he was not in school, in addition to other compensation — an obvious NCAA eligibility violation.

Finding no reason to apply a standard of strict scrutiny, as was done in *Buckton* when the eligibility rules were found to constitute a de facto discrimination against the plaintiff on the basis of national origin, the court determined that the NCAA's eligibility regulations could be found invalid only if they bore no *rational relationship* to the organization's legitimate objectives. Under this standard, the court found no reason to invalidate the eligibility rules, holding that the eligibility regulations did indeed serve to promote amateurism in college athletics.

The court concluded with respect to equal protection that "there is no claim that the NCAA has defined eligibility in terms that operate as an economic penalty, or has imposed costs upon the plaintiff which deprive him of an opportunity to play hockey." The fact that it is more difficult for poor athletes to avoid receiving compensation from semi-professional teams, "is not the type of absolute deprivation which constitutes unconstitutional discrimination on the basis of wealth."

With respect to the antitrust allegations, the court held that the Sherman Act does not apply to the NCAA or its members in the setting of the eligibility standards for intercollegiate athletics. This case, dealing with a student and a voluntary athletic association, did not fit the business scheme that the Sherman Act was constructed to govern. It did not concern the protection of competition in the marketplace. In addition, since the NCAA's eligibility rules were found to be consistent with the association's policy of preserving and advancing amateurism in college athletics, plaintiff's claim of a secondary group boycott failed because it must be shown

that the NCAA's purpose was to exclude a person or group from the market or accomplish some other anticompetitive objective for such a boycott to exist.

The court also held that there was no evidence in this case to show that the NCAA's eligibility decisions were enacted for the purpose of forming a monopoly. A request for a preliminary injunction was denied.

NOTES _____

1. In *Wiley v. National Collegiate Athletic Ass'n.*, 612 F. 2d 473 (10th Cir. 1979), *cert denied*, 446 U.S. 943, 100 S. Ct. 2168, 64 L. Ed. 2d 798 (1980), an action was brought by a student-athlete who was declared ineligible to compete because his financial aid exceeded the amount allowed by the NCAA. Plaintiff had been awarded a full Basic Educational Opportunity Grant (BEOG) in addition to an athletic scholarship. Taken together, they exceeded the financial limitations imposed by the institutions under NCAA regulations and made Wiley ineligible to compete (the court applied a rational basis analysis rejecting a strict scrutiny approach because poverty or wealth is not a suspect classification). The court refused to enjoin the NCAA from enforcing its regulations on the grounds that "unless clearly defined constitutional principles are at issue, suits by student-athletes against high school athletic association or NCAA rules do not present a substantial federal question."

2. In *Buckton v. National Collegiate Athletic Ass'n.*, 366 F. Supp. 1158 (D. Mass. 1973), plaintiff Canadian ice hockey players were denied eligibility because they had received funding from junior league hockey teams in Canada rather than from high schools, as is the custom in the United States. The court enjoined the NCAA from enforcing ineligibility because the rule, in effect, discriminated against plaintiffs on the basis of the suspect criteria of national origin (see Section 1.33).

2.15–1(e) Congressional Concerns over Athletic Scholarships and Eligibility

In June 1984, the Subcommittee on Education, Arts and Humanities of the Committee on Labor and Human Resources of the United States Senate held hearings on the "Oversight on College Athletic Programs." The hearings covered a number of issues, including (1) the exploitation of athletes who clearly have the academic ability to succeed in college but do not because of the time demands placed upon them by athletic pursuits; (2) the dilution of academic standards to accommodate the student-athlete; and (3) the inadequacy of athletic scholarship programs to respond to the educational needs of student-athletes who no longer are able to participate — because of injury, for example — in their college athletic program.

One committee member, Senator Howard Metzenbaum of Ohio, noted during his questioning of witnesses that he was contemplating introducing a bill that would establish federal authority for the regulation of college athletic scholarships. Such legislation would require university athletic departments to maintain an accurate accounting of all athletes under scholarship, broken down by sport, in order that their academic progress could be tracked. The proposed legislation would also require institutions to make an educational commitment to the athlete at the time of the recruitment so that scholarship funding for the athlete's education and eventual graduation would always be available. Time would not be a factor in the scholarship — nor would loss of athletic services due to injury. Penalties would involve some impact on an institution's Title IV funds under the Federal Aid to Education Act.

General reaction to the proposed legislation was negative, with witnesses stating this was not an area of federal government concern. Senator Metzenbaum himself voiced reservations but concluded: ". . . it would be far better if the Government would not be involved, and yet usually you find legislation that comes about because there is a problem and no solution is provided by those who are in a position to provide the solution. And so, out of a sense of frustration, you find a legislative approach."

Edward T. Foote II, president of the University of Miami, noted in his statement before the committee:

The pressures to win are great. They increase more with winning, and even faster with losing. Winning creates excitement, not only in an athletic program but throughout a university. Students like it. Alumni like it. The conventional wisdom is that a winning athletic program generates spinoff benefits, from donations to more freshman applicants.

This is hardly startling news. Winning is no more fun than it was a generation ago. But in recent years, there has been a growing perception throughout higher education that something significant was changing in the equation of major, intercollegiate athletics. It was a dangerous change. If winning wasn't more fun, it was getting much more important to a lot of people. It is not a change of kind, but of intensity and magnitude.

My own view is that the principal reason for the change is television, and especially the money it generates.

During the past generation, as television has woven itself so tightly into the fabric of American life, perhaps no undertakings have been more dramatically affected than athletics, professional and amateur. The money television generates for the successful is immense. The going rate now for a football team's appearance on national television is $675,000, and for a regionally televised game, $350,000. The Orange Bowl paid the University of Miami and the University of Nebraska each $1,800,000 just for showing up. In addition, the University of Miami Football Hurricanes generated $1,094,910 in television income during the fiscal year that ended June 1st. The instant celebrity of athletic stars, made possible by television, translates into cash almost as fast.

Money is not the only temptation presented by television. Amateur athletics are ideal fare for television's capacity to magnify and dramatize. The most mundane sporting event takes on excitement when properly narrated, packaged and hyped. Naturally exciting sports such as football and basketball assume an unnatural magic far larger than mere life itself.

In summary, my message is threefold: first, the American system of big-time intercollegiate athletic competition can and sometimes does distort important educational principles to the detriment of the nation's colleges, universities and students; second, the threat can be resisted successfully by fidelity to those principles, and the world of higher education is stiffening that resistance; third, with all due respect, the forum for addressing and resolving the problem is not the Congress of the United States.

NOTES

1. At the above hearings, Kevin J. Ross, a former Creighton University scholarship basketball player, gave the following testimony:

One cannot possibly earn good grades if they have not been taught to read, and, the only other recourse is to become good in athletics and earn a scholarship to college by proving that you can conquer the world in a pair of gym shoes. Of course, being six foot nine inches helps to bring the college recruiters to your door. If these recruiters feel that you can earn extra monies for the college by lighting up the scoreboards and keeping the crowds yelling it therefore does not become necessary to function in classes.

Creighton knew that I could not read or write well enough for college. In fact they saw the incompletes and poor grades that I had earned in high school. Yet they ignored these grades with the view that I could serve them well on the basketball court.

Had I received a degree from Creighton University I would have been a part of our present national abuse in education ... I would have earned a degree, but it would have not been beneficial to those students that I worked with, nor to society. We must cease the degree factories that give out degrees to people regardless of their achievements.

In fact, not much time is given one to attend classes, since most of an athlete's time is taken up in traveling across the country and in practicing to win on the basketball court.

The athletic director at Creighton University never bothered with the reality that I was an illiterate, he was only concerned with my playing ball for Creighton. The courses were selected for me by the athletic director and coaches at Creighton, and, of course, these courses were easy courses such as the theory of first aid, the theory of tennis and basketball; courses that required not one lofty thought.

If I had a paper to turn in for my classes these were done for me by the secretaries at the college. If I failed a class this was taken care of for me by the coach or athletic director.

Everything is taken care of for you academically unless you have the misfortune of becoming incapacitated to play. I was injured in my junior year, and after having knee surgery I no longer seemed to be able to do anything right. I refused to leave the college without a

degree, or an explanation as to why I was considered good enough to remain at the college until my injury. To appease me the athletic director gave me an option that he knew would ridicule even the strongest of men — the option to return to a grammar school with young children whose skills made me even more inferior. In fact, I thought of suicide many times.

The athletic director called Mrs. Marva Collins of Westside Preparatory School and asked if she would accept me in the school as a student. Mrs. Collins later said that she thought surely it was a joke, but she did indicate that she would let me enroll in the school. Creighton University paid my tuition there for a year with a monthly stipend of $350.00. I, however, dared not take a job, and I had no place to live. I could not afford to work part-time since I had a full-time responsibility of recapturing sixteen years of malpractice and bad education. This was my last chance to breathe literacy.

2. At the hearing, Michael Potts, a former scholarship football player at Northwestern University, noted:

In the spring of 1982 I reinjured my collarbone. I was again told that the x-rays were negative and to return to practice. That was on a Thursday. That Saturday, I asked to see the team doctor. I saw him Monday morning and he told me he wanted to keep me out indefinitely, so I attended practice and watched in my street clothes for the remainder of the spring.

It was at that time that they approached me and asked me to petition the NCAA to not be counted as an athlete, but still receive full grant-in-aid. In the fall of 1982, right before the first term was to begin, I called the student finance office to make sure everything was in order.

The lady told me that she had better check because a handwritten list had been sent over of cancellations of athletes. Upon checking, she informed me that my name was on the list. I tried to find out why; I could not get in touch with anyone.

I called the assistant athletic director, and my mother later called the president's secretary. At about 5 o'clock the athletic director's assistant called, and at about 6 o'clock the athletic director called and they said it was a mistake due to computer coding, after the young lady had told me that a handwritten list was sent over, and they reinstated my scholarship.

At the end of that trimester, the one following the cancellation, they kicked me out of school. Upon asking why, they just basically gave me no reason. I appealed three times. The last time, I took my lawyer and my mother and met with the provost and associate provost and they said, "Here is your transcript; we feel that you are not progressing toward a degree" — when I had taken the courses they told me to take.

I had all my chemistry and calculus out of the way;

one physics course to take. They showed me my grades. I said, those are not my grades. They said, yes, they are. I said, no, they are not. I had two grade changes that went into effect and they had changed those grades, and when they found out I had a copy of the transcript and knew that the grades had been changed, they changed the grades back and sent a letter saying that the grades had been changed back to what they originally should have been.

That is basically it. I feel pressure was put on me in an effort to remove me from my academic program after I was no longer of use to them, football-wise.

I was caught in a coaching change. I was also injured, and so I became, so to speak, damaged goods, and I definitely felt the pressure from it.

3. At the hearings, Harry Edwards, Ph.D., Department of Sociology, University of California, Berkeley, testified:

Collegiate football and basketball players also must adjust not only to playing with pain but to living day in and day out with pain as well as in a constant state of fatigue. Neither condition is very conducive to development of study habits nor requisite levels of mental concentration demanded of students competing in the classrooms of this nation's major universities.

Under existing conditions of medical service and surveillance in intercollegiate sports, this situation seems unlikely to change in the near future. That is, in today's highly competitive collegiate sports enterprise, the line can often be intentionally or unwittingly blurred between playing with pain and playing with an injury or even a significant and life threatening illness. Within the last year alone, I have been contacted by athletes who felt pressured to play with varying medical debilities or lose their athletic grants-in-aid. In one instance, an athlete and his parents contacted me concerning a basketball coach who insisted that the young man play, though he had not fully recovered from two dislocated shoulders. In another instance, I was contacted by attorneys representing a young man who complained to his team physician about a lump on his neck in October only to be told that it was nothing of consequence. Near the end of the season, that same lump was diagnosed as cancerous. This case is now in court.

A major problem here is that team physicians are paid by athletic departments. Also, many institutions either prohibit or make it extraordinarily difficult for a student-athlete to obtain a second medical opinion on an injury or illness and even when second medical opinions are permitted, the team physician opinion prevails — not by credibility or medical convention but by the athletic department rule.

And the two most common problems that I hear from athletes — and I do get a chance to talk to athletes on most of these campuses — is, one, they are being pressured into giving up their scholarships as a result of

injury or as a result of not being the blue chip that the coach thought he would be.

And the second thing that I hear most commonly is a concern about, what happens to me if I am injured. And in numerous cases I find that athletes find out too late that there is a limit on how much the school, the athletic department, will spend for them on an injury.

Virtually, no institution carries catastrophic injury insurance; the NCAA does not require it. I understand that they plan to offer it under circumstances where, I believe, the catastrophic injury — knees, shoulders, and so forth — is up about 18 percent.

In some schools they have actually written into the rules that the school will pay for no second opinions; that the school will not be liable for illness. If this athlete is ill, not as a result of a football or basketball injury, the school will not pay for it.

So, this is a major problem that has simply been swept under the rug, and because you are dealing so often with 17- to 19-year-olds or 19- to 20-year-olds, nobody takes them seriously when they raise these complaints, and they do not know what their rights are under these circumstances.

4. At the hearings, Linda Villarosa, director of the Center for Athletes Rights and Education (Bronx, New York), and Robert Williams, governing officer of the Sports Foundation, Inc., in a joint statement noted:

After talking with scores of Ronnie Ryans, our organizations, the Center for Athletes Rights and Education and the Sports Foundation, came together to uncover just how widespread the problem was. In a survey of seven conferences, we found that nearly half of all senior basketball players did not graduate.

And too many of these young student-athletes are black; in fact, 75 percent of all black college athletes do not graduate, while the rate for all athletes is estimated at a little over 50 percent. Although some 58 percent of *all* students leave college before graduating, athletes represent special cases. In many cases they are actively sought out, brought in and carried through the university system, and then dropped after eligibility has expired and they are no longer useful for attracting gate receipts and TV contracts but before they have been able to accumulate enough credits to earn degrees.

But our role is not to vilify and complain about colleges and universities, but instead we are trying to teach our youngsters how the intercollegiate athletic system functions. We created the Athletes and Parents Counseling Program in 1982, and have presented workshops on college sports to student-athletes in the 19 high schools in the Bronx. A team of five speakers, including former New York Knickerbocker Dean "the Dream" Meminger, discusses recruiting, financial aid, Title IX, Proposition 48, careers and professional sports and also gives each student-athlete an information packet to share with his or her parents. This written material includes a checklist featuring valuable questions that a potential recruit should ask a representative of a college when he or she comes to call. One question, for example, asks whether the university will pay for the remainder of a student-athlete's education in the event of injury or after athletic eligibility is exhausted. We encourage potential recruits to go over the questions with recruiters and then ask them to sign the forms as an informal safeguard against problems that might occur later.

The most important message of both the written materials and the spoken presentation is that a student-athlete can exchange athletic talent for a college education but the exchange is equitable only if he or she attends classes and obtains a degree. We encourage our mainly college-bound audience to take responsibility for their academic futures because colleges generally do not do so, and we warn them not to forsake their educations by sinking their energies into the unrealistic dream of a pro career.

We caution them, too, that being a student-athlete in college is difficult: Working in the classroom and working out on the field or court is stressful, time-consuming and exhausting. In a study conducted at the University of Wisconsin, researchers found that out of 105 waking hours per week, freshman basketball players had nearly every minute occupied attempting to juggle practice, travel, games, studying and attending classes. Preliminary findings of a recent C.A.R.E. study show that the pressure of being a student-athlete takes a heavy toll on young men and women. A survey of 500 male and female basketball players in all divisions indicates that significant numbers take easy classes, choose less demanding majors, have others write term papers, cut classes, miss exams and feel that athletic demands prevent them from being top students.

Along with the workshops, we also offer one-to-one counseling with student-athletes and their parents. We help them sift through different colleges, fill-out forms, contact schools and match their athletic and academic skills with suitable colleges. Although we run the program on a tiny budget, our service is free in New York City where only one high school guidance counselor is available to every 770 students.

5. In February 1983, Senator Arlen Specter (Pa) introduced legislation designed to encourage sports leagues to make student-athletes complete their undergraduate education before turning professional. The legislation, S.610, was entitled "The Collegiate Student-Athlete Protection Act of 1983." The legislation amended the federal antitrust laws so that they would not apply" . . . to a joint agreement by or among persons engaging in or conducting the professional sports of football, baseball, basketball, soccer, or hockey designed to encourage college student-athletes to complete their undergraduate education before

becoming professional athletes." See also, "The Collegiate Student-Athlete Protection Act of 1983," *Hearings Before the Committee on the Judiciary, United States Senate*, 98th Cong., 1st Sess., Serial No. J–98–20, May 17 and 23, 1983.

6. In May 1985, Congressman James Howard (N.J.) introduced legislation designed to encourage the nation's universities to make certain that the majority of the student-athletes graduate from college with a degree. The legislation, H.R. 2620, was entitled "The College Athlete Education and Protection Act of 1985." It was designed to amend the Internal Revenue Code of 1954 to " . . . encourage the graduation of student-athletes by denying the deduction for contributions to athletic departments of schools not meeting certain requirements."

2.15–2   Pay

Under NCAA regulations, student-athletes may not receive pay:

> The term "pay" specifically includes, but is not limited to, receipt directly or indirectly of any salary, gratuity or comparable compensation; division or split of surplus; education expenses not permitted by governing legislation of this Association, and excessive or improper expenses, awards and benefits. Expenses received from an outside amateur sports team or organization in excess of actual and necessary travel and meal expenses for practice and game competition shall be considered pay. [1985–86 *NCAA Manual*, Constitution 3–1–(O.I.2)]

This definition applies to all student-athletes competing under NCAA regulations, whether or not they are attending college on an athletic scholarship. The concept of pay deals directly with the concept of amateurism and should not be confused with employment, which is permitted in certain situations under NCAA regulations (see Section 2.15–2 [a]).

The NCAA also considers a student-athlete ineligible who has received pay in any of the following ways:

1. Has taken pay or accepted the promise of pay, in any form, for participation in a sport.
2. Has participated in a sport with the promise that compensation will be forth-

coming upon the completion of inter-collegiate competition.

3. Has directly or indirectly used athletic skill for pay, including payment for the use of his or her name or photographs promoting commercial products.

4. Has directly or indirectly received a salary, reimbursement of expenses, or any form of financial assistance from a professional organization based on athletic skill or participation.

(1985–86 NCAA Manual, Constitution, 3–1, Principle of Amateurism and Student Partici-pation.)

NOTES _____

1. The NCAA prohibits in its constitution the following practices that are deemed "pay" for participation in intercollegiate athletics:

(1) The award of financial aid to a student-athlete that exceeds commonly accepted educational expenses (i.e., tuition and fees, room and board and required course-related books), other than legitimate loans, based upon a regular repayment schedule, available to all students and administered on the same basis for all students.

(2) Payment of excessive or improper expense allow-ances, including, but not limited to, payment of:

(i) Money to team members of individual competitors for unspecified or unitemized expenses;

(ii) Expenses incurred by a student-athlete which are prohibited by the rules governing an amateur non-college event in which the student-athlete participates, or;

(iii) Expenses incurred by a student-athlete competing in an event that occurs at a time when the student-athlete is not regularly enrolled in a full-time program of studies during the regular academic year, or not eligible to represent the institution, except that expenses may be paid for a student-athlete to compete only in regularly scheduled intercollegiate events and established national championships occurring between terms and during the summer months, provided the student-athlete is representing his or her institution and was eligible for intercollegiate competition the preceding term, and in international competition approved by the NCAA Council.

(3) Awarding complimentary admissions in excess of four per student-athlete per contest and awarding complimentary admissions to student-athletes in sports other than those in which the student-athlete is a participant, except as provided in Constitution 3–1–(h)–(6) and the bylaws. Complimentary admission shall be provided only by a pass list for family members, relatives and fellow students designated by the student-athlete. "Hard tickets" shall not be issued. The student-athlete may not receive any payment from any source for the complimentary admissions and may not exchange them for any item of value.

(4) Payment of expenses of any student-athlete returning home to receive an award for athletic accomplishments or for other personal purposes.

(5) An extra benefit. As used in this subparagraph, the phrase "extra benefit" refers to any special arrange-ment by any institutional employee or representative of the institution's athletics interests to provide the student-athlete, or the student-athlete's relative or friend with a benefit not expressly authorized by NCAA legislation. Receipt of a benefit (including those benefits specifically listed below) by student-athletes or their relatives or other friends is not a violation of this section if it is demonstrated that the same benefit is generally available to the institution's students or their relatives or other friends. Examples of special arrangements that are specifically prohibited include, but are not limited to:

(i) A special discount, payment arrangement or credit on a purchase (e.g., airline ticket, clothing) or service (e.g., laundry, dry cleaning);

(ii) A loan of money;

(iii) A guarantee of bond;

(iv) The use of an automobile;

(v) Transportation to or from a summer job;

(vi) A benefit connected with on-campus or off-campus student-athletes' housing (e.g., individual tele-vision sets or stereo equipment, specialized recreational facilities, room furnishings or appointments of extra quality or quantity);

(vii) Signing or co-signing a note with an outside agency to arrange a loan;

(viii) An institution selling a student-athlete ticket(s) to an athletic event. [*1985–86 NCAA Manual*, Constitution 3–1–(g)]

2. The NCAA is only one of many athletic organizations that require strict compliance on the part of their athletes in order for them to retain their amateur status. United States Swimming, Inc., the Olympic national governing body for swimming, is an athletic organization that requires its amateurs not to capitalize on their athletic fame in any of the following ways:

An amateur cannot convert into cash any award or prize won in swimming competition.

An amateur shall not capitalize on his athletic fame by:

(1) Engaging for pay or other financial benefit,

directly, or indirectly, in any occupation wherein his usefulness or value arises chiefly from the publicity given to the reputation or fame he has achieved from his performance in swimming rather than from his ability to perform the usual acts and duties incidental to such occupation; and

(2) Attaching his name to press or literary contributions which he has not himself written. (*United States Swimming Rules and Regulations 1985*, Part Three, Article 43, Eligibility, Sections 343.7–343.8]

2.15–2(a) Employment

A student-athlete who is receiving a full athletic scholarship from an institution is not eligible for employment during the academic year except during vacation periods and then only until the first day of classes begin. The student-athlete is not eligible for employment because under NCAA regulations, any monies or financial assistance that exceeds commonly accepted educational expenses, such as tuition and fees, room and board, and required course-related books, is classified as pay and renders the student ineligible to compete in NCAA athletics (see Section 2.15–3).

A student-athlete who is receiving only partial financial assistance from an institution, including a partial athletic scholarship, is allowed to receive employment compensation, up to the limit established by the institution, as accepted educational expenses. With some exceptions (see Note 2), any compensation received over commonly accepted educational expenses as set by the individual institution must be deducted from the financial assistance package received by the student-athlete (including athletic scholarships), or else the athlete will be ineligible to compete for the institution.

Student-athletes are limited, incidentally, as to the types of employment they can consider in order to maintain their amateur status and their collegiate eligibility (see Note 3).

NOTES

1. The NCAA distinguishes between pay and employment. Pay deals most directly with a student-athlete's amateur status, while employment is considered basically a segment of the student-athlete's total financial aid package. However, the two terms are closely related and are cross-cited in the NCAA constitution, which notes:

(d) Where a student-athlete's ability is taken into consideration in any degree in awarding unearned financial aid, such aid shall not be awarded for a period in excess of one academic year; and if such aid combined with that received from the following and similar sources exceeds the amount defined in Constitution 3–1–(g)–(1) to (3) and the bylaws, the student-athlete shall not be eligible to participate in intercollegiate athletics.

(1) Employment during semester or term time, which is an all-inclusive period from the opening to the closing of classes of the regular semester, quarter or term, except for the vacation periods properly listed on the institution's official calendar.

(i) An institution shall count income from any employment during the semester or term time, regardless of whether the student-athlete's job is one obtained following completion of eligibility in the student-athlete's senior year; gifts given to a student-athlete following completion of eligibility in appreciation or recognition of the student-athlete's athletic accomplishment; and any bonus or salary from a professional sports organization, or any other income from participation in an athletics event, no matter when received or contracted for.

(ii) A student-athlete receiving aid under this section may, however, obtain a job within seven days prior to the beginning of the institution's Christmas vacation period, provided it is necessary to do so to secure the employment. The income so derived from the additional week's employment need not be computed in determining the maximum allowable financial aid.

(2) Governmental grants for educational purposes, except:

(i) Benefits received by student-athletes under the G.I. Bill of Rights;

(ii) Payments to student-athletes for participation in military reserve training programs (for example, payments by the U.S. government for a student's participation in advanced ROTC or National Guard training shall not be construed under this principle to be "employment" during semester or term time);

(iii) Payments by the U.S. government under the terms of the War Orphans Educational Program, Social Security Insurance Program or Non-Service-Connected Veteran's Death Pension Program; or

(iv) Pell Grants, provided the overall grant total, combining financial aid based on athletic ability and other institutionally administered financial aid and the Pell Grant, does not exceed the value of tuition, fees, room and board and required course-related books, plus $900.

(v) State government awards to disabled veterans provided such awards are approved by the Council by a two-thirds majority of its members present and voting.

(3) Other scholarships and grants-in-aid, except an honorary award for outstanding academic achievement may be received without its being included in the maximum allowable financial aid computation if it is a standing scholarship award published in the institution's catalog, the basis of the award is the candidate's academic record at the awarding institution and the award is determined by competition among the students of a particular class or college of the institution. [*1985–86 NCAA Manual*, Constitution, 3–4–(d)]

2. A student-athlete who is preparing to compete or who has competed in the Olympic Games is entitled to recover any financial losses occurring as a result of absence from employment that is authorized by the United States Olympic Committee. The period involved in recovering the losses must "immediately" precede actual Olympic competition (*1985–86 NCAA Manual*, Constitution 3–[1]–[a]–[3]–[ii]).

3. Student-athletes cannot be employed to teach or coach in their particular sport unless it is part of a general physical education class in which various techniques and skills in several sports are taught. Member institutions are specifically prohibited from hiring student-athletes to coach or teach *any* sport. Student-athletes, enrolled in a student-teacher program, are permitted to be paid traveling expenses if *all* student teachers are eligible and are part of the teacher training program (*1985–86 NCAA Manual*, Constitution 3–1–[f]; see also Section 2.60).

2.15–2(b) Marketing the Athlete with Remaining Eligibility

Once enrolled in an NCAA member institution, student-athletes cannot consent to their names or photos being used to promote commercial products. Doing so results in the loss of eligibility. Such activities prior to enrollment in a member institution, however, do not violate NCAA rules (*1985–86 NCAA Manual*, Constitution 3–[1]–[e]).

Certain activities in the realm of advertising will not jeopardize the student-athlete's eligibility. For example, manufacturers of athletic equipment can donate equipment to a member institution and publicize the school's use of it without endangering any student-athlete's eligibility, provided that no names or photos of team members are used.

Student-athletes whose names or photos are used for commercial purposes without their knowledge or in spite of their refusal are not required to take any action to preserve their eligibility. An individual or team picture can be used in an advertisement only if the primary purpose is to congratulate an achievement. There must be no indication that it is an endorsement of the advertiser's product.

A student-athlete may appear on radio or television because of his or her athletic abilities or performance but may not receive compensation or endorse a product or service. The student-athlete is, however, allowed to receive legitimate and necessary expenses directly related to the appearance (*1985–86 NCAA Manual*, Constitution 3–1–[e]–[1]).

In recent years, the NCAA has begun to enforce its marketing restrictions much more vigorously, without exhibiting the leniency that characterized its earlier efforts. In 1983–84, the NCAA had 19 eligibility cases in which 74 student-athletes were alleged to have promoted commercial products (see Note 2). The cases involved magazine covers, men-on-campus calendars, modeling, television commercials, newspaper advertisements, and personal appearances at commercial businesses and shopping malls.

NOTES

1. The NCAA is not alone among athletic organizations in limiting athletes' involvement in marketing in order to maintain eligibility for competition. The United States Tennis Association (USTA) has marketing restrictions for amateur players who wish to retain their eligibility. In the following USTA rule, an amateur is prohibited from:

(iv) Accepting money or gaining pecuniary advantage:
By permitting the taking of tennis action films or television pictures of himself;

b. By permitting the use of his name as the author of any book or article on tennis of which he is not the actual author;

c. For services which he does not actually render.

(v) Permitting his name or likeness to be placed on tennis equipment or tennis apparel of which he is not the actual manufacturer, wholesaler, retailer or other seller, or to be used in advertising or other sales promotion of such goods;

(vi) Permitting the advertising of his name or likeness as the user of any goods of any manufacturer, wholesaler, retailer or other seller. [*1982 USTA Official Yearbook and Tennis Guide*, Article II, Section E (iv–vi)]

2. In 1984, Olan B. Kollevoll, chair of the NCAA's Eligibility Committee, made the following comments in the *NCAA News* concerning the increase of marketing-related eligibility cases:

In most instances, the committee has felt that the member institutions attempted to inform student-athletes of the prohibition against commercial promotions; however, there is a disturbing number of cases where the student has failed to contact appropriate institutional personnel prior to participation, or misinformed staff members have authorized the promotion.

In past cases, the committee generally has restored a student's eligibility when no compensation has been provided to the student and the involved advertisement or commercial item has been removed immediately from further use or sale.

However, committee members expressed concern that publicity of several cases in which a student's eligibility has been restored without the loss of any opportunities for competition has fostered the erroneous impression that student-athletes can participate in the promotion of commercial products with impunity so long as they are not paid or identified by name.

In response, the Eligibility Committee has determined that, effective with the administration of the 1984–85 student-athlete statement, at which time student-athletes should be informed of the prohibition against involvement in the promotion of a commercial product, any violation of Constitution 3–1–(e) in which the committee concludes the student-athlete knew or should have known of the application of NCAA legislation will result in the student being charged with the loss of competitive opportunities.

Each case will be reviewed individually, based upon the facts of that case, in order to determine whether eligibility should be restored and, if so, after what period of ineligibility. ["Athletes Warned about Commercial Endorsements," *NCAA News*, August 15, 1984, p. 1]

2.15–3   Expenses

The issue of expenses can provide a unique source of trouble for the amateur athlete. In general, any amateur in a position to receive expenses, regardless of the source and prior to receiving the expenses, should distinguish between those that are permissible to receive under the athletic governing body, and more importantly, those that are not. This approach is the safest way for the amateur athlete to safeguard eligibility as an amateur and as a member of a particular athletic association (see Notes 1–3).

In the NCAA, expenses are limited to those that are actual and necessary. Actual and necessary expenses are defined by the NCAA as amounts received for reasonable travel and meals associated with practice and game competition. The NCAA considers any expenses in excess of "reasonable" to be compensation for athletic ability and warns that receipt of same can lead to a loss of eligibility (see Section 2.15–2). Expenses are to be paid on a regular basis and must not be determined by performance or any other incentive plan (see Note 2).

The Athletics Congress of the United States of America (TAC/USA), the national governing body for track and field, road running, and race walking events, has established a trust fund which governs athletes finances for athletic activities while the athlete retains amateur eligibility. TAC/USA refers to this fund as TACTRUST (see Exhibit 2–7). It was passed in 1981 and later approved by the International Amateur Athletic Federation (IAAF). TACTRUST allows an athlete to set up a private trust in which deposits and withdrawals are made in accordance with TAC/USA bylaws. The deposits must consist of monies received by the athlete in the TAC/USA-sanctioned athletic event and donations. The withdrawals must be for training or expenses in connection with the TAC/USA event. TACTRUST-authorized withdrawals are permitted for (1) training, coaching, travel, lodging, equipment, and educational expenses, (2) taxes on athletic earnings, (3) professional fees, and (4) medical and dental bills. The TACTRUST agreement allows the

September 1, 1982

TACTRUST AGREEMENT

TRUST AGREEMENT to establish a trust to be known as TACTRUST by and among the bank, trust company or other fiduciary whose name and address are indicated on Schedule "A" hereof, the individuals whose name or names and addresses are set forth on Schedule "B" hereof, and The Athletics Congress of the USA, Inc., whose address is 155 West Washington Street, Suite 220, Indianapolis, Indiana 46204.

1.0 **PREAMBLE.** The individual parties hereto are athletes who may receive prize money and other financial rewards by virtue and as a result of their athletic activity. The individual parties wish to continue to be eligible to enter and compete in international amateur athletic events notwithstanding their receipt of prize monies or other financial rewards in such competitions. The Athletics Congress of the USA, Inc., as the national governing body for the amateur sport of athletics, pursuant to the Amateur Sports Act of 1978 (36 USC 371) in an effort to reflect the views of such athletes, has obtained the approval of the International Amateur Athletic Federation of the trust to be created hereby as a method of protecting the amateur status of such athletes and all other amateur athletes of the United States of America competing with them.

2.0 **DEFINITIONS.** As used in this trust agreement, the following terms shall have the meanings set forth herein:

2.1 "TACTRUST" shall mean the trust fund created by this trust agreement the full name of which shall be "TAC/USA Athletes' Trust."

2.2 "TAC/USA" shall mean The Athletics Congress of the USA, Inc.

2.3 "Athlete beneficiary" or "athlete beneficiaries" shall mean the individual parties to this trust agreement.

2.4 "IAAF" shall mean the International Amateur Athletic Federation.

2.5 "Trustee" shall mean the bank, trust company, or other fiduciary named on Schedule "A" hereof.

2.6 "Eligibility" shall mean the right under applicable TAC/USA and IAAF rules of an athlete to represent and compete on behalf of the United States of America in the Olympic Games, the Pan-American Games, world championships and to compete in other international athletic meetings involving the athletes of two or more countries.

2.7 "Pro-rata" shall mean the equal allocation among the athlete beneficiaries of TACTRUST of the expenses and income of TACTRUST which allocation shall be apportioned among all athlete beneficiaries of TACTRUST based on the average monthly balance (that is to say, the balance at the beginning of each month plus the balance at the end of each month) divided by two in each athlete beneficiary's account in TACTRUST calculated on a calendar year basis.

Exhibit 2-7   TACTRUST Agreement (*Source:* The Athletic Congress/USA)

2.8 "Domestic Competition" shall mean a competition in which all of the participating athletes are citizens of the United States or if citizens of countries other than the United States participate, such athletes are bona fide athlete members of TAC/USA.

2.9 "International Competition shall mean a competition in which citizens from more than one country participate and all non-U.S. citizens are not bona fide athlete members of TAC/USA.

2.10 Except for the foregoing definitions, any term, word, or phrase used in this trust agreement which is defined in Article 2 of the TAC/USA By-Laws shall have the same definition as provided therein. Any such definition shall and may continue to be amended as, if and when any amendment is effected in the definitions contained in the said By-Laws.

3.0 **PURPOSE.** The purposes of this trust agreement are to

(i) create a trust fund which provides in accordance with IAAF and TAC/USA rules for (a) the receipt of certain financial payments payable to an athlete beneficiary as a result of athletic activity and competition and (b) a method of withdrawals of principal and income therefrom by said athlete beneficiary so that for so long as the athlete beneficiary is a party to this trust agreement, the eligibility of said athlete shall not be impaired solely by virtue of the payment of prize and other monies into TACTRUST for the account of said athlete beneficiary; and

(ii) furnish a model private trust agreement for any athlete who does not wish to become an athlete beneficiary of TACTRUST (or who might wish to be an athlete beneficiary thereof for only a part of the prize money or other financial payments receivable by such athlete) but who nevertheless does wish to establish a private trust agreement for all or part of such prize and other monies to be received, which agreement will protect the eligibility of such athlete to the same extent and in the same manner as such protection is afforded by TACTRUST.

4.0 **CREATION OF TACTRUST.** The parties hereto hereby establish TACTRUST and the trustee hereby accepts a trust consisting solely of such cash as shall be paid or delivered to the trustee by or on behalf of each athlete beneficiary. The trustee shall hold the trust fund in trust and manage and administer it in accordance with the terms and provisions of this trust agreement. The trustee shall accept no property other than that paid or delivered to it pursuant to paragraph 5.0 et seq. hereof.

5.0 **ATHLETE BENEFICIARIES AND PAYMENTS INTO TACTRUST.**
The following provisions describe who may be an athlete beneficiary of TACTRUST and the source and manner of payment of the funds which may be accepted by the trustee pursuant to TACTRUST.

5.1 Any athlete holding a validly issued current TAC/USA membership may, while a TAC/USA member in good standing, become an athlete beneficiary of TACTRUST, provided that no person involved in a sports program subject to NCAA jurisdiction may become a TACTRUST athlete beneficiary until the college or university class of which he or she is a member is graduated.

5.2   Only the following funds shall be paid or delivered to the trustee by or for an athlete beneficiary and the trustee shall not accept any other funds in TACTRUST.

(i) Funds received by an athlete beneficiary for participating in a domestic competition sanctioned by TAC/USA conducted on or after January 1, 1982.

(ii) Funds received by an athlete beneficiary for participating in either a domestic or an international competition sanctioned by either TAC/USA or the appropriate national governing body having jurisdiction thereover, conducted on or after September 1, 1982.

(iii) Funds received by an athlete beneficiary prior to January 1, 1982 for participating in a domestic or international competition provided payment of such funds to the trustee has been specifically approved by TAC/USA.

(iv) Funds received by an athlete beneficiary as donations to TACTRUST, provided such donations are permissible under IAAF rules and are approved by TAC/USA.

5.3   All funds paid or delivered to the trustee pursuant to paragraph 5.2 shall be paid and delivered by good check to the trustee by the athlete beneficiary. Such payment shall represent the entire sum of money payble to the athlete beneficiary for participation in the named athletic competition.

5.4 The athlete beneficiary shall give TAC/USA prompt notice of any proposed payment into TACTRUST. TAC/USA may object to such payment by notifying the athlete beneficiary and the trustee of its objections within thirty (30) days of its actual receipt of such notice. In the event TAC/USA objects to a payment the trustee shall not accept it into TACTRUST.

5.5   As to any payments which are accepted by the trustee into TACTRUST, the athlete beneficiary for whose account said payment is accepted, herein assigns, conveys, transfers, and delivers to the trustee said funds to be administered pursuant to TACTRUST for the purposes herein stated.

6.0   **ATHLETE BENEFICIARY ACCOUNT.** The trustee shall administer the payments received into TACTRUST as follows:

6.1   The trustee (and not TAC/USA) shall administer TACTRUST.

6.2   Each athlete beneficiary shall be assigned, by the trustee, a TACTRUST account number. All payments received by the trustee for the benefit of the athlete beneficiary will be credited to such an account. Any income of TACTRUST allocated to the athlete beneficiary shall also be credited thereto. All withdrawals by the athlete beneficiary of funds from TACTRUST and the pro-rata share of the administrative expenses of TACTRUST shall be deducted therefrom.

6.3   The trustee shall not be required to segregate the funds allocable to each athlete beneficiary's account from the funds of other athlete beneficiaries. The trustee may commingle the entire funds paid into TACTRUST and exercise the investment and the other powers conferred upon the trustee on the entire corpus of TACTRUST or such part of it as it deems appropriate.

6.4 All earnings, income, gains, expenses, losses, fees, and other costs allocable to TACTRUST shall be shared on a pro-rata basis by all the athlete beneficiaries.

6.5 The trustee shall have the right to cause the retention in each athlete beneficiary's account of such sums as it deems appropriate to enable the athlete beneficiary to meet his or her pro-rata share of the expenses and costs of the administration of TACTRUST.

6.6 Unless a different time period is otherwise agreed to between the Trustee and TAC/USA, the athlete beneficiary and TAC/USA shall be sent monthly reports by the trustee of transaction activity in the account of each athlete beneficiary not later than ten (10) days after the close of each calendar month.

7.0 **WITHDRAWALS OF PRINCIPAL, TRANSFERS, AND DISTRIBUTION OF INCOME.** The trustee and each athlete beneficiary may deal with the account standing in the name of the athlete beneficiary in the following manner:

7.1 Amounts due for income taxes which arise out of a payment into or out of TACTRUST for the account or the benefit of an athlete beneficiary may be withdrawn from the principal of the TACTRUST allocated to the account of the affected athlete beneficiary.

7.2 The income of TACTRUST shall be computed on an accrual basis. Within 105 days after the close of each calendar year, the trustee shall allocate the income of TACTRUST to the athlete beneficiaries on a pro-rata basis. The trustee shall apportion the income of TACTRUST on the basis of income received and accrued to that date. The income to be allocated to any athlete beneficiary of TACTRUST shall be the income from the last income allocation made before the death of the athlete beneficiary. The trustee shall not be required to prorate any income payment to the date of the athlete beneficiary's death.

7.3 The athlete beneficiary may withdraw all or any part of the principal sum and any interest or income thereto applicable to the account of the athlete beneficiary by requesting the trustee to pay the same in accordance with Schedule "C" hereof. No withdrawal pursuant to this paragraph 7.3 shall be made prior to obtaining the written consent of TAC/USA to said withdrawal, which consent shall be given or withheld by TAC/USA in its sole discretion applied consistently under TAC/ USA and IAAF rules. The trustee shall pay the requested sum only after TAC/USA's consent thereto is given.

7.4 The athlete beneficiary may withdraw all or any part of the principal sum standing in his or her account by requesting the trustee to pay all or part of said principal sum to the athlete beneficiary or his or her designee without the written consent of TAC/USA for said withdrawal. The trustee shall make such payments only if the athlete beneficiary states in the written request therefor that "This withdrawal is made without the consent of TAC/USA, " and that the athlete beneficiary understands that the withdrawal will result in proceedings to impair his or her eligibility. It shall be a rebuttable presumption that a withdrawal without TAC/USA consent was for a purpose not in conformity with applicable rules and regulations of TAC/USA and IAAF subject to review of the reasons for said withdrawal at a hearing which TAC/USA institutes to review the athlete beneficiaries' eligibility. The trustee shall forthwith notify TAC/USA of any withdrawal at the time thereof by an athlete beneficiary pursuant to this paragraph 7.4.

7.5 The athlete beneficiary initially may establish or may transfer all or any part of the principal in his or her account to a private trust created for a purpose similar to TACTRUST (the "private trust") in which TAC/USA is also a "notify and consent" party as provided in TACTRUST. A copy of such proposed private trust agreement shall be sent to TAC/USA. Upon the consent of TAC/USA to such trust and the actual deposit therein or transfer thereto of all or part of the principal hereof, there shall be no impairment of the eligibility. All private trusts shall have as one of the trustees thereof a bank, trust company or other institution customarily acting in such capacity. This requirement may be waived by TAC/USA on good cause shown. The name of all private trusts shall be substantially as follows: "TAC/USA and (name of trustee or athlete beneficiary), Athlete's Private Trust" and no acronym thereof shall be utilized by any party thereto.

8.0 **ACTS OF REVOCATION AND TERMINATION.** The interest of an athlete beneficiary shall be revoked or terminated in the account standing in his or her name in TACTRUST (or any private trust) upon the happening of any one of the following:

8.1 Upon the death of an athlete beneficiary the interest of said athlete beneficiary shall terminate in TACTRUST and the then entire account standing in the name of the deceased athlete beneficiary shall be paid to the person named in Schedule "D" hereof, and if no person is named therein then to the legal representative of such athlete beneficiary. Any private trust may contain provisions in its initial form or by subsequent amendment which in the event of the death of the athlete beneficiary (a) allows the trust to continue, (b) names successor beneficiaries therein, and (c) terminates the role of TAC/USA in such trust.

8.2 If an athlete beneficiary (a) declares himself or herself in writing to be (i) a professional athlete, (ii) an athlete not wishing to retain eligibility, or (iii) an athlete no longer interested in competing; (b) surrenders for life his or her membership in TAC/USA; (c) is suspended for life as a TAC/USA athlete member; (d) makes any withdrawal of principal pursuant to paragraph 7.4 hereof; (e) accepts prize monies for entering or competing in an athletic competition unless the same are contributed to a trust as provided hereunder; or (f) after January 1, 1983, knowingly competes in an international athletic competition held within the United States not sanctioned by TAC/USA, the interest of the athlete beneficiary in TACTRUST shall be deemed to have been revoked and the trust terminated with respect to said athlete beneficiary. Upon certification to the trustee by TAC/ USA of the happening of any one of such events all monies then in the account of such athlete beneficiary shall be paid by the trustee to the athlete beneficiary. The trustee shall have no responsibility under this paragraph except to act in accordance with the certificate of TAC/USA.

8.3 The entire right to receive all monies in the account of the athlete beneficiary shall be vested in the athlete beneficiary of a TACTRUST account subject only to the provisions of this trust agreement and nothing contained herein shall give TAC/USA or the trustee or either of them any right to any part of TACTRUST, the income or increase thereof, or any residuary rights therein, except that nothing contained herein shall be deemed to prohibit the trustee from receiving its compensation from the corpus of TACTRUST as provided in this trust agreement.

8.4 It is the intent of TAC/USA to create TACTRUST and to provide for payments into and out of TACTRUST (and any private trust) which will permit the most favorable incidents of income taxation permissible under existing law and regulations. To the extent that this instrument requires amendment, or to the extent any private trust requires provisions more suitable to the needs of any particular beneficiary thereof, TAC/USA will effect said amendment or permit the creation of a private trust provided said amendment or transfer trust provisions are allowed by IAAF. TAC/USA makes no representation as to the tax consequences of any payment into or out of TACTRUST or any private trust.

9.0 TAC/USA AND THE ATHLETE BENEFICIARIES OF TACTRUST.
The following provisions are applicable to the relationship of TAC/USA and the TACTRUST athlete beneficiaries:

9.1 TAC/USA shall have no role in the administration of TACTRUST or any private trust except to certify that payments into or out of the particular trust involved are permitted by IAAF and TAC/USA rules.

9.2 TAC/USA shall receive no compensation for its services to or in connection with TACTRUST either directly or indirectly from TACTRUST, the trustee or any athlete beneficiary nor shall any employee, agent, attorney, division or subsidiary of TAC/USA receive direct or indirect compensation therefor from TACTRUST, the trustee or any athlete beneficiary.

9.3 TAC/USA shall not be liable to the trustee or the athlete beneficiary for any loss suffered by TACTRUST or of any impairment of eligibility of an athlete beneficiary resulting from its consent to any payment made into or out of TACTRUST for the account of the athlete beneficiary. Such consent by TAC/USA shall merely signify that based upon the facts certified to TAC/USA at the time of said consent, the payment was in conformity with applicable TAC/USA, IAAF, or TACTRUST rules, regulations or provisions. If the facts certified to TAC/USA are found to be true by TAC/USA after investigation, TAC/USA shall use its best efforts to protect the athlete beneficiary's eligibility before any international body.

9.4 Any withdrawal by an athlete beneficiary not approved by TAC/USA pursuant to 7.4 hereof may result in the loss of eligibility of the said athlete beneficiary under applicable TAC/USA or IAAF rules, but nothing contained herein shall be deemed to deprive an athlete beneficiary of his or her rights pursuant to the By-Laws of TAC/USA.

10.0 INVESTMENT POWERS OF TRUSTEE.
In addition to any powers which the trustee may have under applicable law, the trustee shall have and in its sole and absolute discretion may exercise from time to time and at any time the following powers and authority with respect to TACTRUST:

a. To invest and reinvest trust funds, together with any other assets held by the trustee for the benefit of TACTRUST and its athlete beneficiaries, in shares of stock (whether common or preferred),money market funds, mutual funds, certificates of deposit, IRA funds or other evidences of indebtedness, unsecured or secured by mortgages on real or personal property wheresoever situated (including any part interest in a bond and mortgage or note and mortgage, whether insured or uninsured), and any other property, or part interest in property, real or personal, foreign or domestic, without any duty to diversify and without regard to any restriction placed upon fiduciaries by any present or future applicable law, administrative regulation, rule of court or court decision.

b. To sell, convey, redeem, exchange, grant options for the purchase or exchange of, or otherwise dispose of, any real or personal property, at public or private sale, for cash or upon credit, with or without security, without obligation on the part of any person dealing with the trustee to see to the application of the proceeds of or to inquire into the validity, expediency, or propriety of any such disposition;

c. To borrow from any lender (including the trustee in its individual capacity) money, in any amount and upon any terms and conditions, for purposes of this agreement, and to pledge or mortgage any property held in TACTRUST to secure the repayment of any such loan;

d. To employ in the management of TACTRUST suitable agents, without libility for any loss occasioned by any such agents selected by the trustee with reasonable care, and to compensate any such agent from TACTRUST funds without diminuation of or charging against the commissions or compensation due the trustee hereunder.

e. To consult with counsel, who may be counsel to TAC/USA, on matters relating to the management of the TACTRUST, without liability for taking or refraining from taking action in accordance with the opinion of such counsel; and

f. To do all other acts that the trustee may deem necessary or proper to carry out any of the powers or duties set forth herein or otherwise in the best interests of TACTRUST.

11.0 TAXES, EXPENSES, AND COMPENSATION OF TRUSTEE.

a. The trustee, without direction from any party hereto, shall pay out of the principal of TACTRUST all taxes imposed or levied with respect to TACTRUST and, in its discretion, may contest the validity or amount of any tax, assessment, claim, or demand respecting TACTRUST or any part thereof.

b. The trustee, without direction from any party hereto, shall pay from TACTRUST the reasonable expenses and compensation of counsel and all other expenses of managing and administering TACTRUST, provided that no compensation to or expense of counsel for TAC/USA shall be paid by the trustee from TACTRUST. All expenses paid pursuant to this paragraph "11.0" hereof shall be paid from the principal of TACTRUST except to the extent that the trustee in its discretion shall determine otherwise. The trustee shall receive such compensation for its services as from time to time shall be agreed upon, without necessity of application to or approval by any court. Until otherwise determined by the trustee and TAC/USA, such compensation shall be as set forth in Schedule "E" hereof. All compensation payable to the trustee shall be paid from the principal of TACTRUST unless the trustee in its discretion shall determine otherwise.

12.0 PRINCIPAL AND INCOME ALLOCATION. Allocation as between principal and income accounts shall be as follows: There shall be credited to principal, to the extent that the

same shall constitute principal, all funds received by the trustee from an athlete beneficiary, profits realized on the sale or exchange of investments, and stock dividends or other distributions.   There shall be charged against income all expenses properly chargeable to income, including any taxes and assessments chargeable to the income of TACTRUST pursuant to any statute or regulation.

Dividends or other corporate distributions payable in the stock of the corporation authorizing and declaring the same, however, shall constitute principal and the trustee may apportion extraordinary dividends or other corporate distribution payable in cash or property other than the stock of the corporation authorizing and declaring the same, liquidating dividends, arrears of dividends on preferred stocks, property received in reorganization and other like receipts not constituting ordinary income to principal or income or in part to both in the sole judgment and discretion of the trustee. Premiums paid for the purchase of investments for TACTRUST shall not be amortized.

13.0   **TRUSTEE'S LIABILITY.**   The trustee shall not be liable for the making, retention, or sale of any investment or reinvestment made by it as herein provided nor for any loss to or diminution of TACTRUST, except due to its own negligence, willful misconduct, or lack of good faith.   The trustee shall have no liability or responsibility to investigate the truth or falsity of any certificate, consent, approval or request received by it from TAC/USA or an athlete beneficiary.

14.0   **ACCOUNTS.**   The trustee shall keep accurate and detailed accounts of all its receipts, investments and dis-bursements under this agreement.   Such person or persons as TAC/USA shall designate shall be allowed to inspect the trustee's account relating to the TACTRUST upon request at any reasonable time during the business hours of the trustee. Within 90 days after the close of the fiscal year of TACTRUST or of the removal or resignation of the trustee as provided by this agreement, the trustee shall file with the TAC/USA a written account of its transactions relating to TACTRUST during the period from the submission of its last such account to the close of the fiscal year or the date of the trustee's resignation or removal.   Unless TAC/USA shall have filed with the trustee written exceptions or objections to any such account within 60 days after receipt thereof, TAC/USA shall be deemed to have approved such account; and in such case, the trustee shall be forever released and discharged with respect to all matters and things embraced in such account as though such account had been settled by a court of competent jurisdiction in an action or proceeding to which all persons having a beneficial interest in TACTRUST were parties.   However, should any question be raised at any time by any athlete beneficiary regarding his or her proper share of the income from TACTRUST, the trustee will use its best efforts to supply TAC/USA with the information necessary to resolve the inquiry. Nothing contained in this agreement shall deprive the trustee of the right to have a judicial settlement of its accounts.

15.0   **RESIGNATION OR REMOVAL OF TRUSTEE.**

a. The trustee may resign at any time upon 90 days' written notice to TAC/USA, or upon shorter notice if acceptable to TAC/USA. TAC/USA, by action of its Board of Directors, may remove the trustee at any time upon 120 days written notice to the trustee, or upon shorter notice if acceptable to the trustee.   In the event it resigns or is removed, the trustee shall have its accounts settled as provided in this agreement.

b. Upon the resignation or removal of the trustee, TAC/USA, by action of its Board of Directors, shall appoint a successor trustee to act hereunder after the effective date of such removal or resignation. However, TAC/USA shall not appoint as successor trustee either itself or any athlete beneficiary of TACTRUST. Each successor trustee shall have the powers and duties conferred upon the trustee in this agreement, and the term "trustee" as used in this agreement shall be deemed to include any successor trustee. Upon designation or appointment of a successor trustee, the trustee shall transfer and deliver all trust funds to the successor trustee, reserving such sums as the trustee shall deem necessary to defray its expenses in settling its accounts, to pay any of its compensation due and unpaid, and to discharge any obligation of TACTRUST for which the trustee may be liable; but if the sums so reserved are not sufficient for these purposes, the trustee shall be entitled to recover the amount of any deficiency from a successor trustee. When TACTRUST shall have been transferred and delivered to the successor trustee and the accounts of the trustee have been settled as provided in this agreement, the trustee shall be relased and discharged from all further accountability or liability for TACTRUST and shall not be responsible in any way for the further disposition of TACTRUST or any part thereof.

16.0 COMMUNICATIONS.

a. Any action required by any provision of this agreement to be taken by TAC/USA may be evidenced by a resolution of its Board of Directors certified to the trustee by the secretary or an assistant secretary or equivalent officer of TAC/USA and the trustees shall be fully protected in relying on any resolution so certified to it. Any action of TAC/USA including any approval of or exception to the trustee's accounts with respect to TACTRUST, may be evidenced by a certificate signed by the officer of TAC/USA authorized to do so by resolution by its Board of Directors and the trustee shall be fully protected in relying upon such certificate. The trustee may accept any writing signed by an officer of TAC/USA as proof of any fact or matter that it deems necessary or desirable to have established in the administration of TACTRUST and the trustee shall be fully protected in relying upon the statements in the writing. The trustee shall be entitled conclusively to rely upon any written notice, instruction, direction, certificate, or other communication believed by it to be genuine and to be signed by the proper person or persons, and the trustee shall be under no duty to make investigation or inquiry as to the truth or accuracy of any statement contained therein.

b. Until notice be given to the contrary, communications to the trustee shall be sent to it at its office designated on Schedule "A" hereof; communications to athlete beneficiaries or their legal representatives shall be sent to the addresses furnished to the trustee by the athlete beneficiary and communications to TAC/USA shall b e sent to it at the address set forth in this agreement.

17.0 **AMENDMENT.** TAC/USA expressly reserves the right at any time and from time to time to amend this agreement and the trust created thereby to any extent that it may deem advisable, provided, however, that such amendment shall not increase the duties or responsibilities of the trustee without its consent thereto in writing, and provided further that no such amendment shall be made which retroactively entitles TAC/USA to earn a fee or other compensation out of the funds constituting

TACTRUST or otherwise retroactively reduces the share of any athlete beneficiary to the principal or income of TACTRUST. Such amendment shall become effective upon delivery to the trustee of a written instrument of amendment, duly executed and acknowledged by TAC/USA, and accompanied by a certified copy of a resolution of its Board of Directors authorizing such amendment. An athlete beneficiary of TACTRUST or any private trust pursuant thereto may object to any amendment of the bylaws of TAC/USA (as they affect TACTRUST) or any amendment to TACTRUST by notifying TAC/USA within 30 days of such amendment. If the athlete beneficiary does not waive such objection, the following rules shall apply:

a) For so long as the athlete remains eligible, there should be no further payments into or out of the trust for the account of said athlete beneficiary and the amendment shall be ineffective with respect to the funds in the account of said athlete beneficiary;

b) Any funds thereafter received by the athlete may be placed by him or her in a new TACTRUST account which shall be governed by the amendment, and payments into and out of said account shall be permitted in accordance therewith.

c) Upon the cessation of the athlete beneficiary's eligibility or any act pursuant to paragraph "8.0" hereof, the entire balance, without penalty, standing in the account of the athlete beneficiary in the "frozen" TACTRUST and any other TACTRUST in which said athlete has an interest shall be paid to such athlete in accordance with the terms of the trust involved.

18.0   PROHIBITION OF ASSIGNMENT OF INTEREST. Without the consent of TAC/USA the funds of any athlete beneficiary in his or her account and any interest, right, or claim in or to any part of TACTRUST or any payment therefrom shall not be assignable, transferable, or subject to sale, mortgage, pledge, hypothecation, commutation, anticipation, garnishment, attachment, execution, or levy of any kind, and the trustee shall not recognize any attempt to assign, transfer, sell, mortgage, pledge, hypothecate, commute, or anticipate the same, except to the extent required by law.

19.0   MISCELLANEOUS.

a.   This agreement shall be interpreted, construed, and enforced, and the trust hereby created shall be administered, in accordance with the laws of the state where the trustee is located.

b.   The captions ofthe Articles of this trust agreement are placed herein for convenience only and the agreement is not to be construed by reference thereto.

c.   This agreement shall bind and inure to the benefit of the successors and assigns of TAC/USA, the trustee, and each athlete beneficiary, respectively.

d.   This agreement may be executed in any number of counterparts, each of which shall be deemed to be an original, but all of which together shall constitute but one instrument, which may be sufficiently evidenced by counterpart.

e.   The effective date of this trust agreement shall be as to TAC/USA and the trustee the date set forth next to their signatures and as to each athlete beneficiary, the date said athlete beneficiary causes funds to be paid into TACTRUST for his or her account.

IN WITNESS WHEREOF, the corporate parties hereto have caused this agreement to be executed in their respective names by their duly authorized officers under their corporate seals and the individual parties hereto have executed this agreement and affixed their seals.

The Athletics Congress
of the U.S.A., Inc.

by_____

/s/ The Trustee
(Signing on Schedule "A" hereof)

_____

/s/ The Athlete Beneficiary
(Signing on Schedule "B" hereof)

SCHEDULE A
The Trustee's Signature Page

SCHEDULE B
Athlete Beneficiary Signature Page

SCHEDULE C

1. All requests by athlete beneficiaries for withdrawal of princip[al from TACTRUST shall be made in writing in the form of a certification to TAC/USA stating that the request is made for the purposes set forth therein and for no other purposes and that the facts contained therein are true and correct.

2. TAC/USA shall approve any request for a withdrawal of principal which is certified to be required to meet an emergency which is of such a nature that failure to have use of TACTRUST funds would have life-changing consequences and TAC/USA after investigation agrees with such conclusion.

3. TAC/USA shall approve a request for a withdrawal of principal which is certified to conform to IAAF Rule 14, Rule 15 or Rule 16, a copy of which is annexed hereto as Exhibit 1.

4. Any request for withdrawal under "2" or "3" hereof shall state the amount of such withdrawal in total and shall include a breakdown thereof and an identification of the use to be made or to have been made of the funds requested to have been withdrawn. In the event a withdrawal is requested for a purpose or use to occur after the receipt of funds by the athlete beneficiary, whether said withdrawal is a withdrawal for a specific purpose or in the nature of a periodic stipend, the athlete beneficiary shall report to TAC/USA in writing on the 10th day of each month the actual uses and expenditures incurred by said athlete beneficiary with respect to the funds withdrawn by said athlete beneficiary during the month preceding.

5. TAC/USA shall have the right to require the athlete beneficiary to furnish supporting documents and other satisfactory evidence of the purpose and use of any funds received by the athlete beneficiary from TACTRUST. Each athlete beneficiary agrees to cooperate with TAC/USA in establishing that all withdrawals from TACTRUST by that athlete beneficiary have been for the purposes certified in requesting said withdrawal and a failure to so cooperate shall constitute an act of revocation of TACTRUST by said athlete beneficiary.

SCHEDULE D
Name of Person Entitled to Funds in the Event
of Beneficiary's Death

athlete to withdraw the balance of the trust upon completion of the athlete's amateur career. TAC/USA recommends, however, that athletes involved in NCAA and interscholastic competition contact those organizations before setting up a TACTRUST because the NCAA and many scholastic sanctioning bodies prohibit their athletes from establishing such trusts.

Since the implementation of the TACTRUST program in 1982, over 700 trust fund accounts had been opened by 1983, with more than $2 million passing through the program that year. Since 1983, TAC/USA has allowed athletes to receive money from sources other than track competitions, two notable sources being product endorsements and television competitions such as the ABC network's "Superstars."

NOTES

1. The approaches to expense reimbursement vary among other governing bodies, as can be seen in the following examples:

(a) The United States Soccer Federation (USSF) requires that amateur players may not receive and retain any remuneration for playing, except expenses that have actually been incurred by the player and that are directly related to a game or games (*August 1981 USSF Official Administrative Rulebook*, Section C–[11]–[1102]).

(b) United States Swimming, Inc. eligibility rules require that "An amateur cannot compete, train, coach or give exhibitions for payment received, directly or indirectly, in money or in kind or for material advantage or benefit." However, the organization has instituted regulations that allow for some expense monies to be received by the amateur athlete and which states in part that:

> The amateur status of a swimmer shall not be endangered:
>
> (2) By accepting monetary assistance during approved periods of training, including participation in competitions approved or sanctioned by the Corporation; limited, however, to Olympic Games, World Championships, regional games, continental championships and major international competitions. Such assistance may include payment for food, lodgings, transportation, his sports equipment, coaching, medical care and insurance, and a sum per day for the number of days related to an event as an indemnity against petty expenses.

> (3) By accepting compensation, authorized by the Corporation to cover financial loss resulting from his or her absence from work or basic occupation, related to preparation for and participation in Olympic Games, World Championships, regional games, continental championships and major international competitions approved by the Corporation. Payment, however, shall not be in excess of the sum which the competitor would have earned in the same period of time. [*United States Swimming Rules and Regulations 1985*, Part Three, Article 43, Eligibility, Sections 343.3, 343.11 (2–3)]

(c) The United States Tennis Association (USTA) allows an amateur reasonable expenses actually incurred in connection with participation in a tournament, match, or exhibition (*USTA Official Yearbook and Tennis Guide*, Article II, Section B–I).

2. The NCAA defines permissible expenses that an institution may provide a student-athlete as follows:

(1) Actual and necessary expenses on intercollegiate athletics trips, reasonable trips (within the state in which the member institution is located or a distance not to exceed 100 miles if outside that state) to practice sites other than those of the institution, or to transport a team a reasonable distance (not to exceed 100 miles) to an off-campus site for a post-season team award or recognition meeting; however, it shall be permissible to provide expenses when a team is invited by the President of the United States to be accorded special recognition in the national capital.

O.I.6. Nationally recognized service organizations and church groups (including the Fellowship of Christian Athletes) may underwrite the actual and necessary expenses of student-athletes to attend Fellowship of Christian Athletes encampments. This interpretation specifically excludes member institutions or athletically related organizations from underwriting such expenses.

(2) Actual and necessary expenses incurred by the spouse of a student-athlete in accompanying the student-athlete to a certified post-season football game or an NCAA championship in the sport of football in which the student-athlete is certified eligible to participate, if prescribed by the bylaws of the Association;

(3) Actual and necessary expenses for participation in national championship events; Olympic, Pan American, and World University Games qualifying competition, or bona fide amateur competition during the Christmas and spring vacations as listed on the institution's official calendar. . . . [*1985–86 NCAA Manual*, Constitution 3–1–(h)]

3. Under NCAA regulations, a student-athlete, prior to enrollment at a member institution, may receive one expense-paid, try-out visit from a professional sports

organization (*1985–86 NCAA Manual*, Constitution 3–1–[b]–[1]); see also Section 2.16, Note 2.

4. For further information, see "Amateur Athletes: Some More Equal Than Others," *New York Times*, August 8, 1983, p. C1.

2.16 Professional Contracts

Student-athletes lose their eligibility to participate in an intercollegiate sport if they have agreed to negotiate or have signed a contract to play for a professional sport team (*1985–86 NCAA Manual*, Constitution, 3–1–[b]). For the purposes of this rule, it does not matter if the contract is legally enforceable (see *Shelton v. National Collegiate Athletic Ass'n., infra*). A student-athlete should be wary of a professional team that attempts to circumvent this rule by first indicating that a contract signed by the student-athlete is only legally binding when also signed by a team representative, and then, second, that the team representative promises not to sign the contract until after the student-athlete's college eligibility has expired. Under NCAA rules, legal enforceability is irrelevant; merely signing the contract terminates the student-athlete's eligibility.

The professed goal of the NCAA is the promotion and preservation of amateurism in college athletics. The reasoning behind these eligibility rules is that if the NCAA is to realistically supervise and regulate amateur status, absolute rules are more administratively efficient than ones that require a consideration of mitigating factors. The contract itself does not compromise amateur status; it is the act of signing that is the prohibited first step toward professionalism.

The courts have upheld rules similar to the NCAA rules on professionalism that have been promulgated by private voluntary associations as long as they do not violate the constitutional guarantees of due process or equal protection. The courts have also said they cannot determine the validity of a rule simply because of its unfortunate effects on particular individuals.

Shelton v. National Collegiate Athletic Ass'n., 539 F. 2d 1179 (9th Cir. 1976)

This case involved an appeal by the NCAA from a grant of preliminary injunction which suspended enforcement of its amateur eligibility rule. The rule states that a college athlete who signs a professional contract is ineligible to participate in intercollegiate athletics for the sport involved.

Shelton signed a professional contract with an American Basketball Association (ABA) team and was declared ineligible to play basketball by Oregon State University. Shelton claimed that the contract was unenforceable because he was induced to sign it by fraud and undue influence. He argued that the NCAA rule making him ineligible, despite the alleged defects of the contracts, created an impermissible, overinclusive classification and was thus violative of equal protection. Shelton sought suspension of enforcement while he continued his litigation against the ABA team and participated in the college basketball season.

The appeals court reversed the decision of the lower court, dissolved the preliminary injunction, and rendered Shelton ineligible.

The court decided that in the Shelton case the NCAA rule on eligibility was not in violation of equal protection because the rule rationally furthered some legitimate purpose. An examination of the NCAA's goal of preserving amateurism in intercollegiate athletics legitimized the rule.

In a similar case, *Associated Students, Inc.* v. *National Collegiate Athletic Ass'n.* (see Section 2.11, Note 3), the NCAA eligibility rules were challenged on equal protection grounds. There, as here, no violation of equal protection was found, but the court admitted that "the application of such [eligibility] rules may produce unreasonable results in certain situations." Moreover, though the court recognized that the eligibility rule and its means of enforcement may not be the best way to achieve the objective of ensuring amateurism, it stated: "It is not judicial business to tell a voluntary athletic association how best to formulate or enforce its rules."

Shelton claimed that should he be successful in his case against the ABA team — that is, freeing him of his playing obligation — he would be ineligible to play intercollegiate basketball without ever having been a professional. The court found the NCAA's rule, based on the signing of a contract, whether fulfilled or not, was a sound basis for intercollegiate eligibility. The court believed the rule eliminates any undue work for the institution to determine the validity of the contract. Furthermore, it sets out a clear duty for a college athlete to obey in order to remain eligible for intercollegiate competition.

NOTES

1. In the 1971 NCAA basketball tournament, Villanova finished second and received a tournament share of $68,318.84. After the tournament, it was discovered that one of Villanova's players, Howard Potter, had signed a contract with an agent and also a contract with a professional team. The NCAA ruled that Villanova had to forfeit its second-place finish and return its tournament share.

2. Student-athletes can compete against professional athletes but not as members of a professional team. A student-athlete who plays on a professional team loses eligibility only if that person knew or should have reasonably known he or she was playing on such a team (*1985–86 NCAA Manual*, Constitution 3–[1]–[d]).

A team is considered professional if it is recognized as a member of an organized professional league or if it is supported or sponsored by a professional organization or team (for example, minor league baseball). A student-athlete can play, however, on a team that has a coach who also coaches a professional team (for example, the coach of the U.S. Olympic Hockey Team).

Teams supported by a national amateur sports organization using developmental funds received from professional teams or organizations are not considered to be professional (*1985–86 NCAA Manual*, Constitution 3–[1]–[d]–O.I.4).

The NCAA specifically permits student-athletes to compete in tennis or golf with persons competing for money, but they cannot receive compensation of any kind (for example, PGA tournaments or Pro-Am tournaments).

Eligibility is not lost if, prior to enrollment in college, the student-athlete had a tryout with a professional team, provided it was either (1) at his or her own expense or

(2) consisted of one visit, expenses paid, lasting no longer than 48 hours. The expenses paid must be for actual and necessary expenditures. Student-athletes enrolled in a full-time course of studies cannot try out for a professional team during the academic year, unless their eligibility has been exhausted. Part-time student-athletes are permitted to try out during the academic year, provided no expenses or other compensation is provided from the professional team. It is permissible for the student-athlete to be observed by a professional team representative during a normally scheduled workout, provided the activities observed to evaluate the student-athlete are a normal part of the workout and not conducted specifically for the observer's benefit. Special workouts after the student-athlete's eligibility has expired are permissible and are common practice with potential professional football players. (*1985–86 NCAA Manual*, Constitution 3–[1]–[b]–[2])

3. The United States of America Amateur Boxing Federation defines a professional as follows:

220.9. The designation professional is based on receipt of compensation for competition in any sport. Such compensation will thereafter bar him from competing as an amateur.

220.9(b) Merely signing a contract without receipt of direct or indirect compensation beyond allowed expenses will not ruin eligibility forever. A boxer may be reinstated by the local boxing committee upon proper application. [*USA Amateur Boxing Federation Official Rules 1981–1984*, p. 55]

4. The NCAA recommends the following policies and practices regarding the use of member institutions' facilities by professional sports organizations and the involvement of member institutions' personnel with professional sports:

POLICY 4: Use of Facilities

Section 1. In furtherance of the educational objective of intercollegiate athletics described in Constitution 2–2–(a), member institutions should prohibit the use of their facilities by professional sports teams, it being understood that this does not apply to a professional team's isolated use of college facilities in emergency cases. . . .

POLICY 5: Personnel

Section 1. Member institutions should prohibit an athletics staff member from participating as a player, official or promoter in professional sports such as football, basketball, baseball, soccer, boxing, wrestling and ice hockey. . . . [*1985–86 NCAA Manual*, "Recommended Policies and Practices for Intercollegiate Athletics"]

6. For further information about student-athlete eligibility and professional sports, see the following articles:

(a) "New Pro League Angers Colleges by Signing a Star Before His Senior Year," *Chronicle of Higher Education*, March 2, 1983, p. 15.

(b) "NCAA Rules on Athletes' Contacts with Professional Teams," *Chronicle of Higher Education*, March 2, 1983, p. 15.

6. The following rule was passed by NCAA in 1985 to allow athletes to borrow money against a potential professional contract for the purpose of purchasing a professional disability insurance policy. The purpose behind the rule was to provide an incentive for underclass student-athletes to remain in college and complete their eligibility, while also protecting their potential income as a professional. Under the rule, a student-athlete may:

> (iii) Borrow against his or her future earnings potential from an established, accredited commercial lending institution exclusively for the purpose of purchasing insurance (with no cash surrender value) against a disabling injury that would prevent the individual from pursuing his or her chosen career, provided no third party (including a member institution's athletics department staff members or representatives of its athletics interests) is involved in arrangements for securing the loan.... [*1985–86 NCAA Manual*, Constitution 3–1–(a)–(3)–(iii)]

2.17 Player-Agents

An agent is a person authorized by another person to act in his or her name. The promise of compensation is not required to establish the relationship, although such compensation is usually presumed. The NCAA constitution prohibits college athletes from using an agent, stating:

> Any individual who contracts or who has ever contracted orally or in writing to be represented by an agent in the marketing of the individual's athletic ability or reputation in a sport no longer shall be eligible for intercollegiate athletics in that sport. An agency contract not specifically limited in writing to a particular sport or particular sports shall be deemed applicable to all sports. Securing advice from a lawyer concerning a proposed professional sports contract shall not be considered contracting for representation by an agent under this rule unless the lawyer also represents the student-athlete in negotiations for such a contract.... [*1985–86 NCAA Manual*, Constitution 3–1–(c)]

Because several agents have represented athletes in contract negotiations under the guise of supplying legal advice, the NCAA Council issued a clarification concerning the use of legal counsel by student-athletes. The council asserted that any student-athlete may retain counsel for the purpose of reviewing a contract offered by a professional team. However, the student-athlete who decides to have legal counsel contact a professional team concerning the contract offer has effectively hired counsel as an agent and is no longer eligible. Additionally, the NCAA specifies that a contract which is executed and does not specifically refer to a particular sport will be considered applicable to all sports. Also, any type of agency contract is prohibited, including present contracts for provision of future services. This rule applies at all times, and therefore includes those contracts made prior to matriculation at college.

At its 1984 convention, the NCAA approved a plan, recommended by its Special Committee on Player Agents, under which athletics career counseling panels would be established to assist student-athletes who are contemplating foregoing their remaining college eligibility to pursue a career in professional sports (*1985–86 NCAA Manual*, Constitution 3–1–[h]–[4]). In addition, should the athlete opt for a professional career, the panel would assist in the selection of a competent representative or agent. Representatives would be selected from a list of player-agents who have registered with the NCAA. A player-agent registration form was approved by the NCAA Special Committee on Player Agents in May 1984 (see Exhibit 2–8). The committee is also considering a program of sanctions against registered agents who violate their agreement with the NCAA.

Agents are a relatively recent phenomenon in collegiate sports. The growth of professional leagues, teams, and salaries since the late 1960s has made athlete representation a very lucrative and extremely competitive business. In order to build or protect their own personal

The National Collegiate Athletic Association

Nall Avenue at 63rd Street • Mission, Kansas

Mailing Address: P.O. Box 1906 • Mission, Kansas 66201 • Telephone 913/384-3220

MEMORANDUM

August 24, 1984

TO: Individuals Acting in the Capacity of Player Agent.

SUBJECT: 1984-85 Player Agent Registration Program.

President
JOHN R. DAVIS
Director, Oregon Agricultural
  Experiment Station
Oregon State University
Corvallis, Oregon 97331

Secretary-Treasurer
WILFORD S. BAILEY
Professor
Auburn University
Auburn, Alabama 36849

Division I Vice-President
ARLISS L. ROADEN
President
Tennessee Technological
  University
Cookeville, Tennessee 38505

Division II Vice-President
ADE L. SPONBERG
Director of Athletics
North Dakota State University
Fargo, North Dakota 58105

Division III Vice-President
ELIZABETH A. KRUCZEK
Director of Athletics
Fitchburg State College
Fitchburg, Massachusetts 01420

Executive Director
WALTER BYERS

As you may be aware, the NCAA has become more actively involved during the past 18 months in reviewing the relationships between student-athletes and player agents. Under the authority of the NCAA Council (the elected governing body of the Association), the Special NCAA Committee on Player Agents has created two new avenues by which enrolled student-athletes may obtain accurate information concerning both the opportunity for a future professional athletics career and the selection of honest and competent representation.

The first, a membership-adopted revision of NCAA Constitution 3-1-(h), permits an institution to provide counseling to student-athletes about a professional career through a panel appointed by the institution's chief executive officer from among university employees outside the department of athletics. Each institution's panel will muster information and expertise from a variety of sources (e.g., lawyers, financial consultants, representatives of professional sports teams and player associations, player agents) in an effort to provide objective information about professional career opportunities and to evaluate the various services and proposals extended by player agents.

The second means for generating accurate information is through annual registration of player agents. This voluntary program is intended to foster communication between the Association and individuals acting in the capacity of player agent. An individual registers by supplying requested educational and professional information and returning the signed form to this office. Please note that, in signing the form, you agree to notify the director of athletics (or his or her designated representative) before each contact with an enrolled student-athlete who has eligibility remaining in any sport and before each contact with the student-athlete's coach.

It is also understood that your name may be removed from the registration list if you: (1) engage in any activity prior to a student-athlete's agreement to be represented that would otherwise jeopardize the student-athlete's eligibility, or (2) fail to contact the appropriate individual prior to each contact with an enrolled student-athlete or the student-athlete's coach. A sanctioning body has been established to consider both the circumstances related to an inquiry and the agent's response in each case.

Participation in the registration program will work significantly to your advantage. First, access to university facilities and, more importantly, to student-athlete's will be enhanced. Those individuals on campus who most influence student-athletes (i.e., coaches and directors of athletics) are being urged strongly to advise student-athletes to give consideration only to those individuals who have taken the time to complete a registration form. In addition, the list of registered agents will be a primary reference for institutions' counseling panels. It is anticipated that in assisting student-athletes with the selection of competent representation, panel members will make every effort to recommend registered agents. Institutional counseling panels are also being forwarded information concerning the basic requirements for certification by the National Football League Players Association as a means for providing student-athletes additional points of reference in the selection of competent representation.

5.

Enclosed is a registration form that the Council encourages you to complete and return to this office at the earliest opportunity. Updated lists of those individuals who have completed the registration form will be made available to NCAA member institutions and their counseling panels beginning in September, with updates throughout the academic year. The registration program is an annual procedure, and your participation is applicable to activities and contacts made during the 1984-85 academic year and ensuing summer. Failure to complete the registration form in its entirety will result in your name not being included on the list of registered player agents.

None of the information you provide will be released to any individual or organization outside the Association (e.g., in response to media inquiries), except for a listing of registered agents and the cities in which those individuals reside. Member institutions will be provided answers to specific questions concerning information reported on the registration forms; however, duplicate copies of the completed forms will not be circulated to any institution, organization or individual. Overall statistical profiles applicable to the body of registered agents (e.g., the percentage of registered agents who currently represent athletes in the National Football League) may be generally available at some future point.

Finally, a copy of NCAA legislation of interest to player agents accompanies the registration form. Please review these rules and regulations carefully and feel free to contact this office concerning questions you may have. You may also be interested in obtaining a copy of the NCAA Manual, which contains NCAA rules and regulations, and the NCAA Directory, which lists all NCAA member institutions, as well as the address and telephone numbers of each institution's director of athletics. Copies of both the NCAA Manual (available for $8) and the NCAA Directory (for $6) may be ordered by contacting the NCAA publishing department at the address appearing on this letterhead.

Should you have questions about the information I have provided or the registration process in general, please contact this office.

JOHN H. LEAVENS
Director of Legislative Services

National Collegiate Athletic Association
PLAYER AGENT ANNUAL REGISTRATION FORM
1984-85 ACADEMIC YEAR

I.   General

Name _____ Date of Birth _____ Social Security No. _____

Business Address _____

Business Phone (_____) _____

Home Address _____

Home Phone (_____) _____

II.   Education

High School   School Name _____

                                                          Address _____

                                                          _____

                                                          Month/Year Graduated _____

College (undergraduate)   School Name _____

                                                          Location (City, State) _____

                                                          Degree(s) _____

                                                          Year Graduated _____

Graduate Studies

                                                          College or University _____

                                                          Location (City, State) _____

                                                          Degree(s) _____

                                                          Year Degree(s) Awarded _____

Admitted to Bar? Yes _____   No _____

                                                          If yes, when and what state(s) _____

III.   Experience

Number of years' experience as player agent _____

Sports in which you **currently** represent athletes _____

Exhibit 2-8   Player-Agent Registration Form (*Source:* National Collegiate Athletic Association)

Other sports in which you have represented athletes_____

_____

Total number of athletes you **currently** represent_____

Names of athletes you **currently** represent and, in team sports, the team/league to which the athlete is currently under contract and name of team representative with whom you negotiated this contract. Use back of sheet if additional space is required:

Player Name	Team	League	Team Representative

Past clients (athletes) and their professional teams/leagues

_____

_____

_____

Do you earn income from work performed in some capacity other than player agent?

Yes____   No____

If yes, describe other occupation(s) or service(s) for which you are paid

_____

_____

What approximate percentage of your **total** work time is consumed by your activity as a player agent?_____

_____

IV.   Other Qualifications

Current membership in professional organizations_____

_____

_____

Occupational or professional licenses (e.g., certified public accountant, chartered life underwriter) and date

obtained:

_____

_____

_____

Are you currently certified by the NFLPA? Yes____   No____

General services (other than contract negotiation) performed for client athletes (e.g., financial planning, legal assistance)

_____

_____

If you offer financial planning among your services, names and addresses of individuals, firms or agencies who assist in providing this service

Name_____   Address_____

Name_____   Address_____

Name_____   Address_____

Type of fees and financial terms for your services

_____

_____

V. Previous Employment (last three positions)

Firm_____Position_____

Address_____

Firm_____Position_____

Address_____

Firm_____Position_____

Address_____

VI. References

Name_____Position_____

Address_____

Name_____Position_____

Address_____

Name_____Position_____

Address_____

I certify that the above information is true, correct and complete to the best of my knowledge. Further, I certify that I will notify the director of athletics (or his or her designated representative) before each contact with a student-athlete who has eligibility remaining in any sport and is enrolled in an NCAA member institution or before each contact with the student-athlete's coach and that I have reviewed the NCAA rules and regulations (excerpts from the Association's constitution and selected numbered official interpretations) that accompany this form and will engage in no activity prior to a student-athlete's agreement to be represented that would otherwise jeopardize the student-athlete's eligibility. **I also understand that failure to comply with the terms of this certification may result in removal of my name from the list of registered player agents.**

Signature_____

Date_____

interests, many agents will contact, offer inducements to, and attempt to sign student-athletes with remaining college eligibility. They may also entice athletes to leave college early to join professional teams. Inducements may take the form of cash, "loans," and/or the use of a car or other benefits. This transfer and acceptance of money or other benefits by student-athletes is in direct conflict with the principles of amateurism and specifically violates rules related to receiving compensation or pay and limits on the amount and type of acceptable remuneration (*1985–86 NCAA Manual*, Constitution 3–1).

The "offer sheet" is one method by which agents may attempt to circumvent NCAA rules. An offer sheet is presented by the agent to the student-athlete, who often mistakes it for a contract. The student-athlete signs this form prior to the expiration of college eligibility, but the agent will not sign it until after the student-athlete's eligibility has expired. Since most student-athletes are not versed in the technicalities of the requirements for a binding contract, they often believe they have a contract with the agent and will discontinue dealing with other agents. Agents who use this tactic to reserve players claim the offer sheet is not an agency contract until the representative executes the document at the close of the student-athlete's playing season. Since no contract exists, there can be no violation of NCAA rules. The NCAA, however, disagrees, believing that the substance of its rules clearly prohibits any agreements to provide future services even if the agreement does not constitute an enforceable contract.

NOTES

1. Some agents in the past have argued that because the NCAA does not govern agents, members of the profession are not subject to the association's rules. Furthermore, some agents have gone as far as to publicly acknowledge that their business conduct as an agent is often in "constant and conscious violation of NCAA rules." (See "Some Offers They Couldn't Refuse," *Sports Illustrated*, May 21, 1979, p. 28.)

2. The player's responsibility to the agent upon signing an offer sheet may be an area of contention. In 1979, a suit was filed against O. J. Anderson, a former University of Miami football player. The suit alleged breach of contract and damages in the amount of $52,500. Anderson had signed an offer sheet with an agent before his eligibility had expired. Immediately upon Anderson's expiration of eligibility, the agent signed the offer sheet and had it notarized. Subsequently, Anderson decided that he did not want the agent to represent him, and the agent filed the suit in an attempt to enforce the offer sheet agreement. The suit was settled before trial.

3. When a coach acts as an adviser concerning an athlete's professional prospects, does this make the coach an agent? Is the coach's role thus incompatible with NCAA rules? Technically, any person who agrees to help a student-athlete deal with professional offers is an agent. Therefore, a coach who acts as a buffer between a student-athlete and agents or professional teams, when such action is done with the consent and knowledge of the student-athlete, is arguably an agent, even if no compensation or promise of compensation is involved.

This problem was the focus of an NCAA investigation involving George Rogers, a star running back at the University of South Carolina, and his coach, Jim Carlen. The NCAA decided that Carlen was not acting as Rogers's agent, even though the coach admitted acting as a buffer for Rogers. Carlen had done so to protect Rogers from tempting offers that might affect his playing eligibility. The NCAA did not further clarify the basis for the agent-buffer distinction.

4. Former Iona College (New York) basketball player Jeff Ruland lost his eligibility for his senior year of competition when it was discovered that he had signed a personal management contract with a professional agent. Although both Ruland and his agent initially repudiated the arrangement, the agent later divulged that under the terms of their agreement he was to receive 10 percent of Ruland's gross earnings for the next four years. He also asserted that he had given the basketball player both cash and gifts and had provided financial management services. While Ruland stated publicly that he considered any arrangement with the agent to be null and void, the representative made it clear that any attempt to replace him would be dealt with in court.

During the controversy, Iona College maintained the position that Ruland had been "sweet-talked" into the agreement in violation of NCAA rules. Ruland, who went on to play professional basketball, acknowledged his relationship with the agent a year later. While admitting that his actions had been in violation of NCAA standards, Ruland commented that the practice of dealing with professional agents was commonplace among college athletes.

5. In October 1984, Mike Rozier, former University of Nebraska star running back and 1983 Heisman Trophy

winner, revealed that while still under NCAA eligibility regulations, he accepted money from an agent and negotiated a professional football contract with the USFL's Pittsburgh Maulers. Both acts were violations of NCAA regulations. Rozier accepted a total of $2,400 during his last intercollegiate season. His contract with the Maulers was finalized a few days before the Orange Bowl in Miami, Florida, and was signed hours after the completion of the game. Rozier claimed that he made his revelations because he was ashamed and hoped that young athletes could learn from his mistakes. For further details of this incident, see "The Year the Heisman Went to a Pro," *Sports Illustrated*, October 22, 1984, p. 21.

6. Leigh Steinberg, a leading sports agent and head of the Ethics Committee of the Association of Representatives of Professional Agents, in October 1984, alleged that "At least one third of the top athletes in college football and basketball are signing early every year. It is usually done in return for money payments. It is an open secret that no one wants to talk about. It is unconscionable." Steinberg suggested that increasing scholarship monies awarded by the schools might take some of the pressure off the athletes to sign early with agents. For further information, see the following articles:

(a) "Steinberg: Early Signings Are Common Practice," UPI Wireservice, *Newark Star Ledger*, November 1, 1984, p. 58.

(b) "Agents Have Upper Hand with Top College Players," AP Wireservice, *Newark Star Ledger*, November 1, 1984, p. 109.

7. The following sections of "Athletic Agencies," California Labor Code, Section 1500, enacted first in 1981, are applicable to amateur athletics (see also, Vol. I, Section 4.11):

Section 1530.5. Contents of contract; notice concerning amateur status

The contract shall contain in close proximity to the signature of the athlete a notice in at least 10-point type stating that the athlete may jeopardize his or her standing as an amateur athlete by entering into the contract.

Section 1545. Students; filing copies of certificates and contracts with secondary or postsecondary educational institutions

(a) An athlete agency shall, prior to communicating with or contacting in any manner any student concerning an agency contract or a professional sport services contract, file with the secondary or postsecondary educational institution at which the student is enrolled a copy of the registration certificate of the athlete agency.

(b) An athlete agency shall file a copy of each agency contract made with any student, with the secondary or postsecondary educational institution at which the

student is enrolled, within five days after such contract is signed by the student party thereto.

(c) Filing of the copies required by subdivisions (a) and (b) shall be made with the president or chief administrative officer of the secondary or postsecondary educational institution, or the secretary of such officer, or by registered or certified mail, return receipt requested, directed to such officer.

For further information on agent registration in California, see Sobel, "The Regulation of Player Agents: State of California, NFL Players Association, and NCAA Adopt Rules to Regulate Athletes' Agents," 5 *Entertainment Law Reporter* 10 (March 1984).

8. In 1984, the NCAA Council approved a voluntary player-agent registration program to begin in the 1984–85 academic year. The NCAA's purpose was to provide its member institutions and their student-athletes with a reliable system of gathering information on player-agents so they could make decisions concerning representation. In registering with the NCAA, an agent agrees to notify (as opposed to seek permission from) directors of athletics prior to contacts with enrolled student-athletes.

In conjunction with the registration program, the NCAA also suggested that the member institutions implement counseling panels to help their student-athletes make career decisions (*1985–86 NCAA Manual*, Constitution 3–1–[h]–[4]). The NCAA makes available to member institutions a booklet, "A Career in Professional Sports: Guidelines That Make Dollars and Sense," which they recommend be used as background information for student-athletes.

9. The University of Illinois has the following policy concerning player-agents:

In recent years player agents, with or without knowledge of the NCAA rules and regulations, have prematurely talked with, advised, and signed athletes with remaining eligibility to professional contracts, thus ending a player's collegiate eligibility. Therefore, it is essential that all coaching and administrative personnel be aware of and knowledgeable about NCAA rules and regulations relating to player agents. [*Policy and Procedure Manual*, The Athletic Association of the University of Illinois, 1984, section 1, p. 24(e)]

10. For further information, see the following:
(a) "The Offer Sheet: An Attempt to Circumvent NCAA Prohibition of Representation Contracts," 14 *Loyola University Law Review* 187 (December 1980).
(b) Ruxin, *An Athlete's Guide to Agents*, Indiana University Press, Bloomington, Ind., 1982.
(c) "Agent-Athlete Relationship in Professional and Amateur Sports: The Inherent Potential for Abuse and the Need for Regulation," 30 *Buffalo Law Review* 815 (1981).
(d) Ruxin, "Unsportsmanlike Conduct: The Student-

Athlete, the NCAA, and Agents," 8 *Journal of College and University Law* 347 (1982).

(e) "Athletics Career Counseling Panels," Legislative Assistance (column), *NCAA News*, May 30, 1984, p. 3.

(f) "Attorneys and Professional Contracts," Legislative Assistance (column), *NCAA News*, May 9, 1984, p. 7.

(g) "Regulating the Professional Sport Agent: Is California in the Right Ballpark?" 15 *Pacific Law Review* 1231 (July 1984).

(h) Massey, "The Crystal Cruise Cut Short: A Survey of the Increasing Regulatory Influence over the Athlete-Agent in the National Football League," 1 *Entertainment Sports Law Journal* 53 (1984).

2.18 Individual Eligibility Requirements for Olympic Athletes

The Olympic Games are governed by the International Olympic Committee (IOC), which is located in Geneva, Switzerland. The IOC has run the Olympics since 1896, and it controls all aspects of their operation, including eligibility to participate. The enforcement of eligibility of individual athletes is delegated by the IOC to each participating country's National Olympic Committee (NOC), pursuant to IOC Rule 24, which stipulates that each NOC must enforce the rules and bylaws of the IOC.

The IOC recognizes the United States Olympic Committee (USOC) as the NOC for the United States. The USOC is a corporation chartered by Congress in 1950 (P.L. 81–805 [81st Cong. 2d Sess.] September 21, 1950; 60 Stat. 889). This charter was amended in 1978 by enactment of the "Amateur Sports Act of 1978" (P.L. 95–606 [95th Cong. 2d Sess.] November 8, 1978; 92 Stat. 3045). The principal purpose of the Amateur Sports Act was to establish a means of resolving disputes between American sports organizations seeking to become the national governing body (NGB) for a sport as recognized by the USOC. Congressional intent was to shield amateur athletes from being harmed by these disputes.

The objectives and purposes of the United States Olympic Committee are to:

(a) establish national goals for amateur athletic activities and encourage the attainment of those goals;

(b) coordinate and develop amateur athletic activity in the United States directly relating to international amateur athletic competition, so as to foster productive working relationships among sports-related organizations;

(c) exercise exclusive jurisdiction, either directly or through its constituent members or committees, over all matters pertaining to the participation of the United States in the Olympic Games and in the Pan-American Games, including the representation of the United States in such games, and over the organization of the Olympic Games and the Pan-American Games when held in the United States;

(d) obtain for the United States either directly or by delegation to the appropriate national governing body, the most competent amateur representation possible in each competition and event of the Olympic Games and of the Pan-American Games;

(e) promote and support amateur athletic activities involving the United States and foreign nations;

(f) promote and encourage physical fitness and public participation and amateur athletic activities;

(g) assist organizations and persons concerned with sports in the development of amateur athletic program for amateur athletes;

(h) provide for the swift resolution of conflicts and disputes involving amateur athletes, national governing bodies, and amateur sports organizations, and protect the opportunity of any amateur athlete, coach, trainer, manager, administrator, or official to participate in amateur athletic competition;

(i) foster the development of amateur athletic facilities for use by amateur athletes and assist in making existing amateur athletic facilities available for use by amateur athletes;

(j) provide and coordinate technical information on physical training, equipment design, coaching, and performance analysis;

(k) encourage and support research, development, and dissemination of information in the areas of sports medicine and sports safety;

(l) encourage and provide assistance to amateur athletic activities for women;

(m) encourage and provide assistance to amateur athletic programs and competition for handicapped individuals, including, where feasible, the expansion of opportunities for meaningful participation by handicapped individuals in programs of athletic competition for able-bodied individuals; and

(n) encourage and provide assistance to amateur athletes of racial and ethnic minorities for the purpose of eliciting the participation of minorities in amateur activities in which they are underrepresented.

The IOC also designates one International Federation for each Olympic sport. The International Federations are responsible for setting worldwide eligibility rules for each of their sports. This has a confusing effect since no uniformity exists among the different International Federations as to what constitutes an amateur and an eligible athlete.

NOTES

1. For a fuller discussion on the roles of the different governing bodies in the Olympic Games organizations, see *U.S. Wrestling Federation* v. *Wrestling Division of AAU*, 545 F. Supp. 1053 (N.D. Ohio, E.D. 1982), in which the federal court enjoined one national sports organization from being the designated NGB over another organization pursuant to the Amateur Sports Act of 1978. For further information, see the court of appeals decision in Section 1.22–1. See also, *United States Wrestling Federation* v. *United States Olympic Committee*, Civil Action No. 13460–78 (Super. Ct., D.C. 1978).

2. Another major purpose of the Amateur Sports Act of 1978 was to protect the USOC's ability to raise financial revenue to field American Olympic teams which receive no direct government funding. In *United States Olympic Committee* v. *Intelicense*, 737 F. 2d 263 (2nd Cir. 1984), the U.S. Court of Appeals affirmed the judgment of the district court, which ruled that pursuant to the Amateur Sports Act that the USOC's consent is a prerequisite to marketing the Olympic symbol (five interlocking rings) in the United States.

3. Olympic symbols and trademarks not only are protected by the Olympic symbol protection provision of the Amateur Sports Act of 1978, but also by the Federal Trademark Act (Lanham Act; 15 U.S.C. Sec. 1114) or individual state statutes. See the following cases:

(a) *Stop the Olympic Prison* v. *U.S. Olympic Committee*, 489 F. Supp. 1112 (S.D.N.Y. 1980).

(b) *United States Olympic Committee* v. *Union Sports Apparel*, Civ. Act. No. 82–276–A (E.D. Va. 1983), 220 U.S.P.Q. 526.

(c) *United States Olympic Committee* v. *International Federation of Bodybuilders*, Civ. Act. No. 81–9696 (D.D.C. 1982), 219 U.S.P.Q. 353.

(d) *International Olympic Committee* v. *San Francisco Arts & Athletes*, Civ. Act. No. C–82–4183 (N.D. Cal. 1982) 217 U.S.P.Q. 982.

Martin v. International Olympic Committee, 740 F. 2d 670 (9th Cir. 1984)

Women runners and runners' organizations filed suit against the International Olympic Committee (IOC) seeking to require the IOC to institute 5,000 meter and 10,000 meter track events for women at the 1984 Summer Olympic Games. The U.S. District Court (C.D. Cal.) denied a request for a preliminary injunction. The U.S. Court of Appeals affirmed and stated:

Certain women runners and runners' organizations (the women runners) appeal the denial by the district court of their motion for a preliminary mandatory injunction to require the organizers of the 1984 Los Angeles Summer Olympic Games to include 5,000 meter and 10,000 meter track events for women. The women runners claim that the failure to include these events constitutes gender-based discrimination that violates their equal protection rights under the fifth and fourteenth amendments and the Unruh Civil Rights Act, Cal. Civ. Code section 51 (West 1982) (the Act). The district court ruled that the women runners had not met all of the requirements for preliminary injunctive relief....

According to the women runners, the process used to select new Olympic events has resulted in the continuation of an historical pattern of discrimination against women participants in the Olympic Games. The district court's opinion extensively reviewed the history of women's participation in the Games and concluded that the women runners made a strong showing that the early history of the modern Olympic Games was marred by blatant discrimination against women. The district court also found that women's participation in the Olympics has increased markedly during the past thirty-six years. Although there is not parity between men and women in either the number of competitors or the number of events, the district court found that women were progressing in both of these areas. For example, three new women's track and field events — the 3,000 meters, the 400 meter hurdles, and the marathon — will be included for the first time in the 1984 Games.

Although the pertinent background extends to the beginning of this century, the critical occurrence for this lawsuit occurred in 1949, when the IOC adopted rules to slow the rapid growth in the number of Olympic events within recognized sports. The successor rule of that effort, which is at issue in this litigation, is rule 32 of the 1970 Olympic Charter. It provides:

> The IOC in consultation with the IFs (International Federations) concerned shall decide the events which shall be included in each sport in bearing with the global aspect of the Olympic programme and statistical data referring to the number of participating countries in each event of the Olympic programme, of the world championships, of Regional Games and all other competitions under the patronage of the IOC and the patronage of the IFs for a period of one olympiad (four years).

Under this rule, an event must be recognized internationally through national championships and international competition during the four years before the time it is first considered for inclusion, and the decision on whether to include an event is made four years before the games in which it will first appear. Thus, the critical qualifying time period for races to be run for the first time in 1984 was from 1976 to 1980.

Track and field is a recognized Olympic sport. The IAAF is the body charged with regulating international track and field competition. The IAAF determines which track and field events will be included in international competition and for which events world records will be established. The IOC has also made the IAAF responsible for recommending new track and field events for inclusion in the Olympic Games. To assist in providing more women's events, the Women's Committee of the IAAF was organized. Although the IAAF may recommend new track and field events for inclusion in the games, the final decision on inclusion rests solely with the IOC.

The 5,000 meter and 10,000 meter track races have been a part of the men's Olympic program since 1912. In 1978, the Women's Committee of the IAAF requested that the IAAF grant world record status for women's competition in these two events and include them in international competition. The IAAF recognized an increased interest in the events but rejected the request on the grounds that world-wide participation was not yet on a high enough level. "It was agreed to monitor progress "with a view to . . . recommending their introduction as soon as this was justified." In 1980, the IAAF granted world record status to the two events but did not include them in world championship competition. Because the races were not yet sanctioned by the IAAF for international competition in 1980 when decisions about the 1984 Games were being made, the 5,000 meter and 10,000 meter women's races were not eligible under rule 32 for inclusion in the 1984 Games. . . .

In the present case, the district judge applied the correct legal standard governing the issuance of preliminary injunctions. After citing several of the controlling precedents referred to above, the district judge weighed the women runners' request for injunctive relief under the alternative test. He found that the balance of hardships tipped strongly in favor of the women runners. He reasoned that the inherently brief period of an athlete's peak physical capacity may preclude many of the women runners from ever competing in the Olympic Games if they are not allowed to run in 1984. On the other hand, the district judge found that issuing a mandatory injunction requiring the two races at this late date would impose substantial administrative and logistical difficulties on the Olympics organizations. The district judge determined that the irreparable harm the women runners would suffer if they were not allowed to compete outweighed the incremental administrative burden that would be imposed on the Olympics organizations if they had to organize two additional track and field events for women. Notwithstanding these determinations, which we accept, the district judge denied the requested injunction because he also concluded that the women runners had failed to demonstrate a fair chance of success on the merits of their gender discrimination claims. It is this conclusion which the women runners vigorously challenge and which is the issue before us on this appeal.

Because it will be unnecessary to reach the constitutional question if this appeal can be disposed of on statutory grounds, we turn first to the women runners' claim that the lack of 5,000 meter and 10,000 meter track races for women violates the Act.... The women runners argue that the district judge applied an erroneous legal standard when he found that they had not demonstrated a fair chance of success on the merits of their Unruh Act claim. The judge reasoned that "the Olympic rules for including events are rationally related to the orderly administration of the Games." The women runners contend that the proper standard is whether the rules are justified by a compelling societal interest....

... [We] hold that rule 32's process for adding new events does not operate as a blanket exclusion of any class of persons and is therefore not "arbitrary discrimination." It applies equally to all proposed new events and the would-be Olympic competitors for those events, and, therefore, does not violate the Act. Because the finding by the district court of rational relation is functionally similar to a finding that rule 32 is not discriminatory, no remand to the district court is necessary and we may affirm its judgment.

In addition, we find persuasive the argument that a court should be wary of applying a state statute to alter the content of the Olympic Games. The Olympic Games are organized and conducted under the terms of an international agreement — the Olympic Charter. We are extremely hesitant to undertake the application of one state's statute to alter an event that is staged with competitors from the entire world under the terms of that agreement.

We therefore conclude that the district judge did not abuse his discretion in determining that the women runners have not demonstrated a fair chance of success on the merits of their Unruh Act claim. Having concluded that the state statute does not conclude this appeal, we must now turn to the constitutional claim of the women runners.

The women runners contend that the lack of equal medal opportunities for women in the 1984 Olympic Games violates their equal protec-

tion rights under the fifth and fourteenth amendments. Although the fourteenth amendment predicate of state action is contested by the Olympics organizations, we cannot say, on this record, that the district court erroneously found state action present.

The disproportionate impact of a statute or regulation alone, however, does not violate the equal protection clause. To succeed on their equal protection claim, the women runners must show that the allegedly disproportionate impact of rule 32 on women reflects a discriminatory purpose.... It would be sufficient to show that an invidiously discriminatory purpose was a motivating factor in the challenged actions; it is not necessary to prove that such a discriminatory purpose was the sole basis for limiting women's competition in the Olympic Games....

Rule 32 is facially gender-neutral. It describes the procedures for determining events to be included in the Olympic Games without referring to the competitors' sex....

In the case before us, ... after carefully applying the analysis outlined, the district judge found that rule 32 was neither overtly nor covertly gender-based. He also found that the women runners had failed to show that the unequal impact of rule 32 reflected invidious gender-based discrimination.

The women runners dispute both of these determinations. First, they claim that rule 32 is not in fact gender-neutral because it has been applied almost exclusively to women's events. Because there were a great many more men's events than women's events in 1949 when rule 32's predecessor was enacted, the women runners argue that rule 32 has impacted women athletes disproportionately and is therefore not a gender-neutral classification. They argue that, in essence, they are frozen into a secondary role because the women's events will always be restricted by rule 32. This argument is simply untenable.... Indeed, the women runners' own brief concedes that forty-three new men's events have been added since 1949 — presumably under the process of rule 32 and its predecessors — while forty-eight new events have been added for women competitors during this same period. Thus, the women runners' argument that rule 32 is not gender-netural is unpersuasive.

The women runners also dispute the district

court's determination that they failed to demonstrate a fair chance of proving purposeful discrimination behind the unequal number of Olympic events for men and women. . . . Although an historical background of invidious discrimination is a relevant factor in examining rule 32 for evidence of a discriminatory purpose, . . . it is insufficient alone to create a presumption of purposeful discrimination or to shift the burden of showing discriminatory intent behind this facially neutral regulation.

We express no opinion on whether the women runners will eventually be able to prove intent to discriminate. A full record after a trial will provide the ultimate answer.

We now only decide whether the district judge abused his discretion when he found, based upon this record, that the women runners did not have a fair chance of proving intentional discrimination.

Relying upon the facts we have briefly outlined for purposes of this opinion plus many other detailed findings, the district court concluded that the women runners had not made the requisite showing. After a thorough review of the record, we cannot overrule his determination. Therefore, because the district judge applied the proper legal standard and because we cannot conclude that his findings show a "clear error of judgment," we may not reverse his decision not to issue a preliminary injunction based on the women runners' equal protection claims.

NOTES _____

1. In *Michels* v. *United States Olympic Committee*, 741 F. 2d 155 (7th Cir. 1984), a federal appeals court found that an individual athlete had no private cause of action against the USOC under the Amateur Sports Act of 1978. In reversing the district court's decision, the appeals court noted that the Supreme Court has emphasized congressional intent in ruling on cause-of-action suits and that

[t]he legislative history of the Act clearly reveals that Congress intended not to create a private cause of action under the Act. The Act as originally proposed contained an "Amateur Athlete's Bill of Rights," which included a civil cause of action in federal district court for any athlete against an NGB, educational institution, or other sports organization that threatened to deny the athlete's right to participate in certain events. As the Senate Report explains, this bill of rights provision "met with

strong resistance by the high school and college communities. Ultimately, the compromise reached was that certain substantive provisions on athletes rights would be included in the USOC Constitution, and not in the bill." Congress omitted the bill of rights provision in the Act's final version. Congress thus considered and rejected a cause of action for athletes to enforce the Act's provisions.

2. In *DeFrantz* v. *United States Olympic Committee*, 492 F. Supp. 1181 (D.D.C. 1980), *aff'd without opinion*, 701 F. 2d 221 (D.C. Cir. 1980), the federal district court held that the Amateur Sports Act of 1978 did not establish a cause of action for 25 designated Olympic athletes who sought to enjoin the USOC from barring these American athletes from participating in the 1980 Olympic Games in Moscow. The court noted:

We . . . conclude that the USOC not only had the authority to decide not to send an American team to the summer Olympics, but also that it could do so for reasons not directly related to sports considerations.

We . . . find that the decision of the USOC not to send an American team to the summer Olympics was not state action, and therefore, does not give rise to an actionable claim for the infringements of the constitutional rights alleged.

For further information on this case, see Section 1.22–1.

2.20 Student-Athlete's Individual Rights

The authority an athletic association or a coach has to make decisions regarding an athlete's private life is limited. Generally, the purpose of the rules created and enforced must be reasonably related to the pursuit of the sport itself. Without this reasonable relationship, the rule may be deemed impermissible on constitutional grounds. Even when a reasonable relationship to the association's or coach's purpose does exist, a rule may be impermissible if it infringes on the constitutional rights of liberty and property, which are protected by due process guarantees.

2.21 Freedom of Expression

Freedom of expression is the cornerstone of the Bill of Rights and individual liberty under the Constitution. Freedom of expression is a broad term describing the right to free "speech." The term is used to include non-verbal types of communication that are protected under the first amendment — for example, carrying a sign with a written message. Therefore, while the First Amendment uses the words "Congress shall make no law ... abridging the freedom of *speech*" (emphasis added), a broader range of expression is protected.

For purposes of analysis, expression must be broken down into two component parts. First there is the element of conduct or physical action, which is a necessary part of communicating a message. For example, a demonstration requires conduct by the demonstrators which can be either peaceful or violent. Violence is a noncommunicative aspect of speech that can be regulated since compelling government interests in peace and order are involved. Second, there is the component of the actual message or content of speech. This communicative aspect of speech, which consists of the thoughts or informational content of the communication, can be regulated if there is a clear and present danger of imminent lawless action, as, for example, in a riot.

Williams v. **Eaton**, 468 F. 2d 1079 (10th Cir. 1972)

The plaintiffs were a group of 14 black football players for the University of Wyoming. They had approached head football coach Lloyd Eaton and members of his staff in Memorial Fieldhouse at the university in October 1969, just prior to the Brigham Young game, wearing black armbands to protest the beliefs of the Mormon Church. Coach Eaton immediately informed them that they were dismissed from the team for violating team discipline rules. The President of the University, William D. Carlson, met with coach Eaton, the director of athletics, and the football coaching staff. Coach Eaton agreed to meet with the players individually to discuss the possibility of their return. None of the players chose to do so.

President Carlson had the power to resolve the issue, but following a meeting with the players in which they continued to uphold their right to protest, he decided that the dispute should be presented to the highest governing board at the university, the board of trustees.

At the trustee's meeting, President Carlson and Governor Hathaway spoke independently to the players and asked if there were any considerations other than the Brigham Young game which would prevent them from returning to the team. The players responded that they would not return as long as Coach Eaton was retained. The board of trustees supported Eaton's dismissal of the players on the grounds that if the university were to allow the players to wear the armbands to protest the beliefs of the Mormon Church, the players would be construed as representatives of the university. As such, their actions would place the university in violation of the state constitutional requirement of complete neutrality relating to religion and of the principle of separation of church and state. The board also held that the coach's rule banning protests and demonstrations was for disciplinary purposes and that the players had full knowledge of the rule when they accepted the benefits of a football scholarship at the university. Furthermore, at no time did any of the players now involved protest or complain about this rule. When the players were suspended, none of their scholarships were revoked nor was the revocation of scholarships ever threatened.

Subsequently, the players brought suit in the District Court of the United States in Wyoming. The action was dismissed. The players appealed, and the court of appeals affirmed in part while remanding the case back for further proceedings. On remand, the district court found that the players had refused to play unless they were permitted to wear black armbands and until coach Eaton was dismissed from his position. The court held that the players had been given a full and impartial hearing and that their procedural due process rights had not been violated. The court felt that coach Eaton's rule was not arbitrary or capricious, and up until this time, there had been no complaint concerning the rule by any of the players. In addition, coach Eaton, acting as an agent of the University of Wyoming and the state of Wyoming, was compelled not to allow the players, under the guise of the First Amendment rights of freedom of speech, to undertake a protest demonstration against the religious beliefs of the Mormon Church and Brigham Young University. The demonstration was to have taken place in a tax-supported facility, and had the officials of the university acceded to the demands of the players, such action would have been violative of the First Amendment of the U.S. Constitution.

In conclusion, the court held that the rights of the players to freedom of speech as guaranteed by the First Amendment could not be held paramount to the rights of others to practice their religion free from state-supported protest or demonstration.

NOTES

1. In *Menora v. Illinois High School Ass'n.*, 527 F. Supp. 637 (N.D. Ill. 1981), *vacated*, 683 F. 2d 1030 (7th Cir. 1982), *cert. den.*, 103 S. Ct. 801 (1983), a federal district court ruled that an Illinois High School Association (IHSA) rule that prohibited student-athletes from wearing soft barrets or yarmulkes during basketball games violated their right to freedom of religion guaranteed by the First Amendment. Orthodox Jewish students are required by their religion to keep their head covered at all times except when unconscious, immersed in water, or in imminent danger of loss of life. The IHSA stated that the rule was established to prevent injuries from occurring from slips caused from loose yarmulkes, dropped pins, or clips on the playing floor. The court noted that this reasoning was highly speculative.

On appeal to the U.S. Court of Appeals (7th Cir.), the decision was overturned. The court ruled that the students had no constitutional right to wear yarmulkes during basketball games. The case was remanded back to the lower court with instructions that the students come back to the court with a proposal for a more secure form of head gear. The court noted that Jewish religious law requires that the head only be covered, not specifically by yarmulkes.

The plaintiffs' writ of certiorari was denied by the U.S.

Supreme Court. However, after the courts' decisions, the IHSA changed its rule and allowed yarmulkes to be worn when it was demonstrated that they could be safely secured.

2. In *Marcum v. Dahl*, 658 F. 2d 731 (10th Cir. 1981), plaintiffs, two members of the University of Oklahoma women's basketball team, had their scholarship terminated after publicly voicing opposition to the renewal of the head coach's contract. Plaintiffs contended that such an action in response to their comments was a violation of their right to free speech under the First Amendment of the Constitution. The court found for the defendants, holding that the termination of the scholarships was a result of months of dissension, and not solely a product of the players' comments. The court reasoned that the exercise of a constitutional right does not insulate a person from recrimination for other prior comments.

3. For further information on *Menora*, see "Basketball Players' Free Exercise Rights Compromised — Technical Foul," *Wisconsin Law Review* 1487 (1983).

2.22 Hair Length

Rules regulating the length of hair for males have led to law suits. Most litigation of athletic rules on constitutional grounds is based on allegations of infringement of a property interest; hair length regulations, however, are attacked for being infringements of personal liberty interests. Since these cases present constitutional issues, they are usually litigated in federal court. The Circuit Courts of the United States for the First, Third, Fourth, Seventh, and Eighth Circuits have recognized a student's right to govern personal appearance while attending public school (see *Dunham* v. *Pulsifer, infra*). In the Fifth, Sixth, Ninth, and Tenth Circuits, however, this liberty interest is considered too insubstantial to create the threshold controversy necessary to attain federal jurisdiction (see *Zeller* v. *Donegal, infra*).

Dunham v. Pulsifer, 312 F. Supp. 411 (D. Vt. 1970)

Plaintiff high school student-athlete requested an injunction to stop Brattleboro High School in Brattleboro, Vermont, from enforcing an athletic grooming code. The action developed from the adoption of an athletic dress code enacted in 1969 by the school board:

> In order to enhance esprit de corps, prevent adverse public reaction, prevent dissension on teams, and for the general welfare of teams and participants, the following regulations governing dress and grooming for pupils participating in and traveling to and from interscholastic athletic activities are in effect:
>
> 1. Whenever eating and not traveling in team uniform, male athletes shall wear jacket and tie.
> 2. For males, hair must be cut tapered in the back and on sides of the head with no hair over the collar. Sideburns must be no lower than the earlobe and trimmed.
> 3. Males must be clean shaven and not wear beards and mustaches.
> 4. Females, when not traveling in team uniform, shall wear skirts (no slacks or shorts).
> 5. Cleanliness and neatness shall be maintained at all times.

Alleged violations of this code resulted in dismissal of plaintiff from the school tennis team. The court held for the plaintiffs and noted that although one of the asserted justifications for these rules was the promotion of closer team work and discipline, the tennis team had no such problems prior to the enactment of the dress code. "Outside of uniformity in appearance, no evidence was introduced as to advantages to be derived from the athletic code except the question of discipline for the sake of discipline."

In reviewing this regulation under the equal protection clause, the court stated:

> A regulatory classification which, in addition to the creation of differential treatment, serves to penalize the exercise of a fundamental right must be justified by a compelling governmental interest. . . . The "compelling state interest" standard . . . calls upon the state to show more than a link of reasonableness.

The court then went on to discuss the nature of the right that was being violated. The court decided:

> There are few individual characteristics more basic to one's personality and image than the manner in which one wears his hair. . . . The cut of one's hair style is more fundamental to personal appearance than the type of clothing he wears. Garments can be changed at will whereas hair, once it is cut, has to remain constant for substantial periods of time. Hair style has been shadowed with political, philosophical and ideological overtones.

Once the court established the fundamental nature of the right, it went on to review the asserted justifications for imposing the restriction. It decided that there was "no credible evidence that hair length affects performance . . . [or] that long hair creates dissension." It also noted that "the coach's right to regulate the lives of his team members (under the guise of discipline) does have its limits. A coach may not demand obedience to a rule which does not in some way further other proper objectives of participation and performance." Finally, the court noted that standing alone, "conformity per se is neither a reason or a justification for the hair code in this case . . . uniformity is not a reason in and of itself." The court therefore found that there was no reasonable relation between the rule and the justification. When there is not even a reasonable relationship, "the code falls far short of substantial justification. It is not essential to any compelling interest . . . and its enforcement cannot be upheld."

Zeller v. Donegal School Dist., 517 F. 2d 600 (3rd Cir. 1975)

Plaintiff high school soccer player sought an injunction and monetary damages under the Civil Rights Act for his dismissal from the soccer team for noncompliance with the athletic grooming code regulating length of hair. The district court dismissed the complaint, and plaintiff appealed. The court of appeals held that the nature of constitutional interpretation calls for the making of a value judgment in areas that are regulated by the state and in which federal courts should not intrude: "We hold that plaintiff's contention does not rise to the dignity of a protectable constitutional interest." The court based this decision on the concept that a student's liberties and freedoms are not absolute: "We determine today that the Federal system is ill-equipped to make value judgments on hair-lengths in terms of the constitution." The court concluded that student hair cases should be decided by school regulation, "where the wisdom and experience of school authorities must be deemed superior and preferable to the federal judiciary's."

NOTES _____

1. In *Dostert v. Berthold Public School Dist. No. 54*, 391 F. Supp. 876 (D. N.D. 1975), plaintiff sought relief from a rule regulating hair length. The court held that the school's interest in requiring uniformity was such a compelling part of its public educational mission as to outweigh the constitutionally protected interest of students in regard to personal appearance.

2. In *Long v. Zopp*, 476 F. 2d 180 (4th Cir. 1973), plaintiff high school football player challenged the denial of his football letter because of his hair length. The court held unlawful the coach's regulation of the hair length of his players after the end of the football season. The holding was based on the analysis that it is reasonable for a coach to require short hair during a playing season for health and safety reasons. However, it is not reasonable to deny an athletic award or an invitation to a sports banquet when a male athlete allows his hair to grow long after the season.

3. The following rules are from the dress code of the United States of America Amateur Boxing Federation:

(1) Contestants must be clean, present tidy appearance, cleanly shaved; no goatee or beard will be permitted, however, a thinline mustache on the lip to the edge of the outer corners of the mouth is authorized. Hair shall be cut in such a manner as not to interfere with his vision. . . .

(3) No metal, straps, buckles, necklaces, jewelry of any kind, or any other object which may cause injury to either opponent shall be worn.

(4) The use of any type of grease or other substance on the body is prohibited. [*1981–84 USA/ABF Official Rules for Boxing Competition*, Article 9, "Dress," p. 75]

4. In *Davenport v. Randolph County Bd. of Education*, 730 F. 2d 1395 (11th Cir. 1984), plaintiff high school football student-athletes sought an injunction from the school board's decision to refuse to allow them to participate in athletics unless they complied with the coach's "clean-shaven" policy for football and basketball team members. The U.S. District Court denied the injunction. The students appealed to the U.S. Court of Appeals, which affirmed the lower court's decision.

2.23 High School Marriages

Rules relating to high school marriages have resulted in much litigation. In earlier cases, rules excluding married student-athletes from interscholastic competition were upheld under the rational relationship standard. These rules were considered reasonable because it was believed that exclusion of married students from athletics was necessary to (1) protect unmarried students from bad influences, (2) encourage students to finish high school before marriage, and (3) give married students the opportunity for more time together to develop their family life. Such exclusion was not considered an infringement of a constitutionally protected right since participation in extracurricular activities was not viewed as a property right but as a privilege (see *Estay v. La Fourche Parish School Board, infra*).

More recently, however, such rules have been struck down as invalid and improper invasions of the right to marital property (see *Davis v. Meek, infra*). Marriage rules have also been overturned on the basis of a property interest. The courts have reasoned that such rules deprive students of a chance for a college scholarship and therefore infringe upon their property interest (see *Moran v. School Dist. No. 7, Yellowstone County*, Note 2). Most courts have refused to accept the property interest found by *Moran*, noting that such an interest is too speculative at the high school level to merit legal protection as a property interest.

_____

Estay v. La Fourche Parish School Board, 230 So. 2d 443 (La. Ct. App. 1969)

Plaintiff married high school student challenged his exclusion from all extracurricular participation based on a school board regulation. The court of appeals held that the school board had the authority to adopt the regulation. It found the regulation to be reasonable — not arbitrary or capricious — and enforcement of the rule did not serve to deprive the student of any constitutional rights.

The court held that there was a rational relationship between this rule and its stated objective of promoting completion of high school education prior to marriage. It felt the classification rested on a sound and reasonable basis and that the criteria were applied uniformly and impartially.

The court took note of the fact that the plaintiff might lose the opportunity to obtain a scholarship. It designated that the opportunity for scholarship was only a secondary concern. The school board's responsibility, the court held, covers decisions affecting the extent to which students may participate in extracurricular activities. The supervisory powers of the board, when lawfully exercised, will not be interfered with by the courts so long as the policies are "fair, uniform and based upon sound discretion." The student's right to participate is not absolute and unconditional, and therefore the lower court's decision should be upheld.

Davis v. Meek, 344 F. Supp. 298 (N.D. Ohio 1972)

Plaintiff married high school baseball player challenged his exclusion from the baseball team and all other extracurricular activities. The disputed rule read:

> A. Married pupils are permitted to attend school.
> B. Married pupils are not permitted to participate in school sponsored extracurricular activities including the Junior-Senior Prom.

The plaintiff was aware of the rule prior to his marriage and was informed that it would be enforced against him.

The school board justified the rule by arguing that students who marry usually drop out of school and that the rule had been enacted to decrease this drop-out rate. The rule

was based on the public policy of keeping children in school until graduation from high school. The school board believed that a rule discouraging high school marriage was a proper exercise of its governing authority. The plaintiff contended that he had a constitutional right to be married and that the rule interfered with his civil liberties.

The court noted the uniformity in prior court decisions upholding the right of boards of education to deny students participation in extracurricular activities after they are married. It also noted plaintiff's contention that his constitutional rights had been infringed. The court indicated that traditionally the right to get married was a local matter but after a legal marriage, "marital privacy may not be invaded by the state even for the laudable purpose of discouraging other children from marrying at such an early age." The court then stated that extracurricular activities are an integral part of the total educational program. Therefore, the rule denies the plaintiff an opportunity, which under Ohio statutes, he has a right to receive. The court also noted:

> The state cases upholding the validity of such rules as the one involved here were all decided prior to the case of *Tinker* v. *Des Moines Independent School Dist.*, 393 U.S. 503, 89 S. Ct. 733, 21 L. Ed. 2d 731 (1969). Certainly, where there is no finding and no showing that engaging in the forbidden conduct would materially and substantially interfere with the requirements of appropriate discipline in the operation of the school, the prohibition cannot be sustained.

The issue therefore was "whether defendants may enforce against the plaintiff . . . a rule which will in effect punish him by depriving him of a part of his education." The court held that the defendants should be precluded from imposing this restriction because the deterrent effect is minimal.

NOTES

1. Rules barring married students from participating in extracurricular activities were held constitutionally permis-

sible in the following cases:

(a) In *Kissick* v. *Garland Independent School Dist.*, 330 S.W. 2d 708 (Tex. Civ. App. 1959), the court of appeals ruled against a high school student who was previously married, had received a football letter the prior year, and was looking to an athletic scholarship and college. The court held that the "resolution of school district providing that married students or previously married students should be restricted wholly to classroom work and barring them from participating in athletics or other exhibitions and prohibiting them from holding class offices or other positions of honor other than academic honor — was not arbitrary, capricious, discriminatory, or unreasonable."

(b) In *Starkey* v. *Board of Educ. of Davis County School Dist.*, 14 Utah 2d 227, 381 P. 2d 718 (1963), plaintiff brought an action as a married high school student-athlete to prevent enforcement against him of a school board resolution prohibiting married students from participating in school extracurricular activities. The Utah Supreme Court held that the "rule against participation in extracurricular activities by married students bore a reasonable relationship to the problem of 'drop outs' and did not constitute an abuse of school board's discretion."

(c) In *Cochrane* v. *Board of Educ. of Mesick Consol. School Dist.*, 360 Mich. 390, 103 N.W. 2d 569 (1960), original proceedings were held to compel the board of education to allow married high school students to play football during the year (1958). Upon appeal by plaintiff, the Michigan Supreme Court affirmed the circuit court's decision and held that the "school district did not violate the statute guaranteeing to all students an equal right to public educational facilities by excluding married high school students from participation in co-curricular activities."

(d) In *State ex rel. Baker* v. *Stevenson*, 270 Ohio App. 223, 189 N.E. 2d 181 (1962), the court of common pleas held that rule precluding married high school students from participating in extracurricular activities was valid in its application to prevent the plaintiff, a married high school senior, from playing basketball.

(e) In *Board of Directors of the Independent School Dist. of Waterloo* v. *Green*, 259 Iowa 260, 147 N.W. 2d 854 (1967), an action was brought to enjoin enforcement of a school board rule barring participation in extracurricular activities by married pupils. Upon appeal, the Iowa Supreme Court held that engaging in extracurricular activities, such as basketball, was a privilege that may be enjoyed only in accordance with standards set by the school district. The plaintiff did not have a "right" to participate; therefore, no violation of the equal protection clause occurred. Furthermore, the acts of the board were not arbitrary and unreasonable, so there was no abuse of discretion.

2. A rule barring married students from participating in extracurricular activities was held impermissible in the absence of finding of a rational basis for the rule in *Moran* v. *School District No. 7, Yellowstone County*, 350 F. Supp. 1180 (D. Mont. 1972). In *Moran*, a marriage rule was held invalid because it deprived a student the chance for a college scholarship without showing any evidence that the presence of married students would result in a reasonable likelihood of imposing moral pollution on unmarried students. No rational basis existed upon which to restrict participation.

3. Rules barring married students from participating in extracurricular activities were held impermissible as violative of equal protection standards in the following cases:

(a) In *Hollon* v. *Mathis Independent School Dist.*, 358 F. Supp. 1269 (S.D. Tex. 1973), plaintiff sought a temporary injunction against the enforcement of a school district policy that prohibited married students from engaging in interscholastic league activities. The district court held that the policy was unconstitutional. The court decided "there was no justifiable relationship between the marriage of high school athletes and the overall dropout problem; nor does it appear that preventing a good athlete, although married, from continuing to play ... would in any way deter marriages or otherwise enhance the dropout problem."

(b) In *Romans* v. *Crenshaw*, 354 F. Supp. 868 (S.D. Tex. 1971), plaintiff challenged a public high school regulation which prohibited any married or previously married student from participating in any extracurricular activity. The district court held that "absent factual support for considerations urged by the school district to sustain its regulation, the same denied equal protection," and granted judgment for the plaintiff.

(c) In *Indiana High School* v. *Raike*, 164 Ind. App. 169, 329 N.E. 2d 66 (1975), a public high school rule which prohibited married students from participating in any extracurricular activities was held invalid (see Section 1.33).

2.24 Alcohol and Drug Rules

Another set of rules that are frequently contested are those regulating the use and abuse of alcohol and other drugs. While acknowledging that a school and its coaches have a strong interest in the prevention of drug abuse, the courts have consistently required that any rule established in this area be closely related to the problem of drug abuse. (See Section 5.70 for further information on drug abuse and athletics.)

Bunger v. Iowa High School Athletic Ass'n., 197 N.W. 2d 555 (Iowa 1972)

Plaintiff high school football player brought this action to determine the validity of a good conduct rule promulgated by the Iowa High School Athletic Association (IHSAA). The rule read as follows:

> *Item 2*: In the event a boy pleads guilty or is found guilty of using alcoholic beverages or pleads guilty or is found guilty of the use of dangerous drugs, or the transportation of either such beverages or drugs, he shall be declared ineligible for participation in interscholastic athletic competition for a minimum of six weeks for the first offense. (Individual member schools may exclude a boy for more than six weeks.) For the second offense, the penalty shall be loss of interscholastic athletic eligibility for a period of twelve months. At the end of said period the boy may, upon proper application, be reinstated to eligibility by action of the Board of Control.

In 1971, plaintiff Bunger and three other minors were riding in a car that contained a case of beer. Bunger knew the beer was in the car. The car was stopped by a state police officer, who discovered the beer and issued summonses to all four occupants for possession of beer as minors. Bunger reported the incident to his school, whereupon he was declared ineligible for athletics. Plaintiff then brought suit to enjoin enforcement of the rule. The trial court upheld the rule and plaintiff appealed.

The Supreme Court of Iowa first looked at the association's ability/power to enact the rule. It decided that based on Iowa state law the ability to enact eligibility rules rests with the State Board of Education, not with the IHSAA. Therefore, the rule was invalid because the association had no authority to make an eligibility determination.

The court then went on to discuss the rule on its merits. It acknowledged a school board's right to make rules to control and/or correct incidents or events affecting the operation of the school. It noted in this case, however, that

> we are inclined to think that the nexus . . . [in this situation] is simply too tenuous: outside of football season, beyond the school year, no illegal or even improper use of beer. We cannot find a "direct" effect upon the school here. School authorities in reaching out to control beer in cases like this are entering the sphere of the civil authorities. We hold that the rule in question is invalid as beyond the permissible *scope* of school rules.

The court then discussed the reasonableness of the rule and stated that "school authorities may make reasonable beer rules, but we think this rule is too extreme. Some closer relationship between the student and the beer is required than mere knowledge that the beer is there."

NOTES

1. In *Braesch* v. *DePasquale*, 200 Neb. 726, 265 N.W. 2d 842 (1982), the Nebraska Supreme Court held that a drinking rule serves a legitimate rational interest and directly affects the discipline of student-athletes. Such a rule was held not an arbitrary and unreasonable means to attain the legitimate end of deterrence of alcohol use.

2. In *French* v. *Cornwell*, 202 Neb. 569, 276 N.W. 2d 216 (1979), the Nebraska Supreme Court held that a rule allowing a school official to suspend a student for six weeks after the student admitted to being arrested for intoxication was constitutionally acceptable. The court found that suspension of the student was not in violation of due process because the plaintiff was aware of the rule providing for the suspension and admitted his own violation of the rule.

2.25   Handicapped Student-Athletes

The extent of a school's or association's ability to restrict the ability of athletic participation and opportunities for handicapped students is a problem which can lead to litigation by the handicapped individual seeking athletic participation. Two types of problems commonly arise with handicapped athletes. First, many organizations have rules that prohibit the participation of athletes who have either lost the use of a sense — for example, hearing or sight — or of a limb or organ. Such rules are justified on the theory that a loss of this sort creates a hazard for the affected student as well as for the other participants in that sport.

The second problem stems from a rule common to most high school athletic associations that limits participation to students *19 years old or under.* Handicapped students often do not finish high school until after age 19, due to the extended length of time it might take them to complete a basic education. Age limit rules are designed to prevent the deliberate retention of students to increase a varsity team's advantage and to equalize physical size and maturity of participants in contact sports such as football (see Section 2.14). These rules, however, may seem unreasonable when applied to older handicapped students in a sport like wrestling, in which competitors are matched by weight.

New York Roadrunners Club v. State Division of Human Rights, 432 N.E. 2d 780 (N.Y. Ct. App. 1982)

This case involved an appeal from a judgment of the New York State Supreme Court by the State Division of Human Rights, seeking to overturn the Supreme Court's decision to vacate a previous State Human Rights Appeal Board decision allowing handicapped persons in wheelchairs to participate in the New York City Marathon. The court of appeals reasoned:

> The record reveals no proof to support the Human Rights Division's finding that the respondents, New York Roadrunners Club and its president, Fred Lebow, discriminated against the disabled in violation of section 296 (subd. 2, par. [a]) of the Executive Law (Human Rights Law) when, in organizing and promoting the 1978 New York City Marathon, it required participants to use only their feet, and not wheelchairs, skateboards, bicycles or other extraneous aids. Indeed, as the Appellate Division pointed out, so long as entrants met this qualification, as well as some others the propriety of which are unchallenged, any disabilities unrelated to the

capacity to move on foot would rule out no prospective contestant.

The court noted that the Roadrunners Club had decided to run a "traditional" marathon footrace. The club could have laid down guidelines for other competitors, but as a private, though not-for-profit, organization, it was under no legal compulsion to do so. The court further stated:

> In making these observations, we, of course, are not insensitive to the role athletic activity may play in the rehabilitation and in the lives of the handicapped. Nor do we depart from our appreciation of the special concerns committed to the expertise of the Human Rights Division to combat discrimination in the first instance.... Rather, we simply hold that, under the circumstances, the acts on which the complaint here was posited did not constitute an unlawful discriminatory practice.

The court noted that it had

> had no occasion to reach or decide either the issue of safety or the question as to whether the marathon course was a "place of public accommodation" ... or the legal significance, if any, of the failure of the city to have withdrawn its permit once the respondents had rejected its request that wheelchairs be allowed.

A dissenting opinion felt the majority had ignored the significance of the "place of accommodation" issue and the city's relationship to the marathon. The dissenting opinion further noted that "In failing to consider the city's relationship and the place of public accommodation question, the majority ignores affirmed findings that the New York City Marathon," which respondents organize and sponsor, is "an annual athletic competition open to the public at large, and using public facilities." The dissent pointed out that the 1978 New York City Marathon "took place in or about October, 1978, again using park roads, streets and other public facilities and sponsored by New York City departments and agencies." The dissent went on further to discuss that when such public facilities are used, they must be opened to all persons, including disabled individuals. It noted the many other marathons (Boston, Tampa, Miami, etc.) that allow wheelchairs.

Cavallaro by Cavallaro v. Ambach, 575 F. Supp. 171 (W.D.N.Y. 1983)

Plaintiff, a handicapped 19-year-old wrestler with neurological problems that kept him behind in school, sought a waiver of the interscholastic conference's age rule so that he could participate on the wrestling team in his senior year. After denial of the waiver by the conference's Eligibility Committee, the plaintiff sought judicial relief, arguing that the age rule violated his rights under the equal protection clause of the Fourteenth Amendment.

In denying his claim, the court noted that the plaintiff was not physically impaired but had physical skills superior to most other 19-year-old students. It noted that the age rule was designed to prevent more mature students with experience from injuring younger student-athletes in contact sports such as wrestling. It concluded:

> Daniel was treated identically to other non-physically handicapped 19-year-olds and plaintiffs have not established any likelihood of success in proving a discrimination claim. . . .
>
> Participation in organized sports yields many positive results throughout the formative years particularly as in Daniel's case, where it helped build his confidence and self esteem. But that participation also teaches that there are rules to be followed — by all who play — both on and off the playing field.

NOTES _____

1. In *Colombo v. Sewanhaka Central High School Dist.*, 87 Misc. 2d 48, 383 N.Y.S. 2d 518 (1976), an action was brought by plaintiff high school student to overturn a school district directive which prevented him from participating in football, lacrosse, and soccer. In granting judgment for the school district, the court held that the decision of the school district to follow the advice

of its medical director and AMA guidelines and prohibit the 15-year-old student with a hearing deficiency from athletic participation was justified. The court believed there existed a risk of further injury to the ear, in which there was only partial hearing and to which additional injury could result in irreversible and permanent damage. The court held that the prohibition was neither arbitrary nor capricious.

2. The federal Education of the Handicapped Act, Pub. L. 91–230, Title VI § 601, Apr. 13, 1970, 84 Stat. 175, amended Pub. L. 94–142 § 3(a), Nov. 29, 1975, 89 Stat. 774, guarantees to all handicapped children a free public education that emphasizes special education and special services designed to meet their unique needs. It also guarantees the rights of these children and their parents or guardians. While assisting states to provide such an educational experience, the act is also designed to aid in the assessment of these programs.

3. Section 504 of the Rehabilitation Act of 1973 (Pub. L. 93–112), 29 U.S.C. 706, provides that "no otherwise qualified handicapped individual . . . shall, solely by reason of his handicap, be excluded from the participation in, be denied the benefits of, or be subjected to discrimination under any program or activity receiving federal financial assistance." The regulation defines and forbids acts of discrimination against qualified handicapped persons in employment and in the operation of programs and activities receiving assistance from the Department of Education (DOE). The regulation, which applies to all recipients of federal assistance from DOE, is intended to ensure that their federally assisted programs and activities are operated without discrimination on the basis of handicap.

4. For further information on the rights of disabled athletes see "The Disabled Student-Athlete: Gaining a Place on the Playing Field," 5 *Communications/Entertainment Law Journal* 517 (1983).

2.30   Discipline of Individual Athletes

The NCAA has very specific sanctions for rule violations by individual student-athletes. The association has set strict and often complicated guidelines that student-athletes *must* follow if they are to maintain eligibility for NCAA competition. Deviation from these guidelines may result in sanctions against the athlete, and/or the team, and/or the institution (see Section 1.41).

The major and most common disciplinary action that the NCAA takes against individual student-athletes is to declare them ineligible for intercollegiate competition for a stated period of time. This action is enforced by the individual institutions as part of their responsibilities of memberships in the NCAA (*1985–86 NCAA Manual*, Constitution, 3–2).

Regents of University of Minnesota v. National Collegiate Athletic Ass'n., 422 F. Supp. 1158 (D. Minn. 1976)

The University of Minnesota challenged an NCAA sanction that placed all the university's athletic teams on indefinite probation when the university refused to declare three student-athletes ineligible for intercollegiate competition. A preliminary injunction was sought to enjoin the NCAA's action.

The student-athletes had admitted to the NCAA violations, which consisted of (1) selling complimentary season tickets, (2) accepting an invitation to stay at a cabin with all meals, lodging, and entertainment provided by a member of the booster club, and (3) using a private WATS line to place long-distance calls. After admitting to the violations, the student-athletes donated the proceeds from the sale of the tickets to charity and satisfied the university's committees. However, the NCAA was not satisfied. The NCAA's proposed penalty for Minnesota's not declaring the student-athletes ineligible to compete was a three-year probation and a two-year ban on postseason play and televised games. Additionally, the NCAA imposed a two-year restriction on the granting of athletic scholarships for basketball.

The NCAA argued that the determination of student-athlete eligibility was within its exclusive authority. However, under the requirements of the University of Minnesota Student Conduct Code and a Minnesota state court order, and in accordance with authority granted by the NCAA, Minnesota afforded the three basketball players a hearing before the Campus Committee on Student Behaviors and the Assembly Committee on Intercollegiate Athletics. These committees voted not to declare the athletes ineligible despite the findings of the NCAA's Infraction Committee. The university maintained that it had a superior legal duty to grant its students the rights guaranteed to them by the Fourteenth Amendment's due process clause. This duty took precedence over its membership obligations to the NCAA.

The court, relying on an earlier decision that involved the University of Minnesota, *Behagen v. Intercollegiate Conference of Faculty Rep.* (see Section 1.32–1), found that participation in intercollegiate athletics is a substantial property right entitled to due process guarantees. (The court adopted the rule it believed the Minnesota Supreme Court would adopt.) The opportunity to participate in intercollegiate sports could lead to a very remunerative career and is an important part of the student-athlete's educational experience. Education is a necessary ingredient of economic success in later life. Thus, a student must be afforded due process rights before the right to an education or any substantial element of it can be adversely affected.

The court found that Minnesota was bound by law to provide a hearing for the student-athletes before ruling on their eligibility. The NCAA's action transgressed on the university's legal duty to afford due process hearings to student-athletes and to abide by the results of the hearing. Minnesota also has a federal right to be free from interference in the performance of this duty.

The court was satisfied that the campus committees conducted fair and impartial hearings. The court dismissed the NCAA's arguments about nonuniform "Home Town" decisions and recommended that the NCAA amend its rules to provide for prior due process hearings by independent hearing officers or boards prior to declaring student-athletes ineligible.

The court concluded that the plaintiffs had demonstrated a strong probability of success on the merits and that Minnesota would be irreparably harmed if a preliminary injunction were not issued, while the NCAA would not be harmed. The court directed the NCAA to lift the probation and temporarily enjoined them from imposing further sanctions pending a hearing on the merits of the case.

Regents of University of Minnesota v. National Collegiate Athletic Ass'n., 560 F.2d 352 (8th Cir. 1977)

The NCAA appealed the district court's decision, which granted Minnesota a preliminary injunction from the association's sanction that placed Minnesota's athletic program on indefinite probation for failing to declare three student-athletes ineligible to compete for self-confessed NCAA rule violations.

The district court had affirmed the university's position that its legal duty to grant the student-athletes due process, as guaranteed in the Fourteenth Amendment, outweighed its membership obligations to the NCAA. Based on a hearing held before the university's Campus Committee on Student Behavior and the Assembly Committee on Intercollegiate Athletics, Minnesota had refused to declare the three student-athletes ineligible for intercollegiate athletic competition. The district court had upheld the university's decision, ruling that participation in intercollegiate athletics is a substantial property right entitled to due process guarantees.

The appeals court dissolved the preliminary injunction. The court noted that, as a voluntary member of the NCAA, the university agreed to adhere to association rules, including Constitution 4–2–(a), which required Minnesota "[t]o administer their athletic programs in accordance with the Constitution, the Bylaws and other legislation of the Association . . ." The court further noted that the *NCAA Manual* stated:

> If a student-athlete is ineligible under the terms of the Constitution, Bylaws or other legislation of the Association, the institution shall be obligated immediately to apply the applicable rule to the student-athlete and withhold him from all intercollegiate competition. Subsequent to this action, the member institution may appeal to the NCAA Council, or a subcommittee designated by the Council to act for it, if the member concludes that the circumstances warrant restoration of the student-athlete's eligibility.

The appeals court held that Minnesota had standing to assert its claim of interference from the NCAA with its duty to afford minimum due process; however, the appeals court ruled there was no superior constitutional duty to prevent the university's board of regents from honoring its contractual obligations with the NCAA. The appeals court stated:

> . . . We are convinced, at least on the basis of matters currently of record, that the University, as of May 4, 1976, could have declared each of the three student-athletes ineligible consistently with any constitutional duty it may have owed to them and, conversely stated, without violating any due process rights held by them. With this conclusion, the entirety of the University's unconstitutional interference claim necessarily fails, for it follows almost immediately that (1) the University's contractual obligation to declare the student-athletes ineligible was not subject to any superior constitutional obligation; and (2) the sanctions imposed by Confidential Report No. 118(42) were a legitimate consequence of Association rules established by contract and unimpaired by the Constitution. . . .
>
> We well appreciate that our decision leaves the Association's member institutions with the sometimes delicate task of declaring individuals ineligible when facts are found which reasonably reflect proscribed conduct and with not declaring them ineligible when such facts are not found. We cannot say that this task will always be an easy one, nor can we deny that the member institution will occasionally find itself in a position where fairness to the individual and adherence to contractual obligations may seemingly conflict. We also appreciate that the violations with which at least Winey and Saunders were charged were minor violations and that even Thompson's violation was not particularly serious. Nor have we discovered any basis for doubting the University's good faith belief that the Association was in fact penalizing it for affording Thompson, Winey and Saunders what the University genuinely believed to be required by the Fourteenth Amendment.

On the other hand, the Association seeks to vindicate its own authority to interpret its own rules, an authority which we agree is of the utmost importance to the execution of the Association's salutary goals. In addition, we do not view the Association's dealings with the University as unduly harsh or abusive. . . .

Our authority is confined to adjudicating the constitutional issue before us, and apart from that issue we have no authority to judge whether a voluntary association has chosen the most desirable or efficacious means of enforcing its rules. *Shelton v. NCAA.* . . . Here, we have discerned no unconstitutional interference of the type alleged, and with that conclusion our inquiry necessarily ends.

We hold that the University has not demonstrated a substantial likelihood of success on the merits and that the district court accordingly erred in granting the preliminary injunction herein appealed.

Southern Methodist University v. Smith, 515 S.W. 2d 63 (Tex. Civ. App. 1974)

Southern Methodist University (SMU) appealed an order temporarily enjoining the university from declaring student-athlete Smith ineligible to play intercollegiate football. Smith admitted to receiving financial aid in excess of the amounts allowed under NCAA rules. The NCAA ordered SMU to declare Smith ineligible. Faced with the possibility of losing its membership in the NCAA, SMU notified Smith of his ineligibility after protesting the sanction and exhausting its appeals to the NCAA Council.

Smith filed suit and claimed that he was deprived of due process by being denied notice and a hearing concerning his violations and penalty. The court held that Smith did not have a legal right to a hearing by SMU. In addition, he failed to establish a constitutional or contractual right to claim a benefit or privilege from playing football.

The court also held that the question of Smith's right to a hearing was moot. The

NCAA had sole authority over the eligibility decision, and its rules do not provide for the type of hearing Smith requested. An SMU hearing could not have declared him eligible. Moreover, a hearing could not have afforded any relief in light of Smith's admission that he had violated the rule. The order of the trial court was reversed and the temporary injunction dissolved.

Carlton Walker v. National Collegiate Athletic Ass'n. and Officials at the University of Wisconsin, Madison Case No. E1–C–916 (W.D. Wis. 1981)

Plaintiff Walker was a starting guard for the University of Wisconsin football team. In December 1981, he was declared ineligible to participate in a postseason football game (the Garden State Bowl) due to an investigation of recruiting violations. Previously, in July 1981, the NCAA officially charged the university and its alumni with 20 violations of NCAA regulations and bylaws in connection with Walker's recruitment. Neither the NCAA nor the university charged Walker with any violation.

Walker contended that the threatened injury to him outweighed any injury to defendants, since they would suffer no harm by allowing him to participate in the postseason bowl game. Walker immediately filed a motion for a preliminary injunction in December 1981. He contended that he was not afforded due process in connection with the declaration of ineligibility. Walker also argued that athletic participation was a property right protected by the Constitution. He stated that his prohibition from postseason competition would seriously hamper his chances of playing professional football. Walker's family was allegedly looking to him for support.

The NCAA argued that a student-athlete does not have a constitutionally protected property interest in eligibility for participation in intercollegiate athletics. Drawing upon *Colorado Seminary* v. *National Collegiate*

Athletic Ass'n. (see Section 1.32–2), the NCAA contended that the desire to participate in collegiate athletics does not constitute a property interest protectable by the due process guarantees of the Constitution.

The NCAA also relied upon Bylaw 5–6–(e), which stated that any athlete whose recruitment violated NCAA legislation would be ineligible for an NCAA championship. The NCAA contended that plaintiff knew prior to his first football practice that he would be ineligible to compete in the postseason.

The district court denied Walker's motion for a preliminary injunction. The court said that he failed to establish a reasonable likelihood of success on the merits, a degree of irreparable harm necessary to afford the requested relief, or the inadequacy of remedies for redress at law.

Walker attended the University of Wisconsin from the fall of 1980 to the spring of 1982. He then transferred to the University of Utah and enrolled as a full-time student. In August 1982, pursuant to NCAA Bylaw 5–3–(e), the University of Utah requested a waiver of Walker's one-year loss of eligibility due to his transfer (NCAA Bylaw 5–1–[j]–[7]).

The NCAA Committee on Infractions reviewed the waiver request by Utah. The committee determined from the available evidence that Walker's involvement in the Wisconsin recruiting violations was not inadvertent or innocent. The waiver was denied.

Walker amended his initial complaint in November 1982, and claimed that the NCAA had tortiously and arbitrarily interfered with the contractual relations between Walker and the universities of Wisconsin and Utah, thereby depriving him of the opportunity to compete in collegiate athletics and damaging his ability to secure a professional contract. Walker also claimed in the complaint that the NCAA had monopoly power in the field of collegiate football and the regulation of amateur collegiate football personnel. He stated that the NCAA had directed its power against him by engaging in a group boycott and conspiracy with its member institutions to deprive him from playing collegiate football. Walker claimed that the NCAA had violated Sections 1 and 2 of the Sherman Act and that he was due triple damages pursuant to Section 4 of the Clayton Act.

The NCAA filed a brief in support of a motion to dismiss, or in the alternative for summary judgment. Regarding Walker's due process claims, the NCAA stated that it is well settled that a student possesses no liberty or property interest in intercollegiate athletics (see *Mitchell* v. *Louisiana High School Athletic Ass'n.*, Section 2.14, Note 2 [a]). Therefore, the NCAA argued, the privilege of participating in intercollegiate athletics falls outside the parameters of the due process clause.

In addressing the plaintiff's antitrust claims, the NCAA contended that it is well settled that not every form of combination, which may incidentally restrain trade, falls within the ambit of the Sherman Act. On this point, the NCAA cited *Majorie Webster Junior College Inc.* v. *Middle States Ass'n. of Colleges and Secondary Schools, Inc.*, 432 F. 2d 650 (D.C. Cir. 1970), *cert. denied*, 91 S. Ct. 367, 400 U.S. 965 (1970). The antitrust laws are therefore directed only to those combinations that seek control of the business market by suppression of competition in the marketplace (see *Jones* v. *National College Athletic Ass'n.*, Section 2.15–1[d]). Incidental restraints of trade in the educational sphere, absent intent or purpose to affect its commercial aspects, do not warrant application of the antitrust laws.

The NCAA also argued that the Sherman Act was not designed primarily to protect the individual but to protect the general public economically, and a private party may not recover under the act unless there has been an injury to the general public economically.

NOTES

1. The following are some cases which involved discipline issues relating to athletes in intercollegiate athletics:

(a) In *Samara* v. *National Collegiate Athletic Ass'n.*, 1973 Trade Cases 74,536 (E.D. Va.), the court upheld an NCAA decision that participation by a student-athlete in a noncertified track and field event resulted in ineligibility for further NCAA competition. The court stated that the NCAA rule and its subsequent sanctions were not illegal as applied to the student who participated in a non-certified event. This was true even though the event would have been certified if the Amateur Athletic Union (AAU) had requested the NCAA to provide such authorization.

(b) In *National Collegiate Athletic Ass'n.* v. *Gillard*, 352 So. 2d 1072 (Miss. 1977), sanctions were imposed against a non-NCAA member player who accepted a 20 percent clothing discount. Some evidence suggested that this discount policy was not limited to student-athletes. The NCAA decided there was a rule transgression. The Mississippi Supreme Court held that the plaintiff's rights were adequately protected by the NCAA's procedure and that the player's right to play intercollegiate football was not a property right protected by due process guarantees. An imposed penalty is valid if done with concern for due process requirements (see Section 1.32–2, Note 1a).

(c) In *McDonald* v. *National Collegiate Athletic Ass'n.*, 370 F. Supp. 625 (C.D. Cal. 1974), the court ruled that student-athletes have no right to due process when the NCAA imposes sanctions for bylaw violations (see Section 1.31).

(d) In 1984 a Louisiana state court dismissed a case involving Bruce Smith of Virginia Polytechnic Institute because the eligibility issue involved was moot. Smith had been declared ineligible to participate by the NCAA in the 1984 Independence Bowl under Bylaws 5–1–(i) and 5–6–(e), (which apply to postseason bowl-game eligibility per Bylaw 2–2–(f)), because of infractions of violations in his recruitment. After his ineligibility was affirmed by the NCAA on appeal, Smith sought and received temporary restraining orders from state courts in Virginia and Louisiana to allow him to compete in the bowl game. See "Smith Eligibility Case Dismissed," *NCAA News*, March 26, 1984, p. 1.

(e) See *Hall* v. *University of Minnesota*, 530 F. Supp. 104 (D. Minn. 1982), Section 2.12.

2. The following case involves discipline issues relating to athletes in interscholastic athletics:

(a) In *Florida High School Activities Ass'n.* v. *Bradshaw*, 369 So. 2d 398 (Fla. Dist. Ct. App. 1979), plaintiff high school football player sought to enjoin the state high school activities association from imposing a forfeiture of two of his team's games in which an ineligible player competed. The court upheld the penalty, reasoning that there was an absence of actual harm to the player and that the coach and other team members lacked standing to assert a claim of denial of equal protection. The court also held that the opportunity to participate is a privilege, not a constitutionally protected right; therefore, the court will not intervene in an association's discipline of its members.

3. The following case involves discipline issues relating to the AAU:

(a) In *Santee* v. *Amateur Athletic Union of the U.S.*, 2 Misc. 2d 990, 153 N.Y.S. 2d 465 (1956), the court ruled that the Amateur Athletic Union (AAU) had the authority and the jurisdiction to determine the eligibility of athletes who wished to participate in its sanctioned events. This included selection of squads for the Olympic Games, which were held under the auspices of International Amateur Athletic Federation, from which the AAU received its sanctioning authority (see Section 1.22).

4. For more information on athletic participation as a property right, see J. Weistart and C. Lowell, *The Law of Sports*, The Bobbs-Merrill Company, Inc., Charlottesville, Va. (1979).

2.40 The Buckley Amendment

The Family Educational Rights and Privacy Act of 1974 is generally referred to as the Buckley Amendment. This amendment to the General Education Provisions Act primarily involves athletics in regard to the releasing of information concerning a student-athlete's education records, including academic rank, biographical material, and injury and health records. This type of information is often used in athletic department publications and media releases. Sports information directors, especially, should be aware of the provisions and limitations enacted by the Buckley Amendment.

As a general rule, information concerning student-athletes should not be disclosed unless the student has filled out and signed a consent-disclosure-statement form (see Section 2.50, Note 1). These disclosure forms are intended to protect both parties. Written consent-disclosure statements must include the following information:

1. A specification of the records to be disclosed.
2. The purpose or purposes of the disclosure.
3. The party or class of parties to whom the disclosure may be made.

In addition, the form should contain language that allows for the disclosure of unforeseen events, such as academic ineligibility, injury reports, and sudden illness affecting athletic involvement.

Another section of the Buckley Amendment deals with specific parties that do not have to receive a prior written authorization from the student to see that student's education files. Athletic department personnel fall into the school-official exemption category and can review student-athlete files as needed to evaluate 2.0 qualifiers, academic eligibility, and so forth.

NOTE

1. For an analysis of the effect on athletics of the Family Educational Rights and Privacy Act 1974, see the following articles:
(a) "The Buckley Amendment," *NCAA News*, October 15, 1976, p. 3.
(b) "Court Tells NCAA to Release Papers Sought in Libel Suit," *Chronicle of Higher Education*, June 9, 1982, p. 14.

2.50 Athletes' Lawsuits for Failure to Provide an Education

A new area of litigation is one in which former student-athletes have sued institutions for the failure to provide an education. *Echols* v. *Board of Trustees of the California State University and Colleges, infra*, is an example of such a case. As of 1985, no court had rendered a decision on the merits. However, this area remains one in which litigation may occur in the future.

Echols v. Board of Trustees of the California State University and Colleges (Cal. Supe. Ct.), County of Los Angeles, No. C 266 777 (Settled)

Randall Echols and six other former student-athletes of California State University at Los Angeles (CSULA) brought suit against the board of trustees of CSULA, the president, the athletic director, and the basketball coach of the school for breaches of contract, misrepresentation, and conversion of plain-tiff's property to their own use. Plaintiffs claimed that they attended CSULA with the understanding, based upon claims by univer-sity officials, that they would receive a tuition and cost-free college education in exchange for their participation in the basketball program. They contended that they had been induced to sign documents that defendants had repre-sented as scholar-ship and grant applications. These documents were later discovered to be loan applications, and when the "loan" wording was later questioned by plaintiffs, defendants specifically represented to them that repayment obligations would be assumed by the school's athletic department. Plaintiffs also contended that when "scholarship" checks were given to them, they were induced to sign and return them to the athletic department and did so in the belief that these funds would go directly to the payment of costs for their college educations. This money instead, plain-tiffs claim, was utilized for other purposes.

The suit also included a claim that the defendants did specifically breach their portion of the athletic scholarship contracts by not providing education-related services such as adequate counseling. Plaintiffs were denied access to university counselors and were directed by coaches in the athletic department to enroll in nondegree-requirement courses. They were never informed of various academic and course requirements as were other CSULA students and, as a result, were unaware of degree requirements. Plaintiffs claimed that they were instructed to accept grades for courses they had never attended and were therefore deprived of educational opportunities.

Lastly, plaintiffs claimed that the defendants were at all times "agents and employees" of CSULA and at all times were acting "with-in the course and scope of such agency and with the permission and consent" of the uni-versity.

NOTES

1. In *Apuna v. Arizona State University* (pending 1984), plaintiff football player charged an academic adviser, the president of Arizona State University, and a former football coach with fraud, negligence, and interference with a professional contract as a result of their inducement of the plaintiff to enroll in and accept credit for a "bogus correspondence course." Apuna claims that the resulting scandal, adverse publicity, and his subsequent loss of eligibility caused him to lose his bid to play in three college all-star games and undermined his negotiating position with the National Football League. The suit also charged the university with invasion of privacy in the institution's public disclosure of plaintiff's academic records. For further information, see "Former Linebacker Sues Arizona State Officials for $2.4 Million," *Chronicle of Higher Education*, November 11, 1981.

2. In *Curtis E. Jones, Jr. v. University of Michigan* (pending), a suit was filed by the legal guardian of Curtis E. Jones, Jr. against the University of Michigan, which alleged that Michigan athletic officials helped Jones, a high school basketball star, to enroll in North Idaho Junior College in 1968, with the expectation that Jones would transfer to Michigan after two years. The suit further alleged that Jones's junior college classmates discovered he was illiterate and subjected him to "unrelenting razzing, insults and taunts" that caused a "complete mental breakdown." Jones never attended Michigan.

A Michigan district court held that the University of Michigan was a governmental agency and therefore immune from law suit. The Michigan Court of Appeals overturned the decision and ordered a trial on the merits.

3. For further information on *Echols*, see "Players Who Say They Were Duped on Scholarships Settle Lawsuit with California State U. at Los Angeles," *Chronicle of Higher Education*, June 20, 1984, p. 21.

4. A recurring problem in intercollegiate and interscholastic athletics concerns professors and teachers tailoring courses or course work to keep athletes eligible for competition. See, for instance, "Iowa Geared Classes to Athletes," *New York Times*, June 12, 1984, p. B9.

2.60 Summer Camps and Outside Activities

One of the more recent trends in amateur sports litigation involves high school athletes and their parents challenging rules that prohibit student-athlete participation and attendance at camps that specialize in teaching the skills of a particular sport. The rules prohibiting such attendance are relatively new. They were instituted to control overzealous coaches and parents and to equalize interscholastic competition.

One of the first rules to be challenged was a rule promulgated by the University Interscholastic League in Texas in the case of *Kite v. Marshall, infra.* The plaintiffs attacked the rule on constitutional grounds, claiming that the rule violated the constitutional rights of parents to make decisions for their children. The district court treated the rule as an infringement of a protected right and overturned it. However, the court of appeals reversed and held that the right, although important, was not a fundamental one and that the rule need only meet a rational basis test.

The NCAA has many regulations involving summer camps. These rules involve participation by prospective student-athletes, current student-athletes, and coaching staffs. In drawing up their regulations, the NCAA divides summer camps into two categories: specialized sport camps and diversified sport camps. The specialized camps, which place special emphasis on a particular sport or sports, provide specialized instruction, practice, and usually competition. Diversified camps offer a balanced camping experience, including participation in seasonal summer sports and recreational activities, without emphasis on instruction, practice, or competition in any one sport.

Prospective student-athletes are not allowed to enroll in summer camps that are run by a member institution, either on or off campus, since this would be considered by the association as a tryout (*1985–86 NCAA Manual*, Bylaw 1–6). Neither is it permissible to employ such a prospective student-athlete because this would be considered an inducement to enroll (*1985–86 NCAA Manual*, Bylaw 1–10–[a]) and a tryout. The NCAA defines a prospective student-athlete, in terms of summer camp participation, as one who is eligible for admission to a member institution or who has started classes for the senior year in high school. Junior college student-athletes also are not eligible for employment, and both groups of prospective student-athletes are not allowed to receive free or reduced admission to a camp (*1985–86 NCAA Manual*, Bylaw 1–10–[a]).

In the case of specialized camps in the sports of basketball and football, an institution cannot hire one of its own athletes with eligibility remaining in those sports to work at the camp (*1985–86 NCAA Manual*, Bylaw 1–10). Under special regulations, a specialized camp can hire one student-athlete from another institution (*1985–86 NCAA Manual*, Constitution 3–1–[f]–[1] and Bylaw 1–10). Diversified camps, run at a member institution, can employ one student-athlete, with eligibility remaining, from the basketball and football squads. Private camps may also do this under more stringent regulations (*1985–86 NCAA Manual*, Constitution 3–1–[f]–[3] and Bylaw 1–10).

Kite v. Marshall, 494 F. Supp. 227 (S.D. Tex. 1980)

Parents of high school students brought an action challenging the constitutionality of the "summer camp rule," which was adopted by the defendant University Interscholastic League (UIL), the high school athletic association in Texas. The rule read:

> Any student who attends a special athletic training camp in football, basketball, or volleyball shall be ineligible for a period of one year from the date he enrolls in the camp in the sport or sports for which he attended the camp. This does not apply to bona fide summer camps giving an overall activity program to the participants.

The rationale underlying this rule's adoption was that it would ensure that high school athletes would compete on a relatively equal basis. The UIL defended the rule as being essential for keeping athletics in its proper perspective as merely one part of the total education of a student.

The plaintiffs argued that they had a constitutional right as parents to decide what was best for their family unit and in particular what was best for their minor children. The plaintiffs maintained this right is found in the "family choice doctrine." This doctrine is described by the plaintiffs as a fundamental right to family choice or family privacy recognized as a penumbral right under the First Amendment. Thus, the plaintiff parents objected to the rule because it "requires (the student athletes) to forfeit either the discipline, social interaction and fellowship flowing from a summer basketball camp, or the self-esteem and confidence that follow young people who compete for their varsity school teams."

In weighing the two sides, the court first found the actions of the UIL to constitute state action to the extent necessary to prosecute this case on a constitutional theory. The court went on to discuss various constitutional theories of right to choice in family matters. It decided that

> the decision to send a child to summer basketball camp is important enough to warrant constitutional protection under the family's fundamental right of personal privacy. . . .
>
> Having found a fundamental constitutional right, the remaining inquiries are whether or not the UIL rule in question infringes the right and if so, whether the rule is motivated by compelling state interests and has been narrowly drawn to express only those interests.

In deciding the degree of infringement, the court stated:

> The summer camp rule is, however, directly and purposefully aimed at discouraging a specific parental decision made during the summer months when the school is not acting *in loco parentis*. The interference posed by the UIL rule . . . is neither indirect nor incidental.

In response to defendant's argument that the right to participate in interscholastic athletics is not a fundamental constitutional right and that it therefore falls outside the protection of due process, the court noted:

> This case does not involve a violation of a right to play a sport. Ineligibility for interscholastic athletics is part of the penalty imposed on parents for

deciding to send their child to summer basketball camp. These penalties interfere with the right of a family to make educational and developmental decisions for their minor children and not with any right to participate in athletics.

The court noted that the ostensible objective of the UIL rule is to regulate the educational process. This process includes interscholastic athletics, which must be administered in a fair and efficient manner. It dismissed the proffered rationale that the rule prevents the exertion of peer pressure to attend a camp. It also negated or minimized concerns about the equality of educational opportunity that could be provided by families who were more well off than others. It held that the only legitimate interest that might support this rule was the need to control overzealous coaches.

The court then went on to decide that the UIL failed to meet its burden to show that the rule was narrowly drawn and specifically tailored. The court reasoned: "As it presently reads, the summer camp rule constitutes an overbroad and unreasonable infringement on the right of a family to make decisions concerning the education of its children."

Kite v. Marshall, 661 F. 2d 1027 (5th Cir. 1981)

Defendant UIL appealed a lower court ruling striking down its "summer camp rule." The court of appeals held that the "summer camp rule" does not violate either the due process or the equal protection clauses of the Constitution. It reversed the opinion of the district court.

The appellate court noted the plaintiffs' use of the Supreme Court decisions that purported to "recognize the existence of a private realm of family life which the state cannot enter absent compelling reasons." It noted that many recent Supreme Court decisions have restricted and limited this parental right.

In direct opposition to the district court, the court of appeals found that, "this case implicates no fundamental constitutional right." Upon making this finding, the court subjected the rule to the rational basic analysis:

> It cannot be argued seriously that section 21 is wholly arbitrary and totally without value in the promotion of a legitimate state objective.
>
> Admittedly, section 21 operates to treat student-athletes who attend summer athletic camps differently from those students who do not. But the categorization is not premised on impermissible, suspect grounds. Nor does the classification impinge upon the exercise of fundamental rights. The rule seeks to achieve a balance in interscholastic athletics. It is not unconstitutional.

Texas High School Gymnastics Coaches Ass'n. v. Andrews, 532 S.W. 2d 142 (Tex. Civ. App. 1975)

This suit was brought by plaintiff parents and coaches of gymnasts seeking to overturn a Texas High School Gymnastics Coaches Association rule concerning dual membership. The association rule read as follows:

> A Texas high school gymnast must not work out with, practice with, take lessons with, or compete with a private club, and be eligible for dual, regional or state competition during the school calendar year of their school district.

Plaintiffs' complaint alleged that the rule was an "unfair, unlawful and unconstitutional restriction upon the individual rights of high school students who ... desire to compete in high school gymnastic competition." The plaintiffs went on to charge that the rule was an unfair trade practice and an unreasonable restraint of trade and free enterprise which "not only damages the individual high school students involved, but also damages the private gymnastic clubs." It was also alleged that the rule violated the association's constitution by (1) not perpetuating and improving the sport of gymnastics; (2) discouraging the interest of people in healthful sports through gymnastics; (3) violating the principles, interests and desires of the University of Texas Interscholastic League; and (4) failing to protect the interests of the state of Texas and the athletes.

The plaintiffs requested a judgment that the rule be made void and unenforceable, an injunction preventing the association from enforcing the rule, and damages. The trial court overruled a previously sustained plea of privilege by the association and granted an injunction temporarily enjoining the association from attempting to enforce the rule. The association appealed.

The Court of Civil Appeals of Texas found that the Texas Interscholastic League, while regulating high school athletics, does not regulate gymnastics competition. The association was formed by gymnastics coaches to stimulate interest in the sport of gymnastics and to encourage competitive gymnastics. As part of the association's program, it sponsors various types of gymnastic meets which culminated in the Texas High School Championship Meet. According to its constitution, the association has the power to establish and direct the general policies as they pertain to the conduct of dual, regional, and state gymnastic high school competition until such time as the sport becomes part of the Interscholastic League.

The court noted that while the involvement of the coaches in the association might be sufficient to justify classifying its conduct as state action, there was not sufficient evidence presented by the lower court to support the conclusion that the rule is unreasonable, capricious, or arbitrary. In relying on *Parish* v. *National Collegiate Athletic Ass'n.*, the court held that the rule must be upheld unless it could be shown that the rule bears no rational relationship to the achievement of a legitimate purpose.

In an attempt to determine the reasonableness of the rule governing the eligibility of a student to participate in a specific athletic activity, the court relied on *Brown* v. *Wells* (see Note 4), in which the Supreme Court of Minnesota stated that the question was whether a rule is "so willful and unreasoning, without consideration of the facts and circumstances, and in such disregard of them as to be arbitrary and capricious. Where there is room for two opinions on the matter, such action is 'arbitrary and capricious' even though it may be believed that an erroneous conclusion has been reached.

The court also cited *Art Gaines Baseball Camp, Inc.* v. *Houston* (see Note 2). In *Gaines*, the rule challenged held that any student who attended a camp specializing in one sport for more than two weeks during the summer would lose eligibility to represent the school in that particular sport during the following school year. The Missouri court rejected the challenge to the rule by the operator of a private baseball camp and applied the same reasoning found in *Brown* v. *Wells*. The Texas court found the gymnasts' situation to be very similar to the *Gaines* case in that the purpose of the rule was to help prevent inequality and unfair advantage between students of different economic means and schools located in different areas of economic wealth. Hence, the court could not find any basis at all for finding the rule to be invalid. In addition, there was no evidence supporting the conclusion that there was no rational relationship between the rule and the achievement of these purposes that it considers to be legitimate.

In conclusion, the court found that the injunction against the association was wrongfully granted. The judgment of the trial court was reversed, and the temporary injunction was dissolved.

NOTES

1. At the 1983 NCAA convention, the membership enacted legislation that prohibits a member of a basketball coaching staff from being employed by a basketball camp that has been established, sponsored, or conducted by an individual or organization that provides recruiting or scouting services (*1985–86 NCAA Manual*, Bylaw 1–10–[b]).

2. In *Art Gaines Baseball Camp, Inc.* v. *Houston*, 500 S.W. 2d 735 (Mo. Ct. App. 1973), plaintiff camp sought to restrain Missouri High School Activities Association from enforcing a rule stating that a student who attends a camp specializing in one sport for more than two weeks

during a summer would lose eligibility to represent his or her school in that particular sport the following school year. In affirming judgment for defendants, the court of appeals held that the rule did not infringe on public policy or law and was not unreasonable or arbitrary.

3. In *Dumez* v. *Louisiana High School Athletic Ass'n.*, 334 So. 2d 494 (La. Ct. App. 1976), plaintiffs, parents of high school students declared ineligible to participate in interscholastic baseball athletics by defendant association, sought a permanent injunction to prohibit enforcement of the ruling. In reversing judgment for the plaintiffs, the court of appeals held that determination by the association to declare the students ineligible because they violated the "independent team rule" by participating in practice sessions held by the Babe Ruth Baseball League, was not subject to judicial rescission or modification on the grounds that it constituted a serious "inequity" to the students when similar action was not taken against coaches or schools.

4. In *Brown* v. *Wells*, 284 Minn. 468, 181 N.W. 2d 708 (1970), plaintiff hockey player challenged rules excluding his participation on the high school hockey team if he participated in nonschool hockey, including hockey schools or camps. The court held that when rules are adopted for the purpose of deemphasizing extra-curricular athletics that may detract from student interest in education, the court cannot deem such rules arbitrary or unreasonable. The court found that the school board had the discretion to deal with the issue as it thought best. The courts should not attempt to control the discretion of the school board.

5. The NCAA provides that coaches may not supervise or conduct recognized regional, national, or international training programs or competition, including prospects, unless the coaches' participation meets with the approval of the NCAA Council. If approval is not obtained, it may be considered a tryout by the prospective student-athlete (see *1985-86 NCAA Manual*, Bylaw 1–6–[c]–[5]).

SEX DISCRIMINATION
IN ATHLETICS

3.00   Introduction

As women's athletics enters into a mid-life growth pattern following the initial explosion in women's intercollegiate programs in the 1970s and early 1980s, it faces great uncertainties. The absorption of the defunct Association of Intercollegiate Athletics for Women (AIAW) by the NCAA, the effects of the Supreme Court's *Grove City College* decision on enforcement of Title IX in athletics, the loss of football television revenues by the NCAA and its potential effect on the funding of nonrevenue-producing sports championships, and the failure of the Equal Rights Amendment to be ratified as a federal constitutional amendment all pose serious doubts to those individuals concerned with continued development of women's athletic programs. Barely having had time to reflect on how far and how fast they have come with their programs, women's athletic program administrators face new and increasingly difficult problems to solve.

Many indicators, including increases in participation, spectators, and local and national media coverage, point to the growth in women's athletics. The development of athletic opportunity for women may be attributed, to large extent, to Title IX. Title IX of the Education Amendments of 1972 is a federal statute which prohibits sex discrimination (see Section 3.12).

Before Title IX, women comprised only 5 percent of the total number of athletic participants in high school and 15 percent in college. By 1984, 30.8 percent of all participants in NCAA intercollegiate athletics were women.

As compiled by the NCAA, the average number of women's varsity sports in the association has risen from 5.61 in 1977 to 6.9 in 1984, while the aggregate expenditures for women's intercollegiate athletics have increased from $24.7 million in 1977 to $116 million in 1981 (see Note 1). The AIAW studied the relative amounts of financial aid given to male and female athletes from 1973 to 1982. The AIAW estimated that for 1973–74, NCAA Division I schools spent an average of $1.2 million on men's athletic programs but only $27,000 on women's programs. By the 1981–82 academic year, the institutions expended an average of $1.7 million on men and $400,000 on women. This result was contrary to the predictions made by many opponents of Title IX who thought the increased money spent on women's programs would decrease the amount of money available for men's programs.

This is again demonstrated in that the average NCAA Division I school spent $1.65 million on men's athletics in 1978 — an increase from the $1.2 million spent in 1973. Expenditures during that time for women's athletics increased from a low of $27,000 in 1973 to $276,000 in 1978. Between 1973 and 1978, the amount of money spent on scholarships for men increased 35 percent. At the same time, NCAA Division I operations budgets increased by 40 percent, and salaries for coaches went up 56 percent (see Note 1[b]). Thus, while funding for women's athletics increased dramatically, funding for men's athletics increased as well (see Note 1[c]).

The growth of women's sports has been impressive, as evidenced, for example, by the dramatic increase in women's overall participation. Since 1972, the number of women participating in athletics has more than doubled. By 1980, women comprised slightly less than one-third of all athletic participants (see Note 3). Athletic budgets for women's athletics have also increased. The average women's athletic budget for a Big Ten school in 1974 was $3,500. In 1977–78, it had increased to anywhere from $250,000 to $750,000. In 1974, 60 U.S. colleges offered athletic scholarships for women. In 1981, 500 colleges were offering scholarships to women in such diverse sports as track, tennis, basketball, and volleyball (see Note 4). One example of this extensive growth is the University of Oklahoma women's athletic program budget for 1980, which was $700,000 — a 600 percent increase from 1974. Women's athletics have also developed quickly on the conference level. In the 1983–84 academic year, 28 Division I conferences, 15 Division II, and 17 Division III conferences sponsored women's competition.

Since the adoption in 1981 of the NCAA Governance Plan for women's athletics, the association has opened its committees and services to reflect the change in its structure. In 1984, 187 women occupied 230 different positions on NCAA committees. In 1981–82,

during its first year of operating women's championships, the NCAA sponsored 29 championships in 13 sports. By 1984–85, the NCAA offered 33 women's championships in 15 sports. In 1982–83, the NCAA's subsidy of 30 women's championships was $2.2 million and exceeded its support of 29 men's championships that were nonrevenue-producing by 8.4 percent. In 1983–84, women's athletics received 49 percent of the total $709,200 NCAA promotional budget.

Participation in and funding of women's athletics have increased for many reasons. A major factor is the drastic change in society's attitudes toward women, including a perception by women themselves about their own athletic capabilities and participation. These attitudinal changes have helped increase athletic opportunities for women.

The NCAA has repeatedly stated that it is committed to equal athletic opportunity without regard to sex. Despite its late entry into providing athletic opportunities for women, the NCAA has made significant strides in doing so since 1981. Within the ranks of the NCAA, however, there are disagreements concerning the direction the association should take following the dissolution of the AIAW and the NCAA's assumption of control over women's intercollegiate athletics.

For instance, at a May 1984 meeting of administrators of NCAA women's athletic programs, the representatives present requested that a show of support be indicated in the minutes of the meeting for H.R. 5490, a civil rights legislative proposal in the United States Congress (see Note 1). House bill 5490 and Senate bill 2568 were proposed as a response to the Supreme Court's *Grove City College v. Bell* (see Section 3.22) decision, which ruled that Title IX only applies to the individual programs receiving federal funding at an institution of higher education and not to the entire institution. The proposed bills would ensure that athletic programs would still fall within the parameters of Title IX. Despite the concerns of its women's athletic program administrators, the NCAA filed a statement with the chair of the U.S. House of Representatives Subcommittee on Postsecondary Education supporting the objectives of H.R. 5490 but objecting to the bill's construction. In general, the NCAA believed that the impact of the *Grove City College* decision on women's athletics was overstated, that the bill's authority would be overinclusive, and that the demands of inspection and enforcement would be too burdensome and costly (see Note 4).

Beyond Title IX concerns, athletic administrators are increasingly worried about the funding of women's intercollegiate programs. Some worry that the NCAA made commitments to attract women's athletic programs into the association in the early 1980s that it will find hard to continue. This is especially true in light of the reduced funding that the NCAA will receive from college football television contracts due to the U.S. Supreme Court's decision in *National Collegiate Athletic Ass'n. v. Board of Regents of U. of Oklahoma and U. of Georgia Athletic Ass'n* (see Section 6.32).

At the May 1984 meeting of administrators of NCAA women's athletic programs, John Toner, chair of the session, stated:

> It seems to many who are responsible for generating the dollars to pay intercollegiate athletics costs that there must be some correlation between added program costs and increased revenues to support those costs. It seems to me that it is time for women leaders to concentrate on how they can stimulate and enlarge the income from women's programs.

Title IX and other legislation, initially, were vanguards of changed societal attitudes as well as legal factors that helped bring about substantial change in sex discrimination in the United States. An increased reliance on the legal system to redress sex discrimination developed because of the availability of legal options. Women brought complaints about unequal treatment to court and, even more importantly, were often successful in their litigation. Recently, however, a trend of setbacks has besieged the women's movement. The failure to enact the Equal Rights Amendment and limitations imposed on Title IX enforcement by the U.S. Supreme Court have caused concern among promoters of women's athletics. A direct result of the *Grove City College* decision on intercollegiate athletics was the immediate dropping of 23 Title IX investigations (see Note 5). The retrenchment of programs that were so instrumental in the progress achieved in women's athletics, the absence of an organization such as the AIAW to champion the movement's specific issues, and potential funding problems are at the forefront of concerns facing women's athletics in the late 1980s.

Chapter 3 attempts to distinguish among the various legal theories and principles utilized in sex discrimination cases. The legal principles are discussed in Section 3.10, including equal protection (Section 3.11), Title IX (Section 3.12), and state equal rights amendments (Section 3.13). Section 3.20 takes an in-depth look at the major issues involving Title IX. Section 3.30 covers cases involving individual athletics, organized with the two critical areas in the court's analysis of a sex discrimination case in mind: opportunities for participation and contact/noncontact sports. Sections 3.31, 3.32, and 3.33 include cases that have relied on any or all of the legal theories of equal protection, Title IX, and state equal rights amendments. This grouping makes it easier to identify factors that are important in the court's determination of any violation. Section 3.40 deals with cases involving coaches (Section 3.42), officiating (Section 3.43–1), participation in professional sports (Section 3.43–2), and the media (Section 3.43–3).

NOTES

1. For further information on the increased expenditures for women's intercollegiate athletics, increases in NCAA Division I budgets, and increases in funding of men's athletic budgets, see the following articles:

(a) "Women's Programs List Legislative Priorities," *NCAA News*, June 6, 1984, pp. 1, 12.

(b) "NCAA Members Increase Athletic Budgets by 75 Pct. in 4 Years, Study Finds," *Chronicle of Higher Education*, September 22, 1982, p. 9.

(c) "Title IX at X," *Chronicle of Higher Education*, June 23, 1982, p. 1.

2. Since the emergence of the NCAA as the dominant organization in both men's and women's collegiate sports, there has been a tendency toward combining championships (for example, indoor track and skiing). See "Intercollegiate Skiing Halts Its Downhill Slide — NCAA Combines Men's and Women's Championships to Make Sure Enough Will Be Competing," *Chronicle of Higher Education*, March 9, 1983, p. 18.

3. At NCAA member institutions, the number of female participants in intercollegiate athletics increased from 32,000 in 1971–72 to 64,000 in 1976–77, and rose to 80,000 by 1982–83 — a 150 percent increase in 12 years. During that period 1971–82, the number of NCAA member institutions that sponsored women's intercollegiate sports increased as follows:

	1971 (663 schools)	1982 (753 schools)
Basketball	307	705
Cross country	10	417
Softball	147	416
Swimming	140	348
Tennis	243	610
Track and field	78	427
Volleyball	208	603

4. Some of the information on the growth of women's athletics was compiled by the National Advisory Council on Women's Educational Programs. See "NCAA Files Statement Regarding Civil Rights Legislation," *NCAA News*, June 6, 1984, pp. 1, 3.

5. For further information on the dropping of Title IX investigations, see "23 Cases on Civil Rights Closed after Court Rules," *New York Times*, June 3, 1984, p. 36.

6. Legislation to overturn the Supreme Court's *Grove City College* decision failed to pass through Congress in 1984. The House of Representatives had passed the legislation (H.R. 5490) by a vote of 375–32 in June 1984. However, the Senate version of the legislation (S. 2568) failed to gain passage. Similar legislation was introduced in 1985. See "Bill to Overturn Grove City Rule Killed in Senate," *Chronicle of Higher Education*, October 10, 1984, p. 1.

7. In response to the Supreme Court's *Grove City College* decision, the Women's Sports Foundation instituted a letter-writing campaign to have its membership influence passage of Senate bill 2568. The foundation stressed the importance of Title IX in the development of women's intercollegiate athletics and its continued need for future progress. See "Title IX Needs You," *Women's Sports*, September 1984, p. 49.

8. At the 1985 NCAA Convention Division IA institutions (105 major football-playing institutions) voted to require themselves to each sponsor at least eight women's and eight men's sports programs by the 1986–87 academic year. The vote on the requirement was 74 to 37. Approximately 30 Division IA member institutions did not meet the qualifications at the time of the vote and faced being dropped from the division and being ineligible for championships in 1986. See: "Major Football-Playing Universities Must Field Teams in at Least 8 Women's Sports by 1986, New Rule Says," *Chronicle of Higher Education*, January 30, 1985, p. 29.

9. For further information on sex discrimination in athletics, see the following law review articles:

(a) "Sex Discrimination in High School Athletics: An Examination of Applicable Legal Doctrines," 66 *Minnesota Law Review* 1115 (1982).

(b) "Title IX: Women's Intercollegiate in Limbo," 40 *Washington and Lee Law Review* (1983).

(c) "Case for Equality in Athletics," 22 *Cleveland State Law Review* 570 (Fall 1973).

(d) "Legal Problems of Sex Discrimination," 15 *Alberta Law Review* 122 (1977).

(e) "Sex Discrimination and Intercollegiate Athletics," 61 *Iowa Law Review* 420 (December 1975).

(f) "Sex Discrimination and Intercollegiate Athletics: Putting Some Muscle on Title IX," 88 *Yale Law Journal* 1254 (May 1979).

(g) "Emergent Law of Women and Amateur Sports: Recent Developments," 28 *Wayne Law Review* 1701 (1982).

(h) "Equality in Athletics: The Cheerleader v. The Athlete," 19 *San Diego Law Review* 428 (1974).

(i) "Sex Discrimination in High School Athletics," 47 *University of Missouri at Kansas City Law Review* 109 (Fall 1978).

(j) "Sex Discrimination in Interscholastic High School Athletics," 25 *Syracuse Law Review* 535 (Spring 1974).

(k) "Sex Discrimination in Park District Athletic Programs," 64 *Women's Law Journal* 33 (Winter 1978).

3.10 Legal Principles

Sex discrimination in athletics has been challenged using a variety of legal arguments, including equal protection laws, Title IX of the Education Amendment of 1972, state equal rights amendments, and the Equal Pay Act. Most challenges have been based on either the equal protection laws or Title IX.

Equal protection arguments are based on the Fifth Amendment of the U.S. Constitution, which guarantees equal protection of the law to all persons found within the United States. (See Section 1.33 and Section 3.11 for a further discussion of equal protection.)

Title IX is a relatively recent method of attacking sex discrimination. Although the original legislation was passed in 1972, implementation was delayed for the promulgation of regulations and policy interpretations. Even with the delay, many have claimed the rise in participation by women in athletics was directly related to the passage of Title IX. (See Section 3.12 for a further discussion of Title IX.)

A state equal rights amendment can also be used to attack alleged sex discrimination; however, not all states have passed such legislation. (See Section 3.13 for a further discussion of state equal rights amendments.)

The fourth argument concerns two separate statutes: the Equal Pay Act and Title VII of the Civil Rights Act of 1964. Although neither statute was passed to deal specifically with sex discrimination, both have been used to challenge employment-related discrimination. (See Section 3.41 for a further discussion of these two statutes.)

In a sex discrimination case, the plaintiff usually contends that there is a fundamental inequality, regardless of whether a plaintiff employs an equal protection or Title IX approach. When the court attempts to deal with these claims, it considers three factors. The first is whether or not the sport from which women are excluded is one involving physical contact. Total exclusion from all sports or from any noncontact sport is considered a violation of equal educational opportunity. The second factor the courts consider is the quality and quantity of opportunity available to each sex. The courts compare the number of athletic opportunities available to each sex as well as the amount of money spent on equipment, the type of coaches provided, and the access to school-owned facilities. The third factor the courts consider is age and level

of competition involved in the dispute. The younger the athletes involved, the fewer the actual physiological differences that exist. Without demonstrable physiological differences, the justification of inherent biological differences as a rational basis for the exclusion of one sex from athletic participation is negated.

NOTE

1. In *Pavey* v. *University of Alaska* v. *National Collegiate Athletic Ass'n.*, 490 F. Supp. 1011 (D. Alaska 1980), an action was brought against the University of Alaska, charging the university with discrimination against female student-athletes in the operation of its athletic program in violation of Title IX and the Fourteenth Amendment's due process and equal protection clauses. The university filed a third-party suit against the NCAA and the AIAW, which charged that the two associations' inconsistent rules required the university to discriminate in its athletic program in violation of federal laws. The NCAA and AIAW made motions for dismissal of the suit. In denying the motions, the district court held that the university's suit stated a valid claim, that the university was reasonably trying to avoid a confrontation with the two associations' rules that could cause a disruption in the participation of student-athletes in intercollegiate athletics, and that the facial neutrality of the association's rules did not negate the university's claim that those rules, in combined effect, forced the institution to discriminate in its athletic program.

3.11 Equal Protection

The basic analysis utilized for equal protection questions was discussed in Section 1.33. This section examines more closely the effects of using gender to classify persons for different athletic opportunities.

Historically, sex has been an acceptable category for classifying persons for different benefits and burdens under any given law. In 1872, the Supreme Court, in *Bradwell* v. *State*, 83 U.S. [16 Wall] 130 (1873), opened with the statement that a woman's place was in the home. The Court went on to say that this was part of a "divinely ordained law of nature." In 1908, the Court stated in *Muller* v. *Oregon*, 208 U.S. 412, 28 S. Ct. 324, 52 L.Ed. 551

(1908), that a classification based on gender was a valid constitutional classification. Such a classification was not considered to be a violation of equal protection, regardless of whether it was based on actual or imagined physical differences between men and women. Modern equal protection theories have now gained preeminence, and the use of gender to classify persons is considered less acceptable.

Under traditional equal protection analysis, the legislative gender-based classification must be sustained unless it is found to be patently arbitrary and/or if it bears absolutely no rational relationship to a legitimate governmental interest. Under this traditional rational basis analysis, overturning discriminatory laws is extremely difficult. The implication for sex discrimination sports litigation is such that women may be excluded from athletic participation upon a showing of a rational reason for their exclusion and by providing comparable options for those who are excluded. The rational reason must be factually supported and may *not* be based on mere presumptions about the relative physical and athletic capabilities of women and men. It remains, however, a relatively easy standard for the defendant to meet, as it invokes only the lowest standard of scrutiny by the court.

The courts have not found sex to be a suspect class, which would elevate it to the status held by race, national origin, and alienage. If the court were to decide sex is a suspect class, it would make all rules that classify on the basis of gender subject to strict scrutiny analysis. If this were the standard, the rule makers would have to prove that there are compelling reasons for the classification and that there is no less restrictive alternative. They would also have to prove that the classification was directly related to the constitutional purpose of the legislation and that this purpose could not have been achieved by any less objectionable means. Many rules and laws would fail to meet this high standard, and hence would be judged to be discriminatory.

Some courts have moved away from the broad interpretation of the rational relationship test by increasing the burden on the defendant. This intermediate test, between the rational basis and strict scrutiny test, was first established by the Supreme Court in *Reed* v. *Reed*, 404 U.S. 71, 30 L.Ed. 2d 225, 92 S. Ct. 251 (1971). The Supreme Court established therein that sex-based classifications must be "reasonable, not arbitrary, and must rest upon some ground of difference having a fair and substantial relation to the object of the legislation, so that all persons similarly circumstanced shall be treated alike." The Supreme Court again addressed this issue in *Frontiero* v. *Richardson*, 411 U.S. 677, 36 L.Ed. 2d 583, 93 S. Ct. 1764 (1973); in a plurality opinion, Justice Brennan reasoned that sex-based classifications "serve important governmental objectives and must be substantially related to the achievement of those objectives."

A factual basis for any gender classification must exist. Mere preferences or assumptions concerning the ability of one sex to perform adequately are not acceptable bases for a discriminatory classification. This intermediate test is still one step away from a declaration by the courts that sex is an inherently suspect class.

Because a majority opinion to apply a strict scrutiny analysis in gender-based cases does not yet exist, courts may opt to apply either a rational basis test or the intermediate standard of review. The intermediate standard requires more than an easily achieved rational relationship but less than a strict scrutiny standard would demand. The class must bear a substantial relationship to an important but not compelling governmental interest. Also, the relationship between a classification and a law's purpose must now be founded on fact, not on general legislative views of the relative strengths and/or abilities of the two sexes.

Three key factors commonly are considered in an equal protection analysis of athletic discrimination cases. The first factor is state action. Before any claim can be successfully litigated, a sufficient amount of state action must be present. Without state action, an equal protection argument under the U.S. Constitution is not applicable. This factor has significant ramifications in cases in which the athletic activity is conducted outside the auspices of a state or municipal entity or a public educational institution. Examples include youth sport leagues such as Little League Baseball, Pop Warner Football, and the YMCA's Youth Basketball Association.

The second factor is whether the sport involves physical contact. In contact sports the courts have allowed separate men's and women's teams. This "separate but equal" doctrine is based on considerations of the physical health and safety of the participants. When separate teams do not exist, however, both sexes may have an opportunity to try out and to meet the necessary physical requirements on an individual basis. A complete ban on the participation of one sex will not be upheld if it is based on generalizations about characteristics of an entire sex rather than on a reasonable consideration of individual characteristics. (See *Clinton* v. *Nagy*, in Section 3.31–1.)

The third factor to be considered is whether both sexes have equal opportunities to participate. This "equal opportunity" usually requires the existence of completely separate teams or an opportunity to try out for the one available team. If there are separate teams, however, it is permissible for the governing organization to prohibit co-ed participation. Unlike classifications based on race, when gender is a determining factor, "separate but equal" doctrines may be acceptable. The issue then may become whether the teams are indeed equal. (See *O'Connor* v. *Board of Education of School District No. 23* in Section 3.33–1[a] and *Ritacco* v. *Norwin School Dist.* in Section 3.33.1[b].) Other factors that have been taken into consideration are the age of the participant and the level of the competition. Physical differences between boys and girls below the age of 12 are minimal. Therefore, health and safety considerations that might be applicable to older athletes have not constituted legitimate reasons for restricting young athletes' access to participation. (See *Bednar* v. *Nebraska School Activities Ass'n.* in Section 3.31–2, Note 7.)

The legal analysis of any particular case, however, will depend on the philosophy of the court and the particular factual circumstances presented. (See *Brenden* v. *Independent School District 742* in Section 3.31–2.) Some courts are reluctant to intervene in discretionary decisions made by an association governing athletic events unless there are obvious abuses. (See Section 1.21–1 for a discussion of judicial review.) Other courts have been reluctant to intervene in discretionary decisions because they do not believe they are equipped with the administrative knowledge or time necessary to oversee the administration of sport programs effectively.

Historically, challenging sex discrimination based on the equal protection laws has not been totally effective. The constitutional standard of rational relationship has been a very difficult one for a plaintiff to challenge alleged sex discrimination successfully. The use of the intermediate standard, a more stringent test, is partly attributable to some of the recent successful challenges of alleged sex discrimination. However, the plurality decision of the Supreme Court in *Frontiero* v. *Richardson* lessens the impact of the intermediate standard. A strong decision by the court with respect to the intermediate standard or a finding that sex should be included as a suspect category would greatly assist plaintiffs in attacking alleged sex discrimination.

Another disadvantage of the equal protection laws is that they constitute a private remedy. Therefore, the plaintiff must be in a position to absorb the costs of litigation. This reduces the number of complaints filed and encourages settlement before final resolution of a number of equal protection claims.

NOTES _____

1. In *Ridgefield Women's Political Caucus, Inc.* v. *Fossi,*

458 F. Supp. 117 (D. Conn. 1978), plaintiff girls and tax-payer parents brought claims against town selectmen seeking to enjoin the town from offering public property at a nominal price to a private organization that restricted membership to boys. The district court found for the plaintiffs, ruling that the defendants had no right to offer land at less than fair value to the private organization in question as long as this organization restricted membership and the town failed to offer to girls comparable recreational opportunities equivalent to those provided by the organization in question. Until such services are offered, any conveyance of the property at a nominal fee would constitute governmental support of sex discrimination in violation of the equal protection clause of the Fourteenth Amendment.

2. For further information on athletic participation and equal protection, see: "Sex Discrimination in Secondary School Athletics," 46 *Tennessee Law Review* 222 (Fall, 1978).

3. In *Richards v. United States Tennis Association*, 400 N.Y.S. 2d 267 (Sup. Ct. N.Y. County 1977), an action was brought by a professional tennis player who had undergone a sex-change operation against a professional tennis association which sought a preliminary injunction against the organization to prevent it from requiring the plaintiff to undergo a sex-chromatin test to prove she was a female and eligible to participate in a women's tournament. The court granted the injunction and held the test was grossly unfair, discriminatory and inequitable, and violated the plaintiff's rights under the New York Human Rights Law.

3.12   Title IX

Section 901 (a) of Title IX of the Education Amendments of 1972 provides:

> No person in the United States shall, on the basis of sex, be excluded from participation in, be denied the benefits of, or be subjected to discrimination under any education program or activity receiving Federal financial assistance.

Title IX became law on July 1, 1972, as Public Law 92–318. It specifically and clearly recognizes the problems of sex discrimination and forbids such discrimination in any program, organization, or agency that receives federal funds. A long process of citizen involvement preceded the first set of regulations. In July 1975, the Department of Health, Education & Welfare (HEW) issued the regulations designed to implement Title IX.

These regulations are found in Title 45, Code of Federal Regulations (CFR), section 86 A–F. The regulations were criticized by many as being vague and inadequate. In December 1978, HEW attempted to alleviate the criticism by releasing a proposed policy interpretation, which attempted to explain but did not change the 1975 requirements. However, not until December 1979, seven years after the original passage of Title IX, did the Office of Civil Rights (OCR) (successor to HEW) release the policy interpretation for Title IX. These final guidelines specifically included intercollegiate athletics. Developed after numerous meetings and countless revisions, they reflected comments from universities, legislative sources, and the public.

The policy interpretation contained some very strict guidelines for OCR to apply in assessing Title IX compliance, including the following:

1. The exemption of football and other revenue-providing sports.
2. "Sport-specific" comparisons as the basis for assessing compliance.
3. "Team-based" comparisons (grouping sports by levels of development) as the basis for compliance assessments.
4. Institutional planning that does not meet the provisions of the policy interpretation as applied by OCR.

The policy interpretation also outlined certain "nondiscriminatory factors" to be considered when assessing Title IX compliance. These factors include differences that may result from the unique nature of particular sports, special circumstances of a temporary nature, the need for greater funding for crowd control at more popular athletic events, and differences that have not yet been remedied but which an institution is voluntarily working to correct. In the area of compensation for men's and women's coaches, OCR assessed rates of compensation, length of contracts, experience, and other factors, while taking into account mitigating conditions such as nature of duties, number of assistants to be supervised, number of participants, and level of competition.

The major issues raised regarding Title IX revolve around the scope of the legislation and the programs to which it is applicable. The July 1975 policy regulations issued by HEW covered three areas of activity within educational institutions: employment, treatment of students, and admissions. Several sections of the regulations concerned with the treatment of students included specific requirements for intercollegiate, intramural, and club athletic programs.

One important issue is whether Title IX applies to an entire institution or only to the programs within that institution which receive direct federal assistance. The Supreme Court ruled in *Grove City College* v. *Bell* (see Section 3.22) that only those programs within an institution that receive direct financial assistance from the federal government should be subject to Title IX strictures. This interpretation is often referred to as the "programmatic approach" to the Title IX statute. (See *Othen* v. *Ann Arbor School Board* in Section 3.22.) Others have reached the opposite conclusion, that the receipt of any federal aid to an institution, whether it be limited to only certain programs or indirect (for example, student loan) programs, should place the entire institution under the jurisdiction of Title IX (see *Haffer* v. *Temple University* in Section 3.22). This interpretation is called the "institutional approach" to Title IX.

While Title IX does not require the creation of athletic programs or the same sport offerings to both sexes — for example, a football program for women or a volleyball program for men — it does require equality of opportunity in accommodation of interests and abilities, in athletic scholarships, and in other benefits and opportunities (see *Othen* v. *Ann Arbor School Board* in Section 3.22).

Athletics and athletics programs were not specifically mentioned in Title IX when it first became law in 1972. Congress was generally opposed to placing athletics programs under the realm of Title IX. However, HEW, taking the position that sports and physical education are an integral part of education, specifically included athletics, despite strong lobbying efforts to exempt revenue-producing intercollegiate sports from the Title IX requirements. This specific inclusion of athletics occurred in 1974 and extended from general athletic opportunities to athletic scholarships. The principles governing athletic scholarships included the idea that all recipients of federal aid must provide "*reasonable opportunities*" for both sexes to receive scholarship aid. The existence of "*reasonable opportunities*" is determined by examining the ratio of male to female participants. Scholarship aid must then be distributed according to this participation ratio. (See Title 45, Code of Federal Regulations [CFR], Section 86.13[c].)

Another section of the Title IX regulations specifies requirements for athletic programs (see 45 CFR, Section 86.41[c]). Contact sports are subject to regulations distinct from those governing noncontact sports. The regulations in this section state that separate teams are acceptable for contact sports and for teams in which selection is based on competitive skill. For noncontact sports, if only one team exists, both sexes must be allowed to compete for positions on the team. The Office of Civil Rights, which monitors compliance of Title IX, considers many factors in determining the equality of opportunity, including the following:

1. Selection of sports and the level of competition offered.
2. Facilities available.
3. Equipment and supplies available.
4. Games and practice schedule.
5. Methods of travel and per diem allowances.
6. Coaching (including amount of compensation).
7. Housing.
8. Dining facilities.
9. Publicity.

Equal expenditures are not required (see 45

CFR, Section 86.41[c]), but comparative budgets are often considered in relation to those factors just listed.

The procedures for Title IX analysis are established in special administrative guidelines, which list specific factors that should be examined in determining whether or not equality in athletics exists. The number of sports, the type of arrangements, and benefits offered to women competing in athletics are reviewed. When teams of one sex are favored in such areas as funding, coaching, and facilities, resulting in severely reduced opportunities for the other sex to compete, the courts will closely examine program expenditures, number of teams, and access to facilities to determine if the school is fulfilling the requirements of Title IX. As a general rule, although Title IX does not require the adoption of programs and equivalent funding, increases in either or both may be necessary to redress past discrimination.

The final area of coverage in the regulations is the method of enforcement of Title IX. Compliance with the dictates of the law is monitored by the Office of Civil Rights (OCR) in the Department of Education (formerly part of the Department of Health, Education and Welfare). The procedure to be followed is initiated by the OCR, which makes random compliance reviews and also investigates complaints submitted by individuals. The first step in the process is to examine the records kept by the institution under investigation to review its attempted compliance with Title IX. Following a preliminary review, the OCR has the option to conduct a full hearing or to drop the case.

If the OCR calls a full hearing, the institution has the right to have counsel present and to appeal any adverse decision; the complainant has neither of these rights. The affected individual is not a party involved in the hearing. Instead, the OCR becomes the complainant and pursues the claim. If the OCR finds that there has not been substantial compliance, it may turn its findings over to federal or local authorities for prosecution under the appropriate statutes.

A number of attempts to change Title IX have been made since 1979. Many of the proposals would lessen the impact of Title IX. One of these proposed changes was introduced on June 11, 1981, by Senator Hatch of Utah. His amendment (S. 1361) would have specifically restricted the scope of Title IX to those programs that receive direct funding from the federal government. The amendment was also designed to specify that money received by students in the form of scholarships, grants, or loans does not constitute federal aid for Title IX purposes. Passage of this amendment would have effectively eliminated claims by women in the areas of athletics and other extracurricular activities, health care, guidance counseling, and residential housing, since these programs do not generally receive direct federal funding. It would have also restricted the application of Title IX with respect to employment discrimination claims, therefore relegating employment discrimination problems to the less inclusive legislation of Title VII of the Civil Rights Act of 1964. Supporters of the amendment found merit in the proposal in that it advocated the lessening of federal involvement in education. Furthermore, some educators argued that the slackening of governmental restraint would not necessarily create a situation in which women's athletic programs would suffer. Instead, they claimed, administrators would become more innovative in terms of women's programs once they were freed of the threat of legal action if these programs did not immediately meet the standards of men's programs. Senator Hatch's proposal was not passed, and he subsequently withdrew the legislation.

Another proposed amendment, commonly referred to as the Family Protection Act, advocated the repeal of Title IX. Its provisions would remove from the jurisdiction of federal courts the right to determine whether the sexes should be allowed to intermingle in athletics or in any other school activity. A third effort to restrict the power of Title IX involved a bill (S. 1091) that was introduced by Senators Hatch and Edward Zorinsky of Nebraska. It proposed that institutions be reimbursed by the OCR for expenses incurred during any investigation the OCR conducts of institutional programs or activities. Opponents of this bill argued that should the OCR be required to reimburse schools without a corresponding increase in its own budget, the total budget actually available for enforcement would diminish. They argued that less money for enforcement would restrict the number of investigations initiated by the OCR, thereby limiting the potential deterrent value of the threat of such an investigation.

NOTES _____

1. For further information concerning the institutional and programmatic approaches to Title IX application, see the following articles:
(a) "The Application of Title IX to School Athletic Programs," 68 *Cornell Law Review* 222 (1983).
(b) "The Program-Specific Reach of Title IX," 83 *Columbia Law Review* 1210 (June 1983).

2. For an examination of the legislative history of Title IX in respect to athletics, see the following articles:
(a) Johnson, "The Evolution of Title IX: Prospects for Equality in Intercollegiate Athletics," 11 *Golden Gate University Law Review* 759 (1981).
(b) "Title IX and Intercollegiate Athletics: Adducing Congressional Intent," 24 *Boston College Law Review* 1243 (September 1983).

3. For further information on Title IX, see the following law review articles:
(a) "Half-Court Girls' Basketball Rules: An Application of the Equal Protection Clause and Title IX," 65 *Iowa Law Review* 766 (1980).
(b) "HEW's Final 'Policy Interpretation' of Title IX and Intercollegiate Athletics," 6 *Journal of College and University Law* 345 (1980).
(c) "Implementing Title IX: The HEW Regulations," 124 *University of Pennsylvania Law Review* 806 (1976).
(d) "Intercollegiate Athletics and Title IX," 46 *George Washington Law Review* 34 (1977).
(e) "The Legality and Requirements of HEW's Proposed 'Policy Interpretation' of Title IX and Intercollegiate Athletics," 6 *Journal of College and University Law* 161 (1980).
(f) "Postsecondary Athletics in an Era of Equality: An Appraisal of the Effect of Title IX," 5 *Journal of College and University Law* 123 (1978–79).

(g) "Sex Discrimination in Athletics," 21 *Villanova Law Review* 876 (October 1976).
(h) "Sex Discrimination in Athletics: Conflicting Legislative and Judicial Approaches," 29 *Alabama Law Review* 390 (Winter 1978).
(i) "Title IX and the NCAA," 3 *Western State University Law Review* 185 (Spring 1976).
(j) "Title IX and Intercollegiate Athletics: Scoring Points for Women," 8 *Ohio Northern University Law Review* 481 (Summer 1981).
(k) "Title IX of the Education Amendments of 1972: Change or Continuity?", 6 *Journal of Law and Education* 183 (April 1977).
(l) "Title IX's Promise of Equality of Opportunity in Athletics: Does It Cover the Bases," 64 *Kentucky Law Journal* 432 (1975–76).

3.13 Equal Rights Amendment

Although there are many legal alternatives to allegations of sex discrimination, there has been no nationwide comprehensive prohibition of sex discrimination to date. Supporters of the Equal Rights Amendment (ERA) argued that passage of a constitutional amendment would remedy the lack of such a general prohibition. In order to amend the United States Constitution, the proposed amendment must first be passed by a three-quarters vote of both the United States Senate and the House of Representatives. Then it must be ratified by at least 38 state legislatures. The ERA was passed in both Houses of Congress in 1972, but it did not receive the necessary 38 votes from the state legislatures by the required ratification date of July 1, 1982.

In some instances, individual states have passed their own equal rights amendments. Thus, equal rights amendments have impacted on athletics at the state level, but not at the federal level. Several cases have been decided in favor of the complainant on the basis of a state ERA. All of these cases, however, could have been decided on other arguments in states without ERAs.

In general, the proposed federal ERA absolutely prohibited discrimination based on gender and required that any law using gender as a basis for classification be subject to a strict scrutiny analysis by the courts. Opponents of the ERA claimed that this prohibition was an unnecessary step. They believed that women's rights are sufficiently protected by the U.S. Constitution, state equal protection laws, and other federal legislation such as the Equal Pay Act, Title VII, and Title IX.

Supporters of the ERA argued that without proper enforcement, neither Title IX nor Title VII can alleviate the basic problems of sex discrimination. The strength of Title IX in particular is dependent on federal funding, since a reduction in funding can effectively diminish the OCR's enforcement capabilities. In addition to this financial vulnerability, sex discrimination statutes are also subject to congressional revisions, which may lessen or even negate much of the available protection. It has been argued that a constitutional amendment would be more sheltered from political interests.

Supporters of a constitutional amendment continue to argue that the effectiveness and importance of an equal rights amendment can be demonstrated in *Darrin* v. *Gould, infra*. In *Darrin*, the lower court considered the equal protection argument and ruled in favor of the defendant. The Washington Supreme Court, however, reversed the decision in favor of the plaintiffs, based on the state's equal rights amendment argument. As such, the court's decision may be effectively downgraded with the subsequent passage of limiting legislation to the state ERA. Regardless of the precarious position in which protection against sex discrimination exists, the existence of an equal rights amendment on the state level is often helpful and may even be crucial to the success of sex discrimination cases.

Darrin v. **Gould, 85 Wash. 2d 859, 540 P. 2d 882 (1975)**

This action was an appeal filed by the parents of high school students Carol and Delores Darrin, of a Washington Superior Court decision denying them relief in their class action claim of illegal discrimination against females in interscholastic football competition.

The two sisters wished to play contact football and were deemed to be eligible and physically capable by the Wishkah Valley High School coach. A Washington Interscholastic Activities Association (WIAA) regulation, however, prohibited girls from participating on boys' interscholastic contact football teams. Therefore, the school district ruled that the Darrin girls could not play.

The Washington Supreme Court examined the case under several standards before reversing the lower court's decision. The court discussed the "strict scrutiny" standard applied under the Fourteenth Amendment of the U.S. Constitution to cases of discrimination based on the suspect classifications of race, alienage, and national origin. Despite the inclinations of some courts to include sex in the list of suspect criteria, the court ruled here that since sex was not a suspect category, the appropriate standard to apply was that of rational relationship, not strict scrutiny.

The court found that the school board's denial of permission for the girls to compete constituted "a discrimination by state action based on sex per se, not a classification based on ability to play." Under the due process clause of the Fourteenth Amendment, "performers are entitled to an individualized determination of their qualifications, not a determination based on the qualifications of a majority of the broader class of which the individual is a member."

The supreme court decided that the Darrin girls could participate, based on the provision of Washington's Equal Rights Amendment, which stated "Equality of rights and responsibility under the law shall not be denied or abridged on account of sex." The court stated:

> . . . the WIAA rule discriminating against girls on account of their sex violates Const. art. 31 [of the Washington Constitution], if not the Equal Protection Clause of the Fourteenth Amendment. . . . The overriding compelling state interest as adopted by the people of this state in 1972 is

that: "Equality of rights and responsibility under the law shall not be denied or abridged on account of sex." (Const., art. 31, section 1)

Commonwealth, Packal v. Pennsylvania Interscholastic Athletic Ass'n., 18 Pa. Commw. Ct. 45, 334 A. 2d 839 (1975)

The state of Pennsylvania, acting through its attorney general, filed suit against the Pennsylvania Interscholastic Athletic Association (PIAA), charging that Article XIX, Section 3B of the PIAA bylaws, which stated that "Girls shall not compete or practice against boys in any athletic contest," is in violation of both the Fourteenth Amendment of the U.S. Constitution and Pennsylvania's equal rights amendment. Plaintiff claimed that the association's rule denied to female athletes the same opportunities to practice and compete in interscholastic sports that were afforded male athletes.

Pennsylvania's ERA provided that "Equality of rights under law shall not be denied or abridged in the Commonwealth of Pennsylvania because of the sex of the individual." The court found the association's rule to be "unconstitutional on its face under the ERA" and proclaimed that "none of the justifications for it offered by the PIAA, even if proved could sustain its legality." The court found it unnecessary to consider whether or not the rule also violated the Fourteenth Amendment.

While the PIAA had argued that athletic participation is not a "legally recognizable right" and should not fall under the jurisdiction of the state ERA, the court rejected this argument, finding that the language of the ERA — specifically, "equality of rights under the law" — was broad enough to include public education, in which "state action" was apparent.

The court found that the rule was unconstitutional and ordered that the PIAA permit girls to practice and compete with boys in interscholastic athletics.

Office of the Attorney General of California: Opinion No. SO 76–57, 60 Ops. Cal. Atty. Gen. 326 (September 27, 1977). (Excerpts)

In 1977, the Attorney General of California issued the following opinion concerning interscholastic athletic competition of boys or girls on opposite or mixed teams:

SYLLABUS:

Competition on Opposite or Mixed Teams: California Interscholastic Federation Bylaw 200 is constitutionally permissible and classifications based on sex are only upheld if they serve an important governmental objective and are related to the achievement of that objective. . . .

Does California Interscholastic Federation (hereinafter CIF), Bylaw 200, which sets forth the conditions under which high school students may compete on opposite sex or mixed teams, violate any provision of state or federal law? . . .

California Interscholastic Federation (CIF) Bylaw 200, adopted in November, 1976 provides as follows:

(a) Student Team: Whenever the school provides only . . . [one varsity] team . . . for boys in a particular sport, girls are permitted to qualify for the student team(s).

(b) Boys' Team: Whenever the school provides a [varsity] team . . . for boys and a [varsity] team . . . for girls in the same sport, girls shall not be permitted to qualify for the boys' team(s) in that sport, nor shall boys be permitted to qualify for the girls' team(s) in that sport.

(c) Girls' Team: Whenever the school provides only . . . [one varsity] team . . . for girls in a particular sport, boys shall not be permitted to qualify for the girls' team in that sport unless opportunities in the total sports program for boys in the school have been limited in comparison to the total sports program for girls in that school. Permission for boys to qualify for the girls' team must be secured through petition by the school principal to the State CIF Federated Council.

(d) Mixed Team (Coed): Whenever the school provides a mixed or coed team in a sport in which the game rules designate either a certain number of team participants from each sex or contains an event that designates a certain number of participants from each sex, boys shall not be permitted to qualify for the girls' positions on the mixed team nor shall girls be permitted to qualify for the boys' positions on the mixed team.

(e) These limitations are binding upon all CIF Sections, although not intended to prohibit any student from qualifying for a team for which he or she has previously competed. . . .

The conclusion is:

Classifications based on sex are subject to judicial scrutiny and will be upheld only if they serve an important governmental objective and are substantially related to the achievement of that objective. The important governmental objective served by this regulation is that of providing equal opportunities for girls in high school athletics. CIF has demonstrated a substantial relationship between that objective and the classifications embodied in Bylaw 200. It is therefore concluded that a court would hold that Bylaw 200 is constitutionally permissible.

We also note, however, that there is contradictory evidence of whether there is a demonstrable, substantial relationship between the governmental objective and the classification which prohibits girls from playing on boys' teams, and that the determination of this issue is a close question. Under such circumstances, we suggest that it might be appropriate for CIF to adopt a permissive rule which would allow each school district to determine whether this particular rule is necessary for its district program. . . .

NOTES

1. Until 1970, there were no CIF-sanctioned interscholastic sports events for high school girls at all. Until the advent of Title IX requirements, the budget for girls' sports programs was considerably lower than that for boys, and teachers who coached girls' athletic teams were paid less than those who coached boys' teams. Furthermore, girls were frequently required to use worn, outmoded equipment that had been discared by the boys.

2. In regard to section (b) of Bylaw 200, a CIF representative and athletic director of a California high school stated that the only girls skilled enough to compete on boys' teams are the potential Olympic and professional champions. She believed that these girls, by sharing their unusual talents with other girls, set the standards of

excellence to which other female athletes should aspire. This official asserted that the mere presence of an outstanding girl athlete on a girls' team improves the quality of the other girls' performances (Letter from Barbara Wilson, Assistant Principal, Beverly Hills High School, to Deputy Attorney General Hadassa K. Gilbert, dated February 1, 1977).

3. A 1976 survey conducted by the CIF Southern Section showed that 84 percent of the women coaches supported Bylaw 200. Opposition to the regulation seemed to come from coaches of boys' teams who wanted the top-quality competitors regardless of their sex. See *Report of CIF State Girls' Advisory Committee*, October 1976.

4. Four states responded to Title IX by opening all teams to both sexes. The result was that boys dominated all the teams, and fewer girls than before could compete. In Indiana, the first- and second-place volleyball teams (previously all female) had one and three boys, respectively. In West Virginia, the first-place girls' bowling team was composed of five boys. Michigan was forced to change its rule so that boys could not compete on a statewide level on girls' teams. The CIF was not aware of any girls playing on boys' teams in states that responded in this manner. This information came from reports sent to member organizations by the National Federation of State High School Athletic Associations. (See *National Federation Publications*, Summer 1975 [in-house publication].)

5. According to information supplied by the National Organization for Women, as of 1984, 16 states had enacted their own individual equal rights amendments.

6. In *MacLean* v. *First Northwest Industries of America, Inc.*, 600 P. 2d 1027 (Wash. Ct. App. 1970), a class action lawsuit was brought against the city of Seattle and the corporation operating a professional basketball team that alleged "Ladies Night" price-ticketing policies were violative of the state's equal rights amendment that prohibited sex discrimination. The court of appeals reversed a lower court decision and found the ticket practice a violation of the amendment.

7. For further information on individual state's ERA's see:

(a) "Hawaii's Equal Rights Amendment: Its Impact on Athletic Opportunities and Competition for Women," 2 *University of Hawaii Law Review* 97 (1979).

(b) "Sexual Equality in High School Athletics: The Approach of *Darrin* v. *Gould*," 12 *Gonzaga Law Review* 691 (Summer 1977).

3.20   Title IX and Athletics Programs

Section 3.21 reviews the major legal issues that have resulted from the passage of Title IX. The first challenge to Title IX was brought by the

NCAA. It sought declaratory and injunctive relief for the invalidation of the Title IX regulations promulgated by HEW (see Section 3.21 and *National Collegiate Athletic Ass'n. v. Califano*).

Section 3.22 discusses the scope of application of Title IX to a school's athletic program. The key determination is whether Title IX applies to any program in a school that receives federal financial assistance — the "institutional" approach — or whether Title IX is applicable only to the particular program within the school that receives federal financial assistance — the "programmatic" approach. This determination is extremely important for athletics because few, if any, school athletics departments receive direct federal financial assistance.

Section 3.23 describes the compliance review process used by the Office of Civil Rights to investigate complaints of alleged sex discrimination.

3.21 Legality of Title IX

The Title IX regulations and accompanying policy interpretations were promulgated by the Department of Health, Education and Welfare (HEW) and were not finalized until July 1979 after many revisions and in spite of remaining ambiguities. Many of the questions may eventually be decided by the courts in future interpretations of Title IX.

National Collegiate Athletic Ass'n. v. Califano, 444 F. Supp. 425 (D. Kan. 1978)

This case was brought by the plaintiff NCAA against HEW and its secretary, Califano, seeking declaratory and injunctive relief for the invalidation of the Title IX regulations promulgated by HEW with respect to sex discrimination in athletics. The defendant entered a motion to dismiss and for summary judgment, which was sustained by the district court. The court held that the association:

1. In its own right lacked standing to complain of allegedly vague and indefinite standards with respect to which it had no duty to comply.
2. Could not establish standing on the basis of mere regulatory invalidation of certain of its rules, accompanied by no discernible further ramifications.
3. Could not claim standing on the basis of alleged injuries that would be caused by the conduct of its own members in changing their practices in response to the challenged regulations.
4. Could not claim representational standing on the basis of changes that member institutions be required to make in the organization and operation of individual intercollegiate athletic programs, in absence of allegation as to how member institutions would be adversely affected thereby, nor on the basis of requirements not posing threat of injury to any of the limited interests that plaintiff association was qualified to represent.
5. Challenge to allegedly vague factors, to be considered in determining compliance with antidiscrimination requirements, was not ripe for review.

For the reasons discussed above, the court held that the plaintiff's amended complaint failed to allege any "injuries in fact," both casually related to actions of the defendant and for which the NCAA is an appropriate spokesperson, to any members of the NCAA. Accordingly, in the absence of any alleged injury to the NCAA itself, the court denied the NCAA standing to litigate in a purely representational capacity.

National Collegiate Athletic Ass'n v. Califano, 622 F.2d 1382 (10th Cir. 1980)

The NCAA appealed the decision of the district court. The court of appeals reversed and remanded the decision of the lower court. The appeals court stated:

... The NCAA asserts that HEW, in issuing the

regulations, exceeded its authority under Title IX; that some of the regulations are arbitrary and capricious under the Administrative Procedure Act; that some of the regulations are unconstitutionally vague; and that some of the regulations create a sex-based quota system in violation of Title IX and the Fifth Amendment. Although the NCAA pled these legal theories as separate "counts" of the amended complaint, the amended complaint presents but a single claim, i.e., that the unlawful regulations will injure the NCAA and its members and that enforcement of the regulations should be enjoined. . . .

Standing of the NCAA to Sue for Itself

We agree with the District Court that the NCAA does not have standing to sue in its own right. As the District Court noted, the challenged regulations can only be read to apply to the member colleges and not to the NCAA itself. The NCAA contends it will lose members and be impaired in its athletics rulemaking function (one of its chief functions) due to effects the regulations will have on its members.

All of the injuries are speculative. They might or they might not occur. . . .

As the mechanism of the alleged injuries to itself, the NCAA identifies certain of the HEW regulations which assertedly mandate equal treatment of the sexes in intercollegiate sports generally and sports scholarships in particular. The NCAA concludes that inasmuch as its members follow NCAA rules for men's intercollegiate sports and AIAW rules for women's intercollegiate sports, and the NCAA and the AIAW rules differ, the members must react either by dropping out of the NCAA or by compelling the NCAA to change its rules at its own cost. But even if it is assumed that the colleges' adherence to both the NCAA and the AIAW rules would necessarily violate the challenged regulations, it does not follow that any of the member colleges will adopt a course of action damaging to the NCAA. The colleges might instead compel the AIAW to change its rules to match those of the NCAA. They might even decide to continue their intercollegiate sports programs as before and to incur the sanctions imposed by Title IX. Significantly, the amended complaint contains no allegation that the NCAA has lost a single member, or has led to change a single one of its

rules on account of the HEW regulations. Thus, insofar as injury to the NCAA is concerned, the amended complaint invites a wholly advisory decision from the court, for such injury may never happen.

Standing of the NCAA to Sue for its Member Colleges

With respect to the question of whether the NCAA has standing to sue in behalf of its members, we hold that the amended complaint was sufficient to withstand the motions to dismiss. The amended complaint discloses that the plaintiff's members would have standing to sue in their own right, that the plaintiff's stated purposes as an association make it a suitable proponent of its members' interests in this litigation, and that the issues to be resolved by the suit do not require the individual participation of the members. This is enough to confer standing on the association. . . .

The Members and "Injury in Fact"

The District Court concluded that the members of the NCAA would not have standing if they had brought this suit, and thus it found no basis for standing in the association. . . .

We turn now to an examination of the allegations of the NCAA's amended complaint, which, if accepted as true and given a favorable construction, suffice to show injury to the NCAA's members.

First. According to the amended complaint, the members of the NCAA have committed substantial resources over many years to the intercollegiate athletic programs that today represent the status quo:

> Each of the member institutions of the NCAA maintains a program of intercollegiate athletic competition for student-athletes enrolled at the institution. These programs in general have been built up over a period of many years, and today involve not only major annual expenditures of time and operating funds by the individual institutions, but also the development and maintenance of substantial plant and equipment devoted to athletic programs for both male and female student-athletes.

Second. The amended complaint shows that colleges have limited amounts of money available for the intercollegiate athletics programs. The colleges operate the programs to attract the greatest number of spectators. This enables many NCAA members to subsidize some sports programs with the profits generated by a few popular ones:

> These programs are designed and operated in response to demonstrated student, alumni and spectator interest, within the limits of athletic budget capacity. At many NCAA member institutions, certain intercollegiate sports are entirely self-supporting, and often provide all or most of the funds necessary to operate the entire intercollegiate athletic program for both males and females. . . .

Third. The amended complaint further alleges the colleges now must operate and budget the intercollegiate athletic programs differently. The challenged regulations are the direct cause. The phrase "arbitrary demands" drives home the point that the changes in the status quo are unwanted:

> Application of the Regulations to the member institutions of the NCAA requires that they presently make substantial changes in the organization, operation and budgeting of their individual intercollegiate athletic programs, requires that they presently engage in time-consuming and expensive programs of self-evaluation and affirmative action, and requires that their intercollegiate athletic programs and activities be conducted in compliance with arbitrary demands of a Federally-imposed mandate. . . .

The amended complaint then cites specific provisions of the regulations which tell the colleges when they must obey.

Fourth. In light of the allegation that colleges aim to attract as many spectators as possible under the status quo, the inference must be drawn that changes in the status quo will reduce the colleges' "take" from intercollegiate athletic programs. The NCAA specifically alleges that its members must spend money to obey the regulations and are losing significant liberties:

> The above-quoted directives of the Regulations require the NCAA member institutions immediately to apply substantial amounts of time and money to satisfaction of those directives, to the detriment of other legitimate educational purposes. Such requirements deprive the member institutions of the NCAA of the freedom to determine the education programs most suited to that institution, free from interference or regulation by the Federal Government. . . .

The District Court reasoned that injury to "education programs" generally does not necessarily mean injury to those intercollegiate sports programs that the NCAA is concerned about. Read in context, however, "education programs" is clearly meant to include intercollegiate sports programs. Intercollegiate sports programs are "education programs" under HEW's Title IX regulations (*See* 45 C.F.R. Part 86, Subpart D) and the District Court itself refers to men's intercollegiate sports as an "educational program.". . .

It is equally clear, in our view, that the members of the NCAA would have standing to sue on their own under the Administrative Procedure Act. This is so whether the question is of "legal wrongs" or of "zones of interests.". . .

Contrary to the view of the District Court, we think a cause-and-effect relation appears between the regulations and the changing operation of intercollegiate athletics programs and that invalidation of the regulations would likely preserve part or all of some NCAA members' existing athletics policies. . . .

Suitability of the NCAA as a Representative

Having decided that the member colleges of the NCAA would have standing themselves to challenge HEW's regulation of intercollegiate sports programs, we turn to the issue of whether the NCAA should be permitted to represent its members in this lawsuit. . . .

. . . We hold that when an association does not have standing in its own right, and it is not clear which side of the lawsuit the association's members would agree with, one or more of the members must openly declare their support of the association stance, and they must do so through those officials authorized to bring suit on their behalf. Moreover, if more members of the association declare *against* the association's position than declare in favor of it, the association does not have standing, for then the parties in the lawsuit most likely would not be adverse.

The amended complaint states that "NCAA member institutions, meeting in Convention in January, 1976, were formally advised by the NCAA Council of the possible necessity for bringing this action, and voted to adopt the Report of the Council in which such advice was contained." Favorably construed, this pleading withstands a motion to dismiss. Sham allegations of membership support may be sought out by a motion for summary judgment. . . .

NOTE _____

1. For further information, see the following articles:
(a) Cox, "Intercollegiate Athletics and Title IX," 46 *George Washington Law Review* 34 (November 1977).
(b) "Sex Discrimination in High School Athletics," 47 *University of Missouri at Kansas City Law Review* 109 (Fall 1978).
(c) "Sex Discrimination and Intercollegiate Athletics: Putting Some Muscle on Title IX," 88 *Yale Law Journal* 1254 (May 1979).

3.22 Scope and Applicability of Title IX

A major issue involved in Title IX litigation centers on arguments concerning the scope of Title IX. The question is whether Title IX applies only to the specific departments receiving direct funding (commonly referred to as the "programmatic approach") or extends to any department within an institution that benefits from federal assistance (commonly referred to as the "institutional approach"). The dilemma is often expressed as whether Title IX is, or is not, program-specific. An integral factor in the resultant litigation has been the determination of what constitutes qualifying federal assistance. In some cases, it has been argued that federal student loan programs constitute federal aid to an institution, while other interpretations define federal aid as only those funds specifically earmarked or directly given to a particular program. Therefore, in terms of the scope of Title IX, the questions become very complex: What constitutes federal aid? Is indirect aid or direct aid

required by the statute? Once federal assistance is found, is only the particular program that benefits from the aid or the entire institution subject to Title IX regulation?

The decision in *Grove City College* v. *Bell* (*infra*) has answered some of these questions, but other issues remain to be clarified through further litigation or legislation. Many of the cases preceding *Grove City College* v. *Bell* deal with the "programmatic" versus "institutional" issue. A programmatic approach was taken by the district courts in *Othen* v. *Ann Arbor School Board* (*infra*), *Bennett* v. *West Texas State University* (*infra*), *Hillsdale College* v. *Department of Health, Education and Welfare* (*infra*), and *University of Richmond* v. *Bell* (see Note 2). An institutional approach was taken by the court in *Haffer* v. *Temple University* (*infra*) and the court of appeals in *Grove City College* v. *Bell* (*infra*). The resolution of certain issues in *Grove City College* was extremely important, not only in terms of the potential ramifications for hundreds of schools whose only federal assistance existed in the form of indirect aid or student participation in loan programs, but also in terms of the establishment of a precedent and subsequent settling of contradictory approaches and decisions among the circuit courts.

The decision in *North Haven Board of Education* v. *Bell* (*infra*) had particularly important ramifications for Title IX litigation. While the case did not specifically deal with athletics, the Supreme Court resolved two fundamental questions about the scope of Title IX, which were applicable to athletics. First, it decided that Title IX prevented discrimination against employees as well as against students. Second, it determined that both the power to regulate and to terminate federal assistance are program-specific. Thus, Title IX sanctions are limited to particular programs receiving federal financial assistance.

The issue of "programmatic" versus "institutional" was ultimately decided by the Supreme Court in *Grove City College* v. *Bell* (*infra*). This 1984 decision had an immediate and dramatic impact on then-pending litigation initiated by the Department of Education (successor to HEW and responsible for Title IX enforcement) against colleges and school systems alleged to be in violation of Title IX. The Department of Education had to drop cases in which policies in an athletic department were being challenged if it could not be established that the athletic departments or programs were direct recipients of federal funds. Cases against the University of Alabama, University of Maryland, Penn State University, the New York City school system, and at least 19 other institutions were discontinued or severely narrowed when no such connection could be found.

The Office of Civil Rights (OCR) commenced a proceeding in March 1984, which may be indicative of the strategy the OCR will employ in the future. The OCR informed Auburn University that an investigation had revealed Title IX violations in the Auburn athletics department. The OCR conceded that it no longer had jurisdiction over the athletics department, but charged that its investigation also revealed Title IX violations in the awarding of financial aid. The OCR therefore commenced proceedings to terminate all federal funding for the Auburn financial aid program. Concentration on athletic scholarship policies may be the most effective tool remaining for the OCR unless and until federal legislation reaffirming Title IX's applicability to all of a school's or college's programs is passed.

Such legislation was introduced by a bipartisan coalition of senators and congressmen in April 1984. The legislation proposed to change the wording in Title IV, Title IX, the Rehabilitation Act (rights of the handicapped), and the Age Discrimination Act, to state that discrimination was prohibited in the programs and activities of any "recipient" of federal funds. The bill further defined "recipient" as "any state or political subdivision thereof, . . . or any public or private agency, institution or organization, or other entity . . . to which federal financial assistance is extended (directly or through another entity or a person)."

Yellow Springs Exempted Village School District Board of Education v. Ohio High School Athletic Ass'n., 443 F. Supp. 753 (S.D. Ohio, 1978)

The Yellow Springs Board of Education brought this suit against the Ohio High School Athletic Association (OHSAA) and the Ohio Board of Education to challenge the association's rule excluding girls from participation in contact sports. In 1974, two female students competed for and earned positions on the Morgan Middle School's interscholastic basketball team. The board excluded them from the team and then created a separate girls' basketball team. This action was taken to comply with OHSAA Rule 1, section 6, which prohibited mixed-gender interscholastic athletic competition in contact sports such as basketball. Failure to exclude the girls from the team would have jeopardized the school district's membership in the association, effectively halting the basketball team's interscholastic competition.

The district court ruled on three questions in this case. First, it determined that the Ohio Board of Education was a proper party to the suit; although the Board of Education officer involved in the litigation did not have a duty to enforce the challenged regulation, his position as an ex-officio member of the OHSAA's governing board created a duty to prevent its enforcement. Secondly, the court found that the OHSAA's conduct constituted state action based on these considerations: (1) the association's dependence on the state for operating revenue; (2) the involvement of school officials in the association's decision-making process; (3) the predominance of public schools within association membership; and (4) the association's ability to impose sanctions upon state schools. Third, the court examined the facts in relation to the Due Process clauses of the Fifth and Fourteenth amendments. Two primary conclusions were reached in this area:

> The Association's exclusionary rule deprives school girls of liberty without due process of law. Freedom of personal choice in matters of "education and acquisition of knowledge"... is a liberty interest protected by the due process clause of the Fourteenth Amendment.

The due process clause permits deprivation of a liberty right only when it is predicated on a sufficiently important governmental interest; the court found that no such governmental interest existed in this case. The court also found that Title 45, Code of Federal Regulations (CFR), violated the Fifth Amendment and was unconstitutional to the extent that it authorized federal aid recipients to deny physically qualified girls the right to compete with boys in interscholastic contact sports. Subsection (b) of 45 CFR 86.41 specifies that "a recipient [of federal aid] may operate or sponsor separate teams for members of each sex where selection for such teams is based upon competitive skill or the activity is a contact sport."

Accordingly, the district court issued a permanent injunction enjoining defendants from promulgating or enforcing any rule or regulation barring physically qualified girls from participating with boys in interscholastic sports.

Yellow Springs Exempted Village School District Board of Education v. Ohio High School Athletic Ass'n., 647 F. 2d 651 (6th Cir. 1981)

The Ohio High School Athletic Association (OHSAA) and the Ohio State Board of Education appealed the district court's summary judgment in favor of the school district. Yellow Springs had originally filed suit fearing that compliance with certain OHSAA regulations violated federal law and could lead to loss of federal funds under Title IX.

The appeals court upheld portions of the district court's decision concerning the parties to the suit and state action. The court also ruled that Title IX focuses on "recipients" of federal aid. Since OHSAA was not itself a recipient of federal aid and does not bear the burden of noncompliance, it may not adopt a rule that limits the abilities of recipients to furnish equal athletic opportunities for girls and boys.

The district court had found Regulation 45 CFR Sec. 86.41 of Title IX to be unconstitutional as a violation of substantive due process. OHSAA had asserted that its Rule 1, Section 6 was worded to comply with Sec. 86.41, which proscribes sex discrimination in interscholastic athletics and sets guidelines by which school districts may establish separate boys' and girls' teams while still meeting the criteria of Title IX. The district court found that Rule 1, Section 6 and Sec. 86.41 were identical and declared both unconstitutional. The appeals court disagreed, finding that Sec. 86.41 allowed school boards flexibility in implementing Title IX, while OHSAA Rule 1, Section 6 was a restrictive measure. The appeals court reversed the finding of the district court that 45 CFR Sec. 86.41 was unconstitutional and remanded the case to district court for further proceedings. The school board was granted an injunction enjoining OHSAA from enforcing Rule 1, Section 6.

Othen v. Ann Arbor School Board, 507 F. Supp. 1376 (E.D. Mich., 1981), 699 F. 2d 309 (6th Cir. 1983)

Pamela Othen was a senior at Pioneer High School, and expected to graduate in June 1980. She had been a member of the Pioneer golf team during the 1978 fall season, but after tryouts she was cut from the 1979 team. In order to build the team for the future, the coach had chosen only the top three seniors, the top three juniors, and five sophomores. Othen had finished fifth in the overall tryouts, with three senior boys placing ahead of her.

Her father filed a complaint on her behalf charging the Ann Arbor school board and the golf coach with sex discrimination in violation of Title IX. The plaintiff sought a temporary restraining order immediately restoring Pamela to the 1979 golf team and prohibiting discrimination "against women who want to play on the Pioneer golf team." The complaint also asked for punitive and exemplary damages as well as costs and attorney's fees. The district court denied the motion for an injunction and found the plaintiff failed to demonstrate a likelihood of success on the merits.

One week before the trial came to court in February 1980, the plaintiff sought to broaden the scope of the action by amending the complaint. The amended complaint included Janice Othen, a sophomore who wished to play golf at Pioneer, as an additional plaintiff. It also contained detailed information on all interscholastic athletic programs at Pioneer, including breakdowns of male and female participants. The new complaint dropped all claims for damages, asked for a declaratory judgment that the athletic programs violated Title IX, and "requested a mandatory injunction requiring the school board to work with the plaintiff and women's organizations in Indianapolis, Indiana and Cleveland, Ohio to develop a plan for providing equal opportunity in interscholastic sports for men and women at Pioneer High School." No specific relief was sought for either Pamela or Janice Othen.

The defendant responded to the amended complaint with a motion for summary judgment, stating that none of the athletic programs at Pioneer received federal financial assistance and therefore were not covered by the provisions of Title IX. A school official testified that the only federal financial aid that the board received was "impact aid" in the form of payments to the school systems to compensate for increased enrollments caused by the proximity of federal facilities and the loss of tax revenue resulting from these tax-exempt federal properties. This money is channeled through the Ann Arbor school system's general fund and indirectly aids athletic programs. The defendant also asserted that the golf team had

always been open to both men and women and students were accepted "as their abilities warranted."

In December of 1980, the plaintiff filed an affidavit stating that it was his understanding that there would be a spring golf team at Pioneer for which his daughter Janice could try out. He stated that "these assurances were satisfactory [to] him as settlement of this case," and he withdrew all requests for other remedies except for attorney's fees and costs. The court determined that the award of attorney's fees and costs could only be based on a finding that the plaintiff would have been able to recover under his complaint had it not been voluntarily withdrawn. The district court subsequently ruled on the merits of the case and found the athletic programs at Pioneer received no direct federal assistance and the indirect federal assistance from "impact aid" was "de minimus."

In its ruling, the court was called on to construe Title IX, particularly the portion of the statute reading "under any education program or activity receiving federal financial assistance." While the defendant argued that Title IX's requirements are programmatic in nature — that is, they only apply to those specific programs or activities receiving direct federal financial assistance — the plaintiffs applied an institutional interpretation of Title IX, contending that the statute covers any program or activity of any institution that receives federal financial assistance, *whether or not the particular program under attack receives direct federal funding.* Under the defendant's interpretation, the athletic program that receives no federal assistance would be immune to Title IX regulations and the school would not be required to provide a women's athletic program or activity.

The court carefully examined the interplay between Title IX and the regulations promulgated by HEW with respect to athletics, section 86.41 of CFR, which provides:

No person on the basis of sex, shall be excluded

from participation in, be denied the benefits of ... or otherwise be discriminated against in any ... athletics offered by a recipient, and no recipient shall provide any such athletics separately on such basis.

Although on its face the language of the HEW regulations seems to support an institutional approach to the elimination of sex discrimination, the court found that the specific language chosen by the drafters of Title IX indicated that "the Act's provisions and requirements apply only to the specific class of educational programs or activities which receive direct federal financial assistance." The court noted that congressional rejection of the original version of the law, which would have barred discrimination "under any program or activity conducted by a public institution ... which is a recipient of federal financial assistance for any education program or activity," indicated that the intent of the accepted language was to limit the scope of coverage to only those programs or activities receiving direct aid.

The court's finding that "the clear language of Title IX and the intent of Congress requires that the Act be applied programmatically" had important ramifications in the case. Since it was determined that the athletic programs and activities under the jurisdiction of the Ann Arbor School Board received no direct federal financial assistance, the defendant was not obligated under the law to establish a golf team for girls. Therefore, plaintiff's daughters were not excluded from participation, denied, or discriminated against in violation of Title IX. The court held that no attorneys fees should be awarded to plaintiff. The court of appeals affirmed the lower court decision.

Bennett v. West Texas State University, 525 F. Supp. 77 (N.D. Tex. 1981)

Plaintiffs, six female athletes, filed a class action suit charging West Texas State University (WTSU) with sex discrimination, based on their denial of equal opportunity in the institution's intercollegiate athletic program. Plaintiffs sought both declaratory and injunctive relief to redress violations of their rights as secured under Title IX.

Plaintiffs contended that WTSU had intentionally discriminated against female athletes in the following areas:

1. The allocation of athletic scholarship money.
2. Travel allowances, allocations, and expenditures.
3. Scheduling of games and practice times.
4. The compensation and treatment of coaches.
5. The provision of supplies, equipment, and laundry facilities.
6. The provision of support staff.
7. The provision of locker room, practice and office facilities.
8. Authority to spend in excess of budget allocations.
9. The provision of publicity, promotion, and awards.
10. Perpetuating and aiding assistance to organizations and persons who discriminate on the basis of sex in providing aid, benefit, and service to students and employees.

Plaintiffs stated that the effect of the above policies has been to exclude them from full participation and benefits thereof and subject them to sex discrimination in violation of Title IX.

The District Court for the Northern District of Texas rejected the plaintiffs' contentions, finding that the athletic department of WTSU was not subject to Title IX regulation. Judge Sanders ruled that the language of Title IX showed "the clear intent of Congress" in that the terms "recipient" and "programs" limited Title IX application to only specific programs or activities that receive direct financial assistance. The court rejected the theory that the athletic department benefits from other federal assistance received by WTSU because that government funding frees other WTSU monies for use in other activities, specifically athletics. The court found that this connection was too remote, and if that connection were accepted, the program-specific construction of the statute would be rendered invalid, as every program or activity and thus the entire university itself would be subject to Title IX regulation. The court rejected Title IX jurisdiction and dismissed the action, ruling that plaintiffs had failed to state a claim for which relief could be granted.

Haffer v. Temple University, 524 F. Supp. 531 (E.D. Pa. 1981), *aff'd*, 688 F. 2d 14 (3rd Cir. 1982)

This action is an appeal of a District Court decision denying summary judgment to Temple University on the grounds that its athletic department was not exempt from Title IX regulation. Eight women undergraduates had filed a class action suit charging Temple University with sex discrimination in its intercollegiate athletic program in violation of Title IX. Temple had requested summary judgment arguing that Title IX applied only to those educational programs or activities which receive direct federal funding and that the athletic department at Temple receives no such assistance.

After an extensive examination of the federal funding received by the institution, the district court rejected Temple's request for summary judgment. The court held that (1) "Title IX coverage is not limited to educational programs and activities that receive earmarked federal dollars, but also includes any program that indirectly benefits from the receipt of federal funds; because Temple's athletic program indirectly benefits from the large amounts of federal financial assistance furnished to the University in the form of grants and contract, Title IX is applicable to Temple's athletic program"; and (2) "even if Title IX is construed to require direct federal financing, the Temple athletic program receives and benefits from several hundred thousand dollars worth of annual federal aid, and therefore is covered under Title IX."

Temple appealed the decision, questioning whether the court's inclusion of the athletic program under Title IX jurisdiction was consistent with the wording of the statute which required that the education program or activity receive "Federal financial assistance" as a prerequisite for its inclusion in the realm of Title IX authority.

Citing *Grove City College v. Bell*, 687 F. 2d 684 (3rd Cir. 1982), the appeals court affirmed the lower court's opinion. The appeals court rejected the "program-specific" interpretation put forth by Temple, claiming that the entire institution should be considered the "program." In referring to *Grove City College*, the court suggested that "the legislators [who enacted Title IX] did not contemplate that separate, discrete and distinct components or functions of an integrated educational institution would be regarded as the individual program, to which section 901 ... refer[s]." The court added that "if Temple University as a whole is to be considered the program or activity" for Title IX purposes, it follows that because the University as a whole receives federal monies, its intercollegiate athletic department is governed by Title IX. The court held that the district court's theory that federal monies received by the institution benefited the athletic program because it freed other university money for athletic program-related purposes was consistent with its finding that Title IX was applicable.

Hillsdale College v. Department of Health, Education and Welfare, 696 F. 2d 418 (6th Cir. 1982)

This action was an appeal of an HEW compliance proceeding which would have terminated federal financial aid to Hillsdale College students. The order disqualifying students from participation in federal aid programs had been issued in response to the refusal of Hillsdale's officials to sign an "assurance of compliance" with Title IX. There were no charges of sexual discrimination at the college.

Officials at the institution argued that their compliance with HEW demands would threaten both the college's independence and autonomy and subject the private institution to stringent governmental regulation. Hillsdale also claimed that since it received no direct federal financial assistance — although individual students received federal aid under the National Direct Student Loan, Pell Grant, Supplementary Educational Opportunity and Guaranteed Student Loan programs — it should not be considered a "recipient" of federal financial aid. As a nonrecipient, Hillsdale argued that it should not be subject to Title IX regulation. Therefore, a regulation requiring the execution of the "assurance of compliance" as a prerequisite for continuation of student participation in federal loan and grant programs was inappropriate and invalid. The college also contended that Title IX was program-specific and that an institution could only be required to assure compliance in programs actually receiving federal aid.

HEW contended that Hillsdale was subject to Title IX regulation and it was under the scope of HEW's power as determined in section 902 of Title IX to enforce compliance through the cutting or revoking of federal funding. The position of HEW was that "when an educational institution receives federal financial assistance by virtue of the receipt by its students of federal grants and loans, the entire educational institution constitutes a single 'educational program or activity' . . ." and thus is subject to Title IX regulation.

The U.S. Court of Appeals for the Sixth Circuit rejected the HEW interpretation of "educational program or activity." The court pointed out that the language "educational institution" fails to appear in Title IX. In addition, the court held that because Congress failed to adopt proposals that would have prohibited all discriminatory practices of an institution that receives federal funds, it was clear that, as enacted, Title IX adopts a "programmatic as opposed to institutional approach to discrimination on the basis of sex

in education." The court suggested that Hillsdale as an institution is not a program, but that the "program" in question would be the student loan and grant program. The court did, however, accept HEW's contention that Hillsdale was a "recipient" of financial aid, and stated that "provided that the 'program-specific' limitation in Title IX is met, it would be subject to regulation."

Even though the court found that Hillsdale was subject to Title IX regulation in those programs receiving federal financial assistance, the court felt that while HEW had been given the authority to promulgate regulations for Title IX enforcement, in this case, the order imposed was in excess of statutory authority in that it would subject the entire college, rather than any one program, to the strictures of Title IX.

North Haven Board of Education v. Bell, 102 S. Ct. 1912, 456 U.S. 512, 72, L. Ed. 2d 299 (1982)

In January of 1978, Elaine Dove, a tenured teacher in the North Haven public school system, filed a complaint on her behalf and others with HEW and its secretary, Bell, which alleged that North Haven had violated Title IX by refusing to rehire her after a one-year maternity leave. HEW began to investigate the school board's employment practices and sought from North Haven information regarding policies on hiring, leaves of absence, and so forth. North Haven refused to comply, asserting that HEW lacked authority to regulate employment practices under Title IX.

The North Haven Board of Education received federal funds for its educational programs and activities. Since the 1975–76 school year, North Haven had devoted between 46.8 percent and 66.9 percent of its federal assistance to employees' salaries.

North Haven brought this action in the U.S. District Court of Connecticut after HEW notified the board of education that it was considering administrative enforcement proceedings. The complaint sought a declaratory judgment that Subpart E regulations exceeded the authority conferred on HEW by Title IX, and an injunction forbidding HEW from attempting to terminate the school district's federal funds on the basis of those regulations. Subpart E's general introductory section states:

No person shall, on the basis of sex, be excluded from participation in, be denied the benefits of, or be subjected to discrimination in employment, or recruitment, consideration, or selection therefore, whether full-time or part-time, under any education program or activity operated by a recipient which receives or benefits from federal financial assistance.

The parties filed cross-motions for summary judgment, and in 1979 the district court granted North Haven's motion. The district court agreed that Title IX was not intended to apply to employment practices.

The case was appealed by HEW, and the U.S. Court of Appeals for the Second Circuit reversed (629 F. 2d 773). The court examined Title IX's legislative history and concluded that the provision was intended to prohibit employment discrimination. The court remanded the case to the district court to determine whether North Haven had violated the HEW regulations and, if so, what remedies were appropriate. The school board disputed the department's authority to regulate any employment practices whatsoever, and the court of appeals found this to be in error. However, the school board did not oppose HEW's investigation into its employment practices on the grounds that the complaining employees' salaries were not funded by federal monies, that the employees did not work in an educational program that received federal assistance, or that the discrimination they allegedly suffered did not affect a federally funded program.

The decision of the Second Circuit Court of Appeals was appealed to the United States Supreme Court. The Supreme Court affirmed the appeals court's decision and held that "... petitioners disputed the Department's authority to regulate any employment practices whatsoever, and the District Court adopted that view, which we find to be in error."

Supreme Court Chief Justice Burger, Justice Powell, and Justice Rehnquist all had dissenting opinions. They found the court's interpretation inconsistent with the statutory language involved. They stated that Congress made no reference whatsoever to employees or employer in Title IX, which is in direct contrast to the explicit language found in other statutes regulating employment practices. The dissenters believed that although the court examined the legislative history, it ignored other factors highly relevant to congressional intent, including:

i. Whether the ambiguity easily could have been avoided by the legislative draftsman;
ii. whether Congress had prior experience and a certain amount of expertise in legislating with respect to this particular subject; and
iii. whether existing legislation clearly and adequately proscribed and provided remedies for the conduct in question.

In response to the dissent, the majority argued that if this were a "plain language" case, their points would be unobjectionable. The court recognized, however, that its position could not be sustained solely by the plain language of the statute, and it, therefore, relied heavily on ambiguous oral statements during the statute's enactment made on the Senate floor. The court held that: "Where ambiguity exists it is not 'irrelevant,' to the process of ascertaining the intention of Congress, to consider specifically other statutes on the same subject. Nor must a court shun common sense in resolving ambiguities."

Brief of the Council of Collegiate Women Athletic Administrators as Amicus Curiae in Support of Respondent: Grove City College, petitioner, vs. T. H. Bell, Secretary of the United States Department of Education, Respondent, No. 82–792 (October Term, 1983, August 5, 1983) (Excerpts)

The following are excerpts from an amicus curiae brief which was filed by the Council of Collegiate Women Athletic Administrators

(CCWAA) in support of the Department of Education in *Grove City College* v. *Bell*. The CCWAA was concerned that a narrow interpretation of Title IX in *Grove City College* by the U.S. Supreme Court would have an adverse impact on women's intercollegiate athletic programs. The excerpts indicate the importance of the ramifications of the court's interpretation of Title IX and the case decisions which the CCWAA would support as precedent.

The Council of Collegiate Women Athletic Administrators is a nonprofit professional organization, organized to provide opportunities for women in athletic administration to enhance their professional relationships with colleagues and to provide a forum for discussion of issues affecting collegiate athletic programs. CCWAA members are employed by universities and colleges in administrative positions in intercollegiate athletics, and represent approximately 100,000 female athletes. Members are located in all 50 states.

Because of their professional responsibilities, CCWAA members are vitally concerned that Title IX remains available as a tool for eliminating sex discrimination and for enhancing women's opportunities in intercollegiate athletics. For the reasons explained below, CCWAA members are concerned that the opinion of the Court in this case may have an unanticipated impact on the viability of Title IX in cases dealing with sex discrimination in intercollegiate athletics. . . .

Although this case does not directly involve intercollegiate athletics, the legal arguments made by Grove City College are identical to legal arguments that have been made in other Title IX cases which have involved athletics. As a result, the court's decision in this case could have a direct — even if unintended — effect on intercollegiate athletics.

In three recent cases, Federal District Courts have held that intercollegiate athletics are not covered by Title IX; and all three have used the same reasoning that Grove City College has argued in this case: that the Title IX regulations are invalid where the Department of Education seeks to prohibit discrimination by indirect beneficiaries of federal financial aid or in specific programs that do not receive direct federal financial assistance. . . .

In *Othen* v. *Ann Arbor School Bd.*, 507 F. Supp. 1376 (E.D. Mich. 1981), the court held that Title IX extends only to programs which receive direct financial assistance; and thus, Department regulations bringing athletics within the scope of Title IX are invalid when applied to athletic programs which do not receive direct federal financial assistance.

In *Bennett* v. *West Texas State University*, 525 F. Supp. 77 (N.D. Texas 1981), the court held that Title IX applies only to specific programs or activities which receive direct federal financial assistance; and thus, indirect aid as received by state university athletic programs does not bring them within the ambit of Title IX.

And in *University of Richmond* v. *Bell*, 543 F. Supp. 321 (E.D. Va. 1982), the court held that the Department has no authority to investigate and regulate athletic programs which have not received direct federal financial assistance.

Although the case now before this Court involves federal financial aid to students — and not intercollegiate athletics — if the Court accepts Grove City College's argument and renders a broadly worded decision, more than a decade of painstaking progress in eliminating sex discrimination in intercollegiate athletics could be severely if not fatally undermined. This is so because a broadly worded decision favoring Grove City College would encourage more lower courts to rule that all indirect beneficiaries of federal financial aid, including intercollegiate athletic programs, are outside the scope of Title IX. For the following reasons, such rulings would be in error insofar as intercollegiate athletics are concerned.

TEXT: ARGUMENT

I. Amicus curiae endorses the position of the Department of Education, and urges the court to affirm the decision of the Third Circuit Court of Appeals in this case on the grounds stated by that court.

Amicus Curiae files this brief only in what may turn out to be an excess of concern. . . .

Indeed, if this Court does affirm the Third Circuit, and does so on the grounds stated by that court, it appears that the concerns of the CCWAA will have been satisfied. This is so because in *Haffer* v. *Temple University*, . . . a separate panel of the Third Circuit relied on the ruling below in *Grove City* in holding that Title IX does apply to the intercollegiate athletic program at Temple University, even though that program does not receive direct, earmarked federal funds.

The specific result in *Haffer* v. *Temple University* is the one desired by the CCWAA, and is one which the CCWAA wants to assure is not impliedly overturned by the Court's decision in this case.

II. If the court concludes that it must reverse the Department's victory on the Third Circuit, amicus curiae urges this court to note that the status of intercollegiate athletics under Title IX differs from that of the student financial aid program at issue in this case; and thus amicus curiae urges the court to rule expressly that its decision here should not be interpreted to mean that Title IX is inapplicable to collegiate athletic programs.

A. The legislative history of Title IX clearly indicates that Congress intended Title IX to apply to intercollegiate athletics, even though collegiate athletic programs themselves do not receive direct federal financial assistance. . . .

The Department's interpretation of Title IX displeased some members of Congress, especially Senator John Tower of Texas. As a result, Senator Tower introduced a proposed amendment, Amend. 1343 to S. 1539, 120 Cong. Rec. 15322 (1974), to Title IX which would have exempted "revenue producing" sports from Title IX's coverage. Senator Tower's proposed amendment was killed in Conference. In its place, the Conference Committee substituted an amendment directing the Department to prepare regulations implementing the provisions of Title IX which were to include ". . . with respect to intercollegiate athletic activities reasonable provisions considering the nature of particular sports." Section 844 of the Education Amendments of 1974, Pub. L. No. 93–380, Section 844, 88 Stat. 612 ("Javits Amendment"). . . .

These legislative initiatives show a direct and intense involvement by Congress in planning the scope of Title IX. And such specific inclusions and exclusions by Congress demonstrate that Congress clearly intended Title IX to encompass intercollegiate athletic programs.

B. In response to the statutory mandate of Congress, the Department of Education promulgated detailed regulations prohibiting sex discrimination in intercollegiate athletics.

As required by Title IX generally, the Department drafted a comprehensive set of regulations governing the conduct of federally-assisted schools in a number of areas (45 C.F.R. sections 86.1–71). One section was drafted in response to the Javits Amendment in particular, and it pertains specifically and exclusively to athletics (45 C.F.R. section 86.41).

The athletics regulations provide generally that all intercollegiate athletes, regardless of sex, shall be treated equally (section 86.41(a)). . . .

III. Title IX has been instrumental in the progress that has been made in reducing sex discrimination in collegiate athletics; and any ruling by this court that is interpreted to exempt athletics from Title IX will immediately reverse much if not all of that progress.

A. Prior to the enactment of Title IX in 1972, participation by women in intercollegiate athletics was only a fraction of what it is today. . . .

B. Title IX prodded colleges and universities into responding to the interests and desires of women athletes, and the progress that has been made in reducing sex discrimination in athletics is traceable directly to the adoption of Title IX. . . .

C. The Title IX regulations provide invaluable, specific guidance concerning the particular actions colleges and universities must take to reduce sex discrimination.

D. If the ruling of the Court in this case is interpreted to mean that Title IX does not apply to athletics, the discrimination claims of women athletes will have to be litigated under the broad mandate of the Equal Protection Clause, thus making every such discrimination claim a cumbersome Constitutional law case instead of a more manageable exercise in the interpretation of specific regulations. . . .

If the decision of this Court is interpreted to mean that Title IX does not apply to athletics, the regulations will have no force as law at all. As a result, the ten issues addressed by the regulations will have to be litigated under the 14th Amendment — a prospect which raises the specter of years of Constitutional litigation and literally dozens of cases. For this reason, the efficiency of the Title IX regulations is clear; and the CCWAA urges this Court not to do anything that may call into question the validity of those regulations.

CONCLUSION:

For all of the foregoing reasons, CCWAA as amicus curiae respectfully urges the Court to affirm the decision of the Third Circuit Court of Appeals.

If, however, the Court is unable to affirm, then the CCWAA respectfully urges the Court to expressly indicate that its decision in this case should not be interpreted to mean that Title IX is inapplicable to intercollegiate athletics.

Grove City College v. Bell, 465 U.S. 555, 104 S. Ct. 1211, 79 L. Ed. 2d 516 (1984)

Petitioner Grove City College was a private, coeducational, liberal arts college that has sought to preserve its autonomy by consistently refusing state and federal financial assistance. Grove City therefore declined to participate in the Regular Disbursement Scheme (RDS) of the Department of Education, in which schools are given federal funds and those funds are then distributed to students as financial aid for education on the basis of need. The college does, however, enroll students who receive Basic Educational Opportunity Grants (BEOG) under the Alternate Disbursement System (ADS). Under ADS, institutions make appropriate certifications to the secretary of education, but the secretary calculates and awards disbursements directly to eligible students, and the university has no control over the program.

Title IX of the Educational Amendments of 1972 prohibits sex discrimination in institutions that are recipients of federal funds. The Department of Education determined that Grove City qualified as a recipient of federal funds and requested that the college execute an assurance of compliance as required in Section 106.4 of Title IX. This assurance of compliance requires that the college agrees to "comply, to the extent applicable to it, with Title IX" and ensure that "no person. . . shall, on the basis of sex, be . . . subjected to discrimination under

any education programs or activity for which [it] receives or benefits from federal financial assistance. . . ." Grove City refused to execute an assurance, and the department initiated proceedings to declare the college and its students ineligible to receive BEOGs. The administrative law judge held that the federal financial assistance received by Grove City obligated it to execute an assurance of compliance and ordered federal assistance terminated until Grove City met the requirements of Title IX.

Grove City and four of its students then filed suit in district court. The court ruled that BEOGs constitute federal financial aid but that the department could not terminate the students' aid for failure to execute an assurance of compliance. The court of appeals (687 F. 2d 684 [3rd Cir. 1982]) reversed, holding that indirect as well as direct aid triggered coverage under Title IX. The court also found that although Title IX's language was program-specific, funds flowing to Grove City through its students were similar to nonearmarked aid, and that in such cases the school itself must be the program. Finally, the court held that the department could terminate such aid for failure to execute an assurance of compliance, and that it was not necessary to prove actual discrimination before termination.

Grove City appealed to the U.S. Supreme Court, arguing that neither it nor any of its programs are recipients of federal financial assistance. The court disagreed, holding that BEOGs are a key component of federal financial aid to institutions, since funds are strictly limited to use for educational costs. The court cited language in the Education Amendments of 1972 which states that one purpose of BEOGs is to provide financial assistance to colleges.

On the question of which programs fall under Title IX, the appeals court held that federal funds given to students free up school funds that can be used elsewhere in the institution. Thus, any programs that are recipients of these school funds are subject to

Title IX. The Supreme Court disagreed, holding that in *North Haven Board of Education* v. *Bell*, it had ruled that the language of Title IX made it program-specific, that only those programs directly receiving federal funds were subject to the regulations of Title IX. This ruling applies to schools that participate in the BEOG program through RDS and ADS. Otherwise, one student receiving federal aid would trigger Title IX coverage of the entire institution. This does not square with the program-specific language of the legislation.

Grove City's refusal to execute an assurance of compliance warranted a termination of federal assistance to the student financial aid program and was invalid in that it was not consistent with the program-specific nature of Title IX. The court held that execution of an assurance of compliance does not itself impose institutionwide obligations. Rather, it requires that "each education program or activity . . . which receives or benefits from federal financial assistance" comply with Title IX (34 CFR Section 106.11 [1982]). According to this opinion, only Grove City's financial-aid program is covered by Title IX. Further, Grove City's contention that discrimination must be found before federal assistance to its financial-aid program is cut off is invalid. Section 902 of Title IX clearly states that aid may be cut off for failure to execute an assurance of compliance. The court also found that Grove City's final argument — that conditioning federal assistance on compliance with Title IX infringes First Amendment rights of the college and its students — held little weight. The Supreme Court noted that: "Congress is free to attach reasonable and unambiguous conditions to federal financial assistance that educational institutions are not obligated to accept. . . . Grove City may terminate its participation in the BEOG program and thus avoid the requirements [of Title IX]. Students affected by the Department's action may take either their BEOGs elsewhere or else attend Grove City without federal financial aid. . . . Accordingly, the judgment of the court of appeals is affirmed."

NOTES

1. In *University of Richmond* v. *Bell*, 543 F. Supp. 321 (E.D. Va. 1982), the University of Richmond, a private institution, refused to give the Office of Civil Rights (OCR) investigator access to data requested in conjunction with the investigation of a complaint alleging sex discrimination in the institution's athletic program. The university argued that the agency had no authority to request any information because the athletic department received no federal funding. The OCR argued that because the athletic department benefits from other federal funding received by the university, specifically federal student loan and grant programs, it falls under Title IX jurisdiction.

In its opinion, the court redefined federal student funding as payment for services rendered to the college and as such was not deemed direct assistance to the institution. Even if these funds were construed as aid to educational institutions, the court decided that they do not constitute the requisite direct aid necessary for Title IX jurisdiction as was determined by the Supreme Court's *North Haven Board of Education* v. *Bell* (*supra*) decision, which established the program-specific interpretation of the statute.

2. Although the *Grove City College* decision did not directly involve the application of Title IX to athletics, Justice Brennan (with whom Justice Marshall joined, concurring in part and dissenting in part) noted:

. . . Congress has consistently endorsed the Department's regulation of college athletic programs, and indeed has affirmatively required such regulations. See, e.g. Pub. L. 93–380, Sect. 844, 88 stat. 612 (1974) ("The Secretary shall prepare and publish . . . proposed regulations implementing the provisions of Title IX . . . relating to the prohibition of sex discrimination in federally assisted education programs which shall include with respect to intercollegiate athletics reasonable provisions considering the nature of particular sports.") See also Brief for Council of Collegiate Women Athletic Administrators as *Amicus Curiae* 4–16. Cf. *Haffer* v. *Temple University*. . . . The opinion for the Court, limited as it is to a college that receives only "[s]tudent financial aid . . . [that] is *sui generis*," *ante*, at 16, obviously does not decide whether athletic programs operated by colleges receiving other forms of federal financial assistance are within the reach of Title IX. Cf. 688 F. 2d, at 15, n. 5 (discussing the many forms of federal aid received by Temple University and its athletic department).

Brennan's concur dissent in *Grove City College* v. *Bell*.

3. Immediately following the *Grove City College* decision, the OCR dropped its efforts to cut off federal aid to the University of Maryland and Auburn University for Title IX violations in their athletic departments. The OCR decided it did not have jurisdiction to investigate the

departments because they received no direct federal funding. However, in the case of Auburn University, the OCR decided it would still seek to pursue enforcement on the student financial aid program at Auburn since that program received federal aid. Financial aid was involved because the OCR charged that the institution had failed "to award athletics scholarships and grants-in-aid so as to provide reasonable opportunities for such awards for students of each sex in proportion to the number of students of each sex participating in intercollegiate athletics." For further information, see "Grove City Decision Spurs OCR Actions," *NCAA News*, March 21, 1984, pp. 1, 16.

4. In response to the *Grove City College* decision, legislation was introduced in Congress (H. R. 5490 and S. 2568) in 1984 to reverse the effect of the Supreme Court's ruling (see Section 3.00). For further information on the legislation, see the following articles:

(a) "Bill to Reverse High Court's Grove City Decision Gets Bipartisan Support," *Chronicle of Higher Education*, April 18, 1984, p. 21.

(b) "House Passes Civil Rights Bill," *NCAA News*, July 4, 1984, p. 7.

(c) "House Backs Bill to Counter Supreme Court Ruling in Grove City Case; Senate Unit Postpones Action," *Chronicle of Higher Education*, July 5, 1984, pp. 13, 14.

(d) "NCAA Files Statement Regarding Civil Rights Legislation," *NCAA News*, June 6, 1984, p. 1.

5. While it is notoriously hard to discern trends in Supreme Court decisions, many court observers think that the Burger Court has become more conservative in its legal attitudes. For further information, see "Conservatives on Supreme Court Dominated Rulings of Latest Term," *New York Times*, July 8, 1984, p. 18.

6. For further information on sports-related employment discrimination, see Section 3.40.

7. For articles concerning Title IX see the following:

(a) "Even Colleges That Get Only Indirect Aid Must Obey U.S. Bias Laws, Court Says," *Chronicle of Higher Education*, September 1, 1982, p. 19.

(b) "Ruling Could 'Decimate' Protection Against Sex Bias, Official Says," *Chronicle of Higher Education*, September 1, 1982, p. 20.

(c) "Sports Not Covered by Bias Law Unless U.S. Pays, A Judge Rules," *Chronicle of Higher Education*, March 9, 1981, p. 5.

(d) "Bell Unveils 'Flexible' Approach To Settling Complaints of Sex Bias in College Athletics," *Chronicle of Higher Education*, April 27, 1982, p. 1.

(e) "First Circuit Takes Programmatic View of Title IX," *Sports Law Reporter*, Vol. 4, No. 10, February, 1982, p. 1.

(f) "U. of Richmond Sues To Halt U.S. Probe of Its Sports Programs," *Chronicle of Higher Education*, May 11, 1981, p. 8.

(g) "Judge Says Title IX Doesn't Cover College's Sports Program," *Chronicle of Higher Education*, September 9, 1981, p. 8.

3.23 Office of Civil Rights Title IX Compliance Reviews

The Office of Civil Rights (OCR) is responsible for conducting compliance reviews of Title IX. The OCR selects schools at random to review for Title IX compliance and also reviews schools based on complaints brought by individuals. The OCR begins a Title IX investigation by notifying the schools and then collecting data on the overall athletic program. The information may include the number of teams, scheduling of games and practice times, travel and per-diem allowances, compensation of coaches, provision of facilities, and publicity. Based on a review of the data, the OCR will determine whether or not equivalent treatment, benefits, and opportunities as mandated by Title IX have been afforded to both sexes.

A finding of inequality in a single component of the program is not a basis in and of itself for the OCR to find a school in noncompliance with Title IX. The OCR's approach in investigating and determining compliance with Title IX has been to focus on the *overall* provision of equivalent opportunities in the athletic program. Therefore, the OCR will look to other components of the athletic program before it finds the school to be in noncompliance. In addition, Secretary Terrel H. Bell of the Department of Education adopted a nonconfrontation approach in 1981. Under this policy, the OCR may find schools in compliance with Title IX if the schools agree to rectify any violations of Title IX found through the OCR's investigation.

OCR officials will meet with the administrators of an investigated institution and review the OCR's proposed findings before a letter of noncompliance is issued. If the institution voluntarily forms a committee to adopt a plan to rectify its violations within a reasonable period of time, the institution will be granted a letter of compliance because it is implementing a corrective plan. The Department of Education is then responsible for monitoring the progress of the plan. If the plan is not implemented within the time specified or proves to be an inadequate remedy, the institution will be found in noncompliance and further legal action against the school could be taken.

Office of Civil Rights Title IX Compliance Review of the University of Akron

In 1980 the University of Akron was selected for a Title IX compliance review of its intercollegiate athletics program. Various complaints alleged that the university discriminated against female athletes in selection of sports and levels of competition. For example, the school had no varsity track team for women, and it offered no scholarships for women athletes.

The Office of Civil Rights (OCR) found that the University of Akron provided men and women equivalent treatment in five areas: (1) provision and maintenance of equipment and supplies, (2) travel and per-diem allowances, (3) provision of housing and dining services and facilities, (4) publicity, and (5) support services.

The OCR found that benefits, opportunities, and treatment were not equivalent in the areas of (1) scheduling of games and practice times, (2) opportunity to receive coaching, (3) provision of locker rooms, practice, and competitive facilities, (4) provision of medical and training facilities and services, (5) recruitment of student-athletes, and (6) the accommodation of student interests and abilities. The OCR concluded that these disparities violated Title IX. However, the University of Akron was implementing a plan that would remedy the disparities within a reasonable period of time. Therefore, the university was found to be in compliance with Title IX.

In 1979–80, the University of Akron awarded 95 percent of all financial aid to men and 5 percent to women; men comprised 85 percent of all athletes and women 15 percent. The university acknowledged that this award of aid was disproportionate, but indicated that it was implementing a plan to increase the percentage of aid for the women's program. The OCR concluded that the university's plan would correct the violation within a reasonable period of time. Thus, the OCR found the University of Akron in compliance with 34 CFR 106.37(c).

Office of Civil Rights Title IX Compliance Review of University of Iowa

The sports information director's (SID) staff for the University of Iowa women's program consisted of a full-time director, a quarter-time graduate assistant, two part-time assistants, and one work-study assistant. Time and funding limitations made it difficult for the staff to travel with the women's teams. The men's staff consisted of a full-time director, a full-time assistant director, two part-time assistants, and a student volunteer. It was determined that the provisions of publicity personnel were not equivalent because the lack of professional, travel, and clerical support severely limited the ability of the women's sports information director to perform tasks critical to her job function.

The following problem areas in the Iowa SID operation also were addressed by the OCR:

1. Men's basketball, football, and wrestling received radio and TV coverage. Women's team events were broadcast occasionally on local radio.
2. A newsletter that provided information about men's programs was sent to local high schools from six to eight times a year. No such service was rendered for the women's program.
3. All media guides for the women's pro-

grams were mimeographed on plain paper and contained limited data. No recruitment brochures were provided. Three of the media guides for the men's programs were printed books that contained color photographs. All guides contained a great variety of data on the individual players, the coaches, and the facilities. The disparity present in the provision of publications was found to be of concern because of the impact they have on recruiting and attendance figures.

The following remedial actions were taken by the University of Iowa:

1. A commitment was made to provide equivalent services and publications.
2. A centrally located SID office encompassing a women's SID, a men's SID, and a pooled staff of assistants was established.
3. A marketing assistant for men's minor sports and women's athletics was hired.

Office of Civil Rights Title IX Compliance Review of Central Michigan University

The Central Michigan University Sports Information Director (SID) had concentrated on those events that attracted the greatest spectator and media attention. Public relations luncheons were held only for football and men's basketball. Generally, football and men's basketball were the events that received television broadcasting, although some of the women's basketball tournament also received television coverage.

The SID office produced game programs, season brochures, fact books, and press releases for the football, men's basketball, and baseball teams. Recruitment brochures and player profiles for all other teams (except women's basketball) were inserted in the men's game programs and received additional coverage through press releases only.

The following remedial actions were taken by Central Michigan University to correct deficiencies noted by the OCR review of its athletic publicity operation:

1. SID coverage of away games was increased for all teams.
2. Game programs were provided for women's athletics home events.
3. A factbook was produced for the women's basketball team. (Fact sheets were developed for those women's sports that do not generate sufficient fan and media interest to warrant fact-book production.)
4. Radio and television coverage of women's athletic events was expanded.

NOTE _____

1. The Office of Civil Rights had issued decisions after Title IX compliance reviews on a number of institutions, including the following:
(a) Bentley College
(b) University of Bridgeport
(c) Central Missouri University
(d) University of Hawaii at Manoa
(e) University of Illinois, Urbana Campus
(f) University of Kansas
(g) Kansas State University
(h) Michigan State University
(i) University of Missouri, Kansas City
(j) University of Nevada, Reno
(k) Northwest Missouri State University
(l) Pensacola Junior College
(m) St. Olaf College
(n) Texas A & I University
(o) University of Texas at Arlington
(p) Yale University

3.30   Sex Discrimination

In the following section, the cases have been discussed in terms of the presence or absence of teams available to either sex. Within each category, the cases have been further divided into those dealing with contact and those dealing with noncontact sports. This was done because the approach taken — and sometimes the result reached — is different because of the sports involved.

The division of cases is not by legal theory,

since very often the litigation makes use of one, two, or even three prominent theories — for example, equal protection, Title IX, and state equal rights amendments (in certain states). To distinguish between the cases would therefore entail too much repetition without sufficiently differentiating the decisions.

The courts view contact sports and non-contact sports differently. Thus, in cases involving sex discrimination in athletics, the arguments used will vary depending on whether or not the particular sport is designated a contact sport. Under Title IX, contact sports include boxing, wrestling, rugby, ice hockey, football, basketball, and other sports in which the purpose or major activity involves bodily contact. In some jurisdictions, baseball and soccer have also been labeled contact sports.

In a sport designated "contact," certain arguments are commonly propounded. The most frequent argument raised by defendants is that women, as a group, lack the physical qualifications necessary for safe and reasonable competition against men in a sport in which bodily contact is expected to occur. It is argued that women are more susceptible to injury because they have a higher percentage of adipose (fatty) tissues and a lighter bone structure. Because of these physiological differences, the argument goes, contact sports are dangerous for all women.

Plaintiffs counter this argument by insisting that determinations of physical capability should be made on a case-by-case basis. When there is no other opportunity for participation in a certain sport, a blanket prohibition is overinclusive and violates equal protection by assuming that all women have identical physical structures and that all men are stronger and more athletically capable than women. Indeed, the health and safety rationale behind such total exclusion may fail a court challenge, as has been demonstrated in some cases. In one case, a women who was 5'9" tall and weighed over 200 pounds was denied a chance to play football because her supposedly lighter bone structure would render her more susceptible to injury. There was, however, no height or weight requirement for men, and the court thus found exclusion from participation to be unacceptable. (See *Clinton* v. *Nagy* in Section 3.31–1.)

Although the most important consideration used to substantiate separate teams for contact sports is the health and safety of the participants, this argument does not apply to non-contact sports. Since there is no legitimate and important state interest for allowing exclusion from noncontact sports, citing sex as the sole exclusionary factor would constitute a violation of the U.S. constitutional guarantees of the equal protection clause. Thus, the arguments made by defendants in noncontact sports sex discrimination cases are different.

The most common argument is that if men and women are allowed to compete together and/or against each other, the psychological development of both would be impaired. This stance is generally based on a variation of the "tradition" argument, which says that allowing men and women to compete as equals will irreparably disturb the innate nature of relationships between the sexes.

Another commonly made argument is that if men and women are allowed to compete together, men will dominate the co-ed teams. The underlying rationale here is that since men are inherently stronger and more physically capable than women, co-ed teams will actually limit opportunities for women. Plaintiffs argue that a justification of this sort does not take into account individual differences among participants. It also does not recognize the argument that if women are given opportunities to compete against men from the beginning of their athletic careers, their capabilities would improve and men might not be able to totally dominate the athletic field.

3.31 One Team Only

The general rule in both contact and non-contact sport is that when only one team is available, both sexes must be allowed to try out for and play on that team. Determinations as to the athlete's capability and risk of injury must be made on an individual basis, with the recognition that the contact or noncontact sports designations only make a difference if there is opportunity for athletes of both sexes to compete. If there is ample opportunity for women to compete on their own, courts appear to be less apt to allow women to compete with men in contact sports.

NOTE

1. For further information, see the following articles:
(a) "The Case for Equality in Athletics," 22 *Cleveland State Law Review* 570 (Fall 1973).
(b) "Female High School Athlete and Interscholastic Sports," *Journal of Law and Education* 285 (April 1975).
(c) "The Emergent Law of Women and Amateur Sports: Recent Developments," 28 *Wayne Law Review* 1701 (Summer 1982).

3.31–1 Contact Sports

In cases where contact sports are involved and there is no women's team, there is a split in decisions as to whether to allow a female to play on the men's team. In the majority of cases, as represented by *Clinton* v. *Nagy* (*infra*), the courts have upheld the women's sex discrimination claim and allow participation on the men's team. In some cases, the plaintiff-female was not successful because of the lack of state action (see Notes 1 and 4).

Clinton v. Nagy, 411 F. Supp. 1396 (N.D. Ohio 1974)

Plaintiff, 12-year-old Brenda Clinton, brought this action seeking a temporary restraining order and preliminary and permanent injunction against multiple defendants — the commissioner of the Division of Recreation of the City of Cleveland, the director of the Cleveland Browns Muny Football Association, the director of Class "F" Muny League teams, and the mayor of Cleveland. Plaintiff alleged that defendants deprived her of equal recreational opportunities in refusing to allow her the opportunity to qualify to play recreational league football because of her sex. Pursuant to 42 USC § 1983, plaintiff sought to enjoin defendants from denying her equal recreational opportunities on the basis of sex and to receive a declaratory judgment that "the policies, customs, and practices of the defendants are in violation of the Constitution and laws of the United States."

Clinton wished to play football as a member of the 97th Street Bulldogs of the Cleveland Browns Muny Football Association. Neither her mother nor the Bulldogs' coach objected to her participation. On several game days, plaintiff was suited and ready to play, but on each occasion she was informed by the league director that she could not play because she was female. Mrs. Clinton then signed a waiver, not required of the male participants in the association's program, absolving the city and its agents from liability for any injuries received by the plaintiff. Even after the waiver had been signed, Clinton was told she could not play because that "was the law." Plaintiff then initiated litigation to restrain defendants from denying her an opportunity, solely on the basis of her sex, to qualify to participate as a member of the Bulldogs in the team's last two games of the 1974 season.

The district court stated that the sole issue at the hearing on the motion for a temporary restraining order was whether the plaintiff showed a substantial likelihood of success on the merits of her claim that "defendants should be enjoined from enforcing the city's regulations which exclude females from the opportunity to qualify for participation in Muny league football, a contact sport, because such regulations do not bear a reasonable relationship to any legitimate state purpose." The court held for the plaintiff, issuing a temporary restraining order against defendants. Defendants asserted that the exclusion of females from contact sports was "necessary for their safety and welfare" and that the rule was rationally related to that purpose because at the 10- to 12-year-old level, "boys are beginning to develop speed and greater physical stamina at a faster pace than are girls of those ages." The court rejected this argument since plaintiff did not bring her case as a class action but as an individual seeking the opportunity to qualify to play football. Also, defendants made no claim that Clinton did not meet the standards required of other team members, except for the fact that she was female.

The court rejected the defendants' interpretation of the ruling in *Morris* v. *Michigan State Bd. of Educ.*, 472 F. 2d 1207 (6th Cir. 1973). The defendants had argued:

> . . . although a temporary restraining order was properly granted against the defendants from enforcing a school regulation barring women athletes from participating in non-contact sports [tennis in this case], the issuance of a temporary restraining order against the enforcement of a regulation excluding women from contact sports would be improper since that regulation would bear a reasonable relationship to a legitimate state purpose.

The court noted that in *Morris*, the sixth circuit remanded the case to the district court for modification of the injunctive order to limit its scope to noncontact sports "not because the record supported a finding that the state had a legitimate state purpose in excluding females from contact sports, but rather because there was no case or controversy before the district court in that action regarding the constitutionality of such an exclusion."

The court did, however, adopt the test applied in the *Morris* noncontact sport case — that is, when a regulation is based on a sex-based classification, "the classification is subject to scrutiny under the Equal Protection Clause of the Fourteenth Amendment to ascertain whether there is a rational relationship to a valid state purpose."

Finally, defendants argued that even if Clinton were qualified to play for the team, the temporary restraining order should not be issued because she had not demonstrated that she would suffer irreparable harm if not permitted to play on the team. Again, the court disagreed with defendants' assertion, stating that organized contact sports are considered an opportunity and means of developing strength of character, leadership qualities, etc., "yet, although these are presumably qualities to which we desire all of the young to aspire, the opportunity to qualify to engage in sports activities through which such qualities may be developed has been granted to one class of the young and summarily denied to the other."

NOTES

1. In *Junior Football Ass'n. of Orange County, Texas* v. *Gaudet*, 546 S.W. 2d 70 (Tex. Civ. App. 1976), the trial court granted a temporary injunction allowing plaintiff to play football in the Junior Football Association until she reached puberty. This decision was based on Article 1, Section 3a of the Texas Constitution, which provides: "Equality under the law shall not be denied or abridged because of sex, race, color, creed or national origin."

The association appealed on the basis that there was no state action sufficient to authorize the injunction. The association complained that there was insufficient evidence of state involvement to authorize the temporary injunction and the court agreed. The court noted:

> Not every subversion by the federal or state government automatically involves the beneficiary in "state action," and it is not necessary or appropriate in this case to undertake a precise delineation of the legal rule as it may operate in circumstances not now before the court.

On appeal, the temporary injunction order was reversed and dissolved. Even though the association was chartered by the state of Texas as a nonprofit corporation and the players usually practiced on school grounds and games were played in a park owned by the city of Orange, the court of appeals did not find state action or private conduct closely interrelated in function with state action.

2. *Lavin* v. *Chicago Board of Education*, 73 F.R.D. 438 (1975), *Lavin* v. *Illinois High School Association*, 527 F. 2d 58 (7th Cir. 1977), a class action lawsuit for declaratory, injunctive, and monetary relief against the Chicago Board of Education was instituted because plaintiff Lavin was denied participation in interscholastic athletics based on her sex. Lavin and another classmate tried out for the varsity basketball team at their high school and were denied positions on the squad because of the Illinois State High School Association rules. Plaintiff contended that the Fourteenth Amendment guarantee of equal protection had been violated. The appeals court

reversed and remanded the trial court's summary judgment for defendants and awarded monetary damages to the plaintiffs. On remand the trial court denied the class action claim because plaintiff was no longer a member of the "class" because of graduation. In addition, the court reasoned that she did not present an argument that showed she was qualified enough to make the boys' squad, and therefore was not a member of that particular "class" of girls either. The trial court allowed the plaintiff's individual claim for damages.

3. In *Muscare* v. *O'Malley*, Civil No. 76–C–3729 (N.D. Ill. 1977), an action was brought by a 12-year-old girl who wanted to play tackle football in Chicago Park District football games. There was a touch football program available for girls. In ruling for the plaintiff, the court reasoned that offering a sport for males, yet not to females, is a violation of equal opportunity rights under the Fourteenth Amendment.

4. In *Lincoln* v. *Mid-Cities Pee Wee Football Ass'n.*, 576 S.W. 2d 922 (Tex. Civ. App. 1979), an action was brought by an eight-year-old female who had played on the Pirates, a Mid-City Pee Wee Football team, in 1977. After the season ended, a decision was made to provide a separate league for girls. Because very little interest was shown at registration for the 1978 season, the girls' league was dropped and plaintiff was told she could not play again on a boys' team. Plaintiff then brought an action under the Texas Equal Rights Amendment (ERA) for a permanent injunction preventing the association from enforcing its decision. The appeals court affirmed the trial court's decision to deny the injunction. The court stated that the discrimination complained of must be state action or private conduct that was encouraged, or closely interrelated in function with state action. The court found neither and held that the Texas ERA did not cover purely private conduct.

5. In *Hoover* v. *Meiklejohn*, 430 F. Supp. 164 (D. Colo. 1977), an action was brought by plaintiff Hoover, who wanted to play on her high school soccer team. The Colorado High School Athletic Association limited inter-scholastic soccer team membership to boys. The district court held for Hoover, based on an equal protection analysis. The court held that the appropriate analysis requires a triangular balancing of the importance of the opportunities being unequally burdened or denied against the strength of the state's interests and the character of the group being denied the opportunity. The court found that a complete denial, as in this case, violated Hoover's rights to equal protection.

The court determined that the school had three options. It could allow co-ed teams; it could discontinue the sport for males, or it could field a second, all-female team.

6. In *Leffel* v. *Wisconsin Interscholastic Athletic Ass'n.*, 444 F. Supp. 1117 (E.D. Wis. 1978), plaintiff brought a class action suit charging that an interscholastic athletic association's rule limiting co-educational athletics violated her civil rights as guaranteed under the equal protection clause. The court granted summary judgment for the plaintiff finding that

> exclusion of girls from all contact sports in order to protect female high school athletes from unreasonable risk of injury was not fairly or substantially related to a justifiable government objective in the context of the Fourteenth Amendment, where demand for relief by plaintiffs would be met by establishing separate girls' teams with comparable programs.

Plaintiffs were granted the right to participate in a varsity interscholastic program in any sport in which only a boys' team was provided.

7. In *Simpson* v. *Boston Area Youth Soccer, Inc.*, Case No. 83–2681 (Super. Ct. Mass. 1983) (settled), an action was brought by a sixth-grade female soccer player. Defendant soccer association excluded plaintiff from the all-male soccer team in her town. Plaintiff had played for three years on co-educational teams, and many of her former teammates were on the team. Although the defendant also maintained a girls' league, no team in that league was readily accessible to the plaintiff. Plaintiff was also considered an above-average soccer player and maintained that the girls' league would present inferior competition. The case was settled when defendant soccer league agreed to change its constitution and bylaws to allow females to play on male teams, with such teams being entered in the boys' league.

8. In *Force* v. *Pierce City R-VI School District*, 570 F. Supp. 1020 (W.D. Mo., 1983), a 13-year-old female plaintiff sought injunctive relief to allow her to play on the interscholastic football team. The court granted injunctive relief for the plaintiff and held that:

(1) no sufficiently substantial relationship was shown between blanket prohibition against female participation on a high school football team and Title IX of the Educational Amendments of 1972, the high school activities association rules and regulations, and maintaining athletic educational programs which are as safe for participants as possible, or administrative ease, and (2) under the circumstances, rules and regulations of high school activities association and manner of promulgation and enforcement thereof constituted "state action," thus subjecting association's actions to equal protection clause requirements and, as such, enforcement of a rule which effectively prohibited members of the opposite sex from competing on the same team in interscholastic football was enjoined.

9. Review *Yellow Springs Exempted Village School District Board of Education* v. *Ohio High School Athletic Ass'n.* in Section 3.22 concerning the scope and applicability of Title IX, and *Darrin* v. *Gould* in Section 3.13 concerning the legality of a state equal rights amendment.

10. See Section 1.21–3 for an explanation of the standards required for an injunction.

11. See Section 4.50 for a discussion of waivers and releases of liability. The plaintiff in *Clinton* v. *Nagey,* *supra,* signed one before being allowed to participate.

12. For further information see the following articles:
(a) "Irrebuttable Presumption Doctrine: Applied to State and Federal Regulations Excluding Females from Contact Sports," 4 *Dayton Law Review* 197 (1979).
(b) "Title IX of the Education Amendment of 1972 Prohibits All-Female Teams in Sports Not Previously Dominated by Males," 14 *Suffolk University Law Review* 1471 (Fall 1980).
(c) "Girls' High School Basketball Rules Held Unconstitutional," 16 *Journal of Family Law* 345 (Fall 1978).
(d) "Sexual Equality in High School Athletics: The Approach of *Darrin* v. *Gould,*" 12 *Gonzaga Law Review* 691 (Summer 1977).

3.31–2 Noncontact Sports

In cases where noncontact sports are involved and there is no women's team, the trend and majority of cases allow the women to participate on the men's team. Cases such as *Gilpin* v. *Kansas State High School Activities Ass'n.* (*infra*) and *Brenden* v. *Independent School District 742* (*infra*) allowed women to participate on men's cross-country and tennis teams where there were no women's teams. Some courts have prevented females from participating on the men's teams (see Notes 4 and 5). In cases where private organizations are involved, the plaintiff-women may have difficulty proving state action (see Note 8[b], [c], and [d]).

Gilpin v. Kansas State High School Activities Ass'n., 377 F. Supp. 1233 (D. Kan. 1974)

Plaintiff Gilpin, a junior at Southeast High School in Wichita, Kansas, brought a civil rights suit against the Kansas State High School Activities Association (KSHSAA). Gilpin claimed she was deprived of equal protection by a KSHSAA rule that prevented her from participating in interscholastic cross-country competition solely on the basis of her sex.

In 1973, the board of education of Unified School District #259 (Wichita, Kansas) adopted a policy permitting mixed competition in certain noncontact sports, including cross-country. Plaintiff Gilpin accordingly joined Southeast High's formerly all-male cross-country squad. Prior to the team's first interscholastic meet, however, Gilpin was informed that a KSHSAA rule prohibited her participation. The rule stated that "Boys and girls shall not be members of the same athletic teams in interscholastic contests." Thus, although Southeast High officials did not object to Gilpin's participation, she was not permitted to compete for fear that her doing so would subject the school to disciplinary sanctions from the KSHSAA.

Plaintiff then filed suit seeking preliminary and permanent injunctive relief based on (1) a violation of her constitutional right to equal protection under the Fourteenth Amendment and (2) a denial of her civil rights based on sex. The court issued a temporary restraining order enjoining defendants from interfering with plaintiff's participation.

At the trial, the district court first determined that a cause of action did exist. It found that two essential elements to a cause of action under the Civil Rights Act of 1871 were met: "(1) that the conduct complained of was by a person acting under color of state statutes or local law, custom or usage; who (2) while so acting, deprived another of rights, privileges or immunities secured by the Constitution and laws of the United States."

The court found that although the KSHSAA is not an agency of the state or any local governmental unit, it acts under color of state law, and its actions are therefore subject to judicial scrutiny under the Civil Rights Act for a variety of reasons — for example, the KSHSAA is sanctioned and regulated by Kansas state law, a majority of its members are public schools, and its funds come from membership dues generated largely by interscholastic contexts held in state-owned and state-supplied facilities.

On the subject of whether plaintiff was denied her constitutional rights by defendants' actions, the court discussed two necessary prerequisites: (1) the delineation of the scope of the court's inquiry as limited by plaintiff's pleadings and (2) the determination of the standard of review to be applied in judging the constitutionality of the KSHSAA rule under scrutiny. The court noted that plaintiff brought this suit, not as a class action representative, but as an individual, and stated: "The court's inquiry is therefore limited in scope to the particular factual situation herein obtaining, and its decision will have no broader application."

The court then discussed the rigidity of the two-tier approach to the standard of review in which alleged violations of "fundamental rights" or violations based on a "suspect classification" are subject to the "strict scrutiny" standard, while others employ the "rational relationship" standard analyzing the relationship between the allegedly unconstitutional rule and its objective. The court noted a statement by the U.S. Supreme Court:

> By moving away from the rigidified equal protection approach previously adhered to, the Court has clearly demonstrated a willingness to scrutinize particular classifications based upon the constitutional and societal importance of the interest adversely affected and the recognized invidiousness of the basis upon which the particular classification is drawn in evaluating claims of violations of the Equal Protection Clause. . . .

The court held that plaintiff was entitled to injunctive relief but not to monetary damages. The court made this ruling after examining three basic criteria employed in the evaluation of equal protection claims: "[1] the character of the classification in question; [2] the individual interests affected by the classification; and [3] the governmental interests asserted in support of the classification."

The court, based on legal precedent, decided to subject the sex-based classification alleged in this case to close scrutiny and stated:

> Since sex, like race and national origin, is an immutable characteristic determined solely by

the accident of birth, the imposition of special disabilities upon the members of a particular sex because of their sex would seem to violate "the basic concept of our system that legal burdens should bear some relationship to individual responsibility . . ."

The court agreed that education is a privilege, not a fundamental right. It also concurred, in part, with an eighth circuit decision, *Brenden* v. *Independent School District 742*, that because participation in interscholastic competition is a privilege rather than a right, relief under the Civil Rights Act is inappropriate. The court in *Brenden* held:

> The question . . . is not whether the plaintiffs have an absolute right to participate in interscholastic athletics, but whether the plaintiffs can be denied the benefits of activities provided by the state for male students.

The court found plaintiff Gilpin's interest to be substantial. The importance of interscholastic competition as an integral part of her educational experience and the fact that she was denied the opportunity for the benefits of such competition rendered irrelevant the question of whether participation is characterized as a right or a privilege.

The court also examined defendant KSHSAA's interests in the case. It agreed with the association that the development of a viable girls' interscholastic athletic program was a "desirable and legitimate state interest." The court went on to note:

> Furthermore, in light of the physiological differences between males and females, the Court agrees that the separation of male and female interscholastic competition arguably bears a substantial relation to the advancement of that interest, when separate and substantially equivalent programs for males and females are in fact in existence.

Because Southeast High School offered no cross-country program for girls, however, the KSHSAA rule effectively deprived Gilpin of the opportunity to compete at all. The court held that:

Thus, although the Association's overall objective is commendable and legitimate, the method employed to accomplish that objective is simply over-broad in its reach. It is precisely this sort of overinclusiveness which the Equal Protection Clause disdains.

The district court determined that the KSHSAA rule prohibiting mixed competition was unconstitutional as applied to the plaintiff and accordingly granted plaintiff the requested injunctive relief. The punitive damages sought were denied, however, since no evidence was introduced that she actually suffered any monetary or compensatory damages or that she was subjected to hurt feelings, outrage, embarrassment, or humiliation.

Brenden v. Independent School District 742, 342 F. Supp. 1224 (D. Minn. 1972), *aff'd*, 477 F. 2d 1292 (8th Cir. 1973)

Plaintiff high school students Brenden and St. Pierre brought this action against Independent School District 742, seeking preliminary and permanent injunctive relief from alleged violation of their constitutional rights under the Fourteenth Amendment and Civil Rights Act (42 USC § 1983). Brenden and St. Pierre contended that the Minnesota State High School League rule prohibiting girls from participating in boys' interscholastic athletic competition was arbitrary and unreasonable as applied to their particular situations and thus, constituted a violation of their rights under the equal protection clause of the Fourteenth Amendment.

Brenden was an 18-year-old senior at St. Cloud Technical High School (St. Cloud, Minnesota) and an excellent female tennis player, ranked as the number-one 18-year-old woman player in the area by the Northwestern Lawn Tennis Association. The only opportunity for her to play organized tennis at St. Cloud High School, however, consisted of an extramural program with little coaching and no organized matches. Although there was interscholastic tennis competition for boys at St. Cloud High School, there was no such program for girls.

St. Pierre was a 17-year-old junior at Hopkins Eisenhower High School, which sponsored no girls' teams in her sports of cross-country or skiing. Hopkins High School did offer these programs for boys.

The plaintiffs sought to enjoin defendants from enforcing Article I, section 8 of the Athletic Rules for Boys and Article III, section 5 of the Athletic Rules for Girls of the Minnesota State High School League. Both rules state:

> Girls shall be prohibited from participation in boys' interscholastic athletic programs either as a member of the boys' team or a member of the girls' team playing the boys' team. The girls' teams shall not accept male members.

The court had jurisdiction over this cause of action in accordance with 42 USC § 1983 and 28 USC § 1343. Under the former, any person who suffers the deprivation of civil rights guaranteed by the Constitution by persons acting under color of state law may bring suit for the redress of those deprivations. The court found that the Minnesota State High School League and the defendant school districts were persons within the meaning of 42 USC § 1983 and that defendants had been acting under color of state law.

In response to the assertion by defendant that plaintiffs had not exhausted administrative remedies and therefore were not entitled to relief under 42 USC § 1983, the court concluded: "Where the administrative remedies are plainly inadequate, or where resort to those procedures would be futile, there can be no requirement of exhaustion of remedies." The defendants argued that a court decision would either uphold the league rule preventing mixed interscholastic competition or render the rule void. The court responded that it would not decide whether participation in interscholastic athletics is a fundamental right or whether sex constitutes a suspect classification. The court further stated that the case did not involve a class action and that the court would not decide whether the league rule in question was unconstitutional.

In making this ruling, the court decided to concern itself only with the specific factual situations of Brenden and St. Pierre, including the plaintiffs' high level of competitive skill and the absence of interscholastic competition in the relevant sports at the two high schools. The court was governed by the principles set forth in *Reed* v. *Reed*, 404 U.S. 71, 92 S. Ct. 251 (1971), in determining whether the application of the league rule to Brenden and St. Pierre was valid. It stated:

> A classification must be reasonable, not arbitrary, and must rest upon some ground of difference having a fair and substantial relation to the object of the legislation, so that all persons similarly circumstanced shall be treated alike.

The court examined defendants' contention that a rational relationship existed between the objective sought to be achieved by the rule and the classification utilized in reaching that objective. Defendants cited the rule's objective as promoting equitable competition and that gender is a reasonable basis of classification to reach this objective because of the physiological differences between males and females.

While recognizing the desirability of developing separate competitive interscholastic athletic programs for boys and girls and the existence of physiological differences between males and females, the court believed that the plaintiffs' cases were exceptional, noting that "it is not the rule itself which the court is here questioning, but only its application to the plaintiff in this case."

Because of the circumstances — that is, the girls were capable of competing on the boys' team, that no girls' team existed at their respective schools in the sports in which they wished to participate, and that Brenden and St. Pierre were kept from participation solely on the basis of sex — the court found the application of the rule to be arbitrary and

unreasonable. Because the classification by sex had no fair or substantial relation to the objective of the interscholastic league rule, its application to Brenden and St. Pierre was in violation of the equal protection clause of the Fourteenth Amendment.

The district court granted the requested injunctive relief and enjoined the Minnesota State High School League from imposing sanctions on the schools or any of their opponents stemming from plaintiffs' participation on boys' interscholastic athletic teams.

Reed v. Nebraska School Activities Ass'n., 341 F. Supp. 258 (D. Neb. 1972)

Plaintiff Reed, a student at Norfolk High School in Nebraska, brought this action, which challenged a state high school athletic association's practice of providing a public school golf program for boys, while providing none for girls and prohibiting girls from participation with or against boys. Plaintiff sought a preliminary injunction enjoining the Nebraska School Activities Association and school officials from denying her membership on the boys' golf team.

The district court held for the plaintiff, basing the decision on its findings regarding the requirements for issuance of a preliminary injunction: (1) plaintiff's probability of success on the merits, (2) comparative interests of the parties, and (3) irreparable injury.

The court found that the association's activities constituted state action and were thus subject to the equal protection provisions of the Fourteenth Amendment. Equal protection considerations require that sex classifications bear a rational relationship to the state objective sought to be advanced by the application of the rule in question. While stating that the defendants should have an opportunity to show justification for this sex-based discrimination before the issuance of a permanent injunction, the court ruled that the evidence presented demonstrated sufficient probability of success on the part of the plaintiff to warrant issuing a temporary injunction.

Regarding the comparative interests of the parties, the court determined that Reed's interests, such as the opportunity to enhance her reputation and to receive instruction from the school's coaching staff, far outweighed the state's interest in not allowing the plaintiff to participate "because of enforcement of rules unfettered by student attacks and financial savings."

On the subject of the irreparable nature of the injury to each party upon the granting or denial of injunctive relief, the balance again tipped in the plaintiff's favor. The court stated:

> For Debbie Reed, her benefits are fixed in time to the present golf season and when it ends, so will its benefits to her. The loss, whatever its nature or dimensions, will be irretrievable. It is true that defendants' interest in enforcement of the rules ... will be similarly lost. ... however, that interest is less weighty than those of Debbie Reed in the context of this case.

Accordingly, the district court judge ruled that a preliminary injunction should be issued.

NOTES _____

1. In *Carnes* v. *Tennessee Secondary School Athletic Ass'n.*, 415 F. Supp. 569 (E.D. Tenn. 1976), an action was brought by an 18-year-old girl who wanted to play on the boys' high school baseball team. Plaintiff Carnes sought a preliminary injunction from the court against the Tennessee Secondary Athletic Association rule barring mixed competition in contact sports. Baseball in this case was considered a contact sport.

In granting the preliminary injunction, the district court held that there was a likelihood that Carnes would prevail on the merits of the claim of invalidity of the association's rule and that a denial of injunction would result in irreparable harm to Carnes, whose last opportunity to play high school baseball was drawing to an end.

2. In *Morris* v. *Michigan State Board of Education*, 472 F. 2d 1207 (6th Cir. 1973), plaintiff Morris brought an action against a state high school athletic association rule barring mixed competition in interscholastic sports. Morris and a female friend wanted to play on the high school boys' tennis team. There was no girls' team.

Plaintiff contended a violation of equal protection under the Fourteenth Amendment. The lower court ruled for the plaintiff. The appeals court affirmed the decision but remanded the suit to the lower court to have noncontact sports added to the wording of the order granting the injunction. As a result of the case, Michigan Laws Act 183 were enacted, which permitted women to participate with men on noncontact sports teams.

3. In *Haas* v. *South Bend Community School Corporation*, 259 Ind. 515, 289 N.E. 2d 495 (1972), a suit was brought by a female which sought injunctive relief from a state high school athletic association rule barring mixed competition on sports teams. Plaintiff Haas had made the "B" golf team but was denied the opportunity to play with the "A" team because of the association's rule. The lower court held for the defendant. The decision was later reversed by the appellate court, which held that the rule was a violation of equal protection under the Fourteenth Amendment and the Civil Rights Act. The court found the defendant's arguments to be insufficient justification for barring girls from non-competitive sports or from denying girls the chance to qualify.

4. In *Harris* v. *Illinois High School Ass'n.*, No. S-Civ. 72–75 (S.D. Ill. 1972) (unreported), an action was brought by plaintiff Harris, who wanted to play on her high school boys' tennis team. There was no girls' team. The court ruled for the defendant and held that gender classifications were rational. Plaintiff's claim that she had a "right" to participate in interscholastic sports was denied.

5. In *Gregoria* v. *Board of Educ. of Asbury Park*, Case No. A-1277-70 (N.J. Super. Ct. App. Div. 1971) (unreported), an action was brought by plaintiff Gregoria, who wanted to play on the high school boys' tennis team. There was no girls' team. The board of education would not permit her to play. The trial court ruled in favor of the defendant. The appeals court affirmed the lower court's ruling that the "psychological well-being of girls is a rational reason for exclusion."

6. In *Hollander* v. *Connecticut Interscholastic Athletic Conf., Inc.*, Civil No. 12-49-27 (Conn. Super. Ct., New Haven County, 1971), *appeal dismissed*, mem., 164 Conn. 658, 295 A. 2d 671 (1972), an action was brought by plaintiff Hollander, who wanted to run on the boys' cross-country team at her high school. The Connecticut Intercollegiate Athletic Association barred mixed competition. The court worked out an agreement with the association to allow girls to compete on boys' teams in noncontact sports. Despite that, the court held for defendant association based on Fourteenth Amendment equal protection arguments. The court expressed the opinion that allowing girls to compete on the same teams with boys would bring into question the physical safeguard for girls and the "removal of challenge and incentive for boys to win."

7. In *Bednar* v. *Nebraska School Activities Ass'n.*, 531 F. 2d 922 (8th Cir. 1976), the mother of a high school student brought a civil rights action on behalf of her daughter, who had been denied the opportunity to participate on the boys' cross-country team because of her sex. There was no girls' team. The district court issued a

preliminary injunction enjoining the school from excluding Bednar from competition. The school association appealed the decision, but the court of appeals affirmed, finding that as Bednar was one of the top competitors in her event and her qualification for higher levels of competition was likely, she would be subject to irreparable harm if she were not allowed to compete.

8. The following cases involved suits against Little League Baseball:

(a) In *Rappaport* v. *Little League Baseball, Inc.*, 65 F.R.D. 545 (1975), a group of parents and plaintiff girl filed suit against the Little League because of its policy of excluding girls from participation. The Little League changed its policy after the complaint was filed. The court ruled the case moot.

(b) In *King* v. *Little League Baseball, Inc.*, 505 F. 2d 264 (6th Cir. 1974), an action was brought by a 12-year-old girl who wanted to play on a Little League team. The National Little League Baseball rules excluded girls from competing. However, the Little League Regional Board permitted plaintiff King to try out, and she made the team on the basis of her ability. The team was notified by the National Little League Baseball that if she continued to play or practice with the team, it would lose its charter. King was dropped from the roster, which resulted in the town revoking the team's privilege to use the municipal field for games. King was then put back on the roster, and the team lost its charter.

The case was dismissed and affirmed on appeal. The court held that there was not sufficient state action involved in the defendants' enforcement of the "no girls" rule to bring it under the color of state law. The courts agreed that they did not have jurisdiction over the subject matter in the case.

(c) In *McGill* v. *Avonworth Baseball Conference*, 364 F. Supp. 1212 (W.D. Pa. 1973), an action was brought by a 10-year-old girl against a nonprofit corporation operating a baseball conference, claiming that she was unconstitutionally discriminated against on the basis of sex when the conference refused to permit her to play Little League baseball. The team used public fields, and plaintiff McGill sought an injunction against their use. The district court held for the defendant, stating that the actions of the conference could not be considered state action for purposes of the Civil Rights Act, that the conference's decision was not unreasonable or discriminatory in light of the circumstances, and that the classification was rational where any contact sport was involved.

(d) In *McGill* v. *Avonworth Baseball Conference* 516 F. 2d 1328 (3rd Cir. 1975), the court of appeals affirmed the trial court's decision for the defendant because the plaintiff had failed to show significant state involvement in the league's discrimination. The court reasoned that the waiver of a $25 fee for use of the public playing field was de minimus, that analysis of nature, value, and proportion of state aid to defendants did not end court's inquiry, and that nexus between the state and defendant's allegedly offensive policy was not sufficiently close so that defendant's action could be fairly treated as state action where defendant was granted nonexclusive, scheduled use of four public playing fields, school buildings were used only for once-a-year registration purposes, and no government officials were involved in determining eligibility requirements.

(e) In *Fortin* v. *Darlington Little League, Inc.*, 376 F. Supp. 473 (D. R.I. 1974), *rev'd*, 514 F. 2d 344 (1st Cir. 1975), an action was brought by a 10-year-old girl who was denied the opportunity to try out for Little League baseball solely because of her sex. Plaintiff Fortin argued that the baseball park where the team played was public property, a fact that supplied sufficient proof to find the required state action. The appeals court ruled for the plaintiff, reversing the lower court's decision. The appeals court found that the defendant's preferred dependency upon city baseball diamonds introduced significant state involvement to find state action. The appeals court also rejected defendant's argument that the discrimination was appropriate because females would injure more easily than males, because it was not supported by the facts.

(f) In *National Organization for Women, Essex County Chapter* v. *Little League Baseball, Inc.*, 127 N.J. Super. 522, 318 A. 2d 33 Ct. App. Div. (1974), the Essex County chapter of the National Organization for Women (NOW) filed suit on behalf of 8- to 12-year-old girls who wanted to play Little League baseball. Plaintiff contended this discrimination against girls was a violation of New Jersey's antidiscrimination laws. In affirming a lower court order for the plaintiff, the superior court held that the evidence permitted the finding that girls of the particular age concerned were not subject to greater hazard of injury while playing baseball than boys of the same age group and that the Little League did not fall within any statutory exemptions.

9. In August 1984, a girl was listed on the roster of a team participating in the Little League World Series for the first time in that organization's 38-year-old history. One problem faced by the player, Victoria Roche, was that there was no facility for girls at the stadium complex that housed the world series teams. For further information, see "'One of the Kids,'" *New York Times*, August 5, 1984, sec. 5, p. 13.

10. In August 1983, Mary Decker, Grete Waitz, and 50 other leading female runners filed a sex discrimination suit against the International Olympic Committee, the Los Angeles Olympic Organizing Committee, the International Amateur Athletic Federation, the Athletics Congress, and others. The suit was filed in Los Angeles Superior court, and sought an order that would force the defendants to

include 5,000- and 10,000-meter runs for women at the 1984 Olympic Games in Los Angeles. These events are part of the men's events and were historically excluded from the women's program because of the belief that women could not physically handle the distances. (See Section 2.18, *Martin* v. *International Olympic Committee*, and "Female Runners Sue to Add Long Events," *New York Times*, August 12, 1983, p. A18, c.1.) The request for injunctive relief was denied by the court. The International Olympic Committee later added these events to the women's program for the 1988 Olympic Games in Seoul, S. Korea.

3.32   Women's Team, No Men's Team

The all-women, no-men type of case has arisen only with noncontact sports. In cases where there is a women's team and no men's team for noncontact sports, there is a split in decisions as to whether to allow a male to play on the women's team. In *Gomes* v. *Rhode Island Interscholastic League (infra)*, the court upheld the male's sex discrimination claim and allowed him to play on the women's volleyball team. In *Clark* v. *Arizona Interscholastic Ass'n (infra)*, the court refused to allow boys to compete on the girls' volleyball team. The plaintiff-male may not be successful for a variety of reasons, including lack of state action where a private organization is involved (see Note 2), prohibition of males on women's teams to redress disparate treatment of females in scholastic athletic programs (see Note 3), to promote athletic opportunities for females (see Note 4), and the fact that there are more athletic opportunities for males (see Note 5).

Gomes v. Rhode Island Interscholastic League, 469 F. Supp. 659 (D.R.I. 1979), *vacated as moot*, 604 F. 2d 733 (1st Cir. 1979)

Plaintiff Gomes, a senior at Rogers High School in Newport, Rhode Island, brought this action under the federal civil rights statute. He sought preliminary injunctive relief enjoining school officials from preventing his participation on the girls' volleyball team since the school offered no separate male squad in this sport.

Gomes had played on an all-male volleyball team at his former high school in Pennsylvania, but upon transferring to Rogers High School for his senior year, he was excluded from interscholastic competition on the school's only volleyball team, an all-female one. Rogers High allowed Gomes to join the all-female team but did not use him in Rhode Island Interscholastic League competition for fear of league disqualification.

Consequently, Gomes brought suit against the league at the start of the volleyball season. He alleged that the rule against male participation in volleyball competition violated both the Fourteenth Amendment and Title IX. Without reaching the constitutional issues, the district court ruled in plaintiff's favor, granted a preliminary injunction, and ordered the league to allow Gomes to compete on the volleyball team. The district court's decision was based on a regulation regarding athletics promulgated by the Department of Health, Education and Welfare (HEW) and issued under Title IX:

> . . . where a recipient operates or sponsors a team in a particular sport for members of one sex but operates or sponsors no such team for members of the other sex, and athletic opportunities for members of that sex have previously been limited, members of the excluded sex must be allowed to try-out for the team offered unless the sport involved is a contact sport . . .

In the *Gomes* case, the district court found that the exception for separate-sex teams under Title IX was not applicable since defendants sponsored no boys' volleyball teams and opportunities for boys to play the sport previously had been nonexistent.

The district court decision was rendered in the middle of the volleyball season. Defendants, however, persuaded the appeals court that implementation of the district court's order would disrupt the remainder of the season and that there existed a probability of defendant's success on the merits. The appeals court stayed implementation of the order pending review.

Although the case was expedited, the league's season had ended and Gomes was about to graduate from Rogers High School by the time the case was heard on appeal. The merits of the case were never reached on appeal since the case was dismissed as moot, the judgment vacated, and the case remanded for dismissal. The plaintiff had brought suit as an individual, not as a class action, and thus his case did not fit the "capable of repetition, yet evading review" exception to the usual definition of a "live" case necessary for federal adjudication.

Clark v. Arizona Interscholastic Ass'n., 695 F. 2d 1126 (9th Cir. 1982), *cert. den.*, 104 S. Ct. 79 (1983)

The appellants, plaintiffs below are students in Arizona High Schools, and have demonstrated their prowess in volleyball by participating on national championship teams sponsored by the Amateur Athletic Union. The plaintiffs have not, however, been able to participate on their high school volleyball teams. Their schools only sponsor interscholastic volleyball teams for girls, and a policy of the Arizona Interscholastic Association (the AIA) has been interpreted to preclude boys from playing on girls' teams, even though girls are permitted to participate on boys' athletic teams. The AIA's policy on matters relating to gender discrimination is set forth in its resolution of October 19, 1981:

> That the nondiscrimination policy of the AIA permits participation by girls on boys['] teams in non-contact sports in order to compensate for the girls['] historical lack of opportunity in interscholastic athletics, however, boys are not allowed to play on girls['] teams in non-contact sports since boys historically have had ample opportunity for participation and currently have available to them sufficient avenues for interscholastic participation, and since to allow boys to play on girls['] teams in non-contact sport would displace girls from those teams and further limit their opportunities for participation in interscholastic athletics.

The following stipulation was presented at trial:

Generally, high school males are taller, can jump higher and are stronger than high school females. There are six basic skills necessary in volleyball — serving, passing, setting, digging, hitting and blocking. Of these skills, hitting and blocking are enhanced by physical size, strength and vertical jump. Males generally have the potential to be better hitters and blockers than females and thus may dominate these two skills in volleyball.

A second stipulation indicates that these physiologically-derived differences in athletic potential have real impact on the game of volleyball. Under the rules of the AIA, girls' volleyball teams use a net that is substantially lower than that used by boys' teams. According to the stipulated facts there seems to be no question, then, that boys will on average be potentially better volleyball players than girls.

... The trial court found that the rules and regulations of the AIA do not violate the equal protection clause of the fourteenth amendment. It held that the maintenance of a girls-only volleyball team "is substantially related to and serves the achievement of the important governmental objective" of: (1) promoting equal athletic opportunities for females in interscholastic sports, and (2) redressing the effects of past discrimination. Specifically, the court held:

> [M]ore favorable treatment for females is permissible if such treatment redresses society's longstanding disparate treatment of women.... Precluding male students from becoming members of the girls' volleyball team is a permissible means of redressing the past discrimination against females in high school interscholastic athletic programs.

The only issue presented on appeal is whether the trial court was correct in holding that the AIA's policy of prohibiting boys from playing on girls' volleyball teams did not deprive plaintiffs of equal protection under the fourteenth amendment.

... We believe that while a lack of overall equality of athletic opportunity certainly raises its own problems, the presence of such equality cannot by itself justify specific inequality of opportunity in any given sport. The question, then, is whether denying boys the particular opportunity to compete on a girls' volleyball team, even when boys' overall opportunity is not inferior to girls', can be justified as substantially related to an important governmental interest.

As discussed above, the governmental interest claimed is redressing past discrimination against women in athletics and promoting equality of athletic opportunity between the sexes. There is no question that this is a legitimate and important governmental interest. . . .

The only question that remains, then, is whether the exclusion of boys is substantially related to this interest. The question really asks whether any real differences exist between boys and girls which justify the exclusion; i.e., are there differences which would prevent realization of the goal if the exclusion were not allowed.

The record makes clear that due to average physiological differences, males would displace females to a substantial extent if they were allowed to compete for positions on the volleyball team. Thus, athletic opportunities for women would be diminished. As discussed above, there is no question that the Supreme Court allows for these average real differences between the sexes to be recognized or that they allow gender to be used as a proxy in this sense if it is an accurate proxy. . . .

The AIA is simply recognizing the physiological fact that males would have an undue advantage competing against women for positions on the volleyball team. . . . The situation here is one where there is clearly a substantial relationship between the exclusion of males from the team and the goal of redressing past discrimination and providing equal opportunities for women.

We recognize that specific athletic opportunities could be equalized more fully in a number of ways. For example, participation could be limited on the basis of specific physical characteristics other than sex, a separate boys' team could be provided, a junior varsity squad might be added, or boys' participation could be allowed but only in limited numbers. The existence of these alternatives shows only that the exclusion of boys is not *necessary* to achieve the desired goal. It does not mean that the required substantial relationship does not exist. . . .

In this case, the alternative chosen may not maximize equality, and may represent trade-offs between equality and practicality. But since absolute necessity is not the standard, and

absolute equality of opportunity in every sport is not the mandate, even the existence of wiser alternatives than the one chosen does not serve to invalidate the policy here since it is substantially related to the goal. That is all the standard demands. . . . While equality in specific sports is a worthwhile ideal, it should not be purchased at the expense of ultimate equality of opportunity to participate in sports. As common sense would advise against this, neither does the Constitution demand it.

The appeals court affirmed the lower court decision upholding the rule prohibiting boys from playing on the girls' volleyball team.

NOTES

1. For further information on *Clark* v. *Arizona Interscholastic Ass'n.*, see the following articles:

(a) "Constitutional Law — Equal Protection — Sex Discrimination Against Males in Athletics — Physiological Differences Are Valid Reasons to Exclude Boys From Girls' Athletic Teams," (*Clark* v. *Arizona Interscholastic Ass'n.*), 695 F. 2d 1126 [9th Cir. 1982], cert. den., 104 S. Ct. 79 [1983], 6 *Whittier Law Review* 151 (1984).

(b) "Equal Protection Scrutiny of High School Athletics," (*Clark* v. *Arizona Interscholastic Ass'n.*), 695 F. 2d 1126 [9th Cir. 1982], cert. den., 104 S. Ct. 79 [1983]), 72 *Kentucky Law Journal* 935 (1983–84).

2. In *White* v. *Corpus Christi Little Misses Kickball Ass'n.*, 526 S.W. 2d 766 (Tex. Civ. App. 1975), an action was brought by plaintiff White, a 10-year-old boy who was not allowed to register to play in the girls' kickball association, purely because of his sex. The district court had held for the defendant and the plaintiff appealed. On appeal, plaintiff argued that denial of right to play because of his sex was a denial of equal protection under both federal and state constitutions. The appeals court denied his claim because he had failed to establish the requisite state action. His participation was denied by a private organization acting without any connection to government except that the games were played in a public park.

3. In *Forte* v. *Board of Education, North Babylon Union Free School District*, 431 N.Y.S. 2d 321 (1980), an action was brought by plaintiff Forte on behalf of his son, a 17-year-old high school student who wanted to play on the North Babylon High School Volleyball Team, which was all female. The court held for the defendant. The court reasoned that the rule the school district had enacted was a discernible and permissible means of redressing disparate treatment of females in interscholastic athletic programs.

4. In *Petrie* v. *Illinois High School Ass'n.*, 75 Ill. App. 3d 1980, 31 Ill. Dec, 653, 394 N.E. 2d 855 (1979), an

action was brought by plaintiff Petrie, who wanted to play on the girls' high school volleyball team since the school had no boys' team. The Illinois High School Association would not allow Petrie to play on the girls' team. The appeals court affirmed a lower court decision which upheld the association's rule. The court found no violation of state law and reasoned that the association's rule "substantially related to and served the achievement of the governmental objective of maintaining, fostering, and promoting athletic opportunities for girls."

5. In *Mularadelis* v. *Haldane Central School Board*, 74 A.D. 2d 248, 427 N.Y.S. 2d 458 (1980), an action was brought by plaintiff Mularadelis, a member of the high school's girls' tennis team who was told by the school board that he could no longer play on the team. The appeals court reversed a lower court decision and held for the school board on the basis that Title IX allowed for the exclusion of boys from the girls' team when there were, overall, more athletic opportunities for boys in the community.

6. In *Atty. Gen.* v. *Massachusetts Interscholastic Athletic Ass'n. Inc.*, 378 Mass. 342, 393 N.E. 2d 284 (1979), an action was brought by the state attorney general, who claimed that an athletic association rule excluding boys from competing on a girls' team, even though a girl could play on a boys' team if that sport was not offered for girls, was discriminatory. Injunctive relief was sought.

The Massachusetts Supreme Judicial Court held that the discriminatory classification could not be justified by (1) the theory that the classification was based on inherent biological differences rather than sex, (2) the theory that absolute exclusion on the basis of gender was necessary to protect players' safety, and (3) the theory that such a discriminatory classification would protect "emergent girls' programs from inundation of male athletes." The court found that none of the above were applicable and held that a "rule prohibiting any boy from playing on a girls' team was invalid under the state equal rights amendment and statute barring sex discrimination in the educational sphere." The case was remitted for declaration that the rule was invalid and an issuance of an injunction enjoining its application.

3.33 Women's Teams and Men's Teams

Four different types of arguments are raised in cases in which there are teams for both sexes. The first group are those cases in which the plaintiff women argue that "separate but equal is not equal." The women sue to participate on the men's team because the competition may be better and the women are far superior to the participants on the women's teams. As *O'Connor* v. *Board of Education of School District No. 23* (see Section 3.33–1[b]) illustrates, the court will generally approve "separate but equal" teams and rule against plaintiff females who want to play on boys' teams based on playing ability arguments. The second type of argument is that the separate teams are not equal, especially with respect to the benefits and opportunities provided to the teams. In *Aiken* v. *Lieuallen* (see Section 3.33–1[a]), plaintiff women athletes contended that they were discriminated against in the areas of transportation, officiating, coaching, and the school's commitment to competitive programs. In a similar situation, *Blair* v. *Washington State University* (see Section 3.33–1[a]) the court awarded damages to plaintiff women athletes and ordered equivalent funding for the men's and women's athletic programs.

The third type of case occurs when two teams exist but the women compete under different playing rules than the men (see Section 3.33–2). These situations, challenged on equal protection grounds, have produced mixed results. The trend seems to be away from allowing different rules to exist when those rules are based purely on the gender of the athletes, especially when those rules place those who play under a disadvantage if they want to continue in the sport. The fourth type of case involves different seasons for the same men's and women's sport (see Section 3.33–3). The courts have generally held that separate seasons of play are not a denial of equal protection of the law.

3.33–1 Separate but Equal

The sexes are generally separated when it comes to participation in sports, and the challenges to this practice have been largely unavailing. The doctrine of "separate but equal" remains applicable to sex distinctions, even though it has been rejected for discrimination based on race. Thus, if separate teams exist for men and women, there may be a prohibition against co-ed teams or against women competing against men. The doctrine of "separate but equal" raises the critical question of whether or not such separate teams are substantially equal. The fact that two teams exist does not necessarily satisfy the doctrine. "Separate but equal" is based on the concept that the exclusion of a group is not unconstitutional if the excluded group is provided with comparable opportunities. If women are excluded from the men's basketball team but are provided with an equal one of their own, the school district will not be in violation of Title IX under the "separate but equal" theory. When the sexes are segregated in athletics, there must be an overall equality of expenditures, coaching, and access to facilities. Without this substantial equality, the existence of separate teams and the prohibition of women competing with men is unconstitutional.

Apart from these circumstances, the segregation of the sexes in athletics is generally upheld, although the court is careful to examine the specific circumstances in each case before making a determination. The court usually considers whether or not the particular sport in question is considered to be a contact (Section 3.33–1[a]) or a noncontact sport (Section 3.33–1[b]). Physiological differences between the sexes have been found to be a valid reason for the exclusion of one sex from a contact sport. Contact sports include boxing, wrestling, rugby, ice hockey, football, basketball, and other sports in which the major activity involves bodily contact.

When dealing with noncontact sports, the courts have allowed co-educational participation when only one team is sponsored and athletic opportunities for the excluded sex have previously been limited.

3.33–1(a) Contact Sports

In cases where there are both women's and men's teams in contact sports, the courts have generally not allowed a female to participate on the men's team. In *O'Connor* v. *Board of Education of School District No. 23 (infra)*, the court denied the sex discrimination allegation of a female who wanted to participate in better competition by playing on the men's team. The other issue which may be raised is whether the separate men's and women's teams are in fact equal. Both *Aiken* v. *Lieuallen* and *Blair* v. *Washington State University (infra)* deal with this issue.

O'Connor v. Board of Education of School District No. 23, 645 F. 2d 578 (7th Cir. 1981), cert. den., 454 U.S. 1084, 102 S. Ct. 641, 70 L. Ed. 2d 619 (1981)

This appeal was instituted in response to a district court order granting a preliminary injunction to restrain defendant school board from refusing to permit female plaintiff to try out for the boys' sixth-grade basketball team. The plaintiff argued that the school board's policy of maximizing participation in sports by providing for separate but equal boys' and girls' interscholastic sports teams violated Title IX. The appellate court held that the trial court abused its discretion in granting a preliminary injunction restraining the school board because the plaintiff failed to show a reasonable likelihood of success on the merits.

Plaintiff O'Connor was an 11-year-old sixth-grade student in Illinois, whose school was a member of a junior high school athletic conference. Conference rules required separate athletic teams for boys and girls in contact sports such as basketball. On August 27, 1980, Karen's father requested that she be permitted to try out for the boys' team. On October 10, 1980, the request was denied by the board of education, which suggested she try out for the girls' team. On October 22, 1980, plaintiff filed a complaint and a motion for a temporary restraining order or a preliminary injunction. On October 23, the district court held an adversary hearing and found the school's classification violated plaintiff's fundamental right to develop as an athlete. It also held that "the right to education is a fundamental right and the rights to the constituent elements of an education is a fundamental right [sic]." The court further held that the separate boys' and girls' teams were inherently unequal. This finding was based on the assumption that competition with less skilled females was not as valuable as competition with males of equal or better skills. The court rejected the board's argument that to force the school to open both teams to either sex would ensure domination of all teams by males. The court applied a strict scrutiny analysis. It held that the board had failed to show the program as it existed was the least restrictive alternative.

The court of appeals granted a review of the preliminary injunction. The appeals court noted that to be constitutional, a gender-based discrimination must serve an important governmental objective and the means employed must be substantially related to the achievement of that objective. It noted that in *San Antonio Independent School Dist.* v. *Rodriguez*, 411 U.S. 1, 93 S. Ct. 1278, 36 L. Ed. 16 (1973), the U.S. Supreme Court had expressly rejected the notion that education or the "right to develop" is a fundamental right. The appeals court therefore decided that the main issue was whether the plaintiff had demonstrated a reasonable likelihood that the two-team approach was not substantially related to the objective of maximizing participation in sports. The court decided this was not sufficiently shown and overturned the injunction.

Aiken v. Lieuallen, 39 Or. App. 779, 593 P. 2d 1243 (1979)

Plaintiff taxpayers and parents of athletes on the University of Oregon's women's varsity basketball program appealed from the determination of the chancellor of the State Board of Higher Education that the university was not violating state statute ORS 659.150, which prohibited discrimination on the basis of sex in state-financed educational programs. The statute stated:

No person in Oregon shall be subjected to discrimination ... in any higher education program or service, school or interschool activity where the program, service, school or activity is financed in whole or in part by moneys appropriated by the Legislature Assembly.

The plaintiffs filed a complaint in March 1977, alleging that the following four areas of Oregon's athletic program were in violation of ORS 659.150: transportation, officiating, coaching, and commitment to competitive programs. A contested case hearing was held in October 1977, from which the hearing officer determined that the university was in violation of ORS 659.150. The hearing officer made the following findings:

1. Up until spring 1977, the transportation provided to the women's team was inferior.
2. There were striking differences in pay for officials at men's and women's games. Officials for men's games received $125/game plus mileage and expenses, while officials for the women's games received $20/game plus minor allowances for travel.
3. The number of coaches assigned to each team, the qualifications of the respective coaches, and the salary paid to the coaches and staff indicated that there was an extreme disparity in the level of coaching provided to the teams; and,
4. A disparity existed in the university's commitment to the basketball programs offered for men and women.

These findings and recommendations were issued in March 1978 and were submitted to Oregon's chancellor of higher education for review and entry of an order. The chancellor reversed the hearings officer's decision and found that the university was not in violation of the statute. The plaintiffs filed an appeal in the courts from the final order issued by the chancellor.

The appeals court reversed the chancellor's order and remanded the case for further proceedings. In its decision, the court elaborated on the following points:

1. The Chancellor's findings were inadequate to permit the court to determine what criteria were used.
2. The relevant statute (ORS 659.150) does not provide for a three-year compliance schedule, which is followed in efforts to comply with Title IX.
3. In making the determination regarding compliance with the statute, the chancellor could consider the revenue-generating capability of a sport, the level of interest and ability of the participants, the nature of transportation provided, the amounts paid to contest officials, the level of coaching provided, and the university's commitment to competitive athletic programs.
4. Different treatment could not be based on conference rules.

The court, after reviewing the plaintiffs' allegations of discrimination in the areas of transportation, officiating, coaching, and university commitment, stated that upon remand, the chancellor should address these allegations to determine whether the university's actions have led to "unreasonable differentiation of treatment" under ORS 659.150. Determinations of the unreasonableness of actions should include evaluations of whether or not the action by the university had a disparate effect on opportunity for women to participate in athletics. The court held:

In some instances, the amounts of money budgeted for the men's and women's team may indicate so clearly an unreasonable differentiation that no other evidence will be necessary to evaluate the discriminatory impact. In other instances, testimony of the women athletes themselves as to the impact of certain policies and expenditures on their opportunity to participate in athletics may be essential and its absence fatal to petitioners' case.

Blair v. Washington State University, No. 28816 (Super Ct. Wash.) (unreported)

A class action suit was brought by present and former women athletes at Washington State University, alleging sex discrimination in its athletic programs. The plaintiffs based their claim on the Washington State Equal Rights Amendment. The court held for the plaintiffs and ordered in part increased financial support for women's athletics, noting:

The Court has considered the evidence and arguments of counsel and entered Findings of Fact and Conclusions of Law herein. Based upon said Findings and Conclusions, It Is Now Ordered, Adjudged And Decreed As Follows:

I. Class Designation

The class of student athletes certified pursuant to CR23 (b) (2) is composed of all past, present and future students who have or will participate in the women's intercollegiate athletics program at Washington State University (hereafter referred to as "University") as athletes, student managers, or student assistant coaches since September 12, 1977. Members of this class of athlete plaintiffs are awarded damages suffered between September 12, 1977 and the conclusion of the spring semester 1982.

II. Claims For Damages

A. *Athletes.* Members of the certified class of plaintiff athletes are awarded damages suffered between September 12, 1977 and the conclusion of spring semester, 1982, as follows:

1. *Awards*: Each class member is awarded the reasonable cost of awards for which she would have qualified, under standards reasonably equivalent to those in the Athletic Awards Code of men's intercollegiate athletics.

2. *Practice Clothing*: Each class member is awarded the reasonable cost of such clothing as was furnished by her for practice purposes.

3. *Game Uniforms*: Each class member who participated in varsity tennis is awarded the reasonable cost for such competition apparel.

4. *Claims Procedure*: Each class member will be notified by the defendant no later than

February 1, 1983 by certified mail. This notice will include a summary of the court's decision, an application form for opting out of the class, all necessary claim forms, a full explanation of the claim procedures with instructions for filing claims.

The University alumni newsletter, the *Hilltopics*, will publicize no later than March 1, 1983 the names of the class members described and the appointed contact person(s).

Claims must be filed with the Clerk of the Court. Any claim filed after August 1, 1983 will be barred.

A summary hearing will be held if the defendant contests a claim within sixty (60) days after receipt. Undisputed, unpaid claims shall bear interest at the statutory judgment rate commencing sixty (60) days after receipt by the Court Clerk. Disputed, unpaid claims shall bear interest at the statutory judgment rate commencing thirty (30) days after determination by the Court.

5. *Other Claims for Damages*: All other claims for damages are denied except the following:

(A) *Coaches/Complimentary Cars*: Each plaintiff coach is hereby awarded damages for the :defendants' failure to solicit complimentary cars. The amount of the awards range from $1,200 to $8,600. . . .

III. Injunctive Relief

A. *General.* The defendant and its officers and agents shall cease and desist from the doing of any act related to or affecting the operation of intercollegiate athletic programs, which is prohibited by the Washington State Law Against Discrimination as set forth under RCW 49.60 *et seq.*, and the Washington State Equal Rights Amendment as set forth in Article XXXI of the Washington State Constitution.

B. *Funding.*
1. 37.5% of the University's financial support of the athletic program must be allocated in support of Women's Intercollegiate Athletics for academic year 1982–83.
2. Financial support for women's athletics shall increase, starting the fall semester 1983–84, by 2% until this support reaches a level representing the same percentage as women

represent of the total undergraduate population at the University; provided, however, that the level of University financial support for women's athletics shall not be required to exceed by more than 3% of the actual participation rate of women in intercollegiate athletics at the University excluding football participation.

3. For the academic year 1982–83, 10% of net contributed funds will be allocated between the men's and women's programs on a per capita basis, including football participation. The percentage of net contributed funds to be allocated in this manner will increase by 15% each academic year.

4. In no instance shall the total budget allocated to Women's Intercollegiate Athletics fall below the 1981–82 base budget of $841,145, unless there is a corresponding reduction in expenditures for the men's program.

C. *Scholarships.*
1. For the academic year 1982–83, women athletes shall be allocated 37.5% of the total funds expended for Athletic Scholarships, excluding funds expended for football scholarships. This percentage shall increase by 2% each academic year following 1982–83 until the level of scholarship funds for women athletes reach a level representing the same percentage as women represent of the total University population. The amount of this allocation shall not drop below the 1982–83 base of $236,000, unless there is a corresponding reduction in the men's program.

D. *Participation.* The University shall not take any action which would deny the level of participation of women athletes to reach a level commensurate with the proportion of female undergraduate students at the University. Participation in athletics shall be monitored by the sex equity committee.

E. *Administration.* The sex equity committee shall develop recommendations for written policies concerning matters affecting sex equity. It shall also develop and recommend a uniform definition of the term "participant" to be used for men's and women's sports for the purposes of comparing relative participation rates and monitoring female participation levels. This committee will submit an annual report which summarizes the committee's activities and effectiveness.

NOTES

1. In *Hutchins v. Board of Trustees of Michigan State University*, C.A. No. G79–87 (W.D. Mich. 1979) (unreported), the women's basketball team from the East Lansing campus of Michigan State brought a Title IX complaint against Michigan State University and the Board of Trustees, alleging that the men's team was receiving better treatment. The alleged better treatment included more money for traveling and better facilities. The court held for the plaintiffs and issued a temporary restraining order barring the better treatment of the men's team.

2. In *Petersen v. Oregon State University* (settled 1980), two student-athletes filed a complaint with the Board of Education of the state of Oregon, alleging that Oregon State University (OSU) offered athletic programs of lesser quality to female student-athletes than were offered to their male counterparts. A settlement was reached in July 1980, entitled "OSU Conciliation Agreement for Sex Equality in Intercollegiate Athletics," that implemented a five-year plan at OSU designed to put the men's and women's athletic programs on an equal competitive basis.

3. For further information on *Aiken* and *Petersen*, see "*Aiken v. Lieuallen* and *Petersen v. Oregon State University*: Defining Equity in Athletics," 8 *Journal of College and University Law* 369 (1981–82).

4. In *Michigan Department of Civil Rights, ex rel. Forton v. Waterford Township Department of Parks and Recreation*, 355 N.W. 2d 305 (Mich. Ct. App. 1983), plaintiff brought a Civil Rights Act claim based on defendant's policy of maintaining a gender-based elementary level basketball program. The appeals court reversed the district court's decision and ruled in favor of the plaintiff. The court reasoned that: (1) separate leagues involved were not equal and could not withstand equal protection analysis, and consequently violated the Civil Rights Act, and (2) subsequent modification of policy to allow up to two girls to participate on each boys' basketball team and two boys on each girls' basketball team did not cure the statutory violation.

3.33–1(b) Noncontact sports

In cases where there are both women's and men's teams in noncontact sports, the courts have generally not allowed the female to participate on the men's team. The rationale is that separate but equal is equal, since this enhances athletic opportunities for females.

Ritacco v. Norwin School District, 361 F. Supp. 930 (W.D. Pa. 1973)

Plaintiffs Ritacco, a 1973 graduate of Norwin High School, and her mother filed a class action challenging the Pennsylvania Interscholastic Athletic Association (PIAA) rule, which in effect required separate girls' and boys' teams for interscholastic noncontact sports. The district court ruled in favor of defendant school district. It held that since the school district had not deprived Ritacco of her constitutional rights in violation of the Civil Rights statute, 42 USC § 1983, she was entitled to neither the declaratory judgment nor the injunctive relief.

The court first determined that no proper class action existed because Ritacco had graduated from high school and therefore was no longer a member of the class she sought to represent (Fed. Rules Civ. Proc. rule 23[a]). Without a proper class action, the court found no basis for granting plaintiffs any relief.

The court further ruled that "if [we are] in error in concluding that no proper class action exists, in the alternative, there is no basis for determining that plaintiffs have been denied any constitutional right." The court held that "separate but equal" in the realm of athletic competition is justifiable and permissible when a rational basis for the rule exists, and that sex, unlike race, is not an inherently suspect classification for purposes of determining a denial of equal protection.

Based on these findings, the court concluded that the PIAA rule forbidding co-educational noncontact sports teams did not invalidly and unfairly discriminate against females. In fact, the court felt that this rule had produced positive effects on girls' interscholastic athletics in Pennsylvania since its adoption in 1970. The court cited "a virtual mushrooming of girls' interscholastic sports teams" and was convinced that "the prime purpose behind the no-mixed-sex competition rule is a valid one seeking to enhance the quality, quantity, and calibre of interscholastic sports opportunities for girls and boys in Pennsylvania." Accordingly, the court ruled for the defendant, holding that the PIAA rule under scrutiny in this case was proper and should be allowed to stand.

NOTE _____

1. In *Ruman* v. *Eskew*, 343 N.E. 2d 806 (Ind. Ct. App. 1975), an action was brought by plaintiff Ruman, who wanted to play on the high school boys' tennis team, even though there was a girls' team at her school. The Indiana High School Athletic Association prohibited girls from playing on boys' teams if girls' teams in the same sport exist. The court held for the defendant, and relying on *Haas* v. *South Bend Community School Corporation* (see Section 3.31–2, Note 3), upheld the rule since it was reasonably related to the objective of providing athletic opportunities for both males and females. The court of appeals further stated that "until girls' programs comparable to those established for boys exist, the rule cannot be justified." However, in this case, since the trial court had already decided the issue of "whether the tennis program for girls at Munster High School during the school year 1974–75 was and is comparable to that for boys," the appellate court believed it was in no position to "review the evidentiary basis upon which the facts rest."

3.33–2   Same Sport, Different Rules

Cases and issues in this section have traditionally arisen in basketball because of women's playing rules being different from men's rules. As evidenced by the *Bucha* v. *Illinois High School Ass'n.* (Section 3.33–2[b]), the cases have also evolved from generally disparate treatment of student-athletes rather than from different rules of a sport.

3.33–2(a)   Contact Sports

In cases where there are different playing rules for women's and men's teams in contact sports, there is a split in decisions as to whether the women's rules should be changed to conform with the men's. The plaintiff-women in these cases generally have alleged sex discrimination based on the rule differences with men's sport and also the reduced opportunity to compete against other women (who had the advantage of playing under men's rules) for college scholarships. In *Dodson* v. *Arkansas Activities Ass'n.* (*infra*), the court ruled for the plaintiff, while in *Jones* v. *Oklahoma Secondary School Activities Ass'n.* (*infra*, Note 1) and *Cape* v. *Tennessee Secondary School Athletic Ass'n.* (*infra*, Note 2), the courts ruled for the defendant athletic associations.

_____

Dodson v. Arkansas Activities Ass'n., 468 F. Supp. 394 (E.D. Ark., 1979)

Plaintiff Dodson, a junior high school basketball player in the Arkadelphia, Arkansas, public school system, brought this action in January 1977 against three defendants — the school district, the superintendent, and the Arkansas Activities Association. Her suit challenged the constitutionality of rules for girls' junior and senior high school basketball, which in Arkansas differed from those under which boys played.

In reaching its decision for the plaintiff, the district court examined several issues. For example, the court determined that the difference between the girls' and boys' rules, as established by a voluntary association such as the Arkansas Activities Association, did not violate the federal statute prohibiting sex discrimination in education since there was no evidence that any "education program or activity" involved in the case received federal financial assistance.

The court also determined, however, that although the association was not itself a governmental body, it was largely supported by dues from public school districts and was therefore subject to the equal protection clause of the U.S. Constitution. After noting that the existence of differences in the treatment of girls and boys in the Arkansas schools did not constitute conclusive evidence of deprivation under equal protection laws, the court set out to determine whether there was sufficient justification for the different treatment. Under the equal protection clause of the Fourteenth Amendment, gender-based classification must serve important governmental objectives and must be substantially related to the achievement of those objectives.

The court's examination of the equal protection issue led to its finding that "the rules place girl athletes in Arkansas at a substantial disadvantage compared to boy athletes, that no sufficient justification is offered to justify this disparity, and that the resulting discrimination is unconstitutional." The court cited the fact that Arkansas' rules for six-on-six girls' basketball put female basketball players at a tremendous physical and psychological disadvantage in the transition from high school to college basketball since only three other states played half-court basketball at the secondary school level, and all intercollegiate and international competition follows full-court rules.

The court found that, "none of the reasons proffered [for the rule differentiation] is at all relevant to a gender-based classification." Defendant stated that "no physiological differences between males and females . . . prohibit females from playing five-on-five basketball," and the primary justification given for the sex-based distinction between rules was simply that of tradition.

The court ordered that the defendants be permanently enjoined and restrained from enforcing different rules for girls and boys playing junior and senior high school basketball in Arkansas. It remarked, however, that the case was not about male-female competition or discrimination between programs, and stated that:

The point here is that Arkansas boys are in a position to compete on an equal footing with boys elsewhere, while Arkansas girls, merely because they are girls, are not. . . . Arkansas schools have chosen to offer basketball. Having taken that step, they may not limit the game's full benefits to one sex without substantial justification.

NOTES

1. In *Jones* v. *Oklahoma Secondary School Activities Ass'n.*, 453 F. Supp. 150 (W.D. Okla. 1977), plaintiff Jones sought an injunction to suspend the association's split-court basketball rules, arguing that they created an arbitrary and unreasonable distinction between boys and girls that violated her right to equal protection. The court held for the defendant. Plaintiff's Title IX arguments were dismissed because she did not follow administrative procedures. Her Fourteenth Amendment argument was seen as faulty because her allegations concerning her reduced opportunity to compete in the future and a reduced likelihood for college scholarships did not rise to the level of an equal protection interest. Her claims that such rules interfered with her enjoyment of the game as well as her physical development also did not establish a cognizable equal protection claim.

2. In *Cape* v. *Tennessee Secondary School Athletic Ass'n.*, 424 F. Supp. 732 (E.D. Tenn., N.D. 1976), *rev'd. per curiam*, 563 F. 2d 793 (6th Cir. 1977), plaintiff Cape, a high school student, challenged the "split-court" rules used in women's basketball. These rules, she claimed, denied her the full benefits of the game as well as an athletic scholarship to college. The court held for the defendent and dismissed the plaintiff's arguments, which were based on a private right of action under Title IX and the Fourteenth Amendment. The court held that the plaintiff who sought to challenge regulations must first exhaust all administrative remedies within the Department of Health, Education and Welfare before her suit could be addressed in federal court.

3. In *Russell, Wolf and Enslav* v. *Iowa Girls High School Athletic Union* (pending), three Iowa girls brought a class action suit charging that the state's six-on-six half-court rules violated their rights as guaranteed under the equal protection clause. Noting that intercollegiate and international competition for women is conducted under five-on-five rules, the plaintiffs argued that they were being discriminated against because half-court basketball does not offer the same benefits and experience as the game of basketball available to the boys of Iowa.

4. For further information, see Johnson, "Half Court Girls' Basketball Rules: An Application of the Equal Protection Clause and Title IX," 65 *Iowa Law Review* 766 (March 1980).

3.33–2(b) Noncontact Sports

In *Bucha* v. *Illinois High School Ass'n.* (*infra*), the court allowed different rules for men's and women's noncontact sports. The court applied a rational relationship test and found that the physical and psychological differences between male and female athletes justified the different rules.

Bucha v. Illinois High School Ass'n., 351 F. Supp. 69 (N.D. Ill. 1972)

Plaintiffs, two female students at Hinsdale Center Township High School, brought this class action challenging Illinois High School Association (IHSA) bylaws placing limitations on girls' athletic contests that were not applicable to boys' athletics. Three IHSA bylaws in particular were challenged in this suit:

1. A bylaw that prohibited member schools from conducting interscholastic swimming competition for girls (later amended to permit such meets).
2. A bylaw that placed limitations on girls' athletics that were not applicable to boys' programs, including a prohibition on organized cheering, a one-dollar limitation on the value of awards, and a prohibition on overnight trips in conjunction with contests.
3. A bylaw that completely prohibited competition between members of the opposite sex.

The plaintiffs asked the court to declare these IHSA rules in violation of the equal protection clause of the Fourteenth Amendment and to enjoin the enforcement of the bylaws. They also sought a judgment against all defendants in the amount of $25,000.

The court first determined that the named plaintiffs in this case adequately represented all the members of their class and thus, their standing to bring a class action was affirmed. It stated:

> Although these two girls might have an interest in becoming members of presently all-boy teams, they also have an interest in seeking the development of a "separate but equal" program. . . . The fact that the named plaintiffs have interests which exceed those of some class members will not defeat the class action, so long as they possess interests which are coextensive with those of the class.

The defendants — IHSA, its directors, and the board of education of Hinsdale Township — based their motions to dismiss on three arguments:

1. The IHSA and the board of education were not persons within the meaning of 42 USC § 1983 (1970).
2. The challenged discrimination was not an action under color of state statute, ordinance, regulation, custom or usage.
3. The challenged discrimination did not constitute a deprivation of a right guaranteed by the U.S. Constitution and laws.

Concerning the defendants' first argument, the court held that "all defendants may properly be enjoined as persons under section 1983, but only the individual defendants can be liable for the damages sought," citing several cases in which high school athletic associations such as the IHSA have been treated as persons for injunctive purposes when engaged in activities constituting state action. On the second argument, the court rejected defendants' contention that the acts of the IHSA, which "neither exists by any authority of the State of Illinois nor acts pursuant to any statute in fulfilling its functions," did not amount to state action and therefore could not be reached under section 1938. The court stated:

> The fact that many members of the IHSA are tax supported, public institutions which cannot violate the rights of their students without being subject to judicial review, . . . and the fact that many IHSA sporting events are conducted in facilities constructed, operated, and maintained at taxpayer expense is sufficient involvement to constitute state action under 1983.

On the third and final argument, the court reviewed plaintiffs' complaint that defendants had denied them equal protection, stating that the relevant inquiry was whether the challenged classification based on sex was rational. Because participation in interscholastic athletics is not a constitutionally guaranteed right and the

Illinois courts do not interfere with the policies of a voluntary association such as the IHSA unless it acts "unreasonably, arbitrarily, or capriciously," plaintiffs had asserted their claims based on an equal educational opportunity argument and not the right to interscholastic athletic participation.

The court analyzed the alleged denial of equal protection in this case using the traditional test that identifies the purposes or objective of a legislative scheme and then asks whether the challenged discrimination bears a rational relationship to one of those purposes. The court stated:

> ... what is questioned [in this case] is a matter of degree and professional judgment, that is, given the uncontroverted existence of a statewide athletics program open to all girls, plaintiffs assert that the decision of Illinois' physical educators to conduct separate athletic contests for the sexes and to provide a different program for each sex is not rationally related to the overall educational objectives in sponsoring sporting events....

The court found a factual basis for defendants' claims that the physical and psychological differences between male and female athletes would lead to male domination of coed interscholastic sports and result in decreased female athletic participation should unrestricted competition between the sexes be permitted. It held that:

> ... the uncontroverted existence of a bona fide athletic program for girls coupled with the physical and psychological differences ... also support the rationality of the IHSA's decision to conduct girls' interscholastic sports programs different from the boys'.

Thus, the district court entered summary judgment in favor of all defendants on the basis that the traditional equal protection standard "requires this court to defer to the judgment of the physical educators of the IHSA once a rational relationship has been shown to exist between their actions and the goals of interscholastic athletic competition."

3.33–3 Same Sport, Different Seasons

In *Striebel* v. *Minnesota State High School League (infra)*, the plaintiff women brought suit to move the girls' swimming season to the fall. They challenged the athletic association's policy of scheduling men's swimming in a different season (i.e., fall) from the women's season (i.e., winter). The women claimed they were being discriminated against on the basis of sex. The athletic association's decision was upheld. The court reasoned that there was a reasonable basis for the decision: the lack of available pool time for both women's and men's teams to practice and compete during the same season.

Striebel v. Minnesota State High School League, 321 N.W. 2d 400 (Minn. 1982)

This action was brought by Charlotte Striebel against the Minnesota State High School League (MSHSL), challenging the constitutionality of a MSHSL rule which authorized "separate seasons of play for high school athletic teams separated or substantially separated according to sex." The MSHSL had established separate seasons for boys and girls in tennis and swimming.

The district court held that the league's policy of establishing separate seasons for boys and girls was constitutional and in compliance with the statute. The court found that under the circumstances presented, separating teams by season was a "reasonable means of achieving maximum participation by both sexes in the high school athletic program."

On appeal, the Minnesota Supreme Court held that "where limited athletic facilities made it necessary to schedule high school boys' and girls' athletic teams in two separate seasons, and neither was substantially better than the other, that scheduling decision was not a denial of equal protection of the law."

3.40 Sex Discrimination in Athletic Employment

The following cases focus on sex discrimination in the area of athletic employment. The plaintiff is generally an employee who has been employed as a coach or physical education teacher.

3.41 Equal Pay Act and Title VII

Two separate statutes specifically pertain to discrimination in employment. The first is the Equal Pay Act, which was passed in 1963 (effective date was June 10, 1964). The second is Title VII of the Civil Rights Act of 1964. While the Equal Pay Act deals solely with wages paid to women and men within the same company, Title VII focuses on discriminatory hiring/firing practices and advancement policies within companies. Neither is specific to the issue of sex discrimination; however, they both encompass discrimination on the basis of race, religion, or national origin.

The Equal Pay Act stipulates that an employer must pay equal salaries to men and women holding jobs that require equal skill, effort, and responsibility and that are performed under similar working conditions. The jobs done need not be identical; they must only be substantially equal. For example, if there are differences between jobs, the employer must still pay equal wages if the variations are minor. Different salaries are permissible, however, when they are based not on the sex of the employees but on a bona fide seniority system or on merit increases. Consequently, the Equal Pay Act addresses only the most overt wage discrimination cases and does not apply to problems created by prior discrimination in the workplace.

The Labor Department's Division of Wages and Hours was initially responsible for enforcement of the Equal Pay Act under the Fair Labor Standards Acts (29 USC § 201 *et seq*). In 1979, enforcement was moved to the Equal Employment Opportunity Commission (EEOC). Enforcement procedures consist of routine checks as well as investigations in response to specific complaints. If a claim is substantiated and a violation is found, the complaining party may receive the difference between the wages paid to men and women for a maximum two-year period.

The other statute available to combat employment discrimination is Title VII. Title VII was enacted as a comprehensive prohibition on private acts of employment discrimination. It forbids discriminatory employment practices based on the race, color, religion, sex, or national origin of the applicant. These categories may, however, be used to differentiate between applicants when sex, religion, or national origin is a bona fide occupational qualification (BFOQ). A BFOQ is very narrowly defined as an actual job requirement, not merely a customer or employer preference. For example, race is never considered a BFOQ.

Title VII is applicable to all employers of more than 15 persons and it specifically covers almost all state and local government employees as well as employees of most educational institutions. It is enforced by the Equal Employment Opportunity Commission (EEOC), which has the authority to process and investigate any complaints. The EEOC may also bring suits in federal court if necessary. Enforcement of Title VII is not limited to EEOC actions, however, because the legislation also has individual and class causes of action.

The remedies of both injunctive and affirmative relief are available to the winning party in an employment discrimination suit. The prevailing party may be awarded back pay and attorney's fees as well as an injunction prohibiting the employer's unlawful action.

Both these approaches have limitations. Even taken together, they are not always sufficient to enforce a prohibition against sex discrimination. Although the Equal Pay Act applies to all employers, Title VII has been limited to employers of more than 15 people.

Thus, many smaller businesses are able to escape the mandates of Title VII. The Equal Pay Act is limited in other ways. For example, it is directed only to disrepancies in pay levels once on a job. It does not address the problem of discriminatory hiring or advancement policies. The basic weakness of these acts is that neither is all-encompassing. They fail to address the overall problems of sex discrimination that exist outside of the workplace. Thus, very few of the problems of discrimination encountered in athletics are addressed by either act. This legislation provides potential relief only in athletic employment.

The other major problem in pursuing litigation under these statutes is the cost. Neither provides any guaranteed basis for the eventual recovery of attorneys fees and/or double or triple damages. Thus litigation is not an option for many of those who might wish to file claims. Cases are seldom pursued, and the effectiveness of the legislation diminishes as the chance that an employer will be punished lessens. One last problem is that until recently, courts have been reluctant to interpret the statutes broadly. This reluctance stems from the fact that hiring and salary decisions are well within the area of management prerogatives allotted to employers. The court is reluctant to interfere in any discretionary decision unless there has been a clear abuse of that discretion. Thus, it is very difficult to establish a case based on a complaint regarding practices in either of these areas. Usually, the evidence is open to a variety of interpretations. Such circumstances can make it difficult or even impossible for a plaintiff to prevail in a sex discrimination case under application of the aforementioned statutes.

Kunda v. Muhlenberg College, 621 F. 2d 532 (3rd Cir. 1980)

This action involved an employment discrimination case based on sex. The plaintiff was a female physical education instructor at a private college. She was denied tenure because she lacked a master's degree, whereas three male members of the physical education department who lacked master's degrees were promoted. The court issued an injunction requiring defendant to promote plaintiff with tenure and back pay. The court of appeals affirmed the decision, stating that "Academic institutions' decisions are not *ipso facto* entitled to special treatment under federal laws prohibiting discrimination." The court noted that although the interests of an educational institution in academic freedom are important, academic freedom is not implicated in every academic employment decision.

NOTES

1. In *Caulfield v. Board of Education of City of New York*, 632 F. 2d 999 (2nd Cir. 1980), the court upheld a decision that Title IX applies to athletic hiring practices because discrimination against women's access to supervisory positions has a discriminating effect on the institution's students, the direct beneficiaries of federal financial aid. Coaching and other supervisory positions in athletic programs must be assigned without discrimination, even if the program receives no direct federal aid for funding these positions.

2. In *Cannon v. University of Chicago*, 60 L.Ed. 2d 560 (1979), 99 S. Ct. 1946, 441 U.S. 677, the court held that Title IX should be interpreted as being similar in intent to Title VI of the Civil Rights Act of 1964. The Supreme Court cited cases in which plaintiffs suing officials of the federal government under Title VI secured orders requiring those officials either to aid recipients of federal funds in devising nondiscriminatory alternatives to presently discriminatory programs or cut off aid to those programs. The court held that these rulings applied to Title IX situations as well.

3.42 Coaching

Allegations of discrimination based on sex have often been made in the area of coaching. Many of the claims are based on a lack of parity in pay between the coaches of male and female teams. Often coaches of women's teams — women, usually — are paid less than coaches of men's teams. According to the National Education Association, in the 1977–78 school year, only 28 percent of high school districts paid coaches equally. The justification most often made by school districts for the pay differential is that coaches of men's teams and coaches of women's teams do not do equivalent work. In order to redress the inequality in salary, women must prove they perform substantially equivalent work. Some factors that courts consider in making determinations are the nature of the game, the number of the players being supervised, the length of the playing season, the time taken up in practices, the amount of travel required, and any other responsibilities undertaken by the coach — for example — recruiting, scouting, academic counseling, and so forth.

In cases in which it is difficult for the coach of a women's team to meet the standard of "equivalent work," the argument has been made that the work *is* more difficult. Plaintiff coaches of women's teams have argued that girls have not been as exposed to sports as boys; therefore, coaches of women's teams often spend much more time actually teaching their players. They do not have the luxury of merely retaining the skills of a player who has participated in that sport for a number of years. Instead, they often coach women who have had no experience in the particular sport at all. However, as women's sports programs proliferate at the youth levels, this argument is becoming less effective.

Textor v. Board of Regents of Northern Illinois University, 711 F.2d 1387 (7th Cir. 1983)

Alice Textor, a female women's athletic director and coach, appealed an order of the U.S. District Court (N.D. Ill.) that denied her motion to amend her complaint, which alleged that the Mid-American Conference had practiced sex discrimination in its operation of the intercollegiate athletic conference. The appeals court remanded the case to the district court to allow the plaintiff to file an amended complaint. The appeals court noted in part that:

Plaintiff-appellant Alice Textor appeals the district court's denial of her motion for leave to file an amended complaint while her attorneys appeal the court's award of attorney's fees based on its finding that they were guilty of willful abuse of the judicial process . . .

Plaintiff was employed by defendant Northern Illinois University (NIU) as women's athletic director and coach of women's basketball and tennis. In January of 1980 attorney Deidrich filed this class-action suit on behalf of plaintiff and other similarly situated women against the Mid-America Conference (MAC), member colleges of MAC, and MAC Commissioner Fred Jacoby. The complaint alleged constitutional and statutory violations stemming from defendants' disparate treatment of men's and women's athletics. . . .

Plaintiff attempted to remedy the defects relied upon by the district court in dismissing the out-of-state defendants by amending the complaint to include an allegation that defendants had conspired to discriminate against women's athletics in violation of the Constitution and several federal statutes. Among these allegations were the following:

[Defendants] have engaged in annual and other conference meetings and discussions within Illinois, including DeKalb, Illinois, and have held meetings with the Council of Presidents and the Conference of Deans for such Conference in DeKalb, Illinois, and at such meetings and conferences, issued directives and requests regarding women's athletics.

Said defendants have, in concert with each other, agreed to and followed a pattern in disregard to deprive female athletic directors and coaches of due process of law, equal protection of the laws and of other rights guaranteed in whole or in part by various statutory and constitutional provisions heretofore enumerated; and in furtherance thereof, said defendants acted as described hereinafter described [sic] in Paragraph 22, and that the effect of their actions in conspiracy has been felt by plaintiffs in Illinois and by other females similarly situated.

The alleged effects of the conspiracy included lower pay for women coaches, differences between the length of contracts entered into with men and women coaches, and scheduling inequities. Plaintiff alleged that defendants obtained their objectives because they "acted in concert by joining together by a conspiracy to keep such salaries of plaintiff and others low with a disparate differential."

In paragraph 22 of the amended complaint plaintiff further alleged that:

22. In furtherance of said conspiracy, Defendant Universities in or about August, 1979, did donate and give $1,000.00 dollars each to the Defendant Conference and Commissioner for payment to a lobby in Washington, D.C., for the purpose of urging on behalf of said Defendants that certain athletic endeavors of Defendants be exempted from application and regulations of Title IX, and that said conduct was done without consultation with any of the Plaintiffs and contrary to the philosophy and terms of Title IX and of other statutes and regulations heretofore described herein.

There does not seem to be any question that if plaintiff's complaint alleges an actionable conspiracy then the minimum contacts test has been met. The "conspiracy theory" of personal jurisdiction is based on the "time honored notion that the acts of [a] conspirator in furtherance of a conspiracy may be attributed to the other members of the conspiracy." ...

In denying leave to amend the court analyzed paragraph 22 of the amended complaint and concluded that it failed to allege an actionable conspiracy. We agree. Plaintiff alleges in paragraph 22 that defendants gave financial support to a lobbying effort directed toward legislative change of Title IX. Plaintiff has not explained to us why defendants' support of legislative change is illegal, and we can see no possible basis for holding that this action supports a charge of illegal conspiracy. ...

The inadequacies of paragraph 22 do not necessarily spell defeat for plaintiff. Plaintiff need only present a prima facie showing of personal jurisdiction, and in appraising her allegations we must read the complaint liberally, in its entirety, and with every inference drawn in favor of plaintiff. ...

Read liberally plaintiff's amended complaint alleges that defendants agreed to follow a systematic campaign of discrimination against women's athletics. As defendants were in competition with each other in recruiting women's coaches the success of their plan to keep women's salaries low depended on the cooperation of all MAC members. In furtherance of, and in accordance with, this conspiracy defendant NIU discriminated against female members of the athletic department. The illegal actions of NIU in Illinois are enough to provide the requisite minimum contacts between the remaining members of the conspiracy and the State of Illinois. In addition, it is a fair inference that the treatment of women's athletics was discussed by the conspirators during the alleged meeting in DeKalb, Illinois. Such action is sufficient basis for the exercise of personal jurisdiction and service of process may be affected under the Illinois long-arm statute. ...

Because the district court abused its discretion in denying leave to amend we vacate the order dismissing the out-of-state defendants and order the district court to allow plaintiff to file her amended complaint. We intimate no view on the merits of defendants' remaining arguments concerning standing and certification of the class. Plaintiff, of course, must be prepared to prove the alleged conspiracy at the appropriate time.

Burkey v. Marshall County Board of Education, 513 F. Supp. 1084 (N.D. W. Va. 1981)

Plaintiff Burkey instituted a girl's basketball program at a junior high school in West Virginia during the 1971–72 school year. She posted a career mark of 31–5 in the four years she coached the team. In the 1973–74 season, plaintiff received nominal remuneration for coaching. In keeping with school board policies, plaintiff was paid one-half of the amount given to the coach of the junior high boys' team. Additionally, she was prevented from coaching the boys' team, solely on the basis of her sex.

Plaintiff complained to both state and federal authorities about the alleged discrimination. In 1977, HEW issued a finding that the school district's operation of the girls' athletic program violated the rights of women coaches and female students as protected under Title IX. The Equal Employment Opportunity Commission (EEOC) also found reasonable cause to believe the board's policies constituted unlawful sex discrimination against Burkey. Plaintiff was removed as coach and transferred from the junior high to an elementary school after she filed a complaint with the West Virginia Human Rights Commission.

Plaintiff brought suit against the school board, alleging sexual discrimination in violation of rights granted to her by Title VII, the Civil Rights Act of 1971, and the Equal Pay Act. The court found for the plaintiff and awarded her $1,260 in lost back pay. It also ordered the school board to offer plaintiff the next available vacant physical education teaching position in either the junior or senior high school, and to offer her the head coach's position for girls' basketball at that school.

California Women's Coaches Academy v. California Interscholastic Federation, Case No. 77–1270 LEW (C.D. Cal. 1980) (settled)

In 1977, the California Women's Coaches Academy and three individual members of the academy filed a class action on behalf of themselves and certain other female coaches and officials for girls' high school interscholastic athletic contests. Defendants were the California Interscholastic Federation (CIF); the Federated Council, Northern Section, North Coast Section, San Joaquin Section, San Francisco City Section, Central Coast Section, Central Section, Los Angeles City Section, Southern Section, and San Diego Section, which are the regional subdivisions of the CIF; the California Department of Education; and Wilson Riles, the superintendent of public instruction and director of education for the state of California.

Plaintiffs made certain allegations of unlawful sex discrimination, including charges that the defendants:

1. Excluded women from participating in the Federated Council.
2. Established fewer interscholastic sports for girls than for boys.
3. Established shorter seasons for girls than for boys.

4. Discriminated on the basis of sex in the hiring of persons to appoint officials for girls' contests.
5. Discriminated on the basis of sex in the hiring of officials for girls' contests.
6. Established lower rates of pay for officials of girls' interscholastic athletics.

Defendants CIF, Federated Council, and member sections denied all charges against them. Defendants State Department and Wilson Riles made the following admissions:

1. The opportunity for females to act as voting members of CIF and the governing bodies of member sections was limited by the policy of allowing only superintendents, high school principals, and members of high school administrative staffs to participate as voting members.
2. The rules and regulations of all defendants provided for a smaller number of approved sports for girls than for boys.
3. The rules and regulations allowed girls' athletics to be scheduled for shorter seasons and fewer contests per season than boys' interscholastic athletics, the effect of which was to provide fewer employment opportunities for female coaches and officials than for their male counterparts.

The litigation proceeded, pursuant to Rule 23(b)–(2) of the Federal Rules of Civil Procedure, as a class action on behalf of the following class of persons:

All females in the State of California who are qualified by training and experience to coach or officiate for pay at girls high school interscholastic athletic contests sponsored by any of the defendants.

The settlement between plaintiffs and defendants State Department and Wilson Riles included the following conditions:

1. Each secondary school will be required to conduct a survey to determine the interest of its students in participating in and

supporting teams for interscholastic sports.

2. Females will be given substantial opportunities to participate as voting members of the governing structure for interscholastic athletics.
3. Discrimination between boys and girls in interscholastic programs will not be allowed.
4. The settlement is to be implemented in the 1980–81 academic year.
5. Plaintiffs agree not to seek attorney's fees or costs.
6. The State Department will obtain annually from each member Section of CIF its rules and regulations and assurances of compliance with the provisions of the settlement.

The settlement between plaintiffs and defendant Los Angeles City Section included the following conditions:

1. Discrimination between boys and girls in interscholastic athletic programs will not be allowed.
2. The settlement is to be implemented in the 1980–81 academic year.
3. Plaintiffs agree not to seek attorney's fees.

The settlement between plaintiffs and CIF, Federated Council, and member sections included the following conditions:

1. CIF defendants will not assume the responsibility of policing compliance by individual schools with the law in regard to sex discrimination.
2. In the event of a court determination that a member of CIF is in noncompliance with applicable sex discrimination laws, CIF will undertake suspension or other sanctions deemed appropriate.
3. CIF defendants agree to pay $7,500 to plaintiffs' counsel toward plaintiffs' attorneys' fees, costs, and expenses.

The following is a summary of the terms and conditions that were common to all three of the settlements:

1. The number of sports available to female athletes will equal approximately the same number as those available to male athletes.
2. Levels of competition and scheduling will be determined without regard to the sex of the athlete.
3. Facilities will be made available without regard to the sex of the athlete.
4. The length of the season in identical sports will consist of an equal number of weeks.
5. Appointments to officiate and rates of officials' pay for identical sports will be determined without regard to the sex of the athletes or the officials.
6. Plaintiffs and class members will relinquish any claims they had for lost wages and lost employment opportunities due to past discrimination by defendants.
7. Defendants need not schedule identical sports during the same season as long as it is not to the detriment of one sex over another.

NOTES

1. In *Jackson* v. *Armstrong School District*, 430 F. Supp. 1050 (W.D. Pa. 1977), an action was brought by plaintiffs Jackson and Pollick, who were women's basketball coaches. They claimed the school district had violated Title VII and the Pennsylvania Human Relations Act by paying them significantly less than the male coaches of the men's basketball team. There were four men and four women within the district coaching women's basketball who were all paid equally. The court ruled in favor of the defendant, finding that it lacked jurisdiction under the State Human Relations Act and that the plaintiffs' claim was not valid.

2. In *Kenneweg* v. *Hampton Township School District*, 438 F. Supp. 575 (W.D. Pa. 1977), plaintiffs Kenneweg and Love sued the Armstrong School District on grounds of sex discrimination. They were both coaches and claimed they were paid less because of their sex. The court held that because the charge filed with the Equal Employment Opportunity Commission had dealt only with the question of pay, the complaint could not be amended to allege discrimination with respect to working conditions. The

court also held that the actions of the school district in paying female coaches of female sports less than male coaches of male sports did not constitute discrimination based on sex. The court decided for the defendant, stating that the claim was based on a Title VII argument and "disparity in treatment not based on plaintiffs' sex is not a valid claim under Title VII."

3. In *State Division of Human Rights* v. *Syracuse City Teachers Ass'n.*, 412 N.Y.S. 2d 711 (App. Div. 1979), an action was brought by two female coaches who had filed a complaint with the State Division of Human Rights. The women had agreed to coach the junior high girls' basketball team as volunteers and were not paid. The women later found that the male basketball coach was receiving $308 to coach the boys' team. The commissioner of the Human Rights Division found that the board of education had discriminated against the women and ordered equal payment.

The court overturned the commission's decision and held for the defendant. It found no discrimination in employment by the board. The court reasoned that both the male and female coaches were treated equally and that the unequal pay schedule was reasonable because the job responsibilities and time commitment differed.

4. In *United Teachers of Seaford* v. *New York State Human Rights Appeal Board*, 414 N.Y.S. 2d 207 (App. Div. 1979), the court held that a union has the obligation to represent its member coaches fairly and impartially and may not discriminate on the basis of race or sex. The fundamental purpose of a union is to provide for its members the bargaining power that unity creates; when a union fails to exercise that power in the bargaining process and permits an employer to discriminate against union members, it discriminates against them as surely as if it proposed the inequitable agreement. Evidence proved that the union was aware of the unduly low salaries and that the union had settled for an agreement that grossly discriminated against female coaches.

5. In *Kings Park Central School District No. 5* v. *State Division of Human Rights*, 424 N.Y.S. 2d 293 (App. Div. 1980), the petitioners asked the court to review a decision of the State Division of Human Rights finding unlawful discrimination by the petitioner in paying coaches of boys' teams more than girls' teams. The court granted the petition and found no discrimination by the school district. Although the skill, effort, and responsibility were equal, coaching boys' teams required greater coaching time and travel.

6. For further information on *Textor*, see the district court opinion in *Textor* v. *Board of Regents*, 87 F.R.D. 751 (N.D. Ill. 1980).

7. For further information, see "Equal Pay for Coaches of Female Teams: Finding a Cause of Action under Federal Law," 55 *Notre Dame Law Review* 751 (June 1980).

3.43   Sports-Related Employment Discrimination

While Title IX has been available as a basis to contest sex discrimination in coaching, attacks on perceived inequalities in other sports-related employment have largely consisted of allegations of the denial of equal protection rights. Cases regarding discrimination in officiating, refereeing, and media coverage have stemmed from charges that employment practices, and specifically exclusionary rules, are arbitrary, are related to no legitimate purpose, and are therefore violations of the plaintiffs' constitutional rights.

3.43–1   Officiating

Arbitrary height and weight requirements for umpires and referees may act unlawfully to discriminate against women. When such requirements are not sufficiently related to the job, they may be deemed to be arbitrary and thus impose unconstitutional restrictions.

New York State Division of Human Rights v. New York–Pennsylvania Professional Baseball League, 36 App. Div. 2d 364, 320 N.Y.S. 2d 788 (1971), *aff'd.*, 29 N.Y. 2d 921, 279 N.E. 2d 856, 329 N.Y.S. 2d 920 (1972)

In this sex discrimination case, the plaintiff, acting upon a complaint of female umpire Bernice Gera, charged the defendant with a violation of a state statute (Sec. 296, Executive Law) prohibiting employment discrimination. The New York Supreme Court, Appellate Division, held that league rules requiring an umpire to stand at least 5′10″ tall and weigh at least 170 pounds "were not justified by the claim that umpires must command respect of big men or by factors relating to increased size of professional catchers, physical strain, travel conditions and length of games, and that the standards were inherently discriminatory against women." The league was ordered to cease and desist such discrimination.

3.43–2 Participation in Professional Sports

Although females have competed with males on all levels of amateur athletics, relatively few women have entered as participants into professional sports. Sex discrimination cases litigated in regard to female participation in professional sports have largely concerned professional wrestling. These cases have not centered on the right to participate with men but rather on the constitutionality of rules that refuse women the right to petition for and receive a professional wrestling license. Plaintiffs have relied on equal protection claims to challenge these exclusionary rules.

Calzadilla v. Dooley, 29 App. Div. 2d 152, 286 N.Y.S. 2d 510 (1968)

This discrimination suit was brought by a woman wrestler, who alleged the refusal by the state's athletic commission to grant her a professional wrestling license constituted a violation of the Fourteenth Amendment's equal protection clause. In arguing that "a great deal of latitude and discretion must be accorded the State Athletic Commission," the court held that the commission's rule against granting wrestling licenses to women was not "an unjust and unconstitutional discrimination against women." The court reasoned that no one had an inherent right to participate in public wrestling exhibitions.

NOTES ―――――――――――――――

1. In *Hesseltine* v. *State Athletic Commission*, 126 N.E. 2d 631 (Ill. 1955), plaintiff Hesseltine (also known as Rose Roman) applied through normal procedures for a permit to wrestle. The Illinois State Athletic Commission rejected her application. She appealed to the circuit court and won. The commission appealed. The appeals court affirmed the lower court decision. The defendant's adoption of a rule excluding women from wrestling within the state was seen as arbitrary and therefore invalid.

2. In *State* v. *Hunter*, 208 Ore. 282, 300 P. 2d 455 (1956), defendant Hunter, a female wrestler, was prosecuted by the state for competing in a wrestling match that was held in violation of a statutory ban on women's

wrestling. The court ruled in favor of the state, holding that the ban on women's participation in wrestling was not unconstitutional.

3. In *Whitehead* v. *Krulewitch*, 25 App. Div. 2d 956, 271 N.Y.S. 2d 565 (1966), plaintiff Whitehead appealed a ruling of the New York Special Term Court denying her a professional wrestling license. The New York Supreme Court, Appellate Division affirmed the decision.

4. For further information, see the following law review article: "Employment and Athletics Are Outside HEW's Jurisdiction," 65 *Georgetown Law Journal* 49 (October 1976).

3.43–3 The News Media

Barring members of the news media has been an area of concern for many sports organizations. If a barred reporter is female (see *Ludtke* v. *Kuhn, infra*), and male members of the news media are not similarly restricted, she may allege a violation of equal protection of the laws under the Fourteenth Amendment. In all Fourteenth Amendment cases, the plaintiff must demonstrate that state action is involved before relief under the Fourteenth Amendment can be considered (see Section 1.31). The court in *Ludtke* found such state action because the New York Yankees had leased their stadium from the city of New York, a subdivision of the state. Private universities that lease stadiums from the state, municipal, or local governments could face a similar result. When public institutions such as state universities are involved, a court is likely to find state action without the need for such a relationship with a facility. A court is likely to have difficulty finding state action when a private institution (for example, the Boston Red Sox) does not lease from a governmental entity but instead owns its playing facility.

The *Ludtke* decision is the only reported case involving a rule barring female reporters from a male locker room. One important issue — the players' right to privacy — remains unanswered after *Ludtke*. In *Ludtke*, the court found that the players' right to privacy had been negated by the presence of television cameras in the locker room. If the right of privacy is not negated in a future case, the court will have to strike a balance between the players' right to privacy and the female reporters' right not to be discriminated against.

Ludtke v. Kuhn, 461 F. Supp. 86 (S.D.N.Y. 1978)

This civil rights action suit sought an injunction by plaintiff Ludtke, a female reporter for *Sports Illustrated* magazine. The plaintiff sought an order "enjoining defendants, the New York Yankees, from enforcing a policy determination made by Baseball Commissioner Kuhn, and approved by American League President MacPhail, which required that accredited female sports reporters be excluded from the locker room of the Yankee clubhouse in Yankee Stadium." Defendants admitted that accredited male sports reporters could enter the locker room after a ball game for the purpose of interviewing ballplayers and that such fresh-off-the-field interviews were important to the work of sports reporters.

The court was asked to decide whether the Kuhn policy determination

> constitutes state action within the contemplation of the Fourteenth Amendment to the Federal Constitution and, if so, whether it violates (1) plaintiff Ludtke's right to the equal protection of the laws guaranteed by that Amendment, (2) the right of both plaintiffs to freedom of the press guaranteed by the First Amendment, or (3) plaintiff's rights under the state's equal accommodations statute.

The court found that there was no genuine issue as to the material fact and that plaintiff is entitled to judgment as a matter of law.

The defendants argued that women reporters were excluded from the locker rooms "in order (1) to protect the privacy of those players who are undressed or in various stages of undressing and getting ready to shower; (2) to protect the image of baseball as a family sport; and, (3) preservation of traditional notions of decency and propriety."

The court ruled on the basis of *Burton* v. *Wilmington Parking Authority*, 365 U.S. 715, 81 S.Ct. 856, 6 L.Ed. 2d 45 (1961), and *Gilmore* v. *City of Montgomery*, 417 U.S. 556, 94 S.Ct. 2416, 41 L. Ed. 2d 304 (1974), that the city of New York's ownership of Yankee Stadium and the lease arrangement with the Yankees were such as to make the Kuhn policy determination state action within the contemplation of the Fourteenth Amendment. The court held that Yankee Stadium, where the discriminatory acts occurred, is publicly owned and leased pursuant to special legislative provisions to the Yankees.

Having found state action, the court then decided that the total exclusion of women from the Yankees' locker room infringed upon both the equal protection and due process rights of Ludtke. In discussing equal protection, the court stated:

> On the basis of the undisputed facts, plaintiff Ludtke, while in pursuit of her profession as a sports reporter, was treated differently from her male counterparts (other properly accredited sportswriters) solely because she is a woman. . . . The court holds that defendants' policy of total exclusion of women sports reporters from the locker room at Yankee Stadium is not substantially related to the privacy protection objective and thus deprives plaintiff Ludtke of that equal protection of the laws which is guaranteed her by the Fourteenth Amendment.

In regard to due process, the court stated:

> An analysis of these same facts from the perspective of substantive due process leads us to an identical result. The right to pursue one's profession is a fundamental "liberty" within the meaning of the Fourteenth Amendment's due process guarantee. . . .
>
> . . . [T]he Kuhn policy substantially and directly interferes with the right of plaintiff Ludtke to pursue her profession as a sports reporter. Her male counterparts are able to get to the ballplayers fresh-off-the-field when comments about plays may still be in progress, for example.
>
> When a statutory classification significantly interferes with the exercise of a fundamental right, it cannot be upheld unless it is supported by sufficiently important state interests and is closely tailored to effectuate only those interests.

The undisputed facts show that the Yankees' interest in protecting ballplayer privacy may be fully served by much less sweeping means than that implemented here. The court holds that the state action complained of unreasonably interferes with plaintiff Ludtke's fundamental right to pursue her profession in violation of the due process clause of the Fourteenth Amendment.

The other two interests asserted by defendants, maintaining the status of baseball as a family sport and conforming to traditional notions of decency and propriety, are clearly too insubstantial to merit serious consideration. Weighed against plaintiff's right to be free of discrimination based upon her sex, and her fundamental right to pursue her profession, such objectives cannot justify the defendants' policy under the equal protection or due process clauses of the Fourteenth Amendment.

Since plaintiff Ludtke has been deprived, under color of the authority of the state, of rights secured to her by both the due process and equal protection clauses of the Fourteenth Amendment to the Federal Constitution, 42 U.S.C. § 1983, she is entitled to the injunctive relief sought and to an award of counsel fees. . . .

NOTES ————————————————————

1. Counsel for Kuhn and Major League Baseball decided not to appeal *Ludtke* v. *Kuhn*, since they believed that the decision was not a damaging precedent. (See *NCAA Public Relations and Promotions Manual*, NCAA publication, Mission, Kansas, 1983, Appendix C.)

2. Most major league sports teams routinely allow female sports writers into their locker rooms. A few leagues — for example, the National Basketball Association and the United States Football League — have written policies that give women equal access with men to the locker room. Other leagues allow individual teams to set locker-room policies. For further information, see "Women Sports Writers Gaining in Struggle for Equality, Respect," *NCAA News*, December 28, 1983, pp. 3, 5.

3. The NCAA requires that its championship teams open locker rooms to all certified members of the media after a 10-minute cooling-off period. See, for instance, *1983 Men's and Women's Soccer National Collegiate Championships Handbook*, NCAA publication, Mission, Kansas, 1983, p. 49.

4. In March 1985, Major League Baseball Commissioner Peter Ueberroth issued a directive to all clubs, "Club/Media Procedures — 1985," in which he noted that in the past MLB has had excellent cooperation with the media, but that, "An exception has been in the area of access permitted accredited women reporters. We now are saying that clubhouses will be open and all accredited members of the media will be given the same access." For further information, see "Baseball Adopts Open-Door Policy," *New York Times*, March 22, 1985, p. A23.

5. For further information on media access to locker rooms, see "Civil Rights in the Locker Room," 2 *Journal of Communication and Entertainment Law*, 645 (Summer 1980).

Chapter 4

TORT LIABILITY

4.00   Tort Liability and Its Relationship to Sports

Tort liability is a major concern today in both professional and amateur sports. Chapter 4 sets forth a number of the problems and issues that face both professional and amateur sports organizations and associations as well as the various individuals who are associated with sports. The material this chapter presents could have been organized by legal principles involved, by possible defendants, or by possible plaintiffs. As a compromise, the chapter is organized by both legal principles and possible defendants. Therefore, an organization by potential plaintiffs was not deemed practical since such an arrangement would have simply been a reorganization of the cases contained in the defendants' section. Chapter 4 differs in its organization from the other chapters in that Section 4.10, "Legal Principles in Tort Law," presents a separate section on basic principles of tort law. This has been done to give the nonlawyer/nonlaw student a basic introduction to tort law and to give the reader a cross-referencing device to search for cases by legal theory. In order to reduce repetition, note cases are used in most of the subsections in Section 4.10.

Sections 4.11 to 4.17 discuss the basic legal principles of tort law that are most often involved in sports. The legal principles defining the intentional torts of assault and battery are set forth in Section 4.11. Section 4.12 discusses negligence, which is the most common theory found in sports tort cases. The theory of vicarious liability, often used in tort cases to sue an employer for the negligence of an employee, follows in Section 4.13. Sections 4.14, 4.15 and 4.16 cover the torts of defamation, invasion of privacy, and intentional infliction of emotional distress. Finally, Section 4.17 presents the basic principles of products liability law. A further discussion and application of products liability to the sports world appears in Section 4.30.

The format for Section 4.20, as previously mentioned, differs from the first part of Chapter 4 in that the subsections are organized by possible defendants in sports tort cases. Section 4.21 discusses the potential liabilities of a participant in a sporting event. Section 4.22 explores the potential liabilities of coaches and physical education teachers in the areas of supervision (Section 4.22–1), instruction and training (Section 4.22–2), medical assistance (Section 4.22–3), and vicarious liability for actions of fans and players (Section 4.22–4). The legal theory most commonly used in this area is negligence.

Section 4.23 focuses on the potential liabilities of administrators, schools, and universities. Administrators, for example, may be found negligent in hiring personnel (perhaps a coach or physical education teacher) or in supervising personnel (Section 4.23–1). An administrator may also be found vicariously liable for the negligence of an employee who attempts to render medical assistance (Section 4.23–2). Finally, the administrator may be found negligent for not providing equipment, or vicariously liable if an employee did not furnish equipment or furnished ill-fitting or defective equipment (Section 4.23–3). Schools and universities can be sued under a vicarious liability theory for the negligence of any of their employees in the areas of supervision and personnel (Section 4.23–1), medical assistance (Section 4.23–2), and equipment (Section 4.23–3). A possible defense for the administrator, school, or university — the doctrine of sovereign immunity — is discussed in Section 4.23–4.

Section 4.24 investigates the liability of professional teams and leagues and focuses primarily on their potential liability for the actions of their players. Although this may be a potential liability area for schools and universities, there are no reported cases to date. Another area that is covered in Section 4.24 is spectator injury from projectiles leaving the playing area. In most cases in which a team has been sued, however, there are other potential defendants, including the athlete, the security guards, and the facility owner and possessor.

Section 4.25 covers the liability of facility owners and possessors, including liability from defects in a building or negligent supervision of a crowd. Section 4.26 discusses the liability of medical personnel for negligent treatment of an injured athlete or fan. Section 4.27 explores a newly developing area of sports torts, the potential liabilities of officials, referees, and umpires. Some officials, for example, have been sued for injuries to athletes that have allegedly resulted from a failure to take corrective action to remedy an injury-causing situation. Such situations may include failing to stop a game during inclement weather conditions or allowing objects or spectators to be too close to the playing area. Officials, referees, and umpires have also been sued for incorrectly applying games rules and making incorrect judgment calls.

Section 4.30 presents cases involving defects in equipment. Section 4.40 discusses liability insurance and how high school athletic associations and high schools are purchasing insurance to combat the rising number of tort claims being made by those associated with sports activities. The National Collegiate Athletic Association is also endorsing liability insurance, beginning in the 1985–86 academic year. The final topic discussed in the chapter is the waiver and releases of liability (see Section 4.50).

Tort law is an important area of sports law. The number of cases filed that are based on intentional or nonintentional tort theories is on the increase. (See *Gaspard* v. *Grain Dealers Mutual Insurance* Co. and *Hackbart* v. *Cincinnati Bengals, Inc.* in Section 4.21.) There are many reasons for this upward trend, including the astronomical rise in medical costs that injured players are unable to meet, along with a prevailing notion that one who injures deliberately or negligently should pay for such action when it creates catastrophic consequences.

Civil law provides the injured individual with a cause of action by which one may be compensated or "made whole" through the recovery of damages. This cause of action comes under the general heading of "torts." A tort is a private (or civil) wrong or injury, other than a breach of contract, suffered by an individual as the result of another person's conduct. The law of torts deals with the allocation of losses arising from human activities and provides for the adjustment of these losses via the compensation of the individual for injuries sustained as the result of another's conduct.

Civil law and criminal law share the common end of inducing people to act for the benefit of society by preventing behavior that negatively affects society or by encouraging behavior that has a positive effect. Civil law and criminal law differ, however, in their means of achieving this similar end. The purpose of criminal law is to protect the public from harm through the punishment of conduct likely to cause harm. Tort law, on the other hand, aims to compensate (to "make whole") an injured party for the harm suffered as a result of another person's conduct.

Varying interpretations of criminal and civil offenses lead to divergent methods of action in these two areas of law. Criminal actions emphasize the immorality or bad intentions of the defendants. Tort actions, on the other hand, seek to achieve desirable social results by resolving the conflicting interests of individuals. Society tends to distinguish criminal wrongs from civil wrongs by condemning or judging the morality of the criminal more severely than that of the tortious wrongdoer. Once a crime has been discovered, the state or a subdivision of the state, in its capacity as protector of the public interest, brings an action against the accused (see Chapter 5 on criminal law). In a tort action, however, the injured party institutes the action as an individual in an effort to recover damages as compensation for the injury received.

The following seven areas are covered by the law of torts, and each can be further defined either by the nature of the defendant's conduct or by the nature of the harm resulting to the plaintiff:

1. Intentional harm to the person
2. Intentional harm to tangible property
3. Negligence
4. Nuisance
5. Strict liability
6. Harm to tangible personal interests
7. Harm to tangible property interests

The most common tort actions arising from the area of sports law result from intentional harm to the person, negligence, and strict liability. Therefore, the emphasis in this chapter is on these areas. The area (civil or criminal) under which the action will be brought is determined by the relationship of the potential plaintiff to the potential defendant and by the nature of the action or nonaction that caused the injury.

Common problems are faced by the majority of sports-related tort cases. The first is the difficulty of determining exactly what a tort is in a sports context (see Section 4.11–3[a] on consent and Section 4.12–5[d] on assumption of risk). The second problem, a public-policy consideration, is whether court interference with sports destroys amateur athletics and unreasonably restricts the free play of sports. The third common problem is that litigation may discourage participation in the more dangerous sports.

NOTE

1. For further information, see the following articles:
(a) "Compensating Injured Professional Athletes: The Mystique of Sport versus Traditional Tort Principles," 55 *New York University Law Review* 971 (1980).
(b) "Property Rights, Risk Sharing, and Player Disability in Major League Baseball," 25 *Journal of Law and Economics* 343 (October 1982).
(c) "Sports Torts and School Athletics," 37 *Washington State Business News* 21 (October 1983).
(d) "Compensation for Injuries Due to Sport," 54 *Australian Law Journal* 588 (October 1980).

4.10 Legal Principles in Tort Law

The distinction between intentional and nonintentional torts is important in the area of tort law. The degree of the defendant's intent toward the plaintiff (intent to harm) can be differentiated on the following three "levels":

1. *Intentional tort* (for example, assault and battery): intent to commit the act and intent to harm the plaintiff (see *Tomjanovich* v. *California Sports, Inc.* in Section 4.24).
2. *Reckless misconduct*: intent to commit the act but no intent to harm the plaintiff. This is often called gross negligence (see *Hackbart* v. *Cincinnati Bengals* in Section 4.21).
3. *Negligence*: no intent to commit the act and no intent to harm the plaintiff — a failure to exercise reasonable care (see Section 4.12).

On a continuum ranking the three types of torts, gross negligence falls somewhere between intentional torts and mere ordinary negligence. It differs from negligence in degree rather than in substance. One single act may be seen as either negligent or grossly negligent, depending on the intent of the actor.

NOTE _____

1. For further information, see the following article and book:
   (a) "Comment, a Proposed Legislative Solution to the Problem of Violent Acts by Participants during Professional Sporting Events," 7 *University of Dayton Law Review* 91 (1981).
   (b) J. Weistart and C. Lowell, *The Law of Sports* (Charlottesville, Virginia, 1979).

4.11   Assault and Battery

The torts of assault and battery are usually linked in criminal law. Most state statutes broadly define criminal assault to include both attempted and actual battery. Such is not the case in civil law where assault and battery are more specifically defined and where the two actions constitute separate and distinct torts. Further elaboration will clarify the distinction between the criminal and civil law views of assault and battery. A civil law battery is an unpermitted touching of another person while

assault is the apprehension of imminent harmful contact. For civil assault and battery, as for all intentional torts, there does not have to be harm to the plaintiff to establish a charge of assault and/or battery. The harm will, however, be important in assessing monetary damages.

In torts involving intentional harm to the person, the plaintiff may recover for lost earning capacity, medical expenses, pain and suffering, and the loss of consortium. These are termed actual damages. Unlike negligence, however, it is not necessary in an intentional tort case to prove actual damages to recover. The plaintiff may recover substantial damages even though he does not prove specific bodily injuries. Torts involving intentional harm allow for recovery of damages for emotional suffering (for example, humiliation, indignity, or injury to feelings) as long as this suffering was proximately caused by the defendant's conduct. Certain conduct on the part of the plaintiff that is not sufficient to constitute a defense to the action may be considered in mitigation or moderation of damages. For instance, although provocative words by the plaintiff do not justify the defendant's use of force, these words may be considered in mitigation of the damages awarded to the plaintiff.

Intentional torts such as assault and battery are actions characterized by focusing on the defendant's state of mind. An intentional tort includes a wrong perpetrated on a person or on intangible or real property. There does not have to be an actual injury to recover for the wrong done. The mere fact that a person has done and intended to do a prescribed action will suffice to provide at least nominal damages. In the sports setting, the intentional torts most often encountered are assault and battery.

In addition to actual damages, a plaintiff may recover exemplary or punitive damages when the defendant has acted willfully or has exhibited outrageous conduct. These damages are awarded on the theory that they may help to deter future wrongful conduct. They have also been justified on the theory that they help remedy the lack of money available to pay for plaintiff's litigation expenses, which are normally unavailable under American civil procedure. Punitive damages are awarded, not according to the tort committed (although they are often given for assault and battery), but for the defendant's intentional conduct. Punitive damages are available only for intentional tort cases and are not awarded in negligence cases.

4.11–1 Assault

For an action to constitute assault, three elements must be present: the intent to cause harm by the defendant, the apprehension of immediate harm by the plaintiff, and the lack of consent by the plaintiff. With the first element, the plaintiff does not have to prove that the defendant intended to inflict bodily harm. With the second element, the apprehension to the plaintiff must be reasonable. For example, claims that a plaintiff is extraordinarily timid will not lower the court's standard of reasonable apprehension. However, the defendant will be held responsible when the defendant knows of the plaintiff's timidness.

The *apparent* ability to carry out a threat as opposed to *actual* ability to do so is what the court relies on in determining assault. The defendant who claims that he had no intention of carrying out a threat will not be successful. For example, a claim by the defendant that the gun was not loaded will not be a successful defense when the reasonable person would be placed in apprehension of immediate harm by the defendant's actions. The reasoning is that the plaintiff had no way of knowing whether or not the gun was loaded.

The third element required in an assault action is lack of consent, which means that a plaintiff has not consented to the alleged assault. The consent issue is extremely important in sports cases in which the court may have difficulty in distinguishing between consented to contact, such as apprehension and intimidation, as opposed to unconsented to activities.

Actual contact between the defendant and the plaintiff need not occur for assault to have been committed; however, the plaintiff must be aware of the possibility of contact. The distinction between actual physical contact and the mere apprehension of it marks the dividing line between assault and battery.

4.11–2 Battery

For an action to constitute battery, three elements must be present: the intent to touch by the defendant, actual touching, and the lack of consent to the contact by the plaintiff. With the first element, the plaintiff does not have to prove that the defendant intended the specific harm that the victim incurred. The rationale is that the defendant is presumed to have intended the natural and probable consequences of the act. However, a touching that results from a reflex action is not considered intentional.

With the second element, the mere apprehension of contact is not sufficient; rather, actual contact must occur for a plaintiff to prove that a defendant's action constituted battery. The plaintiff's awareness of the contact or force at the time of the battery is not essential. Plaintiffs have made successful battery claims in cases in which the contact occurred when they were asleep or under anesthesia. Contact does not necessarily have to be harmful but may instead be offensive, such as spitting at another person. The act must cause and be intended to cause an unconsented contact by the defendant.

The third element required in a battery action is lack of consent to the contact by the plaintiff. The determination of whether or not consent existed is often difficult; factors such as the time of the act and the place in which it occurred must be considered. The element of consent is crucial to both assault and battery, especially in the sports setting. In contact sports, force is expected to be used by the participants because it is one of the necessary terms and conditions of the game. The contact is justified if it is reasonable under the circumstances. Many of the contacts that occur in the sports setting would be considered batteries in a nonsports setting. However, the key distinction in sports battery cases is the determination of whether a particular contact has been consented to by the participant. If the finder of fact concludes that consent was given and the contact was reasonable, a plaintiff will not be successful in a battery case.

If consent was not given or if the contact was unreasonable, then the type of contact initiated by the defendant will determine the type of damages available to the plaintiff. Any proven intentional tort provides at least nominal damages. Outrageous or extremely offensive contact will, in addition to the nominal damages, provide a basis on which to support punitive damages that may greatly increase the plaintiff's award. (See Section 4.12 for further information concerning negligence damages.)

NOTES _____

1. In *Bourque* v. *Duplechin*, 331 So. 2d 40 (La. Ct. App. 1976), the plaintiff sued defendant for an intentional battery that occurred during a softball game. Defendant ran into plaintiff after plaintiff second baseman had completed his throw to first base. On appeal, the court held that it was not an intentional tort because the defendant had no intent to harm the plaintiff (see Section 4.21).

2. In *Griggas* v. *Clauson*, 128 N.E. 2d 363 (Ill. App. Ct. 1955), Griggas sued Clauson for assault and battery for injuries received when the defendant struck the plaintiff in the face several times in a basketball game. The court found that Griggas was subjected to wanton, unprovoked, and unanticipated assault and battery and held for Griggas (see Section 4.21).

3. In *Averill* v. *Luttrell*, 311 S.W. 2d 812 (Tenn. Ct. App. 1957), plaintiff batter, angered by the pitcher's intentionally thrown beanball, which struck him, threw his bat in the direction of the mound. The defendant catcher then stepped behind the batter and hit him with his fist. The batter sued both the catcher and the catcher's club. The court held for the plaintiff batter and found that the defendant catcher had committed assault and battery (see Section 4.24).

4. In *Manning* v. *Grimsley*, 643 F. 2d 20 (1st Cir. 1981), defendant pitcher was sued for assault and battery for throwing a baseball from the bullpen into the stands and hitting a spectator (see Section 4.21).

5. In *Hackbart* v. *Cincinnati Bengals*, Inc., 435 F. Supp. 352 (D. Colo. 1977), plaintiff football player was precluded from suing for assault and battery by the statute of limitations (see Section 4.21).

6. For further information, see the following articles:
(a) "Professional Sports and Tort Liability: A Victory for the Intentionally Injured Player," *Detroit College of Law Review* 687 (Summer 1980).
(b) "Torts in Sports — Deterring Violence in Professional Athletics," 48 *Fordham Law Review* 764 (April 1980).

4.11–3   Defenses for Assault and Battery

The three defenses available to the defendant in an intentional harm-to-the-person action, such as assault or battery, are consent, privilege, and immunity. Consent, when given by a plaintiff, does not excuse a tort (see Section 4.11–3[a]). However, because its absence is an essential element of an intentional tort, its presence will totally negate the claim of liability since the plaintiff will not be able to establish the three required elements. On the other hand, both privilege (see Section 4.11–3[b]) and immunity (see Section 4.11–3[c]), in effect, excuse the commission of a tort after its occurrence.

4.11–3(a)   Consent

Consent is a voluntary yielding of one's will to the dictates of another. It is an act of reason, accompanied by deliberation, which is made by an individual possessed of sufficient mental capacity to make an intelligent choice. To be effective, consent must be an act unclouded by fraud or duress. Consent may be expressed, or it may be reasonably implied by the circumstances surrounding the situation.

The element of consent presents a special problem in the realm of sports in general and for athletic participants in particular. The traditional interpretation in many assault and battery cases in the sport setting has been that the athlete, by participating in a given event, consents to the degree of contact commonly found within the rules of the sport. A special problem arises in the area of sports because it is often difficult to determine the extent or scope of the implied consent given. Consent implied from participation in athletic events is not a blanket consent that protects athletes from the consequences of their actions under all circumstances. Instead, many plaintiffs argue that the scope of consent is limited to acts that occur in the ordinary and normal conduct of the game.

The difficulty arises from the determination of what is "ordinary and normal conduct" in a particular game. For example, the consent defense might be employed in a sports-related assault and battery action. The defendant could claim that no tort was committed based on the nature of the relationship between himself and the plaintiff, who by his very participation in the contest consents to a certain degree of contact. Indeed, the difficulty in maintaining a tort action in a sports case is the difficulty of ascertaining, in the context of a game in which physical contact is allowed, exactly when or how a tort occurs.

NOTES _____

1. For information concerning scope of consent, see section 40 Criminal Liability, Defense of Consent.

2. In *Tavernier* v. *Maes*, 242 Cal. App. 2d 532, 51 Cal. Rptr. 575 (1966), plaintiff sought recovery for injuries sustained during a family softball game. Plaintiff alleged defendant deliberately slid into him in an attempt to break up a double play. The court held that the scope of the implied consent created by plaintiff's participation, as well as the question of whether the defendant's conduct exceeded the scope of the consent given, was a matter for the jury to decide.

4.11–3(b) Privilege

A privilege is a particular, limited benefit enjoyed by an individual or class that extends beyond the common advantages of other citizens. In certain situations a privilege is more appropriately classified as an exemption from a burden rather than as a benefit to be enjoyed. A privilege is commonly enjoyed in

situations in which the defendant has acted in defense of his or her person or property. The defendant who is successful in using the defense of privilege must bear the burden of proof to establish that a privilege existed and that the force used pursuant to the privilege was reasonable under the circumstances. The defense is denied, and the defendant will be held liable if the force used is found to be excessive or unreasonable. The defense of privilege commonly encompasses these six types of behavior:

1. Self-defense
2. Defense of third persons
3. Corporal punishment
4. Defense of property
5. Effecting an arrest
6. Arrest without a warrant

The privilege most commonly utilized in sports cases is that of self-defense. In order to successfully argue self-defense, the defendant must prove that no more force than was reasonably necessary was used to repel an attack.

4.11–3(b)–i Self-Defense

The self-defense privilege rests on the policy that allows a person being attacked to come to his or her own defense. The privilege extends to the use of all reasonable force needed to prevent harmful bodily contact. The privilege arises when danger exists or there is a reasonable belief that danger is imminent. It is limited to the use of force that is or that appears to be necessary for adequate protection. There is never any privilege to use force when the immediate danger is past. (See *Polonich* v. *A.P.A. Sports, Inc.* and *Agar* v. *Canning* in Section 4.21, Notes 6 and 12.)

4.11–3(b)–ii Defense of Third Persons

The defense of third persons is also a potentially viable legal argument for defending against an action for assault or battery. In order for the defense to be effective, certain requirements must be met. First, the privilege extends only to the reasonable force necessary to defend another from imminent harm. The defense must occur in reaction to events as they exist at the time of the threat. There is no privilege for physical reactions to future threats or past attacks.

The privilege of third-person defense is available to anyone who reasonably defends another. There does not have to be any special relationship between the two. Some courts require that the third party take the risk that the person being defended would not be privileged to defend himself. The preferred view, however, is that an honest mistake as to the necessity for the defensive action will relieve the defendant of liability.

4.11–3(c)   Immunity

Immunity is a condition that protects against a tort action. It exists because of the particular position of the defendant, and not because of any action taken by the defendant. This defense may exist either because of a relationship between the plaintiff and the defendant, or because of the capacity of the defendant. Examples of relationships that in some states permit a defense of immunity in intentional torts include those between husband and wife or between parent and child. Charitable corporations, federal, state and municipal governments, and public officials may use this defense because of their role as protectors and defenders of the public welfare. (See Section 4.23–4 on sovereign immunity.)

4.12   Negligence

Negligence is an unintentional tort that focuses on an individual's conduct or actions. Negligence must be distinguished from intentional torts such as assault and battery that revolve around the individual's state of mind or intent. Negligent conduct is defined as that which falls below the standard established by law for the protection of others against an unreasonably great risk of harm. The ability of the injured party to sue and to recover damages for negligence is based on the idea that one who acts should anticipate the consequences that might involve unreasonable danger to others. (See Sections 4.12–1[d] and [e] for a discussion of damages.)

A person must only take precautions against unreasonable risks of harm. Unreasonable risks are those in which danger is apparent or should be apparent to one in the position of the actor. The law, however, does not seek to burden the freedom of human action with excessive or unreasonable demands and restraints. Therefore, one is not expected to guard against situations or occurrences that are unlikely to happen. The standard of care required is measured by reference to the reasonable person standard. This hypothetical reasonable person is one who selects a course of action that would be selected by a reasonable person residing in the affected community. The law excuses all persons from liability for accidents that are either unavoidable or unforeseeable.

The court commonly examines three factors to aid in its determination of whether or not a defendant's action constitutes negligence: (1) the extent and nature of the risk involved, (2) the social value and utility of the interest advanced, and (3) the availability of an alternative course of action. With the first factor, the greater the risk of a particular action (for example, the risk of death), the greater the extent of precautions required by the actor. Knowing that as the gravity of the potential harm of a given action increases, the apparent likelihood of the occurrence lessens, does not preclude precaution regarding an action involving great risk. In other words, if the potential risk is significant (if death is likely to occur), the court will weigh less heavily the rarity of the event and will demand a higher degree of precaution despite the low probability of the particular harm in question. For example, a school bus may be required to stop at all railroad crossings. The chance of the bus being hit is extremely small; yet if collision occurs, the consequences may be devastating. Thus, the court would demand a high degree of precaution, even if this standard were not set by state statute. In sports, the degree of care required for archery might exceed the degree required for softball. Even though there might be the same likelihood of injury, the potential gravity of the harm in archery (death) is so much greater than for softball (broken bones) that the degree of care required may be greater.

In examining the second factor to determine negligence, the court will balance a consideration of the potential harm of an action and the probability of its occurrence against social value or utility in the interest that the actor seeks to advance. Certain factory machinery, for example, poses significant potential harm to employees utilizing it. Its introduction or continued use, however, may be justified in the public interest because of the tremendous quantity and/or quality of its output. Instead of banning the use of such machinery, federal or state governments may enact and impose safety regulations for its use. If the safety regulations are met and an injury occurs, the defendant will not be found negligent. Likewise, any sport must be found to have some social value or utility that will permit its continuance despite the potential for serious injury. Thus, one problem is that of defining the extent or existence of a social value for a sport such as football, which may cause catastrophic injuries.

The third factor used to determine whether or not an act is negligent is the availability to the actor of alternative courses of action. Different persons in the same situation may have a variety of courses of action available to them based on their age, knowledge, and/or experience. Acts will be negligent if the action taken is not one that is acceptable under a "reasonable person" standard, and if there is an alternative available. For example, when confronted with a burning house, a person has

many alternatives. He may call the fire department or attempt to extinguish the blaze single-handedly. However, it may not always be reasonable to attempt to put out a fire without help, and a person who does so may be negligent if the fire gets out of control and causes more damage than if the fire department had been called. This point leads to a discussion of the various elements and standards involved in the theory of negligence.

Four specific elements must be proven by the plaintiff in order for an action to be considered negligent: (1) duty between parties, (2) breach of duty, (3) actual and proximate causation, and (4) damages. These elements are discussed in detail in Sections 4.12–1(a) through (d) after a further discussion of the reasonable person standard.

4.12–1 Reasonable Person Standard

Even if a particular relationship does not exist between parties, a person owes to others the duty of exercising reasonable care in his or her activities. The courts "measure" the conduct in each negligence case against the "reasonable person" standard — that is, how a person of ordinary sense using ordinary care and skill would react under similar circumstances. It is important to note that the conduct of the "reasonable person" is not necessarily "perfect" conduct, but that of a prudent and careful individual. As employed by the courts, the standard of reasonableness takes into account the risk apparent to an actor, the capacity of the actor to meet the risk, and the circumstances under which the person must act.

The reasonable person is held to possess a minimum level of knowledge common to the community where the injury occurs. A negligent defendant who possesses superior knowledge, skill, or intelligence, however, will be held to higher standards of care — that is, conduct which conforms to that of others with similar knowledge and/or skills. For example, a surgeon performing an operation would be held to the same standard of skill and conduct exhibited by other surgeons in the field performing similar operations. When the reasonable person standard entails a degree of skill or knowledge higher than that of a judge or the lay person sitting on a jury, qualified expert testimony is utilized to establish the proper standard of care for the defendant in question. Again, using the case of a surgeon sued for negligence, both parties would probably call as witnesses other qualified surgeons who would testify as to how the operation is usually performed and what precautions or steps are taken under normal circumstances. This expert testimony would help establish the standard of care for the particular situation. The jury would then determine whether the defendant surgeon met the standard of care.

The reasonable person is deemed to possess physical characteristics identical to those of the defendant in question. If the actor is exceptionally strong, for example, the standard of care demands that the person exhibit conduct which parallels that of a reasonably prudent person of like strength under similar circumstances. The reasonable person standard does not take into account the temperament or emotions of the individual actor. The law seeks objectivity and not subjectivity based on a person's mental attributes or states. There are several reasons for this. First, it would be extremely difficult, if not impossible, to prove what was in an individual's mind at the time of the particular conduct. Second, the harm caused by a negligent act is not changed by the actor's particular thoughts or feelings. Finally, the courts have determined that a person must learn to conform to the standard of the community or pay for any violation of those standards.

It is argued that in extreme cases of mental deficiency the actor cannot comprehend the danger inherent in certain conduct. The courts, however, have still applied the reasonable person standard when dealing with insane defendants. This is based on the public-policy consideration of promoting the responsibility of guardians for those in their care. The

sanction for civil liability involves monetary compensation and not personal liberty. Therefore, the courts and the legislature have determined that protecting the public from harm, or at least requiring those responsible to pay for their own harm, is a goal of sufficient importance to justify distinguishing between civil liability and moral culpability. A "greater degree of care" standard may be applicable when dealing with an inherently dangerous object or an activity where it is reasonably foreseeable that an accident or injury may occur (see Note 5).

NOTES

1. In *Johnson* v. *Krueger*, 36 Colo. App. 242, 539 P. 2d 1296 (1975), plaintiff sought recovery in negligence for injuries sustained when he ran onto defendant's land while playing football and fell over a stump 10 inches high and 6 inches in diameter. In affirming judgment for the landowner, the court of appeals held that the landowner did not act unreasonably in leaving the stump on his land. It was not reasonably foreseeable that a child would run from a football game onto an adjacent lot, a considerable distance onto landowner's property, and fall on the stump, which was clearly visible, even when owner knew children often played football on the adjacent lot.

2. In *Rabiner* v. *Rosenberg*, 176 Misc. 885, 28 N.Y.S. 2d 533 (City Ct. 1941), plaintiff spectator sued for damages sustained when a fish slipped off defendant fisherman's hook, causing the hook to snap back and become embedded in the plaintiff's eye. The trial court, in rendering judgment for the defendant, held that the fisherman acted as any prudent fisherman would have and was not liable.

3. In *Reddick* v. *Lindquist*, 484 S.W. 2d 441 (Tex. Civ. App. 1972), plaintiff widow sued in wrongful death for loss of her husband, who was killed when defendant's boat ran over him after he fell while water-skiing. In affirming judgment for the defendant, the court of civil appeals held that deceased's negligence in attempting a maneuver which an ordinarily prudent skier would not have tried was the proximate cause of the fatal accident.

4. In *Stehn* v. *Bernarr MacFadden Foundation, Inc.*, 434 F. 2d 811 (6th Cir. 1970), the court held that the standard for the safe teaching of wrestling during physical education class may be determined by the jury when the evidence proffered provided ample documentation about wrestling instruction. This documentation would allow a jury to compare the quality of instruction and the supervision of the teacher and the conduct of the activities provided by the defendant, thus establishing a standard

applicable to a "reasonable wrestling program." (See Section 4.23–1, Note 4.)

5. In *Smith* v. *Vernon Parish School Bd.*, 442 So. 2d 1319 (La. Ct. App. 1983), plaintiff sued the school board, a physical education teacher, and the insurer of teachers for damages suffered in a trampoline activity during a high school physical education class. The court held that the teacher exercised reasonable supervision and that the "greater degree of care" standard was not applicable.

4.12–1(a) Duty

The plaintiff's initial step in a negligence case is to establish the duty of care owed to him by the defendant. Duty is divided into two categories: (1) duty to act and (2) duty not to act in an unreasonable manner.

A duty of care is an obligation, recognized by law, which requires an individual or a group to conform to a particular standard of conduct toward another. The duty of care required of an individual is established by reference to any special qualifications. In the case of a professional (for example, a doctor or an athletic trainer), a duty of care is determined by reference to uniform requirements that establish minimum standards of behavior. All professionals are judged not as individuals in society at large but as members of a specified class. When acting in a professional capacity, the professional person will be judged by the professional standards in existence at the time.

The concept of legal duty is based on the relationship that exists between the parties involved. Certain relationships, such as employer-employee, principal-agent, teacher-student, and coach-athlete, establish a legal duty to act. An employer, for example, has the duty to render aid and assistance to an employee who is injured during the course of employment. In the absence of a duty-imposing relationship, an individual is not liable for an omission to act. A moral obligation to act does not create a legal duty to act, and hence the individual who fails to act cannot be held liable in negligence. However, the person without a duty to act who does undertake to

act may be held liable if he acts negligently. By acting, one can create a duty between oneself and another that may not have previously existed. The person who undertakes to rescue another may not abandon that attempt if it becomes inconvenient. By acting, the would-be rescuer has created a duty to continue to aid the person in trouble. In sports cases, duty is often described as the "reasonable care" necessary to avoid creating risks that may result in injuries to players or spectators.

Often liability will rest on whether the court designates the act or nonact as misfeasance, nonfeasance, or malfeasance. Misfeasance is the term applied to lawful conduct that is improperly done. Nonfeasance is an omission of an action that ought to have been taken. Malfeasance is the doing of an act that is illegal. In *Cantwell* v. *University of Massachusetts*, the case turned on whether the coach's improper spotting position constituted misfeasance or nonfeasance. If the coach's act was misfeasance, he would have been personally liable for the injury suffered as a result of his action. If, however, his action was in effect nonfeasance, there would be no personal liability (see Section 4.23–4).

NOTES

1. In *Nabozny* v. *Barnhill*, 31 Ill. App. 3d 212, 334 N.E. 2d 258 (1975), the court decided the first sports case that found that players have a legal duty to one another to refrain from reckless misconduct actions in a game (see Section 4.21).

2. In *Hackbart* v. *Cincinnati Bengals, Inc.*, 435 F. Supp. 352 (D. Colo. 1977), 601 F.2d 516 (10th Cir. 1979), the lower court found no duty existed between two professional football players for actions in a game. However, on appeal, the court found that there was a duty on the part of one professional football player to another to refrain from reckless misconduct (see Section 4.21).

3. In *Townsley* v. *Cincinnati Gardens, Inc.*, 39 Ohio App. 353, 83 N.E. 2d 616 (1949) and *Benjamin* v. *State*, 115 Misc. 2d 71, 453 N.Y.S. 2d 329 (Ct. Cl. 1982), the court discussed duty and standard of care in a sports arena (see Section 4.25).

4. In *Lynch* v. *Board of Education of Collingsville Community School District*, 390 N.E. 2d 526 (Ill. Ct. App. 1979), the court discussed the duty of a teacher to a

student (see Section 4.22–1).

5. In *Wells* v. *Minneapolis Baseball & Athletic Ass'n.,* 122 Minn. 327, 142 N.W. 706 (1913), the court discussed duty and standard of care (see Section 4.24).

6. In *Berman by Berman* v. *Philadelphia Board of Education,* 456 A. 2d 545 (Pa. Super. Ct. 1983), an action was brought by plaintiff student, who was injured during a school-sponsored floor hockey game that was supervised by a physical education instructor. A mouthguard would have prevented the injury, but Amateur Hockey Association (AHA) rules did not require them at the time. The court, however, held that the board of education could not escape its duty of care for the welfare of students because of a lack of AHA rules and standards.

7. In *Hunt* v. *Scotia-Glenville Central School District,* 460 N.Y.S. 2d 205 (1983), the court held that a basketball coach and school district were under no legal obligation to submit timely recommendations for a student applying for a college athletic scholarship. The court reasoned that there was no statute or regulation mandating such a recommendation, and that the student's civil rights were not violated.

8. For further information, see "School Liability for Athletic Injuries: Duty, Causation and Defense," 21 *Washburn Law Journal* 315 (Winter 1982).

4.12–1(b)   Breach of Duty

A plaintiff who has demonstrated that a duty of care was owed to him by the defendant must also prove that the defendant violated this duty. The burden of proof requires that the party on whom it rests establish the validity of the claim being made. The plaintiff may sustain this burden of proof by showing direct evidence of negligence, violation of a statute, and res ipsa loquitur.

Direct evidence of negligence is evidence that tends to establish actual factual occurrences through proof they occurred. An example of direct evidence is eyewitness testimony. When direct evidence is not available, certain procedural devices are used to enable a plaintiff to prove a case. One of these is presumptions. Presumptions are a legal fiction that requires the judge or jury to assume the existence of one fact, based on the existence of another fact or group of facts. They are used in the absence of sufficient evidence to prove the fact itself. The classic example is the presumption that a person who has been missing for seven years is dead.

Violation of a statute is sometimes referred to as negligence per se. Negligence per se means that upon finding a violation of an applicable statute, there is a conclusive presumption of negligence. This conclusive presumption requires that a jury find for the plaintiff. It does not allow the jury to weigh all the evidence and independently determine the relative liabilities of the parties. Although in some states the violation of a valid statute may be considered negligence per se, in other states, the violation of a statute, ordinance, or even an administrative regulation is deemed only evidence of negligence. The current trend is away from viewing violations of statutes as negligence per se. When a violation is treated as evidence of negligence, it is accorded a different weight. A jury will not be required to draw any specific conclusion from the violation. Instead, a violation merely establishes an inference of negligence that may or may not be accepted by the jury.

For a statutory violation to provide evidence of negligence, two points must be established by the complaining party. First, the statutory violation must be causally related to the plaintiff's harm. If an individual's taillights are not working in violation of a statute, that violation may only be used to establish negligence when the failure of the taillights causes an accident. The second factor to be considered is that the harm must be the kind sought to be prevented by the statute. If an individual's car pushes another car into a wall, the fact that the pusher's car taillights do not work in violation of a motor vehicle safety statute is of little or no significance.

The last method of establishing the negligence of the defendant is through the use of the legal doctrine of res ipsa loquitur. Res ipsa loquitur permits the fact-finder to infer both negligence and causation from circumstantial evidence. It is, in effect, another type of presumption. The plaintiff must establish that it is more likely than not that the harm suffered was a result of the defendant's negligence. To defeat the application of this doctrine, the defendant must establish that there is another, equally believable explanation for plaintiff's injury.

Res ipsa loquitur is strictly a procedural device designed to allow a plaintiff to establish an otherwise unprovable case. In negligence cases, direct evidence of the defendant's negligence is sometimes not available. This doctrine allows a plaintiff to recover on the basis of what probably happened. (See *Grauer* v. *State of New York* in Note 1 and in Section 4.25.)

Presumptions may be rebuttable, depending on the situation. If rebuttable, the defendant or plaintiff may counter the presumption raised by the opposition through the introduction of alternative evidence tending to dispute the validity of the presumption.

NOTES _____

1. In *Grauer* v. *State of New York*, 15 Misc. 2d 471, 181 N.Y.S. 2d 994 (Ct. Cl. 1959), defendant was found negligent under res ipsa loquitur (see Section 4.25).

2. In *Jordan* v. *Loveland Skiing Corp.*, 503 P. 2d 1034 (Colo. Ct. App. 1972), plaintiff skier sought to recover for injuries sustained in a fall from defendants' ski lift. In affirming judgment for the defendant, the court of appeals held that the issues of the lift operator's negligence and proximate cause were properly submitted to the jury, and the doctrine of res ipsa loquitur did not apply.

4.12–1(c) Proximate Cause

The primary issue in the area of causation is that of proximate cause — that is, whether the defendant's negligent act was connected to the plaintiff's harm to such an extent as to be considered the legal cause of it. Before any determination of proximate cause can be made, however, the defendant's conduct must be shown to be the actual cause of the plaintiff's harm. If the same harm would have resulted had the negligent act never occurred, then the act is not the actual cause of the harm. This is sometimes referred to as the "but for" test, meaning that the particular harm in question would not have been suffered "but for" the negligent act of the defendant.

After establishing the existence of actual causation between the plaintiff's harm and the defendant's act, recovery requires that it be demonstrated that the latter is also the proximate cause of the former. Proximate cause is tested by determining whether or not the harm that resulted to the plaintiff was a reasonably foreseeable consequence of the defendant's act. To demonstrate proximate cause, it is sufficient to show that the probable consequence of the defendant's act was harm of the same general character as that which befell the plaintiff. It is not necessary to show that the harm to the plaintiff in its precise form or particular manner should have been foreseen by the defendant.

One last problem of determining causation occurs when there is more than one cause of injury. In some cases, when a combination of causes leads to the damage, a defendant can defeat claims of liability by showing that there was an unforeseeable intervening cause. An intervening cause is one that comes into existence after the negligent action of the defendant and that somehow affects the "result."

Often there may be more than one cause for any given injury. In such cases, no liability will be assigned to individual causes unless the individual cause was a "substantial factor" in the creation of the ultimate result. This substantial factor test precludes liability for inadvertent or minor causational factors. The test is predicated on the theory that any cause should not be held partly or totally liable for the injury unless it substantially causes harm.

NOTES _____

1. In *Parmentier* v. *McGinnis*, 157 Wis. 596, 147 N.W. 1007 (1914), plaintiff administrator of the estate of a deceased boxer sought a recovery from his opponent and the fight promoter. The plaintiff's theory was based on the violation of a statute forbidding prize fights. The court decided that because the fight was not for a prize, the statute did not apply. Recovery based on a negligence per se theory was not allowed.

2. Intervening negligence will not relieve an original wrongdoer of liability unless it is both unforeseeable and causes an unforeseeable result, as evidenced in *Freeman* v.

United States, 509 F. 2d 626 (6th Cir. 1975), where plaintiff brought an action against the United States for the wrongful death of parachutists. In affirming judgment for plaintiffs, the court of appeals held that the air controller owed a duty of care to the parachutists, that they were not contributorily negligent in jumping through a cloud cover into Lake Erie, and that the intervening negligence of the pilot and jump master in directing a jump through a cloud cover did not relieve the government of liability.

3. In *Kallish* v. *American Baseball Club of Philadelphia*, 138 Pa. Super. 602, 10 A. 2d 831 (1940), plaintiff spectator sought recovery for injuries sustained by his four-year-old-son, who fell from an overcrowded parapet in defendant's ballpark. In affirming judgment for the defendant, the superior court held that there was no circumstance from which it could be inferred that the conduct of other patrons could have been foreseen and controlled by the club or that the club had knowledge or constructive notice that patrons were standing upon the parapet or that their conduct was disorderly, which was the proximate cause of injury to the boy.

4. In *Gaspard* v. *Grain Dealers Mutual Insurance Co.*, 131 So. 2d 831 (La. Ct. App. 1961), the court held that an accident caused by a bat slipping from a player's hands was unavoidable. The defendant claimed he was unaware of the plaintiff's presence. Defendant's ignorance was found not to be the proximate cause of the injury (see Section 4.21).

5. In *Barrett* v. *Phillips*, 29 N.C. App. 220, 223 S.E. 2d 918 (1976), the court held that a violation of a safety rule prohibiting players over 18 years of age from high school sports was not the proximate cause of player's death, which occurred after a collision with 20-year-old opponent (see Section 4.21, Note 5).

6. In *Toone* v. *Adams*, 262 N.C. 403, 137 S.E. 2d 132 (1964), the court held that a coach's abuse of an umpire was not the proximate cause of an injury which resulted from a fan's attack on the umpire (see Section 4.22–4).

7. In *Schofield* v. *Wood*, 170 Mass. 415, 49 N.E. 636 (1898), plaintiff spectator sought recovery for injuries sustained when the rail he was leaning on gave way. Plaintiff contended that the rail had been negligently maintained. In affirming a jury verdict for plaintiff, the supreme judicial court held that the fact that other spectators pushed plaintiff did not relieve defendant of liability for negligent maintenance of the rail.

8. For further information, see "School Liability for Athletic Injuries: Duty, Causation and Defense," 21 *Washburn Law Journal* 315 (Winter 1982).

4.12–1(d) Damages

Damages are a pecuniary compensation given by courts to any person who suffered an injury through the unlawful act, omission, or negligence of another. Damages may be compensatory and punitive. Compensatory damages consist of money given to the injured party and are measured by the amount of actual injury incurred. Compensatory damages are usually awarded in negligence cases, where the plaintiff must establish that the damage was suffered as a result of the defendant's conduct. The plaintiff may seek recovery of damages in any or all of the following four areas: (1) pain and suffering, past, present and future; (2) medical expenses, past, present and future; (3) diminution of earning capacity, past, present and future; and (4) loss of consortium (right to a spouse's companionship).

In intentional tort actions, when no actual injury has occurred, nominal damages may still be awarded. These damages are a minimal amount given when no real loss or injury can be proven but when a right has been infringed. Generally, they are one dollar or less. However, punitive damages may be awarded to an injured party as punishment for outrageous conduct and to deter future transgressions. They are awarded to a plaintiff in an amount over and above the amount given to compensate for the loss, when the wrong committed was aggravated by violence, oppression, malice, fraud, or excessively wicked conduct. Punitive damages are intended to comfort the plaintiff for mental anguish, shame, or degradation suffered. In addition, punitive damages serve to punish the defendant and to set an example for other wrongdoers. They are based on entirely different policy considerations than are compensatory damages, which merely reimburse a plaintiff for any actual loss suffered. (See *Tomjanovich* v. *California Sports, Inc.* in Section 4.24.)

NOTES

1. In *Lynch* v. *Board of Education of Collingsville Community School District*, 390 N.E. 2d 526 (Ill. Ct. App. 1979), the court discussed the different reasonings for damages (see Section 4.22–1).

2. In *Benjamin* v. *State*, 115 Misc. 2d 71, 453 N.Y.S.

2d 329 (Ct. Cl. 1982), the court awarded compensatory damages (see Section 4.25).

4.12–1(e) Wrongful Death Statutes

Wrongful death statutes exist in all states. They provide a statutory cause of action in favor of the decedent's personal representative for the benefit of certain beneficiaries (for example, a spouse, parent, or child), and against the person who negligently caused the death of the spouse, parent, or child. The enactment of such statutes changed the common-law rule that the death of a human being was not a proper civil cause of action. The cause of action established in wrongful death statutes was for the wrong to the beneficiaries for their loss of companionship and suffering — not for any harm committed against the decedent.

The majority of the wrongful death statutes award compensatory damages to the decedent's beneficiaries. These compensatory damages attempt to evaluate the monetary worth of the individual and award money based on that determination. In a minority of jurisdictions, the statutes measure damages by the level of culpability shown by the negligent party. The damages awarded are greater for injuries inflicted intentionally than for those inflicted merely negligently. A few states enacted statutes which employ a combination of the two above methods to determine damages. For example, Massachusetts enacted statutes which can be seen in the following passage from the Massachusetts General Laws:

A person who (1) by his negligence causes the death of a person, or (2) by willful, wanton or reckless act causes the death of a person under such circumstances that the deceased could have recovered damages for personal injuries if his death had not resulted, or (3) operates a common carrier of passengers and by his negligence causes the death of a passenger, or (4) operates a common carrier of passengers and by his willful, wanton or reckless act causes the death of a passenger under such circumstances that the deceased could have recovered damages for personal injuries if his death had not resulted, or (5) is responsible for a breach of warranty arising under Article 2 of chapter one hundred and six which results in injury to a person that causes death, shall be liable in damages in the amount of: (1) the fair monetary value of the decedent to the persons entitled to receive the damages recovered, as provided in section one, including but not limited to compensation for the loss of the reasonably expected net income, services, protection, care, assistance, society, companionship, comfort, guidance, counsel, and advice of the decedent to the person entitled to the damages recovered; (2) the reasonable funeral and burial expenses of the decedent; (3) punitive damages in an amount of no less than five thousand dollars in such case as the decedent's death was caused by the malicious, willful, wanton or reckless conduct of the defendant or by the gross negligence of the defendant; except that (1) the liability of an employer of a person in his employment shall not be governed by this section, (2) a person operating a railroad shall not be liable for negligence in causing the death of a person while walking or being upon such railroad contrary to law or to the reasonable rules and regulations of the carrier, and (3) a person operating a street railway or electric railroad shall not be liable for negligence for causing the death of a person while walking or being upon that part of the street railway or electric railroad not within the limits of a highway. A person shall be liable for the negligence or the willful, wanton or reckless act of his agents or servants while engaged in his business to the same extent and subject to the same limits as he would be liable under this section for his own act. Damages under this section shall be recovered in an action of tort by the executor or administrator of the deceased. An action to recover damages under this section shall be commenced within three years from the date of death or within such time thereafter as is provided by section four, four B, nine or ten of chapter two hundred and sixty. [Actions for Death and Injuries Resulting in Death, Massachusetts General Laws Chapter 229, Section 2, Wrongful death; damages]

NOTES _____

1. Massachusetts General Laws Ch. 106. Title 3 to Civil

Actions Section 377. Wrongful death of adults or certain minors; parties; right of action; damages; consolidation of action, which states that:

> When the death of a person not being a minor, or when a death of a minor person who leaves surviving him either a husband or wife or child or children or father or mother, is caused by the wrongful act or neglect of another, his heirs, and his dependent parents, if any, who are not heirs, or personal representatives on their behalf may maintain an action for damages against the person causing the death, or in case of death of such wrongdoer, whether the wrongdoer dies before or after the death of the person injured. If any other person is responsible for any such wrongful act or neglect, the action may also be maintained against such other person, or in case of his death, his personal representatives.

2. In New York and some other states, an action for injury to person or property survives despite death of person in whose favor or against whom cause of action existed:

(a) Action against personal representative for injury to person or property.

(1) No cause of action for injury to person or property is lost because of the death of the person liable for the injury. For any injury, an action may be brought or continued against the personal representative of the decedent, but punitive damages shall not be awarded nor penalties adjudged in any such action brought to recover damages for personal injury. This section extends to a cause of action for wrongfully causing death and an action therefore may be brought or continued against the personal representative of the person liable thereafter.

(2) Where death or an injury to person or property, resulting from a wrongful act, neglect or default, occurs simultaneously with or after the death of a person who would have been liable therefore if his death had not occurred simultaneously with such death or injury or between the wrongful act, neglect or default and the resulting death or injury, an action to recover damages for such death or injury may be maintained against the personal representative of such person.

(b) Action by personal representatives for injury to person or property. No cause of action for injury to person or property is lost because of the death of the person in whose favor the cause of action existed. For any injury an action may be brought or continued by the personal representatives of the decedent, but punitive damages shall not be awarded nor penalties adjudged in any such action brought to recover damages for personal injury. On the trial of any such action, which is joined with an action for causing death, the contributory negligence of the decedent is a defense, to be pleaded

and proved by the defendant. No cause of action for damages caused by an injury to a third person is lost because of the death of the third person. [New York Kinney Consolidated Laws, Estate, Powers and Trusts, Art. 11, Section 11–3.2]

3. In *Barrett v. Phillips*, 29 N.C. App. 220, 223 S.E. 2d 918 (1976), a wrongful death action was brought by parents on behalf of their son, who died in a football game as a result of a collision with another football player. The action was brought against the high school and the athletic association (see Section 4.21, Note 5).

4. In *Mogabgad v. Orleans Parish School Bd.*, 239 So. 2d 456 (La. Ct. App. 1970), an action was brought against a coach, school principal, and school district for the death of a football player from heat exhaustion (see Section 4.22–3, Note 1).

5. In *Truelove v. Wilson*, 285 S.E. 2d 556 (Ga. Ct. App. 1981), an action was brought for the wrongful death of a student who was fatally injured when he struck a metal soccer goal post during a physical education class. Punitive damages and damages for maintenance of a nuisance were also sought. The DeKalb Superior Court granted summary judgment to the defendants.

The court of appeals held that (1) punitive damages were not available in wrongful death actions, (2) the county board of education and the county school district were entitled to the defense of sovereign immunity, and (3) the individual defendants who were school employees and members of the county board of education were entitled to the defense of sovereign immunity.

Certiorari was denied by the Georgia Supreme Court in 1981.

4.12–2 Standard of Care for Children

Children as defendants in a negligence case present an important exception to the reasonable person standard. Children are not held to the same objective standard of duty that is applied to adults. The courts recognize that at young age levels, there exists a wide range of mental capabilities and experiences. The law attempts to accommodate this variety by viewing the reasonable child as one who exercises in his or her actions a degree of care that is reasonably to be expected of children of like age, intelligence, and experience. Thus, under this more subjective standard, it follows that if a six-year-old boy has intelligence vastly superior to that of his peers, the child will be held to that standard of care encompassing his superior knowledge. Several states have established age brackets that purport to distinguish childhood from adulthood. This method has been criticized, however, because of the problems inherent in setting an accurate age-level guideline regarding mental capabilities.

An exception to the application of this subjective standard for children occurs when a child engages in an activity normally reserved for adults, such as driving an automobile or hunting with a gun. In cases such as these, the courts in many jurisdictions will apply the reasonable person standard for adults without any special consideration of the fact that the individual is a child.

NOTES _____

1. In *Gaspard v. Grain Dealers Mutual Insurance Co.,* 131 So. 2d 831 (La. Ct. App. 1961), a 12-year-old boy was injured by an 11-year-old boy in a baseball game and the court applied the standard of care for children (see Section 4.21).

2. In *Vendrell v. School District No. 26C, Malheur County,* 233 Or. 1, 376 P. 2d 406 (1962), plaintiff high school football player was injured as a result of a football coach's negligence in not properly training an allegedly inexperienced player. The defendant argued contributory negligence and assumption of the risk. The court found the plaintiff to be an experienced football player and held for the defendant (see Section 4.22–2).

3. In *Benjamin v. State,* 115 Misc. 2d 71, 453 N.Y.S. 2d 329 (Ct. Cl. 1982), an 11-year-old spectator was injured by a hockey puck that left the rink. The court held that the plaintiff was not guilty of contributory negligence (see Section 4.25).

4. In *Berman by Berman v. Philadelphia Board of Education,* 456 A. 2d 545 (Pa. Super. 1983), a student was injured in a school-sponsored floor hockey game (see Section 4.12–1[a], Note 6).

4.12–3 Standard of Care for Owners and Possessors of Property

The legal responsibility for injuries that have occurred in connection with the use of land has been quite rigidly segregated by the law into specific categories of duty. The duty that the owner or possessor of the land owes varies, depending on the characterization of the party who was injured while upon the premises.

The status of a spectator or athlete at a sports event in legal terms is that of a business invitee. A business invitee is a visitor who brings a pecuniary benefit to the person in possession of the property by his presence. A business invitee is also a person whom the possessor encourages to enter onto the property, and by such encouragement implicitly represents that the premises are safe to enter. The possessor of the property undertakes an affirmative duty to protect business invitees from known dangers and to protect them against dangers which, in the exercise of ordinary care, the possessor might reasonably discover.

The possessor of a sports arena or stadium is subject to liability for known dangers or dangers that could be identified based on an inspection. The possessor must maintain the facility in a reasonably safe condition, inspect the facility, and supervise the conduct of persons on the premises to prevent harm. However, it must be emphasized that this is based on a negligence theory and not a strict liability theory. The operator is not an insurer of safety to the fans and need only take reasonable precautions to prevent unreasonable risks of harm. In addition, the doctrines of contributory negligence (see Section 4.12–5[b]), comparative negligence (see Section 4.12–5[c]), and assumption of risk (see Section 4.12–5[d]) may bar recovery or reduce the damages awarded to the plaintiff when the spectator knows of the risks.

Persons who have entered the property of another have been divided into three categories. In addition to business invitees (discussed above), the other two categories are trespassers and licensees. These two categories are beyond the scope of this text as they do not involve the sports industries in any unique way. Trespassers enter property without consent and are owed very little care. Licensees are guests who are present with permission for a nonbusiness purpose and are generally owed no more than a duty to be warned of known defects by the property owner.

4.12–3(a) Lessors of Land

In the eyes of the law, when land is leased, it is, in effect, sold for a period of time. Thus the lessee (person leasing the land) assumes the responsibilities of the lessor (person who has leased the land) to those who enter the land. A lessor still has a duty, however, to disclose any concealed or dangerous conditions. These hidden defects are termed latent defects. The duty to disclose such defects extends to lessees, their families, their guests, and others reasonably expected to be on the premises. In order for this duty to attach, the lessor does not have to believe that the condition is dangerous or to have definite knowledge of the defect. Instead, it is sufficient that the lessor be informed of facts from which a reasonable person would conclude that there is a possible danger. The lessor has no obligation to inspect or to investigate in the absence of some reason to believe that there is danger. In addition, there is no duty to warn about patent defects, which are defined as known, open, or obvious conditions.

When land is leased for a purpose that includes admission to the public, the lessor has an affirmative duty to exercise reasonable care to inspect and to repair the leased property. This duty is imposed to prevent an unreasonable risk to the public. The duty exists whether or not members of the public actually enter the premises. Liability will extend, however, only to parts of the premises open to the public and to invitees who enter for the purpose for which the place was leased. (See Section 4.12–3[c].)

NOTES _____

1. A lessor will not be liable for injuries caused by faulty equipment in the absence of notice as to the defect. In *Schimenti* v. *Nansen Properties, Inc.*, 20 App. Div. 2d 653, 246 N.Y.S. 2d 273 (1964), plaintiff baseball player sought recovery from lessor of the ball field for injuries sustained when he slid into a spike-secured base. In denying recovery, the trial court held that in the absence of a showing that the lessor knew that the spike connection had become loose within sufficient time prior to ball-player's injuries to have permitted lessor to remedy the condition, lessor was not liable.

2. A lessor who does not remedy unreasonably dangerous conditions after receiving notice of such conditions will be liable. In *Fitchett* v. *Buchanan*, 2 Wash. App. 2d 695, 472 P. 2d 623 (1970), plaintiffs, racetrack patrons, sought recovery from lessor of racetrack for injuries sustained when a wheel became dislodged from a race car and flew into the stands. In affirming judgment for the plaintiffs, the court of appeals held that the lessor did not concern himself with the safety of the spectators despite previous fatalities from such occurrences, which are not uncommon to the sport. The unreasonably dangerous conditions, coupled with the principle that the lessor is liable if he has actual or constructive knowledge of a defect in his premises, was sufficient to find liability.

3. A lessor who retains control of the property will be liable for negligence causing injury. In *Ward* v. *United States*, 208 F. Supp. 118 (D. Colo. 1962), plaintiffs, parents of a minor who drowned in a lake leased to a private operator by defendant United States, sued for wrongful death for failure to adequately supervise the area and the lifeguards employed when the leased area invited public use. In granting the relief, the district court held that the government's failure to provide reasonable supervision of swimming facilities leased to the association constituted negligence and that the government was not relieved of liability because the lease provided that the government would retain control of the premises.

4.12–3(b) Licensees and Invitees

To establish a duty for owners, operators, supervisors, or possessors of land, the status of the person injured must be determined. Generally, there are two classes of persons: licensees and invitees. A licensee is one who enters upon land of another, with the owner's consent, for the licensee's own purposes. Included in this category are people who cut across another person's land for their own benefit (for example, people going fishing or hunting). When one is a licensee, the occupier of the land owes only a duty of ordinary care. This means there is no obligation to inspect the area to discover dangers currently unknown. There is also no duty to warn of conditions that are known or should be obvious to the licensee. The occupier or owner of land owes a licensee a duty to warn only when a risk is known or should have been known under the reasonable person standard, which the licensee does not know about. In addition, the owner must refrain from causing any intentional injury or injury caused by willful, wanton, or reckless misconduct.

An invitee, on the other hand, is owed a higher degree of care by the owner, operator, supervisor, or occupier of the land. There is an affirmative duty to be protected from known defects as well as from defects that would be discovered by the exercise of reasonable care. The basis of liability is the implied representation at the time of the invitation that the premises are safe to enter. The invitation does not have to be extended personally for an individual to fall into this category. An invitee may be found whenever an owner encourages others to enter somewhere for the owner's purpose. The invitation implies that reasonable care has been exercised for the safety of the invitees.

The owner or possessor of land is not, however, an insurer of the safety of invitees. That is, the owner does not guarantee safety under all possible circumstances. Instead, the owner or possessor must only exercise reasonable care for the invitee's protection. (See *Townsley* v. *Cincinnati Gardens, Inc.* in Section 4.25.)

In addition, this standard of reasonable care only extends to the invitation itself. The invitee may not exceed the scope of the invitation without becoming at the most a licensee, with the correspondingly lower standard of care required of the owner. Thus, visitors to a sports arena are owed an affirmative duty of reasonable care as long as they stay in the area designated for the crowds. If they wander off into an area where they are not allowed and expected to be, only a duty of ordinary care is owed.

The distinction between licensee and invitee is important because the different standards of care that may be applied can be decisive in determining the outcome of a lawsuit.

NOTES _____

1. In *Watford* v. *Evening Star Newspaper Co.*, 211 F. 2d 31 (D.C. Cir. 1954), plaintiff minor spectator sued defendant promoters for recovery for injuries received when he was struck by a racer at a soapbox derby. In reversing the district court's judgment for the defendants, the court of appeals held that the district court should have instructed the jury that defendant promoters as a matter of law occupied the status of invitors to the plaintiff, chargeable with the duty to exercise reasonable care.

2. A defendant cannot avoid liability by claiming plaintiff is a licensee when the public is invited or enticed onto land owned or controlled by the defendant. In *Stroud* v. *Bridges*, 275 S.W. 2d 503 (Tex. Civ. App. 1955), plaintiffs sought recovery for death of a minor who fell from the top of grandstand at defendant's ballpark. In affirming the jury verdict for plaintiffs, the court of civil appeals held that because park lessees and the owners of the club sponsored an advertising plan whereby any boy under 12 who bought and wore baseball club T-shirt would be admitted free, the defendant could not avoid liability on the grounds that since no ticket was purchased, the boy was a "licensee."

3. The duty of invitors attaches even to temporary owners or users of land. In *Isler* v. *Burman*, 232 N.W. 2d 818 (Minn. 1975), a snowmobile passenger sought recovery from the driver and church for injuries sustained in a snowmobile accident. In affirming judgment against the church, the Minnesota Supreme Court held that the church, which invited snowmobilers for a party and secured permission from the owner of the land to use the property, had assumed the duty of a landowner and was therefore responsible for making an adequate inspection of the land so that any dangerous conditions could be discovered.

4. A licensee will not recover unless intentionally or recklessly injured. In *Grahn* v. *Northwest Sport*, 310 P. 2d 306 (Or. 1957), plaintiff spectator sought recovery from defendant racetrack corporation for injuries sustained when he was struck by a race car while he stood on the track inside the crash rail. In affirming judgment for the defendant, the Oregon Supreme Court held that because the racetrack owner had instructed employees that there was to be no practice racing that day, the plaintiff, who was invited by the owner of the racing car to watch the practice, was a mere licensee and not an invitee of the racetrack owner.

5. In *Wells* v. *Minneapolis Baseball & Athletic Ass'n*, 122 Minn. 327, 142 N.W. 706 (1913), the court discussed invitees and licensees at a professional baseball game, at which a spectator was injured by a foul ball (see Section 4.24).

6. In *Townsley* v. *Cincinnati Gardens, Inc.*, 39 Ohio App. 353, 83 N.E. 2d 616 (1949), the court discussed invitees and licensees at an indoor facility at which a minor spectator was assaulted in the men's room (see Section 4.25).

4.12–3(c)   Patent and Latent Defects

In any discussion of the liability of owners and possessors of sports facilities, a distinction must be made between patent and latent defects. Both are potentially injury-causing defects, but an owner or operator cannot be held liable for undiscovered and undiscoverable defects. There is no strict liability standard (see Section 4.25) imposed for allowing persons to enter onto land under control by the owner. An owner or operator must only exercise "reasonable care" to discover defects in order to satisfy the required standard of care.

A *patent defect* is one that is plainly visible or that could be discovered during an ordinary and prudent inspection. A facility owner is liable for obvious defects, such as old debris on steps, that create a hazard if they cause an injury. Other examples of patent defects are steps missing from bleachers, nails protruding upward into seating, or ice on a sidewalk that is not cleared in a reasonable time.

A *latent defect* is a hidden or concealed defect that could not be discovered by reasonable or customary inspection. It is a defect of which the owner has no knowledge, or of which, in the exercise of reasonable care, the owner should not have had knowledge. Since owners must exercise only reasonable care, they are generally not liable for injuries caused by defects of this type unless as owners they have not met their obligation of periodic inspections. An example of a latent defect would be a structural defect in bleachers, which would not be readily apparent.

Whether or not a lessor of property is liable for injuries caused by defects is a question of fact. The fact-finder (judge or jury) will determine the type of defect. This determination will then be used to choose the rule of law to be applied. The general rule is that lessors will not be liable for injuries caused by patent defects but may be liable if they had sufficient knowledge of a latent defect. Lessees may be liable if they had control of the property for a period of time sufficient to reasonably discover any potentially injury-causing latent defect.

NOTES

1. Plaintiffs cannot recover for injuries caused by a lack of reasonable care for their own safety. In *Waxenberg* v. *Crystal Baths*, 129 N.Y.S. 2d 71 (Sup. Ct. 1954), plaintiff handball player sought recovery from defendant handball court owner in negligence action for injuries sustained when playing partner tripped on defective section of the floor. In granting a directed verdict for the defendant, the trial court held that the plaintiff could not recover in absence of a showing that the defect was obscure or hidden and could not have been discovered through exercise of reasonable care.

2. Lessee will not be liable for injuries caused by latent defects that could not be detected through a reasonably careful inspection. In *Greene* v. *Seattle Athletic Club*, 60 Wash. 300, 111 P. 157 (1910), plaintiff spectator sought recovery from defendant athletic club for injuries sustained when a railing, which appeared to be safe, gave way because of a latent structural defect. In affirming judgment for the defendant, the Washington Supreme Court held that since defendant had leased the newly constructed armory for one night only, the defendant was only required to exercise reasonable care.

3. Plaintiffs may not recover for injuries caused by a defect defendants could not have discovered through the exercise of reasonable care. In *Wright* v. *Mt. Mansfield Lift*, 96 F. Supp. 786 (D. Vt. 1951), plaintiff skier sued defendant ski resort for injuries sustained as a result of his striking a snow-covered stump. The district court, in directing a verdict for the defendant, held that in absence of evidence of any dangers existing on the ski trail, which reasonable prudence by defendants would have foreseen and corrected, the plaintiff was merely accepting a danger that was inherent to the sport of skiing.

4. In *Dudley Sports Co.* v. *Schmitt*, 151 Ind. App. 217, 29 Ind. Dec. 285, 279 N.E. 2d 266 (1972), the court found a defect in a pitching machine to be a latent defect (see Section 4.30).

5. In *Heldman* v. *Uniroyal, Inc.*, 371 N.E. 2d 557 (Ohio Ct. App. 1977), the court found a synthetic tennis playing surface to be a patent defect (see Section 4.30).

4.12–3(d)   Common Carriers

A common carrier is any carrier required by law to convey passengers or freight without refusal if the approved fee or charge is paid. A common carrier is different from a private or contract carrier, which has a right to refuse a load.

Common carriers have a duty to their passengers to use the utmost care in providing a safe environment (see Note 3). The standard of care imposed on common carriers is higher than the reasonable care standard owed to invitees. However, it is a lesser standard than the strict liability standard in which the defendant is responsible for all injuries. Carriers are responsible for all negligence but are not insurers of passengers' safety — that is, if there is an unavoidable or unforeseeable accident, a common carrier will not be held liable.

NOTES

1. Common carriers are held to a high standard. In *Fischer* v. *Mt. Mansfield Co., Inc.*, 283 F. 2d 533 (2nd Cir. 1960), plaintiff skier sought recovery for injuries sustained while riding on defendant's ski lift. In affirming judgment for plaintiff, the court of appeals held that the ski lift was a "common carrier" and its operator was required to exercise the highest degree of care for the passengers' safety.

2. A common carrier does not assume the role of insurer to all potential plaintiffs. The common carrier is not liable unless it is somehow negligent itself. In *Vogel* v. *State*, 204 Misc. 614, 124 N.Y.S. 2d 563 (1953), 136 N.Y.S. 2d 376 (App. Div. 1953), plaintiff skier sued state to recover for injuries incurred while getting off a moving chair lift. The court of claims held that the state was a common carrier but had exercised the requisite degree of care. The skier's own negligence was the proximate cause of her injuries.

3. Plaintiff invitee will recover if a common carrier falls below the standard of "utmost care." In *Grauer* v. *State of New York*, 15 Misc. 2d 471, 181 N.Y.S. ed. 994 (1959), plaintiff skier sought recovery for injuries sustained when ski-lift chair, operated by defendant state, struck him as he attempted to board. In granting judgment for the plaintiff, the court of claims held that as a common carrier, the state owed plaintiff highest duty of care and that it was negligent in allowing an approaching chair to tip or swing in such a way that injury was foreseeable (see Section 4.25).

4.12–4 Reckless Misconduct

Reckless misconduct or gross negligence falls between the unintentional tort of negligence and the intentional torts of assault and battery. Behavior in the category of reckless misconduct is characterized by intent on the part of the defendant to commit the act but no intent to harm the plaintiff by the act. Reckless mis-conduct means the actor has intentionally performed an act in disregard of a known risk, when the risk is so great as to make the harm highly probable. It must usually be accompanied by a conscious disregard of the circumstances. Reckless misconduct is particularly important in the area of participant-against-participant tort cases. Only recently have courts found a duty between sports participants to refrain from reckless misconduct toward another player (see Section 4.21).

To find reckless misconduct, an action must be more than ordinary inadvertence or inattention but less than conscious indifference to the consequences. It may be defined as an action that is willfull, wanton, or reckless. Reckless misconduct is not an intentional action. However, the degree of care exercised is so far below the usual standard that in effect it is treated as intentional action. Reckless misconduct encompasses action that evidences an extreme departure from the ordinary degree of care required from the actor in the particular circumstances.

The legal principles in establishing negligence or gross negligence are the same, but the damages awarded in a gross negligence case may be greater because punitive damages may be awarded.

NOTES

1. The court has applied the standard of reckless misconduct in the following cases, which involve one participant suing another participant:
(a) *Nabozny* v. *Barnhill*, 334 N.E. 2d 258 (Ill. Ct. App. 1975), (see Section 4.21).
(b) *Hackbart* v. *Cincinnati Bengals Inc.*, 601 F. 2d 516 (10th Cir. 1979) (see Section 4.21).
(c) *Bourque* v. *Duplechin*, 331 So. 2d 40 (La. Ct. App. 1976) (see Section 4.21).
For a further discussion on the theory of reckless misconduct, see *Restatement (Second) of Torts*, section 500.

3. For further information, see
(a) "Comment, Compensating Injured Professional Athletes: The Mystique of Sport versus Traditional Tort Principles," 55 *New York University Law Review* 971 (November 1980).
(b) "Federal Jurisdiction — Torts — Federal District

Court in Diversity Suit May Not Refuse Jurisdiction Over Professional Football Player's Claim for Damages Resulting from Blow Intentionally Inflicted," 11 *Rutgers-Camden Law Journal* 497 (Spring 1980).

(c) "Negligence — A Professional Football Player Owes a Duty to All Participants to Refrain from Reckless Misconduct in the Course of a Professional Football Game," 15 *Gonzaga Law Review* 867 (1980).

4.12–5   Defenses for Negligence

Once the four elements essential to a negligence action have been presented by the plaintiff, the defendant can employ a number of common defenses in such lawsuits. The most common defenses employed by defendants in tort actions for negligence are as follows:

1. No negligence (see Section 4.12–5[a])
2. Contributory negligence (see Section 4.12–5[b])
3. Comparative negligence (see Section 4.12–5[c])
4. Assumption of risk (see Section 4.12–5[d])
5. Immunity, statute of limitations, and Good Samaritan statutes (see Section 4.12–5[e])

4.12–5(a)   No Negligence

A defendant in a tort lawsuit will usually attempt to prove that his behavior did not constitute negligence. This can be approached in two ways. The defendant can dispute the negligence claim by either attacking one or more of the four previously discussed requirements for negligence (see Section 4.12) or by proving that reasonable care in his actions was exercised as specified by the reasonable person standard (see Section 4.12–1). Thus a defendant may defend a charge of negligence by asserting that he had no duty toward the plaintiff. Even a defendant who had a duty toward the plaintiff would not be liable if that duty was not breached. Therefore, if the defendant owed the plaintiff a duty of reasonable care and properly discharged that duty, any harm to the plaintiff would not be actionable negligence on the part of the defendant.

NOTES

1. In *Wells* v. *Minneapolis Baseball & Athletic Ass'n.*, 122 Minn. 327, 142 N.W. 706 (1913), the defendant facility possessor was held to be not negligent when a foul ball struck a spectator and caused injuries. The court held that the defendant's behavior met the standard of care required in the situation (see Section 4.24).

2. In *Townsley* v. *Cincinnati Gardens, Inc.*, the defendant facility owner was held to be not negligent when a young boy was beaten up in the men's room. The court held that the defendant's behavior met the standard of care required in the situation (see Section 4.25).

4.12–5(b)   Contributory Negligence

Any act of the plaintiff that amounts to a lack of ordinary care and contributes to the proximate cause of the injury is contributory negligence. Contributory negligence is, in essence, a departure from the standard of reasonableness required of all people, including plaintiffs. There does not have to be an actual appreciation of the risk involved. There need only be a risk that is known or should be known and avoided by a reasonable person. A plaintiff has a duty to exercise ordinary care, and if he does not, plaintiff may be to some degree contributorily negligent.

In a jurisdiction that recognizes the defense of contributory negligence, a finding of contributory negligence effectively bars the plaintiff from any recovery from the defendant. The success of the defense of contributory negligence rests on the defendant's ability to prove that the plaintiff failed to exercise due care for personal safety and that this lack of due care was the proximate cause of the plaintiff's injury. In contributory negligence theory, as in negligence theory, the standard of care for children is reasonable care. The child's age, intelligence, and experience, however, are relevant to the issue of whether reasonable care was exercised (see Section 4.12–2). With respect to both negligence and contributory negligence, there are situations in which the negligent conduct of one party may be imputed to a second party under the doctrine of respondeat superior (see Section 4.13).

NOTES _____

1. The plaintiff in the following cases was precluded from recovery because of a successful contributory negligence defense.

(a) In *Juntila* v. *Everett School Dist. No. 24*, 48 P. 2d 613 (Wash. 1935), plaintiff spectator sought recovery for injuries sustained when the guard railing on which he was seated while watching a football game collapsed. In affirming dismissal, the Washington Supreme Court held that the plaintiff, who sat on railing knowing it was not intended as a seat, was contributorily negligent as a matter of law. (See also Section 4.25.)

(b) In *Powless* v. *Milwaukee Co.*, 94 N.W. 2d 187 (Wis. 1959), plaintiff spectator sought recovery for injuries suffered because she was struck by a foul ball. In affirming the trial court's dismissal, the Wisconsin Supreme Court held that even if owners were negligent under the state's "safe-place" statute, the plaintiff's choice of seat and failure to react to noise and excitement around her after hearing the bat hit the ball made her liable of contributory negligence.

(c) In *Shields* v. *Van Kelton Amusement Corp.*, 228 N.Y. 396, 127 N.E. 261 (Ct. App. 1920), plaintiff ice skater sought recovery for injuries sustained when she fell as a result of a soft spot on defendant's outdoor skating rink. In reversing judgment for the plaintiff, the court of appeals held that plaintiff, an experienced skater, was aware that the ice was melting and that defendant's placement of benches near the soft spot to prevent access was sufficient to notify patrons of dangerous areas. The court found that the plaintiff was contributorily negligent.

(d) In *Pierce* v. *Murnick*, 145 S.E. 2d 11 (N.C. 1965), plaintiff, a ring-side spectator at defendant promoter's wrestling match, sought recovery for injuries sustained when a wrestler fell on him from the ring. In affirming judgment for defendant, the North Carolina Supreme Court held that the promoter was not required to take steps for the safety of invitees that would reasonably impair enjoyment of exhibition by usual patrons, and that even if defendant was negligent in failing to take precaution to protect plaintiff, plaintiff was barred by contributory negligence in choosing the ring-side seat.

(e) In *Polsky* v. *Levine*, 243 N.W. 2d 503 (Wis. 1976), plaintiff, a minor, sought recovery for injuries sustained while water skiing on defendant camp operator's lake. In affirming judgment for defendants, the Wisconsin Supreme Court held that since plaintiff could have kicked the rope and tow bar free and avoided injury but

did not do so because he would have fallen and received unsuccessful marks, he failed to exercise ordinary care for his own safety and could not recover.

(f) See *Gaspard* v. *Grain Dealers Mutual Insurance Co.*, 131 So. 2d 831 (La. Ct. App. 1961), in Section 4.21.

2. The defense of contributory negligence was not successful in the following cases:

(a) In *Bourque* v. *Duplechin*, 331 So. 2d 40 (La. Ct. App. 1976), an action involved a collision in a softball game between a runner and the second baseman (see Section 4.21).

(b) In *Nabozny* v. *Barnhill*, 334 N.E. 2d 258 (Ill. Ct. App. 1975), an action involved a collision between a goalie and a forward in a high school soccer game (see Section 4.21).

(c) In *Benjamin* v. *State*, 115 Misc. 2d 71, 453 N.Y.S. 2d 329 (Ct. Cl. 1982), a spectator at a hockey game was injured by a hockey puck (see Section 4.25).

3. In *Harrison* v. *Montgomery County Board of Education*, 456 A. 2d 894 (Md. Ct. App. 1983), a suit was brought by an eighth grader who was rendered a quadraplegic while attempting a running front flip during a "free exercise" day in the gymnasium. The Maryland court refused to abandon the doctrine of contributory negligence in favor of comparative negligence. The court found little dissatisfaction with the doctrine of contributory negligence in Maryland case law, and said any such change should be left to the legislature to enact.

4.12–5(c) Comparative Negligence

Comparative negligence is a statutory rule adopted in many states in an effort to alleviate the harshness of the contributory negligence doctrine. Comparative negligence statutes seek to divide the responsibility between the two negligent parties. Under a comparative negligence statute, the jury or fact-finder determines the proportionate degree of negligence that is to be attributed to all parties involved. The damages are then assessed pro rata.

In states adopting the doctrine of comparative negligence, contributory negligence on the part of the plaintiff is not necessarily a complete bar to plaintiff's recovery. Generally, two rules are applied under the theory of comparative negligence in most states:

1. If the plaintiff's negligence as compared with total negligence of all defendants is greater than 50 percent, plaintiff is totally barred from recovery. For example, the

plaintiff who is determined to be 60 percent at fault will not be able to recover against the defendant.

2. If the plaintiff's negligence as compared with the total negligence of all defendants is 50 percent or less, plaintiff's damages are reduced in proportion to plaintiff's negligence. For example, the plaintiff who suffers $100,000 in damages and whose negligence is determined to be 40 percent recovers $60,000 (his 40 percent responsibility is subtracted from the damages of $100,000).

NOTES _____

1. The following example is a comparative negligence statute from the Massachusetts General Laws:

Contributory negligence shall not bar recovery in any action by any person or legal representative to recover damages for negligence resulting in death or in injury to person or property, if such negligence was not greater than the total amount of negligence attributable to the person or persons against whom recovery is sought, but any damages allowed shall be diminished in proportion to the amount of negligence attributable to the person for whose injury, damage or death recovery is made. In determining by what amount the plaintiff's damages shall be diminished in such a case, the negligence of each plaintiff shall be compared to the total negligence of all persons against whom recovery is sought. The combined total of the plaintiff's negligence taken together with all of the negligence of all defendants shall equal one hundred per cent.

The violation of a criminal statute, ordinance or regulation by a plaintiff which contributed to said injury, death or damage shall be considered as evidence of negligence of that plaintiff, but the violation of said statute, ordinance or regulation shall not as a matter of law, and for that reason alone, serve to bar a plaintiff from recovery.

The defense of assumption of risk is hereby abolished in all actions hereunder.

The burden of alleging and proving negligence which serves to diminish a plaintiff's damages or bar recovery under this section shall be upon the person who seeks to establish such negligence, and the plaintiff shall be presumed to have been in the exercise of due care. [Massachusetts General Laws Chapter 231, Section 85. Comparative negligence; limited effect of contributory negligence as defense]

2. In *Duffy* v. *Midlothian Country Club et al.*, No. 75 L12096 (Ill. Cir. Ct. 1982), the court found the plaintiff to be 10 percent negligent and therefore reduced the award granted by 10 percent (see Section 4.24, Note 2[f]).

3. In *Harrison* v. *Montgomery County Board of Education*, 456 A. 2d 894 (Md. Ct. App. 1983), the court refused to apply the doctrine of comparative negligence instead of contributory negligence. The court indicated that any change must be made by the legislature and not the judiciary system (see Section 4.12–5[b], Note 3).

4. In *Van Stry* v. *State*, 479 N.Y.S. 2d 258 (App. Div. 1984), the court found the state 60 percent liable for the injury suffered by a student who slipped in a puddle of water in a locker room. (See Section 4.25, Note 1[j].)

5. For further information, see the following articles: "*Akis* v. *Glens Falls City School District*; A Crack in the Wall of Comparative Negligence," 46 *Albany Law Review* 1533 (Summer 1982).

4.12–5(d) Assumption of Risk

Assumption of risk means that the plaintiff has given prior consent to what would normally be an unpermitted, potentially injury-causing action. This consent effectively relieves defendant's obligation of any standard of care toward the plaintiff. Legal duty no longer exists between the two and therefore negligence cannot be found (see Section 4.12–1[a]).

Assumption of risk requires that the plaintiff know and fully appreciate the risks involved in pursuing the course of action to which he is committed. In addition to knowing and appreciating the risk, the plaintiff must also carefully and reasonably agree to assume whatever risk is involved.

The defense of assumption of risk may be utilized in those states that have not passed a comparative negligence statute (see Section 4.12–5[c]) to supplement the contributory negligence statute (see Section 4.12–5[b]). In such states, the defendant may claim that the plaintiff, by assuming the risk of injury, is barred from any recovery. Under the comparative negligence statute, however, partial recovery is allowed in many situations in which the plaintiff's contributory negligence proximately contributed to plaintiff's injury. This does not reconcile with the previous legal interpretation under which no recovery was allowed to a plaintiff who was found to have assumed the risk, even when such assumption of risk was considered reasonable under the circumstances. In states in which assumption of risk has been abolished as a defense in negligence actions, a plaintiff is entitled to full recovery if the assumption of risk was reasonable. If such assumption of risk was unreasonable, comparative negligence may exist and recovery is therefore governed by the state's contributory negligence statute. In sports cases, assumption of risk is an important concept because its action may negate a plaintiff's case. If the plaintiff is deemed to have assumed the risk, there may be a valid excuse for a tort that may have been committed.

NOTES

1. In the following cases, the plaintiff was precluded from recovery because of a successful assumption-of-risk defense:

(a) In *Schentzel v. Philadelphia National League Club*, 96 A. 2d 181 (Pa. Super. Ct. 1953), plaintiff female spectator, who was viewing a baseball game for the first time, sought recovery for injuries sustained when she was struck by a foul ball while seated in the upper deck near first base. In reversing the trial court's refusal to enter judgment notwithstanding the verdict for defendant, the court held that the plaintiff knew or should have known that foul balls sometimes go astray, that she had assumed the risk, and that the defendant was not negligent in failing to provide screens for the upper deck.

(b) In *Richmond v. Employers' Fire Ins. Co.*, 298 So. 2d 118 (La. Ct. App. 1974), plaintiff college baseball player sought recovery from the defendant college coach and insurance company for injuries sustained during practice in which the coach was allegedly negligent in allowing a bat to fly from his hands. In affirming a finding for the defendants, the court of appeals held that the coach was not negligent and that the player had assumed the risk of injury inherent in a baseball practice session.

(c) In *Stevens v. Central School Dist. No. 1*, 270 N.Y.S. 2d 23 (App. Div. 1966), plaintiff sought recovery for injuries sustained when playing basketball in defendant's school building, his momentum carried him through a glass window in a door just behind the basket. In affirming a verdict for defendant, the court held the plaintiff had assumed the risk of the dangerous condition caused by the use of ordinary window glass in the door.

(d) In *Hackbart v. Cincinnati Bengals*, 435 F. Supp. 352 (D. Colo. 1977), the defendant raised the defense of assumption of risk involving an alleged tort that occurred on the football field (see Section 4.21).

(e) In *Gaspard v. Grain Dealers Mutual Insurance Co.*, 131 So. 2d 831 (La. Ct. App. 1961), the defendant successfully raised the defense of assumption of risk involving a baseball bat that slipped out of the hands of one boy and struck another boy (see Section 4.21).

(f) In *Heldman v. Uniroyal, Inc.*, 371 N.E. 2d 557 (Ohio Ct. App. 1977), plaintiff professional tennis player was imputed to have a higher degree of knowledge and awareness than the average non-professional tennis player about synthetic playing surfaces (see Section 4.30).

(g) In *Wells v. Minneapolis Baseball & Athletic Association*, 122 Minn. 327, 427 N.W. 706 (1913), a spectator at a baseball game was held to have assumed the risk of injury caused by a foul ball (see Section 4.24).

2. In the following cases, the defense of assumption of risk was not successful:

(a) In *Nabozny v. Barnhill*, 334 N.E. 2d 258 (Ill. Ct. App. 1975), the case involved a collision between a goalie and a forward in a high school soccer game (see Section 4.21).

(b) In *Bourque v. Duplechin*, 331 So. 2d 40 (La. Ct. App. 1976), the case involved a collision in a softball game between a runner and the second baseman (see Section 4.21).

(c) In *Duffy v. Midlothian Country Club et al.*, No. 75 L 12096 (Ill. Cir. Ct. 1982), the case involved a spectator who was hit in the eye by a golf ball (see Section 4.24, Note 2[f]).

3. In *Rutter v. Northeastern Beaver County School District*, 437 A. 2d 1198 (Pa. 1981), the Pennsylvania Supreme Court joined a growing number of states in abolishing the doctrine of assumption of risk. The plaintiff had suffered a detached retina as a result of an injury that occurred during a summer football practice supervised by the high school coaches. The plaintiff was playing a type of touch football known as jungle football when he was injured.

The court found on the facts of the case two possible types of assumption of risk that might apply. The first implied from the plaintiff's voluntary entering into a relationship with the defendant that he knew it involved the type of risk that caused the injury. Because of the voluntariness of the plaintiff's conduct, he was found to have agreed through implication to relieve the defendant-coach of responsibility. In entering into the player-coach relationship, the plaintiff in *Rutter* would be viewed as having assumed the ordinary risks encountered in football. The second type of assumption of risk is implied from the plaintiff's knowingly and voluntarily encountering the hazard created by the defendant. Thus, by participating voluntarily in jungle football, without protective gear, the plaintiff in *Rutter* could be subject to a defense of assumption of the risk.

The court abolished the doctrine of assumption of the risk because of the extreme difficulty in applying the doctrine and because the doctrine was duplicative of two other concepts — the scope of the defendant's duty and the plaintiffs' contributory negligence.

4. For further information, see the following articles:

(a) "*Rutter* v. *Northeastern Beaver County School District*," 21 *Duquesne Law Review* 815 (Spring 1983).

(b) "Non-professional Sport-Related Injuries and Assumption of Risk in Pennsylvania: Is There Life after Rutter?" 54 *Pennsylvania Bar Association Quarterly* 43 (January 1983).

(c) "Assumption of the Risk of Vicarious Liability in Personal Injury Actions Brought by Professional Athletes," *Duke Law Journal* 742 (September 1980).

(d) "Assumption of Risk after *Sunday* v. *Stratton Corporation*, 390 A. 2d 398 (Vt.): The Vermont Sports Injury Liability Statute and Injured Skiers," 3 *Vermont Law Review* 129 (1978).

5. The following is a statement issued by the NCAA Committee on Competitive Safeguards and Medical Aspects of Sports. It discusses the student-athletes assumption of risk and his or her responsibility to promote sport safety.

SHARED RESPONSIBILITY FOR SPORT SAFETY
A statement of the NCAA Committee on Competitive Safeguards and Medical Aspects of Sports (August 1978, Reissued March 1979)

Participation in sport requires an acceptance of risk of injury. Athletes rightfully assume that those who are responsible for the conduct of sport have taken reasonable precautions to minimize the risk of significant injury. Periodic analysis of injury patterns continuously lead to refinements in the rules and/or other safety guidelines. However, to legislate safety via the rule book and equipment standards, while often necessary, is seldom effective in and by itself. To rely on officials to enforce compliance with the rule book is as insufficient as to rely on warning labels to produce behavioral compliance with safety guidelines. By compliance is meant respect on everyone's part for the intent and purpose of a rule or guideline, not merely technical satisfaction with some of its phrasing.

Some sport safety problems lend themselves readily to identification and solution (e.g., heat stroke and the administration of liquids freely during early football practice). Some safety problems may be less clearly identified (e.g., head injuries), and solutions may be developed on selected assumptions and the premise that measurable standards are better understood than qualitative rhetoric (e.g., purchase a helmet manufactured in accordance with NOCSAE standards instead of purchase the "best helmet possible"). Some safety problems remain problems because of questionable

compliance with the legislated solutions (e.g., dental mouthguards).

Other sports and other concerns can be similarly approached. Coaches should acquaint athletes appropriately with the risks of injury and the rules and practices they are employing to minimize his/her risk of significant injury while pursuing the many benefits of sport.

The athlete and the athletic program have a mutual need for an informed awareness of the risk being accepted and for sharing the responsibility for controlling those risks.

4.12–5(e) Other Defenses: Immunity, Statute of Limitations, and Good Samaritan Statutes

Additional defenses that the defendant may raise when appropriate are those of immunity, statute of limitations, and Good Samaritan statutes. The immunity defense that may be raised in a negligence case is similar to the defense that may be raised in an assault and battery case (see Section 4.11–3[c]). Immunity may exist because of the relationship between the plaintiff and defendant or because of the capacity of the defendant. (See also sovereign immunity in Section 4.23–4.)

The statute-of-limitations defense may be raised when the plaintiff has not filed a complaint within the state's prescribed time period after a right to bring suit has accrued. A successful statute-of-limitations defense is a complete bar to recovery by the plaintiff. However, there may be different statutes of limitations for various torts, and the plaintiff may bring suit under a different tort theory if the statute of limitations has already expired on another (see Note 1).

The third defense involves Good Samaritan statutes. The Good Samaritan doctrine as a matter of law precludes negligence liability for one who sees and attempts to aid another person who has been placed in imminent and serious peril through the negligence of a third person. This exemption exists provided the attempt is not recklessly or rashly made. The negligence of a volunteer must actually worsen the position of a person in distress before liability will be imposed. The exemption is provided by statute in most states. Many states have statutes that specifically encourage medical personnel to render voluntary assistance either by exempting them from liability (see Note 3) or by establishing a standard of gross negligence (see Note 2). In addition, certain classes of nonmedical personnel who may be in a position to render medical assistance may be covered by statute (see Note 3[c]).

NOTES

1. In *Hackbart v. Cincinnati Bengals Inc.*, 435 F. Supp. 352 (D. Colo. 1977), plaintiff did not sue under an assault and battery theory because he did not file his action within the one-year statute of limitations. However, the plaintiff was able to bring suit under a reckless misconduct theory, since the statute of limitations was longer for that type of claim (see Section 4.21).

2. The following example is a Good Samaritan statute from the New York Laws:

Notwithstanding any inconsistent provision of any general, special or local law, any licensed dentist who voluntarily and without the expectation of monetary compensation renders first aid or emergency treatment at the scene of an accident or other emergency, outside of a hospital or any other place having proper and necessary medical equipment, to a person who is unconscious, ill or injured shall not be liable for damages for injuries alleged to have been sustained by such person or for damages for the death of such person alleged to have occurred by reason of an act or omission in the rendering of such first aid or emergency treatment unless it is established that such injuries were or such death was caused by gross negligence on the part of such dentist. Nothing in this subdivision shall be deemed or construed to relieve a licensed dentist from liability for damages for injuries or death caused by an act or omission on the part of a dentist while rendering professional services in the normal and ordinary course of practice. [New York Laws, Title 8 Art. 133 Education Law. Section 6611]

3. The following examples are Good Samaritan statutes from the Massachusetts General Laws:

No physician duly registered . . . and no hospital shall be liable in a suit for damages as a result of acts or omissions related to advice, consultation or orders given in good faith to ambulance operators and attendants who . . . under emergency conditions and prior to arrival of the patient at the hospital, clinic, office or other health facility from which the emergency communication to the ambulance operators or attendant is made shall be liable in a suit for damages as result of his said acts or omissions based upon said advice, consultations or orders . . . [Massachusetts General Laws Chapter 112A Section 13. Liability of doctors, nurses, hospitals, ambulance operators and attendants]

A physician employed by a school committee or a person who has completed a full course in emergency medical care as provided in section six of chapter one hundred and eleven C shall be assigned to every interscholastic football game played by any team representing a public secondary school in the Commonwealth, and the expenses of such physician or person shall be paid by the school committee of the city, town or district wherein such football game is played. [Massachusetts General Laws Chapter 71, Section 54A. Physician or person trained in emergency medical care; assignment to interscholastic football games]

No member of a ski patrol duly registered in the National Ski Patrol system, who, in good faith, renders emergency care or treatment to a person who has become injured or incapacitated at a place or in an area where an emergency rescue can be best accomplished by the members of such a ski patrol together with their special equipment, shall be liable in a suit for damages as a result of his acts or omissions, either for such care or treatment or as a result of providing emergency transportation to a place of safety, nor shall he be liable to a hospital for its expenses if, under such emergency conditions, he causes the admission of such injured or incapacitated person. [Massachusetts General Laws Chapter 231, Section 85. Emergency care, etc. of injured persons by members of ski patrols; exemption from civil liability]

4.13 Vicarious Liability

The doctrine of vicarious liability imposes liability for a tortious act upon a person who was not personally negligent, but is held liable because of his relationship with the individual who committed the tort. The most typical relationships that give rise to vicarious liability are master-servant, employer-employee, and principal-agent. Vicarious liability is also known as the doctrine of "respondeat superior," which means "look to the man higher up."

Vicarious liability imposes liability for a negligent act by A to B, because of some legal relationship between A and B, such as employer-employee. Under the doctrine of vicarious liability, B is liable to C, the party injured by A, even though B was not himself negligent and did not aid or encourage the negligence of A, and even if B attempted to prevent harm to C. For example, if the groundskeeper of a baseball stadium fails to fix a hole on the front of the pitcher's mound and injury results, the owner-employer may be held vicariously liable if the pitcher is injured as a result of the hole.

The justification for the doctrine of vicarious liability has been a topic of debate since the doctrine first appeared in the mid-1700s. The catalyst for the introduction of vicarious liability was the industrial revolution, which complicated commerce and industry. The rationale behind the doctrine is based on public-policy considerations. Since the servant is furthering the master's employment, the master should be responsible for the servant's actions. This places an increased burden on the master, but the master is in a better position to bear the risks of injuries to others. A master is in a better position to cover risks by being self-insured. The master is also responsible for supervision and correcting a servant's actions that lead to a tort. Finally, this doctrine allows an innocent plaintiff to recover from a "deep pocket" — that is, one who has the ability to pay the damage award.

Under vicarious liability, the employer may be held responsible when the employer exercises control and discretion over the employee, and the employee is negligent while acting within the scope of his employment. Vicarious liability is usually imposed when an employee has been involved in unreasonable or grossly negligent conduct. As a general rule, liability is not imposed on the employer for intentional torts committed by the employee. An intentional tort is usually considered beyond the scope of authority of the employer, not under control of the employer, and not in the furtherance of the employer's business. However, an employer may be held responsible for an intentional tort committed by an employee if the employee was under the authority and control of the employer and the tort was committed in the furtherance

of the employer's business purpose. These same general rules apply to vicarious liability claims in sports-related cases.

The doctrine of vicarious liability is widely applicable to tort actions for negligence in the sports setting. For example, a coach may be held liable for the actions of the players, a school district may be held liable for the actions of a coach or a teacher, or front-office personnel may be liable for the actions of a coach. For an employer to be held liable in these situations, the employee must first be found negligent under the primary standard of reasonable care, and then the action must be determined to have been within the scope of the defendant's employment.

In a tort case involving a monetary award for damages, it is common practice to sue in the alternative — that is, to sue each party involved in the alleged incident of negligence. This practice serves three primary purposes:

1. It allows the plaintiff to determine exactly who is responsible for the particular injury.
2. It allows the plaintiff to determine which party involved in the suit has money sufficient to pay the damages award ("deep pocket").
3. It prevents multiple suits on the same cause of action directed against the various defendants.

NOTES

1. Promoters of athletic events may be held liable for negligent actions of their supervisory personnel. In *Rosenberger* v. *Central Louisiana Dist. Livestock Show, Inc.*, 312 So. 2d 300 (La. 1975), plaintiff bareback bronco rider sought recovery from defendant rodeo promoters and defendant employees for injuries sustained at the rodeo. In reinstating the trial court verdict for plaintiff, the Louisiana Supreme Court held that the negligence of the rodeo supervisor in failing to check whether the gate of rodeo facility was closed resulted in plaintiff's injuries and that promoters were liable under the doctrine of respondeat superior.

2. An owner of a facility may be held liable for the negligence of an employee if the employee is acting within the scope of his job. In *Johnson* v. *County Arena, Inc.*, 349

A. 2d 643 (Md. Ct. App. 1976), plaintiff sought recovery in wrongful death for a roller skater who was struck from behind and knocked down by a skating guard while the guards were playing tag. In reversing a directed verdict for defendant arena owner, the court of special appeals held that the evidence on the issue of whether the guard had exercised the amount of care and prudence in the performance of his duties commensurate with his relationship with patron required submission to the jury.

3. In *Fustin* v. *Board of Education of Community Unit Dist. No. 2*, 242 N.E. 2d 308 (Ill. Ct. App. 1968), plaintiff high school basketball player sought recovery for injuries sustained when struck in the face by the fist of an opposing player. In affirming judgment for the defendant school board, the court of appeals held that employee's lack of negligence prevented application of respondeat superior and the fact that the board had taken out liability insurance did not in any way make the board liable (see Section 4.23–1, Note 5).

4. In *Hackbart* v. *Cincinnati Bengals Inc.*, 435 F. Supp. 352 (D. Colo. 1977), a football team was sued under the theory of respondeat superior for the alleged reckless misconduct of one of its players (see Section 4.21).

5. In *Mogabgab* v. *Orleans Parish School Board*, 239 So. 2d 456 (La. Ct. App. 1970), the court held that the school district and principal were not liable for the death of a football player who died from heat exhaustion, although the coach had actively denied medical assistance to the player for over two hours (see Section 4.23–2, Note 1).

6. In *Toone* v. *Adams*, 262 N.C. 403, 137 S.E. 2d 132 (1964), a baseball manager was held not responsible for the action of a fan since he had not directly incited the fan to commit a violent act (see Section 4.22–4).

7. In *Averill* v. *Luttrell*, 311 S.W. 2d 812 (Tenn. Ct. App. 1957), the court held that the baseball club was not liable for an intentional tort committed by its employee against an opposing player since the employee's action was not within the scope of his employment or working to further his employer's business (see Section 4.24).

8. In *Domino* v. *Mercurio*, 17 A.D. 2d 342, 234 N.Y.S. 2d 1011 (1962), *aff'd* 13 N.Y. 2d 922, 193 N.E. 2d 893 (1963), the school district was held responsible for the injuries caused to a player who fell over the bench. The school district was held liable under the doctrine of respondeat superior for the negligence of its employees, who allowed spectators at a softball game to push a bench too close to the playing surface (see Section 4.22–1, Note 1).

9. In *Rosensweig* v. *State of New York*, 146 N.Y.S. 2d 589 (Ct. Cl. 1955), several doctors employed by the state boxing commission where held to be agents and servants of the state (see Section 4.26).

10. In *Welch* v. *Dunsmuir Joint Union High School District*, 326 P. 2d 633 (Cal. Ct. App. 1958), the court held that the team doctor was an independent contractor and therefore the school district was not responsible for his actions (see Section 4.22–3).

11. In *Morris* v. *Union High School District A., King County*, 294 P. 998 (Wash. 1931) and *Vargo* v. *Svitchan* 301 N.W. 2d 1 (Mich. Ct. App. 1980), the defendant school districts were held vicariously liable for the negligence of their employee, the football coach (see Section 4.22–1).

12. In *Tomjanovich* v. *California Sports, Inc.*, No. H-78-243 (S.D. Tex. 1979), the defendant basketball team was held vicariously liable for the violent actions of one of its players (see Section 4.24).

13. For further information, see the following articles:
(a) "Professional Sports and Tort Liability: A Victory for the Intentionally Injured Player," *Detroit College of Law Review* 687 (Summer 1980).
(b) "Torts in Sports — Deterring Violence in Professional Athletics," 48 *Fordham Law Review* 764 (April 1980).

4.13–1 Independent Contractors

The problems raised by the existence of independent contractors are important in understanding the scope of the doctrine of vicarious liability. An independent contractor is a person who, although in some way is connected to the employer, is not under the employer's control. Thus, if such a person is determined to be an independent contractor, no vicarious liability may be imposed.

To determine the status of any person, the degree of control that the employer has over the employee's actions must be examined. The person who was hired for a specific, limited purpose, with no direct supervision, and who works without allowing the employer to have control over his actions is most likely an independent contractor. Once a determination has been made that the person is an independent contractor, the employer may not be held liable for negligence committed by that independent contractor. As a general rule, a doctor who is provided by a school that is hosting a football game is considered to be an independent contractor. Here, although paid by the school district, the doctor is not in any way under their control when making medical decisions. Thus, the doctrine of vicarious liability would not be applicable, and the school would not be liable for the doctor's medical negligence.

NOTES _____

1. A plaintiff's recovery against an employer is based on the defendant being found to be an employee rather than an independent contractor. In *Gross* v. *Pellicane*, 167 A. 2d 838 (N.J. Super. Ct. App. Div. 1961), petitioner, a free-lance jockey, sought worker's compensation for injuries sustained while riding defendant's horse in a race. In affirming the award, the trial court held that petitioner was an employee of the horse trainer, due to the control the trainer exercised over his duties, rather than an independent contractor.

2. In *Cramer* v. *Hoffman*, 390 F. 2d 19 (2nd Cir. 1968), the court held that a physician's negligence could not be imputed to the university when the plaintiff first alleged that the doctor was an agent of the hospital and not of the university. By not raising this issue until the trial, plaintiffs unfairly surprised the defendants. Also, there was no evidence to show that the defendant doctor was an agent of the hospital (see Section 4.23–2).

4.14   Defamation Law

Defamation law concerns the protection of personal reputation. The law in most states strongly protects and guards a person's reputation. The focus of a defamation action is on the alleged defamatory statement and its impact on third persons. The *Restatement (Second) of Torts*, section 559, defines a defamatory communication as one that "tends to harm the reputation of another as to lower him in the estimation of the community or to deter third persons from associating or dealing with him."

To establish liability for defamation there must be (1) a false and defamatory statement concerning another, (2) publication to a third person, (3) some degree of fault on the defendant's part, and (4) damages. A defamatory statement is also one that exposes the plaintiff to public hatred, shame, contempt, or ridicule. The reputation that is protected by the law of defamation is the opinion of others. The plaintiff must show that his reputation was injured in the eyes of a respectable group of the community.

Defamation is an intentional tort in that the defendant need only intend to make the publication of the statement or material. It does not matter that the defendant did not intend to harm the reputation of the plaintiff; defendant will still be accountable if the defamatory statement was intentional.

Defamation is divided into libel and slander. *Libel* is the publication of defamatory matter by writing, and *slander* is the publication of defamatory matter by spoken words. There are three kinds of libelous materials: (1) materials that are obviously defamatory (libel per se), (2) materials that could be taken as defamatory or as not defamatory, and (3) materials that are not obviously defamatory but when taken with other facts become libelous.

The basic elements of libel are a defamatory statement, publication, and damages. Truth is a defense to a libel action; however, it is only a qualified defense, not an absolute defense. The defendant has the burden of proving the truth of the communication if truth is the defense. If the libel is not true, the plaintiff has the burden of proving that it was published with malice. The level of malice required to defeat the defendant's proof of truth and to make the defamatory matter actionable in spite of the truth is hatred, ill will, or malevolent intention. The plaintiff must also prove that a third person was exposed to the publication. Finally, the plaintiff must prove actual damages. There are two basic forms of damages in this context: general and special damages. General damages include damages to reputation, as well as emotional pain and suffering. Special damages are those which are the natural but not the necessary result of the alleged wrong and must be supported by specific proof. The defendant may be able to mitigate damages by making a retraction or taking some other measure.

Slander is publication of defamatory matter by spoken words. There must be a publication, and the plaintiff must be held up to scorn and ridicule as a result of the defamatory statement. A statement is slanderous per se if it falls into one of the following categories:

1. Accuses the plaintiff of criminal conduct.
2. Accuses the plaintiff of having a loathsome disease.
3. Accuses the plaintiff of being unchaste.
4. Accuses the plaintiff of misconduct in public office.
5. Tends to injure plaintiff in plaintiff's profession, business, or trade.

Truth is an absolute defense to a slander action. Again, however, the plaintiff must show that the statement was heard and understood by a third person. To show damages, plaintiff must prove that it was slanderous per se or must prove special damages.

The United States Supreme Court has put forth standards that apply in libel and slander sections. In these decisions, the Court balanced the competing interests of protecting the reputation of an individual against freedom of the press. In the first of these decisions in 1964 the Court held in *New York Times Co. v. Sullivan*, 376 U.S. 254, 84 S. Ct. 710, 11 L. Ed. 2d 686 (1964), that the constitutional guarantee of free press requires a public official to prove actual malice in the publication of a defamatory falsehood in order to recover for defamation. Then, in 1967 the constitutional privilege in *Curtis Publishing Co. v. Butts, infra* was extended to public figures as well as to public officials. Finally, in *Gertz v. Robert Welch Inc.*, 418 U.S. 323, 94 S. Ct. 2997, 41 L. Ed. 2d 789 (1974), the Court extended the "actual malice" standard. A public official or public figure who has been defamed must prove that the defendant published the statement with actual malice — that is, knowing that the material was false or in reckless disregard of whether or not it was false.

Defamation should be distinguished from both invasion of privacy (See Section 4.15) and intentional infliction of emotional distress (see Section 4.16). Intentional infliction of emotional distress concerns the impact on the individual plaintiff without regard to third persons. Defamation involves the element of publication to third persons, as well as the requirement that the material be taken by the third persons as damaging. Defamation must also be distinguished from the tort of invasion of privacy. An action for invasion of privacy concerns one's peace of mind and comfort, while the action for defamation involves the plaintiff's character or reputation. Invasion of privacy can also be distinguished from defamation in that truth is a defense to the defamation action, but truth is not a defense to an invasion of privacy action.

Curtis Publishing Co. v. Butts, 388 U.S. 130, 87 S. Ct. 1975, 18 L. Ed. 2d 1094 (1967)

The Curtis Publishing Company, publishers of the *Saturday Evening Post*, printed an article in which it was alleged that Wallace Butts, athletic director at the University of Georgia, had supplied to Paul Bryant, head football coach at the University of Alabama, information concerning Georgia's plays and preparations for its upcoming game with Alabama, thus throwing the game in Alabama's favor. The article revealed that George Burrett, an Atlanta insurance salesman, had accidentally overheard a telephone conversation between Butts and Bryant one week prior to the game, in which Butts outlined Georgia's offensive and defensive plays, mentioning plays and players by name. The article contended that the Georgia players and sideline observers were aware that their plays were known to Alabama and that Georgia "took a frightful physical beating." The article concluded by announcing Butts's resignation from Georgia for health and business reasons. Butts brought an action for libel in federal court, seeking $5 million in compensatory and $5 million in punitive damages. The jury found for Butts and awarded $60,000 in general damages and $3 million in punitive damages. The trial judge reduced the total to $460,000.

At the time the *Curtis Publishing Co.* case

was being tried, the U.S. Supreme Court was hearing the case of *New York Times Co.* v. *Sullivan*. After *Curtis Publishing Co.* was concluded in district court, the Supreme Court handed down a decision in *New York Times Co.* v. *Sullivan*. The Supreme Court held that a public official may not recover damages for libel relating to official conduct unless plaintiff can prove that the statement was made with actual malice — that is, with knowledge that it was false or with reckless disregard for whether it was false or not.

Curtis Publishing Co. was appealed to the United States Supreme Court. The Court's decision focused on Curtis Publishing Company's contention that Butts, while not a public official, was a public figure and thus fell under the stricter guidelines of *Sullivan*. The Court held that public officials usually hold a protection against libel judgments for their utterances, and that *Sullivan* had given like protection to the press in its comment on the official actions of such persons. The thrust of this decision was to ensure free debate of ideas by allowing both the press and public officials freedom from the ordinary standards of libel. Butts, on the other hand, enjoyed no such protection for his utterances, but did hold a position that commanded a substantial amount of public interest at the time of the publications — indeed, as much interest as the plaintiff in *Sullivan* commanded. The Court found that libel action involving public figures cannot be left entirely to state libel laws, but also held that "the rigorous federal requirements of *Sullivan* are not the only appropriate accommodation of the conflicting interests at stake." The Court held that a public figure who is not a public official may recover damages for a defamatory falsehood that is obviously damaging to reputation, on a showing that the conduct of the publisher was highly unreasonable and constituted an extreme departure from the standards of investigation and reporting ordinarily adhered to by responsible publishers. The Court then dealt with Curtis's contention that it could not be assessed punitive damages because an unlimited punitive award against a magazine publisher constitutes an effective prior restraint by giving the jury the power to destroy the publisher's business. The Court rejected this argument on the grounds that publishers engage in a wide variety of activities, which may lead to tort suits in which punitive damages are a possibility. The mere fact that a company is in the business of publishing does not exempt it from an imposition generally expected from other members of the community. The constitutional guarantees of freedom of speech and freedom the press are served by judicial control over jury awards. In addition, when a publisher engages in misconduct severe enough to strip it of such constitutional guarantees, it is to the public's benefit that the company be assessed punitive damages as a deterrent to a repetition of its misdeeds.

Having set forth the standard by which the constitutionality of damage awards in this case must be judged, the Court then turned to a review of the facts of the case. The Court found that the evidence and findings of the lower court met that standard, and thus affirmed the judgment of the court of appeals in favor of Butts.

Chuy v. Philadelphia Eagles Football Club, 431 F. Supp. 254 (E.D. Pa., 1977), *aff'd*, 595 F. 2d 1265 (3rd Cir. 1979)

A pro football player brought an action against his team, the Philadelphia Eagles, which was based on breach of contract, intentional infliction of emotional distress, and defamation. Chuy's defamation claim was founded on an allegedly false statement made by a team physician who had falsely reported to the press that Chuy had a rare blood disease, which would permanently prevent him from playing football. The first issue that the court addressed was the legal status of Chuy in a defamation case. Applying the standard set forth in *Gertz* v. *Robert Welch, Inc.*, 418 U.S. 323, 94 S. Ct. 2997, 41 L. Ed. 2d 789 (1974), the court found that Chuy was a public figure.

He was a prominent starting player on a professional team, and he had voluntarily placed himself in the public eye. The court noted that the United States Supreme Court had established two types of public figures. In *Gertz* the Supreme Court had stated:

> For the most part those who attain public figure status have assumed roles of special prominence in the affairs of society. Some occupy positions of such persuasive power and influence that they are deemed public figures for all purposes. More commonly those classed as public figures have thrust themselves to the forefront of public controversies in order to influence the resolution of the issues. [*Gertz* v. *Robert Welch, Inc.*, 418 U.S. 323, 345 (1974)]

The court concluded that Chuy was a public figure. The court noted that a person who chooses to engage in a profession that is of public interest invites discussion and that there is a tremendous public interest in professional football.

Since it was established that Chuy was a public figure, Chuy had to meet the "actual malice" test established in *New York Times Co.* v. *Sullivan* in order to be successful in his claim. Although the evidence showed that the doctor knew the statement was false, Chuy was not allowed to recover, since he was unable to meet the actual malice test.

The court held for the Eagles on the defamation claim because Pennsylvania law provided that the newspaper columnist had to understand the statement as defamatory for there to be liability. Since Chuy could not prove that the reporter understood the statement in a defamatory way, Chuy was barred from recovery.

An interesting part of this case was that the court found the Eagles football club to be protected by the requirement that false comments about public figures must be made in knowing or in reckless disregard for the truth. The court held that the Eagles were protected by this standard even though they were a private, nonmedia defendant.

NOTES

1. In Chuy, the plaintiff also sued for intentional infliction of emotional distress (see Section 4.16).

2. Chuy also sued the Philadelphia Eagles and the National Football League on antitrust grounds based on the facts arising out of the same situation. See *Chuy* v. *Philadelphia Eagles*, 407 F. Supp. 717 (E.D. Pa. 1977), *aff'd*, 595 F. 2d 1235 (3rd Cir. 1979).

3. See *Rutledge* v. *Arizona Board of Regents*, 660 F. 2d 1345 (9th Cir. 1981), *aff'd*, 103 S. Ct. 148 (1982), in which a football coach was sued for defamation by one of his players (see Section 4.22–2).

4. In *Paul Hornung* v. *National Collegiate Athletic Ass'n.*, No. 82 CI–06769 (Jefferson Cir. Ct., Ky., 1982), (pending), a multimillion dollar lawsuit was brought by former Green Bay Packer and Heisman Trophy winner Hornung against officials who represented the NCAA. Hornung, who since his retirement in 1967, had an extensive broadcast career, including coverage of many college games, was under an agreement in principle with Turner Broadcasting to provide color commentary for 19 college games in 1982. However, a representative of the NCAA sent a letter to Turner Broadcasting, which contained the following statement:

> Paul Hornung was not approved for 1982. The committee believes he is closely identified with professional football, that he had at least one undesirable public situation while a professional player and that the image which he projects or is projected for him does not personify college football.

Hornung stated that the accusations made in the letter were false and were published by the NCAA with actual malice and in reckless disregard of the true facts. Hornung alleged, that as a result of the letter, defamation and interference with contractual relationships occurred. Hornung sought actual, direct, and consequential damages of $1 million. In addition, he sought punitive damages of $2 million.

In 1985, Hornung was finally allowed to telecast games for WTBS through the individual NCAA institutions and allied athletic conferences, since the NCAA no longer controlled college football games on television. Shortly thereafter, Hornung's case came to trial, and a Kentucky state court ruled in his favor. Hornung, who had sought $3 million in damages, was awarded $1.5 million from the jury, including $150,000 in compensatory damages and $1 million in punitive damages.

For further information, see the following articles:

(a) "Hornung Back in Booth," *USA Today*, August 20, 1985, p. C3.

(b) "Big Gain for Hornung," *New York Times*, August 25, 1985, sec. 5, p. 9.

(c) "Names: Hornung a Winner vs. NCAA," *Boston Globe*, August 25, 1985, p. 71.

5. Tom Meyer, men's basketball coach at the University of Illinois at Chicago, filed a $1-million lawsuit in 1983 against the University's board of trustees and three staff members, which claimed a breach of contract as well as irreparable damage to his reputation. The individuals named in the suit were the university's vice-chancellor, Richard Ward; the athletic director, William Roetzheim, and an assistant coach, Willie Little. Meyer was dismissed as coach by Mr. Roetzheim following accusations by several players that he had neglected their personal and academic needs. He was then reinstated as coach, first by a court order and then by the university. As a result of this, Mr. Meyer contended that the entire incident had impaired his professional reputation so that it would be difficult for him to secure another coaching job. The case was settled.

6. In *Carlen v. University of South Carolina*, No. 83–379–0 (D.S.C. 1983), (pending), plaintiff, former head football coach at the University of South Carolina, brought suit against the university, in part, under a defamation theory. He alleged that his termination and breach of his contract permanently damaged his reputation as a major college football coach, irreparably impairing his ability to obtain another position.

7. A former team doctor for the San Diego Chargers football team, in a book he wrote about his experiences, stated that the Chargers players thought wide receiver Dave Williams was "chicken" because he allegedly was afraid of short patterns to mid-field where the tackling was most severe. Williams filed suit for libel and was awarded $300,000 by the jury.

8. Pam Parsons, former women's basketball head coach at the University of South Carolina, filed suit in U.S. District Court seeking $75 million in damages for libel after a *Sports Illustrated* article stated that she resigned her position when confronted with information concerning a lesbian affair she had with one of her players. The jury, in 1984, found for the defendant after ruling that the story was "substantially true." See "Stormy Weather at South Carolina," *Sports Illustrated*, February 8, 1982, p. 30. Parsons and a former player who testified on her behalf were later convicted of perjury.

9. In *Institute of Athletic Motivation* v. *University of Illinois*, 170 Cal. Rptr. 411, 114 Cal. App. 3d 1 (1980), the developer of a questionnaire administered to coaches and athletes purporting to identify certain personality traits predictive of athletic success brought action for defamation against a university physical education professor who wrote a letter critical of the questionnaire and sent it to many professional athletic associations and organizations and to some sports magazines. The trial court entered judgment on general verdict to defendant University of Illinois. The institute appealed the decision. The court of appeals upheld the lower court's decision. It noted that, "Whether an allegedly defamatory statement constituted fact or opinion is a question of law, to be determined in light of the nature

and content of the communication taken as a whole." The court of appeals ruled that the letter(s) was a privileged communication to interested persons under the Civil Code and as such did not constitute grounds for a defamatory action.

10. In *Woy v. Turner*, 573 F. Supp. 35 (N.D. Ga. 1983), plaintiff William "Bucky" Woy, a sports agent for Bob Horner, a baseball player with the Atlanta Braves, filed a libel and slander suit against team owner Ted Turner. Turner had made statements to the effect that Woy's negotiation tactics on behalf of his client had contributed to the death of Braves' general manager Bill Lucas.

The United States District Court found that Woy was a public figure under the *New York Times Co.* v. *Sullivan* standard, and as such, Woy must show that Turner's statements were made with actual malice before being allowed to recover. The court applied a three-pronged test:

a. Did the plaintiff voluntarily thrust himself into the vortex of this particular controversy?

b. What was the nature and extent of the plaintiff's participation in the particular controversy?

c. Did the plaintiff encourage the public's attention in an attempt to influence the outcome of a particular controversy?

The court noted in discussing whether Woy was a public figure that:

Upon careful consideration of the aforementioned factors and after listening to the testimony in this case, oral argument of counsel, and viewing the various documents in evidence, the court finds that during the period of the contractual dispute up until the time when the defendant made the alleged defamatory statements (January–June 1979), the plaintiff had voluntarily thrust himself into the forefront of the contractual dispute. The plaintiff was in contact with the press, television stations, and sports magazines regarding the contractual dispute, several times upon his own initiation.

11. In *Smith v. McMullen*, 589 F. Supp. 642 (S.D. Tex. 1984), Tal Smith, former general manager of the Houston Astros baseball team, brought an action for slander against John J. McMullen, chairman of the board and owner of the Astros. McMullen had been quoted in Houston newspapers as calling Smith a "despicable human being" and questioning his managerial abilities. In ruling that McMullen's statements were actionable under Texas law the United States District Court noted that:

In the case at bar the Court concludes that defendant's remarks pertaining to plaintiff were hybrid in nature and were not pure opinion. The Court further finds that defendant failed to set forth any facts in support of his assertion that plaintiff had nothing to do with the apparent success of the Astros during his tenure as general manager. Thus, inasmuch as defendant's statements were no more than conclusory statements of unsupported fact, they are not privileged as opinion.

Therefore, McMullen's motion for judgment on the pleadings was denied.

12. In *King* v. *Burris*, 588 F. Supp. 1152 (D. Colo. 1984), Dick King, president and general manager of the Wichita Aeros, filed a defamation suit against Jim Burris, president and general manager of the Denver Bears, for remarks Burris made at the 1981 winter meetings of the American Association of Professional Baseball Clubs. Burris called King a "damn fat fag," "fatso," and "liar," among other epithets. King alleged that as a direct result of Burris' actions, he resigned from the Aeros and sought medical assistance. The United States District Court, applying Florida law, held that Burris' comments stated a cause of action for defamation, but was subject to dismissal without prejudice due to King's failure to notify Burris of his intent to sue. In a colorful opinion, the court stated that in sport abusive language and insult are common, noting:

> See e.g., There is no reason why the field should not try to put the batsman off his stroke at the critical moment by neatly timed disparagements of his wife's fidelity and his mother's respectability. (George Bernard Shaw)
>
> (H)is head was full of larceny, but his feet were honest. ("Bugs" Bear on outfielder Ping Bodie, 1917)
>
> Call me anything, call me M——— F———, but don't call me Durocher. A Durocher is the lowest form of living matter. (Harry Wendelstedt, 1974)
>
> The more we lose, the more Steinbrenner will fly in. And the more he flies, the better chance there will be a plane crash. (Graig Nettles, 1977)
>
> (Charlie Finley) would want to know why there were fourteen uniforms dirty when only ten men got in the game. (Frank Ciensczk, Oakland equipment manager, 1972)
>
> I have often called Bowie Kuhn a village idiot. I apologize to all the village idiots of America. He is the nation's idiot. (Charlie Finley, 1981)
>
> The best way to test a Timex would be to strap it to (Earl) Weaver's tongue. (Marty Springstead, umpire)
>
> As a lifetime Cubs fan, I was used to players who, as the sportswriters say, "can do it all." In the case of the Cubs, "doing it all" means striking out, running the wrong way, falling down, dropping the ball. (Mike Royko, writer)

13. In *Barry* v. *Time, Inc.*, 584 F. Supp. 1110 (N.D. Cal. 1984), plaintiff failed to prove actual malice with sufficient specificity against defendant publisher and one of its magazines, *Sports Illustrated*, and defendant professional basketball player Quintin Dailey, when the magazine republished accusations made against the plaintiff. The district court held that the plaintiff was a limited public figure and that the publisher was constitutionally protected by the privilege of neutral reportage.

14. In *Stabler* v. *New York Times*, et al., No. M8-85 (S.D.N.Y. 1984) (settled), former NFL quarterback Ken Stabler brought a libel action against the *New York Times* and the National Broadcasting Company (NBC-TV), which had published and broadcast a news story that Stabler had been linked to a convicted bookmaker and organized crime figure. To prepare for the suit, both the plaintiff and defendants sought information contained in NFL security files. The NFL refused to turn over information in its files. The district court held that the files were not privileged materials and that the NFL must allow discovery of relevant material specifically limited to the purpose of the litigation.

15. Stabler later dropped his suit. A *New York Times* attorney noted that: "Stabler's withdrawal confirms what has been the *Time's* position all along, that our story was accurate and that this lawsuit should never have been filed.... I think Stabler was thrown for a loss on this one." See "Stabler Drops *Times* from a Libel Action, "*New York Times*, July 25, 1985, p. B11. For more information on the Stabler case, see *Stabler* v. *New York Times*, 569 F. Supp. 1131 (S.D. Tex. 1983).

16. In *Bell* v. *Associated Press*, 584 F. Supp. 128 (D.D.C. 1984), a libel action was brought by a professional football player against defendant news service for an erroneous report that stated plaintiff was arrested for lewdness. The district court held that plaintiff could not prove malice when the plaintiff conceded that the news service "thought it was me," based on the arrested individual's claim to be Bell.

17. In 1985, Louisiana State University (LSU) basketball coach Dale Brown lost a $4 million libel suit filed against the *Leesville Leader*, in which he claimed that the newspaper had written a story with reckless disregard for the truth when it stated that Brown had a disagreement with LSU academic adviser Mike Mallet over LSU player Derrick Taylor. See "Coaches' Corner," *Sporting News*, July 29, 1985, p. 51.

18. In *Cepeda* v. *Cowles Magazines and Broadcasting, Inc.*, 392 F. 2d 417 (9th Cir. 1968), *cert. denied* 393 U.S. 840 (1968), plaintiff baseball player filed a defamation suit against defendant magazine that said he was "not a team man" and was "temperamental, uncooperative and underproductive." Although when Cepeda brought the suit in 1963 he was under no obligation to prove actual malice, the legal developments during the five-year span of the case eventually dictated that he needed to prove actual malice. Unable to do so, Cepeda lost the suit.

19. In *Dempsey* v. *Time, Inc.*, 43 Misc. 2d 754, 252 N.Y.S. 2d 186 (1964), plaintiff heavyweight boxer Jack Dempsey brought a defamation suit against defendant magazine for suggesting in its article that plaintiff used

"loaded gloves" in a victory over Jess Willard in 1919. The court denied defendant's motion to dismiss, holding that plaintiff provided sufficient evidence of actual malice. In this case, as well as the *Cepeda* case, the court viewed the sports celebrity as a public figure for defamation purposes, especially since these cases involved accounts relating to the athlete's performance.

20. For further information, see the following articles:

(a) "Defamation: A Guide to Referees' Rights," 16 *Trial* 42 (January 1980).

(b) "Professional Football — Are Three One-Year Agreements Signed at one Sitting Actually One Contract? Are Players 'Public Figures'?" 10 *Connecticut Law Review* 350 (1978).

4.15   Invasion of Privacy

An action for invasion of privacy is designed to protect a person's mental peace and/or comfort. Invasion of privacy is an intentional tort. The laws prohibiting invasion of privacy are intended to protect the purely private matters of a person. Some intrusions into a person's life are expected and must be tolerated in society, but when the intrusions become excessive or unjustified, a cause of action exists for invasion of privacy.

The *Restatement (Second) of Torts*, section 652, determines the ways in which one may tortiously invade the privacy of another. That section provides:

> One who gives publicity to a matter concerning the private life of another is subject to liability to the other for invasion of his privacy, if the matter publicized is of a kind that
> (a) would be highly offensive to a reasonable person; and
> (b) is not of legitimate concern to the public.

Prosser, in *Law of Torts*, section 117 (1971), names four distinct ways for one to invade the privacy of another:

(1) intrusion upon one's physical solitude;

(2) public disclosure of private facts;

(3) putting one in false light in the public eye; and

(4) appropriation of some element of another's personality for commercial gain.

In an action for invasion of privacy, the intrusion must be substantial, and it must be into an area for which there is an expectation of privacy. For example, simply staring at a person would not generally amount to an intrusion. Wiretapping or phone tapping would amount to an intrusion of privacy.

The plaintiff must also show that the publication of private matters involved a matter that in fact was truly private. Newsworthy, public-interest matters or public facts are not considered to be of a purely private nature. Court records, for example, are open to the public and are therefore not viewed as private facts.

The United States Supreme Court in *Time, Inc.* v. *Hill*, 385 U.S. 374, 87 S.Ct. 534, 17 L.Ed. 2d 456 (1967), held that the First Amendment to the Constitution protects reports of newsworthy matters. These matters can be publicized unless actual malice is shown (see Section 4.14 on Defamation Law). The actual malice standard may be applied even though a plaintiff was a private person who did not want the publicity.

In *Bilney* v. *Evening Star Newspaper Co., infra*, members of the University of Maryland basketball team brought suit against two newspapers. The newspapers published an article concerning certain players whose academic standing was threatening their eligibility. The newspapers printed that the players were in danger of academic dismissal and gave details of their academic records. The players based their action, in part, on theory of invasion of privacy. The court, basing its decision on the *Restatement (Second) of Torts*, section 652, held that the players were public figures. The court found that there was widespread public interest in Maryland basketball. When the players' academic standing threatened their eligibility, the privacy of those facts then lessened. The court stated that "the publication of their eligibility-threatening status was not unreasonable and did not trample community mores" of what is legitimate public interest.

The court relied primarily on the reasoning

of the *Restatement (Second) of Torts*, section 652D. A public figure cannot complain about receiving publicity that has been sought even though it may be unfavorable. The *Restatement (Second) of Torts* also states that the publicity of public figures "is not limited to the particular events that arouse the interests of the public" (section 652D, comment). The legitimate public interest of these figures extends into some of their private matters. The court also held that the right to make public the private facts of a public figure is not an unlimited right. The court held that what is allowable is determined by community mores: "The line is to be drawn when the publicity ceases to be the giving of information to which the public is entitled and becomes a morbid and sensational prying into private lives" (section 652, comment).

The *Bilney* case typifies the difficult burden an athlete or any private figure has in winning an invasion of privacy action. The Maryland players were unsuccessful because the news article did not invade a "private" area. The opinion reflects how difficult it is for a person classified as a public figure to recover for invasion of privacy. Public figures must put up with more publicity of their private lives than one who is not a public figure. Most pro athletes and the majority of big-time college athletes would probably be classified as public figures; therefore, for them to recover under the theory of invasion of privacy would be extremely difficult.

Bilney v. Evening Star Newspaper Co., 406 A. 2d 652 (Md. Ct. App. 1979)

Six members of the University of Maryland basketball team brought suit over articles which appeared in the November 1, 1977 editions of the *Washington Star* and the University of Maryland's student publication, the *Diamondback*. A late-morning edition of the *Star* printed two articles concerning four of the players who brought suit. Pictures of the four players were prominently displayed on page one, and underneath the pictures were their names and this caption: "The University of Maryland's basketball program is in danger of collapse because of poor school work. The *Star* has learned that four of eight returning players — Larry Gibson, Jo Jo Hunter, Billy Bryant and John Bilney — are on academic probation and in danger of flunking." A full story appeared on page one of the sports section. The article stated that the *Star* had learned from university records that the four named players were on academic probation and in danger of flunking at the end of the fall semester. The information had actually come from two student reporters of the *Diamondback*, who had received it from a volunteer source.

On the same day — November 1, 1977 — the *Diamondback* printed a story reporting that Bilney, Bryant, Gibson, and Hunter were on probation and in danger of being academically dismissed. The story included the players' grade averages and a brief academic history of two of the players. The six players then brought suit against the publishers of the *Star* and the *Diamondback*, the editor and sports editor of the *Star*, the two authors of the *Diamondback* article, and a stringer and staff reporter for the *Star*. Their complaint alleged invasion of privacy and intentional infliction of emotional distress in that the actions of the defendants constituted a willful, wrongful, and malicious invasion of the players' confidential university records and facts concerning their private lives. Both tort actions were based on facts concerning their private lives, the unlawful obtaining of confidential school records, and the unlawful publication of such records. The Circuit Court for Prince George's County in Maryland granted summary judgment in favor of the defendants, and the players then appealed to the Maryland Court of Special Appeals.

In handing down its decision, the court took note of the fact that basketball at the University of Maryland was a big-time sport that generated a great deal of interest and excitement among students and fans in the Baltimore-Washington area. The court also noted Maryland basketball also generates a great deal of money — legally for the school and the Atlantic Coast Conference, and illegally through gambling. The team receives a great deal of coverage, and naturally this interest in the team spills over to the individual players. A great deal of notoriety is given to their recruitment and individual performances. The court went on to note that the players admitted in court documents that they were, by virtue of their status as members of the basketball team, "public figures" — that as team members they were the subject and object of widespread public interest.

The court affirmed the lower court decision. Plaintiffs had based their appeal on two major issues: (1) that the evidence did not support the lower court's conclusion that the defendants did not intentionally invade a private area of the players' lives and (2) that the defendants had no right to publicize the players' academic standing even if they were public figures. The appeals court disagreed with the plaintiffs' contentions and found that the players had failed to show that the defendants had personally invaded and inspected confidential university files or solicited a third party to obtain information. The information regarding the players was gratuitously given to the *Diamondback* reporters by a volunteer source, whose identity, under the aegis of the Maryland Shield Law, the reporters declined to reveal. The Maryland Shield Law provides that persons connected with or employed by a newspaper "may not be compelled to disclose, in any legal proceeding . . . the source of any news or information procured or obtained by him for and published in the newspaper" with which he or she is connected. The court also stated that the *Star* did not invade the student records when it paid the student reporters the standard fee for their contribution to the story. The court concluded that the information, though emanating ulti-

mately from confidential university records, was not obtained by any personal act of invasion or intrusion on the part of any of these appellees.

The court next dealt with the players' allegation that the publication of their scholastic standing was an invasion of privacy. In its holding, the court referred to sections 652A–652L of the *Restatement (Second) of Torts*, which recites the ways in which one may tortiously invade the privacy of another. One way, which is listed in section 652D, notes that:

> One who gives publicity to a matter concerning the private life of another is subject to liability to the other for invasion of his privacy, if the matter publicized is of a kind that
> (a) would be highly offensive to a reasonable person, and
> (b) is not of legitimate concern to the public.

A comment to this section deals with "voluntary public figures" and stated:

> One who voluntarily places himself in the public eye, by engaging in public activities or by assuming a prominent role in institutions or activities having general economic, cultural, social or similar public interest, or by submitting himself or his work for public judgment, cannot complain when he is given publicity that he has sought, even though it may be unfavorable to him. . . . In such a case, however, the legitimate interest of the public in the individual may extend beyond those matters which are themselves made public, and to some reasonable extent may include information as to matters that would otherwise be private.

Another comment relating to this case stated:

> Permissible publicity to information concerning either voluntary or involuntary public figures is not limited to the particular events that arouse the interest of the public. That interest, once aroused by the event, may legitimately extend, to some reasonable degree, to further information concerning the individual and to facts about him, which are not public and which, in the case of one who had not become a public figure, would

be regarded as an invasion of his purely private life. . . .

The extent of the authority to make public private facts is not, however, unlimited. . . . In determining what is a matter of legitimate public interest, account must be taken of the customs and conventions of the community; and in the last analysis what is proper becomes a matter of community mores. The line is to be drawn when the publicity ceases to be the giving of information to which the public is entitled, and becomes a morbid and sensational prying into private lives for its own sake, with which a reasonable member of the public, with decent standards, would say that he had no concern. The limitations, in other words, are those of common decency, having due regard to the freedom of the press and its reasonable leeway to choose what it will tell the public, but also due regard to the feelings of the individual and the harm that will be done to him by exposure. Some reasonable proportion is also to be maintained between the event or activity that makes the individual a public figure and the private facts to which publicity is given.

In acknowledging the status of players as public figures solely by virtue of their membership on the university basketball team, the court held that their possible exclusion from the team, whether for academic or any other reason, was therefore a matter of legitimate public interest. Bilney and the others were not in the same posture as other students, whose scholastic standing in its entirety was purely of private concern. When their academic standing reached the point of affecting their eligibility to play basketball for Maryland, the privacy of their status became somewhat reduced. The publication of their eligibility-threatening status was not unreasonable and did not trample on community mores. The players had sought and basked in the limelight by virtue of their membership on the team and they could not be allowed to complain when the light focused on their potentially imminent withdrawal from the team.

The judgment of the lower court in favor of the defendants was affirmed.

NOTES

1. The Commonwealth of Massachusetts has a statute governing invasion of privacy. It provides: "A person shall have a right against unreasonable, substantial or serious interference with his privacy" (Massachusetts General Laws Chapter 214, Section 113). This statute allows for legal as well as equitable relief. It also appears broad enough to cover the four distinct ways to invade the privacy of another.

2. The following exhibit is a publicity waiver form used by the University of Illinois in regard to the potential release of a student-athlete's personal and medical information:

MEMO TO: All Student-Athletes
FROM: Terry W. Cole, Director of Academic Services
SUBJECT: Release of Personal and Medical Information, and Acknowledgment of Physical Examinations and Athletic Association Policies

It is important to read this carefully before signing. If you have questions, I will be glad to discuss them.

As most of you are aware, current laws protect your right to privacy and your right to be made adequately aware of policies and procedures. The following statements outline the policies of the Athletic Association regarding the gathering and release of information, physical examination procedure, and your acknowledgment you have received a copy of the "Statement of Policy Governing Intercollegiate Athletics" and realize the importance of reading and understanding this document.

I. I give my authorization to the registrar, the dean of my college, and my course instructors to release my official transcript and academic records to the Athletic Association with the understanding the Athletic Association will release this information only in cases of academic awards and/or in responding to NCAA or Big Ten Conference requests.

II. I authorize the information contained in the Sports Information Office questionnaire to be used by the Athletic Association for press releases, press guide brochures, and official programs. I further permit this information to be released to members of the media.

III. I do —— do not —— give my consent for the team physician, athletic trainers, or other medical personnel of the University of Illinois, Urbana-Champaign, to release such information regarding my medical history, record of injury or surgery, record of serious illness, and rehabilitation results as may be requested by the scout or representative of any professional or amateur athletic organization or business organization seeking such information.

IV. I understand the Athletic Association has adopted the NCAA policy regarding medical examinations which indicates a full medical examination should be required only under the student-athlete's initial entrance into an institution's intercollegiate program and provided there is a continuous awareness of the health status of the athlete the traditional annual physical examination is not deemed necessary. I further understand if I encounter any medical or orthopedic problems that would exempt me from competing in any Athletic Association sponsored sport. Should I encounter any problems, I will contact the athletic training staff immediately.

V. By signing this form I acknowledge I have been given a copy of the "Statement of Policy Governing Intercollegiate Athletics" at the University of Illinois at Urbana-Champaign and realize the importance of reading and understanding this document.

_____
Student's Name (Signature) Social Security Sport Date

3. In *Spahn* v. *Julian Messner, Inc.*, 43 Misc. 2d 219, 250 N.Y.S. 2d 529 (1964), plaintiff Spahn, Hall of Fame baseball player, sued the defendant, publisher of an unauthorized fictional biography of Spahn, to enjoin publication and for compensatory damages for the invasion of privacy. The trial court ruled in favor of Spahn, finding that the defendants had (1) intruded upon the plaintiff's solitude and into his private affairs, (2) disclosed embarrassing "facts" about plaintiff, (3) placed plaintiff in a false light in the public eye, and (4) appropriated, for defendant's advantage, the plaintiff's name and likeness. Spahn was awarded injunctive relief and damages of $10,000.

4. In *Namath* v. *Sports Illustrated*, 48 A.D. 2d 487, 371 N.Y.S. 2d 10 (1975), plaintiff Namath, a star NFL quarterback, sued defendant magazine for its use of plaintiff's picture in advertisements to promote the sale of new subscriptions. Plaintiff claimed a violation of his right of privacy. The court granted defendant's motion to dismiss, holding that use of plaintiff's photograph was incidental advertising of defendant's magazine in which plaintiff had earlier been properly and fairly depicted. The court added that, since the language of the advertisements did not indicate plaintiff's endorsement of the magazine, it was again not violative of New York's Civil Rights Law.

5. For further information concerning the right of privacy, see Section 6.40.

4.16 Intentional Inflication of Emotional Distress

The tort of intentional infliction of emotional distress is designed to protect a person's emotional tranquility. Simple minor disturbances and infringements are not actionable.

The provoking conduct must be outrageous for the plaintiff to have an action for intentional infliction of emotional distress. An increasing number of states are recognizing intentional infliction of emotional distress as an independent tort. The recent trend of states that recognize the tort has been to adopt principles from the *Restatement (Second) of Torts*, section 46, in which the following four requirements are set forth:

1. The conduct must be extreme and outrageous.
2. The conduct must be intentional or reckless.
3. The conduct must cause emotional distress.
4. The distress must be severe.

The intent required under section 46(2) is simply the intent to engage in the conduct. Section 46, however, does not require that the defendant have a criminal or tortious intent, or even an intent to cause emotional distress. It is enough if the conduct has

> been so outrageous in character and so extreme in degree as to go beyond all possible bounds of decency and to be regarded as atrocious, and utterly intolerable in a civilized community. [*Restatement (Second) of Torts*, section 46, comment (d)]

Thus, if the defendant is joking and informs the plaintiff that her son has been killed, and the plaintiff suffers emotional distress, the defendant will be liable. Or if a doctor falsely or recklessly makes it known to a person that he is suffering from a fatal disease, then the doctor will be liable (see *Chuy* v. *Philadelphia Eagles Football Club, infra*). The plaintiff has an initial burden of showing enough evidence for reasonable persons to find extreme and outrageous conduct. Comment (j) to section 46 requires that the plaintiff prove that he or she suffered severe distress and that this distress was not unreasonable, exaggerated, or unjustified.

Chuy v. Philadelphia Eagles Football Club, 431 F. Supp. 254 (E.D. Pa. 1977), aff'd, 595 F. 2d 1265 (3rd Cir. 1979)

Plaintiff professional football player brought suit against the Philadelphia Eagles Football Club and the National Football League (NFL) seeking to recover the balance of his salary allegedly due on his contract and for damages for defamation and intentional infliction of emotional distress.

Chuy had suffered a serious injury while playing football. A week later the injury was diagnosed to have caused the development of an acute pulmonary embolism. After hospitalization and treatment, the embolus was dissolved.

Chuy also claimed that although the NFL believed he had signed three separate contracts, each guaranteeing him a salary of $30,000 per year, the three one-year contracts were in effect a three-year deal for $90,000. He brought suit for $60,000, which he claimed he was owed for the remaining two years of his contract.

Chuy's claims for emotional distress and defamation were based on a statement a team physician made in a media interview. The doctor reported that Chuy had contracted a rare blood disease, which would prevent him from playing football. Chuy, having no prior knowledge of the existence of such a condition, claimed that on hearing the report, he was put under incredible emotional anguish and that he anticipated death.

Chuy's claim for intentional infliction of emotional distress was based on section 46 of the *Restatement (Second) of Torts*, which states that: "one who by extreme and outrageous conduct intentionally or recklessly causes emotional distress to another is liable for such emotional distress."

The court referred to the elements required for the intentional infliction of emotional distress: (1) an intentional act, (2) extreme and outrageous conduct, (3) causing *severe* emotional distress, and (4) by one not privileged. The court held that the doctor's conduct was sufficiently outrageous. The court found that the doctor intentionally told news reporters that Chuy was suffering from a blood disease knowing that this was in fact not true. Chuy recovered $10,000 in compensatory damages for this intentional infliction of emotional distress. He also recovered $60,000 in punitive damages, an amount that was affirmed on appeal as not being excessive.

The court also found the Eagles to be liable. The medical doctor was viewed by the court as an employee of the defendant Philadelphia Eagles Football Club. One crucial factor was that the doctor was acting within the control and discretion of the Eagles when he made statements to the press.

Chuy recovered $40,000 on his breach on contract claim but was unsuccessful with his defamation action.

NOTES _____

1. Although doctors are generally viewed as independent contractors (see Section 4.26), in *Chuy* the doctor was found to be an employee, and the employer was held vicariously liable (see Section 4.13). It should be noted that the doctor's negligence was his statements to the press and not his medical decisions. In this situation, the court reasoned that an employer should be able to control a doctor's statement to the press.

2. In the same case, Chuy also sued for defamation (see Section 4.14).

3. Chuy also sued the Philadelphia Eagles and the National Football League on antitrust grounds for restraint of trade for imposing a contract without adequate injury compensation, based on facts arising out of the same situation. See *Chuy* v. *Philadelphia Eagles Football Club*, 407 F. Supp. 717 (E.D. Pa. 1977), aff'd 595 F. 2d 1235 (3rd Cir. 1979).

4. In *Bilney* v. *Evening Star Newspaper* Co., 406 A. 2d 652 (Md. Ct. App. 1979), the plaintiffs unsuccessfully sued for intentional infliction of emotional distress and invasion of privacy (see Section 4.15).

4.17 Products Liability Law

Products liability is an expansive area of tort law that allows a party who has been injured by a product that is defectively designed, manufactured, or distributed to recover under one of several possible causes of action. The causes of action in products liability cases are negligence, breach of warranty, and strict liability in tort.

The possible defendants in a products liability action are numerous. Everyone involved in a product's chain of distribution is potentially liable, from the manufacturer to the seller or lessor to those who service or install the product. In *Halbrook* v. *Oregon State Univ.* (see Section 4.30, Note 7), the defendants included the Astroturf manufacturer, the Astroturf installer, the asphalt subsurface manufacturer, the asphalt installer, and the university responsible for the selection, maintenance, and repair of the field.

A product is any item of personal property — most commonly consumer goods — and includes the container in which it is sold. Even vacant land that is altered by earth-moving equipment to form a baseball diamond could be a "product," so that the manufacturer (the earth mover) could be liable for injuries caused by holes or bumps in the surface.

The plaintiff in a products liability case must show that a defect existed at the time the product left the control of the defendant and that the injury was caused by the defect. Courts have most frequently applied a definition of defect from the *Restatement (Second) of Torts*, section 402A, which states that a product is in a defective condition if it is "unreasonably dangerous to the user." Comment (i) of section 401A further defines a defect:

> The article sold must be dangerous to the extent beyond that which would be contemplated by the ordinary consumer who purchases it, with the knowledge common to the community as to its characteristics.

NOTES _____

1. See *Byrns* v. *Riddell, Inc.*, 550 P. 2d 1065 (Ariz. 1976) and other cases in Section 4.30 for further discussion of products liability law.
2. For further information, see the following articles:
(a) "Sports Products Liability: It's All Part of the Game — or Is It?" 17 *Trial* 58 (1981).

(a) "The Liability Path to Safer Helmets," 13 *Trial* 38 (January 1977).
(c) "In Defense of Artificial Turf," 13 *Trial* 38 (January 1977).

4.17–1 Products Liability: Negligence

In products liability law, a manufacturer of a product must meet legal standards of safety and care in the product's design, manufacture, and use. In addition, the supplier of the product and the seller may be liable for negligence if they have not exercised reasonable care. For the basic discussion of the principles underlying the legal theories of negligence, see Sections 4.12–(1–5). (See also *Dudley Sports Co.* v. *Schmitt* and *McCormack* v. *Lowe & Campbell Athletics Goods Co.* [Note 12) in Section 4.30.) The courts generally balance the probability and gravity of the potential harm against the social value of the product and the inconvenience of taking precautions, to determine whether or not a duty of care has been breached.

The standard of care involved in manufacturing is one of reasonable care in both the manufacture and design of the product to ensure that it will be reasonably safe when used in the manner for which it was intended. In addition, when a product may be dangerous even when properly used, a manufacturer may have a duty to warn users about the hazard. (See *Dudley Sports Co.* v. *Schmitt* and *McCormack* v. *Lowe & Campbell Athletic Goods Co.* [Note 12] in Section 4.30.) The manufacturer, however, is not required to make the safest or best possible product, even though the product will be compared to similar products. Similar products will be used to help determine what a "reasonably" safe product is.

Sellers, the retailers of a product, are also subject to liability for negligence under some circumstances. A seller of a product which the seller knows to be dangerous has a duty to warn a purchaser who has no knowledge of the dangerous nature of the product. A seller may also have a duty to inspect a product manufactured by another, if the seller knows or has reason to know that the product is likely to be hazardous.

Advertisers and marketers of a product also have a duty to exercise reasonable care. When a product appears on the market, a warning about the dangers associated with the product must accompany it. This warning must be adequate and must disclose the dangers from an improper design as well as dangers that are possible even when the product is properly used. The warning must also be sufficient to protect third parties who might reasonably be expected to come into contact with the product.

Suppliers, the wholesalers of a product, must also exercise reasonable care. A supplier has a duty to use reasonable care to make a product safe. In addition, if the supplier knows or has reason to know that the product is dangerous and that the user is not likely to realize the danger, the supplier must exercise reasonable care to notify the user of the potential danger.

4.17–2 Products Liability: Strict Liability

The strict liability cause of action requires that one who sells a product that is unreasonably dangerous because of a defect (whether in design or manufacture) be held liable for any physical harm proximately caused by use of the product. The seller will be liable to the ultimate user or customer, provided that the product has not been changed from its initial state or condition. Liability can be found only if the product has been used in the manner and for the purposes intended by the sellers; therefore, a seller will not be liable for harm resulting from unforeseeable, abnormal use of the product. This strict liability standard applies despite the fact that the seller may have exercised all the care necessary in and appropriate for the preparation and sale of the product.

The theory behind strict liability is that the seller who markets the product for use and consumption by the public assumes a special responsibility to any member of the public for any injury caused by the product. The public has the right to expect that the seller will provide a reasonably safe product. There is a strong public policy supporting the demand that the burden of accidental injuries caused by a seller's products be placed on those who marketed them. The theory is that the cost inherent in the assumption of responsibility can be insured, treated as a cost of production, and added to the cost of the item. Therefore, the court's policy is for the consumer to receive the maximum possible protection from unreasonably dangerous products from the people in the best position to provide this protection — those who market and profit from the products. (See *Nissen Trampoline Company* v. *Terre Haute First National Bank* in Section 4.30.)

Most courts have applied the *Restatement (Second) of Torts*, section 402A, definition of strict tort liability, which states that:

(1) One who sells any product in a defective condition unreasonably dangerous to the user or consumer or to his property is subject to liability for physical harm thereby caused to the ultimate user or consumer, or to his property; if:

(a) the seller is engaged in the business of selling such a product, and

(b) it is expected to and does reach the user or consumer without substantial change in the condition in which it is sold.

(2) The rule stated in subsection (1) applies although:

(a) the seller has exercised all possible care in the preparation and sale of his product, and

(b) the user or consumer has not bought the product from or entered into any contractual relation with the seller.

4.17–3 Products Liability: Warranties

A cause of action for products liability may be based on a breach of warranty claim against a manufacturer. This is basically an adaption of contract law to tort problems. First, the plaintiff has to establish that there was an express or implied warranty in the product purchased. Second, the plaintiff has to prove that the warranty was breached by the defendant. The advantage to a claim based on warranty principles is that the plaintiff does not have to prove that the product was defective in its design.

An express warranty is an affirmation of material fact concerning the nature and fitness of a particular product upon which the buyer might reasonably rely. An example is the case of *Heldman* v. *Uniroyal, Inc.* (see Section 4.30), in which it was alleged that the seller of a "roll-away" tennis surface expressly warranted that it was free of dents, hollows, or soft spots.

An implied warranty does not arise from any words of the seller, either oral or in writing, but is a rule of law that has been enacted by every state. The rule is embodied in section 2–314 of the Uniform Commercial Code, which states: "A warranty that the goods shall be merchantable is implied in a contract for their sale if the seller is a merchant with respect to goods of that kind." Once again, see *Heldman* v. *Uniroyal, Inc.* (Section 4.30), in which the plaintiff also alleged an implied warranty of merchantability that the tennis court was safe and fit for the ordinary purpose for which it was intended.

4.20   Application of Legal Principles to Persons Involved in Sports

The legal principles which were discussed in previous sections are applied to different groups of persons involved in sports. This section has been organized by potential defendant. For example, Section 4.21 discusses the ways in which a participant may be sued and Section 4.22 discusses ways in which coaches and physical education teachers may be sued.

4.21   Liability of Participants

The liability stemming most directly from sports activity is that for injuries to participants. Until recently, most sports-related injuries were viewed as a natural outgrowth of the competitive and physical nature of sports. This attitude was supported by the traditional belief that a participant assumes the dangers inherent in the sport and is therefore precluded from recovery for an injury caused by another participant. Although this theory has some merit, it fails to address injuries occurring within a game that are not necessarily an outgrowth of competitive spirit.

This traditional attitude has been strictly scrutinized in recent decisions which clearly establish that a player does not necessarily assume the risk of all injuries resulting from gross recklessness on the part of another player. Nor does a participant necessarily consent to intentional attacks falling outside the recognized rules of the sport. Thus, the traditional defenses of assumption of risk and consent must be reviewed on a case-by-case basis to determine whether or not they are applicable in a particular instance (see Sections 4.11–3[a] and 4.12–5[d]).

This change in legal attitude has occurred in part due to an increase in the number of serious injuries to sports participants. The increased volume of sports participation resulting from the involvement of boys and girls, and men and women, in unprecedented numbers has produced a corresponding increase in the number of sports-related injuries. It is estimated that in a single football season alone, there are approximately 1 million injuries at 20,000 high schools (50 per school), and 70,000 injuries at 900 colleges and universities (78 per institution). On the average, there is one injury per player per year in the National Football League.

A second reason for the change in attitude is that professional sports and to some extent intercollegiate and amateur athletics are now viewed as businesses. Because of this, people are more inclined to see the situation as one in which a lawsuit is a viable option. In addition, with greatly increased salaries, a player has much more at stake, and owners have increased revenues and "deep pockets" from which to pay large awards. A third reason is that legal precedents have been established that allow injured athletes recovery. Finally, the rise in sports-related lawsuits is a result of society becoming increasingly reliant on the judicial system for the resolution of disputes.

As mentioned previously, the increase in lawsuits filed by sports participants charging negligence and other tortious conduct has paralleled the rising number of sports injuries in recent years. One factor behind the rise in participant-versus-participant lawsuits is the steady erosion of the athlete's traditional reluctance to sue fellow participants. The increasing recognition of the dangers involved in playing a game against an opponent who does not follow an accepted safety rule has also increased the likelihood of a lawsuit. Players are refusing to accept injury-provoking actions of opponents when the actions are not sanctioned by the rules of the game. There is some legal precedent which recognizes that each player has a legal duty to refrain from unreasonably dangerous acts.

Courts have found that many sports, including soccer, softball, and football, have created safety rules to help define the often unclear line between legal and illegal behavior on the field. A safety rule is one that is initiated to protect players and to prevent injuries rather than to make the game more exciting or interesting. The existence of safety rules mandates that in many situations a player is charged with a legal duty to every other player involved in the activity. This legal duty requires the player to refrain from conduct, proscribed by such rules, which is likely to cause harm. In cases involving the alleged violation of a safety rule, the courts have held that a player is liable for tort action if his or her conduct displays deliberate, willful, or reckless disregard for the safety of other participants and results in injury to another participant.

Thus, a participant may recover for either intentional torts (see Section 4.11) or for

reckless misconduct (see Section 4.12–4). Actions based on ordinary negligence are still difficult to establish in athletic cases. However, case law indicates that there are situations in sports for which the commonly accepted defenses of contributory negligence and assumption of risk (see Sections 4.12–5[b] and 4.12–5[d]) are not adequate to bar recovery by the plaintiff. For example, criminal charges have been brought in hockey fights where stick swinging resulting in serious injuries has occurred. Criminal liability issues are covered in Chapter 5.

Bourque v. Duplechin, 331 So. 2d 40 (La. Ct. App. 1976)

On June 9, 1974, Jerome Bourque was playing second base on a softball team sponsored by Boo Boo's Lounge. Adrien Duplechin was a member of the opposing team. During the game, Duplechin was on first base when a teammate hit a ground ball. Duplechin started for second base as the shortstop threw the ball to Bourque, who stepped on second base and then stepped away from second base to throw the ball to first and complete a double play. After Bourque had thrown the ball to first base, Duplechin ran full speed into Bourque and brought his left arm up under Bourque's chin. Bourque suffered a fractured jaw and seven broken teeth. When Duplechin made contact with Bourque, Bourque was standing 5 feet away from second base. As a result of his conduct, the umpire ejected Duplechin from the game. Bourque brought suit against Duplechin and his liability insurer, Allstate Insurance Company. The lower court found for Bourque, and Duplechin appealed to the Court of Appeals of Louisiana.

The court of appeals rejected Duplechin's argument that when Bourque voluntarily participated in the softball game he assumed the risk of injury. Citing *Benedetto v. Travelers' Insurance Company*, 172 So. 2d 354 (La. Ct. App. 1965) and *Richmond* v. *Employers' Fire*

Insurance Company, 298 So. 2d 118 (La. Ct. App. 1974), the court stated that although Bourque did assume the risk of those injuries, which were common incidents of baseball and softball, he did not assume the risk of Duplechin breaching his duty to play softball in the ordinary fashion without unsportsmanlike conduct and inflicting wanton injury to his fellow players. Although Bourque did assume the risk of being hit with a ball or bat or being spiked, he did not assume the risk of his fellow players acting in an unsportsmanlike manner by displaying a reckless lack of concern for the other participants. In support of its position, the court cited *Carroll* v. *Aetna Casualty & Surety Company*, 301 So. 2d 406 (La. Ct. App. 1974) and *Hawayek* v. *Simmons*, 91 So. 2d 49 (La. Ct. App. 1956). The court of appeals also concluded that there was no evidence in the record to indicate contributory negligence on Bourque's part.

Allstate Insurance Company claimed on appeal that there was no coverage under their policy because Duplechin's actions were an intentional tort, and he should have expected injury to occur. On this issue, the court quoted William Prosser from the *Law of Torts*, 4th edition:

> . . . the mere knowledge and appreciation of a risk, short of substantial certainty, is not the equivalent of intent. The defendant who acts in the belief or consciousness that he is causing an appreciable risk of harm to another may be negligent, and if the risk is great his conduct may be characterized as reckless or wanton, but it is not classed as an intentional wrong.

Thus, in the court's opinion, Duplechin did not commit an intentional tort because he was not motivated by a desire to injure Bourque. Duplechin's conduct was negligent and was thus covered under the Allstate policy. Because Bourque had suffered a fractured jaw and had to have six teeth crowned, one tooth replaced by a bridge, and his chin repaired by plastic surgery, the court of appeals found the lower court's award of $12,000 for pain and suffering and $1,496 for special damages not to be

excessive. The judgment of the trial court was affirmed.

Griggas v. Clauson, 128 N.E. 2d 363 (Ill. Ct. App. 1955)

Robert Griggas was a 19-year-old member of the Rockford Athletic Club Basketball Team. On the night of November 15, 1953, he played in a game against the Blackhawk Athletic Club Basketball Team and was guarded by La Verne Clauson. During the game, while Griggas had his back to Clauson and was about to receive a pass from a teammate, Clauson pushed him and then struck him in the face with his fist. As Griggas fell, Clauson again struck him, which knocked him unconscious. Clauson swore profusely and made statements to the effect that he was going to teach Griggas a lesson and that one of the two of them was going to play basketball in the city and the other was not.

Griggas was hospitalized for about three weeks. His right temple near the eye was badly bruised and swollen and his mouth was lacerated, with both lips cut and swollen. After the incident, he began to have headaches, and his vision deteriorated to the extent that he began to wear glasses. Griggas filed suit against Clauson. The court found that Griggas suffered "an injury to his face and head and by reason of said injury became sick, sore, lame and disoriented and has suffered and will continue to suffer in the future pain by reason of said injuries and has been unable because of said injuries to go about his affairs and duties . . ." Prior to the injury, Griggas neither had headaches nor had to wear glasses. Griggas missed four and a half weeks of school. As a result, he dropped out of school and lost his basketball scholarship at DePaul University. At the time of the trial, Griggas had transferred to the University of Minnesota on a partial scholarship. The jury in the lower court found in favor of Griggas and awarded him $2,000 damages. Clauson appealed on the grounds that the verdict was incongruous given the manifest weight of the evidence, and furthermore, he claimed that the award was excessive.

The appellate court of Illinois affirmed the decision and award of the lower court. It held that the evidence in the record supported the finding that Griggas had been subjected to a wanton and unprovoked battery and was struck at a time when he had his back to Clauson. There was ample testimony to rebut Clauson's contention that Griggas was injured while they were both going for the ball. Based on the severity of the attack, the injuries sustained, the expenses associated with the incident, and the pain and suffering, the award was ruled not to be excessive.

Nabozny v. Barnhill, 334 N.E. 2d 258 (Ill. Ct. App. 1975)

During an amateur soccer game involving two teams composed of high school players in Winnetka, Illinois, defendant David Barnhill, who was playing a forward position for the Winnetka team, kicked plaintiff Julian Nabozny, the goaltender for the Hansa team, in the head while Nabozny was in possession of the ball. The resultant injury left the plaintiff with permanent skull and brain damage.

The play developed when a Winnetka player kicked the ball over midfield, and two players, one for Hansa and the defendant, chased after the loose ball in the Hansa defensive half of the field. The Hansa player reached the ball first. He passed the ball back to his goaltender, Nabozny, because he was closely pursued by the defendant. The Hansa player turned upfield to receive a pass from Nabozny, who went down on one knee to receive the ball, which he pulled to his chest. The defendant did not cease his charge when the Hansa player turned upfield but continued to advance toward the plaintiff and kicked the plaintiff's head, inflicting the severe injuries.

Witnesses concurred that plaintiff was in clear possession of the ball when the defendant struck him and that the contact could and

should have been avoided. Contact with a goaltender who is in possession of the ball is a violation of the FIFA (International Association Football Federation) — soccer's international governing body — rules that govern soccer competition.

Plaintiff brought suit against the defendant to recover damages for personal injuries caused by the defendant's negligence. At the close of the plaintiff's case, the trial court directed a verdict in favor of the defendant. Plaintiff appealed the ruling.

Plaintiff contended on appeal that the trial judge erred in granting defendant's motion for a directed verdict and that the plaintiff's actions as a participant did not prohibit the establishment of a prima facie case of negligence. The defendant argued in support of the trial court's ruling that he was free from negligence as a matter of law (lacking duty to the plaintiff) and that plaintiff was contributorily negligent as a matter of law.

The appeals court examined both of the defendant's arguments. It reviewed whether such a relationship existed between the parties that the court should impose a legal duty upon one for the benefit of the other.

The court did not wish to "place unreasonable burdens on the free and vigorous participation in sports by our youth," but also stated that "athletic competition does not exist in a vacuum." Therefore, the court found that a player is charged with a legal duty to every other player on the field to refrain from conduct proscribed by a safety rule. The court found a legal duty where the athletes are engaged in athletic competition and the teams involved are trained and coached by knowledgeable personnel; a recognized set of rules governs the conduct of the competition; and a safety rule is involved, which is primarily designed to protect players from serious injury. Then, if the safety rule is violated, this reckless disregard for the safety of other players cannot be excused.

The court stated that it had "carefully drawn" this duty rule "in order to control a new field of personal injury litigation." The court noted that the facts as presented in this case clearly warranted such a duty.

In summary, the court noted that a player is liable for tort action if player's conduct is such that it is either deliberate, willful, or with reckless disregard for the safety of other players so as to cause injury to another player, and that this is a question of fact for a jury to decide.

The court disagreed with the defendant's claim that the plaintiff was contributorily negligent. The evidence presented tended to show that the plaintiff exercised ordinary care for his own safety. He did what was expected of a goaltender in the given situation. Plaintiff had no reason to know of the danger created by the defendant. Without this knowledge, it cannot be said that the plaintiff unreasonably exposed himself to such danger or failed to discover or appreciate the risk.

Gaspard v. Grain Dealers Mutual Insurance Co., 131 So. 2d 831 (La. Ct. App. 1961)

Andrus Gaspard brought this suit for damages for personal injuries on behalf of his son Ronnie, following an injury to the boy in a playground baseball game. Defendant Grain Dealers Mutual Insurance Co. had issued a comprehensive liability policy to Alfred Viator, the father of the boy responsible for plaintiff's injury.

Twelve-year-old Ronald Gaspard and 11-year-old Ronald Viator had been participating in a supervised baseball game during school recess on a hot summer day. Gaspard stood near the players' bench while defendant took his turn at bat using a heavy, worn bat, which was a favorite among the boys. As Viator swung at a pitch and missed, the bat slipped from his hands and struck Gaspard on the head. Gaspard was not seriously injured as evidenced by his success as a Little League pitcher that same season.

At the trial court level, defendant denied any negligence on the part of Ronald Viator and pleaded assumption of risk as a bar to plaintiff's recovery. In the alternative, defendant alleged contributory negligence on the part of Ronnie Gaspard. Following a decision in defendant's favor, plaintiff filed an appeal.

The appeals court based its affirmation of the lower court's ruling for the defendant based on two findings. The first involved the general rule on the standard of care required of children in a determination of negligence. The court noted that ". . . the Viator boy was not negligent, that is, he exercised that degree of care to be reasonably expected from a boy of his age engaged in such an athletic contest." The second reason for denial of recovery by Gaspard was defendant's successful application of the assumption-of-risk defense. The district court noted and the appeals court affirmed that ". . . generally a participant in a lawful game or contest assumes the danger inherent in that game or contest with consequent preclusion from recovery for injury or death resulting therefrom."

Both courts found that young Viator's action did not constitute negligence because he exercised a reasonable degree of care. The court held that Gaspard assumed the risk as he "knew of the danger and clearly acquiesced or proceeded in the face of danger by voluntarily playing the game." Accordingly, the appeals court denied Gaspard's appeal and affirmed judgment for the defendant.

Hackbart v. Cincinnati Bengals, Inc., 435 F. Supp. 352 (D. Colo. 1977)

The Cincinnati Bengals and the Denver Broncos were playing a National Football League (NFL) exhibition game in Denver, on September 8, 1973. During the first half of that game, Dale Hackbart, a free safety for the Denver Broncos with 13 years of professional experience, was covering Booby Clark, a rookie running back for the Cincinnati Bengals, on an end-zone pattern. The intended pass was intercepted by the Broncos at the goal line. Hackbart attempted to block Clark, and in doing so, fell to the ground. Hackbart then turned, while still with one knee on the ground, to look upfield at the play. Acting out of anger and frustration, but without a specific intent to injure, Clark stepped forward and struck a blow with his right forearm to the back of the kneeling plaintiff's head with sufficient force to cause both players to fall forward to the ground. Both players returned to play during the second half of the game.

The next day the plaintiff was unable to keep a golf date because of pain which persisted for some time. Despite the pain, the plaintiff continued to play on specialty teams for the Broncos for two weeks following the injury but was thereafter dropped from the team. Not having sought medical attention until after his release, the plaintiff found out that he had sustained a serious neck injury. Hackbart received his full payment for the 1973 season pursuant to an injury clause in his contract.

Hackbart filed suit against Clark on two theories of liability. First, the plaintiff contended that Clark's foul was so far outside the rules of play and acceptable practices of pro football that it should be characterized as reckless misconduct. The theory of intentional misconduct was not claimed by the plaintiff, since it was barred by the statute of limitations. Reckless misconduct had been recognized in the case of *Nabozny v. Barnhill*, in which the reckless disregard for safety of a goalkeeper in a schoolboy soccer game was the basis of recovery. Second, plaintiff contended that his injury was at least the result of a negligent act by the defendant. Both of these theories relied on a definition of duty between the parties and on an objective standard of conduct based on the hypothetical, reasonably prudent person. Thus, the question was, what would a reasonably prudent professional football player be expected to do under the circumstances that confronted Charles Clark in this incident? Plaintiff did not bring an assault and battery claim, since the one-year statute of limitations had passed.

The trial court ruled in favor of the defendant and held that it was unable to establish the existence of a duty between the parties or to determine the proper conduct of an NFL player during a game, based upon any recognized standard of reasonableness. Additionally, even if a duty did exist between the parties, the court stated that no recovery would be awarded due to the assumption-of-risk doctrine.

The court noted that football is an inherently violent game, but that it is self-regulatory in its play. Officials on the field during a game enforce the rules and regulations, and several infractions occur in each game that warrant penalties, usually assessed by yardage lost. However, the court admitted that some violations pass by the officials undetected.

Pregame preparation by players consists of charging themselves up emotionally to levels of "controlled rage." Large crowds at football games contribute to the high emotional levels of the players. Fighting between players on the field during a football game is not uncommon. The coaches of both teams involved in the case, Paul Brown of Cincinnati and John Ralston of Denver, admitted that the coaching and instructing of pro football players does not include any training with respect to a responsibility or even any regard for the safety of opposing players.

Due to the violent nature of the game and the total lack of training or consideration for the safety of other players, the court found that it was:

> . . . wholly incongruous to talk about a professional football player's duty of care or the safety of opposing players when he has been trained and motivated to be heedless of injury to himself. The character of NFL competition negates any notion that the playing conduct can be circumscribed by any standard of reasonableness.

In examining the question of assumption of risk, the court listened to testimony of several former players who denounced the defendant's actions as not customary or accepted football practice. Yet, the court noted, though the game films clearly showed the incident between the plaintiff and the defendant, those who viewed it did not consider it a matter requiring attention from a football standpoint. All of the witnesses with playing or coaching experience in the NFL agreed that players are urged to avoid penalties. The emphasis on the avoidance of penalties is on the unfavorable effects of the yardage lost, and not on the safety of the other players. It was undisputed that no game is without penalties and that players frequently lose control of their tempers in surges of emotion. Therefore, the court concluded that the level of violence and the frequency of emotional outbursts in NFL games are such that the plaintiff must have recognized and accepted the risk that he would be injured by an act such as that committed by the defendant.

Several other arguments by the plaintiff were found inapplicable by the court. For example, the plaintiff claimed that the standard player contract, which calls for players to abide by the rules and regulations of the game, was for his protection. The court dismissed this claim on the grounds that such a broad interpretation would "create a potential for contract liability for every infraction of every playing rule." The plaintiff had also asserted that Clark was guilty of outrageous conduct. Plaintiff described outrageous conduct as being the basis for liability where severe emotional distress resulted from some behavior that was considered to be so far from societal norms as to be regarded as atrocious and utterly intolerable. The court stated that Hackbart did not suffer any such emotional distress nor was Clark's action outside applicable norms for the NFL. Relief on the basis of outrageous conduct was denied.

The plaintiff also sought recovery for interference with a contract. To prove that such a tort was committed, the plaintiff had to prove as necessary elements an intent to cause a breach of contract and some action which did induce a breach. The court held that neither was shown in the evidence. The Broncos fully performed the Hackbart contract and an intent

to interfere with it was certainly not what caused the blow by Clark. Finally, the Cincinnati Bengals were held free from liability under the doctrine of respondeat superior, since their liability depended on the liability of Clark. Since Clark was not found liable, neither were the Bengals.

The court also examined the application of tort principles to pro football as a question of social policy. Likening the occupation of a pro football player to positions in coal mining and railroading as far as potential danger to human health and welfare were concerned, the court noted that legislation had been enacted to protect the interests of coal miners and railroad workers:

> The only protection which NFL contract players have beyond self-defense and real or threatened retaliation is that which is provided by the League rules and sanctions. It may well be true that what has been provided is inadequate and that these young athletes have been exploited and subjected to risks which should be unacceptable in our social order.

The court held that had the litigated incident been "in the context of common community standards there can be no question that Mr. Clark's blow here would generate civil liability. It would involve a criminal sanction if the requisite intent were present."

The court called upon the legislature to decide which restraints should be made applicable to the game of football, stating that the courts "are not well suited" to that task. The court further stated:

> The NFL rules of play are so legalistic in their statement and so difficult of application because of the speed and violence of the play that the difference between violations which could fairly be called deliberate, reckless or outrageous and those which are "fair play" would be so small and subjective as to be incapable of articulation. The question of causation would be extremely difficult in view of the frequency of forceful collisions. The volume of such litigation would be enormous and it is reasonable to expect that the court systems of the many states in which

NFL games are played would develop differing and conflicting principles of law. It is highly unlikely that the NFL could continue to produce anything like the present games under such multiple systems of overview by judges and juries.

Finally, the court noted that its decision regarding the inability of the civil courts to control violence in pro football was limited by the facts of the case before it. It considered only a claim for an injury resulting from a blow, without weaponry, delivered emotionally without a specific intent to injure, in the course of regular play in a league-approved game involving adult, contract players. The court noted that football as a commercial enterprise was something quite different from athletics as an extension of the academic experience and that its decision may have no applicability in other areas of physical competition.

Hackbart v. Cincinnati Bengals Inc., 601 F. 2d 516 (10th Cir. 1979)

Dale Hackbart, plaintiff-appellant, brought this appeal after he was denied judgment in federal district court. The trial court's reasons for rejecting the appellant's claim were that professional football is a species of warfare and that so much physical force is tolerated and the magnitude of the force exerted is so great that it renders injuries not actionable in court. Even intentional batteries were held beyond the scope of judicial process. The trial court rendered this decision despite the fact that the defendant Charles Clark admitted that the blow which had been struck was not accidental and that it was intentionally administered. The trial court ruled as a matter of law that the game of professional football is basically a business which is violent in nature, and that the available sanctions are imposition of penalties and expulsion from the game. Notice was taken of the fact that many fouls are overlooked, that the game is played in an emotional and noisy environment, and that incidents such as the one complained of are not unusual.

The trial court spoke as well of the reasonableness of applying the laws and rules that are part of tort law to the game of professional football, noting the unreasonableness of holding that one player has a duty of care for the safety of others. It also talked about the concept of assumption of risk and contributory negligence as applying and concluded that Hackbart had accepted the risk that he would be injured by such an act.

The appeals court examined two key issues, among others, which had a bearing on the case: (1) whether the trial court erred in ruling that as a matter of policy the principles of law governing the infliction of injuries should be entirely rejected when the injury took place in the course of a game; and (2) whether the evidence justified consideration by the court of the issue of reckless misconduct as it is defined in *Restatement (Second) of Torts*, section 500, since (admittedly) the assault and battery theory was not available because that tort was governed by a one-year statute of limitations.

The appeals court reversed the trial court. The court held that jurisdiction existed to hear and rule on the case. While the court of appeals affirmed that there are certain recognized limitations on federal court, none of these limitations permit a court to exercise discretion such as the trial court had exercised.

The appeals court concluded that the trial court did not decide the case on the evidence bearing on the defendant's liability, but rather decided the case as a matter of social policy that the game was so violent and unlawful that valid lines could not be drawn. The appeals court held that this was not a proper issue for determination and that the plaintiff was entitled to have the case tried on an assessment of his rights and whether they had been violated.

The evidence at the trial uniformly supported the proposition that the intentional striking of a player in the head from the rear is not an accepted part of the playing rules or the general custom of an NFL game. In fact, the evidence showed that the NFL rules, Article I, Item I, subsection c, stated: "All players are prohibited from striking on the head, face or neck with the heel, back or side of the hand, wrist, forearm, elbow or clasped hand."

The district court recognized that if Clark's actions had taken place away from the football field, they would have generated civil liabilities. However, since the injury was inflicted during a professional football game, the district court held that the act should not be subject to the restraints of the law because to do so would place unreasonable impediments and restraints on the activity of pro football players. While the district court acknowledged that the potential threat of legal liability has a significant deterrent effect, and further that private civil actions constitute an important mechanism for societal control of human conduct, the court reasoned that the need to expand the law of liability to this area of sports should be accomplished by legislation and administrative regulation — not through court decision.

The appeals court reversed the trial court on this position and stated that there are no principles of law that allow a court to rule out certain tortious conduct by reason of general roughness of the game or any difficulty in administering the law. To determine whether Charles Clark's action warranted a claim of reckless misconduct, the appeals court examined the *Restatement (Second) of Torts*, section 500, wherein reckless misconduct and negligent misconduct are distinguished. Reckless misconduct differs from negligence in that negligence consists of mere inadvertence, lack of skillfulness, or failure to take precautions. Reckless misconduct, on the other hand, involves a choice or adoption of a course of action, either with knowledge of the danger or with knowledge of facts that would disclose the danger to a reasonable person. Reckless misconduct also differs in that it consists of intentionally carrying out an act with knowledge not only that it contains a risk of harm to others (as does negligence), but also that it actually involves a risk substantially greater in magnitude than is necessary in the case of negligence. The difference, therefore, is in the degree of risk.

The *Restatement (Second) of Torts*, subsection (f), also distinguished between reckless misconduct and intentional wrongdoing. To be reckless the act must have been intended by the actor. But the actor does not intend to cause the harm which results from it. It is enough that the actor realized, or from the facts should have realized, that there was a strong probability that harm would result, even though the actor might have hoped or expected that this conduct would prove harmless. Nevertheless, the existence of a probability is different from substantial certainty, which is an ingredient of intent to cause the harm that results from the act. Therefore, reckless misconduct exists when the person knows that the act is harmful but fails to realize that it will produce the extreme harm which it did produce. It is in this respect that recklessness and intentional conduct differ in degree.

The appeals court noted that the defendant Clark admittedly acted impulsively and in the heat of anger, and even though it could be concluded from the admitted facts that he intended the act, it could also be concluded that he did not intend to inflict the serious injury which resulted from the blow he struck.

In ruling that recklessness is the appropriate standard and that assault and battery is not the exclusive one, the appeals court held that these two liability concepts are not necessarily opposed to each other. Rather, recklessness under the *Restatement (Second) of Torts*, section 500, might be regarded, for the purpose of analysis at least, a lesser included act.

Assault and battery, having originated in a common-law writ, is narrower than recklessness in its scope. In essence, two definitions enter into it. The assault is an attempt, coupled with the present ability, to commit a violent harm against another. Battery is the unprivileged or unlawful touching of another. Assault and battery, then, calls for an intent, as does recklessness. In recklessness, however, the intent is to do the act, but without an intent to cause the particular harm. It is enough if the actor knows that there is a strong probability that harm will result.

The appeals court found enough justification for a retrial before a jury to determine the liability of defendant Charles Clark on a charge of reckless misconduct.

Manning v. Grimsley, 643 F. 2d 20 (1st Cir. 1981)

The plaintiff, a Boston Red Sox fan, was seated in the bleachers at Fenway Park behind the visiting pitcher's bullpen. The defendant, a pitcher for the visiting Baltimore Orioles, had become visibly irritated at the fans in the bleachers, who were constantly heckling the Orioles. The defendant had been warming up in the bullpen when, after his catcher had left the plate, he threw a hard pitch at a 90 degree angle from the direction of the plate. The ball passed through a wire fence that separated the stands from the bullpen and struck the plaintiff.

The plaintiff brought suit in federal district court against the pitcher and his employer, the Baltimore Baseball Club, Inc., with one count for battery and one count for negligence. The district judge directed a verdict for the defendant on the battery count, under the theory that no reasonable jury could find that the defendant intended to throw in the direction of the hecklers, to cause the spectators to fear imminent harm, or to act in response to verbal abuse which was affecting his ability to prepare to play. On the negligence count, the jury returned a verdict in favor of the defendant pitcher and his employer.

The court of appeals held that the trial judge was in error to have directed the verdict in favor of the defendants on the battery count. The court reasoned that because the defendant was an expert pitcher who appeared angry at the hecklers, and considering the fact that the ball traveled at a right angle to the plate, the jury could reasonably have found for the plaintiff on the battery count. The evidence taken as a whole could have supported a finding by the jury that the defendant threw the ball intentionally.

The court of appeals also held that the plaintiff was not precluded from maintaining the battery count due to the jury verdict in favor of the pitcher on the negligence count. The directed verdict was also reversed with respect to the defendant baseball club. Under Massachusetts tort law, an employer may be held liable for an employee's assault when the employee's act was in response to conduct of the plaintiff, which was an affirmative attempt to prevent an employee from carrying out his assignments. In this case, the heckling could have so irritated the pitcher that he could not effectively warm up.

Vacated and remanded.

NOTES

1. In *Hackbart* v. *Cincinnati Bengals Inc.*, 601 F. 2d 516 (10th Cir. 1979), the appeals court remanded the case to the district court, with instructions regarding the existence of a duty between the players. However, the case was settled for a reported $200,000 before it was retried in the district court.

2. For further information on the reckless misconduct theory and its relationship to sports torts case, see the following articles:

(a) "*Hackbart* v. *Cincinnati Bengals, Inc.*," 10 *Connecticut Law Review* 365 (Winter 1978).

(b) "Tort Law: Reckless Misconduct in Sports," 19 *Duquesne Law Review* 191 (Fall 1980).

(c) "Judicial Scrutiny of Tortious Conduct in Professional Sports: Do Professional Athletes Assume the Risk of Injuries Resulting from Rule Violations? *Hackbart* v. *Cincinnati Bengals, Inc.* (601 F. 2d 516)," 17 *California Western Law Review* 149 (Fall 1980).

(d) "Torts — Assumption of Risk — A Professional Football Player Assumes the Risk of Receiving a Blow, Delivered Out of Anger and Frustration But Without Specific Intent to Injure, During a Game," 12 *Georgia Law Review* 380 (Winter 1978).

3. In *Tomjanovich* v. *California Sports, Inc.*, No. H-78-243 (S.D. Tex. 1979), the injured player, Tomjanovich, did not sue the other player, Kermit Washington. However, a lawsuit was brought against Washington's employer for injuries received when Washington punched Tomjanovich in the face during the professional basketball game (see Section 4.24).

4. For a discussion of potential criminal liability for intentional acts of players, see Chapter 5.

5. In *Barrett* v. *Phillips*, 223 S.E. 2d 918 (N.C. Ct. App. 1976), a wrongful death suit against a high school and an athletic association was brought when plaintiff's son was killed in a collision during a high school football game with a player over 20 years old. The defendants were in

violation of a rule prohibiting players over 19 from playing. The court reasoned that the rule's purpose was not for the safety of the players, and that there was no actionable negligence because there was no causal connection between the death and the violation of the rule.

6. In *Polonich* v. *A.P.A. Sports, Inc.*, No. 74635 (E.D. Mich. filed Nov. 12, 1982), former Detroit Red Wings hockey player Dennis Polonich sued Wilf Paiement and the owner of Paiement's team, A.P.A. Sports, Inc., for "using excessive force" after Paiement hit Polonich with a "baseball-like swing" of his hockey stick across the face during a scuffle between the two during a Red Wings–Colorado Rockies contest in 1978. A federal jury awarded Polonich $500,000 in actual damages and $350,000 in exemplary damages. Neither team was a party to the suit.

7. In *Averill* v. *Luttrell*, 311 S.W. 2d 812 (Tenn. Ct. App. 1957), plaintiff baseball player successfully sued another baseball player for assault and battery (see Section 4.24).

8. In *Osborne* v. *Sprowls*, 419 N.E. 2d 913 (Ill. 1981), a bystander sued participant for injuries incurred during a game called "tackle-the-football." In this game, which is a combination of football, keep-away, and soccer, the players chase the person with the football until that person is tackled or kicks or throws the ball away. The Supreme Court of Illinois determined that an ordinary negligence standard would apply because the plaintiff was neither a participant nor was located in an area where the game was or could be in progress. The court determined the defendant owed the plaintiff the duty to select an area free from the presence of nonparticipating individuals.

9. Injuries suffered in sports, even in a violent game such as hockey, will not normally give rise to a negligence action, even though such injury resulted from a violation of the rules, because players willingly assume the risk of harm. But a retaliatory blow, even if provoked, may go beyond the immunity normally conferred by this principle and give rise to actionable negligence, as was the case in *Agar* v. *Canning*, 54 W.W.R. 302 (Manitoba 1965), aff'd, 55 W.W.R. 384 (1966).

10. In *State* v. *Forbes*, No. 76–602398 (Mich. Cir. Ct.), after the criminal suit ended in a hung jury (see Section 5.22), the civil case was settled out of court.

11. In August 1965, Juan Marichal, a pitcher for the San Francisco Giants, was batting against the Los Angeles Dodgers. Marichal hit John Roseboro, the catcher of the Dodgers, over the head with his baseball bat. Marichal claimed that when Roseboro threw the ball back to the pitcher, it grazed Marichal's ear. Marichal was fined $1,750 and suspended for eight games by the National League. Roseboro brought a civil action against Marichal. The case was reportedly settled out of court for $7,500. See R. Horrow, *Sports Violence: The Interaction Between Private Lawmaking and the Criminal Law* (Arlington, Va.: Carrollton Press, Inc., 1980), p. 210, n. 821. See also "The Battle of San Francisco," *Sports Illustrated*, August 30, 1965, p. 12.

12. In *Rhodes* v. *Kansas City Kings* (1980) (unreported case), Richard Rhodes, a former player for the Chicago Bulls, won $125,000 in damages from the Kansas City Kings and Lucius Allen. Allen, a player on the Kings, had broken Rhodes's jaw with a punch during an exhibition game.

13. For further information on torts and sports in general, see the following articles:

(a) "Sports Lawsuits Erupt," *National Law Journal*, February 1981, p. 30, col. 1.

(b) "Torts in Sports — I'll See You in Court!" 16 *Akron Law Review* 537 (Winter 1983).

(c) "Comment, A Proposed Legislative Solution to the Problem of Violent Acts by Participants during Professional Sporting Events," 7 *University of Dayton Law Review* 91 (1981).

14. For further information, see the following articles:

(a) "Professional Sports and Tort Liability: A Victory for the Intentionally Injured Player," 1980 *Detroit College of Law Review* 687 (Summer 1980).

(b) "Torts in Sports — Deterring Violence in Professional Athletics," 48 *Fordham Law Review* 764 (April 1980).

(c) "Participant's Liability for Injury to a Fellow Participant in an Organized Athletic Event," 53 *Chicago-Kent Law Review* 97 (November 1976).

(d) "Sports, Torts, Courts: Responsibility Is Also Part of the Game," 13 *Trial* 21 (January 1977).

(e) "Tort Liability for Players in Contact Sports," 45 *University of Missouri-Kansas Law Review* 119 (Fall 1976).

(f) "Tort Liability in Professional Sports," 44 *Albany Law Review* 696 (April 1980).

(g) "Tort Liability in Professional Sports: Battle in the Sports Arena," 57 *Nebraska Law Review* 1128 (1978).

(h) "Torts — Civil Liability of Athletes — Professional Football Player May Have Tort Claim for Injuries Intentionally Inflicted During Football Game, *Hackbart* v. *Cincinnati Bengals, Inc.*, 601 F. 2d 516 (10th Cir. 1979)," 84 *Dickinson Law Review* 753 (Summer 1980).

(i) "Injuries Resulting from Non-Intentional Acts in Organized Contact Sports: The Theories of Recovery Available to the Injured Athlete," 12 *Indiana Law Review* 687 (April 1979).

(j) "Liability in Professional Sports: An Alternative to Violence?" 22 *Arizona Law Review* 919 (1980).

(k) "Torts: Athlete States Cause of Action for Injury During a Professional Football Game," 19 *Washburn Law Journal* 646 (Spring 1980).

(l) "Torts — Participant in Athletic Competition States Cause of Action for Injuries Against Other Participant," 42 *Missouri Law Review* 347 (Spring 1977).

4.22 Liability of Coaches and Physical Education Teachers

Coaches and physical education teachers may be held personally liable for any intentional torts they commit in their capacity as coaches or teachers (see Section 4.11) and are generally not shielded by the defenses of consent, privilege, and immunity from liability by virtue of their position (see Section 4.11–3 [a]–[c]).

The coach is judged by the standard of a "reasonable coach" and the teacher by the standard of a "reasonable physical education teacher." There are some limited exceptions in which the coach or teacher is held to a lower standard of care and will not be held liable unless deemed to be grossly negligent. One situation involves coaches or teachers who are given the status "in loco parentis" — that is, the coach or teacher is placed in the position of the parents of the student (see *Lynch* v. *Board of Education of Collingsville Community School District, infra*).

A coach or a physical education teacher who becomes involved in a court action has a number of defenses available against a negligence claim (see Sections 4.12–5[a–e]). Since a minor is often involved in this area, note should be taken that certain defenses, such as contributory negligence, comparative negligence, and assumption of risk (see Sections 4.12–5[b]–[d] may be affected by the different standard of a care for children (see Section 4.12–2). The defense of sovereign immunity is a particularly important one for coaches and physical education teachers (see Sections 4.12–5[e] and 4.23–4). As a general rule, the coach or physical education teacher cannot be sued individually when the school district is protected under sovereign immunity. However, this protection is limited and may not cover the coach who is not acting within the scope of employment or who has been misfeasant (see *Cantwell* v. *University of Massachusetts* in Section 4.23–4).

Not much litigation has been brought against coaches and physical education teachers as a result of the sovereign immunity protection and the reluctance by potential plaintiffs to bring lawsuits. This was especially true in the case of coaches and physical education teachers who were often members of the community they were employed by and highly respected for their work. Coaches and physical education teachers are more likely to be sued today, since injured student-athletes are more likely to bring suit and the sovereign immunity doctrine is being eroded.

In many of the cases, the institution has been sued under the theory of respondeat superior for the coach's or teacher's negligence, and the coach has not been a named defendant (see *Morris* v. *Union High School District A, King County, infra*). However, the basis for the litigation is the negligence of the coach or physical education teacher, and he may be sued individually in a later case.

This section has been divided by the areas of responsibility for which a coach or physical education teacher may be sued: supervision (Section 4.22–1), instruction and training (Section 4.22–2), medical assistance (Section 4.22–3), and vicarious liability for actions of fans and players (Section 4.22–4).

4.22–1 Supervision

The coach and the physical education teacher are responsible for providing reasonable supervision to the student-athletes under their direction. However, they are not insurers of the safety of everyone under their supervision.

The coach and the physical education teacher may be sued for failing to provide adequate supervision. An allegation may include such diverse areas as negligent supervision at a football game or the failure to provide the proper equipment for the game (see *Lynch* v. *Board of Education of Collingsville Community School District, infra*). It may also include improper supervision of an off-season weight training program (see *Vargo* v. *Svitchan, infra*) or the coercing of an injured student to play (see *Morris* v. *Union High School District A,*

King County, infra). An additional responsibility for the coach and the physical education teacher is to check the playing area to ensure that it is in proper playing condition and that nothing is on or near the playing area that may cause injury, including objects such as benches and persons such as students or spectators (see *Domino* v. *Mercurio, infra*, Note 1).

Finally, the coach and the teacher may be sued for nonplaying-field activities, such as supervising the student-athlete in going to or from the playing field. The coach and teacher are responsible for providing reasonable supervision (see *Kersey* v. *Harbin, infra*, Note 4).

Any supervisory capacity carries with it the responsibility to exercise due care — that is, the care of a "reasonable supervisor" (see Section 4.12–1) for the safety of anyone who is likely to or actually does come into contact with the area under supervision. The duty entails using reasonable care in either rectifying dangerous situations or warning those who may encounter them of the possible hazards. The supervisor is not generally liable for an intentional act of his employees unless he was negligent in choosing the employee(s) involved. A school district or supervisor is liable in such instances only if the institution or one for whom it is legally responsible breaches the requisite standard of reasonable care. If the supervisor is not negligent himself, liability will be assessed only if the employee and the action taken satisfy the requirements of respondeat superior (see Section 4.13). Also, the doctrine of sovereign immunity may bar the action unless the state involved has specifically abrogated its immunity under this doctrine (see Section 4.23–4).

A supervisor must only exercise reasonable care in carrying out his assigned duties. Unless there is information or notice to the contrary, the supervisor is entitled to assume that all under his supervision will also be exercising due care. Thus, a spectator who is injured by another spectator may not enforce a claim against a school district or its administrators unless the school district or administrator had notice that the other spectator was likely to cause an unreasonably dangerous condition and failed to take steps to prevent the injury (see *Bearman* v. *Notre Dame*, Section 4.25). Past experience, however, will be considered when assessing liability. For example, if the same spectator appeared at another contest and injured a fellow spectator, the school district might be held liable, because the first situation provided warning of the person's potentially dangerous nature. The duty of care required may depend on the type of event being supervised. Rock concerts, for example, may require more security and precautions by a supervisor than do track and field events.

Morris v. **Union High School District A, King County, 294 P. 998 (Wash. 1931)**

Lowell Morris was a 17-year-old student at Union High School. On September 4, 1928, he began to train and practice as a member of the football team. On September 7, 1928, Morris received injuries to his back and spine while practicing with the team. On September 21, 1928, he was still suffering from his injuries, which the coach was aware of (or should have become aware of in the exercise of reasonable care). On this date, Morris was "permitted, persuaded and coerced by his coach to play" football in a regular game. As a result of his participation in the game, he suffered serious injuries to his back and spine, along with internal injuries that required a number of major operations to correct. A suit was brought by Morris against the school district. It alleged that the district was liable for the negligence of its coach, who had negligently allowed, persuaded, and coerced Morris to play. The lower court granted a motion in favor of the school district and dismissed the action. Morris appealed the decision.

The Washington Supreme Court held that a school district is liable for the negligent acts or omissions of its officers and agents acting within the scope of their authority. Therefore, the court held that if a school district organized and maintained a football team and used one of its teachers as a coach, and the coach knew that a student was physically unable to play football, or in the exercise of reasonable care should have known it, but nevertheless permitted, persuaded, and coerced the student to play and this resulted in injury to the student, the district would be liable. In its opinion, the court cited *Mokovich v. Independent School Dist. of Virginia, No. 222,* 177 Minn. 446, 225 N.W. 292 (1929), in which a student playing a football game was injured when he was thrown to the ground and his face was forced into the lime used to mark the field. The lime got into his eyes and caused the loss of sight in one eye and seriously damaged the other. While there was no liability in this case because of the common-law rule of governmental immunity, it was clearly indicated that were it not for the common law, the district would have been liable. In Washington, a statutory rule of liability superseded the common-law rule of immunity.

The court reversed the lower court decision against Morris and held the school district liable for negligence by its officers and agents, who were acting within the scope of their authority.

Vargo v. Svitchan, 301 N.W. 2d 1 (Mich. Ct. App. 1980)

Plaintiff high school football player, while participating in a summer weight-training program at the high school gymnasium, attempted to lift a 250- to 300-pound weight, fell, and received injuries resulting in paraplegia. Plaintiff's lawsuit charged the school's athletic director, principal, and superintendent with negligent supervision of the football coach in allowing him "to abuse students and to threaten and pressure them into attempting athletic feats beyond their capabilities . . ." The complaint further alleged that the gymnasium's facilities were inadequate and defective because of a lack of sufficient ventilation, which caused plaintiff to perspire excessively,

contributing to his injuries.

The trial court granted an accelerated judgment to the defendants on the grounds of governmental immunity. On appeal, the court found the principal should not be covered by the cloak of governmental immunity for "personal neglect" in maintaining inadequate school facilities, in allowing an illegal summer weight-lifting program, and in providing insufficient supervision. Similarly, "since the plaintiff was injured in the course of an athletic injury, a trier of fact could find that defendant [athletic director] abused a personal and direct duty to provide a safe weight-lifting program. Defendant [athletic director] is not entitled to the protection of the governmental immunity statute." On the other hand, the possible negligence of the coach and other employees could not be imputed to the school superintendent merely because he was in a supervisory position. In absence of a charge of "personal neglect," he is protected by governmental immunity. The plaintiff's allegation against defendant school district for providing unsafe facilities was found to be protected under the governmental immunity statute. Further, "it appears from the facts that the lack of supervision, not a defect in the building, was the cause of the plaintiff's injuries."

The trial court's accelerated judgments to defendant athletic director and school principal on the grounds of government immunity were reversed; those granted to defendant school district and superintendent were affirmed.

Lynch v. Board of Education of Collingsville Community School District, 390 N.E. 2d 526 (Ill. Ct. App. 1979)

Cynthia Lynch, prior to her junior year in high school, was a friendly, outgoing, well-liked student according to her parents and friends. That year she participated in an informal, tackle "powderpuff" football game between the junior and senior classes. Prior to the contest, two teachers held five or six practices with the junior class, although minimal instruction on football rules was given and no equipment was provided.

During the course of the game, which the seniors won 52–0, quarterback Lynch passed the ball downfield. Subsequently, a senior pass rusher struck her in the face and knocked her to the ground — a blatant "roughing the passer" transgression. Her face bloodied, her nose broken, and having smacked the back of her head against the ground, Lynch had to be assisted to the sidelines.

Several months later she underwent a dramatic personality change. By her own admission, she could no longer get along with people. She ran away from home in Collingsville, Illinois, after taking her father's car, and was taken into custody by Wyoming police after she wrecked the vehicle. Her parents brought a negligence suit against the school district. Plaintiff alleged ordinary negligence on the part of the defendant in failing to provide adequate equipment and willful and wanton misconduct on defendant's part in failing to adequately supervise the powderpuff football game.

An Illinois statute delimits the duty a teacher owes to its students: "[They] stand in the relation of parents and guardians to the pupils." This relationship extends to all activities connected with the school program and may be exercised at any time for the safety and supervision of the pupils in the absence of their parents or guardians (Ill. Rev. Stat. 1973, ch. 122, Par. 24). Thus, in a negligence suit against a teacher, concerning improper supervision, a plaintiff must allege willful and wanton misconduct rather than mere negligence on the teacher's part.

In its defense, the school district argued that it was not negligent since the game was not authorized by the school. Further, defendant argued it was not liable for inadequate supervision amounting to willful and wanton misconduct since plaintiff's parents were spectators at the game.

In affirming the $600,000 award to the plaintiff, the appeals court stated that since the

teams' coaches were teachers and the field on which the contest was played was fenced and could have been locked to keep students out, there was sufficient evidence for the jury to conclude that the game was authorized by the school. Further, in light of public-policy considerations, the court held that the presence of the plaintiff's parents did not obviate the school's duty to provide adequate equipment.

NOTES

1. In *Domino* v. *Mercurio*, 17 A.D. 2d 342, 234 N.Y.S. 2d 1011 (1962), *aff'd* 13 N.Y. 2d 922, 193 N.E. 2d 893 (1963), a negligence suit was brought by plaintiff father against the local board of education and its playground supervisors who were employees of the board for injuries sustained by plaintiff's son, who, while playing softball on school playground, fell over a bench that was too close to the basepath. The court held for the plaintiff and reasoned the board could be held liable for the negligence of the playground supervisors who allowed spectators to congregate too close to the third-base line and moved the bench into a dangerous position near that line. It was not necessary that the board itself be found guilty of negligence in its selection of playground supervisors.

2. In *Foster* v. *Houston General Insurance Company*, 407 So. 2d 759 (La. Ct. App. 1981), an action was brought on behalf of a mentally retarded student who was killed en route to an off-campus facility to attend basketball practice. Decedent Foster attended a school for the mentally retarded and was a member of his school's Special Olympics basketball team. On the way to basketball practice, Foster dashed in front of a car and was struck and killed while under the supervision of one teacher. This teacher had assumed responsibility for the 11 players because the other teacher involved was detained in class. The trial court ruled that the defendant teachers owed Foster a legal duty, and they breached their duty by failing to act reasonably under the circumstances. Defendants (1) failed to provide an adequate number of supervisory personnel and (2) they were negligent in the selection of the safest possible walk route. The defendant school board was not liable for independent negligence. The trial court's decision was affirmed on appeal.

3. See *Cantwell* v. *University of Massachusetts*, 551 F. 2d 879 (1st Cir. 1977), in Section 4.23–4, and *Larson* v. *Independent School District No. 314*, 289 N.W. 2d 112 (Minn. 1979), in Section 4.23–1, Note 12, in which plaintiffs contended that they were improperly spotted during gymnastics and tumbling routines.

4. In *Kersey* v. *Harbin*, 591 S.W. 2d 745 (Mo. Ct. App. 1979), a negligence suit was filed against various defendant school officials for fatal injuries sustained by plaintiff's son

during gym class. Decedent Kersey engaged in a brief scuffle after a fellow student deliberately and persistently stepped on Kersey's heels. During the scuffle, Kersey sustained a skull fracture, which occurred on the stairway leading from the locker room to the gymnasium. Plaintiff alleged the school authorities were possessed of actual or constructive knowledge of quarrelsome propensities on the part of a fellow student and, despite such knowledge, failed to take appropriate measures to prevent injury by exercising ordinary care. In reversing a summary judgment of governmental immunity granted the defendants, the appeals court held that supervisory public school employees and teachers are not immune from tort liability for inadequate supervision of their students but that such liability is highly subjective and the scope of their duties is extremely narrow. Further, the court held that whether ordinary care was exercised was a question of fact precluding summary judgment: ". . . compliance with a legislative enactment or an administrative regulation does not preclude a finding of negligence where a reasonable man would take additional precaution."

5. In December 1983, 15-year-old Ronald Dorko and his father, John, filed suit seeking $325,000 in damages from Medina (Ohio) Buckeye High School football coach Kenneth Woodruff, assistant coach Scott Tipton, and the Buckeye School District Board of Education. The complaint alleged that Ronald Dorko missed practice on August 29 and was punished in a "shedding" drill on August 30. Dorko, in uniform, was ordered to stand 25 feet from 30 teammates, also in uniform. In three-second intervals, the players ran full speed at Dorko and either tackled him or blocked him. Dorko claimed that muscles in his upper right arm were damaged during the drill. For further information, see *USA Today*, December 23, 1983, p. Cl.

6. In *DeMauro v. Tusculum College, Inc.*, 603 S.W. 2d 115 (Tenn. 1980), the court discussed an institution's duty of supervision and instruction (see Section 4.23–1).

7. A coach may also be sued for not providing proper equipment. See *Vendrell v. School District No. 26C, Malheur County*, 233 Or. 1, 376 P. 2d 406 (1962), in Section 4.22–2.

4.22–2 Instruction and Training

The coach and the physical education teacher are responsible for providing proper instruction and training to the student-athletes. The coach and the teacher should be qualified to teach the particular activity (see *DeMauro v. Tusculum College, Inc.*, Note 3). In addition, the coach must properly instruct the student-athletes on the activity, the safety rules, and the proper method of playing. In a number of cases involving football-related injuries, the injured

player has alleged that the coach or teacher did not provide proper instruction and training concerning tackling (see *Vendrell v. School District No. 26C, Malheur County, infra*). In addition, a proper preseason conditioning program should be provided. This may be an issue in places where football practice begins in August, where in some instances players have died from heat exhaustion.

It has been recommended that coaches and physical education teachers keep detailed records of their instruction and training. They should also be aware of any new developments in their sport. In addition, some companies have started producing instruction and training films to assist coaches and teachers in preparing their student-athletes.

A final area of potential liability for the coach or the teacher is a claim by a player of assault and battery. Several issues are raised in *Rutledge v. Arizona Board of Regents, infra*, and *Hogenson v. Williams*, Note 2. Is there a defense of privilege? Is the standard of care "reasonable care" or "gross negligence"? Does sovereign immunity protect the coach and the teacher? Can force be used to involve compliance with commands and punishment for prohibited conduct? Can force be used when the player has not performed adequately?

Vendrell v. School District No. 26C, Malheur County, 233 Or. 1, 376 P. 2d 406 (1962)

Louis Vendrell brought this action against the school district for damages from a neck injury he sustained while playing in a football game for the Nyssa High School team. The trial court entered a judgment of $25,000 in favor of Vendrell.

Vendrell, upon entering his freshman year of high school, registered to participate in the school's football program. He had played football the previous two years at Nyssa Junior High School. Vendrell was issued football equipment with the rest of the team in the presence of the team's coaches. After receiving equipment, the team began practice and conditioning in preparation for the season.

About six weeks later, Vendrell was playing the position of running back for Nyssa High School in a game against Vale High School. On a certain play, Vendrell carried the ball, and when he saw two Vale players in front of him, he lowered his head and collided with them. The collision caused Vendrell to sustain a fractured neck at the fifth vertebrae. Plaintiff Vendrell contended that when he was injured he was an inexperienced player, that the equipment he had been issued was unsatisfactory, and that he was improperly trained.

In its discussion of the case, the Supreme Court of Oregon found each of Vendrell's contentions to be without merit. With regard to Vendrell's assertion of "inexperience," the court held that the plaintiff was not an inexperienced player in that he had played football for two years in junior high school, and during those years received substantial football training from competent coaches. Vendrell competed in several junior varsity football games and played the same position in those games that he played at the time of his injury.

With regard to the plaintiff's contention that he was issued unsatisfactory equipment, the court held that since the coaches were present when the equipment was given out to hear any questions or complaints from the players, and since the plaintiff had the privilege of returning any of his equipment and selecting a substitute, the contention could not be sustained by the facts.

In his final contention, Vendrell argued that he was provided with improper training. The court held that the game of football is an inherently rough sport in which body contact and some degree of injury is inevitable and that no player needs to have this explained. In order to minimize the possibility of injury to players, as well as to enhance the players' football skills, coaches employ extensive instruction and exercise sessions. The coaching staff at Nyssa High School held such sessions. Football coaches from schools other than

Nyssa High but familiar with Nyssa's training program testified that Nyssa's practice and conditioning program was a good one and similar to programs at many other schools.

Furthermore, regarding plaintiff's argument that the coaches did not tell him that if he lowered his head as a battering ram he could sustain a neck injury, the court held that it was the player's right, in fact duty, to inquire of his coaches about any matter of which he was not clear. The coaches also had the right to assume that the plaintiff possessed normal intelligence for his age, and that plaintiff knew of the potential for injury if he used his head as a battering ram.

The Supreme Court of Oregon reversed the decision of the trial court and ordered that judgment be entered in favor of the defendant.

Rutledge v. Arizona Board of Regents, 660 F. 2d 1345 (9th Cir. 1981), aff'd, 460 U.S. 719, 103 S. Ct. 148, 75 L.Ed 2d 413 (1983)

Kevin Rutledge sued Coach Frank Kush for assault and battery, demotion, harassment, embarrassment, defamation and deprivation of his scholarship. He claimed that on October 28, 1978, Kush took Rutledge's helmeted head between his hands, shook it from side to side, yelled obscenities, and then struck Rutledge's mouth with his fist. Rutledge filed suit in Arizona state court but was denied relief. He then filed suit in federal district court. The court dismissed the complaint and Rutledge appealed. On appeal, the Ninth Circuit Court of Appeals held that the university, the board of regents, and the athletic director were entitled to at least partial immunity. The coaches were not entitled to immunity, and the athletic director was not immune on the charge he failed to properly supervise the coach.

The court, however, dismissed Rutledge's assault and battery complaint from federal court because it had already been litigated in state court. The complaint based on the deprivation of scholarship was dismissed because Rutledge was held to have no right to maintain his position on the team. The court also held that his intercollegiate participation was not a protectable property right (see Sections 2.10–2.13–1).

NOTES

1. In *Pirkle v. Oakdale Union Grammar School Dist.*, 253 P. 2d 1 (Cal. 1953), an action was brought by an eighth grade student against the school district for injuries received when he was blocked during a touch football game that was being played without supervision. The court held for the defendants on appeal, ruling that the players had been selected according to skill and by a reasonable means of classification. They were properly instructed, experienced, and proficient, and they participated in the game only if they chose to do so. The court also held that plaintiff's injuries could not have been readily apparent to a layman since the activity was not an inherently dangerous one. In addition, the court held that no further damage resulted from a delay in receiving medical treatment.

2. In *Hogenson v. Williams*, 542 S.W. 2d 456 (Tex. Civ. App. 1976), an action for assault was brought when a coach, displeased with the blocking of a seventh grade player, grabbed him by the face mask and knocked him to the ground. This resulted in a severe cervical sprain. The jury found for the defendant, but the appeals court held that the trial judge had improperly interpreted the rule of "privileged force" granted to a teacher when he instructed the jury that "intent to injure is the gist of an assault." Rather, a teacher or coach can use force necessary to invoke compliance with his commands or to punish the child for prohibited conduct. A coach cannot use force merely because the student-athlete's performance is inadequate, even though the coach may consider such violence to be constructive. The jury verdict was reversed and remanded.

3. In *DeMauro v. Tusculum College, Inc.*, 603 S.W. 2d 115 (Tenn. 1980), the college was sued under the theory of respondeat superior, when the instructor of a golf class assigned a class to a teaching assistant who was an inexperienced golfer. A student was injured in the class supervised by the teaching assistant (see Section 4.23–1).

4. In *Larson v. Independent School District No. 314*, 289 N.W. 2d 112 (Minn. 1979), plaintiff contended that the teacher was negligent in teaching a headspring (see Section 4.23–1, Note 12).

5. In *Kluka v. Livingston Parish School Board*, 433 So. 2d 302 (La. Ct. App. 1983), a basketball coach was held not liable for injuries to a student who caught his foot between two mats while wrestling the coach in a friendly match. The court reasoned that the student initiated the match and knew that wrestling could lead to injury.

6. Rutledge has also been unsuccessful in pursuing a claim against his former coach on the state level. In 1985,

an Arizona Court of Appeals upheld a lower court decision for Kush. Rutledge's attorney planned to appeal the civil suit to the state's supreme court. See "Kush Wins Again," *USA Today*, May 24, 1985, p.Cl.

4.22–3 Medical Assistance

A common risk encountered in the area of sports is the risk of serious injury. When an injury to an athlete or spectator appears to be serious, those in charge of the activity are under a duty to use reasonable efforts to obtain reasonably prompt and capable medical assistance. At the same time, there is a duty to refrain from actions that could aggravate an injury in situations in which a reasonable person would know of the risk.

The coach and the physical education teacher are held to a standard of "reasonable care" when rendering medical assistance to an injured student-athlete. They are not expected to provide the assistance of a doctor or one with medical training (see Section 4–23–2). In fact, some of the obligations of a coach and teacher have shifted to others. For example, many states have passed statutes requiring that medical personnel be in attendance at games (see Section 4.23–2, Note 1).

The institution may be the responsible party if medical personnel have not been provided. In addition, the institution may be responsible for having medical personnel "reasonably" available even when it is not statutorily mandated. With medical personnel available, the care of the injured athlete may not have to be undertaken by the coach or teacher.

Therefore, in most situations, the main responsibilities of the coach and physical education teacher are twofold. First, they may have to render assistance before the medical personnel arrive. First-aid training may be helpful in preventing situations such as a coach improperly moving an injured student-athlete (see *Welch* v. *Dunsmuir Joint Union High School District, infra*). The second responsibility is to exercise reasonable care in sending an injured athlete for medical treatment. The following two cases illustrate the potential liability of the coach and the teacher when medical assistance is not provided (see *Mogabgab* v. *Orleans Parish School Board*, Note 1 and *Stineman* v. *Fontbonne College*, Note 2).

Welch v. Dunsmuir Joint Union High School District, 326 P. 2d 633 (Cal. Ct. App. 1958)

A high school football player who was injured during a scrimmage between two high school teams brought a civil suit against the school district. The injured student, Anthony Welch, had been proclaimed physically fit by a doctor prior to the start of school. The teams were participating in a controlled scrimmage with no officials. Instead, the coaches were on the field supervising the activity. The plaintiff was a quarterback for one of the teams. During one play, he took the ball on a "quarterback sneak" and was tackled shortly after he went through the line. As he was falling forward, another player was going in to make the tackle and fell on top of him. After this play, the plaintiff was lying on his back on the field and unable to get to his feet. Coach Reginato of the Dunsmuir team suspected that Welch might have a neck injury and had him take a hold of his hands to see if there was any grip in them. Welch was able to move his hands at the time.

The evidence is conflicting as to whether or not Doctor Saylor, who was admittedly present at the scrimmage, examined the plaintiff before he was moved to the sidelines. Evidence indicates, however, that plaintiff was carried from the field by eight boys, four on each side, without the aid of a stretcher or board or any other solid structure beneath him.

The undisputed and only medical testimony was that the plaintiff was a permanent quadriplegic, caused by damage to the spinal cord at the level of the fifth cervical vertebra; that there was a fracture of this vertebra without significant displacement; that the fracture was the result of severe trauma; and that the removal of the plaintiff from the field without the use of a stretcher was an improper medical practice in view of the symptoms. The doctor testified that movement of the fingers, hands, and feet are the most important indicators of a spinal injury of the type suffered by the plaintiff. After the plaintiff was moved off the field to the sidelines, he was unable to move his fingers, hands, or feet. With these circumstances in mind, a doctor who testified as an expert witness, stated that in his opinion the plaintiff must have sustained additional damage to the spinal cord while being moved.

When the original case was decided, the jury returned a verdict in favor of the plaintiff in the sum of $325,000. The defendant filed a motion for a new trial, which was denied. The defendant appealed the judgment, contending that the court erred in giving the following instructions to the jury:

> Because of the great danger involved in moving an injured human being a person of ordinary prudence will exercise extreme caution when engaged in such an activity. Hence, it is the duty of anyone managing or participating in such an activity to exercise extreme caution.

Defendant claimed that this instruction was prejudicial because it set up a false standard of conduct and placed on the defendant a burden that is not consistent with existing laws. The appeals court rejected defendant's claim. The court held that the challenged instruction, read with the other instructions, correctly informed the jury that the standard of care required of the defendant was that of ordinary care under the circumstances. Immediately preceding this instruction, the court had given the following instruction:

> Inasmuch as the amount of caution used by the ordinarily prudent person varies in direct proportion to the danger known to be involved in the undertaking, it follows that in the exercise of ordinary care, the amount of caution required will vary in accordance with the nature of the act and the surrounding circumstances.
>
> To put the matter in another way, the amount of caution involved in the exercise of ordinary care, and hence required by law, increases or

decreases as does the danger that reasonably should be apprehended.

The appeals court ruled that this standard was still one of ordinary care — that is, of a person of ordinary prudence, in which the factual situation shows that great danger was involved in the activity. There was evidence in the case that the moving of a person with suspected grave injuries is inherently a hazardous activity.

The defendant had requested that the following instructions be given to the jury and claimed the court erred in failing to do so:

(1) If you find that Dr. Saylor attended the plaintiff after the accident and before the plaintiff was moved from the place where he was injured; then, in that event, I instruct you that the responsibility of the coach to render first aid ended when the doctor's responsibility began.

(2) I instruct you that the evidence in this case did not establish that Dr. Saylor was an agent, servant, or employee of the Dunsmuir Joint Union High School District and if you find that the doctor was negligent, such negligence is not chargeable to the defendant.

The first of the above refused instructions was taken substantially from the Red Cross textbook, which says: "The responsibilities of the first aider stop when the physician's begin. First aid tells what to do until the doctor comes." The defendant claimed that the instruction would have given the jury a measuring stick from which they could have determined when the responsibility of the coach ended and the responsibility of the doctor commenced. The second instruction was proposed on the theory that the doctor alone was negligent. In lieu thereof, the court gave the following instruction, which the defendant claimed was prejudicial:

When the negligent acts or omissions of two or more persons, whether committed independently or in the course of a jointly directed conduct, contribute concurrently and as proximate cause to the injury of another, each of such persons is liable. This is true regardless of the relative degree of the contribution. It is no defense for one of such persons that some other person, not joined as a defendant in the action, participated in causing the injury even if it should appear to you that the negligence of that other person was greater in either its wrongful nature or its effect.

Under the evidence in this case, the jury could reasonably have inferred that both the doctor and the coach were negligent in the removal of the plaintiff from the field to the sidelines — the coach in failing to wait for the doctor and allowing the plaintiff to be moved, and the doctor in failing to act promptly after plaintiff's injury. Therefore, the appeals court held that the trial court properly gave the instructions to the jury and properly refused defendant's proposed instructions.

NOTES

1. In *Mogabgab* v. *Orleans Parish School Board*, 239 So. 2d 456 (La. Ct. App. 1970), an action was brought by parents for the wrongful death of their son, a high school football player who died as a result of heatstroke and exhaustion following a practice. The plaintiff sued the coach, the school principal, and the school district on the theory that the school was negligent in not making sure the coach was properly trained. They argued that the school was negligent in making arrangements for the proper care of sick and injured players. The court held that the coach who actively denied student access to medical treatment for two hours after symptoms of heatstroke and shock appeared was guilty of negligence. It did not find negligence attributable to the principal or the district, however, because they were either unaware of the events or on vacation.

2. In *Stineman* v. *Fontbonne College*, 664 F. 2d 1082 (8th Cir. 1981), an action was brought by Patricia Stineman, a deaf student who had played on the Fontbonne College softball team. Her softball coaches were aware of her deafness. Stineman had also signed an authorization for emergency medical treatment in the event of an injury. During the course of practice, plaintiff was struck in the eye with a ball. Although she was in great pain, a coach merely applied ice and advised Stineman to go to her room and rest. Neither of the coaches who were present suggested that she seek medical attention. No immediate professional medical attention was given, even though the school infirmary was across the street. Permanent eye damage resulted from the injury.

The trial court awarded Stineman $800,000 in damages for the negligence of the defendant in failing to provide medical assistance. The Court of Appeals affirmed the decision, finding the college vicariously liable; however, the court reduced the award to $600,000.

4.22–4 Vicarious Liability for Actions of Fans and Players

The coach and the physical education teacher may be sued under a vicarious liability theory for either an unintentional or an intentional tort. The case of *Toone* v. *Adams, infra,* illustrates the problems a plaintiff will have in winning a case on a vicarious liability theory. In *Toone* v. *Adams,* an umpire was injured by a fan, and the umpire sued, among others, the manager of the team for inciting the fan to act. The court held for the manager and found that the manager's actions were not the proximate cause of the umpire's injuries.

The nexus between the coach and the injury may be more easily established in other fact situations that have occurred but that have not resulted in a reported decision. For example, a coach who orders a player to fight or to attempt to injure an opposing player may be liable under the vicarious liability theory if injuries occur.

Toone v. Adams, 262 N.C. 403, 137 S.E. 2d 132 (1964)

Plaintiff baseball umpire John Toone brought suit against baseball fan Baxter Adams, baseball manager Ken Deal, and Raleigh Baseball, Inc. (RBI), owner of a baseball team in the Carolina League, after Toone was assaulted by Adams while on the way to the dressing room following a game.

Several times during the game on June 16, 1968, between the Raleigh Caps and a minor league rival, the Greensboro Yankees, controversies arose over calls by Toone, who was the field umpire. Each time, Deal charged onto the field to argue the call vehemently. His second time out, Deal warned Toone that if he made another decision with which he disagreed, Deal would act in such a manner that Toone would be forced to eject him, the result of which would be extreme hostility toward Toone on the part of the partisan Caps fans. During the ninth inning, another controversy

developed, and Deal again charged out onto the field to protest. While the argument continued, two Yankee players scored and another runner advanced a base. The Raleigh players began to shove Toone, and when Toone requested Deal to control his players, Deal deliberately disregarded his request. Deal was ejected from the game but continued to argue for ten minutes before leaving. When the game ended, Toone passed unharmed toward the dressing room until Adams, without any cause or provocation and without warning, struck Toone on his head, injuring him.

Plaintiff contended that the defendants Deal and RBI owed him the duty to conduct themselves so as not to incite the fans against him and also to provide him with safe passage from the playing field "either by police or by agents of the corporation" immediately after the game. Plaintiff alleged that these duties were breached and that his injuries were proximately caused by the joint "willful, wanton and malicious negligence of the defendants" Adams and Deal, for which RBI was also liable under the doctrine of respondeat superior. Plaintiff sought compensatory and punitive damages.

When the action came to trial, defendants Deal and RBI objected to the complaint because it failed to state a cause of action in that (1) the alleged acts of Deal did not constitute a breach of any legal duty that the defendants owed to the plaintiff; (2) the alleged facts showed no causal relation between the conduct of Deal and the assault by Adams; and (3) Deal could not reasonably have foreseen an assault by a spectator. The court sustained the motion, and the plaintiff appealed. The defendant Adams, who had failed to file an answer before the trial, was not a party to the appeal, having had judgment by default and inquiry rendered against him.

On the appeal, the Supreme Court of North Carolina affirmed the lower court's decision. The major consideration was whether the plaintiff stated a cause of action against defendants for damages proximately caused by the breach of a duty arising out of the contractual relationship between them.

The Supreme Court found that umpires are used to having their calls disputed and that disagreements, as such, were not a major problem. The plaintiff was well escorted on his way to the dressing room, and though the guards themselves could have been a bit more diligent, lack of police protection was not a proximate *cause* of the plaintiff's injury.

On the question of whether Deal's conduct on the field was a proximate cause of Adams's assault on the plaintiff, the Supreme Court found that it was not. The Court stated that the "law imposes upon every person who enters upon an active course of conduct the positive duty to use ordinary care to protect others from harm and a violation of that duty is negligence." Though the liability for assault and battery can be extended to others who procure, instigate, or incite the tort, one "is not responsible for a beating inflicted by another, however wrongful it may be, simply because he thinks the punishment deserved, or is pleased at it, or thinks well of it. He must do something more." Plaintiff made no allegations that there was ever any personal contact or concert of action between Deal and Adams. Instead, plaintiff claimed that Deal attempted to incite the entire audience with only Adams being moved to act. The Court asserted that Deal did not actually intend or could not reasonably have anticipated that one or more persons would assault the plaintiff as a result of his conduct.

To describe the action of inciting, the Court noted that: "In order that one may incite another, that is, to move another to action, to spur him on, persuade him, it is necessary that he be present at the scene of the action; otherwise, he is directing, ordering or procuring." Since Deal had been ejected from the game and was nowhere near the area when Adams assaulted Toone, Deal could not be said to have incited Adams. Since Adams's attack came well after the antics of Deal on the field and since Deal had no knowledge of the

intentions of Adams toward the plaintiff, to state that Deal's conduct was a proximate cause of the assault would be pure speculation. Any number of other reasons, including Adams's own disgust with Toone's call, or even the challenge of another fan, could have spurred Adams on.

The Court concluded by stating that Adams was acting voluntarily and of his own accord when he injured the plaintiff, and noted that:

> The mere fact that both Adams and Deal may have become simultaneously enraged with the plaintiff for the same cause does not establish a concert of action. It would be an intolerable burden upon managers of baseball teams to saddle them with responsibility for the action of every emotionally unstable person who might arrive at the game spoiling for a fight and become enraged over an umpire's call which the managers had protested.

NOTES

1. For further information on the liability of game officials in sports, see Section 4.27.

2. For a case in which a basketball official successfully sued a merchant for selling T-shirts with the official's likeness printed on them with a noose around his neck, see *Bain* v. *Gillespie*, 357 N.W. 2d 47 (Iowa Ct. App. 1984), in Section 4.27.

4.23 Liability of Administrators, Schools, and Universities

Sports-related injuries that take place within the confines of an educational institution raise the issue of an institution's legal accountability. From the perspective of the seriously injured plaintiff, it may be highly desirable to obtain a judgment against an institution rather than against an individual coach or physical education instructor because the institution is much more likely to have a "deep pocket."

If an administrator or institution is subject to liability, the standards to which it will be held are the same as in similar areas of tort law. An administrator or institution is required to exercise reasonable care to prevent reasonably foreseeable risks and to make safe foreseeably dangerous conditions by repairing or warning. If an institution fails to maintain a reasonable standard of care, it may be sued for negligence (see Section 4.12). An administrator or institution should establish rules for the safe use of its facilities, provide supervision of its athletic activities (see Section 4.23–1), hire qualified personnel (see Section 4.23–1), provide proper medical assistance (see Section 4.23–2), provide proper equipment (see Section 4.23–3), and properly maintain equipment and facilities (see Section 4.23–3). Institutions cannot guarantee the safety of students, but they are subject to liability when the institution or someone for whom the institution is legally responsible does not meet the standard of care that the law requires.

The administrator, school, or university may also be sued under the theory of vicarious liability for the alleged negligence of an employee (see Section 4.13). For example, an administrator may be sued as the supervisor of a coach or teacher. An institution may be sued in its role as the employer of an administrator, coach, teacher, referee, doctor, or owner or possessor of a facility.

One roadblock in the path of the potential plaintiff against a school or its administrators, however, is the sovereign immunity doctrine. This doctrine is a rule of law, which in many states exempts public schools and universities from private suit. Sovereign immunity has been an established legal principle for centuries, but in recent years the doctrine's applicability has eroded. In states in which sovereign immunity has been partially abrogated, there are usually special rules of procedure that the plaintiff must carefully follow in bringing suit (see Section 4.23–4).

NOTE

1. For further information, see the following articles:
(a) "The Student-Athlete and the National Collegiate Athletic Association: The Need for a Prima Facie Tort Doctrine," 9 *Suffolk University Law Review* 1340 (Summer 1975).
(b) "Controlling Crowds at Basketball Games: Persistent Problem for Coaches, Officials," *Chronicle of Higher Education*, February 27, 1985, pp. 33, 36.

4.23–1 Supervision and Personnel

The administrator is the supervisor of the coach or physical education teacher, and may be held liable for negligence in failing to exercise reasonable care in fulfilling this responsibility. Many of the administrator's duties and responsibilities are similar to the supervisory duties of the coach or physical education teacher in dealing with student-athletes (see Section 4.22–1).

In dealing with personnel, administrators may be held liable if they have not exercised reasonable care in hiring coaches and physical education teachers with proper skills and qualifications (see *Cook v. Bennet, infra*) and in ensuring that properly qualified personnel are supervising an activity (see *DeMauro v. Tusculum College, Inc., infra*, and *Stehn v. Bernarr MacFadden Foundations, Inc.*, Note 4).

Schools and universities are generally sued on a vicarious liability theory, in which the negligence of their employee is imputed to the employer. The negligent individual may be an administrator, a teacher, a coach, a substitute teacher, a student teacher, or a referee. However, any of these individuals and the school or university may be immune from lawsuit under a sovereign immunity defense (see Section 4.23–4).

Carabba v. Anacortes School District No. 103, 435 P. 2d 936 (Wash. 1967)

Stephen Carabba, a high school wrestler, brought this suit against defendant Anacortes and Oak Harbor school districts to recover damages for injuries he sustained in a wrestling match.

Carabba was a member of the Anacortes High School varsity wrestling team. On January 13, 1963, his team was engaged in a wrestling meet with Oak Harbor High School. Near the end of Carabba's match against Roger Anderson, in the 145-pound weight class, the referee, noticing that a side protective mat had separated from the main wrestling mat, moved to bring the side mat closer to the main mat. At this point, while the referee's attention was briefly diverted from the ongoing match, Anderson applied a wrestling hold to Carabba called a "full nelson" where Anderson, being behind Carabba, put his arms under Carabba's arms and placed his hands on the back of Carabba's neck or head and applied pressure forcing Carabba's head down. The whistle sounded to end the match almost immediately after the full nelson was applied. But when Anderson released Carabba, Carabba slumped to the mat, paralyzed below the neck due to the substantial severance of his spinal cord.

The superior court found that the referee was an agent of the school district and instructed the jury in this regard. However, the court decided in favor of the school district and Carabba appealed. The supreme court of Washington agreed with the superior court that the referee was an agent for the school district. The court reasoned that a school district's authority is not limited to curricular activities, as evidenced by their employment of athletic coaches, band directors, and even debate coaches, to control and supervise extracurricular activities because of their educational and cultural value. Furthermore, the match was "under the auspices" of the school district, and since the school district provided the wrestling program, the coaches, a place to practice, the equipment, and, in fact, encouraged student participation in wrestling, the court held that the school district owed a duty to the student participants to provide protection from injury. Therefore, the instruction to the jury in regard to the referee's agency relationship with the school district was proper.

The case was reversed and remanded to the superior court on other grounds.

Cook v. Bennett, 288 N.W. 2d 609 (Mich. Ct. App. 1979)

Plaintiff elementary school student was seriously injured while playing "kill" during recess. In the game of "kill," all participants attempt to obtain the ball by tackling the lone participant who has it. At trial, a summary judgment based on governmental immunity was granted to defendant teacher and principal who had been sued for negligence.

On appeal, the court affirmed summary judgment for the teacher, since the teacher was absent from school the day of the accident "and that any duty imposed by law was owed (to the plaintiff) by the substitute teacher who was in charge." In regard to defendant principal, the court held "the extent to which a school principal is protected by immunity is dependent on whether the act complained of falls within the principal's discretionary or ministerial powers." Since inadequate supervision is not a discretionary function and is not protected by governmental immunity, the appeals court reversed the summary judgment granted the principal.

DeMauro v. Tusculum College, Inc., 603 S.W. 2d 115 (Tenn. 1980)

Donna DeMauro, the plaintiff, was an 18-year-old freshman at Tusculum College. In partial fulfillment of her physical education requirement, she took an introductory course spring semester in golf. Prior to taking the course, Donna had never played the sport in her life.

James Hunter was a 22-year-old senior attending Tusculum College on a basketball scholarship. As a physical education major, Hunter signed up for a class in the department entitled "Teaching Assistant." The class requirement was to "assist in all aspects of the instruction of an activity course, and, on occasion, to conduct the class." Even though he had not played much golf since taking a similar introductory course in golf his freshman year, Hunter was the teaching assistant for DeMauro's golf class.

After a few classes indoors, the students traveled to a local country club for their first session on a golf course. At the No. 5 tee,

Hunter attempted to demonstrate hitting a golf ball for a foursome of freshmen women in the class, one of whom was DeMauro. Hunter apparently "shanked" the shot, which struck DeMauro in the face. She received severe injuries which required two surgical operations.

DeMauro sued the college for negligence, and the jury returned a verdict in her favor. The court of appeals, in a split decision, reversed and dismissed, holding that there was no material evidence of causative negligence. The Supreme Court of Tennessee overruled the decision of the court of appeals and held that jury issues were presented on the question of defendant's liability. More specifically, the court believed three major issues were raised in the trial that were matters for the jury:

1. Whether Hunter was an authorized representative of the college in instructing the class.
2. Whether the actual instructor of the class, a Dr. Shasby, and through him the college, was negligent in placing Hunter, an inexperienced golfer, in such a position where his lack of experience was a factor which made injury to DeMauro foreseeable and hence that the school had breached its duty of proper supervision and instruction owed to DeMauro
3. Whether DeMauro was aware of the risks associated with golf, whether she assumed such risks, and whether the action was completely unavoidable.

In refuting defendant's claim that it had no duty or responsibility to DeMauro because she was struck by a fellow student rather than a servant of the college, the supreme court stated:

> Under some circumstances, of course, this may be correct. It is ... true that participants in sporting activities occupy a somewhat different legal position from mere observers or passers-by. Where, however, students are novices and are receiving courses of instruction in sports ... by an educational institution, a duty of supervision

and instruction arises from the relationship which is not terminated or abrogated merely by reason of the fact that one student participant injures another.

Reversed and remanded for a new trial.

NOTES

1. In *Germond* v. *Board of Educ. of Central School Dist. No. 1*, 197 N.Y.S. 2d 548 (1960), plaintiff student sought recovery from defendant board and defendant teacher for injuries sustained when struck in the face by a bat swung by an older student during a softball game on the school's playground.

The trial court's decision against the board was affirmed by the court of appeals. The court reasoned that the board assumed responsibility for the individual negligence of a teacher. The board's failure to reasonably enforce adequate rules with respect to playing of games on the playground and the failure to provide adequate supervision were sufficient evidence to justify a verdict against the board. The evidence presented sustained a finding of no cause of action against the school teacher who had been supervising play. The appellate court ruled that "the mere presence of the older girls would not necessarily alert a reasonable and careful teacher of young children to danger."

2. A college is not liable for failure to supervise in absence of notice of potential for serious injury. In *Rubtchinsky* v. *State University of New York at Albany*, 46 Misc. 2d 679, 260 N.Y.S. 2d 256 (1965), plaintiff sought recovery from university based on university's alleged failure to supervise a pushball game. (Pushball is similar to rugby in type of contact between players.) The court granted judgment for the defendant, holding that the university had no duty to supervise since the game had been played for 38 years without serious injury.

3. In *Mogabgab* v. *Orleans Parish School Board*, 239 So. 2d 456 (La. Ct. App. 1970), the school district and principal were held not liable for failure to provide adequate medical training for the coach when all were unaware of the events that caused the death of the player (see Section 4.22–3, Note 1).

4. In *Stehn* v. *Bernarr MacFadden Foundations, Inc.*, 434 F. 2d 811 (6th Cir. 1970), plaintiff argued that the owner of the private school was negligent in not providing proper instructions to and not properly supervising a new physical education teacher who taught the segment on wrestling, during which plaintiff was injured. Defendant appealed after the lower court found for the plaintiff, but the decision was affirmed (see Section 4.12–1, Note 4).

5. In *Fustin* v. *Board of Education of Community Unit Dist. No. 2*, 242 N.E. 2d 308 (Ill. Ct. App. 1968), the plaintiff argued that the board of education, which controlled and managed the basketball gymnasium and provided for supervision of the games by its agents, was

liable for the acts and omissions of its agents, including the failure to properly control and supervise. The board defended in part by stating that it could not be liable under respondeat superior for the conduct of an opposing player in absence of notice as to his violent proclivity (see Section 4.13, Note 3).

6. In *Brahatcek v. Millard School District No. 17*, 273 N.W. 2d 680 (Neb. 1979), an action was brought for the death of a ninth grade student who was accidentally struck by a golf club during physical education class. The court held that the school district and its instructors were negligent in not supervising and that the lack of supervision was the proximate cause of the student's death. The instructors should have foreseen the intervening negligent act of the ninth grade student who fatally struck a classmate. If there had been proper supervision, the death would not have occurred, and therefore the intervening negligence of the classmate did not preclude the district from liability for the death.

7. In *Kersey v. Harbin*, 591 S.W. 2d 745 (Mo. Ct. App. 1979), the plaintiff alleged that school administrators were negligent in not preventing a scuffle which resulted in injury (see Section 4.22–1, Note 4).

8. In *Crohn v. Congregation B'nai Zion*, 317 N.E. 2d 637 (Ill. Ct. App. 1974), a negligence suit was brought by plaintiff father against defendant summer day camp for injuries sustained when his 7-year-old-daughter was struck in the face by a baseball bat being swung by a boy, age 10, during an activity supervised by a 15-year-old counselor. The trial court directed a verdict in favor of defendant. On appeal, the court held the evidence did not overwhelmingly favor the defendants on the question of whether the camp provided a safe place and adequate supervision for children's activities. Judgment was reversed and remanded.

9. In *Morris v. Union High School District A, King County*, 294 P. 998 (Wash. 1931), the school district was sued on the theory of respondeat superior for a football coach's negligence in persuading, coercing, and allowing an injured football player to play (see Section 4.22–1).

10. In *Domino v. Mercurio*, 17 A.D. 2d 342, 234 N.Y.S. 2d 1011 (1962), *aff'd* 13 N.Y. 2d 922, 193 N.E. 2d 893 (1963), the court discussed the issue of an employer's responsibility in the selection of employees (see Section 4.22–1, Note 1).

11. In *Foster v. Houston General Insurance Company*, 407 So. 2d 759 (La. Ct. App. 1981), defendant school board was held not liable for negligence (see Section 4.22–1, Note 2).

12. In *Larson v. Independent School District No. 314*, 289 N.W. 2d 112 (Minn. 1979), plaintiff brought an action against the superintendent of the school district, the principal of the high school, a physical education teacher, and the school district for injuries received in an eighth grade physical education class.

In April 1971, Steven Larson was severely injured while performing a "headspring over a rolled mat," by landing on his head and breaking his neck, resulting in quadriplegic paralysis. He argued that the teacher was negligent in teaching the exercise and in spotting and that the principal and superintendent were negligent because they had not properly developed and supervised the curriculum and the instructor. The teacher involved was new and had replaced another teacher who was called for military duty, and the principal did not properly supervise one with so little experience.

The court held, inter alia, that (1) the superintendent was not sufficiently involved in actions or inactions to be found negligent, (2) the judgment used by the physical education instructor was not a decision entitled to protection under the doctrine of discretionary immunity and therefore the instructor was personally liable for negligent spotting and teaching of exercise, and (3) the principal who abdicated his responsibility of developing and administering the teaching of physical education curriculum was not engaged in decision making at a planning level, and therefore his liability for negligent discharge of that responsibility was not precluded by discretionary immunity. The dissent argued that it was not reasonable to hold the principal responsible for the negligence of the physical education teacher when the principal was not experienced in the area and also had to supervise the entire school.

13. In *Lynch v. Board of Education of Collingsville Community School District*, 390 N.E. 2d 526 (Ill. Ct. App. 1979), the school district was sued for the alleged negligence of its teachers (see Section 4.22–1).

14. In *Lockard v. Leland Stanford Junior University*, No. 774–201, (Cal. Super. Ct. 1980) (settled), an action was brought by a student at the university who suffered serious injuries while using a trampoline in the school's gymnasium. The case is worthy of note because of the interesting theory of liability set forth in the complaint. The defendants were a broad group, including the university, the manufacturer of the trampoline, and some 50 "John Does" who were in some way connected to the university. The plaintiff's theory was that the defendants were negligent in the operation, maintenance, repair, design, inspection, and servicing of the trampoline. In addition, the complaint cited the lack of supervision or training of the plaintiff in his exercises and failure to provide spotters. The plaintiff reportedly received a multimillion dollar settlement.

15. In *Vargo v. Svitchan*, 301 N.W. 2d 1 (Mich. Ct. App. 1980), the principal, athletic director, and school district were sued in addition to the coach (see Section 4.22–1).

16. In 1984, two years after falling off a human pyramid and fracturing her skull on national TV, a former Syracuse University cheerleader sued the school for $1 million. Michelle Burkhart fell from the top of a three-level human pyramid while performing at a basketball game at the Carrier Dome in January 1982. Burkhart, who

returned to the cheerleading squad 11 months after the accident, charged the university with failing to provide cheerleaders with adequate training, supervision, and safety devices. She also claimed the school allowed her to "participate in an inherently dangerous activity," which caused her permanent injury. Syracuse University denied the charges and attributed the accident to Burkhart's "culpable conduct." (Pending)

17. For further information, see the following articles:
(a) "Gymnastics Litigation: Meeting the Defenses," 16 *Trial* 34 (August 1980).
(b) "Gymnastics Litigation: The Standard of Care," 16 *Trial* 24 (August 1980).
(c) "Responsibility Is Also a Part of the Game," 13 *Trial* 22 (January 1977).
(d) "Sports Torts and School Athletics," 37 *Washington State Business News* 21 (October 1983).

18. For further information on the application of tort law to physical education, see the following texts by Herb Appengeller, all published by The Michie Company, Charlottesville, Virginia:
(a) Sports and the Courts (1980).
(b) Physics Education and the Law (1978).
(c) Athletics and the Law (1975).
(d) From the Gym, To the Jury (1970).

4.23–2 Medical Assistance

Administrators, schools, and universities are generally not responsible for providing direct medical treatment to an injured student, student-athlete, or spectator. However, the administrator, school, or university may be sued on the theory of respondeat superior for negligent medical treatment by a coach (see Section 4.22–3) or athletic trainer. The administrator, school, or university will generally not be held responsible for the medical malpractice of a doctor, since in most cases the doctor is held to be an independent contractor and not an employee (see *Cramer v. Hoffman, infra*). However, the administrator, school, or university may be held responsible for the negligent selection, supervision, or hiring of medical personnel. There may also be potential liability for the administrator, school, or university if the administrator was negligent in not providing medical personnel at a game or practice. Many states have rules that require medical personnel to be present at certain events such as football or basketball games (see Note 1). And finally, the school or university may be held responsible on the theory of vicarious liability (see Section 4.13) if the administrator is found to be negligent in the selection or supervision of medical personnel.

O'Brien v. Township High School District No. 214, 392 N.E. 2d 615 (Ill. Ct. App. 1979)

Plaintiff O'Brien alleged negligence by the school district for permitting an incompetent and untrained student to administer medical and surgical treatment, for failing to properly carry out treatment, and for failing to secure parental consent. The trial court granted the school district's motion to dismiss the student's complaint, and O'Brien appealed.

O'Brien argued that the district court had erred in its decision because (1) "neither the School Code (Ill. Rev. Stat. 1971, Ch. 122, pars 1–1 et seq.) nor the Local Government and Governmental Employees Tort Immunity Act (Ill. Rev. Stat. 1971, Ch. 85, pars 1–101 et seq.) gives the defendants immunity from their negligent actions"; and (2) the facts of the case constitute willful and wanton misconduct.

The court found that an educator's immunity under the School Code should not bar O'Brien's complaint alleging that the school district, through its agents, undertook to have plaintiff's injury treated by an untrained student in a negligent fashion. The court reasoned that the treatment of injuries or medical conditions does not fall into the realm of action "necessary for the orderly conduct of schools and maintenance of a sound learning atmosphere" and as such were subject to ordinary negligence claims. "To hold school districts to an ordinary care standard in this area does not appear unduly burdensome." The court, however, did affirm the trial court's opinion that the facts of the case did not represent a "reckless disregard for safety of others" and thus did not constitute willful and wanton misconduct.

Cramer v. Hoffman, 390 F. 2d 19 (2d Cir. 1968)

Plaintiff was a football player at St. Lawrence University in New York. He was hospitalized for treatment of German measles during the school year. Within a few days of his discharge, the plaintiff participated in a football practice and was seriously injured while making a tackle. Cervical injuries, which the plaintiff alleged were a consequence of negligence in moving and treating him, resulted in paralysis.

Several defendants settled prior to trial, but the case was heard with the university, coach, and the treating physician as defendants. The doctor was alleged to be negligent in the treatment of plaintiff's cervical injuries. The plaintiff in his complaint sought to hold the university liable for the negligence of the doctor under an agency theory.

At trial, however, the judge ruled as a matter of law that the alleged negligence of the doctor could not be imputed to the university. The ruling was based upon the plaintiff's failure to set forth any substantial facts to prove an agency relationship between the doctor and the university.

The court of appeals upheld the lower court on this issue. Its decision was based upon New York law, which holds that an institution is not responsible for the negligence of physicians who are independent contractors exercising their own discretion. The only evidence introduced as to the relationship between the doctor and the university was that a dean of the university had said that the doctor was "the college or contract physician" at a deposition. If he was a "contract" physician, this evidence actually goes against the plaintiff's contentions, as it would show the status of the doctor was that of an independent contractor. If there is not sufficient evidence to put agency at issue, the decision is one of law for the court to decide and not for the jury to consider.

NOTES

1. Massachusetts requires a physician or person trained in emergency medical care to be assigned to all inter-scholastic football games (see Massachusetts General Laws Chapter 112, section 54A and section 10.12–5[e]).

2. In *Welch* v. *Dunsmuir Joint Union High School District*, 326 P. 2d 633 (Cal. Ct. App. 1958), the school district was held vicariously liable for the negligence of a football coach who improperly rendered first-aid assistance (see Section 4.22–3).

3. In *Mogabgab* v. *Orleans Parish School Board*, 239 So. 2d 456 (La. Ct. App. 1970), plaintiff sued the school district on the theory that it was negligent for not properly training a coach who denied medical treatment to an athlete (see Section 4.22–3, Note 1).

4. In *Stineman* v. *Fontbonne College*, 664 F. 2d 1082 (8th Cir. 1981), the college was held vicariously liable for the negligence of its coach in failing to provide proper medical assistance (see Section 4.22–3, Note 2).

5. The NCAA has the following policy regarding medical (physical) examinations:

> A preparticipation medical examination should be required upon a student-athlete's initial entrance into an institution's intercollegiate athletic program. This initial examination should include a review of the student-athlete's health history and relevant general and orthopedic physical examination. Medical records maintained during the student-athlete's collegiate career should include a record of injuries and illnesses sustained during the competitive season and off-season, medical referrals, subsequent care and clearances and a completed yearly health status questionnaire. Provided there is a continuous awareness of the health status of the athlete, the traditional annual preparticipation physical examination for all student-athletes is not deemed necessary.

(1985–86 NCAA Manual, Recommended Policy 9, Medical Examinations)

4.23–3 Equipment

The failure to provide equipment or the failure to provide satisfactory equipment has been the basis for a number of lawsuits brought against administrators, schools, and universities. The individuals who are involved with equipment vary from institution to institution; they may be the coach, the teacher, an equipment manager, a business manager who purchases the equipment, an athletic director, and/or other administrators. All of the aforementioned individuals are employees of the institution, and the institution may be responsible for their negligent acts under the theory of vicarious liability (see Section 4.13).

While lawsuits filed against institutions regarding equipment have mostly been unsuccessful, they do indicate potential liability areas. The first consideration is to purchase appropriate equipment for the athletic activities offered. The second consideration is to purchase satisfactory equipment. For example, with respect to football helmets, the institution should adhere to NOCSAE guidelines (see Section 4.30, Note 8). The third consideration is to provide equipment for the athletic activities in which equipment is necessary. For example, the plaintiff in *Lynch* v. *Board of Education of Collingsville Community School District* (see Note 1 and Section 4.22–1) alleged that the defendant school district was negligent in not providing equipment for a football game. The fourth consideration is to provide proper-fitting equipment to the participants. In *Gerrity* v. *Beatty, infra,* the plaintiff alleged that his football equipment did not fit properly and that it was the proximate cause of his injuries. The last consideration is to periodically inspect the equipment and recondition when necessary. Again, the NOCSAE guidelines are useful, since helmets may be decertified and reconditioning guidelines have been established (see Section 4.30, Note 8).

Gerrity v. **Beatty, 373 N.E. 2d 1323 (Ill. 1978)**

Plaintiff high school football player brought personal injury action against football helmet manufacturer, attending physician, hospital, city, and school district for injuries he sustained while making a tackle in a high school football game. Gerrity's complaint alleged that the defendant school district carelessly and negligently (1) permitted and allowed the plaintiff to wear an ill-fitting and inadequate football helmet, (2) refused to furnish adequate and proper football equipment upon plaintiff's request, and (3) furnished and provided the plaintiff with an ill-fitting and inadequate football helmet when it knew or in the exercise of ordinary care should have known said helmet was improper and likely to cause plaintiff injury.

The school district claimed, relying on *Kobylanski* v. *Chicago Board of Education,* 347 N.E. 2d 705 (Ill. 1976), that Gerrity needed to prove "willful and wanton misconduct on the part of school personnel" as a condition for recovery of damages. The *Kobylanski* decision, which involved maintaining order and discipline within the schools, had likened the student-teacher relationship to that of parent-child. The school district argued that this principle of limited parental immunity, which denies children a cause of action against parents except for cases of willful and wanton misconduct, was extended to all teachers and certified educational employees. Failing to find such "willful and wanton misconduct," the trial court in *Gerrity* held for the defendants.

On appeal, the decision was reversed. The Supreme Court of Illinois distinguished *Kobylanski* from the facts of the *Gerrity* case. *Kobylanski* applied only to negligence claims arising out of matters relating to the teacher's personal supervision and control of conduct or physical movement of a student. Therefore, the court held that the school district in *Gerrity* was not immune. The court found that the furnishing of equipment to students was a separate and distinguishable function. In addition, the court stated that "public policy considerations argue rather strongly against any interpretation [of the Illinois immunity statute] which would relax a school district's obligation to insure that equipment provided for students ... is fit for the purpose." Furthermore, the court held that to hold school districts to the duty of ordinary care in such matters would not be unduly burdensome or inconsistent with the purpose of the Illinois statute. The action was remanded to the circuit court, with orders to reinstate the cause of action against the defendant school district.

NOTES

1. In *Lynch* v. *Board of Education of Collingsville Community School District,* 390 N.E. 2d 526 (Ill. Ct. App. 1979), the school district was held negligent for not providing equipment for a football game (see Section 4.22–1).

2. In *Vendrell v. School District No. 26C, Malheur County*, 233 Or. 1, 376 P. 2d 406 (1962), plaintiff Vendrell alleged that the school district provided unsatisfactory equipment, which resulted in a severe injury. The court held for the school district and found that Vendrell could have questioned, complained, or returned the equipment (see Section 4.22–2).

3. In *Berman by Berman v. Philadephia Board of Education*, 456 A. 2d 545 (Pa. Super. Ct. 1983), the court held the school district liable for an injury to a student in a floor hockey game, even though Amateur Hockey Association rules did not require the equipment that would have prevented the injury (see Section 4.12–1[a], Note 6).

4. In *Turner v. Caddo Parish School Board*, 252 La. 810, 214 So. 2d 153 (1968), plaintiff spectator grandmother sued defendant school authorities for negligence when she was injured by a football player who intentionally ran out of bounds. The Louisiana Supreme Court, in reinstating the trial court's dismissal, held that defendant was not negligent in failing to anticipate spectators who did not know that plays are often designed to carry the ball out of bounds. The court also held that defendant was not negligent in its failure to provide a barricade.

5. University of Illinois has the following sport safety notice form, which is distributed to its student-athletes:

NOTICE: *TO ALL ATHLETES PARTICIPATING IN THE INTERCOLLEGIATE ATHLETIC PROGRAM FOR THE UNIVERSITY OF ILLINOIS, ATHLETIC ASSOCIATION:*
FROM: Neale Stoner, Director of Athletics

_____is a sport that could cause you serious injury. Participation in the sport is an acceptance of some risk of injury. In order to minimize this risk, it is necessary that you as a participant be aware of and abide by certain safety rules and guidelines.

Any abuse of your equipment or any equipment relating to your sport could cause serious injury to you, your teammates, or your opponents if used improperly.

For example, the football helmet is not to be used to but, ram or spear an opposing player. This is in violation of NCAA football rules and such use can result in severe head or neck injuries, paralysis, or death to you and possible serious injury to your opponent. No football helmet can prevent all head or neck injuries that a player might receive while participating in football.

Used in a proper manner, all your equipment can be valuable.

You must also report all injuries and any illness to the athletic trainers or team physicians as soon as they become evident to you.

In consideration of the opportunity to participate in the intercollegiate athletic program at the University of Illinois during my entire period of eligibility for the

program, I hereby certify that I have read and understand the above statement, that I have had an opportunity to ask for explanation or clarification of any portion I did not understand, and that I agree to observe these and other rules and practices which may be employed to minimize my risk of serious injury while pursuing the benefits of this sport.

Signed_____

Date_____

4.23–4 Sovereign Immunity

An immunity is a condition which protects against tort liability regardless of the circumstances and is based on the status or position of the potential defendant. It does not deny the tort, but rather the resulting liability. This is to be distinguished from a privilege or justification that operates to excuse the commission of tort under specific conditions. Sovereign immunity is the type of immunity most often encountered in a sports setting, although charitable immunity may, in some instances, be a consideration.

Historically, all states had sovereign immunity laws, but some state courts and state legislatures have recently determined that the state can be sued in certain situations for certain activities. In order to determine if an entity is immune from legal recourse, one must first determine whether it is a governmental entity. Governmental entities may be federal, state, or local governments, municipalities, or any activity that is under the control of any of the above. This may include state universities, public high schools, and quasi-public associations such as high school athletic associations.

There are public-policy considerations that underlie the establishment of sovereign immunity. One rationale is that public agencies have limited funds and should expend them only for public purposes. To allow an individual to sue a public entity unfairly restricts the amount that should be devoted to the public welfare. Another rationale for sovereign immunity is the idea that the state can do no wrong. This is a vestige of the historical policy that a king could do no wrong and was the original basis for the establishment of sovereign immunity. Other reasons include the idea that the public cannot be held responsible for the torts of their government employees and that public bodies themselves have no authority to commit torts. Many feel that the aforementioned policy considerations are not compelling, and the trend in many jurisdictions is to repeal or limit the immunity granted to governments.

Sovereign immunity rests on the concept that a state must give consent to be sued. Most states have given such consent either in the form of a statute which authorizes an individual to sue or by providing special courts and procedures to be followed when an instrumentality of the state is responsible for an injury (i.e., federal court of claims). These statutes are strictly construed, but they have been extended to agencies related to but not part of the actual state government. Public high schools and high school athletic associations may be included as part of the list of agencies whose traditional sovereign immunity may be abrogated by statutes of this kind.

In those states governed by a sovereign immunity statute, the distinction between governmental and proprietary activities presents an important legal issue. A governmental activity is one that can only be performed by the state, and as such, is commonly protected from lawsuits on the grounds of sovereign immunity. Education is a governmental activity. A proprietary activity is one that is done by the state but could be undertaken by the private sector and is therefore not given the protection of sovereign immunity. An example is when a town leases a facility for a professional sporting event.

The court is often asked to determine whether the activity on which the plaintiff's case against the state entity is based is a governmental or proprietary activity. If the activity is found to be a governmental one, the action brought by the plaintiff is automatically dismissed, based on the sovereign immunity statute protecting the governmental body. A determination that the activity is proprietary in nature, however, permits the continuation of the case and possible recovery of damages by the plaintiff. Naturally, then, in the initial stages of a case involving the state, the defendant commonly argues that the activity in question was governmental, while the plaintiff claims it was proprietary.

The distinction between governmental and proprietary functions is often very difficult to make. A school's sports facility may be involved in either a proprietary or a governmental function, depending on the circumstances in existence at any given time. If the public school is using its own sports facility, the courts have usually found that the holding of athletic contests is part of the educational function of the state and is therefore a governmental function that is protected by the sovereign immunity doctrine. If the facility is leased for use by the private sector, the courts have concluded that it is conducting a proprietary activity and therefore may be held liable for injuries sustained as a result of any negligent maintenance of the facility.

Cantwell v. University of Massachusetts, 551 F. 2d 879 (1st Cir. 1977)

Diane Cantwell was a nationally known gymnast and a member of the University of Massachusetts gymnastics team. At practice one day, the defendant assistant coach directed her to do her mount onto the uneven parallel bars. Cantwell alleged in her complaint that it was the coach's duty to stand next to the gym equipment as a "spotter" in order to catch anyone who fell. As Cantwell began her run to the bars, she saw the coach standing in the spotter's position inside the guy wires attached to the equipment. During the first part of her mount, she fell and suffered severe injuries. As Cantwell was falling, she saw the coach outside the guy wires and beyond reach. The district court dismissed her action against the university on the basis of sovereign immunity. The court also ruled that because the coach was a public official, he was immune from liability for nonfeasance. Cantwell appealed this decision.

The court of appeals held that while there was some movement in the direction of abolishing sovereign immunity, it had not been done so either judicially or by the legislature in Massachusetts and thus the lower court was correct in dismissing the action against the university. In reversing the action against the individual coach, the court cited *Oeschger* v. *Fitzgerald*, 314 N.E. 2d 444 (Mass. App. Ct. 1974), which held that a public officer engaged wholly in the performance of public duties is personally liable only for his own acts of misfeasance. The court went on to say that the distinction between misfeasance and non-feasance in Massachusetts law is not always clear and noted that:

> Negligence which amounts to nothing more than an omission or nonfeasance creates no liability. . . . While nonfeasance is the omission of an act which a person ought to do, misfeasance is the improper doing of an act which a person might lawfully do.

In the opinion of the court of appeals, the coach would not be liable for the mere failure to spot just because it was his duty to spot. However, if he had, by affirmative action, reasonably led Cantwell to believe that he would spot her throughout the routine, and, in addition, she had reasonably relied thereon, a jury could find his failure to perform to be misfeasance rather than mere nonfeasance. The court could not say that the record precluded the possibility of such findings. The judgment for the coach was vacated and remanded for further proceedings consistent with the findings.

NOTES _____

1. Generally, liability of school districts and colleges for tortious acts or omissions of its officers, agents, or servants is determined according to the normal rules of tort law. Some states by statute have made their public agencies immune to suits in tort. The following two cases are ones where the doctrine of sovereign immunity was applied:

(a) In *Clary* v. *Alexander County Board of Education*, 19 N.C. App. 637, 199 S.E. 2d 738 (1973), *aff'd*, 285 N.C. 188, 203 S.E. 2d 820 (1974), a North Carolina student who was injured when he crashed into glass panel doors at the end of a basketball court was denied any recovery for his injuries. The doors did not have safety glass, and as evidence of the unsafe structure, there was shown to have been several previous collisions with the doors. However, the North Carolina Supreme Court found statutory immunity and stated that the purchase of liability insurance was not enough to abrogate the immunity (see also Section 4.25, Note 1[e]).

(b) In *Zawadzki* v. *Taylor*, 246 N.W. 2d 161 (Mich. Ct. App. 1976), the court denied recovery to a student who sustained eye injuries when struck by a tennis ball in physical education class. The court reasoned that the school district was protected by a statute granting immunity from tort liability for government agencies.

2. The liability of a school district will not be sustained in the absence of a statute allowing the state and its subdivisions to be sued for such liability. For example, in *Perkins* v. *Trask*, 23 P. 2d 982 (Mont. 1933), plaintiff parent sued defendant school district for negligence in the drowning of her son in defendant's swimming pool. In affirming the trial court's dismissal, the Montana Supreme Court held that school districts are not liable for injuries caused by negligence of officers, agents, or employees unless liability is imposed by statute.

3. Sovereign immunity, even if not expressly abrogated, will not protect a state from all liability. In *Johnson* v. *Municipal University of Omaha*, 187 N.W. 2d 102 (Neb. 1971), Jack Johnson, a pole vaulter, brought a personal injury action through his father against Municipal University of Omaha to recover damages for injuries he sustained while attempting a vault during a track meet in Municipal University's stadium. Johnson was a pole vaulter for Fort Hays College. During the meet Johnson did not run fast enough to get the momentum necessary to carry him up and over the crossbar. Instead, he fell backward and landed on one of the wooden boxes used to support the uprights. The uprights hold the crossbar which measures the height of the vault.

The trial court found that the evidence was insufficient to find the college negligent and gave judgment in favor of the defendant university. The Supreme Court of Nebraska affirmed the trial court's decision and held that where a reasonable person would perceive an act to involve risk of harm to another, such risk will be negligent and unreasonable only when the risk is so great it outweighs the utility of the act or the manner in which it is performed. The court found that the wooden boxes used by the university to hold the uprights served a useful purpose in that they expedited the event, made officiating easier, and did not restrict the level of the crossbar to a maximum height of 15 feet. Since the court found that the utility of the boxes outweighed the risk of harm caused by them, it found no negligence on the part of the university.

4. A school will not be liable if its exercise of a governmental function causes any injury. In *Rhoades v. School Dist. No. 9, Roosevelt County*, 142 P. 2d 890 (Mont. 1943), plaintiff, a visiting spectator at defendant high school's basketball game, sought recovery for injuries sustained when an improperly maintained stairway collapsed. In affirming the dismissal, the Montana Supreme Court held that the school district was exercising a "government function" so that it could not be held liable. See also, *Fetzer v. Minor Park District*, 138 N.W. 2d 601 (N.D. 1965).

5. When a school district is immune as a governmental agency, its employees will avoid liability if they are performing discretionary duties. For example, in *Hall v. Columbus Board of Educ.*, 290 N.E. 2d 580 (Ohio Ct. App. 1972), plaintiff elementary school student sought recovery from the board of education and school officials for an injury sustained in a fall from a sliding board on the school playground. In affirming the dismissal, the court of appeals held that the board of education was immune as a governmental agency of the state, and the school officials were not liable for torts committed by them in performance of duties involving judgment and discretion.

6. Immunity for a school board will not guarantee immunity for individuals. In *Short v. Griffiths*, 255 S.W. 2d 479 (Va. 1979), plaintiff sued the school board, the athletic director, the baseball coach, and the buildings and grounds supervisor for injuries he sustained by falling on broken glass while running laps around the school's outdoor track facility. Defendants claimed immunity. The court held that the athletic director and the buildings and grounds supervisor were not entitled to immunity even though their employer (school board) had immunity. The court reasoned that the employees of a local government agency should be answerable for their own acts of simple negligence, even though they were working for an immune employer because to hold otherwise would be to unacceptably widen the role of sovereign immunity.

7. In the following cases, the court found no liability for discretionary decisions:

(a) In *Larson v. Independent School District No. 314*, 289 N.W. 2d 112 (Minn. 1979), the court held that the principal who abdicated his responsibility of overseeing physical education curriculum was not engaged in decision making at a planning level, and therefore his liability for negligent discharge of that responsibility was not precluded by discretionary immunity (see Section 4.23–1, Note 12).

(b) In *Cook v. Bennett*, 288 N.W. 2d 609 (Mich. Ct. App. 1979), the plaintiff was injured at recess during a dangerous, unsupervised, quasi-football game called "kill." The principal's alleged liability for playground injury was based on her negligent performance of supervisory powers. The extent to which a school principal is protected under sovereign immunity is dependent upon whether the act complained of falls within the principal's discretionary or ministerial powers. The court held that "even though the supervisory powers of the school principal are incident to her public function, she has a duty to exercise these powers in such a way as to minimize injury to students in her charge. Where the principal negligently performs this duty, government immunity does not operate to insulate her from all liability" (see Section 4.23–1).

(c) In *Brown v. Wichita State University*, 219 Kan. 2, 547 P. 2d 1015 (1976), plaintiffs sought to recover as third-party beneficiaries after a charter airplane carrying the school football team crashed. The court made the distinction between a governmental function and proprietary function and held the team a commercial activity. Therefore, since the court found it to be a proprietary function, the action could be maintained against the university. See also, *Shriver v. Athletic Commission of Kansas State University*, 222 Kan. 216 (1977).

8. The availability of insurance will not abrogate immunity as can be seen in the following cases:

(a) In *Weinstein v. Evanston Township Community Consolidated School District 65*, 40 Ill. App. 3d 6, 351 N.E. 2d 236 (1976), the purchase of liability insurance did not waive general immunity of the school district, and no damages were awarded to a junior high school student who was injured while exercising on the parallel bars.

(b) In *Merrill v. Birhanzel*, 310 N.W. 2d 522 (S.D. 1981), plaintiff sued the teacher, who was in charge of a required wrestling class at the time of his injury. During the match, the plaintiff was thrown to the ground, and his left ankle was broken. The court stated:

> School districts are state agencies exercising and wielding a distributive portion of the sovereign power of the state, and the officers of school districts are the living agencies through whom the sovereign state act is carried into effect. A school district officer in the performance of his duties acts in a political capacity, as much so as the Governor of the state, and is not liable for negligent acts of omission occurring in the performance of such political or public duties, unless the sovereign power of the state has authorized and consented to a suit for such negligence.

The plaintiff argued that this case law was not applicable because the school district had waived immunity by purchasing liability insurance. The court stated that it failed to find any permission for the district to be sued: "Authority to purchase, and the purchase of liability insurance does not provide that permission. . . . We have consistently held that if there is to be a departure from the immunity rule, the policy must be declared and the extent of liability fixed by the legislature."

9. Charitable immunity may have the same effect as sovereign immunity, as can be seen in the following cases:

(a) In *Southern Methodist University* v. *Clayton*, 142 Tex. 179, 176 S.W. 2d 749 (1943), a negligence suit was brought in which plaintiff spectator Clayton sought recovery from defendant Southern Methodist University (SMU) for injuries sustained when a temporary bleacher collapsed during the SMU–Texas A & M football game in 1940. The court held that SMU, a private, charitable institution, was immune from liability for torts of its agents unless the injured party was an employee of the charity. The Supreme Court of Texas reasoned: "It is better for the individual to suffer injury without compensation than for the public to be deprived of the benefit of the charity." Judgment for SMU was affirmed.

(b) In *Pomeroy* v. *Little League Baseball of Collingswood*, 362 A. 2d 39 (N.J. Super. Ct. App. Div. 1976), plaintiff, a spectator at defendant Little League's game, sought recovery for injuries received when the bleacher collapsed. In affirming judgment for the defendant, the superior court held that the league had been established purely for educational purposes — that is, to build character and sportsmanship — and that the charitable immunity statute prevented plaintiff from recovery from defendant.

10. In *Holzer* v. *Oakland University Academy of Dramatic Arts*, 313 N.W. 2d 124 (Mich. Ct. App. 1981), Holzer brought suit against the university seeking to recover damages based on an injury sustained while attempting to perform an exercise in a "movement" class. The Oakland County Circuit Court entered a summary judgment for the defendant. On appeal it was held that the operation of a state university was a governmental function that was immune from tort liability.

11. For cases dealing with the issue of sovereign immunity, see *Rutledge* v. *Arizona Board of Regents*, 660 F. 2d 1345 (9th Cir. 1981), *aff'd*, 103 S. Ct. 148 (1983), in Section 4.22–2, *Vargo* v. *Svitchan*, 301 N.W. 2d 1 (Mich. Ct. App. 1980), and *Kersey* v. *Harbin*, 591 S.W. 2d 745 (Mo. Ct. App. 1979), in Section 4.22–1, and *O'Brien* v. *Township High School District No. 214*, 392 N.E. 2d 615 (Ill. Ct. App. 1979), in Section 4.23–2.

12. A great deal of variation is evident in a review of cases in which the courts have been called upon to determine whether the governmental entity was involved in governmental or proprietary activities. The following two cases are representative of this variation:

(a) In *Crone* v. *City of El Cajon*, 24 P. 2d 846 (Cal. Ct. App. 1933), the court found the city to be involved in a governmental activity in the operation of a swimming pool where a person drowned, even though swimmers were charged an admission fee.

(b) In *Ide* v. *City of St. Cloud*, 8 So. 2d 924 (Fla. 1942), the court found the city to be involved in a proprietary activity and held the city liable for a drowning death at a public beach in a city park.

4.24 Liability of Professional Teams and Leagues

Professional teams and leagues have been sued under both the theories of negligence (see Section 4.12) and vicarious liability (see Section 4.13). The plaintiffs have included athletes, teams, spectators, and umpires.

The professional team may be sued in its capacity as the employer of an athlete, a coach, a doctor, or a trainer. As an employer, professional teams may be responsible for injuries caused by the negligence of their employees if they either encourage or do not discourage improper action(s) on the part of their employee (see *Tomjanovich* v. *California Sports, Inc., infra*). A team may also be liable for negligence in its selection of a coach who may not be qualified for the job or in its failure to properly supervise the coach's activities (see *Toone* v. *Adams* in Section 4.22–4). Thus, for example, even if a team does not condone excessive violence, it may be liable if it does not supervise the coach so as to prevent such violence.

The professional team may also be sued under the theory of vicarious liability for the negligence or recklessness of its players. However, the team generally will not be held responsible for an intentional tort committed by its employee. (See *Averill* v. *Luttrell, infra*, *Hackbart* v. *Cincinnati Bengals, Inc.*, Note 1[b] and in Section 4.21, and *Rhodes* v. *Kansas City Kings*, Note 1[g] and in Section 4.21, Note 8.)

The professional team may also be sued as the employer of a doctor or trainer under the theory of vicarious liability (see Section 4.26). Or, a professional team may be sued by another professional team for the loss of services of an employee (see *Tomjanovich* v. *California Sports, Inc., infra*). Finally, a professional team may also be sued in its capacity as owner or possessor of a facility under the theories of negligence or vicarious liability (see Section 4.25). While most professional teams lease their facilities, a few own their facilities. Although most facility-related liability issues are covered in section 4.25, one liability issue is covered here: lawsuits brought by injured spectators against teams for items of the game that have left the field, court, or rink, including bats, balls, pucks, sticks, and players, either intentionally or unintentionally.

Since the earliest beginnings of sports, spectators have often been injured when activity within the arena has spilled over into the stands. In England, during the formative period of common law, spectators at a cricket match were certainly well aware of the risk that they could be injured by a batted ball which traveled beyond the field of play. The common law's response to spectator injuries was not at all surprising. The general rule which has been followed in the United States is that the spectator assumes the risk of injury from projectiles that leave the playing area in the normal course of the game (see *Wells* v. *Minneapolis Baseball & Athletic Ass'n., infra*). The court reasoned that the possibility of injury was known to any reasonable person, and spectators who voluntarily chose to attend a sporting event could not recover for those reasonable risks they knowingly assumed. The assumption-of-risk defense is as strong today as it ever was and presents a major obstacle to a successful tort action brought by a spectator (see Section 4.12–5[d]).

The plaintiff, in order to overcome the assumption-of-risk defense, must show that the risk of injury was not within or beyond the scope of the game. In other words, given all the facts of the particular case, the relevant question is, Was the type and severity of the injury to be reasonably expected to occur during the type of event taking place? If there are facts showing that negligence on the part of a defendant player, club, or facility owner directly contributed to the injury, the plaintiff has some hope of recovery. For example, if a baseball park erects a screen behind home plate to protect the fans but fails to properly maintain the screen and a ball passes through a hole in the screen and injures a spectator, the owners of the park may be held liable. Other lawsuits have been brought under the theory that the projectile did not leave the playing area in the normal course of the game (see *Manning* v. *Grimsley* in Section 4.21 and *Guttenplan* v. *Boston Professional Hockey Ass'n., Inc.,* Note 2[d]).

Wells v. Minneapolis Baseball & Athletic Ass'n., 122 Minn. 327, 142 N.W. 706 (1913)

The defendant, Minneapolis Baseball & Athletic Association, maintained grounds in Minneapolis where baseball games were held. The public was invited to attend these games for an admission price, although on some days ladies were admitted free of charge. The spectators sat in the grandstand that encircled the field. A screen, which was placed in front of the grandstand behind the home plate area, covered 65 feet of exposed area laterally and extended from to the base of the grandstand to the rooftop. The screen was constructed so that baseballs could not pass through it and was positioned in the area most vulnerable to foul balls or wild throws.

The plaintiff alleged that on July 9, 1910, she was struck by a foul ball with sufficient force to fracture her collar bone. She stated that she took a seat about 10 feet inside one end of the screen and about 10 to 12 feet back from the screen. She sat there even though there were vacant seats even more protected. Her companion confirmed their sitting position. Neither the plaintiff nor her companion claimed that the ball passed through the screen but rather that it curved around the end of it. Thirteen other witnesses testified that the plaintiff was seated outside the screen when she was struck by the ball. No one claimed that the ball hit something else before striking the plaintiff.

Plaintiff also claimed that even though the

defendant had placed a screen for the protection of the patrons, the defendant had negligently constructed the screen of insufficient size to furnish such protection and that she was ignorant of the fact that the screen was of insufficient size and that batted balls might pass the screen and strike spectators in the grandstand. Defendant's answer was that the injury was accidental and, further, that the plaintiff was injured through her own negligence and that she assumed the risk of injury from flying balls.

The Minnesota Supreme Court, in evaluating the case, determined that the position of the plaintiff when she was struck was instrumental in deciding the case and that it should be left to a jury to make that determination on the evidence. The trial court had instructed the jury to find for the defendant if the defendant's claim as to where plaintiff was sitting was correct. The supreme court held that it was inconceivable that a baseball, when fouled by a batter, could curve around the end of the screen and reach plaintiff in the manner described by the plaintiff. The defendant was not an insurer against all perils, nor was it guilty of negligence in failing to guard against improbable dangers. Since the defendant had an obligation to exercise reasonable care, its duty would have been fulfilled in the event that such an unforeseeable occurrence brought about the plaintiff's injury. In the event that the plaintiff sat outside the screen as the witnesses claimed she did, and she may have been mistaken as to where she sat, then the court would not be able to direct a verdict.

The court established the duty of the defendant by quoting from the case of *Crane v. Kansas City Baseball & Exhibition Co.*, 153 S.W. 1076 (Mo. Ct. App. 1913), which noted that:

> Defendants were not insurers of the safety of spectators; but, being engaged in the business of providing a public entertainment for profit, they were bound to exercise reasonable care — i.e., care commensurate to the circumstances of the

situations — to protect their patrons against injury.... In view of the fact that the general public is invited to attend these games, that hard balls are thrown and batted with great force and swiftness, and that such balls often go in the direction of the spectators, we think the duty of defendants towards their patrons included that of providing seats protected by screening from wildly thrown or foul balls, for the use of patrons who desire such protection.

It has been frequently held that one who invites the public to places of amusement, such as theaters, shows, or exhibitions, must exercise a high degree of care for the safety of those invited. But this rule must be modified when applied to an exhibition or game that is necessarily accompanied by some risk to the spectators. Baseball is not free from danger to those witnessing the game. But the perils are not so imminent that due care on the part of the management required all spectators to be screened in. In fact, a large part of those who attend prefer to sit where no screen obscures their view. The defendant has a right to cater to their desires. The Supreme Court Held that management cannot be held negligent when it provided a choice between a screened-in and an open seat, the screen being reasonably sufficient as to extent and substance. The supreme court also asserted that the question of the defendant's negligence did not depend on the extent to which the screen should extend beyond the place the plaintiff chose for her seat, but rather on whether the screen furnished was one that the ordinarily prudent person would deem of sufficient size to afford reasonable protection. As a result, the court stated that the determination of what precaution the ordinary prudent person, furnishing a public amusement of this kind, should take to warn and protect the spectators from the attendant dangers of which they may be ignorant, is a question for the jury.

The supreme court also discussed whether the issue of the screen tied into evidence that was not permitted to be entered in district court concerning signs that were posted at the entrance and in the grandstands in conspicuous positions stating that the management would not be responsible for injuries received from thrown or batted balls. The supreme court ruled that this evidence was pertinent to the case and should have been introduced. The issue of the signs raised two further questions. One was whether the signs were considered informative only in nature or whether they were also intended to serve as warnings that flying balls could cause injuries. The supreme court found that the signs did indeed convey a message of warning about possible injuries. The other question was whether or not the plaintiff saw any signs of this nature during her visit to the game.

The signs, as well as the screens, bore upon the defendant's conduct with respect to precautions taken for the safety of the spectators, and they also bore upon the question of the plaintiff's assumption of risk. If the signs conveyed a warning or information, their mere posting in conspicuous places in the grandstand made the plaintiff's observation of them a question for the jury, without direct proof that she saw them. Although the defendant stated that it could not prove that the plaintiff saw these notices, the jury might conclude that in posting these notices and screening a part of the stand for the use of those who sought protection, the defendant had performed its full duty to its patrons. As a result, the court held that there was no negligence and no recovery, regardless of the plaintiff's actual knowledge of such notices.

Averill v. Luttrell, 311 S.W. 2d 812 (Tenn. 1957)

Plaintiff Lyle Luttrell, a professional baseball player with the Chattanooga Lookouts, was struck by a pitch while batting against the Nashville Vols. In reacting to having been intentionally struck after dodging three earlier pitches, Luttrell threw his bat in the direction of the pitcher's mound, whereupon Nashville's catcher, defendant Earl Averill, Jr., stepped up

behind plaintiff and struck him with a hard blow on the side or back of the head with his fist. The force of the blow rendered Luttrell unconscious, and falling face first to the ground, he fractured his jaw.

Plaintiff brought this action against Averill and his employer, Nashville Baseball Club (NBC), for compensatory and punitive damages. Defendants separately filed pleas of general issue and numerous special pleas denying liability. At the conclusion of plaintiff's proof, motions for directed verdicts made on behalf of both defendants were overruled. NBC, electing to stand on its motion, introduced no evidence. The jury trial returned a verdict for the plaintiff against both defendants for $5,000. Defendant's motion for a new trial was overruled. NBC appealed the decision.

In the initial court case, plaintiff relied on the fact that Averill was "acting within the scope of his employment as the agent, servant, or employee of the Nashville Baseball Club, and the furtherance of its said business," to hold NBC liable for damages. By assignment of error, the appeals court held that the trial court should have sustained NBC's motion for a directed verdict because plaintiff introduced no evidence that the assault committed by Averill was within the scope of his employment or in the prosecution and furtherance of the business of NBC.

It was conceded by the parties that the assault made by Averill "was no part of the ordinary risks expected to be encountered in sportsmanlike play." Nor was there any proof showing that the assault was other than a willful, independent act on Averill's part, entirely outside the scope of his duties. The assault was neither incident to nor in the furtherance of his employer's business. As a result, the court ruled that NBC was not liable under the doctrine of respondeat superior. The applicable rule is stated in 57 C.J.S. Master and Servant:

> It is not ordinarily within the scope of a servant's authority to commit an assault on a third party,

and, in the absence of a non-delegable duty, such as that imposed by the relationship of carrier and passenger, or hotel and guest, if the assault committed by the servant was outside the scope of his employment and was made in a spirit of vindictiveness or to gratify personal animosity, or to carry out an independent purpose of his own, the master is not liable, unless the servant's conduct is ratified by the master. [Section 575, p. 341]

Accordingly, the judgment against NBC was reversed.

Tomjanovich v. California Sports, Inc., No. H-78-243 (S.D. Tex. 1979)

In a 1977 National Basketball Association (NBA) game between the Los Angeles Lakers and the Houston Rockets, Rockets center Kevin Kunnert pulled down a defensive rebound and in the process hit Laker forward Kermit Washington in the face with an elbow. Washington responded with a series of punches, during which several other players from both teams ran to assist their respective teammates. As Rocket forward Rudy Tomjanovich sprinted toward the scuffle from the backside of Washington, Washington sighted Tomjanovich's red jersey out of the corner of his eye, pivoted, and threw one right-hand punch that crashed into Tomjanovich's face. The force of the blow knocked Tomjanovich backward onto the court, where he lay motionless for several minutes bleeding from the mouth and nose. Rushed to the intensive-care ward of a hospital, Tomjanovich recovered, though he had suffered fractures of the nose, jaw, and skull, facial lacerations, a brain concussion, and leakage of spinal fluid from the brain cavity.

Both Tomjanovich and the Rockets sued the Los Angeles Lakers, but not Washington personnally, under the doctrine of respondeat superior. Tomjanovich alleged Washington had dangerous tendencies since he was known as an "enforcer." Tomjanovich supported this contention with a *Sports Illustrated* article which highlighted the "enforcers" in the NBA.

Washington was highlighted as one of several enforcers. The Lakers were sued on the theory that as the employer of Washington, they were responsible for curbing his "dangerous tendencies," and that the Lakers had failed to do so. Tomjanovich sued for $2.6 million in damages. During the federal jury trial, the surgeon who operated on Tomjanovich described the medical operation as rebuilding his face as if it were "a jigsaw puzzle." He added, rather graphically, "it was like trying to put a cracked egg back together with Scotch tape." After the jury awarded Tomjanovich $3.3 million in damages, the Lakers appealed. In 1981, California Sports, Inc., the Lakers' parent company, and Tomjanovich settled out of court for an undisclosed amount. The Rockets also sued the Lakers for the loss of Tomjanovich's services. After the Tomjanovich-Laker settlement, the Rockets and Lakers settled out of court for an undisclosed amount.

NOTES

1. The following lawsuits were brought by players:
(a) In 1978, Bill Walton demanded that he be traded from the Trail Blazers to the Golden State Warriors. This demand resulted from what Walton contended was negligent medical treatment. He believed that he might not have fractured a bone in his left foot had the team provided proper medical care. Walton also charged the team with the misuse of certain pain-modifying and anti-inflammatory drugs. Coach Jack Ramsay had this to say: "I would never allow a player to play if I thought he was risking serious injury. But listen, this is their job. A professional basketball player is capable of deciding for himself whether he should take an injection or none. He knows the risks involved. If he doesn't, he should ask." (See "Off on a Wronged Foot," *Sports Illustrated*, August 21, 1978, p. 18.) See also, Section 4.26, Note 6.
(b) In *Hackbart v. Cincinnati Bengals, Inc.*, 435 F. Supp. 352 (D. Colo. 1977), the plaintiff sued Booby Clark and his employer, the Cincinnati Bengals, on the theory that the team was responsible for player Clark's actions, as they had prior knowledge of his dangerous propensities (see Section 4.21).
(c) In a 1978 NFL game between the New England Patriots and the Oakland Raiders, the New England quarterback overthrew wide receiver Darryl Stingley, who was running a short "post" pattern into the middle of the field. Stingley sprung into the air in an obviously

futile attempt to catch the pass and was still airborne when Raider safety Jack Tatum smashed into him. The blow broke Stingley's neck between the fourth and fifth vertebrae and compressed his spinal cord, leaving the wide receiver a quadriplegic. Stingley is still partially paralyzed. Stingley threatened to sue the Raiders, the other 27 NFL teams, and the NFL for not preventing these dangerous activities. Stingley received a settlement before any action was commenced.

(d) In *Chuy* v. *Philadelphia Eagles Football Club*, 431 F. Supp. 254 (E.D. Pa. 1977), aff'd, 595 F. 2d 1265 (3rd Cir. 1979), (see Sections 4.14 and 4.16), plaintiff football player successfully brought a lawsuit against the defendant club. The Court held the club vicariously liable for the negligence of the team doctor.

(e) In *Robitaille* v. *Vancouver Hockey Club*, 3 W.W.R. 481 (Ct. App. B.C. 1981), the club was held to be vicariously liable for the negligence of the team doctors (see Section 4.26, Note 10).

(f) In *Gregory Taylor* v. *New England Patriots Football Club, Inc., and Norwood Hospital*, (Mass. Dist. Ct.), an action was brought by former New England Patriots football player Gregory Taylor against both the New England Patriots football club and the Norwood Hospital for their role in concealing the serious nature of a leg injury he sustained during a game with the Baltimore Colts. Plaintiff requested and received an examination by the training staff and was advised that he had suffered a "bone bruise." Taylor was directed to return to the game, although he complained of pain and was visibly impaired. Taylor was later removed from the game by the coaching staff.

The next morning, Taylor, at the direction of the trainer, and accompanied by the assistant trainer, reported to Norwood Hospital for x-rays, a thorough examination, and treatment. Plaintiff contended that said x-rays revealed a fracture of the right fibula bone and that these results were relayed to the trainer, who failed to inform him of the seriousness of the injury. Taylor was directed to continue playing until the severity of his injury forced his removal from practice. Four days later, Taylor was placed on waivers and signed by the Montreal Concordes, who discovered and reported to Taylor the true nature of his injury. Plaintiff claimed that both the New England Patriots and the Norwood Hospital willfully concealed the severity of his injury, and as a result of such willful concealment, he sustained a severe and permanent injury and would continue to incur substantial expense and loss of earnings as both parties have "effectively deprived [him] of successful career as a professional football player."

(g) In *Rhodes* v. *Kansas City Kings* (unreported case), the plaintiff successfully sued defendant player and team for an intentional punch (see Section 4.21).

2. The following lawsuits were brought against facility owners and possessors by spectators:

(a) Plaintiff spectator David Brown sued the New York Rangers and former Rangers hockey player Greg Polis, claiming he became an epileptic after Polis struck him on the head with a hockey stick at the conclusion of a Rangers–Penguins game in Pittsburgh in 1978. Brown admitted to shouting obscenities at several Rangers during the contest; Polis admitted "tapping" Brown on the head. The parties reportedly settled out of court for $27,500.

(b) In *Ratcliff* v. *San Diego Baseball Club of the Pacific Coast League*, 81 P. 2d 625 (Cal. Ct. App. 1938), an action was brought for injuries sustained when a bat slipped out of a baseball player's hands and flew into the stands. In affirming the trial court's judgment for plaintiff, the district court of appeals held that while screens for all seats are not required, those in charge of professional baseball games are required to exercise ordinary care to protect patrons from injuries, and the question of whether defendant exercised such care since plaintiff was struck with a bat in the aisle on the way to a seat was for the jury to decide.

(c) In *Iervolino* v. *Pittsburgh Athletic Co.*, 243 A. 2d 490 (Pa. Super. Ct. 1968), plaintiff spectator sought recovery for an injury sustained after being struck by a foul ball. In reversing the trial court decision in favor of the plaintiff, the superior court held that in absence of proof that the operator of the game had deviated from ordinary standards in the erection or maintenance of ballpark, it was an error to permit the jury to determine what safety measures, if any, operator should have taken for the protection of its customers and that plaintiff assumed the risk of injury from foul balls.

(d) In *Guttenplan* v. *Boston Professional Hockey Ass'n., Inc.*, No. 80–415 (S.D. N.Y. 1981), four hockey fans sued nine individual Boston Bruins hockey players, the Bruins, the New York Rangers, Madison Square Garden, Inc., the National Hockey League, and the city of New York for $7 million in damages for injuries suffered when a players' brawl on the ice spilled over into the stands in December 1979. The suit charged that the plaintiffs were "stomped" by the Bruins players, while league and arena security personnel "merely observed and made no attempt to prevent or stop" the altercation. Criminal charges against individual Bruin players were dropped due to conflicting evidence and testimony that indicated fans had provoked the players. A federal judge dismissed the civil damage suit on jurisdictional grounds.

(e) In *Philpot* v. *Brooklyn Nat'l. League Baseball Club*, 303 N.Y. 116, 100 N.E. 2d 164 (1951), plaintiff spectator sought recovery for injuries sustained when she was struck by a broken bottle in defendant's ballpark. In reversing judgment for defendants, the court of appeals held that the question of whether defendant had provided a sufficient means of protecting plaintiff from the reasonably foreseeable risk of harm from bottles, since no waste receptacles were provided and since the park seats were slanted so as to allow bottles to roll, was a question for the jury to decide.

(f) In *Duffy v. Midlothian Country Club, et al.*, No. 75 L 12096 (Ill. Cir. Ct. 1982), plaintiff Duffy was struck by a golf ball at the 1972 Western Open and lost an eye. She was standing in the rough between the first and 18th holes, watching play on the first hole. She was hit by a golfer playing the 18th hole, 200 to 250 yards away. Duffy was found 10 percent at fault when her negligence was compared to the tournament sponsors, and therefore awarded $450,000. The court barred the assumption-of-risk defense.

(g) In *Rogers v. Miami Dolphins, Ltd.*, 469 So. 2d 852 (Fla. Ct. App. 1985), plaintiff filed suit for injuries sustained when leaving the Orange Bowl Stadium and walking across an adjacent parking lot, he slipped and fell over some railroad ties which had been concealed by tall grass and shrubbery. The plaintiff alleged that the Dolphins were liable for his injuries. The Dolphins moved for summary judgment on the grounds that the city of Miami owned and controlled the parking lot. The trial court held for the Dolphins, and the appeals court affirmed the decision.

3. In *Toone v. Adams*, 262 N.C. 403, 137 S.E. 2d 132 (1964), plaintiff Toone, a baseball umpire, sued not only the coach and the fan but also the club as the employer of the coach, for injuries received when the umpire was attacked by a fan following a game. The plaintiff's theory was that the club was responsible for controlling and restraining its coach so that the coach would not incite the fans to violence (see Section 4.22–4).

4. For further information, see the following articles:

(a) "Assumption of Risk and Vicarious Liability in Personal Injury Actions Brought by Professional Athletes," *Duke Law Journal* 742 (September 1980).

(b) "Tort Liability in Professional Sports," 44 *Albany Law Review* 696 (April 1980).

4.25 Liability of Facility Owners and Possessors

Facility owners and posessors have a duty to exercise reasonable care in maintaining the premises and in supervising the conduct of others at the facility. They are, however, entitled to assume that participants will obey the rules and that employees will not be negligent in absence of notice to the contrary. Thus, their duty does not include protecting consumers from unlikely occurrences. An unlikely occurrence is one such that the probability of injury is outweighed by the burden of taking adequate precautions (see Section 4.21–1).

The general rule is that facility owners and possessors are liable for conditions on their premises that cause physical harm if they know or should reasonably have known about the existence of the dangerous condition when such a condition poses an unreasonable risk to an invitee (see Section 4.12–3). The requirement of reasonable care is supported by the assumption that a spectator, like a participant assumes all the ordinary and inherent risks of the particular sport (see Section 4.12–5[d]). These inherent risks are those commonly associated with the sport in question. The application of this common knowledge rule will depend on the circumstances. No invitee, whether a player or a spectator, assumes the risk that an owner will fail to meet a duty of reasonable care.

A facility owner and possessor's duty of reasonable care can be divided into three parts. The first is the duty to protect invitees from injurious or defective products. An owner and possessor must exercise reasonable care in the selection of equipment necessary for the operation of the facility (see *Benjamin v. State, infra*). Second, owners and possessors must exercise reasonable care in the maintenance of both the facility itself and any equipment in the facility. Standards of safety, suitability, and sanitation must be maintained. In addition, if an invitee uses any of the equipment and the facility owner or possessor is supervising, then the facility owner or possessor is held to a standard of reasonable care (see *Grauer v. State of New York, infra*). The third part of an owner and possessor's duty is to guard against foreseeable harmful risks caused by other invitees (see *Townsley v. Cincinnati Gardens, Inc., infra*). A breach of any of these duties may subject a facility owner or operator to liability for negligence. (See Exhibit 4–1.)

Promoters and other sports event organizers often use a facility for a day or a few days. They usually do not own the facility, and they are not in a long-term lease situation; therefore,

LEASE AGREEMENT
NASSAU VETERANS MEMORIAL COLISEUM
HYATT MANAGEMENT CORPORATION OF NEW YORK, INC.
UNIONDALE, NEW YORK 11553

Lease _____

THIS AGREEMENT made this _____ day of _____ , 19____ between Hyatt Management Corporation of New York,

Inc., d/b/a Nassau Veterans Memorial Coliseum (hereinafter referred to as COLISEUM) and _____

(hereinafter referred to as LESSEE) whose address is _____

_____

WITNESSETH:

AREA RENTED—DATES RESERVED
1.   In consideration of the sums hereinafter specified, COLISEUM grants to the LESSEE the use of the following facilities in the
Nassau Veterans Memorial Coliseum:

ARENA ☐   EXHIBITION HALL ☐   OTHER ☐

SQUARE FOOTAGE RENTED:

_____

for the following program and/or event: _____

on the following dates: _____

_____

_____

RENT
2.   (a)   The LESSEE agrees to pay by check, payable to Hyatt Management Corporation of New York, Inc., as rent for said space
the following: _____

_____

A non-refundable deposit of $_____ shall be paid when this agreement is executed and the balance as
follows:_____

_____

(b)   For purposes of this agreement, "gross receipts" shall mean the entire proceeds from the sale of tickets of admission, less
any admissions taxes.

(c)   Final settlement between LESSEE and COLISEUM of all monies owing under this agreement shall be effected on or
before: _____

(d)   (I) If the LESSEE cancels this agreement or otherwise fails to comply with its terms, the aforesaid non-refundable deposit,
at the option of COLISEUM, shall be retained by COLISEUM without any claim therefor by the LESSEE. COLISEUM,
however, has the option to elect to commence a suit or other action against the LESSEE by reason of such cancellation or
failure to perform, for the balance of any unpaid rent plus any resulting damages.
(II) In case suit or other action is instituted by COLISEUM against LESSEE as a result of LESSEE'S failure to comply with
the terms of this agreement, COLISEUM shall recover all damages provided by law, all costs and disbursements provided
by statute and all costs usually incurred, including reasonable attorney's fees.

(e)   LESSEE assumes full responsibility for all customer's checks returned by the bank because of insufficient funds and the
total sum thereof shall be charged against LESSEE'S share of the gross receipts.

BOX OFFICE/TICKETS
3.   The LESSEE must use the COLISEUM Box Office and only ticket agencies approved by COLISEUM. LESSEE will reimburse
COLISEUM for such Box Office use. (See "Rules, Regulations and Conditions for Lessees of the Coliseum."

INSURANCE AND INDEMNITY OF LESSEE
The LESSEE shall be liable for all damages to building and equipment, normal wear and tear excepted, and agrees to
indemnify and hold COLISEUM harmless from any claims or suits arising out of injury or death to any person or damage to
property resulting from use of said building. LESSEE will be required to furnish an appropriate certificate of insurance
showing that there is in effect, and will remain in effect throughout the term of the Lease, comprehensive general liability
insurance, including public liability and property damage, written by an insurer, authorized to do business in the State of New
York, in the following amounts:

Comprehensive General Liability — (Including Personal Injury, Contractual, and Products Liability)_____

Bodily Injury (each occurrence) _____ Property Damage (each occurrence)_____

Aggregate_____ Workmen's Compensation (Statutory) _____

Exhibit 4-1

The LESSEE shall name as additional insured, Hyatt Management Corporation of New York, Inc., its officers, agents, employees and the County of Nassau. At least fourteen (14) days prior to the commencement of this Lease, the LESSEE shall deliver to COLISEUM certificates of insurance, with the limits specified above, evidencing that the policies hereby required by LESSEE will be in full force and effect through the lease term. COLISEUM may obtain said policies at LESSEE'S expense or cancel subject event(s).

ASSIGNMENT

The LESSEE shall not assign or sublet to others the space covered by this Lease Agreement without written consent of COLISEUM.

COMPLIANCE WITH LAWS AND REGULATIONS

(a) Compliance with Laws: LESSEE shall comply with all laws of the United States, of the State of New York, and all local statutes and ordinances, and all rules and regulations established by any authorized officer or department of said entities; LESSEE will not suffer or permit to be done anything on said premises in violation of any laws, statutes, ordinances, rules; or regulations.

(b) Licenses: LESSEE shall obtain all necessary permits or licenses required by such laws, statutes, ordinances, rules and regulations. If proper required licenses and permits are not obtained by LESSEE, then COLISEUM may obtain same and LESSEE will be responsibile for reimbursement of all associated costs.

(c) Compliance with Rules and Regulations: LESSEE shall, and shall cause its servants, agents, employees, licensees, patrons and guests, to abide by such reasonable rules and regulations as may from time to time be adopted by COLISEUM for the use, occupancy and operation of the COLISEUM.

CONCESSIONS SALES

Except as specifically provided for herein, COLISEUM reserves unto itself, or its assigned agents, the sole rights: (a) to sell or dispense programs, librettos, periodicals, books, magazines, newspapers, soft drinks, flowers, tobacco, candies, food, novelties, or any related merchandise commonly sold or dispensed in the auditorium; (b) to rent and/or sell opera glasses, cushions and other articles; (c) to take and/or sell photographs; (d) to operate the parking lots and checkrooms.

HANDLING FUNDS

In the handling, control, custody and keeping of funds, whether the same are received through the box office or otherwise, COLISEUM is acting for the accommodation of LESSEE, and as to such funds, COLISEUM shall not be liable to LESSEE nor to any other person for any loss, theft, or defalcation thereof, whether such loss, theft or defalcation is caused or done by employees of COLISEUM or otherwise; nor shall any officer, agent, employee or servant of COLISEUM be liable for any loss, theft, or defalcation of such funds unless he willfully caused or permitted to be caused the same or unless it was proximately caused by his own gross negligence.

CONTROL OF BUILDING

The COLISEUM and premises, including keys thereto, shall be at all times under the control of the General Manager, and he or other duly authorized representatives of COLISEUM shall have the right to enter the premises at all times during the period covered by this contract. The entrances and exits of said premises shall be locked and unlocked at such times as may be reasonably required by LESSEE for its use of the COLISEUM; but LESSEE, at its own expense, must at all times place proper watchmen at all entrances and exits when the same are unlocked.

LICENSOR/LICENSEE

(a) It is expressly understood that COLISEUM shall not be construed or held to be a partner, agent or associate by joint venture or otherwise of LESSEE in the conduct of its business, it being expressly understood that the relationship between the parties hereto is and shall remain at all times that of licensor and licensee.

(b) It is understood and agreed that no agent, servant, or employee of LESSEE or any of its subcontractors shall under any circumstances be deemed an agent, servant or employee of COLISEUM.

COMPLIMENTARY TICKETS

LESSEE agrees that COLISEUM is entitled to receive and retain, for its own use or for the use of others, complimentary tickets to the Event in locations to be designated by COLISEUM; provided however, that the number of such complimentary tickets should not exceed one-half of one percent (0.5%) of the total number of tickets printed.

EXISTING UTILITIES

The rental includes the permanently attached electric lights, heat and/or air conditioning needed for the presentation of the attraction; however, failure to furnish any of the foregoing from circumstances beyond the control of the COLISEUM shall not be construed a breach of agreement.

OCCUPANCY DISRUPTION

In the event the COLISEUM or any part thereof shall be destroyed or damaged by fire, act of God, or any other cause, or if any other casualty or unforeseen occurrence of any kind shall render the fulfillment of this contract by COLISEUM reasonably or practically impossible, including without limitation thereto, the requisitioning of the premises by the United States Government, or any arm thereof, or by reason of labor diputes, then and thereupon, this contract shall terminate and LESSEE shall pay rental for said premises only up to the time of such termination, at the rate herein specified, and LESSEE hereby waives any claim for damages or compensation should this contract be so terminated.

COLISEUM'S RIGHT TO TERMINATE

It is agreed that without prejudice to any other rights and remedies that may be available to COLISEUM, in the event of the breach by LESSEE of one or more of the provisions of this Lease Agreement of any misrepresentations in obtaining said Lease Agreement, COLISEUM may refuse to allow the LESSEE to take possession of the premises, or if LESSEE is already in such possession, may stop all activities of LESSEE on premises and oust LESSEE therefrom. COLISEUM and its agents and employees shall in no way be responsible to the LESSEE for doing any or all of the things authorized by this paragraph.

THIS AGREEMENT IS SUBJECT TO EACH AND EVERY TERM AND CONDITION OF THE FOLLOWING:

(a) Agreement of Lease between the County of Nassau and Hyatt Management Corporation of New York, Inc. dated October 15, 1979, on file with the Nassau County Board of Supervisors;

(b) Any Rider annexed to this agreement and made a part thereof;

(c) All rules, regulations, terms and conditions set forth in a booklet entitled: "NASSAU VETERANS MEMORIAL COLISEUM RULES, REGULATIONS AND CONDITIONS FOR LESSEES OF THE COLISEUM" delivered to the LESSEE at the time of the execution of this agreement. Receipt of booklet is acknowledged by the LESSEE by the execution of this agreement.

(a) Unless this contract is returned duly executed by LESSEE to COLISEUM on or before _____ , it shall be deemed to be outstanding, and the contract becomes null and void and of no force and effect.

(b) This contract shall not be effective or binding upon COLISEUM until such time as it has been duly executed by an authorized officer of COLISEUM and an executed copy thereof delivered to the LESSEE.

This agreement shall be construed under the laws of the State of New York.

IN WITNESS WHEREOF, the parties have affixed their signatures as follows:

LESSEE: HYATT MANAGEMENT CORPORATION OF NEW YORK, INC.

_____   _____
(SIGNATURE OF AUTHORIZED OFFICER)   (SIGNATURE)

ADDENDUM TO LEASE AGREEMENT

NASSAU VETERANS MEMORIAL COLISEUM
HYATT MANAGEMENT CORPORATION OF NEW YORK, INC.
UNIONDALE, NEW YORK 11553

This addendum hereby becomes a part of Lease Agreement Number: _____

between Hyatt Management Corporation of New York, Inc. and _____

_____

whose address is _____

_____

dated _____ of _____ 19____.

LESSEE: _____   HYATT MANAGEMENT CORPORATION OF NEW YORK, INC.
                SIGNATURE OF AUTHORIZED OFFICER

_____   BY: _____
(COMPANY)

they are not considered a permanent tenant. Some examples of events that are usually not in long-term lease situations are a boxing match, the Harlem Globetrotters, and the Ice Capades. The promoter owes a duty of reasonable care in the maintenance and supervision of the facility. With respect to maintenance, a promoter is more likely to be responsible for patent defects he does not correct, while the facility owner is responsible for latent defects (see Section 4.12–3[c]). With respect to supervision, the promoter is responsible for reasonable care in the running of the event, and the determination of reasonable care may differ depending on the type of event. For example, the amount and type of security may differ for a family event as opposed to a rock concert. The promoter, however, is not responsible for unique or unforeseeable events causing injury in the absence of notice that an injury is apt to occur. Therefore, courts have often refused to find liability for patrons' injuries caused by other spectators. A promoter is only required to exercise reasonable precautions. However, to protect itself in the event that an invitee is successful in a claim against a promoter, the facility owner or possessor may require a promoter to execute a lease agreement, which will usually require the promoter to obtain general liability insurance and agree to indemnify and hold harmless the facility owner or possessor. (See clause 3 of Exhibit 4–1.)

Benjamin v. State, 115 Misc. 2d 71, 453 N.Y.S. 2d 329 (Ct. Cl. 1982)

Eleven-year-old Thomas Benjamin, on the evening of November 16, 1979, went to a college hockey doubleheader at Romney Arena, a state facility on the campus of the State University of New York at Oswego. He and his brother found seats in the second or third row of bleachers along the sidelines. They were seated behind the protective fence, 10 to 15 feet north of the nearest players' bench. While there, an errant puck found its way through the open area in front of the players' bench, passed behind the protective fence, and struck Thomas on the left side of the forehead. He was administered first aid and taken to the local hospital from which he was later discharged. The following morning he awoke feeling nauseous and began to vomit. He was taken to a medical center, where a palpable depression in the left frontal area was revealed. Surgery was performed, and he was discharged on November 29, 1979. He returned to school, but his activities were limited, and he complained of intermittent headaches. In gym classes he wore a protective helmet.

The plaintiff brought action against the state, seeking compensation for injuries, alleging that the state failed to provide adequate protection for the safety of spectators seated in the arena. The New York Court of Claims stated: "The State, like any other owner or occupier of land, is only under a duty to exercise 'reasonable care under the circumstances' to prevent injury to those who come to watch games played at its facility."

In determining whether the state had fulfilled its duty, the court was guided by the claim of an expert, who testified that in similar facilities it was the usual and customary practice to protect the area around the players' bench. In the absence of such protection, it was the usual and customary practice to restrict seating in an arena outside the zone of danger. Since neither course of action was chosen, the judge stated that the state failed to provide Thomas with adequate protection. The court found that the failure of the state to provide for the safety of Thomas in the protected seating area constituted negligence and that such negligence was a substantial factor in bringing about the injuries.

In addition, the court found that the accident and the injuries sustained by Thomas were not attributable to any culpable conduct on his part. When he took his seat in the protected area on the sidelines, he had the right to assume that every reasonable care had been taken for his safety. Although he admitted to being aware that the area in front of the players' bench was unprotected, it cannot be said that a reasonably prudent person of Thomas's years, intelligence, and degree of development would have fully appreciated the danger and, hence, could have been said to have assumed the risk.

The court found that Thomas had been damaged in the sum of $24,000 (all compensatory), and an award was made accordingly.

Grauer v. State of New York, 181 N.Y.S. 2d 994 (Ct. Cl. 1959)

Claimant, a private citizen, sought recovery for personal injuries sustained when the chair he was about to sit on at the chair lift at Belleayre State Park swung or was tipped in such a way that it struck the back of his right leg, fracturing it. The court found sufficient evidence to establish that the state was negligent in permitting the accident to happen and therefore rendered judgment for the claimant in the amount of $5,880 ($3,000 for personal injuries, $2,500 for loss of earnings, and $380 for medical expenses).

Belleayre State Park operated a chair lift, which was used by skiers in the winter and sightseers in the summer. On August 6, 1955, claimant rode the lift to the top of the mountain and went sight-seeing with his family and friends. However, on the return trip, claimant testified that while waiting on the platform, he was struck on the right leg and thrown bodily into the chair traveling downward. He claimed that he was given no instructions on how to stand on the platform and that he merely followed the crowd and stood as others did. He did not see what struck him.

The chair lift is a constantly moving chain of 85 to 90 chairs, moving at approximately 3 or 4 miles an hour. Chairs are attached to the running cable in such a way that they can swing from front to back and from side to side. An attendant at the lift guides the chairs to each waiting patron, preparing each chair so that the patron can access the chair easily.

Arthur G. Draper, superintendent at Belleayre, testified that normally nothing on a chair could strike a waiting patron on the right foot. Certain exaggerated motions by the chair could force the footrest to strike a patron's leg, but it would hit higher on the body than in this particular case. He further stated that if the footrest were open, it would close upon striking a patron, making it impossible for the patron to sit in the chair. Only if the shaft of the footrest struck the patron could the footrest remain open.

An engineer for the company that designed the chair lift testified that if the safety bar on the chair were open, it would be possible for the chair to be moved in such a way that a standing passenger could be struck below the right calf and still be seated. He also stated that if a patron were careless and dragged a foot along the ground while being seated, an injury could occur.

To determine the degree of care to be exercised by the state in the operation of the chair lift, the court had to consider the status of the state. Claimant maintained that the state was a common carrier. A common carrier's duty to its passengers is to use the utmost foresight as to possible dangers and the utmost prudence in guarding against them. A common carrier of goods is one "who, by virtue of his calling, undertakes, for compensation, to transport personal property from one place to another for all who may choose to employ him, and everyone who undertakes to carry for compensation all persons indifferently is, as to liability, to be deemed a common carrier." According to the court, the difference between a common carrier and others is that the common carrier holds himself out to the public "in common, that is, to all persons who choose to employ him, as ready to carry for hire."

Here, the service offered by the chair lift was transportation of passengers for which a fee was charged. The service was offered to the public "in common." The revenue obtained from the operation of the chair lift went to the state, which operated it for the purposes of receiving such revenues. Although the state suggested that riding the chair lift was similar to "riding a merry-go-round, steeple chase, roller coaster or similar device," becoming rather an "uncommon carrier," the court rejected this claim and stated that the lift was used for transportation, not amusement or thrills. Therefore, the court found that the state was a common carrier in the operation of the chair lift, ascribing the aforementioned duty to it, stating also that the "degree of care to be exercised should be commensurate with the danger to be avoided."

Claimant, in attempting to prove that the state had breached a duty owed to him, invoked the res ipsa loquitur doctrine. In making out a prima facie case, res ipsa loquitur:

> . . . relieves a plaintiff from the burden of producing direct evidence of negligence, but it does not relieve a plaintiff from the burden of proof that the person charged with negligence was at fault. . . . It requires evidence which

shows at least probability that a particular accident could not have occurred without legal wrong by the defendant . . .

The doctrine applies when there is control by the person charged with negligence and when there is improbability of the occurrence having happened if the person had been reasonably careful. The court noted that: "It is familiar law that in applying the doctrine of res ipsa loquitur there is required proof 'of absence of any action on the part of the plaintiff contributing to the accident. Its purpose, of course, is to eliminate the possibility that it was the plaintiff who was responsible . . .'"

Since the claimant made out a prima facie case, the state was obligated to come forward with an explanation of the accident so as to overcome the implication resulting from the proof of the claimant. The state's defense rested on a motion picture of the chair lift in operation, the testimony of the engineer who stated that a careless person could drag and injure a foot while being seated, and the testimony of the attendant on duty at the time of the accident who stated that he did not swing the chair in which the claimant sat.

The court stated that what the state had done was to offer an inference that the claimant caught his foot under the footrest as he sat down in the chair; thereby it failed in its duty to offer an adequate explanation of the accident.

The court held for the claimant.

Townsley v. Cincinnati Gardens, Inc., 314 N.E. 2d 409 (Ohio Ct. App. 1974)

A minor, who was a business invitee of the defendant, attended a Harlem Globetrotters' exhibition at Cincinnati Gardens and was assaulted in a washroom by a group of boys when he told them he had no money to give them. A suit for damages was brought against the Gardens for negligence for the injuries of the boy and for the doctor and medical bills sustained by the father.

The trial court held for the plaintiff, stating that

where an incident such as the instant matter occurred in a large metropolitan sports arena with approximately 5,000 persons present; where such incident took place in an isolated, dimly lighted public restroom; where, on the night of such incident, the security guard was made up of five patrolmen; where two of such patrolmen were stationed on the main level and; where the responsibilities of the other three included supervising the entire remainder of the Gardens, the defendant either knew, or, in the exercise of ordinary care, should have known of the danger which victimized the plaintiff.

On an appeal by the defendant, the court sustained the appeal and reversed the decision of the trial court. The defendant relied on the case of *Howard* v. *Rogers*, 249 N.E. 2d 804 (Ohio 1969), and the appeals court agreed. In that case, it was established that the occupier of a premise for business purposes is not an insurer of the safety of any business invitees while they are on those premises; and the occupier of a premise is not liable for damages when a business invitee is injured by a danger of which, in the exercise of ordinary care, the occupier could not have known.

The testimony of the security guard captain revealed that the type of event dictated the number of guards needed to secure the Gardens. Since the Globetrotters' exhibition was a family-type program, as opposed to a boxing match or a rock concert, it was determined that five guards were all that was necessary. Also, there had never been an incident in the Gardens in which a boy was beaten up in a washroom by other boys for refusing to give them money. The court concluded that there was no duty on the part of the defendant to have anticipated such an occurrence.

The appeals court ruled that there was no evidence to indicate that the defendant could have anticipated, or reasonably have known of, the danger to the plaintiff. Therefore, the trial court should have entered a judgment for the defense. The court stated that since this incident had happened, there would be no reason not to expect it in the future, so more guards in the washroom areas, or at least more frequent visits to those areas by the guards, would be in order.

Eddy v. Syracuse University, 433 N.Y.S. 2d 923 (App. Div. 1980)

Thomas Eddy was an "ultimate frisbee" player for a team of Harpur College students. In March 1977, the team traveled to Syracuse University to play against a group of Syracuse students, although the latter team was neither officially recognized nor sponsored by the defendant. During the course of an "ultimate frisbee" game played in the basketball gymnasium, plaintiff, running toward one of the goal lines and looking back over his shoulder for a thrown frisbee, crashed through a glass window in a door, severely lacerating his arm.

Plaintiff sued defendant for negligence. Defendant argued that since it had not authorized use of the gym, had no foreknowledge of the plaintiff's use, could not have foreseen that students would use the basketball courts for an "ultimate frisbee" game, and that the gym was not defective in design or construction for its ordinary purposes, there was lack of evidence to even submit the issue of negligence. The judge disagreed, and the jury found for the plaintiff.

In affirming the verdict for the plaintiff, the appeals court held that the case was properly sent to the jury and that the jury's findings were reasonable. The court noted: "Surely the jury could have concluded that ... on the campus of a large university ... some of its students, and their guests, might use the facility without express permission." Also properly left to the jury was the question of whether the glass doors, located as they were in a building intended to be used for strenuous physical activity, constituted a dangerous condition and whether the risk presented by the glass doors could have been alleviated without imposing an undue burden upon the university.

Bearman v. University of Notre Dame, 453 N.E. 2d 1196 (Ind. Ct. App. 1983)

Plaintiff sued the University of Notre Dame for injuries she suffered as she left a Notre Dame home football game. The injury occurred in the stadium's parking lot when a third party, who was "tailgating," became involved in a fight, fell onto the plaintiff, and broke her leg. The plaintiff sued Notre Dame and claimed that the school had "a duty to protect her from injury caused by the acts of other persons on the premises," since she was a business invitee. Notre Dame argued that it could not be held liable for the act of a third person since it had no knowledge or notice of any danger to the woman. The trial court granted Notre Dame's motion for judgment on the evidence, and the plaintiffs appealed.

The Court of Appeals of Indiana noted that the issue involved two different factors. An operator of a place of public entertainment generally "owes a duty to keep the premises safe for its invitees." Conversely, "an invitor is not the insurer of invitee's safety and before liability may be imposed on invitor, it must have actual or constructive knowledge of the danger." The court reasoned that Notre Dame was aware of the tailgate parties in the parking areas around the stadium and the fact that drinking occurred. It recognized that while Notre Dame did not have particular knowledge of any danger for the plaintiff, it was aware that intoxicated people pose a threat to the safety of patrons at the games.

The appeals court therefore reversed the lower court's decision and held that Notre Dame had a duty to do all it could reasonably do to protect those people who attend the games from injury inflicted by the acts of third parties. It remanded the case for a jury to consider on the question of whether protective measures were lacking and, if so, if this inadequacy contributed to the plaintiff's injury.

On the remand, the trial court ruled for the plaintiff and awarded her $53,500 in damages.

NOTES

1. The following lawsuits were brought against facility owners and possessors by participants:

(a) In *Kaiser* v. *State*, 55 Misc. 2d 576 285 N.Y.S. 2d 874 (1967), *rev'd*, 30 App. Div. 2d 482, 294 N.Y.S. 2d 410 (1968), plaintiff bobsledder sought recovery for injuries sustained when his bobsled crashed on the state's bobsled run. In granting summary judgment for plaintiffs, the court of claims held that evidence established that the state was negligent in failing to close the run, although it had actual notice of a gash in the wall in sufficient time to suspend operations before bobsledders' injuries.

(b) In *Praetorius* v. *Shell Oil Co.*, 207 So. 2d 872 (La. Ct. App. 1968), plaintiff baseball player sought recovery from a defendant baseball diamond owner for injuries sustained by stepping in a hole while running from home plate to first base. In reversing the trial court's judgment for the plaintiff, the court of appeals held that defendants were not negligent in failing to properly maintain area in batter's box where small holes and depressions were dug by batters' cleats during the course of a softball game.

(c) In *Ardoin* v. *Evangeline Parish School Board*, 376 So. 2d 372 (La. Ct. App. 1979), an action was brought on behalf of a boy, who, while playing softball during a physical education class at his elementary school, tripped over a 12-inch square piece of concrete that was embedded in the base path between second and third base. His father brought a negligence suit against the school, alleging that the concrete slab, which protruded at least a half inch above ground, constituted such a hazardous condition that it was a breach of the required standard of care on the part of the school board which failed to remove it from the playing field. The school district argued that it had no actual knowledge of the concrete slab.

In affirming the trial court's finding of negligence on the part of the school authorities, the appeals court held that the school board had constructive knowledge of the hazardous condition since it should have anticipated and discovered the potential danger and eliminated it before allowing students to use the field during physical education classes.

(d) In *Sykes* v. *Bensinger Recreation Corp.*, 117 F. 2d 964 (7th Cir. 1941), plaintiff bowler sought recovery under the Wisconsin "safe place" statute for injuries sustained as a result of catching his foot in a 2-inch space between the floor of the alley and the bottom of a return, through which he slipped and fell on the alley. In reversing judgment for plaintiff, the court of appeals held that a proprietor is not an insurer of bowlers' safety and that the mere fact that such an accident happened does not prove the place was unsafe. "Safe" is a relative term, and what is safe depends on the facts and conditions of each case.

(e) In *Clary* v. *Alexander County Board of Education*, 19 N.C. App. 637, 199 S.E. 2d 738 (1973), *aff'd*, 285 N.C. 188, 203 S.E. 2d 820 (1974), plaintiff senior on the high school basketball team suffered severe lacerations when he collided with some glass panels along one wall of the gymnasium while running wind sprints. Plaintiff's suit alleged negligence on the part of the school board for permitting breakable glass to be used in the gym and in permitting the coaches to direct the players to run wind sprints toward the glass panels.

The trial court granted a directed verdict for the defendant. On appeal, the appeals court held that the evidence indicated the plaintiff was contributorily negligent and affirmed the decision. The court reasoned that the plaintiff had run similar wind sprints in the gym during his three previous years in the basketball program: "Yet he chose to run at the panel at full speed without slowing down until he was within three feet of the glass. Anyone [doing such] . . . would be compelled by his momentum to crash into the wall and suffer injury." Plaintiff contended he was excused from contributory negligence because he was acting under the instructions of his coach. The court disagreed, since the reasonable person disregards orders when the compliance with such orders could result in injury. The North Carolina Supreme Court affirmed the decision (see Section 4.23–4, Note 1[a]).

(f) In *Friedman* v. *State*, 54 Misc. 2d 448, 282 N.Y.S. 2d 858 (1967), plaintiff skier sought recovery for injuries sustained in a fall from an aerial ski lift at a ski center owned by state. In granting judgment for the plaintiff, the court of claims held that the state was negligent in the placement of signs relating to the time of chair lift operation, the size of the signs, and the failure to use a loudspeaker to announce that lift was closed for the night, and that such negligence was the proximate cause of injuries sustained when plaintiff fell from the lift after it had stopped for the night while she was still descending.

(g) In *Ragni* v. *Lincoln-Devon Bounceland, Inc.*, 234 N.E. 2d 168 (Ill. App. Ct. 1968), plaintiff trampoline user sought recovery for injuries sustained in landing on the frame of defendant's trampoline. In affirming a directed verdict for the defendant, the appellate court held that the owner had no duty to warn plaintiff, who had received instruction on indoor trampolines in college, that the mat in the middle of the trampoline was the only safe place to land.

(h) In *Mokovich* v. *Independent School District*, 225 N.W. 292 (Minn. 1929), plaintiff alleged that the lime used to make lines on the football field caused player the loss of sight in one eye and seriously injured the other eye. However, the court ruled in favor of the defendant, since it was exercising one of its governmental functions of education.

(i) In *Maddox* v. *City of New York*, 455 N.Y.S. 2d 102 (N.Y. App. Div. 1982), 467 N.Y.S. 2d 972, 121 Misc. 2d 358 (N.Y. App. Div. 1983), *rev'd*, 487 N.Y.S. 2d 354 (N.Y. App. Div. 1985), an action was brought by former Yankee center fielder Elliot Maddox against the owner, maintenance company, and designer of Shea Stadium for an injury that occurred when Maddox slipped on the wet field in Shea Stadium. In ruling for the plaintiff on defendant's motion for a summary judgment, the court found that Maddox did not assume the risk of playing on a dangerous field when, as an employee, he was under the orders of his superiors. On appeal, the trial court's decision was reversed. The appeals court held that the doctrine of assumption of the risk completely barred recovery.

(j) In *Van Stry* v. *State*, 479 N.Y.S. 2d 258 (App. Div. 1984), plaintiff student slipped and fell in men's locker room while changing for his badminton class. Plaintiff testified that he fell on the edge of a puddle of water, approximately ⅛ of an inch deep, 4 to 5 feet in diameter, and 20 to 30 feet from the showers. The trial court found the state 60% liable for the injury and the New York Supreme Court, Appellate Division, affirmed the lower court's ruling. The court found that, "...a persistent accumulation of wetness created a foreseeable risk, that the state had notice of the condition through its employees and that the state did not use reasonable care to eliminate the hazard."

2. The following lawsuits were brought against facility owners and possessors by spectators involving actions of other spectators:

(a) In *Weldy* v. *Oakland High School Dist. of Alameda County*, 65 P. 2d 851 (Cal. Ct. App. 1937), plaintiff, a spectator at a football game supervised by agents of defendant school district, sued in negligence for injuries sustained when struck by a bottle thrown by a fellow student. The appeals court held that plaintiff had failed to state a cause of action. The complaint did not allege that defendant should have foreseen the rowdyism of the student nor that the defendant's servants were responsible for some act or omission amounting to negligence.

(b) In *Porter* v. *California Jockey Club*, 285 P. 2d 60 (Cal. Ct. App. 1955), plaintiff, a racetrack spectator, sought recovery from defendant track operator for injuries sustained when she was violently knocked down by another spectator. In affirming a judgment of nonsuit, the district court of appeals held that in absence of facts which would reasonably put defendant on notice that one spectator would run violently into another so as to put the duty upon defendant to guard

against it, there was no question of negligence.

(c) In *Parker* v. *Warren*, 503 S.W. 2d 938 (Tenn. Ct. App. 1973), plaintiff spectator sued defendant promoter when the bleacher on which she was to view a wrestling match collapsed. In affirming a jury verdict for the plaintiff, the court of appeals held that the evidence made a submissible case for res ipsa loquitur. Therefore, the promoter was required to use ordinary care with respect to the bleacher conditions and had a duty to inspect them, and that patrons were entitled to assume that premises were in safe condition.

(d) In *Wells* v. *Minneapolis Baseball & Athletic Ass'n.*, 122 Minn. 327, 427 N.W. 706 (1913), a spectator at a baseball game was injured by a foul ball and brought suit against the possessor of the facility (see Section 4.24).

3. The following lawsuits were brought against facility owners and possessors by spectators involving actions of participant:

(a) In *Wiersma* v. *Long Beach*, 106 P. 2d 45 (Cal. Ct. App. 1940), plaintiff, who purchased a ticket to watch a wrestling match held in defendant's municipal auditorium, sought recovery for injuries sustained when one of the wrestlers deliberately hit him with a chair. In affirming a directed verdict for defendant, the district court of appeals held that since the city had leased the auditorium to a promoter, it was not responsible to plaintiff for the misconduct of its tenant.

(b) In *Silvia* v. *Woodhouse*, 248 N.E. 2d 260 (Mass. 1960), plaintiff wrestling spectator sought recovery for injuries sustained when wrestler, who had been ejected from the ring, was knocked back into him while trying to reenter. In affirming judgment against defendant auditorium operator, the Massachusetts Supreme Judicial Court held that the defendant, who had seen such jostling before, was negligent in either failing to warn patrons or in failing to move seats back to a safer distance.

(c) In *Perry* v. *Seattle School Dist. No. 1*, 405 P. 2d 589 (Wash. 1965), plaintiff spectator sued defendant school district in negligence when she was injured by a football player who was pushed out of bounds over her. The Supreme Court of Washington, in affirming the trial court's verdict for defendant, held that even though defendant did not charge admission and could have roped off the area, it was not negligent.

(d) In *Turner* v. *Caddo Parish School Board*, 252 La. 810, 214 So. 2d 153 (1968), plaintiff spectator grandmother sued defendant school authorities in negligence after she was run down on a football play intended to carry out of bounds. The Louisiana Supreme Court, in reinstating the trial court's dismissal, held that defendant was not negligent in failing to anticipate spectators who did not know that football players are often carried out of bounds or for failing to erect a barricade.

(e) In *Rich* v. *Madison Square Garden Corp.*, 266 N.Y.S. 288, 149 Misc. 123 (Sup. Ct. 1933), *aff'd*, 241 A.D. 722, 270 N.Y.S. 915 (1934), plaintiff spectator sought recovery for injuries sustained when struck by a hockey stick during a game at defendant's rink. In directing a verdict for defendant, the trial court held that defendant was not required to foresee that a hockey stick would fly into the stands and was therefore not liable for failure to have constructed protective screens.

(f) In *Ramsey* v. *Kallio*, 62 So. 2d 146 (La. Ct. App. 1952), plaintiff spectators sought recovery from the operator of wrestling arena for damages incurred when a wrestler jumped out of the ring and assaulted them. In affirming the trial court's dismissal, the court of appeals held that the operator had no reason to expect that wrestler would jump from the ring and assault spectators and therefore was not liable.

4. The following lawsuits were brought against facility owners and possessors involving the equipment and building:

(a) In *Taylor* v. *Hardee*, 232 S.C. 338, 102 S.E. 2d 218 (1958), plaintiff spectator sought recovery from injuries sustained when a bleacher, constructed by defendant speedway owner, collapsed under him. The South Carolina Supreme Court held that evidence of how the bleachers were constructed was sufficient on the issue of racetrack owner's negligence to send the question to the jury.

(b) In *Rockwell* v. *Hillcrest Country Club*, 181 N.W. 2d 290 (Mich. Ct. App. 1970), plaintiff golf spectators sought recovery from injuries sustained while watching a golf tournament. They were standing on a suspension bridge that collapsed, and they fell into the river below. In affirming the trial court's judgment for plaintiffs, the court of appeals held that the plaintiffs had established a prima facie case of negligence in that the bridge capacity was 25 people, that 80 to 100 people were on the bridge when it collapsed, and that no warning signs or supervisors were present.

(c) In *Woodring* v. *Board of Education of Manhasset*, 435 N.Y.S. 2d 52 (App. Div. 1981), plaintiff brought a wrongful death suit against the school district after a platform railing in the gymnasium gave way, throwing decedent to his death. In affirming the $1.4 million award to plaintiff, the appeals court found that the school district (1) lacked a preventive maintenance program, (2) improperly constructed the platforms, (3) failed to regularly inspect its gymnasium facilities, and (4) should have known — given the extensive use of the platforms by students — that injury was foreseeable if the railings were not properly maintained or constructed. These findings sustained the jury's determination of the defendant's negligence.

(d) In *Novak* v. *City of Delavan*, 143 N.W. 2d 6 (Wis. 1966), the court ruled that a school district was not liable for injuries caused by facilities over which they had no control but merely used from time to time. This ruling was handed down in an action that was brought against a city and a school district for injuries sustained as a result of a bleacher collapse at an athletic event. The court found in favor of the school district because the school district used the facility for only seven football games. The school district did not purport to inspect the bleachers or perform any maintenance services, and it was the city, not the school employees, who attended to any bleacher problems. Without control or custody of the facility, the school board was not obligated to repair the bleachers, and the school district could not be held liable when a footboard gave way.

(e) In *Whitfield* v. *Cox*, 52 S.E. 2d 72 (Va. 1949), plaintiff, a spectator at defendant promoter's wrestling match, sought recovery in negligence for injuries sustained when she was struck by a whiskey bottle thrown by another spectator. In reversing a jury verdict for plaintiff, the Virginia Supreme Court of Appeals held that the defendant was not required to search patrons for objects that could be used to injure other patrons.

(f) In *Witherspoon* v. *Haft*, 106 N.E. 2d 296 (Ohio 1952), plaintiff spectator at a football game sued for injuries sustained when plaintiff fell from last row of temporary bleachers that defendant installer had negligently fastened. In affirming the court of appeal's reversal of the trial court's directed verdict for defendant, the Ohio Supreme Court held that reasonable minds could conclude that failure of defendants to fasten the top plank seat securely could result in the serious hazard to plaintiff.

(g) In *Williams* v. *Strickland*, 112 S.E. 2d 533 (N.C. 1960), plaintiff racetrack patron sued defendant racetrack owner in negligence for injuries sustained when a wheel came off a race car and struck her. In reversing the trial court's dismissal, the North Carolina Supreme Court held that racetrack operators could be held liable for failure to exercise care commensurate with known or reasonably foreseeable dangers incident to motor vehicles racing at high speeds, in that no seats were provided and no ropes were strung to indicate where patrons could stand to view races safely.

(h) In *Thurman* v. *Clune*, 125 P. 2d 59 (Cal. Ct. App. 1942), plaintiff spectators sought recovery for injuries sustained when hit with a flying puck in defendant's unscreened ice rink. In affirming the trial court's judgment for the defendant, the district court of appeals held that the question of whether the defendant was negligent in failing to warn of the danger of flying pucks or in failing to provide protective screens was for the jury to decide.

5. For further information, see the following articles:

(a) "Tort Liability and Recreational Use of Land," 28 *Buffalo Law Review* 767 (Fall 1979).

(b) "Owner Liability for Intentional Torts Committed

by Professional Athletes Against Spectators," 30 *Buffalo Law Review* 565 (Summer 1981).

(c) "Liability for Injured Baseball Spectators Under *Rudnick* v. *Golden West Broadcasters*: Still Playing the Same Old Game? (*Rudnick* v. *Golden West Broadcasters*, 156 Cal. App. 3d 793 [1984])," 12 *Western State University Law Review* 345 (Fall 1984).

(d) "The Sports Spectator as Plaintiff," 16 *Trial* 26 (March 1980).

(e) Wong and Ensor, "Torts and Tailgating," *Athletic Business*, Vol. 9, No. 5 (May 1985), p. 46.

(f) "Anatomy of a Recreational Tort Case," 5 *American Journal of Trial Advocacy* 457 (Spring 1982).

(g) "Good Sports and Bad Lands: The Application of Washington's Recreational Use Statute Limiting Landowner Liability," 53 *Washington Law Review* 1 (December 1977).

(h) "Liability for Ski Injuries Caused by Defective Bindings," 27 *Federation of Insurance Counsel Quarterly* 311 (Spring 1977).

(i) "Utah's Inherent Risks of Skiing Act: Avalanche from Capitol Hill," 1980 *Utah Law Review* 355 (Spring 1980).

(j) "Ski Area Liability for Downhill Injuries," 49 *Insurance Counsel Journal* 36 (January 1982).

(k) "Ski Liability," 32 *Federation of Insurance Counsel Quarterly* 223 (January 1982).

(l) "Swimming Pool Liability," 14 *Trial* 24 (June 1978).

(m) "Continuing Changes in Colorado Ski Law," 13 *Colorado Law* 407 (March 1984).

(n) "Ski Operators and Skiers — Responsibility and Liability," 14 *New England Law Review* 260 (Fall 1978).

(o) "Update: Torts and Tailgates," *Athletic Business* (August 1985), p. 8.

4.26 Liability of Medical Personnel

A person or an organization in charge of a sports activity has a duty to provide reasonable medical assistance to participants as well as to spectators. To determine if this duty has been met, both the quality and the speed of the treatment must be considered. The quality of the treatment will be assessed by looking at the qualifications of the provider and the type of treatment offered. The speed of the treatment may be determined by the availability of medical personnel.

There are many different levels of healthcare providers within the American medical system. With respect to athletic events, these providers may be doctors or nurses, but more often they are trainers or emergency medical technicians (EMTs). The standard of care required of each person is based on training and qualifications (see Section 4.12–1). A higher standard of care is established if the class of medical personnel has skills and training beyond what is expected of the reasonable lay person. For example, the standard of care imposed upon the medical profession is that the doctor must have met the level of skill and knowledge common to the profession in general or common to the profession within the nearby geographical area.

In the case of a specialist, however, the duty has increasingly become more stringent. A specialist must act with the skill and knowledge that is reasonable within the specialty. Thus, while in the past little has distinguished medical malpractice cases involving athletes from other cases, the growing ranks of doctors practicing sports medicine will certainly lead to a higher standard of care for sports medicine specialists in negligence lawsuits brought by injured athletes. The standard of care is usually established by expert testimony. A doctor may be negligent when others of lesser skill and expertise would not be. The standard of care for any other medical personnel is applied in a similar fashion.

Generally, medical personnel are considered independent contractors rather than employees (see Section 4.13–1), even though they are usually paid by a school district, facility owner, or other supervisory body (see *Cramer* v. *Hoffman*, Note 2). As independent contractors, even if they are found to have been negligent, their employers cannot be held liable under the doctrine of vicarious liability (see Section 4.13–1). To determine if a doctor or other medical person is an independent contractor, the court considers the degree of control exercised by the employee's supervisor over actual medical decisions. While the general rule is that medical personnel are independent contractors, there have been cases in which the employer has been held liable under the doctrine of vicarious liability. For example, in *Rosensweig v. State of New York, infra,* and *Chuy v. Philadelphia Eagles Football Club,* Note 1, the court found that the employer exercised sufficient control and discretion over the medical personnel to be held liable.

There are some special considerations for a doctor involved in the area of athletics. The first concerns the relationship between a doctor and patient. Typically, the doctor is paid by the patient. However, in sports, the doctor is hired and paid by the team's management or the athletic organization. Normally, a confidential relationship exists between doctor and patient. When the doctor is employed by a third party, however, a different relationship is established. In effect, the team doctor has two masters to serve: the team management or athletic organization and the player-patient. And, although both the team and player are concerned with restoring the player to full health, there are situations in which the team may seek a shorter rehabilitation program than the more cautious recovery time frame favored by the player. The team doctor is placed in the middle. The doctor's dilemma is highlighted by suits against team doctors brought by players who contended that the doctor did not place their long-term recovery before the team's interests.

In addition to this potential conflict, the normal confidential relationship between doctor and patient is changed. When a third party, the team or athletic organization, pays the doctor, it typically has full access to the medical records. The team also discusses with the doctor the appropriate treatment for the injured athlete. In some situations, the team has access to the medical records and the athlete does not. Rafael Septien, a former place-kicker with the Dallas Cowboys, sued the Cowboys for full access to his medical records. Despite the difference in the doctor-patient relationship in athletics as opposed to the normal doctor-patient relationship, the doctor still has certain obligations to the athlete-patient — for example, the doctor's release of accurate information to the public (see *Chuy v. Philadelphia Eagles Football Club,* Note 1).

Another consideration for the doctor in athletics concerns the prescribing of painkilling drugs to enable the athlete to continue playing for the benefit of the team but to the potential detriment of the player's career. The cases involving Bill Walton (see Note 6) and Dick Butkus (see Note 11) raise the issue of the responsibility a doctor has to a player-patient and to the doctor's employer — the team.

One final consideration is that even though doctors may be negligent in their handling of an injured player, they may not be legally liable under normal tort analysis. When a player is injured through intentional or negligent actions on the part of a coach, referee, player, spectator, or anyone else, subsequent negligent action will not usually relieve the original negligent party from liability created by the original action. The doctor may, however, be liable as an additional defendant if the doctor's conduct is found to be a substantial factor in the injury or if additional injuries occurred because of the doctor's negligence. Subsequent medical negligence is generally not an unforeseeable, unreasonable cause that would relieve the original party from liability.

Rosensweig v. State of New York, 146 N.Y.S. 2d 589 (Ct. Cl. 1955)

Rosensweig, acting as administrator for the estate of George Flores, brought a claim against the state of New York for the conscious pain and suffering, hospital and medical expenses, and wrongful death of a professional prize fighter, Flores. Rosensweig based his claim upon the alleged negligence of the State Athletic Commission in permitting Flores to fight after he had been the victim of two knockouts within a five-week period.

The court held that the evidence established that the decedent's prefight brain injury should have been discovered or reasonably anticipated by the doctors examining him, and that the doctors were the servants of the State Athletic Commission. The court found in favor of Rosensweig.

Flores fought Johnny Corky on July 24, 1951, and the referee awarded Corky a technical knockout (TKO) in the second round after Flores absorbed a series of punches to his head. Three weeks later, on August 14, after passing the standard prefight physical exam, Flores fought Roger Donoghue and again lost by a TKO, this time in the eighth round. Dr. Bockner, who had administered the prefight exam, examined Flores after the fight, both in the ring and later in the dressing room. He testified that he found nothing physically wrong with Flores.

On August 15, Flores attempted to have a rematch with Donoghue approved by Deputy Commissioner Duberstein. Knowing that Flores had lost by TKOs twice within a three-week period, Duberstein demanded that Flores pass an electroencephalogram (EEG) before he would approve the bout. On August 16, Flores had an EEG taken by a technician, and Dr. Kaplan found the test results to be "within normal limits." Duberstein then approved the rematch, which was scheduled for August 29. At noon on the day of the fight, Flores was given a prefight examination by Dr. Vincent Nardiello. Made aware of the results of Flores's last two fights, Nardiello voiced concern to Flores about fighting again that day. Despite his concern, Nardiello certified that Flores was physically fit to fight.

In the eighth round of the fight, Donoghue knocked out Flores's mouthpiece. With the next punch, Flores went down. Unconscious as he fell, Flores hit his head on the mat. Dr. Nardiello examined the fighter in the ring but took no further action. Flores walked to his dressing room and very soon after lapsed into a coma. He was rushed to a hospital and placed under a neurosurgeon's care. At midnight, a brain operation was performed, which revealed two pertinent facts. First, the absence

of a massive hemorrhage ruled out the possibility that the injury had resulted from a single blow. Second, the amount of edema present at this early stage was not in keeping with the elapsed time. The edema could only have been accounted for by an injury to the brain prior to the last fight. Flores never regained consciousness; he died on September 3, five days after the fight.

In deciding the case in favor of the decedent, the court had to arrive at affirmative answers to these two questions: Should Flores's brain injury have been discovered or reasonably anticipated by the doctors examining him? and Is the negligence of the doctors attributable to the state of New York? Responding positively on the first question, the court received medical testimony that concluded that the results of a single EEG taken at the time that Flores's EEG was taken were inconclusive with regard to the discovery of possible brain injury. Good medical practice required that a person who had been knocked out or received a severe beating about the head be kept quiet and inactive for a period of from six weeks to two months.

Each doctor who examined Flores from the time of the Corkey fight on July 24 to the second Donoghue fight on August 29 had the power to suspend Flores or to recommend his suspension to the commissioner. The fact that this was not done was found to be an indictment of each of the doctors. Dr. Nardiello claimed that it is the practice of the commission's doctors to leave the question of suspension to the doctor who attends the fighter's last fight. Suspensions are not levied during prefight examinations. The court stated that this type of reasoning opens the door to tragic and foreseeable consequences and that it was a negligent practice.

Though Flores was the one who stepped into the ring of his own volition, he cannot be said to have assumed the risk in this case. If no other forces intervened, then a boxer is said to have assumed the risk of injury of death through the accumulation of blows over a series of fights. However, the court concluded that the negligence on the part of the doctors was an intervening factor that conditioned Flores's appreciation of the risk such that he could not be found to have assumed the risk.

In determining that the doctor's negligence was attributable to the state of New York, the court examined pertinent statutes, which revealed that boxing in the state was stringently regulated by the state government — more so, in fact, than any other field of activity known to the court. The State Athletic Commission, which regulated boxing in the state, appointed the doctors to a panel from which the boxing promoters would pick doctors to handle examination for their bouts. The commission designated the form and character of the examinations and the fee to be paid to the doctors by promoters.

The court stated that direction and control are the criteria for determining the existence of a master-servant relationship creating liability for the master — not merely the authority to designate time and place of work and wages paid. The court found that the type of control exercised by the State Athletic Commission left no doubt that the doctors were its servants, with the state being liable for the injuries caused by their negligence.

NOTES

1. In *Chuy* v. *Philadelphia Eagles Football Club*, 431 F. Supp. 254 (E.D. Pa. 1977), *aff'd*, 595 F. 2d 1265 (3rd Cir. 1979), plaintiff, a former professional football player, sought damages from his club for "intentional infliction of emotional distress." The court held that there was sufficient evidence to support the jury's determination that the team physician had intentionally or recklessly inflicted mental distress on the plaintiff. The physician had made a false statement to the press about a supposedly fatal disease from which plaintiff was suffering. The club was held liable under the doctrine of respondeat superior (see Sections 4.14 and 4.16).

2. A team physician has been sued for failure to provide good, sound, reasonable medical care. The plaintiff in *Bayless* v. *Philadelphia National League Club*, 472 F. Supp. 625 (E.D. Pa. 1979), argued that he had been given pain-killing drugs without knowledge of their potential side effects. The court determined that the plaintiff's exclusive remedy for an action was under the state worker's compensation act and not the court's legal jurisdiction.

3. A professional sports team may be liable for negligence of any medical assistance provided by its staff to spectators. In *Fish* v. *Los Angeles Dodgers Baseball Club*, 128 Cal. Rptr. 807 (1976), plaintiffs sought recovery from defendant club and its physician for the death of their son, who died as a result of allegedly negligent diagnosis after being struck by a foul ball. In reversing judgment, the court of appeals held for the plaintiffs, finding that the negligence of the ballpark doctor in failing to ascertain decedent's symptoms necessitated the emergency surgery which resulted in death. This resulted in converting decedent from a patient who probably would have survived without emergency surgery to a patient who had little hope of recovery. The verdict for the club was also reversed by the court of appeals for consideration of the issue of the agency relationship between the parties.

4. In *Cramer* v. *Hoffman*, 390 F. 2d 19 (2nd Cir. 1968), the court found, based on New York law, that an institution was not liable for the negligence of a physician who was an independent contractor exercising his own discretion. The court concluded that there was not an automatic agency relationship established between the university and its physician (see Section 4.23–2).

5. In *Deaner* v. *Utica Community School Dis.*, 297 N.W. 2d 625 (Mich. Ct. App. 1980), an action was brought for damages suffered by plaintiff during wrestling class when a vertebrae injury resulted in his quadriplegia. The circuit court granted summary judgment for the defendant school district and the defendant doctor who had examined and approved plaintiff for wrestling. On appeal, the court held that summary judgment could not be granted to the doctor because issues of fact had to be decided. The court also ruled that the school district was immune from tort liability.

6. Bill Walton sued the NBA Portland Trail Blazers' team doctor, Dr. Robert Cook, and 20 other unnamed physicians of the Oregon City Orthopedic Clinic. The suit alleged medical malpractice in failure to diagnose a foot fracture, negligent prescription of drugs, and failure to provide Walton with information concerning the true nature and extent of the injury. The suit asked for $632,000 in lost wages and medical expenses and $5 million in general damages. The Trail Blazers were not a party to the suit, which was finally settled out of court for an undisclosed amount.

In another case arising from Walton's injuries during his tenure with the Trail Blazers, the owner of the San Diego Clippers, Irv Levin, sued Walton and his two physicians, who certified the center's fitness when Walton signed a multimillion dollar contract with the Clippers in 1979. In his suit, which sought $17 million in damages, Levin alleged that Drs. Ernest Vanderweghe and Anthony Daly knew or should have known of a congenital bone defect in Walton's left foot before certifying the center's fitness for the NBA.

Levin sought repayment of Walton's salary for the time he was on the Clipper's roster; relief from the obligation to honor the rest of the contract (at the time Levin filed his suit, Walton had retired from the league due to his injuries); $2 million for the loss of Kermit Washington and Kevin Kunnert, the players sent by the Clippers to the Trail Blazers in compensation for signing free-agent Walton; and $10 million in punitive damages (see Section 4.24, Note 1).

7. For potential tort liability of hospitals and athletic trainers, see *Gregory Taylor* v. *New England Patriots Football Club, Inc. and Norwood Hospital* (Mass. Dist. Ct.) (see Section 4.24, Note 1[f]).

8. In *Welch* v. *Dunsmuir Joint Union High School District*, 326 P. 2d 633 (Cal. Ct. App. 1958), a doctor at a high school football game was sued for negligence (see Section 4.22–3).

9. Otis Armstrong, a former running back with the Denver Broncos of the National Football League, filed suit against Dr. James F. McElhinney and six other doctors. Armstrong hurt his neck in a 1980 game, and the examining doctors concluded that he suffered from a congenital deformity of the spine. Since this condition could lead to paralysis, Armstrong took the doctor's advice and retired from football. Armstrong subsequently contended that the doctors fraudulently concealed Armstrong's real injuries. These were discovered in an extensive neurological examination in February 1983, which revealed a cranial fracture, three fractures of the cervical spine, a fractured spinal column, and five rib fractures. For further information, see *New York Times*, November 3, 1983, p. 21.

10. In *Robitaille* v. *Vancouver Hockey Club*, 3 W.W.R. 481 (Ct. App. B.C. 1981), a personal injury suit was brought by a professional hockey player against his club for injuries incurred while playing hockey. A shoulder injury had caused the plaintiff recurring problems, which the club's management and physicians attributed to mental rather than physical causes. The plaintiff was ordered to play while injured and sustained a minor spinal-cord injury during a game. He requested medical attention, but his requests were ignored since he was perceived as having mental problems. Further play aggravated the minor injury, and the plaintiff suffered a spinal-cord injury that left him permanently disabled.

On appeal, the court upheld the award of damages to the plaintiff against the defendant club. The court reasoned that the club had breached its duty to ensure the fitness, health, and safety of its players. The club was also found to have exercised sufficient control over the doctors to make the doctors employees of the club. Therefore, the club was liable for the acts of the doctors.

11. Hall of Fame linebacker Dick Butkus sued the Chicago Bears in 1974 for breach of contract, claiming club management did not provide him with the medical and hospital care promised him in his contract with the team. In his suit, Butkus charged that the team had been negligent in the treatment of his right knee by prescribing extensive injections of cortisone that caused irreparable damage to his knee.

Butkus also sued five physicians, including the Bears' team physician, for negligent treatment of his right knee. He charged the doctors "carelessly, negligently and improperly over-prescribed and over-administered various drugs and medications" and that it was known or should have been known that such treatments "would further aggravate the knee and/or endanger the chance of recovery." Butkus and the Bears settled out of court for $600,000 in 1976.

12. Bill Enyart, a former NFL player, sued the Oakland Raiders team physician for alleged malpractice during the 1973 football season. Enyart alleged that the team and its physicians allowed him to continue playing instead of prescribing surgery. The case was settled out of court.

13. Paul Hofer, a former NFL player, sued the San Francisco team physician for alleged malpractice during the 1982 football season. Hofer alleged that the team and its physicians improperly treated his knee, which caused him to end his career prematurely. The case was settled out of court.

14. In *Gillespie* v. *Southern Utah State College*, 669 P. 2d 861 (Utah 1983), plaintiff sought recovery against the college for its trainer's negligence in treating a sprained ankle. The court held that the trainer was not a "guarantor" of good results, because that standard would result in anyone treating an injury to be "strictly" liable for any adverse consequences resulting from the treatment.

15. For further information, see the following articles:
(a) "Malpractice on the Sidelines: Developing a Standard of Care for Team Sports Physicians," 2 *Journal of Communication and Entertainment Law* 579 (Spring 1980).
(b) "Duty and Standard of Care for Team Physicians," 18 *Houston Law Review* 657 (May 1981).

4.27 Liability of Officials, Referees, and Umpires

Officials, referees, and umpires of athletic contests may incur tort liability as a result of their actions or inactions on the playing field. There have been two distinct areas in which suits against officials, referees, and umpires have been filed. The first is the personal injury area in which the official, referee, or umpire is sued for negligence. The second is the judicial review of a decision by an official, referee, or umpire. Since only a handful of cases have been filed, and many of those have been settled, there are only a few reported cases. However, this area has the potential for increased litigation.

In the personal injury area, the official, referee, or umpire may be sued for negligence in a number of different situations. The first is when there has been a failure to inspect the premises. In *Thompson* v. *University of South Carolina*, the plaintiff contended that the referee should have inspected the line stripe to determine whether it had chemical content, which later caused injury to the plaintiff. The second situation is when the official, referee, or umpire fails to keep the playing area free of equipment and/or spectators. For example, an official, referee, or umpire may be held liable when a ball or bat is left on the playing field, and a player trips, falls, and is injured by the equipment. Another possible case involves an injured spectator who might contend that the official, umpire, or referee should have stopped play on the field and moved the spectators from the playing area. A player who is injured by running into a spectator might contend that the official, referee, or umpire should have moved the spectator away from the playing area. The third situation involves weather conditions; an injured player may contend that the official, referee, or umpire should not have started the game or that the game should have been stopped due to potentially hazardous conditions.

The fourth situation involves equipment that causes injury to a player. It could be argued that the official, referee, or umpire has the responsibility to prevent a player from participating with obviously ill-fitting equipment. An area that is more likely to result in successful litigation is when a referee does not enforce a rule, such as a new "no jewelry" rule in basketball. This litigation may be successful because it involves a "safety rule." The fifth and final situation involves a potential claim that the official, referee, or umpire did not

properly enforce the rules of the game. For example, the plaintiff may allege that because the basketball referees failed to control the game by not calling fouls or technical fouls, a much rougher game was played, which was the proximate cause of the injuries suffered by the plaintiff.

The area of judicial review of an official's, referee's, or umpire's playing-field decision is one that has been infrequently litigated. The general rule is that courts are reluctant to review playing-field decisions, whether they have been judgmental errors or a misapplication of a rule. An example of a judgmental error occurred in *Georgia High School Ass'n.* v. *Waddell* (see Section 4.27–3); however, the court refused to reverse a referee's critical error in a football game. An example of a misapplication of a rule and incorrect scorekeeping occurred in Missouri, where a suit was brought by players against officials. The players contended that they were deprived of an opportunity to show their skills to college coaches and that therefore their chances of obtaining a college scholarship were reduced. Plaintiffs have not been successful in this area, and the courts may continue to show their reluctance to become involved in decisions on the playing field, unless fraud or corruption can be found (see *Wellsville-Middleton School Dist.* v. *Miles*, in Section 4.27–3, note 4).

4.27–1 Intentional and Negligent Injury

Dillard v. Little League Baseball Inc., 390 N.Y. 2d 735 (App. Div. 1977)

Plaintiff Harold L. Dillard was requested by defendant Lyncourt Little League to umpire Little League baseball games on a volunteer basis. On May 22, 1970, he was asked to umpire a game for which he was provided an umpire's mask and chest protection but no shin guards or groin protection. During the course of the game, after plaintiff had called time out and while plaintiff was looking away, the pitcher threw a pitch in the direction of home plate, which struck the plate, bounced upward, and struck plaintiff in the groin, causing serious injuries. Plaintiff asserted negligence on behalf of Little League Baseball for failing to provide him with the proper protective equipment and negligence on the part of the nine-year-old pitcher, John Rotondo, for failing to heed his call for time out and for pitching the ball while plaintiff's attention was turned from the plate.

The New York Appellate Division affirmed the dismissal of the claims against each of the parties on the grounds that Dillard had assumed the risk of such injury when he volunteered to umpire the game. The court relied on *McGee* v. *Board of Education of City of New York*, 226 N.Y.S. 2d 329 (App. Div. 1962), and other cases in which the courts had held that voluntary participants assume the risk of those dangers that are inherent in the sport and to any open and obvious condition of the place in which the sport is carried on. Quoting *McGee*, at 331, the court held that "Players, coaches, managers, referees and others who, in one way or another, voluntarily participate must accept the risks to which their roles expose them."

The court found that awareness of the general scope of the risk, combined with the skill and experience of the actor, are primary factors that influence whether the assumption-of-risk doctrine will be applied. In this regard, Dillard had coached Little League two years before his injury. The court found that he must have been aware of the wild pitches and errant play of nine-year-olds. It could not be said that it would be a total surprise for a nine-year-old to throw a pitch after the umpire had called time out and before the umpire had called for a resumption of play. This kind of mistake, error, inadvertence, or lack of attention was, in the court's view, to be fully expected during

the heat of a game from so young a player.

The court found no merit in Dillard's claim against Little League Baseball, Inc. for failing to provide him with a protective cup. The court found that the risk of being struck in the groin while umpiring is reasonably foreseeable. It also found that it was not the common practice for the Little League to provide a protective cup, nor in light of the fact that such equipment is usually personal to the wearer, not unreasonable for them not to do so. Additionally, the court noted that Dillard could have provided himself such protection at little expense.

Carroll v. State of Oklahoma, 620 P. 2d 416 (Crim. App. 1980)

Jerry Carroll was the assistant coach for the losing team at a baseball tournament. After the game, the home plate umpire was at the trunk of his car in the parking lot changing uniforms in preparation for the next game and surrounded by a group of players from the losing team who were criticizing his calls. Carroll approached the group, exchanged words with the umpire, and struck him on the jaw with his fist. For this, Carroll was convicted of "assault upon a sports officiary" under Oklahoma Laws 1978, chapter 204, paragraph 1 and sentenced to pay a fine of $425 plus costs. The statute provided:

> Every person who, without justifiable or excusable cause and with intent to do bodily harm, commits any assault, battery, assault and battery upon the person of a referee, umpire, timekeeper, coach, player, participant, official, sports reporter or any such person having authority in connection with any amateur or professional athletic contest is punishable by imprisonment in the county jail not exceeding six (6) months or a fine not exceeding Five Hundred Dollars ($500) or by both such fine and imprisonment.

Carroll challenged the statute on the grounds of being unconstitutionally vague. The Oklahoma Court of Criminal Appeals, however, held that the statute clearly indicated which persons were covered and also apprised the public of what particular conduct was deemed punishable, for which reasons the court found the statute neither unconstitutionally vague and indefinite nor void for uncertainty.

The appeals court also held that the trial court did not err in excluding evidence of a letter from the district attorney's office stating that Carroll would not be prosecuted for this charge as irrelevant. The issue of relevance is discretionary with the trial court, and without a showing of abuse of that discretion, the appeals court held that the allegation was without merit.

McGee v. Board of Education of City of New York, 226 N.Y.S. 2d 329 (App. Div. 1962)

Plaintiff James T. McGee was a high school teacher employed by defendant board of education. He was assigned by the school principal to assist the regular coach of the student baseball team. While conducting a practice session on fielding bunts, McGee stood behind the pitcher's mound and advised the pitcher what to do. The practice session was conducted on a temporary diamond, and the bases were only about 80 feet apart instead of the regulation 90. As a result, the pitcher stood on a direct line between first and third bases. McGee was hit in the face by a ball thrown to third base by the first baseman, who made the throw when the head coach called out for him to "Get the man at third." The first baseman had not on previous occasions during the practice routine thrown the ball to third base, but rather had returned the ball to home plate for the next bunt.

Plaintiff brought suit against the board of education on the grounds that their employee, the head coach, was negligent in conducting the practice session on a diamond of non-regulation size, without adjusting precautions, and in suddenly directing a departure from the practice routine while plaintiff's attention was distracted, thereby exposing him to the hazard of being hit by a thrown ball.

In reversing a lower court judgment for the plaintiff, the appeals court held that, generally, players, coaches, managers, referees, and others who voluntarily participate in an athletic event must assume the risks to which their roles expose them. Though there may be occasions when a participant's conduct amounts to such careless disregard for the safety of others as to create risks not fairly assumed, what the scorekeeper may regard as an "error" was not, according to the court, the equivalent, in law, of negligence.

The court rejected plaintiff's contention that the nonregulation size and layout of the diamond materially increased the hazards to which plaintiff was exposed. On the contrary, the court found, had plaintiff been standing in the same relative position on a regulation diamond, he would have been even closer to a direct line between the two bases. In any event, the court found, because of the prospect of inaccurate or wild throws by these high school players, it could not be said that the position taken by plaintiff appreciably affected the hazards involved.

The court also rejected plaintiff's contention that the head coach's calling out to "Get the man on third" when plaintiff was unprepared amounted to actionable negligence. The court found that the head coach had no occasion to warn plaintiff, or anyone else, to watch out for the throw. In such situations, the court held, the athlete's maxim, "keep your eye on the ball" applies.

Moreover, the court found that, even in supervising relatively inexperienced players, the head coach had no reason to expect that the first baseman would follow his instructions blindly and throw the ball in the direction of one who was visibly inattentive. It might, in the court's view, have been reasonably anticipated that the first baseman would shout out to alert plaintiff as he threw. But in the excitement of the play, the court held, even the first baseman's action can hardly be deemed negligent. His failings, at least, can only be deemed an "error," albeit an unfortunate one.

NOTES _____

1. In *McHugh* v. *Hackensack Public Schools*, Docket No. 1–2542–81 (N.J. Super. Ct. 1983), the plaintiff high school basketball referee was attacked by an unknown fan after a state tournament game and sought damages from the public school system because it did not provide a safe place to work, safe entry and exit before and at the conclusion of the game, or proper supervision of the crowd. The Superior Court of New Jersey, Law Division, granted a summary judgment because the school was immune under the New Jersey Tort Claims Act. Defendant appealed, but the decision was affirmed. The effect of the decision was to leave New Jersey sports officials without legal remedy from unknown attackers at games they officiate.

2. In *Toone* v. *Adams*, 262 N.C. 403, 137 S.E. 2d 132 (1964), an umpire brought suit against a coach and a club for injuries received from an attack by a fan (see Section 4.22–4).

4.27–2   Liability for Player Injury

Cap v. Bound Brook Board of Education (N.J. Super. Ct.), (Settled 1984)

New Jersey high school football officials were sued for permitting a game to be played on a field that was in an unsafe and unplayable condition, which allegedly was a factor in a player's being paralyzed from an injury suffered during the contest. The case was dismissed against the officials and settled with the other co-defendants.

Nash v. Borough of Wildwood Crest, Docket No. 1–6624–77 (N.J. Super. Ct.) (Settled 1983)

Recreational softball catcher was injured when he was struck in the eye by a softball while catching without wearing a protective mask. In slo-pitch softball, a catcher is not required to wear a mask. Player sued and alleged that the umpire should have given him his mask and then officiated from behind the pitcher's position rather than from behind home plate. The case was settled prior to trial with the plaintiff receiving $24,000.

Pantalowe v. Lenape Valley Regional High School, Docket No. L–40828–26 (N.J. Super. Ct.) (Settled 1976)

A New Jersey high school wrestling referee was sued for allegedly allowing a wrestler to continue an illegal hold on his opponent, which resulted in a paralyzing injury. The case was settled, with a monetary award, before coming to trial.

Smith v. National Football League, No. 74–418 Civ. T–K (D. Fla.)

Bubba Smith, an All-Pro and former National Football League (NFL) Lineman-of-the-Year, sued the head linesman and one of the attendants of the down markers, along with the Tampa Bay Sports Authority and the NFL, for $2.5 million. Smith alleged that a collision he had with the down marker caused a serious knee injury that ended his career. He claimed that the collision was a result of neglect on the part of the defendants, including the failure of the sports official to properly supervise and move the markers and the use of dangerous equipment. The jury in the case's second trial found no liability on the part of the defendants, after an earlier trial ended in a mistrial because the jury was deadlocked (5–1) for the defendants.

NOTES _____

1. In *Carabba* v. *Anacortes School Dist. No. 103*, 435 P. 2d 936 (Wash. 1967), a referee was found negligent for failure to detect an illegal wrestling hold (a full-nelson), which caused serious injury. The court held that the referee was an employee of the school district (see Section 4.23–1).

2. Referees may be liable for failure to supervise. See *Crohn* v. *Congregation B'nai Zion*, 317 N.E. 2d 637 (Ill. Ct. App. 1974), in Section 4.23–1, Note 8.

3. An umpire may be liable for allowing a game to proceed on an unfit playing surface. For example, in *Forkash* v. *City of New York*, 277 N.Y.S. 2d 827 (1966), *cert. denied*, 87 S. Ct. 1482 (1977), plaintiffs sought recovery for injuries sustained in a collision in the outfield during a city-sponsored softball game. In reversing the trial court's dismissal, the appellate division held that whether the players could recover was a question for jury determination. The evidence presented proved that the collision took place after one plaintiff tripped over a piece of glass. The umpire furnished by the city had been advised that the outfield was not in playing condition but had directed that the game proceed.

4. Promoters will not be liable for all actions of a referee employed by them. For example, in *Ulrich* v. *Minneapolis Boxing and Wrestling Club, Inc.*, 129 N.W. 2d 288 (Minn. 1964), plaintiff, a 77-year-old wrestling spectator, sought recovery from defendant promoter for injuries sustained when a referee, hired by the defendant, whirled about and struck him. In reversing the trial court's judgment for the plaintiff, the Minnesota Supreme Court held that the injury was not proximately caused by the promoter's alleged failure to provide adequate crowd supervision, by the exposure of the referee to plaintiff when he left the ring, or by the employment of a referee with dangerous propensities.

4.27–3   Review of Officials' Decisions

Bain v. **Gillespie, 357 N.W. 2d 47 (Iowa Ct. App. 1984)**

James Bain was one of the referees for the Big Ten Conference basketball championship game between the University of Iowa and Purdue University. Bain made a controversial call late in the game that allowed a Purdue player to make a free throw that gave his team a last-minute victory.

John and Karen Gillespie operated the Hawkeye John's Trading Post, a novelty store in Iowa City. The Gillespie's store specialized in University of Iowa sporting goods and souvenirs. A few days after the elimination of Iowa from the basketball championship of the Big Ten Conference, the Gillespie's began

selling T-shirts in their store, ". . . showing a man with a rope around his neck and was captioned 'Jim Bain Fan Club'."

Bain sued the Gillespie's for injunctive relief, and for actual and punitive damages for their sale and marketing of the T-shirts. The Gillespie's counterclaimed and alleged that Bain's officiating of the Iowa–Purdue game was, ". . . below the standard of competence required of a professional referee. As such it constituted malpractice. . . ." The Gillespie's claimed actual damages for loss of potential earnings and exemplary damages, ". . . because Bain's calls as a referee were baneful, outrageous, and done with a heedless disregard for the rights of the Gillespies."

The trial court which granted summary judgment to Bain found that the Gillespies had no rights and dismissed their counterclaim. The trial court stated that:

This is a case where the undisputed facts are of such a nature that a rational fact finder could only reach one conclusion — no foreseeability, no duty, no liability. Heaven knows what uncharted morass a court would find itself in if it were to hold that an athletic official subjects himself to liability every time he might make a questionable call. The possibilities are mind-boggling. If there is a liability to a merchandiser like the Gillespies, why not to the thousands upon thousands of Iowa fans who bleed Hawkeye black and gold every time the whistle blows? It is bad enough when Iowa loses without transforming a loss into a litigation field day for "Monday Morning Quarterbacks." There is no tortious doctrine of athletic official's malpractice that would give credence to Gillespie's counterclaim.

The Gillespies appealed the lower court ruling. The National Association of Sports Officials filed an amicus curiae brief on Bain's behalf. The Iowa Appeals Court upheld the lower court's grant of summary judgment. The court noted that:

. . . we find the trial court properly granted the summary judgment against the claim. It is beyond credulity that Bain, while refereeing a game, must make his calls at all times perceiving that a wrong call will injure Gillespies' business or one similarly situated and subject him to liability. The range of apprehension, while imaginable, does not extend to Gillespies' business interests. Referees are in the business of applying rules for the carrying out of athletic contests, not in the work of creating a marketplace for others. In this instance, the trial court properly ruled that Bain owed no duty. Gillespies have cited no authority, nor have we found any, which recognizes an independent tort for "referee malpractice." Absent corruption or bad faith, which is not alleged, we hold no such tort exists.

Georgia High School Ass'n. v. Waddell, 285 S.E. 2d 7 (Ga. 1981)

The Georgia Supreme Court ruled that it does not possess authority to review the decision of a high school football referee. The high school referee admitted that he made an error in not awarding an automatic first down on a roughing-the-kicker penalty, which might have been determinative of the final outcome for the game.

The trial court had overturned the referee's ruling, based on a school's property right that the game of football be played according to the rules. The court ordered the game to be replayed from the point of the referee's error.

In reversing, the Georgia Supreme Court reasoned: "We now go further and hold that courts for equality in this state are without authority to review decisions of football referees because those decisions do not present judicial controversies."

NOTES

1. In *Tilelli* v. *Christenberry*, 1 Misc. 2d 139, 120 N.Y.S. 2d 697 (1953), a New York court upheld the decision of a boxing referee and a ringside judge. The New York Athletic Commission had ordered that the voting card of the judge who they suspected was involved in an illegal gambling scheme be changed. The New York court overruled the commission and upheld the referee's decision and held that the suspicion of illegality was not sufficient enough grounds for the court to intercede in the decision and substitute its judgment for that of the assigned judge.

2. In *State* v. *State Athletic Commission*, 272 Wis. 191, 75 N.W. 2d 451 (1956), the Wisconsin Supreme Court upheld the State Athletic Commission's decision that under its rules it had no authority to reverse a boxing referee's alleged failure to properly administer the "knock-down" rule.

3. In *Wellsville-Middleton School District* v. *Miles* (Mo. Cir. Ct. 1982) (Unreported), a Missouri circuit court dismissed, for failure to state a claim, a lawsuit filed by the plaintiff school district against the Missouri State High School Activities Association. The plaintiff claimed that the official scorer in a state tournament basketball game had made a mistake in scoring, which ultimately led to plaintiff's team losing the contest.

4. In *Wellsville-Middleton School District* v. *Miles*, Docket No. 406570 (Mo. Cir. Ct. 1982) (Unreported), a companion case to above case was filed by three players on the affected high school team. The plaintiffs alleged that the referee negligently failed to follow proper procedures, which ultimately affected their opportunity to secure college athletic scholarships. The plaintiffs dropped their suit after dismissal of the companion suit.

4.27–4 Worker's Compensation

Gale v. Greater Washington Softball Umpires Ass'n., 311 A. 2d 817 (Md. Ct. App. 1973)

The court found that an umpire is not an employee of an umpire association, but an "independent contractor," thereby precluding the umpire from receiving worker's compensation under Maryland law.

Ehehalt v. Livingston Board of Education, 371 A. 2d 752 (N.J. App. Div. 1977)

The court held that a basketball official is not an employee of the school he or she regularly officiates at but an "independent contractor," thereby precluding the official from recovering worker's compensation under New Jersey law.

Ford v. Bonner County School District, 612 P. 2d 557 (Idaho 1980)

The Idaho Supreme Court found that a high school football official injured while officiating is an employee of the school district and entitled to worker's compensation under Idaho law.

Daniels v. Gates Rubber Co., 479 P. 2d 983 (Colo. Ct. App. 1970)

The Colorado Court of Appeals found that a member of the Umpires Association of Colorado, who was struck in the eye by a softball while umpiring a corporate recreational league game, was not an employee of the corporation for purposes of the Colorado worker's compensation statute. The appeals court thus affirmed a lower court decision, which had overturned a worker's compensation judge's decision to award the umpire compensation.

Warthen v. Southeast Oklahoma State University, 641 P. 2d 1125 (Okla. Ct. App. 1981)

The court held that a university drama professor, who was also a licensed basketball referee and was asked by a dean to referee an intramural fraternity game, had sustained a compensable injury when he died while officiating the game.

NOTES ————————————————————

1. In California, the issue of worker's compensation for officials has been dealt with legislatively by specifically excluding amateur sports officials from eligibility for compensation. An "employee" excludes:

(j) Any person, other than a regular employee, performing officiating services relating to amateur sporting events sponsored by any public agency or private, nonprofit organization, who receives no remuneration for these services other than a stipend for each day of service no greater than the amount established by the State Board of Control as a per diem expense for employees or officers of the state pursuant to Section 13920 of the Government Code. The stipend shall be presumed to cover incidental expenses involved in officiating, including, but not limited to, meals, transportation, lodging, rule books and courses, uniforms, and appropriate equipment.

(k) Any student participating as an athlete in amateur sporting events sponsored by any public agency, public or private nonprofit college, university or school, who receives no remuneration for such participation other than the use of athletic equipment, uniforms, transportation, travel, meals, lodgings, scholarships, grants-in-aid, or other expenses incidental thereto. [California Labor Code S 3352 (j) and (k)]

2. For a further discussion of tort issues and the officiating, see the following:

(a) "Liability for Injury to or Death of Umpire, Referee, or Judge of Game or Contest," 10 *ALR* 3d 446.

(b) "Tort Liability of Public Schools and Institutions of Higher Learning for Injuries Resulting from Lack or Insufficiency of Supervision," 38 *ALR* 3d 830.

(c) "Tort Liability of Public Schools and Institutions of Higher Learning for Accidents Occurring during School Athletic Events," 35 *ALR* 3d 725.

(d) "Modern Status of Doctrine of Sovereign Immunity as Applied to Public Schools and Institutions of Higher Learning," 33 *ALR* 3d 703.

3. For further information, see the following articles:

(a) Dedopoulos and Narol, "A Guide to Referee's Rights and Potential Liability," 16 *Trial* 18 (March 1980).

(b) Dedopoulos and Narol, "Kill the Umpire: A Guide to Referee's Rights," 15 *Trial* 32 (March 1979).

(c) "Sports Violence Lawsuits Erupt," *National Law Journal*, February 9, 1981, p. 1.

(d) Narol and Dedopoulos, "The Official's Right to Sue for Game-Related Injuries," *National Law Journal*, June 7, 1982, p. 26.

(e) "A Worker's Compensation Casebook," *Referee*, September 1983.

(f) "The Official's Potential Liability for Injuries in Sporting Events," *National Law Journal*, September 6, 1982, p. 20.

(g) "Sports Liability: Blowing the Whistle on the Referees," 12 *Pacific Law Journal* 937 (1981).

(h) Narol, "Player Injuries: Baseball Umps' Potential Liability," *Referee*, February 1984.

(i) "Jury Awards Damages to Referee in Suit Against T-Shirt Firm," *NCAA News*, April 3, 1985, p. 12.

(j) "A Better Game Heightens Pressure on Officials," *New York Times*, March 3, 1985, p. J1.

(k) "Knight Suspended for Game," *New York Times*, March 3, 1985, p. J7.

4.30 Application of Legal Principles to Defects in Equipment

The "failure to warn" theory is established upon the finding of a manufacturer's duty to warn of known latent and potentially injury-causing defects in the design of equipment. The extent of the duty is based on the age and experience of the user and of the reasonably foreseeable use of the product.

In order to maintain a suit based on a theory of a "failure to warn," the plaintiff must prove that the product is defective in design. The test most commonly used to determine the defectiveness of a product design was adopted from *Barker* v. *Lull Engineering*, 10 Cal. 3d 413 (1978). The test itself has two distinct prongs. The first prong involves looking at the product to see if it has failed to perform as safely as an ordinary consumer would expect. The determination would include whether the product was used as intended, was misused, or was tampered with. If the plaintiff cannot directly establish that the product failed to perform adequately, this part of the test may be satisfied by the second prong, which involves proving that the product's defective design proximately caused the injury and that the benefits of the challenged design do not outweigh the inherent risk of danger created by the design. To aid in its determination as to both defectiveness and resultant liability, the court will also consider factors such as the nature of the sport, the type of injury, the amount of use or foreseeable misuse, the degree to which the particular risk is greater due to the defect, and the current state of the art in designing an absolutely safe product.

Dudley Sports Co. v. Schmitt, 151 Ind. App. 217, 29 Ind. Dec. 285, 279 N.E. 2d 266 (1972)

Dudley Sports Co. filed this appeal of a personal injury products liability case after a jury had awarded $35,000 to the plaintiff Schmitt.

On March 24, 1965, Danville High School purchased an automatic baseball pitching machine, which was designed and manufactured by Commercial Mechanism, Inc. for Dudley Sports Co. The machine consisted of a frame and an open-extended metal throwing arm. No protective shield guarded the throwing arm. When the arm reached a 10 o'clock energized position and it received a ball, energy was released from the coiled spring and transmitted to the arm to pass through a clockwise pitching cycle at a high rate of speed, coming to rest in a 4 o'clock position. The machine was capable of delivering a powerful blow when in the 10 o'clock position, even when it was unplugged.

The machine, when uncrated, included a parts list, assembly instructions, and a tool to deactivate the spring. The only warning instruction contained in the crate was a general warning tag that said: "Warning! *Safety First.* STAY CLEAR OF THROWING ARM AT ALL TIMES. No operating instructions were included in the crate.

The machine was stored, unplugged and behind locked doors in a locker room. However, the two adjoining locker rooms, with inside entrances to the locker room where the machine was stored were not secured and allowed access to the machine.

The day after the pitching machine was delivered, Schmitt, a student, was sweeping the locker room where the machine was stored, as he had done in the past at the request of the coaching staff. He stated that as he approached the front of the machine, he heard a whistling noise and a pop. He was hit in the face by the throwing arm and received extensive facial injuries. The injuries consisted of deep cuts and lacerations on Schmitts's upper lip, nose, and above his right eyebrow, a partially severed nose, a crushed left sinus cavity, skull bone exposure, and two chipped teeth.

Schmitt brought action against the high school, Em-Roe, the sporting goods retail company, and Dudley alleging negligence. A verdict of $35,000 was reached by the jury in favor of Schmitt. Dudley appealed the case.

It was the court's opinion that a vendor that holds itself out as the manufacturer of a product and labels the product as such must be held to the same standard of care as if it were in fact the manufacturer. When a vendor puts its name exclusively on a product, in no way indicating that it is a product of another, the public is induced to believe that the vendor was the manufacturer of the product. The mechanism manufactured by Commercial Mechanism, Inc., of Kansas City, bore Dudley's name only, as did the advertising material.

The court also found that Dudley was negligent in the design, manufacture, and sale of the machine. The ability to operate the machine while unplugged as a result of even a slight vibration was considered a latent danger, which could only be discovered through an examination of the machine, combined with knowledge of the engineering principles that produce the action of the machine. This knowledge is not ordinarily possessed by a 16-year-old high school boy, especially one who had never seen the machine before.

The court held that the law required a supplier of an imminently dangerous product to warn all who may come in contact with it of any concealed danger, regardless of whether privity of contract applies. Dudley did include a general warning tag in the shipping crate, but no warning was given of the latent dangers of the machine. Dudley also stressed that the pitching machine was stored behind locked doors in a locker room. However, the court held that Dudley overlooked that the hallway doors to adjacent locker rooms, with inside entrances to the room with the machine, were unlocked.

The decision of the trial court was affirmed.

Heldman v. Uniroyal, Inc., 53 Ohio App. 2d 21, 371 N.E. 2d 557 (1977)

A professional women's tennis player, Julie Heldman, injured her knee during the Wightman Cup tennis championships between Great Britain and the United States and brought suit for damages against Uniroyal, Inc., which supplied the tennis court surface for the matches.

Heldman claimed that the defendant made certain representations and warranties, both expressed and implied, (1) that its Roll-a-Way tennis court was free of dents, hollows, soft or rough spots and was safe and fit for its intended use as a tennis court playing surface; and (2) that Uniroyal installed and maintained one of these surfaces for the Wightman Cup, but contrary to their representations and warranties, the court began to blister and come

loose at the seams, making footing uncertain and play unreasonably hazardous. Heldman, who represented the United States, further alleged that while she was engaged in a tennis match with Virginia Wade of Great Britain on August 21, 1971, she suffered severe injury to her left knee as a direct and proximate result of the defective condition of the playing surface and the breach of the representations and warranties of Uniroyal. Heldman's second claim for relief was in the form of a negligence action.

Uniroyal's answer was in the form of a general denial. The company also alleged that any injury to Heldman was proximately caused or contributed to by her own negligence and also was the result of Heldman's assuming the consequences of a known risk.

The Wightman Cup matches were held August 21, 22, and 23, 1971, with three days of practice sessions preceding the competition. Heldman testified that during her practice sessions on August 19, 20, and 21, she noted bubbles on the court and bad bounces as a result. She complained to her team captain, Carol Graebner, who attempted to have the problem solved.

Graebner corroborated Heldman's testimony as to the condition of the court and stated that the problematic condition persisted through the week of competition. Graebner stated in her opinion that the court was hazardous and asked Uniroyal to fix the surface. She later allowed her players to play on the court, however, because she had been assured by Uniroyal that the court had been repaired.

Heldman added that she did not refuse to play because she was a professional and the show must go on; she thought the bubbles would simply produce bad bounces, but did not consider them to be an injury risk. She stated that she had spoken to Graebner and had been advised that the court was fixed but was never told that the court was hazardous.

Rain was a major contributor to the problem with the court surface. According to the expert witness for the plaintiff, the rainfall of .04

inches on August 21 before the Wade–Heldman match was sufficient to put water under the tennis court if total adhesion of the surface had not been accomplished. An additional .33 inches of rain fell after the Wade–Heldman match.

Wade testified for Heldman through deposition, but the defense counsel objected to the testimony because it related to events occurring two days subsequent to the accident. Conditions had changed so dramatically between the date of the accident (August 21) and August 23 as to make the testimony of Wade irrelevant and highly prejudicial. Wade did not expressly testify in regard to the condition of the court on August 21 other than to state that there were bubbles and bad bounces. Most of her testimony was concerned with conditions of the court on August 23.

The trial court overruled the objection on the grounds that the dramatic changes referred to were issues for the jury to decide and that the condition of the court two days subsequent to the event upon which the case was brought was relevant in that it tended to show what the condition was on the date of the accident.

The Uniroyal representative present at the Wightman Cup Matches, in testifying for the defense, revealed that he had inspected the court before the Wade–Heldman match and found no bubbles or dead spots. He stated that there was some moisture present, but all puddles had been soaked by towels. He did admit, however, that rain had flooded the court before the Wade-Heldman match on August 23 and that the presence of bubbles and dead spots on the court would be dangerous for the players.

The jury returned a verdict for Heldman in the amount of $67,000, stating that Uniroyal was negligent for failing to properly secure the tennis surface it provided and that this negligence was a proximate cause of Heldman's injury.

The appeals court reversed the decision of the trial court and remanded the case. Two key errors were cited. Foremost was the failure of the trial court to instruct the jury on the defense of assumption of risk. In order for the trial court to be required to charge the jury on assumption of risk, there must be evidence that the plaintiff either had actual knowledge of the danger or that the danger was so patently obvious that the party may be taken to have knowledge of it and there must be a voluntary exposure to the hazard. The appeals court ruled that there was sufficient evidence to raise a jury question as to whether Heldman assumed the risk by playing in the match with Wade. The court came to this conclusion based on the fact that (1) Graebner testified that she told all the members of her team that the court was in a dangerous condition, (2) Heldman was a professional tennis player and is presumed to know the various risks attendant with playing on different types of surfaces, and (3) a higher degree of knowledge and awareness is imputed to professional tennis players than to average non-professional tennis players as to the dangers in playing on a synthetic tennis court having obvious bubbles on the playing surface.

The other major error centered on the Wade testimony. The appeals court ruled that the admission of the Wade evidence regarding the condition of the court on August 23 was a prejudicial error. The general rule is that testimony of conditions of a place subsequent to the date of an accident is not admissible into evidence to demonstrate conditions at the time of the accident unless the conditions were the same on both dates. The appeals court held that the large additional rainfall after the Wade–Heldman match significantly altered the conditions of the tennis court and allowed the jury to speculate or infer that the conditions were the same on August 21 as on August 23, without any evidence to demonstrate that the conditions were the same.

Byrns v. Riddell, Inc., 113 Ariz. 264, 550 P. 2d 1065 (1976)

Plaintiff Kevin Byrns brought a products liability action against Riddell, Inc., a manufacturer of football helmets, after he sustained a head injury in an interscholastic football contest in October 1970. The case reached the Supreme Court of Arizona in 1976, following a directed verdict for Riddell at the superior court level and an appeal in which the court of appeals' decision was vacated.

Byrns, a member of the Alhambra High School football team, was injured in a play in which he received an "on-side" kick. Originally, the Phoenix Union High School District was included as one of the defendants, but Byrns's complaint was later amended to include Riddell and to dismiss the claim against the school district.

The Arizona Supreme Court examined evidence relating to proof of strict liability in tort to determine whether the trial court properly granted Riddell's motion for a directed verdict. Byrns alleged that the helmet manufactured by Riddell was defective by design and manufacture and was therefore inherently dangerous to the user. Byrns also claimed that Riddell failed to provide a warning of the defects.

Two witnesses for Byrns stated that the helmet was defective and unreasonably dangerous in that it "bottomed out" or transmitted the energy of the blow to the wearer's head without absorbing a sufficient amount of energy within the helmet-cushioning system itself. The witnesses testified that the forehead, rear, and temporal areas of helmet model TK–2 had failed a crash-helmet standard known as Z90.1. Riddell countered with evidence relating to the inapplicability of the Z90.1 standard to the testing of football helmets. Riddell further argued on its motion for a directed verdict that there was neither proof of a defect in the TK–2 helmet nor proof that any such a defect caused Byrns's injury.

The parties also disagreed on the location of Byrns's head injury. Byrns's physicians believed that the injury — a swelling of the right temporal lobe of the brain — resulted from a blow in front of the right ear and behind the right eye, or from a blow to the opposite side

of the head. Riddell argued — and the trial court agreed — that the game films showed a top-of-helmet to top-of-helmet impact. Riddell concluded, therefore, that since the top of the helmet was not defective and since the film showed a blow to the top of the head, the injury was not caused by a defect in the helmet. Based on these findings, the trial court directed a verdict for defendant, holding that "since the strongest (top) portion of the helmet was not tested, it would be mere speculation on the part of the jury to determine that the top of the helmet was defective."

The supreme court's decision to reverse and remand the trial court's directed verdict for Riddell was based on an analysis of the term "unreasonably dangerous," as applied to the theory of strict liability set forth in the *Restatement (Second) of Torts*, section 402A (1965). The court in this case finally subscribed to a factor analysis approach developed in *Dorsey v. Yoder Co.*, 331 F. Supp. 753 (E.D. Pa. 1971), *aff'd.*, 474 F. 2d 1339 (3rd Cir. 1973). To determine if a defect is unreasonably dangerous, it considered:

... (1) the usefulness and desirability of the product, (2) the availability of other and safer products to meet the same need, (3) the likelihood of injury and its probable seriousness, (4) the obviousness of the danger, (5) common knowledge and normal public expectation of the danger (particularly for established products), (6) the avoidability of injury by care in use of the product (including the effect of instructions or warnings), and (7) the ability to eliminate the danger without seriously impairing the usefulness of the product or making it unduly expensive.

The supreme court found that the doubts raised by Byrns as to the possibility of a defect in the design of the TK–2 helmet, the place of impact, and the presence of the defect at the time the helmet left the seller's hands merited a ruling in his favor. Accordingly, it held that the trial court had erred in directing a verdict in Riddell's favor and thus reversed and remanded the case.

Everett v. Bucky Warren, Inc., 380 N.E. 2d 653 (Mass. 1978)

Plaintiff Everett was a student at the New Prep School and a member of its hockey team. Owen Hughes, the hockey coach at New Prep, distributed helmets to the team that were of a three-piece design, consisting of three plastic pieces. One piece covered the back of the head, one the forehead, and one the top of the head. The pieces were attached to each other by elastic straps. The straps expanded, depending on the size of the wearer's head, leaving gaps as large as ¾ of an inch. Other helmets available on the market were of one-piece design and had no gaps. The helmets in question were purchased by Hughes, the authorized representative of New Prep School, from Bucky Warren, Inc., a sporting-goods retailer. Warren had purchased the helmets from T. E. Pender, the designer and manufacturer.

During a game with the Brown University freshman team, Everett threw himself in front of a Brown player's shot in an attempt to block it. The puck penetrated a gap in the helmet, struck Warren above the right ear, and caused a skull fracture. The injury required placement of a steel plate in Warren's skull and caused recurring headaches. Warren brought suit against the school, manufacturer, and retailer for negligence, and against the manufacturer and retailer on the grounds of strict liability. The trial court jury found for the plaintiff on all counts and awarded $85,000 in damages. However, the trial court judge then directed a verdict in favor of the defendants on the negligence counts, holding that as a matter of law, Everett assumed the risk of injury. The judge did, however, enter a judgment for the plaintiff of $85,000 on the strict liability counts. Plaintiff then appealed the court's finding on the negligence counts, while defendants Pender and Warren appealed the court's finding on the strict liability counts.

The appeals court first dealt with the negligence counts, finding that Pender should have known that a puck could penetrate the gaps in the helmet and was therefore negligent in the design of the helmet. The court also held that New Prep school was negligent since the coach, Hughes, was a person with substantial experience in the game of hockey who should be held to a higher standard of care. Hughes should also have been aware of the availability of one-piece helmets, which he conceded in his testimony were safer than the Pender helmets. Warren had not appealed on this point.

Having upheld the jury's decision, the appeals court then dealt with the trial court's finding that Everett had assumed the risk of injury. The appeals court found that it could not be clearly established that Everett was aware of the possible injuries that could result from the gaps in the helmet, and therefore had not assumed the risk of injury. The directed verdict in favor of defendants on the negligence counts was reversed with instructions.

On the question of strict liability, the court first held that Pender and Warren could be found liable for manufacturing the helmet with an "unreasonably dangerous design." The court stated that factors that should be weighed when determining whether a particular design was reasonably safe included:

> . . . the gravity of the danger posed by the challenged design, the likelihood that such danger would occur, the mechanical feasibility of a safer alternative design, the . . . cost of an improved design, and the adverse consequences to the product and the consumer that would result from an alternative design.

The court held that the gravity of the danger was demonstrated by Everett's injuries, that helmets of the one-piece design were safer than the Pender model and were being manufactured prior to Everett's injury, and that while more expensive than the Pender helmets, the one-piece helmets were not economically unfeasible. The court upheld the finding of strict liability in favor of plaintiff.

Garcia v. Joseph Vince Co., 148 Cal. Rptr. 843 (Cal. Ct. App. 1978)

Plaintiff Garcia brought a products liability suit in California Superior Court against Joseph Vince Co. and American Fencers Supply Co., seeking damages for an eye injury suffered during a college fencing match. The court entered a judgment of nonsuit, from which plaintiff appealed.

Garcia's injury occurred during a fencing match when the sabre of his opponent penetrated Garcia's face mask and caused an eye injury. Although Garcia's suit sought damages from American Fencers Supply Co. as the manufacturer of the blade, the supplier of the sabre in question was not clearly known, because the opponent's team purchased equipment from both defendant firms. Following the injury, the sabre was placed in a bag, along with the rest of the team's equipment, thus making it impossible to identify. Immediately following the injury, the coach of each team examined the tip of the blade, with one coach declaring that the blade tip was much thinner than regulation, and the other asserting that it complied with regulations then in effect.

Because of the failure to identify the blade, the identity of the manufacturer was also unclear, although it could reasonably be asserted to be one of the defendant firms. In an annotation in 51 A.L.R. 3d, 1344, 1349 on product liability, the applicable rule stated in part, "Regardless of the theory which liability is predicated upon . . ., it is obvious that to hold a manufacturer, or seller liable for injury caused by a particular product, there must first be proof that the defendant produced, manufactured, sold, or was in some way responsible for the product . . ." Since it could not be clearly established which firm was the supplier of the blade, neither could be held responsible.

Plaintiff argued that *Summers* v. *Tice*, 33 Cal. 2d 80, 199 P. 2d 1 (Cal. 1948), established a precedent whereby the defendants bore the burden of proving nonliability. The court held that *Summers* differed in that the defendants in that case had both been shown to have acted negligently and thus had both violated a legal duty to Summers. Garcia had failed to show that either manufacturer had violated a duty to him, thus creating a fundamental difference with *Summers*. The court held instead that *Wetzel* v. *Eaton Corp.*, 62 F.R.D. 22 (D.C. Minn. 1973), in which the court held for the defendants because the failure to identify the manufacturer invited a ruling based on conjecture, correctly stated the appropriate rule.

In regard to the face mask, the court held that it was clearly established that Vince was the manufacturer. The mask was a three-weapon mask — that is, it could be used for foil, epee, or sabre fencing. The interior of a three-weapon mask has horizontal and vertical bars that supply added protection for the wearer. A sabre mask has no such protection; it has only a wire mesh covering, which is also found on the three-weapon mask. The mask worn by the plaintiff was found to comply with the specifications for international and lesser competitions; it not only met but exceeded the requirements for strength and durability. Two experts testified that the mask in question had no defects in manufacture and that penetration could not be effected by a legal, standard weapon. Another expert further testified that a sabre with sharp corners could penetrate any legal fencing mask. None of the expert testimony was rebutted.

In view of a lack of evidence suggesting any defect in the manufacture of the mask, plaintiff's case rested solely on an allegation of a defective design. In order to establish a prima facie case based on defective design, the plaintiff must establish that (1) the product was used in an intended or reasonably foreseeable manner and (2) the product design was the proximate cause of the injury. The court found that the mask was not intended to serve as protection against a sharp-tipped blade and that no evidence was presented to indicate that the mask was the proximate cause of the injury. In addition, the court found that a fencer had knowledge that fencing is a dangerous sport and thus assumed the risk of injury.

A judgment of nonsuit may be granted only when, after plaintiff's evidence is given all the value to which it is legally entitled, there is still insufficient substantiality to support a verdict for the plaintiff. The court held that plaintiff had failed to meet this test and affirmed the lower court's ruling.

Nissen Trampoline Company v. Terre Haute First National Bank, 332 N.E. 2d 820 (Ind. Ct. App. 1975)

An action was brought by Terre Haute on behalf of a thirteen-year-old boy who was injured on a small circular trampoline which was used instead of a diving board. The boy landed with only one foot on the trampoline, and the other foot became entangled in the cables supporting the bed of the trampoline. Eventually, the boy's leg had to be amputated above the knee. The product was marketed without any warnings or instructions for use.

The trial court jury ruled for Nissen, but the judge overruled and awarded Terre Haute a new trial. The court of appeals affirmed the trial judge's decision. The court reasoned that:

> Under the doctrine of strict tort liability as expressed in Restatement (2d) Torts, § 402A, and adopted in Indiana, it is well established that a product, although virtually faultless in design, material, and workmanship, may nevertheless be deemed defective so as to impose liability upon the manufacturer for physical harm resulting from its use, where the manufacturer fails to discharge a duty to warn or instruct with respect to potential dangers in the use of the product. Generally, the duty to warn arises where the supplier knows or should have known of the danger involved in the use of its product, or where it is unreasonably dangerous to place the product in the hands of a user without a suitable warning. However, where the danger or potentiality of danger is known or should be known to the user, the duty does not attach . . .

NOTES _____

1. Liability for failure to warn can be based on constructive knowledge. For example, in *Filler* v. *Rayex Corp.*, 435 F. 2d 336 (7th Cir. 1970), plaintiff baseball player sued defendant sunglass manufacturer in negligence, strict liability, and breach of implied warranty of fitness for a particular purpose, when the glasses shattered into his eye. The court of appeals, in affirming the district court, held that the defendant, who advertised the glasses as protection against baseballs, had constructive knowledge of the danger and was liable for failure to warn and for breach of warranty of fitness for a particular purpose.

2. There may be no duty to warn of known dangers. For example, in *Garrett* v. *Nissen Corp.*, 498 P. 2d 1359 (N.M. 1972), plaintiff, an experienced trampoline user, sued defendant trampoline manufacturer in negligence for *failure to warn* of the danger involved in landing incorrectly. The New Mexico Supreme Court affirmed summary judgment for defendant, holding there is no duty to warn of dangers known to a user of a product, either in strict liability or negligence.

3. There may also be a duty to warn of known dangerous conditions. In *Pleasant* v. *Blue Mount Swim Club*, 128 Ill. App. 2d 277, 262 N.E. 2d 107 (1970), plaintiff diver sought recovery from defendant pool owner for injuries sustained in hitting the bottom of the pool after diving off a diving board. In affirming the trial court's judgment in favor of plaintiff, the appellate court held that the evidence supported a finding that the water level of the pool had been lowered to an extent that it constituted a dangerous condition, which was brought about by defendant's back-floating process and that manager and lifeguards were negligent for failure to warn of the danger present.

4. The following two cases are examples of negligent design:

(a) In *Standard* v. *Meadors*, 347 F. Supp. 908 (N.D. Ga. 1972), plaintiff water-skier sought recovery from defendant designer and manufacturer of speed boat for injuries sustained when the boat propeller severed her leg while she was in the water waiting to be towed. In denying defendant's motion for summary judgment, the district court held that the allegation that the boat was negligently designed so that the prow (front of the boat) obscured the forward view of the operator and that propeller was manufactured so that it would not stop upon contacting a person in the water, stated a claim upon which relief could be granted under Georgia law.

(b) In *Hauter* v. *Zogarts*, 120 Cal. Rptr. 681 (1975), plaintiff sought recovery for injuries sustained when he was hit on the head by a golf ball following a practice swing with a golf training device that was described by the manufacturer as "completely safe, ball will not hit player." In affirming the decision for the plaintiff, the California Supreme Court held that the plaintiff was entitled to recover on theories of false representation, breach of express and implied warranties, and strict liability in tort based on defective design.

5. A mere change in design is not sufficient to establish

the existence of a defect. In addition, misuse of a product may preclude liability. In *Gentemen* v. *Saunders Archery Co.*, 355 N.E. 2d 647 (Ill. Ct. App. 1976), plaintiff archer sought recovery under strict products liability against the manufacturer of "string silencers," which broke when he used them and injured him. In affirming a jury verdict for the defendant, the appellate court held that the evidence was sufficient to warrant a reasonable belief that the change in design did not establish the existence of a defect in the product and that the plaintiff had misused it.

6. A breach of warranty can cause liability. For example, in *Salk* v. *Alpine Ski Shop*, 115 R.I. 309, 342 A. 2d 622 (1975), plaintiff skier sought recovery from defendant ski manufacturers for injuries sustained in a fall. In affirming a directed verdict for defendant, the Rhode Island Supreme Court held that there was no jury question presented as to the negligence of ski manufacturer, since there was no competent evidence that the failure of the bindings to release actually caused the injury. Furthermore, the plaintiff failed to show a breach of express warranty where the skier did not establish that the advertisement of the manufacturer warranted that its bindings would release in every situation presenting a danger to the user's limbs.

7. In *Halbrook* v. *Oregon State University*, Case No. 16–83–04631, (Or. Cir. Ct. 1983) (pending), an action was brought by the estate of Scott O. Halbrook for $2,500,000 in actual and $2 million in punitive damages against a number of defendants.

On March 2, 1982, Halbrook was participating in an Oregon State University baseball practice on an Astroturf field when he collided with another player, fell to the ground, and struck his head. As a result of his injuries, Halbrook died on March 5, 1982.

Plaintiff alleged that defendants Oregon State University and the Oregon State Board of Higher Education were responsible for the proper selection, installation, maintenance, and repair of the athletic field surface. More specifically, they failed to hire a competent and qualified installer for the Astroturf, they failed to adequately supervise the activities of the installer hired, and they failed to perform adequate shock absorbency tests upon the Astroturf when they knew or should have known that continued use would diminish its shock absorbency characteristics.

Plaintiff alleged that the Astroturf sold by defendant Monsanto was in a defective condition, was unreasonably dangerous, and created an unreasonable risk of harm because it was too hard and without adequate cushioning effect. In addition, Monsanto marketed it without adequate warnings to the average user. Plaintiff also sued Matrecon, who sold the asphalt which was placed under the Astroturf, under many of the same theories that were alleged against Monsanto.

8. The National Operating Committee on Standards for Athletic Equipment (NOCSAE) was organized to research

and test equipment to develop new standards and improve existing ones. It was founded in 1969 in an effort to reduce death and injuries through the adoption of standards and certification for athletic equipment. Fatalities decreased by more than 50 percent by 1977, after a 37-year high of 36 deaths in 1968. The number of cases of permanent quadriplegia from neck injuries in the early 1970s averaged 35 per year, and these were reduced to 7 in 1977, 9 in 1978, and 7 in 1979.

The helmet standards were published in 1973, and manufacturers and reconditioners have improved their equipment to meet NOCSAE standards.

An area of recent study was face masks for ice hockey helmets. Research in the future may include helmets for lacrosse and equestrian competition.

9. In *Harper* v. *Liggett Group, Inc.*, No. 246, 652, (La. Dist. Ct. 1983) (unreported), plaintiff was blinded when his opponent's racquet separated from its safety strap. He sued the manufacturer, importers, distributors, and "K-Mart," and was awarded $924,300.

10. In May 1984, a New Jersey high school football player, who had been paralyzed in a 1979 game, settled a lawsuit for at least $1.3 million. The plaintiff, who had been injured from a head-first tackle, had brought the suit against the board of education, his former head football coach, and Riddell, Inc., of Illinois, manufacturer of the helmet plaintiff was wearing. The plaintiff had contended that there was a lack of any requirements or standards in the hiring of the football coach. The plaintiff was awarded $50,000 a year for the rest of his life, as well as a one-time payment of $247,000 and another $550,000 payment to be distributed over a 25-year period. See "Paralyzed Man Settles for $1 Million-Plus in High School Football Tragedy," *Newark Star Ledger*, May 1, 1984, p. 13.

11. In 1973, there were 17 manufacturers of football helmets. However, by 1983, this number had dropped to four manufacturers. The primary cause for the decline in manufacturers was attributed to insurance costs, litigation costs, and the view that manufacturers have unlimited "deep pockets" to be used for injury awards. See "Helmet Lawsuits Threaten Prep Football," *Sporting News*, July 4, 1983, pp. 13, 34.

12. In *McCormack* v. *Lowe & Campbell Athletic Goods Co.*, 144 S.W. 2d 866 (Mo. Ct. App. 1940), plaintiff, a high school pole vaulter, was seriously injured when a pole vault manufactured by defendant broke during a vault. Plaintiff alleged that the defendant was negligent in its failure to inspect and test the pole. The court of appeals affirmed the trial court decision in favor of plaintiff. The court held that if defendant had tested the pole in a reasonably careful manner, the defect would have been discovered and the injury averted. The court noted that the manufacturer of a product was under a duty to exercise ordinary care to test the product to determine whether or not it had a defect that rendered it unsafe when applied to its intended use. The court also noted that a

failure to perform such duty rendered the manufacturer liable to a person injured in consequence of such failure while using such article in the ordinary and usual manner.

  13. For further information, see the following articles:
  (a) "Torts on the Courts," 14 *Trial* 28 (June 1978).
  (b) "Sports Products Liability: It's All Part of the Game — Or Is It?" 17 *Trial* 58 (November 1981).

4.40   Insurance

This section examines two topics that athletic administrators should be aware of and concerned with: liability insurance and the NCAA's catastrophic injury plan.

4.41   Liability Insurance

Liability insurance is a form of indemnity whereby the insurer undertakes to indemnify or pay the insured for a loss resulting from legal liability to a third person. It is based on contract law principles. Liability insurance protects the insured against financial loss resulting from lawsuits brought against them for negligent behavior. Common subjects for liability insurance are risks from use of the premises, from faulty products, from use of vehicles, and from the practice of professions.

Insurance is effective even if the insured has committed a minor violation of the criminal law. A minor violation will not invalidate the insurance or deprive the defendant of protection. An insurance policy may be invalidated, however, if the insured's conduct was so outrageous that it would be against public policy to indemnify it. The policy may also be invalidated if the insured misrepresented a material fact at the time of the application for the policy.

One of the standard provisions in any insurance policy requires the insured to fully cooperate with the insurance company by providing full and accurate information about the accident. It may also require the insured to attend any trial, to take part in a trial if required, and to do nothing for the injured party that would harm the insurance company. A violation of any of the above requirements would relieve the insurance company of liability to the injured third party.

The term "subrogation" is oftentimes found in tort cases. Subrogation is the right of a party who has paid legal obligation of a third party to recover from payment from the third party who has benefited. As an example, suppose a fan is injured at a baseball stadium by a foul ball that passed through a hole in the netting behind home plate, and the hole was there because of the negligence of a third-party contractor who damaged the screen during installation. If the liability insurer for the stadium pays the injured fan, it has a right, under subrogation, to sue the installer for negligence, just as if the insured stadium owner had filed suit.

Typically, insurance policies contain a clause that entitles the insurer to be subrogated to its insured cause of action against any party who caused a loss which the insurer paid. The insurer can also be entitled to subrogation in the absence of an express contractual provision. This is called equitable subrogation. In some states, however, an insurance company must prove it was not a gratuitous payment in order to recover under equitable subrogation.

One response by institutions and sports associations to the increasing number of lawsuits brought under a tort liability theory is to use insurance. The National Federation of High School Associations and many state high school athletic associations and their member schools have adopted a liability/lifetime catastrophe medical plan. The plan covers the National Federation of State High School Associations, the state high school athletic/activities association, their member schools and school districts, and member school administrators, athletic directors, coaches, and trainers. This type of insurance allows the student-athlete who suffers a catastrophic injury to waive suit and opt for life-long medical, rehabilitation, and work-loss benefits. The philosophy behind the insurance plan is to provide needed benefits to the injured student-athlete without the time, costs, and risks that accompany litigation. If the injured student-athlete opts for the benefits provided by the insurance policy, the institution saves time, expense, and a possible award in favor of the plaintiff. The NCAA attempted to implement a similar policy for the 1984–85 academic year, but it was subsequently delayed. The NCAA implemented an insurance policy beginning in the 1985–86 academic year.

NOTES

1. In *Strong* v. *Curators of the University of Missouri*, 575 S.W. 2d 812 (Mo. Ct. App. 1979), plaintiff parents sued for the drowning death of their six-year-old child in a swimming pool run by defendant university. The defense of sovereign immunity was raised, and the plaintiffs countered with the argument that insurance precluded the necessity for and therefore abrogated the doctrine of sovereign immunity. The court held that the purchase of liability insurance will not, by itself, abrogate the doctrine.

2. In *Fustin* v. *Board of Education of Community Unit Dist. No. 2*, 242 N.E. 2d 308 (Ill. Ct. App. 1968), the court held that the purchase of insurance did not waive immunity and that the availability of insurance did not affect liability in any way (see Section 4.13, Note 3).

3. In *Bourque* v. *Duplechin*, 331 So. 2d 40 (La. Ct. App. 1976), an injured softball player sued for personal injuries, and the defendant insurance company defended on the grounds that its policy did not cover the policyholder for intentional injury to others. The court ruled that the company was liable, however, because the policyholder had acted negligently in injuring the plaintiff while attempting to break up a double play, even though he did not intend to injure (see Section 4.21).

4. In *Gaspard* v. *Grain Dealers Mutual Insurance Co.*, 131 So. 2d 831 (La Ct. App. 1961), the court applied the doctrine of subrogation. The insurer successfully defended a suit against the minor son of its policyholder on assumption-of-risk grounds (see Section 4.21).

5. Seattle Public Schools liability insurance coverage and premiums from 1975–76 through 1981–82 are as follows:

Year	Coverage	Premium
1975–76	$5,500,000	$143,935
1976–77	3,500,000	201,429
1977–78	3,500,000	120,000
1978–79	3,500,000	249,000
1979–80	5,500,000	185,000
1980–81	20,500,000	191,500
1981–82	30,500,000	117,500

6. For more information on the National Federation of State High School Associations' insurance plan, see "Injured Athletes Face Dilemma: Cash or Court?" *Wall Street Journal*, March 22, 1985, Sec. 2, p. 27.

4.42 The NCAA's Catastrophic Insurance Plan

The NCAA has instituted a catastrophic injury protection insurance plan. The NCAA's plan, which can be adopted by institutions on an individual basis, should accomplish two important objectives. First, by having this type of insurance, it should reduce — if not eliminate — the number of worker's compensation cases filed against NCAA member institutions (see Section 2.15–1[b]). The NCAA's insurance policy is similar to worker's compensation in that it provides benefits to catastrophically injured student-athletes, regardless of fault. And the benefits offered by the NCAA program may be more attractive than a successful worker's compensation claim. For instance, a student-athlete's claim for worker's compensation benefits may have to be litigated. Second, the NCAA insurance policy assists the catastrophically injured student-athlete by providing benefits immediately, without time delays, without the costs of litigation, and without the uncertainties involved in litigation. The benefits are provided for the lifetime of the student-athlete, and the plan is extremely helpful to the student-athlete who is injured without fault. The student-athlete who is catastrophically injured as a result of negligence of an institution or one of its employees still has the alternative of litigating the case and not collecting the benefits provided by the NCAA policy.

The injured student-athlete and his representative must weigh the possibility of success in litigation, which goes to the ultimate issue of whether the employee(s) and/or institution was negligent, the likely amount of the award, the time delay involved in litigating the case (since the student-athlete may be without benefits until a decision is rendered in his favor and all appeals are exhausted), and the adverse impact of going through the litigation process for the injured student-athlete and his family (see NCAA Catastrophic Injury Policy, Exhibit 4–2).

NOTE _____

1. For a detailed, year-by-year account of the NCAA's efforts to develop a catastrophic injury insurance policy, see "Membership Gets Enrollment Forms for Catastrophic Injury Insurance," *NCAA News*, March 6, 1985, pp. 1, 16.

4.50   Waiver and Release of Liability

In the law, there are often competing legal theories in a given situation. The resolution of this type of situation is usually based on the preeminent public policies existing at the time the conflict arises. In the area of waivers and releases of liability, the principles underlying tort law and contract law conflict. Waivers or exculpatory agreements are contracts that alter the ordinary negligence principles of tort law. Contract law is based on the concept that any competent party should have the absolute right to make a binding agreement with any other competent party. The only limit to this right to make such agreements is that a contract is invalid if it violates public policy. For example, a contract in which the parties agree to commit a crime would violate an important public policy of preventing crime.

Tort law, on the other hand, is based on the concept that a party should be responsible for negligent or intentional actions that cause injury to another person. Waivers then create a conflict between the right to enter into contracts and the policy that one should be held responsible for injury-causing negligent actions. The conflict between contract and tort law principles has been resolved in favor of the general rule that waivers and releases of liability will be enforceable unless they would frustrate an important public policy or unless the party getting the waiver was unfairly dominant in the bargaining process. This resolution is based on the general contract law principle that a party is bound by the signing of a contract unless there is evidence of fraud, misrepresentation, or duress.

In order to determine if fraud, misrepresentation or duress exists, a court will consider whether the party waiving rights knew or had an opportunity to know the terms. This does not mean that merely failing to read or to understand a waiver and release of liability will invalidate it. The terms must be conspicuous and not be hidden in fine print so that a careful reader is unlikely to see it. The waiver and release of liability must also result from a free and open bargaining process. If one party forces the other to agree to a waiver, it may not be enforceable. The last consideration is whether the express terms of the waiver and release of liability are applicable to the particular conduct of the party whose potential liability is being waived. In other words, the language of the waiver must be clear, detailed, and specific (see Exhibits 4–3 through 4–7).

A waiver and release of liability will not be enforceable if it attempts to insulate one party from wanton, intentional, or reckless misconduct. Therefore, only liability for negligent actions can be waived.

If the person signing the waiver and release of liability is a minor, other issues are raised. Under basic contract principles, a minor may repudiate an otherwise valid contract. A problem may also arise when parents sign waivers for their children (see *Doyle v. Bowdoin College v. Cooper International, Inc., infra*). Courts are attempting to define whether the rights of minors may be waived by their parents.

For competent adult participants in sports activities, waivers and releases of liability are generally upheld. However, questions are frequently litigated in the area of auto racing. Courts have reasoned that a driver is under no compulsion to race; therefore the driver has the ability to make a decision whether to race and to assume all the risks inherent in auto racing. This may include risks that arise as a result of negligence on the part of the event's promoters. Courts are generally more reluctant to enforce a waiver and release of liability signed by spectators, based on the theory that they may not be as familiar with the risks of auto racing or that they are entitled to assume that the premises are reasonably safe.

Doyle v. Bowdoin College v. Cooper International, Inc., 403 A. 2d 1206 (Me. 1979)

Leonard Doyle brought this action on behalf of his son Brian, who was injured while playing floor hockey at a clinic sponsored by defendant college and directed by the school's agents, Sidney Watson and Charles Holt, Jr. Plaintiff alleged that the defendant's negligence resulted in his son's injury when a plastic hockey blade flew off the end of another boy's stick, hitting Brian in the eye, shattering his glasses, and damaging his retina so as to leave him partially blind.

The case was tried before a jury, which concluded that the negligent conduct of defendants Bowdoin College and Holt proximately caused Brian's injuries and thus awarded plaintiff $50,000 in damages. The defendants appealed this judgment, contending that the presiding justice erred in ruling (1) that certain documents were *not* releases relieving defendants of all liability for future injuries Brian might suffer as a result of defendants' negligent conduct and (2) that another document was not a contract of indemnification obligating Brian's mother to reimburse defendants for any liability they might incur regarding injuries sustained by Brian at the clinic.

The Maine Supreme Judicial Court affirmed the trial court's decision. First, it noted that courts have traditionally disfavored contractual exclusions of negligence liability, citing Prosser, *Law of Torts*, section 68: "If an express agreement exempting the defendant from liability for his negligence is to be sustained, it must appear that its terms were brought home to the plaintiff . . ." The court found that the documents executed by Leonard and Margaret Doyle contained no express reference to defendants' liability for their own negligence. The court noted that: "Though the documents state that Bowdoin College will not 'assume' or 'accept' any 'responsibility' for injuries sustained by Brian . . . whether 'assumed' or 'accepted,' or not, Bowdoin College has such responsibility in any event because the *law* had imposed it."

The court applied the same rationale in its interpretation that the second document was *not* an agreement to indemnify Bowdoin College, its employees, or its servants for injury or damages caused by their negligence. The court held that: "The majority view is that such indemnity agreements should not be executed to indemnify the indemnitee's own negligence unless the language is clear and unambiguous." Because of the fact that the document executed by Brian's mother did not contain such terms as "indemnify," "reimburse," or "hold harmless" and the prevailing unfavorable judicial attitude toward indemnification of a party for damage (injury) caused by that party's own negligence, the court held that this document was not an agreement of indemnity.

Based on its review of the exclusion of liability and indemnification documents, the appeals court denied defendants' appeal and affirmed the lower court's judgment in the Doyles's favor.

Williams v. Cox Enterprises, Inc., 283 S.E. 2d 367 (Ga. Ct. App. 1981)

Plaintiff Williams had entered a 10,000-meter Georgia Peachtree Road Race and brought a class action lawsuit charging sponsors of the event with negligence in failing to adequately warn participants of the inherent dangers involved in running the race. In the 1977 race, Williams suffered heat stroke, heat prostration, renal failure, and other disorders, which resulted in the permanent impairment of some of his motor functions.

STATE MUTUAL LIFE
ASSURANCE COMPANY OF AMERICA

440 LINCOLN STREET

WORCESTER · MASSACHUSETTS 01605

(Hereinafter Called The Company)

certifies the Participating School named in the Specifications below is insured under Policy No. 59004 issued to The National Collegiate Athletic Association (NCAA) (herein called the Policyholder).

Subject to all the provisions of the policy, the Company will pay the benefits described in this Certificate.

This Certificate replaces any certificate previously issued covering the Participating School.

The provisions of this and the following pages are part of this Certificate.

SPECIFICATIONS

Policy No.: 59004

Participating
School:_____   Certificate No.:_____

Effective Date of Participation:_____

Initial Coverage Period:_____

School Classification (Premium Class):_____

Initial Premium for Coverage Period:_____

Richard J. Baker   *Frederick Leslie*

Secretary   President

SECTION 1

Insurance Provided

The Company will pay Net Economic Loss sustained by an Insured Person arising out of a Covered Accident.

Exhibit 4-2

SECTION 2

Insured Person

An Insured Person is a student who is:

(a) attending a school which (i) is a member of The National Collegiate Athletic Association (NCAA), and (ii) has, by payment of the premium, and submission of a completed Enrollment Form, elected to participate under the policy; and

(b) participating as (i) a player on an athletic team in an Intercollegiate Sport sanctioned and recognized by the Participating School, or (ii) a student coach, student manager or student trainer of such a team formally listed as such on the official roster, or (iii) a cheerleader officially recognized as such by the Participating School.

"Intercollegiate Sport" means a sport: (1) which has been accorded varsity status by the Participating School; (2) which is administered by such School's department of intercollegiate athletics; (3) for which the eligibility of the participating student athletes is reviewed and certified in accordance with NCAA legislation, rules or regulations and (4) which entitles qualified participants to receive the Participating School's official awards.

Effective Date of Participation By School

Insurance under this policy will become effective for a School on:

(a) August 1, 1985 if the School has paid the required annual premium; or

(b) if later, the date the properly completed Enrollment Form and required annual premium are received by the Company; or

(c) if elected by the School in the Enrollment Form, on the August 1st next following the date the completed Enrollment Form and the required annual premium are received by the Company;

except that, a School may elect, by completing an Enrollment Form and paying the required premium in advance, to become insured hereunder prior to August 1, 1985, subject to approval by the Company. The actual Effective Date of Participation will be as indicated in the SPECIFICATIONS in the Certificate of Insurance issued to the Participating School.

SECTION 3

Covered Accident

A Covered Accident is an accident:

(a) which occurs to an Insured Person while insured under the policy; and

(b) which results in bodily injury sustained by the Insured Person during his or her participation in scheduled games or organized supervised practice sessions or official team or group travel in connection therewith (but excluding any personal travel to and from practice sessions or games); and

(c) on account of which the Insured Person, within one year of the date of the accident (i) incurs Medical or Dental Expenses in an amount exceeding $25,000 or (ii) sustains Presumptive Disability.

In no event will a Covered Accident be construed to include an illness or disease, or natural causes, (except where the illness or disease results from the Covered Accident).

Presumptive Disability

If an Insured Person suffers one or more of the losses shown below as a result of, and within one year of the date of, an accident which meets the requirements of (a) and (b) of the definition of Covered Accident above, such accident will be considered a Covered Accident under the policy, and the Deductible Amount will be presumed satisfied.

The losses which will create Presumptive Disability are the entire and irrecoverable loss of:

(a) speech; or
(b) hearing in both ears; or
(c) sight of both eyes; or
(d) use of both hands; or
(e) use of both feet; or
(f) use of one hand and one foot.

Ancillary Illness or Injury

If an Insured Person, during the period he or she is receiving benefits hereunder in connection with a Covered Accident, incurs Medical Expenses for unrelated accidental bodily injuries which are sustained, or illness which first manifests itself, while he or she is receiving benefits hereunder in connection with a Covered Accident, such Medical Expenses, which are in excess of the Deductible set forth below, will be considered Medical Expense as defined herein, and will be reimbursed as Medical Expense, subject, however, to the Deductible and the Maximum Lifetime Benefit set forth below:

Deductible (Each Ancillary Illness or Injury):

(a) $5,000 of Medical Expense applicable to each ancillary illness or injury; or
(b) the total of Other Collectible Benefits applicable to the ancillary illness or injury;
whichever is greater.

Maximum Lifetime Benefit for all Ancillary Illnesses or Injuries:

$100,000 of reimbursement for Medical Expense.

SECTION 4

Net Economic Loss

Net Economic Loss means Economic Loss minus: (a) the Deductible Amount, or (b) Other Collectible Benefits, whichever is greater.

"Economic Loss" means Medical Expense, Dental Expense, Miscellaneous Expense, Lost Earnings, Rehabilitation Expense, and Special Expenses covered under this policy.

A Medical, Dental or Rehabilitation Expense will be an Economic Loss covered under the policy only if it is incurred on the recommendation or approval of a doctor attending the Insured Person; it must be medically necessary; and the provider of service must be acting within the scope of his or her license.

A charge for any Economic Loss (except Miscellaneous Expense and Lost Earnings) will be covered under the policy only to the extent it is reasonable. A charge is reasonable if it is not more than is charged when there is no insurance and it is not more than the prevailing charge in the locality for a like service or supply. A like service is one of the same nature and duration, requiring the same skill and performed by one of similar training and experience. A like supply is one which is the same or substantially equivalent. Locality is the city or town where the service or supply is obtained, if it is large enough so that a representative cross-section of like services or supplies can be obtained. In large cities, it may be a section or sections of the city, if the above criteria can be met. In smaller urban or rural areas it may have to be expanded to include surrounding areas to meet the criteria.

An expense will be deemed incurred when the service or supply is rendered or provided.

"Medical Expense" means the charges: (a) of a professional ambulance service to and from a hospital; (b) of a doctor for medical care; (c) for medical and/or surgical services and medical supplies commonly used for therapeutic purposes and prescribed by a doctor; (d) of a hospital for inpatient services, outpatient services, and emergency room services; and (e) of a qualified nurse for nursing care, including a practical nurse, if under the supervision of a registered graduate nurse, for Home Health Care which follows a period of hospital confinement and which is prescribed by a physician, but only to the extent that such charges do not exceed $30,000 each calendar year; and (f) of an Extended Care Facility for inpatient services which follow a period of hospital confinement of at least five (5) days, provided the confinement in the Extended Care Facility results from the need for further and indefinite medical care and the attending doctor certifies the confinement is medically necessary.

Charges for the treatment of a mental or nervous condition shall be treated as a medical expense only to the extent that the charges do not exceed $50 per visit, and limited to one visit per day and 50 visits per calendar year.

"Dental Expense" means expenses only for repair to sound natural teeth, provided such care is recommended and given by a doctor operating within the scope of his or her license.

"Miscellaneous Expense" means for an Insured Person who is Totally Disabled by a Covered Accident:

> $200 per month (a) commencing on the date the Insured Person becomes Totally Disabled, and (b) continuing so long as the Insured Person is Totally Disabled until his or her Academic Class graduates or if later the end of the academic year in which he or she becomes Totally Disabled by a covered accident.

"Lost Earnings", means for an Insured Person who is Totally Disabled by a Covered Accident:

(1) $1,500 per month increasing at an annual rate of 4%;
(2) commencing on the date the Insured Person's Academic Class graduates or, if later the end of the academic year in which he or she becomes Totally Disabled by a Covered Accident; and
(3) continuing so long as the Insured Person's Total Disability continues.

"Lost Earnings" means for an Insured Person who is Partially Disabled immediately following a period of Total Disability caused by a Covered Accident:

(1) $1,000 per month:

> (a) increasing at an annual rate of 4%;
>
> (b) commencing on the last to occur of:
>
> > (i)   the date the Insured Person's Academic Class graduates, if the Insured Person is then Partially Disabled;
> >
> > (ii) the end of the academic year during which the Insured Person becomes Totally Disabled if the Insured Person is Partially Disabled on the date such academic year ends; or
> >
> > (iii) the date the Insured Person becomes Partially Disabled; and
>
> (c) continuing so long as the Insured Person's Partial Disability continues.

"Other Collectible Benefits" means any reimbursement for or recovery of any element of Economic Loss available from any source whatsoever, excepting gifts and donations, but including, without limitation:

> (a) any group, blanket, franchise, policy of accident and health insurance;
>
> (b) any prepaid service arrangement such as Blue Cross or Blue Shield, individual or group practice plans, or health maintenance organization;
>
> (c) any amount payable for hospital, medical, or other health services for accidental bodily injuries arising out of a motor vehicle accident to the extent such benefits are payable under any medical expense payment provision (by whatever terminology used -- including such benefits mandated by law) of any automobile insurance policy;

(d) any amount payable for services for injuries or diseases related to the Insured Person's job to the extent he actually receives benefits under a Workers' Compensation Law. If the Insured Person enters into a settlement giving up his rights to recover future medical benefits under a Workers' Compensation Law, the policy will not pay those medical benefits that would have been payable except for that settlement;

(e) Social Security disability benefits, except that other collectible benefits shall not include any increase in Social Security disability benefits payable to an Insured Person after he becomes disabled while insured hereunder;

(f) fifty percent (50%) of any recovery from any alleged third-party wrongdoer (including the School at which the Insured Person was a student and any agents thereof), provided, however, this setoff shall not apply to Insured Persons residing in Kansas or attending Participating Schools located in Kansas and shall not apply to Insured Persons residing in other states or attending Participating Schools in other states where this setoff is prohibited by law;

(g) any plan or program solely or largely provided by or through any government action or law to the extent that benefits are payable under such plan or program.

If an Insured Person receives benefits or services from any source described as an "Other Collectible Benefit" for any element of Economic Loss for which he was paid benefits under this policy, the Company shall be entitled to reimbursement in amount equal to the benefit received from such source.

Whether Other Collectible Benefits are available shall be determined as if this policy did not exist and shall not depend upon whether or not timely application therefore is made.

Provided, however, if an Insured Person is covered under a group catastrophic policy issued by another insurance carrier which provides substantially similar benefits to those provided herein and has a deductible applicable to the Insured Person of not less than $25,000, any benefits payable under such policy shall not be treated as other collectible benefits.

"Doctor" means a medical practitioner who provides services or treatment which are within the scope of his license to provide.

"Home Health Care" means nursing care and treatment of an Insured Person in his home as part of an overall extended treatment plan. To qualify, the plan must (a) be established on and approved in writing by the attending physician; (b) the care and treatment must be provided by a hospital certified to provide home health services or by a certified home health care agency; (c) the plan must commence within seven (7) days of discharge from a hospital; and (d) be preceded by a hospital confinement of five (5) days or more.

SECTION 5

Proof and Payment of Claims

Notice of Claim. Written notice of claim must be given to the Company within

30 days after the occurrence or commencement of any loss covered by the policy or as soon thereafter as is reasonably possible. Notice given by or on behalf of the claimant to the Company at its Home Office, Worcester, Massachusetts, or to any authorized agent of the Company, with information sufficient to identify the Insured Person, shall be deemed notice to the Company.

Claim Form. The Company, upon receipt of a written notice of claim, will furnish to the claimant such forms as are usually furnished by it for filing proofs of loss. If such forms are not furnished within 15 days after the giving of such notice, the claimant shall be deemed to have complied with the requirements of the policy as to proof of loss upon submitting, within the time fixed in the policy for filing proofs of loss, written proofs covering the occurrence, the character and the extent of the loss for which claim is made.

Proofs of Loss. Written proof of loss must be furnished to the Company within 90 days after the date of such loss. Failure to furnish such proof within the time required shall not invalidate nor reduce any claim if it was not reasonably possible to give proof within such time, provided such proof is furnished as soon as reasonably possible, and in no event, except in the absence of legal capacity, later than one year from the time proof is otherwise required.

Time of Payment of Claims. Indemnities payable under the policy for any loss other than for Lost Earnings shall be paid as they accrue immediately upon receipt of due written proof of such loss. Subject to due written proof of loss, all accrued Lost Earnings benefits shall be paid monthly.

Payment of Claims. All indemnities payable under the policy will be payable to the Insured Person.

minus

(2) one-half of the gross monthly compensation for personal services earned by the Insured Person during each month in excess of $500.

"Rehabilitation Expense" means reasonable and necessary expenses for physical or occupational rehabilitation.

"Special Expense" means expenses that are approved by a doctor as being appropriate to accommodate physical disability sustained by the Insured Person on account of a Covered Accident, such as expenses for transportation (including a vehicle) or housing adaptation, up to a maximum of $100,000 during the first decade of disability and $50,000 for each subsequent decade of disability.

Provided, however, any amount payable hereunder to or on behalf of an Insured Person for any loss sustained to a vehicle or housing adapted to accommodate the Insured Person's physical disability shall be reduced to the extent of any amount paid or payable to or on behalf of an Insured Person for such loss under any automobile, housing or homeowners insurance policy.

"Totally Disabled" or "Total Disability" means (a) for the period ending with the date the Insured Person's Academic Class graduates, or if later the date the Insured Person ceases attending a Participating School as a full-time student, the inability of the Insured Person to engage in the usual and customary activities of other persons of the same age, and (b) thereafter, it means the inability of the Insured Person to engage in any gainful occupation for which he or she is or may become reasonably fitted by education, training or experience.

Only Total Disability which starts while a person is insured under the policy and which results from a Covered Accident will be covered.

"Partially Disabled" or "Partial Disability" means that although the Insured Person is engaging in some occupation:

    (a) he or she is able to perform some but not all of the important duties of that occupation; and

    (b) he or she is earning less than $2,500 monthly.

No Partial Disability will be deemed to exist so long as the Insured Person's Academic Class has not graduated or he or she is attending School as a full-time student.

Partial disability will be deemed to end when:

    (a) the Insured Person becomes able to perform all the important duties of an occupation in which he is engaged; or

    (b) the Insured Person's average gross monthly income for 6 consecutive months amounts to $2,500 or more per month.

EXCEPT THAT, with respect to an Insured Person who sustained Presumptive Disability, if after recovering from Partial Disability, such person's average gross monthly income falls below $2,500 monthly for three (3) consecutive months, he or she will be regarded as Partially Disabled again and shall qualify for the Lost Earnings monthly indemnity benefit payable for Partial Disability at the same benefit level as the last such benefit paid to the Insured Person hereunder.

"Hospital" means an institution which meets these requirements:

    (a) it is licensed as a hospital;

    (b) it provides facilities for medical and surgical treatment either:

        (1)   on its premises; or

        (2)   through formal written arrangements with other hospitals.

    (c) it provides said treatment primarily to patients confined for more than 24 hours;

    (d) it provides 24 hour nursing services supervised by registered graduate nurses;

    (e) all treatment and services are supervised by doctors; and

    (f) it charges patients for its services.

"Inpatient Services" includes room and board, and hospital services and supplies. The maximum room and board charge that will be considered a medical expense for purposes of this provision will be the hospital's normal semi-private room charge.

"Outpatient Services" includes services and supplies provided by hospital staff in the Outpatient Department of the hospital and where no overnight confinement is required and no room and board charges made.

"Academic Class" means the designation given to an incoming Freshman Class which assumes the members of the Class will complete the course credits required for an undergraduate degree in four (4) consecutive years of undergraduate work.

"Extended Care Facility" means an institution operating pursuant to law which is engaged in providing, for compensation from its patients, skilled nursing care and related services, including physical therapy services, to persons convalescing from illness and who are confined for the purpose beyond 24 hours, and which has facilities for ten (10) or more in-patients, and provides such facilities under the supervision of a doctor and a registered graduate nurse and maintains clerical records on all its patients.

"Deductible Amount" means $25,000 of Medical or Dental Expense incurred by the Insured Person within one year of a Covered Accident for which no benefits will be payable.

Physical Examination and Autopsy. The Company at its own expense shall have the right and opportunity to have the Insured Person, whose injury is the basis of claim, examined by a medical doctor when and as often as it may reasonably require during the pendency of a claim under the policy, and to make an autopsy in case of death where it is not forbidden by law.

Legal Actions. No action at law or in equity shall be brought to recover on the policy prior to the expiration of 60 days after written proof of loss has been furnished in accordance with the requirements of the policy. No such action shall be brought after the expiration of 3 years after the time written proof of loss is required to be furnished.

SECTION 6

General Provisions

Modification. The Policyholder and the Company may modify the policy by rider or endorsement thereon or by an amendment thereto. Consent of Participating Schools or Insured Persons to any modification shall not be required.

Information Required. The Policyholder and Participating School shall furnish to the Company all information which the Company may reasonably require with regard to matters pertaining to the insurance afforded by the policy. All documents, books and records which may have a bearing on the insurance or premiums under the policy shall be open for inspection by the Company at all reasonable times during the continuance of the policy and within one year after its final termination.

Clerical Error. Failure of the Policyholder or Participating School to furnish to the Company proper records of an Insured Person shall not deprive the Insured Person of any insurance; but upon discovery of any such failure, all necessary information shall be furnished and an equitable adjustment of the premiums will be made.

Conformity with State Statutes. Any provision of the policy which, on its effective date, is in conflict with the statutes of the state in which this policy was delivered or issued for delivery is hereby amended to conform to the minimum requirements of such statute.

Workers' Compensation. The policy does not affect any requirement for Workers' Compensation benefits and cannot be used in lieu thereof.

Assignment. The benefits provided hereunder shall not be assigned, transferred, or encumbered without the consent of the Company, and to the extent permitted by law shall be exempt from attachment and otherwise free from claims of creditors of the Insured Person.

Individual Terminations. Insurance with respect to an Insured Person will terminate on termination of the policy for any reason whatsoever or when the Insured Person ceases to be eligible for insurance, whichever first occurs, provided however, that such termination shall be without prejudice to any claim originating prior thereto.

Termination of Participation. Participation in this insurance by the Participating School and all of its Insured Persons shall terminate upon the earlier of:

(1) the termination of the policy by the Company or the Policyholder; and

(2) ten (10) days after the premium due date for which the School has failed to pay the required annual premium.

Williams appealed the trial court's summary judgment in favor of Cox Enterprises, which had argued in court that Williams had assumed risk of injury and that he had signed a waiver-of-liability form. Participants in the race had been required to sign the form, which contained the following language:

In consideration of acceptance of this entry, I waive any and all claims for myself and my heirs against officials or sponsors of the 1977 Peachtree Road Race, for injury or illness which may directly or indirectly result from my participation. I further state that I am in proper physical condition to participate in this event.

The application also described the course as "one of the most difficult 10,000-meter courses in America. . . . Heat and humidity, in addition to hills, make this a grueling 10,000-meter race."

Williams argued that the waiver was invalid because given the size of the event and the fact that the race was so well publicized, it was the public duty of the sponsor to provide and insure the safety of participants. Williams also contended that the waiver was invalid due to the disparity in bargaining positions between runners and race officials. Williams claimed that because running had become so popular and because the Peachtree Road Race was "the only road race of its kind in the Atlanta area," he and other athletes were under "enormous pressure to enter it on whatever terms were offered to them."

The court held that a contractual waiver of liability is valid unless the waiver violates public policy. The court held that a contract cannot be held to be contrary to public policy in Georgia unless it is (1) declared so by the General Assembly, (2) is contrary to good morals and law, or (3) is entered into for an illegal purpose. Since the contract signed by Williams met none of these conditions, it was valid. The court also held that Williams signed the waiver without duress; thus, his claim of disparity in bargaining positions was not valid. The court noted that the application signed by Williams described the race as "grueling" due to heat and humidity. Since Williams admitted to having read the warning and being aware of the danger, the court held that recovery was precluded under the assumption of risk doctrine.

NOTES

1. In *Hewitt* v. *Miller*, 11 Wash. App. 72, 521 P. 2d 244 (1974), a release was held valid when plaintiff scuba diver had read conspicuous language.

2. In *Garretson* v. *United States*, 456 F. 2d 1017 (9th Cir. 1972), a release was held valid when plaintiff amateur ski jumper had read conspicuous language and previously signed similar forms.

3. In *Winterstein* v. *Wilcom*, 16 Md. App. 130, 293 A. 2d 821 (1972), a release signed by the plaintiff drag racer was held valid when the release had been freely entered into and bargained for by two equal parties.

4. Releases by race car drivers are not against public policy. See *French* v. *Special Services, Inc.*, 107 Ohio App. 435, 159 N.E. 2d 785 (1958); *Gervasi* v. *Holland Raceway, Inc.*, 40 App. Div. 2d 574, 334 N.Y.S. 2d 527 (1972); *Solodar* v. *Watkins Glen Grand Prix Corp.*, 36 App. Div. 2d 552, 317 N.Y.S. 2d 228 (1971); and, *Gore* v. *Tri-County Raceway, Inc.*, 407 F. Supp. 489 (M.D. Ala. 1974).

5. Releases are not valid when they are not clearly stated. In *Hertzog* v. *Harrison Island Shores, Inc.*, 21 App. Div. 2d 859, 251 N.Y.S. 2d 164 (1964), plaintiff beach and yacht club member sought recovery for injuries received in a fall from the gangplank leading to the dock on club premises. In granting judgment for plaintiff, the appellate division held that the provision of a membership application, provided that, if accepted, plaintiff would waive his claim for any loss to personality or for personal injury while a member of club was *not sufficiently clear* or explicit to absolve club of its own negligence in regard to plaintiff's fall.

6. Waiver and release form used by the National Football League (see Exhibit 4–3).

7. Waiver and release form which has been used by a National Basketball Association team (see Exhibit 4–4).

8. A second waiver and release form which has been used by a National Basketball Association team (see Exhibit 4–5).

9. Student information and parent approval form used by Seattle Public Schools (see Exhibit 4–6).

10. Student information and parent approval form for football used by Seattle Public Schools (see Exhibit 4–7).

11. An off-season participation consent form from the National Basketball Association Operation Manual, para. 134.3 (see Exhibit 4–8).

12. Parent/Guardian Permission and Release Form Used by the Central Massachusetts Youth Athletic Association (see Exhibit 4–9).

13. University of Illinois Fighting Illini Summer Camps Medical Statement and Release Form (see Exhibit 4–10).

WAIVER AND RELEASE

1. I have been informed by the Club physician that I have the following physical condition(s).

2. The physical condition(s) set forth above existed prior to the date of the physical examination for the current season.

3. I have received a full explanation from the Club physician that to continue to play professional football may result in deterioration or aggravation of such pre-existing physical condition(s) rendering me physically unable to perform the services required of me by my NFL Player Contract executed this date.

4. I fully understand the possible consequences of playing professional football with the physical condition(s) set forth in paragraph 1 above. Nevertheless, I desire to continue to play professional football and hereby assume the risk of the matters set forth in paragraph 3 above.

5. Because I desire to play professional football for the Club, I hereby waive and release the Club, the Club physician, its trainers and the National Football League from any and all liability and responsibility in the event I become physically unable to perform the services required of me by my NFL Player Contract executed this date because of a deterioration or aggravation of the physical condition(s) set forth in paragraph 1 above.

Date:

_____
Player

_____
Club Physician

Exhibit 4-3

WAIVER OF LIABILITY

SAMPLE: Professional Basketball Team Release and Waiver of Liability Form

<u>R E L E A S E   &   W A I V E R</u>

STATE OF _____

COUNTY OF _____

For and in consideration of ___team name___ a ___State___ Limited

Partnership inviting and permitting the undersigned to attend and participate

in the ___team name___ Rookie/Free Agent Tryout Camp for the 1978-'79

basketball season and for and in the further consideration of round trip

travel expenses, hotel room, per diem and travel from the hotel to the

tryout facility, I, the undersigned individual, being of lawful age, now

and forever, fully and finally, for myself, my heirs, my administrators,

executors, successors, and assignes, agree to waive all claims of whatever

nature, and forever release, remise, acquit, discharge, and hold harmless

the ___team name___ and ___name of facility___ and any other facility

used for this Rookie/Free Agent Tryout Camp, and their respective officers,

agents, employees, successors, assigns, and assureds, all other persons,

firms, corporations, associations or partnerships associated therewith,

for all claims, demands, actions or causes of action arising out of any

losses or injuries to my person or property, or both, which may result,

be sustained, or be received by me as a result of my attending and

participating in the above Rookie/Free Agent Tryout Camp for the 1978-'79

basketball season.

Exhibit 4-4

The undersigned fully understands that by executing this Release
and Waiver, he agrees to completely release, acquit, discharge and hold
harmless forever the ____team name____ and ____name of facility____ and any
other facility used for this Rookie/Free Agent Tryout Camp for all
claims of whatever kind, nature and description arising in any manner
whatever from his attendance and participation in the aforementioned
Rookie/Free Agent Tryout Camp, or from any travel or other activity
associated therewith.

The undersigned further understands that by signing this Release
and Waiver, he covenants and agrees that he, as well as his heirs,
executors, administrators, successors, and assigns, will never instiutute
any suit or action at law or otherwise against the ____team name____
or ____name of facility____ or any other facility used for this Rookie/Free Agent
Tryout Camp or in any way aid in the institution or prosecution of any
claim, demand, action or cause of action for damages, costs, loss of
services, expenses or compensation for or on account of any damage, loss
or injury either to his person, property or both, which may result from
the undersigned's attendance and participation at the aforementioned
Rookie/Free Agent Tryout Camp, or any travel or other activity associated
therewith.

The undersigned acknowledges that by attending the above-mentioned
Rookie/Free Agent Tryout Camp he voluntarily assumes all risks and
dangers known or unknown, foreseen or unforeseen, attendant to his
attendance and participation in said camp. The undersigned further
declares and represents that no promise, inducement or agreement not
herein expressed has been made to the undersigned, and that his release
contains the entire agreement between the parties to this release and
that the terms of this release are contractual and not a mere recital.

The undersigned has read the foregoing release and fully understands it.

Witness my hand and seal this ____ day of _____, 1978.

Signature _____

Address   _____

           _____

SWORN to and Subscribed before me

this _____ day of _____, 1978.

_____
NOTARY PUBLIC

Team Name

I, _____ , in consideration of

_____Team Name_____ (the "Club") giving to me an opportunity to earn a

position on the Club's roster, agree that, notwithstanding the provisions

of Paragraph 6(b) of the NBA Uniform Player Contract, the Club shall not

be liable for any damage or injury sustained by me as a result of may

participation in the Club's Trial Camp held at _____name of facility_____

in location of _____facility_____ from

_____date_____ through _____date_____ .

_____   _____
Date   Signature

Exhibit 4-5

SEATTLE PUBLIC SCHOOLS

1982-83 STUDENT INFORMATION AND PARENTAL APPROVAL FORM

A.   STUDENT INFORMATION

  1. Student's Name_____Birth Date_____ Age_____

  2. Name of Parent(s) _____

  3. Address of Parent(s)_____

  4. Name of Person(s) with whom Student Resides_____

  5. Address of Person(s) with whom Student Resides_____

  6. If this student does not reside with a parent, supply the following information:

     (a) How long has the student resided with this person(s)?_____

     (b) Has a legal guardianship been appointed by the courts? Yes_____ No____
          (If the answer is "yes", submit a certified copy of the court order or
          letter of guardianship.)

  7. School attended last year_____ City _____

  8. Grade level completed last June_____

  9. Did student pass in at least four (4) full-time subjects in the immediately
      preceding semester/trimester and receive the maximum credit given? Yes___No___

  10. Describe any physical limitations or problems that should be known by the coach:

      _____

      _____

B.   STUDENT RIGHTS

     Students participating in the Interscholastic Athletic program are governed by
the rights, protection and responsibilities as prescribed by the Washington Interscholastic Activities Association Handbook, the Metropolitan League By-Laws, and
their respective schools.

     Students and/or their parent(s)/guardians may make application for exceptions
to League and WIAA eligibility regulations and may appeal any decisions relative to
such requests through their school principal.

C.   STUDENT RESPONSIBILITIES

     Participants are required to conform to the rules and regulations of their school,
Metropolitan League, and the WIAA, and to conduct themselves in a safe and sportsmanlike manner. Violators are subject to probation, suspension or expulsion.

D.   STUDENT ELIGIBILITY REQUIREMENTS

  1. Prior to participation in practice of athletic contests a student must:

     (a) PHYSICAL EXAMINATION - During the 12-month period prior to first partici-
          pation in interscholastic athletics in a middle school, a junior high school,
          and prior to participation in a high school, a student shall undergo a medical
          examination and be approved for interscholastic athletic competition by a

Exhibit 4-6

medical authority licensed to perform a physical examination. Prior to each subsequent year of participation, a student shall furnish a statement, signed by a medical authority licensed to perform a physical examination, which provides clearance for continued athletic participation.

The school in which this student is enrolled must have on file a statement (or prepared form) from a medical authority licensed to give a physical examination, certifying that his/her physical condition is adequate for the activity or activities in which he/she participates.

To resume participation following an illness and/or injury serious enough to require medical care, a participating student must present to the school officials a physician's written release.

(b) be covered by the school's athletic injury insurance or have on file in the school office a properly signed League Insurance Waiver form.

(c) Seattle school students must have paid for the school's Catastrophic Insurance coverage.

(d) have on file in the school office a signed Student Information and Parental Approval form.

2. To be eligible to participate in an Interscholastic contest a student must:

(a) be under twenty (20) years of age on September 1 for the Fall sport season; on December 1 for the Winter sport season; and March 1 for the Spring sport season.

(b) have passed in at least four (4) full-time subjects in the immediately preceding semester/trimester and earned the maximum credit given for each subject.

(c) be enrolled in and currently passing at least four full credit subjects.

(d) reside with their parents, the parent with legal custody, or a court appointed guardian who has acted in such a capacity for a period of one year or more.

(e) not miss practices or games for the purpose of participating in non-school athletic activities.

(f) not accept cash awards in any amount or merchandise of more than $100.00 in value, or have ever signed a contract with or played for a professional athletic organization.

3. Students shall be entitled to four consecutive years of participation after entering the ninth (9th) grade.

4. A student completing the highest grade offered in an elementary or middle school is eligible for athletic participation upon entering a public or non-public high school. After starting his/her attendance in a high school, a student who transfers voluntarily or involuntarily to another high school shall become ineligible unless he/she obtains a signed Transfer Form from the principal of the high school from which he/she transfers, indicating that the transfer was not for athletic or disciplinary reasons.

5. Be in attendance a full day of school on any game date which falls on a school day.

6. Your athletic eligibility can be adversely affected by:
   (a) Providing misleading or false information relative to factors which affect your eligibility. (Loss of minimum of one year of eligibility.)
   (b) Missing a game or practice to participate in an out-of-school athletic activity.
   (c) Participating in an athletic activity under a false name.
   (d) Disruptive behavior during practice and/or contests.
   (e) Irregular attendance at school or practice.
   (f) Committing and/or aiding or abetting in the commission of any physical abuse or attack upon any person associated with athletic practices or contests.
   (g) Using a school uniform in a non-school athletic event or failure to maintain proper care or return of athletic equipment.

We have read, understand, and agree to abide by the Student Rights and Responsibilities and Student Eligibility Requirements listed in this form.

Date:_____, 19____ Signed_____
                                    Parent or Guardian

                         Signed_____
                                    Student

         WARNING, AGREEMENT TO OBEY INSTRUCTIONS, RELEASE, ASSUMPTION
                OF RISK, AND AGREEMENT TO HOLD HARMLESS

(Both the applicant student and a parent or guardian must read carefully and sign.)

SPORT (check applicable box):

☐ Football	☐ Basketball	☐ Track
☐ Volleyball	☐ Wrestling	☐ Baseball
☐ Cross-Country	☐ Gymnastics	☐ Softball
☐ Soccer	☐ Swimming	☐ Tennis
☐ Golf		

STUDENT

I am aware playing or practicing to play/participate in any sport can be a dangerous activity involving MANY RISKS OF INJURY. I understand that the dangers and risks of playing or practicing to play/participate in the above sport include, but are not limited to, death, serious neck and spinal injuries which may result in complete or partial paralysis, brain damage, serious injury to virtually all internal organs, serious injury to virtually all bones, joints, ligaments, muscles, tendons, and other aspects of the muscular skeletal system, and serious injury or impairment to other aspects of my body, general health and well-being. I understand that the dangers and risks of playing or practicing to play/participate in the above sport may result not only in serious injury, but in a serious impairment of my future abilities to earn a living, to engage in other business, social and recreational activities, and generally to enjoy life.

Because of the dangers of participating in the above sport, I recognize the importance of following coaches' instructions regarding playing techniques, training and other team rules, etc., and to agree to obey such instructions.

In consideration of the Seattle School District permitting me to try out for the _____ High School _____team and to engage in all
                                              (indicate sport)
activities related to the team, including, but not limited to, trying out, practicing or playing/participating in that sport, I hereby assume all the risks associated with participation and agree to hold the Seattle School District, its employees, agents, representatives, coaches, and volunteers harmless from any and all liability, actions, causes of action, debts, claims, or demands of any kind and nature whatsoever which may arise by or in connection with my participation in any activities related to the _____ High School _____ team. The terms hereof shall
                                    (indicate sport)
serve as a release and assumption of risk for my heirs, estate, executor, administrator, assignees, and for all members of my family.

The following to be completed only if sport is <u>football</u>, <u>wrestling</u>, <u>gymnastics</u>, or <u>baseball</u>:

I specifically acknowledge that _____ is
                                          (indicate sport)
a VIOLENT CONTACT SPORT involving even greater risk of injury than other sports._____
                              (initial)

Date:_____, 19____   _____
                                       Signature of Student

I, _____, am the parent/legal guardian of

_____(student). I have read the above warning and release and understand its terms. I understand that all sports can involve many RISKS OF INJURY, including, but not limited to, those risks outlined above.

In consideration of the Seattle School District permitting my child/ward to try out for the _____ High School _____ team and
                                                    (indicate sport)
to engage in all activities related to the team, including, but not limited to, trying out, practicing, or playing/participating in _____, I hereby agree
                                                    (indicate sport)
to hold the Seattle School District, its employees, agents, representatives, coaches, and volunteers harmless from any and all liability, actions, causes of action, debts, claims, or demands of every kind and nature whatsoever which may arise by or in connection with participation of my child/ward in any activities related to the _____ High School_____team. The terms hereof shall
                        (indicate sport)
serve as a release for my heirs, estate, executor, administrator, assignees, and for all members of my family.

> The following to be completed only if sport is <u>football</u>, <u>wrestling</u>, <u>gymnastics</u>, or <u>baseball</u>:
>
> I specifically acknowledge that _____ is
>   (indicate sport)
> a VIOLENT CONTACT SPORT involving even greater risk of injury than other sports._____
>   (initial)

Date:_____, 19____

_____
Signature of Parent or Legal Guardian

10/82

WARNING, AGREEMENT TO OBEY INSTRUCTIONS, RELEASE, ASSUMPTION OF RISK, AND AGREEMENT TO HOLD HARMLESS

(Both the applicant student and a parent or guardian must read carefully and sign.)

I am aware that tackle football is a violent contact sport and that playing or practicing to play tackle football will be a dangerous activity involving MANY RISKS OF INJURY. I understand that the dangers and risks of playing or practicing to play tackle football include, but are not limited to, death, serious neck and spinal injuries which may result in complete or partial paralysis, brain damage, serious injury to virtually all internal organs, serious injury to virtually all bones, joint, ligaments, muscles, tendons, and other aspects of the muscular skeletal system and serious injury or impairment to other aspects of my body, general health and wellbeing. I understand that the dangers and risks of playing or practicing to play tackle football may result not only in serious injury, but in a serious impairment of my future abilities to earn a living, to engage in other business, social and recreational activities, and generally to enjoy life.

Because of the dangers of tackle football, I recognize the importance of following coaches' instructions regarding playing techniques, training and other team rules, etc., and to agree to obey instructions.

In consideration of the Seattle School District permitting me to try out for the _____ High School football team and to engage in all activities related to the team, including but not limited to trying out, practicing, or playing tackle football, I hereby assume all the risks associated with tackle football and agree to hold the Seattle School District, its employees, agents, representatives, coaches, and volunteers harmless from any and all liability, actions, causes of action, debts, claims, or demands of any kind and nature whatsoever which may arise by or in connection with my participation in any activities related to the _____ High School football team. The terms hereof serve as a release and assumption of risk for my heirs, estate, executor, administrator, assignees, and for all members of my family.

DATE _____, 1982   _____
                                          Signature of student

I, _____, am the parent/legal guardian of _____(student). I have read the above warning and release and understand its terms. I understand that tackle football is a VIOLENT CONTACT SPORT involving many RISKS OF INJURY, including but not limited to those risks outlined above.

In consideration of the Seattle School District permitting my child/ward to try out for the _____ High School tackle football team and to engage in all activities related to the team, including, but not limited to, trying out, practicing, or playing tackle football, I hereby agree to hold the Seattle School District, its employees, agents, representatives, coaches, and volunteers harmless from any and all liability, actions, causes of action, debts, claims, or demands of every kind and nature whatsoever which may arise by or in connection with participation of my child/ward in any activities related to the _____ High School football team. The terms hereof shall serve as a release for my heirs, estate, executor, administrator, assignees, and for all members of my family.

DATE:_____, 1982   _____
                                          Parent or Legal Guardian

Exhibit 4-7

OFF-SEASON PARTICIPATION CONSENT FORM

The _____ ("Team") hereby grants permission for _____ ("Player") to
    (Team Name)   (Player)

participate in a game or exhibition of basketball in _____ from (or on) _____ to
                                           Location   Date

_____. It is acknowledged that the Player's participation is not part of an NBA or team event.
    Date

Although the Team's consent for the Player to participate, as required under paragraphs 6 and 17 of the NBA

Uniform Player Contract or any amendments or modifications thereof, is being given to the Player, such consent is

granted solely on the condition that:

> THE PLAYER WAIVES ANY AND ALL LIABILITIES AND OBLIGATIONS WHICH ARE
> REQUIRED OF THE TEAM UNDER PARAGRAPH 6 OF THE CONTRACT OR ANY
> AMENDMENT OR MODIFICATION THEREOF, AND THE PLAYER FURTHER WAIVES
> ANY PROTECTIONS OR GUARANTEES ENTITLING THE PLAYER TO THE
> PAYMENT OF SALARY, BONUS AND/OR DEFERRED COMPENSATION UNDER
> PARAGRAPH 2 OR 20 OF THE CONTRACT OR ANY AMENDMENT OR
> MODIFICATION THEREOF, SHOULD INJURIES TO THE PLAYER RESULT FROM
> PARTICIPATION IN SAID EVENT.

The Player understands and acknowledges this waiver. Should any injury occur to keep the Player from playing

basketball next season, the Team will not be responsible for paying any medical expenses or for paying the Player's

contract that season or any other season for which the Player cannot play basketball.

_____   _____
        Player   Date

_____   _____
    Team Representative   Date

Valid upon Team's receipt of Player's signature.

Exhibit 4-8

**CENTRAL MASSACHUSETTS
YOUTH ATHLETIC ASSOCIATION**
P. O. Box 321 ● Southboro, Mass. 01772

CHILD'S NAME_____

ADDRESS_____

TOWN_____ ZIP_____

PHONE NO._____ GRADE_____

DATE OF BIRTH_____ AGE_____

DATE OF LAST PHYSICAL_____ DR._____

PHYSICAL RESTRICTIONS: Yes ⧄   No ⧄
    (If yes, please explain below.)

_____ DIV.____
Franchise area   Team Name

PARENT/GUARDIAN PERMISSION AND RELEASE FORM

I, as parent/guardian of the above named child, do hereby give my approval to his/her participation in the game of _____ under the direction of the Central Massachusetts Youth Athletic Association, Inc. (CMYAA). I assume all risks and hazards incidental to such participation including transportation to and from the activities, and I do hereby waive, release, absolve, indemnify and agree to hold harmless the CMYAA and each town participating in CMYAA programs and the organizers, supervisors, coaches, participants and persons transporting my child to or from activities for any claim arising out of any injury to my child, except to the extent and in the amount covered by the accident or liability insurance provided through the CMYAA

I assume all responsibility and certify that my child is in good physical health and is capable of participation in the above mentioned sport.

I agree to return upon request any uniforms and/or equipment which may be issued in as good condition as when received except for normal wear and tear.

I will also furnish upon request a certified birth certificate and/or doctor's health certificate as may be required by the CMYAA or the town in which my child is a participant.

Parent/Guardian_____ Date_____
              Signature

(Describe physical restrictions, if any, or any other information which you may feel would be appropriate.)

Exhibit 4-9

Health Information Record

FIGHTING ILLINI SUMMER CAMPS MEDICAL STATEMENT & RELEASE

(Please Print)

We are enrolling our son/daughter _____ in the
(Name)

FIGHTING ILLINI _____ Camp to be held in Champaign on
(Name of Sport)

_____.
(Date of Camp)

I state to you that my son/daughter is in excellent physical condition
and that in no way should his/her activities be limited, or participation
hindered because of any physical ailment. I assume full responsibility for
my son's/daughter's physical condition and you should proceed with him/her
in all activities with full confidence in my statement. If my son's/daugh-
ter's physical condition should change between the time of this statement
and the time your camp begins, I will notify you. During the time that my
son/daughter is at your camp, if any emergency arises involving the physical
well being of my son/daughter, I give you full permission and authority to
take such steps as are reasonably necessary, in your own good judgement, to
protect and assist my son/daughter. I ask that you proceed in the way you
would if your own son/daughter were involved, and I release you from all responsibility for such actions. I agree that I will pay any hospital expenses, doctor bills, or any other expenses that my be incurred as a fesult
of treatment given my son/daughter for camp related injuries in excess of
that provided by the "Camper's Insurance."* I understand that the "Camper's
Insurance" does not cover any expenses incurred as a result of illness. I
make these statements and commitments as consideration for your allowing my
son/daughter to be enrolled in your camp and to take part in all of its
activities.

*Camper's Insurance	(Signature of Parent/Guardian)
$1,000.00 maximum Accidental Injury	
$ 150.00 maximum Dental Injury	

(Date Signed)

THIS STATEMENT MUST BE PROPERLY SIGNED AND RETURNED BEFORE THE FIRST DAY CAMP

Home Address _____
(Street)   (City)   (State)   (Zip)

Telephone Number ( ) - _____ Date of Birth _____
Parent/Guardian _____
(Name)   (Business Phone)
Occupation _____
(Street)   (City)   (State)   (Zip)
Name of Family Physician _____ Telephone Number( ) -

Medical History:

	Yes	Year		Yes	Year		Yes	Year
Heart Condition			Epilepsy			Allergies		
Asthma			Diabetes			Other		

1. Injuries and/or operations during the past year?_____
(Include Dates)
2. Has your physical activity been restricted during the past year?_____
(Reasons & Duration)
_____
3. Is your son/daughter taking any medication?_____
   If yes, why?_____ Name of medication_____
4. Has your son/daughter ever taken any sulfa drugs?_____
5. Adverse reactions to any drugs?_____
6. Date of last tetanus immunization?_____

Exhibit 4-10

Chapter 5

CRIMINAL LAW
AND SPORTS

5.00 Introduction and General Considerations

Violence within the context of professional sports is a familiar subject to nearly every sports fan. Many of the incidents of violent conduct in sports go beyond the reasonable scope of risks associated with sport. For example, acts that are clearly criminal in the nonsports context seem to be licensed if they take place on the playing field. Many people consider the punishments of fines and suspensions for violent action on the field to be minor when compared with the nature of the conduct. Several well-publicized incidents within the past several years in professional hockey, football, and basketball illustrate the potential problems of uncontrolled, excessive violence.

The most frequent and brutal acts have occurred in professional hockey. In 1969, Ted Green of the Boston Bruins suffered severe injuries from a blow to his unprotected head off the stick of Wayne Maki of the St. Louis Blues (see Section 5.22). Another incident, in 1975, involving Dave Forbes of the Boston Bruins and Henry Boucha of the Minnesota North Stars, set the stage for the only criminal prosecution in contemporary American legal history of a professional athlete for conduct

during a game. Forbes was prosecuted for striking Boucha in the face with the butt end of his stick and then pounding Boucha's face into the ice as he lay bleeding and stunned. The trial ended in a hung jury, however, and the case was not retried (see *State* v. *Forbes* in Section 5.22). Violence during a hockey game has not always been confined to the ice. In 1980, in a game between the Bruins and the New York Rangers, all but two of the Bruins players entered the stands to engage in a general melee with some Rangers fans. All criminal and civil charges against the players and the Boston Bruins were later dropped after an investigation disclosed that the fans had instigated the fight by punching a Bruins player and throwing a stick at the players (see *Guttenplan* v. *Boston Professional Hockey Ass'n., Inc.* in Section 4.24, Note 2[d]).

Professional football, a very "physical" sport to begin with, has also had its share of violent incidents. One well-publicized example occurred in 1976 during a game between the Oakland Raiders and the Pittsburgh Steelers. In that game, Raiders safety George Atkinson flattened Steeler receiver Lynn Swann with a vicious forearm clout to the back of Swann's helmet at the base of his neck. Swann suffered a concussion and was out of action for two weeks. Although violent hits are a part of football, this blow was delivered some 15 yards away from the play to an unsuspecting Swann. Commissioner Pete Rozelle remarked that he had never seen a more flagrant foul when players were not involved in the play than Atkinson's clubbing of Swann's head.

Even "permissible" hits under the rules of football have occasionally had disastrous consequences. During the 1977–78 season, Jack Tatum of the Oakland Raiders struck Darryl Stingley in the neck area with his helmet with such force that Stingley became paralyzed. No penalty flag for a late or illegal hit was thrown on the play. After reviewing the films, NFL's supervisor of officials, Art McNally, called the play a legal hit, even though Stingley had little chance of catching the pass.

Professional basketball, which many consider to be less physical than hockey or football, has not been without violence in recent years. For example, Los Angeles Lakers' all-star center Kareem Abdul-Jabbar broke his right hand in 1977 when he threw a blind-side punch at Milwaukee center Kent Benson. Benson was struck near the eye and suffered a concussion. The most brutal act in basketball, however, occurred later that same season when Kermit Washington of the Lakers threw a hard punch at an on-rushing Rudy Tomjanovich of the Houston Rockets. Tomjanovich suffered severe facial injuries with multiple fractures and a concussion (see *Tomjanovich* v. *California Sports, Inc.* in Section 4.24).

Examples of violent conduct such as these may have been subject to criminal prosecution had they not taken place during a sports event. In fact, no criminal charges were filed in any of these cases. Thus, the ability of the leagues to control violence with their sanctions (see Section 5.40) has been questioned. Many people believe that legislative action is needed (see Section 5.50) and others believe that criminal law sanctions should be invoked.

Criminal law is based on society's need to be free from harmful conduct. Criminal law defines criminal conduct and prescribes the punishment to be imposed on a person convicted of engaging in such conduct. In addition to its broad aim of preventing injury to the health, safety, morals, and welfare of the public, criminal law is also designed to protect society's broader notions of morality.

Understanding the basis of criminal law makes it easier to understand why violent and possibly criminal behavior is looked on differently when the violence occurs in a sporting event. All the harm and violence are confined to the participants, who know and assume the risks of the game. The public, while sitting in the stands or watching on television, is not subjected to any risk of physical harm. This may be an underlying reason why society treats sports violence differently from violence in the streets.

Opponents of sports violence argue that this approach overlooks the interests of society as a whole in protecting society's notions of morality. Opponents contend that the incidents just cited evoke a sense of moral outrage and a feeling that some kind of punishment should be exacted. The existence in sporting events of socially unacceptable conduct that is treated with impunity conflicts with society's overall concept of good and bad conduct that has been long espoused by educational and religious institutions. However, violent conduct in sports continues to be punishable only by league sanctions that are arguably much less severe than punishments that would be ordered in criminal court (see Section 5.40).

In order to determine whether or not criminal law sanctions should be imposed in incidents of sports violence, it is useful to examine the rationale behind criminal punishment. Prison terms are imposed for a purpose, and unless some of the same reasons apply in cases of sports violence, then treating sports violence as a crime may not make any sense. A primary rationale for criminal sanctions is the prevention theory — that is, punishment will keep a criminal from becoming a repeat offender. The theory's aim is to rehabilitate the offender in the criminal justice system. In sports, rehabilitation would be a desirable goal if treating the offending athlete as a criminal would actually prevent the repetition of dangerous conduct.

A second theory behind punishment for criminal conduct is the deterrence theory: that exacting punishment for bad conduct deters others from committing crimes, lest they suffer the same fate. This, too, could perhaps have valuable applications in the area of sports violence. Athletes would in theory be less likely to engage in violent conduct that is outside the scope of the risks of the sport if they feared criminal punishment.

One final theory that is relevant to sports violence is the education theory of punishment, which states that the publicity that surrounds a criminal trial and the subsequent punishment of criminals serves to educate the public as to the nature of right and wrong. This theory may be the strongest one for treating sports violence as a criminal act. By failing to treat violent acts as crimes simply because they take place in the limited area of sports, society is sending out a contradictory message and perhaps educating the public, especially the younger public, that violent acts are permissible under certain circumstances.

The number of criminal prosecutions of participant-perpetrators of violent acts during the course of sports events is very small. The number of published decisions from cases that have gone to trial is even smaller. In fact, no American case has ever made it as far as the appellate process, where decisions are usually published. The only published opinions are a few Canadian cases (see *Regina* v. *Maki*, *Regina* v. *Green*, *Regina* v. *Maloney*, and *Regina* v. *Leyte* in Section 5.22).

One American case, *State* v. *Forbes* (see Section 5.22), involved a serious injury that resulted from a stick-swinging incident in a professional hockey game. It was extensively publicized, although the trial resulted in a hung jury, and the prosecutor decided against pursuing a second trial. The prosecutor believed that the expense of a second trial was pointless when weighed against the strong likelihood of another hung jury.

In this chapter, the elements of the "crimes" that are most likely to occur in a sports event are discussed in order to acquaint the reader with criminal law (see Section 5.10). The application of these specific crimes, such as assault and battery, to sports violence is then examined (see Section 5.20). Common defenses to these crimes are discussed in Sections 5.21 and 5.22. Section 5.30 covers the applicability of such crimes as conspiracy and solicitation to the area of sports violence. Section 5.40 examines the disciplinary procedures of professional sports leagues and amateur organizations. Section 5.50 discusses proposed legislative solutions to sports violence. Section 5.60 on drug abuse and Section 5.70 on gambling examine subjects that are criminal law matters which have increasingly involved both amateur and professional sports in the United States. Finally, Section 5.80 looks at ticket scalping, which some states are trying to prevent by passing criminal sanctions against the practice.

NOTES

1. For the most comprehensive books and articles on the subject of sports violence and criminal law, see the following:
(a) Horrow, *Sports Violence: The Interaction Between Private Lawmaking and the Criminal Law* (Arlington, Va.: Carrollton Press, 1980).
(b) "Violence in Professional Sport," *Wisconsin Law Review* 771 (1975).
(c) Hechter, "Criminal Law and Violence in Sports," 19 *Criminal Law Quarterly* 425 (1977).
(d) "Sports Violence: A Matter of Societal Concern," 55 *Notre Dame Law Review* 796 (June 1980).
(e) "Controlling Violence in Professional Sport," 2 *Glendale Law Review* 323 (1978).
(f) Perelman, "Violence in Professional Sports: Is It Time for Criminal Penalties?" 2 *Loyola Entertainment Law Journal* 75 (1982).
(g) Tatum and Kushner, *They Call Me Assassin*, (paperback ed., 1979).
2. For a discussion of the Kermit Washington–Rudy Tomjanovich incident, see Halberstam, *The Breaks of the Game* (New York: Alfred A. Knopf, 1981).

5.10   Defining a Crime

In order to apply criminal law sanctions for undesirable conduct, the act that will incur penalties must first be defined — and in a way that insures predictability. This issue is especially difficult in the area of sports violence. Certain sports involve a great deal of physical contact and intimidation. Therefore, a certain amount of very physical but legal contact may be considered part of the game. The problem is in drawing a neat and predictable line as to when an act goes beyond the scope of the game and becomes criminal in nature.

The crime of battery is the offense that most often applies to sports violence. A battery can be defined as an unlawful application of force to the person of another resulting in bodily injury. The requirement that the battery be "unlawful" is the key to the exemption of sports-related batteries. Although the issue is often couched in such legal terms as consent or assumption of risk, the crux of the problem in distinguishing sports violence from criminal acts is unlawfulness. Society has seemingly exempted sports violence from the criminal law by treating it as lawful. The elements of a battery are (1) a "guilty" state of mind, (2) an act, (3) a physical touching or harming of a victim, and (4) causation — that is, the act must cause the touching or harm. The state of mind for a battery does not require actual intent. An extreme conscious disregard of known serious risks, called criminal negligence, will suffice. The criminal statutes in most states also define some acts as aggravated battery and punish them as felonies. For example, the use of a deadly weapon or the causing of serious bodily injury are examples of an aggravated battery. Interestingly enough, ordinary objects can qualify as deadly objects if they are used in a way that can cause death. Hockey sticks, baseballs, and football helmets may qualify as deadly objects.

Battery, of course, is not necessarily the only crime that might occur in the sports world. In what is possibly the only reported American decision involving a crime committed during a sporting event, a boxer in 1895 was acquitted of manslaughter charges in New York for the death of his sparring partner during an exhibition match (see *People* v. *Fitzsimmons* in Section 5.22). The violence that occurs in sports events today clearly meets certain elements of battery in some cases. The unique factor is that the acts occur within the confines of athletics, which underscores the difficult issue of determining when an act within the confines of sports becomes a crime.

5.20   Defining a Criminal Act in Athletic Competition

Sports violence presents difficult issues in drawing the line between conduct that is accidental or within the rules of the game and conduct that is criminal. The problem is that certain sports are extremely physical, and violent physical contact is condoned under the rules. Thus, recalling the legal definition of a criminal battery as discussed previously, the act which is a crime on the streets becomes legal in the arena, and the illegality element of the definition of battery is negated. Only the most heinous acts that occur in contact sports such as football, hockey, and basketball fall beyond any possible justification under the scope of the game that legalizes violent contact.

Unfortunately, the extreme violence that is legal under the rules of some sports can have tragic consequences. The incident in which Jack Tatum of the Oakland Raiders paralyzed Darryl Stingley of the New England Patriots with a "legal" hit is an example that demonstrates the problem of defining a crime in the arena of sports violence (see Sections 5.00 and 4.24, Note 1[c]). In a biography that was published after the incident, Tatum stated that he made the hit viciously with the intent to put a player out of commission.

The seriousness of sports violence has received attention from Congress. In 1980, Representative Ronald M. Mottl of Ohio

96TH CONGRESS
2D SESSION
H.R. 7903

To amend title 18 of the United States Code to provide penalties
for excessive violence during professional sports events.

IN THE HOUSE OF REPRESENTATIVES

July 31, 1980

Mr. MOTTL introduced the following bill; which was referred to
the Committee on the Judiciary

A BILL

To amend title 18 of the United States Code to provide penalties
for excessive violence during professional sports events.

*Be it enacted by the Senate and House of Representa-
tives of the United States of America in Congress assembled,*
That this Act may be cited as the "Sports Violence Act of
1980".

SEC. 2. Chapter 7 of title 18 of the United States Code
is amended by adding at the end the following:

"**§115. Excessive violence during professional sports
events**

"(a) Whoever, as a player in a professional sports event,
knowingly uses excessive physical force and thereby causes a
risk of significant bodily injury to another person involved in
that event shall be fined not more than $5,000 or imprisoned
not more than one year, or both.

"(b) As used in this section, the term—

"(1) 'excessive physical force' means physical
force that—

"(A) has no reasonable relationship to the
competitive goals of the sport;

"(B) is unreasonably violent; and

"(C) could not be reasonably foreseen, or
was not consented to, by the injured person, as a
normal hazard to such person's involvement in
such sports event; and

"(2) 'professional sports event' means a paid admission contest, in or affecting interstate or foreign
commerce, of players paid for their participation.".

Sec. 3. The table of sections for chapter 7 of title 18 of
the United States Code is amended by adding at the end the
following new item:

"115. Excessive violence during professional sports events."

Exhibit 5-1   Sports Violence Act of 1980

---

introduced the "Sports Violence Act" (see
Exhibit 5–1), which addressed itself to the
issue of defining crime in a sports contest:

(a) Whoever, as a player in a professional
sports event, knowingly uses excessive physical
force and thereby causes a risk of significant
bodily injury to another person involved in that
event shall be fined not more than $5,000 or
imprisoned not more than one year, or both.

(b) As used in this section, the term ...
excessive physical force means physical force that
has no reasonable relationship to the competitive
goals of the sport; is unreasonably violent; and
could not be reasonably foreseen, or was not
consented to, by the injured person, as a normal
hazard of such person's involvement in such
sports event.

The Mottl bill never made it out of committee
in the 96th Congress. Congressman Mottl was
not reelected, and the bill was never passed. A
bill was introduced in the 98th Congress called
the "Sports Violence Arbitration Act of 1983"
(see Exhibit 5–2). It was introduced by Repre-

sentative Thomas A. Daschle of South Dakota
and addressed the same issues as the "Sports
Violence Act," although the new bill substituted
civil sanctions for criminal sanctions (see
Section 5.50).

5.21   Justification and Excuse

Two major defenses are available to a defendant in a criminal prosecution involving sports
violence: consent and self-defense. Consent is
not normally a defense to a criminal act. The
general rule is that one cannot consent to be
the victim of a crime, and this rule is true
except for certain specific exceptions; those
exceptions are crimes in which a lack of
consent forms one of the elements of the crime.
For example, a successful prosecution for rape
must include proof that there was a lack of
consent on the part of the victim.

Sports violence, specifically the crime of
battery, falls in a more difficult area to define
compared with nonsports-related violence.

H. R. 4495

To provide for the establishment of an arbitration system to reduce the number and costs of injuries resulting from the use of excessively violent conduct during professional sports events.

IN THE HOUSE OF REPRESENTATIVES

NOVEMBER 18, 1983

Mr. DASCHLE introduced the following bill; which was referred to the Committee on Education and Labor

---

A BILL

To provide for the establishment of an arbitration system to reduce the number and costs of injuries resulting from the use of excessively violent conduct during professional sports events.

Be it enacted by the Senate and House of Representatives of the United States of America in Congress assembled,

SHORT TITLE

SECTION 1. This Act may be cited as the "Sports Violence Arbitration Act of 1983".

STATEMENT OF PURPOSE

SEC. 2. It is the purpose of this Act to reduce the number and costs of injuries resulting from the use of excessively violent conduct during professional sports events by establishing an arbitration system empowered to settle grievances resulting from such conduct.

DEFINITIONS

SEC. 3. As used in this Act, the term—

(1) "arbitration board" means any arbitration board established pursuant to section 4(a);

(2) "excessively violent conduct" means physical force or contact employed during a professional sports event which creates a risk of injury and which—

(A) is unnecessary for effective participation in the sport consistent with the competitive goals of that sport;

(B) is intended to injure; or

(C) is intended to create a threat of injury;

(3) "management representative" means any person or persons charged with the responsibility of representing professional sports club owners in collective-bargaining matters;

(4) "player" means any individual who receives remuneration from a professional sports club for direct participation as a contestant in professional sports events; but such term does not include any manager or coach of a professional sports club, or any other individual employed by a professional sports club who does not directly participate in professional sports events as a contestant;

(5) "player representative" means any person or persons charged with the responsibility of representing players in collective-bargaining matters;

(6) "professional sports club" means any professional baseball, basketball, football, hockey, or soccer club which employs players who regularly participate in professional sports events;

(7) "professional sports event" means any paid admission event in which players engage in athletic contests, competitions, or games which occur in or affect interstate or foreign commerce;

(8) "professional sports league" means any association of professional sports clubs whose members participate in professional sports events on a regular basis; and

(9) "league game official" means any individual who participates in professional sports events as an official, referee, or umpire and who has the responsibility at such events of enforcing the rules of play at such event.

ESTABLISHMENT OF ARBITRATION SYSTEMS

SEC. 4. (a) Each professional sports league shall establish an arbitration system in accordance with this Act for the

Exhibit 5-2   Sports Violence Arbitration Act of 1983

arbitration of grievances resulting from the use of excessively violent conduct.

(b) Each arbitration system established pursuant to subsection (a) of this section shall comply with the following terms and requirements:

(1) The league will establish an arbitration board, which shall consist of three members, none of whom may be officers or employees of the Federal Government or of any State or local government.

(2) The management representative and player representative of each professional sports league shall select the arbitration board members by mutual agreement.

(3) The system shall include procedures for the investigation and arbitration of grievances, consistent with the requirements of section 5 of this Act.

(4) The system shall establish policies and rules relating to compensation awards, as defined in section 5(c)(1), which may be made by the arbitration board.

(5) The system shall establish policies and rules relating to disciplinary sanctions, as defined in section 5(c)(2), which may be imposed by the arbitration board.

ARBITRATION OF GRIEVANCES

SEC. 5. (a) Any player or professional sports club which sustains injury as the result of excessively violent conduct, or is the object of excessively violent conduct, may bring a grievance before the arbitration board against the player who allegedly engaged in such excessively violent conduct and the professional sports club which employed such player.

(b) Any person who acted as a league game official at a professional sports event may bring a grievance before the arbitration board against any player who allegedly engaged in excessively violent conduct during such professional sports event and against the professional sports club which employed such player.

(c) Upon the bringing of any grievance, the arbitration board shall conduct an investigation and hold proceedings in accordance with the policies, rules, and procedures established by the Federal Mediation and Conciliation Service pursuant to section 8 of this Act. Upon the completion of such proceedings, the arbitration board shall issue a written decision and order. Such decision and order may include the following:

(1) An award of compensation to any party which sustained injury as a result of the excessively violent conduct which is the subject of the grievance. The award of compensation shall be paid by the professional sports club which employed the player who engaged in such excessively violent conduct.

(2) The imposition of disciplinary sanctions against the player who engaged in such excessively violent conduct, against the professional sports club which employed such player, or against both such player and such professional sports club. The disciplinary sanctions which may be imposed include fines, suspension from play without pay, and loss of a draft choice.

(d) The factors which the arbitration board shall take into account in fixing the amount of compensation awarded under subsection (c)(1) of this section shall include—

(1) the extent of any injuries sustained by any player injured as a result of such excessively violent conduct;

(2) the duration of any period during which such injured player was unable to participate in professional sports events as a result of such injuries;

(3) the amount of salary paid to such injured player by the professional sports club which employs such player during that period which such player was unable to participate in professional sports events as a result of such injuries;

(4) the amount of any medical or other expenses incurred by such injured player or the professional sports club which employs such player as a result of such injuries; and

(5) any other factors which the arbitration board may deem relevant.

(e) The factors which the arbitration board shall take into account in imposing disciplinary sanctions under subsection (c)(2) of this section shall include—

(1) the extent of any injuries sustained by any player injured as a result of conduct;

(2) the duration of any period during which such player was unable to participate in professional sports events as a result of such injuries;

(3) the risk of serious injury which was created by the use of such excessively violent conduct, whether or not such conduct actually resulted in injuries;

(4) any prior history of excessively violent conduct on the part of the player who engaged in such excessively violent conduct;

(5) the apparent intent on the part of the player who engaged in such excessively violent conduct to cause injury; and

(6) any other factors which the arbitration board may deem relevant.

(f) Any fines assessed by an arbitration board under subsection (c)(2) of this section shall be used to defray any expenses incurred in the administration of the arbitration system.

(g) The provisions of title 9, United States Code, shall apply to proceedings under this section to the extent that the provisions of such title are consistent with the provisions of this Act. Where the provisions of title 9 are inconsistent with the provisions of this Act, this Act shall control.

REVIEW OF ARBITRATION ORDERS

SEC. 6. (a) Not later than sixty days after the issuance of an order by an arbitration board under section 5 of this Act, any person adversely affected by such order may file a petition with the United States Court of Appeals for the circuit in which such person resides or has his or her principal place of business, for judicial review of such order.

(b) Upon the filing of a petition under subsection (a) of this section, the court shall have jurisdiction to review the order issued by the arbitration board in accordance with chapter 7 of title 5 of the United States Code. The court shall have authority to grant appropriate relief as provided in such chapter.

(c) For purposes of this section, an arbitration board shall be considered to be an agency within the meaning of section 701(b)(1) of title 5, United States Code.

ADDITIONAL REMEDIES

SEC. 7. Any player or professional sports club bringing an action before an arbitration board under section 5(a) of this Act shall not, by reason of such action, be barred from instituting a civil action in any court of competent jurisdiction based upon the occurrence which is the subject of the action brought before the arbitration board, except that any compensation awarded by the arbitration board under section 5(c)(1) of this Act shall be reduced by an amount equal to the amount for any monetary settlement or award in any such civil action.

THE FEDERAL MEDIATION AND CONCILIATION SERVICE

SEC. 8. The Federal Mediation and Conciliation Service established pursuant to section 202 of the Labor Management Relations Act, 1947 (29 U.S.C. 172), is authorized and directed to establish policies, rules, and procedures applicable to arbitration proceedings under this Act.

ENFORCEMENT BY THE SECRETARY OF LABOR

SEC. 9. The Secretary of Labor is authorized and directed to bring an action in United States district court to enforce the requirements of this Act.

○

Battery is not a crime that has lack of consent of the victim as an element, but in certain battery cases the unlawful-application-of-force element is not present because of consent. A consented-to application of force is not unlawful. The Model Penal Code, Section 2.11, provides:

> [W]hen conduct is charged to constitute an offense because it causes or threatens bodily harm, consent to such conduct or to the infliction of such harm is a defense if: (a) the bodily harm consented to or threatened by the conduct consented to is not serious; or (b) the conduct and the harm are *reasonably foreseeable hazards* of joint participation in a *lawful* athletic contest or competitive sport (emphasis added).

The most difficult issue concerning the consent defense is drawing a line between reasonably foreseeable hazards that may be consented to and unreasonably foreseeable hazards that are not consented to. One of several different approaches on how to draw the line concerns looking at the normal violence associated with the sport. This means defining the scope of consented-to physical contact in a particular sport so that a participant in that sport would not be deemed to consent to acts that go beyond that scope.

The rules-of-the-game test is an alternative approach to the consent issue. A participant-victim would not be deemed to have consented to acts that were illegal under the rules of the sport. This is a much weaker standard that would lessen the types of violence subject to a successful consent defense. On the other hand, the rules-of-the game approach is also an easier test to apply.

Some courts apply a test that looks toward the seriousness of the injury for a solution. This is a simplistic approach which reasons that the victim cannot be said to have consented to a grave injury. Another approach is "the reasonable foreseeability test," which is commonly used in the area of torts. Under this test, a participant would only be held to have consented to those acts of violence that were considered a reasonably foreseeable part of the sport.

Finally, it should be noted that in addition to the above tests, the assumption-of-risk doctrine of tort law is often discussed in the area of consent to criminal acts (see Section 4.12[d]). Assumption of risk is very similar to the consent defense. A participant in a contact sport assumes the risk of violent contact and consents to the contact. But any injury that is serious enough to raise the specter of criminal prosecution should exceed the risk assumed by the participant. Therefore, the assumption-of-risk doctrine does not really add any useful analysis to the problem of the consent defense to battery.

The second major defense to a charge of battery is self-defense. The nonaggressor in a violent incident may use a reasonable amount of force against the aggressor when there is reason to believe that an immediate danger of harm is imminent and that the use of force is required to avoid this danger. In the area of sports violence such a defense may not be available for a number of reasons.

A successful showing of self-defense must prove that the force used by the nonaggressor was no greater than that used against him. Usually, for example, a case will involve escalating violence, such as when a hockey player punches an opponent and the opponent strikes back with his stick. This may cause some difficulty in determining when "reasonable force" has been used. Another problem is the requirement that the defendant have the honest belief that danger of immediate, serious, bodily injury is imminent. In many cases, the possibility of an honest belief is discredited because often the defendant provoked the attack, and this negates a self-defense argument. Finally, some jurisdictions would further limit the defense to those cases in which the defendant had no reasonable means of retreat. Therefore, a player who could have avoided seriously injuring another by breaking off the confrontation would not be able to plead self-defense.

NOTES

1. In *Agar* v. *Canning*, 54 W.W.R. 302 (Manitoba 1965), *aff'd* 55 W.W.R. 386 (1966), the Canadian courts held that in sports situations the consent defense must be viewed on a case-by-case basis.
2. For further information, see the following articles:
(a) "Consent Defense: Sports, Violence, and the Criminal Law," 13 *American Criminal Law Review* 235 (Fall 1975).
(b) "Consent in Criminal Law: Violence in Sports," 75 *Michigan Law Review* 148 (1976).
(c) "Criminal Law: Consent as a Defense to Criminal Battery — The Problem of Athletic Contests," 28 *Oklahoma Law Review* 840 (Fall 1975).

5.22 Responsibility for the Act

Other factors can relieve a defendant of responsibility for a crime, even though they are not true "defenses." Thus, even though the prosecution proves each and every element of the crime charged, the defendant can escape punishment by showing that he acted in the heat of passion or was intoxicated. A person who acts as the result of an involuntary action may not have the mental element that is required under the definition of the crime. For example, murder that occurs under extenuating circumstances, such as discovering one's spouse in bed with another, will be reduced to the lesser charge of voluntary manslaughter. Under certain circumstances, the heat of passion aroused in the defendant diminishes the responsibility for the criminal act.

The diminished responsibility theory has been used by the defense in criminal cases involving sports violence. Defense counsels in *Regina* v. *Maki*, *Regina* v. *Green*, and *State* v. *Forbes* raised the defense of involuntary action (*infra*). Each defendant argued that players received training in the "skills" and the mental attitude necessary for a successful hockey player. Because of this training, the defendant's actions were not voluntary but merely instinctual responses or reflex actions. The question in these cases was whether or not the action causing the injury was a normal or regular part of the game, or whether it was an unreasonable response considering the training each player had received.

Regina v. Maki, 14 D.L.R. 3d 164 (1970)

A criminal lawsuit was brought against Wayne Maki, a professional ice hockey player with the St. Louis Blues of the National Hockey League (NHL), by the Province of Regina for assault causing bodily harm. This incident occurred when Maki intentionally struck another NHL player, Ted Green of the Boston Bruins, with his stick in an exhibition match played in Ottawa, Canada. The blow caused serious injury to Green.

The incident occurred when Maki and Green both went into the corner of the rink to chase the puck. They collided, and Green pushed or punched Maki in the face with his glove, apparently causing injury to Maki's mouth. The referee signaled a delayed penalty on Green, meaning that the whistle would be blown once Boston got possession of the puck. The players were said to have separated, but there was some evidence that Maki speared Green with his stick before they did. The court found this fact to be in considerable doubt.

The players then came together again swinging their sticks. Green first struck Maki with his stick on the neck or shoulder. Maki responded with a chopping blow, meaning a vertical swing as opposed to a baseball-like swing; it glanced off Green's stick, which Green still held high and brandished at Maki. Maki then struck Green about the side of the head, causing the serious injury.

Maki was charged with assault causing bodily harm. Maki's plea was that his action was self-defense. The Canadian Criminal Code reads:

> Anyone who is unlawfully assaulted and who causes death or grievous bodily harm in repelling the assault is justified if (a) he causes it under reasonable apprehension of death or grievous bodily harm from the violence with which the assault was originally made or with which the

assailant pursues his purposes, and (b) he believes, on reasonable and probable grounds, that he cannot otherwise preserve himself from death or grievous bodily harm.

Canadian law requires an acquittal on a charge of assault causing bodily harm if the court cannot rule out self-defense beyond all doubt. The court must consider the reasonableness of the force used under the circumstances and the state of mind of the accused at the time in question. An examination of the evidence pertaining to Maki's emotional state during the incident showed that he was not angry at Green nor retaliatory in his action. It appeared that he was just trying to protect himself and prevent Green from doing anything further to him. A number of witnesses, including the referee, could not assess the severity of the blow which caused the injury to Green. The defense argued that when the means of defense used is not disproportionate to the severity of the assault, a plea of self-defense is valid.

The court dismissed the charges against Maki, stating that it could not say beyond any doubt that Maki intended to injure Green, that Maki was not under any reasonable apprehension of bodily harm, or that Maki used excessive force under the circumstances. Though it did not enter into the court's decision, the defense of consent was addressed by the court since it had been raised. The court said that no sports league, no matter how well organized or self-policed, could render its players immune from criminal prosecution. The court admitted that all players who step onto a playing field or an ice surface assume certain risks and hazards of the sport, and in most cases the defense of consent (assumption of the risks) would be applicable. However, no athlete should be presumed to accept malicious, unprovoked, or overtly violent attacks as part of playing a sport. The court stated that in the Maki situation a defense of consent alone would have failed.

Regina v. Green, 16 D.L.R. 3d 137 (Ont. Prov. Civ. 1970)

This case arose from the same incident as in *Regina* v. *Maki*, and involved criminal charges of common assault against Ted Green, an NHL player with the Boston Bruins, who hit another player with both his glove and stick. The action from which the charges arose took place in a National Hockey League (NHL) exhibition match played in Ottawa, Canada, in September 1969. In deciding the case, the court stated that it found it difficult to envision an offense of common assault as opposed to assault causing actual bodily harm, which could readily stand on facts produced from incidents occurring in a professional hockey game. Citing statute 230 of the Canadian Criminal Code, which reads "A person commits an assault, when without the consent of another person . . . (a) he applies force intentionally to the person of the other, directly or indirectly," the court reasoned that professional hockey players consent to a great number of "assaults" due to the speed, force, and vigor with which the game of hockey is played.

Maki admitted that he had been struck in the face by an opposing player's glove hundreds of times while playing hockey. The court found that this common episode in the course of an ice hockey game, which would be considered assault outside the context of an NHL game, was not an assault but simply one of the risks a professional ice hockey player assumes when playing the game. In the course of a hockey game, the court stated, a player does not examine each potential action to determine if it is an assault. The roughness of the game has to permit certain actions that would be considered an assault outside the confines of an NHL contest.

The court concluded that the most serious blows struck during the incident were by Maki. Green's blow to Maki's shoulder was found to be instinctive, for Maki admitted that if he did indeed spear Green, he could expect an immediate retaliation. The court stated that Green's blow with his stick was meant only as a warning and was for his own protection, and not an attempt to commit an assault. If Maki had not speared Green — if only the glove to the face had taken place — then there would have been no cause for retaliation by Green. A penalty would have been called, and that might have been the end of the incident. The court found Green not guilty.

The court did discuss whether given other circumstances and another set of facts, a charge of common assault could be successfully argued. The court stated, however, that although common assaults are difficult to establish in an NHL contest, unprovoked, savage attacks in which serious injury results would come under the heading of assault causing bodily harm, as opposed to common assault.

State v. Forbes, No. 63280 (Minn. Dist. Ct. 1975)

In December 1974, an NHL hockey game was played in Minnesota between the Boston Bruins and the Minnesota North Stars. Early in the first period, Henry Boucha, closely followed by David Forbes, chased a loose puck against the boards. Forbes proceeded to check Boucha, using his elbows as offensive weapons as is commonly done by hockey players. After being elbowed, Boucha turned and knocked Forbes down. The referee penalized both players for a total of seven minutes. Once in their respective penalty boxes, they exchanged threats. Upon their return to the ice, Boucha had started to skate toward the North Star bench when Forbes said, "Okay, let's go now" and took a swing at Boucha. Forbes missed him with his hand but connected with his stick just above Boucha's right eye. Boucha dropped to the ice covering his injured face. Forbes then discarded his stick and gloves, jumped on top of Boucha, and proceeded to bang Boucha's head on the ice until he was forcibly removed.

Boucha was taken from the ice to the hospital, where 25 stitches were required to close the cut beside his right eye. When the patch was removed five days later, Boucha complained of double vision in the injured eye and underwent remedial surgery to repair a small fracture in the floor of the right eye socket.

After hearing evidence about the incident, NHL Commissioner Clarence Campbell suspended Forbes for ten games. Then, on January 15, 1975, Forbes was indicted by a Minnesota grand jury and charged with violating Minnesota statute, section 609.25, aggravated assault, which stated:

> Subdivision 1. Whoever assaults another and inflicts great bodily harm may be sentenced to imprisonment for not more than ten years or to payment of a fine of not more than $10,000 or both.
> Subdivision 2. Whoever assaults another with a dangerous weapon but without intent to inflict great bodily harm may be sentenced to imprisonment for not more than five years or to payment of a fine of not more than $5,000 or both.

At trial, the prosecution argued that Forbes had committed an aggravated assault on Boucha. The argument made was that criminal assault was a crime whether it was done in public or under game conditions. The defense argued a variation on the temporary insanity defense, basing its argument on the theory that from the age of four years, hockey players are taught not to let other players intimidate them. Coaches emphasize the need for physical violence against other players and crowds cheer the sight of fighting and blood. The defense argued that given these circumstances, hockey, and not David Forbes, should be on trial. The trial ended in a 9 to 3 hung jury in favor of the assault conviction. The prosecutor decided not to retry the case because he felt that the deep split in public opinion would make a required unanimous verdict virtually impossible.

Regina v. Maloney, 28 CCC 2d 323 (1976)

In November 1975, Daniel Maloney committed

an assault on Brian Glennie during the course of a hockey game. Maloney's action caused serious bodily harm to Glennie in violation of the Canadian Criminal Code. One of the issues raised in this suit was whether or not the victim consented by participation in athletics to serious harm or injury when the assailant intended to injure.

The court ruled that in this case, some consent could be implied. It stated: "Implied consent would be that consent which Glennie agrees to when he agrees to play the game. He agrees to those assaults which are inherent in and reasonably incidental to the normal playing of the game of hockey. . . . Bear in mind that regardless of implied or expressed consent, there are legal limitations to the consent that a person can give." The court reviewed cases for the possible scope of consent and noted that if the intentional nature of the crime is established, consent is not a viable defense. The case was sent to the jury, which acquitted Maloney of all charges.

Regina v. Leyte, 13 C.C.C. 2d 458 (Ont. Prov. Ct. Crim. Div. 1973)

Plaintiff and accused were on opposing teams engaged in a play-off game of handball. The accused, who was in the defensive position, fouled the plaintiff by pushing him. The plaintiff turned with his hands raised to ward off further blows. Interpreting this as an aggressive act, the defendant swung twice at the plaintiff. The first blow caused no damage, but the second broke his nose. The court, in reviewing assault charges against the accused, held that:

> Players in competitive sport such as this game must be deemed to enter into such sport knowing that they may be hit in one of many ways and must be deemed to consent thereto so long as the reactions of the players are instinctive and closely related to the play. . . . However, where there is a significant time interval between the termination of play and the blows struck and where the players . . . have . . . ceased to be aggressive so that their subsequent actions should no longer be

instinctive, then the players cannot be deemed to consent to assaults at that stage.

The charge was dismissed.

Regina v. Watson, Provincial Court (Criminal Division), Durham Judiciary District, Ontario, May 21, 1975

The defendant in this case, which involved an assault committed during a hockey game, used the consent theory to defend himself against the criminal charges. The court said:

> The consent implied by a person's participation generally in a game such as hockey is limited to the routine bodily contact in the game. . . . In any event, since the degree of force used was such as to be likely to, and did in fact, cause bodily harm, any consent by the victim would be immaterial and not excuse the accused.

The defendant was convicted, but the judge refused to impose criminal sanctions, granting him an absolute discharge. This is because it was the first case of its kind to be decided by a Canadian court. The judge believed that the defendant had not been given sufficient notice that he might be subject to criminal sanctions and that consequently, it would not be fair to impose the available sanctions in this situation.

People v. Fitzsimmons, 34 N.Y.S. 1102 (1895)

This case was a prosecution for manslaughter against a professional fighter for causing the death of another fighter in a sparring match. The jury found the defendant innocent. The defendant and the victim had given a sparring exhibition in Syracuse, New York. Prize fighting was a crime under New York law at the time, but exhibitions were legal. The exhibition match became quite heated, and the defendant struck the victim in the jaw. The victim fell to the floor, and after being unconscious for five hours, died.

The defense offered three theories to negate the defendant's criminal responsibility for the death. The first was that the homicide was excusable under the New York Penal Code.

The code provided: "Homicide is excusable when committed by accident and misfortune, in doing any lawful act, by lawful means, with ordinary caution and without any unlawful intent." It was argued that under the code the defendant's responsibility for his sparring partner's death was negated.

The second defense was that the homicide was justifiable under the theory of self-defense. The fatal blow, it was argued, was delivered in response to the provocation of the defendant. There was testimony that the victim had escalated the intensity of the sparring match.

The third and primary defense was the consent defense. The defendant maintained that the victim took his chances in engaging in the contest, whatever the consequences might be.

NOTE _____

1. For a further discussion of *State* v. *Forbes*, see Flakne and Caplan, "Sports Violence and the Prosecution," 13 *Trial* 33 (January 1977).

5.30   The Scope of Criminal Liability

One very interesting aspect of criminal liability for sports violence has never been explored in the criminal courts and that is the role that owners and coaches play in condoning violent conduct. Theoretically, criminal law could be applied to bring charges against them. For instance, Fred Shero, coach of the Philadelphia Flyers hockey team in the 1970s, was severely criticized for his strategy of intimidation. The team was nicknamed the "Broad Street Bullies" because of tactics that included fighting to take opposing players out of a game.

Crimes involving condoning a criminal activity already exist. They have not, however, been applied to sports. These crimes are the general class of offenses known as the anticipatory offenses, such as solicitation, conspiracy, and accomplice liability. Solicitation is committed when a person, with intent that another person commit a crime, advises, incites, or orders another to commit an offense. A coach or owner who orders a player to physically take an opposing player out of the game would be committing the crime of solicitation, even if the player never acted on the request. Conspiracy is a crime that consists of (1) an agreement between two or more persons and (2) an intent to achieve an unlawful objective or a lawful objective by unlawful means. Thus, an agreement between a coach and a player or coaches and players to intimidate the opposing team by fighting could be prosecuted under a conspiracy theory. Accomplice liability is a common-law doctrine which holds that certain persons who aid and abet a crime are liable for the same punishment as the principal. This type of criminal liability could, in theory, be applied to the sports violence situation to reach coaches or players who aid and abet a criminal battery during a sports event.

Although theoretically these offenses could be applied to the area of sports violence, it is not very likely to occur. The application of criminal punishment to the athlete is so infrequent that the possibility of criminal charges being brought against remote parties to the violence is even more unlikely.

NOTE _____

1. For further information, see the following articles:
(a) "Violence in Professional Sport," *Wisconsin Law Review* 771 (1975).
(b) Hechter, "Criminal Law and Violence in Sport," 19 *Criminal Law Quarterly* 425 (Spring 1977).

5.40   League Disciplinary Procedure and Sanctions

The professional sports leagues have their own internal procedures for punishing excessive violence and other rules violations. These procedures run the gamut from well-developed written rules of conduct to a completely discretionary power to discipline that resides in the hands of one person — the league commissioner or president. Internal league discipline is extremely important, for, unless prosecutors or legislators become more involved in the sports violence area, league discipline is the only method presently used to control sports violence.

Internal procedures for maintaining discipline have been established by all professional sports leagues and most amateur sports organizations (the NCAA, for example) to avoid the entanglement of civil and criminal court procedures. The power to discipline is commonly concentrated in the offices of the commissioner or president — persons who wield immense discretionary powers when it comes to determining violations and punishments. The leagues or organizations derive their power from the consent of the players, who have little choice but to submit to the rules. In professional sports, players unions have been uniformly unsuccessful in reducing the power of the commissioner in the area of player discipline. Athletes are generally given an internal means of appealing a commissioner's or president's decision and, in limited situations, may be able to take an appeal to the courts. However, these cases are difficult for athletes to win because of the commissioner's and president's immense discretionary power.

In professional sports, the standard player contract and/or collective bargaining agreement is the instrument that gives the league its disciplinary control. These agreements generally contain a clause stating that the player consents to be bound by the constitution, rules, and bylaws of the league. The league uses the consent obtained by this clause to impose fines and/or suspensions for violations of a rule. Examples of these clauses appear in the notes.

The procedures the leagues follow in imposing punishment for rule infractions often lack any fundamental due process. In the National Basketball Association (NBA), for example, the commissioner has complete discretionary power to discipline a player by way of a fine or suspension. Kermit Washington

received a 60-day suspension without pay for his brutal blow to Rudy Tomjanovich's face (see Section 4.24), while some 25 years earlier, Jack Molinas was suspended for life by the NBA commissioner for gambling (see Volume 1, Chapter 4). Many contracts contain a clause that allows the commissioner to discipline a player for acts that are contrary to the "best interests of the game."

NOTES

1. The following excerpt is from the National Football League's Standard Player Contract, clause 15:

Integrity of Game. Player recognizes the detriment to the League and professional football that would result from impairment of public confidence in the honest and orderly conduct of NFL games or the integrity and good character of NFL players. Player therefore acknowledges his awareness that if he accepts a bribe or agrees to throw or fix an NFL game; fails to promptly report a bribe offer or an attempt to throw or fix an NFL game; bets on an NFL game; knowingly associates with gamblers or gambling activity; uses or provides other players with stimulants or other drugs for the purpose of attempting to enhance on-field performance, or is guilty of any other form of conduct reasonably judged by the League Commissioner to be detrimental to the League or professional football, the Commissioner will have the right, but only after giving Player the opportunity for a hearing at which he may be represented by counsel of his choice, to fine Player in a reasonable amount, to suspend Player for a period certain or indefinitely; and/or to terminate this contract.

2. Major League Baseball is governed, in part, by Major League Rule 21, "Misconduct," which states in part:

Violence or Misconduct in Interleague Games. In case of any physical attack or other violence upon an umpire by a player, or by an umpire upon a player, or of other misconduct by an umpire or a player, during or in connection with any interleague Major League game or any exhibition game of a Major League Club with a club or team not a member of the same league, the Commissioner shall impose upon the offender or offenders such fine, suspension, ineligibility or other penalty, as the facts may warrant in the judgment of the Commissioner.

Other Misconduct. Nothing herein contained shall be construed as exclusively defining or otherwise limiting acts, transactions, practices or conduct not to be in the best interests of Baseball; and any and all other acts, transactions, practices or conduct not to be in the best interests of Baseball are prohibited and shall be subject to such penalties including permanent ineligibility, as the facts in the particular case may warrant.

3. The Collective Bargaining Agreement between the National Hockey League and the National Hockey League Players Association, in Article 15.01, "Intentional Injury," states:

The Clubs shall promulgate on an experimental basis a rule requiring immediate suspension of any hockey player who receives a match penalty for intentionally injuring any other hockey player. Such suspension shall remain in effect until a determination with respect to the match penalty has been made by the President of the National Hockey League. Any hearing which the President decides to hold with respect to the matter shall be held as promptly as is practicable under the circumstances, and reasonable efforts shall be made to hold any such hearing not later than one week after the date of the suspension.

4. The following excerpt is from the *National Basketball Association's Administrative Manual*, Sec. 330, pp. 2–3: *Position of NBA and Its Teams Regarding Violence on the Basketball Court:*

Violence has no place in the game of basketball and violent behavior cannot be tolerated under any circumstances.

You are highly skilled and highly trained athletes. Your physical well-being is of paramount importance to you, your team, and the NBA. Violence can and often does result in serious physical injury. Such injury could seriously impair your future as an athlete as well as others who may be involved in such violent conduct.

The NBA and all of its teams abhor violence and condemn its existence in our sport. As a player in the NBA, you are hereby advised that violent conduct will not be tolerated under any circumstances. Nothing which occurs during a game can justify an act of willful violence.

The NBA and your team will take immediate and appropriate action against any player who engages in such conduct and all personnel are advised that violence must be avoided at all times. There will be no variance from this express statement of policy.

This avoidance of violence is to your benefit as well as to the benefit of all players and teams in the NBA. *You must comply.*

5. In March 1971, NFL Commissioner Peter Rozelle proposed the following rule to the team owners, which they accepted: *Any player leaving the bench area while a fight is in progress on the field will be fined $200.* Rozelle wanted to curtail injuries to players from violence on the football field. However, the NFL Players Association

challenged the rule and the court agreed that the rule change constituted an unfair labor practice. See *National Football League Players Ass'n. v. National Labor Relations Board and National Football League Management Council,* 503 F. 2d 12 (8th Cir. 1974).

6. In 1985, the umpires in the Puerto Rican Winter League threatened to strike when Vic Power, manager of the Caguas team, punched an umpire during a game and was only suspended for the remainder of the season. The umpires wanted a minimum one-year suspension. See "Umpires Protest," *New York Times,* January 12, 1985, p. 30.

7. For further information, see the following articles:
(a) "Comment, Discipline in Professional Sports: The Need for Player Protection," 60 *Georgetown Law Journal* 771 (1972).
(b) "Contract Matters and Disciplinary Procedures in Professional Sport," 39 *Saskatchewan Law Review* 213 (1974).
(c) "The Professional Athlete: Liberty or Peonage?" 13 *Alberta Law Review* 212 (1975).
(d) Schneiderman, "Professional Sport: Involuntary Servitude and the Popular Will," 7 *Gonzaga Law Review* 63 (Fall 1971).

5.50   Proposed Legislative Solutions to Sports Violence

As a result of the general dissatisfaction with the amount of violence in sports and the ineffectiveness of both league disciplinary rules and criminal sanctions in preventing needless injuries, a few legislative solutions have been proposed to bring the problem under control. One major proposal in this area was the Sports Violence Act (see Exhibit 5–1 in Section 5.20). The Sports Violence Act was proposed by Congressman Ronald M. Mottl and was introduced before the House of Representatives in both 1980 (H.R. 7903) and 1981 (H.R. 2263). The bill never made it to the floor of the House, and Congressman Mottl was not reelected in 1982.

The act would have made it a criminal offense for professional athletes to engage in excessive violence. Under the act, a player who "knowingly uses excessive physical force and thereby causes a risk of significant bodily injury to another person involved in that event" could be punished. Excessive physical force was defined as that which was unreasonably violent, had no reasonable relationship to the game, and could not have been reasonably foreseen or consented to.

A federal criminal statute covering sports violence was seen as necessary because of the interstate nature of modern professional sports leagues and the lack of local enforcement of criminal statutes by the states where professional athletes were involved in bahavior that could be classified as a crime. Local assault and battery prosecutions, based on commonlaw notions of crime, had no relevancy to the issues of sports violence because of the special problems of assumption of risk, consent, and self-defense that are present in sports cases.

Although the Sports Violence Act died in Congress due to the absence of its chief sponsor, another bill was subsequently introduced which would have established an arbitration board as an independent disciplinary body to handle sports violence incidents. Entitled the "Sports Violence Arbitration Act of 1983" (see Exhibit 5–2 in Section 5.20), this bill was introduced before the 98th Congress in 1983 by Congressman Thomas A. Daschle of South Dakota; however, it also was not passed.

The bill was intended to allow the professional leagues to control incidents of excessive violence more effectively without direct intervention by the federal government. Instead of a federal criminal statute, such as the Sports Violence Act proposed, the Sports Violence Arbitration Act required each professional league to establish an arbitration panel that would have had the power to punish teams and players for conduct found to be inconsistent with the competitive goals of the sport. Proposed sanctions against the guilty player's team included payment of the injured player's salary and medical expenses, payment of compensatory damages if the player's career had ended, and/or payment of damages or relinquishment of a draft choice to the injured player's club for loss of the player's services and fines. The guilty player would have been subjected to severe fines and lengthy suspensions at the discretion of the arbitration board. The act provided for a full evidentiary hearing process. The sponsor of the bill believed that its positive impact on the level of violence in professional sports would have great influence on play at the amateur level.

If the level of serious violence remains high in professional sports and the leagues cannot control it, Congress may continue to consider different types of federal legislation to eliminate the problem. The use of criminal statutes, however, has been and probably will be vigorously opposed by the professional leagues.

NOTES

1. The idea behind the Sports Violence Arbitration Act was first presented by Carlsen and Walker in "Sports Court: A Private System to Deter Violence in Professional Sports," 55 *University of Southern California Law Review* 399 (1982).

2. See Hearings Before the Subcommittee on Crime of the Committee on the Judiciary, House of Representatives 96th Congress (2nd Session) on H.R. 7903, *Excessive Violence in Professional Sports*, Serial No. 76 (1981).

3. For further information, see the following articles:

(a) "Controlling Violence in Professional Sports: Rule Reform and the Federal Professional Sports Violence and Commission," 21 *Duquesne Law Review* 843 (Summer 1983).

(b) "Proposed Legislative Solution to the Problem of Violent Acts by Participants during Professional Sporting Events: The Sports Violence Act of 1980," 7 *University of Dayton Law Review* 91 (Fall 1981).

4. On May 29, 1985, a riot broke out in Brussels, Belguim, before the finals of the European Cup soccer match that had a team from Liverpool, England, playing a team from Turin, Italy. In the riot, 38 people died, 31 of them Italians. Because of fears of further fan violence, the match was still played as stretcher bearers carried off the dead and injured. In June 1985, the International Soccer Federation (FIFA) placed an indefinite worldwide ban on English soccer clubs competing in matches. In July 1985 FIFA modified its ban to exclude English clubs only from competition in Europe. For further information on this subject, see the following articles:

(a) "Why Soccer Serves as a Vehicle for Fan Violence," *New York Times*, June 2, 1985, sec. 5, p. 2.

(b) "Source of Pride Now a Source of Liverpool Sorrow," *New York Times*, June 15, 1985, p. 2.

(c) "Ban Is Modified on British Soccer," *St. Louis Post Dispatch*, July 12, 1985, D4.

(d) "Britain Acts on Soccer 'Hooligans,'" *Boston*

Globe, July 25, 1985, p. 2.

5. Many experts fear that violence similar to the Brussel's soccer incident could occur in this country if proper control is not exercised at sports facilities. For further information, see the following articles:

(a) "Rowdies Everywhere Beware," *USA Today*, May 9, 1985, pp. C1, 2.

(b) "Dark Signs Exist in the U.S., Too," *New York Times*, June 2, 1985, sec. 5, p. 2.

(c) "Unruliness an Ugly Pastime for Some Baseball Fans," *New York Times*, June 16, 1985, sec. 5, pp. 1, 10.

5.60 Drug Abuse, Testing, and Enforcement

The problem of drug abuse has grown at all levels of athletic competition over the last 20 years at a frightening speed, from the interscholastic to the Olympic and professional levels of competition. In the United States, the increased instances of drug abuse in athletics reflect a like increase and, to a degree, acceptance of drugs among the general populace. It is a serious issue that includes health considerations, law enforcement problems, and moral/ethical questions for athletes, coaches, and sport managers.

In June 1984, U.S. Attorney General William French Smith announced a drug-abuse prevention program designed to reach 5.5 million interscholastic athletes (see Note 1). According to the attorney general, athletes "can provide the leadership needed to create a peer-pressure strongly against drug use. They can help cut the demands in our society for illicit drugs." The recognition by the nation's highest law enforcement official of this problem at the high school level of athletics underscores the degree to which drug abuse has become a concern in American society.

In this section, drug-abuse problems in athletics will be examined primarily in the area of detection and penalty methods used by the collegiate, professional, and Olympic governing bodies. The case law in this area generally deals with criminal sanctions imposed by the courts on athletes and is not a concern of this text. One exception is *Shoemaker et al.* v. *Handel, infra*, which examines questions relating to the constitutionality of drug testing for individuals involved in sports.

Shoemaker et al. v. Handel, Civil Action No. 85-1770 (D.N.J. 1985)

This action involved plaintiff jockeys William Shoemaker (President of the Jockey's Guild), Angelo Cordero, Jr., William McCauley, Philip Grove, and Vincent Bracciole who on behalf of the Jockey's Guild brought suit against the New Jersey Racing Commission under 42 U.S.C. Section 1983 and sought a preliminary injunction against the defendant from enforcement of the commission's regulations requiring breathalyzer and urine tests for licensed jockeys (N.J.A.C. 13:70–14A.10 and 13:70–14A.11). The suit was filed in April 1985, and in May 1985 the district court made the following finding of facts and conclusions of law:

I. FINDINGS OF FACT

... 5. The New Jersey State Legislature has established a New Jersey Racing Commission, vested with the broad "powers necessary or proper to enable it to carry out fully and effectually all the provisions and purposes of this act," including jurisdiction over "any and all persons, partnerships, associations or corporations which shall hereafter hold or conduct any meeting within the State of New Jersey whereat horse racing shall be permitted for any stake, purse, or reward." N.J.S.A. 5:5-22.

6. The Racing Commission promulgated N.J.A.C. 13:70-14A.10 and 14A.11 pursuant to its authority granted by N.J.S.A. 5:5-30. These regulations permit the use of breathalyzer and urine tests to detect the presence of alcohol or controlled substances as defined in N.J.S.A. 24:21-1 *et seq.* They were proposed on June 18, 1984, 16 N.J.R. 1457(a), adopted on January 14, 1985, 17 N.J.R. 470, effective on February 19, 1985, and operational on April 1, 1985.

7. N.J.A.C. 13:70-14A.10 provides that a State Steward may direct officials, jockeys, trainers and grooms to submit to a breathalyzer test. If the result of that test shows a reading of .05 percent

of alcohol in the blood, "such person shall not be permitted to continue his duties." The Steward "may fine or suspend any participant who records a blood alcohol reading of .05 percent or more." Second or repeat offenders "shall be subject to expulsion, or such penalty as the stewards may deem appropriate."

8. N.J.A.C. 13:70-14A.11 provides, *inter alia*, that "[e]very jockey for any race at any licensed racetrack may be subjected to a post-race urine test, or other non-invasive fluid test at the direction of the State Steward in a manner prescribed by the New Jersey Racing commission. Any jockey who fails to submit to a urine test when requested to do so by the State Steward shall be liable to the penalties provided in N.J.A.C. 13:70-31." N.J.A.C. 13:70-14A.11(b). The regulation further provides that a "positive" drug test result be reported in writing to the Executive Director of the Racing Commission or his designee. N.J.A.C. 13:70-14A.11(d).

9. N.J.A.C. 13.70-14A.11 also provides that "[t]he results of any urine test shall be treated as confidential, except for their use with respect to a ruling issued pursuant to this rule, or any administrative or judical hearing with regard to such a ruling. Access to the reports of any "positive" results shall be limited to the Commissioners of the New Jersey Racing Commission, the Executive Director and/or his designee and the subject jockey, except in the instance of a contested matter." N.J.A.C. 13:70-14A.11(e).

10. N.J.A.C. 13:70-14A.11 also provides that "[n]o jockey shall use any Controlled Dangerous Substance as defined in the 'New Jersey Controlled Dangerous Substance Act,' N.J.S.A. 24:21-1, *et seq.* or any prescription legend drug, unless such substance was obtained directly, or pursuant to a valid prescription or order from a licensed physician, while acting in the course of his professional practice. It shall be the responsibility of the jockey to give prior notice to the State Steward that he is using a Controlled Dangerous Substance or prescription legend drug pursuant to a valid prescription or order from a licensed practitioner." N.J.A.C. 13:70-14A.11 (a).

11. On April 1, 1985, a meeting was held in the jockey's room at the Garden State Park, Cherry Hill, New Jersey, among representatives of the Racing Commission, jockeys, and representatives of the National Jockeys Guild, the purpose of which was to explain the new regulations.

12. The Jockeys Guild requested that the Racing Commission defer implementation of these regulations until a court challenge to their validity could be mustered. The Racing Commission declined to defer enforcement.

13. Defendants have forced or threatened to force plaintiffs to undergo breathalyzer and/or urine testing pursuant to N.J.A.C. 13:70-14A.10 and 14A.11.

14. Defendants have forced or threatened to force plaintiffs to fill our certain forms requiring the disclosure of personal medical data and other information pursuant to N.J.A.C. 13:70-14A.11(a).

II. CONCLUSIONS OF LAW

1. The following Conclusions of Law, insofar as they may be considered Findings of Fact, are so found by this court to be true in all respects....

5. Plaintiffs allege that N.J.A.C. 13:70-14A.10 and 14A.11 violate their rights guaranteed by the Fourth, Fifth, and Ninth Amendments and the Due Process and Equal Protection Clauses of the Fourteenth Amendment to the United States Constitution. Specifically, plaintiffs argue that defendants:

(a) subject jockeys to unreasonable searches and seizures;

(b) require the disclosure of private medical information, potentially relevant to violations of the criminal law of the State of New Jersey, without adequate safeguards for maintaining its confidentiality.

(c) fail to provide a hearing during which plaintiffs can challenge the results of the breathalyzer and urine tests; and

(d) discriminate against jockeys as a group by singling them out for breathalyzer and urine testing.

The court will address the strength of the plaintiffs' claims *seriatim.*

6. *The Search and Seizure Claim.* The Fourth Amendment provides that "[t]he right of the people to be secure in their persons ... against unreasonable searches and seizures, shall not be violated, and no Warrants shall issue, but upon probable cause, supported by Oath or affirmation, and particularly describing the place to be searched, and the persons or things to be seized." The essential purpose of the proscriptions in the

Fourth Amendment is to "impose a standard of 'reasonableness' upon the exercise of discretion by government officials," including law enforcement agents and state regulatory personnel, in order to "safeguard the privacy and security of individuals against arbitrary intrusions. . . ." (cites omitted). Thus, the Fourth Amendment protects individuals from "unreasonable government intrusions into their legitimate expectations of privacy." . . . (cites omitted)

Except in certain carefully limited classes of cases, a search of private property or person without consent is "unreasonable" unless it has been authorized by a valid search warrant. . . . An exception to the search warrant requirement has been recognized for "pervasively regulated business" and for "closely related" industries "long subject to close supervision and regulation." . . .

Horse racing meets *both* exceptions to the search warrant requirement. . . . This industry has been subject to "pervasive *and* long standing regulation by New Jersey." *State v. Dolce*, 178 N.J. Super. 275, 283-85 (App. Div. 1981) (emphasis added).

> The State has had and continues to have a vital interest in the horse racing industry, particularly with respect to maintaining its integrity. *Jersey Downs, Inc. v. New Jersey Racing Commission*, 102 N.J. Super. 451, 457 (App. Div. 1968). Consequently, our legislature has established the Racing Commission and vested in it the power and duty to govern all aspects of horse racing in this State, including all those working in the industry. N.J.S.A. 5:5-22. To this end, the Racing Commission was granted broad rule-making powers to protect the state's interest in the industry and to carry out its statutory mandate. N.J.S.A. 5:5-30.

. . . While horse racing comes within the recognized exception to the administrative search warrant rule, the court must still address whether the state's regulations which provide for the use and administration of breathalyzer tests and urinalyses meet the "reasonableness" test of the Fourth Amendment. As the Supreme Court has noted,

> [Reasonableness] is not capable of precise definition or mechanical application. In each case it requires a balancing of the need for the particular search against the invasion of personal rights that the search entails. Courts must consider the scope of the particular intrusion,

the manner in which it is conducted, the justification for initiating it, and the place in which it is conducted.

The courts have used this standard to differentiate between levels and degrees of intrusiveness among searches and seizures. As measured by the degree of invasion, inspections of personal effects are generally least intrusive, while breaches of the "integrity of the body" result in the greatest invasion of privacy. The court, of course, must also consider an individual's reasonable expectations of privacy under the circumstances. In other words, the court must balance the competing interests involved on a case-by-case basis. . . .

The court finds that plaintiffs fail to demonstrate that the Racing Commission's breathalyzer testing and urinalysis program is not closely tailored to further the state's legitimate interest in reducing the use of alcoholic beverages and drugs, thereby promoting the safety and integrity of horse racing and protecting the public.

First, the regulations contested by plaintiffs were promulgated for the specific purpose of combatting and hopefully eliminating the perceived and actual use of alcohol and drugs which plagues this sport, as well as so many others. Use of drugs and alcohol by jockeys increases significantly the probability that serious injuries and death will occur during the race, as a result of single and multi-horse accidents. The state argues that the testing regimen previously used proved ineffective and failed to stop or reduce the use of these substances. As a result, the state has issued new regulations which may increase the likelihood of success and which provide for such testing at the direction of the State Steward when it appears most efficacious — at the track, proximate to race time. In this respect, the court notes that "substantially identical regulations are in effect for the testing of harness drivers" in New Jersey. The harness breathalyzer rule has been in effect for several years. Harness drivers have been required to submit to random post-race urine tests since January 1985. . . . From June, 1982 to the present, 385 tests have been conducted on harness drivers on a random basis, using the Enzyme Multiplied Immunoassay Technique System of analysis. Thirty-five of these tests, more than eight percent, proved positive. Readings ranged from marijuana to heroin use. . . .

Second, these tests as applied to jockeys are not

unique. Boxing is also a heavily regulated industry in New Jersey, with boxers being subject to stringent regulations and testing as to their physical fitness to compete. All boxers must undergo physical examinations on the day of the bout "both at weigh in and in the evening, a short while before the boxing program commences." These tests include blood samples, and "[i]n all cases . . . a thorough ophthalmological and neurological examination and a urinalysis." N.J.A.C. 13:46-12.2(a). A boxer may be disqualified for any medical reason. N.J.A.C. 13:46-12.2(b). The boxer "must submit to any prefight or postfight urinalysis or other laboratory procedure ordered by the physician appointed by the Commissioner to detect the presence of any drug. Refusal to submit to such testing shall result in the immediate disqualification of the boxer from the match and an indefinite suspension from boxing. N.J.A.C. 13:46-12.3.

Third, while the Supreme Court has refrained from drawing bright lines among searches, breathalyzer tests and urinalyses are considered less intrusive than body cavity and strip searches and those searches which have been identified as intruding upon the "integrity of the body," . . .

While breathalyzer and urine tests require the individual involved to "give up" something, the intrusion is less than the involuntary securing of a blood sample or other searches into which an intrusion into the body is required.

Fourth, jockeys have diminished expectations of privacy as to these job related searches and seizures. The jockeys admit to the pervasive historical regulation of their industry:

Jockeys, like other athletes have always been subject to medical examinations or testing where they exhibited some physical symptomatology indicating a potential problem with their riding performance. . . .

. . . The state's regulations go one step further by permitting the random examination of jockeys at the direction of the Steward. Jockeys are licensed by the State to race in New Jersey, subject to the extensive and detailed conditions and regulations in effect. By securing their licensure, jockeys accept the unique benefits as well as the burdens of their trade. They have notice that the state has regulations which concern aspects of their physical and mental fitness to ride. This includes alcohol and drug use

which impedes their riding performance. The state has a legitimate interest in ensuring the health and safety of all participants and in preserving the integrity of the gambling industry as a whole. . . .

. . . By adopting these regulations the state has embarked upon a unique regulatory program, rehabilitative rather than penal in nature.

The court is reluctant, without a greater showing by plaintiffs, to enjoin part of an extensive state regulatory scheme, especially when such action may be perceived by the public as undermining the ability of the Racing Commission to adequately police this industry or the public's confidence in the Racing Commission's ability to do its job. The court finds that, at this point, plaintiffs have failed to meet their burden to demonstrate a probability of success on the merits, that plaintiffs will suffer any irreparable harm as a result of continued testing during the duration of this litigation, and that the public interest in the integrity and safety of thoroughbred racing will be served by an injunction. Therefore, the court denies plaintiffs' motion for a preliminary injunction preventing the enforcement of N.J.A.C. 13:70-14A.10 and 13:70-14A.11.

7. The Privacy Claim. The state forbids plaintiffs from using any Controlled Dangerous Substances, as defined by N.J.S.A. 24:21-1 *et seq.*, or prescription legend drugs, unless obtained directly or pursuant to a valid prescription or order from a licensed physician. Plaintiffs must give the State Steward notice of such use. N.J.A.C. 13:70-14A.11(a). Plaintiffs must fill out a form . . . which asks for the names of prescribed medications, the names of the persons who prescribed them, what each prescription treats, and the date and time of the last dosage of each medication taken. The form also requires that plaintiffs provide the names of over-the-counter medications used, what these medications treat, and the date and time of the last dosage. Plaintiffs argue that the regulation (1) forces jockeys to divulge private, personal medical information without sufficient justification, (2) forces jockeys to divulge information which could incriminate them under the laws of New Jersey, and (3) fails to provide adequate provisions and safeguards to prevent the disclosure of such information to the public and members of their profession.

While the constitution does not explicitly state that there is a right to privacy, a constitutional doctrine has been established and expanded "variously described as recognizing a right to privacy." . . .(cites omitted). There is a privacy interest in avoiding disclosure to government agents of personal medical information. . . . (cite omitted). However, this privacy interest is not absolute and must be balanced against the legitimate interest of the state in securing such information. The regulations must be narrowly tailored to "express only those compelling state interests." . . . (cites omitted). The extent of the plaintiffs' privacy interests must be judged in light of the statutory safeguards against disclosure. . . . (cite omitted). The state must use the narrowest means consistent with the maintenance of its legitimate interests. . . . (cites omitted).

The state's disclosure form, by asking jockeys to provide the nature of the illness requiring treatment by prescription drug, is more intrusive . . . For example, if a jockey takes antipsychotic medications, he would be required to divulge, if applicable, that he suffers from certain mental illnesses or diseases. The court recognizes that the Racing Commission has a legitimate safety interest in preventing the use of Dangerous Controlled Substances by jockeys. The disclosure of certain medical information, and the forms utilized for that disclosure, furthers that stated purpose. The court does not find persuasive the state's arguments that it has tailored the disclosure form so as to avoid unnecessarily intruding into private medical matters which are not germaine to the furtherance of the state's articulated interests. These medical forms require jockeys to disclose within the sections marked "For Treatment Of" the illness or conditions for which a particular drug has been prescribed or used. The regulation is designed to prevent the illicit use of drugs and to aid in the proper detection of that use. The court questions whether such disclosure will further the state's professed goals. In fact, such disclosure is not required on the face of the regulations issued by the Racing Commission. The state argues that the jockeys may, at their option, choose to leave the "For Treatment Of" sections blank when they complete these forms. Consistent with the state's representations as to this aspect of the controversy, the court directs the Racing Commission to insert the word "optional" in the "For Treatment Of" sections of the disclosure form, thereby clearly indicating to jockeys that they may leave the objectionable sections empty.

Plaintiffs also argue that the regulations do not clearly safeguard against the disclosure of information obtained by the testing program or the medical forms. The regulations do provide that the results of urine tests shall be treated as confidential "*except* for their use with respect to a ruling issued pursuant to this rule." Access to the results of "positive" urine tests "shall be limited to the Commissioners of the New Jersey Racing Commission, the Executive Director and/or his designee and the subject jockey, *except* in the instance of a contested matter." N.J.A.C. 13:70-14A.11(a) & (e) (emphasis added). The defendants have represented to this court that they wish to do everything possible to preserve the confidentiality of the medical information collected pursuant to the regulations. The Racing Commission will not share any data collected with any state agency charged with the enforcement of New Jersey's criminal laws. Such information is gathered with "rehabilitative" and not "penal" purposes in mind.

Under the circumstances, plaintiffs have failed to persuade the court that they are likely to prevail on the merits of their privacy claims. Therefore, the court will deny plaintiffs' motion for a preliminary injunction . . .

8. *The Due Process Claim*. Plaintiffs also allege that the regulations fail to provide a hearing at which plaintiffs can challenge the results of the breathalyzer and urine tests. The Racing Commission does provide a hearing, however, for jockeys wishing to challenge the results of the tests — at the jockeys' request. . . .

9. *The Equal Protection Claim*. Plaintiffs also allege that the regulations discriminate against jockeys by singling them out as a group for breathalyzer and urine testing, without a rational basis or compelling interest to do so. The state has a legitimate safety interest in testing the jockeys in order to reduce the possibility of accidents and even death while racing.

10. *Conclusion*. In summary, the court denies plaintiffs' motion for a preliminary injunction in its entirety. The court orders defendants to insert the word "optional" in the "For Treatment Of" sections of the medical disclosure form.

NOTES _____

1. The plan announced by Attorney General William French Smith was essentially a drug-abuse education program in which prevention materials were provided by the Drug Enforcement Administration (DEA) to participating schools. It was developed as a joint project of the National High School Athletic Coaches Association (48,000 members in 20,000 schools) and the DEA. Its focus was on the special bond of trust and mutual respect that exists between young athletes and their coaches. For further information, see "U.S. School Drug Plan," *New York Times*, June 28, 1984, p. 11.

2. Jack Lawn, Deputy Director of the Drug Enforcement Administration, testified before the U.S. Senate Subcommittee on Alcoholism and Drug Abuse on September 25, 1984. The following statement is excerpted from his testimony:

The Sports Drug Abuse Awareness Program we have recently launched is designed to do exactly that — to focus on the demand for drugs. What is probably most important about this program is that it is a joint undertaking involving the teamwork of DEA and the National High School Athletic Coaches Association, with support and participation from the IACP, the NFL and the NFL Players Association, and the Office of Juvenile Justice and Delinquency Prevention — and this teamwork is what will make this new initiative successful.

Our goal is to prevent drug abuse among school-age youth, with a special emphasis on the role of the coach and the student athlete. We want to reach, and intend to reach, the 48,000 men and women coaches in 20,000 high schools across the country who can, in turn, help us reach five and one-half million student athletes. And then we hope there will be a snow-balling effect to reach millions of other students who look up to our athletes.

As I mentioned, our first task is to involve the coaches. They are, for the most part, born leaders and have earned respect and loyalty from their athletes. And they have contact with more than half of their student bodies. With the help and involvement of the coaches, we feel that student athletes can be trained to act as role models, using positive peer pressure to dissuade other students from using drugs.

Key elements that we intend to accomplish during the first year of the project include the following:

- Distribution of a brochure that provides information to coaches on the need for high school prevention programs involving student athletes.
- Distribution of a packet of materials containing an

action plan and guidelines on how to start a drug-abuse prevention program for student athletes. Kits containing both the brochure and the action plan are currently being distributed to every high school coach in the country.

- DEA presentations and technical assistance for coaches in district clinics nationwide. Special Agent teams, representing DEA's finest athletes, will be assisted by professional football players at each clinic. Their presentations and assistance will deal with such elements as drug recognition; what signs to look for in determining whether athletes are using drugs; what to do about it and how to counsel young people with respect to what they are doing to themselves and their teammates.

The brochure and action plan that have been developed for this project represent what we believe is the best thinking currently available on how to combat school drug use and abuse. Besides those organizations I mentioned earlier who are participating, we also have under study the involvement of professional baseball, basketball, hockey and colleges, as well as some major national organizations such as the National Federation of Parents for Drug Free Youth.

The task of teaching the athletes to serve as positive role models will take the dedication and commitment of each person and organization involved throughout the country. As a former high school coach, I am convinced we can achieve positive results.

3. In September 1984, the U.S. Senate Subcommittee on Alcoholism and Drug Abuse held hearings concerning drug abuse in athletics. Senator Paula Hawkins of Florida, the subcommittee chair, stated:

Today we examine the impact of illegal drugs on sports and the national efforts of sports figures to fight youth drug abuse.

Almost every kind of professional sports, and amateur athletics, can be exciting for the spectator, though punishing for the participant. Until recently, however, it was not thought that the tragedy of drug abuse had entered the game, but more and more disturbing information is emerging of the tragic correlation between the pressures of play, both physical and emotional, and resulting drug use.

While there is no reliable scientific data available detailing the amount of drug use by athletes, all indications are that a larger proportion of athletes than non-athletes, both amateur and professional, are abusing drugs and/or alcohol.

One of the most tragic aspects of this situation is, as

one sports figure poignantly states: ". . . the saddest thing about an athlete having a drug problem is that the kids see it." We Americans take our sports, and our sports figures, seriously, and expect those involved to be above suspicion, not only of bribery and manipulation, but also of such aberrational behavior as drug abuse. When a major sports figure is found to be drug dependent, even though he may be an involuntary role model, he disappoints and hurts many more people than just himself. It can be devastating not only for the athlete, who throws away the precious gifts of supreme athletic ability and achievement, but also for the young person who idolizes and often emulates him.

Organized sports, both amateur and professional, should be alert to the potential for the corruption that exists in drug use, most importantly because no anti-drug program can be successful, whether it stresses education, prevention or treatment, unless it commands the support and participation of the players.

4. In 1984, at the Meadowlands Sports Complex, the New Jersey Sports and Exposition Authority implemented new policies to control alcohol abuse and rowdiness at events:

> (a) Beer vendors are not allowed to sell beer to customers in their seats. To purchase beer, a customer will have to leave his seat and go to the concession stand.
> (b) At football games, sales of beer are discontinued at the beginning of the third quarter.
> (c) The largest capacity beer sold is limited to twenty ounces, eliminating the thirty-two ounce "big beers."
> (d) Football season ticket holders may lose their ticket rights for subsequent seasons if they become involved in fights or other such rowdy behavior.
> (e) Low-alcohol and no-alcohol beers are offered for sale. See "Rowdy Football Fans at Meadows Will Put Season Tickets in Jeopardy," *Newark Star Ledger*, July 21, 1984, p. 1.

5. Similarly, Sullivan Stadium in Foxboro, Massachusetts, home of the New England Patriots, began offering low-alcohol beer during the 1984 season. Tiger Stadium, home of the Detroit Tigers, began offering low-alcohol beer for the 1985 season. The Metrodome in Minneapolis sells only 3.2 beer at its events, while at Pittsburgh's Three Rivers Stadium fans can sit in an alcohol-free family section. At other facilities, such as Shea Stadium in New York, low-alcohol beers were offered for sale for the first time ever in 1985, with half the vendors assigned to sell the product. See "Sports Fans Face Curbs on Excessive Drinking" (AP Wireservice), *Newark Star Ledger*, March 14, 1985, p. 50, and "Clubs Trying to Halt Drunkenness in Stands," *Dallas Times Herald*, March 14, 1985, p. C9.

6. Commenting on *Shoemaker*, Harold G. Handel,

executive director of the New Jersey Racing Commission, noted that: "The idea [drug testing of jockeys] is supposed to be a rehabilitative thing; to identify a problem and get them into some kind of treatment." See "Judge to Decide Fate of New Jersey Rules," *USA Today*, April 18, 1985, p. C8.

7. For further information on *Shoemaker*, see the following articles:

(a) "Jockeys Lose Challenge Against State Tests for Drugs, Alcohol," *Newark Star Ledger*, May 17, 1985, p. 28.

(b) "Jockeys Press Court to Bar State from Making Drug Tests at Tracks," *Newark Star Ledger*, June 19, 1985, p. 29.

5.61 Intercollegiate Athletics: Drug Abuse and Enforcement

In its 1983 publication, *NCAA Sports Medicine Handbook*, the NCAA made its position on drug abuse quite clear:

Policy No. 12: Nontherapeutic drugs

> Section 1. The NCAA condemns the employment of nontherapeutic drugs in any of its member institutions or affiliated organizations by staff members who authorize or allow their student-athletes to use such drugs and by student-athletes who do use such drugs.
>
> Section 2. All member institutions, their athletic staffs and their student-athletes should assert aggressively their wholesome influences in combating usages of non-therapeutic drugs among the nation's youth.

Policy 12 was a recommendation by the NCAA Committee on Competitive Safeguards and Medical Aspects of Sport. The committee develops "pertinent information regarding desirable training methods, the prevention and treatment of sports injuries and the utilization of sound safety measures on the college level." The committee was established in August 1982, because one of the NCAA's responsibilities is to recommend sports safety policies for the guidance of member institutions.

Before the 1980s, the NCAA had only minimal involvement concerning the presence of drugs in its intercollegiate athletic programs. It prohibited the use of drugs at athletic events, but the focus was more on spectators than on college athletes. As incidents of abuse became more frequent, however, and as the chief executive officers of member institutions became more vocal about the problem, the NCAA began to investigate the area of drugs and sports. One of the NCAA's first actions was to publish a Big Ten Conference Study on drug abuse conducted under the auspices of the NCAA Drug Committee with recommendations from the NCAA's newly formed Committee on Competitive Safeguards and Medical Aspects of Sport. The following excerpts are from this study:

CASE STUDY: NCAA Drug Use Pilot Study
August 15, 1982

General Comments

A questionnaire on drug use was prepared by the Drug Education Committee of the NCAA. The Big Ten Conference was chosen for a pilot study on substance use among college athletes.

Over 1,000 responses were obtained. The questionnaires were distributed by the team physicians and the students sealed them in unmarked envelopes which were sent to NCAA offices in Shawnee Mission, Kansas. There was no way to identify the responses of each school since it was felt that to receive confidential responses, no method of identifying individual schools should be provided.

Only male athletes in football, basketball, track and swimming were surveyed. No women's sports were surveyed. A revised questionnaire is being prepared for other NCAA schools or conferences wishing to expand this type of survey to other sports and to women's sports.

The purpose of the survey was to try to identify the extent of substance use and to assess the extent of the problem. From this, specific suggestions will be sent to member schools from the Drug Education Committee of the NCAA.

CASE STUDY: Program Recommendations to NCAA Member Institutions from the NCAA Drug Education Committee
April 16, 1982

Data from a recent pilot study of drug use by student-athletes conducted by the NCAA Drug Education Committee, and from other sources in the scientific literature, indicate that while the use of drugs such as heroin, LSD or the smoking of cigarettes is not a major problem among student-athletes, the use of alcohol has become by far the predominant drug problem within this group. The committee also is concerned particularly about the use of marijuana and the recent increase in the use of smokeless (chewing) tobacco. Results from the committee's pilot study also indicate that student-athletes would

Percentage of Big 10 Athletes Who Use Drugs

	First-year students	Upperclass-men	By Sport			
			Football	Track	Swimming	Basketball
Illegal substances						
Heroin	0.0%	0.2%	0.0%	1.0%	0.0%	0.0%
LSD-PCP	0.0	1.5	1.0	1.0	3.0	0.0
Downers (Quaaludes)	1.0	3.0	2.0	2.0	3.0	1.0
Amphetamines	3.0	6.0	6.0	3.0	5.0	4.0
Cocaine	2.0	7.0	7.0	4.0	5.0	4.0
Marijuana	13.0	22.0	22.0	16.0	19.0	10.0
Controlled substances						
Anabolic steroids	1.0	2.0	2.0	3.0	1.0	1.0
Other substances						
Alcohol	60.0	65.0	63.0	62.0	72.0	42.0
Smokeless tobacco	15.0	18.0	20.0	5.0	11.0	9.0
Cigarettes	1.0	2.0	1.0	2.0	3.0	0.0

like more guidance in this area from their athletic departments and their coaches.

Therefore, the NCAA Drug Education Committee strongly urges athletic departments at all member institutions to implement the following minimal elements of a drug education program for their student-athletes:

1. Schedule at the beginning of each school year a course of drug and alcohol awareness for all men and women athletes. Rather than trying to develop their own program, it is suggested that each institution utilize the resources and expertise already available in most communities. These programs should be aimed particularly at the new student-athlete and should emphasize the deleterious effects of drugs on athletic performance as well as on other aspects of life. If possible, a former athlete who has had a drug problem should be used for maximum impact. It also is suggested that a minimum of three sessions be scheduled: one dealing with alcohol; a second with other drugs; and a third with the legal aspects of drug use, and any other problems reasonably unique to the student-athlete that the institution might wish to cover (e.g., gambling).

2. Each member institution should develop and have in place a plan for treatment of student-athletes with drug or alcohol-related problems. Such plans should utilize treatment centers and programs available in the local community, and should emphasize rehabilitation rather than punishment. It is obviously more prudent to have such a plan in place before rather than after a problem develops.

3. Coaches should become more aware of potential drug-related problems in student-athletes, and specifically should be an available source of support if a student-athlete does develop a drug or alcohol-related problem.

4. In relation to recommendation #3, the athletic department at each member institution should schedule training sessions for all coaches, trainers and team physicians to present information on how to recognize and handle drug and alcohol-related problems.

The NCAA Drug Education Committee is developing a list of available written materials and videotapes for distribution to member institutions to provide help in implementing the above recommendations.

At the 1984 NCAA convention, Proposal No. 163 was adopted. It mandated the NCAA to develop a drug-testing program that could be enacted at the January 1985 convention. At the 1985 convention, however, the NCAA membership voted not to implement any drug testing program for at least one year until costs and legal problems could be further studied. Specifically, the 1984 convention resolution, sponsored by the Pacific-10 Conference, directed the development of a plan to test student-athletes for "controlled substances" (e.g., marijuana, LSD, heroin and alcohol) and alleged "performance-enhancing" drugs, which refer to central nervous system stimulants such as the amphetamine group, cocaine, and the various anabolic steroids and related compounds. It also directed preparation of a list of the NCAA "banned" drugs.

CASE STUDY: Proposed NCAA Three-Part Drug Testing Plan
June 28, 1984

1. The NCAA would be responsible for testing at NCAA championships for purported performance-enhancing drugs, primarily stimulants such as amphetamines, cocaine, and other psychomotor and central nervous system stimulants. At selected events, anabolic steroids would be included. This same approach would be used at postseason football games.

2. Because testing at specific events would not necessarily be an effective deterrent to the use of anabolic steroids (the student-athlete may cease using the steroids one or two months prior to the championship and escape detection), the committee is suggesting that the NCAA institute a random, on-campus testing program throughout the academic year. Within a specified number of years, all member institutions would be visited at least once by specimen-collection teams, and student-athletes in specified sports would be selected randomly to be tested for anabolic steroids. Other performance-enhancing drugs also could be included in the on-campus testing. It is contemplated that this part of the program would be a cooperative, integrated effort involving the institutions, its conference (if so affiliated) and the NCAA.

3. Testing for other controlled substances (e.g., marijuana, LSD, heroin), which are not considered in the performance-enhancing category, would be the responsibility of each institution. The special committee proposes to provide guidelines to assist those institutions choosing to develop a locally arranged drug-testing program to cover this category.

The committee believes that a drug-testing program in which the NCAA tested for drugs that generally are not believed to affect athletic performance or to impair the health of the student-athlete would be difficult to justify legally because it could be argued that such testing does not fall within the purview of an athletics governing body.

The committee encourages all member institutions to develop local drug-education programs for student-athletes and staff, as recommended in 1982 by the NCAA Drug Education Committee. In addition, it proposes an educational program, if a drug-testing plan is adopted at the 1985 Convention, to inform student-athletes and staff of the purposes and methods of the plan and the responsibilities of all parties in implementing the program.

Sanctions

The Administrative Committee is continuing to study the sanctions to be applied if a prohibited drug is used by a student-athlete. Among the possibilities are these:

- Forfeiture of an institution's contests if a student-athlete tests positive in the NCAA testing program (not the institutional program).
- Permanent loss of eligibility (subject to existing appeal opportunities) of the student-athlete testing positive in the NCAA program (not the institution's own program).
- Application of the "show cause" provision of the enforcement procedure if an athletics department staff member is found to have been involved, directly or indirectly, in arrangements to provide prohibited drugs to student-athletes.

Costs

The special committee continues to investigate cost factors. While no specific cost figure is available at this time, the committee currently estimates that the proposed program would cost $700,000 to $1 million for the first year.

Proposed NCAA List of Banned Drugs

The following list has been developed by the Special Committee on Drug Testing after consideration of a similar list developed for Olympics purposes. The list includes drugs generally purported to be performance-enhancing drugs and/or potentially harmful to the health and safety of the student-athlete.

The committee believes that a student-athlete who may be subject to drug testing should take no drug or medication without checking specifically on it status. A substance on the NCAA's banned list, even though it may be prescribed by a physician or dentist, would remain a banned substance in sports. In most instances, there are appropriate alternatives that can be prescribed that do not contain banned substances.

1. Psychomotor stimulant drugs. The amphetamines and cocaine represent this category within the list. Ritalin and preludin are among the drugs in relatively common clinical use that are on the banned list.

2. Sympathomimetic drugs. The ephedrines are in this category, and they are found in many medicines for upper-respiratory illnesses, congestion, and asthma.

Proposed Banned Drug List with Examples

Psychomotor stimulants:

amphetamine	methylphenidate
benzphetamine	norpseudoephedrine
chlorphentermine	pemoline
cocaine	phendimetrazine
diethylproplon	phenmetrazine
dimethylamphetamine	phentermine
ethylamphetamine	pipradol
fencamfamin	prolintane
meclofenoxate	and related compounds
methylamphetamine	

Sympathomimetic amines:

chlorprenaline	isoetharine
ephedrine	isoprenaline
etafedreine	methoxyphenamine

methylephedrine   and related compounds
phenylpropanolamine

Miscellaneous central nervous system stimulants:

amiphenazole	ethamivan
bemigride	leptazol
caffeine[1]	nikethamide
cropropamide	picrotoxine
crolethamide	strychnine
dozapram	and related compounds

Anabolic steroids:

clostebol	norethandrolene
dehydrochlormethyl-	oxandrolone
testosterone	oxymesterone
fluoxymesterone	oxymetholone
mesterolone	stanozolol
methenolone	testosterone[2]
methandienone	and related compounds
nandrolone	

Substances banned for specific sports:
Rifle:

alcohol	pindolol
atenolol	propranolol
metoprolol	timolol
nadolol	and related compounds

Diuretics:

bendroflumethiazide	hydroflumethiazide
benzthiazide	methyclothiazide
bumetanide	metolazone
chlorothiazide	polythiazide
chlorthalidone	quinethazone
cyclothiazide	spironolactone
ethacrynic acid	triameterene
flumethiazide	trichlormethiazide
furosemide	and related compounds
hydrochlorothiazide	

Definition of positive depends on the following:
[1] for caffeine: if the concentration in urine exceeds 15 micrograms/ml.
[2] for testosterone: if the ratio of the total concentration of testosterone to that of epi-testosterone in the urine exceeds 6.

CASE STUDY: *NCAA Guidelines for Member Institutions Planning Drug Testing of Student-Athletes*
February 1, 1984

These guidelines were developed after the NCAA Drug Education Committee began receiving questions from member institutions about how to proceed in local drug screening. More information is available from Eric D. Zemper, research coordinator, at the NCAA national office.

Suggested guidelines for drug screening are:

1. A member institution considering drug screening of student-athletes should involve the institution's legal counsel at an early stage, particularly in regard to right-to-privacy statutes, which may vary from one state and locale to another. With the use of proper safeguards such as those listed below, drug screening is considered legally acceptable; however, the legal aspects involved at each individual institution should be clarified.

2. Before initiating drug-screening activity, a specific written policy on drug screening should be developed, distributed and publicized. The policy should include such information as: (a) a clear explanation of the purposes of the drug-screening program; (b) who will be screened and by what methods; (c) the drugs to be screened, how often and under what conditions (i.e., announced, unannounced or both), and (d) the actions, if any, to be taken against those who test positive. (It is advisable that a copy of such a policy statement be given to all student-athletes entering the institution's intercollegiate athletic program and have them confirm in writing that they have received and read the policy.)

3. At many institutions, student-athletes sign waiver forms regarding athletics departments' access to academic and medical records. It is recommended that specific language be added to such waiver forms wherein the student-athlete agrees to submit to drug screening at the request of the institution in accordance with the published guidelines.

4. An institution considering drug screening should develop a list of drugs for which the student-athlete will be tested. The Drug Education Committee recommends the following categories as a minimum group of drugs for this purpose:

a. amphetamines;
b. anabolic steroids (including testosterone and epitestosterone); and
c. "street drugs" (e.g., marijuana, cocaine, LSD, PCP, quaaludes, heroin).

Alcohol, although by far the most commonly used and abused drug by student-athletes, is not included in this list primarily because it is cleared from the body quite rapidly. Therefore, testing for alcohol generally would be futile; however, if unannounced tests are part of an institution's screening policy, alcohol should be included.

5. Any institution considering drug screening of student-athletes must confront several logistical, technical and economic questions. Among them are:

a. When and how samples will be collected, secured and transported.

b. What laboratory should be used.

c. How samples will be stored, and for how long before analysis.

d. What methods of screening should be utilized in the laboratory.

e. What costs are involved.

f. How accurate are the tests. What are the false-positive and false-negative rates. (These will vary from one type of test to another and from one laboratory to another.)

g. How will false-positives be confirmed and handled.

h. Who will get the results and how will the results be used.

Many of these issues cannot be dealt with at this time because answers will vary from one institution to another. The NCAA Drug Education Committee recommends that each institution considering drug screening of student-athletes appoint a committee of representatives from various relevant academic departments and disciplines (e.g., biochemistry, chemistry, medicine) to deal with the issues.

The question of where the samples will be analyzed is critical. No matter where the analyses are done, data on false-positives and false-negative rates for the specific tests to be used should be provided. If the laboratory cannot provide such information, another laboratory should be considered.

Costs obviously will be a factor in deciding where analyses will be done, how many tests will be conducted and how often they will be done. The cost of a test is not necessarily directly proportional to its accuracy, which is critical. Institutional committee members familiar with the equipment and analysis procedures can be invaluable in this regard.

How the results of drug screening will be handled should be specified before any screening program is begun. Of particular importance is the question of how any student-athlete with a positive test will be handled. Again, it is recommended that specific written policies be formulated. Member institutions are referred to the Drug Education Committee's recommendations concerning drug education and treatment programs that were published in the June 16, 1982, edition of the *NCAA News*. Such programs should emphasize rehabilitation rather than punishment.

As the 1984 academic year began, over 30 schools had developed drug-testing programs in preparation for anticipated NCAA testing. At least 12 of the schools had plans in effect during the 1983 academic year. "The fact that someone knows they're going to be tested will discourage even occasional use of drugs," noted Edward E. Bozik, athletic director at the University of Pittsburgh, which in 1984 began checking members of its football and basketball teams for such drugs as barbiturates, cocaine, marijuana, and anabolic steroids, a prescription drug used by some athletes to build their muscle bulk and strength. Pittsburgh plans to extend the test to all athletes in all sports starting with the 1985 academic year.

The University of Georgia implemented a plan that involves weekly tests of athletes selected at random. Administrators believe it has dramatically curbed experimentation with street drugs and excessive drinking. Georgia is one of a few institutions that uses a breathalyzer test to check for alcohol abuse. "We feel we've cut social experimentation of drugs from 50 percent to less than 1 percent in one year," noted Warren Morris, the university's head trainer.

Ohio State University tests coaches, trainers, and managers, in addition to athletes in all sports, to make certain no one is unfairly singled out for the tests. Other institutions, such as Pennsylvania State University, test only their football players.

NOTES _____

1. The costs of drug-testing programs are very high. The following excerpt is from "Testing Athletes for Drugs Now Common as Colleges Try to Deter Experimentation," *Chronicle of Higher Education*, September 12, 1984, pp. 31–32.

Each test performed on an athlete at the University of Pittsburgh and sent to a private laboratory for analysis costs the athletic department $15. If the analysis includes examination for anabolic steroids, the cost is $45. Because several screenings and checks are performed on the athletes during season, Mr. Bozik estimates the total cost of the program will be $18,000 to $20,000 this year, and $50,000 to $60,000 next year when the tests are extended to all athletes. He adds, though, that the price for the tests is not excessive when its benefits are considered.

"You afford what you have to afford," Mr. Bozik says. "If there is just one young life that might be saved from drug addiction or disease, then it's worth the cost."

Some institutions — such as Purdue University, where a drug screening for marijuana costs $9 — have kept down expenses by using their on-campus pharmacies or medical schools to conduct the analyses.

Others, such as the University of Georgia, have purchased their own drug-screening analyzers, which the athletic trainers themselves can operate.

Mr. Morris of Georgia says his department purchased a $35,000 analyzer last year when it began its drug testing program. He plans to purchase a second one, costing $15,000, this year, when athletes will be selected at random each week to be tested.

Because of the high costs, on-campus drug testing of collegiate athletes has generally been limited to large institutions — particularly those with major football teams — that have substantial athletic budgets.

All eight universities in the Big Eight Conference, for example, adopted testing programs after the conference sponsored a drug-education program last year. The Big Eight includes Iowa State, Kansas State, and Oklahoma State Universities, and the Universities of Colorado, Kansas, Missouri, Nebraska, and Oklahoma.

None of the eight universities in the Big Sky Athletic Conference, which plays football in the NCAA's less competitive Division I-AA, have drug-testing programs, the conference said.

In the Pacific-10 Conference, only Arizona State University and the University of Oregon have adopted drug-testing programs, according to a conference official, even though the other eight institutions have healthy athletic budgets and major football teams.

"Quite frankly," says the official, David Price, "I think some of the schools are concerned about protecting the civil rights of their student athletes."

2. The above article continues, now on the subject of civil rights:

In addition to their high cost, some lawyers believe the tests could be challenged in court as an unlawful invasion of privacy.

"We can't really do compulsory drug testing because of state regulations," says William Combs, team physician at Purdue University, which this fall tested its football players, trainers, and coaches for marijuana use and plans to test athletes in 16 other sports later this year.

Dr. Combs says the university's lawyers advised him that requiring a drug test would be a violation of the state's privacy act. "But we got almost 100-percent participation from athletes to conduct the test," he adds.

Elizabeth Simons, a staff lawyer for the American Civil Liberties Union in Washington, which opposes the testing of athletes as an unlawful search, notes that the drug-testing equipment often used by local authorities and some universities to analyze the urine samples can give "false positives" that could lead to the suspension and embarrassment of an innocent individual.

Last September the ACLU won a preliminary injunction from a District of Columbia Superior Court judge to stop the arbitrary testing of police officers there for drug use.

"Urine tests are a search, and you can't do a search without a warrant," Ms. Simons says.

Because universities in most instances lack probable suspicion that an athlete is on drugs when he or she is tested, Ms. Simons says, they cannot require drug tests in the same way a police officer can require an alcohol test from a motorist who has been observed speeding or driving erratically.

"That's different from testing 35 members of a football team who probably have never seen marijuana," she says.

Ms. Simons says that the civil-liberties group has been worried that the same rationale that many athletic directors use to justify their drug-testing programs — to protect the health of their athletes — could be used to test any employee or student at the university.

"What's to prevent them from going to a dorm and testing all the students in the dorm by saying that if the students take drugs, they might fall down the stairs?" she asks.

Other lawyers disagree.

"I don't think it's anymore of a violation of an athlete's privacy to go over to a doctor's office and require him to take a physical before he plays than requiring a drug test," says Theodore Ayers, general counsel for the University of Colorado, one of the institutions that have made drug tests for athletes mandatory this fall.

Colorado's program, like others recently instituted,

imposes drug counseling for first-time offenders, a one-week suspension for a second positive test, and a one-year suspension from participation in intercollegiate athletics for a third positive test.

"What's the difference between that and following a coach's curfew, not smoking, or making a certain time in a 100-yard dash?" asks Mr. Ayers.

James Googe, executive assistant to the attorney general of Georgia, notes that a distinction also exists between a student at the university and an athlete.

"The testing is a condition of participation in a sport which is voluntary," he says. "Participation in a sport is not a condition for attendance at a university."

But if institutions place penalties on athletes because of a drug test, notes Daniel Hanley, an adjunct professor of medicine at the Dartmouth College Medical School who serves on the NCAA's drug-testing committee, "they'd better make sure it's accurate."

3. Drug abuse on an athletic team can have serious consequences on an institution's good name and reputation (see "2 Incidents Still Haunt Maryland," *New York Times*, February 27, 1984, p. C7, which concerned the arrest and conviction of star basketball player Adrian Branch on misdemeanor charges of possession of marijuana).

4. "The Substances Athletes Use," *Chronicle of Higher Education*, September 1, 1982, p. 26, contains a list of some of the substances that athletes use to improve their sports performance, their weight, cope with pain, or handle the emotional pressures of competition.

- Alcohol is used in small amounts by marksmen to steady their aim, by wrestlers as a diuretic, and by distance runners to replace carbohydrates after a long run. It is also used by athletes to reduce pain, overcome fear and pain, increase self-esteem, and relax their muscles. Even in small amounts, however, alcohol decreases coordination, reaction time, depth perception, and muscle strength.
- Amphetamines and other psychomotor stimulants, including cocaine and benzphetamine, reduce pain and delay exhaustion. Some athletes believe these stimulants allow them to perform at higher levels for longer periods. Others believe they make athletes more vicious. These drugs can be addictive and can cause hypertension, loss of appetite, intracranial hemorrhage, and death.
- Anabolic steroids, androgenic hormones, and testosterone-like synthetic drugs are used by weight throwers, body builders, swimmers, and football players to increase strength and muscle mass.

The American College of Sports Medicine says in a position paper that use of steroids neither helps nor hinders athletic performance, and most physicians questioned by the *Chronicle* agree with that assessment. However, David R. Lamb, director of the exercise-physiology laboratory at Purdue University, says about half of the well-conducted scientific studies published verify that steroids do increase strength slightly — by about eight to ten kilograms in the bench press, for example.

Mr. Lamb says that while he believes steroids may help some people and have no effect on others, "I wouldn't advise anybody to take them, because of the side effects." These include a decrease in sperm production and in the size of testicles in men, infertility and baldness in women, liver problems, and acne.

- Aspirin, as well as other non-narcotic analgesics and anti-inflammatory drugs, are used by athletes to reduce pain and to make it possible to perform with an injury. However, some of those drugs cause stomach problems, confusion, and lethargy.
- Caffeine has gained popularity as an easily obtained cardiac and respiratory stimulant that is claimed to increase muscle efficiency and decrease fatigue. The drug, however, can cause nervousness, insomnia, and rapid heartbeat.
- Nicotine, such as that obtained by chewing tobacco, is sometimes used as a stimulant, but actually decreases athletic performance.
- Tranquilizers and other sedatives, such as barbiturates, are sometimes used to counteract nervousness before an athletic event or to promote sleep. By slowing response and reaction time, however, they increase the risk of injury. They are also addictive and can cause death.
- While not usually considered drugs, protein supplements and large amounts of vitamins B, C, and E are thought to promote athletic performance. Some athletes believe an excessive consumption of protein will increase strength and build muscle. However, the body does not store protein, and more energy is used to digest it than it produces. In addition, vitamins B, C, and E, according to physicians, do not improve endurance, muscle efficiency, or motor performance.

5. Hertzinger and Associates was formed by Ronald Hertzinger and his brother Donald. Initially, they began by providing drug education services to the University of Wisconsin. Now they offer a nationwide program on drug abuse, education, and eradication. For further information, see "Athletes Can Get Drug Counseling," *Chronicle of Higher Education*, September 1, 1982, p. 28.

6. The following comment was made in "The College Game," *New York Times*, September 16, 1984, Sec. 5, p. 3.

"Our lawyers tell us we have a legitimate right to test for drugs that enhance performance," said Eric Zemper, the NCAA staff member in charge of drug programs. "But the committee feels it is a little unfair for us to recommend penalizing students for what their non-athletic peers are not being tested for."

7. At a workshop sponsored by the National Association of College and University Lawyers in November 1984, it was noted that in dealing with drug testing for athletes the following questions may be raised:

- Would waiver forms signed by athletes stand up in court?
- Will random selection of athletes be vulnerable to charges that athletes in bad graces were chosen?
- If an athlete kills himself because of a test result is the institution liable?
- What about errors or breaches of confidentiality, do they lead to litigation?

It was noted that:
- Testing should be mandatory and athletes should sign a consent form. Even if contested there are legal arguments that the signing was voluntary.
- Stress drug education aspects of testing.
- Establish a notification program about drug test results, who is to be informed, and disciplinary actions to be levied.
- Check state laws since they may impact on testing ability of institution.
- Inform all parties that there is no coach-player privilege, or right to refuse to divulge confidential information.

For further information, see "Mandatory Drug Tests for College Athletes May Face Court Challenges, Lawyers Warn," *Chronicle of Higher Education*, November 7, 1984, p. 31.

8. A study of drug use among intercollegiate athletes, commissioned by the NCAA and released in 1985, showed that among the 2,000 athletes questioned on 10 teams at 11 campuses across the country in the fall of 1984, 82% had used alcohol, 27% had used marijuana, 12% had used cocaine, and 3% had used steroids. See the following articles for further information:
(a) "NCAA Surveys Drug Use," *New York Times*, March 17, 1985, Sect. 5, p. 3.
(b) "Most-Used Drug Is Alcohol, NCAA Study Shows," *NCAA News*, January 9, 1985, p. 12.

9. In 1985, two former coaches at Clemson University (South Carolina) pleaded guilty to charges of distributing steroids and other prescription drugs to athletes. The coaches were fined and placed on probation by the court. See the following articles for further information.
(a) "Two Ex-Clemson Coaches Receive Fines, Probation," *Boston Herald*, March 12, 1985, p. 56.
(b) "No Defense," *New York Times*, January 17, 1985, p. B14.
(c) "Grand Jury Indicts Ex-Coaches Linked to Clemson Drug Probe," *USA Today*, March 5, 1985, p. C4.
(d) "Grand Jury Hears Results of Clemson Drug Probe," *USA Today*, March 4, 1985, p. C9.
(e) "Drug Use Believed to Extend Beyond Two Schools

in South," *New York Times*, January 20, 1985, Sec. 5, p. 9.
(f) "2 Former Clemson U. Track Coaches Placed on Probation," *Chronicle of Higher Education*, March 20, 1985, p. 36.

10. The controversy at Clemson University began with a coroner's investigation into the death of Clemson runner Augustinius Jaspers, who died as a result of congenital heart disease but whose autopsy disclosed the drug phenylbutazone, an anti-inflammation drug, in his system. As an indirect result of the investigation, Clemson University president William Atchley resigned when the institution's Board of Trustees refused to remove H. C. McClellan as athletic director. Atchley had held McClellan responsible for the many problems that Clemson had experienced in their athletic program including NCAA sanctions. See the following articles for further information:
(a) "Clemson Head Says He Quit Over Lack of Support," *New York Times*, March 7, 1985, p. B9.
(b) "Drug Scandal Forces Out Clemson Head," *New York Times*, March 3, 1985, Sec. 5, p. 1.
(c) "Drug Scandal at Clemson Linked to Obsession to Win," *USA Today*, March 12, 1985, p. C4.
(d) "What Is at Stake When an Athletic Scandal Hits," *New York Times*, March 10, 1985, Sec. 5, p. 2.
(e) "New Troubles in Tiger Country: This Time, Clemson U.'s President Becomes the Victim," *Chronicle of Higher Education*, March 13, 1985, p. 27.

11. In 1985, as a result of the Clemson drug scandal, an investigation was begun at Vanderbilt University (Tennessee) involving the strength coach at Vanderbilt, who was a former football player at Clemson. It was alleged there was a link in use of drugs at both programs. See "Vanderbilt Steroid Sale Cited," *New York Times*, January 12, 1985, p. 27.

The Vanderbilt strength coach was indicted in April 1985 of selling steroids to athletes, including 32 current and former football players who were named as unindicted co-conspirators. Vanderbilt had by then initiated a random drug-testing program for its athletes. See "Vanderbilt's Drug Fight," *New York Times*, April 28, 1985, Sec. 5, p. 11.

12. For further information on the Vanderbilt drug scandal, see the following articles:
(a) "Vanderbilt Is Chagrined by Steroid Investigation," *Boston Globe*, February 10, 1985, p. 55.
(b) "3 Men Indicted for Conspiracy to Distribute Drugs to Athletes," *Chronicle of Higher Education*, March 1, 1985, pp. 31, 33.

13. NCAA officials are worried that there may be a link between drugs and gambling at some of the NCAA members institutions. In 1985, John R. Davis, president of the NCAA, noted at hearings on gambling conducted in New York City that:

We at the NCAA have no hard information that there is a direct link between organized crime, on the one hand, and drugs and gambling on the college scene . . . But, from our conversations with Federal law enforcement authorities, we believe this is simply a possibility that cannot be ignored.

See, "Davis Gives Views at U.S. Hearing," *NCAA News*, July 3, 1985, pp. 1, 12.

14. In 1985, it was disclosed that members of the Arizona State University baseball team had been using Nardil, a mood-altering drug, on the advice of a psychiatrist who acted as a consultant to the team and prescribed the drug. The ensuing scandal led to the resignation of the school's athletic director. See the following articles for further information:

(a) "Sinking Sun Devils," *New York Times*, March 14, 1985, p. 25.

(b) "Use of Drug Questioned," *New York Times*, March 23, 1985, p. 45.

(c) "Athletic Director Quits at Arizona State," *New York Times*, March 27, 1985, p. B14.

(d) "More Drug Tests," *New York Times*, August 15, 1985, p. B14.

15. At the 1985 NCAA Convention the membership voted to defer a decision on whether to establish a uniform drug-testing procedure for athletes. It was felt that the proposal was too general and that there was no inexpensive way to test for the 75 banned drugs. See "NCAA Shelves Drug Plan," *New York Times*, January 16, 1985, p. B8.

16. The NCAA has the following recommended policy concerning alcohol use and abuse:

Policy 14: Use of Alcoholic Beverages

Member institutions should prohibit athletic department staff members and student-athletes from having in their possession or consuming alcoholic beverages at the site of athletics competition before, during, or after a contest or at other times while wearing the institution's athletics uniform.

17. The Athletic Association of the University of Illinois has the following policy concerning drug and alcohol abuse:

(1) Education Phase:
Each athlete will listen to a presentation on this topic once a year. A handout on drug and alcohol abuse as well as other topics covered in the presentation is distributed. Included are specific instructions as to what should be done if the athlete has a problem in this area or knows of another athlete with a problem.

Each coach in all sport programs will also listen to a presentation on this topic once a year.

(2) Identification Phase:
An athlete with a drug or alcohol problem should go directly to his/her trainer or the sport psychologist. These individuals will immediately refer the athlete to the substance abuse expert at McKinley Health Center. If the athlete desires, the coach *does not* need to be informed about the problem.

If a coach suspects that an athlete has a problem in this area, this suspicion should be made known to the sport psychologist. The coach can then recommend that the individual visit with the sport psychologist. Confrontation of the athlete by the psychologist on the issue is handled in a very non-threatening manner.

(See *Policy and Procedures Manual*, Sec. I, p. 23, [d].)

18. In 1985, John L. Toner, immediate past president of the NCAA, director of athletics at the University of Connecticut, and chair of the Special NCAA Committee for National Drug Testing Policy, noted that:

I believe it's inevitable we will have drug testing. Ideally, if we could conduct tests before an NCAA championship, we could conduct a championship free of drugs. This would nullify the advantage a user would have over a non-user, and it would prevent a non-user from feeling forced to use drugs just to feel competitive.

See, "Drug Tests for College Athletics Called Inevitable," *Boston Globe*, June 21, 1985, p. 52.

19. For further information, see the following articles:

(a) "Executive Committee Approves Drug Testing," *NCAA News*, May 9, 1984, pp. 1, 12.

(b) "Athletes Warned on Hormone," *New York Times*, June 14, 1984, pp. D1, 25.

(c) "Colleges Urged to Teach Athletes, Coaches the Dangers of Drug Abuse and 'Doping,'" *Chronicle of Higher Education*, September 1, 1982, p. 25.

(d) "Drug Testing in College Intensifies," *USA Today*, August 30, 1983, p. 1.

(e) "Colleges Giving New Type of Test," *USA Today*, November 26, 1984, p. C1.

(f) "Psychologists, Counselors Cite Complex Drug-Test Problems," *Chronicle of Higher Education*, March 6, 1985, p. 32.

(g) "How to Avoid Legal Pitfalls in Setting Up Drug Tests for Athletes," *Chronicle of Higher Education*, March 6, 1985, p. 33.

(h) "Drugs, Athletes, and the NCAA: A Proposed Rule for Mandatory Drug Testing in College Athletics," 18 *John Marshall Law Review* 205 (Fall 1984).

(i) "Colleges Learn That Testing Athletes for Steroids Won't Be Easy or Cheap," *Chronicle of Higher Education*, May 8, 1985, pp. 27, 28.

(j) "Experts Say Steroids Offer Few Benefits, Pose Great Risks," *Chronicle of Higher Education*, May 8, 1985, pp. 27, 29.

(k) "LSU: Drug Program Proves Positive Step," *USA Today*, May 13, 1985, p. C8.

(l) "Drug Testing at Championships, Bowl Games May Begin in '86," *USA Today*, June 21, 1985, p. C9.

(m) "NCAA Panel Refining Drug-Testing Plan, Hopes to Begin Checking Athletes in 1986," *Chronicle of Higher Education*, July 3, 1985, p. 19.

(n) "Illinois Planning Spot Drug Tests," *St. Louis Post Dispatch*, July 8, 1985, p. C7.

20. In 1985, former NCAA president John Toner noted that, "I think it's about time we all took our heads out of the sand. Face it — drugs are being used on the college level." See, "Colleges Face Test," *Boston Globe*, August 17, 1985, p. 32.

5.62 Professional Sports: Drug Abuse and Enforcement

Athletes playing professional team sports in the United States face great temptations in the form of drugs. Often idolized by their fans and courted by "groupies," athletes can all too easily fall into a lifestyle where drugs are free and easy. The temptation to live life in the fast lane, coupled with the alternating grueling demands of professional athletic competition and excess time between games, has caused many of today's pros to fall victim to drug abuse.

Jean S. Fugett, Jr., a former professional football player for the Dallas Cowboys and Washington Redskins (1972–1979), noted:

> In America, achievement usually brings rewards. Unlike success in most trades and professions, success for the professional athlete also brings the reward of publicity.
>
> The professional athlete is the same athlete fans rooted for in high school, he's the same player fans cheered for during his college career, and now he is idolized as a pro. He is the player many youths hope to grow up and become. He is the all-American boy, and that is the problem.
>
> Publicity presents a problem for the professional athlete who desires privacy in public without the pressure of always being perfect. Living up to the standard of perfection expected by the public causes problems for athletes. It also presents a problem for our youth who, while growing up, often perceive reality in terms of black and white, and then are confronted with the harsh, stark realization that their "heroes" are not all they're cracked up to be.

(See Fugett, "Higher Standards, Not Higher Liability," *New York Times*, December 4, 1983, Sec. 5, p. 2.)

Given such circumstances, it is important to realize that professional athletes often pay a higher penalty for their crimes than the average citizen. Ewing M. Kauffman, chairman of the board of the Kansas City Royals, a baseball team that experienced great problems with cocaine abuse in the early 1980s, noted:

> The question arises: How should society treat baseball players accused of misdeed or misadventure? Should their standing as stars be a part of the calculation of punishment?
>
> Let's look first at the average baseball player, whether star or superstar (although it would seem a player of greater skills and higher reputation might be said to be held to a higher, more stringent level of behavior).
>
> Let's say that, whether he likes it or not, he is in the position of a role model. He knows he is held in great affection by multitudes of fans. He is aware of the relationship. He knows such support can be a source of inspiration in his performance on the field. He seeks such support. And usually is grateful for it.
>
> And, too, the public is ever happy to shower its love and attention upon its heroes.
>
> Must he, therefore, acknowledge and respond to this extraordinary relationship with the public?
>
> I think he must.
>
> A major league player wears a crown with a special import. It may (and I insist it does) rest heavily upon his head.
>
> Noblesse, oblige!
>
> Let's take the thought a step further. There is no doubt in my mind that such loyalty, bordering almost on fealty, inspires some young men to shape ambitions along the lines of a favorite player. One may be reluctant to admit such attitudes are to be encouraged. Still, in the present system, the greater the player's reputation, the sadder the consequences of his misdeeds.
>
> I cannot honestly say that I know how all these factors might influence a court of law in rendering judgment on an offending player.
>
> Should the court treat him as an ordinary citizen, brushing aside his professional prestige? Should the court remove the tether that binds the player, imposed upon him by a loving public?
>
> In the recent drug matter involving a few of our players, the United States magistrate rendered a kind of obiter in speaking to the defendants: As a professional athlete in our society, there are

special obligations you must live up to.

At that particular moment, one can feel how sensitive and complex the situation is, a player being punished in part for something that is separate from his misdeed, something that involves an ancient loyalty between fan and player and the deep pleasure the public experiences in its embrace of the player.

In such circumstances, it may take a Solomon to render a judgment that honors all the equities. Perhaps there is one that must be acknowledged: The player-hero is held to a higher degree of behavior. How to translate that element into concrete terms in a court of law, I am happy to leave to more judicial minds.

For good or ill, the player is saddled with that duty to the public.

He knows, or should know, that it comes with the territory.

(See Kauffman, "They Must Defer to a Duty to the Public," *New York Times*, December 4, 1983, Sec. 5, p. 22.)

Timothy D. Plant, manager of Employee Assistance Services for the Hazelden Foundation, claims that the following major points must be confronted in dealing with the problem of drug and alcohol abuse among athletes:

- *Athletes can benefit from treatment*. Athletes, like other special populations, present unique needs at the treatment setting, such as dietary and exercise facilities. While we need to accommodate these needs, experience so far indicates that athletes do well in a treatment environment which is peer-oriented and includes a population with diverse backgrounds. Most important, athletes must be assessed and treated as individuals, recognizing the uniqueness of each person.

- *Intensive intervention assistance must be available*. All professional groups are a challenge when it comes to motivating a dependent person to look at the need for treatment. Athletes are no exception. While "self-referral" will occur under the right circumstances, most referrals require an intervention process, usually including the employer, family, and professionals.

- *Residential assessment is a useful model for case entry*. Few treatment centers yet offer a separate, structured, residential component. In this program, an individual questioning his chemical abuse/dependency completes an intensive, multi-disciplinary evaluation over a period of five to seven days. This is a good starting point for the athlete, as it is for others, because it affords an honest assessment process and lessens the need for numerous outside intervention sessions, which often contain subjective data and threaten client's confidentiality.

- *Trust is an issue for the athlete making professional contact*. The athlete has much riding on the outcome of any professional contact. Fame, wealth, and cultural issues are a few of the potential barriers to developing a trusting relationship with a professional. While treatment centers teach self-responsibility, value conflict is likely. The athlete comes from an environment where his success is viewed as too important for him to be allowed to make his own mistakes.

- *Media attention can be a detriment*. Public exposure is extremely counterproductive during treatment. Not only does it distract the patient, but it jeopardizes the confidentiality of other patients in the center. Press conferences and interviews following treatment, even when at the sole discretion of the athlete, increase pressure on the newly-recovering person.

- *Aftercare must be well structured*. An ongoing recovery program of a treated chemically dependent athlete should offer consequences for failure to follow the aftercare plan.

Ron Hertzinger, president of Hertzinger & Associates, a Wisconsin-based drug-abuse consulting firm that specializes in athletes suggests that comprehensive drug abuse and prevention programs for athletes need to address the following areas:

- *Advertising*. How much does an organization support alcohol advertising and use their staff to focus on the subject? Do they have special alcohol and drug-oriented functions? Are chemicals readily available in the clubhouse or locker rooms? One organization recently had juices and fruit substituted for beer and soda after the games and the players' response was positive. Things such as this do change behaviors. If a player starts to drink alcohol after a game, he is more likely to continue when he leaves the locker room.

- *Administrative support.* Organizations at all levels (professional, collegiate, high school) should not see these programs for athletes only. They should be organizational-wide, inclusive programs. The organization's commitment has to be 100% behind these efforts. Monies should be allocated and valuation mechanisms developed. In addition to this support, abuse incidents which are tolerated as "celebrations or parties" should be re-examined and evaluated as to their potential implications for conveying a "condonement" message.

- *Education.* The most important part of these approaches is education. Prevention has proven successful. I still am amazed during presentations at how little people know about alcohol and other drug abuse. Educational sessions should be developed for all segments of an organization (management, players, staff, coaches, and family members). Each group serves a different role and needs to be informed about the signs of abuse and stages of dependency. The field is becoming sophisticated enough to hire consultants who deal specifically with athletes on this topic and not someone who only is versed in alcohol and other drugs.

- *Family programs.* Family members have been underused as an asset regarding the alcohol and drug abuse problem. Traditionally, they are the first to be aware of problems and also the first to cover up, deny, or enable, thereby furthering the progression of problems. Comprehensive educational programs for family members may also mean that they need assistance. When I worked in treatment, more family members initiated the treatment process before any other potential reference source, and certainly before the person with the problem.

- *Crisis hotline.* Many organizations have initiated this step. An 800 toll-free hotline serves three functions. It provides confidentiality for those concerned about concealing their identity. It provides a confidential way to seek information towards receiving assistance for a problem. And, a range of service resources can be offered on a national level given the transient nature of the professional athlete's lifestyle.

- *Intervention.* Each organization should have an individual to intervene in situations where problems exist. Most sports organizations have an in-house doctor, psychologist, or outside consultant for this purpose. This person should be educated beyond the educational sessions provided by the team and should be versed on confrontation and intervention approaches.

- *Testing.* Alcohol and other drug testing is an important tool for the total program only if players and management agree on its parameters. It has yet to be tested in the courts. Some organizations have used this as an end all to a total program. They will discover that it will not solve the chemical problem in itself.

- *Treatment.* Treatment should consist of three major areas: detoxification, in-patient and/or out-patient treatment, and aftercare. Each of these is needed depending upon the severity of the problem. Many athletes fail in their commitment to remain abstinent due to poor follow-up provided by treatment programs, partially understandable due to the athlete's transience.

NOTES

1. For further information, see the following articles:
(a) "What Obligations Do Pro Athletes Have to the Fans," *New York Times*, December 4, 1983, sec. 5, p. 2, which goes the viewpoints of an owner ("They Must Defer to a Duty to the Public," by Ewing M. Kauffman) and a former player ("Higher Standards, Not Higher Liability," by Jean S. Fugett, Jr.).
(b) Point-Counterpoint, "Reducing Alcohol and Drug Abuse Among Athletes — Is Treatment Enough?" *U.S. Journal of Drug and Alcohol Dependents*, January 1984, p. 7.
2. In July 1982, the House Select Committee on Narcotics Abuse and Control held closed meetings with professional sports commissioners Bowie Kuhn and Pete Rozelle and representatives of players' unions. The committee was chaired by Les C. Zeferetti (Democrat, New York), and it was reported that the purpose of the meetings was "to pursue the possibility of getting the parties together on a good drug program." For further information, see "Congress Holds Drug Hearings," *Washington Post*, July 22, 1982, p. B1.
3. The following exerpt is from "How Drugs Threaten to Ruin Pro Sports," *U.S. News & World Report*, September 12, 1983, pp. 64–65:

Life on a fast track often means that a young athlete comes into contact with fans who offer drugs to ingratiate themselves. Carl Eller, a former Minnesota Vikings star whose NFL career was ended by cocaine, says that his first exposure to the drug came at a party with friends.

Now an NFL consultant on drug and alcohol abuse,

Eller says that sometimes unrelenting job pressures lead a player to drugs. "There is no security," he says. "A guy knows his job can be over at any time."

Yet another factor is the coddling of athletes. Dr. Pursch says that some players get special treatment from the time they show star potential. If that mind-set is reinforced at home, players think "they can make their own rules," and drug abuse may lie ahead.

4. For information on drug abuse in boxing, see the following article: "20% of Active Pros Said to Have Tried It," *New York Daily News*, January 15, 1984, pp. 99, 100.

5. For information on drug abuse in the NFL, see the following article: "Don Murdock," *Boston Globe*, January 28, 1979, p. 46.

5.62–1 National Basketball Association

In September 1983, the National Basketball Association (NBA) and the NBA Players Association (NBAPA) announced a comprehensive and precedent-setting drug program (see Exhibits 5–3 and 5–4). It called for the following provisions:

Any player convicted of or who pleads guilty to a crime involving the use or distribution of heroin or cocaine will immediately be permanently dismissed from the NBA.

Without penalty, any player can voluntarily seek drug rehabilitation through the Life Extension Institute, a health firm which provides counseling services to NBA players. The treatment will be paid for by the player's team and he will continue to be paid.

After being treated for drug use once, a player who voluntarily seeks drug rehabilitation again will be suspended without pay while undergoing treatment.

If a player seeks help a third time, even voluntarily, he will be permanently dismissed from the NBA.

If the NBA or players association is informed that a player might be using illegal drugs, that information will be given to a yet unnamed, independent drug expert. Suspected player will be identified by code numbers and not by name.

If the drug expert suspects drug use, he will give the NBA permission to administer several drug tests to the player. If drug use is discovered, or if the player refuses to take the test, he will be dismissed from the NBA.

Any player who has been dismissed from the league can apply for reinstatement after a two-year absence.

An amnesty period was in effect until Dec. 31, 1982, during which the program was explained to NBA players.

The program is taking effect on Jan. 1, 1984.

Larry O'Brien, commissioner of the NBA, and Larry Fleisher, general counsel for the NBA Players Association, designed the innovative program to ensure that illegal drugs would not be used in the NBA. The agreement was signed by O'Brien and by Bob Lanier of the Milwaukee Bucks, president of the NBAPA (see Exhibit 5–3). "Drugs are a problem in our society, one we in the NBA cannot and will not ignore," declared O'Brien. He added:

This program, which provides clear-cut penalties for any player who is found to be involved in the illegal use of drugs, now gives us every element of the package — education, rehabilitation and enforcement. This complete approach to the problem clearly serves the best interests of our players as well as our fans, whose confidence in the sport of pro basketball must never be compromised. We are pleased that our far-sighted Players Association shares our view on this matter. . . .

Lanier had this to say:

There is no question that professional basketball players are role models for young people all over the country and particularly in inner cities. By telling the world that we as professional players will not tolerate the use of illegal drugs we are setting a new standard, something that is absolutely essential in today's environment. . . .

O'Brien continued:

We have included the provision that permits players to step forward and seek treatment, using the resources of the Life Extension Institute, a program which we have had in place for the last three years. Both parties involved in this agreement recognized, however, that the illegal use of drugs is inconsistent with competing in the NBA and would threaten the image of the game and its athletes. Therefore, it was felt that anyone

AGREEMENT made this ____ day of October, 1983, by
and between the National Basketball Association ("NBA") and
the National Basketball Players Association ("Players Association").

WHEREAS, the NBA and the Players Association recognize
that the illegal use and abuse of drugs has become a serious
problem in our society and in professional sports, in particular;
and

WHEREAS, the illegal use of drugs can adversely affect
the performance of NBA players and threatens the image of and
public confidence in NBA basketball; and

WHEREAS, the NBA and the Players Association have
agreed that the illegal use of drugs is inconsistent with competing in the NBA and that anyone found to have engaged in the
use of the substances set forth in Exhibit 1, annexed hereto,
ought properly to forfeit any opportunity to play in the NBA;

NOW, THEREFORE, the NBA and the Players Association
have agreed upon the following program, the purpose of which
is to eliminate the illegal use of drugs in the NBA:

1. Dismissal and Permanent Disqualification. Any player who
has been convicted of or has pled guilty to a crime involving
the use, possession, or distribution of any of the substances
set forth in Exhibit 1, annexed hereto (the "prohibited
substances") or has been found through the procedures set
forth in Paragraphs 6 or 7 below to have used, possessed, or
distributed any of the prohibited substances, shall, without

Exhibit 5-3   National Basketball Association Collective Bargaining Agreement: Exhibit C

exception, immediately be dismissed and permanently disqualified from any further association with the NBA or any of its
teams. Such dismissal and permanent disqualification shall be
mandatory and may not be rescinded or reduced by the player's
club or the NBA.

2. <u>Amnesty</u>. (a) From the date hereof through December 31, 1983
(the "Amnesty Period"), no player will be subject to the penalty
set forth in Paragraph 1 hereof. During the Amnesty Period,
the NBA and the Players Association will use their best efforts
to inform all players, in writing and in person at team and/or
individual meetings, of the details of this Agreement, including
the procedures to be utilized and the penalties provided.
In addition, the parties may notify certain player(s) that one
or both of the parties has reason to believe that such player(s)
may have used, possessed, or distributed a prohibited substance.

(b) During the term of this Agreement, any
player, except a player referred to in Paragraph 10 below, who
comes forward voluntarily to seek treatment of a problem
involving the use of drugs, will be provided with appropriate
counselling and medical assistance, at the expense of his club.
No penalty of any kind will be imposed on such a player and,
provided he complies with the terms of his prescribed treatment,
he will continue to receive his salary during the term of his
treatment, for a period of up to 3 months of in-patient care
in a facility approved by the Life Extension Institute and such
out-patient care as is required in a program approved by the
Life Extension Institute.

3. <u>Appointment of Independent Expert</u>. The NBA and the Players Association shall jointly appoint an Independent Expert (the "Expert") who shall be a person experienced in the field of drug abuse detection and enforcement. The Expert shall serve for the duration of the Collective Bargaining Agreement, dated October 10, 1980, between the NBA and the Players Association, as amended by the Memorandum of Understanding, dated April 18, 1983 (the "Collective Bargaining Agreement"); provided, however, that as of each September 1, either the NBA or the Players Association may discharge the Expert by serving 30 days' prior written notice upon him and upon the other party. In the event the parties do not reach an agreement, within 45 days, as to who shall serve as the Expert, each party shall appoint a person who shall have no relationship to or be affiliated with that party. Such persons shall then have fifteen days to agree on the appointment of an Expert. The Expert's fees shall be paid in equal shares by the NBA and the Players Association.

4. <u>Authorization for Testing</u>. In the event that either the NBA or the Players Association has information which gives it reasonable cause to believe that a player may have been engaged in the use, possession, or distribution of a prohibited substance at a time after the conclusion of the Amnesty Period, such party shall request a conference with the other party and the Expert, which shall be held within 24 hours or as soon thereafter as the Expert is available. Upon hearing the information presented, the Expert shall immediately decide whether there is reasonable cause to believe that the player in question may have been engaged in the use, possession, or distribution of a prohibited substance. If the Expert decides that such reasonable

cause to believe exists, the Expert shall thereupon issue an
Authorization for Testing with respect to such player in the
form annexed hereto as Exhibit 2.

5. Sources of Information. In evaluating the information presented to him, the Expert shall be entitled to use his independent
judgment based upon his experience in drug abuse detection and
enforcement. The parties acknowledge that the type of information
to be presented to the Expert is likely to consist of reports
of conversations with third parties of the type generally considered by law enforcement authorities to be reliable sources,
and that such sources might not otherwise come forward if their
identities were to become known. Accordingly, neither the
NBA nor the Players Association shall be required to divulge
to each other or to the Expert the names of their sources of
information regarding the use, possession, or distribution of
a prohibited substance, and the absence of such identification
of sources shall not be considered by the Expert in determining
whether to issue an Authorization for Testing with respect to
a player. In conferences with the Expert, the player involved
shall not be identified by name until such time as the Expert
has determined to issue an Authorization for Testing with
respect to such player.

6. Testing. Immediately upon the Expert's issuance of an
Authorization for Testing with respect to a particular player,
the NBA shall arrange for such player to undergo the testing
procedures, as set forth in Exhibit 3, annexed hereto, no more
than four times during the six-week period commencing with the
issuance of the Authorization for Testing. Such testing pro-

cedures may be administered at any time, in the discretion of the NBA, without prior notice to the player. In the event that any of the testing procedures produces a positive result, the player shall be deemed to have used a prohibited substance and shall suffer the penalty set forth in Paragraph 1, above, and shall be so notified by the Commissioner. Any player refusing to submit to a testing procedure, pursuant to an Authorization for Testing, at the time set by the NBA, shall be deemed to have produced a positive result for such testing procedure and shall suffer the penalty set forth in Paragraph 1, above.

7. Dismissal Without Testing. In the event that either the NBA or the Players Association determines that there is sufficient evidence to demonstrate that a player has engaged in the use, possession, or distribution of a prohibited substance at a time after the conclusion of the Amnesty Period, it may, in lieu of requesting the testing procedure set forth in Paragraphs 4 through 6, request a hearing on the matter before the Impartial Arbitrator under the Collective Bargaining Agreement. If the Impartial Arbitrator concludes that the player has used, possessed, or distributed a prohibited substance at a time after the conclusion of the Amnesty Period, the player shall suffer the penalty set forth in Paragraph 1, above, notwithstanding the fact that the player has not undergone the testing procedure set forth in Paragraph 6.

8. Confidentiality. The NBA and the Players Association agree that neither of them will divulge to any other party, including their respective members and the player and team involved (other than as required by the Testing Procedure set forth in Paragraph 6 above):

i)   that it has received information
regarding the use, possession, or distribution
of a prohibited substance by a player;

ii)   that it is considering requesting
has requested, or has had a conference with
the Expert;

iii)   any information disclosed to the
Expert; and

iv)   the results of any conference with
the Expert.

9. Amendment to Uniform Player Contract. All forms of the
Uniform Player Contract attached to the Collective Bargaining
Agreement as exhibits and, in cases where a player and a
Member are parties to a currently effective Uniform Player
Contract each such contract, shall, upon execution of this
Agreement, be deemed amended to include a new Paragraph 6(d),
which shall provide as follows:

"The Player acknowledges that, in the
event he is found, in accordance with the
terms of the Agreement between the Association and the National Basketball Players
Association, dated October ____, 1983 to have
engaged in the use, possession, or distribution of a "prohibited substance" as defined
therein, it will result in the termination
of this contract and the Player's immediate
dismissal and permanent disqualification
from any employment by the Association and
any of its teams. Notwithstanding any terms
or provisions of this contract (including any
amendments hereto) in the event of such termination, all obligations of the Club, including
obligations to pay compensation, shall cease,
except the obligation of the Club to pay the
Player's earned compensation (either current
or deferred) to the date of termination.

The Player hereby releases and waives every
claim he may have against the Club, the
Association, the National Basketball Players
Association, and each of their respective
members, directors, governors, officers,
stockholders, trustees, partners, and
employees, arising out of or in connection
with the testing procedures or the imposition
of any penalties set forth in the Agreement
between the Association and the National
Basketball Players Association dated as of
October ___, 1983.

10. Second Treatment. Any player who, after previously

requesting and receiving treatment for a drug problem, again

comes forward voluntarily to seek such treatment, shall be

suspended without pay during the period of such treatment, but

shall not suffer the penalty set forth in Paragraph 1, above.

Any subsequent use, possession, or distribution of a prohibited

substance, even if voluntarily disclosed, shall result in the

imposition of the penalty set forth in Paragraph 1, above.

11. Application for Reinstatement. Notwithstanding the pro-

visions of Paragraph 1 above, after a period of at least two

years from the time of a player's dismissal and permanent

disqualification, such player may apply for reinstatement as

a player in the NBA. However, such player shall have no right

to reinstatement under any circumstance and the reinstatement

shall be granted only with the prior approval of both the

Commissioner and Players Association. The approval of the

Commissioner and the Players Association shall rest in their

absolute and sole discretion, and their decision shall be

final, binding and unappealable. Among the factors which may

be considered by the Commissioner and the Players Association

in determining whether to grant reinstatement are (without

limitation): the circumstances surrounding the player's dis-

missal and permanent disqualification, whether the player has
satisfactorily completed a treatment and rehabilitation program,
the player's conduct since his dismissal, including the extent
to which the player has since comported himself as a suitable
role model for youth, and whether the player is judged to possess
the requisite qualities of good character and morality. The
granting of an application for reinstatement may be conditioned
upon periodic testing of the player or such other terms as may
be agreed upon by the NBA and the Players Association. A player
who has been reinstated pursuant to this paragraph shall, immediately upon such reinstatement, notify the Club for which he
last played. Such Club shall have 30 days to notify the player
that it is prepared to accept his playing services under the
terms and conditions of that portion of the term of the player's
last player contract, for which services were not rendered because
of such player's dismissal and permanent disqualification. If the
Club notifies the player that it is prepared to accept his employment under such terms and conditions, the Club and the player
shall immediately enter into a new Uniform Player Contract in
accordance with those terms and conditions. If the Club does not
so notify the player, the player shall be deemed to have completed
the services called for under his last player contract and
shall immediately be free to negotiate and sign an Offer Sheet
with any NBA team, subject to the Right of First Refusal set
forth in Article XXII, Section 1(d) of the Collective Bargaining
Agreement.

12. <u>Incorporation in Collective Bargaining Agreement</u>. This
Agreement shall be incorporated in and extend through the term
of the Collective Bargaining Agreement.

13.   Limitation on Other Testing.   Except as expressly provided in Paragraph 6, above, there shall be no other screening
or testing for the prohibited substances conducted by the NBA
or NBA clubs, and no player shall be required to undergo such
screening or testing.   Notwithstanding the foregoing, any
player who has acknowledged the use of a prohibited substance
by entering a treatment program, shall be subject to such
screening or testing as may be determined by the Life Extension
Institute.   The frequency and duration of any screening or
testing, as determined by the Life Extension Institute hereunder,
shall not exceed 3 times a week or a period of more than one
year following in-patient treatment.   Any player refusing to
submit to a screen or test pursuant to this paragraph or for
whom such screen or test produces a positive result, shall be
subject to the provisions of Paragraph 10, above, as a player
who "again comes forward voluntarily."

IN WITNESS WHEREOF, the parties have entered into
this Agreement as of the day and year first written above.

NATIONAL BASKETBALL ASSOCIATION

By _____
          Commissioner

NATIONAL BASKETBALL PLAYERS ASSOCIATION

By _____
          President

EXHIBIT 1

LIST OF PROHIBITED DRUGS

Cocaine

Heroin

EXHIBIT 2

AUTHORIZATION FOR TESTING

TO: _____
      (Player)

Please be advised that on _____, you were the subject of a conference held pursuant to the Agreement between the NBA and Players Association, dated _____ ("Agreement"). Following the conference, I authorized the NBA to conduct the testing procedures set forth in the Agreement, and you are hereby directed to submit to those testing procedures, on demand, no more than 4 times during the next six weeks.

Please be advised that your failure to submit to these procedures, will result in your dismissal and permanent disqualification from the NBA.

_____
Independent Expert

Dated:

EXHIBIT 3

TESTING PROCEDURES

Urinalysis. To be screened and tested through scientifically accepted analytical techniques, such as chromatography (gas and/or thin-layer), spectrophoto fluorometry, EMIT, and/or TLC.

Each club trainer, in cooperation with his team's physician, shall institute and maintain the following procedures with regard to drug administration and control:

Take a complete inventory of all prescription drugs on hand and submit a list of such drugs by name and quantity to Jack Joyce, Director of Security, to be received no later than the week prior to the start of the regular season. As the stock of such drugs is depleted and replenished, or new drugs are purchased, the inventory list must be amended and the NBA Security Office must be mailed a revised report. At the end of the season or following your final game in the playoffs, a complete inventory of all prescription drugs on hand must also be submitted to the League Office.

When any prescription drug is dispensed or administered to a player, an appropriate notation must be recorded in the player's medical file and in the team's medical log, specifying the date, time, drug, dosage, prescribing physician's name and his reason for administering the drug. In the team's medical log, the player's name should be coded, and the code should be maintained by the team physician.

On the first day of each month, the medical log from the previous month will be sent to the NBA Security Office and a new monthly record will commence. Each monthly team medical log must be received in the NBA Office no later than the 15th of each month. If no prescription drugs are dispensed during the month, a notation to this effect must be reported. The inventory and medical log will be subject to audit by the NBA.

All prescription drugs stored in home arenas must be in

Exhibit 5-4   National Basketball Association Administrative Manual, Section 310: Drug Control

a metal cabinet under lock and key, and the team physician must be registered with the Drug Enforcement Administration (DEA) in that location. Team trainers must not dispense prescription drugs at home without a doctor's authorization for a specific player and no prescription drugs can be taken by the trainer on the road unless they have been authorized by a physician for specific players. Such prescription drugs must be secured under lock and key.

All home team physicians must insure that in urgent situations, visiting teams will have access to a 24-hour hospital/pharmacy in their city. In addition, to facilitate the dispensing of standard medications to visiting team players, all teams must stock the following prescription drugs in their arena:

>Actifed
>Dimetapp
>Tetracycline 500
>Penicillin G - 400,000 units
>Darvon Compound 65
>Lomotil
>Empirin #3
>Kenalog Cream
>Pontocaine Eye gtts
>Donnatal
>Mycolog Cream
>Entex
>Butazolidin Alka 100 mg.

All of the above recordings and reporting procedures must be followed when a home team physician prescribes, administers or dispenses prescription drugs to a visiting team player.

The General Manager of each club will be held responsible for the implementation and maintenance of the foregoing administrative procedures and controls. The General Manager, Coaches, and Trainer must report to each other and discuss any concern, suspicion or allegation involving the alleged use of drugs by team personnel. Prior to January 1, of the given year, the

General Managers must then report to Mr. Joyce that such a meeting
was held and state the identity of those in attendance as well
as any information developed. Failure to comply with these
procedures or to submit a prescription inventory on or before
October 15, of the given year, will result in a minimum fine
of $10,000.

Please note that Dr. Torrey C. Brown is a medical
consultant to the NBA on drug education and control, and
he is available to discuss any matters relating to drugs,
on a confidential basis, with any NBA personnel. He may
be contacted by mail or by telephone at:

>   The John Hopkins Medical Institutions
>   Baltimore, Maryland 21218
>
>   Telephone: (301) 955-3353

found to have engaged in the illegal use of drugs ought properly to forfeit any opportunity to play in the NBA.

I stress that this is just one aspect of our approach to the problem posed by drug abuse. For more than 10 years we have had regularly scheduled meetings among players, team physicians and law enforcement personnel to educate players of the dangers and consequences of drug involvement. And the Life Extension Institute for the past several years has provided players with crisis counseling, on a completely confidential basis, as well as long-range programs for dealing with drug, alcohol or other personal problems. We also recognize that these problems do not start for athletes at the professional level, and urge the NCAA and its member colleges to develop similar programs, especially when it comes to educating student athletes about the dangers of drug abuse.

Lanier emphasized the players' support in this effort:

The Players Association strongly believes that this program will help those of our players who may have a drug problem to eliminate their problem. It will also help the overwhelming number of players who are not involved with drugs by strengthening public confidence in them and developing a better image for professional basketball. We also believe that working closely together with the NCAA and its member colleges, this program will convince present and future college players to stay away from illegal drugs, since there will be no place for them in the NBA.

CASE STUDY: Michael Ray Richardson

On February 6, 1983, the New Jersey Nets of the National Basketball Association (NBA) acquired Michael Ray Richardson from Golden State. On April 1, 1983, a New York newspaper ran a story, "Nets' Michael Ray: Says He Used Drugs." The story noted in part:

"Michael Ray Richardson has a drug problem." So says one of Richardson's best friends, Butch Beard, the Knicks' TV color commentator.

"Michael Ray has a drug problem — and he knows that I know." So says Richardson's wife, Rene, who has filed for divorce.

"The odds are, he might've, you know, played around with this stuff." So says Joe Taub, president of the Nets, the team for which Michael (Sugar) Ray Richardson plays.

Richardson denies he has ever used any drug. . . .

But the story of the 27-year-old Richardson's NBA career, which includes four years with the Knicks, has not always been a laughing matter. It's a story of erratic play. Missed practices. Musical agents (five agents in his five-year career). Financial disarray ("Michael's strong suit is not saving money," says one former agent). A $600,000 lawsuit (filed against Richardson and his present agent by his former agent, Don Cronson). And, always, there were the suspicions, the whispers, that cocaine was at the core of Richardson's problems.

In response to the story, the Nets issued the following statement:

The New Jersey Nets have issued the following statement in response to a story that appeared in today's *New York Daily News*, concerning Michael Ray Richardson:

The New Jersey Nets disapprove of drug use by anyone, especially professional athletes. The New Jersey Nets will not condone drug use by any NBA players and we fully support actions of the NBA in this regard.

Let us not, however, convict Michael Ray Richardson or anyone else on the basis of unsubstantiated allegations of third parties. Let us judge him, rather, on the available evidence which includes his current conduct on and off the court.

In this light, the New Jersey Nets will continue to support Michael Ray Richardson in any way that we can.

In May 1983, reports began circulating in New York newspapers that Richardson had checked himself into a six- to eight-week drug rehabilitation program at Fair Oaks Hospital in New Jersey. In June, Richardson checked himself out of the program. Richardson entered the Hazelden Foundation in August 1983 for another attempt at controlling his cocaine abuse. This attempt also ended short of completion.

In September 1983, Richardson called a press conference on the day that the NBA announced its new drug rules. He openly talked about his drug abuse problems and claimed he was cured. A week later, on October 5, Richardson missed training camp practice. After three days, he returned and agreed to enter another drug rehabilitation program. On October 11, he refused to enter the program, and the Nets placed him on irrevocable waivers. The next day, Richardson's agent Pat Healy filed a grievance against the Nets and the NBA. Healy wanted his client paid fully during emotional rehabilitation and, upon completion of a program, wanted Richardson reinstated in the NBA. On October 13, Richardson cleared waivers, unclaimed by any other NBA team.

In December 1984, under pressure from the NBA, the Nets reinstated Richardson. In their press release discussing the return of Richardson to active play, the NBA outlined the following:

Michael Ray Richardson will be reinstated by the New Jersey Nets under the terms of an agreement reached at the urging of NBA Commissioner Larry O'Brien and Players Association counsel Larry Fleisher. The agreement provides that Richardson will drop his arbitration proceeding and submit to the provisions and penalties of the NBA's new anti-drug program even though the circumstances arose prior to the effective date of the program.

Richardson will be dealt with as a player who voluntarily sought treatment for a drug problem a second time. Under such circumstances, the player is automatically suspended without pay. Having now completed his treatment, Richardson will be reinstated by the Nets effective immediately, but he forfeits his salary for all time missed this season. In addition, Richardson must undergo daily testing for drug usage, and should he fail any such test, he would then be permanently dismissed from the NBA.

"Although the facts of the Richardson case arose prior to the implementation of our new anti-drug agreement, it was important to the NBA and the Players Association that this matter be settled to the satisfaction of all parties so that we can move forward with the anti-drug program on January 1 with equal applicability to all players and without any confusion relating to a prior incident," said O'Brien. "Therefore, Larry Fleisher and I urged both sides to make every effort to settle this dispute, and the Nets have demonstrated a willingness to place the interests of the League and its new anti-drug program above their own contractual rights."

"Even though the penalty provisions of our new anti-drug program do not take effect until January 1, Richardson and the Nets have voluntarily agreed to implement all of the agreement's terms immediately with respect to Richardson. We think this is an appropriate resolution of the matter and one that is consistent with our goals of voluntary rehabilitation, if possible, but with permanent dismissal where necessary."

Under the new anti-drug program, an amnesty period is in effect until January 1, and no player can be banned from the League prior to that date. After January 1, a procedure for drug testing will be in operation and any player failing such a test will be permanently dismissed from the NBA. However, if a player comes forward voluntarily to seek treatment for a cocaine problem, he will be treated the first time at club expense with no loss of pay. A player who comes forward voluntarily a second time is suspended without pay while undergoing treatment. Any player who has a third recurrence, whether disclosed voluntarily or not, will be permanently dismissed.

Richardson completed the 1983–84 NBA season without any more difficulties. He had to undergo urinalysis four times a week, meet with a psychiatrist once a week, and attend group sessions with other former drug abusers twice a week.

NOTES _____

1. For further information, see the following magazine article: "I'm at the Edge of a Cliff," *Sport*, April 1, 1984, p. 104.

2. For further information, see the following newspaper articles:

(a) "NBA and Its Players Association Announce New Drug Program," *NBA Press Release*, September 28, 1983, pp. 1–3.

(b) "NBA Drug Program," *USA Today*, September 29, 1984, p. C1.

(c) "NBA, Players Association Unite to Drive Out Drug Abusers," *Boston Globe*, September 29, 1983, p. 45.

(d) "NBA Will Urge Drug Test," *Washington Post*, July 2, 1982, p. C1.

(e) "Richardson Reconstructs Life Shredded by Cocaine," *USA Today*, April 4, 1984, p. C7.

5.62–2   National Football League

The 1982 National Football League (NFL) Collective Bargaining Agreement between the league and the NFL Players Association (NFLPA) contains the following language concerning drug and alcohol abuse:

Article XXXI: Player's Rights
to Medical Care and Treatment

Section 6. Chemical Dependency Program: The parties agree that it is the responsibility of everyone in the industry to treat, care for and eliminate chemical dependency problems of players. Accordingly, the parties agree to jointly designate Hazelden Foundation, Center City, Minnesota or its successor if such becomes necessary, to evaluate existing facilities to assure the highest degree of care and treatment and to assure the strictest observance of confidentiality. Any treatment facility which does not meet standards of adequacy will be eliminated and a successor facility in the same metropolitan area chosen solely by Hazelden. Hazelden will be responsible for conducting an ongoing education program for all players and Club personnel regarding the detection, treatment and after-care of chemically dependent persons. The cost of retaining Hazelden will be paid by the clubs.

Section 7. Testing: The club physician may, upon reasonable cause, direct a player to Hazelden for testing for chemical abuse or dependency problems. There will not be any spot checking for chemical abuse or dependency by the club or club physician.

Section 8. Confidentiality: All medical bills incurred by any player at a local treatment facility will be processed exclusively through Hazelden which will eliminate all information identifying the patient before forwarding the bills to any insurance carrier for payment. Details concerning treatment any player receives will remain confidential within Hazelden and the local chemical dependency facility. After consultation with Hazelden and the player, the facility will advise the club of the player's treatment and such advice will not in and of itself be the basis for any disciplinary action. No information regarding a player's treatment will be publicly disclosed by Hazelden, the facility or the club.

As a result of this agreement, the program that is outlined in the following case study was implemented.

CASE STUDY: The NFL/NFLPA Alcohol and Other Drugs Program

Your Program:
- Is supported by both the Players Association and the management of all 28 NFL clubs.
- Is covered by the 1982 collective bargaining agreement.
- Supports the idea that everyone in the industry is responsible to treat, care for and eliminate alcohol and drug abuse problems of players.
- Designates the Hazelden Foundation to give you the "highest degree of care and treatment."

Points to Remember

Alcohol and drug dependency is:
1. A disease — not a question of weakness or will power.
2. It must be dealt with first before other problems can be resolved.
3. It affects the individual and everyone close — both team and family members alike.
4. Your knowledge and concern can make a big difference.
5. Your alcohol and drug abuse program is the gateway to help.

How Does It Work?

If you, a family or team member has a problem, you simply pick up the phone and call the toll-free 800 number for help:
- Call 800–328–5000 and ask for the NFL counselor.
- You'll get immediate information, which can lead to professional, face-to-face help.

What Kind of Help Will I Get?

Assessment is one possibility. If you're not sure there's a problem, a personal assessment will help determine what problems exist, whether alcohol/drug-related or other personal difficulties.

Treatment is another possibility. Hazelden has approved a coast-to-coast network of resource centers which treat alcohol and drug problems.

Aftercare help is provided no matter what the problem may have been. This follow-up support aids the lifelong recovery process — no one ever cures a drinking or drug problem.

	800 Number
Information	Professional Help
CD Problems	Assessment
Treatment	Other Problems

How Is My Privacy Protected?

- Your 800 number call is confidential — between you and a trained professional who can guide you.
- If you receive assessment or treatment, the collective bargaining agreement guarantees that this information will not be publicly disclosed by Hazelden, the treatment facility, or the club.
- If you want your treatment kept confidential from your club, there is always the option of bearing the cost for treatment yourself.
- If your treatment is covered through your NFL insurance, your identity will be kept confidential from the insurance company and the club accounting office.
- If paid for through NFL insurance, a designated staff member at your club will be advised of all treatment, but the bargaining agreement states that such knowledge, "will not in and of itself be the basis for disciplinary action."

How Does Insurance Coverage Work?

All costs for care are covered by your NFL insurance and your club. If you choose NFL insurance coverage, you will sign a release authorizing Hazelden to notify a designated person at your club. (Again, your identity is kept confidential from the insurance company and the club accounting office.)

Who Can Use the Program?

Call the 800 number. It could be your key to recovery.

• Throughout the year, the program is available to any insured player, coach or team employee and eligible members of their families for any alcohol or drug-related problem. (During training camp, the program is also available to rookies.)

• The collective bargaining agreement recognizes that upon reasonable cause, a club official may direct a player to Hazelden for alcohol/drug problems.

• If you're worried about your alcohol/drug use, or that of a family or team member, this program is for you. It's also for you if you're recovering and need to know you're not alone.

NOTES

1. For a personal account of how drugs can destroy an NFL career, see Don Reese's story, "I'm Not Worth A Damn," Special Report, *Sports Illustrated*, June 14, 1982, pp. 1, 66–82. The following is an excerpt from that article:

Cocaine arrived in my life with my first-round draft into the National Football League in 1974. It has dominated my life, one way or another, almost every minute since. Eventually, it took control and almost killed me. It may yet. Cocaine can be found in quantity throughout the NFL. It's pushed on players, often from the edge of the practice field. Sometimes it's pushed *by* players. Prominent players. Just as it controlled me, it now controls and corrupts the game, because so many players are on it. To ignore this fact is to be short-sighted and stupid. To turn away from it the way the NFL does — the way the NFL turned its back on me when I cried for help two years ago — is a crime . . .

2. The following excerpt is from "A Test with Nothing But Tough Questions," *Sports Illustrated*, August 9, 1982, p. 24.

Now that it has become evident that drug abuse is a pervasive problem in the National Football League, battle lines have been drawn on the explosive issue of how best to deal with it — and specifically on whether players should be tested. The debate involves heated disagreement over the question of privacy, the subject of testing techniques and, indeed, matters of honor. At present the opposition sides are far apart. San Diego Coach Don Coryell says, "Anybody who won't take a drug test just doesn't want to play football." Gene Upshaw, the Raiders' veteran lineman and president of the NFL Players Association, asserts, "To suggest urinalysis (the standard method of detecting drugs) for players is an insult to our integrity. We will not participate."

3. For further information, see the following articles:
(a) "De Saulnier Says NFL Ignoring Drug Abuse," *Boston Globe*, June 13, 1982, p. 80.
(b) "NFL and Drugs," *Boston Globe*, March 8, 1981, p. 57.
(c) "Drugs in NFL: No Answer in Sight," *Washington Post*, July 4, 1982, p. E1.
(d) "Redskins: Drug Allegations Give Players a Bad Image," *Washington Post*, July 13, 1982, p. D1.
(e) "Drug Testing for Redskins under Study," *Washington Post*, July 20, 1982, p. D1.
(f) "Redskins: No Special Drug Tests," *Washington Post*, July 21, 1982, p. D1.
(g) "Redskins Avoided Drug-Test Showdown," *Washington Post*, July 22, 1982, p. B1.
(h) "Adviser Suspects NFL Steroid Use," *New York Times*, August 28, 1983, Sec. 5, p. 1.
(i) "Steroids: Discovery in Face of Disbelief," *New York Times*, August 28, 1983, Sect. 5, p. 1.
4. One tragic example of how drug abuse can affect a pro football player's career involves former ALL-PRO Chuck Muncie, who was suspended from the NFL for continued substance abuse. See the following:
(a) "Muncie Fails Test, Voiding His Trade," *New York Times*, September 15, 1984, p. 43.
(b) "Muncie Ineligible in Rozelle Ruling," *New York Times*, November 17, 1984, p. 44.
(c) "Chargers Drop Muncie," *New York Times*, March 29, 1985, p. A30.
5. In 1985, NFL commissioner Pete Rozelle reinstated Muncie, who was then traded from San Diego to Minnesota. Rozelle noted that:

We met recently with Chuck Muncie and reviewed all the factors in his case . . . We also reviewed the medical views of physicians involved in his rehabilitation and after-care program.

According to the information available to me, Chuck has made sustantial progress in working out his problems and establishing his true priorities while remaining drug free. He fully understands the consequences of further drug use, non-compliance with his program or any other conduct detrimental to the integrity of NFL football or public confidence in it. See "Muncie Reinstated and Traded," *Daily Hampshire Gazette* (AP Wireservice), July 20, 1985, p. 16.

6. In November 1984, the NFL ordered Cincinnati Bengals running back Stanley Wilson to undergo a drug evaluation or else face immediate suspension. He was barred from playing until completion of the ordered treatment. Wilson's drug problem was detected by urinalysis. Previously, the Bengals had sent Wilson to drug detoxification centers three times, including two sessions at the Hazelden Foundation. When drugs were again detected, the NFL took over jurisdiction of the problem from the Bengals. Wilson was a second-year player from Oklahoma University.

7. In 1984, Les Steckel, coach of the Minnesota Vikings, stated that he had been ordering surprise drug tests on players who, he said, had agreed to the tests. Such tactics were in violation of the NFL's collective bargaining agreement with the NFLPA, which prohibits spot checking for drug abuse. See "Viking Drug Issue," *New York Times*, November 14, 1984, p. A30.

8. In 1985, the New York Giants used urinalysis to test players on the team for use of illegal drugs. NFL Players' Association general counsel Richard Berthelsen called the spot tests a "clear violation of the collective bargaining agreement." For further information, see the following articles:

(a) "NFLPA to Probe Giant Tests," *New York Post*, February 20, 1985, p. 55.

(b) "Drug Tests," *USA Today*, February 18, 1985, p. C1.

9. In 1983, NFL Commissioner Pete Rozelle suspended four players for four games because of cocaine use. For further information, see the following articles:

(a) "Rozelle Suspends 4 for Drug Use," *New York Times*, July 26, 1983, p. B5.

(b) "Rozelle Suspends 4 Players," *USA Today*, July 26, 1983, p. C1.

5.62–3   Major League Baseball

In June 1984, Major League Baseball (MLB) and the MLB Players Association ratified a drug-abuse program. Even though the program was more lenient than the National Basketball Association's plan, professional baseball had trouble getting the union to agree to terms, partially due to past problems in the area of drug abuse and to penalties that had previously been levied by the commissioner of baseball. Commissioner Bowie Kuhn called the plan a "dramatic breakthrough in labor relations and sports." Baseball had thus become the second major American team sport to set in place a management-union program to deal comprehensively with drug abuse.

The baseball program excludes marijuana, amphetamines, and alcohol. Players who are found to be abusing these substances will continue to be subject to action by the commissioner, and the union will continue to have the right to file grievances in such cases. Referring to the excluded drugs, Lee MacPhail, president of the owners' Player Relations Committee, noted: "At the present time, politically, we are not able to cover all things. We're trying to take this one step at a time. We know this is an area we might want to expand at a later date." Until then, the program will be aimed almost exclusively at cocaine, currently the most serious problem.

A cornerstone of the new agreement was a salary abatement procedure to penalize players who continued to use drugs. A player who asks for help with a drug problem will receive full pay for the first 30 days of treatment and half pay for the next 30 days. Beyond 60 days, if kept on the major league roster by the club, the player will be paid at a rate of $60,000 a year, the minimum salary.

A club that suspects a player of drug involvement can ask the person to undergo examination. If the player refuses, the evidence will be presented to a review council, a panel that includes drug counselors. The members of this council are selected by a joint committee of owners and players. If the council recommends that the player undergo testing or treatment and the player refuses, he will be subject to disciplinary action by the commissioner.

The agreement between the MLB and the MLBPA was deemed insufficient in 1985 by the MLB's new commissioner Peter Ueberroth. Reacting in part to a major federal investigation centered in Pittsburgh, which was investigating drug dealing in professional baseball and involved players throughout the league, Ueberroth called for a comprehensive mandatory drug-testing program for the MLB, including the commissioner's office, the club's front office staffs and employees, umpires, as well as the players. Ueberroth was able to get quick agreement and implement testing for all the groups except the players, who rejected his plan. The decision of the players, announced through the MLBPA, was made despite mounting evidence that drug abuse had in the near past affected player performances on the field. John McHale, president of the Montreal Expos, in particular blamed cocaine for his franchise's failure to win a close pennant race in 1982. McHale noted: "We felt we should've won in '82. When we all woke up to what was going on, we found that there were at least eight players on our club who were into this thing." At least one player admitted that on a close play at a base he would dive head first into the bag to avoid being tagged out, but more importantly, to protect the glass container of cocaine in his back pocket.

NOTES _____

1. For further information, see the following articles:
(a) "Baseball Approves Program on Drugs," *New York Times*, June 22, 1984, p. A20.
(b) "Approval of Drug Program Was a Must," *USA Today*, June 25, 1984, p. C8.
(c) "Cocaine Use Called Common by Moffett," *New York Times*, February 23, 1984, p. B20.
(d) "Angry Hernandez Threatens to Sue," *New York Daily News*, February 24, 1984, p. 72.
(e) "Kuhn Announces Tough Drug Rules," *USA Today*, June 29, 1984, p. C9.
(f) "Baseball Meeting on Drugs Cancelled," *New York Times*, November 30, 1983, p. B13.
(g) "Drug Problem Is Testing Sports," *Boston Globe*, May 9, 1985, pp. 53, 55.
(h) "ACLU Calls Drug Plan 'Invasion of Privacy,'" *Boston Globe*, May 9, 1985. p. 55.
(i) "First Drug Tests Are Set for Baseball," *New York Times*, June 19, 1985, pp. B11, 13.
(j) "Players Balk at Drug Tests," *USA Today*, April 9, 1985, pp. A1, 2.
(k) "Baseball Backs Big Drug Plan," *USA Today*, May 8, 1985, p. C1.
2. The following excerpt is from "Doubleday Calls Drugs Baseball's Biggest Threat," *New York Daily News*,

March 3, 1984, p. 30:

"There are some severe problems in baseball and it is important we put our shoulder to the wheel together — management and players," New York Mets owner Nelson Doubleday said.

"The single largest problem in baseball is drugs. It is a lot more serious than people [are aware of], and it has been shoved under the rug at times. I think it's time for the players and baseball to work together. We've got to stop the 'we' and the 'they.' I don't think it's too late. Maybe it is but I am an optimist."

3. Former MLB Commissioner Bowie Kuhn announced that players who are convicted of drug-related crimes face a minimum one-year suspension from MLB and could be barred for life. See "Kuhn Announces Rules on Drug Crimes," *New York Times*, June 29, 1984, p. A18.
4. In 1985, MLB negotiations for a new collective bargaining agreement (CBA) with the Players' Association came to a halt when the MLBPA learned that the Dodgers were inserting clauses into their players' contracts calling for mandatory drug testing in contravention to the drug agreement announced in 1984. The clause was later withdrawn by the Dodgers, in anticipation of it being negotiated in the next CBA. For further information, see the following articles:
(a) "Baseball Talks Are Snagged," *New York Times*, January 24, 1985, p. B7.
(b) "Dodgers' Decision Defuses a Conflict," *New York Times*, January 26, 1985, p. 29.
(c) "Baseball Settles Drug Issues," *New York Times*, January 30, 1985, p. A16.
5. In 1985, Yankees' owner George Steinbrenner announced the establishment of a drug abuse program for his minor league system whereby voluntary spot-check testing is allowed. First-time offenders would be fined $500, while second-time offenders would face a full-scale rehabilitation program or immediate suspension. See Steinbrenner Strikes Out at Drugs," *New York Post*, April 23, 1985, p. 9.
6. For more information on player drug problems facing MLB commissioner Peter Ueberroth, see the following four-part series published by the *New York Times*:
(a) "Baseball and Cocaine: A Deepening Problem," *New York Times*, August 19, 1985, pp. A1, C6.
(b) "Cocaine Disrupts Baseball from Field to Front Office," *New York Times*, August 20, 1985, pp. A1, B8.
(c) "Talking Baseball, Snorting Cocaine," *New York Times*, August 21, 1985, pp. A21, 23.
(d) "Battling Drugs: Approaches Vary," *New York Times*, August 22, 1985, pp. D21, 22.

5.63 Olympic Games: Drug Abuse and Enforcement

At the 1984 Summer Olympic Games in Los

Angeles, the most intensive program of drug testing of athletes ever developed was implemented. Dr. Anthony F. Daly, Jr., an orthopedist and sports-medicine specialist from Inglewood, California, and vice president and medical director of the Los Angeles Olympic Organizing Committee noted:

> There's no way to mask the drugs. The testing equipment is so sensitive that it can pick up one part in a billion. It's more sensitive than the equipment used last summer in the Pan American Games in Caracas. Our goal is to protect the athlete from himself and from gaining an unfair advantage. We want a drug-free Olympics where the athlete relies on his natural ability.

The International Olympic Committee and the international federations that govern each Olympic sport ban more than 60 generic drugs. They fall into five classes: psychomotor stimulants (including amphetamines and cocaine); central nervous system stimulants (including caffeine); sympathomimetic amines (including ephedrine); narcotic analgesics (including codeine and heroin); and anabolic steroids (including testosterone). Many over-the-counter remedies for colds, congestion, hay fever, and allergies contain drugs on the list.

Only about 1,500 of the roughly 8,500 Olympic competitors were required to submit to drug tests. The selected athletes included the four top performers (or teams) in each event, plus others selected at random. The Olympic drug-testing program, however, was not foolproof. For example, athletes who used steroids could possibly have escaped detection. An athlete's urine usually is free of steroids if the oral doses were stopped three to four weeks before testing or if injectable steroids were halted three to four months beforehand.

Testosterone, which, like a steroid, speeds muscle regeneration in injured people, was added to the banned list for the first time at the Los Angeles Olympic Games. Because the hormone occurs in the body naturally, Olympic officials tested for excessive levels. Although the definition of excessive levels is high enough

to allow some suspected illicit users to escape disqualification, it was established at that level to protect innocent athletes.

"It's possible that someone could go around the [drug testing] system," medical director Daly said. "But we keep closing loopholes, as we have with stimulant drugs. ... If we keep closing every little loophole that develops, then pretty soon we'll reach the ultimate goal, which is a drug-free Olympics."

Although estimates vary considerably there was little disagreement that use of anabolic steroids has been extensive among Olympic athletes, at least in certain sports. "In the weightlifting events and probably in track and field, it's a fairly high percentage," Daly said, acknowledging some estimates that up to 95 percent of weightlifters use the drugs. "It's probably a relatively low percentage — lower than people think — in the other events," he added.

Different tests were used to detect various drugs, but the major testing devices at Los Angeles were eight gas chromatograph-mass spectrometers. These machines break down a substance into its component parts, which show up on a graph as a unique chemical "fingerprint," even if the concentration of a drug in urine is as little as one part per billion.

The tests were conducted so that after a competition ended, the athletes to be tested reported to the testing facility. There, they chose a code number and beaker for their urine specimen. Under observation, they produced a sample, a process that sometimes took an hour or two because of dehydration. The athlete then poured equal amounts of the sample into two bottles. As the athlete watched, the crew chief capped the bottles, sealed them with wax and labeled them "A" and "B."

Both bottles were then taken to the testing laboratory at UCLA. Specimen B was set aside, and Specimen A was tested. If no banned substance was found, the test was over. If a banned substance turned up, another sample from Specimen A was checked. If that also tested positive, the athlete and the head of the athlete's national delegation were notified. In that event, Specimen B was tested within ten days in the presence of the athlete and medical representatives from the delegation. The result of the Specimen B test was final. An athlete whose final test was positive was disqualified, lost his or her medal, and faced suspension by the sport's international federation. Of all the athletes tested at the Olympic Games in 1984, only five were found to be using drugs and disqualified.

NOTES ————————————————————

1. For further information, see the following articles:
(a) "The Other Game: Testing for Drugs," *New York Times*, July 24, 1984, p. B7.
(b) "Drug Free Olympics Is Goal," (AP Wireservice), *Newark Star Ledger*, July 17, 1984, p. 36.
(c) "Overcoming the Drug Mentality," *Boston Globe*, July 15, 1984, p. 41.
(d) "USOC to Seek More Tests for Drugs," *New York Times*, March 24, 1985, Sec. 5, p. 1.
(e) "USOC to Get Drug Plan," *Washington Post*, February 9, 1985, p. D1.
2. At the 1984 Summer Olympic Games, the International Olympic Committee (IOC) began a four-year research project in sports medicine and drug abuse. The following excerpt is from "Drug Plan to Start at Games," *New York Times*, June 29, 1984, p. A16.

Prince Alexandre de Merode, president of the IOC's Medical Commission, said that the program would continue the testing of athletes for use of illegal drugs and seek to expand the number of laboratories from the current 15. Also, he said the project would examine training techniques to help athletes find ways to improve their performances without having to rely on drugs.

The program, called the International Olympic Association for Research and Sports Medicine, will be funded by health-care organizations. Prince Alexandre said it would have a budget the first four years of more than $2.9 million.

He did not elaborate on what sort of health-care organizations would be asked to contribute, but an IOC health committee official suggested this might include corporations in the medical and health-care fields that would have access to the project's publications and films.

"The Olympic Games in Los Angeles will provide the first opportunities for analysis of top athletes' biomechanical and physiological techniques in actual competition and training," Prince Alexandre said in a statement. "It is hoped that this analysis will lead to healthy alternatives which should render doping agents unattractive to athletes."

3. In 1983, at the Pan-American Games, over 20 medals were forfeited by participating countries because of drug detection among those countries' athletes. The large numbers of athletes involved was attributed to advances in the equipment for detection of drugs, which the athletes were unaware of when they entered the Games. The results of this detection program served to forewarn athletes entering the 1984 Olympic Games. For further information, see the following articles:
(a) "Detection Takes Drugs Out of Game," *USA Today*, August 24, 1983, p. C1.
(b) "Commission to Question Track Athletes," *USA Today*, September 14, 1983, p. C1.
(c) "Drug Control Brings Controversy," *New York Times*, November 14, 1983, p. D4.
4. In November 1984, the International Amateur Athletic Federation (IAAF) confirmed lifetime bans on six athletes for drug-related infractions. The IAAF governs international track competition. Athletes could appeal the bans through their national federations but would still face a minimum 18-month suspension if reinstated on that level. See "Track Group Bans 6," *New York Times*, November 27, 1984, p. B10.
5. In 1985, the United States Cycling Federation announced that some Olympic cyclists had used "blood doping" treatments before competing at the 1984 Summer Olympic Games in Los Angeles. This treatment involves the transfusing of red blood cells into an athlete's body. It supposedly helps in a meet because it allows an athlete's bloodstream to carry more oxygen. While the procedure had not been banned by the IOC, it was considered unethical by the USOC. For further information see the following articles:
(a) "Triumphs Tainted with Blood," *Sports Illustrated*, January 21, 1985, p. 62.
(b) "Authorities Split on 'Blood Doping' Benefits," *Philadelphia Inquirer*, January 11 1985, p. C7.
(c) "Blood-Doping Unethical, U.S. Olympic Official Says," *New York Times*, January 13, 1985, Sec. 5, p. 3.
(d) "Unit Says Cyclists Used Blood Doping," *New York Times*, January 19, 1985, p. 27.
(e) "USOC Sets Penalties for Blood Doping," *USA Today*, June 17, 1985, p. C1.
6. In 1985, the British Amateur Athletic Board announced it would implement a stricter drug policy for track and field and would ask all potential Olympic athletes to sign a waiver allowing random drug testing. See "British Tighten Drug Rules," *New York Times*, February 13, 1985, p. B15.
7. In 1985, at the National Sports Festival in Baton Rouge, Louisiana, the USOC began a program of drug testing for all athletes who seek to compete on 1988 U.S.

Olympic teams. The $800,000 program involves testing athletes who are competing in pre-Olympic events and athletes who are residing at the USOC's Olympic Training Center in Colorado Springs, Colorado. The USOC reported that in 1983–84, it tested 2,500 athletes for drug abuse and noted that no American athlete failed a drug test at the 1984 Winter or Summer Olympic Games. For further information, see the following articles:

(a) "USOC to Begin Testing," *New York Times*, June 25, 1985, p. A21.

(b) "Anti-Drug Programs Growing," *USA Today*, July 26, 1985, p. C8.

5.70   Gambling

The problems associated with illegal gambling and the influence it may exert on professional and intercollegiate sports are of special concern to athletic administrators and others since gambling affects the integrity of the games, the games themselves, and the public confidence in athletes and sports. Some argue that betting on games is encouraged by the press, which prints the "spread" on games in its sports pages, as well as advertisements on weekly tip sheets and betting aids.

Although some contend that betting on athletics is enjoyable and is a form of entertainment, others contend that illegal gambling has a negative impact on society and sports. Many sports managers have taken steps to combat the dangers of illegal gambling in an effort to preserve the integrity of their schools, conferences, and leagues.

NOTES _____

1. John Thompson, basketball coach of the 1984 NCAA champion Georgetown University team, made the following remarks during an appearance before the District of Columbia Citizen's Gambling Study Commission.

My opinion then, as now, is that it's not a question of whether gambling should be legal or not, but of being consistent. To legalize some forms of gambling, like lotteries, and to run betting lines in newspapers and broadcast them on television, is a kind of "entrapment."

It's like putting heroin all over the street and advertising it in the newspapers, then arresting somebody for using it. By creating an atmosphere of permissiveness,

it tells a kid it's okay to gamble because we've gone public with it.

2. Tony Vaccarino, an agent in the FBI's Criminal Investigations Division, says that coaches should study tapes of all games and talk with players to make sure they are all performing properly. He thinks a coach should get in touch with the FBI "if he feels his team is not performing the way it should." Vaccarino claims the FBI is opposed to legalizing sports gambling of any sort: "We say it would create situations where people get involved in gambling who would normally not get involved. It exposes them to involvement with organized-crime figures — with loan sharks, for instance, to pay off gambling debts."

3. In June 1985, at hearings held by the President's Commission on Organized Crime, John R. Davis, president of the NCAA, testified that the association would be in favor of a law that prohibited the printing of "point spreads" in newspapers, "were it not for apparent constitutional limitations." Davis also called for a federal law banning gambling on amateur sports. At the same hearings, Vince Doria, assistant managing editor for sports at the *Boston Globe*, testified that he thinks "most newspapers have come to the conclusion that gamblers are readers too. . . . In fact, they are extremely avid readers of the sports pages. I think most of us believe that those readers deserve to be serviced." See "Davis Gives Views at U.S. Hearing, *NCAA News*, July 3, 1985, pp. 1, 12.

5.71   Intercollegiate Athletics and Gambling

Estimates are that gambling on college athletics is currently a $1 billion a year industry. Problems associated with and arising from wagering, however, have continually plagued college athletics. In 1945, five Brooklyn College basketball players were expelled from school after they admitted to accepting bribes to lose a game. In 1951, 37 players at 22 schools were caught shaving points (trying to win by fewer points than bookmakers predict) in 44 games. Recently, a gambling scandal at Boston College during the 1978–79 season led to the conviction of basketball player Rick Kuhn, who was sentenced to ten years in prison on federal gaming charges (*infra*).

More recently, in 1985, a gambling and drug scandal was uncovered at Tulane University. That incident, which involved a number of basketball players, led to the institution's dropping the sport from competition at the intercollegiate level (*infra*, note 12).

The NCAA has continued to add to its investigating staff to keep tabs on the gambling problem. Many NCAA investigators are former FBI agents who attempt to maintain contacts with bookmakers both in Nevada, where sports gambling is legal, and in other states where it is not. The unorthodox relationship between bookmakers and NCAA investigators is based on mutual concern that sporting events not be rigged to reach a predetermined outcome. The bookmakers cannot afford a rigged game for economic reasons, for their winning percentages and profit margins are based on a "point spread," which they formulate on the theory that the game is not rigged. The NCAA and the individual schools' concerns are based on the integrity of the game and on their own reputations.

The bookmakers usually alert NCAA investigators if there is a sizable change in the point spread on a particular game. Such a change is suspicious and may indicate that bettors have placed large wagers on a team. Of course, heavy betting may occur for other reasons, such as a coach's announcement of injury to a key player. If no legitimate reasons are found, however, it increases the possibility that gamblers have "fixed" the game by bribing a coach, player, or official. Remember, bribes are not necessarily made to ensure that a team loses — just that it wins by fewer points than the predicted point spread. Once suspicions are aroused, college officials such as the president and athletic director are then informed by the NCAA. They may also be notified if investigators hear "street talk" about "something funny" going on somewhere in their institution's athletic program.

United States v. Burke, 700 F. 2d 70 (2d Cir. 1983)

Rick Kuhn, a former Boston College basketball player, was charged (along with four co-defendants) and convicted of racketeering by conspiring to fix at least six games, on sports bribery and violation of the Interstate Travel and Aid to Racketeering statutes.

In sentencing Kuhn to ten-years imprisonment, the court noted:

The crimes in this case are especially significant in view of the ramifications which they have had on the world of sports, college basketball in particular. A group of gamblers and career criminals were able to band together and successfully bribe and influence college athletes. Their motivation was simple and clear — financial gain. The crime, however, reminds millions of sports fans that athletics can be compromised and are not always merely honest competition among dedicated athletes.

While it is true that only one or possibly two athletes were compromised, the effect remains basically the same. Every college athlete may now come under suspicion by fans and coaches. This suspicion has existed previously due to earlier scandals dating back several years, and it is now renewed as a result of [this] offense.

This 26-year-old defendant undoubtedly assumed one of the more essential roles in this offense. While it may be true that his performance during games was not particularly pivotal, his actions away from the basketball court are of significant importance. He was a member of the 1978–79 Boston College team who initially agreed to participate and thereafter recruited other players, maintained contact with the gamblers and accepted their payments.

It is interesting to note that there was not testimony introduced at the trial which indicated a reluctance on the part of the defendant to participate [in point shaving] or a desire to terminate his involvement. Rather, he emerges as somewhat of a greedy individual who was more interested in collecting money from his criminal associates than he was in winning basketball games.

The defendant is a product of a stable and supporting working-class family. From a young age, he developed natural abilities in athletics and was essentially successful in signing a professional baseball contract in 1973 and in attending college on a basketball scholarship three years later. Various individuals who have been (associated) with the defendant in his home town of Swissville, Pennsylvania, have described him in very positive terms. The reasons therefore as to why he became involved in this offense remain unclear.

On final analysis, deterrence emerges as the most important sentencing objective. A strong argument can be offered that the substantial term of incarceration imposed on this defendant will be recalled in the future by another college athlete who may be tempted to compromise his performance.

NOTES

1. The NCAA followed the Kuhn case with great interest and followed up the conviction with the account below, which was published in the *NCAA News*. It shows the interesting sequence of events and the interaction with organized crime that led to Kuhn's ten-year sentence.

The government's case on the Boston College point-shaving case sought to prove that the scandal was a calculated and prolonged undertaking. The following picture of what occurred emerged from the trial.

The investigation began when Henry Hill, who was cooperating with prosecuting authorities and was a participant in the Federal Witness Protection Program, outlined the scheme to the Federal Bureau of Investigation.

Hill, an acknowledged narcotics dealer and truck hijacker, told FBI agents that he and several of his associates had given money and drugs to various members of the Boston College basketball team during the 1978–79 season. In return, the players agreed to "shave points" or deliberately lose games so that Hill and his associates would win large amounts of money by wagering on the games.

The government alleged the plan took shape in the summer of 1978 when Anthony Perla, his brother, Rocco, and Paul Mazzei met with Rick Kuhn, a member of the Boston College basketball team. During these early discussions, Anthony Perla told Kuhn he could earn substantial sums of money if he agreed to participate in a "point-shaving" scheme. After indicating an interest in cooperating, Kuhn was given drugs and other items by the Perla brothers and Mazzei for the rest of the summer.

In September, realizing the group could not handle the plan alone, Mazzei approached Hill. Hill was valuable in that he would be able to contact Jimmy Burke, an organized crime figure with the necessary influence to make the plan succeed. Burke would be able to provide protection from disgruntled bookmakers who might discover the "fix" and lose large sums of money, and he also would be able to arrange for those involved in the scheme to maximize the amount of money that could be wagered and therefore won.

In October, Hill proposed the plan to Burke, who was enthusiastic about it. Burke expressed a desire to meet Mazzei and said he would use only his most trusted bookmakers.

During the first week of November, Mazzei traveled to New York to meet with Burke. Burke reiterated his interest in the plan, but now he said he would like to meet Anthony Perla, who was the principal contact with Kuhn. Mazzei and Perla came to New York November 16 and met with Burke, who then directed Hill to Boston to meet with the players.

About this time, Kuhn proposed the plan to Boston College captain Jim Sweeney. Sweeney and Kuhn met with Hill, Mazzei and Anthony Perla on November 16, with Mazzei telling the players they would have to lose games directly if instructed to do so and that influential people from New York were backing up the scheme.

Shortly thereafter, Kuhn was given $500 and some cocaine, and it was agreed that the team's December 6 game against Providence would be a "trial run."

The test did not go well. Boston College was favored by six to eight points, but it won by 19. Since the group was wagering against Boston College, the group lost. The large margin of victory resulted from the refusal of Sweeney to go along with the plan and from an excellent game by Ernie Cobb, the star of the team.

Hill described Burke as being furious. Rather than abandon the plan, however, the group instructed Kuhn to recruit Cobb. Kuhn and Sweeney later told FBI agents that Cobb was in fact recruited, but Cobb denied receiving any money and never was indicted.

The next significant game was against Harvard on December 16. Burke told Hill to go to Boston for the game and tell the players that the group was not going to tolerate the "foolishness" that was exhibited in the Providence game.

By now, Kuhn had attempted to recruit starting center Joe Beaulieu. Beaulieu, however, refused to go along.

Hill, Anthony Perla, Rocco Perla, Paul Mazzei and Judy Wicks (Hill's girlfriend) attended the Harvard game. They saw Boston College win by three points, well under the gambling line of 12. Having bet against Boston College, the group won. After the game, Hill paid Kuhn $3,000 and told him there was more to come in a few days. Another $2,000 was sent to Kuhn by Rocco Perla via Western Union several days later.

The next game that was "fixed" was the December 23 UCLA game. UCLA was a 15-point favorite and Kuhn told the Perla brothers that Boston College was incapable of winning the game. When Boston College lost by 22 points, the group had won again and on January 8, Kuhn received a Western Union money order for $2,000.

During the next week, Boston College traveled to Honolulu for a holiday tournament. Although no proof exists that the BC games in the event were fixed, gambling lines did shift dramatically (reflecting heavy betting). Also, telephone records show that Burke contacted both Henry Hill and Anthony Perla during the tournament.

The group won again with the January 10 game against Rhode Island, but by the time a January 17 rematch against Rhode Island arrived, the group realized that bookmakers were becoming suspicious. To allay those concerns, the group bet heavily on Boston College to win. The Eagles won the contest, the members of the group won their bets and Kuhn collected another $2,000 from Rocco Perla. By late January, Kuhn — according to his former girlfriend — was in constant telephone contact with Rocco and Anthony Perla discussing games that were to be fixed.

Boston College played Fordham on February 3. It was an important game to the group because it involved a New York team, which meant that large amounts of money could be wagered without raising suspicion. BC was favored by 13 but won by only seven. Rocco Perla attended in place of his brother and provided Kuhn with $1,000 and a stereo system.

Three nights later, Boston College visited New York for a game against St. John's. The Eagles were a nine point underdog, and they lost by nine, resulting in a "push" (a tie). Afterwards, Kuhn's girlfriend said Kuhn was concerned that Cobb was unreliable, but the group wanted his cooperation more than ever.

The next game, a February 10 contest against Holy Cross, was important because it was regionally televised, which again meant that large amounts of money could be wagered without causing concern. Kuhn told the group he would make up for the St. John's game, and Anthony Perla traveled to Las Vegas to bet with legal bookmakers. Hill, who claimed that Burke wagered between $30,000 and $50,000 on the game, watched the contest with Burke. The point spread had Holy Cross by seven, but Boston College lost by only two. The group lost as well. Kuhn himself reportedly lost $10,000 on the game.

The entire series of events might have gone undetected had not Hill come under suspicion in a 1978 robbery of $5.8 million from the Lufthansa Airlines freight terminal at New York's Kennedy International Airport. A federal attorney asked Hill where he was on a certain date, and Hill said he had been in Boston. When the attorney asked Hill what he had been doing there, Hill said, "Fixing some Boston College basketball games."

On September 8, 1980, the FBI interviewed Kuhn. He admitted he was recruited to shave points, lose games and recruit others to go along. He is thought to have received about $10,500. Another $10,000 was promised to him, but he never received it because he bet it on the Holy Cross game and lost. See "Boston College: A Gamble That Didn't Pay Off," *NCAA News*, February 15, 1982, p. 3.

2. In 1984, a federal court acquitted Ernie Cobb, a teammate of Kuhn's, of charges arising out of the same violations as those that convicted Kuhn. Cobb admitted accepting $1,000 in 1979 from one of the men convicted but claimed it was not for fixing games but only for giving advice as to which teams Boston College was likely to beat. See "Former College Players Acquitted on Basketball Gambling Charge," *Chronicle of Higher Education*, April 4, 1984, p. 28.

3. In January 1983, the Second U.S. Circuit Court of Appeals unanimously upheld the Kuhn case convictions. In making its ruling, the court upheld the right of newsmen to keep confidential their information and sources in criminal cases. In the appeal, the defense had contended the convictions should be overturned because the trial court would not allow access to press information that was considered vital in cross-examining Henry Hill, the key prosecution witness. The defendants wanted the documents and tapes that were used by *Sports Illustrated* in a February 1981 article and were purported to be Hill's first-hand account of the point-shaving scheme. (See "How I Put the Fix In," *Sports Illustrated*, February 16, 1981, p. 14.) The appeals court concluded that interest did not outweigh the public interest in preserving the confidentiality of journalists' sources. "Reporters," the appeals court said, "are to be encouraged to investigate and expose — free from unnecessary government intrusion — evidence of criminal wrongdoing."

The appeals court in its review said that trial evidence showed the point-shaving scheme was the brainchild of the Perla brothers, who were described as "small-time gamblers with big-time ideas."

4. In October 1983, the U.S. Supreme Court upheld the Kuhn case convictions. It rejected the appeal without comment. (See "Rick Kuhn Sentenced to 10 years," *New York Times*, February 6, 1982, p. 17.)

5. In May 1983, in the wake of disclosures made to the FBI by Baltimore Colts quarterback Art Schlichter that while at Baltimore he had run up in four months gambling debts of $389,000, his alma mater, Ohio State, began an investigation into his alleged gambling while a student-athlete. "It would only be prudent administration for us to know what took place," said Ohio State associate athletic director James Jones. For further information, see the following articles:

(a) "NFL Player Admits Placing Sports Bets," *Boston Globe*, April 8, 1983, p. 1.

(b) "Has It All Been Thrown Away?" *Sports Illustrated*, April 18, 1983, p. 40.

(c) "A Big Loss for a Gambling Quarterback," *Sports Illustrated* May 30, 1983, p. 30.

6. Schlichter later admitted he had been gambling for years — in high school, at Ohio State, and while with the Colts. Schlichter was indefinitely suspended from the NFL by Commissioner Pete Rozelle and was reinstated 14 months later. See "Schlichter Enters the Next Phase Along

the Way Back," *New York Times*, July 23, 1984, p. C1.

7. In March 1985, three Tulane University basketball players were arrested and charged with fixing the outcome of games, the first point-shaving scandal to involve intercollegiate athletics since the Boston College incident during the 1978–79 season. It was alleged that the point-shaving scheme involved cocaine purchases for the athletes. In the wake of the scandal all Tulane basketball coaches resigned, the basketball program was terminated, and the athletic director resigned. For further information, see the following articles:

(a) "2 at Tulane Held in Basketball Fix," *New York Times*, March 27, 1985, p. B11.

(b) "2 More at Tulane Charged in Fix," *New York Times*, March 28, 1985, p. B11.

(c) "5th Tulane Student Arrested," *New York Times*, March 29, 1985, p. A27.

(d) "The Darkest Blot," *New York Times*, March 29, 1985, p. A27.

(e) "DA Terms Cocaine Point-Shaving Lure," *New York Daily News*, March 29, 1985, p. 93.

(f) "Cops: Tulane Fixed at Least Two Games," *New York Daily News*, March 27, 1985, p. 53.

(g) "Tulane Ends Basketball," *New York Times*, February 19, 1985, p. A26.

(h) "Tulane Student Pleads Not Guilty," *New York Times*, February 11 1985, p. B15.

(i) "Two Plead Guilty in Point-Shaving Investigation at Tulane," *NCAA News*, April 10, 1985, p. 3.

(j) "Tulane U., Beset by Recruiting Violations, Gambling Allegations, to Drop Basketball," *Chronicle of Higher Education*, April 10, 1985, p. 31.

(k) "Blowing the Whistle on Men's Basketball at Tulane U.," *Chronicle of Higher Education*, April 17, 1985, pp. 27, 28.

8. In August 1985, the first of the Tulane basketball players to go on trial, John 'Hot Rod' Williams, had a mistrial called after a few days of testimony when the judge ruled that the state's prosecutor had withheld valuable evidence from the defendant's attorney during pretrial discovery. For further information, see the following articles:

(a) "Trial Starts Today for Tulane Star," *New York Times*, August 12, 1985, p. C8.

(b) "Tulane Fix Meeting Recalled," *New York Times*, August 13, 1985, p. A19.

(c) "Tulane Trial Is Halted by Judge," *New York Times*, August 14, 1985, p. B9.

(d) "Williams' Defense Wins a Key Issue," *New York Times*, August 15, 1985, p. B11.

(e) "Mistrial Declared for Ex-Tulane Star," *New York Times*, August 16, 1985, p. A19.

(f) "Mistrial Order Opposed," *New York Times*, August 17, 1985, p. 12.

9. The Tulane basketball players were charged under Louisiana's Bribery of Sports Participants law (L.S.A. — R.S. 14:118.1) which states:

A. Bribing of sports participants is the giving or offering to give, directly or indirectly, anything of apparent present or prospective value to any professional or amateur baseball, football, hockey, polo, tennis or basketball player or boxer or any person or player who participates or expects to participate in any professional or amateur game or sport or any contest of skill, speed, strength or endurance of man or beast or any jockey, driver, groom or any person participating or expecting to participate in any horse race, including owners of race tracks and their employees, stewards, trainers, judges, starters or special policemen, or to any owner, manager, coach or trainer of any team or participant in any such game, contest or sport, with the intent to influence him to lose or cause to be lost, or corruptly to affect or influence the result thereof, or to limit his or his team's or his mount or beast's margin of victory in any baseball, football, hockey or basketball game, boxing, tennis or polo match or horse race or any professional or amateur sport or game in which such player or participant or jockey or driver is taking part or expects to take part, or has any duty in connection therewith.

The acceptance of, or the offer to accept directly or indirectly anything of apparent present or prospective value under such circumstances by any of the above named persons shall also constitute bribery of sports participants.

Whoever commits the crime of bribery of sports participants is guilty of a felony and shall be punished by a fine of not more than ten thousand dollars and imprisoned for not less than one year nor more than five years, with or without hard labor, or both.

B. The offender under this Section, who states the facts under oath to the district attorney charged with the prosecution of the offense, and who gives evidence tending to convict any other offender under that Section, may, in the discretion of such district attorney, be granted full immunity from prosecution in respect to the offense reported, except for perjury in giving such testimony.

10. See also *Louisiana* v. *Angelo Trosclair, III*, 443 So. 2d 1098 (La. 1984), for a Louisiana Supreme Court decision which examined the Louisiana Bribery Sports Participant law in relation to horse racing.

11. The NCAA has the following recommended policy in regards to gambling:

POLICY 8

Gambling and Bribery

Section 1. College administrators should redouble their efforts in counseling the student body at large and athletes in particular as to the seriousness of the gambling problem. This is an unending and continual challenge and one to which college athletics administrators must constantly rededicate themselves.

Section 2. All institutions should warn their athletics squads regularly against the threat and corruption attached to the activities of gamblers; cite existing and applicable Federal, state and local laws; review the tragedy that has struck some students, and post pertinent messages on this subject to remind the student-athletes of these facts.

Section 3. Institutional rules should provide that any student (athlete or nonathlete) shall be expelled from college and any staff member shall be terminated as an employee for failure to report a solicitation to be a party to sports bribery; further, institutional regulations should provide that a student shall be expelled or a staff member shall be terminated if the individual becomes an agent of the gambling industry through the process of distributing handicap information or handling bets. [Note: Institutions should encourage local authorities to enact and enforce laws prohibiting this type of activity on the part of any citizen.]

Section 4. Institutional rules should provide for the termination of employment for life of any staff member who knowingly continues association with known gamblers or bookmakers after being advised by the institution's chief executive officer to discontinue such association.

Section 5. Any additional steps that can be taken to make it more difficult for the briber to gain information or to make contact at the campus level should be undertaken.

Section 6. In those states that do not have antibribery laws or where existing laws are inadequate, member institutions should take the leadership in petitioning state legislatures to pass strong legislation to deal with this subject.

Section 7. No press credentials should be issued to representatives of any organization that regularly publishes, or otherwise promotes the advertising of, "tout sheets" or "tip sheets" or other advertising designed to encourage gambling on college sports events.

See *1985–86 NCAA Manual*, Policy 8.

12. As a result of the investigation surrounding the Tulane University "point shaving" scandal, Memphis State University also became the target of a gambling probe. For further information, see the following articles:

(a) "Rumors Worry Head of Memphis State," *New York Times*, February 27, 1985, p. 42.

(b) "Probe by Memphis State U. Fails to Turn Up Any Evidence to Support Gambling Rumors," *Chronicle of Higher Education*, July 31, 1985, pp. 23, 26.

13. See "Gambling on College Games Said to Be Up Dramatically," *Chronicle of Higher Education*, March 2, 1983, pp. 1, 16–18. The following excerpt is from that article:

The Commission on the Review of the National Policy Toward Gambling recommended in its 1976 report, *Gambling in America*, "that there be an absolute prohibition against the inclusion of wagering on amateur sporting events [if betting on professional sports is legalized]. While the commission recognizes that some amateur events already are the objects of illegal wagering nationwide, it cannot condone the utilization for wagering purposes of educational institutions and similar organizations dedicated to the improvement of youth.

This opinion is in part predicated on the fact that young athletes of high school and college age are far more impressionable and therefore are in greater danger of being subjected to the temptations of player corruption. Additionally, unlike professional sports leagues, particularly the [National Football League], amateur athletic associations do not have enforcement or investigative capabilities which would enable them to maintain sufficient safeguards.

14. Billy Packer and Al McGuire, TV broadcast personalities, have produced a film called "Sell Out," which warns athletes of the dangers associated with gambling. (The film was produced by TPC Communication and financed by Nike, Inc.)

15. Nevada, which is the only state in the nation to allow legal sports gambling, does not permit betting on college games involving public or private institutions located in the state, whether the contest is being played inside or outside state borders. The regulation was enacted in 1972 by the Nevada Gambling Control Board.

16. Most athletic conferences, if they address the problem of gambling at all, do so in a manner to disclaim responsibility. The following excerpt is from the *1984–85 Pacific-10 Conference Handbook*, p. 26:

8. Instruction Re: Gambling, Pro Contracts. Each member institution shall carry out its own procedures to inform and instruct its student-athletes on their responsibilities in protecting themselves and their sports from gambling interests.

5.72 Professional Sports and Gambling

Sean McWeeney, of the FBI's Organized Crime Division, stated in 1983 that the FBI estimates that over $25 billion is gambled annually in the United States on sports. Most of this money is bet illegally and according to McWeeney, "There is a connection between organized crime and gambling in this country. The major metropolitan areas, where we have our traditional [crime] families, have controlled sports bookmaking for years."

The threat posed by gambling and organized crime to the image and integrity of professional football has caused the NFL to warn its members each year to have no associations whatsoever with known gamblers. To maintain the integrity of the game, the NFL employs its own security and enforcement division.

One notable incident involving association with known gamblers concerned Joe Namath, a Hall of Fame quarterback and now an ABC-TV commentator, who played for the New York Jets during the late 1960s. Namath was forced to sell his restaurant, Bachelor's III, because it had become an alleged hangout for bookies and gamblers. NFL Commissioner Rozelle said of the Namath incident: "If they're going to associate with individuals that are clearly on the outskirts of society, they're going to be a discredit to themselves, to the league . . ."

The connection between gambling and professional sports is not a recent occurrence in America. The decision to appoint the first commissioner of baseball, Kennesaw Mountain Landis, was   direct result of the Chicago Black   fix of the 919 World Series. *The*   *Diamond*, be   wenfish and Lupien,   inted because of   hicago "Black

k So   ndal has been   Eight Men   sing of the   d led the   all parks.   ularities.   rs were

     ers of   n a Chicago   ny was rising for the play   ...ns of Charles Comiskey's stinginess. "The magnates led the public to believe that the ballplayers got about $10,000 a year . . . when they got as little as $2,600," defense attorney Ben

Short declared to the jury. "At the end of the season, they have nothing left but a chew of tobacco, a glove, and a few pairs of worn-out socks."

It was a strange trial. The owners recognized that airing the game's dirty linen was not in their best interests. Therefore, they decided to provide good attorneys to aid in the players' defense. Later, baseball would punish its sinners by extra-legal weapons in its arsenal.

Powerful New York gambler Arnold Rothstein, deeply implicated in the scandal as the man who gave the go-ahead, greatly helped the owners' strategy by arranging for the theft of the players' confessions from the Chicago district attorney's office. Unable to use its most damning evidence in the trial, the prosecution was doomed. On August 2, 1921, the jury acquitted all the players.

Some of the Black Sox dreamed of reinstatement for the duration of the 1921 season. Commissioner Landis, in office since March, quickly crushed that hope. He pronounced, "Regardless of the verdict of juries, no player that entertains proposals or promises to throw a game; no player that sits in a conference with a bunch of crooked players and gamblers where the ways and means of throwing games are discussed, and does not promptly tell his club about it, will never play professional baseball." [Lowenfish and Lupien, *The Imperfect Diamond* (New York: Stein & Day, 1980), pp. 96, 103–104.]

CASE STUDY: Excerpts from "Inquiry into Professional Sports," Final Report of the Select Committee on Professional Sports, United States House of Representatives (January 3, 1977)

Part G: Gambling

. . . The Federal interest in gambling activity is substantial. Not only does the U.S. Code contain an assortment of criminal, tax, lottery, and miscellaneous statutes relating to gambling, but the Congress even created the Commission on the Review of the National Policy Toward Gambling to study gambling activity in the United States.

Fortunately, the Committee's inquiry was well-timed to take advantage of the Gambling Commission's study results. The Commission was created in the Organized Crime Control Act of 1970 (Public Law 91–452) to conduct a comprehensive legal and factual study of gambling including Federal, State, and local policy practices regarding legal prohibition and taxation of gambling activities.

The Committee did not have sufficient time to hear from proponents of legalized sports gambling; therefore, primary reliance is placed on the objective analysis of the Gambling Commission's study and Committee staff research.

Representatives of league sports clearly opposed legalization. Internal Revenue Service and Federal Communication Commission representatives also presented their views on specific aspects of sports gambling.

Scope and Type of Sports Gambling

According to the Gambling Commission, a national survey showed that about 61 percent of all adult Americans participated in some form of gambling during 1974 — 13 percent wagering with friends in a social setting and 48 percent patronizing legal or illegal commercial gambling. The survey also estimated that during that year at least $22 billion was wagered — $17 billion legally and $5 billion illegally of which $2.5 billion was attributed to illegal sports cards and sports bookmaking. The Commission gives credence to the $17 billion figure, but challenges the illegal amount estimated. The $5 billion was considered by Commission officials to be understated because heavy bettors "may tend to lie" to survey-takers and may not keep track of their total transactions but instead just the amount they are ahead or behind. . . .

Illegal Gambling

Illegal sports gambling takes the form of book-making and card wagering. The Commission reports that in terms of gross volume of betting, sports wagering is today the number one form of illegal gambling in the United States. Whether sports bets are placed with a bookie or between social acquaintances, they are most often placed on football, baseball, basketball, and hockey games and less frequently on events such as prizefighting and golf. Although sports book-making used to be a sideline with horserace

bookmakers, radio and television broadcasting of sports contests has reversed this emphasis to where sports wagering is dominant.

A sports bookmaker has been defined as a broker bringing together money on both sides of a sports contest, hopefully in such a manner that the losers' money will be more than sufficient to cover payments to winners. The general format of a bookmaking business begins with a bettor utilizing either the telephone or a middleman to place his bet with a bookmaker. Middlemen generally work on a percentage basis. In a large bookmaking operation, clerks may man telephones at different locations to avoid electronic surveillances, and a telephone system of communication is the most essential element of the sports wagering business.

Sports card wagering, according to the Commission, is a variation of standard sports betting involving pool, sports, or parlay cards. This gambling technique is attractive to the small bettor who, because of the low dollar volume of his bets, is rejected as a client by the sports bookie. Runners are used as agents to pass out cards, collect wagers and card stubs, and make payoffs to winners.

The Gambling Commission's survey indicated that the "typical" customer of illegal bookies resides in a Northeastern or North Central state, is a white male between the ages of 18 and 44, has a college degree or some college education, and earns more than $10,000 a year. It also showed that the average amount wagered per bettor is higher for sports betting than for any other form of gambling. In addition, only 20 percent of the population favored legalization of betting on sports events with a bookie, while 32 percent favored legalization of sports card betting. Finally, the survey respondents perceived all sports as generally honest, but saw a greater danger of corruption of sports events when betting is legalized than with legalization of any other kind of gambling.

Positions of Proponents and Opponents

Proponents of legalized gambling have pointed to the pervasiveness and large dollar volume of illegal sports gambling to show that people want to gamble. Even the Gambling Commission reports that gambling, generally, is an activity that is practiced, or tactily endorsed, by a substantial majority of Americans, and in other words is inevitable. The proponents also argue that current laws are unenforceable and are therefore corrupting the criminal justice system. They are even persuaded that the benefits to be derived from legalization would be added sources to tax revenues and in combating organized crime.

As a means of expressing these arguments, the following excerpts were taken from the summaries of testimony of witnesses who appeared before the Gambling Commission in February 1975 advocating legalized sports gambling:

Sports betting should be legalized, but whether it is legalized or not, it will continue to exist. . . . Sports lotteries have their place and should be legalized as well, but they are a separate business that has little in common with the average bookmaker and that attracts only a fraction of the sports betting volume. . . . The sports bettor already has formed his habits: Thus, to be effective, legislation changes must be made to accommodate these habits. If it does not, he will continue to bet illegally. . . . It is safe to say illegal betting has not affected the integrity of sports events. . . . Sports betting has been conducted in dozens of countries, and none of them has been swallowed up in moral decay. Gambling in moderation is a healthy recreational outlet with numerous financial and psychological rewards. . . [Kelso Sturgeon, Author of *Guide to Sports Betting*, and President of Gambling Research, Inc., in testimony before the Gambling Commission, February 20, 1975]

Sports betting should be legalized but only if it is structured in such a way that it does not endanger sports. . . . People want to gamble and the laws prohibiting them from doing so cannot be enforced. The resultant social contradictions are familiar: bribed law enforcement agents, with a resulting loss of public confidence; plea bargaining and miniscule fines that mock and overcrowd the courts; and the enrichment of organized crime. . . . The government would benefit in numerous ways if it licensed bookmakers. A state or municipal licensing board could screen applicants and determine qualifications or licenses. Revenue could be generated from license fees, taxes on profits, the creation of jobs, and the unburdening of law enforcement agencies. It could possibly drive organized crime out of gambling, and legitimize the independent bookmakers who would like to operate in the open as ordinary businessmen. [Larry Merchant, Sports Columnist, *New York Post*, and Author of *The National Football Lottery*, in testimony before the Gambling Commission, February 20, 1975]

Legalized gambling must not be viewed as the solution to government budgetary problems, but it can be one of the many useful devices employed to balance a budget in a manner politically acceptable to the public and at socially acceptable cost. . . . To prohibit such legalization would be a de facto acceptance that the illegal game cannot and should not be competed against, thus insuring a monopoly for the illegal enterprise. . . . To the extent that sports can be contaminated by betting, the contamination is already present. To the extent that benefits can be derived from legalized sports betting, the present situation contributes virtually no plusses and all minuses. The time is appropriate for controlled experimentation with legalized sports betting, hopefully with the cooperation and participation of those directly involved with the administration of sports. [Paul Screvane, President, New York City Off-Track Betting Corporation, in testimony before the Gambling Commission, February 20, 1975]

Whatever the individual motives in urging legalized sports gambling, public interest in gambling seems to be rising. As one news account reports, the evolution of the "public gaming industry" has also produced an expanding list of private corporations to serve it — consultants, equipment suppliers, printers, advertising agencies, computer houses, and designers of new games. [George Lardner, Jr., "Betting Business Booms and Seeks to Get Bigger," *The Washington Post*, October 18, 1976, p. A1]

Opponents of legalized sports gambling presented numerous arguments before the Gambling

Commission in February 1975, and some of these concerns were re-emphasized in testimony before the Committee. Excerpts of summaries of opponents' testimonies are presented below.

The National Football League Commissioner pointed out that:

> Professional football depends for its survival on the public's perception of the integrity of the games, owners, and players. . . . The pressure on players and club and league personnel from increased numbers of people seeking inside information would quickly become intolerable. . . . Legal sports betting would seriously erode public confidence in the games. It would create a generation of cynical fans, obsessed with point spreads and pari-mutuel tickets and constantly suspicious of the moves of players and coaches. . . . A State-run monopoly on team sports betting would be administratively burdensome and extremely expensive to oversee, with only dubious prospects of ultimate financial reward. . . . There is serious doubt that legal State-run gambling could compete effectively with illegal gambling. [NFL, commissioner Pete Rozelle in testimony before the Gambling Commission, February 19, 1975]

The Football Commissioner told the Select Committee that he was especially concerned about players. He stated that players have a sufficient burden, a pressure on them from the fans and media representatives and that public suspicions could be generated if it were known that a player or his relative bet against the team, even though the league has rules against players gambling on a game. Possible public suspicions could also arise under the following conditions: Team A is favored to beat Team B by four points. The score is tied at the game's end requiring sudden death overtime. Team A moves to within three yards of the goal line where a three-point field goal would be a near certainty to win the game. However due to lack of confidence in the field goalkicker, the decision is to pass. The pass is successful and Team A wins by six points. If team A had kicked the field goal, Team A bettors would have lost because of not winning by at least four points. However, the pass play could be interpreted as an attempt to ensure that the team went over the point spread.

Losing bettor would probably question the motives of whoever called for the pass play.

Football team officials stated:

> The impact of legal betting on organized crime and the revenues derived from such legalization would be too insignificant to offset the great harm that could be done to sports. . . . The integrity, success, and future of football would be jeopardized if gambling were legalized. The number of bettors — both social and compulsive — would increase dramatically. More fans would have a financial stake in the outcome of the game and hence little or no interest in its competitive value. . . [Pittsburgh Steelers President Arthur J. Rooney, in testimony before the Gambling Commission, February 19, 1975]

The Commissioner of Baseball informed the Gambling Commissioner that ever since the Black Sox scandal in 1919, the commissioners of baseball have traditionally considered the maintenance of the sport's integrity as their most important function. He stated that any form of gambling, legal or illegal, imposes a threat to the integrity of baseball, exposes it to grave economic danger, and is a disservice to the public interest. He further expressed his views that:

> No government operation can effectively compete with the illegal bookmaker. Organized crime would be able to exploit the market of newly initiated gamblers that legalized gambling would make available to it. . . . The legalization of gambling on team sports will not provide an important new source of revenue for government. . . . The legalization of sports betting could also lead to the licensing and government control of owners, players, and game conditions, as is the case in horseracing.

The Baseball Commissioner explained to the Select Committee that:

> . . . If you start out with pool gambling, you are going to open the door to other kinds of gambling. I think it is absolutely as inevitable as can be that you will see local forces moving to enlarge the area of municipal gambling if you have pool gambling. . . . Even with pool

gambling it is the little edge that makes the difference to the professional gambler and if, with pool gambling, he can affect the outcome of one game he has an edge and we know from our experience with soccer in Europe that legalized pool gambling has not prevented attempted fixes. . . . I think we have to put the heat on the enforcement people, where I think it belongs, to enforce the laws we have on the books. . . [MLB Commissioner Bowie K. Kuhn in testimony before the Gambling Commission, February 19, 1975]

The position of the President of the National Hockey League was that:

The NHL is not in the hockey business to provide a medium for conducting an activity that potentially threatens the integrity of the sport. Ever since two players were expelled from the league in 1948 for gambling on NHL games, the National Hockey League has been free from any gambling scandal. . . . The legalization of sports betting would not only increase that potential danger of a gambling scandal in the NHL, but would also greatly increase the expense of maintaining proper surveillance over the league. . . . Most people still attach a stigma to illegal gambling. If this stigma is removed, and gambling is given an aura of respectability and social acceptability, a whole new generation of gamblers will be created. [NHL President Clarence Campbell in testimony before the Gambling Commission, February 19, 1975]

The former Commissioner of the National Basketball Association testified:

Legalized sports betting would not compete effectively with its illegal counterpart, would not produce significant revenue, would have minimal impact on organized crime, and would place government in the role of promoting an activity that encourages gambling by those who can least afford it. . . . The legalization of sports betting would make every adult citizen a potential gambler rather than just a fan. A new generation of fans would be more concerned with the margin of defeat rather than with who wins or loses the game. Every missed basket, poor play, choice

of strategy, or substitution would become an economic factor; cynicism would replace family fun. . . . The potential abuses are endless and would lead to the destruction of professional sports in this country because of the irreplaceable loss of confidence in the integrity of competition [Former NBA Commissioner J. Walter Kennedy in testimony before the Gambling Commission, February 20, 1976]

In summary, the opponents of legalized gambling expressed that the integrity of professional sports would be jeopardized due to attempted or reportedly attempted fixes (bribes), increased dangers of scandals, people seeking inside information, cynical fans who may question key plays, and a general eroding of public confidence. They also questioned the ability of legalized sports betting activities to compete with illegal gambling; believed State-run activities would be expensive to operate and doubted the financial gains to be derived; and predicted that government controls would be burdensome on the sports industry.

Views of the Gambling Commission

The Gambling Commission's principal conclusion regarding a national gambling policy is that the State should have the primary responsibility for determining what forms of gambling may legally take place within their borders and that the only role of the Federal Government should be to prevent interference by one State with the gambling policies of another and to protect identifiable national interests with regard to gambling issues. It recommends that a Federal statute be enacted to ensure the States continued power to regulate gambling, and that the Federal Government, in exercising its regulatory and tax powers, take care not to hinder State efforts to compete with illegal gambling operations.

In regard to the concern that legalized sports gambling would jeopardize the integrity of the game, the Commission believes that with the intensity of illegal wagering that exists today, primarily in professional football, this should already be of concern to sports officials. The Commission rejects the concern that an attempted "fix" would be any more possible with a legal betting system than an illegal one, and characterizes this expressed fear as an exaggeration.

The Commission criticizes the sports industry for not assuming its proper role of leadership in controlling peripheral activities that enhance illegal wagering. It points to pregame discussions by sports personalities and broadcasters who attempt to predict the outcome of games and discuss point spreads, weather conditions, injury reports, and other factors that might influence the outcome. This practice, according to Commission officials, does little to discourage the attention of a bettor with an illegal wager at stake, and even creates an appetite for wagering. They are convinced that the National Football League's publication of player injury reports are inextricably involved with point spreads.

The Commission reported that despite these inconsistencies in the announced positions of the sports industry, it does not favor legalizing sports-by-event wagering, but for different reasons than those put forth by sports officials. It claims that enormous problems would result from this type of State-sponsored wagering. First the Commission contends that the take-out rate (the money retained by the operator) is much lower in illegal single event sports betting than in other types of wagering, and any attempt by a State to increase their take above the rates used by bookmakers would drastically reduce the State's ability to compete. The reported take-out rate in the illegal marketplace averages 4.6 percent, and a survey conducted by the Commission estimated that the maximum take-out sports bettors would tolerate would be 7 percent before returning to the higher payouts (lower take-outs) offered by the illegal game. Second, it is claimed that other competitive elements such as extension of credit and telephone betting could not be readily provided by State-run bookmaking operations. Third, a major Commission conclusion is that existing Federal tax policies are said to constitute the largest single obstacle to a competitive sports bookmaking operation . . .

The Commission did share two concerns of sports officials. First, if a state decided to implement sports betting there is a question of certain proprietary rights of sports teams (The National Football League reportedly argued this point in a recent suit against the State of Delaware to stop sports betting in that State),

and whether states should compensate team owners or the league. This is a matter for the courts, but as the Commission suggested, the multi-state system of sports franchises is of National concern, and further activity in this area may deserve Congressional attention. Second, the Commission suggested that involvement of governments in legalized sports gambling would probably result in some type of licensing operation. Based on experience in other forms of licensed gambling such as horseracing, and dog racing, athletes could be subjected to pregame or postgame drug testing (as horses and dogs are), or they could be licensed themselves as jockeys currently are. . . .

Conclusion

The three-year study on gambling in America conducted by the Gambling Commission was without doubt a comprehensive task. The final report is revealing in that the section or primary interest to this Committee shows that sports gambling is today the greatest single form of illegal gambling. In dollar volume it exceeds the illegal gambling activity in horseracing, numbers, and casinos on a one-for-one basis. The problem is how to contend with it.

The proponents of legalized gambling generally argue that it will be a source of tax revenue and a means of combating organized crime. There were no different views expressed about legalizing sports gambling. Opponents shudder at the thought of the gambling influence which could cast suspicions on the integrity of the sports industry, and could bring on increasing government regulation. The Gambling Commission expresses a practical view about legalizing sports gambling in that states could not effectively compete with illegal gamblers unless basic changes are made to the Federal income tax laws as they relate to gambling. The Internal Revenue Service is obviously opposed to such changes. This will certainly require a congressional solution as to the merits of permitting states to effectively compete versus restructuring the tax laws.

There appears to be inconsistencies in the Federal Communications Commission policy toward broadcasting information that may aid illegal gamblers. This area is in need of further analysis as to the scope of the FCC's authority in this area.

Recommendations

The Committee agrees with the conclusions and recommendations of the Gambling Commission that states not legalize single-event sports wagering under the present Federal tax structure as it relates to gambling; that if the Federal tax policies are amended, legalized sports wagering should be subject to extensive debate to allow the voting public to form an educated opinion; that states should prohibit wagering on amateur sports contests in the event sports wagering is legalized; and that states choosing to institute sports card wagering (sport pools) should only do so after voter approval rather than unilaterally incorporating such a betting scheme under existing lottery programs. However, the Committee recommends that Congress thoroughly explore the implications of amending Federal tax laws as they relate to gambling before accepting the Gambling Commission's recommendations concerning sports.

NOTES ─────────────────────

1. See "Gambling in America," *Final Report of the Commission on the Review of the National Policy Toward Gambling*, Washington, D.C., October 15, 1976.

2. See Lowenfish and Lupien, *The Imperfect Diamond* (New York: Stein and Day, 1980).

3. The following excerpts are from the "Unauthorized History of the NFL," *Frontline*, Transcript No. 101, 1983 WGBH–TV Educational Foundation.

NARRATOR: No owner had more dubious associations than the late Carroll Rosenbloom.

In the late 1950s he invested in this Cuban casino. In those days Cuba's dictator, Batista, had thrown his country open to Mafia-run gambling interests.

Batista welcomed Rosenbloom's partners, men like Mike McLaney, a stock swindler and tax evader, and Lou Chesler, a sometimes associate of mobster Meyer Lansky.

Rosenbloom shared Chesler's passion for betting on football. He used to bet against his own team, the Baltimore Colts, and was even accused of fixing games by leaving key players at home.

In 1972 Rosenbloom sold the Colts and bought the Los Angeles Rams. But he continued to play with fire, placing huge bets with Mafia-linked bookies. [T. p. 13]

NARRATOR: Carroll Rosenbloom. His way of life raises questions about how he died.

Rosenbloom left some unfinished business behind him. According to a sworn deposition, Rosenbloom and two other team owners had been scalping Super Bowl tickets for years. The year he died the Rams had 27,000 superbowl tickets to sell.

Rosenbloom's widow, Georgia, has denied newspaper stories that she scalped any tickets. Nevertheless, *Frontline* has learned that the IRS is investigating the ticket-scalping racket. IRS inquiries have centered on a Los Angeles hoodlum called Jack Catain. [T. p. 15]

NARRATOR: Davis had come to an attorney's office in San Mateo, California to make a long, sworn deposition. *Frontline* obtained complete transcripts of this deposition. It details Davis's relationship with the casino owner, Allan Glick.

At the age of thirty-two, Glick bought himself four casinos in Las Vegas with the help of a one hundred million dollar loan from the Mafia-dominated Central States Teamster's Pension Fund. FBI wiretaps showed Glick to be little more than a front man for Mafia chieftains like Joey Aiuppa.

An FBI affidavit says, "Allan R. Glick is merely a straw party controlled by the organized crime syndicate and designated by them to be the licensee on paper in the state of Nevada."

From this office building in La Jolla, California, Glick concluded several real estate deals with Al Davis. But one of the partners suspected she'd been swindled by Glick, so Tamara Rand threatened to go to the FBI. [T. p. 17]

NARRATOR: All Davis's partnership with Allan Glick has been criticized by Pete Rozelle.

Press Conference

AL DAVIS: Well, I don't have that much respect for Pete Rozelle.

NARRATOR: But Davis has done nothing to sever the relationship.

Tom Mechling founded the National Commission on Gambling Information. It's an anti-gambling pressure group. Mechling's research has led him to delve into the business backgrounds of a number of football team owners. He talked to us about Davis's dealings with Glick.

TOM MECHLING: The best deal that Glick ever made with Al Davis was to give him a quarter interest in a twenty-five million dollar teamster-funded shopping center: thirty-three acres, eighty-five stores and so forth for $5,000. One quarter interest in a twenty-five million dollar shopping center for $5,000?

PETE ROZELLE: Mr. Glick has never been convicted of anything, nonetheless because of the Las Vegas casino connection, and intense federal investigation of him, we, I suggested to Al Davis that it'd be best if he divorced himself from a shopping mall Mr. Glick was involved in, I think in Oakland. But Al Davis has chosen to retain his association to the best of my knowledge, in this East Mall in Oakland. [T. p. 18]

NARRATOR: But Davis was by no means the only NFL member in business with Glick, Davis's sworn deposition lists a number of players. Quarterback John Hadl and receiver Lance Allworth were two of fifteen who were for a while enticed into dealing with Glick.

According to depositions, several coaches struck bargains with Glick. Don Shula was one. When he found out about Glick, he severed the connection. But several unnamed owners had also formed limited partnerships with Allan Glick.

The American public is largely unaware that some football team owners have associations that might be frowned on in a player.

Edward DeBartolo was considered an unsuitable owner by major league baseball.

TOM MECHLING: DeBartolo was turned down by Bowie Kuhn. He's very sensitive as a Commissioner of Baseball to gambling interests, racetrack interests and so forth.

NARRATOR: But the NFL allowed DeBartolo to buy the '49ers and turn it over to his son. Al Davis was paid a $100,000 finder's fee.

TOM MECHLING: Strangely enough, since he swung four times and never made a connection with a major league baseball team, he was able to make a very quick connection to become the owner of the San Francisco '49ers.

NARRATOR: San Diego is the home of the Chargers. The owner is Eugene Klein. Eugene Klein has owned many buildings and properties through the years.

TOM MECHLING: One of the strangest building places he had, along with some very strange people, was a small resort hotel at Acapulco, Mexico, called Acapulco Towers.

NARRATOR: Sidney Korshak was one of Klein's partners in the Acapulco venture. He started his career

in Chicago giving legal advice to a member of Al Capone's gang. [T. p. 19]

NARRATOR: For 30 years Carlos Marcello has been the boss of the New Orleans underworld. Though he claims to be nothing more than an innocent tomato salesman.

NARRATOR: Marcello's influence stretches into every aspect of New Orleans life. And in the past that has included the football team. Gamblers and bookies associated with Marcello drew the new, young owner of the Saints into a series of joint investments.

TOM MECHLING: Mecom is the very rich son of a very rich father who was given the franchise at the age of 27, and then almost immediately got entwined with real estate deals — they all seem to get into real estate deals — which was being fronted by several people that were really Marcello's people.

NARRATOR: You make a statement, NFL Commissioner Pete Rozelle's reaction to disclosures of the nature you just made were typical "Rozelle-esque." What does that mean?

TOM MECHLING: There seems to be a double standard operating in the National Football League. A commissioner is thought of as commissioner of all the league: the players, the fans and the owners. But frankly, Rozelle, who has been in the office a long time, was hand-picked by Carroll Rosenbloom and others and they can fire him at any time, and it seems like he constantly tilts for the interests of the owners. For example, he seems to look the other way when these funny associations in business and otherwise of his owners become. Lamar Hunt, who owns the Kansas City Chiefs, put it quite pointedly. He said, "a commissioner can be fired." [T. p. 21]

Jessica Savitch/Pete Rozelle Interview

SAVITCH: Do you ever feel there's a conflict of interest?

ROZELLE: Not as long as you have a long-term contract.

SAVITCH: Are you confident as the NFL is currently constructed you could investigate owners thoroughly with regard to associations with gamblers?

ROZELLE: Why, absolutely.

SAVITCH: Do you have the power to tell an owner to divest himself of a questionable property the same way you would a player?

ROZELLE: I don't have the power to force either to necessarily, but in extreme circumstances, I could test that power. It would probably mean a court case.

SAVITCH: Do you think it might be necessary at this time to get some outside help with regard to policing the game and gambling?

ROZELLE: I think it would be very difficult to say, you have a federal agency, which I assume is what you're suggesting, get involved in sports because it wouldn't just be the NFL. It would be basketball, hockey, baseball. And I think that we just have to enforce these things ourselves. I don't see that a government agency could really help.

NARRATOR: More money will ride on this year's Super Bowl than ever before. If the NFL fails to enforce its own rules, the sport will be ripe for corruption. Because gamblers will do anything they can to get an inside edge. That is one sure bet. [T. p. 22]

Update

JESSICA SAVITCH: Since *Frontline* interviewed Commissioner Rozelle, two new allegations have been made. One: John Piazza's charge that he helped fix four games a year in 1968, 1969, and 1970. Commissioner Rozelle told me he never heard of Piazza . . . and that to his knowledge, there were no games fixed in that period. Two: as to ticket scalping, Commissioner Rozelle told me Anthony Capozolla brought him no new information. But he would neither confirm nor deny that the NFL is currently investigating the scalping of Super Bowl tickets.

As we prepared this "Frontline" investigation, we contacted NFL owners mentioned for their comments. Some did not respond: Davis of the Raiders, DeBartolo, Jr. of the '49ers, Murchison of the Cowboys, and Frontiere of the Rams.

A spokesman for Mecom of the Saints told *Frontline* that Mr. Mecom severed his business ties with a notorious gambler at the request of Pete Rozelle, and that he had never knowingly done business with Marcello Associates. Klein of the Chargers spoke personally to *Frontline*. He told us he never knew the late Meyer Lansky. As to Sidney Korshak, he acknowledged Korshak had represented the team in one matter. But he said he did not know that Korshak was one of his limited partners in the Acapulco Towers.

But this story, as of tonight, continues on other fronts.

Art Modell, owner of the Cleveland Browns, is the subject of a four-part series that began yesterday in the Akron *Beacon Journal*. Part two (it's on the newsstands today) focuses on Mr. Modell's long history of gambling associations.

Leonard Tose, the owner of the Philadelphia Eagles, announced last week he was considering selling part of the franchise and turning over part to his daughter. It was alleged this was due to heavy gambling losses. Tose told me that his losses at the Sands Hotel in Las Vegas were somewhere near a million dollars last year, and his losses in New Jersey casinos in excess of that amount. But he told me his debts are paid and the sale and transfer are for estate purposes only.

Now, in all of these cases, we remind you, this is not a question of guilt by association, but rather whether questionable associations violate the NFL's own rules. As to illegal activities, a highly-placed official in the Justice Department told me today that there are investigations into drugs, gambling, and pro football. The NFL, of course, is concerned about its own vulnerability. And Commissioner Pete Rozelle told me he has stepped up his vigilence on the sidelines.

4. In May, 1982, Art Schlichter, a quarterback and 1982 first-round draft pick of the Baltimore (Indianapolis) Colts, was suspended by NFL Commissioner Pete Rozelle for gambling activities. Shortly before the decision, Schlichter had turned himself in to federal agents, reporting that he had lost $389,000 in wagers and was heavily in debt to Baltimore bookmakers. He admitted placing large bets on at least ten NFL games in 1982. As part of his suspension, Schlichter underwent treatment for compulsive gambling at South Oaks Hospital in Amityville, New York. In June 1984, after a 13-month suspension, Commissioner Rozelle lifted his suspension of Schlichter. Rozelle had this to say:

We met twice recently with Art Schlichter and reviewed all the factors in his case. . . . We also reviewed the medical views of physicians qualified in the care of compulsive gambling. Art has faced a long and difficult rehabilitation this past year in terms of dealing with his gambling pathology and its underlying psychological causes. . . . It is of central importance to both Art and the NFL that the doctors believe that Art's condition is under control and that his chances for a relapse are minimal.

See "Schlichter Suspension Lifted by Rozelle," *New York Times*, June 23, 1984, p. 31, and "Schlichter Enters the Next Phase Along the Way Back," *New York Times*, July 23, 1984, p. C1.

5. In 1985, MLB Commissioner Peter Ueberroth announced that Mickey Mantle and Willie Mays would be allowed to associate with MLB teams again despite their affiliation as representatives of legal gambling in Atlantic City, New Jersey. Ueberroth's predecessor

Bowie Kuhn had barred them from MLB. Mantle and Mays, *Sports Illustrated*, March 25, 1985, p. 62.

6. The National Basketball Association, in its *Administrative Manual*, Section 380, addresses the issue of gambling as follows:

Notwithstanding any provisions of the Constitution or of the By-Laws of the Association, it is agreed that if the Commissioner of the Association shall, in his sole judgment, find that the player has bet or has offered or attempted to bet, money or anything of value on the outcome of any game participated in by any club which is a member of the Association, the Commissioner shall have the power in his sole discretion to suspend the player indefinitely or to expel him as a player for any member of the Association and the Commissioner's finding and decision shall be final, binding, conclusive and unappealable. The player hereby releases the Commissioner and waives every claim he may have against the Commissioner and/or the Association, and against every member of the Association, and against every director, officer, stockholder, trustee and partner of every member of the Association, for damages and for all claims and demands whatsoever arising out of or in connection with the decision of the Commissioner.

It is your responsibility to immediately report to your coach any attempt to have you influence the outcome of a game. Failure to do so will mean immediate suspension.

5.80 Ticket Scalping

A growing area of criminal law that many pro teams, intercollegiate athletic departments, and stadium and arena facility operators must deal with is ticket scalping. Ticket scalping is the resale of tickets at prices over the face value purchase amount. It is a big underground economic enterprise. It has been estimated that in 1981, the NFL's Super Bowl Championship in the New Orleans Superdome generated nearly $7 million in ticket scalping revenue, with about 25,000 fans (75,000 total attendance) paying inflated prices between $150 to $500 for a ticket that had a face value of $50. Similarly, at Super Bowl XIX in San Francisco, ticket scalpers were getting between $500 to $1,000 for tickets originally priced at $60, and at the 1984 NBA Championship in Boston, ticket scalpers were receiving $300 for a $22 ticket.

The problems associated with ticket scalping

are not limited to professional sports. Before a 1984 NCAA regular season game between Big East Athletic Conference opponents St. John's University and Georgetown University at Madison Square Garden in New York City, scalpers were getting up to $300 per ticket. Indicative of the problems that ticket scalping poses to intercollegiate athletics is a situation that involved the University of Southern California, which in 1982 was placed on probation by the NCAA for generating illegal cash payments to its student-athletes through an elaborate ticket scalping operation that ran from 1971 to 1979 and was controlled by the coaching staff.

In the terminology of ticket scalping, the persons who stand in line to purchase tickets are termed "diggers." The diggers work for ticket scalpers and may wait in line for tickets for hours at a time.

Many states and local municipalities have attempted to regulate the sale of scalped tickets. These regulations generally attempt to control the scalping problem by regulating resale of tickets, by regulating ticket resellers through licensing procedures (ticket brokers), or by regulating both the resale of tickets and the licensing of brokers. Some states make a special exemption for a computerized ticket agency that contracts with a stadium or sports authority to distribute their tickets for a fee (e.g., Ticketron, Ticket World, Chargit). The vast majority of recent litigation challenging state or local regulation of ticket scalping has been decided in favor of the enacted legislation.

State v. Spann, 623 S.W. 2d 272 (1981)

Spann had been convicted in a Tennessee county criminal court of scalping twenty tickets to the NCAA 1980 National Basketball Tournament regional and final rounds. The face values of the involved tickets were $16 for a regional game and $30 for the finals. Spann had offered to sell the tickets at $75 for the regionals and $250 for the finals. Spann argued that the scalping legislation was violative of both Tennessee's and the federal Constitution's due process clauses. While conceding that the state can exercise its police power to reasonably regulate resale of tickets, Spann contested the state's total prohibition on the scalping of tickets.

In rejected Spann's arguments and affirming the lower court's decision, the Tennessee Supreme Court stated that:

> This in our opinion is a fallacious argument. The statute in question does not prohibit the resale of a ticket at all. It does, however, prohibit such resale for a premium or a profit, and we believe that this is a regulation which is entirely reasonable and within the police power of the General Assembly.

The court noted that the regulation of public events like the one for which Spann was scalping tickets was traditionally a state concern. The court viewed as a legitimate state objective, the "equal and fair opportunity" for the public to attend entertainment events. The court stated that while this legislation might interfere with private property rights, that such regulation was reasonable when the "public welfare" was involved.

NOTES

1. For cases in which the courts have upheld the constitutionality of ticket scalping laws, see the following:
(a) In *State v. Major*, 243 Ga. 255, 253 S.E.2d 724 (1979), the defendant was convicted of scalping tickets to the Atlanta Falcons' NFL game. The Georgia Supreme Court in affirming the conviction held that "this statute puts all sports fans on an equal footing in the race to the ticket window."
(b) In *State v. Yonker*, 36 Or. App. 609, 585 P.2d (1978), the defendant was convicted of scalping Portland Trail Blazers' NBA playoff tickets. The Oregon Court of Appeals in affirming the conviction reasoned that the Portland ordinance was designed to make tickets easily available, without interference from scalpers, to the citizens whose tax dollars built and continued to support the municipal arena.
(c) In *People v. Shepherd*, 141 Cal. Rptr. 379, 74 Cal.3d 334 (1977), *cert. den.*, 436 U.S. 917 (1978), the court reasoned that the ticket scalping ordinance was designed not only to regulate ticket re-sales but to control all business activity on the grounds of public property designed for recreational use.
2. For a case in which a ticket scalping law was struck down as unconstitutional, see *Estell v. Birmingham*, 291 Ala. 680, 286 So.2d 872 (1973), in which Estell, who had been convicted of scalping tickets to the annual Alabama-Auburn football game, had his conviction reversed by the Alabama Supreme Court, which found Estell's action not to be ". . . so affected with a public interest as to be the subject of a price fixing regulation under the police power of the City of Birmingham."
3. For examples of ticket scalping statutes, see the following:
(a) The Georgia ticket scalping statute, Ga. Code Ann. §96–602 (1985) reads:
> It shall be unlawful for any person to sell, or offer for sale, any ticket of admission or other evidence of the right of entry to any football game, basketball game, baseball game, soccer game, hockey games, or golf tournament for a price in excess of the price printed on the ticket: Provided, however, that a service charge, not to exceed $1, may be charged when tickets or other evidences of the right of entry are sold by an authorized ticket agent through places of established businesses licensed to do business by the municipality or county, where applicable, in which such places of business are located.
(b) The Tennessee ticket scalping statute, Tenn. Code Ann. §39–4101 (1984) reads:
> Scalping admissions tickets — Penalty. It is unlawful for any person to scalp an admission ticket, pass or admission card to any theater, auditorium stadium dance hall, rink, athletic field or any other place to which tickets, passes or admission cards are required as a condition upon admittance thereto; or to offer or to attempt to scalp any such admission ticket, pass or admission card. . . .
4. For further information on ticket scalping, see the following articles:
(a) "Super Bowl XV, Football's Little Bighorn?" *Sports Illustrated*, January 26, 1981, p. 33.
(b) "Ticket to the Big Game," *Money*, February, 1983, p. 110.
(c) "NFL Concerned by Scalping," *New York Times*, January 17, 1985, p. B10.
(d) ". . .And as Complicated as Trying to Find a Ticket," *New York Times*, January 17, 1985, p. B5.
(e) "Making Cost-Of-Living and Other Allowances for Cheating at USC," *Sports Illustrated*, May 10, 1982, p. 27.
(f) "Hot Ticket, Celtic Scalpers Plot $300-A-Seat Killing," *Boston Herald*, June 12, 1984, pp. 1, 2.
(g) Cobb, "Validity of State and Local Regulation Dealing with Resale of Tickets to Theatrical or Sporting Events," 81 *A.L.R.*, 655 (1977).
(h) "Ticket Scalping: Legislative Review," 4 *Pacific Law Review*, 376 (1973).
(i) Bershad and Ensor, "New Jersey's Ticket Scalping Law: A Case Study," *Seton Hall Legislative Journal* (Summer 1985).

Chapter 6

SPORTS AND
THE MEDIA

6.00   The "Product" of the Game

Sports have moved beyond the mere playing of the game. Fans flock to stadiums and arenas in record numbers. The print media report not only the action but the scenes behind the action. Radio has long been a vehicle to bring the game to those unable to attend and to remind everyone of where the action can be found. Television first appeared in the late 1930s and now is almost larger, economically, than the games themselves. The influences of the media on sports are unquestioned, but the nature of the influences are perhaps not so readily ascertained.

It has long been assumed that the people who stage the game — the owners or promoters — also control the product as it is disseminated in the media, at least as to the actual oral or visual depiction of the game. Although one early case held against this ownership interest (see *National Exhibition Co.* v. *Teleflash, Inc.* in Section 6.11), later precedent clearly established that those who stage the game own the ancillary product. Whether that is still the case, in light of developing technologies and players' demands that they have an ownership interest, is one subject this chapter focuses on.

So that we might understand where the legal and business problems involving sports and the media may be headed, we examine in Section 6.10 the nature of rights in the transmission and description of the game. Section 6.20 then concentrates on the assertion of rights that parties may presently make and those they may predictably make in the future.

Two other areas demand investigation. One deals with the attempts of professional and amateur sports leagues and associations to band together in their contract dealings with networks and stations. Section 6.30 addresses the impacts of antitrust laws on these attempts. The other area concerns the rights of the media to cover sports events and to report on sports figures. To the extent that a right exists, there is arguably an erosion of the concept of ownership of the product discussed above. Section 6.40 covers several facets of the news function.

6.10   Nature of Rights in Transmission and Description

The initial assertions of rights in the transmission and description of a sports event resided in common-law concepts. As technologies developed, however, it became clear that other protections might be needed. Thus federal laws dealing with communications and copyright came into existence. This section explores cases, statutes, and federal regulations. All are important, but more important is to understand the interrelationship among the various concepts and to know when one set of concepts applies and others arguably do not. Careful attention must be paid to the wording of the statutes and the details of the regulations.

NOTE ─────────────────

1. The single best source for understanding the legal relationships between sports and sports broadcasting is Garrett and Hochberg, "Sports Broadcasting and the Law," 59 *Indiana Law Journal* 155 (1984).

6.11 Common Law: Misappropriation of Property, Breach of License, Unfair Competition

The courts began grappling with the ownership of sports broadcast rights in the 1930s. The first two cases discussed below (*National Exhibition Co. v. Teleflash, Inc.* and *Pittsburgh Athletic Co. v. KQV Broadcasting Co.*) illustrate the complexities immediately confronting the courts. Various legal concepts are discussed in both cases, and opposite results are reached. It is interesting to note that the *National Exhibition* case was not reported until the *Pittsburgh Athletic* case arose two years later. They appear consecutively in 24 Federal Supplement. The background is that, at the time of the decision in *National Exhibition*, its full significance was not apparent. However, the major league baseball owners were appalled by the decision and sought out a situation where they believed they could focus their full forces to obtain a different result. They found this situation in Pittsburgh.

The decision in *Pittsburgh Athletic Co. v. KQV Broadcasting Co.* emerged as the one usually followed in later legal disputes. Even so, questions lingered and matters have not

been completely resolved in the owners' favor, even to the present day. Thus, such later cases as *Loeb* v. *Turner* and *National Exhibition Co.* v. *Fass* must be studied as well to gain appreciation of the background leading to disputes that continue and are discussed throughout this chapter.

─────────────────

National Exhibition v. Teleflash, Inc., 24 F.Supp. 488 (S.D. N.Y. 1936)

Plaintiff producers of baseball games sought an injunction preventing defendants from transmitting play-by-play descriptions over the telephone while the game was being played. The district court granted the defendants' motion to dismiss, since plaintiff did not demonstrate an exclusive right to describe games play by play.

To begin with, plaintiff's assertion that it had an exclusive right was not grounded on contract since there was no contractual relation between plaintiff and those reporting the information. The ticket was a complete license to see the game and contained no notice of objection to what was being done.

Second, it did not appear that there was a continuing trespass which interfered with the control of plaintiff's grounds. Third, the court found no unfair competition. What the plaintiff owned was the instrumentalities through which the game was produced, while the defendants conveyed to their listeners what they had seen. There was no competition between the game itself and the words concerning it used by the defendants.

Finally, while there was damage to the plaintiff in its failure to derive income from the Western Union Telegraph Company for the privilege of announcing the results and from reduced ticket sales, the court could find no right that was violated. The court, holding that the defendants were free to convey what they saw to telephone listeners, dismissed the complaint for failure to state a cause of action.

Pittsburgh Athletic Co. v. KQV Broadcasting Co., 24 F.Supp. 490 (W.D. Pa. 1938)

The complaint asked for a preliminary injunction to restrain defendant from broadcasting play-by-play reports and descriptions of baseball games played by the Pittsburgh Pirates. The defendant claimed that it secured the news of the Pittsburgh games it broadcast from observers whom it stationed outside the playing field.

Plaintiff had a contract with General Mills, which gave General Mills an exclusive right to broadcast the play-by-play descriptions or accounts of the games. NBC had a contract with General Mills to broadcast the play-by-play descriptions of the games over the radio. Socony-Vacuum Oil Company purchased from General Mills a one-half interest in its contract.

The court held that the exclusive right to broadcast play-by-play descriptions of the games is a property right of the plaintiff with which the defendant was interfering. Plaintiff and defendant were using baseball news as material for profit. Plaintiff, by reason of its creation of the game, its control of the park, and its restriction of the dissemination of news therefore, had a property right in such news and the right to control the use thereof for a reasonable time following the games. Defendant was practicing *unfair competition* by violating the plaintiff's property rights. The communication of news by plaintiff was not a general publication.

Loeb v. Turner, 257 S.W. 2d 800 (Tex. Civ. App. 1953)

Appellant owner and operator of radio station KRIZ in Phoenix, Arizona, sought damages and a permanent injunction to restrain appellees, the owner and announcer of radio station KLIF in Dallas, Texas, from broadcasting accounts of stock car automobile races held in Phoenix. A lap-by-lap description of the races was broadcast over Phoenix station KRIZ, which was heard within a 40-mile radius. The Dallas station placed an agent within the broadcast area who listened to the broadcast and then communicated the bare facts in abbreviated form via long-distance telephone to KLIF. The announcer then presented to his listeners a re-creation of the race, embellishing the account with details of his own imagination and sound effects.

The court affirmed the lower court's denial of the injunction. Since it was uncontested that the Dallas station had a right to broadcast the portion of the program that was original and imaginative on the part of the announcer, the only question was whether it had a right to incorporate the news that had been picked up from the appellant's factual broadcast. The court held that after the Phoenix station communicated gratuitously the events of the races, the news became available for comment and use. Under the law of Texas, as a result of such publication, the material became available to everyone since it was uncopyrighted. Any attempt to obtain exclusive control of the dissemination of news would be a violation of the law against monopolies in restraint of trade. The pertinent fact was that the Dallas agent was not within the confines of the raceway and thus had the right to inform his fellow agent at Dallas of the facts pertaining to the races.

The court further dismissed appellant's argument that he was entitled to judgment on the grounds of unfair competition. After examining the record and taking judicial notice of the fact that Phoenix is over a thousand miles from Dallas, the court failed to find any evidence of competition between the parties.

National Exhibition Co. v. Fass, 143 N.Y.S. 2d 767 (Sup. Ct. 1955)

Plaintiff owner of the New York Giants professional baseball team sought an injunction against defendant, an independent news gatherer and professional sports reporter who listened to the broadcasts of the baseball games outside the Polo Grounds where the games were played and then transmitted teletype re-creations of the games to other radio stations without plaintiff's permission. The defendant asserted that the broadcasts constituted news in the public domain, published in interstate commerce, and that he was thus privileged under both the U.S. Constitution and the constitution of the state of New York.

The New York Supreme Court, however, held that plaintiff, as owner and producer of a professional baseball exhibition, had the proprietary right to sell to others the communication of reports, descriptions, and accounts of the games. These property rights were of great value to the plaintiff, and defendant's actions in transmitting re-creations without the consent of the plaintiff and without consideration deprived the plaintiff of the just benefits of its labors and expenditures. Additionally, defendant's actions had injured plaintiff's goodwill and reputation with those stations it had contracted with to broadcast the games and had made it impossible for the plaintiff to realize in full the benefits of its rights, thereby causing great and irreparable loss.

6.12   Communications Law

The Federal Communications Act was passed in 1934. It has been amended several times since then, but its original purpose to regulate the broadcast industries has continued. As the depiction of sports events became integral to radio and later to television, the act's provisions, as enforced by the agency created under the act, the Federal Communications Commission (FCC), assumed great influence in affecting the growth and development of the sports themselves. Even later, as new technologies have developed, this influence has become still more pronounced.

There are constant challenges that question the FCC's proper role in the regulation of the broadcast industries. *Malrite TV of N.Y. v. FCC*, discussed below, examines the delicate task the FCC faces in responding to pressures from various interested parties. Often at issue is a balancing of the provisions of the com-

munications act and the copyright statutes.

Malrite TV of N.Y. v. FCC, 652 F. 2d 1140 (2d Cir. 1981)

This suit attempted to set aside the FCC's order to deregulate the cable television industry by rescinding rules relating to syndicated program exclusivity and distant signal coverage that restricted cable systems in their use of copyrighted works. The FCC's actions were in response to the 1976 Copyright Act, which provided a system of partial copyright liability for cable television with a compulsory licensing scheme. This scheme eliminated the need of cable operators to obtain the consent of or to negotiate licenses with copyright owners by requiring the payment to the owners of a prescribed royalty fee. Upon inquiry, the FCC found that its copyright protections, the distant signal and syndicated exclusivity, should be eliminated since Congress had resolved the copyright issue. Furthermore, the impact on broadcast stations from the FCC's deregulation would be negligible, and consumers would in fact benefit from increased viewing options.

The petitioners, among them the professional sports leagues, argued that the FCC's action misconstrued the mandate of the 1976 Copyright Act and was arbitrary and capricious. The court rejected the contention that the act was premised on maintenance of the regulatory framework or that a retransmission consent requirement should be adopted. First, in establishing the Copyright Royalty Tribunal, responsible for collecting and distributing the royalty fees, Congress had clearly provided that that entity could readjust the royalty rate if the FCC altered its cable restrictions. Second, the adoption of a retransmission consent rule would undermine Congress' compulsory licensing scheme since it would function no differently from full copyright liability.

The court also did not believe that the FCC overlooked any of the contentions by pertinent segments of the industry that the FCC's action were arbitrary and capricious. For example, the professional sports leagues contended that cable television, by making available more broadcasts of games from distant cities, would decrease game receipts, threaten the league by hurting the weaker franchises, and ultimately lead to less sports programming. The leagues, however, did not produce any evidence that the number of sports broadcasts by home clubs was reduced in existing areas of high cable penetration. The court held it was not arbitrary for the FCC to conclude that sports programming required no special protection after the repeal of the distant signal rules, especially in light of the fact that the primary means of sports protection, the home broadcast blackout rules (47 C.F.R. § 76.67 [1980]), would continue to exist.

The court concluded that the widespread participation of all industry segments and the comprehensive evaluation of data reflected the "rational weighing of competing policies" that Congress intended to be exercised by the FCC, and upheld the rescission of the rules deregulating the cable industry.

NOTES _____

1. In *Springfield Television Corp.* v. *Federal Communications Commission*, 609 F. 2d 1014 (1st Cir. 1979), plaintiff television station challenged an order of defendant FCC, which permitted a cable television system to telecast baseball games after a two and one-half hour delay, although plaintiff had exclusive rights to them. The court of appeals held that so long as the FCC's position was reasonable after considering each pertinent factor, it had no power to reverse the order.

2. The following excerpts from FCC regulations underscore the importance and complexity of determining which stations are permitted to telecast live sports events. As technologies develop, the demands for increased surveillance over unauthorized broadcasts multiply. The foregoing *Malrite* case cited these following regulations as primary protections for home broadcast blackout rules.

Federal Communications Commission Regulations, 47 C.F.R. Section 76.67 (1983).
Section 76.67   Sports broadcasts.

(a) No community unit located in whole or in part within the specified zone of a television broadcast station licensed to a community in which a sports event

is taking place, shall, on request of the holder of the broadcast rights to that event or its agent carry the live television broadcast of that event if the event is not available live on a television broadcast signal carried by the community unit pursuant to the mandatory signal carriage rules of this part. For the purposes of this section, if there is no television station licensed to the community in which the sports event is taking place, the applicable specified zone shall be that of the television station licensed to the community with which the sports event or local team is identified, or, if the event or local team as not identified with any particular community, the nearest community to which a television station is licensed. . . .

(c) Notifications given pursuant to this section must be received, as to regularly scheduled events, no later than the Monday preceding the calendar week (Sunday–Saturday) during which the program deletion is to be made. Notifications as to events not regularly scheduled and revisions of notices previously submitted must be received within twenty-four (24) hours after the time of the telecast to be deleted is known, but in any event no later than twenty-four (24) hours from the time the subject telecast is to take place.

(d) Whenever, pursuant to this section, a community unit is required to delete a television program on a signal regularly carried by the community unit, such community unit may, consistent with the rules contained in Subpart F of this part, substitute a program from any other television broadcast station. A program substituted may be carried to its completion, and the community unit need not return to its regularly carried signal until it can do so without interrupting a program already in progress. . . .

6.12–1   Negative Enforcement: Threat of Loss of Licence

Since the early days of its existence, the FCC has acted on requests for license renewal. In a few instances, radio and television stations have lost their licenses because of improper activities. No license has actually been revoked because of improprieties connected with sports. However, as the FCC's opinion *In the Matter of A. E. Newton (WOCL)* emphasizes, a realistic threat of revocation exists and cannot be ignored.

The following opinion is by the Broadcast Division of the FCC.

In the Matter of A. E. Newton (WOCL), 2 F.C.C. 281 (1936)

This proceeding arose upon the application of A. E. Newton, licensee of Radio Station WOCL, at Jamestown, New York, for renewal of license, (B1–R–234), filed September 26, 1934. . . .

Said renewal application was designated for hearing to determine the nature and character of certain programs broadcast by the station, and to determine whether the station had violated Section 325 of the Communications Act of 1934, which prohibits the rebroadcasting, by any station, of the program or any part thereof, of another broadcasting station, without the express authority of the originating station, and to determine whether the continued operation of the station would serve public interest, convenience, and necessity. . . .

The issue directly presented for determination is whether an account of a World Series baseball game, which was carried over the station in 1934, was a violation of said Section 325 of the Communications Act of 1934, as above indicated.

The station is located in the dwelling where the applicant resides. It appears that a radio receiver was placed in the dining room of dwelling of the applicant. The transmitter for the broadcast station was located in the basement of applicant's dwelling, directly beneath the dining room. The radio set was tuned in so as to receive the signal from Station WGR, and by means of wires running from said receiving set in the room above, to a pair of ear phones at the announcer's station in the room below, the announcer of Station WOCL listened to the station and gathered the information from the receiving set tuned to Station WGR. The announcer of Station WOCL by this means gave a running account of the World Series baseball game to the listeners of Station WOCL. It was also in the evidence that the information announced was supplemented from other sources than that received over the receiving set from Station WGR; that some of said information was secured from a scoreboard to which the station had access; and from other broadcast stations; and from the information gained from the scoreboard and from the use of the receiving set the running account was given.

It does not appear that the announcer of Station WOCL repeated verbatim the broadcast of Station WGR, but it appears that he gathered enough information from the broadcast of Station WGR and other stations, including the use of the scoreboard, to make a fair report of the ball game. It appears that there was no transmission of the broadcast signals of any other station.

The evidence shows that by the means mentioned, the announcer of Station WOCL was able to, and did, follow the details of the game, and announced same from the beginning practically until the end, covering a period of an hour and a half or two hours. No announcement was made by Station WOCL as to the origin of the program and the audience of Station WOCL was not informed that the program was not originating with that station.

There appears to have been no court ruling on the matter involved, but a decision of the Federal Radio Commission, with which this Commission is in accord, dealt with issues which appear to be quite similar to the facts involved here, in ruling on the application of Radio Station WCOT, to which reference is made in the Second Annual Report of the Federal Radio Commission, at Page 153. The conclusion of that Commission, in that case, on the construction of Section 28 of the Radio Act of February 27, 1927, which carries the same language as Section 325 of the Communications Act of 1934, was that rebroadcasting meant that the station engaged therein actually reproduced the signal of another station mechanically or by some other means, such as feeding the program received directly into a microphone. From a strict standpoint, the receiving of a program of another station over an ordinary receiving set and then restating the information thus received over the microphone does not constitute a violation of Section 325 of the Communications Act.

However, it is not inappropriate to observe that the production of programs by a radio station calls for the exercise of creative faculties and the outlay of funds for the employment of talent — the preparation and planning of the broadcast and the employment of persons trained and qualified for their particular duties. When, therefore, a station engages in the practice here involved, its conduct is inconsistent with fair dealing, is dishonest in nature, and amounts to an unfair utilization of the results of another's labor. Moreover, the practice is deceptive to the public upon the whole, and contrary to the interests thereof.

While the Commission has experienced difficulty in reaching a determination in this case, it concluded, upon consideration of the entire record, the general qualifications shown and the apparent fact that the practice engaged in is not shown to have occurred more than the instance referred to, that public interest, convenience, and necessity will be served by the granting of a renewal of the licence. . . .

6.12–2 Positive Enforcement: Protection of Private Transmissions

The foregoing case (*In the Matter of A. E. Newton*) illustrates the negative enforcement powers that the FCC can potentially use to revoke a station's license. The following statutory provision, an amendment to the Federal Communications Act, presents opportunities for *both* governmental and individual responses to communications violations. Private transmissions, not intended for public reception, are protected under the provisions.

UNITED STATES CODE TITLE 47
Section 605. Unauthorized publication or use of communications
(a) Practices prohibited

No person not being authorized by the sender shall intercept any radio communication and divulge or publish the existence, contents, substance, purport, effect, or meaning of such intercepted communication to any person. No person not being entitled thereto shall receive or assist in receiving any interstate or foreign communication by radio and use such communication (or any information therein contained) for his own benefit or for the benefit of another not entitled thereto. No person having received any intercepted radio communication or having become acquainted with the contents, substance, purport, effect, or meaning of such communication (or any part thereof), knowing that such communication was intercepted, shall divulge or publish the existence, contents, substance, purport, effect, or meaning of such

communication (or any part thereof) or use such communication (or any information therein contained) for his own benefit or for the benefit of another not entitled thereto. This section shall not apply to the receiving, divulging, publishing, or utilizing the contents of any radio communication which is transmitted by any station for the use of the general public, which relates to ships, aircraft, vehicles, or persons in distress, or which is transmitted by an amateur radio station operator or by a citizens band radio operator.

(b) Exceptions

The provisions of subsection (a) of this section shall not apply to the interception or receipt by any individual, or the assisting (including the manufacture or sale) of such interception or receipt, of any satellite cable programming for private viewing if—

(1) the programming involved is not encrypted; and

(2)(A) a marketing system is not established under which—

(i) an agent or agents have been lawfully designated for the purpose of authorizing private viewing by individuals, and

(ii) such authorization is available to the individual involved from the appropriate agent or agents; or

(B) a marketing system described in subparagraph (A) is established and the individual receiving such programming has obtained authorization for private viewing under that system.

(c) Definitions

For purposes of this section—

(1) the term "satellite cable programming" means video programming which is transmitted via satellite and which is primarily intended for the direct receipt by cable operators for their retransmission to cable subscribers;

(2) the term "agent," with respect to any person, includes an employee of such person;

(3) the term "encrypt," when used with respect to satellite cable programming, means to transmit such programming in a form whereby the aural and visual characteristics (or both) are modified or altered for the purpose of preventing the unauthorized receipt

of such programming by persons without authorized equipment which is designed to eliminate the effects of such modification or alteration;

(4) the term "private viewing" means the viewing for private use in an individual's dwelling unit by means of equipment, owned or operated by such individual, capable of receiving satellite cable programming directly from a satellite; and

(5) the term "private financial gain" shall not include the gain resulting to any individual for the private use in such individual's dwelling unit of any programming for which the individual has not obtained authorization for that use.

(d) Penalties; civil actions; remedies; attorney's fees and costs; computation of damages; regulation by State and local authorities

(1) Any person who willfully violates subsection (a) of this section shall be fined not more than $1,000 or imprisoned for not more than 6 months, or both.

(2) Any person who violates subsection (a) of this section willfully and for purposes of direct or indirect commercial advantage or private financial gain shall be fined not more than $25,000 or imprisoned for not more than 1 year, or both, for the first such conviction and shall be fined not more than $50,000 or imprisoned for not more than 2 years, or both, for any subsequent conviction.

(3)(A) Any person aggrieved by any violation of subsection (a) of this section may bring a civil action in a United States district court or in any other court of competent jurisdiction.

(B) The court may—

(i) grant temporary and final injunctions on such terms as it may deem reasonable to prevent or restrain violations of subsection (a) of this section;

(ii) award damages as described in sub-paragraph (C); and

(iii) direct the recovery of full costs, including awarding reasonable attorneys' fees to an aggrieved party who prevails.

(C)(i) Damages awarded by any court under this section shall be computed, at the election of the aggrieved party, in accordance with either of the following subclauses;

(I) the party aggrieved may recover the actual damages suffered by him as a result of the violation and any profits of the violator that are attributable to the violation which are not taken into account in computing the actual damages; in determining the violator's profits, the party aggrieved shall be required to prove only the violator's gross revenue, and the violator shall be required to prove his deductible expenses and the elements of profit attributable to factors other than the violation; or

(II) the party aggrieved may recover an award of statutory damages for each violation involved in the action just a sum of not less than $250 or more than $10,000, as the court considers just.

(ii) In any case in which the court finds that the violation was committed willfully and for purposes of direct or indirect commercial advantage or private financial gain, the court in its discretion may increase the award of damages, whether actual or statutory, by an amount of not more than $50,000.

(iii) In any case where the court finds that the violator was not aware and had no reason to believe that his acts constituted a violation of this section, the court in its discretion may reduce the award of damages to a sum of not less than $100.

(4) The importation, manufacture, sale, or distribution of equipment by any person with the intent of its use to assist in any activity prohibited by subsection (a) of this section shall be subject to penalties and remedies under this subsection to the same extent and in the same manner as a person who has engaged in such prohibited activity.

(5) The penalties under this subsection shall be in addition to those prescribed under any other provision of this subchapter.

(6) Nothing in this subsection shall prevent any State, or political subdivision thereof, from enacting or enforcing any laws with respect to the importation, sale, manufacture, or distribution of equipment by any person with the intent of its use to assist in the interception or receipt of radio communications prohibited by subsection (a) of this section.

(e) Rights, obligations and liabilities under other laws unaffected

Nothing in this section shall affect any right, obligation, or liability under Title 17, any rule, regulation, or order thereunder, or any other applicable Federal, State or local law.

6.13   Copyright

A companion to the communications provisions in the U.S. Code are copyright provisions pertinent to broadcasts. Note below Section 102(6), which extends basic copyright protection to "motion pictures *and other audiovisual works*" (emphasis added), if "fixed in any tangible medium of expression." If the transmitted sports event is recorded on tape, and thus fixed tangibly, it is protected by the copyright laws.

Section 106 accords the copyright owner the control over the various ways that a copyrighted product can be reproduced, adapted, distributed, performed, and displayed publicly. Obviously, sections 102(6) and 106, taken together, provide substantial benefits and protections for sports broadcasts. In and of themselves, they do not determine who actually owns the copyright or other interests in the product. This question, already considered in part earlier in this chapter (see Section 6.11), is examined in detail in Section 6.20 and its several subsections.

Another important section of the copyright laws is Section 111, which deals with a cable system's ability to retransmit intercepted conventional signals without violating the copyright of the stations sending the signal. This lengthy and complex provision is not reproduced but is discussed in various cases throughout this chapter.

17 United States Code

Section 102. Subject matter of copyright: In general

(a) Copyright protection subsists, in accordance with this title, in original works of authorship fixed in any tangible medium of expression, now known or later developed, from which they can be perceived, reproduced, or otherwise communicated, either directly or with the aid of a machine or device. Works of authorship include the following categories:

(1) literary works;
(2) musical works, including any accompanying words;
(3) dramatic works, including any accompanying music;
(4) pantomimes and choreographic works;
(5) pictorial, graphic, and sculptural works;
(6) motion pictures and other audiovisual works; and
(7) sound recordings.

(b) In no case does copyright protection for an original work of authorship extend to any idea, procedure, process, system, method of operation, concept, principle, or discovery, regardless of the form in which it is described, explained, illustrated, or embodied in such work.

Section 106. Exclusive rights in copyrighted works

Subject to sections 107 through 118, the owner of copyright under this title has the exclusive rights to do and to authorize any of the following:

(1) to reproduce the copyrighted work in copies or phonorecords;
(2) to prepare derivative works based upon the copyrighted work;
(3) to distribute copies or phonorecords of the copyrighted work to the public by sale or other transfer of ownership, or by rental, lease, or lending;
(4) in the case of literary, musical, dramatic, and choreographic works, pantomimes, and motion pictures and other audiovisual works, to perform the copyrighted work publicly; and
(5) in the case of literary, musical, dramatic, and choreographic works, pantomimes, and pictorial, graphic, or sculptural works, including the individual images of a motion picture or other audiovisual work, to display the copyrighted work publicly.

6.20   Parties' Assertions of Rights to the Product

The decision in *Pittsburgh Athletic Co. v. KQV Broadcasting Co.* (see Section 6.11) established that club owners could sell the rights in the transmission and description of a game and could protect their interests by restraining others from infringing on that right. Concepts of misappropriation of property and unfair competition were used to substantiate the owners' rights. We have also examined how provisions of the communications and copyright statutes give protections to both owners and other parties regarding the transmission and descriptions of a sports event. However, what seemed simple and straightforward at one time is no longer. New technologies have created varied possibilities for transmission, and new parties in interest have emerged.

This section and its many subsections expand on the complexities that surround sports and the media today. The analysis proceeds from one party in interest to the next, creating an extensive chain of rights and responsibilities. The cases examined are at times somewhat arbitrarily assigned to illustrate a particular party's interests. In fact, such cases often deal with the concerns of several competing parties. This should not detract from the overall emphasis of the section.

Beginning with a look at new dimensions concerning owner rights in the broadcast of sports events (Section 6.21), the analysis then weaves through a maze of other asserted interests — those of players (Section 6.22), broadcasters in general (Section 6.23), conventional television (Section 6.24), regular cable (Section 6.25), pay cable and STV (Section 6.26), superstations and satellite transmissions (Section 6.27), and finally the consumers, the fans (Section 6.28).

Not all interests in the broadcast product are equal. Some rights are clearly more extensive than others. They are more valuable and safeguarded by greater legal protections.

Sorting out who has what rights and how these rights translate into financial rewards are a central concern of this section. As we shall see, however, there is no simple solution. The ownership of rights and the establishment of protected interests propel the inquiry into complex legal and business considerations. In many instances, there are as yet no definitive solutions.

6.21   Sports Teams and Leagues: Recent Complications

Teams in a professional sports league formulate rules that provide, where no network broadcast is involved, for each team's rights to broadcast its own "home" and "away" games, at least in its own territory. Teams in the league do not interfere with each other's rights, since each desires to retain exclusivity in its own home territory.

On the college level, the scene is not so orderly. Even schools in the same conference have been selling rights that have the effect of invading another school's home territory. The cases are still developing in this area, and those which follow involving Wichita State and Michigan State Universities may be harbingers.

While professional leagues have set up orderly procedures for dividing television broadcast rights, this does not prevent outsiders from contesting the exclusivities created. *Management TV Systems, Inc. v. NFL* is only one example of an attempt to break into the inner circle. Other cases are detailed throughout this chapter.

Wichita State University Intercollegiate Athletic Ass'n., Inc. v. Swanson Broadcasting Co., Case No. 81C130 (Sedgwick City, Kan. Dist. Ct., Jan. 3, 1981)

Wichita State University (WSU) entered a contract with a Wichita radio station to broadcast WSU football and basketball games. Another Wichita radio station, however, contracted with WSU's opponents to broadcast WSU's "away" games into the Wichita area. WSU sought to enjoin these broadcasts, citing common law principles of misappropriation and interference with a contractual relationship.

Faced with the question of which team owns the right to transmit the accounts and descriptions of a game, the court in a bench ruling concluded that a team has an exclusive right to broadcast the sports event into its own home territory, regardless of whether the game is home or away. Therefore, WSU had the exclusive right to determine with whom it would contract to broadcast both its "home" and "away" games in the Wichita area. WSU did not have the right to determine who would broadcast an "away" game into other areas.

A preliminary injunction was issued against the defendant broadcasting the WSU "away" games in the Wichita area.

Gross Telecasting Co., Inc. v. Michigan State University, No. G81–712–CA6, U.S. Dist. Ct. (W.D. Mich., filed Sept. 15, 1981) (settled)

Plaintiff Gross Telecasting Co., unsuccessful in its attempts to negotiate television rights to Michigan State athletic events, obtained the rights to broadcast certain of Michigan State's "away" basketball games from three other Big Ten schools. Gross claimed that Michigan State coerced the other Big Ten schools into refusing to grant similar rights. Gross thus sued Michigan State, claiming antitrust violations, state law business tort liabilities, and abridgment of First Amendment rights.

During early arguments in the case, the parties agreed that defendant Michigan State would bring a motion before the court to raise the specific issue of whether the university had a legally cognizable property right in the "away" game telecasts of its Big Ten basketball games. Before this motion was filed, however, the case was dismissed on plaintiff's motion, with prejudice.

Management TV Systems, Inc. v. National Football League, 52 F.R.D. 162 (E.D. Pa. 1971)

Plaintiff, who operated a closed-circuit television system, sued the National Football League, the league members, and three national television networks alleging that there was a conspiracy to exclude plaintiff from the market by refusing to deal with it. On plaintiff's motion to maintain the action as against an unincorporated association, the district court held that the action could be maintained as a class action under Rule 23.2, since the NFL and those clubs properly named and served represent all 26 members of the league.

The court held that Rule 23.2 was applicable since all clubs comprising the NFL were adequately represented by qualified counsel appearing for the representative defendants. Next, the plaintiff made an adequate showing that the distribution of television rights was a matter of league policy and that, if there were agreements, all clubs participated or acquiesced. Finally, the judgment binding on all members did not offend due process, since steps could be taken during the proceedings to ensure the protection of the members, especially in the light of the manageable size of the class.

6.22 Players

Players in certain leagues have recently become more militant concerning their rights in the broadcast or telecast of a sports event in which they participate. Although no resolution of this matter has been forthcoming, it is anticipated that this will be an issue in the future in most major sports leagues, particularly those in which the players' associations become involved.

An early indicator of this trend was sounded in June 1979, when NBA players on behalf of all players in the league filed suit in the United States District Court of the Southern District of New York. This was the case of *Silas et al. v. Manhattan Cable Television, and Teleprompter Corp.*, 79 Civ. 3025, filed June 8,

1979. The complaint read in part:

5. Of the tens of thousands of highly skilled basketball players in the United States only the best 242 are skilled enough to play in the NBA. Plaintiffs have been and continue to be among the most skilled of this limited number of professional basketball players and each plaintiff has devoted many years to the development of a nationally recognized reputation as such a highly skilled professional basketball player. As a result, plaintiffs possess property rights of substantial commercial or trade value in their names, pictures and performing ability. . . .

11. Defendants have used plaintiffs' names, pictures and performances for advertising and for purposes of trade by advertising, selling and broadcasting such names, pictures and performances by cable television to defendants' subscribers in New York and elsewhere. . . .

WHEREFORE, Plaintiffs . . . each demand judgment against each of the defendants as follows:

(a) a declaration that defendants' use of plaintiffs' names, pictures and performances in connection with defendants' cable television business violates §§ 50 and 51 of the Civil Rights Law of the State of New York.

(b) a declaration that defendants' use of plaintiffs' names, pictures and performances in connection with defendants' cable television business constitutes an unlawful misappropriation of plaintiffs' valuable proprietary interests in their names, pictures, performances and the publicity thereof.

(c) damages . . .

(d) an injunction permanently enjoining defendants from further violations of the rights of the plaintiffs . . .

This suit was later withdrawn when the players' association and the league reached a new collective bargaining agreement in 1980. The withdrawal was made, however, only after a clause was included in the collective agreement recognizing that the league and the players were in disagreement as to ownership rights in certain televised products. That dispute continues, as witnessed by the following provision contained in the amendments to the 1980 agreement, as agreed to by NBA management and labor in 1983.

National Basketball Association, 1983 Memorandum of Agreement, Article IV

The NBA and the Players Association disagree as to whether the NBA or any Team has the right to use, distribute, or license any performance by the players, under this Memorandum or the Uniform Player Contract, for Pay TV, any form of cassette or cartridge system, or other means of distribution known or unknown. By entering into this Memorandum, the parties specifically reserve any rights, legal or otherwise, on this point that they may own.

Notwithstanding the foregoing, the parties agree that for the term of this Memorandum, the NBA and its Teams shall have the right to use, distribute, or license any performance by the players under this Memorandum or the Uniform Player Contract, for Pay TV, Cable TV, any form of cassette or cartridge system, or other means of distribution, known or unknown.

6.23   Broadcasters

Broadcasters expend large sums to obtain the rights to transmit sports events. The successful bidder usually obtains exclusivity as to the immediate broadcast, but whether others can intercept the signals and retransmit has become an important inquiry as the technological ability to retransmit has developed. We saw in *Malrite TV of N.Y.* v. *FCC* (see Section 6.12) that companies have extensive rights under the copyright statute to engage in passive retransmission. This is done at a price, the price being the payment of a statutorily mandated fee to the Copyright Tribunal, which in turn redistributes the funds received to the copyright owners.

The Copyright Tribunal found itself in the middle of substantial controversy when it had to determine how the royalty "pie" was to be divided. It was hardly surprising that the tribunal's eventual determination would be challenged in court. This occurred in *National Ass'n. of Broadcasters* v. *Copyright Royalty Tribunal*, discussed below. Of special note are the percentages accorded the various parties involved in a televised product. This includes, of course, all television and not just sports.

The bottom line is that the act of broadcasting is not seen as creating a substantial copyright interest. The great share goes to the basic producers (owners) of the product. In sports, these are the leagues and clubs and, on the amateur level, the universities and their conferences. It is *not* the broadcasters.

National Association of Broadcasters v. Copyright Royalty Tribunal, 675 F. 2d 367 (D.C. Cir. 1982)

Congress enacted the Copyright Act of 1976 in part to compensate copyright owners for retransmission of their works by cable systems. The act invested the Copyright Royalty Tribunal, whose function was to make an annual distribution of the royalty fees paid by cable television operators, with broad discretion in apportioning the fees among the copyright owners. Accordingly, specific awards were reversible only if the agency's decision was not supported by "substantial evidence" or was "arbitrary, capricious, and abuse of discretion or otherwise not in accordance with law."

These consolidated cases arose out of the first royalty distribution for the 1978 calendar year. The $15 million fund was distributed in the following proportions:

Program syndicators and	
movie producers	75.00%
Sports leagues	12.00
Television broadcasters	3.25
Public television	5.25
Music claimants	4.50

The tribunal, after hearing arguments and examining data advanced by the parties, had determined that the following criteria would guide its allocation of the shares:

1. The harm caused to copyright owners by secondary transmissions of copyrighted works by cable systems.
2. The benefit derived by cable systems from the secondary transmissions of certain copyrighted works.
3. The marketplace value of the works transmitted.

Among the secondary factors were:

1. The quality of copyrighted program material.
2. Time-related considerations.

The U.S. Court of Appeals upheld the tribunal's decisions in all but one instance; it reversed the tribunal's decision to award $50,000 to National Public Radio (NPE). The court was troubled by apparent procedural flaws in its reconsideration and decision to rescind the award to NPR and remanded only that portion. As to the other claimants — the National Association of Broadcasters; the Joint Sports Claimants, a group including professional baseball, basketball, hockey, and soccer leagues; ASCAP, an unincorporated membership association of music publishers and writers; and the Canadian Broadcasting Corporation — the court was satisfied that the tribunal's resolution was reasonable and comported with congressional intent. The court recognized that it was impossible to satisfy all the cliamants, whose combined requests totaled roughly three times more than the finite amount of the fund. However, the administrative record provided rational support for the distribution of the royalty shares, and the tribunal's allocation was upheld.

6.24 Conventional Television

Stations and networks engaged in standard broadcasts to the general public must constantly guard against unauthorized interceptions of their signals. While conventional television interests have lost the battle to exclude *all* retransmissions, they nevertheless still can protect against certain unauthorized interceptions.

National Broadcasting Co. v. Athena Cablevision of Corpus Christi, Inc., No. C–83–120 (S.D. Tex., filed June 16, 1983) (pending)

NBC and its Corpus Christi, Texas, affiliate brought an action against a cable system which retransmitted to its subscribers the satellite "clean feed" of the 1983 Super Bowl XVII. The plaintiffs alleged copyright infringement under the theory that the NFL transferred to NBC the exclusive live U.S. television rights to the Super Bowl, and NBC in turn transferred to its affiliate the exclusive right to televise the game in the Corpus Christi area. The complaint also alleged violations of section 605 of the Communications Act of 1934 and a comparable Texas statute.

The defendant claimed that its carriage of the transmission was inadvertent. Apparently, NBC and the NFL had authorized Home Box Office (HBO), a pay cable programming service, to transmit a separate feed of the game to HBO executives in Puerto Villarta, Mexico. In doing so, HBO used a satellite transponder, which normally carried another programming service. The defendant, who was a subscriber to this other service, claimed it had failed to "turn off" the earth station when that service was not on the air and hence did not know that its earth station was carrying the Super Bowl live.

The case raises the issue of whether cable systems have any affirmative obligations to ensure that they do not engage in the unauthorized interception of satellite transmissions. To date, no ultimate resolution of the case has been reached.

NOTES ————————————————

1. In *NFL* v. *The Alley Inc.*, No. 83–0701 CIV–JWIC (S.D. Fla., filed March 25, 1983), the NFL and the Miami Dolphins brought suit against a number of commercial establishments, including bars and restaurants, which used

earth stations to intercept satellite transmissions of the Dolphins' home games in an attempt to attract sports-minded patrons. The plaintiffs objected to this practice because some of the telecasts had been blacked out in the Miami home territory and because the intercepted transmissions were a "clean feed" and did not contain any commercials. The NFL and the Dolphins claimed copyright infringement under the 1976 Copyright Act and violations of section 605 of the Communications Act of 1934, as well as violations of state laws regarding the team's right of publicity.

The district court held for the plaintiffs on their copyright and section 605 counts, rejecting defendants' claim that the telecasts of sports events are noncopyright-able news in the public domain and that the showing of the telecasts did not constitute an actionable public performance. Additionally, the court failed to find as defendants had claimed that the display was exempt under 17 U.S.C., section 110(5), which exempts displays of works by a "single receiving apparatus of a kind commonly used in private homes." The plaintiffs had established that earth stations did not fall within the limitation. The court entered a preliminary injunction.

2. In *NFL* v. *Campagnolo Enter., Inc.*, No. 83–1205–Civ.–T–13 (M.D. Fla., filed Sept. 22, 1983), the NFL and Tampa Bay Buccaneers filed a lawsuit against several Tampa area bars that intercepted satellite transmissions of Tampa Bay games by the use of earth stations. These transmissions were not intended for broadcast in the Tampa area because of the blackout rule. The case, which was similar to the one filed by the NFL and the Miami Dolphins, was settled by the parties.

6.25   Cable

Earlier discussion has focused on the general ability of cable systems to intercept over-the-air transmissions and rebroadcast them. There are limits to this right, and the FCC has issued extensive regulations as to the ability of a cable system to duplicate programming that is being seen on conventional television in the same locale where the cable system wishes to transmit. Appearing below are excerpts from FCC regulations that indicate the complexity that confronts both stations and cable systems in determining whether a station's signal can be intercepted and its programming duplicated within a certain defined zone.

Federal Communications Commission Regulations, 47 C.F.R. Sections 76.92–76.95

Section 76.92 Stations entitled to network program nonduplication protection

(a) Any community unit which operates in a community located in whole or in part within the 35-mile specified zone of any commercial television broadcast station or within the secondary zone which extends 20 miles beyond the specified zone of a smaller market television broadcast station (55 miles altogether), and which carries the signal of such station shall, except as provided in paragraphs (e) and (f) of this section, delete, upon request of the station licensee or permittee, the duplicating network programming of lower priority signals in the manner and to the extent specified in §§ 76.94 and 76.95.

(b) For purposes of this section, the order of nonduplication priority of television signals carried by a community unit is as follows:

(1) First, all television broadcast stations within whose specified zone the community of the community unit is located, in whole or in part;

(2) Second, all smaller market television broadcast stations within whose secondary zone the community of the community unit is located, in whole or in part. . . .

(e) Any community unit which operates in a community located in whole or in part within the specified zone of any television broadcast station or within the secondary zone of a smaller market television broadcast station is not required to delete the duplicating network programming of any 100-watt or higher power television translator station which is licensed to the community of the community unit.

(f) Any community unit which operates in a community located in whole or in part within the secondary zone of a smaller market television broadcast station is not required to delete the duplicating network programming of any major market television broadcast station whose reference point (See § 76.53) is also within 55 miles of the community of the community unit. . . .

Section 76.94 Notification requirements and extent of protection

(a) Where the network programming of a television station is entitled to nonduplication protection, a community unit shall, upon request of the station licensee or permittee, refrain from simultaneously duplicating any network program broadcast by such station only if the community unit has received the information required in paragraphs (a)(1) and (2) of this section:

(1) Notification of the date and time of the programming to be protected and date and time of the programming to be deleted must, at a minimum, be received on a monthly basis. If the station licensee or permittee elects to provide such notification on a monthly basis, it must be submitted no later than six (6) days preceding the calendar month during which nonduplication is requested. If the station licensee or permittee elects to provide such notification on a weekly basis, notice shall be given no later than the Monday preceding the calendar week (Sunday–Saturday) during which nonduplication protection is sought.

(2) Changes in the monthly notification request required by paragraph (a)(1) must be submitted six (6) days preceding the broadcast of the programming to be protected: *Provided, however,* that the licensee or permittee of the television station otherwise entitled to nonduplication protection must notify the affected community unit as soon as possible. . . .

(b) Where a community unit is required to provide same-day network program nonduplication protection, either pursuant to specific Commission order or pending Commission action on a broadcast station petition for special relief filed pursuant to the procedures described in paragraph 25 of the *Second Report and Order in Docket 19995,* FCC 75–820, 54 FCC 2d 229 (1975), the following provisions shall be applicable:

(1) A community unit need not delete reception of a network program if, in so doing, it would leave available for reception by subscribers, at any time, less than the programs of two networks (including those broadcast by any stations whose signals are being carried and whose programming is being protected pursuant to the requirements of this section);

(2) A community unit need not delete reception of a network program which is scheduled by the network between the hours of 6 and 11 p.m., eastern time, but is broadcast by the station requesting deletion, in whole or in part, outside of the period which would normally be considered prime time for network programming in the time zone involved.

Section 76.95   Exceptions

(a) Notwithstanding the requirements of §§ 76.92 and 76.94, a community unit need not delete reception of any program which would be carried on the community unit in color but will be broadcast in black and white by the station requesting deletion.

(b) The provisions of §§ 76.92 and 76.94 shall not apply to a community unit having fewer than 1,000 subscribers. Within 60 days following the provision of service to 1,000 subscribers, each such community unit shall file a notice to that effect with the Commission and shall send a copy thereof to all television broadcast and translator stations carried by the community unit.

(c) Network nonduplication protection need not be extended to a higher priority station for one hour following the scheduled time of completion of the broadcast of a live sports event by that station or by a lower priority station against which a cable community unit would otherwise be required to provide nonduplication protection following the scheduled time of completion.

(d) The Commission will give full effect to private agreements between operators of community units and local television stations which provide for a type or degree of network program nonduplication protection which differs from the requirements of §§ 76.92 and 76.94. . . .

6.26   Pay Cable and STV

The FCC has clear and undisputed authority to control the public airwaves through regulatory authority over radio and television stations using those airwaves. By extension, this authority controls the actions of other carriers, whether their use be public or private. Even so, this does not mean all actions by the FCC go without challenge. The following cases examine the FCC's rule making authority as it applies to sports programming and pay television.

WWHT, Inc. v. FCC, 656 F. 2d 807 (D.C. Cir. 1981)

In 1968, the FCC established a nationwide over-the-air subscription television broadcasting service and adopted rules designed to ensure the integration of the new STV service into the total television broadcasting service. No further action, however, was taken with respect to the 1968 rule-making proceeding until September 21, 1978, when the commission terminated the proceeding without adopting the proposed amendments. The following day, Blonder-Tongue Laboratories petitioned the commission to institute rule-making proceedings to amend its mandatory cable carriage rules to include the carriage of STV signals. Comments in favor of the petition were also submitted by the Motion Picture Association of America and the NBA, jointly with the NHL.

After reviewing the comments, the commission denied the request for rule making, setting forth reasons justifying the denial and concluding that it was "appropriate that STV operators and cable television operators be left free to bargain in their own best interests for cable carriage." The commission also denied Suburban Broadcasting Corporation's request for a declaratory ruling on the scope of the existing cable carriage rules. Suburban had argued that the commission's rules already required mandatory STV carriage. The FCC in reply declared that it had "publicly, clearly, and consistently" over the preceding 12 years neither intended nor enforced its rules to require STV carriage.

The court's review of the record indicated that no procedural infirmity marred the actions of the FCC, and the court had before it a challenge to the factual and policy determinations of the FCC. The court held that under 5

U.S.C., section 706(2)(A) it had the jurisdiction to review actions committed to agency discretion, but the scope of review should be extremely narrow. The court found that the explanations given by the FCC were adequate to explain the facts and policy concerns it had relied on, and there was nothing to indicate that the opinions of the commission were unlawful, arbitrary, capricious, or wholly irrational. The interest sought to be protected by petitioners was primarily economic and did not present unusual or compelling circumstance to justify overturning the FCC's decision. Moreover, the policy determinations as to the relative merits of mandatory cable carriage of STV signals were not suitable for determination by the court and thus were well within the discretion of the agency.

National Ass'n. of Theatre Owners v. FCC, 420 F. 2d 194 (D.C. Cir. 1969)

On the basis of its 17-year inquiry into the feasibility of over-the-air subscription television (STV), the FCC issued its Fourth Report and Order concluding that STV would provide a beneficial supplement to free broadcasts. In its report, the commission imposed a number of restrictions governing technical specifications and modus operandi of the operations but rejected the suggestion that direct regulation of the rates was necessary to prevent "gouging" of the public.

The petitioners advanced arguments in support of their contention that the commission exceeded the proper bounds of its power and also raised equal protection and First Amendment issues. After examining the language and history of the Communications Act of 1934, the court found that the act was a broad grant of general licensing authority that had been affirmed by subsequent court challenges. The act also did not preclude the commission from approving a system of direct charges to the public as a means of financing broadcasting services; rather it was designed to foster diversity in the financial organization of broadcasting stations. Therefore, the commission did not exceed its authority in concluding that STV was consistent with its goals.

As to the petitioners' argument that the FCC's decision not to employ rate-making measures was arbitrary and capricious, the court found that in its 144-page Fourth Report, the commission had adequately determined that a substantial amount of economic competition would exist between STV and other forms of entertainment, making regulation unnecessary. The court noted that it was very reluctant to declare that free market forces must be supplanted by rate regulation when neither Congress nor the FCC had deemed it essential.

The court also found no merit to the petitioners' constitutional claims. The authorization of nationwide STV would not result in unconstitutional discrimination against people in low-income groups. The public's access to the broadcast media had never been wholly free, since it is necessary to procure and maintain the necessary apparatus. Moreover, under the regulations, any deprivation of access would be slight; at most, one out of five stations serving a community would be devoted to STV, and that station would be required to carry at least 28 hours of free programming per week. Finally, when the net effect of the program restrictions was considered, it was likely that the public in STV areas would receive more rather than less diversity of expression in television programming, thus refuting petitioners' contention that STV would be a prior restraint on free speech in violation of the First Amendment.

In fashioning the remedy in equity, the court granted a permanent injunction against defendant's actions. Furthermore, because the defendant realized proceeds of $1,432.50 through the conversion and disposition to its own use of the property rights of the plaintiff, the amount was deemed to be held in constructive trust for the plaintiff, and plaintiff was held entitled to that sum.

Home Box Office, Inc. v. FCC, 567 F. 2d 9 (D.C. Cir. 1977)

SYLLABUS

These 15 consolidated cases challenge four orders of the Federal Communications Commission which, taken together, regulate and limit the program fare cablecasters and subscription broadcast television stations may offer to the public for a fee set on a per-program or per-channel basis. Acting under its rulemaking authority, the Commission in 1975 issued rules which prohibited pay exhibition of: (1) feature films more than three, but less than 10, years old; (2) specific sports events (*e.g.,* the World Series) shown on broadcast television within the previous five years; (3) more than the minimum number of non-specific (*i.e.,* regular season) sports events which had not been broadcast in any of the five preceding years, and in some cases only half that number; and (4) all series programs (*i.e.,* programs with interconnected plot or substantially the same cast of principal characters). In addition, the Commission prohibited commercial advertising in conjunction with pay exhibition of programming and limited the overall number of hours of pay operation which could be devoted to sports and feature films to 90% of total pay operations. *See* 47 C.F.R. §§ 73.643, 76.225 (1975). By subsequent orders in the same rulemaking, the series programming restriction was removed and recordkeeping requirements were imposed on feature film programming. The stated purpose of these rules was to prevent competitive bidding away of popular program material from the free television service to a service in which the audience would have to pay a fee to see the same material. Such competitive bidding, or "siphoning," is said to be possible because the money received from pay viewers is significantly more for some programs than money received from advertisers to attach their messages to the same material. For this reason, even a relatively small number of pay viewers could cause a program to be siphoned regardless of the wishes of a majority of its free viewers.

Held:

1. Review of the rulemaking record indicates that the pay cable television regulations must be considered separately from those regulating subscription broadcast television. Because the Commission has exceeded its authority over cable television in promulgating the pay cable rules and because there is no evidence to support the need for regulation of pay cable television, these rules must be vacated. Pp. 29–67.

a. The Communications Act of 1934, 47 U.S.C. § 151 *et seq.,* contains no provision expressly authorizing the Commission to regulate cable television. The Supreme Court has nonetheless sanctioned regulation of cable television under § 2(a) of the Act, 47 U.S.C. § 152(a), but only where the ends to be achieved were "long established" in the field of broadcast television or were "congressionally approved." *See United States* v. *Midwest Video Corp.,* 406 U.S. 649, 667–668 (1972); *United States* v. *Southwestern Cable Co.,* 392 U.S. 157, 173–176 (1968). These cases and considerations of administrative consistency further indicate that in most instances the proper test for Commission jurisdiction over pay cable television is whether the ends proposed to be achieved by Commission regulations are also well understood and consistently held ends for which broadcast television could be regulated. *See United States* v. *Midwest Video Corp., supra,* 406 U.S. at 667–668; *cf. Greater Boston Television Corp.* v. *FCC,* 143 U.S. App. D.C. 383, 394, 444 F. 2d 841, 852 (1970), *cert. denied,* 403 U.S. 923 (1971). *See also Hampton* v. *Mow Sun Wong,* 426 U.S. 88, 116 (1976). Pp. 30–34.

b. Under the standard set out above, the Commission has exceeded its jurisdiction and its rules must be vacated as unauthorized by law insofar as they regulate cable television. Pp. 34–48.

c. Even if the Commission had jurisdiction to promulgate its anti-siphoning rules, there is no evidence in the record supporting the need for regulation. Consequently, the rules must be vacated since a "regulation perfectly reasonable and appropriate in the face of a given problem [is] highly capricious if that problem does not exist." *City of Chicago* v. *FPC,* 147 U.S. App. D.C. 312, 323, 458 F. 2d 731, 742 (1971), *cert. denied,* 405 U.S. 1074 (1972). Pp. 48–60.

d. Moreover, although the Commission properly recognized the need to balance the benefits of regulation against the detriment to unfettered competition, it proceeded incorrectly. Contrary to the Commission's position, *United States* v. *Southwestern Cable Co., supra,* does not sanction regulation of cable television to prevent "unfair competition," but even if it did, the "unfairness" recognized in *Southwestern Cable* is not present here. Moreover, the balance between regulation and competition is not to be resolved on the basis of legal precedent, but by a considered decision upon the record in each rulemaking. Pp. 60–67.

2. The cable television rules are inconsistent with the First Amendment. Even though substantially similar rules which applied to broadcast television were upheld by this court in *National Ass'n. of Theatre Owners (NATO)* v. *FCC,* 136 U.S. App. D.C. 352, 420 F. 2d 194 (1969), *cert. denied,* 397 U.S. 922 (1970), that case is not controlling since "differences in the characteristics of news media justify differences in the First Amendment standards applied to them." *Red Lion Broadcasting Co.* v. *FCC,* 395 U.S. 367, 386 (1969). Pp. 67–83.

a. The constitutional question in *NATO* was straightforward: whether a grant of a broadcast license could be conditioned on terms which made reference to the kind and content of programs being offered to the public. Phrased this way, the question was identical to that resolved in the affirmative over 25 years before *NATO* in *National Broadcasting Co.* v. *United States,* 319 U.S. 190, 212–217, 226–227 (1943). Although *NATO* did not itself cite *National Broadcasting Co.,* there was no need for it to break new First Amendment ground and a reading of *NATO* shows that it did not do so. The conflict among speakers using the electromagnetic spectrum which justified Commission regulation in *NATO* and *National Broadcasting Co.* is absent from cable television, however. For this reason, the conventional justification for Commission regulation of broadcast speakers cannot be applied to regulation of cable television. Pp. 67–72.

b. The absence in cable television of the physical limitations of the electromagnetic spectrum does not automatically lead to the conclusion that no regulation of cable television is valid under the First Amendment. Because "the right of free speech . . . does not embrace a right

to snuff out the free speech of others," *Red Lion Broadcasting Co.* v. *FCC, supra,* 395 U.S. at 387, government may adopt reasonable regulations separating broadcasters competing and interfering with each other for the same audience. In determining whether such regulations comport with the First Amendment, the proper test is that set out in *United States* v. *O'Brien,* 391 U.S. 367, 377 (1968). Pp. 73–77.

c. Analysis of the Commission's stated reasons for promulgating the anti-siphoning rules indicates that the rules are intended to remove a conflict between those with and those without access to pay cable television. This purpose is unrelated to the suppression of free expression as required by *O'Brien.* Nonetheless, the rules are invalid because the record here will not support the conclusion that there is in fact conflict between these groups. Moreover, the restraints imposed by the rules are greater than necessary to further any legitimate government interest, and this overbreadth is not cured by the waiver provisions associated with the rules since the procedures established for obtaining a waiver are fundamentally at odds with the standards set out in *Freedman* v. *Maryland,* 380 U.S. 51 (1965). Pp. 77–83.

3. During the pendency of the rulemaking proceeding before the Commission, and even after the rulemaking record was supposed to be closed while the Commission deliberated, there were numerous *ex parte* contacts made between the parties to the rulemaking and various commissioners and Commission employees. Although this court *sua sponte* ordered the Commission to prepare and submit a list of all "*ex parte* presentations together with the details of each," it is still not possible to determine the effect of such communications on the integrity of the rulemaking. As a result, the elaborate public discussion in the dockets here under review may be a sham and a fiction. Our fundamental notions of judicial review require that reviewing courts have access to "the full administrative record" that was presumably before an agency when it exercised its discretion and promulgated rules. *See Citizens to Preserve Overton Park, Inc.* v. *Volpe,* 401 U.S. 402, 415–420 (1971). Where there have been frequent *ex parte* contacts, it is simply not possible to know the contents of the

"full administrative record." Moreover, *ex parte* contacts violate fundamental notions of fairness implicit in due process. *Sangamon Valley Television Corp.* v. *United States*, 106 U.S. App. D.C. 30, 269 F. 2d 221 (1959). For these reasons, it is imperative that agency officials involved in the decisional process of a rulemaking shun *ex parte* contacts on the subject matter of the rulemaking from the time a notice of proposed rulemaking issues until a final decision in the proceeding. If *ex parte* contacts nonetheless occur, the substance of the contacts must be reduced to writing and put in a public file. Pp. 84–101.

4. Rules substantially similar to the subscription broadcast television rules were affirmed by this court over six years ago in *NATO* v. *FCC*, *supra*. At that time the commission acted on an elaborate rulemaking record containing data generated in trial operations of a subscription broadcast station at Hartford, Connecticut. It appears that few, if any, subscription stations have begun operation in the interim. Accordingly, the best information available with respect to subscription broadcast television is that reviewed in *NATO*, which has not been called into question in the instant rulemaking. For this reason, *NATO* requires affirmance of the rules promulgated in the dockets here under review to the extent that such rules apply to subscription broadcast television, subject, however, to further review upon completion of additional hearings regarding *ex parte* contacts as ordered herein. Pp. 101–104. *Remanded.*

NOTE _____

1. The foregoing report of *HBO* v. *FCC* is a summary of the federal court's findings and was written by the court itself. This syllabus appears at the beginning of the court's decision and can be found at 567 F. 2d 13–15.

6.27 Superstations and Satellite Transmissions

Each new technological development adds a perplexing dimension to the efforts of sports owners and traditional broadcast interests to control their product. When cable systems expanded beyond their original role of importing signals into remote areas where normal television reception was difficult, their move was to bring multi-channel programming into populous metropolitan centers, including the importation of distant signals. These signals often were of sports contests from other cities. This circumstance caused great consternation to sports owners and conventional television interests. The frustration mounted as the so-called superstations developed, beaming programming to a satellite and thus making it available to cable systems nationwide.

Some television stations have voluntarily become superstations. Others, despite their protests, have found their signals beamed to satellites. Both types of superstations nevertheless have one thing in common: They carry a large amount of sports programming. It was inevitable that the ability to show live sports events nationwide would be challenged, since this was seen as an invasion of the network's exclusive contracts concerning national broadcasts and of sports teams' territorial rights as to exclusive local broadcasts.

The reported cases which follow do not resolve all issues by any means. Upon becoming Commissioner of Baseball, Peter Ueberroth in late 1984 declared that the superstations and their use of satellite transmissions constituted a great threat to the economic stability of major league baseball. However, instead of seeking further legal redress against the superstations, the commissioner sought an accommodation that would have the stations purchasing broadcast rights from the leagues. Whether the stations are legally obligated to pay for the rights, beyond a statutory copyright fee, is debatable, as the following cases reveal. But there have been indications that such an accommodation may be acceptable, rather than further litigation. Even so, the matters are not completely resolved, and the legal principles enunciated by the cases provide the underpinning for any eventual actions taken.

Cox Broadcasting Corp. v. National Collegiate Athletic Ass'n., 297 S.E. 2d 733 (Ga. 1982)

ABC and Cox Broadcasting Company filed an action seeking to restrain the NCAA from an alleged breach of contract concerning the broadcast of its college football games. The NCAA had decided to sell the rights to telecast live NCAA football via free over-the-air television for the 1982 season to two networks instead of one and began negotiating with ABC Sports in July of 1981 for one of the packages. Additionally, the NCAA planned to sell the rights to televise a Supplementary Series "via such media as cable and/or pay over-the-air television."

When ABC learned that Ted Turner, owner of the WTBS superstation, was one of the bidders, it tried to negotiate into its draft contract language to indicate that ABC's television rights were exclusive. It objected to the fact that if the series were awarded to Turner, it would be shown free over-the-air in Atlanta before being retransmitted via satellite to its cable system customers. The NCAA, however, refused to incorporate this language into the contract.

Turner's bid was accepted by the NCAA on January 27, 1982, and two days later ABC sent a telegram protesting the origination of the series free over-the-air. At this time, ABC and the NCAA were in the process of reaching a final written contract. ABC signed the agreement on February 11, 1982, but sent a letter conditioning its acceptance on the express understanding that ABC's right was exclusive and that there could not be "any local-like over-the-air broadcast of college football of the type planned in Atlanta by WTBS."

The NCAA indicated that it could not accede to the construction of the contract which ABC wished to impose. The two parties then agreed that the contract should be signed with the understanding that each party would preserve its differing position.

ABC and the NCAA continued to argue over whether Turner could telecast the Supplemental Series free over-the-air in the Atlanta area, and this disagreement led to the filing of the suit. The lower court issued an injunction against Turner for the 1983 through 1985 seasons, and ABC appealed from its refusal to enjoin the 1982 season.

The Supreme Court of Georgia reversed the lower court in its finding that there was no meeting of the minds on the rights and obligations relating to the Supplemental Series. When the contract was executed, the NCAA envisioned that the language did not prohibit it from contracting with Turner, and this understanding was conveyed to ABC. Conversely, ABC envisioned the language to provide it with rights that precluded the NCAA from contracting with Turner, and this understanding was clearly conveyed to the NCAA. Consequently, the court found that the NCAA and ABC had no agreement or justifiable expectations relating to how the series could be presented. Therefore, ABC had no contractual rights pursuant to which injunctive relief could be granted.

Eastern Microwave, Inc. v. Doubleday Sports, Inc., 691 F. 2d 125 (2d Cir. 1982)

Plaintiff Eastern Microwave, Inc. (EMI), licensed by the FCC as a communication common carrier, retransmits the entire original signals of WOR-TV, including the New York Mets baseball games, to cable television (CATV) systems, which then distribute the signals to subscribers in markets outside the service area of WOR-TV. As owners of the New York Mets, Doubleday Sports, Inc., notified EMI that it believed the retransmission of the Mets games infringed on its copyright. The dispositive issue in this suit was whether EMI was a passive carrier exempt from copyright liability under 17 U.S.C., section 111(a)(3) of the Copyright Act of 1976.

The first requirement for exemption is that the carrier must be passive, exercising no control over either the content of the primary transmission or the recipients of its transmission. The court held that EMI's choice to carry WOR-TV's signals rather than those of other stations merely reflected EMI's limitation to one technical facility. EMI in its role as an intermediary link between WOR-TV programming and the various subscriber cable systems thus had no selective control over the content. In addition, the record indicated that no reasonable request for EMI's services was ever refused by EMI, demonstrating that it did not exercise control over its CATV customers.

EMI also met the requirement that it merely provide wires, cables, or other communications channels for the use of others. The court found that EMI transmits nothing of its own creation and sells only its transmission services for the use of others within the meaning of the statute.

Because retransmission activities such as EMI's were developed after Congress had enacted the Copyright Act of 1976, the court looked to the common sense of the statute and the practical consequences of the suggested interpretation to divine and apply the intent of Congress. Congress, recognizing that a system requiring each CATV system to obtain the consent of or negotiate with numerous individual copyright owners would be unworkable, enacted a compulsory licensing scheme. Television broadcast stations like WOR-TV continue to pay license or royalty fees to copyright owners like Doubleday, while CATV systems pay a license fee to the Copyright Office in accordance with a formula based on percentages of gross receipts from subscribers, which are then distributed to copyright owners (17 U.S.C. § 111[d][2][B]). The court held that to require a separate entity like EMI, which provides intermediary services, to also pay the copyright owners for the right to retransmit their works would produce a result never intended by Congress — namely, a substantially increased royalty payment to copyright owners with no increase in the number of viewers. The court concluded that EMI's activities fell within the exemption from copyright liability in 17 U.S.C., section 111(a)(3).

Hubbard Broadcasting, Inc. v. Southern Satellite Systems, Inc., No. 3–81–Civ. 330, Slip Opinion (D. Minn. Aug. 23, 1984)

In this copyright infringement action, plaintiff claimed it had the exclusive right to televise certain works in particular geographic areas and that defendants, Southern Satellite Systems and Turner Broadcasting, allegedly showed the same works in this areas. In order to make a prima facie showing of copyright infringement, plaintiff first had to establish these five elements:

1. The originality and authorship of the compositions involved.
2. Compliance with all formalities required to secure a copyright under 17 U.S.C., section 101 et seq.
3. That plaintiff is the proprietor of the copyrights of the compositions involved.
4. That the compositions were publicly performed for profit.
5. That the defendants have not received permission from plaintiff or its representatives for such performance.

Since the first three elements were not in dispute, the only issues before the court were whether the works were performed publicly by both Turner and Southern, and in lieu of permission from plaintiffs, whether defendants were entitled to an exemption under 17 U.S.C., section 111. The court found that plaintiff met its burden of proving that the works were publicly performed for profit under the broad definition of section 101 of the Copyright Act, which stated that to perform or display a work "publicly means to transmit or otherwise communicate a performance or display of the work . . . to the public, by means of any device or process, whether the members of the public capable of receiving the performance or display receive it in the same place or in separate places and at the same home or at different times." Plaintiff argued that under this definition, it was clear that the act was intended to cover indirect as well as direct transmissions.

Turner originated performance of the works, and Southern's retransmission was independently a public performance. Defendants, however, argued that the works were not public because Southern's transmissions were to other cable systems, and the cable subscribers, not the cable systems, constituted the public. The court found this argument nonpersuasive and inconsistent with other portions of the act, particularly the passive carrier exemption of section 111(a)(3) and the compulsory licensing system of section 111(c). Additionally, there was no basis for excluding certain transmitters from copyright liability solely on their position in the distribution chain. The court thus found that works were publicly performed for profit.

The defendants agreed that they did not seek or receive permission from plaintiff under the fifth element of a copyright infringement, but argued that several subparts of section 111 justified their actions. The court first considered whether, under section 111(b), the secondary transmissions were actionable as acts of infringement and hence, precluded from qualifying for any exemptions. Plaintiffs had contended that Turner's practice of commercial substitution, whereby technicians could select national rather than local commercials, resulted in the application of section 111(b) because the primary transmission was no longer made for the public at large. The court, however, found that section 111(b) did not apply to this case, since in effect, Southern only received and retransmitted one signal — either the microwave or UHF. The commercial substitution on one of these signals constituting only 40 percent of the nonprogramming content did not require the application of section 111(b).

The defendants contended that Southern qualified for exemption under section 111(a) (3), the passive-carrier exemption, and that Southern had met all five of the necessary requirements. The court agreed. First, Southern was a carrier since it was licensed by the FCC as a resale common carrier. Second, the retransmissions were merely secondary trans-

missions of primary transmissions of the works. Third, Southern did not have direct or indirect control over the content or selection of the primary transmission. The court agreed with the Second Circuit in *Eastern Microwave, Inc. v. Doubleday Sports, Inc.*, 691 F. 2d 125 (2d Cir. 1982), that the technologically mandated initial choice of the broadcaster's signal to retransmit does not constitute selection. Except for the practice of commercial substitution, Southern is indistinguishable from EMI. Fourth, the court also agreed with the reasoning of EMI in finding that Southern did not exercise control over the particular recipients of the secondary transmission. The recipients were cable systems that complied with Southern's FCC tariff. Finally, Southern met the fifth requirement that the carrier's activities must consist solely of providing wires, cables, or other communications channels for the use of others. The court agreed with the EMI decision that this section did not prohibit normal business activities such as marketing and promotional efforts. The use of material inserted in the empty space of Turner's video signal also did not disqualify Southern from the exemption, primarily because plaintiff did not have a copyright interest in this space. Thus the court concluded that Southern met the requirements for a section 111(a)(3) carrier's exemption and that there was no basis for copyright infringement.

Plaintiff's final argument was that the practice of commercial substitution prevents the application of the section 111(c) compulsory license to Southern's cable system customers, and thus the dual goals of section 111 were circumvented. Section 111, by allowing an exemption to passive carriers and creating a compulsory licensing system, was designed to effect a compromise between encouraging the development of the cable TV industry and at the same time protecting local broadcasters and copyrighted works. The court found that the practice of commercial substitution did not result in the loss of the compulsory license for Southern's cable customers, since it did not change the nature of the transmission. The court was persuaded that the application of the carrier exemption was compatible with the compulsory license system and, in fact, furthered the dual goals embodied in section 111.

Thus Southern, as a matter of law, was not liable for copyright infringement, nor was Turner liable as a contributory infringer. Defendants' motion for a summary judgment was granted.

6.28 Consumers

Sports consumers do not own direct property rights in the events played or depicted through broadcasts. Even so, types of rights have been obtained in two instances.

The first area, where the fans benefit indirectly, is the ability of television stations to circumvent blackouts by teams and leagues of local telecasts where a game is sold out 72 hours in advance of its occurrence. For a time in the 1970's, anti-blackout provisions were mandated by federal law. At present, with the expiration of the federal statute, blackouts are lifted only through voluntary compliance of clubs and leagues. As the cases in Section 6.28–1 reveal, there is little legal precedent to force the lifting of blackouts, absent specific statutory prescription. Consequently, so long as fans must rely on voluntary compliance by leagues and clubs, the possibility that blackouts will be restored remains.

The second area relates to home taping of television programming. The principal case to date is *Sony Corp.* v. *Universal Studios, Inc.*, discussed at length in Section 6.28–2.

6.28–1 Blackouts

In *Blaich* v. *NFL*, 212 F. Supp. 319 (S.D. N.Y. 1962), an early attempt was made to force the lifting of a television blackout. The plaintiff sought a preliminary injunction to prevent the NFL from enforcing a blackout of its professional championship game (the term used before the NFL and AFL merged to put on the "Super Bowl"). In denying the injunction, the court held that the federal statutory provisions (15 U.S.C., sections 1291–1295), which authorized a league to sell its games as a package to networks and stations, also allowed it to restrict the televising of particular games in the home territory of a team on a day when that club was playing at home. The court held this applied to championship games, as well as to regular season contests.

The cases that follow represent numerous other attempts, largely unsuccessful, to lift blackouts. Of course, the fans were victorious to some extent when 47 U.S.C., section 331 was enacted, and blackouts were lifted in certain situations. Although that law has expired, sports leagues still adhere to its strictures on a voluntary basis. How long that will continue can be questioned. In any event, the holdings in the following cases continue to be important.

Campo v. NFL, 334 F. Supp. 1181 (E.D. Pa. 1971)

Plaintiff John Campo sought an injunction against the National Football League, alleging the league was in violation of the Clayton Act because of its television broadcast policies for the 1972 Super Bowl. The NFL, adhering to Article X of its constitution, prohibited any television station within 75 miles of the city where the game was being played from broadcasting the game. Plaintiff, a major stockholder of two motels within 75 miles of New Orleans, the site of the Super Bowl, brought the action before the date of the game.

The court cited the material facts and noted there was no dispute as to their accuracy. The Super Bowl, jointly owned by all 26 NFL member teams, was to be played in New Orleans on January 16, 1972, and it was to be broadcast by CBS television. Article X of the NFL constitution gave the NFL commissioner control over all radio and television rights. Following the uniform practice of 20 years, the commissioner chose to black out the game in accordance with section 10.5, calling for a blackout within a 75-mile radius of New Orleans. Plaintiff was apparently claiming that since his hotels were within the radius, he was suffering an injury. The court, however, found no injury.

The court never reached the substantive merits of the claim because it held plaintiff had no standing to bring the action. His injury as a stockholder in the hotel corporation had to be direct, not merely consequential or derivative, and he failed to show any injury at all. Furthermore, the court held that plaintiff was not typical of a class of motel owners and would not adequately protect the interests of the class. The corporation had no standing because it was not within the area of the economy that would be endangered by a breakdown of competitive conditions, not having shown it would suffer any damages. Plaintiff acknowledged hotels would be full that weekend. The action was dismissed.

Hertel v. City of Pontiac, 470 F. Supp. 603 (E.D. Mich. 1979)

Two residents of the metropolitan Detroit area challenged the constitutionality on equal protection grounds of defendant NFL's blackout rule, which prohibits television broadcasts of "home" football games in areas within 75 miles of the home stadium. The district court held that since the city of Pontiac subleased to the Detroit Lions and received revenues from ticket sales, parking, and concessions, the conduct of the defendant city should be treated as state action, subject to Fourteenth Amendment review.

The classification drawn was geographic, and not based on a suspect class or fundamental interest triggering strict scrutiny. Therefore, the standard of review was the rational relation test. The court held that the operation of a profitable stadium was a legitimate public purpose, and the blackout rule, designed to increase home game attendance, was rationally

related to the profitable operation of the Silverdome.

WTWV, Inc. v. NFL, 678 F. 2d 142 (11th Cir. 1982)

Plaintiff television station, located 96 miles north of Miami, Florida, penetrated its signal 40 miles into the Miami Dolphins home territory. The plaintiffs brought suit when defendant NFL refused to authorize a broadcast of the Dolphins' home game, which was not sold out, based on the NFL bylaw defining home territory for the purpose of the blackout as 75 miles from the club's city.

The plaintiff claimed that in 15 U.S.C.A., section 1292, "televising" meant originating a signal, thus permitting blackout only when the transmitter is located inside Dolphins territory. The court, however, stated that to hold as the plaintiffs alleged would destroy the purpose of the statute. Congress intended to preserve the existence of the NFL by shielding its clubs from a decline in game attendance due to television coverage in the area from which spectators are drawn. Technological advances that permit a station such as the plaintiff's to be physically located outside the prescribed area, yet transmit its signal into the home territory, would undermine the protective shield.

The court, holding that signal penetration rather than station location determines whether a station is televising within the home territory, thus upheld the blackout.

6.28–2 Home Taping

In *Sony Corp. v. Universal Studios, Inc.*, discussed below, sports interests were not directly involved in bringing or framing the arguments in the suit. However, there is clear overlap between the concerns expressed by motion picture producers, fighting to control the copying of their product, and sports owners, seeking to preserve films of their games for their own future financial advantages. At the same time, there are differences. The timeliness of a sports event does make it of lesser lasting quality than a classic motion picture.

Despite this, other interests involved in the telecasting of sports events will argue that home taping has an adverse effect. Sponsors of the televised event, for example, feel that viewers watching a tape will "fast forward" the advertisements, causing the message to be lost. Thus, there is need to read the *Sony* case with great care, considering the sports interests, as well as those more directly articulated in the decision.

In the *Sony* case, the U.S. Supreme Court obviously struggled with the issues. At one point, the Court ordered reargument of the case. Only after several months' deliberation did the Court reach its decision.

Sony Corp. v. Universal City Studios, Inc., 464 U.S.—, 78 L. Ed. 574 (1984)

The two respondents, Universal Studios and Walt Disney Productions, brought a copyright infringement action against Sony Corporation, the manufacturer of Betamax video tape recorders (VTRs). The suit alleged that some individuals had used the VTRs to record certain of respondents' copyrighted works, which had been exhibited on commercially sponsored television. The respondents did not seek relief against any Betamax consumer, but rather maintained that Sony was liable for the copyright infringement because of its marketing of the product. Respondents sought money damages and an equitable accounting of profits as well as an injunction against the manufacture and marketing of the Betamax VTR.

Both parties had conducted surveys of the way the Betamax machine was used during a sample period in 1978. Essentially, both surveys showed that the primary use of the machine for most owners was "time-shifting" — the practice of recording a television show to view it once at a later time and then erasing it. Additionally, a substantial number of inter-

viewees had also accumulated libraries of tapes. After a lengthy trial, the district court concluded that this noncommercial home use recording of a broadcast over the public airwaves was a fair use and did not constitute copyright infringement, primarily because there was no accompanying reduction in the market for plaintiff's original work. As an independent ground of decision, the decision court also concluded that Sony could not be held liable as a contributory infringer since "Sony merely sold a product capable of a variety of uses, some of them allegedly infringing." Finally, the court concluded that an injunction was wholly inappropriate because any harm to petitioners was outweighed by the fact that the VTR could still legally be used, and an injunction would deprive the public of the use of the Betamax for noninfringing recording.

The court of appeals, however, reversed the district court's judgment, concluding as a matter of law that the home use of a VTR was not a fair use because it was not a productive use. On the issue of contributory infringement, the court rejected the district court's reliance on Sony's lack of knowledge that home use constituted infringement, and held Sony chargeable with knowledge because the reproduction of copyrighted works was either the "most conspicuous use" or the major use" of the Betamax product. The court of appeals concluded that statutory damages might be appropriate and in remanding to the district court, referred to "the analogous photocopying area" and suggested that a continuing royalty pursuant to a judicially created compulsory license might be an acceptable resolution of the relief issue.

In fashioning its decision, the U.S. Supreme Court first generally noted that the basic purpose of the copyright law — to stimulate artistic creativity for the general good — must be kept in mind as new technological innovations alter the market and render the terms of copyright law ambiguous. The judiciary thus should be reluctant to expand the protections of the copyright without explicit legislative guidance.

The specific issue before the Court was whether users of the Betamax had infringed respondents' copyrights and whether Sony should be held responsible for that infringement. In both copyright and patent law, this contributory infringement doctrine is grounded on the recognition that adequate protection of a monopoly may require that courts look beyond the actual duplication to the product that makes such duplication possible. However, there is a balance to be struck between the protection of the monopoly and the rights of others to engage freely in substantially unrelated areas of commerce. No contributory infringement thus existed if the Betamax was found capable of substantial noninfringing uses.

Relying on the district court's findings of fact, the Supreme Court held that the private, noncommercial, time-shifting use in the home was a substantial, commercial significant use of the Betamax. This use satisfied the standard because (1) respondents had no right to prevent other copyright holders from authorizing its use, and (2) even the unauthorized, home time-shifting was a legitimate fair use.

First, the district court's findings of fact indicated that sports, religious, educational, and other programming welcomed the practice of time-shifting and would continue to authorize it in the future. In an action for contributory infringement, copyright holders may not prevail unless the relief they seek affects only their programs, or unless they speak for virtually all copyright holders with an interest in the outcome. The record from the district court clearly showed that many producers of local and national programs found nothing objectionable in the practice, as it would enlarge the size of the television audience. Thus, Sony could not be a contributory infringer since respondents could not prevent other copyright holders from authorizing its legitimate use.

As to the unauthorized time-shifting, the Court supported the district court's conclusion that home time-shifting was a "fair use." The general rule in copyright law is that an unlicensed use is not an infringement unless it conflicts with one of the specific exclusive rights conferred by the copyright statute. Specifically, in 17 U.S.C., section 107, the legislature endorsed the doctrine of fair use, enabling a court to consider the commercial or nonprofit character of the activity and the effect of the use on the potential market for or value of the copyrighted work.

The district court's findings had clearly established that the time-shifting was a noncommercial, nonprofit activity. Respondents had failed to carry their burden of proof with regard to a showing that some meaningful likelihood of future harm existed, and respondents had admitted that no actual harm to their copyrights had occurred to date. Furthermore, to the extent that time-shifting expanded public access to freely broadcasted programs, it yielded societal benefits. Since the Betamax was capable of substantial noninfringing uses, Sony's sale of the VTR to the general public did not constitute contributory infringement of respondents' copyrights.

The dissent, written by Justice Blackman and joined by justices Marshall, Powell, and Rehnquist, criticized the majority's narrow standard of contributory infringement and stated that the Court has "once again" confused the issue of liability with that of remedy. Under the dissent's analysis, the home taping of television programs did not fall within the fair use exemption, since the user simply reproduces an entire work and uses it with no added benefit to the public. A productive use is at the crux of the fair use doctrine; copied works that are used for socially laudable purposes, such as by scholars or researchers, result in some added benefit to the public beyond that produced by the first author's work. Such a benefit was not presented by Betamax owners. Nor was the harm to the authors de minimis; the respondents and their *amici* had demonstrated that they had been deprived of the ability to exploit the potential market of viewers who use time-shifting. Finally, the dissent agreed with the court of appeals that Sony had induced and materially contributed to the infringing conduct of Betamax owners.

6.30 Limitations on Teams Dealing Through Cooperative Ventures

In the formative years of broadcast sports, the accepted procedure was that a team (professional or college) would sell its broadcast rights to a local station or, at times, a corporate sponsor. It was a one-to-one venture, with the buyer of the rights then seeing if any sort of networking with other stations could be achieved. The umbrella organizations — leagues on the professional level and conferences and associations on the amateur — largely stayed out of the process. Each team made its best deal.

As the technologies developed and the potential financial rewards grew, it became apparent that the then prevailing system of doing business might not be optimal. If teams pooled their product, even greater monies could be realized. There was not complete unanimity supporting this approach, since some teams did very well on their own. Accommodations were made for them, however, leaving some local territorial rights.

A larger hurdle was whether the pooling of rights was (or is) legal. This chapter examines three major developments of the past 25 years. The first (Section 6.31) deals with professional sports teams' attempts to deal on a league-wide basis with the networks.

This is followed (Section 6.32) by the corollary occurrence in intercollegiate sports, where the National Collegiate Athletic Association assumed almost total control over televising college football. This led to several legal challenges, culminating in *NCAA v. Board of Regents*, which is set forth below.

The final consideration of the chapter (Section 6.33) concerns the most recent development. Clubs in different professional sports, but located in the same geographical area, are

entering the broadcast business themselves. Typically, a company is formed with the sports clubs, two or more, participating as part owners in the venture. As the considerations reveal, the legality of the ventures will be challenged.

6.31 Pooling Rights in Professional Sports

Professional sports leagues determined early that certain controls would have to be placed on member clubs to prevent one club invading another's home territory with unwanted broadcasts of games. The rules adopted by the National Football League were typical and also led to legal challenge in *U.S. v. NFL* (Part I), discussed below. This case did not directly concern the pooling of rights for purposes of contracting as a league. It dealt only with a league's ability to circumscribe the activities of its members and their contracting parties.

Within a few years of the first *U.S. v. NFL* decision, the league determined its best future lay in the teams dealing collectively with one or more networks to obtain a wide-ranging agreement for televising NFL games. The league first thought it prudent to return to the same federal court that had heard its earlier case to determine if dealing on a league-wide basis were permitted by the court's 1953 decree. The court, however, decided that its earlier decree did not permit such dealing (see *U.S. v. NFL*: Part II below). This left the NFL and other sports leagues in a quandary as to what action to take next.

The answer was to approach members of Congress to seek a change in the antitrust laws to permit league-wide dealing. In a remarkably short time, Congress responded affirmatively. Though conditions were attached to the legislation that would later hamper certain leagues' desired courses of action, a broad exemption to negotiate on league-wide bases was accorded professional football, basketball, hockey, and baseball. The latter of course was already exempt because of earlier court decisions, such as *Federal Baseball Club of Baltimore v. National League of Professional Baseball*

Clubs, 259 U.S. 200 (1922) and *Toolson* v. *New York Yankees*, 346 U.S. 356 (1953). (See Volume I, Chapter 2, Section 2.22.) Even so, an express immunity could only strengthen baseball's position.

The statutory provisions in question are 15 U.S.C. Sections 1291–1294, set forth below. They have been amended since their passage in 1961. Notable is the provision in Section 1291, adding language that allowed the merger of the National and American Football Leagues in the late 1960's.

The provisions of 15 U.S.C. Sections 1291–1294 should be analyzed closely, along with cases that have examined the statute's application. That the process is an on-going one is highlighted by the announcement by the U.S. Justice Department in late 1984 that it would approve the televising of United States Football League games on Saturdays when that league went to a fall schedule in 1986. It is a mystery where the Justice Department finds the authority to ignore the clear and unqualified restrictions of Section 1293. As they say in broadcasting, "stay tuned — it's not over yet."

United States v. NFL, 116 F. Supp. 319 (E.D. Pa. 1953) (NFL: Part 1)

The government filed this antitrust action seeking an injunction against the enforcement of certain provisions of Article X of the bylaws of the National Football League. Three restrictions of Article X effectively prevented live broadcasts or telecasts of practically all "outside games" in all home territories. The fourth provision gave the football commissioner unlimited power to prevent the broadcasting or televising of any or every game. The U.S. argued that each provision was an illegal restraint of trade or commerce under the Sherman Act, 15 U.S.C., Section 1.

The court found that the provision which prevented the telecasting of outside games into the home territories of other teams on days when the other teams are playing at home was not illegal. The restriction was a restraint of trade; it allocated marketing territories among competitors. But a restraint of trade must be unreasonable to be illegal.

Professional football is a unique type of business. This provision aimed to protect home game gate attendance, the greatest source of a club's income. Telecasts of a more popular team's game in another team's home game territory could adversely affect gate attendance. Unrestricted competition in this area would cause the winning and wealthier teams to get richer, while the weaker teams suffered financial failure. Without sufficient teams, there would be no league.

The court found that this restriction reasonably promoted competition more than it restrained it; its immediate effect was to protect the weak teams, and its ultimate effect was to preserve the league itself.

The second provision restricted the telecasting of outside games in home territories when the home teams were playing away games. The court admitted that the simultaneous telecasting of an outside game and an away game in the away team's home area would result in a division of the television audience. There was no evidence, however, that this would have a subsequent effect on the home team's gate attendance or receipts. The courts chose to measure the reasonableness of a restriction by its effect on the attendance and gate receipts. When a team plays away, there is no gate to protect. Thus, this provision was an unreasonable and illegal restraint of trade, which merely enabled clubs in the home territories to sell monopoly television rights.

The third provision restricted the radio broadcasting of outside games in home territories on days when the home teams were playing at home and on days when the home teams were playing away games and were either televising or broadcasting them in their home territories. The court found it apparent that no club felt that such radio broadcasting had any significant adverse effect on gate attendance since each club permitted the radio broadcasting of *all* its games in its home area.

The restriction enhanced the value of monopoly broadcast rights but had no significant effect on attendance. Thus, the court found that territorial restrictions on the sale of radio broadcast rights were illegal under the Sherman Act.

Article X gave the football commissioner the unlimited and arbitrary power to prevent the broadcasting and televising of any and every game. If the court did not restrict the commissioner's power, he could circumvent its rulings on the provisions deemed illegal.

The NFL argued that the action should be dismissed because professional football is not commerce or interstate commerce. The court rejected this argument as immaterial since the case concerned the league's restraint of interstate commerce in the radio and television industries.

The court dismissed the government's claim for injunctive relief with respect to the restraint-of-trade. The court enjoined the restriction of the sale of rights for the telecasting of outside games in a club's home territory on a day when the home club is permitting the telecast of its away game in its home territory, all territorial restrictions on the sale of radio broadcasting rights, and the exercise of the commissioner's power under Article X to enforce the provisions now deemed illegal.

United States v. NFL, 196 F. Supp. 445 (E.D. Pa. 1961) (NFL: Part 2)

Defendants sought a construction of the final judgment entered in this case (116 F. Supp. 319 [see Part I]) to the effect that a contract dated April 24, 1961, between the National Football League (NFL) and the Columbia Broadcasting System (CBS) does not violate the judgment.

The contract granted CBS the sole and exclusive right to televise all league games for two years, with limited exceptions. After certain deductions, the league was to distribute the $4,650,000 annual license fee equally among the 14 NFL teams.

Prior to this contract, each club individually negotiated and sold the television rights to its games. Each club pooled its television rights and authorized the commissioner to sell its television rights as a package, which he did under the 1961 NFL–CBS contract. In effect, by agreement, the clubs eliminated competition among themselves.

The contract granted CBS the sole authority to determine which games would be televised and where. But the final judgment enjoined the NFL from making any agreement "having the purpose or effect of restricting the areas within which broadcasts or telecasts of games . . . may be made." Thus, the court held that the final judgment did prohibit the execution and performance of the NFL–CBS contract.

15 United States Code, Chapter 32, "Telecasting of Professional Sports Contests"

Section 1291. *Exemption from antitrust laws of agreements covering telecasting of sports contests and combining of professional football leagues*

The antitrust laws, as defined in section 12 of this title or in the Federal Trade Commission Act, as amended, shall not apply to any joint agreement by or among persons engaging in or conducting the organized professional team sports of football, baseball, basketball, or hockey, by which any league of clubs participating in professional football, baseball, basketball, or hockey contests sells or otherwise transfers all or any part of the rights of such league's member clubs in the sponsored telecasting of the games of football, baseball, basketball, or hockey, as the case may be, engaged in or conducted by such clubs. In addition, such laws shall not apply to a joint agreement by which the member clubs of two or more professional football leagues, which are exempt from income tax under section

501(c)(6) of Title 26, combine their operations in expanded single league so exempt from income tax, if such agreement increases rather than decreases the number of professional football clubs so operating, and the provisions of which are directly relevant thereto.

Section 1292. *Area telecasting restriction limitation*

Section 1291 of this title shall not apply to any joint agreement described in the first sentence in such section which prohibits any person to whom such rights are sold or transferred from televising any games within any area, except within the home territory of a member club of the league on a day when such club is playing a game at home.

Section 1293. *Intercollegiate and interscholastic football contest limitations*

The first sentence of section 1291 of this title shall not apply to any joint agreement described in such section which permits the telecasting of all or a substantial part of any professional football game on any Friday after six o'clock postmeridian or on any Saturday during the period beginning on the second Friday in September and ending on the second Saturday in December in any year from any telecasting station located within seventy-five miles of the game site of any intercollegiate or interscholastic football contest scheduled to be played on such a date if—

(1) such intercollegiate football contest is between institutions of higher learning, both of which confer degrees upon students following completion of sufficient credit hours to equal a four-year course, or

(2) in the case of an interscholastic football contest, such contest is between secondary schools, both of which are accredited or certified under the laws of the State or States in which they are situated and offer courses continuing through the twelfth grade of the standard school curriculum, or the equivalent, and

(3) such intercollegiate or interscholastic football contest and such game site were announced through publication in a newspaper of general circulation prior to August 1 of such year as being regularly scheduled for such day and place.

Section 1294. *Antitrust laws unaffected as regards to other activities of professional sports contests*

Nothing contained in this chapter shall be deemed to change, determine, or otherwise affect the applicability or nonapplicability of the antitrust laws to any act, contract, agreement, rule, course of conduct, or other activity by, between, or among persons engaging in, conducting, or participating in the organized professional team sports of football, baseball, basketball, or hockey, except the agreements to which section 1291 of this title shall apply.

Colorado High School Activities Ass'n. v. NFL, 711 F. 2d 943 (10th Cir. 1983)

Plaintiff school districts and interscholastic competition governing board brought this action against the NFL, Commissioner Pete Rozelle, and NBC and CBS, alleging state and federal antitrust violations by virtue of defendants' broadcasts of particular professional football games in 1977, 1978, and 1979.

An exception to the antitrust laws, 15 U.S.C., section 1291 (1976), enabled member clubs to pool together and sell a package of rights to telecast their games to a television network. This exemption, however, was limited by 15 U.S.C., section 1293 (1976), which was enacted to prevent such package contracts from impairing high school and college gate receipts. Schools could invoke the limitation by announcing the game site through publication in a newspaper of general circulation prior to August 1 of that year. If this limitation was thus invoked, NFL games could not be broadcast from any television station within 75 miles of the game site.

During the three years at issue, plaintiffs attempted to comply by announcing that the state championship games would be played "in Denver," or "in the Denver metropolitan area," when in fact, in 1977 and 1978, the game was held in Boulder and in 1979, in Lakewood. Professional football games were telecast in Denver on all three dates.

Plaintiffs contended that because championship games were played on the home field of one of the finalists, and the finalists were not known until shortly before the final game, plaintiffs gave the best game site designation possible by August 1 of the relevant years. To require a more specific game site identification would frustrate the congressional purpose of protecting high school gate receipts.

The court resolved the issue using the fundamental principle of statutory construction: if the statutory language is unambiguous, in the absence of a clearly expressed legislative intent to the contrary, the language is conclusive. The common sense, unambiguous meaning of "game site" was that particular football field or stadium where the game was to be played. This construction fulfilled the purpose underlying the statutory scheme, which was to provide a specific, fixed point from which to establish the 75-mile blackout rule. In view of the plain meaning of the statute, the court was unwilling to readjust the balance of competing interest struck by Congress.

Henderson Broadcasting Corp. v. Houston Sports, 541 F. Supp. 263 (S.D. Tex. 1982)

Plaintiff radio station KYST-AM sued Houston Sports Association, the owner of the Houston Association, the owner of the Houston Astros baseball team, and the owner of the KENR-AM radio station, charging violations of the Sherman Act and breach of contract. The gist of the complaint was that the Astros canceled KYST's contract to broadcast the Astro's baseball games and entered into a conspiracy with KENR to divide and allocate audiences in the Houston-Galveston radio market and eliminate competition. Defendants moved to dismiss for lack of subject matter jurisdiction and failure to state a claim on the grounds that defendants' actions fell within the baseball exemption from the antitrust laws.

The court, however, held that defendants' alleged actions were not exempt. First, the line of U.S. Supreme Court cases had implied that broadcasting was not central enough to baseball to be encompassed in the baseball exemption. After reviewing *Federal Baseball Club of Baltimore, Inc.* v. *National League of Professional Baseball Clubs*, 259 U.S. 200 (1922), *Toolson* v. *New York Yankees*, 346 U.S. 356 (1953), and *Flood* v. *Kuhn*, 407 U.S. 258 (1972), the court concluded that the stare decisis basis for the exemption was an aberration that was narrow in scope. Courts consistently have refused to extend the exemption to other sports, in part because the interstate broadcasting of the sports thrust them into interstate commerce. The court found it perplexing that broadcasting on one hand had subjected other pro sports to the antitrust laws, but on the other hand had not affected the baseball exemption. However, because radio broadcasting is not a part of the sport in the way players, league structure, and the reserve system are, the court concluded that defendants' actions were not within the baseball exemption.

The court next found that Congress clearly had not extended the exemption to cover other businesses related to baseball. In refusing to extend the exemption to other sports, Congress had recognized that professional organized sports are involved in extraneous business activities. To extend the exemption would contravene the federal antitrust laws. Moreover, on the question of exemption of the television broadcast of sports from the antitrust laws, Congress had legislated no differently with regard to baseball than it had with football, basketball, and hockey.

Finally, an examination of judicial application of the baseball exemption showed that in antitrust actions involving baseball teams and nonexempt business enterprises, no court had granted a dismissal on the grounds that baseball was somehow implicated. The court thus concluded that the baseball exemption as it stands today is an anachronism in light of the changes in the economics of the sport and that defendants had not presented a reason to extend it.

6.32   Amateur Sports Pooling Arrangements

The total picture in the broadcast of amateur sports is a complex one. A variety of approaches are taken. It is noteworthy that the exempting language of 15 U.S.C. Sections 1291–1294, allowing teams to deal collectively, is restricted to *professional* sports leagues (see Section 6.31). Whether members of Congress, in specifying only professional sports, were of the opinion that amateur sports were not commerce and thus were not affected by the federal antitrust laws is unknown.

What is clear is that today the televising of amateur sports, particularly men's intercollegiate football and basketball, has become a big-money business. While the National Collegiate Athletic Association largely left decisions as to televising basketball to the individual schools and conferences, the NCAA placed tight controls over the televising of intercollegiate football. It was inevitable that a major lawsuit would result at some point.

National Collegiate Athletic Ass'n. v. Board of Regents of U. of Oklahoma and U. of Georgia Athletic Ass'n., 468 U.S. ——, 82 L. Ed. 70 (1984)

Justice Stevens delivered the opinion of the Court.

The University of Oklahoma and the University of Georgia contend that the National Collegiate Athletic Association has unreasonably restrained trade in the televising of college football games. After an extended trial, the District Court found

that the NCAA had violated § 1 of the Sherman Act and granted injunctive relief. 546 F. Supp. 1276 (W.D. Okla. 1982). The Court of Appeals agreed that the statute had been violated but modified the remedy in some respects. 707 F. 2d 1147 (C.A.10 1983). We granted certiorari, 464 U.S. —— (1983), and now affirm.

I

The NCAA

Since its inception in 1905, the NCAA has played an important role in the regulation of amateur collegiate sports. It has adopted and promulgated playing rules, standards of amateurism, standards for academic eligibility, regulations concerning recruitment of athletes, and rules governing the size of athletic squads and coaching staffs. In some sports, such as baseball, swimming, basketball, wrestling and track, it has sponsored and conducted national tournaments. It has not done so in the sport of football, however. With the exception of football, the NCAA has not undertaken any regulation of the televising of athletic events.

The NCAA has approximately 850 voting members. The regular members are classified into separate divisions to reflect differences in size and scope of their athletic programs. Division I includes 276 colleges with major athletic programs; in this group only 187 play intercollegiate football. Divisions II and III include approximately 500 colleges with less extensive athletic programs. Division I has been subdivided into Divisions I-A and I-AA for football.

Some years ago, five major conferences together with major football-playing independent institutions organized the College Football Association (CFA). The original purpose of the CFA was to promote the interests of major football-playing schools within the NCAA structure. The Universities of Oklahoma and Georgia, respondents in this Court, are members of the CFA.

History of the NCAA Television Plan

. . . The plan adopted in 1981 for the 1982–1985 seasons is at issue in this case. This plan, like each of its predecessors, recites that it is intended to reduce, insofar as possible, the adverse effects of live television upon football game attendance. It provides that "all forms of television of the football games of NCAA member institutions during the Plan control periods shall be in accordance with this Plan." App. The plan recited that a television committee has awarded rights to negotiate and contract for the telecasting of college football games of members of the NCAA to two "carrying networks." . . . In addition to the principal award of rights to the carrying networks, the plan also describes rights for a "supplementary series" that had been awarded for the 1982 and 1983 seasons, as well as a procedure for permitting specific "exception telecasts."

In separate agreements with each of the carrying networks, ABC and the Columbia Broadcasting System (CBS), the NCAA granted each the right to telecast the 14 live "exposures" described in the plan, in accordance with the "ground rules" set forth therein. Each of the networks agreed to pay a specified "minimum aggregate compensation to the participating NCAA member institutions" during the 4-year period in an amount that totaled $131,750,000. In essence the agreement authorized each network to negotiate directly with member schools for the right to televise their games. The agreement itself does not describe the method of computing the compensation for each game, but the practice that has developed over the years and that the District Court found would be followed under the current agreement involved the setting of a recommended fee by a representative of the NCAA for different types of telecasts, with national telecasts being the most valuable, regional telecasts being less valuable, and Division II or Division III games commanding a still lower price. The aggregate of all these payments presumably equals the total minimum aggregate compensation set forth in the basic agreement. Except for differences in payment between national and regional telecasts, and with respect to Division II and Division III games, the amount that any team receives does not change with the size of the viewing audience, the number of markets in which the game is telecast, or the particular characteristic of the game or the participating teams. Instead, the "ground rules" provide that the carrying networks make alternate selections of those games they wish to televise, and thereby obtain the exclusive right to submit

a bid at an essentially fixed price to the institutions involved.

The plan also contains "appearance requirements" and "appearance limitations" which pertain to each of the 2-year periods that the plan is in effect. The basic requirement imposed on each of the two networks is that it must schedule appearances for at least 82 different member institutions during each 2-year period. Under the appearance limitations no member institution is eligible to appear on television more than a total of six times and more than four times nationally, with the appearances to be divided equally between the two carrying networks. . . . The number of exposures specified in the contracts also sets an absolute maximum on the number of games that can be broadcast.

Thus, although the current plan is more elaborate than any of its predecessors, it retains the essential features of each of them. It limits the total amount of televised intercollegiate football and the number of games that any one team may televise. No member is permitted to make any sale of television rights except in accordance with the basic plan.

Background of this Controversy

Beginning in 1979 CFA members began to advocate that colleges with major football programs should have a greater voice in the formulation of football television policy than they had in the NCAA. CFA therefore investigated the possibility of negotiating a television agreement of its own, developed an independent plan, and obtained a contract offer from the National Broadcasting Co. (NBC). This contract, which it signed in August 1981, would have allowed a more liberal number of appearances for each institution, and would have increased the overall revenues realized by CFA members. . . .

In response the NCAA publicly announced that it would take disciplinary action against any CFA member that complied with the CFA-NBC contract. The NCAA made it clear that sanctions would not be limited to the football programs of CFA members, but would apply to other sports as well. On September 8, 1981, respondents commenced this action in the United States District Court for the Western District of

Oklahoma and obtained a preliminary injunction preventing the NCAA from initiating disciplinary proceedings or otherwise interfering with CFA's efforts to perform its agreement with NBC. Notwithstanding the entry of the injunction, most CFA members were unwilling to commit themselves to the new contractual arrangement with NBC in the face of the threatened sanctions and therefore the agreement was never consummated. . . .

Decision of the District Court

After a full trial, the District Court held that the controls exercised by the NCAA over the televising of college football games violated the Sherman Act. The District Court defined the relevant market as "live college football television" because it found that alternative programming has a significantly different and lesser audience appeal. . . . The District Court then concluded that the NCAA controls over college football are those of a "classic cartel.". . .

The District Court found that competition in the relevant market had been restrained in three ways: (1) NCAA fixed the price for particular telecasts; (2) its exclusive network contracts were tantamount to a group boycott of all other potential broadcasters and its threat of sanctions against its own members constituted a threatened boycott of potential competitors; and (3) its plan placed an artificial limit on the production of televised college football. . . .

Decision of the Court of Appeals

The Court of Appeals held that the NCAA television plan constituted illegal *per se* price fixing. . . . It rejected each of the three arguments advanced by the NCAA to establish the procompetitive character of its plan. First, the court rejected the argument that the television plan promoted live attendance, noting that since the plan involved a concomitant reduction in viewership the plan did not result in a net increase in output and hence was not procompetitive. Second, the Court of Appeals rejected as illegitimate the NCAA's purpose of promoting athletically balanced competition. It held that such a consideration amounted to an argument that "competition will destroy the market" — a position inconsistent with the policy of the

Sherman Act. Moreover, assuming *arguendo* that the justification was legitimate, the court agreed with the District Court's finding "that any contribution the plan made to athletic balance could be achieved by less restrictive means." . . .

Third, the Court of Appeals refused to view the NCAA Plan as competitive justified by the need to compete effectively with other types of television programming, since it entirely eliminated competition between producers of football and hence was illegal *per se*.

Finally, the Court of Appeals concluded that even if the television plan were not *per se* illegal, its anticompetitive limitation on price and output was not offset by any procompetitive justification sufficient to save the plan even when the totality of the circumstances was examined. . . .

II

There can be no doubt that the challenged practices of the NCAA constitute a "restraint of trade" in the sense that they limit members' freedom to negotiate and enter into their own television contracts. In that sense, however, every contract is a restraint of trade, and as we have repeatedly recognized, the Sherman Act was intended to prohibit only unreasonable restraints of trade.

It is also undeniable that these practices share characteristics of restraints we have previously held unreasonable. The NCAA is an association of schools which compete against each other to attract television revenues, not to mention fans and athletes. As the District Court found, the policies of the NCAA with respect to television rights are ultimately controlled by the vote of member institutions. By participating in an association which prevents member institutions from competing against each other on the basis of price or kind of television rights that can be offered to broadcasters, the NCAA member institutions have created a horizontal restraint — an agreement among competitors on the way in which they will compete with one another. A restraint of this type has often been held to be unreasonable as a matter of law. Because it places a ceiling on the number of games member institutions may televise, the horizontal agreement places an artificial limit on the quantity of televised football that is available to broadcasters and consumers. By restraining the quantity of television rights available for sale, the challenged practices create a limitation on output; our cases have held that such limitations are unreasonable restraints of trade. Moreover, the District Court found that the minimum aggregate price in fact operates to preclude any price negotiation between broadcasters and institutions, thereby constituting horizontal price fixing, perhaps the paradigm of an unreasonable restraint of trade.

Horizontal price-fixing and output limitation are ordinarily condemned as a matter of law under an "illegal *per se*" approach because the probability that these practices are anti-competitive is so high; a *per se* rule is applied when "the practice facially appears to be one that would always or almost always tend to restrict competition and decrease output." *Broadcast Music, Inc. v. CBS*, 441 U.S. 1, 19–20 (1979). In such circumstances a restraint is presumed unreasonable without inquiry into the particular market context in which it is found. Nevertheless, we have decided that it would be inappropriate to apply a *per se* rule to this case. This decision is not based on a lack of judicial experience with this type of arrangement, on the fact that the NCAA is organized as a nonprofit entity, or on our respect for the NCAA's historic role in the preservation and encouragement of intercollegiate amateur athletics. Rather, what is critical is that this case involves an industry in which horizontal restraints on competition are essential if the product is to be available at all.

As Judge Bork has noted: "[S]ome activities can only be carried out jointly. Perhaps the leading example is league sports. When a league of professional lacrosse teams is informed, it would be pointless to declare their cooperation illegal on the ground that there are no other professional lacrosse teams." R. Bork, "The Antitrust Paradox" 278 (1978). What the NCAA and its member institutions market in this case is competition itself — contests between competing institutions. . . . Thus, the NCAA plays a vital role in enabling college football to preserve its character, and as a result enables a product to be marketed which might otherwise be unavailable. In performing this role, its actions widen consumer choice — not only the choices available to sports fans but also those available to athletes — and hence can be viewed as procompetitive.

Broadcast Music squarely holds that a joint selling arrangement may be so efficient that it will increase sellers' aggregate output and thus be procompetitive. . . . Similarly, as we indicated in *Continental T.V., Inc. v. GTE Sylvania Inc.*, 433 U.S. 36, 51–57 (1977), a restraint in a limited aspect of a market may actually enhance market-wide competition. Respondents concede that the great majority of the NCAA's regulations enhance competition among member institutions. Thus, despite the fact that this case involves restraints on the ability of member institutions to compete in terms of price and output, a fair evaluation of their competitive character requires consideration of the NCAA's justifications for the restraints. . . .

III

Because it restrains price and output, the NCAA's television plan has a significant potential for anticompetitive effects. The findings of the District Court indicate that this potential has been realized. The District Court found that if member institutions were free to sell television rights, many more games would be shown on television, and that the NCAA's output restriction has the effect of raising the price the networks pay for television rights. Moreover, the court found that by fixing a price for television rights to all games, the NCAA creates a price structure that is unresponsive to viewer demand and unrelated to the prices that would prevail in a competitive market. And, of course, since as a practical matter all member institutions need NCAA approval, members have no real choice but to adhere to the NCAA's television controls.

The anticompetitive consequences of this arrangement are apparent. Individual competitors lose their freedom to compete. Price is higher and output lower than they would otherwise be, and both are unresponsive to consumer preference. This latter point is perhaps the most significant, since "Congress designed the Sherman Act as a 'consumer welfare prescription.'" *Reiter* v. *Sonotone Corp.*, 442 U.S. 330, 343 (1979). A restraint that has the effect of reducing the importance of consumer preference in setting price and output is not consistent with this fundamental goal of antitrust law. Restrictions on price and output are the paradigmatic examples of restraints of trade that the Sherman Act was intended to prohibit. See *Standard Oil Co.* v. *United States*, 221 U.S. 1, 52–60 (1911). At the same time, the television plan eliminates competitors from the market, since only those broadcasters able to bid on television rights covering the entire NCAA can compete. Thus, as the District Court found, many telecasts that would occur in a competitive market are foreclosed by the NCAA's plan.

Petitioner argues, however, that its television plan can have no significant anticompetitive effect since the record indicates that it has no market power — no ability to alter the interaction of supply and demand in the market. We must reject this argument for two reasons, one legal, one factual.

As a matter of law, the absence of proof of market power does not justify a naked restriction on price or output. To the contrary, when there is an agreement not to compete in terms of price or output, "no elaborate industry analysis is required to demonstrate the anticompetitive character of such an agreement." *Professional Engineers*, 435 U.S., at 692. Petitioner does not quarrel with the District Court's finding that price and output are not responsive to demand. Thus the plan is inconsistent with the Sherman Act's command that price and supply be responsive to consumer preference. We have never required proof of market power in such a case. This naked restraint on price and output requires some competitive justification even in the absence of a detailed market analysis.

As a factual matter, it is evident that petitioner does possess market power. The District Court employed the correct test for determining whether college football broadcasts constitute a separate market — whether there are other products that are reasonably substitutable for televised NCAA football games. Petitioner's argument that it cannot obtain supracompetitive prices from broadcasters since advertisers, and hence broadcasters, can switch from college football to other types of programming simply ignores the findings of the District Court. It found that intercollegiate football telecasts generate an audience uniquely attractive to advertisers and that competitors are unable to offer programming that can attract a similar audience. These findings amply support its conclusion that the NCAA possesses market

power. Indeed, the District Court's subsidiary finding that advertisers will pay a premium price per viewer to reach audiences watching college football because of their demographic characteristics is vivid evidence of the uniqueness of this product. Moreover, the District Court's market analysis is firmly supported by our decision in *International Boxing Club* v. *United States*, 358 U.S. 242 (1958), that championship boxing events are uniquely attractive to fans and hence constitute a market separate from that for non-championship events. . . . Thus, respondents have demonstrated that there is a separate market for telecasts of college football which "rest[s] on generic qualities differentiating" viewers. *Times-Picayune Publishing Co.* v. *United States*, 345 U.S. 594, 613 (1953). It exorably follows that if college football broadcasts be defined as a separate market — and we are convinced they are — then the NCAA's complete control over those broadcasts provides a solid basis for the District Court's conclusion that the NCAA possesses market power with respect to those broadcasts. . . .

Thus, the NCAA television plan on its face constitutes a restraint upon the operation of a free market, and the findings of the District Court establish that it has operated to raise price and reduce output. Under the Rule of Reason, these hallmarks of anticompetitive behavior place upon petitioner a heavy burden of establishing an affirmative defense which competitively justifies this apparent deviation from the operations of a free market. . . . We turn now to the NCAA's proffered justifications.

IV

Relying on *Broadcast Music*, petitioner argues that its television plan constitutes a cooperative "joint venture" which assists in the marketing of broadcast rights and hence is procompetitive. While joint ventures have no immunity from the antitrust laws, as *Broadcast Music* indicates, a joint selling arrangement may "mak[e] possible a new product by reaping otherwise unattainable efficiencies." *Arizona* v. *Maricopa County Medical Society*, 457 U.S. 332, 365 (1982) (Powell J., dissenting) (footnote omitted). The essential contribution made by the NCAA's arrangement is to define the number of games that may be televised, to establish the price for each exposure, and to define the basic terms of each contract between the network and a home team. The NCAA does not, however, act as a selling agent for any school or for any conference of schools. The selection of individual games, and the negotiation of particular agreements, is a matter left to the networks and the individual schools. Thus, the effect of the network plan is not to eliminate individual sales of broadcasts, since these still occur, albeit subject to fixed prices and output limitations. Unlike *Broadcast Music*'s blanket license covering broadcast rights to a large number of individual compositions, here the same rights are still sold on an individual basis, only in a noncompetitive market.

The District Court did not find that the NCAA's television plan produced any procompetitive efficiencies which enhanced the competitiveness of college football television rights; to the contrary it concluded that NCAA football could be marketed just as effectively without the television plan. There is therefore no predicate in the findings for petitioner's efficiency justification. Indeed, petitioner's argument is refuted by the District Court's finding concerning price and output. If the NCAA's television plan produced procompetitive efficiencies, the plan would increase output and reduce the price of televised games. The District Court's contrary findings accordingly undermine petitioner's position. . . . No individual school is free to televise its own games without restraint. The NCAA's efficiency justification is not supported by the record.

Neither is the NCAA's television plan necessary to enable the NCAA to penetrate the market through an attractive package sale. Since broadcasting rights to college football constitute a unique product for which there is no ready substitute, there is no need for collective action in order to enable the product to compete against its nonexistent competitors. This is borne out by the District Court's finding that the NCAA's television plan *reduces* the volume of television rights sold.

V

Throughout the history of its regulation of intercollegiate football telecasts, the NCAA has indicated its concern with protecting live attendance. This concern, it should be noted, is not with protecting live attendance at games which *are* shown on television; that type of interest is not at issue in this case. Rather, the concern is that fan interest in a televised game may adversely affect ticket sales for games that will not appear on television.

Although the NORC studies in the 1950's provided some support for the thesis that live attendance would suffer if unlimited television were permitted, the District Court found that there was no evidence to support that theory in today's market. Moreover, as the District Court found, the television plan has evolved in a manner inconsistent with its original design to protect gate attendance. Under the current plan, games are shown on television during all hours that college football games are played. The plan simply does not protect live attendance by ensuring that games will not be shown on television at the same time as live events.

There is, however, a more fundamental reason for rejecting this defense. The NCAA's argument that its television plan is necessary to protect live attendance is not based on a desire to maintain the integrity of college football as a distinct and attractive product but rather on a fear that the product will not prove sufficiently attractive to draw live attendance when faced with competition from televised games. At bottom the NCAA's position is that ticket sales for most college games are unable to compete in a free market. The television plan protects ticket sales by limiting output — just as any monopolist increases revenues by reducing output. By seeking to insulate live ticket sales from the full spectrum of competition because of its assumption that the product itself is insufficiently attractive to consumers, petitioner forwards a justification that is inconsistent with the basic policy of the Sherman Act. "[T]he Rule of Reason does not support a defense based on the assumption that competition itself is unreasonable." . . .

VI

Petitioner argues that the interest in maintaining a competitive balance among amateur athletic teams is legitimate and important and that it justifies the regulations challenged in this case. We agree with the first part of the argument but not the second.

Our decision not to apply a *per se* rule to this case rests in large part on our recognition that a certain degree of cooperation is necessary if the type of competition that petitioner and its member institutions seek to market is to be preserved. It is reasonable to assume that most of the regulatory controls of the NCAA are justifiable means of fostering competition among amateur athletic teams and therefore procompetitive because they enhance public interest in intercollegiate athletics. The specific restraints on football telecasts that are challenged in this case do not, however, fit into the same mold as do rules defining the conditions of the contest, the eligibility of participants, or the manner in which members of a joint enterprise shall share the responsibilities and the benefits of the total venture.

The NCAA does not claim that its television plan has equalized or is intended to equalize competition within any one league. The plan is nationwide in scope and there is no single league or tournament in which all college football teams compete. There is no evidence of any intent to equalize the strength of teams in Division I-A with those in Division II or Division III, and not even a colorable basis for giving colleges that have no football program at all a voice in the management of the revenues generated by the football programs at other schools. The interest in maintaining a competitive balance that is asserted by the NCAA as a justification for regulating all television of intercollegiate football is not related to any neutral standard or to any readily identifiable group of competitors.

The television plan is not even arguably tailored to serve such an interest. It does not regulate the amount of money that any college may spend on its football program, nor the way in which the colleges may use the revenues that are generated by their football programs, whether derived from the sale of television rights, the sale of tickets, or the sale of concessions or program advertising. . . .

Perhaps the most important reason for rejecting the argument that the interest in competitive balance is served by the television plan is the District Court's unambiguous and well supported finding that many more games would be televised in a free market than under the NCAA plan. The hypothesis that legitimates the maintenance of competitive balance as a procompetitive justification under the Rules of Reason is that equal competition will maximize consumer demand for the product. The finding that consumption will materially increase if the controls are removed is a compelling demonstration that they do not in fact serve any such legitimate purpose.

VII

The NCAA plays a critical role in the maintenance of a revered tradition of amateurism in college sports. There can be no question but it needs ample latitude to play that role, or that the preservation of the student-athlete in higher education adds richness and diversity to intercollegiate athletics and is entirely consistent with the goals of the Sherman Act. But consistent with the Sherman Act, the role of the NCAA must be to *preserve* a tradition that might otherwise die; rules that restrict output are hardly consistent with this role. Today we hold only that the record supports the District Court's conclusion that by curtailing output and blunting the ability of member institutions to respond to consumer preference, the NCAA has restricted rather than enhanced the place of intercollegiate athletics in the Nation's life. Accordingly, the judgment of the Court of Appeals is affirmed.

Justice White, with whom Justice Rehnquist joins, dissenting.

I

. . . In affirming the Court of Appeals, the Court first holds that the television plan has sufficient redeeming virtues to escape condemnation as a per se violation of the Sherman Act, this because of the inherent characteristics of competitive athletics and the justifiable role of the NCAA in regulating college athletics. It nevertheless affirms the Court of Appeals' judgment that the NCAA Plan is an unreasonable restraint of trade because of what it deems to be the plan's price-fixing and output-limiting aspects. As I shall explain, in reaching this result, the Court traps itself in commercial antitrust rhetoric and ideology and ignores the context in which the restraints have been imposed. But it is essential at this point to emphasize that neither the Court of Appeals nor this Court purports to hold that the NCAA may not (1) require its members who televise their games to pool and share the compensation received among themselves, with other schools, and with the NCAA; (2) limit the number of times any member may arrange to have its games shown on television; or (3) enforce reasonable blackout rules to avoid head-to-head competition for television audiences. As I shall demonstrate, the Court wisely and correctly does not condemn such regulations. What the Court does affirm is the Court of Appeals' judgment that the NCAA may not limit the number of games that are broadcast on television and that it may not contract for an individual price that has the effect of setting the price for individual game broadcast rights. I disagree with the Court in these respects.

II

. . . As I have said, the Court does not hold, nor did the Court of Appeals hold, that this redistributive effect alone would be sufficient to subject the television plan to condemnation under § 1 of the Sherman Act. Nor should it, for an agreement to share football revenues to a certain extent is an essential aspect of maintaining some balance of strength among competing colleges and of minimizing the tendency to professionalism in the dominant schools. Sharing with the NCAA itself is also a price legitimately exacted in exchange for the numerous benefits of membership in the NCAA, including its many-faceted efforts to maintain a system of competitive, amateur athletics. For the same reasons, limiting the number of television appearances by any college is an essential attribute of a balanced amateur athletic system. Even with shared television revenues, unlimited appearances by a few schools would inevitably give them an insuperable advantage over all others and in the end defeat any efforts to maintain a system of athletic competition among amateurs who measure up to college scholastic requirements.

The Court relies instead primarily on the District Court's findings that (1) the television plan restricts output; and (2) the plan creates a noncompetitive price structure that is unresponsive to viewer demand. These findings notwithstanding, I am unconvinced that the television plan has a substantial anticompetitive effect.

First, it is not clear to me that the District Court employed the proper measure of output. I am not prepared to say that the District Court's finding that "many more college football games would be televised" in the absence of the NCAA controls, is clearly erroneous. To the extent that output is measured solely in terms of the number of televised games, I need not deny that it is reduced by the NCAA's television plan. But this measure of output is not the proper one. The District Court found that eliminating the plan would reduce the number of games on network television and increase the number of games shown locally and regionally. It made no finding concerning the effect of the plan on total viewership, which is the more appropriate measure of output or, at least, of the claimed anti-competitive effects of the NCAA plan. . . .

Second, and even more important, I am unconvinced that respondents have proved that any reduction in the number of televised college football games brought about by the NCAA's television plan has resulted in an anticompetitive increase in the price of television rights. The District Court found, of course, that "the networks are actually paying the large fees because the NCAA agrees to limit production. If the NCAA would not agree to limit production, the networks would not pay so large a fee." Undoubtedly, this is true. But the market for television rights to college football competitions should not be equated by the markets for wheat or widgets. Reductions in output by monopolists in most product markets enable producers to exact a higher price for *the same product*. By restricting the number of games that can be televised, however, the NCAA creates *a new product* — exclusive television rights — that are more valuable to networks than the products that its individual members could market independently. . . .

Third, the District Court's emphasis on the prices paid for particular games seems misdirected and erroneous as a matter of law. The distribution of the minimum aggregate fees among participants in the television plan is, of course, not wholly based on a competitive price structure that is responsive to viewer demand and is only partially related to the value those schools contribute to the total package the networks agree to buy. But as I have already indicated, . . . this "redistribution" of total television revenues is a wholly justifiable, even necessary, aspect of maintaining a system of truly competitive college teams. As long as the NCAA cannot artificially fix the price of the entire package and demand supercompetitive prices, this aspect of the plan should be of little concern. And I find little, if anything, in the record to support the notion that the NCAA has power to extract from the television networks more than the broadcasting rights are worth in the marketplace. . . .

IV

Finally, I return to the point with which I began — the essentially noneconomic nature of the NCAA's program of self-regulation. Like Judge Barrett, who dissented in the Court of Appeals, I believe that the lower courts "erred by ubjugating the NCAA's educational goals (and, coincidentally, those which Oklahoma and Georgia insist must be maintained in any event) to the purely competitive commercialism of [an] 'every school for itself' approach to television contract bargaining." Although the NCAA does not enjoy blanket immunity from the antitrust laws, cf. *Goldfarb* v. *Virginia State Bar*, 421 U.S. 773 (1975), it is important to remember that the Sherman Act "is aimed primarily at combinations having commercial objectives and is applied only to a very limited extent to organizations . . . which normally have other objectives." *Klor's, Inc.* v. *Broadway-Hale Stores, Inc.*, 359 U.S. 207, 213, n. 7 (1959).

The fact that a restraint operates on nonprofit educational institutions as distinguished from business entities is as "relevant in determining whether that particular restraint violates the Sherman Act" as is the fact that a restraint affects a profession rather than business. . . .

NOTE

1. The NCAA television case has evoked substantial commentary. See, for example, Gulland, Byrne and Steinbach, "Intercollegiate Athletics and Television Contracts: Beyond Economic Justifications in Antitrust Analysis

of Agreements Among Colleges," 52 *Fordham Law Review* 717 (1984); and Rowe, "NCAA v. Board of Regents [104 S. Ct. 2948]: A Broadening of the Rule of Reason," 11 Journal of College and University Law 377 (1984).

Warner Amex Cable v. American Broadcasting Companies, Inc., 499 F. Supp. 537 (S.D. Ohio 1980)

Plaintiff Warner Amex Cable Communications alleged that ABC and the NCAA prevented it from cablecasting the 1980 Ohio State University football games on its QUBE system in violation of the Sherman Act. Warner had previously cablecasted OSU games in 1978 and 1979 due to an agreement reached with the NCAA to avert an earlier suit. ABC, however, protested, and in 1980, the agreement was that cablecasts were to be permitted only when all other college games in the same geographic area were sold out. The plaintiff was unable to secure this condition and moved for a preliminary injunction.

The court held that Warner Amex had failed to meet the court standards necessary to issue the injunction. The plaintiff did not prove a probability of success on the merits of the claim, since under the rule of reason, it was not shown that the NCAA television regulations lacked any redeeming virtue. Plaintiff also did not prove irreparable injury. The court held it was problematic whether plaintiff would suffer substantial harm, and the plaintiff could put a price tag on its potential damages by computing what it would cost to buy out the conflicting games in order to cablecast OSU's games.

The court next found that a preliminary injunction would pose a substantial harm to other parties since ABC would suffer erosion of its valuable exclusivity, which it had contracted for, and the diminution of gate receipts in the Columbus area would threaten small schools. Finally, the court concluded that in the light of Warner Amex's uncertain probability of success on the merits, considerations of public interest such as protection of private contractual rights and preservation of amateur athletics weighed against the issuance of the preservation of amateur athletics weighed against the insurance of the preliminary injunction. The motion was denied.

Ass'n. for Intercollegiate Athletics for Women v. National Collegiate Athletic Ass'n., 558 F. Supp. 487 (D.D.C. 1983)

In its suit against the NCAA and its entry into the market for women's sports, the AIAW charged that the contract between the NCAA and CBS for the purchase of the rights to televise the NCAA's Division I men's basketball championship was "tied" to the television rights to its newly instituted women's basketball championships.

The evidence strongly suggested that it was the overall attractiveness of CBS's total offer rather than its willingness to telecast the women's game that induced the NCAA to accept it. In fact, CBS had offered less for the women's game than its competitor NBC. The AIAW conceded that it had no personal knowledge of NCAA's intent to condition the purchase of the men's championships upon its sale of the women's counterpart, and the court concluded that the sale of the women's championship was merely collateral to a much larger transaction that would have gone forward with or without the women's event.

With respect to the AIAW's claim that the NCAA interfered with its commercial relationship with NBC, the NCAA asserted that NBC's decision not to televise the AIAW championship was motivated by the fact that most of the "name" schools that had participated in the previous AIAW tournament had expressed an intent to participate only in the NCAA tournament in 1982. The court held that the evidence as to this alleged predatory act was at best equivocal and became dispositive when the plaintiff failed to prove specific intent necessary to sustain its monopoly claim.

6.33   New Ventures in Professional Sports

The growth of cable systems in major metropolitan areas has made it feasible for sports teams to move their product to pay cable channels. One method of doing this is to have two or more clubs in the same geographical area combine in a venture to market their games jointly. A virtue of this approach is that something approaching year-round sports programming can be offered.

When two teams pool their broadcast opportunities, however, this reduces the possibilities that a station which wishes to obtain a sports broadcasting contract will be successful. The market has been reduced substantially, since there are only a few professional sports franchises in a given geographical area. If only two teams enter a joint venture, a reduction of the market of up to 50 percent can nevertheless occur.

Midwest Communications, Inc. v. Minnesota Twins, Inc. et al., 1983–2 CCH Trade Cases ¶65719 (D.C. Minn. 1983)

The baseball Minnesota Twins and the hockey Minnesota North Stars formed a third company (TwinStar) to market as a package the television rights to both the Twins and North Stars games. One of the losers in bidding for the package was Midwest Communications, Inc. (WCCO), which then instituted an antitrust action against the clubs, their TwinStar company, and the cable system that successfully bid for the television rights. At trial before a jury, the defendants prevailed on certain theories, but lost on a jury finding that the actions undertaken constituted an illegal tying arrangement. The excerpts from the U.S. District Court's post-trial memorandum and order, set forth below, discuss defendants' motions to overturn the illegal tie findings.

   1. *Two Products In One Market.* Defendants push three arguments founded upon the structure of the local pay sports programming market, any one of which, if accepted, would strangle the

finding of an illegal tie. Intertwined, their contentions construct one product standing alone in one market.

Defendants first renew their claim that Twin-Star's offer of the Twins and North Star's telecast rights as a year-round package constitutes the sale of a single product. Both teams' broadcasts, defendants claim, are integral to the success of the programming. Business demands, in other words, compelled the creation of a new product.

All agree that two products must be sold in order to create a tying arrangement. *E.g., Times Picayune Publishing Co. v. United States*, 345 U.S. 594, 614 (1953); *Rosebrough Monument Co. v. Memorial Park Cemetery Ass'n.*, 666 F. 2d 1130, 1140 (8th Cir. 1981). The jury was so instructed. . . . Fatal to defendants' claim, therefore, is the jury's finding that the Twins' and North Stars' telecasts formed two distinct products.

The jury's findings depended on two determinations: (1) defining the products and (2) deciding whether the two products are distinct. It had before it conflicting testimony as to the nature of TwinStar's pay sports offering. The evidence provided ample room to refuse to treat the two products as inevitably intermingled and to conclude that TwinStar packaged two products which could be sold separately. TVQ, for instance, wanted only North Stars' telecast rights. Defendants' expert on pay sports, moreover, conceded that a number of existing and planned pay sports channels have seasonal rather than year-round programming. Mr. Guth, plaintiff's expert, added that the "tying" violation caused serious economic dislocation by preventing the sale of the teams' telecast rights on their own merits.

WCCO offered its most convincing evidence in support of its two-product theory, however, when it attacked defendants' defense of business justification. As defendants, in their post-trial briefs, concede, the task of product definition spawned a subsidiary inquiry into whether the TwinStar enterprise could survive if each team's telecasts stood on its own. Although extended an opportunity to adopt this perspective on the local pay sports programming industry, . . . the jury believed WCCO's evidence to the contrary. It rejected again the notion that business success

required joint sales or one synergistic product.

Defendants' last two structural arguments contesting the illegality of the tie hinge upon the jury's answer to special verdict question no. 1 where it found that the two clubs' broadcasts stood alone in the same relevant market. They deny that tying could be found when TwinStar marketed two products in the same relevant market. They also argue that since the teams' telecasts co-exist in one market *and* possess monopoly power in that market, there can be no anticompetitive effect from the tie. The court rejects both arguments.

Although courts traditionally refer to tying and tied products, an illegal tie does not demand that the two goods fall into separate relevant markets. As long as the products are distinct, they need not also come from markets which do not compete with one another. That is, two separate products which normally compete may comprise an illegally tied package. For instance, in *United States v. Loew's*, 371 U.S. 38 (1962), and *United States v. Paramount Pictures, Inc.*, 334 U.S. 131 (1948), the Supreme Court proscribed the blocked book sale of feature films to exhibitors despite the competition amongst the films for the same dollar. Although found within the same market, the films could not be sold together; each had to stand on its own economic footing.

The confusion stems from ambiguity surrounding product versus market definition. The task of defining both products and markets admittedly often devolves into a normative inquiry with product lines blurring with market boundaries. Nevertheless, an illegal tie requires two products, not two markets. The confusion typically manifests itself when two distinct components from different markets are aggregated and sold as a unit by one company. The inquiry into whether separate markets exist involves whether the two components comprise but a single product. In other words, courts speak of distinct markets but their ultimate concern is product differentiation. . . .

Defendants next argue that the package sale of the two clubs' broadcasts cannot be illegal since the two products are the only products in the market. Where the market is already monopolized, they insist, a tie can have no anticompetitive effect.

Monopoly power, however, will not save TwinStar's otherwise illegal tie. A joint venture cannot immunize a tie-in from the antitrust laws simply by having all competing sellers participate in the scheme. This is true even where there would be no adverse effect on any existing competitors. WCCO, however, presented the jury with sufficient evidence to warrant the conclusion that TwinStar's tie required the purchaser to accept terms that could not be exacted in a completely competitive market. . . . Purchasers could not individually bid for each team's telecast rights. In short, the tie-in raised barriers to entry into the pay sports market for purchasers and for other potential sports entities wishing to tap into this emerging broadcast market.

In focusing on the lack of injury to individual competitors, defendants overlook the purposes of the tying laws, including protection of purchasers, potential competitors, and overall competition. These manifest themselves particularly as to the single-product issue, the business justification defense, the economic power issue and the concern with foreclosure. Each, in other words, tests the competitive effect, and thus the legality, of the practice. . . .

Despite the absence of existing competitors in the TwinStar market, therefore, the jury had considerable evidence to allow it to conclude that the TwinStar tying arrangement is anticompetitive. WCCO's evidence shows that the tie could be seen as requiring purchasers to accede to burdensome terms, foreclosing emerging competitors from launching into this pioneer market, and endangering long-run efficiency in this new field. . . .

TwinStar's market power cannot be cast as an unexpected savior against these anticompetitive evils. In *Driskell* v. *Dallas Cowboys Club, Inc.*, 498 F. 2d 321 (5th Cir. 1974), the Ninth Circuit did reject a tying claim by a Cowboys season ticket holder who alleged he was compelled to purchase preseason tickets if he wanted to obtain regular season tickets. The tie in the restricted market for stadium seating simply infringed on consumer choice. Here, however, the jury examined a tie in an emerging market where the two products could have been in keen competition with each other and with other potential entrants. The impact could portend a stagnation of the pay sports market, a market whose long-run characteristics could easily be found by a factfinder to differ substantially from Dallas Cowboys season ticket sales.

2. *Coercion*. Defendants next assert that the court erred in failing to give defendants proposed coercion and unbundling instructions, crucial here, they argue, because their evidence shows that WCCO wanted both teams' telecast rights. But despite defendants' protestations to the contrary, the court finds the instructions to be complete, particularly in light of TwinStar's market power, the jury's rejection of claims of business justification and defense counsel's own arguments to the jury. . . .

This court declines to upset the jury's conclusions. Defense counsel emphasized throughout the trial, including closing arguments, that WCCO wanted both teams. The instructions did not undercut those claims. To the contrary, the court included the essential elements of the defense request in its instructions and left it to counsel to elaborate. With so many issues before the jury, the court did not then, nor does it now, consider defendants' requested instructions appropriate.

Finally, the court notes that neither the Supreme Court nor the Eighth Circuit have focused on the necessity of showing actual coercion in a tie-in case, stating only that tie-ins are coercive. . . .

Here, the court's instructions as to the required proof of "coercion," and the manner in which counsel cast the evidence for the jurors, support a finding that WCCO did not want to bargain for a dual package. Nevertheless, proof of coercion may well have been unnecessary in light of TwinStar's market power over potential entrants and purchaser's bid for a two-product package, and the economic analysis allowing the jury to determine if this tie made economic sense. . . .

3. *Standing*. Defendants also argue that WCCO's tying claim should be dismissed for lack of standing due to failure to incur antitrust injury. To maintain an action for treble damages under section 4 of the Clayton Act, WCCO must be "injured in [its] business or property by reason of anything forbidden in the antitrust

laws." Antitrust standing requires not only injury to WCCO's business but that WCCO's actual injury be attributable to something the antitrust laws were designed to prevent. *J. Truett Payne Co. v. Chrysler Motors Corp.*, 451 U.S. 557, 562 (1981).

The determination of whether WCCO is a proper party to bring suit, therefore, hinges upon "an evaluation of the plaintiff's harm, the alleged wrongdoing by the defendants, and the relationship between them." . . .

In discussing the impact of the tie-in on the pay sports cable market, defendants consistently confine those to be protected to actual purchasers and existing competitors. Traditionally, it is true that tying laws provide a remedy for purchasers who must buy the dual package at inflated prices or competing suppliers denied free access to the market. See, e.g., *Kypta* v. *McDonald's Corp.*, 671 F. 2d 1282, 1285 (11th Cir. 1983); *Heatransfer Corp.* v. *Volkswagenwerk*, 553 F. 2d 964 (5th Cir. 1977). However, in this case, where we have a novel venture in an emerging market, the scope defendants recommend for tying protections is too narrow. To insure proper regulation of this infant industry, the court must also protect TwinStar's potential competitors from entry barriers constructed by the tie.

WCCO, however, has not suffered this antitrust injury. Giving WCCO the benefit of all inferences reasonably to be drawn in its favor, the harm it incurred is the lost business opportunity to potentially purchase the Twins and/or North Stars' broadcast rights. A potential purchaser, however, can hardly be said to have standing to challenge the TwinStar tie.

Although the evidence allowed the jury to conclude that the tie prevented WCCO from purchasing property it wanted to purchase, more than a violation in the market and harm to WCCO must be shown. . . .

The injury here occurred because another bidder in the market, Spectrum, obtained the available property, albeit at a price which arguably differs from that earned through individual sale. WCCO had both the desire and the capability to enter the pay sports market. Absent the tie, in other words, WCCO may have found itself in Spectrum's place. This result, however, is not the type which Congress sought to rectify. TwinStar's claimed market restraint directly injured only potential competition. Its indirect impact upon WCCO's business at another level of the market structure is too remote to allow it to recover threefold damages or to invoke this court's injunctive power.

It becomes clear that antitrust standing cannot be given to frustrated potential purchasers when one contemplates the difficulties in fashioning a remedy in damages. If WCCO has standing, so also would all potential distributors of sports programming in the Twin Cities, or at least those who spoke to the teams about pay TV. The result would be duplicative recoveries, a traditional tying concern. . . .

The denial of standing is all the more prudent here since the damages to be awarded WCCO would, of necessity, be speculative. Even if WCCO were prepared to purchase telecast rights if sold individually, a chance to participate in a process subjected to the "competitive stresses of the open market" would not guarantee a successful bid. If such rights would have been obtained, moreover, WCCO would yet have to prove it could survive in the cable market and project profits. Such an amount could be but conjecture.

To avoid such ruinous recoveries, standing must be limited to actual or potential competitors foreclosed from the market and to buyers who actually enter the tying arrangement and are damaged by an increased price. . . .

6.40   Rights of the Media Through the News Function

The media provide a variety of functions. News is reported and analyzed, information is conveyed, education is attempted, and an audience is entertained. Some undertakings by the media focus on one element — such as a straight news report on a public occurrence. Even then, other functions are involved. The fact is that most of what the media do cuts across the several concerns — news, information, education, and entertainment. This causes difficulties.

Conflicts between the media and other interests are inevitable. Our scheme of rights under the U.S. and state constitutions and under federal and state laws seeks to protect an individual's privacy, rights of publicity, freedom from unfair competition, and protection against libel and slander. At the same time, freedoms of speech and press are central to our concepts of ordered liberty. One is tempted to say we cannot have it both ways, but that is exactly what we attempt to accomplish under a balancing of interests that occurs in the many cases reaching the courts.

There are multiple dimensions to balancing the interests of an individual against general freedoms. This section examines several different ways in which the asserted rights come into conflict.

First is the question of a party's property right in a name and image versus another party's right to earn a living by performing. Freedom of artistic expression is central to the court's concerns. See, below, the discussion of *KGB, Inc.* v. *Ted Giannoulas.*

Conflicts develop within the media. A television station does battle with a company which controls a sports event, but the real dispute is between the station and a network that has an exclusive to tape the performances for showing at a later time. The station wishes to tape on its own for its nightly news show. Again, a property right is raised against freedom of the press. See, below, *Post Newsweek* v. *Travelers Ins. Co.* Closely attending that problem is a station having an exclusive on live sports broadcasts insisting on the right to sell news clips to others. See, below, *New Boston Television, Inc.* v. *Entertainment Sports Program Network.*

In a case of a performer wishing to prevent a television station from showing his fifteen-second act on the evening news, the performer confronts the station's assertions of freedom of speech and of the press. See, below, *Zacchini* v. *Scripps-Howard Broadcasting.*

Finally, an athlete complains of the manner in which he is depicted in a work of fiction. A right of privacy and complaint of libel must contend with the latitude allowed those who write about public figures. The case proceeds through several stages, two of which are set forth in detail in this chapter. See, below, *Spahn* v. *Julian Messner, Inc.*

These situations do not exhaust the possibilities. Note should be made of the female reporter demanding and obtaining access to the male locker room in *Ludtke* v. *Kuhn*, 461 F. Supp. 86 (S.D.N.Y. 1978). This case is discussed in this volume in Chapter 3, Sex Discrimination. In exploring the problems of representing the professional athlete (see Volume One, Chapter 4), several cases touch on the conflict between the rights of the press and the individual. Particularly of note are *Namath* v. *Sports Illustrated*, 371 N.Y.S. 2d 10 (N.Y. App. Div. 1975), and *Ali* v. *Playgirl, Inc.*, 447 F. Supp. 723 (S.D. N.Y. 1978).

Valuable property rights come from many sources in sports. One is the right to stage the event. Another is the event's depiction and description. Yet others are the ancillary rights arising from the players' names and images. But sports events are also news, and the athletes who play the games are newsworthy subjects. As the monies increase, the property rights becomes more valuable; but the news interests also escalate. The cases in this section explore the dimensions of the problems arising to date.

KGB, Inc. v. Ted Giannoulas, 104 Cal. App. 3d 844, 164 Cal. Rptr. 571 (1980)

Radio station KGB employed Ted Giannoulas to make public appearances dressed as a chicken bearing the KGB initials. Giannoulas soon became well known for his comic performances as the KGB chicken at the San Diego Padres baseball games. When Giannoulas stopped working for KGB and appeared in the chicken suit without the KGB insignia, KGB brought suit alleging breach of the employment contract, unfair competition, and service-mark infringement. KGB also obtained an injunction preventing Giannoulas from appearing in a chicken suit either with the KGB initials or any costume substantially similar, and Giannoulas was further restrained from appearing in any chicken suit in San Diego County or where any team from San Diego appeared.

The court of appeals found those provisions of the injunction that prevented Giannoulas from appearing in any chicken suit to be invalid in that they restricted Giannoulas's right to earn a living and to express himself as an artist. Not only was there judicial reluctance to impose any restraints on one pursuing a living, but a California statute expressly dictates an absolute bar to postemployment restraints (Business and Professional Code, section 16600). Underlying this policy is recognition of the unequal bargaining position of the average employee, who often is in no position to object to the boilerplate restrictive covenants placed before him or her, and the general reluctance to enforce agreements or injunctions that preclude employees from earning a living. While there was authority for enjoining employee performance for breach of an entertainment contract under California Civil Code, section 3423, dictum in recent cases expressed grave doubts about whether the injunction would be legal beyond the term of the contract. Here, Giannoulas's term of employment expired on September 15, 1979.

In addition, the court recognized Giannoulas's artistry in performing as a chicken and cited cases that protect the personal freedom of artistic expression under the First Amendment. Any injunction inhibiting Giannoulas's self-expression thus would be inappropriate and possibly unconstitutional.

However, an injunction which restricted these vital rights could be justified if KGB could prove irreparable injury under unfair competition, breach of the employment contract, or service-mark infringement. The court held that KGB failed to prove any of these.

The court first held that Giannoulas's performances in the unmarked chicken suit did not constitute unfair competition. The essence of unfair competition is that one takes another's labor and exploits it to one's own advantage.

The evidence of the case did not establish any misappropriation by Giannoulas of KGB's labor. Recognizing Giannoulas's artistic contribution to the fluid role of the character, the court held that only the costume, with its fixed KGB logo, could be attributed to the radio station. By permitting that part of the injunction, which prevents Giannoulas from using the KGB initials on the chicken suit, the court was protecting KGB's interest.

The employment contract also did not give KGB the right to prevent Giannoulas from performing at all. The most pertinent provision only referred to preventing Giannoulas from working for another radio station. Other contractual provisions which stated that the KGB chicken character was the exclusive property of KGB did not create a contract monopoly of all appearances by Giannoulas in a chicken suit. Again, the specific chicken referred to was the KGB chicken, and the court permitted the restriction on appearing as the KGB chicken to stand.

Finally, the court held that a person appearing in a chicken costume cannot be a service mark, as it is an activity and not a stationary, unchanging mark. As the court had previously reasoned, there was no exploitation, as Giannoulas had not pirated the fruits of KGB's labor.

While the court agreed with the trial court that a costumed chicken at a sports event is associated with KGB in the public mind and that Giannoulas's appearances could cause confusion, such appearances do not show any harm to KGB to warrant a prohibitory injunction restricting the right to pursue a living and the freedom of artistic expression. For these reasons only, the portions of the injunction that prohibited Giannoulas from appearing in the defined KGB chicken costume were allowed to stand.

Post Newsweek v. Travelers Inc. Co., 510 F. Supp. 81 (D. Conn. 1981)

Plaintiff Post Newsweek Stations-Connecticut,

Inc. objected to the defendant's insistence that the plaintiff execute an indemnity agreement before entering the Hartford Civic Center Coliseum with television cameras to report on the 1981 World Figure Skating Championships. The indemnity provision resulted from the grant of exclusive television rights to Candid Production, Inc., associated with ABC television network, by the International Skating Union, which controls world-class skating competition.

The defendant Skating Club of Hartford was awarded the bid to hold the 1981 Championships in Hartford subject to this agreement, and it sent advisory letters containing the proposed indemnity agreement to area television stations. The agreement stated that in consideration for entrance to the Hartford Civic Center Coliseum, the television station was to agree to refrain from broadcasting television footage of the event until ABC concluded its entire telecast of the championships. The television station was also to agree to indemnify the Skating Club and other parties from costs and attorney fees resulting from any violation of the agreement. As a local television station, plaintiff claimed that the indemnity agreement represented unconstitutional attempts to restrict its First and Fourteenth Amendment rights to provide immediate reporting of a newsworthy event and sought a restraining order and preliminary injunction against the defendants.

A primary issue was whether the plaintiff had a special right of access to information. The court held the plaintiff's reliance on *Zacchini* v. *Scripps-Howard Broadcasting Co.*, 433 U.S. 562 (1977), was misplaced, as the parties in that case agreed that one could contract to protect the commercial value of an entertainment act. Likewise, the International Skating Union had a legitimate commercial stake in the championship and was entitled to contract to protect it by imposing certain restrictions on all those who would attend the event. In this case, the press had no constitutional right of special access to an event such

as a skating championship but was offered access like the rest of the general public if it conformed to contractual restrictions.

The court then turned its attention to the plaintiff's claim that the indemnity clause was unduly burdensome to its First and Fourteenth Amendment rights because state action existed in the city of Hartford's operation of the Civic Center Coliseum. The court found that the city was functioning in a proprietary rather than governmental capacity since the Civic Center was a commercial venture in competition with other similar facilities and was not intended as a nonprofit venture. Federal restrictions imposed on a proprietor were less harsh, and the constitutional guide instead was whether their restrictions were arbitrary or capricious.

In weighing the balance, the court considered that the forum was being used for an exposition of athletic exercise rather than for political speech, and that the information was not completely censored. The court also found that the restrictions were not arbitrary, but were necessary to protect the commercial value of the uniquely visual part of figure skating. The plaintiff's motion for a restraining order and preliminary injunction were thus denied.

NOTE _____

1. In *Chavez* v. *Hollywood Post No. 43*, 16 U.S. L.W. (Cal. Sup. Ct. 1948), a prizefighter sought a preliminary injunction to restrain a television station from broadcasting his bout, claiming that it would be an invasion of his right of privacy. The court denied his motion, and in an oral opinion said: "A prizefighter who participates in a public boxing match waives his right of privacy to that fight. Unless the fighter in his contract reserves television rights, the promoter owns those rights because the promoter dictates who may and who may not use a television camera on the premises."

_____

New Boston Television, Inc. v. **Entertainment Sports Programming Network, Inc.**, 1981, CCH Copyright Law Decisions § 25,293 at 16,625 (D. Mass. 1981)

Plaintiff owner and operator of WSBK-TV

owned the exclusive right to televise Boston Red Sox baseball and Bruins hockey games in the greater Boston area. On September 4, 1979, Entertainment Sports Programming Network (ESPN) proposed to exchange segments of ESPN's programs in return for segments of WSBK's sports broadcasts. WSBK declined that proposal, instead offering to authorize use of highlights upon payment of a fee. This offer was rejected by ESPN on October 17, 1979, in a letter in which ESPN announced its intention to copy and use its copies of WSBK's broadcasts without payment or authorization. After informing ESPN of its protest and attempting to settle the dispute out of court, plaintiffs brought an action claiming that ESPN's conduct in videotaping, excerpting, and distributing portions of WSBK's copyrighted films and in broadcasting these excerpts constituted an infringement of their exclusive copyright under federal law, entitling them to an injunction.

Defendants admitted to videotaping, excerpting, and rebroadcasting plaintiff's copyrighted films but opposed the motion on three grounds. First, they asserted that their use of the excerpts was a fair use because it was a de minimis use for news purposes only. Second, defendants contended that plaintiffs failed to demonstrate a market effect sufficient to rise to the level of irreparable harm necessary to sustain an injunction. Finally, they argued that plaintiffs were barred by the doctrine of laches.

The court rejected defendant's arguments and granted plaintiff's motion for a preliminary injunction. In response to defendant's assertion that their use was primarily for "news" purposes and hence should be protected by the fair use doctrine, the court held that while protection of the public right of access was a primary justification for the fair use doctrine, this right was sufficiently protected merely by enabling defendants to report the underlying facts. It did not, however, permit defendants to appropriate the plaintiff's expression of that information by copying the plaintiff's films. Additionally, the fact that plaintiffs had not attempted to market their product within the cablefield did not permit defendants to appropriate plaintiff's material. It was for the plaintiffs to determine the time and manner in which to exploit their copyright. This factor, plus evidence of revenue from three major networks, lent credence to plaintiff's claim that defendant's use deprived them of substantial additional revenue.

The court further held that plaintiffs had shown sufficient injury to warrant injunctive relief. In addition to the general rule that a copyright holder is presumed to suffer irreparable harm when his or her right to the exclusive use of the copyright is invaded, plaintiff also established that defendants threatened to preclude them from a substantial potential market — a harm not compensable by monetary damages. As to defendants claim of laches, which was based on their assertion that plaintiffs unreasonably delayed filing suit, the court concluded that the delay was due in part to plaintiff's efforts to reach an out-of-court resolution and in part by the fact that ESPN was a new organization and its initial efforts posed an insufficient threat to WSBK. Plaintiffs acted promptly after they became aware of ESPN's rapid growth and the improbability of a negotiated solution.

Zacchini v. Scripps-Howard Broadcasting Co., 433 U.S. 562 (1977)

Mr. Justice White delivered the opinion of the Court.

> Petitioner, Hugo Zacchini, is an entertainer. He performs a "human cannonball" act in which he is shot from a cannon into a net some 200 feet away. Each performance occupies some 15 seconds. In August and September 1972, petitioner was engaged to perform his act on a regular basis at the Geauga County Fair in Burton, Ohio. He performed in a fenced area, surrounded by grandstands, at the fair grounds. Members of the public attending the fair were not charged a separate admission fee to observe his act.

On August 30, a freelance reporter for Scripps-Howard Broadcasting Co., the operator of a television broadcasting station and respondent in this case, attended the fair. He carried a small movie camera. Petitioner noticed the reporter and asked him not to film the performance. The reporter did not do so on that day; but on the instructions of the producer of respondent's daily newscast, he returned the following day and videotaped the entire act. This film clip, approximately 15 seconds in length, was shown on the 11 o'clock news program that night, together with favorable commentary.

Petitioner then brought this action for damages, alleging that he is "engaged in the entertainment business," that the act he performs is one "invented by his father and . . . performed only by his family for the last fifty years," that respondent "showed and commercialized the film of his act without consent," and that such conduct was an "unlawful appropriation of plaintiff's professional property." . . . Respondent answered and moved for summary judgment, which was granted by the trial court.

The Court of Appeals of Ohio reversed. The majority held that petitioner's complaint stated a cause of action for conversion and for infringement of a common-law copyright, and one judge concurred in the judgment on the ground that the complaint stated a cause of action for appropriation of petitioner's "right of publicity" in the filming of his act. All three judges agreed that the First Amendment did not privilege the press to show the entire performance on a news program without compensating petitioner for any financial injury he could prove at trial.

Like the concurring judge in the Court of Appeals, the Supreme Court of Ohio rested petitioner's cause of action under state law on his "right to publicity value of his performance." 47 Ohio St. 2d 224, 351 N.E. 2d 454, 455 (1976). The opinion syllabus, to which we are to look for the rule of law used to decide the case, declared first that one may not use for his own benefit the name or likeness of another, whether or not the use or benefit is a commercial one, and second that respondent would be liable for the appropriation, over petitioner's objection and in the absence of license or privilege, of petitioner's right to the publicity value of his performance. *Ibid.* The court nevertheless gave judgment for

respondent because, in the words of the syllabus:

> A TV station has a privilege to report in its newscasts matters of legitimate public interest which would otherwise be protected by an individual's right of publicity, unless the actual intent of the TV station was to appropriate the benefit of the publicity of some non-privileged private use, or unless the actual intent was to injure the individual. *Ibid.*

We granted certiorari, 429 U.S. 1037 (1977), to consider an issue unresolved by this Court: whether the First and Fourteenth Amendments immunized respondent from damages for its alleged infringement of petitioner's state-law "right of publicity." Pet. for Cert. 2. Insofar as the Ohio Supreme Court held that the First and Fourteenth Amendments of the United States Constitution required judgment for respondent, we reverse the judgment of that court. . . .

The Ohio Supreme Court held that respondent is constitutionally privileged to include in its newscasts matters of public interest that would otherwise be protected by the right of publicity, absent an intent to injure or to appropriate for some nonprivileged purpose. If under this standard respondent had merely reported that petitioner was performing at the fair and described or commented on his act, with or without showing his picture on television, we would have a very different case. But petitioner is not contending that his appearance at the fair and his performance could not be reported by the press as newsworthy items. His complaint is that respondent filmed his entire act and displayed that film on television for the public to see and enjoy. This, he claimed, was an appropriation of his professional property. The Ohio Supreme Court agreed that petitioner had "a right of publicity" that gave him "personal control over commercial display and exploitation of his personality and the exercise of his talents." This right of "exclusive control over the publicity given to his performances" was said to be such a "valuable part of the benefit which may be attained by his talents and efforts" that it was entitled to legal protection. It was also observed, or at least expressly assumed, that petitioner had not abandoned his rights by performing under the circumstances present at the Geauga County Fair Grounds.

The Ohio Supreme Court nevertheless held that the challenged invasion was privileged, saying that the press "must be accorded broad latitude in its choice of how much it presents of each story or incident, and of the emphasis to be given to such presentation. No fixed standard which would bar the press from reporting or depicting either an entire occurrence or an entire discrete part of a public performance can be formulated which would not unduly restrict the 'breathing room' in reporting which freedom of the press requires." 47 Ohio St. 2d, at 235, 351 N.E. 2d, at 461. Under this view, respondent was thus constitutionally free to film and display petitioner's entire act.

The Ohio Supreme Court relied heavily on *Time, Inc.* v. *Hill*, 385 U.S. 374 (1967), but that case does not mandate a media privilege to televise a performer's entire act without his consent. Involved in *Time, Inc.* v. *Hill* was a claim under the New York "Right to Privacy" statute that *Life Magazine*, in the course of reviewing a new play, had connected the play with a long-past incident involving petitioner and his family and had falsely described their experience and conduct at that time. The complaint sought damages for humiliation and suffering flowing from these nondefamatory falsehoods that allegedly invaded Hill's privacy. The Court held, however, that the opening of a new play linked to an actual incident was a matter of public interest and that Hill could not recover without showing that the *Life* report was knowingly false or was published with reckless disregard for the truth — the same rigorous standard that had been applied in *New York Times Co.* v. *Sullivan*, 376 U.S. 254 (1964).

Time, Inc. v. *Hill*, which was hotly contested and decided by a divided Court, involved an entirely different tort from the "right of publicity" recognized by the Ohio Supreme Court. As the opinion reveals in *Time, Inc.* v. *Hill*, the Court was steeped in the literature of privacy law and was aware of the developing distinctions and nuances in this branch of the law. The court, for example, cited W. Prosser, *Law of Torts* 831–832 (3d ed. 1964), and the same author's well-known article, "Privacy," 48 Calif. L. Rev. 383 (1960), both of which divided privacy into four distinct branches. The Court was aware that it was adjudicating a "false light" privacy case involving a matter of public interest, not a case involving "intrusion," 385 U.S., at 384–385, n. 9, "appropriation" of a name or likeness for the purposes of trade, *id.*, at 381, or "private details" about a non-newsworthy person or event, *id.*, at 383 no. 7. It is also abundantly clear that *Time, Inc.* v. *Hill* did not involve a performer, a person with a name having commercial value, or any claim to a "right of publicity." This discrete kind of "appropriation" case was plainly identified in the literature cited by the Court and had been adjudicated in the reported cases.

The differences between these two torts are important. First, the State's interests in providing a cause of action in each instance are different. "The interest protected" in permitting recovery for placing the plaintiff in a false light "is clearly that of reputation, with the same overtones of mental distress as in defamation." Prosser, *supra*, 48 Calif. L. Rev., at 400. By contrast, the State's interest in permitting a "right of publicity" is in protecting the proprietary interest of the individual in his act in part to encourage such entertainment. As we later note, the State's interest is closely analogous to the goals of patent and copyright law, focusing on the right of the individual to reap the reward of his endeavors and having little to do with protecting feelings or reputation. Second, the two torts differ in the degree to which they intrude on dissemination of information to the public. In "false light" cases the only way to protect the interests involved is to attempt to minimize publication of the damaging matter, while in "right of publicity" cases the only question is who gets to do the publishing. An entertainer such as petitioner usually has no objection to the widespread publication of his act as long as he gets the commercial benefit of such publication. Indeed, in the present case petitioner did not seek to enjoin the broadcast of his act; he simply sought compensation for the broadcast in the form of damages. . . .

The broadcast of a film of petitioner's entire act poses a substantial threat to the economic value of that performance. As the Ohio court recognized, this act is the product of petitioner's own talents and energy, the end result of much time, effort, and expense. Much of its economic value lies in the "right of exclusive control over the publicity given to its performance"; if the public can see the act free on television, it will be less willing to pay to see it at the fair. The effect of a public broadcast of the performance is similar to preventing petitioner from charging an admission fee. "The rationale for [protecting the right of publicity] is the straightforward one of preventing unjust enrichment by the theft of good will. No social purpose is served by having the defendant get free some aspect of the plaintiff that would have market value and for which he would normally pay." Kalven, "Privacy in Tort Law — Were Warren and Brandeis Wrong?" 31 Law & Contemp. Prob. 326, 331 (1966). Moreover, the broadcast of petitioner's entire performance, unlike the unauthorized use of another's name for purposes of trade or the incidental use of a name or picture by the press, goes to the heart of petitioner's ability to earn a living as an entertainer. Thus, in this case, Ohio has recognized what may be the strongest case for a "right of publicity" — involving, not the appropriation of an entertainer's reputation to enhance the attractiveness of a commercial product, but the appropriation of the very activity by which the entertainer acquired his reputation in the first place.

Of course, Ohio's decision to protect petitioner's right of publicity here rests on more than a desire to compensate the performer for the time and effort invested in his act; the protection provides an economic incentive for him to make the investment required to produce a performance of interest to the public. This same consideration underlies the patent and copyright laws long enforced by this Court. . . . The laws perhaps regard the "reward to the owner [as] a secondary consideration," *United States* v. *Paramount Pictures*, 334 U.S. 131, 158 (1948), but they were "intended definitely to grant valuable, enforceable right" in order to afford greater encouragement to the production of works of benefit to the public. *Washingtonian Publishing Co.* v. *Pearson*, 306 U.S. 30, 36 (1939). The Constitution does not prevent Ohio from making a similar choice here in deciding to protect the entertainer's incentive in order to encourage the production of this type of work. Cf. *Goldstein* v. *California*, 412 U.S. 546 (1973). . . .

There is no doubt that entertainment, as well as news, enjoys First Amendment protection. It is also true that entertainment itself can be im-

portant news. *Time, Inc.* v. *Hill.* But it is important to note that neither the public nor respondent will be deprived of the benefit of petitioner's performance as long as his commercial stake in his act is appropriately recognized. Petitioner does not seek to enjoin the broadcast of his performance; he simply wants to be paid for it. . . .

We conclude that although the State of Ohio may as a matter of its own law privilege the press in the circumstances of this case, the First and Fourteenth Amendments do not require it to do so. *Reversed.*

Justice Powell, with whom Mr. Justice Brennan and Mr. Justice Marshall join, dissenting.

Disclaiming any attempt to do more than decide the narrow case before us, the Court reverses the decision of the Supreme Court of Ohio based on repeated incantation of a single formula: "a performer's entire act." The holding today is summed up in one sentence:

> Wherever the line in particular situations is to be drawn between media reports that are protected and those that are not, we are quite sure that the First and Fourteenth Amendments do not immunize the media when they broadcast a performer's entire act without his consent.

I doubt that this formula provides a standard clear enough even for resolution of this case. In any event, I am not persuaded that the Court's opinion is appropriately sensitive to the First Amendment values at stake, and I therefore dissent.

Although the Court would draw no distinction, *ante*, at 575, I do not view respondent's action as comparable to unauthorized commercial broadcasts of sporting events, theatrical performances, and the like where the broadcaster keeps the profits. There is no suggestion here that respondent made any such use of the film. Instead, it simply reported on what petitioner concedes to be a newsworthy event, in a way hardly surprising for a television station — means of film coverage. The report was part of an ordinary daily news program, consuming a total of 15 seconds. It is a routine example of the press' fulfilling the informing function so vital to our system.

The Court's holding that the station's ordinary news report may give rise to substantial liability has disturbing implications, for the decision could lead to a degree of media self-censorship. Cf. *Smith* v. *California*, 361 U.S. 147, 150–154 (1959). Hereafter, whenever a television news editor is unsure whether certain film footage received from a camera crew might be held to portray an "entire act," he may decline coverage — even of clearly newsworthy events — or confine the broadcast to watered-down verbal reporting, perhaps with an occasional still picture. The public is then the loser. This is hardly the kind of news reportage that the First Amendment is meant to foster. . . .

In my view the First Amendment commands a different analytical starting point from the one selected by the Court. Rather than begin with a quantitative analysis of the performer's behavior — is this or is this not his entire act? — we should direct initial attention to the actions of the news media: what use did the station make of the film footage? When a film is used, as here, for a routine portion of a regular news program, I would hold that the First Amendment protects the station from a "right of publicity" or "appropriation" suit, absent a strong showing by the plaintiff that the news broadcast was a subterfuge or cover for private or commercial exploitation. . . .

Since the film clip here was undeniably treated as news and since there is no claim that the use was subterfuge, respondent's actions were constitutionally privileged. I would affirm.

Justice Stevens filed a separate dissenting opinion.

NOTE _____

1. In *Vanderbury* v. *Newsweek, Inc.*, 507 F. 2d 1024 (5th Cir. 1975), plaintiff-appellant college track coach sued defendant magazine publisher in libel action for allegedly publishing inaccurate statements dealing with the black power movement and its effects on university athletics that were obtained from a professor organizing a boycott of a track meet. In affirming the district court's judgment notwithstanding the verdict, the court of appeals held that plaintiff was required to show actual malice but failed.

Spahn v. Julian Messner, Inc., 250 N.Y.S. 2d 529 (N.Y. Sup. Ct. 1964)

Plaintiff Warren Spahn, a baseball pitcher of wide renown and acclaim, seeks an injunction against the unauthorized publication of a book purporting to be his biography, *The Warren Spahn Story*, written by Milton J. Shapiro and published by Julian Messner, Inc., and damages for injuries sustained by reason of said publication and distribution.

Spahn alleges that the defendants are "taking pecuniary advantage of plaintiff's name, photographs, and likeness and private life to create for profit a fictionalized and dramatic story, fanciful, and sensational in nature, designed primarily and exclusively for entertainment value, and to thrill, adventurize, amuse and inspire [defendants'] reading public." The present lawsuit is thus predicated upon the contention that the fictionalization of his life story, the inclusion in the book of aspects of his private life and the concomitant commercial exploitation of his name and likeness constitute an infringement of plaintiff's "Right of Privacy."

Defendants urge that *The Warren Spahn Story* is not, and cannot, consistent with Article I, section 8 of the Constitution of the State of New York and the First Amendment to the Constitution of the United States, be deemed to be, within the proscriptions of Article 5 (sections 50 and 51) of the Civil Rights Law.

While the essence of the right of privacy eludes precise verbal definition, it comprehends, in its pure form, the individual's absolute dominion and control over his "inviolate personality" — the individual's property right in his very being, whether manifested by his actions, his thoughts, his character, his appearance, his name. . . .

New York law recognizes Article 5 of the Civil Rights Law as the fountainhead of the right to legal redress for the invasion, appropriation and commercial exploitation of the individual's personality (*Gautier* v. *Pro-Football, Inc.*, 304 N.Y. 354, 358, 107 N.E. 2d 485, 487; *Hill* v. *Hayes*, 18 A.D. 2d 488, 240 N.Y.S. 2d 286, 289). . . .

During its early formative years, the right of privacy was shaped to meet the protection needed against the excesses of "yellow journalism" and the unauthorized practices of advertising, then in their embryonic stages. Today, the right must be construed in the context of a society that cannot cavalierly dismiss the pragmatic realities of our day. Scientific advances have multiplied the potential for infringement of the individual's sanctity, and the demands of our highly complex industrialized society dangerously engulf and threaten the perimeter of man's evershrinking sphere of personal liberty.

These constant and increasing pressures upon the individual's right to inviolate personality and dignity have awakened in us an acute awareness that even as against the State, the right of privacy represents but another facet of the fundamental rights to life, liberty and the pursuit of happiness — that the inalienable right of life must comprehend more than the antithesis of biological death; the right of liberty, more than the absence of physical restraint. If, in 1928, it required the prophetic perception of Mr. Justice Brandeis to discern that "[t]he makers of our Constitution . . . conferred, as against the government, the right to be let alone — the most comprehensive of rights and the right most valued by civilized men" (dissenting in *Olmstead* v. *United States*, 277 U.S. 438, 478, 48 S. Ct. 564, 572, 72 L.Ed. 944), the temper of our times has aroused a now receptive and understanding judiciary and public. Great rights, if not created, are perceived by man when he is threatened with their loss. . . .

This does not mean that the right of privacy is absolute. "A legal system attains its end by recognizing certain interests — individual, public, and social — by defining the limits within which these interests shall be recognized legally . . . and by endeavoring to secure the interests so recognized within the defined limits" (Pound, "Interests of Personality," 28 Harv.L.Rev. 343). The case by case delineation of the sphere of the individual's right of privacy has been the handiwork of the judicial process.

In drawing this fine line of demarcation, the courts have been singularly aware that society's interest in the preservation of the inviolate personality conflicts with the public interest in the free and unimpeded dissemination of news and of information (paraphrasing *Gautier* v. *Pro-Football, Inc.*, 278 App. Div. 431, 436, 106 N.Y.S. 2d 553, 558, affd. 304 N.Y. 354, 107 N.E. 2d 485). Defendants maintain (especially in

the light of the recent pronouncement of the United States Supreme Court in *New York Times Co.* v. *Sullivan*, 376 U.S. 254, 84 S.Ct. 710, 11 L.Ed. 2d 686), that Freedom of the Press is absolute and unconditional and that sections 50 and 51 of the Civil Rights Law, if applied to the author and publisher of a biography, are "unconstitutional since they would violate the rights of Freedom of the Press under article 1, section 8 of the Constitution of the State of New York and the First Amendment to the Constitution of the United States."

Any contention that the matter now before this Court falls within the purview of the Supreme Court interdiction in the *New York Times Company* v. *Sullivan*, *supra*, case, must be dismissed. The Supreme Court in that case explicitly limited its decision. "We hold today," the Court said at 283 of 376 U.S., at 727 of 84 S.Ct., "that the Constitution delimits a State's power to award damages for libel in actions brought by *public officials* against critics of their *official conduct*." (emphasis supplied). . . .

The right of privacy — the right in the "inviolate personality" — inheres in each individual. Of particular significance to a public figure is that facet of the right of privacy which, as the obverse of the right of withdrawal from the glare of public scrutiny, embraces the "right of publicity," the exclusive property interest in one's name, portraiture and picture (*Haelan Laboratories* v. *Topps Chewing Gum*, 2 Cir., 202 F. 2d 866, 868, cert. den. 346 U.S. 816, 74 S.Ct. 26, 98 L.Ed. 343). . . .

Indeed, the very purpose of sections 50 and 51 is the prevention of "the use of an individual's name [portraiture or picture] for commercial purposes without his consent" (*Orsini* v. *Eastern Wine Corp.*, 190 Misc. 235, 236, 73 N.Y.S. 2d 426, 427). . . .

The unauthorized use of another's name and picture can no more be countenanced by the law than can the illegal appropriation for profit of any other form of another's property. A prominent figure's "right of publicity" (*Haelan Laboratories* v. *Topps Chewing Gum*, *supra*), the exclusive interest in the financial worth of one's personality, constitutes a legally protected property interest. "[W]here a cause of action under the Civil Rights statute has been established, damages may include recovery for a so-called 'property' interest inherent and inextricably interwoven in the individual's personality." (Shientag, J., in *Gautier* v. *Pro-Football, Inc.,* 278 App.Div. 431, 438, 106 N.Y.S. 2d 553, 560; see *Manger* v. *Kree Institute of Electrolysis,* 2 Cir., 233 F. 2d 5, 9; *Redmond* v. *Columbia Pictures Corp.,* 277 N.Y. 707, 14 N.E. 2d 636.)

The public figure's right of privacy is, however, far from absolute.

"Anyone becoming involved in matters of news interest must submit to the resulting publicity. Those seeking notoriety will be said to have waived, and those having it thrust upon them to have lost, their right to personal seclusion" (Hofstadter, "The Development of the Right of Privacy in New York," 39 [1954]) and to the exclusive property interest in the other facets of personality. . . .

Manifestly, precise delineation of the line of demarcation between the private and the public areas of a public figure's life and the concomitant finding of statutory protection or waiver must be determined upon each factual pattern.

Even as to those aspects of one's life deemed to be within the legitimate interest of the public, the use of an individual's name, portrait or picture is legally restricted. Since the rationale of waiver or loss of the protection afforded by the right of privacy postulates the public's right to know, the privilege of using another's name, portrait or picture without permission exists only within the strict confines of the vindication of this public interest. An individual's *pro tanto* waiver of his exclusive property interest and right of his personality is precisely commensurate with the extent of the legitimate interest of society. . . .

Application of the aforestated juridical criteria to the testimony and evidence adduced at the trial establishes beyond cavil that publication of the book, *The Warren Spahn Story,* constitutes a violation of the prohibitions of section 51 of the Civil Rights Law. The breadth and depth of the offending characteristics of the book are so all-pervasive as to render impracticable their complete recitation without inordinately extending the length of this opinion. Accordingly, the court has limited itself to reference to but relatively few examples of the violating contents. The critical significance of even this small portion of the record emerges clearly when viewed within the perspective of the general nature of the book

itself, for the whole tenor of *The Warren Spahn Story* is gauged to project a supposed close association with the hero and the format can best be characterized as a series of vividly picturesque and detailed incidents profusely highlighted with dialogue.

Two chapters of the book are devoted to Spahn's experiences in World War II. The book mistakenly states that Warren Spahn had been decorated with the Bronze Star. In truth, Spahn had not been the recipient of this award, customarily bestowed for outstanding valor in war. Yet the whole tenor of the description of Spahn's war experience reflects this basic error. Plaintiff thus clearly established that the heroics attributed to him constituted a gross non-factual and embarrassing distortion as did the description of the circumstances surrounding his being wounded. Sergeant Spahn was not in charge of "supervision of the repairs" (p. 10) of the Bridge at Remagen; Spahn did not go "from man to man, urging them on" (p. 9); Sergeant Spahn did not go "into the town of Remagen to check with his company commander on his orders for the day" (p. 11) and, consequently, the whole description thereof is imaginary; Spahn had not "raced out into the teeth of the enemy barrage" (p. 13); and in addition to other untruthful statements surrounding his being wounded, Spahn was not "rolled . . . a stretcher" (p. 14); but remained ambulatory at all times after treatment in the First Aid Station.

In addition, Spahn successfully contested the accuracy of many salient factors regarding his experiences at Camp Gruber.

In like manner, the theme of those chapters which pertain to Spahn's boyhood and teen-age life inaccurately portrays the dominant role of Spahn's father in the selection of and training for a baseball career for plaintiff and the near symbiotic relationship between the two. Plaintiff successfully repudiated the purported factual bases presented in the book for this implication, e.g., the concentrated afternoon pitching practice sessions did not take place as described; it was not true that "daily baseball sessions with his father were the rule during the season" (p. 16) nor consequently was the lengthy portrayal of these sessions accurate; the story of Ed Spahn's promise and gift to Spahn of a new first baseman's mitt never occurred; Spahn's father did not teach the boy to pitch; plaintiff never consulted his father concerning the signing of his first baseball contract; his mother, not his father, signed the necessary legal papers. As a consequence, the lengthy and vividly descriptive scenes describing the author's misconceptions of the foregoing basic facts must be classified as fictional.

As a further manifestation of the author's invented conception of the relationship between Spahn and his father, the author devotes Chapter Four to a grim portrayal of the supposed grave psychological effect of Spahn's injury to his elbow (which the author erroneously and repeatedly describes as a shoulder injury) upon the elder Spahn.... Plaintiff categorically controverted the express references and innuendoes concerning his father's illness which plaintiff described as a normal postoperative recovery, and defendants were unable to rebut his position. Consistent therewith, he unequivocally denied that the aforesaid scene or any resemblance thereto had, or could ever have, taken place. Consequently, the dramatic portrayal of the "guilt-ridden" son represents but another of the book's interesting, artistic but undeniable flights into fantasy.

With respect to the plaintiff's courtship and marriage, most aspects of the author's presentation were emphatically branded by plaintiff as untrue; e.g., Spahn's reaction to his now wife at their first meeting, the dramatization of supposed obstacles to their marriage plans and other difficulties. . . .

Concerning the depiction of his baseball career, plaintiff rightfully took exception to a multitude of factual errors, distortions, and recitations out of context, which are so extensive and varied that in the interest of keeping the size of this opinion within the bounds of propriety, reference must be made to the record in the case. The court, however, feels that mention must be made of the fact that scenes and dialogue were invented by the author, inaccurately depicting plaintiff's professional relationship with Casey Stengel, Jackie Robinson, Lew Burdette, Phil Masi and with his teammates as a whole.

While untrue statements do not necessarily transform a book into the category of fiction, the all-pervasive distortions, inaccuracies, invented dialogue, and the narration of happenings out of context, clearly indicate, at the very least, a careless disregard for the responsibility of the press and within the context of this action, an abuse of the public's limited privilege to inquire into an individual's life.

An equal degree of departure from any factual basis is presented by the introspective revelations and feelings on the part of the plaintiff, which passages are liberally sprinkled throughout the book. The plaintiff denies that he ever entertained these thoughts. . . .

At the trial, the author testified that with regard to the writing of "The Warren Spahn Story," he had never interviewed Mr. Spahn, any member of his family, friends, or any baseball player who knew the subject of the instant "biography," nor did he attempt to obtain information from the Milwaukee Braves, the baseball team of which plaintiff was, and is, a member. Newspaper articles, magazine stories and general background books constituted the sole source of the author's factual bases for his work. The author admitted that he relied upon the "accuracy" and "competency of the people whose articles I read." Of even more crucial significance, the author stated, "I created dialogue based upon a secondary source."

That the foregoing procedure outlined by the author constitutes the customary practice affords no basis for legal justification of defendants' transgression and appropriation of plaintiff's name, portraiture and picture for purposes of trade. Nor, especially in view of the multitude of overlapping offending characteristics of the book, does the contract in which Spahn agreed "that his picture may be taken for still photographs, motion pictures or television at such times as the Club may designate and agrees that all rights in such pictures shall belong to the Club and may be used by the Club for publicity purposes in any manner it desires" efface, insofar as the defendants are concerned, the line of demarcation between the permissible and forbidden areas of unauthorized publicizing of Spahn's life. . . .

The book, jacket and pictures were all published without Spahn's consent. The court also finds that the record unequivocally establishes that the book publicizes areas of Warren Spahn's personal and private life, albeit inaccurate and distorted, and consists of a host, a preponderant percentage, of factual errors, distortions and fanciful passages, only relatively few illustrative portions of which are specifically set forth herein. Although so tightly interwoven as to defy extrication of the one from the other, the offending characteristics of the book comprehend a non-factual novelization of plaintiff's alleged life story and an unauthorized intrusion into the private realms of the baseball pitcher's life — all to Spahn's humiliation and mental anguish.

The subject purported biography transgresses the bounds of legitimate public interest by its breadth of reportorial coverage of those areas of plaintiff's life which defy classification as public, i.e., his deeply personal relationships with members of his immediate family and his introspective thoughts. Quantitatively, these trespasses upon plaintiff's private life represent a substantial portion of the book now under scrutiny. Qualitatively, the colorful portrayal of the intimate facets of Mr. Spahn's relationship with his father and his wife and the revelations of his innermost thinking (e.g., the plaintiff's crucial role in the highly emotional and psychological atmosphere enveloping his father's illness, the detailed intimate courtship scenes and difficulties, plaintiff's reaction to his wife's troublesome pregnancy) in many instances places the reader in the uncomfortable position of an embarrassed interloper upon another's private and personal domain. . . .

Evaluation of the literary attainments of this work falls beyond the judicial province, but critically pivotal to the determination that the book violates the interdiction of Article 5 of the Civil Rights Law is the compelling conclusion that the writing constitutes a product — a creation, both in *form* and *content* — of the author's artistic imagination.

In effect then, the defendants have used Spahn's name and pictures to enhance the marketability and financial success of the subject book of which approximately 16,000 copies were sold at the retail price of $3.25 per copy. (For a discussion of appropriation — unjust enrichment, see Gordon, "Right of Property in Name, Likeness, Personality and History," 55 Northwestern University L.R. 553.) . . .

Accordingly, plaintiff is entitled to the relief sought; to wit, injunctive relief preventing the further publication and distribution of *The Warren Spahn Story* in all its aspects and phases

and is entitled to damages against both defendants in the sum of Ten Thousand Dollars ($10,000) and costs.

NOTE ————————————————————

1. The lower court opinion, set forth in the foregoing, was unanimously affirmed by the New York Court of Appeals. See 260 N.Y.S. 2d 451 (1965). The case then went on appeal to the United States Supreme Court. In a brief per curiam note, the Court held: "The judgment is vacated and the case is remanded to the Court of Appeals of New York for further consideration in light of *Time, Inc.* v. *Hill*, 385 U.S. 374." See 387 U.S. 239 (1967).

————————————————————————

Spahn v. Julian Messner, Inc., 233 N.E. 2d 840 (N.Y. Ct. Apps. 1967)

Again before us is this appeal by the defendant — author, Milton Shapiro, and his publisher, the defendant Julian Messner, Inc., from an order of the Appellate Division (First Department) unanimously affirming a judgment of the Supreme Court (Markowitz, J.) enjoining the publication and dissemination of the book *The Warren Spahn Story* and awarding the plaintiff $10,000 in damages.

On July 7, 1967, in conformance with the mandate of the Supreme Court of the United States, we vacated our prior order of affirmance (18 N.Y. 2d 324, 274 N.Y.S. 2d 877, 221 N.E. 2d 543) and ordered that the case be set down for reargument in light of *Time, Inc.* v. *Hill*, 385 U.S. 374, 87 S.Ct. 534, 17 L.Ed. 2d 456.

Upon reconsideration of the appeal, we adhere to our original determination and again affirm the order appealed from. . . .

The remand of this appeal by the Supreme Court gives us an opportunity to construe the statute so as to preserve its constitutionality (*People* v. *Epton*, 19 N.Y. 2d 496, cert. den. 281 N.Y.S. 2d 9, 227 N.E. 2d 829) and to review the appeal in light of the standards set forth in *New York Times Co.* v. *Sullivan* (*supra*) and *Time, Inc.* v. *Hill*, 385 U.S. 374, 87 S.Ct. 534, 17 L.Ed. 2d 456 (*supra*).

We hold in conformity with our policy of construing sections 50 and 51 so as to fully protect free speech, that, before recovery by a public figure may be had for an unauthorized presentation of his life, it must be shown, in addition to the other requirements of the statute, that the presentation is infected with material and substantial falsification and that the work was published with knowledge of such falsification or with a reckless disregard for the truth.

An examination of the undisputed findings of fact below as well as the defendants' own admission that "[i]n writing this biography, the author used the literary techniques of invented dialogue, imaginary incidents, and attributed thoughts and feelings" (brief for appellants, p. 10) clearly indicates that the test of *New York Times Co.* v. *Sullivan* (*supra*) and *Time, Inc.* v. *Hill* (*supra*) has been met here.

The Trial Judge found gross errors of fact and "all-pervasive distortions, inaccuracies, invented dialogue, and the narration of happenings out of context" (43 Misc. 2d 219, 230, 250 N.Y.S. 2d 529, 541). These findings were unanimously affirmed by the Appellate Division. The court wrote: "[I]t is conceded that use was made of imaginary incidents, manufactured dialogue and a manipulated chronology. In short, defendants made no effort and had no intention to follow the facts concerning plaintiff's life, except in broad outline and to the extent that the facts readily supply a dramatic portrayal attractive to the juvenile reader. This liberty . . . was exercised with respect to plaintiff's childhood, his relationship with his father, the courtship of his wife, important events during their marriage, and his military experience." (23 A.D. 2d 216, 219, 260 N.Y.S. 2d 451, 454.)

Exactly how it may be argued that the "all-pervasive" use of imaginary incidents — incidents which the author knew did not take place — invented dialogue — dialogue which the author knew had never occurred — and attributed thoughts and feelings — thoughts and feelings which were likewise the figment of the author's imagination — can be said not to constitute knowing falsity is not made clear by the defendants. Indeed, the arguments made here are, in essence, not a denial of knowing falsity but a justification for it.

Thus the defendants argue that the literary techniques used in the instant biography are customary for children's books. To quote from their brief (p. 11): "The use of manufactured dialogue was characterized as 'mandatory' by a noted critic, teacher and author of children's

books. She explained that the dialogue is 'created, and based on probable facts and possible dialogue, which the biographer, through his association with his subject, through the vast amount of research that is necessary, can assume might have happened. It's not a falsification in that sense of the word at all.' Basically a juvenile biography 'has to be a lively story to catch a youngster away from television and all other distractions. . . . You cannot make it straight narrative. It can't list a great many facts or details which you can find in an encyclopedia or "Who's Who".'"

Even if we were to accept this explanation as a defense to this kind of action (cf. note, 67 Col. L. Rev. 926, 942), the defendants could not succeed here. The author of *The Warren Spahn Story* had virtually no association with the subject. He admitted that he never interviewed Mr. Spahn, any member of his family, or any baseball player who knew Spahn. Moreover, the author did not even attempt to obtain information from the Milwaukee Braves, the team for which Mr. Spahn toiled for almost two decades. The extent of Mr. Shapiro's "vast amount of research" in the case at bar amounted, primarily, to nothing more than newspaper and magazine clippings, the authenticity of which the author rarely, if ever, attempted to check out.

To hold that this research effort entitles the defendants to publish the kind of knowing fictionalization presented here would amount to granting a literary license which is not only unnecessary to the protection of free speech but destructive of an individual's right — albeit a limited one in the case of a public figure — to be free of the commercial exploitation of his name and personality. . . .

For the reasons stated the order appealed from should be affirmed, with costs.

Bergan, Judge (dissenting).

Had the Supreme Court agreed with our decision at 18 N.Y. 2d 324, 274 N.Y.S. 2d 877, 221 N.E. 2d 543, upholding the constitutional validity of sections 50 and 51 of the Civil Rights Law as applied to Spahn's case, it would normally have affirmed in due course. Instead, it remanded the case back here for further consideration in view of *Time, Inc.* v. *Hill*, 385 U.S. 374, 87 S.Ct. 534, 17 L.Ed. 2d 456.

This seems to imply that on the present record

the court disagrees with out earlier determination to sustain the statute against the argument of defendants that, as invoked by Spahn, it invades the constitutionally protected freedom of the press.

Of course, the converse is also true, that the court could have reversed on the present record if it could see that the case could not be re-examined according to different criteria. But it could not necessarily see that and would then leave it open to the State court to re-examine.

Therefore, one alternative open to us is to remit the case to the trial court to examine and decide the right of plaintiff to recover on showing "calculated falsehood" against which "the constitutional guarantees can tolerate sanctions" (*Hill*, p. 389, 87 S.Ct. p. 543); or a "'reckless disregard of the truth'" (id., p. 390, 87 S.Ct. p. 543) which is treated similarly. (See, further, *New York Times Co.* v. *Sullivan*, 376 U.S. 254, 84 S.Ct. 710, 11 L.Ed. 2d 686; *Garrison* v. *State of Louisiana*, 379 U.S. 64, 85 S.Ct. 209, 13 L.Ed. 2d 125.)

These specific criteria were neither pleaded nor established on this record which essentially rests on an asserted violation of the statute by an actionable invasion of privacy in fictionalized biographical material relating to plaintiff.

The theory of the case, as presented, was that fictionalization relating to plaintiff's life was itself actionable under the statute as the New York courts have construed it. . . .

The case was not based, therefore, on a consideration of "reckless disregard of the truth" or "calculated falsehood" in the sense the Supreme Court used these terms. If, upon re-examination it were found that the material complained of was merely "innocent or negligent" in writing and publication, it would seem then to be necessary to give judgment for defendants (*Hill*, 385 U.S. p. 389, 87 S.Ct. p. 543). There seems to be no suggestion that the publication would be proved on a further examination to be more than that.

Even though the fictionalized parts were literally not true, the writer seems to have regarded the fiction as consistent with Spahn's life and possible or even likely. As to certain dialogue complained of, for example, both sides stipulated in the record that it "was written by the author to interpret what he thought the facts were."

The direction of movement of the cases interpreting the constitutionally shielded freedom of the press suggests that the protection to defendants should now be more broadly based than either the narrow grounds that would rest on the *Hill* criteria, or those laid down by our prior decisions. It does not seem probable, reading *Hill* and *New York Times* together, that fiction alone concerning a public figure, actionable under the New York statute as construed, is any longer actionable.

Spahn is a public figure by his own choice. He is not a public official coming literally within *New York Times* or *Garrison*, but the right to print and publish material about a public figure rests on similar policy considerations even though they are not chosen at ·elections after public debate on their merits. A vast area of public discussion would be closed off if the press could speak much less freely of public figures than of public officials.

At least no good reason exists for imposing sharp discrimination. The material complained of here is not much more a "purely private defamation" than writing false statements about State officers (*Garrison*, *supra*, 379 U.S. p. 76, 85 S.Ct. p. 216).

Therefore, it should be held that as to a public figure willingly playing that role, the New York privacy statute gives no protection against fictionalization not shown to hurt him and not shown designed to hurt him . . .

NOTE _____

1. The final chapter in the Warran Spahn saga occurred with the defendants once again filing notice of appeal from the foregoing New York Court of Appeals decision. The appeal was docketed and then dismissed. See 393 U.S. 1046 (1967). Apparently, the dismissal was by motion of the defendants.

TABLE OF CASES

A.P.A. Sports, inc., Polonich v., 4.21: 330

ABC League v. Missouri State High School Activities Ass'n., 2.14-1: 130

Adams, Toone v., 4.12-1(c), 4.13, 4.22-4, 4.24: 290, 305, 340*, 359

Aetna Casualty & Surety Company, Carroll v., 4.21: 322

Agar v. Canning, 4.21, 5.22: 330, 428

Aiken v. Lieuallen, 3.33-1(a): 258*

Alabama High School Athletic Ass'n. v. Rose, 1.22-3: 30

Alabama High School Athletic Ass'n., Taylor v., 132-1, 1.32-2: 58, 62

Albach v. Odle, 1.21-1, 213-2: 5, 125

Alexander County Board of Education, Clary v., 4.23-4, 4.25: 351, 367

Alpine Ski Shop, Salk v., 4.30; 389

Amateur Ahtletic Union, Santee v., 1.22, 2.30: 8*, 203

Amateur Hockey Ass'n. of the United States, Tondas v., 1.24: 46*

Amateur Softball Ass'n. of America v. United States, 1.24: 46*, 47

Ambach, Cavallaro by Cavallaro v., 2.25: 198*

American Baseball Club of Philadelphia, Kallish v., 4.12-1(c): 290

American Broadcasting Companies, Inc., Warner Amex Cable v., 6.32: 535*

Anacortes School District No. 103, Carabba v., 4.23-1, 4.27-2: 342*, 378

Andrews, Texas High School Gymnastics Coaches Ass'n. v., 260: 207*

Ann Arbor School Board, Othen v., 3.22: 230*

Apuna v. Arizona State University, 2.50: 205

Ardoin v. Evangeline Parish School Board, 4.25: 367

Arizona Board of Regents, Rutledge v., 4.14, 4.22-2, 4.23-4: 309, 336*, 353

Arizona Interscholastic Ass'n., Clark v., 3.32-1: 254*

Arizona State University, Apuna v., 2.50: 205

Arkansas Activities Ass'n., Dodson v., 3.33-2(a): 262*

Arkansas Activities Ass'n., Wright v., 1.31, 1.32-1, 1.42: 55, 58, 93

Arkansas Gazette v. Southern State College, 1.23-1: 37*

Arlosoroff v. National Collegiate Athletic Ass'n., 1.31: 53*

Armstrong School District, Jackson v., 3.42: 271

Art Gaines Baseball Corp. v. Houston, 2.60: 208

Askew v. Macumber, 2.15-1(b): 144

Ass'n. for Intercollegiate Athletics for Women v. National Collegiate Athletic Ass'n., 6.32: 536*

Assmus v. Little League Baseball, Inc., 1.21-2: 6

Associated Press, Bell v., 4.14: 311

Associated Students, Inc., v. National Collegiate Athletic Ass'n., 1.31: 55

Associated Students, Inc. v. National Collegiate Athletic Ass'n., 2.11: 109

Associated Students, Inc. v. National Collegiate Athletic Ass'n., 2.16: 175

Athena Cablevision of Corpus Christi, Inc., National Broadcasting Co. v., 6.24: 508*

Athletic Commission of Kansas State University, Shriver v., 4.23-4: 352

Athletic Council of Iowa State University, Greene v., 1.23: 32

Atlantic Coast Conference, Kupec v., 1.21-3, 2.14-1: 7, 128*

Attorney General v. International Marathons, Inc., 1.23-3: 42*, 43

Atty. Gen. v. Massachusetts Interscholastic Athletic Ass'n. Inc., 3.32-1: 256

---

* Asterisk indicates full text of case given.

Averill v. Luttrell, 4.11-2, 4.13, 4.21, 4.24: 282, 305, 330, 356

Avonworth Baseball Conference, Magill v., 3.31-2: 252

Bain, Gillespie v., 4.22-4, 4.27-3: 341, 380*

Baker v. Carr, 1.22-3: 28

Baltic Independent School District No. 115 v. South Dakota High School Activities Ass'n., 1.33: 66

Barker v. Lull Engineering, 4.30: 382

Barnes, Thompson v., 1.21-3: 7

Barnhill, Nabozny v., 4.12-1(a), 4.12-4, 4.12-5(b), 4.12-5(d), 4.21: 287, 297, 299, 301, 323

Barnhorst v. Missouri State High School Athletic Ass'n., 1.31: 55

Barrett v. Phillips, 4.12-1(c), 4.12-1(e), 4.21: 290, 292, 329

Barry v. Time, Inc., 4.14: 311

Bayless v. Philadelphia National League Club, 4.26: 373

Bearman v. University of Notre Dame, 4.25: 366*

Beatty, Gerrity v. 4.23-3: 348

Bednar v. Nebraska School Activities Ass'n., 3.31-2: 251

Begley v. Corporation of Mercer Univ., 2.15-1(a): 138*

Behagan v. Intercollegiate Conference of Faculty Representatives, 1.32-1, 1.32-2, 2.30: 55, 62, 199

Bell v. Associated Press, 4.14: 311

Bell v. University of South Carolina, 1.41-2: 82

Bell, Grove City College v., 3.00, 3.22: 211, 214, 228, 233, 237*, 239–240

Bell, North Haven Board of Education v. 3.22: 228, 234*, 238

Bell, University of Richmond v., 3.22: 239

Benedetto v. Travelers' Insurance Company, 4.21: 321

Benjamin v. State, 4.12-1(d), 4.12-2, 4.12-5(b), 4.25: 290, 293, 299, 363

Bennett v. West Texas State University, 3.22: 232*

Bennett, Cook v., 4.23-1, 4.23-4: 343*, 352

Bensinger Recreation Corp., Sykes v., 4.25: 367

Berman by Berman v. Philadelphia Board of Education, 4.12-1(a), 4.12-2, 4.23-3: 288, 293, 349

Bernard MacFadden Foundation, Inc., Stehn v., 4.12-1, 4.23-1: 286, 344

Berst v. Chipman, 1.23-1, 1.41-3: 34*, 36*, 85

Berthold Public School Dist. No. 54, Dostert v., 2.22: 193

Big Eight Conference, Stanley v., 1.32-1, 1.41-2: 56*, 81

Bike Athletic Co., et al., Harry v., 1.42: 93

Bilney v. Evening Star Newspaper Co., 4.15, 4.16: 313, 317

Bingler v. Johnson, 2.15-1(a): 138

Birhanzel, Merrill v., 4.23-4: 352

Birmingham Post, Seal v., 1.23-1, 1.41-3: 33*, 85

Birmingham, Estell v., 5.80: 493

Blaich v. NFL, 6.28-1:518

Blair v. Washington State University, 3.33-1(a): 259

Blue Mount Swim Club, Pleasant v., 4.30: 388

Blue v. University Interscholastic League, 2.14-2: 134

Board of Directors of the Independent School Dist. of Waterloo v. Green, 2.23: 195

Board of Educ. of Asbury Park, Gregoria v., 3.31-2: 251

Board of Educ. of Central School Dist. No. 1, Germon v., 4.23-1: 344

Board of Educ. of Davis County School Dist., Starkey v., 2.23: 195

Board of Educ. of Mesick Consol. School Dist., Cochrane v., 2.23: 195

Board of Education of City of New York, McGee v., 4.27-1: 376–377

Board of Education of City of New York, Caulfield v., 3.41: 267

Board of Education of Collingsville Community School District, Lynch v., 4.12-1(a), 4.12-1(d), 4.22-1, 4.23-1, 4.23-3: 387, 290, 333*, 345, 348

Board of Education of Community Unit Dist. No. 2, Fustin v., 4.13, 4.23-1, 4.41: 305, 344, 391

Board of Education of Manhasset, Woodring v., 4.25: 369

Board of Education of School District No. 23, O'Connor v., 1.32-1, 3.33-1(a): 58, 257*

Board of Education, Irwin v., 1.41-2: 82

Board of Education, North Babylon Union Free School District, Forte v., 3.32-1: 255

Board of Regents of Northern Illinois University, Textor v., 3.42: 268*

Board of Regents of U. of Oklahoma and U. of Georgia Athletic Ass'n., National Collegiate Athletic Ass'n. v., 1.24, 3.00, 6.32: 48, 213, 527

Board of Regents v. Roth, 1.32-2: 60

Board of Regents, University of Oklahoma v. National Collegiate Athletic Ass'n., 1.24, 1.41-2: 48, 80*

Board of Trustees of Michigan State University, Hutchins v., 3.33-1(a): 261

Board of Trustees of the California State University and Colleges, Echols v., 2.50: 204

Board of Trustees of University of Ark., McMahon v., 1.23-1: 37

Bonner County School District, Ford v., 4.27-4: 380*

Borough of Wildwood Crest, Nash v., 4.27-2: 378*

Boston Area Youth Soccer, Inc., Simpson v., 3.31-1: 246

Boston Athletic Ass'n. v. International Marathons Inc., 1.23-3: 40*

Boston Professional Hockey Ass'n., Guttenplan v., 4.24: 358

Bound Brook Board of Education, Cap v., 4.27-2: 378*

Bourque v. Duplechin, 4.11-2, 4-12-4, 4.12-5(b), 4.12-5(d), 4.21, 4.41: 282, 297, 299, 301, 321*, 391

Bowdoin College v. Cooper International, Inc., Doyle v., 4.50: 393*

Boyd, Gulf South Conference v., 1.32-2, 2.13-1: 62, 120*

Bradshaw, Florida High School Activities Ass'n. v., 1.21-2, 1.21-3, 1.42, 2.30: 6, 7, 93, 203

Bradwell v. State, 3.11: 215

Braesh v. DePasquale, 2.24: 196

Brahatcek v. Millard School District No. 17, 4.23-1: 345

Brenden v. Independent School District 742, 3.31-2: 248, 249

Bridges, Stroud v., 4.12-3(b): 295

Brooklyn Nat'l. League Baseball Club, Philpot v., 4.24: 358

Brown v. Wichita State University, 4.23-4: 352

Brown v. Wells, 2.60: 208, 209

Brown, Kriss v., 2.13-2: 126

Bruce v. South Carolina High School League, 2.13-2: 122, 125

Bryant, Florida High School Activities Ass'n. v., 2.14-1: 129

Bucha v. Illinois High School Ass'n., 3.33-2(b): 264*

Buchanan, Fitchett v., 4.12-3(a): 294

Buckton v. National Collegiate Athletic Ass'n., 1.31, 1.32-2, 1.33, 2.15-1(d): 54, 61, 68*, 154

Buckey Warren, Inc., Everett v., 4.30: 386

Bunger v. Iowa High School Athletic Ass'n., 1.21-1, 2.24: 4, 196*

Burke, United States v., 5.71: 478*

Burkey v. Marshall County Board of Education, 3.42: 269*

Burman, Isler v., 4.12-3(b): 295

Burris, King v. 4.14: 311

Burton v. Wilmington Parking Authority, 3.43-3: 274

Butts v. National Collegiate Athletic Ass'n., 2.14-2: 130*

Butts, Curtis Publishing Co. v., 4.14: 307*

Byrns v. Riddell, Inc., 4.17, 4.30: 318, 384*

Cabrillo Community College Dist. of Santa Cruz County v. California Junior College Ass'n., 2.14-1: 129

Caddo Parish School Board, Turner v., 4.23-3, 4.25: 349, 368

Califano, National Collegiate Athletic Ass'n. v., 1.21-2, 3.21: 6, 225*

California Interscholastic Federation, California Women's Coaches Academy v., 3.42: 270*

California Jockey Club, Porter v., 4.25: 368

California Junior College Ass'n. Cabrillo Community College Dist. of Santa Cruz County v., 2.14-1: 129

California Sports, Inc., Tomjanovich v., 4.13, 4.21, 4.24: 305, 329, 357*

California State University, Hayward v. National Collegiate Athletic Ass'n., 1.21-1, 1.41-1: 4, 71*

California Women's Coaches Academy v. California Interscholastic Federation, 3.42: 270*

Calzadilla v., Dooley, 3.43-2: 273*

Campagnola Enter., Inc., NFL v., 6.24: 508

Campo v., NFL, 6.28-1: 518*

Canning, Agar v., 4.21, 5.22: 330, 428

Cannon v. University of Chicago, 3.41: 267

Cantwell v. University of Massachusetts, 4.12-1(a), 4.23-4: 287, 350*

Cap v. Bound Brook Board of Education, 4.27-2: 378*

Cape v. Tennessee Secondary School Athletic Ass'n., 3.33-2(a): 263

Carabba v. Anacortes School District No. 103, 4.23-1, 4.27-2: 342*, 378

Carlen v. University of South Carolina, 4.14: 310

Carnes v. Tennessee Secondary School Athletic Ass'n., 3.31-2: 251

Carr, Baker v., 1.22-3: 28

Carroll v. Aetna Casualty & Surety Company, 4.21: 322

Carroll v. State of Oklahoma, 4.27-1: 376*

Caulfield v. Board of Education of City of New York, 3.41: 267

Cavallaro by Cavallaro v. Ambach, 2.25: 198*

Central Louisiana Dist. Livestock Show, Inc., Rosenberger v., 4.13: 304

Central School Dist. No. 1, Stevens v., 4.12-5(d): 301

Cepeda v. Cowles Magazines and Broadcasting, 4.14: 311

Chabert v. Louisiana High School Athletic Ass'n., 2.13-2: 125

Chavez v. Hollywood Post No. 43, 6.40: 542

Cheatham v. Workers' Compensation Appeals Board, 2.15-1(b): 143

Chicago Board of Education, Lavin v., 3.31-1: 245

Chicago Board of Education, Lavin v., 3.31-1: 245

Chipman, Berst v., 1.23-1: 34*

Chipman, Berst v., 1.23-1, 1.41-3: 36*, 85

Christenberry, Tilelli, v., 4.27-3: 380

Christian Brothers Institute v. North New Jersey Interscholastic League, 1.22-3: 29

Chuy v. Philadelphia Eagles Football Club, 4.14, 4.16, 4.24, 4.26: 308*, 309, 317*, 358, 373

Cincinnati Bengal's Inc., Hackbart v., 4.21, 4.11-2, 4.12-1(a), 4.12-4, 4.12-5(d), 4.12-5(e), 4.13, 4.21, 4.24: 324*, 327*, 282, 287, 297, 301, 303, 305, 329, 357

Cincinnati Gardens, Inc., Townsley v., 4.12-1(a), 4.12-3(b), 4.12-5(a), 4.25: 287, 295, 298, 365

City of Delavan, Novak v., 4.25: 369

City of El Cajon, Crone v., 4.23-4: 353

City of Montgomery, Gilmore v., 3.43-3: 274

City of New York, Forkash v., 4.27-2: 379

City of New York, et al., Maddox v., 4.25: 368

City of Pontiac, Hertel v., 6.28-1: 519*

City of St. Cloud, Ide v., 4.23-4: 353

Clark v. Arizona Interscholastic Ass'n., 3.32-1: 254*

Clary v. Alexander County Board of Education, 4.23-4, 4.25: 351, 367

Clauson, Griggas v., 4.11-2, 4.21: 282, 322*

Clay v. U.S., 1.22-4: 31

Clayton, Southern Methodist University v., 4.23-4: 353

Clinton v. Nagy, 3.31-1: 244*

Clune, Thurman v., 4.25: 369

Cochrane v. Board of Educ. of Mesick Consol. School Dist., 2.23: 195

Coleman v. Western Michigan University, 2.15-1(b): 144

College Athletic Placement Services, Inc., v. National Collegiate Athletic Ass'n., 1.24: 45*

Colombo v. Sewanhaka Central High Shcool Dist., 2.25: 198

Colorado High School Activities Ass'n. v. NFL, 6.31: 525*

Colorado Seminary v. National Collegiate Athletic Ass'n., 1.21-1, 1.32-2, 2.30: 5, 61*, 201

Columbus Board of Educ., Hall v., 4.23-4: 352

Commonwealth, Packel v. Pennsylvania Interscholastic Athletic Ass'n., 3.13: 223*

Congregation B'nai Zion, Crohn v., 4.23-1: 345

Connecticut Interscholastic Athletic Conf., Inc., Hollander v., 3.31-2: 251

Cook v. Bennett, 4.23-1, 4.23-4: 343*, 352

Copyright Royalty Tribunal, National Ass'n. of Broadcasters v., 6.23: 507

Cornwell, French v., 2.24: 196

Corporation of Mercer Univ., Begley v., 2.15-1(a): 138*

Corpus Christi Little Misses Kickball Ass'n., White v., 3.32-1: 255

County Arena, Inc., Johnson v., 4.13: 304

Cowles Magazines and Broadcasting, Cepeda v., 4.14: 311

Cox Broadcasting Corp. v. National Collegiate Athletic Ass'n., 6.27: 515*

Cox Enterprises, Inc., Williams v., 4.50: 393*

Cox, Whitfield v., 4.25: 369

Cox, Tennessee Secondary School Ass'n. v., 1.21-1: 4

Cramer v. Hoffman, 4.13-1, 4.23-2, 4.26: 306, 347*, 373

Crane v. Kansas City Baseball & Exhibition Co., 4.24: 355

Crenshaw, Romans v., 2.23: 195

Crohn v. Congregation B'nai Zion, 4.23-1: 345

Crone v. City of El Cajon, 4.23-4: 353

Crystal Baths, Waxenberg v., 4.12-3(c): 296

Cumberland Valley School Dist., Dallam v., 2.13-2: 125

Curators of the University of Missouri, Strong v., 4.41: 391

Curtis E. Jones, Jr. v. University of Michigan, 2.50: 205

Curtis Publishing Co. v. Butts, 4.14: 307*

Dahl, Marcum v., 1.32-1, 2.21: 58, 191

Dallam v. Cumberland Valley School Dist., 2.13-2: 125

Dallas Cowboys Club, Inc., Driskell v., 6.33: 538

Daniels v. Gates Rubber Co., 4.27-4: 381*

Darlington Little League, Inc., Fortin v., 3.31-02: 252

Darrin v. Gould, 3.13: 222*

Davenport v. Randolph County Bd. of Education, 2.22: 193

David v. Louisiana High School Athletic Ass'n., 2.14-1: 129

Davis v. Meek, 2.23: 194*

Deaner v. Utica Community School District, 4.26: 373

DeFrantz v. United States Olympic Committee, 1.22-1, 2.18: 112, 189

DeMauro v. Tusculum College, Inc., 4.22-2, 4.23-1: 337, 343

Dempsey v. Time, Inc., 4.14: 312

Denis J. O'Connell High Sch. v. Virginia High Sch., 1.22-3: 27*

Department of Health, Education and Welfare, Hillsdale College v., 3.22: 233*

DePasquale, Braesch v., 2.24: 196

Dillard v. Little League Baseball Incorporated, 4.27-1: 375*

Division of State Athletic Commission of Department of State of N.Y., Muhammad Ali v., 1.22-4: 31, 32

Dodson v. Arkansas Activities Ass'n., 3.33-2(a): 262

Domino v. Mercurio, 4.13, 4.22-1, 4.23-1: 305, 334, 345

Donegal School Dist., Zeller v., 2.22: 192*

Dooley, Calzadilla v., 3.43-2: 273*

Dorsey v. Yoder Co., 4.30: 385

Dostert v. Berthold Public School Dist. No. 54, 2.22: 193

Doubleday Sports, Inc., Eastern Microwave, Inc., v., 6.27: 515*

Doyle v. Bowdon College v. Cooper International, Inc., 4.50: 393

Driskell v. Dallas Cowboys Club, Inc., 6.33: 538

Dudley Sports Co. v. Schmitt, 4.12-3(c), 4.30: 296, 382

Duffley v. New Hampshire Interscholastic Athletic Ass'n., 1.32-1, 2.14-1: 58, 129

Duffy v. Midlothian Country Club, et al., 4.12-5(c), 4.12-5(d), 4.24: 300, 301, 359

Dumex v. Louisiana High School Athletic Ass'n., 2.60: 209

Dunham v. Pulsifer, 1.21-1, 2.22: 4, 191

Dunsmuir Joint Union High School District, Welch v., 4.13, 4.22-3, 4.23-2, 4.26 305, 338*, 347, 374

Duplechin, Bourque v., 4.11-2, 4.12-4, 4.12-5(b), 4.12-5(d), 4.21, 4.41: 282, 297, 299, 301, 321*, 391

Eastern College Athletic Conference, Weiss v., 2.13-1: 121

Eastern Microwave, Inc. v. Doubleday Sports, Inc., 6.27: 515

Eaton Corp., Wetzel v., 4.30: 387

Eaton, Williams v., 2.21: 190

Echols v. Board of Trustees of the California State University and Colleges, 2.50: 204*

Eddy v. Syracuse University, 4.25: 366*

Ehehalt v. Livingston Board of Education, 4.27-4: 380*

Employers' Fire Ins. Co., Richmond v., 4.12-5(d), 4.21: 301, 321

English v. National Collegiate Athletic Ass'n., 2.13-1: 118*

Entertainment Sports Programming Network, Inc., New Boston Television, Inc., v., 6.40: 542*

Eskew, Ruman v., 3.33-1(b): 262

Estay v. LaFourche Parish School Bd., 1.21-1, 2.23: 4, 193*

Estell v. Birmingham, 5.80: 493

Evangeline Parish School Board, Ardoin v., 4.25: 367

Evans, Guelker v., 1.22-3: 29

Evanston Township Community Consolidated School District 65, Weinstein v., 4.23-4: 352

Evening Star Newspaper Co., Watford v., 4.12-3(b): 295

Evening Star Newspaper Co., Bilney v., 4.15, 4.16: 313*, 317

Everett School Dist. No. 24, Juntila v., 4.12-5(b): 299

Everett v. Bucky Warren, Inc., 4.30: 386

Fass, National Exhibition Co. v., 6.11: 497*

FCC, Malrite TV of N.Y. v., 6.12: 498*

FCC, National Ass'n. of Theatre Owners v., 6.26: 513

FCC, WWHT, Inc. v. 6.26: 510*

FCC, National Ass'n. of Theatre Owners v., 6.26: 511*

FCC, Home Box Office, Inc. v., 6.26: 512*

Federal Baseball Club of Baltimore v. National League of Professional Baseball Clubs, 6.31: 522, 526

Federal Communications Commission, Springfield Television Corp. v., 6.12: 499

Fetzer v. Minor Park District, 4.23-4: 352

Filler v. Rayex Corp., 4.30: 388

First Northwest Industries of America, MacLean v., 3.13: 224

Fischer v. Mt. Mansfield Co., Inc., 4.12-3(d): 297

Fish v. Los Angeles Dodgers Baseball Club, 4.26: 373

Fitchett v. Buchanan, 4.12-3(a): 294

Fitzgerald, Oeschger v., 4.23-4: 351

Fitzsimmons, People v., 5.22: 431*

Flood v. Kuhn, 6.31: 526

Florida High School Activities Ass'n. v. Bradshaw, 1.21-2, 1.21-3, 1.42, 2.30: 6, 7, 93, 203

Florida High School Activities Ass'n. v. Bryant, 2.14-1: 129

Florida High School Activities Ass'n. v. Lee, 2.14-1: 129

Florida High School Activities Ass'n. v. Thomas, 1.42: 92*

Florida State University, University of Washington v., 1.50: 95

Florida State University, Tookes v., 2.15-1(b): 143

Fluitt v. University of Nebraska, 1.32-2: 61*

Fontbonne College, Stineman v. 4.22-3, 4.23-2: 339, 347

Forbes, State v., 4.21, 5.22: 330, 430*

Force v. Pierce City R-VI School District, 3.31-1: 246

Ford v. Bonner County School District, 4.27-4: 380*

Forkash v. City of New York, 4.27-2: 379

Forte v. Board of Education, North Babylon Union Free School District, 3.32-1: 255

Fortin v. Darlington Little League, Inc., 3.31-2: 252

Fossi, Ridgefield Women's Political Caucus, Inc. v., 3.11: 217–218

Foster v. Houston General Insurance Company, 4.22-1, 4.23-1: 334, 345

Freeman v. United States, 4.12-1(c): 289–290

French v. Special Services, Inc., 4.50: 404

French v. Cornwell, 2.24: 196

Friedman v. State, 4.25: 367

Frontiero v. Richardson, 3.11: 216–217

Fustin v. Board of Education of Community Unit Dist. No. 2, 4.13, 4.23-1, 4.41: 305, 344, 391

Gale v. Greater Washington Softball Umpires Ass'n., 4.27-4: 380*

Garcia v. Joseph Vince Co., 4.30: 387*

Garland Independent School Dist., Kissick v., 2.23: 195

Garretson v. United States, 4.50: 404

Garrett v. Nissen Corp., 4.30: 388

Gaspard v. Grain Dealer Mutual Insurance Co., 4.12-1(c), 4.12-2, 4.12-5(b), 4.12-5(d), 4.21, 4.41: 290, 293, 299, 301, 324*, 391

Gates Rubber Co., Daniels v., 4.27-4: 381*

Gaudet, Junior Football Ass'n. of Orange County, Texas v., 3.31-1: 245

Gautier v. Pro-Football, Inc, 6.40: 547–548

Gentemen v. Saunders Archery Co., 4.30: 389

Georgia High School Athletic Ass'n. v. Waddell, 1.21-2, 2.27-3: 6, 380

Germond v. Board of Educ. of Central School Dist. No. 1, 4.23-1: 344

Gerrity v. Beatty, 4.23-3: 348*

Gertz v. Robert Welch Inc., 4.14: 307–308

Gervasi v. Holland Raceway, Inc., 4.50: 404

Giannoulas, KGB, Inc. v., 6.40: 540*

Gilbert, Sult v., 1.50: 95*

Gillard, National Collegiate Athletic Ass'n. v., 1.32-2, 2.30: 62, 203

Gillespie v. Bain, 4.22-4, 4.27-3: 341, 380*

Gillespie v. Southern Utah State College, 4.26: 374

Gilmore v. City of Montgomery, 3.43-3: 274

Gilpin v. Kansas State High School Activities Ass'n., 3.31-2: 247*

Gomes v. Rhode Island Interscholastic League, 3.32-1: 253*

Gore v. Tri-County Raceway, Inc, 4.50: 404

Gould, Darrin v., 3.13: 222*

Grahn v. Northwest Sport, 4.12-3(b): 295

Grain Dealers Mutual Insurance Co., Gaspard v., 4.12-1(c), 4.12-2, 4.12-5(b), 4.12-5(d), 4.21, 4.41: 290, 293, 299, 301, 324, 397

Grauer v. State of New York, 4.12-1(b), 4.12-3(d), 4.25: 289, 297, 363*

Greater Washington Softball Umpires Ass'n., Gale v., 4.27-4: 380*

Green, Regina v., 5.22: 429*

Green, Board of Directors of the Independent School Dist. of Waterloo v., 223: 195

Greene v. Seattle Athletic Club, 4.12-3(c): 296

Greene v. Athletic Council of Iowa State University, 1.23: 32*

Gregoria v. Board of Educ. of Asbury Park, 3.31-2: 251

Griffiths, Short v., 4.23-4: 352

Griggas v. Clauson, 4.11-2, 4.21: 282, 322*

Grimsley, Manning v., 4.11-2, 4.21: 282, 329*

Gross Telecasting Co., Inc. v. Michigan State University, 6.21: 505*

Gross v. Pellicane, 4.13-1: 306

Grove City College v. Bell, 3.00, 3.22: 211, 214, 228, 233, 237*, 239–240

Guelker v. Evans, 1.22-3: 29

Gulf South Conference v. Boyd, 1.32-2, 2.13-1: 62, 120

Guttenplan v. Boston Professional Hockey Ass'n., 4.24: 358

Haas v. South Bend Community School Corporation, 3.31-2, 3.33-1(b): 251, 262

Hackbart v. Cincinnati Bengals, Inc., 4.11-2, 4.12-1(a), 4.12-4, 4.12-5(d), 4.12-5(e), 4.13, 4.21, 4.24: 282, 287, 297, 301, 303, 305, 324*, 327*, 329, 357

Hackensack Public School, McHugh v., 4.27-1: 378

Haffer v. Temple University, 3.22: 233*

Haft, Witherspoon v., 4.25: 369

Halbrook v. Oregon State University, 4.16, 4.30: 318, 389

Haldane Central School Board, Mularadelis v., 3.32-1: 256

Hall v. Columbus Board of Educ., 4.23-4: 352

Hall v. University of Minnesota, 1.21-3, 1.32-2, 1.41-3, 2.12: 7, 62, 85, 111*

Hamilton v. Tennessee Secondary Athletic Ass'n., 1.32-1: 58

Hamilton, Williams v., 1.22-2, 2.13-1: 19*, 121

Hampton Township School District, Kenneweg v., 3.42: 271

Handel, Shoemaker, et al. v., 5.60: 436

Harbin, Kersey v. 4.22-1, 4.23-1, 4.23-4: 334, 345, 353

Hardee, Taylor v., 4.25: 369

Harper v. Liggett Group, Inc., 4.30: 389

Harris v. Illinois High School Ass'n., 3.31-2: 251

Harrison Island Shores, Inc., Hertzog v., 4.50: 404

Harrison v. Montgomery County Board of Education, 4.12-5(b), 4.12-5(c): 299, 300

Harry v. Bike Athletic Co., et al., 1.42: 93

Hauter v. Zogarts, 4.30: 388

Hawayek v. Simmons, 4.21: 322

Hayes, Hill v., 6.40: 547

Heldman v. Uniroyal, Inc., 4.12-3(c); 4.12-5(d), 4.17-3, 4.30: 296, 301, 320, 383

Henderson Broadcasting Corp. v. Houston Sports, 6.31: 526*

Hennessey v. National Collegiate Athletic Ass'n., 1.24, 1.41-2: 48, 81

Hertel v. City of Pontiac, 6.28-1: 519*

Hertzog v. Harrison Island Shores, Inc., 4.50: 404

Hesseltine v. State Athletic Commission, 3.43-2: 273

Hewitt v. Miller, 4.50: 404

Hill v. Hayes, 6.40: 547

Hill, Time, Inc. v., 4.15, 6.40: 312, 545

Hillcrest Country Club, Rockwell v., 4.25: 369

Hillsdale College v. Department of Health, Education and Welfare, 3.22: 233*

Hoffman, Cramer v., 4.13-1, 4.23-2, 4.26: 306, 347*, 373

Hogenson v. Williams, 4.22-2: 337

Holland Raceway, Inc., Gervasi v., 4.50: 404

Hollander v. Connecticut Interscholastic Athletic Conf., Inc., 3.31-2: 251

Hollon v. Mathis Independent School Dist., 2.23: 195

Hollywood Post No. 43, Chavez v., 6.40: 542

Holzer v. Oakland University Academy of Dramatic Arts, 4.23-4: 353

Home Box Office, Inc. v. FCC, 6.26: 512*

Hoover v. Meiklejohn, 3.31-1: 246

Hopkins County Board of Education, Kentucky High School Athletic Ass'n. v., 1.21-1, 1.31, 2.13-2: 4, 51, 122, 125

Hornung, Paul v. National Collegiate Athletic Ass'n., 3.10: 390

Houston General Insurance Company, Foster v., 4.22-1, 4.23-1: 334, 345

Houston Sports, Henderson Broadcasting Corp. v., 6.31: 526*

Houston, Art Gaines Baseball Corp. v., 2.60: 208

Howard University v. National Collegiate Athletic Ass'n., 1.31, 1.33: 52*, 66

Howard v. Rogers, 4.25: 365

Hubbard Broadcasting, Inc. v. Southern Satellite Systems, Inc., 6.27: 516*

Hunt v. Scotia-Glenville Central School District, 4.12-1(a): 288

Hunter, State v., 3.43-2: 273

Hutchins v. Board of Trustees of Michigan State University, 3.33-1(a): 261

Ide v. City of St. Cloud, 4.23-4: 353

Iervolino v. Pittsburgh Athletic Co., 4.24: 358

Illinois High School Ass'n., Robinson v., 1.32-2: 62

Illinois High School Ass'n., Kulovitz v., 2.13-2: 125

Illinois High School Ass'n., Menora v., 2.21: 191

Illinois High School Ass'n., Lavin v., 3.31-1: 245

Illinois High School Ass'n., Harris v., 3.31-2: 251

Illinois High School Ass'n., Petrie v., 3.32-1: 255

Illinois High School Ass'n., Bucha v., 3.33-2(b): 264*

Independent School Dist. of Virginia, No. 222, Mokovich v., 4.22-1, 4.25: 333, 367

Independent School District 742, Brenden v., 3.31-2, 3.31-2: 248, 249*

Independent School District No. 314, Larson v., 4.22-2, 4.23-1, 4.23-4: 337, 345, 352

Indiana High School Athletic Ass'n. v. Raike, 1.33, 2.23: 65, 195

Indiana State University Board of Trustees, Rensin v., 2.15-1(b): 141*, 142

Industrial Accident Commission, Van Horn v., 2.15-1(a–b), 138, 143

Industrial Comm'n., State Compensation Ins. Fund v., 2.15-1(b): 144

Institute of Athletic Motivation v. University of Illinois, 4.14: 310

Intelicense, United States Olympic Committee v., 2.18: 186

Intercollegiate (Big Ten) Conference, Etc., Wilson v., 2.12: 111

Intercollegiate Conference of Faculty Rep, Behagen v., 1.32-1, 1.32-2, 2.30: 55*, 62, 199

International Federation of Bodybuilders, United States Olympic Committee v., 2.18: 186

International Marathons Inc., Boston Athletic Ass'n. v., 1.23-3: 40*

International Marathons, Inc. v. Attorney General, 1.23-3: 42, 43

International Olympic Committee v. San Francisco Arts & Athletes, 2.18: 186

International Olympic Committee, Martin v., 1.22-1, 2.18: 14, 186*

Iowa District Court of Stony County, Knight v., 1.23: 33*

Iowa Girls High School Athletic Union, Russell, Wolf and Enslav v., 3.33-2(a): 263

Iowa High School Athletic Ass'n., Bunger v., 1.21-1, 2.24: 4, 196*

Irwin v. Board of Education, 1.41-2: 82

Isler v. Burman, 4.12-3(b): 295

Jackson v. Armstrong School District, 3.42: 271

Johnson v. Kruger, 4.12-1: 286

Johnson v. County Arena, Inc., 4.13: 304

Johnson v. Municipal University of Omaha, 4.23-4: 351

Johnson, Bingler v., 2.15-1(a): 138

Jones v. National Collegiate Athletic Ass'n., 1.24, 2.15-1(d): 48, 153*

Jones v. Wichita State University, 2.11: 108*

Jones v. Oklahoma Secondary School Activities Ass'n., 3.33-2(a): 263

Jordan v. Loveland Skiing Corp., 4.12-1(b): 289

Joseph Vince Co., Garcia v., 4.30: 387*

Judges of Court of Common Pleas, State v., 1.21-1, 1.22-3: 5, 30

Julian Messner, Inc., Spahn v. 4.15, 6.40: 316, 547*, 551*

Junior Football Ass'n. of Orange County, Texas v. Gaudet, 3.31-1: 245

Juntila v. Everett School Dist. No. 24, 4.12-5(b): 299

Justice v. National Collegiate Athletic Ass'n., 1.22-2: 18*

Kaiser v. State, 4.25: 367

Kallio, Ramsey v., 4.25: 369

Kallish v. American Baseball Club of Philadelphia, 4.12-1(c): 290

Kansas City Baseball & Exhibition Co., Crane v., 4.24: 355

Kansas City Kings, Rhodes v., 4.21, 4.24: 330, 358

Kansas State High School Activities Ass'n., Gilpin v., 3.31-2: 247*

Kelly v. Metropolitan County Board of Education of Nashville, 1.32-1, 1.42: 58, 93

Kenneweg v. Hampton Township School District, 3.42: 271

Kentucky High School Athletic Ass'n. v. Hopkins County Board of Education, 1.21-1, 2.13-2: 4, 122, 125

Kersey v. Harbin, 4.22-1, 4.23-1, 4.23-4: 334, 345, 353

KGB, Inc., v. Ted Giannoulas, 6.40: 540*

Kilpatrick, Scott v. 1.32-2, 2.13-1: 62, 121

King v. Burris, 4.14: 311

King v. Little League Baseball, Inc., 3.31-2: 252

Kings Park Central School District No. 5 v. State Division of Human Rights, 3.42: 272

Kissick v. Garland Independent School Dist., 2.23: 195

Kite v. Marshall, 2.60: 206*, 207*

Kluka v. Livingston Parish School Board, 4.22-2: 337

Knight v. Iowa District Court of Stony County, 1.23: 33*

Kobylanski v. Chicago Board of Education, 4.23-3: 348

KQV Broadcasting Co., Pittsburgh Athletic Co. v., 6.11: 497*

Kriss v. Brown, 2.13-2: 126

Krueger, Johnson v., 4.12-1: 286

Krulewitch, Whitehead v., 3.43-2: 273

Kuhn, Flood v. 6.31: 526

Kuhn, Ludtke v., 3.43-3: 274*

Kulovitz v. Illinois High School Ass'n., 2.13-2: 125

Kunda v. Muhlenberg College, 3.41: 267*

Kupec v. Atlantic Coast Conference, 1.21-3, 2.14-1: 7, 128*

LaFourche Parish School Bd., Estay v., 1.21-1, 2.23: 4, 193*

Larson v. Independent School District No. 314, 4.22-2, 4.23-1, 4.23-4: 337, 345, 352

Lavin v. Chicago Board of Education, 3.31-1: 245

Lavin v. Illinois High School Ass'n., 3.31-1: 245

Lee v. Florida High School Activities Ass'n. Inc., 2.14-1: 129

Leffel v. Wisconsin Interscholastic Athletic Ass'n., 3.31-1: 246

Leland Stanford Junior University, Lockard v., 4.23-1: 345

Lenape Valley Regional High School, Pantalone v., 4.27-2: 378*

Lester v. Public Building Authority of County of Knox, 1.23-2: 39*

Levine, Polsky v., 4.12-5(b): 299

Leyte, Regina v., 5.22: 431*

Lieuallen, Aiken v., 3.33-1(a): 258*

Liga Athletica Interuniversitaria, Rivas Tenorio v., 1.22-2, 1.31, 1.33: 19, 54, 66

Liggett Group, Inc., Harper v., 4.30: 389

Lincoln v. Mid-Cities Pee Wee Football Ass'n., 3.31-1: 246

Lincoln-Devon Bounceland, Inc., Ragni v., 4.25: 367

Lindquist, Reddick v., 4.12-1: 286

Little League Baseball Incorporated, Dillard v., 4.27-1: 375*

Little League Baseball of Collingswood, Pomeroy v., 4.23-4: 353

Little League Baseball, Inc., Assmus v., 1.21-2: 6

Little League Baseball, Inc., Rappaport v., 3.31-2: 252

Little League Baseball, Inc., King v., 3.31-2: 252

Little League Baseball, Inc., National Organization for Women, Essex County Chapter v., 3.31-2: 252

Livingston Board of Education, Ehehalt v., 4.27-4: 380*

Livingston Parish School Board, Kluka v., 4.22-2: 337

Lockard v. Leland Stanford Junion University, 4.23-1: 345

Loeb v. Turner, 6.11: 497*

Lohrke v. University of Louisville, 2.15-1(a): 140

Long Beach, Wiersma v., 4.25: 368

Long v. Zopp, 2.22: 193

Los Angeles Dodgers Baseball Club, Fish v., 4.26: 373

Louisiana High School Athletic Ass'n., Chabert v., 2.13-2: 125

Louisiana High School Athletic Ass'n., David v., 2.14-1: 129

Louisiana High School Athletic Ass'n., Dumex v., 2.60: 209

Louisiana High School Activities Ass'n., Mitchell v., 1.22-3, 1.31, 1.32-1, 2.14-1: 28, 54, 58, 66, 129

Louisiana High School Athletic Ass'n., Sanders v., 1.21-1: 5

Louisiana High School Athletic Ass'n., Walsh v., 1.22-3, 2.13-2: 29, 123

Louisiana High School Athletic Ass'n., Watkins v., 1.21-2: 6

Love & Campbell Athletic Goods Co., McCormack v., 4.30: 389

Loveland Skiing Corp., Jordan v., 4.12-1(b): 289

Ludtke v. Kuhn, 3.43-3: 274*

Lull Engineering, Barker v., 4.30: 382

Luten, State ex rel National Junior College Athletic Ass'n. v., 1.21-1: 4

Luttrell, Averill v., 4.11-2, 4.13, 4.21, 4.24: 282, 305, 330, 356*

Lynch v. Board of Education of Collingsville Community School District, 4.12-1(a): 287

Lynch v. Board of Education of Collingsville Community School District, 4.12-1(d): 290

Lynch v. Board of Education of Collingsville Community School District, 4.22-1: 333*

Lynch v. Board of Education of Collingsville Community School District, 4.23-1: 345

Lynch v. Board of Education of Collingsville Community School District, 4.23-3: 348

MacLean v. First Northwest Industries of America, 3.13: 224

Macumber, Askew v., 2.15-1(b): 144

Maddox v. City of New York, et al., 4.25: 368

Madison Square Garden Corp., Rich v., 4.25: 369

Maes, Tavernier v., 4.11-3(a): 283

Magill v. Avonworth Baseball Conference, 3.31-2: 252

Mahan, Sturrup v., 2.13-2: 125

Maki, Regina v., 5.22: 428*

Maloney, Regina v., 5.22: 430*

Malrite TV of N.Y. v. FCC, 6.12: 498*

Management TV Systems, Inc. v. National Football League, 6.21: 505*

Manhattan Cable Television and Teleprompter Corp., Silas et al. v., 6.22: 505

Manning v. Grimsley, 4.11-2, 4.21: 282, 329*

Marcum v. Dahl, 1.32-1, 2.21: 58, 191

Marino v. Waters, 1.21-1, 2.13-2: 4, 126

Majorie Webster Junior College Inc. v. Middle States Ass'n. of Colleges and Secondary Schools, Inc., 2.30: 202

Marshall County Board of Education, Burkey v., 3.42: 269*

Marshall, Kite v., 2.60: 206*, 207*

Martin v. International Olympic Committee, 1.22-1, 2.18: 14, 186*

Maryland, McGowan v., 1.22-3: 28

Massachusetts Interscholastic Athletic Ass'n. Inc., Atty. Gen. v., 3.32-1: 256

Mathis Independent School Dist., Hollon v., 2.23: 195

McCormack v. Love & Campbell Athletic Goods Co., 4.30: 389

McDonald v. National Collegiate Athletic Ass'n., 1.31, 2.30: 51*, 52, 203

McGee v. Board of Education of City of New York, 4.27-1: 376, 377*

McGinnis, Parmentier v., 4.12-1(c): 289

McGowan v. Maryland, 1.22-3: 28

McHugh v. Hackensack Public School, 4.27-1: 378

McMahon v. Board of Trustees of University of Ark., 1.23-1: 37

McMullen, Smith v., 4.14: 310

Meadors, Standard v., 4.30: 388

Meek, Davis v., 2.3: 194*

Meiklejohn, Hoover v., 3.31-1: 246

Menora v. Illinois High School Ass'n., 2.21: 191

Mercurio, Domino v., 4.13, 4.22-1, 4.23-1: 305, 334, 345

Merrill v. Birhanzel, 4.23-4: 352

Metropolitan County Board of Education of Nashville, Etc., Kelley v., 1.32-1, 1.42: 58, 93

Miami Dolphins, Ltd., Rodgers v., 4.24: 359

Michels v. United States Olympic Committee, 2.18: 189

Michigan Department of Civil Rights, ex rel. Forton v. Waterford Township Department of Parks and Recreation, 3.33-1(b): 261

Michigan State Board of Education, Morris v., 3.31-1, 3.31-2: 245, 251

Michigan State University, Gross Telecasting Co., Inc., v., 6.21: 505*

Mid-Cities Pee Wee Football Ass'n., Lincoln v., 3.31-1: 246

Middle States Ass'n. of Colleges and Secondary Schools, Inc., Majorie Webster Junior College Inc. v., 2.30: 202

Midget, Oklahoma Secondary School Activities Ass'n. v., 1.42: 93

Midlothian Country Club, et al., Duffy v., 4.12(c), 4.12-5(d), 4.24: 300, 301, 359

Midwest Communications, Inc. v. Minnesota Twins, Inc. et al., 6.33: 536*

Miles, Wellsville-Middleton School of District v., 4.27-3: 380

Millard School District No. 17, Brahatcek v., 4.23-1: 345

Miller, Hewitt v., 4.50: 404

Milwaukee Co., Powless v., 4.12-5(b): 299

Minneapolis Baseball & Athletic Ass'n., Wells v., 4.12-1(a), 4.12-3(b), 4.12-5(a), 4.12-5(d), 4.24, 4.25: 288, 295, 298, 301, 354*, 368

Minneapolis Boxing and Wrestling Club, Inc., Ulrich v., 4.27-2: 379

Minnesota State High School League, Stribel v., 3.33-3: 265*

Minnesota Twins, Inc. et al., Midwest Communications, Inc. v., 6.33: 536*

Minor Park District, Fetzer v., 4.23-4: 352

Missouri State High School Activities Ass'n., ABC League v., 2.14-1: 130

Missouri State High School Athletic Ass'n., Barnhorst v., 1.31: 55

Mitchell v. Louisiana High School Athletic Ass'n., 1.22-3, 1.31, 1.32-1, 1.33, 2.14-1: 28, 54, 58, 66, 129

Mogabgab v. Orleans Parish School Board, 4.12-1(e), 4.13, 4.22-3, 4.23-1, 4.23-2: 292, 305, 339, 344, 347

Mokovich v. Independent School Dist. of Virginia, No. 222, 4.22-1, 4.25: 333, 367

Montgomery Country Board of Education, Harrison v., 4.12-5(b), 4.12-5(c): 299, 300

Moran v. School District #7, Yellowstone County, 1.32-2, 1.33, 2.23: 63, 65, 195

Moreland v. Western Pa. Interscholastic, Etc., 1.33: 66

Morris v. Union High School District A, King County, 4.13, 4.22-1, 4.23-1: 305, 332*, 345

Morris v. Michigan State Bd. of Educ., 3.31-1, 3.31-2: 245, 251

Mt. Mansfield Co., Inc., Fischer v., 4.12-3(d): 297

Mt. Mansfield Lift, Wright v., 4.12-3(c): 296

Muhammad Ali v. Division of State Athletic Commission of Department of State of New York, 1.22-4: 31, 32

Muhlenberg College, Kunda v., 3.41: 267*

Mularadelis v. Haldane Central School Board, 3.32-1: 256

Muller v., Oregon, 3.11: 215

Municipal University of Omaha, Johnson v., 4.23-4: 351

Murnick, Pierce v., 4.12-5(b): 299

Murtaugh v. Nyquist, 2.14-1: 129

Muscare v. O'Malley, 3.31-1: 246

Nabozny v. Barnhill, 4.12-1(a), 4.12-4, 4.12-5(b), 4.12-5(d), 4.21: 287, 297, 299, 301, 323*

Nagy, Clinton v., 3.31-1: 244*

Namath v. Sports Illustrated, 4.15: 316

Nansen Properties, Inc., Schimenti v., 4.12-3(a): 294

Nash v. Borough of Wildwood Crest, 4.27-2: 378*

National Ass'n. of Theatre Owners v. FCC, 6.26: 513

National Ass'n. of Broadcasters v. Copyright Royalty Tribunal, 6.23: 507*

National Ass'n. of Theatre Owners v. FCC, 6.26: 511*

National Broadcasting Co. v. Athena Cablevision of Corpus Christi, Inc., 6.24: 508*

National Collegiate Athletic Ass'n., Parish v., 2.11, 2-60: 107*, 208

National Collegiate Athletic Ass'n. v. Board of Regents of U. of Oklahoma and U. of Georgia Athletic Ass'n., 1.24, 3.00, 6.32: 48, 213, 527*

National Collegiate Athletic Ass'n. v. Califano, 1.21-2, 3.21: 6, 225*

National Collegiate Athletic Ass'n. v. Gillard, 1.32-2, 2.30: 62, 203

National Collegiate Athletic Ass'n., Arlosoroff v., 1.31: 53*

National Collegiate Athletic Ass'n., Ass'n. for Intercollegiate Athletics for Women v., 1.24, 6.32: 48, 536*

National Collegiate Athletic Ass'n.., Associated Students, Inc. v., 1.31, 2.11, 2.16: 55, 109, 175

National Collegiate Athletics Ass'n., Board of Regents, University of Oklahoma v., 1.24, 1.4-2: 48, 80*

National Collegiate Athletic Ass'n., Buckton v., 1.31, 1.32-2, 1.33, 2.15-1(d): 54, 61, 65, 154

National Collegeiate Athletic Ass'n., Butts v., 2.14-2: 130*

National Collegiate Athletic Ass'n., California State University, Hayward v., 1.21-1, 1.4-1: 4, 71*

National Collegiate Athletic Ass'n., Colorado Seminary v., 1.21-1, 1.32-2, 2.30: 5, 61*, 207

National Collegiate Athletic Ass'n., College Athletic Placement Services, Inc. v., 1.24: 45*

National Collegiate Athletic Ass'n., Cox Broadcasting Corp. v., 6.27: 515*

National Collegiate Athletic Ass'n., English v., 2.13-1: 118*

National Collegiate Athletic Ass'n., Hennessey v., 1.24, 1.41-2: 48, 81

National Collegiate Athletic Ass'n., Howard University v., 1.31, 1.33: 52*, 66

National Collegiate Athletic Ass'n., Jones v., 1.24, 2.15-1(d): 48, 153*

National Collegiate Athletic Ass'n., Justice v., 1.22-2: 18*

National Collegiate Athletic Ass'n., McDonald v., 1.31, 2.30: 51*, 52, 203

National Collegiate Athletic Ass'n., Parish v., 1.21-2, 1.31: 6, 52, 54

National Collegiate Athletic Ass'n., Paul Hornung v., 4.14: 309

National Collegiate Athletic Ass'n., Regents of the University of Minnesota v., 1.31, 1.32-1, 2.30: 54, 58, 199*, 200

National Collegiate Athletic Ass'n., Samara v., 1.21-3, 2.30: 7, 230

National Collegiate Athletic Ass'n., Shelton v., 1.21-1, 2.16: 5, 175*

National Collegiate Athletic Ass'n., Spath v., 2.14-2: 130

National Collegiate Athletic Ass'n., Wiley v., 2.11, 2.15-1(d): 108, 154

National Exhibition Co. v., Fass, 6.11: 497*

National Exhibition v. Teleflash, Inc., 6.11: 496*

National Football League Players Ass'n. v. National Labor Relations Board and National Football League Management, 5.40: 434

National Football League, Management TV Systems, Inc. v., 6.21: 505*

National Football League, Smith v., 4.27-2: 378*

National Hockey League, San Francisco Seals, Ltd. v., 1.24: 47

National Labor Relations Board and National Football League Management, National Football League

Players Ass'n. v., 5.40: 434

National League of Professional Baseball Clubs, Federal Baseball Club of Baltimore v., 6.31: 522, 526

National Organization for Women, Essex County Chapter v. Little League Baseball, Inc., 3.31-2: 252

NCAA and Officials at the University of Wisconsin, Madison, Walker Carlton v., 2.30: 201*

Nebraska School Activities Ass'n., Reed v., 3.31-2: 250*

Nebraska School Activities Ass'n., Bednar v., 3.31-2: 251

Nelson, Pegram v., 1.32-1: 58

Nemeth, University of Denver v., 2.15-1(a), 2.15(b): 138, 143

New Boston Television, Inc. v. Entertainment Sports Programming Network, Inc., 6.40: 542*

New England Patriots Football Club, Inc. and Norwood Hospital, Gregory Taylor v., 4.24: 358

New Hampshire Interscholastic Atheltic Ass'n., Duffley v., 1.32-1, 2.14-1: 58, 129

New Hampshire Interscholastic, Etc., Snow v., 1.22-3: 29

New York Roadrunners Club v. State Division of Human Rights, 2.25: 197*

New York State Division of Human Rights v. New York-Pennsylvania Professional Baseball League, 3.43-1: 272*

New York State Human Rights Appeal Board, United Teachers of Seaford v., 3.42: 272

New York Times Co. v. Sullivan, 4.14, 6.40: 307, 308, 309, 310, 548

New York Times, et. al., Stabler v., 4.14: 311

New York Yankees, Toolson v., 6.31: 523, 526

New York-Pennsylvania Professional Baseball League, New York State Division of Human Righs v., 3.43-1: 272*

Newsweek, Inc., Vanderbury v., 6.40: 547

NFL v. Campagnolo Enter., Inc., 6.24: 508

NFL v. The Alley Inc., 6.24: 508

NFL, Blaich v., 6.28-1: 518

NFL, Campo v., 6.28-1: 518*

NFL, WTWV, Inc., v., 6.28-1: 519*

NFL, United States v., 6.31: 522, 523*, 524*

NFL, Colorado High School Activities Ass'n. v., 6.31: 525*

Niles v. University Interscholastic League, 2.13-2: 126

Nissen Corp., Garrett v., 4.30: 388

Nissen Trampoline Company v. Terre Haute First National Bank, 4.30: 388

North Haven Board of Education v. Bell, 3.22: 228, 234*, 238

North New Jersey Interscholastic League, Christian Brothers Institute v., 1.22-3: 29

Northeastern Beaver County School District, Rutter v., 4.12-5(d): 301

Northwest Sport, Grahn v., 4.12-3(b): 295

Norwin School District, Ritacco v., 3.33-1(b): 261*

Novak v. City of Delavan, 4.24: 369

Nyquist, Murtaugh v., 2.14-1: 129

O'Brien v. Township High School District No. 214, 4.23,-2, 4.23-4: 346*, 353

O'Connor v. Board of Education, 1.32-1, 3.33-1(a): 58, 257*

O'Malley, Muscare v., 3.31-1: 246

Oakdale Union Grammar School Dist., Pirkle v., 4.22-2: 337

Oakland High School Dist. of Alameda County, Weldy v., 4.25: 368

Oakland University of Academy of Dramatic Arts, Holzer v., 4.23-4: 353

Odle, Albach v., 1.21-1, 2.13-2: 5, 125

Oeschger v. Fitzgerald, 4.23-4: 351

Ohio High School Athletic Ass'n., Yellow Springs Exempted School District v., 1.31, 3.22: 55, 229*, 230

Oklahoma Secondary School Activities Ass'n., Jones v., 3.33-2(a): 263

Oklahoma Secondary School Activities Ass'n. v. Midget, 1.42: 93

Oregona State University, Halbrook v., 4.16, 4.30: 318, 389

Oregon State University, Petersen v., 3.33-1(a): 261

Oregon, Muller v., 3.11: 215

Orleans Parish School Bd., Mogabgad v., 4.12-1(e), 4.13, 4.22-3, 4.23-1, 4.23-2: 292, 305, 339, 344, 347

Osborne v. Sprowls, 4.21: 330

Othen v. Ann Arbor School Board, 3.22: 230*

Pa. Interscholastic Athletic Ass'n., School District of the City of Harrisburg v., 1.42: 93

Pantalone v. Lenape Valley Regional High School, 4.27-2: 378*

Parish v. National Collegiate Athletic Ass'n., 1.21-2, 1.31, 2.11, 2.60: 6, 52, 54, 107, 208

Parker v. Warren, 4.25: 368

Parmentier v. McGinnis, 4.12-1(c): 289

Pavey v. University of Alaska and National Collegiate Athletic Ass'n., 3.10: 215

Pegram v. Nelson, 1.32-1: 58

Pellicane, Gross v. 4.13-1: 306

Pennsylvania Interscholastic Athletic Ass'n., Commonwealth, Packel v., 3.13: 223*

People v. Fitzsimmons, 5.22: 431*

People v. Shepherd, 5.80: 493

Perkins v. Trask, 4.23-4: 351

Perry v. Seattle School Dist. No. 1, 4.25: 368

Petersen v. Oregon State University, 3.33-1(a): 261

Petrie v. Illinois High School Ass'n., 3.32-1: 255

Philadelphia Board of Education, Berman by Berman v., 4.12-1(a), 4.12-2, 4.23-3: 288, 293, 349

Philadelphia Eagles Football Club, Chuy v., 4.14, 4.16, 4.24, 4.26: 308*, 309, 317, 358, 373

Philadelphia National League Club, Schentzel v., 4.12-5(d): 301

Philadelphia National League Club, Bayless v. 4.26: 373

Phillips, Barrett v., 4.12-1(c), 4.12-1(e), 4.21: 290, 292, 329

Philpot v. Brooklyn Nat'l. League Baseball Club, 4.24: 358

Pierce City R-VI School District, Force v., 3.31-1: 246

Pierce v. Murnick, 4.12-5(b): 299

Pirkle v. Oakdale Union Grammar School Dist., 4.22-2: 337

Pittsburgh Athletic Co. v. KQV Broadcasting Co., 6.11: 497*

Pittsburgh Athletic Co., Iervolino v., 4.24: 358

Pleasant v. Blue Mount Swim Club, 4.30: 388

Polonich v. A.P.A. Sports, Inc., 4.21: 330

Polsky v. Levine, 4.12-5(b): 299

Pomeroy v. Little League Baseball of Collingswood, 4.23-4: 353

Porter v. California Jockey Club, 4.25: 368

Post Newsweek v. Travelers Inc. Co., 6.40: 541*

Powless v. Milwaukee Co., 4.12-5(b): 299

Praetorius v. Shell Oil Co., 4.25: 367

Pro-Football, Inc., Gautier v., 6.40: 547–548

Public Building Authority of County of Knox, Lester v., 1.23-2: 39*

Pulsifer, Dunham v. 1.21-1, 2.22: 4, 191*

Rabiner v. Rosenberg, 4.12-1: 286

Ragni v. Lincoln-Devon Bounceland, Inc., 4.25: 367

Raike, Indiana High School Athletic Ass'n. v., 1.33, 2.23: 65*, 195

Ramsey v. Kallio, 4.25: 369

Randolph County Bd. of Education, Davenport v., 2.22: 193

Rappaport v. Little League Baseball, Inc., 3.31-2: 252

Ratcliff v. San Diego Baseball Club of the Pacific Coast League, 4.24: 358

Rayex Corp., Filler v., 4.30: 388

Re U.S. Ex Rel. Missouri State High School, Etc. 2.13-2: 126

Reddick v. Lindquist, 4.12-1: 286

Reed v. Reed, 3.11: 216

Reed v. Nebraska School Activities Ass'n., 3.31-2: 250*

Reed v. Reed, 3.11, 3.31-2: 216, 250

Regents of the University of Minnesota v. National Collegiate Athletic Ass'n., 1.31, 1.32-1, 2.30: 54, 58, 199*, 200

Regina v. Green, 5.22: 429*

Regina v. Leyte, 5.22: 431*

Regina v. Maki, 5.22: 428*

Regina v. Maloney, 5.22: 430*

Regina v. Watson, 5.22: 431*

Rensing v. Indiana State University Board of Trustees, 2.15-1(b): 141*, 142

Rhodes v. School Dist. No. 9, Roosevelt County 4.23-4: 352

Rhode Island Interscholastic League, Gomes v., 3.32-1: 253*

Rhodes v. Kansas City Kings, 4.21, 4.24: 330, 358

Rich v. Madison Square Garden Corp., 4.25: 369

Richards v. United States Tennis Association, 3.11: 218

Richardson, Frontiero v. 3.11: 216, 217

Richmond v. Employers' Fire Ins. Co., 4.12-5(d), 4.21: 301, 321

Riddell, Inc., Byrns v., 4.17, 4.30: 310, 384*

Ridgefield Women's Political Caucus, Inc. v. Fossi, 3.11: 217–218

Riggall v. Washington County Medical Society, 2.30: 129

Ritacco v. Norwin School District, 3.33-1(b): 261*

Rivas Tenorio v. Liga Athletica Interuniversitaria, 1.22-2, 1.31, 1.33: 19, 54, 66

Robert Welch Inc., Gertz v., 4.14: 307, 308

Robinson v. Illinois High School Ass'n., 1.32-2: 62

Robitalle v. Vancouver Hockey Club, 4.24, 4.26: 358, 374

Rockwell v. Hillcrest Country Club, 4.25: 369

Rodgers v. Miami Dolphins, Ltd., 4.24: 359

Rodriguez, San Antonio Independent School District v., 1.22-3, 3.33-1(b): 28, 258

Rogers, Howard v., 4.25: 365

Romans v. Crenshaw, 2.23: 195

Rose, Alabama High School Athletic Ass'n. v., 1.22-3: 30

Rosenberg, Rabiner v., 4.12-1; 286

Rosenberger v. Central Louisiana Dist. Livestock Show, Inc., 4.13: 304

Rosensweig v. State of New York, 4.13, 4.26: 305, 371*

Roth, Board of Regents v., 1.32-2: 60

Rubtchinsky v. State University of New York at Albany, 4.23-1: 344

Ruman v. Eskew, 3.33-1(b): 262

Russell, Wolf and Enslav v. Iowa Girls High School Athletic Union, 3.33-2(a): 263

Rutledge v. Arizona Board of Regents, 4.14, 4.22-2, 4.23-4: 309, 336*, 353

Rutter v. Northeastern Beaver County School District, 4.12-5(d): 301

Salk v. Alpine Ski Shop, 4.30: 389

Samara v. National Collegiate Athletic Ass'n., 1.21-3, 2.30: 7, 203

San Antonio Independent School District v. Rodriguez, 1.22-3, 3.33-1(b): 28, 258

San Diego Baseball Club of the Pacific Coast League, Ratcliff v., 4.24: 358

San Francisco Arts & Athletes, International Olympic Committee v., 2.18: 186

San Francisco Seals, Ltd. v. National Hockey League, 1.24: 42

Sanders v. Louisiana High School Athletic Ass'n., 1.21-1: 5

Santee v. Amateur Athletic Union, 1.22: 2.30: 8*, 203

Saunders Archery Co., Gentemen v., 4.30: 389

Schentzel v. Philadelphia National League Club, 4.12-5(d): 301

Schimenti v. Nansen Properties, Inc., 4.12-3(a): 294

Schmitt, Dudley Sports Co. v. 4.12-3(c), 4.30: 296, 382

Schofield v. Wood, 4.12-1(c):290

School Dist. No. 9, Roosevelt County Rhoades v., 4.23-4: 352

School District #7, Yellowstone County, Moran v., 1.32-2, 1.33, 2.23: 63, 65, 195

School District No. 26C, Malheur County, Vendrell v., 4.12-2, 4.22-2, 4.23-3: 293, 335*, 349

School District of the City of Harrisburg v. Pa. Interscholastic Athletic Ass'n., 1.42: 93

Scotia-Glenville Central School District, Hunt v., 4.12-1(a): 288

Scott v. Kilpatrick, 1.31-2, 2.13-1: 62, 121

Scripps-Howard Broadcasting Co., Zacchini v., 6:40: 542, 543*

Seal v. Birmingham Post, 1.23-1, 1.41-3: 33*, 85

Seattle Athletic Club, Greene v., 4.12-3(c): 296

Seattle School Dist. No. 1, Perry v., 4.25: 368

Sewanhaka Central High School Dist., Colombo v., 2.25: 198

Shell Oil Co., Praetorius v., 4.25: 367

Shelton v. National Collegiate Athletic Ass'n., 1.21-1, 2.16: 5, 175*

Shepherd, People v., 5.80: 493

Shields v., Van Kelton Amusement Corp., 4.12-5(b): 299

Shoemaker, et al. v. Handel, 5.60: 436

Short v. Griffiths, 4.23-4: 352

Shriver v. Athletic Commission of Kansas State University, 4.23-4: 352

Silas et al. v. Manhattan Cable Television and Teleprompter Corp., 622: 505

Silvia v. Woodhouse, 4.25: 368

Simmons, Hawayek v., 4.21: 322

Simpson v. Boston Area Youth Soccer, Inc., 3.31-1: 246

Smith v. Vernon Parish School Bd., 4.12-1: 287

Smith v. McMullen, 4.14: 310

Smith v. National Football League, 4.27-2: 378*

Smith, Southern Methodist University v., 1.32-1, 2.30: 58, 201*

Snow v. New Hampshire Interscholastic, Etc., 1.22-3: 29

Solodar v. Watkins Glen Grand Prix Corp., 4.50: 404

Sony Corp. v. Universal City Studios, Inc., 6.28-2: 520*

South Ben Community School Corporation, Haas v. 3.31-2, 3.33-1(b): 251, 262

South Carolina High School League, Bruce v. 2.13-2: 122, 125

South Dakota High School Activities Ass'n., Baltic Independent School District No. 115 v., 1.33: 66

Southeast Oklahoma State University, Warthen v., 4.27-4: 381*

Southern Methodist University v. Clayton 4.23-4: 353

Southern Methodist University v. Smith, 1.32-1, 2.30: 58, 201

Southern Satellite Systems, Inc., Hubbard Broadcasting, Inc. v., 6.27: 516*

Southern State College, Arkansas Gazette v., 1.23-1: 37*

Southern Utah State College, Gillespie v., 4.26: 374

Spahn v. Julian Messner, Inc., 4.15, 6.40: 316, 547*, 55*

Spann, State v., 5.80: 493

Spath v. National Collegiate Athletic Ass'n., 2.14-2: 130

Special Services, Inc., French v., 4.50: 404

Sports Illustrated, Namath v., 4.15: 316

Springfield Television Corp. v. Federal Communications Commission, 6.12: 499

Sprowls, Osborne v., 4.21: 330

St. Mary's Inter-Parochial School of Salem, South Dakota High School Interscholastic Activities Ass'n. v., 1.23-3: 30

Stabler v. New York Times, et al., 4.14: 311

Standard v. Meadors, 4.30: 388

Stanley v. Big Eight Conference, 1.32-1, 1.41-2: 56*, 81

Starkey v. Board of Educ. of David County School Dist., 2.23: 195

State Athletic Commission, State v., 4.273-380

State Athletic Commission, Hesseltine v., 3.43-2: 273

State Compensation Ins. Fund v. Industrial Comm'n, 2.15-1(b): 144

State Division of Human Rights v. Syracuse City Teachers Ass'n., 3.42: 272

State Division of Human Rights, New York Roadrunners Club v., 2.25: 197

State Division of Human Rights, Kings Park Central School District No. 5 v., 3.42: 272

State ex rel. Baker v. Stevenson, 2.23: 195

State ex rel. National Junior College Athletic Ass'n. v. Luten, 1.21-1

State of New York, Grauer v., 4.12-1(b), 4.12-3(d), 4.25: 289, 297, 363*

State of New York, Rosensweig v. 4.13, 4.26: 305, 371*

State of Oklahoma, Carroll v., 4.271: 376

State University of New York at Albany, Rubtchinsky v., 4.23-1: 344

State v. Forbes, 4.21, 5.22: 330, 430*

State v. Major, 5.80: 493

State v. Spann, 5.80: 493

State v. Yonker, 5.80: 493

State v. State Athletic Commission, 4.27-3: 380

State v. Judges of Court of Common Pleas, 1.21-1, 1.22-3: 5, 30

State v. Hunter, 3.43-2: 273

State, Benjamin v., 4.12-1, 4.12-2, 4.12-5(b), 4.25: 290, 293, 299, 363*

State, Vogel v., 4.12-3(d): 297

State, Van Stry v., 4.12-5(c), 4.25: 300, 368

State, Kaiser v., 4.25: 367

State, Friedman v., 4.25: 367

State, Bradwell v., 3.11: 215

Stehn v. Bernarr MacFadden Foundation, Inc., 4.12-1, 4.23-1: 286, 344

Stevens v. Central School Dist. No. 1, 4.12-5(d): 301

Stevenson, State ex rel. Baker v., 2.23: 195

Stineman v. Fontbonne College, 4.22-3, 4.23-2: 339, 347

Stock v. Texas Catholic Interscholastic League, 1.32-2: 62

Stop the Olympic Prison v. U.S. Olympic Committee, 2.18: 186

Strickland, Williams v., 4.25: 369

Striebel v. Minnesota State High School League, 3.33-3: 265*

Strong v. Curators of the University of Missouri, 4.41: 391

Stroud v. Bridges, 4.12-3(b): 295

Sturrup v. Mahan, 2.13-2: 125

Sullivan v. University Interscholastic League, 2.13-2: 125

Sullivan, New York Times Co. v., 4.14, 6.40: 307–310, 548

Sult v. Gilbert, 1.50: 95*

Summers v. Tice, 4.30: 387

Svitchan, Vargo v. 4.22-1, 4.23-1, 4.23-4: 333, 345, 353

Swanson Broadcasting Co., Wichita State University Intercollegiate Athletic Ass'n., Inc. v., 6.21: 504*

Sykes v. Bensinger Recreation Corp., 4.25: 367

Syracuse City Teachers Ass'n., State Division of Human Rights v., 3.42: 272

Syracuse University, Eddy v., 4.25: 366*

Tarkanian v. University of Nevada, Las Vegas, 1.23-3, 1.41-2: 44, 80*, 81

Tarkanian, University of Nevada v., 1.21-3, 1.41-3: 7, 83

Tavernier v. Maes, 4.11-3(a): 283

Taylor v. Hardee, 4.25: 369

Taylor v. Alabama High School Athletic Ass'n., 1.32-1, 1.32-2: 58, 62

Taylor, Gregory, v. New England Patriots Football Club, Inc., and Norwood Hospital, 4.24: 358

Taylor v. Wake Forest University, 2.15-1(a): 139*

Taylor, Zawadzki v., 4.23-4: 351

Teleflash, Inc., National Exhibition v., 6.11: 496*

Temple University, Haffer v., 3.22: 233*

Tennessee Secondary Athletic Ass'n., Hamilton v., 1.32-1: 58

Tennessee Secondary School Ass'n. v. Cox, 1.21-1: 4

Tennessee Secondary School Athletic Ass'n., Carnes v., 3.31-2: 251

Tennessee Secondary School Athletic Ass'n., Cape v., 3.33-2(a): 263

Terre Haute First National Bank, Nissen Trampoline Company v., 4.30: 388

Texas Catholic Interscholastic League, Stock v., 1.32-2: 62

Texas High School Gymnastics Coaches Ass'n. v. Andrews, 2.60: 207*

Textor v. Board of Regents of Northern Illinois University, 3.42: 268*

The Alley Inc., NFL v., 6.24: 508

Thomas, Florida High School Activities Ass'n. v., 1.42: 92*

Thompson v. University of South Carolina, 4.27: 375

Thompson v. Barnes, 1.21-3: 7

Thurman v. Clune, 4.25: 369

Tice, Summers v., 4.30: 387

Tilelli v. Christenberry, 4.27-3: 380

Time, Inc. v. Hill, 4.15, 6.40: 312, 545

Time, Inc., Barry v., 4.14: 311

Time, Inc., Dempsey v., 4.14: 312

Tomjanovich v. California Sports, Inc., 4.13, 4.21, 4.24: 305, 329, 357*

Tondas v. Amateur Hockey Ass'n. of the United States, 1.24: 46*

Tookes v. Florida State University, 2.15-1(b): 143

Toolson v. New York Yankees, 6.31: 523, 526

Toone v. Adams, 4.12-1(c), 4.13, 4.22-4, 4.24: 290, 305, 340*, 359

Township High School District No. 214, O'Brien v. 4.23-2, 4.232-4: 346*, 353

Townsley v. Cincinnati Gardens, Inc., 4.12-1(a), 4.12-3(b), 4.12-5(a), 4.25: 287, 295, 298, 365*

Trask, Perkins v., 4.23-4: 351

Travelers Inc. Co., Post Newsweek v., 6.40: 541*

Travelers' Insurance Company, Benedetto v., 4.21: 321

Tri-County Raceway, Inc., Gore v., 4.50: 404

Truelove v. Wilson, 4.12-1(e): 292

Turner v. Caddo Parish School Board, 4.23-3, 4.25: 349, 368

Turner, Loeb v., 6.11: 497*

Turner, Woy v., 4.14: 310

Tusculum College, Inc., De Mauro v., 4.222, 4.231: 337, 343*

U.S. Olympic Committee, Stop the Olympic Prison v., 2.18: 186

U.S. Wrestling Federation v. Wrestling Division of AAU, 1.22-1: 13*

U.S., Clay v., 1.22-4: 31

Ulrich v. Minneapolis Boxing and Wrestling Club, Inc., 4.27-2: 379

Union High School District A, King County, Morris v. 4.13, 4.22-1, 4.23-1: 305, 332*, 345

Union Sports Apparel, United States Olympic Committee v., 2.18: 186

Uniroyal, Inc., Heldman v. 4.12-3(c), 4.12-5(d), 4.17-3, 4.30: 296, 301, 320, 383

United States Olympic Committee v. Intelicense, 2.18: 186

United States Olympic Committee v. International Federation of Bodybuilders, 2.18: 186

United States Olympic Committee v. Union Sports Apparel, 2.18: 186

United States Olympic Committee, Defranz v. 1.22-1, 2, 18: 12*, 189

United States Olympic Committee, United States Wrestling Federation v., 2.18: 186

United States Olympic Committee, Michels v., 2.18: 189

United States Tennis Association, Richards v., 3.11: 218

United States v. NFL, 6.31: 522, 523*, 524*

United States v. Burke, 5.71: 478*

United States Wrestling Federation v. United States Olympic Committee, 2.18: 186

United States Wrestling Federation v. Wrestling Division of the AAU, 2.18: 186

United States, Freeman v., 4.12-1(c): 289-90

United States, Ward v., 4.12-3(a): 294

United States, Garretson v., 4.50: 404

United States, Amateur Softball Ass'n. of America v., 1.24: 46*, 47

United Teachers of Seaford v. New York State Human Rights Appeal Board, 3.42: 272

Universal City Studios, Inc., Sony Corp. v., 6.28-2: 520*

University Interscholastic League, Sullivan v., 2.13-2: 125

University Interscholastic League, Niles v., 2.13-2: 126

University Interscholastic League, Blue v., 2.14-2: 134

University of Alaska and National Collegiate Athletic Ass'n., Pavey v., 3.10: 215

University of Chicago, Cannon v., 3.41: 267

University of Denver v. Nemeth, 2.15-1(a), 2.15-(b): 138, 143

University of Illinois, Institute of Athletic Motivation v., 4.14: 310

University of Louisville, Lohrke v., 2.15-1(a): 140

University of Massachusetts, Cantwell v., 4.12-1(a), 4.23-4: 287, 350*

University of Michigan, Curtis E. Jones, Jr. v., 2.50: 205

University of Minnesota, Hall v. 1.21-3, 1.32-2, 1.41-3, 2.12: 7, 62, 85, 111*

University of Nebraska, Fluitt v., 1.32-2: 61*

University of Nevada v. Tarkanian, 1.21-3, 1.41-3: 7, 83

University of Nevada, Las Vegas, Tarkanian v., 1.23-3, 1.41-2: 44, 80*

University of Notre Dame, Bearman v., 4.25: 366*

University of Richmond v. Bell, 3.22: 239

University of South Carolina, Carlen v., 4.14: 310

University of South Carolina, Thompson v., 4.27: 375

University of South Carolina, Bell v., 1.41-2: 82

University of Washington v. Florida State University, 1.50: 95

Utica Community School District, Deaner v., 4.26: 373

Van Horn v. Industrial Accident Commission, 2.15-1(a), 2.15-1(b): 138, 143

Van Kelton Amusement Corp., Shields v., 4.12-5(b): 299

Van Stry v. State, 4.12-5(c), 4.25: 300, 368

Vancouver Hockey Club, Robitaille v., 4.24, 4.26: 358, 374

Vanderbury v. Newsweek, Inc., 6.40: 547

Vargo v. Svitchan, 4.22-1: 333*

Vargo v. Svitchan, 4.23-1, 4.23-4: 345, 353

Vendrell v. School District No. 26C, Malheur County, 4.12-2, 4.22-2, 4.23-3: 293, 335, 349

Vernon Parish School Bd., Smith v., 4.12-1: 287

Virginia High Sch., Denis J. O'Connell High Sch. v., 1.22-3: 29*

Vogel v. State, 4.12-3(d): 297

Waddell, Georgia High School Athletic Ass'n. v. 1.21-2, 4.27-3: 6, 380*

Walker Carlton v. NCAA and Officials at the University of Wisconsin, Madison, 2.30: 201

Wake Forest University, Taylor v., 2.15-1(a): 139*

Walsh v. Louisiana High School Athletic Ass'n., 1.22-3, 2.13-2: 29, 123*

Ward v. United States, 4.12-3(a): 294

Warner Amex Cable v. American Broadcasting Companies, Inc., 6.32: 535*

Warren, Parker v., 4.25: 368

Warthen v. Southest Oklahoma State University, 4.27-4: 381*

Washington County Medical Society, Riggall v., 2.30: 129

Washington State University, Blair v., 3.33-1(a): 259*

Waterford Township Department of Parks and Recreation, Michigan Department of Civil Rights, ex rel. Forton v., 3.33-1(b): 261

Waters, Marino v., 1.21-1, 2.13-2: 4, 126

Watford v. Evening Star Newspaper Co., 4.12-3(b): 295

Watkins Glen Grand Prix Corp., Solodar v., 4.50: 404

Watkins v. Louisiana High School Athletic Ass'n., 1.21-2: 6

Watson, Regina v., 5.22: 431*

Waxenberg v. Crystal Baths, 4.12-3(c): 296

Weinstein v. Evanston Township Community Consolidated School District 65, 4.23-4: 352

Weiss v. Eastern College Athletic Conference, 2.13-1: 121

Welch v. Dunsmuir Joint Union High School District, 4.13, 4.22-3, 4.23-2, 4.26: 305, 338*, 347, 374

Weldy v. Oakland High School Dist. of Alameda County, 4.25: 368

Wells v. Minneapolis Baseball Athletic Ass'n., 4.12-1(a), 4.12-3(b), 4.12-5(a), 4.12-5(d), 4.24, 4.25: 288, 295, 298, 301, 354*, 368

Wells, Brown v., 2.60: 208, 209

Wellsville-Middleton School District v. Miles, 4.27-3: 380

West Texas State University, Bennett v., 3.22: 232*

Western Michigan University, Coleman v., 2.15-1(b): 144

Western Pa. Interscholastic, Etc., Moreland v., 1.33: 66

Wetzel v. Eaton Corp., 4.30: 387

White v. Corpus Christi Little Misses Kickball Ass'n., 3.32-1: 255

Whitehead v. Krulewitch, 3.43-2: 273

Whitfield v. Cox, 4.25: 369

Wichita State University Intercollegiate Athletic Ass'n., Inc. v. Swanson Broadcasting Co., 6.21: 504*

Wichita State University, Brown v., 4.23-4: 352

Wichita State University, Jones v., 2.11: 108*

Wiersma v. Long Beach, 4.25: 368

Wilcom, Winterstein v., 4.50: 404

Wiley v. National Collegiate Athletic Ass'n., 2.11, 2.15-1(d): 108, 154

Williams v. Strickland, 4.25: 369

Williams v. Cox Enterprises, Inc., 4.50: 393

Williams v. Hamilton, 1.22-2, 2.13-1: 19*, 121

Williams v. Eaton, 2.21: 190

Williams, Hogenson v., 4.22-2: 337

Wilmington Parking Authority, Burton v., 3.43-3: 274

Wilson v. Intercollegiate (Big Ten) Conference, Etc., 2.12: 111*

Wilson, Truelove v., 4.12-1(e): 292

Winterstein v. Wilcom, 4.50: 404

Wisconsin Interscholastic Athletic Ass'n., Leffel v., 3.31-1: 246

Witherspoon v. Haft, 4.25: 369

Wood, Schofield v. 4.12-1(c):290

Woodhouse, Silvia v., 4.25: 368

Woodring v. Board of Education of Manhasset, 4.25: 369

Workers' Compensation Appeals Board, Cheatham v., 2.15-1(b): 143*

Woy v. Turner, 4.14: 310

Wrestling Division of AAU, U.S. Wrestling Federation v. 1.22-1: 13*

Wrestling Division of the AAU, United States Wrestling Federation v., 2.18: 186

Wright v. Mt. Mansfield Lift, 4.12-3(c): 296

Wright v. Arkansas Activities Ass'n., 1.31, 1.32-1, 1.42: 55, 58, 93

WTWV, Inc. v. NFL, 6.28-1: 519

WWHT, Inc. v. FCC, 6.26: 510*

Yellow Springs Exempted School District v. Ohio High School Athletic Ass'n., 1.31, 3.22: 55, 229*, 230*

Yoder Co., Dorsey v., 4.30: 385

Yonker, State v., 5.80: 493

Zacchini v. Scripps-Howard Broadcasting Co., 6.40: 542, 543*

Zawadzki v. Taylor, 4.23-4: 351

Zeller v. Donegal School Dist., 2.22: 192*

Zogarts, Hauter v., 4.30: 388

Zopp, Long v., 2.22: 193

INDEX

Agents (*see* Player-agents)

Alcohol and drugs (in amateur athletics), 195–196

Amateur athlete
  academic performance rules
    high schools, 29
    NCAA, 71–73
  antitrust issues in regulation of, 45–50
  Buckley Amendment, 203–204
  Collegiate Athlete Education and Protection Act of 1985, 158
  Collegiate Student-athlete Protection Act of 1983, 158
  Constitutional rights, 12–13, 50–66
    due process, 55–63
    equal protection, 63–66
    state action, 50–55
  definitions of amateur, 1–2
  discipline, 198–203
  eligibility
    academic progress, 109–114
    college transfer rules, 114–122
    grade point average, 107–109
    high school transfer rules, 122–126
    improper education claims, 106
    longevity, 130–134
    Olympic athletes, 185–189
    postseason competition (NCAA), 10
    redshirting, 127–130
    statement of eligibility form, 106
  expenses, 162–175
  financial aid, 134–158
  handicapped, 196–198
  improper education claims, 204–205
  individual rights of
    alcohol and drugs, 195–196
    freedom of expression, 189–191
    grooming, 191–193
    high school marriages, 193–195
  pay
    employment, 160–161
    marketing, 161–162
    NCAA rules, 158–160
  player-agents, 177–185
  professional contracts, 175–177
  recruitment, 83–92
  scholarships
    congressional concerns, 154–158
    as contracts, 137–140
    excessive financial aid, 152–154
    letter of intent, 145–152
  summer camps, 205–209

Amateur athletic associations (*see also* Amateur Athletic Union; Amateur Sports Act of 1978; Olympics)
  antitrust, 45–50
  authority, 67–94
  broadcast pooling arrangements, 527–539
  definitions of amateur, 1–2
  disclosure cases, 33–38
  funding of public facilities, 38–40
  grievance procedures, 58–59
  judicial approach toward, 8–10
  legal principles
    due process, 55–63
    equal protection, 63–66
    injunctions, 6–7
    judicial review, 3–5
    standing, 5–6
    state action requirement, 50–54

liability insurance, 390–392
public broadcast rights, 45
public responsibility of
   delegation of authority, 40–45
   funding of public facilities, 38–40
   open meeting laws, 32–33
scheduling, 94–97
waiver of liability, 392–417
Amateur Athletic Union (AAU)
authority, 13–14
definition of amateur, 2
discipline of athletes, 8–10
Amateur Sports Act of 1978
establishment of USOC, 10–11
judicial review, 12–13
NCAA rules, 45–46
purposes, 186
Sherman Act, 45–50
Antitrust
amateur athletics, 45–50
blackouts, 518–519
broadcast pooling arrangements
   amateur athletics, 527–539
   pro sports, 504–505, 522–527
NCAA rules, 45–46
Sherman Act, 45–50
Assault and battery
baseball, 324, 329, 356–357
baseball umpires, 376–377
basketball, 322–323
boxing, 431–432
defenses
   assumption of risk, 427
   consent, 282, 423–427
   immunity, 284
   involuntary action, 428
   privilege, 283–284
   self-defense, 423–427
defined, 422
hockey cases, 428–431
legal theory, 280–282
professional football, 324–329
soccer, 323–324
softball, 321–322
Assumption of risk
defense to assault and battery, 427
legal theory, 300–302
participant injury defense
   baseball, 324
   professional football, 324–329

soccer, 323–324
softball, 321–322
tennis, 383–384
spectator injury defense
   baseball, 354–356
   golf, 359
Automobile racing
copyright infringement of broadcast rights, 497
waiver of liability, 404

Baseball
assault and battery
   on game officials, 340–341, 376–377
   on participants, 324
   on spectators, 329
broadcast rights
   antitrust, 526–27, 536–39
   application to superstations, 515–518
   ownership, 496–498
drug abuse and enforcement in professional, 473–474
intentional torts
   defamation, 310
   invasion of privacy, 316
liability of franchise/leagues
   for fan disturbances, 340–341
   for participant injury, 324, 330, 356–358
   for spectator injury, 354–356, 358, 373
   for umpire injury, 340–341, 367, 375–376
products liability, 382–383, 389
sex discrimination
   interscholastic, 251
   Little Leagues, 252
   officiating, 272
violence (major league disciplinary procedure), 433
Basketball
amateur
   academic eligibility, 107–109
   academic progress, 111, 113
   longevity, 130–132
   professional contracts, 175–176
   scholarships as contracts, 138–139
   worker's compensation, 143
amateur athletics
   due process, 55–56, 199–201
   right of freedom of expression, 191
   right of transfer rules, 126
   state action requirement, 51–52
   Tarkanian, Jerry, 80–81, 83–84

University of San Francisco, 87–89
assault and battery, 322–323
broadcast rights (NBA players suit), 505–506
drug abuse and enforcement in professional, 455–470
gambling
    amateur athletics, 478–479, 481
    professional, 492
game officials
    liability for injury, 367, 378
    review of decisions during event, 379–380
    worker's compensation, 380, 381
liability of franchise/leagues
    participant injury, 330, 357
liability of school district
    game officials injury, 367, 378
NBA waiver and release forms, 406–409
sex discrimination
    in coaching, 269–270, 271, 272
    intercollegiate (funding), 258–259
    interscholastic, 229–230, 245, 257–258, 262–263
violence
    NBA stance on, 434
    in professional basketball, 420, 433
Battery (*see* Assault and battery)
Boston Marathon, 40–44
Bowling (liability for participant injury), 367
Boxing
    Ali, Muhammad, 31–32
    liability of medical personnel, 371–373
        defamation, 312
        review of referee decision, 380
    licensing, 31–32
    State Commission Authority, 31–32
    USA Amateur Boxing Federation
        "Athletes Bill of Rights," 94
        definition of professional, 176
        objectives, 93
Breach of warranty (*see* Products liability law)
Broadcasting
    amateur athletics, 45
    blackouts, 499, 518–519
    broadcasters' rights, 506–507
    cable systems, 498–499, 508–510
    common law, 496–498
    communications law, 498–503
    consumer rights, 518–522
    copyright
        Copyright Act of 1976, 498–499, 507
        Copyright Royalty Tribunal, 498–499, 506–07
        laws, 503

exclusivity rights, 504–505
FCC regulations, 498–499, 508–510
Federal Communications Act of 1934, 498–499
Federal Communications Commission
    authority, 510–514
    licensing, 499–501
    private transmissions, 501–503
home taping, 519–522
licensing renewal, 499–501
media rights, 539–553
    entertainment as news, 541–547
    exclusivity, 539–541
    "right of privacy law," 547–553
ownership of broadcast rights, 496–498, 504–505
pay TV and STV, 510–514, 536–539
players' rights, 505–506
pooling arrangements
    amateur sports, 527–539
    professional sports, 522–527
protection of private transmissions, 501–503
superstations, 514–518
Buckley Amendment, 203–204

Common carriers
    liability of owner/operators, 363–365
    standard of care, 296–297
Comparative negligence, 298–299
Contracts
    professional, 175–177
    scholarships as, 137–140
Contributory negligence, 299–300
copyright (*see* Broadcasting)
copyright Act of 1976, 498–499, 507 (*see also*
    Broadcasting)
Criminal laws
    assault and battery, 419–422
    drug abuse, testing, and enforcement, 436–441
    gambling, 477–492
    ticket scalping, 492–493
Cross country, sex discrimination in, 247–249,
    251

Defamation law
    judicial review, 307–312
    libel, 306
    slander, 306–307
Doctors, liability of, 370–374
Drug abuse and enforcement
    intercollegiate athletics, 442–452
    Olympics, 474–477

professional sports, 452–477
  abuse and prevention programs, 453–455
  Major League Baseball, 473–474
  National Basketball Association, 455–470
  National Football League, 470–473
Due process
  defined, 55
  discipline of amateur athletes, 198–203
  procedural rights in amateur athletics, 55–60
  property interest in intercollegiate and interscholastic
    athletics, 62
  substantive rights in amateur athletics, 18–20, 60–63

Equal protection
  amateur athletics, 63–66
  defined, 63–66
  strict scrutiny, 63

Federal Communications Act of 1934, 498–499,
  499–503 (*see also* Broadcasting)
Federal Communications Commission (FCC), 498–499,
  508–510, 510–514 (*see also* Broadcasting)
Fencing (product liability), 387–388
Football
  amateur
    academic progress, 111–113
    redshirting, 128–129
    scholarships as contracts, 139–140
    transfer rules, 118–121, 126
    worker's compensation, 5–7, 141–143
  amateur athletes
    antitrust, 80
    due process, 56–58, 201–202, 203
    scheduling, 95–96
  amateur athletes, rights of
    alcohol and drugs, 196
    freedom of expression, 190–191
    grooming, 193
    marriage, 195
  assault and battery, 324–329
  broadcast issues involving NCAA
    antitrust, 527–36
    superstations, 515
    territorial rights, 504–505
  broadcast issues involving NFL
    blackouts, 518–519
    copyright protection, 507–508
    pooling rights, 522–526
  drug abuse and enforcement in professional, 470–473
  gambling in professional, 489–491

game officials
  liability for participant injury, 378
  review of decision during event, 380
intentional torts
  defamation, 308–09, 310
  infliction of emotional distress, 317
  invasion of privacy, 316
liability for defective equipment injuries, 348,
  384–385
liability for insurance, 390–392
liability for participant injuries
  franchise/leagues, 324–329, 357–358
  game officials, 378
  medical personnel, 338–339, 347, 358
  schools/coaches, 331–339, 347, 368
liability for spectator injuries, 349, 368
NCAA sanctions, 18–20
NFL waiver and release form, 405
sex discrimination
  interscholastic, 222–223, 246
  youth leagues, 244–245, 246
violence (NFL sanctions), 434
waiver of liability, 410–414

Gambling
  intercollegiate athletics, 477–482
  professional sports, 482–492
Game officials
  independent contractors as, 380
  liability for injury
    to game officials, 340–341, 375–377, 378
    to participants, 374–376, 378–379
  review of decisions during event, 379–380
  worker's compensation, 380–381
Golf
  liability for participant injury, 343–344, 345, 388
  liability for spectator injury, 369
  sex discrimination, interscholastic, 229–232, 250–251
Good Samaritan statutes, 302–303
Gymnastics, liability for injury in
  coaches, 350–351
  equipment defect, 388
  facility owner, 367

Handicapped athletes, 196–198
High school athletic associations
  academic performance rules, 29
  administration, 23–27
  authority, 92–93
  broadcasting, 525–526

constitutional rights
  due process, 58, 62–63
  equal protection, 27–29, 65–66
  state action, 51
discipline of athletes (due process rights), 203
drug abuse education programs, 436–441
enforcement activities, 92–93
Equal Rights Amendment, application of, 221–224
handicapped, 196–198
judicial review, 27–30
purposes, 26–27, 92
regulations on marriage, 65–66
rules and regulations
  alcohol and drugs, 195–196
  freedom of expression, 191
  grooming, 191–193
  marriages, 193–195
  redshirting, 129
  summer camps, 206–209
  transfers, 122–126
scheduling, 95
sex discrimination, 243–265
  coaches, 269–272
  participants, 242–265
structure, 25
Title IX, application of, 228–232, 234–237
Transfer rules, 4–5
Hockey
  amateur
    excessive financial aid, 152–153
    longevity, 132–134
  amateur organizations
    AHAUS definition of amateur, 2
    antitrust, 46–47
  battery cases in professional, 428–431
    due process, 61
    equal protection, 65
  liability for defective equipment injury, 386
  liability for injury to spectators, 363, 369
  NHL disciplinary procedure in professional, 434

Independent contractors (*see* Vicarious liability)
Injunctions (*see also* Amateur Athletics)
  defined, 6
  judicial review, 7
Insurance
  liability for injury, 390–391
    NCAA allowance for, 177
    NCAA Catastrophic Injury Plan, 391–392
International Olympic Committee (IOC)

definition of amateur, 2
drug abuse, testing, and enforcement, 465–476
eligibility of professionals, 2
recognized international sports federations, 17
Invasion of privacy, 312–316
Invitees, duty to, 294–295

Jockeys (drug abuse and testing), 436–441

Letter of Intent, 145–152
Liability for injury
  coaches, 331–341, 350–351
  common carriers, 296–297, 363–365
  equipment
    defects, 381–390
    facility owners/possessors, 369
    products liability law, 317–320
    schools/universities, 347–349
  facility owners/operators, 358, 359–370
  game officials, 375–379
  general principles
    assault and battery, 280–284
    negligence, 284–306
    reckless misconduct, 297–298
    standard of care, 284–297
    vicarious liability, 303–305
  independent contractors, 305–306
  intentional torts
    infliction of emotional distress, 316–317
    invasion of privacy, 312–316
    libel and slander, 306–312
  medical care, 337–339, 346–347, 370–374
  to participants by
    coaches/teachers, 331–341
    facility owners/possessors, 359–370
    game officials, 374–381
    medical personnel, 370–374
    participants, 320–330
    product manufacturers, 381–390
    professional teams/leagues, 353–359
    schools/universities, 341–353
  professional teams and leagues, 353–359, 373
  promoters, 304, 379
  property owners/possessors, 293–297
  school programs
    liability of institution, 341–353
    liability of teacher/coach, 331–339
  sovereign and charitable immunity, 349–353
  spectators, 329, 349, 358, 363, 365–366, 368, 369
    (*see also*, Game officials; Independent contrac-

tors; Insurance; Medical care; Professional
    sports; Spectators; Waivers of liability)
Libel and slander (*see* Defamation law)
Liberty interest (*see* Due process)
Licensees, duty to, 294–295
Little Leagues
    liability for injury
        charitable immunity as bar to recovery, 353
        to game officials, 375–376
    sex discrimination
        baseball, 252
        football, 244–245

Media
    property rights, 539–547
    right of privacy, 547–553

National Association of Intercollegiate Athletics
    (NAIA), 19–20
National Collegiate Athletic Association (NCAA)
    academic eligibility, 71–73
    antitrust, 45–46, 48–50
    budget, 24
    Byers, Walter, 20–22
    constitutional rights
        due process, 55–58, 59–60, 60–62
        equal protection, 63–66
        state action, 50–54
    definition of amateur, 2
    discipline of athletes, 198–203
    disclosure cases, 33–38
    drug abuse and enforcement, 442–452
    drug testing, 444–445, 446–452
    due process, 18–19
    eligibility for postseason competition, 10
    enforcement activities, 67–92
    funding of women's athletics, 211–213
    gambling, 477–482
    infractions procedure, 67–71
    liability insurance
        catastrophic insurance plan, 391–392
        certificate of insurance, 394–403
    marketing of athletes, 161–162
    negligence defenses, 298–303
        assumption of risk, 300–302
        comparative negligence, 299–300
        contributory negligence, 298–299
        Good Samaritan statutes, 302–303
        not negligent, 298

statute of limitations, 302–303
    payment of athletes, 158–162
    payment of expenses, 162, 174
    player-agents, 177–185
    professional contracts, 175–177
    purposes, 16–17
    regulation
        coaches and personnel, 79–83
        recruiting, 83–92
    rules and regulations
        academic progress, 109–114
        eligibility, 101–106
        grade point average, 107–109
        longevity, 130–134
        redshirting, 126–130
        scholarships/financial aid, 134–158
        transfer rules, 114–122
    scheduling, 96
    standard of care, 285–298
        breach of duty, 288–289
        children, 288, 292, 324, 335–336, 363
        damages, 290–291
        duty, 287–288
        owners/possessors, 293–297
        proximate cause, 289–290
        wrongful death statutes, 291–292
    structure, 22–23
    summer camps, 205–206, 208
    ticket scalping, 492–493
    Title IX, implementation and application, 211–214,
        215, 225–228
    University of Illinois Infractions Report, 74–79
    University of San Francisco Case Study, 87–89
    vicarious liability, 303–305
    (*see also* Assumption of risk; Standard of care;
        Vicarious liability)

Olympics
    Amateur Sports Act of 1978, 103
    drug abuse and enforcement, 474–477
    International Olympic Committee (IOC)
        boycott of 1980, 12–13
        definition of amateur, 2
        eligibility of professionals, 2
        eligibility requirements, 185–189
        establishment, 10–12
        job opportunity programs, 2, 16
        purposes, 10–12, 185–186

Player-agents, NCAA regulation of, 177–185
Procedural due process of law (*see* Due process)
Product liability law
  breach of warranty, 319–320, 383–384, 389
  negligence, 317–319, 381–383, 386–390
  strict liability, 319, 384–385, 388
Professional sports
  broadcast rights
    antitrust, 505
    media interests, 539–543
    ownership, 496–498
    pay cable, 498–499, 536–539
    pooling, 522–526
  drug abuse, testing and enforcement, 452–477
  gambling, 482–492
  liability for injury
    game officials, 340–341
    medical care, 370–374
    participants, 353–354, 356–358, 368
    spectators, 354–356, 358
  sex discrimination
    media coverage, 273–275
    officials, 272
    participants, 218
    participation in, 274
  violence, 419–427
    common defenses, 423–428
    congressional review, 422–426
    criminal liability, 427–432
    defining a crime, 422–428
    legislative actions, 422–426, 434–435
    liability of owners, coaches, 432
    manslaughter, 431–432
    professional league sanctions, 432–434
Property interest (*see* Due process)

Reckless misconduct
  judicial review, 320–329
  legal theory, 297
Restraint of trade (*see* Antitrust; Sherman Act)

Scheduling (amateur athletics), 94–97
Sex discrimination
  amateur athletics, participation in
    contact/noncontact sports, 242–265
    same sport, different seasons, 265
  amateur athletics, separate but equal, 256–262
  amateur athletics, same sport, different rules, 262–265
  athletic employment

    Equal Pay Act, 266–267
    Title VII, 266–267
  coaching, 267–272
  game officials, 272
  legal principles
    equal protection, 215–218
    Equal Rights Amendments, 221–224
  Little Leagues, 244–45, 252
  media, 273–275
  professional sports, participation in, 273
  Title IX, scope and applicability, 224–242 (*see also,*
    NCCA; Specific sports, Title IX)
Skiing (liability for injury)
  breach of warranty, 389
  participants, 286, 367, 388
Soccer
  amateur athletes, rights of, *re* grooming, 192–193
  assault and battery, 323–324
  sex discrimination
    interscholastic, 246
    youth leagues, 246
  spectator violence, 435
  United States Soccer Federation (USSF), 171
Softball
  amateur organizations (antitrust), 46
  assault and battery, 321–322
  game officials (liability for injury), 378
Sovereign and charitable immunity
  colleges and universities, 336–337, 350–353
  legal theory, 349–350
  school districts, 333, 334, 343, 345, 346, 351–353
Spectators
  disturbances by, 340–341, 358
  liability for injury to, 354–356, 358, 363, 365–366,
    368
  violence *re* alcohol sales restrictions, 442
Sports Violence Act of 1980, 423, 434–435
Sports Violence Arbitration Bill of 1983, 423–426, 435
Stadiums and arenas
  liability for injury
    facility owner/possessors, 359–370
  liability for spectator injury
    franchise/leagues, 358
    owner/possessors, 358, 368, 369
Standard of care
  owner/possessors of property
    common carriers, 296–297
    lessors of land, 294
    licensees and invitees, 294–295

reasonable person standard, 285–292
   children, 292–293
State action (*see* Amateur athletic associations)
State athletic commissions
   authority, 31–32
   licensing, 31–32
   rules based on sex, 100, 273
   structure, 31
Statute of limitations, 302–303
Strict liability, 319, 384–385, 388
Student-athlete (*see* Amateur athlete)
Swimming
   definition of amateur, 2
   sex discrimination, interscholastic, 265
   United States Swimming Association (USSA)
      hearing and appeals process, 58–59
      restrictions on expenses, 171
      restrictions of payment, 159–160

TAC Trust, 162–171
Tailgating, liability for injury, 366
Tennis
   amateur athletics (transfer rule), 121
   definition of amateur, 2
   liability for injuries (defective surface), 383–384
   sex discrimination, interscholastic, 249–250, 251,
) 256, 262
   United States Tennis Association (USTA)
      definition of amateur, 2
      restrictions on payment, 161
      restrictions on expenses, 171
Ticket scalping, 492–493
Title IX of Educational Amendments of 1972
   compliance reviews, 240–242
   legality of, 225–228
   passage, 218–221
   scope and applicability, 228–240
      coaching, 267–272
      employment practices, 267
Track and field
   amateur athletics, NCAA regulation of, 203
   amateur organizations
      amateur status, 8–10
      The Athletics Congress (TAC), 2
      commercialization, 2
      due process, 61–62

United States Olympic Committee (USOC)
   definition of amateur, 2

directory of member organizations, 15
drug testing, 476
job opportunity programs, 2, 16
judicial review, 12–14
purposes, 10–11, 185–186
United States Tennis Association (USTA)
   sex discrimination, 218

Vicarious liability, 303–306
   independent contractors
      legal theory, 305–306
      jockeys, 306
      medical personnel (football), 347
      medical personnel (boxing), 371–373
   legal theory, 303–306
   professional teams
      baseball, 340–341, 354–357
      basketball, 357
      football, 324–329
   respondent superior, 303
   school districts
      coaches, 332–333
      medical care, 338–339
Violence in sports (*see also,* Assault and battery)
   assumption of risk defense, 427
   consent defense, 423, 427
   criminal laws, 419–422, 432
   hockey cases, 428–431
   involuntary action defense, 428, 430
   league discipline, 432–434
      legislative action, 422–426, 434–435
      liability of coaches/owners, 432
   liability for game official injury
      coaches, 376–77
      franchise/leagues, 340–341
   liability for participant injury
      franchise/leagues, 356–358
   liability for spectator injury
      franchise/leagues, 358
      owner/possessors, 358, 368, 369
   Model Penal Code, 427
   self-defense, 423, 427–29
   Sports Violence Act of 1980, 422–23, 434–435
   Sports Violence Arbitration Act of 1983, 423–26, 435
Volleyball, sex discrimination in interscholastic, 253–255

Waivers of liability
   judicial review, 393
   legal theory, 392–393

waiver and release of liability forms, 394–417
Worker's compensation
    amateur athletics, 140–145
    game officials, 380–381
Wrestling
    amateur athlete
        handicapped, eligibility for competition, 198
        worker's compensation, eligibility for, 143

liability for participant injury
    game officials, 378
    school/coaches, 342–343, 344, 352
liability for spectator injury (facility owner/possessor), 368, 369
sex discrimination (professional licensing), 273
United States Wrestling Federation (USWF)
    amateur status, 13–14